Collins easy learning

French Dictionary

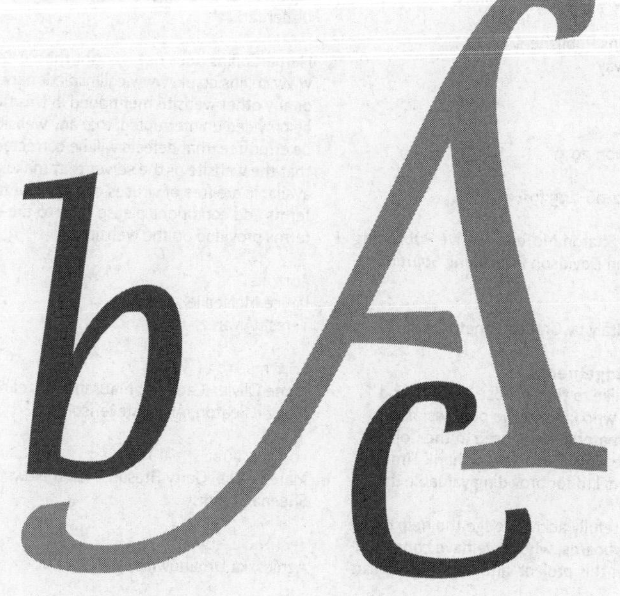

HarperCollins Publishers
Westerhill Road
Bishopbriggs
Glasgow
G64 2QT

Eighth Edition 2019

10 9 8 7 6 5 4 3 2

ISBN 978-0-00-830025-8

Collins® is a registered trademark of HarperCollins Publishers Limited

www.collins.co.uk
www.collinsdictionary.com

A catalogue record for this book is available from the British Library

HarperCollins Publishers
195 Broadway
New York
NY10007

Eighth Edition 2019

ISBN 978-0-06-295391-9

Typeset by Sharon McTeir Creative Publishing Services and Davidson Publishing Solutions, Glasgow

Printed in Italy by Grafica Veneta S.p.A.

Acknowledgements
We would like to thank those authors and publishers who kindly gave permission for copyright material to be used in the Collins Corpus. We would also like to thank Times Newspapers Ltd for providing valuable data.

Collins gratefully acknowledge the help of the examining boards, whom we have consulted throughout this project, and whose word lists and exam papers we carefully studied when compiling this dictionary in order to ensure appropriate coverage and support for GCSE and other exams of a similar level.

EDITORS
Janice McNeillie
Teresa Álvarez

CONTRIBUTORS
Marie Olivier-Caudray, Maurane Prezelin, Maggie Seaton, Anna Stevenson

FOR THE PUBLISHER
Maree Airlie, Gerry Breslin, Helen Newstead, Sheena Shanks

TECHNICAL SUPPORT
Agnieszka Urbanowicz

MIX
Paper from responsible sources
FSC™ C007454

This book is produced from independently certified FSC™ paper to ensure responsible forest management.

For more information visit: www.harpercollins.co.uk/green

In order to ensure that this resource offers high-quality support for the associated Pearson qualification, it has been through a review process by the awarding body. This process confirms that this resource fully covers the teaching and learning content of the specification or part of a specification at which it is aimed. It also confirms that it demonstrates an appropriate balance between the development of subject skills, knowledge and understanding, in addition to preparation for assessment.

Endorsement does not cover any guidance on assessment activities or processes (e.g. practice questions or advice on how to answer assessment questions), included in the resource nor does it prescribe any particular approach to the teaching or delivery of a related course.

While the publishers have made every attempt to ensure that advice on the qualification and its assessment is accurate, the official specification and associated assessment guidance materials are the only authoritative source of information and should always be referred to for definitive guidance.

Pearson examiners have not contributed to any sections in this resource relevant to examination papers for which they have responsibility.

Examiners will not use endorsed resources as a source of material for any assessment set by Pearson.

Endorsement of a resource does not mean that the resource is required to achieve this Pearson qualification, nor does it mean that it is the only suitable material available to support the qualification, and any resource lists produced by the awarding body shall include this and other appropriate resources.

Abbreviations used in this dictionary

aux = auxiliary (for verbs that use être in the perfect tense)

E = indicates that a verb uses être in the perfect tense

fem = feminine

masc = masculine

pl = plural

sing = singular

Contents

Glossary of grammar terms

Adjective

a 'describing' word that tells you more about a person or thing, such as their appearance, colour, size or other qualities, for example, *pretty*, *blue*, *big*, and, in French, grand, alphabétique, génial.

> une solution **éventuelle** a possible solution
> l'équipe **irlandaise** the Irish team

Adverb

a word usually used with verbs, adjectives or other adverbs that gives more information about when, where, how or in what circumstances something happens or to what degree something is true, for example, *quickly*, *happily*, *now*, *extremely*, *very*. Some adverbs in French are: mieux, naturellement, ainsi.

> Il l'a fait **autrement**. He did it differently.
> Je suis **très** fatiguée. I'm very tired.

Article

a word like *the*, *a* and *an*, which is used in front of a noun. In French the words le, la, un or une are articles.

> **les** filles the girls
> **un** journal a newspaper

Conjunction

a word such as *and*, *because* or *but* that links two words or phrases of a similar type or two parts of a sentence, for example, *Diane and I have been friends for years; I left because I was bored*. Common French conjunctions are donc, ou, mais.

> la voiture **et** la maison the car and the house
> Réfléchis bien **car** c'est important. Think carefully because it's important.

Noun

a 'naming' word for a living being, thing or idea, for example, *woman*, *desk*, *happiness*, *Andrew* and, in French, maison, chien, ville.

la **capital** capital
le **chocolat** chocolate

Preposition

a word such as *at*, *for*, *with*, *into* or *from*, which is usually followed by a noun, pronoun or, in English, a word ending in *-ing*. Prepositions show how people and things relate to the rest of the sentence, for example, *She's at home; a tool for cutting grass*; *It's from Nadia*. Some French prepositions are contre, dans, de.

dès le début right from the start
Il marchait **devant**. He was walking in front.

Pronoun

a word which you use instead of a noun, when you do not need or want to name someone or something directly, for example, *it*, *you*, *none* and, in French, elle, leur, même.

Ce vélo-là, c'est le **mien**. That bike's mine.
Prends **ceci**, tu en auras besoin. Take this, you'll need it.

Verb

a 'doing' word which describes what someone or something does, is, or what happens to them, for example, *be*, *sing*, *live*. Some common verbs in French are aimer, prendre, être.

Elle n'a pas beaucoup **changé**. She hasn't changed much.
Je cherche mes **clés**. I'm looking for my keys.

In order to provide additional practice with dictionary skills, free downloadable resources are now available for teachers and learners of French at **www.collins.co.uk/easylearningresources**

Guide to entries

Number refers to where verb is conjugated in full

Star symbol indicates core vocabulary

Verb tables for common irregular verbs

Translations underlined to find them quickly

Examples show how the translation is used

Important phrases set out separately

Article to show gender of French noun

Numbers clearly point out different senses

Look at the main verb to find out about common irregular verb forms

Less common plural forms given for nouns

Cultural notes offer additional information

★ **devoir** VERB [26]

PRESENT TENSE

je dois	nous devons
tu dois	vous devez
il/elle doit	ils/elles doivent

PAST PARTICIPLE

dû

▷ *see also* **devoir** NOUN

1 to have to
□ Je dois partir. I've got to go.

2 must
□ Tu dois être fatigué. You must be tired.

3 to be due to
□ Le nouveau centre commercial doit ouvrir en mai. The new shopping centre is due to open in May.

■ **devoir quelque chose à quelqu'un** to owe somebody something □ Combien est-ce que je vous dois? How much do I owe you?

★ le **devoir** MASC NOUN

▷ *see also* **devoir** VERB

1 exercise

■ **les devoirs** homework

■ **un devoir sur table** a written test

2 duty
□ Aller voter fait partie des devoirs du citoyen. Voting is part of one's duty as a citizen.

disent, disiez, disions VERB ▷ *see* **dire**

★ le **drapeau** (PL les **drapeaux**) MASC NOUN

flag
□ le drapeau français the French flag □ le drapeau tricolore the French flag

DID YOU KNOW...?
le drapeau tricolore is the French flag: its three colours are blue, white and red.

Guide to entries

★ **nice** ADJECTIVE

1 gentil (FEM gentille) (*kind*)

□ Your parents are very nice. Tes parents sont très gentils. □ It was nice of you to remember my birthday. C'était gentil de ta part de te souvenir de mon anniversaire.

■ **to be nice to somebody** être [35] gentil avec quelqu'un

2 joli (FEM jolie) (*pretty*)

□ That's a nice dress! Qu'est-ce qu'elle est jolie, cette robe! □ Aix is a nice town. Aix est une jolie ville.

> **WORD POWER**
> You can use a number of other words instead of **nice** to mean 'pretty':
> **attractive** séduisant
> □ an attractive girl une fille séduisante
> **beautiful** beau
> □ a beautiful painting un beau tableau
> **lovely** charmant
> □ a lovely surprise une charmante surprise
> **pretty** joli
> □ a pretty dress une jolie robe

to **depart** VERB

partir [57E]

★ **doubt** NOUN

▷ *see also* **doubt** VERB

le doute *masc*

□ I have my doubts. J'ai des doutes.

★ to **doubt** VERB

▷ *see also* **doubt** NOUN

douter [28] de

■ **I doubt it.** J'en doute.

■ **to doubt that** douter [28] que

> **douter que** has to be followed by a verb in the subjunctive.

□ I doubt he'll agree. Je doute qu'il soit d'accord.

Star symbol indicates core vocabulary

Word classes written out in full

Feminine form of adjectives shown

Words in brackets identify the meaning given

Word Power boxes help build vocabulary

English text always in black

French text always in blue

'E' indicates verbs that use être in the perfect tense

Reminder to check other word classes of the same word

Language Tip notes give key grammar points

Numbers

1	un(e)	21	vingt et un(e)
2	deux	22	vingt-deux
3	trois	30	trente
4	quatre	40	quarante
5	cinq	50	cinquante
6	six	60	soixante
7	sept	70	soixante-dix
8	huit	71	soixante et onze
9	neuf	72	soixante-douze
10	dix	80	quatre-vingts
11	onze	81	quatre-vingt-un(e)
12	douze	90	quatre-vingt-dix
13	treize	91	quatre-vingt-onze
14	quatorze	100	cent
15	quinze	101	cent un(e)
16	seize	300	trois cents
17	dix-sept	301	trois cent un(e)
18	dix-huit	1,000	mille
19	dix-neuf	2,000	deux mille
20	vingt	1,000,000	un million

Examples

Il habite au dix.	He lives at number ten.
à la page dix-huit	on page eighteen
au chapitre sept	in chapter seven
neuf fois sur dix	nine times out of ten

Years

1764	mille sept cent soixante-quatre
1988	mille neuf cent quatre-vingt-huit
2019	deux mille dix-neuf

Fractions

½	un demi
⅓	un tiers
⅔	deux tiers
¼	un quart
⅕	un cinquième

0.5 zéro virgule cinq (0,5)
3.4 trois virgule quatre (3,4)
10% dix pour cent
100% cent pour cent

1st premier (1er), première (1re)
2nd deuxième (2e)
3rd troisième (3e)
4th quatrième (4e)
5th cinquième (5e)
6th sixième (6e)
7th septième (7e)
8th huitième (8e)
9th neuvième (9e)
10th dixième (10e)
11th onzième (11e)
12th douzième (12e)
13th treizième (13e)
14th quatorzième (14e)
15th quinzième (15e)
16th seizième (16e)
17th dix-septième (17e)
18th dix-huitième (18e)
19th dix-neuvième (19e)
20th vingtième (20e)
21st vingt et unième (21e)
22nd vingt-deuxième (22e)
30th trentième (30e)
100th centième (100e)
101st cent unième (101e)
1000th millième (1000e)

Examples

Il habite au cinquième (étage).	He lives on the fifth floor.
Il est arrivé troisième.	He came in third.
C'est la deuxième fois que je viens en France.	It's the second time I've been to France.

Time

Quelle heure est-il? Il est ... **What time is it? It's ...**

une heure

une heure dix

une heure et quart

une heure et demie

deux heures moins vingt

deux heures moins le quart

A quelle heure? **At what time?**

à minuit

à midi

à une heure (de l'après-midi)

à huit heures (du soir)

à 11h15 *or* onze heures quinze

à 20h45 *or* vingt heures quarante-cinq

In French times are often given in the twenty-four hour clock.

Aa

★ **a** VERB ▷ *see* **avoir**

a should not be confused with the preposition à.

■ **Il a beaucoup d'amis.** He has a lot of friends.
■ **Il a mangé des frites.** He had some chips.
■ **Il a neigé pendant la nuit.** It snowed during the night.
■ **il y a** **1** there is □ Il y a un bon film à la télé. There's a good film on TV. **2** there are □ Il y a beaucoup de monde. There are lots of people. **3** ago □ Je l'ai rencontré il y a deux ans. I met him two years ago.
■ **Qu'est-ce qu'il y a?** What's the matter?
■ **Il n'y a qu'à partir plus tôt.** We'll just have to leave earlier.

★ **à** PREPOSITION

à should not be confused with the verb form a. See also **au** (= à + le) and **aux** (= à + les).

1 at
□ être à la maison to be at home □ à trois heures at 3 o'clock
2 in
□ être à Paris to be in Paris □ habiter au Portugal to live in Portugal □ habiter à la campagne to live in the country □ au printemps in the spring □ au mois de juin in June
3 to
□ aller à Paris to go to Paris □ aller au Portugal to go to Portugal □ aller à la campagne to go to the country □ donner quelque chose à quelqu'un to give something to somebody □ Cette veste appartient à Marie. This jacket belongs to Marie. □ Je n'ai rien à faire. I've got nothing to do.
■ **Ce livre est à Paul.** This book is Paul's.
■ **Cette voiture est à nous.** This car is ours.
4 by
□ à bicyclette by bicycle □ être payé à l'heure to be paid by the hour
■ **à pied** on foot
■ **C'est à côté de chez moi.** It's near my house.
■ **C'est à dix kilomètres d'ici.** It's 10 kilometres from here.
■ **C'est à dix minutes d'ici.** It's 10 minutes from here.
■ **cent kilomètres à l'heure** 100 kilometres an hour
■ **À bientôt!** See you soon!
■ **À demain!** See you tomorrow!
■ **À samedi!** See you on Saturday!
■ **À tout à l'heure!** See you later!

abandonner VERB [28]
1 to abandon
□ Il a abandonné son chien. He abandoned his dog.
2 to give up
□ J'ai décidé d'abandonner la natation. I've decided to give up swimming.

★ l'**abeille** FEM NOUN
bee

abîmer VERB [28]
to damage
■ **s'abîmer** to get damaged

l'**abonnement** MASC NOUN
1 season ticket
2 subscription (*to magazine*)

s'**abonner** VERB [28]
■ **s'abonner à une revue** to take out a subscription to a magazine
■ **être abonné sur Twitter** to be on Twitter

★ l'**abord** MASC NOUN
■ **d'abord** first □ Je vais rentrer chez moi d'abord. I'll go home first.

aboyer VERB [53]
to bark

★ l'**abri** MASC NOUN
shelter
■ **être à l'abri** to be under cover
■ **se mettre à l'abri** to shelter

★ l'**abricot** MASC NOUN
apricot

s'**abriter** VERB [28]
to shelter

★ l'**absence** FEM NOUN
absence
■ **Il est passé pendant ton absence.** He came while you were away.

★ **absent** (FEM **absente**) ADJECTIVE
absent

★ = core vocabulary

French-English

a

★ **absolument** ADVERB
absolutely

l'**abus** MASC NOUN
abuse
■ **abus de confiance** breach of trust
■ **abus de pouvoir** abuse of power
■ **abus sexuels** sexual abuse

l'**accélérateur** MASC NOUN
accelerator

★ **accélérer** VERB [34]
to accelerate

★ l'**accent** MASC NOUN
accent
□ Il a l'accent de Marseille. He has a Marseille accent.
■ **un accent aigu** an acute accent
■ **un accent grave** a grave accent
■ **un accent circonflexe** a circumflex

accentuer VERB [28]
to stress

★ **accepter** VERB [28]
to accept
■ **accepter de faire quelque chose** to agree to do something

★ l'**accès** MASC NOUN
access
□ avoir accès à quelque chose to have access to something
■ **'Accès aux quais'** 'To the trains'

l'**accessoire** MASC NOUN
1 accessory
□ les accessoires de mode fashion accessories
2 prop

★ l'**accident** MASC NOUN
accident
□ un accident de la route a road accident
□ Elle a eu un accident de ski. She had a skiing accident.
■ **par accident** by chance

★ **accompagner** VERB [28]
to accompany

accomplir VERB [38]
to carry out
□ Il n'a pas réussi à accomplir cette tâche. He didn't manage to carry out this task.

★ l'**accord** MASC NOUN
agreement
■ **être d'accord** to agree □ Tu es d'accord avec moi? Do you agree with me?
■ **se mettre d'accord** to come to an agreement
■ **D'accord!** OK!

l'**accordéon** MASC NOUN
accordion
□ Mathieu joue de l'accordéon. Mathieu plays the accordion.

l'**accoudoir** MASC NOUN
armrest

l'**accrochage** MASC NOUN
collision

★ **accrocher** VERB [28]
■ **accrocher quelque chose à** 1 to hang something on □ Il a accroché sa veste au portemanteau. He hung his jacket on the coat rack. 2 to hitch something up to □ Ils ont accroché la remorque à leur voiture. They hitched the trailer up to their car.
■ **s'accrocher à quelque chose** to get caught on something □ Sa jupe s'est accrochée aux ronces. Her skirt got caught on the brambles.

s'**accroupir** VERB [38]
to squat down

★ l'**accueil** MASC NOUN
welcome
□ Il nous a remerciés de notre accueil. He thanked us for our welcome.
■ **Elle s'occupe de l'accueil des visiteurs.** She's in charge of looking after visitors.
■ **'Accueil'** 'Reception'

★ **accueillant** (FEM **accueillante**) ADJECTIVE
welcoming
□ Ses parents ont été très accueillants. Her parents were very welcoming.

★ **accueillir** VERB [22]
to welcome

accumuler VERB [28]
to accumulate
■ **s'accumuler** to pile up

l'**accusation** FEM NOUN
accusation

l'**accusé** MASC NOUN
accused
□ L'accusé a déclaré que ... The accused stated that ...
■ **un accusé de réception** an acknowledgement of receipt

l'**accusée** FEM NOUN
accused

★ **accuser** VERB [28]
to accuse
□ accuser quelqu'un de quelque chose to accuse somebody of something

★ l'**achat** MASC NOUN
purchase
■ **faire des achats** to do some shopping

★ **acheter** VERB [1]
to buy
□ J'ai acheté des gâteaux à la pâtisserie. I bought some cakes at the cake shop.
■ **acheter quelque chose à quelqu'un** 1 to buy something for somebody □ Qu'est-ce que tu lui as acheté pour son anniversaire? What did you buy him for his birthday? 2 to

buy something from somebody □ J'ai acheté des œufs au fermier. I bought some eggs from the farmer.

★ **acide** (FEM **acide**) ADJECTIVE
▷ *see also* **acide** NOUN
acid
□ Ce pamplemousse est trop acide. This grapefruit is too acid.

★ l'**acide** MASC NOUN
▷ *see also* **acide** ADJECTIVE
acid

l'**acier** MASC NOUN
steel

l'**acné** FEM NOUN
acne
□ Il a de l'acné. He has acne.

acquérir VERB [2]
to acquire

acquis VERB ▷ *see* **acquérir**

acquitter VERB [28]
to acquit
□ L'accusé a été acquitté. The accused was acquitted.

l'**acte** MASC NOUN
act
■ **un acte de naissance** a birth certificate

★ l'**acteur** MASC NOUN
actor
□ Il est acteur. He's an actor. □ un acteur de cinéma a film actor

★ **actif** (FEM **active**) ADJECTIVE
active
■ **la population active** the working population

l'**action** FEM NOUN
action
■ **une bonne action** a good deed

s'**activer** VERB [28]
1 to bustle about
□ Elle s'activait à préparer le repas. She bustled about preparing the meal.
2 to get moving
□ Allez! Active-toi! Come on! Get moving!

★ l'**activité** FEM NOUN
activity

★ l'**actrice** FEM NOUN
actress
□ Elle est actrice. She's an actress. □ une actrice de cinéma a film actress

★ l'**actualité** FEM NOUN
current events
■ **un problème d'actualité** a topical issue
■ **les actualités** the news

actuel (FEM **actuelle**) ADJECTIVE
present
□ le système actuel the present system
■ **à l'heure actuelle** at the present time

BE CAREFUL!
actuel does not mean **actual**.

★ **actuellement** ADVERB
at present

BE CAREFUL!
actuellement does not mean **actually**.

l'**adaptateur** MASC NOUN
adaptor

★ l'**addition** FEM NOUN
1 addition
□ l'addition et la soustraction addition and subtraction
2 bill
□ L'addition, s'il vous plaît! Can we have the bill, please?

additionner VERB [28]
to add up

★ l'**adhérent** MASC NOUN
member

★ l'**adhérente** FEM NOUN
member

adhésif (FEM **adhésive**) ADJECTIVE
■ **le ruban adhésif** sticky tape

adieu EXCLAMATION
farewell!

l'**adjectif** MASC NOUN
adjective

admettre VERB [47]
1 to admit
□ Il refuse d'admettre qu'il s'est trompé. He won't admit that he made a mistake.
2 to allow
□ Les chiens ne sont pas admis dans le restaurant. Dogs are not allowed in the restaurant.

l'**administration** FEM NOUN
administration
■ **l'Administration** the Civil Service

admirable (FEM **admirable**) ADJECTIVE
admirable

l'**admirateur** MASC NOUN
admirer

l'**admiratrice** FEM NOUN
admirer

★ **admirer** VERB [28]
to admire

admis VERB ▷ *see* **admettre**

l'**ado** MASC/FEM NOUN
teenager
■ **un camp d'ados** a youth camp

l'**adolescence** FEM NOUN
adolescence

★ l'**adolescent** MASC NOUN
teenager

★ l'**adolescente** FEM NOUN
teenager

French-English

a

★ = core vocabulary

French-English

a

adopter VERB [28]
to adopt

adorable (FEM **adorable**) ADJECTIVE
lovely

★ **adorer** VERB [28]
to love
□ Elle adore le chocolat. She loves chocolate.
□ J'adore jouer au tennis. I love playing tennis.

★ l'**adresse** FEM NOUN
address
■ **une adresse web** a Web address
■ **mon adresse électronique** my email address

adresser VERB [28]
■ **adresser la parole à quelqu'un** to speak to someone
■ **s'adresser à quelqu'un** **1** to speak to somebody □ C'est à toi que je m'adresse. It's you I'm speaking to. **2** to go and see somebody □ Adressez-vous au patron. Go and see the boss. □ Adressez-vous aux renseignements. Ask at the enquiry desk. **3** to be aimed at somebody □ Ce film s'adresse surtout aux enfants. This film is aimed mainly at children.

l'**ADSL** MASC NOUN (= *asymmetric digital subscriber line*)
ADSL
■ **On a l'ADSL à la maison.** We have broadband at home.

★ l'**adulte** MASC/FEM NOUN
adult

l'**adverbe** MASC NOUN
adverb

l'**adversaire** MASC/FEM NOUN
opponent

aérien (FEM **aérienne**) ADJECTIVE
■ **une compagnie aérienne** an airline

l'**aérobic** MASC NOUN
aerobics
□ Teresa fait de l'aérobic. Teresa does aerobics.

l'**aérogare** FEM NOUN
terminal

★ l'**aéroglisseur** MASC NOUN
hovercraft

★ l'**aéroport** MASC NOUN
airport

★ l'**affaire** FEM NOUN
▷ *see also* **affaires** NOUN
1 case
□ une affaire de drogue a drugs case
2 business
□ Son affaire marche bien. His business is doing well.
■ **une bonne affaire** a real bargain
■ **Ça fera l'affaire.** This will do nicely.
■ **avoir affaire à quelqu'un** to deal with somebody

★ les **affaires** FEM PL NOUN
▷ *see also* **affaire** NOUN
1 things
□ Va chercher tes affaires! Go and get your things!
2 business
□ Les affaires marchent bien en ce moment. Business is good at the moment. □ Mêle-toi de tes affaires. (*informal*) Mind your own business.
■ **un homme d'affaires** a businessman
■ **le ministre des Affaires étrangères** the Foreign Secretary

l'**affection** FEM NOUN
affection

★ **affectueusement** ADVERB
affectionately

affectueux (FEM **affectueuse**) ADJECTIVE
affectionate

★ l'**affiche** FEM NOUN
poster

afficher VERB [28]
to put up
□ Ils ont affiché les résultats dehors. They've put the results up outside.
■ **'Défense d'afficher'** 'Post no bills'

affilée
■ **d'affilée** ADVERB at a stretch □ Il a travaillé douze heures d'affilée. He worked 12 hours at a stretch.

★ l'**affirmation** FEM NOUN
assertion

affirmer VERB [28]
to claim
□ Il a affirmé que c'était la vérité. He claimed it was the truth.
■ **s'affirmer** to assert oneself □ Il est trop timide, il faut qu'il s'affirme. He's too shy, he should assert himself.

★ l'**affluence** FEM NOUN
■ **les heures d'affluence** the rush hour

s'**affoler** VERB [28]
to panic
□ Ne t'affole pas! Don't panic!

affranchir VERB [38]
to stamp

★ **affreux** (FEM **affreuse**) ADJECTIVE
awful

affronter VERB [28]
to face
□ L'Allemagne affrontera l'Italie en finale. Germany will face Italy in the final.

afin de CONJUNCTION
■ **afin de faire quelque chose** so as to do something □ Je me suis levé très tôt afin

d'être prêt à temps. I got up very early so as to be ready on time.

afin que CONJUNCTION
so that

> **afin que** is followed by a verb in the subjunctive.

□ Il m'a téléphoné afin que je sois prêt à temps. He phoned me so that I'd be ready on time.

★ **africain** (FEM **africaine**) ADJECTIVE, NOUN
African
■ **un Africain** an African (*man*)
■ **une Africaine** an African (*woman*)

★ l'**Afrique** FEM NOUN
Africa
■ **en Afrique** 1 in Africa 2 to Africa
■ **l'Afrique du Sud** South Africa

★ **agacer** VERB [12]
■ **agacer quelqu'un** to get on somebody's nerves □ Tu m'agaces avec tes questions! You're getting on my nerves with all your questions!

★ l'**âge** MASC NOUN
age
■ **Quel âge as-tu?** How old are you?

★ **âgé** (FEM **âgée**) ADJECTIVE
old
□ Son père est âgé. His father's old. □ Il est âgé de dix ans. He's 10 years old.
■ **les personnes âgées** elderly people

★ l'**agence** FEM NOUN
1 agency
□ l'agence pour l'emploi the employment agency
■ **une agence de voyages** a travel agency
2 office
□ l'agence de Londres the London office
■ **une agence immobilière** an estate agent's

l'**agenda** MASC NOUN
diary
□ J'ai perdu mon agenda. I have lost my diary.

> **BE CAREFUL!**
> The French word **agenda** does not mean **agenda**.

s'**agenouiller** VERB [28]
to kneel down

l'**agent** MASC NOUN
■ **un agent de police** a police officer
■ **un agent d'entretien** a cleaner

l'**agglomération** FEM NOUN
town
■ **l'agglomération parisienne** Greater Paris

aggraver VERB [28]
to make worse
■ **s'aggraver** to worsen

★ **agir** VERB [38]
to act
□ Il a agi par vengeance. He acted out of vengeance.
■ **Il s'agit de ...** It's about ... □ Il s'agit du club de sport. It's about the sports club. □ De quoi s'agit-il? What is it about?
■ **Il s'agit de faire attention.** We must be careful.

agité (FEM **agitée**) ADJECTIVE
1 restless
□ Les élèves sont agités. The pupils are restless.
2 rough
□ La mer est agitée. The sea is rough.
■ **un sommeil agité** broken sleep

★ **agiter** VERB [28]
to shake
□ Agitez la bouteille. Shake the bottle.

★ l'**agneau** (PL les **agneaux**) MASC NOUN
lamb

l'**agrafe** FEM NOUN
staple (*for papers*)

l'**agrafeuse** FEM NOUN
stapler

★ **agrandir** VERB [38]
1 to enlarge
□ J'ai fait agrandir mes photos. I've had my photos enlarged.
2 to extend
□ Ils ont agrandi leur jardin. They've extended their garden.
■ **s'agrandir** to expand □ Leur magasin s'est agrandi. Their shop has expanded.

★ **agréable** (FEM **agréable**) ADJECTIVE
nice

★ **agréer** VERB [18]
■ **Veuillez agréer, Monsieur, l'expression de mes sentiments les meilleurs. Jean** Ormal. Yours sincerely, Jean Ormal.

agressif (FEM **agressive**) ADJECTIVE
aggressive

l'**agressivité** FEM NOUN
aggression
■ **faire preuve d'agressivité envers quelqu'un** to be aggressive to somebody
■ **l'agressivité au volant** road rage

★ **agricole** (FEM **agricole**) ADJECTIVE
agricultural
□ le matériel agricole agricultural machinery
■ **une exploitation agricole** a farm

★ l'**agriculteur** MASC NOUN
farmer
□ Il est agriculteur. He's a farmer.

★ l'**agricultrice** FEM NOUN
farmer

★ l'**agriculture** FEM NOUN
farming

ai VERB ▷ *see* **avoir**
■ **J'ai deux chats.** I have two cats.
■ **J'ai bien dormi.** I slept well.

★ l'**aide** FEM NOUN
1 help
□ J'ai besoin de ton aide. I need your help.
□ appeler quelqu'un à l'aide to call to somebody for help
■ **À l'aide!** Help!
2 aid
□ une aide financière financial aid
■ **à l'aide de** using □ J'ai réussi à ouvrir la boîte à l'aide d'un couteau. I managed to open the tin using a knife.

★ **aider** VERB [28]
to help

l'**aide-soignant** (PL les **aides-soignants**) MASC NOUN
auxiliary nurse
□ Il est aide-soignant. He's an auxiliary nurse.

l'**aide-soignante** (PL les **aides-soignantes**) FEM NOUN
auxiliary nurse
□ Léa est aide-soignante. Léa is an auxiliary nurse.

aie VERB ▷ *see* **avoir**

aïe EXCLAMATION
ouch!

aigre (FEM **aigre**) ADJECTIVE
sour

★ **aigu** (FEM **aiguë**) ADJECTIVE
sharp (*pain*)
□ une douleur aiguë a sharp pain
■ **e accent aigu** e acute

l'**aiguille** FEM NOUN
needle
□ une aiguille à tricoter a knitting needle
■ **les aiguilles d'une montre** the hands of a watch

★ l'**ail** MASC NOUN
garlic

l'**aile** FEM NOUN
wing

aille VERB ▷ *see* **aller**

★ **ailleurs** ADVERB
somewhere else
■ **partout ailleurs** everywhere else
■ **nulle part ailleurs** nowhere else
■ **d'ailleurs** besides

★ **aimable** (FEM **aimable**) ADJECTIVE
kind

l'**aimant** MASC NOUN
magnet

★ **aimer** VERB [28]
1 to love
□ Elle aime ses enfants. She loves her children.
2 to like
□ Tu aimes le chocolat? Do you like chocolate?
□ J'aime bien ce garçon. I like this boy.
□ J'aime bien jouer au tennis. I like playing tennis. □ J'aimerais aller en Grèce. I'd like to go to Greece.
■ **J'aimerais mieux ne pas y aller.** I'd rather not go.

★ **aîné** (FEM **aînée**) ADJECTIVE
▷ *see also* **aîné** NOUN
elder
□ mon frère aîné my big brother

★ l'**aîné** MASC NOUN
▷ *see also* **aîné** ADJECTIVE
oldest child
□ C'est l'aîné. He's the oldest child.

★ l'**aînée** FEM NOUN
▷ *see also* **aîné** ADJECTIVE
oldest child
□ C'est l'aînée. She's the oldest child.

★ **ainsi** ADVERB
in this way
□ Il faut faire ainsi. This is the way to do it.
■ **C'est ainsi qu'il a réussi.** That's how he succeeded.
■ **ainsi que** as well as
■ **et ainsi de suite** and so on

★ l'**air** MASC NOUN
1 air
□ l'air chaud warm air
■ **prendre l'air** to get some fresh air
2 tune
□ Elle a joué un air au piano. She played a tune on the piano.
■ **Elle a l'air fatiguée.** She looks tired.
■ **Il a l'air d'un clown.** He looks like a clown.

l'**aire de jeux** FEM NOUN
playground

★ l'**aire de repos** FEM NOUN
rest area (*on motorway*)

l'**aise** FEM NOUN
■ **être à l'aise** to be at ease □ Elle est à l'aise avec tout le monde. She's at ease with everybody.
■ **être mal à l'aise** to be ill at ease
■ **se mettre à l'aise** to make oneself comfortable

ait VERB ▷ *see* **avoir**

★ **ajouter** VERB [28]
to add

l'**alarme** FEM NOUN
alarm
□ donner l'alarme to raise the alarm

l'**Albanie** FEM NOUN
Albania

l'**album** MASC NOUN
album

★l'**alcool** MASC NOUN
alcohol
□ Je ne bois pas d'alcool. I don't drink alcohol.
■ **les alcools forts** spirits

★**alcoolisé** (FEM **alcoolisée**) ADJECTIVE
alcoholic
■ **une boisson non alcoolisée** a soft drink

les **alentours** MASC PL NOUN
■ **dans les alentours** in the area
■ **aux alentours de Paris** in the Paris area
■ **aux alentours de cinq heures** around 5 o'clock

l'**algèbre** FEM NOUN
algebra

Alger NOUN
Algiers

★l'**Algérie** FEM NOUN
Algeria

★**algérien** (FEM **algérienne**) ADJECTIVE, NOUN
Algerian
■ **un Algérien** an Algerian (*man*)
■ **une Algérienne** an Algerian (*woman*)

l'**algue** FEM NOUN
seaweed

l'**aliment** MASC NOUN
food

★l'**alimentation** FEM NOUN
1 groceries
□ le rayon alimentation du supermarché the grocery department in the supermarket
2 diet
□ Elle a une alimentation saine. She has a healthy diet.

★l'**allée** FEM NOUN
1 path
□ les allées du parc the paths in the park
2 drive (*in street names*)
■ **les allées et venues** comings and goings

allégé (FEM **allégée**) ADJECTIVE
low-fat
□ un yaourt allégé a low-fat yoghurt

★l'**Allemagne** FEM NOUN
Germany
■ **en Allemagne** 1 in Germany 2 to Germany

★**allemand** (FEM **allemande**) ADJECTIVE, NOUN
German
□ Elle parle allemand. She speaks German.
■ **un Allemand** a German (*man*)
■ **une Allemande** a German (*woman*)
■ **les Allemands** the Germans

★**aller** VERB [3, *aux* **être**]

PRESENT TENSE	
je vais	nous allons
tu vas	vous allez
il/elle va	ils/elles vont
PAST PARTICIPLE	
allé	

▷ *see also* **aller** NOUN
to go
□ Je suis allé à Londres. I went to London. □ Je dois y aller. I've got to go. □ Elle ira le voir. She'll go and see him. □ Je vais me fâcher. I'm going to get angry.
■ **s'en aller** to go away □ Je m'en vais demain. I'm going tomorrow.
■ **aller bien à quelqu'un** to suit somebody □ Cette robe te va bien. This dress suits you.
■ **Allez! Dépêche-toi!** Come on! Hurry up!
■ **Comment allez-vous? — Je vais bien.** How are you? — I'm fine.
■ **Comment ça va? — Ça va bien.** How are you? — I'm fine.
■ **aller mieux** to be better

★l'**aller** MASC NOUN
▷ *see also* **aller** VERB
1 outward journey
□ L'aller nous a pris trois heures. The journey there took us three hours.
2 single (*ticket*)
□ Je voudrais un aller pour Angers. I'd like a single to Angers.
■ **un aller simple** a single
■ **un aller retour** 1 a return ticket □ Je voudrais un aller retour pour Londres. I'd like a return to London. 2 a round trip □ Il a fait l'aller retour en dix heures. He did the round trip in ten hours.

allergique (FEM **allergique**) ADJECTIVE
■ **allergique à** allergic to □ Je suis allergique aux poils de chat. I'm allergic to cat hair.

★**allô** EXCLAMATION
hello!
□ Allô! Je voudrais parler à Monsieur Simon. Hello! I'd like to speak to Mr Simon.

> **allô** is only used when talking to someone on the phone.

★l'**allocation** FEM NOUN
allowance
■ **les allocations chômage** unemployment benefit

s'**allonger** VERB [45]
to lie down
□ Il s'est allongé sur son lit. He lay down on his bed.

★**allumer** VERB [28]
1 to switch on
□ Tu peux allumer la lumière? Can you switch the light on? □ Allume la radio. Switch on the radio.
2 to light
□ Elle a allumé une cigarette. She lit a cigarette.
■ **s'allumer** (*light*) to come on □ La lumière s'est allumée. The light came on.

★ l'**allumette** FEM NOUN
match
□ une boîte d'allumettes a box of matches

l'**allure** FEM NOUN
1 speed
□ à toute allure at top speed
2 look
□ avoir une drôle d'allure to look odd

l'**allusion** FEM NOUN
reference

★ **alors** ADVERB
1 then
□ Tu as fini? Alors je m'en vais. Have you finished? I'm going then.
2 so
□ Alors je lui ai dit de partir. So I told him to leave.
■ **Et alors?** So what?
3 at that time
□ Il habitait alors à Paris. He was living in Paris at that time.
■ **alors que** 1 as □ Il est arrivé alors que je partais. He arrived just as I was leaving.
2 while □ Alors que je travaillais dur, lui se reposait. While I was working hard, he was resting.

★ les **Alpes** FEM PL NOUN
Alps
□ dans les Alpes in the Alps

l'**alphabet** MASC NOUN
alphabet

alphabétique (FEM **alphabétique**) ADJECTIVE
alphabetical
□ par ordre alphabétique in alphabetical order

★ l'**alpinisme** MASC NOUN
mountaineering

l'**alpiniste** MASC/FEM NOUN
mountaineer

l'**Alsace** FEM NOUN
Alsace

l'**amande** FEM NOUN
almond
■ **la pâte d'amande** marzipan

l'**amant** MASC NOUN
lover

★ **amateur** (FEM **amatrice**) ADJECTIVE
▷ *see also* **amateur** NOUN
amateur
□ Elle est pianiste amateur. She's an amateur pianist.

★ l'**amateur** MASC NOUN
▷ *see also* **amateur** ADJECTIVE
amateur
■ **en amateur** as a hobby □ Il fait de la photo en amateur. He takes photos as a hobby.
■ **C'est un amateur de musique.** He's a music lover.

★ l'**amatrice** FEM NOUN
▷ *see also* **amateur** ADJECTIVE
amateur

l'**ambassade** FEM NOUN
embassy

l'**ambassadeur** MASC NOUN
ambassador

★ l'**ambiance** FEM NOUN
atmosphere
□ Je n'aime pas l'ambiance ici. I don't like the atmosphere here. □ Il y a de l'ambiance dans ce café. This café has a lively atmosphere.
■ **la musique d'ambiance** background music

ambitieux (FEM **ambitieuse**) ADJECTIVE
ambitious

★ l'**ambition** FEM NOUN
ambition
□ Il a l'ambition de devenir Premier ministre. His ambition is to be Prime Minister.
■ **Il a beaucoup d'ambition.** He's very ambitious.

★ l'**ambulance** FEM NOUN
ambulance

l'**âme** FEM NOUN
soul

★ l'**amélioration** FEM NOUN
improvement

★ **améliorer** VERB [28]
to improve
■ **s'améliorer** to improve □ Le temps s'améliore. The weather's improving.

★ l'**amende** FEM NOUN
fine
□ une amende de cinquante euros a 50 euro fine

★ **amener** VERB [43]
to bring
□ Qu'est-ce qui t'amène? What brings you here? □ Est-ce que je peux amener un ami? Can I bring a friend?

★ **amer** (FEM **amère**) ADJECTIVE
bitter

★ **américain** (FEM **américaine**) ADJECTIVE, NOUN
American
■ **un Américain** an American (*man*)
■ **une Américaine** an American (*woman*)

★ l'**Amérique** FEM NOUN
America
■ **en Amérique** 1 in America 2 to America
■ **l'Amérique du Nord** North America
■ **l'Amérique du Sud** South America

★ l'**ami** MASC NOUN
friend
■ **C'est son petit ami.** He's her boyfriend.

■ **ajouter quelqu'un à sa liste d'amis** to friend somebody (*social networks*)
■ **supprimer quelqu'un de sa liste d'amis** to unfriend somebody (*social networks*)

★ **amical** (FEM **amicale**, MASC PL **amicaux**) ADJECTIVE
friendly

★ **amicalement** ADVERB
in a friendly way
■ **Amicalement, Pierre.** (*in letter*) Best wishes, Pierre.

★ l'**amie** FEM NOUN
friend
■ **C'est sa petite amie.** She's his girlfriend.

★ l'**amitié** FEM NOUN
friendship
■ **Fais mes amitiés à Paul.** Give my regards to Paul.
■ **Amitiés, Lucie.** (*in letter*) Best wishes, Lucie.

★ l'**amour** MASC NOUN
love
■ **faire l'amour** to make love

amoureux (FEM **amoureuse**) ADJECTIVE
in love
□ être amoureux de quelqu'un to be in love with somebody

l'**amour-propre** MASC NOUN
self-esteem

l'**amphithéâtre** MASC NOUN
lecture theatre

amplement ADVERB
■ **Nous avons amplement le temps.** We have plenty of time.

★ l'**ampoule** FEM NOUN
1 light bulb
2 blister
□ J'ai une ampoule au pied. I've got a blister on my foot.

★ **amusant** (FEM **amusante**) ADJECTIVE
amusing

les **amuse-bouches** MASC PL NOUN
party nibbles

★ **amuser** VERB [28]
to amuse
■ **s'amuser** 1 to play □ Les enfants s'amusent dehors. The children are playing outside. 2 to enjoy oneself □ On s'est bien amusés. We really enjoyed ourselves.

★ l'**an** MASC NOUN
year
■ **le premier de l'an** New Year's Day
■ **le nouvel an** New Year

l'**analyse** FEM NOUN
1 analysis
2 test (*medical*)
□ une analyse de sang a blood test

★ l'**ananas** MASC NOUN
pineapple

l'**ancêtre** MASC/FEM NOUN
ancestor

l'**anchois** (PL les **anchois**) MASC NOUN
anchovy

★ **ancien** (FEM **ancienne**) ADJECTIVE
1 former
□ C'est une ancienne élève. She's a former pupil.
2 old
□ notre ancienne voiture our old car
3 antique
□ un fauteuil ancien an antique chair

l'**ancre** FEM NOUN
anchor

Andorre FEM NOUN
Andorra

l'**âne** MASC NOUN
donkey

l'**ange** MASC NOUN
angel
■ **être aux anges** to be over the moon

l'**angine** FEM NOUN
throat infection

★ **anglais** (FEM **anglaise**) ADJECTIVE, NOUN
English
□ Est-ce que vous parlez anglais? Do you speak English?
■ **un Anglais** an Englishman
■ **une Anglaise** an Englishwoman
■ **les Anglais** the English

l'**angle** MASC NOUN
1 angle
□ un angle droit a right angle
2 corner
□ à l'angle de la rue at the corner of the street

★ l'**Angleterre** FEM NOUN
England
■ **en Angleterre** 1 in England □ J'habite en Angleterre. I live in England. 2 to England □ Je suis allée en Angleterre le mois dernier. I went to England last month.

anglo- PREFIX
anglo-
■ **les îles Anglo-Normandes** the Channel Islands

anglophone (FEM **anglophone**) ADJECTIVE
English-speaking

angoissé (FEM **angoissée**) ADJECTIVE
stressed
□ Il a l'air angoissé. He looks stressed.

★ l'**animal** (PL les **animaux**) MASC NOUN
animal

★ l'**animateur** MASC NOUN
1 host
□ Il est animateur à la télé. He's a TV host.

French-English

a

2 youth leader
□ Pierre est animateur au centre sportif. Pierre is a youth leader at the sports centre.

★ l'**animatrice** FEM NOUN
1 host
□ Elle est animatrice à la télé. She's a TV host.
2 youth leader
□ Cécile est animatrice au centre sportif. Cécile is a youth leader at the sports centre.

★ **animé** (FEM **animée**) ADJECTIVE
lively
□ Cette rue est très animée. This is a very lively street.
■ **un dessin animé** a cartoon

l'**anis** MASC NOUN
aniseed

l'**anneau** (PL les **anneaux**) MASC NOUN
ring

★ l'**année** FEM NOUN
year
□ l'année dernière last year □ l'année prochaine next year

★ l'**anniversaire** MASC NOUN
1 birthday
□ C'est l'anniversaire de Marion. It's Marion's birthday.
2 anniversary
□ un anniversaire de mariage a wedding anniversary

★ l'**annonce** FEM NOUN
advert
□ J'ai lu votre annonce dans le journal. I saw your advert in the newspaper. □ passer une annonce to place an advert
■ **les petites annonces** the small ads

★ **annoncer** VERB [12]
to announce
□ Ils ont annoncé leurs fiançailles. They've announced their engagement.

★ l'**annuaire** MASC NOUN
phone book

★ **annuel** (FEM **annuelle**) ADJECTIVE
annual

★ **annuler** VERB [28]
to cancel

★ **anonyme** (FEM **anonyme**) ADJECTIVE
anonymous

★ l'**anorak** MASC NOUN
anorak

l'**Antarctique** MASC NOUN
Antarctic

★ l'**antenne** FEM NOUN
1 aerial
■ **antenne parabolique** satellite dish
■ **être à l'antenne** to be on the air
2 antenna

l'**antibiotique** MASC NOUN
antibiotic

l'**antidépresseur** MASC NOUN
antidepressant
□ Elle est sous antidépresseurs depuis un mois. She's been on antidepressants for a month.

l'**antigel** MASC NOUN
antifreeze

les **Antilles** FEM PL NOUN
West Indies
■ **aux Antilles** 1 in the West Indies 2 to the West Indies

antipathique (FEM **antipathique**) ADJECTIVE
unpleasant
□ Je le trouve plutôt antipathique. I find him rather unpleasant.

antipelliculaire (FEM **antipelliculaire**) ADJECTIVE
■ **shampooing antipelliculaire** anti-dandruff shampoo

l'**antiquaire** MASC/FEM NOUN
antique dealer
□ Elle est antiquaire. She's an antique dealer.

l'**antiquité** FEM NOUN
antique
□ un magasin d'antiquités an antique shop
■ **pendant l'Antiquité** in classical times

★ **antiseptique** (FEM **antiseptique**) ADJECTIVE
▷ *see also* **antiseptique** NOUN
antiseptic

★ l'**antiseptique** MASC NOUN
▷ *see also* **antiseptique** ADJECTIVE
antiseptic

antivirus MASC NOUN
antivirus (program)

l'**antivol** MASC NOUN
1 lock (*on bike*)
2 steering lock (*on car*)

anxieux (FEM **anxieuse**) ADJECTIVE
anxious
■ **Il est anxieux de nature.** He's a born worrier.

★ **août** MASC NOUN
August
■ **en août** in August

★ **apercevoir** VERB [67]
to see
□ J'aperçois la côte. I can see the shore.
■ **s'apercevoir de quelque chose** to notice something
■ **s'apercevoir que ...** to notice that ...

★ l'**apéritif** MASC NOUN
aperitif
□ Venez donc prendre l'apéritif ce soir! Come round for drinks this evening!

 Numbers in brackets refer to verb tables on pages 650 to 658

apparaître VERB [56]
to appear

★ l'**appareil** MASC NOUN
device
■ **un appareil dentaire** a brace (*for teeth*)
■ **les appareils ménagers** domestic appliances
■ **un appareil photo** a camera
■ **Qui est à l'appareil?** Who's speaking? (*on phone*)

apparemment ADVERB
apparently

l'**apparence** FEM NOUN
appearance

l'**apparition** FEM NOUN
appearance
□ Il n'a fait qu'une brève apparition. He only appeared briefly.

★ l'**appartement** MASC NOUN
flat

★ **appartenir** VERB [83]
■ **appartenir à quelqu'un** to belong to somebody

apparu VERB ▷ *see* **apparaître**

★ l'**appel** MASC NOUN
1 cry
□ un appel au secours a cry for help
2 phone call
■ **faire appel à quelqu'un** to appeal to somebody
■ **faire l'appel** to call the register (*in school*)
■ **faire un appel de phares** to flash one's headlights

★ **appeler** VERB [4]
to call
□ Elle a appelé le médecin. She called the doctor. □ J'ai appelé Richard à Londres. I called Richard in London.
■ **s'appeler** to be called □ Comment ça s'appelle? What is it called?
■ **Elle s'appelle Muriel.** Her name's Muriel.
■ **Comment tu t'appelles?** What's your name?

l'**appendicite** FEM NOUN
appendicitis

★ **appétissant** (FEM **appétissante**) ADJECTIVE
appetizing

★ l'**appétit** MASC NOUN
appetite
■ **Bon appétit!** Enjoy your meal!

applaudir VERB [38]
to clap (*applaud*)

les **applaudissements** MASC PL NOUN
applause *sing*

l'**appli** FEM NOUN
app

appliquer VERB [28]
1 to apply
2 to enforce
□ appliquer la loi to enforce the law
■ **s'appliquer** to apply oneself

★ **apporter** VERB [28]
to bring

★ **apprécier** VERB [19]
to appreciate

appréhender VERB [28]
to dread
□ J'appréhende cet examen. I'm dreading this exam.

★ **apprendre** VERB [65]
1 to learn
□ apprendre quelque chose par cœur to learn something by heart
■ **apprendre à faire quelque chose** to learn to do something □ J'apprends à faire la cuisine. I'm learning to cook.
2 to hear
□ J'ai appris son départ. I heard that she had left.
■ **apprendre quelque chose à quelqu'un**
1 to teach somebody something □ Ma mère m'a appris l'anglais. My mother taught me English. □ Elle lui a appris à conduire. She taught him to drive. **2** to tell somebody something □ Vincent m'a appris la nouvelle. Vincent told me the news.

★ l'**apprentissage** MASC NOUN
learning
□ On dit que l'apprentissage de l'arabe est très difficile. Learning Arabic is said to be very difficult.

appris VERB ▷ *see* **apprendre**

l'**approbation** FEM NOUN
approval
□ donner son approbation to give one's approval

★ **approcher** VERB [28]
■ **approcher de** to approach □ Nous approchons de Paris. We are approaching Paris.
■ **s'approcher de** to come closer to □ Ne t'approche pas, j'ai la grippe! Don't come too close to me, I've got flu!

★ **approprié** (FEM **appropriée**) ADJECTIVE
suitable
□ une tenue appropriée suitable clothes

★ **approuver** VERB [28]
to approve of
□ Je n'approuve pas ses méthodes. I don't approve of his methods.

approximatif (FEM **approximative**) ADJECTIVE
1 approximate
□ un prix approximatif an approximate price

2 rough
□ un calcul approximatif a rough calculation

l'**appui** MASC NOUN
support
□ J'ai besoin de votre appui. I need your support.

★ **appuyer** VERB [53]
1 to press
□ appuyer sur un bouton to press a button
2 to lean
□ Elle a appuyé son vélo contre la porte. She leaned her bike against the door.
■ **s'appuyer** to lean □ Elle s'est appuyée contre le mur. She leaned against the wall. □ Il s'est appuyé sur la table. He leaned on the table.

★ **après** PREPOSITION, ADVERB
1 after
□ après le déjeuner after lunch □ après son départ after he had left □ après qu'il est parti after he left □ Nous viendrons après avoir fait la vaisselle. We'll come after we've done the dishes.
2 afterwards
□ aussitôt après immediately afterwards
■ **après coup** afterwards □ J'y ai repensé après coup. I thought about it again afterwards.
■ **d'après** according to □ D'après lui, c'est une erreur. According to him, that's a mistake.
■ **après tout** after all

★ **après-demain** ADVERB
the day after tomorrow

★ l'**après-midi** MASC/FEM NOUN
afternoon

★ l'**après-rasage** MASC NOUN
aftershave

l'**aquarium** MASC NOUN
aquarium

arabe (FEM **arabe**) ADJECTIVE, NOUN
1 Arab
□ les pays arabes the Arab countries
2 Arabic
□ la littérature arabe Arabic literature □ Il parle arabe. He speaks Arabic.
■ **un Arabe** an Arab (*man*)
■ **une Arabe** an Arab (*woman*)

l'**Arabie Saoudite** FEM NOUN
Saudi Arabia

l'**araignée** FEM NOUN
spider

★ l'**arbitre** MASC NOUN
1 referee
2 umpire

★ l'**arbre** MASC NOUN
tree
■ **un arbre généalogique** a family tree

l'**arbuste** MASC NOUN
shrub

l'**arc** MASC NOUN
bow
□ son arc et ses flèches his bow and arrows

l'**arc-en-ciel** (PL les **arcs-en-ciel**) MASC NOUN
rainbow

l'**archéologie** FEM NOUN
archaeology

l'**archéologue** MASC/FEM NOUN
archaeologist
□ Elle est archéologue. She's an archaeologist.

l'**archipel** MASC NOUN
archipelago

★ l'**architecte** MASC/FEM NOUN
architect
□ Elle est architecte. She's an architect.

l'**architecture** FEM NOUN
architecture

l'**Arctique** MASC NOUN
Arctic

l'**ardoise** FEM NOUN
slate

l'**arène** FEM NOUN
bullring
■ **des arènes romaines** a Roman amphitheatre
■ **l'arène politique** the political arena

l'**arête** FEM NOUN
fish bone

★ l'**argent** MASC NOUN
1 silver
□ une bague en argent a silver ring
2 money
□ Je n'ai plus d'argent. I haven't got any more money.
■ **l'argent de poche** pocket money
■ **l'argent liquide** cash

argentin (FEM **argentine**) ADJECTIVE, NOUN
Argentinian
■ **un Argentin** an Argentinian (*man*)
■ **une Argentine** an Argentinian (*woman*)

l'**Argentine** FEM NOUN
Argentina

l'**argile** FEM NOUN
clay

l'**argot** MASC NOUN
slang

★ l'**arme** FEM NOUN
weapon
■ **une arme à feu** a firearm

★ l'**armée** FEM NOUN
army
■ **l'armée de l'air** the Air Force

l'**armistice** MASC NOUN
armistice

★ l'**armoire** FEM NOUN
wardrobe

l'**armure** FEM NOUN
armour
□ un chevalier en armure a knight in armour

arnaquer VERB [28] (*informal*)
to con

l'**arobase** FEM NOUN
@ symbol
■ **Mon adresse e-mail, c'est 'lola arobase europost point fr'.** My email address is 'lola@europost.fr'.

aromatisé (FEM **aromatisée**) ADJECTIVE
flavoured

l'**arôme** MASC NOUN
1 aroma
2 flavouring (*added to food*)

arpenter VERB [28]
to pace up and down
□ Il arpentait le couloir. He was pacing up and down the corridor.

arrache-pied
■ **d'arrache-pied** ADVERB furiously
□ travailler d'arrache-pied to work furiously

arracher VERB [28]
1 to take out
□ Le dentiste m'a arraché une dent. The dentist took one of my teeth out.
2 to tear out
□ Arrachez la page. Tear the page out.
3 to pull up
□ Elle a arraché les mauvaises herbes. She pulled up the weeds.
■ **arracher quelque chose à quelqu'un** to snatch something from somebody

★ **arranger** VERB [45]
1 to arrange
□ arranger des fleurs dans un vase to arrange flowers in a vase
2 to suit
□ Ça m'arrange de partir plus tôt. It suits me to leave earlier.
■ **s'arranger** to come to an agreement
□ Arrangez-vous avec le patron. You'll have to come to an agreement with the boss.
■ **Je vais m'arranger pour venir.** I'll organize things so that I can come.
■ **Ça va s'arranger.** Things will work themselves out.

l'**arrestation** FEM NOUN
arrest
□ en état d'arrestation under arrest

★ l'**arrêt** MASC NOUN
stop
□ un arrêt de bus a bus stop
■ **sans arrêt** 1 non-stop □ Elle travaille sans arrêt. She works non-stop. 2 continually □ Ils se disputent sans arrêt. They quarrel continually.

★ **arrêter** VERB [28]
1 to stop
■ **Arrête!** Stop it!
■ **arrêter de faire quelque chose** to stop doing something
2 to switch off
□ Il a arrêté le moteur. He switched the engine off.
3 to arrest
□ Mon voisin a été arrêté. My neighbour's been arrested.
■ **s'arrêter** to stop □ Elle s'est arrêtée devant une vitrine. She stopped in front of a shop window.
■ **s'arrêter de faire quelque chose** to stop doing something □ Il s'est arrêté de fumer. He stopped smoking.

★ les **arrhes** FEM PL NOUN
deposit *sing*
□ verser des arrhes to pay a deposit

★ l'**arrière** MASC NOUN
▷ *see also* **arrière** ADJECTIVE
back
□ l'arrière de la maison the back of the house
■ **à l'arrière** at the back
■ **en arrière** behind □ Ils sont restés en arrière. They stayed behind.

★ **arrière** (FEM+PL **arrière**) ADJECTIVE
▷ *see also* **arrière** NOUN
back
□ le siège arrière the back seat □ les roues arrière the rear wheels

l'**arrière-grand-mère** (PL les **arrière-grands-mères**) FEM NOUN
great-grandmother

l'**arrière-grand-père** (PL les **arrière-grands-pères**) MASC NOUN
great-grandfather

★ l'**arrivée** FEM NOUN
arrival

★ **arriver** VERB [5, *aux* **être**]
1 to arrive
□ J'arrive à l'école à huit heures. I arrive at school at 8 o'clock.
2 to happen
□ Qu'est-ce qui est arrivé à Thomas? What happened to Thomas?
■ **arriver à faire quelque chose** to manage to do something □ J'espère que je vais y arriver. I hope I'll manage it.
■ **Il m'arrive de dormir jusqu'à midi.** I sometimes sleep till midday.

arrogant (FEM **arrogante**) ADJECTIVE
arrogant

★ l'**arrondissement** MASC NOUN
district

DID YOU KNOW...?
Paris, Lyon and Marseille are divided into numbered districts called **arrondissements**.

★ **arroser** VERB [28]
to water
□ Daphné arrose ses tomates. Daphné is watering her tomatoes.
■ **Ils ont arrosé leur victoire.** They had a drink to celebrate their victory.

l'**arrosoir** MASC NOUN
watering can

l'**art** MASC NOUN
art

l'**artère** FEM NOUN
1 artery
2 thoroughfare
■ **les grandes artères de Paris** the main roads of Paris

l'**artichaut** MASC NOUN
artichoke

★ l'**article** MASC NOUN
1 article
□ un article de journal a newspaper article
2 item
□ les articles en promotion items on special offer

l'**articulation** FEM NOUN
joint
□ l'articulation du genou the knee joint

articuler VERB [28]
to pronounce clearly

artificiel (FEM **artificielle**) ADJECTIVE
artificial

l'**artisan** MASC NOUN
self-employed craftsman

★ l'**artiste** MASC/FEM NOUN
1 artist
2 performer

artistique (FEM **artistique**) ADJECTIVE
artistic

as VERB ▷ *see* **avoir**
▷ *see also* **as** NOUN
■ **Tu as de beaux cheveux.** You've got nice hair.

l'**as** MASC NOUN
▷ *see also* **as** VERB
ace
□ l'as de trèfle the ace of clubs

★ l'**ascenseur** MASC NOUN
lift

l'**Ascension** FEM NOUN
Ascension

asiatique (FEM **asiatique**) ADJECTIVE
Asiatic
■ **la cuisine asiatique** Oriental cooking
■ **le Sud-Est asiatique** South East Asia

★ l'**Asie** FEM NOUN
Asia
■ **en Asie** 1 in Asia 2 to Asia

l'**aspect** MASC NOUN
appearance

l'**asperge** FEM NOUN
asparagus

★ l'**aspirateur** MASC NOUN
vacuum cleaner
■ **passer l'aspirateur** to vacuum

★ l'**aspirine** FEM NOUN
aspirin

assaisonner VERB [28]
to season

l'**assassin** MASC NOUN
murderer

assassiner VERB [28]
to murder

assembler VERB [28]
to assemble
■ **s'assembler** to gather □ Une foule énorme s'était assemblée. A huge crowd had gathered.

★ s'**asseoir** VERB [6]
to sit down
□ Asseyez-vous! Sit down! □ Assieds-toi! Sit down!

★ **assez** ADVERB
1 enough
□ Nous n'avons pas assez de temps. We don't have enough time. □ Est-ce qu'il y a assez de pain? Is there enough bread?
■ **J'en ai assez!** I've had enough!
2 quite
□ Il faisait assez beau. The weather was quite nice.

★ l'**assiette** FEM NOUN
plate
□ une assiette creuse a soup plate □ une assiette à dessert a dessert plate
■ **une assiette anglaise** assorted cold meats

★ **assis** (FEM **assise**) ADJECTIVE
sitting
□ Il est assis par terre. He's sitting on the floor.

★ **assis** VERB ▷ *see* **asseoir**

l'**assistance** FEM NOUN
1 audience
□ Y a-t-il un médecin dans l'assistance? Is there a doctor in the audience?
2 aid
□ l'assistance humanitaire humanitarian aid
3 assistance
□ avec l'assistance de quelqu'un with the assistance of somebody

l'**assistant** MASC NOUN
assistant
□ Il était assistant d'anglais à Tourcoing. He

was an English assistant in Tourcoing.
■ **un assistant social** a social worker

l'**assistante** FEM NOUN
assistant
□ Elle est assistante de français à Oxford. She's a French assistant in Oxford.
■ **une assistante sociale** a social worker

★ **assister** VERB [28]
■ **assister à un accident** to witness an accident
■ **assister à un cours** to attend a class
■ **assister à un concert** to be at a concert

l'**association** FEM NOUN
association

l'**associé** MASC NOUN
partner (*in business*)

l'**associée** FEM NOUN
partner (*in business*)

s'**associer** VERB [19]
to go into partnership

assommer VERB [28]
to knock out
□ Il l'a assommé avec une bouteille. He knocked him out with a bottle.

l'**Assomption** FEM NOUN
Assumption

assorti (FEM **assortie**) ADJECTIVE
1 matching
□ des couleurs assorties matching colours
2 assorted
□ des chocolats assortis assorted chocolates
■ **être assorti à quelque chose** to match something □ Son sac assorti à ses chaussures. Her bag matches her shoes.

l'**assortiment** MASC NOUN
assortment

★ l'**assurance** FEM NOUN
1 insurance
□ une assurance maladie medical insurance
2 confidence
□ parler avec assurance to speak with confidence

★ **assurer** VERB [28]
1 to insure
□ La maison est assurée. The house is insured. □ être assuré contre quelque chose to be insured against something
2 to assure
□ Je t'assure que c'est vrai! I assure you it's true!
■ **s'assurer de quelque chose** to make sure of something □ Il s'est assuré que la porte était fermée. He made sure the door was shut.

l'**asthme** MASC NOUN
asthma
□ une crise d'asthme an asthma attack

l'**astronaute** MASC/FEM NOUN
astronaut

l'**astronomie** FEM NOUN
astronomy

astucieux (FEM **astucieuse**) ADJECTIVE
clever

★ l'**atelier** MASC NOUN
1 workshop
2 studio (*artist's*)

Athènes NOUN
Athens

l'**athlète** MASC/FEM NOUN
athlete

★ l'**athlétisme** MASC NOUN
athletics
□ un championnat d'athlétisme an athletics championship

★ l'**Atlantique** MASC NOUN
Atlantic

l'**atlas** MASC NOUN
atlas

l'**atmosphère** FEM NOUN
atmosphere

atomique (FEM **atomique**) ADJECTIVE
atomic
□ la bombe atomique the atomic bomb

l'**atout** MASC NOUN
1 asset
□ L'atout principal de ce joueur, c'est sa vitesse. This player's main asset is his speed.
2 trump card
□ J'avais quatre atouts dans mon jeu. I had four trump cards in my hand.

atroce (FEM **atroce**) ADJECTIVE
terrible

attachant (FEM **attachante**) ADJECTIVE
lovable

★ **attacher** VERB [28]
to tie up
□ Elle a attaché ses cheveux avec un élastique. She tied her hair up with an elastic band.
■ **s'attacher à quelqu'un** to become attached to somebody
■ **une poêle qui n'attache pas** a non-stick frying pan

★ **attaquer** VERB [28]
to attack

atteindre VERB [60]
to reach

★ **attendant**
■ **en attendant** ADVERB in the meantime

★ **attendre** VERB [7]
to wait
□ attendre quelqu'un to wait for someone
□ J'attends d'avoir un appartement à moi. I'm waiting until I've got a flat of my own.

★ = core vocabulary

French-English

a

□ Attends qu'il ne pleuve plus. Wait until it's stopped raining.
■ **attendre un enfant** to be expecting a baby
■ **s'attendre à** to expect □ Je m'attends à une surprise. I'm expecting a surprise.

BE CAREFUL!
attendre does not mean **to attend**.

l'**attentat** MASC NOUN
■ **un attentat à la bombe** a terrorist bombing

l'**attente** FEM NOUN
wait
□ deux heures d'attente two hours' wait
■ **la salle d'attente** the waiting room

attentif (FEM **attentive**) ADJECTIVE
attentive

★ l'**attention** FEM NOUN
attention
□ à l'attention de for the attention of
■ **faire attention** to be careful
■ **Attention!** Watch out! □ Attention, tu vas te faire écraser! Watch out, you'll get run over!

attentionné (FEM **attentionnée**) ADJECTIVE
thoughtful

★ **atterrir** VERB [38]
to land

l'**atterrissage** MASC NOUN
landing (*of plane*)

attirant (FEM **attirante**) ADJECTIVE
attractive

★ **attirer** VERB [28]
to attract
□ attirer l'attention de quelqu'un to attract somebody's attention
■ **s'attirer des ennuis** to get into trouble □ Si tu continues, tu vas t'attirer des ennuis. If you keep on like that, you'll get yourself into trouble.

l'**attitude** FEM NOUN
attitude

l'**attraction** FEM NOUN
■ **un parc d'attractions** an amusement park

★ **attraper** VERB [28]
to catch

attrayant (FEM **attrayante**) ADJECTIVE
attractive

attrister VERB [28]
to sadden

★ **au** PREPOSITION ▷ *see* **à**

au is the contracted form of **à** + **le**.

□ au printemps in the spring

l'**aube** FEM NOUN
dawn
□ à l'aube at dawn

★ l'**auberge** FEM NOUN
inn
■ **une auberge de jeunesse** a youth hostel

l'**aubergine** FEM NOUN
aubergine

★ **aucun** (FEM **aucune**) ADJECTIVE, PRONOUN
1 no
□ Il n'a aucun ami. He's got no friends.
□ Aucun enfant ne pourrait le faire. No child could do that.
2 none
□ Aucun d'entre eux n'est venu. None of them came. □ Aucune de mes amies n'aime le foot. None of my female friends like football. □ Tu aimes ses films? — Je n'en ai vu aucun. Do you like his films? — I haven't seen any of them.
■ **sans aucun doute** without any doubt

au-delà ADVERB
■ **au-delà de** beyond □ Votre ticket n'est pas valable au-delà de cette limite. Your ticket is not valid beyond this point.

★ **au-dessous** ADVERB
1 downstairs
□ Ils habitent au-dessous. They live downstairs.
2 underneath
■ **au-dessous de** under □ au-dessous du pont under the bridge
■ **dix degrés au-dessous de zéro** ten degrees below zero

★ **au-dessus** ADVERB
1 upstairs
□ J'habite au-dessus. I live upstairs.
2 above
■ **au-dessus de** above □ au-dessus de la table above the table

audiovisuel (FEM **audiovisuelle**) ADJECTIVE
audiovisual

l'**auditeur** MASC NOUN
listener (*to radio*)

l'**auditrice** FEM NOUN
listener (*to radio*)

★ l'**augmentation** FEM NOUN
rise

★ **augmenter** VERB [28]
to increase

★ **aujourd'hui** ADVERB
today
□ Il travaille aujourd'hui. He's working today.

★ **auparavant** ADVERB
first
□ Vous pouvez utiliser l'ordinateur, mais auparavant vous devez taper le mot de passe. You can use the computer, but first you have to key in the password.

auquel (MASC PL **auxquels**, FEM PL **auxquelles**) PRONOUN

auquel is the contracted form of **à** + **lequel**.

□ l'homme auquel j'ai parlé the man I spoke to

aura, aurai, auras, aurez, aurons, auront VERB ▷ *see* **avoir**

l'**aurore** FEM NOUN
daybreak

ausculter VERB [28]
■ **Le médecin l'a ausculté.** The doctor listened to his chest.

★**aussi** ADVERB
1 too
□ Dors bien. — Toi aussi. Sleep well. — You too. □ Lui aussi parle espagnol. He speaks Spanish too.
2 also
□ J'aimerais aussi que tu achètes le journal. I'd also like you to get the paper. □ Je parle français et aussi allemand. I speak French and also German.
■ **aussi ... que** as ... as □ aussi grand que moi as big as me

★**aussitôt** ADVERB
straight away
□ aussitôt après son retour straight after his return
■ **aussitôt que** as soon as □ aussitôt que tu auras fini as soon as you've finished

★l'**Australie** FEM NOUN
Australia
■ **en Australie** 1 in Australia 2 to Australia

★**australien** (FEM **australienne**) ADJECTIVE, NOUN
Australian
■ **un Australien** an Australian (*man*)
■ **une Australienne** an Australian (*woman*)

★**autant** ADVERB
■ **autant de** 1 so much □ Je ne veux pas autant de gâteau. I don't want so much cake. 2 so many □ Je n'ai jamais vu autant de monde. I've never seen so many people.
■ **autant que** as much as □ Elle travaille autant que moi. She works as much as I do.
■ **autant ... que** 1 as much ... as □ J'ai autant d'argent que toi. I've got as much money as you have. 2 as many ... as □ J'ai autant d'amis que lui. I've got as many friends as he has.
■ **d'autant plus que** all the more since □ Elle est d'autant plus déçue qu'il le lui avait promis. She's all the more disappointed since he had made her a promise.
■ **d'autant moins que** even less since
□ C'est d'autant moins pratique pour lui qu'il doit changer deux fois de train. It's even less convenient for him since he has to change trains twice.

★l'**auteur** MASC NOUN
author

★l'**auto** FEM NOUN
car

★l'**autobus** MASC NOUN
bus
□ en autobus by bus

★l'**autocar** MASC NOUN
coach
□ en autocar by coach

★**autocollant** (FEM **autocollante**) ADJECTIVE
▷ *see also* **autocollant** NOUN
self-adhesive
□ une étiquette autocollante a self-adhesive label
■ **une enveloppe autocollante** a self-seal envelope

★l'**autocollant** MASC NOUN
▷ *see also* **autocollant** ADJECTIVE
sticker

★l'**auto-école** FEM NOUN
driving school

automatique (FEM **automatique**) ADJECTIVE
automatic

★l'**automne** MASC NOUN
autumn
■ **en automne** in autumn

★**automobile** (FEM **automobile**) ADJECTIVE
▷ *see also* **automobile** NOUN
■ **une course automobile** a motor race

★l'**automobile** FEM NOUN
▷ *see also* **automobile** ADJECTIVE
car

★l'**automobiliste** MASC/FEM NOUN
motorist

l'**autoradio** MASC NOUN
car radio

l'**autorisation** FEM NOUN
1 permission
□ Il m'a donné l'autorisation de sortir ce soir. He's given me permission to go out tonight.
2 permit
□ Il faut une autorisation pour camper ici. You need a permit to camp here.

autoriser VERB [28]
to give permission for
□ Il m'a autorisé à en parler. He's given me permission to talk about it.

autoritaire (FEM **autoritaire**) ADJECTIVE
authoritarian

l'**autorité** FEM NOUN
authority

★l'**autoroute** FEM NOUN
motorway

★l'**auto-stop** MASC NOUN
■ **faire de l'auto-stop** to hitchhike

l'**auto-stoppeur** MASC NOUN
hitchhiker

l'**auto-stoppeuse** FEM NOUN
hitchhiker

★ **autour** ADVERB
around
□ autour de la maison around the house

★ **autre** (FEM **autre**) ADJECTIVE, PRONOUN
other
□ Je viendrai un autre jour. I'll come some other day. □ J'ai d'autres projets. I've got other plans.
▪ **autre chose** something else
▪ **autre part** somewhere else
▪ **un autre** another □ Tu veux un autre morceau de gâteau? Would you like another piece of cake?
▪ **l'autre** the other □ Non, pas celui-ci, l'autre. No, not that one, the other one.
▪ **d'autres** others □ Je t'en apporterai d'autres. I'll bring you some others.
▪ **les autres** the others □ Les autres sont arrivés plus tard. The others arrived later.
▪ **ni l'un ni l'autre** neither of them
▪ **entre autres** among other things □ Nous avons parlé, entre autres, de nos projets de vacances. We talked about our holiday plans, among other things.

★ **autrefois** ADVERB
in the old days

★ **autrement** ADVERB
1 differently
□ Il l'a fait autrement. He did it differently.
2 otherwise
□ Je n'ai pas pu faire autrement. I couldn't do otherwise.
▪ **autrement dit** in other words

★ l'**Autriche** FEM NOUN
Austria
▪ **en Autriche** **1** in Austria **2** to Austria

★ **autrichien** (FEM **autrichienne**) ADJECTIVE, NOUN
Austrian
▪ **un Autrichien** an Austrian (*man*)
▪ **une Autrichienne** an Austrian (*woman*)

l'**autruche** FEM NOUN
ostrich

★ **aux** PREPOSITION ▷ *see* **à**

> **aux** is the contracted form of **à** + **les**.

□ J'ai dit aux enfants d'aller jouer. I told the children to go and play.

auxquelles PL PRONOUN

> **auxquelles** is the contracted form of **à** + **lesquelles**.

□ les revues auxquelles il est abonné the [illegible] which he sub[illegible]es

auxquels PL PRONOUN

> **auxquels** is the contracted form of **à** + **lesquels**.

□ les enfants auxquels il a parlé the children he spoke to

avaient, avais, avait VERB ▷ *see* **avoir**
▪ **Il y avait beaucoup de monde.** There were lots of people.

l'**avalanche** FEM NOUN
avalanche

★ **avaler** VERB [28]
to swallow

★ l'**avance** FEM NOUN
▪ **être en avance** to be early
▪ **à l'avance** beforehand □ réserver longtemps à l'avance to book well beforehand
▪ **d'avance** in advance □ payer d'avance to pay in advance

avancé (FEM **avancée**) ADJECTIVE
advanced
□ à un niveau avancé at an advanced level
▪ **bien avancé** well under way □ Les travaux sont déjà bien avancés. The work is already well under way.

avancer VERB [12]
1 to move forward
□ Il avançait prudemment. He was moving forward cautiously.
2 to bring forward
□ La date de l'examen a été avancée. The date of the exam has been brought forward.
3 to put forward
□ Il a avancé sa montre d'une heure. He put his watch forward an hour.
4 to be fast (*watch*)
□ Ma montre avance d'une heure. My watch is an hour fast.
5 to lend
□ Peux-tu m'avancer dix euros? Can you lend me 10 euros?

★ **avant** (FEM+PL **avant**) PREPOSITION, ADJECTIVE
▷ *see also* **avant** NOUN
1 before
□ avant qu'il ne pleuve before it rains □ avant de partir before leaving
2 front
□ la roue avant the front wheel □ le siège avant the front seat
▪ **avant tout** above all

★ l'**avant** MASC NOUN
▷ *see also* **avant** PREPOSITION, ADJECTIVE
front
□ l'avant de la voiture the front of the car
▪ **à l'avant** in front
▪ **en avant** forward □ Il a fait un pas en avant. He took a step forward.

★ l'**avantage** MASC NOUN
advantage

l'**avant-bras** (PL les **avant-bras**) MASC NOUN
forearm

avant-dernier (FEM **avant-dernière**, MASC PL **avant-derniers**) ADJECTIVE
last but one
□ l'avant-dernière page the last page but one □ Ils sont arrivés avant-derniers. They arrived last but one.

★ **avant-hier** ADVERB
the day before yesterday
□ Il est arrivé avant-hier. He arrived the day before yesterday.

★ **avare** (FEM **avare**) ADJECTIVE
▷ *see also* **avare** NOUN
miserly

★ l'**avare** MASC/FEM NOUN
▷ *see also* **avare** ADJECTIVE
miser

★ **avec** PREPOSITION
with
□ avec mon père with my father
■ **Et avec ça?** Anything else? (*in shop*)

★ l'**avenir** MASC NOUN
future
■ **à l'avenir** in future □ À l'avenir, essayez d'être à l'heure. Try to be on time in future.
■ **dans un proche avenir** in the near future

★ l'**aventure** FEM NOUN
adventure

★ l'**avenue** FEM NOUN
avenue

★ l'**averse** FEM NOUN
shower (*of rain*)

★ **avertir** VERB [38]
to warn
■ **avertir quelqu'un de quelque chose** to warn somebody about something

★ l'**avertissement** MASC NOUN
warning

★ **aveugle** (FEM **aveugle**) ADJECTIVE
blind

★ l'**avion** MASC NOUN
plane
■ **aller en avion** to fly □ Il est allé en Italie en avion. He flew to Italy.
■ **par avion** by airmail

l'**aviron** MASC NOUN
rowing

★ l'**avis** MASC NOUN
1 opinion
□ J'aimerais avoir ton avis. I'd like to have your opinion.
■ **à mon avis** in my opinion
2 notice
□ jusqu'à nouvel avis until further notice
■ **changer d'avis** to change one's mind □ J'ai changé d'avis. I've changed my mind.

★ l'**avocat** MASC NOUN
1 lawyer
□ Il est avocat. He's a lawyer.
2 avocado

★ l'**avocate** FEM NOUN
lawyer
□ Elle est avocate. She's a lawyer.

l'**avoine** FEM NOUN
oats
□ les flocons d'avoine porridge oats

★ **avoir** VERB [8]

PRESENT TENSE	
j'ai	nous avons
tu as	vous avez
il/elle a	ils/elles ont
PAST PARTICIPLE	
eu	

1 to have
□ Ils ont deux enfants. They have two children. □ Il a les yeux bleus. He's got blue eyes. □ J'ai déjà mangé. I've already eaten. □ Est-ce que tu as vu ce film? Have you seen this film?
■ **Je lui ai parlé hier.** I spoke to him yesterday.
■ **On t'a bien eu!** (*informal*) You've been had!
2 to be
□ Il a trois ans. He's three. □ J'avais dix ans quand je l'ai rencontré. I was ten when I met him.
■ **il y a** **1** there is □ Il y a quelqu'un à la porte. There's somebody at the door. **2** there are □ Il y a des chocolats sur la table. There are some chocolates on the table. **3** ago □ Je l'ai rencontré il y a deux ans. I met him two years ago.
■ **Qu'est-ce qu'il y a?** What's the matter?
■ **Il n'y a qu'à partir plus tôt.** We'll just have to leave earlier.

l'**avortement** MASC NOUN
abortion

avouer VERB [28]
to admit

★ **avril** MASC NOUN
April
■ **en avril** in April

ayez, ayons VERB ▷ *see* **avoir**

Bb

le **baby-foot** MASC NOUN
table football
□ jouer au baby-foot to play table football

★ le **baby-sitting** MASC NOUN
■ **faire du baby-sitting** to babysit

★ le **bac** MASC NOUN = **baccalauréat**

★ le **baccalauréat** MASC NOUN
A levels
□ Elle a passé son baccalauréat l'année dernière. She did her A levels last year.

> **DID YOU KNOW...?**
> The French **baccalauréat**, or **bac** for short, is taken at the age of 17 or 18. Students have to sit one of a variety of set subject combinations, rather than being able to choose any combination of subjects they want. If you pass you have the right to a place at university.

bâcler VERB [28]
to botch up
□ Je déteste le travail bâclé! I hate botched work!

le **bagage** MASC NOUN
luggage
■ **faire ses bagages** to pack
■ **les bagages à main** hand luggage □ un bagage à main a piece of hand luggage

la **bagarre** FEM NOUN
fight
□ Une bagarre a éclaté à la fermeture du pub. A fight broke out when the pub closed.

se **bagarrer** VERB [28]
to fight
□ Il s'est encore bagarré avec son frère. He's been fighting with his brother again.

★ la **bagnole** FEM NOUN (*informal*)
car

★ la **bague** FEM NOUN
ring

★ la **baguette** FEM NOUN
1 stick of French bread
2 chopstick
□ manger avec des baguettes to eat with chopsticks
■ **une baguette magique** a magic wand

★ la **baie** FEM NOUN
bay

la **baignade** FEM NOUN
■ **'baignade interdite'** 'no swimming'

se **baigner** VERB [28]
to go swimming
□ Si on allait se baigner? Shall we go swimming?

★ la **baignoire** FEM NOUN
bath (*bathtub*)

bâiller VERB [28]
to yawn

★ le **bain** MASC NOUN
bath
□ prendre un bain to take a bath
■ **prendre un bain de soleil** to sunbathe

★ le **baiser** MASC NOUN
kiss

la **baisse** FEM NOUN
fall
□ la baisse du taux de chômage the fall in the unemployment rate
■ **être en baisse** to be falling
■ **revoir les chiffres à la baisse** to revise figures downwards

★ **baisser** VERB [28]
1 to turn down
□ Il fait moins froid, tu peux baisser le chauffage. It's not so cold, you can turn down the heating.
2 to fall
□ Le prix des jeux vidéo a baissé. The price of video games has fallen.
■ **se baisser** to bend down □ Il s'est baissé pour ramasser son mouchoir. He bent down to pick up his handkerchief.

★ le **bal** MASC NOUN
dance
□ un bal populaire a local dance

la **balade** FEM NOUN (*informal*)
walk
□ faire une balade to go for a walk

se **balader** VERB [28] (*informal*)
to wander around
□ J'adore me balader dans les rues de Paris. I love to wander around the streets of Paris.

★ le **baladeur** MASC NOUN
▪ **un baladeur numérique** an MP3 player

le **balai** MASC NOUN
broom
▪ **Je vais donner un coup de balai dans la cuisine.** I'm going to sweep the kitchen.

la **balance** FEM NOUN
scales *pl* (*for weighing*)
▪ **la Balance** Libra □ Todd est Balance. Todd is Libra.

se **balancer** VERB [12]
to swing

la **balançoire** FEM NOUN
swing

balayer VERB [59]
1 to sweep
□ Clément a balayé la cuisine. Clément swept the kitchen.
2 to sweep up
□ Va balayer les feuilles sur la terrasse. Go and sweep up the leaves on the terrace.

le **balayeur** MASC NOUN
roadsweeper

balbutier VERB [19]
to stammer

★ le **balcon** MASC NOUN
balcony

la **baleine** FEM NOUN
whale

★ la **balle** FEM NOUN
1 ball
□ une balle de tennis a tennis ball
2 bullet

la **ballerine** FEM NOUN
1 ballet dancer
2 ballet shoe
□ une paire de ballerines rouges a pair of red ballet shoes

le **ballet** MASC NOUN
ballet

★ le **ballon** MASC NOUN
1 ball
□ lancer le ballon to throw the ball
▪ **un ballon de foot** a football
2 balloon

balnéaire (FEM **balnéaire**) ADJECTIVE
▪ **une station balnéaire** a seaside resort

banal (FEM **banale**) ADJECTIVE
1 commonplace
□ La violence est devenue banale à la télévision. Violence has become commonplace on television.
2 hackneyed
□ L'intrigue du film est très banale. The plot of the film is very hackneyed.

★ la **banane** FEM NOUN
1 banana
2 bumbag
□ Mes clés sont dans ma banane. My keys are in my bumbag.

★ le **banc** MASC NOUN
bench

★ **bancaire** (FEM **bancaire**) ADJECTIVE
▪ **une carte bancaire** a bank card

le **bandage** MASC NOUN
bandage

★ la **bande** FEM NOUN
1 gang
□ une bande de voyous a gang of louts
2 bunch
□ C'est une bande d'idiots! They are a bunch of idiots!
3 bandage
□ une bande Velpeau® a crepe bandage
▪ **une bande dessinée** a comic strip

> **DID YOU KNOW...?**
> Comic strips are very popular in France with people of all ages.

▪ **une bande magnétique** a tape
▪ **la bande sonore** the sound track
▪ **Elle fait toujours bande à part.** She always keeps to herself.

le **bandeau** (PL les **bandeaux**) MASC NOUN
headband

bander VERB [28]
to bandage
□ L'infirmière lui a bandé la jambe. The nurse bandaged his leg.

le **bandit** MASC NOUN
bandit

★ la **banlieue** FEM NOUN
suburbs
□ Pauline habite en banlieue. Pauline lives in the suburbs.
▪ **les lignes de banlieue** suburban lines
▪ **les trains de banlieue** commuter trains

★ la **banque** FEM NOUN
bank
▪ **une banque alimentaire** a food bank

le **banquet** MASC NOUN
dinner

★ la **banquette** FEM NOUN
seat
□ la banquette arrière de la voiture the back seat of the car

le **banquier** MASC NOUN
banker

le **banquière** FEM NOUN
banker

★ le **baptême** MASC NOUN
christening
□ le baptême de notre fille our daughter's christening
▪ **C'était mon baptême de l'air.** It was the first time I had flown.

★le **bar** MASC NOUN
bar

la **baraque** FEM NOUN (*informal*)
house
□ Elle habite dans une belle baraque. She lives in a beautiful house.

★**barbant** (FEM **barbante**) ADJECTIVE (*informal*)
boring
□ Il est vraiment barbant! He's so boring!

barbare (FEM **barbare**) ADJECTIVE
barbaric

★la **barbe** FEM NOUN
beard
□ Il porte la barbe. He's got a beard.
■ **Quelle barbe!** (*informal*) What a drag!
■ **la barbe à papa** candyfloss

le **barbecue** MASC NOUN
barbecue

barbouiller VERB [28]
to daub
□ Les murs étaient barbouillés de graffitis. The walls were daubed with graffiti.
■ **J'ai l'estomac barbouillé.** (*informal*) I'm feeling queasy.

barbu (FEM **barbue**) ADJECTIVE
bearded
□ un grand barbu a big, bearded man

barder VERB [28] (*informal*)
■ **Ça va barder!** There's going to be trouble!

le **baromètre** MASC NOUN
barometer

la **barque** FEM NOUN
rowing boat
■ **Ils sont allés faire une promenade en barque.** They've gone for a row.

le **barrage** MASC NOUN
dam
■ **un barrage de police** a police roadblock

la **barre** FEM NOUN
bar (*metal*)
□ une barre de fer an iron bar

le **barreau** (PL les **barreaux**) MASC NOUN
bar (*on window*)
□ Il s'est retrouvé derrière les barreaux. He ended up behind bars.

barrer VERB [28]
to block
□ Il y a un tronc d'arbre qui barre la route. There's a tree trunk blocking the road.
■ **se barrer** (*informal*) to clear off □ Barre-toi! Clear off!

la **barrette** FEM NOUN
hair slide

★la **barrière** FEM NOUN
fence

le **bar-tabac** (PL les **bars-tabacs**) MASC NOUN

DID YOU KNOW...?
A **bar-tabac** is a bar which also sells cigarettes, lottery tickets and sometimes stamps; you can tell a **bar-tabac** by the red diamond-shaped sign outside it.

★**bas** (FEM **basse**) ADJECTIVE, ADVERB
▷ *see also* **bas** NOUN
low
□ parler à voix basse to speak in a low voice
■ **en bas 1** down □ Ça me donne le vertige de regarder en bas. I get dizzy if I look down.
2 (down) at the bottom □ Son nom est tout en bas. His name is down at the bottom. □ Il y a un supermarché en bas de la rue. There's a supermarket at the bottom of the street.
3 downstairs □ Elle habite en bas. She lives downstairs.

★le **bas** MASC NOUN
▷ *see also* **bas** ADJECTIVE, ADVERB
1 bottom
□ en bas de la page at the bottom of the page
□ en bas de l'escalier at the bottom of the stairs □ Le bas de mon pantalon est plein de boue. The bottom of my trousers is full of mud.
2 stocking
□ une paire de bas a pair of stockings

le **bas-côté** MASC NOUN
verge
□ Il s'est garé sur le bas-côté de la route. He parked his car on the verge.

la **bascule** FEM NOUN
■ **un fauteuil à bascule** a rocking chair

la **base** FEM NOUN
base
□ la base de la pyramide the base of the pyramid
■ **de base** basic □ Le pain et le lait sont des aliments de base. Bread and milk are basic foods.
■ **à base de** made from □ des produits de beauté à base de plantes cosmetics made from plants
■ **une base de données** a database

le **basilic** MASC NOUN
basil

★le **basket** MASC NOUN
basketball
□ jouer au basket to play basketball

★les **baskets** FEM PL NOUN
trainers
□ une paire de baskets a pair of trainers

BE CAREFUL!
The French word **baskets** does not mean **baskets**.

basque ADJECTIVE, NOUN
Basque

□ Elle parle basque. She speaks Basque.
■ **un Basque** a Basque (*man*)
■ **une Basque** a Basque (*woman*)

basse FEM ADJECTIVE ▷ *see* **bas**

la **basse-cour** (PL les **basses-cours**) FEM NOUN
farmyard

★ le **bassin** MASC NOUN
1 pond
□ Il y a un bassin à poissons rouges dans le parc. There's a goldfish pond in the park.
2 pelvis
□ une fracture du bassin a fractured pelvis

la **bassine** FEM NOUN
bowl (*for washing*)

le **bas-ventre** MASC NOUN
lower abdomen
□ Elle se plaint de douleurs dans le bas-ventre. She is complaining of pains in her lower abdomen.

★ la **bataille** FEM NOUN
battle

★ le **bateau** (PL les **bateaux**) MASC NOUN
boat

★ le **bateau-mouche** (PL les **bateaux-mouches**) MASC NOUN
pleasure boat

bâti (FEM **bâtie**) ADJECTIVE
■ **bien bâti** well-built

★ le **bâtiment** MASC NOUN
building

★ **bâtir** VERB [38]
to build

le **bâton** MASC NOUN
stick
□ un coup de bâton a blow with a stick

le **battement** MASC NOUN
■ **J'ai dix minutes de battement.** I've got ten minutes free.

★ la **batterie** FEM NOUN
1 battery
□ La batterie est à plat. The battery is flat.
2 drums
□ jouer de la batterie to play the drums
■ **la batterie de cuisine** the pots and pans

le **batteur** MASC NOUN
drummer

★ **battre** VERB [9]
to beat
□ Quand je le vois, mon cœur bat plus vite. When I see him, my heart beats faster.
■ **se battre** to fight □ Je me bats souvent avec mon frère. I fight a lot with my brother.
■ **battre les cartes** to shuffle the cards
■ **Battre les blancs en neige.** Beat the egg whites until stiff.
■ **battre son plein** to be in full swing □ A minuit, la fête battait son plein. At midnight, the party was in full swing.

★ **bavard** (FEM **bavarde**) ADJECTIVE
talkative

★ **bavarder** VERB [28]
to chat

baver VERB [28]
to dribble

baveux (FEM **baveuse**) ADJECTIVE
runny
□ une omelette baveuse a runny omelette

la **bavure** FEM NOUN
blunder
□ une bavure policière a police blunder

le **bazar** MASC NOUN
general store
■ **Quel bazar!** (*informal*) What a mess!

BCBG (FEM+PL **BCBG**) ADJECTIVE (= *bon chic bon genre*)
posh

la **BD** (PL les **BD**) FEM NOUN (= *bande dessinée*)
comic strip
□ Marguerite adore les BD. Marguerite loves comic strips.

béant (FEM **béante**) ADJECTIVE
gaping
□ un trou béant a gaping hole

★ **beau** (FEM **belle**, MASC PL **beaux**) ADJECTIVE, ADVERB

> The masculine singular form **beau** changes to **bel** before a vowel and most words beginning with 'h'.

1 lovely
□ un bel été a lovely summer □ une belle journée a fine day
2 beautiful
□ C'est une belle femme. She is a beautiful woman.
3 good-looking
□ C'est un beau garçon. He is a good-looking boy.
4 handsome
□ un bel homme a handsome man
■ **Il fait beau aujourd'hui.** It's a nice day today.
■ **J'ai beau essayer, je n'y arrive pas.** However hard I try, I just can't do it.

★ **beaucoup** ADVERB
1 a lot
□ Il travaille beaucoup. He works a lot.
2 much
□ Elle n'a pas beaucoup d'argent. She hasn't got much money. □ Louise est beaucoup plus grande que moi. Louise is much taller than me.
■ **beaucoup de** a lot of □ Il y avait beaucoup de monde au concert. There were a lot of

people at the concert. □ Elle fait beaucoup de fautes. She makes a lot of mistakes.
■ **J'ai eu beaucoup de chance.** I was very lucky.

★ le **beau-fils** (PL les **beaux-fils**) MASC NOUN
1 son-in-law
2 stepson

★ le **beau-frère** (PL les **beaux-frères**) MASC NOUN
brother-in-law

★ le **beau-père** (PL les **beaux-pères**) MASC NOUN
1 father-in-law
2 stepfather

la **beauté** FEM NOUN
beauty

les **beaux-arts** MASC PL NOUN
fine arts

les **beaux-parents** MASC PL NOUN
in-laws

★ le **bébé** MASC NOUN
baby

le **bec** MASC NOUN
beak

la **bécane** FEM NOUN (*informal*)
bike

la **bêche** FEM NOUN
spade

bêcher VERB [28]
to dig
□ Il bêchait son jardin. He was digging the garden.

bégayer VERB [59]
to stammer

beige (FEM **beige**) ADJECTIVE
beige

le **beignet** MASC NOUN
1 fritter (*savoury or sweet batter*)
□ les beignets aux pommes apple fritters
2 donut (*sweet dough*)

bel MASC ADJECTIVE ▷ *see* **beau**

★ **belge** (FEM **belge**) ADJECTIVE, NOUN
Belgian
■ **un Belge** a Belgian (*man*)
■ **une Belge** a Belgian (*woman*)

★ la **Belgique** FEM NOUN
Belgium
■ **en Belgique** 1 in Belgium 2 to Belgium

le **bélier** MASC NOUN
ram
■ **le Bélier** Aries □ Marine est Bélier. Marine's Aries.

★ **belle** FEM ADJECTIVE ▷ *see* **beau**

la **belle-famille** (PL les **belles-familles**) FEM NOUN
in-laws

★ la **belle-fille** (PL les **belles-filles**) FEM NOUN
1 daughter-in-law
2 stepdaughter

★ la **belle-mère** (PL les **belles-mères**) FEM NOUN
1 mother-in-law
2 stepmother

★ la **belle-sœur** (PL les **belles-sœurs**) FEM NOUN
sister-in-law

la **bénédiction** FEM NOUN
blessing

le **bénéfice** MASC NOUN
profit
□ La société réalise de gros bénéfices. The company is making big profits.

★ **bénévole** (FEM **bénévole**) ADJECTIVE
voluntary
□ du travail bénévole voluntary work

bénir VERB [38]
to bless

bénit (FEM **bénite**) ADJECTIVE
consecrated
■ **l'eau bénite** holy water

la **béquille** FEM NOUN
crutch
□ Il marche avec des béquilles. He walks on crutches.

le **berceau** (PL les **berceaux**) MASC NOUN
cradle

bercer VERB [12]
to rock

la **berceuse** FEM NOUN
lullaby

le **béret** MASC NOUN
beret

la **berge** FEM NOUN
bank (*of river*)

le **berger** MASC NOUN
shepherd

la **bergère** FEM NOUN
shepherdess

★ le **besoin** MASC NOUN
need
■ **avoir besoin de quelque chose** to need something □ J'ai besoin d'argent. I need some money. □ J'ai besoin d'y réfléchir. I need to think about it.
■ **une famille dans le besoin** a needy family

le **bétail** MASC NOUN
livestock

★ **bête** (FEM **bête**) ADJECTIVE
▷ *see also* **bête** NOUN
stupid

★ la **bête** FEM NOUN
▷ *see also* **bête** ADJECTIVE
animal

★ la **bêtise** FEM NOUN
■ **faire une bêtise** to do something stupid
□ J'ai fait une bêtise. I've done something stupid.
■ **dire des bêtises** to talk nonsense □ Tu dis des bêtises! You're talking nonsense!

★ le **béton** MASC NOUN
concrete
■ **un alibi en béton** a cast-iron alibi

la **betterave** FEM NOUN
beetroot
□ la salade de betterave beetroot salad

le/la **beur** MASC/FEM NOUN (*informal*)

DID YOU KNOW...?
A **beur** is a young person of North African origin born in France.

★ le **beurre** MASC NOUN
butter
□ une sauce au beurre a sauce made with butter

beurrer VERB [28]
to butter

Beyrouth NOUN
Beirut

le **bibelot** MASC NOUN
ornament

le **biberon** MASC NOUN
baby's bottle

la **Bible** FEM NOUN
Bible

le/la **bibliothécaire** MASC/FEM NOUN
librarian

★ la **bibliothèque** FEM NOUN
1 library
□ emprunter un livre à la bibliothèque to borrow a book from the library
2 bookcase
□ une bibliothèque en chêne massif a bookcase made of solid oak

★ le **bic**® MASC NOUN
Biro®

la **biche** FEM NOUN
doe

★ la **bicyclette** FEM NOUN
bicycle

★ le **bidet** MASC NOUN
bidet

★ le **bidon** MASC NOUN
▷ *see also* **bidon** ADJECTIVE
can
□ un bidon d'essence a can of petrol

★ **bidon** (FEM+PL **bidon**) ADJECTIVE (*informal*)
▷ *see also* **bidon** NOUN
phoney
■ **Son histoire est complètement bidon.** His story is a complete load of rubbish.

le **bidonville** MASC NOUN
shanty town

la **Biélorussie** FEM NOUN
Belarus

★ **bien** (FEM+PL **bien**) ADJECTIVE, ADVERB
▷ *see also* **bien** NOUN
1 well
□ Marie travaille bien. Marie works well. □ Je me sens bien. I feel fine. □ Je ne me sens pas bien. I don't feel well.
2 good
□ Ce restaurant est vraiment bien. This restaurant is really good.
3 quite
□ bien assez quite enough
■ **Je veux bien le faire.** I'm quite willing to do it.
■ **bien mieux** much better
■ **J'espère bien y aller.** I very much hope to go.
4 right
□ Ce n'est pas bien de dire du mal des gens. It's not right to say nasty things about people.
□ Il croyait bien faire. He thought he was doing the right thing.
■ **C'est bien fait pour lui!** It serves him right!

★ le **bien** MASC NOUN
▷ *see also* **bien** ADJECTIVE, ADVERB
1 good
□ le bien et le mal good and evil □ Jean m'a dit beaucoup de bien de toi. Jean told me a lot of good things about you. □ C'est pour son bien. It's for his own good.
■ **faire du bien à quelqu'un** to do somebody good □ Ses vacances lui ont fait beaucoup de bien. His holiday has done him a lot of good.
2 possession
□ son bien le plus précieux his most treasured possession

le **bien-être** MASC NOUN
well-being
□ une sensation de bien-être a feeling of well-being

la **bienfaisance** FEM NOUN
charity
■ **une œuvre de bienfaisance** a charity

bien que CONJUNCTION
although

bien que is followed by a verb in the subjunctive.

□ Il fait assez chaud bien qu'il n'y ait pas de soleil. It's quite warm although there's no sun.

★ **bien sûr** ADVERB
of course

★ **bientôt** ADVERB
soon
□ À bientôt! See you soon!

★ le **bienvenu** MASC NOUN
■ **Vous êtes le bienvenu!** You're welcome!
□ Vous êtes tous les bienvenus! You're all welcome!

★ la **bienvenue** FEM NOUN
welcome
□ Bienvenue à Paris! Welcome to Paris!
□ Vous êtes la bienvenue! Welcome!

★ la **bière** FEM NOUN
beer
■ **la bière blonde** lager
■ **la bière brune** brown ale
■ **la bière pression** draught beer

★ le **bifteck** MASC NOUN
steak

le **bigoudi** MASC NOUN
roller (*in hair*)

★ le **bijou** (PL les **bijoux**) MASC NOUN
jewel

★ la **bijouterie** FEM NOUN
jeweller's

le **bijoutier** MASC NOUN
jeweller

la **bijoutière** FEM NOUN
jeweller
□ Elle est bijoutière. She's a jeweller.

le **bilan** MASC NOUN
■ **faire le bilan de quelque chose** to assess something □ Il faut faire le bilan de la situation. We need to assess the situation.

bilingue (FEM **bilingue**) ADJECTIVE
bilingual

le **billard** MASC NOUN
billiards
■ **le billard américain** pool

la **bille** FEM NOUN
marble (*toy*)
□ jouer aux billes to play marbles

★ le **billet** MASC NOUN
1 ticket
□ un billet d'avion a plane ticket □ un billet électronique an e-ticket
2 banknote
□ un billet de dix euros a 10 euro note

bio (FEM+PL **bio**) ADJECTIVE
organic
□ Je préfère les produits bio. I prefer organic produce.

le **biocarburant** MASC NOUN
biofuel

★ **biodégradable** ADJECTIVE
biodegradable

la **biographie** FEM NOUN
biography

★ la **biologie** FEM NOUN
biology

biologique (FEM **biologique**) ADJECTIVE
1 organic
□ des légumes biologiques organic vegetables
2 biological
□ des armes biologiques biological weapons

★ le **bip** MASC NOUN
beep
■ **bip sonore** tone □ Veuillez laisser votre message après le bip sonore. Please leave your message after the tone.

la **Birmanie** FEM NOUN
Burma

bis ADVERB
▷ *see also* **bis** NOUN
■ **Il habite au douze bis rue des Fleurs.** He lives at 12A rue des Fleurs.

le **bis** MASC NOUN
▷ *see also* **bis** ADVERB
encore

la **biscotte** FEM NOUN
toasted bread (*sold in packets*)

★ le **biscuit** MASC NOUN
biscuit
■ **un biscuit de Savoie** a sponge cake

★ la **bise** FEM NOUN (*informal*)
kiss
□ Grosses bises de Bretagne. Love and kisses from Brittany.
■ **faire la bise à quelqu'un** to give somebody a kiss on the cheek □ Elle m'a fait la bise. She gave me a kiss on the cheek.

DID YOU KNOW...?
Between friends and family members, the normal French way of saying hello and goodbye is with two kisses, usually one on each cheek, but sometimes three or even four depending on the region. Men and boys often shake hands instead.

le **bisou** MASC NOUN (*informal*)
kiss
□ Viens faire un bisou à maman! Come and give Mummy a kiss!

bissextile (FEM **bissextile**) ADJECTIVE
■ **une année bissextile** a leap year

★ le **bistrot** MASC NOUN (*informal*)
café

DID YOU KNOW...?
Cafés in France sell both alcoholic and non-alcoholic drinks.

★ **bizarre** (FEM **bizarre**) ADJECTIVE
strange

la **blague** FEM NOUN (*informal*)
1 joke
□ raconter une blague to tell a joke
■ **Sans blague!** No kidding!
2 trick
□ Antoine nous a encore fait une blague! Antoine has played a trick on us again!

blaguer VERB [28] (*informal*)
to joke

le **blaireau** (PL les **blaireaux**) MASC NOUN
1 badger
2 shaving brush

★ **blâmer** VERB [28]
to blame

le **Blanc** MASC NOUN
white man

★ **blanc** (FEM **blanche**) ADJECTIVE
▷ *see also* **blanc** NOUN
1 white
□ un chemisier blanc a white blouse
2 blank
□ une page blanche a blank page

★ le **blanc** MASC NOUN
▷ *see also* **blanc** ADJECTIVE
1 white
□ habillé tout en blanc dressed all in white
2 white wine
□ un verre de blanc a glass of white wine
3 blank
□ Remplissez les blancs. Fill in the blanks.
■ **un blanc d'œuf** an egg white
■ **un blanc de poulet** a chicken breast

la **Blanche** FEM NOUN
white woman

★ **blanche** FEM ADJECTIVE ▷ *see* **blanc**

la **blanchisserie** FEM NOUN
laundry

le **blé** MASC NOUN
wheat

★ **blessé** (FEM **blessée**) ADJECTIVE
▷ *see also* **blessé** NOUN, **blessée** NOUN
injured

★ le **blessé** MASC NOUN
▷ *see also* **blessé** ADJECTIVE
injured person
□ L'accident a fait trois blessés. Three people were injured in the accident.

★ la **blessée** FEM NOUN
▷ *see also* **blessé** ADJECTIVE
injured person

★ **blesser** VERB [28]
1 to injure
□ Il a été blessé dans un accident de voiture. He was injured in a car accident.
2 to hurt
□ Il a fait exprès de le blesser. He hurt him on purpose.
■ **se blesser** to hurt oneself □ Je me suis blessé au pied. I've hurt my foot.

> **BE CAREFUL!**
> **blesser** does not mean **to bless.**

★ la **blessure** FEM NOUN
injury

★ **bleu** (FEM **bleue**) ADJECTIVE
▷ *see also* **bleu** NOUN
1 blue
□ une veste bleue a blue jacket
■ **bleu marine** navy blue
2 very rare (*steak*)

★ le **bleu** MASC NOUN
▷ *see also* **bleu** ADJECTIVE
1 blue
□ J'aime le bleu. I like blue.
2 bruise
□ Il a un bleu au front. He's got a bruise on his forehead.

le **bleuet** MASC NOUN
cornflower

le **bloc** MASC NOUN
pad
□ un bloc de papier à lettres a pad of writing paper
■ **le bloc opératoire** the operating theatre

le **bloc-notes** (PL les **blocs-notes**) MASC NOUN
note pad

★ le **blog** MASC NOUN
blog

★ le **bloggeur** MASC NOUN
blogger

★ **bloguer** VERB [28]
to blog

★ le **blogueur** MASC NOUN
blogger

★ la **blogueuse** FEM NOUN
blogger

★ **blond** (FEM **blonde**) ADJECTIVE
blond
■ **blond cendré** ash blond □ Simon a les cheveux blond cendré. Simon has ash blond hair.

bloquer VERB [28]
to block
□ bloquer le passage to block the way
■ **être bloqué dans un embouteillage** to be stuck in a traffic jam

se **blottir** VERB [38]
to huddle
□ Ils étaient blottis l'un contre l'autre. They were huddled together.

la **blouse** FEM NOUN
overall

★ le **blouson** MASC NOUN
jacket
□ un blouson en cuir a leather jacket

le **bob** MASC NOUN
cotton sunhat

la **bobine** FEM NOUN
reel
□ une bobine de fil a reel of thread

le **bocal** (PL les **bocaux**) MASC NOUN
jar

★ le **bœuf** MASC NOUN
1 ox
2 beef
□ un rôti de bœuf a joint of beef

★ **bof** EXCLAMATION (*informal*)
■ **Le film t'a plu? — Bof! C'était pas terrible!** Did you like the film? — Well ... it wasn't that great!
■ **Comment ça va? — Bof! Pas terrible.** How is it going? — Oh ... not too well actually.

le **bohémien** MASC NOUN
gipsy

la **bohémienne** FEM NOUN
gipsy

★ **boire** VERB [10]
to drink
■ **boire un coup** (*informal*) to have a drink

★ le **bois** MASC NOUN
wood
■ **en bois** wooden □ une table en bois a wooden table
■ **avoir la gueule de bois** (*informal*) to have a hangover

★ la **boisson** FEM NOUN
drink
□ une boisson chaude a hot drink □ une boisson non alcoolisée a soft drink

★ la **boîte** FEM NOUN
1 box
□ une boîte d'allumettes a box of matches
■ **une boîte aux lettres** a letter box
■ **une boîte postale** a PO Box
■ **une boîte vocale** voice mail
2 tin
□ une boîte de sardines a tin of sardines
■ **une boîte de conserve** a tin
■ **en boîte** tinned □ des petits pois en boîte tinned peas
■ **une boîte de nuit** a night club
■ **sortir en boîte** to go clubbing

boiter VERB [28]
to limp

★ le **bol** MASC NOUN
bowl
■ **en avoir ras le bol** (*informal*) to be fed up □ J'en ai ras le bol de ce boulot. I'm fed up with this job.

bombarder VERB [28]
to bomb

la **bombe** FEM NOUN
1 bomb
2 aerosol
□ du déodorant en bombe aérosol aerosol deodorant

★ **bon** (FEM **bonne**) ADJECTIVE, ADVERB
▷ *see also* **bon** NOUN
1 good
□ un bon restaurant a good restaurant □ Le tabac n'est pas bon pour la santé. Smoking isn't good for you. □ être bon en maths to be good at maths
■ **sentir bon** to smell nice
■ **Bon anniversaire!** Happy birthday!
■ **Bon courage!** Good luck!
■ **Bon voyage!** Have a good trip!
■ **Bon week-end!** Have a nice weekend!
■ **Bonne chance!** Good luck!
■ **Bonne journée!** Have a nice day!
■ **Bonne nuit!** Good night!
■ **Bonne année!** Happy New Year!
■ **Bonnes vacances!** Have a good holiday!
2 right
□ Il est arrivé au bon moment. He arrived at the right moment. □ Ce n'est pas la bonne réponse. That's not the right answer.
■ **Il fait bon aujourd'hui.** It's nice today.
■ **de bonne heure** early
■ **bon marché** cheap □ Les fraises ne sont pas bon marché en hiver. Strawberries aren't cheap in winter.
■ **Ah bon?** Really? □ Je pars aux États-Unis la semaine prochaine. — Ah bon? I'm going to the States next week. — Really?
■ **J'aimerais vraiment que tu viennes! — Bon, d'accord.** I'd really like you to come! — OK then, I will.
■ **Est-ce que ce yaourt est encore bon?** Is this yoghurt still OK?

★ le **bon** MASC NOUN
▷ *see also* **bon** ADJECTIVE, ADVERB
voucher
□ un bon d'achat a voucher
■ **pour de bon** **1** for good □ Il est parti pour de bon. He's gone for good. **2** for real □ Cette fois, on le fait pour de bon. Let's do it for real this time.
■ **Il est fâché pour de bon.** He's really angry.

★ le **bonbon** MASC NOUN
sweet

bondé (FEM **bondée**) ADJECTIVE
crowded

bondir VERB [38]
to leap

★ le **bonheur** MASC NOUN
happiness
■ **porter bonheur** to bring luck

★ le **bonhomme** (PL les **bonshommes**) MASC NOUN
■ **un bonhomme de neige** a snowman

★ **bonjour** EXCLAMATION
1 hello!
□ Donne le bonjour à tes parents de ma part. Say hello to your parents for me.
2 good morning!
3 good afternoon!

bonjour is used in the morning and afternoon; in the evening **bonsoir** is used instead.

■ **C'est simple comme bonjour!** It's easy as pie!

bonne FEM ADJECTIVE ▷ *see* **bon**

le **bonnet** MASC NOUN
hat
□ un bonnet de laine a woolly hat
■ **un bonnet de bain** a bathing cap

★ **bonsoir** EXCLAMATION
good evening!

la **bonté** FEM NOUN
kindness

★ le **bord** MASC NOUN
1 edge
□ le bord de la table the edge of the table
2 side
□ Jeanne a garé sa voiture au bord de la route. Jeanne parked her car on the side of the road.
■ **au bord de la mer** at the seaside
■ **au bord de l'eau** by the water
■ **monter à bord** to go on board
■ **être au bord des larmes** to be on the verge of tears

le **bordeaux** MASC NOUN
▷ *see also* **bordeaux** ADJECTIVE
Bordeaux wine
■ **du bordeaux rouge** claret

bordeaux (FEM+PL **bordeaux**) ADJECTIVE
▷ *see also* **bordeaux** NOUN
burgundy
□ une jupe bordeaux a burgundy skirt

border VERB [28]
1 to line
□ une route bordée d'arbres a tree-lined street
2 to trim
□ un col bordé de dentelle a collar trimmed with lace
3 to tuck in
□ Sa mère vient la border tous les soirs. Her mother comes and tucks her in every night.

la **bordure** FEM NOUN
border
■ **une villa en bordure de mer** a villa right by the sea

la **borne** FEM NOUN
terminal (*of computer*)

la **Bosnie** FEM NOUN
Bosnia
■ **la Bosnie-Herzégovine** Bosnia-Herzegovina

la **bosse** FEM NOUN
bump
□ Nicolas a une grosse bosse au front. Nicolas has got a big bump on his forehead.
■ **La route est pleine de bosses.** The road is very bumpy.

bosser VERB [28]
to work (*informal*)
■ **bosser un examen** to study for an exam

le **bossu** MASC NOUN
hunchback

la **bossue** FEM NOUN
hunchback

botanique (FEM **botanique**) ADJECTIVE
▷ *see also* **botanique** NOUN
botanic
□ le jardin botanique the botanic gardens

la **botanique** FEM NOUN
▷ *see also* **botanique** ADJECTIVE
botany

★ la **botte** FEM NOUN
1 boot
□ une paire de bottes a pair of boots
■ **les bottes en caoutchouc** Wellington boots
2 bunch
□ une botte de radis a bunch of radishes

le **bottin**® MASC NOUN
phone book

le **bouc** MASC NOUN
1 goatee beard
2 billy goat
■ **un bouc émissaire** a scapegoat

★ la **bouche** FEM NOUN
mouth
■ **le bouche à bouche** the kiss of life
■ **une bouche d'égout** a manhole
■ **une bouche de métro** an entrance to the underground

la **bouchée** FEM NOUN
mouthful
■ **une bouchée à la reine** a chicken vol-au-vent

★ **boucher** VERB [28]
▷ *see also* **boucher** NOUN
1 to fill
□ boucher un trou to fill a hole
2 to block
□ L'évier est bouché. The sink is blocked. □ J'ai le nez bouché. My nose is blocked.

★ le **boucher** MASC NOUN
▷ *see also* **boucher** VERB
butcher
□ Il est boucher. He's a butcher.

★ la **bouchère** FEM NOUN
butcher
□ Elle est bouchère. She's a butcher.

★ la **boucherie** FEM NOUN
butcher's

★ le **bouchon** MASC NOUN
1 top (*of plastic bottle*)

2 cork (*of wine bottle*)
3 hold-up
□ Il y avait beaucoup de bouchons sur l'autoroute. There were a lot of hold-ups on the motorway.

★ la **boucle** FEM NOUN
curl (*of hair*)
■ **une boucle d'oreille** an earring □ une paire de boucles d'oreille a pair of earrings

★ **bouclé** (FEM **bouclée**) ADJECTIVE
curly

le **bouclier** MASC NOUN
shield

le/la **bouddhiste** MASC/FEM NOUN
Buddhist

bouder VERB [28]
to sulk

le **boudin** MASC NOUN
■ **le boudin noir** black pudding
■ **le boudin blanc** white pudding

la **boue** FEM NOUN
mud

la **bouée** FEM NOUN
buoy
■ **une bouée de sauvetage** a life buoy

boueux (FEM **boueuse**) ADJECTIVE
muddy

la **bouffe** FEM NOUN (*informal*)
food
□ La bouffe est infecte à la cantine. The food in the canteen is revolting.

la **bouffée** FEM NOUN
■ **une bouffée d'air frais** a breath of fresh air

bouffer VERB [28] (*informal*)
to eat

le **bougeoir** MASC NOUN
candlestick

★ **bouger** VERB [45]
to move

la **bougie** FEM NOUN
candle

la **bouillabaisse** FEM NOUN
fish soup

bouillant (FEM **bouillante**) ADJECTIVE
1 boiling
□ Faites cuire les pâtes à l'eau bouillante. Cook the pasta in boiling water.
2 piping hot
□ La soupe est bouillante. The soup is piping hot.

bouillir VERB [11]
to boil
□ L'eau bout. The water's boiling.
■ **Je bous d'impatience.** I'm bursting with impatience.

la **bouilloire** FEM NOUN
kettle

le **bouillon** MASC NOUN
stock
□ du bouillon de légumes vegetable stock

la **bouillotte** FEM NOUN
hot-water bottle

★ le **boulanger** MASC NOUN
baker
□ Il est boulanger. He's a baker.

★ la **boulangère** FEM NOUN
baker
□ Elle est boulangère. She's a baker.

★ la **boulangerie** FEM NOUN
baker's

★ la **boule** FEM NOUN
ball
□ une boule de cristal a crystal ball
■ **une boule de neige** a snowball
■ **jouer aux boules** to play bowls

DID YOU KNOW...?
boules is played on rough ground, not smooth grass. The balls are smaller than those used in bowls, and are made of metal.

★ le **boulevard** MASC NOUN
boulevard

bouleverser VERB [28]
1 to move deeply
□ Cette histoire déchirante m'a bouleversée. This heartbreaking story moved me deeply.
2 to shatter
□ La mort de son ami l'a bouleversé. He was shattered by the death of his friend.
3 to turn upside down
□ Cette rencontre a bouleversé sa vie. This meeting turned his life upside down.

★ le **boulot** MASC NOUN (*informal*)
1 job
□ Anita a trouvé du boulot. Anita has found a job.
2 work
□ J'ai beaucoup de boulot en ce moment. I've got a lot of work to do at the moment.

★ la **boum** FEM NOUN (*informal*)
party

le **bouquet** MASC NOUN
bunch of flowers
□ un bouquet de roses a bunch of roses

le **bouquin** MASC NOUN (*informal*)
book

bouquiner VERB [28] (*informal*)
to read

bourdonner VERB [28]
to buzz

le **bourg** MASC NOUN
small market town

bourgeois (FEM **bourgeoise**) ADJECTIVE
middle-class
□ un quartier bourgeois a middle-class area

le **bourgeon** MASC NOUN
bud

la **Bourgogne** FEM NOUN
Burgundy

bourré (FEM **bourrée**) ADJECTIVE
■ **bourré de** stuffed with □ un portefeuille bourré de billets a wallet stuffed with banknotes
■ **être bourré** (*informal*) to be plastered □ Il était complètement bourré. He was completely plastered.

le **bourreau** (PL les **bourreaux**) MASC NOUN
executioner
■ **C'est un véritable bourreau de travail.** He's a real workaholic.

bourrer VERB [28]
to stuff
□ bourrer une valise de vêtements to stuff clothes into a case

★ la **bourse** FEM NOUN
grant
■ **la Bourse** the Stock Exchange

bous VERB ▷ *see* **bouillir**

la **bousculade** FEM NOUN
crush
□ la bousculade dans les grands magasins au moment des soldes the crush in the big stores at sale time

bousculer VERB [28]
1 to jostle
□ être bousculé par la foule to be jostled by the crowd
2 to rush
□ Je n'aime pas qu'on me bouscule. I don't like to be rushed.

la **boussole** FEM NOUN
compass

★ **bout** VERB ▷ *see* **bouillir**

★ le **bout** MASC NOUN
1 end
□ Elle habite au bout de la rue. She lives at the end of the street. □ Marie est assise en bout de table. Marie is sitting at the end of the table.
2 tip
□ le bout du nez the tip of the nose
3 bit
□ un petit bout de fromage a bit of cheese
■ **un bout de papier** a scrap of paper
■ **au bout de** after □ Au bout d'un moment, il s'est endormi. After a while he fell asleep.
■ **Elle est à bout.** She's at the end of her tether.

★ la **bouteille** FEM NOUN
bottle
□ une bouteille d'eau gazeuse a bottle of sparkling water
■ **une bouteille de gaz** a gas cylinder

★ la **boutique** FEM NOUN
shop

★ le **bouton** MASC NOUN
1 button
2 spot (*on skin*)
□ J'ai un bouton sur le nez. I've got a spot on my nose.
3 bud
□ un bouton de rose a rosebud
■ **un bouton d'or** a buttercup

★ le **bowling** MASC NOUN
1 tenpin bowling
2 bowling alley

la **boxe** FEM NOUN
boxing

le **boxeur** MASC NOUN
boxer

le **bracelet** MASC NOUN
bracelet

le **bracelet-montre** (PL les **bracelets-montres**) MASC NOUN
wristwatch

le **brancard** MASC NOUN
stretcher

le **brancardier** MASC NOUN
stretcher-bearer

★ la **branche** FEM NOUN
branch

★ **branché** (FEM **branchée**) ADJECTIVE
(*informal*)
trendy
□ avoir un look branché to look trendy

★ **brancher** VERB [28]
1 to connect
□ Le téléphone est branché? Is the phone connected?
2 to plug in
□ L'aspirateur n'est pas branché. The hoover isn't plugged in.

★ le **bras** MASC NOUN
arm

la **brasse** FEM NOUN
breaststroke
□ nager la brasse to do the breaststroke

★ la **brasserie** FEM NOUN
café-restaurant

brave (FEM **brave**) ADJECTIVE
nice
□ C'est un brave type. He's a nice enough fellow.

★ **bravo** EXCLAMATION
bravo!

le **break** MASC NOUN
estate car

la **brebis** FEM NOUN
ewe
■ **le fromage de brebis** sheep's cheese

★ **bref** (FEM **brève**) ADJECTIVE, ADVERB
short
□ Sa lettre était brève. His letter was short.
■ **en bref** in brief □ l'actualité en bref the news in brief
■ **Bref, ça s'est bien terminé.** To cut a long story short, it turned out all right in the end.

le **Brésil** MASC NOUN
Brazil

★ la **Bretagne** FEM NOUN
Brittany

la **bretelle** FEM NOUN
strap
□ La bretelle de son soutien-gorge dépasse. Her bra strap is showing.
■ **les bretelles** braces □ Il porte des bretelles. He's wearing braces.

breton (FEM **bretonne**) ADJECTIVE, NOUN
Breton
□ Ils parlent breton. They speak Breton.
■ **un Breton** a Breton (*man*)
■ **une Bretonne** a Breton (*woman*)
■ **les Bretons** the Bretons

brève FEM ADJECTIVE ▷ *see* **bref**

le **brevet** MASC NOUN
certificate

le **brevet des collèges** MASC NOUN

> **DID YOU KNOW...?**
> The **brevet des collèges** is an exam you take at the end of **collège**, at the age of 15.

★ le **bricolage** MASC NOUN
DIY
□ Elle aime le bricolage. She likes doing DIY.
□ un magasin de bricolage a DIY shop

la **bricole** FEM NOUN (*informal*)
■ **J'ai acheté une bricole pour le bébé de Sabine.** I've bought a little something for Sabine's baby.
■ **J'ai encore quelques bricoles à faire avant de partir.** I've still got a few things to do before I go.

★ **bricoler** VERB [28]
to do DIY
□ Pascal aime bricoler. Pascal loves doing DIY.

le **bricoleur** MASC NOUN
DIY enthusiast

la **bricoleuse** FEM NOUN
DIY enthusiast

le **bridge** MASC NOUN
bridge (*game*)
□ Guillaume adore jouer au bridge. Guillaume loves playing bridge.

★ **brièvement** ADVERB
briefly
□ Expliquez-moi brièvement ce qui s'est passé. Tell me briefly what happened.

la **brigade** FEM NOUN
squad (*of police*)
□ la brigade des stups (*informal*) the drugs squad

brillamment ADVERB
brilliantly
□ Il a réussi brillamment à son examen. He did brilliantly in the exam.

brillant (FEM **brillante**) ADJECTIVE
1 brilliant
□ une brillante carrière a brilliant career □ Ses notes ne sont pas brillantes. His marks aren't brilliant.
2 shiny
□ des cheveux brillants shiny hair

★ **briller** VERB [28]
to shine

le **brin** MASC NOUN
■ **un brin d'herbe** a blade of grass
■ **un brin de muguet** a sprig of lily of the valley

la **brindille** FEM NOUN
twig

la **brioche** FEM NOUN
brioche bun

★ la **brique** FEM NOUN
brick

le **briquet** MASC NOUN
cigarette lighter

la **brise** FEM NOUN
breeze

se **briser** VERB [28]
to break
□ Le vase s'est brisé en mille morceaux. The vase broke into a thousand pieces.

★ le/la **Britannique** MASC/FEM NOUN
Briton
■ **les Britanniques** the British

★ **britannique** (FEM **britannique**) ADJECTIVE
British

la **brocante** FEM NOUN
junk
□ un magasin de brocante a junk shop

le **brocanteur** MASC NOUN
dealer in second-hand goods

la **brocanteuse** FEM NOUN
dealer in second-hand goods

la **broche** FEM NOUN
brooch
□ une broche en argent a silver brooch
■ **à la broche** spit-roasted □ un poulet à la broche a spit-roasted chicken

la **brochette** FEM NOUN
skewer
■ **les brochettes d'agneau** lamb kebabs

★ la **brochure** FEM NOUN
brochure

broder VERB [28]
to embroider

la **broderie** FEM NOUN
embroidery

la **bronchite** FEM NOUN
bronchitis
□ avoir une bronchite to have bronchitis

le **bronze** MASC NOUN
bronze

★ **bronzer** VERB [28]
to get a tan
□ Il est bien bronzé. He's got a good tan.
■ **se faire bronzer** to sunbathe

★ la **brosse** FEM NOUN
brush
■ **une brosse à cheveux** a hairbrush
■ **une brosse à dents** a toothbrush
■ **Il est coiffé en brosse.** He's got a crew cut.

★ **brosser** VERB [28]
to brush
■ **se brosser les dents** to brush one's teeth
□ Je me brosse les dents tous les soirs. I brush my teeth every night.

la **brouette** FEM NOUN
wheelbarrow

★ le **brouillard** MASC NOUN
fog
■ **Il y a du brouillard.** It's foggy.

le **brouillon** MASC NOUN
first draft
□ Ce n'est qu'un brouillon. It's just a first draft.

les **broussailles** FEM PL NOUN
undergrowth *sing*

brouter VERB [28]
to graze (*animals*)

broyer VERB [53]
to crush
■ **broyer du noir** to be down in the dumps

le **brugnon** MASC NOUN
nectarine

★ le **bruit** MASC NOUN
1 noise
□ J'ai entendu un bruit. I heard a noise. □ faire du bruit to make a noise
■ **sans bruit** without a sound
2 rumour
□ Des bruits circulent à son sujet. There are rumours going round about him.

brûlant (FEM **brûlante**) ADJECTIVE
1 blazing
□ un soleil brûlant a blazing sun
2 boiling hot
□ Marie boit son café brûlant. Marie drinks her coffee boiling hot.

le **brûlé** MASC NOUN
smell of burning
□ Ça sent le brûlé. There's a smell of burning.

★ **brûler** VERB [28]
to burn
■ **se brûler** to burn oneself

la **brûlure** FEM NOUN
burn
■ **des brûlures d'estomac** heartburn

★ la **brume** FEM NOUN
mist

★ **brumeux** (FEM **brumeuse**) ADJECTIVE
misty

★ **brun** (FEM **brune**) ADJECTIVE
brown
■ **Elle est brune.** She's got dark hair.

le **brushing** MASC NOUN
blow-dry
□ une coupe et un brushing a cut and blow-dry

brusque (FEM **brusque**) ADJECTIVE
abrupt
■ **d'un ton brusque** brusquely

brusquer VERB [28]
to rush
□ Il ne faut pas la brusquer. You mustn't rush her.

brut (FEM **brute**) ADJECTIVE
■ **le champagne brut** dry champagne
■ **le pétrole brut** crude oil
■ **son salaire brut** his gross salary

brutal (FEM **brutale**, MASC PL **brutaux**) ADJECTIVE
brutal

★ **brutaliser** VERB [28]
to knock about
□ Il a été brutalisé par la police. He was knocked about by the police.

★ **Bruxelles** NOUN
Brussels

bruyamment ADVERB
noisily

★ **bruyant** (FEM **bruyante**) ADJECTIVE
noisy

la **bruyère** FEM NOUN
heather

bu VERB ▷ *see* boire

la **bûche** FEM NOUN
log
■ **la bûche de Noël** the Yule log

DID YOU KNOW...?
la bûche de Noël is what is usually eaten in France instead of Christmas pudding.

French-English

b

le **bûcheron** MASC NOUN
woodcutter

★ le **budget** MASC NOUN
budget

★ le **buffet** MASC NOUN
1 sideboard
□ un buffet en chêne an oak sideboard
2 buffet
□ un buffet froid a cold buffet

★ le **buisson** MASC NOUN
bush

la **Bulgarie** FEM NOUN
Bulgaria

la **bulle** FEM NOUN
bubble
□ une bulle de savon a soap bubble

★ le **bulletin** MASC NOUN
1 bulletin
■ **le bulletin d'informations** the news bulletin
2 report
□ Ton bulletin n'est pas fameux. Your school report isn't very good.
■ **le bulletin météorologique** the weather report
■ **un bulletin de salaire** a pay slip
■ **un bulletin de vote** a ballot paper

★ le **bureau** (PL les **bureaux**) MASC NOUN
1 desk
□ Posez le dossier sur mon bureau. Put the file on my desk.
2 office
□ Il vous attend dans son bureau. He's waiting for you in his office.
■ **un bureau de change** a bureau de change
■ **le bureau de poste** the post office
■ **le bureau de tabac** the tobacconist's
■ **le bureau de vote** the polling station

★ **bus** VERB ▷ *see* **boire**

★ le **bus** MASC NOUN
bus

le **buste** MASC NOUN
bust

★ **but** VERB ▷ *see* **boire**

★ le **but** MASC NOUN
1 aim
□ Ils n'ont pas de but dans la vie. They have no aim in life.
■ **Quel est le but de votre visite?** What's the reason for your visit?
■ **dans le but de** with the intention of □ Je suis venue dans le but de vous aider. I came with the intention of helping you.
2 goal
□ marquer un but to score a goal

le **butane** MASC NOUN
Calor gas®

le **butin** MASC NOUN
loot
□ Les cambrioleurs se sont partagé le butin. The burglars shared the stolen goods.

buvais, buvait VERB ▷ *see* **boire**

le **buvard** MASC NOUN
blotter

Cc

c' PRONOUN ▷ *see* **ce**

★ **ça** PRONOUN

1 this

□ Est-ce que vous pouvez me donner un peu de ça? Can you give me a bit of this?

2 that

□ Regarde ça là-bas. Look at that over there.

3 it

□ Ça ne fait rien. It doesn't matter.

■ **Comment ça va?** How are you?

■ **Ça alors!** Well, well!

■ **C'est ça.** That's right.

■ **Ça y est!** That's it!

★ **çà** ADVERB

■ **çà et là** here and there

la **cabane** FEM NOUN

hut

le **cabillaud** MASC NOUN

cod

★ la **cabine** FEM NOUN

cabin (*on a ship*)

■ **une cabine d'essayage** a fitting room

★ le **cabinet** MASC NOUN

surgery (*of doctor, dentist*)

■ **une chambre avec cabinet de toilette** a room with washing facilities

★ les **cabinets** MASC PL NOUN

toilet *sing*

★ le **câble** MASC NOUN

cable

■ **la télévision par câble** cable television

cabosser VERB [28]

to dent

la **cacahuète** FEM NOUN

peanut

■ **le beurre de cacahuète** peanut butter

le **cacao** MASC NOUN

cocoa

■ **le beurre de cacao** cocoa butter

cache-cache MASC NOUN

■ **jouer à cache-cache** to play hide-and-seek

le **cachemire** MASC NOUN

cashmere

le **cache-nez** (PL les **cache-nez**) MASC NOUN

long woollen scarf

★ **cacher** VERB [28]

to hide

□ J'ai caché les cadeaux sous le lit. I hid the presents under the bed. □ Tu me caches quelque chose! You're hiding something from me!

■ **se cacher** to hide □ Elle s'est cachée sous la table. She's hidden under the table.

★ le **cachet** MASC NOUN

1 tablet

■ **un cachet d'aspirine** an aspirin

2 fee (*for performer*)

□ Il a touché un gros cachet pour ce concert. He got a big fee for the concert.

■ **le cachet de la poste** the postmark

la **cachette** FEM NOUN

hiding place

■ **en cachette** on the sly □ Il est sorti en cachette sans réveiller ses parents. He crept out on the sly without waking his parents.

le **cachot** MASC NOUN

dungeon

le **cactus** MASC NOUN

cactus

le **cadavre** MASC NOUN

corpse

le **Caddie**® MASC NOUN

supermarket trolley

★ le **cadeau** (PL les **cadeaux**) MASC NOUN

present

□ un cadeau d'anniversaire a birthday present

□ un cadeau de Noël a Christmas present

■ **faire un cadeau à quelqu'un** to give somebody a present

le **cadenas** MASC NOUN

padlock

★ **cadet** (FEM **cadette**) ADJECTIVE

▷ *see also* **cadet** NOUN, **cadette** NOUN

1 younger (*brother, sister*)

□ ma sœur cadette my younger sister

2 youngest (*son, daughter*)

□ son fils cadet his youngest son

★ le **cadet** MASC NOUN

▷ *see also* **cadet** ADJECTIVE

youngest

□ C'est le cadet de la famille. He's the youngest of the family.

★ la **cadette** FEM NOUN
▷ *see also* **cadet** ADJECTIVE
youngest
□ C'est la cadette de la famille. She's the youngest of the family.

★ le **cadre** MASC NOUN
1 frame
□ un cadre en bois a wooden frame
2 surroundings
□ L'hôtel est situé dans un très beau cadre. The hotel is set in beautiful surroundings.
3 executive
□ un cadre supérieur a senior executive

le **cafard** MASC NOUN
cockroach
■ **avoir le cafard** (*informal*) to be feeling down □ J'ai le cafard. I'm feeling down.

★ le **café** MASC NOUN
1 coffee
□ un café au lait a white coffee □ un café crème a strong white coffee
2 café

> **DID YOU KNOW...?**
> Cafés in France sell both alcoholic and non-alcoholic drinks.

★ le **café-tabac** (PL les **cafés-tabacs**) MASC NOUN

> **DID YOU KNOW...?**
> A **café-tabac** is a bar which also sells cigarettes, lottery tickets and sometimes stamps; you can tell a **café-tabac** by the red diamond-shaped sign outside it.

★ la **cafétéria** FEM NOUN
cafeteria

★ la **cafetière** FEM NOUN
1 coffee maker
2 coffeepot

★ la **cage** FEM NOUN
cage
■ **la cage d'escalier** the stairwell

la **cagoule** FEM NOUN
balaclava

★ le **cahier** MASC NOUN
exercise book
□ mon cahier de brouillon my rough book

la **caille** FEM NOUN
quail

le **caillou** (PL les **cailloux**) MASC NOUN
pebble

★ la **caisse** FEM NOUN
1 box
□ une caisse à outils a tool box
2 till
□ le ticket de caisse the till receipt
3 checkout
□ J'ai dû faire la queue à la caisse. I had to queue at the checkout.

★ le **caissier** MASC NOUN
cashier

★ la **caissière** FEM NOUN
cashier

le **cake** MASC NOUN
fruit cake

★ le **calcul** MASC NOUN
1 calculation
□ Je me suis trompé dans mes calculs. I made a mistake in my calculations.
2 arithmetic
□ Je ne suis pas très bon en calcul. I'm not very good at arithmetic.

★ la **calculatrice** FEM NOUN
calculator

★ **calculer** VERB [28]
to work out
□ J'ai calculé combien ça allait coûter. I worked out how much it was going to cost.

la **calculette** FEM NOUN
pocket calculator

la **cale** FEM NOUN
wedge

calé (FEM **calée**) ADJECTIVE (*informal*)
■ **Elle est calée en histoire.** She's really good at history.

le **caleçon** MASC NOUN
boxer shorts

le **calendrier** MASC NOUN
calendar

le **calepin** MASC NOUN
notebook

caler VERB [28]
to stall
□ La voiture a calé dans une côte. The car stalled on a hill.

câlin (FEM **câline**) ADJECTIVE
▷ *see also* **câlin** NOUN
cuddly

le **câlin** MASC NOUN
▷ *see also* **câlin** ADJECTIVE
cuddle
□ faire un câlin à quelqu'un to give somebody a cuddle

le **calmant** MASC NOUN
tranquillizer

★ **calme** (FEM **calme**) ADJECTIVE
▷ *see also* **calme** NOUN
1 quiet
□ un endroit calme a quiet place
2 calm
□ Elle est restée très calme. She stayed very calm.

★ le **calme** MASC NOUN
▷ *see also* **calme** ADJECTIVE
peace and quiet
□ J'ai besoin de calme pour travailler. I need peace and quiet to work.

calmer VERB [28]
to soothe
□ Cette pommade calme les démangeaisons. This ointment soothes itching.
■ **se calmer** to calm down □ Calme-toi! Calm down!

la **calorie** FEM NOUN
calorie

★ le/la **camarade** MASC/FEM NOUN
friend
■ **un camarade de classe** a school friend

★ le **cambriolage** MASC NOUN
burglary

★ **cambrioler** VERB [28]
to burgle

le **cambrioleur** MASC NOUN
burglar

la **cambrioleuse** FEM NOUN
burglar

la **camelote** FEM NOUN (*informal*)
junk
□ C'est vraiment de la camelote. It's absolute junk.

★ la **caméra** FEM NOUN
camera (*cinema, TV*)
■ **une caméra numérique** a digital camera

★ le **caméscope®** MASC NOUN
camcorder

★ le **camion** MASC NOUN
lorry

★ la **camionnette** FEM NOUN
van

le **camionneur** MASC NOUN
lorry driver

la **camomille** FEM NOUN
camomile tea

le **camp** MASC NOUN
camp
□ un camp de prisonniers a prison camp □ un camp de vacances a holiday camp

★ la **campagne** FEM NOUN
1 country
■ **à la campagne** in the country □ Nous passons nos vacances à la campagne. We spend our holidays in the country.
2 campaign
□ une campagne de marketing a marketing campaign

★ **camper** VERB [28]
to camp

★ le **campeur** MASC NOUN
camper

★ la **campeuse** FEM NOUN
camper

★ le **camping** MASC NOUN
camping
□ faire du camping to go camping
■ **un (terrain de) camping** a campsite

★ le **Canada** MASC NOUN
Canada
■ **au Canada** 1 in Canada 2 to Canada

★ **canadien** (FEM **canadienne**) ADJECTIVE, NOUN
Canadian
■ **un Canadien** a Canadian (*man*)
■ **une Canadienne** a Canadian (*woman*)

le **canal** (PL les **canaux**) MASC NOUN
canal

★ le **canapé** MASC NOUN
1 sofa
2 open sandwich

★ le **canard** MASC NOUN
duck

le **canari** MASC NOUN
canary

★ le **cancer** MASC NOUN
cancer
□ le cancer du poumon lung cancer
■ **le Cancer** Cancer □ Sabine est Cancer. Sabine's Cancer.

★ le **candidat** MASC NOUN
1 candidate (*in exam, election*)
2 applicant (*for job*)

★ la **candidate** FEM NOUN
1 candidate (*in exam, election*)
2 applicant (*for job*)

la **candidature** FEM NOUN
■ **poser sa candidature à un poste** to apply for a job □ Il a posé sa candidature à des dizaines de postes. He has applied for dozens of jobs.

le **caneton** MASC NOUN
duckling

la **canette** FEM NOUN
■ **une canette de bière** a small can of beer

le **caniche** MASC NOUN
poodle

la **canicule** FEM NOUN
scorching heat

★ le **canif** MASC NOUN
penknife

le **caniveau** (PL les **caniveaux**) MASC NOUN
gutter

la **canne** FEM NOUN
walking stick
■ **une canne à pêche** a fishing rod

la **cannelle** FEM NOUN
cinnamon

le **canoë** MASC NOUN
1 canoe
2 canoeing
□ faire du canoë to go canoeing

le **canon** MASC NOUN
1 gun
2 cannon

le **canot** MASC NOUN
dinghy
□ un canot pneumatique a rubber dinghy
■ **un canot de sauvetage** a lifeboat

la **cantatrice** FEM NOUN
opera singer

★ la **cantine** FEM NOUN
canteen

le **caoutchouc** MASC NOUN
rubber
■ **des bottes en caoutchouc** Wellington boots

le **cap** MASC NOUN
cape (*land*)

capable (FEM **capable**) ADJECTIVE
■ **Elle est capable de marcher pendant des heures.** She can walk for hours.
■ **Il est capable de changer d'avis au dernier moment.** He's capable of changing his mind at the last minute.

la **cape** FEM NOUN
cape (*garment*)

le **capitaine** MASC NOUN
captain

★ la **capitale** FEM NOUN
capital
□ la capitale de la France the capital of France

le **capot** MASC NOUN
bonnet (*of car*)

la **capote** FEM NOUN (*informal*)
condom

la **câpre** FEM NOUN
caper (*food*)

le **caprice** MASC NOUN
■ **faire des caprices** to make a fuss □ Il n'aime pas les enfants qui font des caprices. He doesn't like children who make a fuss.

capricieux (FEM **capricieuse**) ADJECTIVE
■ **un enfant capricieux** an awkward child

le **Capricorne** MASC NOUN
Capricorn
□ Hélène est Capricorne. Hélène's Capricorn.

captivant (FEM **captivante**) ADJECTIVE
fascinating

la **captivité** FEM NOUN
captivity
□ en captivité in captivity

capturer VERB [28]
to capture

la **capuche** FEM NOUN
hood
□ un manteau à capuche a coat with a hood
■ **un pull à capuche** a hoodie

le **capuchon** MASC NOUN
cap (*of pen*)

la **capucine** FEM NOUN
nasturtium

★ le **car** MASC NOUN
▷ *see also* **car** CONJUNCTION
coach
■ **un car scolaire** a school bus

★ **car** CONJUNCTION
▷ *see also* **car** NOUN
because
□ Réfléchis bien car c'est important. Think carefully because it's important.

la **carabine** FEM NOUN
rifle

★ le **caractère** MASC NOUN
personality
□ Il a le même caractère que son père. He's got the same personality as his father.
■ **Il a bon caractère.** He's good-natured.
■ **Elle a mauvais caractère.** She's bad-tempered.
■ **Il n'a pas un caractère facile.** He isn't easy to get on with.

★ **caractéristique** (FEM **caractéristique**) ADJECTIVE
▷ *see also* **caractéristique** NOUN
characteristic

★ la **caractéristique** FEM NOUN
▷ *see also* **caractéristique** ADJECTIVE
characteristic

★ la **carafe** FEM NOUN
jug
□ une carafe d'eau a jug of water

les **Caraïbes** FEM PL NOUN
Caribbean Islands

le **caramel** MASC NOUN
1 caramel
□ la crème caramel crème caramel
2 toffee

★ la **caravane** FEM NOUN
caravan

★ **carbonique** (FEM **carbonique**) ADJECTIVE
■ **le gaz carbonique** carbon dioxide

le **carburant** MASC NOUN
fuel

cardiaque (FEM **cardiaque**) ADJECTIVE
■ **une crise cardiaque** a heart attack
■ **Ma tante est cardiaque.** My aunt has heart trouble.

le **cardigan** MASC NOUN
cardigan

le/la **cardiologue** MASC/FEM NOUN
heart specialist

le **carême** MASC NOUN
Lent

la **caresse** FEM NOUN
stroke
□ faire des caresses à un chat to stroke a cat

caresser VERB [28]
to stroke

la **carie** FEM NOUN
tooth decay
■ **J'ai une carie.** I've got a hole in my tooth.

★ **caritatif** (FEM **caritative**) ADJECTIVE
■ **une association caritative** a charity

le **carnaval** MASC NOUN
carnival

★ le **carnet** MASC NOUN
1 notebook
2 book
□ un carnet d'adresses **an address book** □ un carnet de chèques **a cheque book** □ un carnet de timbres **a book of stamps** □ un carnet de tickets **a book of tickets**

> **DID YOU KNOW...?**
> In the Paris metro it is cheaper to buy tickets in a book of ten, known as a **carnet**.

■ **mon carnet de notes** my school report

★ la **carotte** FEM NOUN
carrot
□ les carottes râpées **grated carrots**

★ **carré** (FEM **carrée**) ADJECTIVE
▷ *see also* **carré** NOUN
square
■ **un mètre carré** a square metre

★ le **carré** MASC NOUN
▷ *see also* **carré** ADJECTIVE
square

le **carreau** (PL les **carreaux**) MASC NOUN
1 check
□ une chemise à carreaux **a checked shirt**
2 tile (*on floor, wall*)
□ des carreaux de terre cuite **terracotta tiles**
3 pane
□ Il a cassé un carreau. **He broke a windowpane.**
4 diamonds (*cards*)
□ l'as de carreau **the ace of diamonds**

★ le **carrefour** MASC NOUN
junction

le **carrelage** MASC NOUN
tiled floor

carrément ADVERB
1 completely
□ C'est carrément impossible. **It's completely impossible.**
2 straight out
□ Dis-lui carrément ce que tu penses. **Tell him straight out what you think.**

★ la **carrière** FEM NOUN
career
■ **un militaire de carrière** a professional soldier

la **carrure** FEM NOUN
build
□ Il a une carrure d'athlète. **He has an athletic build.**

★ le **cartable** MASC NOUN
satchel

★ la **carte** FEM NOUN
1 card
■ **une carte d'anniversaire** a birthday card
■ **une carte postale** a postcard
■ **une carte de vœux** a Christmas card

> **DID YOU KNOW...?**
> The French send greetings cards (**les cartes de vœux**) in January rather than at Christmas, with best wishes for the New Year.

■ **une carte de vœux électronique** an e-card
■ **une carte bancaire** a cash card

> **DID YOU KNOW...?**
> **Carte Bleue** is a major French debit card.

■ **une carte de crédit** a credit card
■ **une carte de fidélité** a loyalty card
■ **une carte d'embarquement** a boarding card
■ **une carte d'identité** an identity card
■ **une carte de séjour** a residence permit
■ **un jeu de cartes** 1 a pack of cards 2 a card game
2 map
□ une carte de France **a map of France** □ une carte routière **a road map**
3 menu
□ la carte des vins **the wine list**
■ **manger à la carte** to eat à la carte □ Nous allons manger à la carte. **We'll choose from the à la carte menu.**

★ le **carton** MASC NOUN
1 cardboard
□ un morceau de carton **a piece of cardboard**
2 cardboard box
■ **un carton à chaussures** a shoe box

la **cartouche** FEM NOUN
cartridge
■ **une cartouche de cigarettes** a carton of cigarettes

★ le **cas** (PL les **cas**) MASC NOUN
case
□ plusieurs cas **several cases**
■ **ne faire aucun cas de** to take no notice of
■ **en aucun cas** on no account
■ **en tout cas** at any rate
■ **au cas où** in case □ Prends un sandwich au cas où la cantine serait fermée. **Take a sandwich in case the canteen's closed.**
■ **en cas de** in case of □ En cas d'incendie, appelez ce numéro. **In case of fire, call this number.**

la **cascade** FEM NOUN
waterfall

le **cascadeur** MASC NOUN
stuntman

★ la **case** FEM NOUN
1 square (*in board game*)
2 box (*on form*)

la **caserne** FEM NOUN
barracks

cash ADVERB
■ **payer cash** to pay cash

le **casier** MASC NOUN
locker

★ le **casque** MASC NOUN
1 helmet
2 headphones

★ la **casquette** FEM NOUN
cap

cassant (FEM **cassante**) ADJECTIVE
■ **Il m'a parlé d'un ton cassant.** He spoke to me curtly.

★ le **casse-croûte** (PL les **casse-croûte**, les **casse-croûtes**) MASC NOUN
snack

le **casse-noix** (PL les **casse-noix**) MASC NOUN
nutcrackers

★ **casse-pieds** (FEM+PL **casse-pieds**) ADJECTIVE (*informal*)
■ **Il est vraiment casse-pieds!** He's a real pain in the neck!

★ **casser** VERB [28]
to break
□ J'ai cassé un verre. I've broken a glass.
■ **se casser** to break □ Il s'est cassé la jambe au ski. He broke his leg when he was skiing.
■ **se casser la tête** (*informal*) to go to a lot of trouble □ Ne te casse pas la tête pour le dîner. Don't go to a lot of trouble over dinner.

★ la **casserole** FEM NOUN
saucepan

le **casse-tête** (PL les **casse-têtes**) MASC NOUN
■ **C'est un vrai casse-tête!** It's a real headache!

★ le **cassis** MASC NOUN
blackcurrant

le **castor** MASC NOUN
beaver

le **catalogue** MASC NOUN
catalogue

★ la **catastrophe** FEM NOUN
disaster

le **catch** MASC NOUN
wrestling

le **catéchisme** MASC NOUN
catechism

la **catégorie** FEM NOUN
category

catégorique (FEM **catégorique**) ADJECTIVE
firm
■ **un refus catégorique** a flat refusal

★ la **cathédrale** FEM NOUN
cathedral

catholique (FEM **catholique**) ADJECTIVE
▷ *see also* **catholique** NOUN
Catholic

le/la **catholique** MASC/FEM NOUN
▷ *see also* **catholique** ADJECTIVE
Catholic

★ le **cauchemar** MASC NOUN
nightmare
□ faire un cauchemar to have a nightmare

★ la **cause** FEM NOUN
cause
■ **à cause de** because of □ Je suis puni à cause de toi. I've been punished because of you.

★ **causer** VERB [28]
1 to cause
□ La tempête a causé beaucoup de dégâts. The storm caused a lot of damage.
2 to chat
□ Nous n'avons pas beaucoup eu le temps de causer. We didn't have much time to chat.

la **caution** FEM NOUN
1 bail
2 deposit

le **cavalier** MASC NOUN
1 rider
2 partner (*at dance*)

la **cavalière** FEM NOUN
rider

★ la **cave** FEM NOUN
cellar

★ la **caverne** FEM NOUN
cave

★ le **CD** (PL les **CD**) MASC NOUN
CD

★ le **CDD** MASC NOUN (= *contrat de durée déterminée*)
temporary contract

★ le **CDI** MASC NOUN (= *contrat de durée indeterminée*)
permanent contract

le **CD-ROM** (PL les **CD-ROM**) MASC NOUN
CD-ROM

★ **ce** (FEM **cette**, PL **ces**) ADJECTIVE
▷ *see also* **ce** PRONOUN

> The masculine singular form **ce** changes to **cet** before a vowel and most words beginning with 'h'.

1 this
□ Tu peux prendre ce livre. You can take this

book. □ cet après-midi this afternoon □ cet hiver this winter
■ **ce livre-ci** this book
■ **cette voiture-ci** this car
2 that
□ Je n'aime pas du tout ce film. I don't like that film at all.
■ **ce livre-là** that book
■ **cette voiture-là** that car

★ **ce** PRONOUN
▷ *see also* **ce** ADJECTIVE

ce changes to **c'** before the vowel in **est**, **était** and **étaient**.

it
□ Ce n'est pas facile. It's not easy.
■ **c'est** **1** it is □ C'est vraiment trop cher. It's really too expensive. □ Ouvre, c'est moi! Open the door, it's me! **2** he is □ C'est un peintre du début du siècle. He's a painter from the turn of the century. **3** she is □ C'est une actrice très célèbre. She's a very famous actress.
■ **ce sont** they are □ Ce sont des amis de mes parents. They're friends of my parents.
■ **Qui est-ce?** Who is it?
■ **Qu'est-ce que c'est?** What is it?
■ **ce qui** what □ C'est ce qui compte. That's what matters.
■ **tout ce qui** everything that □ J'ai rangé tout ce qui traînait par terre. I've tidied up everything that was on the floor.
■ **ce que** what □ Je vais lui dire ce que je pense. I'm going to tell him what I think.
■ **tout ce que** everything □ Tu peux avoir tout ce que tu veux. You can have everything you want.

ceci PRONOUN
this
□ Prends ceci, tu en auras besoin. Take this, you'll need it.

céder VERB [34]
to give in
□ Elle a tellement insisté qu'il a fini par céder. She went on so much that he eventually gave in.
■ **céder à** to give in to □ Je ne veux pas céder à ses caprices. I'm not going to give in to her whims.

★ le **cédérom** MASC NOUN
CD-ROM

la **cédille** FEM NOUN
cedilla

★ la **ceinture** FEM NOUN
belt
□ une ceinture en cuir a leather belt
■ **une ceinture de sauvetage** a lifebelt
■ **votre ceinture de sécurité** your seatbelt

★ **cela** PRONOUN
1 it
□ Cela dépend. It depends.
2 that
□ Je n'aime pas cela. I don't like that.
■ **C'est cela.** That's right.
■ **à part cela** apart from that

★ **célèbre** (FEM **célèbre**) ADJECTIVE
famous

★ **célébrer** VERB [34]
to celebrate

le **céleri** MASC NOUN
■ **le céleri-rave** celeriac
■ **le céleri (en branche)** celery

célibataire (FEM **célibataire**) ADJECTIVE
▷ *see also* **célibataire** NOUN
single

★ le/la **célibataire** MASC/FEM NOUN
▷ *see also* **célibataire** ADJECTIVE
single person
■ **un célibataire** a bachelor
■ **une célibataire** a single woman

celle PRONOUN ▷ *see* **celui**

celles PRONOUN ▷ *see* **ceux**

la **cellule** FEM NOUN
cell

celui (FEM **celle**, MASC PL **ceux**, FEM PL **celles**) PRONOUN
the one
□ Prends celui que tu préfères. Take the one you like best. □ Je n'ai pas d'appareil photo mais je peux emprunter celui de ma sœur. I haven't got a camera but I can borrow my sister's. □ Je n'ai pas de webcam mais je peux emprunter celle de mon frère. I haven't got a webcam but I can borrow my brother's.
■ **celui-ci** this one
■ **celle-ci** this one
■ **celui-là** that one
■ **celle-là** that one

la **cendre** FEM NOUN
ash

★ le **cendrier** MASC NOUN
ashtray

censé (FEM **censée**) ADJECTIVE
■ **être censé faire quelque chose** to be supposed to do something □ Vous êtes censé arriver à l'heure. You're supposed to get here on time.

★ **cent** NUMBER
a hundred
□ cent euros a hundred euros

cent is spelt with an **-s** when there are two or more hundreds, but not when it is followed by another number, as in 'four hundred and two'.

□ trois cents ans **three hundred years** □ cent deux kilomètres **a hundred and two kilometres** □ trois cent cinquante kilomètres **three hundred and fifty kilometres** □ trois cent mille kilomètres **three hundred thousand kilometres**

la **centaine** FEM NOUN
about a hundred
□ Il y avait une centaine de personnes. **There were about a hundred people.**
■ **des centaines de** hundreds of □ Des centaines de réfugiés se sont présentés à l'ambassade. **Hundreds of refugees came to the embassy.**

le **centenaire** MASC NOUN
centenary

centième (FEM **centième**) ADJECTIVE
hundredth

le **centilitre** MASC NOUN
centilitre

★ le **centime** MASC NOUN
cent (*one hundredth of a euro*)
□ un centime d'euro **a euro cent**

> **DID YOU KNOW...?**
> The euro is divided into 100 **centimes**.

★ le **centimètre** MASC NOUN
centimetre

central (FEM **centrale**, MASC PL **centraux**) ADJECTIVE
central

la **centrale** FEM NOUN
power station
□ une centrale nucléaire **a nuclear power station**

★ le **centre** MASC NOUN
centre
■ **un centre commercial** a shopping centre
■ **un centre d'appels** a call centre
■ **un centre de recyclage** a recycling centre

★ le **centre-ville** (PL les **centres-villes**) MASC NOUN
town centre

★ **cependant** ADVERB
however

★ le **cercle** MASC NOUN
circle
□ Entourez d'un cercle la bonne réponse. **Put a circle round the right answer.**
■ **un cercle vicieux** a vicious circle

le **cercueil** MASC NOUN
coffin

★ la **céréale** FEM NOUN
cereal
□ un bol de céréales **a bowl of cereal**
■ **un pain aux cinq céréales** a multigrain loaf

la **cérémonie** FEM NOUN
ceremony

le **cerf** MASC NOUN
stag

le **cerf-volant** (PL les **cerfs-volants**) MASC NOUN
kite

★ la **cerise** FEM NOUN
cherry

le **cerisier** MASC NOUN
cherry tree

cerné (FEM **cernée**) ADJECTIVE
■ **avoir les yeux cernés** to have shadows under one's eyes □ Elle avait les yeux cernés. **She had shadows under her eyes.**

cerner VERB [28]
■ **J'ai du mal à le cerner.** I can't figure him out.

★ **certain** (FEM **certaine**) ADJECTIVE
1 certain
□ Je suis certain que je l'ai remis en place. **I'm certain that I put it back.** □ Ce n'est pas certain. **It's not certain.**
2 some
□ Certaines personnes n'aiment pas la crème. **Some people don't like cream.**
■ **un certain temps** quite some time □ Ça m'a pris un certain temps. **It took me quite some time.**

★ **certainement** ADVERB
1 definitely
□ C'est certainement le meilleur film que j'ai vu cette année. **It's definitely the best film I've seen this year.**
2 of course
□ Est-ce que je peux t'emprunter ton stylo? — Mais certainement! **Can I borrow your pen? — Of course!**

certains (FEM **certaines**) PL PRONOUN
1 some
□ certains d'entre vous **some of you**
□ certaines de ses amies **some of his friends**
2 some people
□ Certains pensent que le film est meilleur que le roman. **Some people think that the film is better than the novel.**

certes ADVERB
certainly
□ Nous nous connaissons, certes, mais nous ne sommes pas amis. **We know each other, certainly, but we are not friends.**

★ le **certificat** MASC NOUN
certificate

le **cerveau** (PL les **cerveaux**) MASC NOUN
brain

la **cervelle** FEM NOUN
brain

Numbers in brackets refer to verb tables on pages 650 to 658

■ **se creuser la cervelle** (*informal*) to rack one's brains

★ le **CES** MASC NOUN (= *collège d'enseignement secondaire*)
secondary school

★ **ces** PL ADJECTIVE
1 these
□ Tu peux prendre ces photos si tu veux. You can have these photos if you like.
■ **ces photos-ci** these photos
2 those
□ Ces montagnes sont dangereuses en hiver. Those mountains are dangerous in winter.
■ **ces livres-là** those books

cesse
■ **sans cesse** ADVERB continually □ Elle me dérange sans cesse. She continually interrupts me.

★ **cesser** VERB [28]
to stop
□ cesser de faire quelque chose to stop doing something

le **cessez-le-feu** (PL les **cessez-le-feu**) MASC NOUN
ceasefire

★ **c'est-à-dire** ADVERB
that is
□ Nous partons lundi prochain, c'est-à-dire le quinze. We're leaving next Monday, that's the 15th.

cet ADJECTIVE ▷ *see* ce

★ **cette** ADJECTIVE ▷ *see* ce

ceux (FEM PL **celles**) PL PRONOUN
the ones
□ Prends ceux que tu préfères. Take the ones you like best. □ Je n'ai pas de skis mais je peux emprunter ceux de ma sœur. I haven't got any skis but I can borrow my sister's. □ Je n'ai pas de jumelles mais je peux emprunter celles de mon frère. I haven't got any binoculars but I can borrow my brother's.
■ **ceux-ci** these ones
■ **celles-ci** these ones
■ **ceux-là** those ones
■ **celles-là** those ones

★ **chacun** (FEM **chacune**) PRONOUN
1 each
□ Il nous a donné un cadeau à chacun. He gave us each a present. □ Nous avons chacune donné dix euros. We each gave 10 euros.
2 everyone
□ Chacun fait ce qu'il veut. Everyone does what they like.

le **chagrin** MASC NOUN
■ **avoir du chagrin** to be very upset □ Elle a eu beaucoup de chagrin à la mort de sa tante. She was terribly upset by the death of her aunt.

le **chahut** MASC NOUN
bedlam
□ Il y avait du chahut dans la classe. There was bedlam in the classroom.

★ la **chaîne** FEM NOUN
1 chain
□ une chaîne en or a gold chain
2 channel (*on TV*)
□ Le film passe sur quelle chaîne? Which channel is the film on?
■ **une chaîne hi-fi** a hi-fi system
■ **une chaîne stéréo** a music centre
■ **travailler à la chaîne** to work on an assembly line

la **chair** FEM NOUN
flesh
■ **en chair et en os** in the flesh □ J'ai vu Kate Winslet en chair et en os. I saw Kate Winslet in the flesh.
■ **avoir la chair de poule** to have goose pimples

★ la **chaise** FEM NOUN
chair
■ **une chaise longue** a deckchair

le **châle** MASC NOUN
shawl

★ la **chaleur** FEM NOUN
1 heat
2 warmth

chaleureux (FEM **chaleureuse**) ADJECTIVE
warm
□ un accueil chaleureux a warm welcome

se **chamailler** VERB [28] (*informal*)
to squabble
□ Elle se chamaille sans cesse avec son frère. She's always squabbling with her brother.

★ la **chambre** FEM NOUN
1 bedroom
□ Il y a trois chambres. There are three bedrooms.
2 room
□ C'est la chambre de Camille. This is Camille's room.
■ **une chambre d'amis** a spare room
■ **une chambre simple** a single room
■ **une chambre pour une personne** a single room
■ **une chambre double** a double room
■ **une chambre pour deux personnes** a double room
■ **une chambre de famille** a family room
■ **'Chambres d'hôte'** 'Bed and Breakfast'

★ le **chameau** (PL les **chameaux**) MASC NOUN
camel

★ le **champ** MASC NOUN
field

le **champagne** MASC NOUN
champagne

★ le **champignon** MASC NOUN
mushroom
□ une omelette aux champignons a mushroom omelette
■ **un champignon de Paris** a button mushroom

★ le **champion** MASC NOUN
champion

★ le **championnat** MASC NOUN
championship
□ le championnat du monde the world championship

★ la **championne** FEM NOUN
champion

★ la **chance** FEM NOUN
1 luck
■ **Bonne chance!** Good luck!
■ **par chance** luckily
■ **avoir de la chance** to be lucky □ Tu as de la chance de partir au soleil! You're lucky, going off to the sun!
2 chance
□ Il n'a aucune chance. He's got no chance.
□ Il a des chances de réussir son examen. He's got a good chance of passing his exam.

le **change** MASC NOUN
exchange
□ le taux de change the exchange rate

★ le **changement** MASC NOUN
change
□ Il n'aime pas le changement. He doesn't like change.
■ **le changement climatique** climate change

★ **changer** VERB [45]
to change
□ Il n'a pas beaucoup changé. He hasn't changed much. □ J'ai changé les draps ce matin. I changed the sheets this morning.
□ J'ai changé trois cents euros. I changed 300 euros.
■ **se changer** to get changed □ Je vais me changer avant de sortir. I'm going to get changed before I go out.
■ **changer de** to change □ Je change de chaussures et j'arrive! I'll change my shoes and then I'll be ready!
■ **changer d'avis** to change one's mind
□ Appelle-moi si tu changes d'avis. Give me a ring if you change your mind.
■ **changer de chaîne** to change the channel

★ la **chanson** FEM NOUN
song

le **chant** MASC NOUN
singing
□ des cours de chant singing lessons
■ **un chant de Noël** a Christmas carol

le **chantage** MASC NOUN
blackmail
□ faire du chantage à quelqu'un to blackmail somebody

★ **chanter** VERB [28]
to sing

★ le **chanteur** MASC NOUN
singer

★ la **chanteuse** FEM NOUN
singer

★ le **chantier** MASC NOUN
building site

la **chantilly** FEM NOUN
sweetened whipped cream

chantonner VERB [28]
to hum

★ le **chapeau** (PL les **chapeaux**) MASC NOUN
hat

la **chapelle** FEM NOUN
chapel

le **chapitre** MASC NOUN
chapter

★ **chaque** (FEM **chaque**) ADJECTIVE
1 every
□ chaque année every year
2 each
□ Ces verres coûtent cinq euros chaque. These glasses cost 5 euros each.

le **char** MASC NOUN
tank (*military*)

le **charabia** MASC NOUN (*informal*)
gibberish
□ Je n'y comprends rien: c'est du charabia. I don't understand any of it: it's gibberish.

la **charade** FEM NOUN
1 riddle
2 charade
□ jouer aux charades to play charades

★ le **charbon** MASC NOUN
coal
■ **le charbon de bois** charcoal

★ la **charcuterie** FEM NOUN
1 pork butcher's

> **DID YOU KNOW...?**
> A **charcuterie** sells cuts of pork and pork products such as sausages, salami and pâté, as well as various cooked dishes and salads.

2 cold meats

★ le **charcutier** MASC NOUN
pork butcher

★ la **charcutière** FEM NOUN
pork butcher

le **chardon** MASC NOUN
thistle

Numbers in brackets refer to verb tables on pages 650 to 658

★ **charger** VERB [45]
to load
■ **charger quelqu'un de faire quelque chose** to tell somebody to do something
□ Paul m'a chargé de vous dire que la clé est sous le paillasson. Paul told me to tell you that the key's under the mat.

le **chargeur** MASC NOUN
charger

★ le **chariot** MASC NOUN
trolley (*at supermarket*)

★ **charmant** (FEM **charmante**) ADJECTIVE
charming

le **charme** MASC NOUN
charm

charmer VERB [28]
to charm

la **charrue** FEM NOUN
plough

★ la **chasse** FEM NOUN
1 hunting
□ un chien de chasse a hunting dog
2 shooting
□ la chasse au canard duck shooting
■ **tirer la chasse d'eau** to flush the toilet

le **chasse-neige** (PL les **chasse-neiges**, les **chasse-neige**) MASC NOUN
snowplough

★ **chasser** VERB [28]
1 to hunt
□ Mon père chasse le lapin. My father hunts rabbits.
2 to chase away
□ Ils ont chassé les cambrioleurs. They chased away the robbers.
3 to get rid of
□ Ouvre donc la fenêtre pour chasser les odeurs de cuisine. Open the window to get rid of the cooking smells.

le **chasseur** MASC NOUN
hunter

★ le **chat** MASC NOUN
1 cat
■ **appeler un chat un chat** to call a spade a spade
2 chat

This word has two pronunciations. **chat** meaning **cat** is pronounced 'shah', and the internet one is pronounced the same as in English.

la **châtaigne** FEM NOUN
chestnut

le **châtaignier** MASC NOUN
chestnut tree

★ **châtain** (FEM+PL **châtain**) ADJECTIVE
brown
□ J'ai les cheveux châtain. I've got brown hair.

★ le **château** (PL les **châteaux**) MASC NOUN
1 castle
■ **un château fort** a castle
2 palace
□ le château de Versailles the palace of Versailles

le **chaton** MASC NOUN
kitten

chatouiller VERB [28]
to tickle

chatouilleux (FEM **chatouilleuse**) ADJECTIVE
ticklish

★ la **chatte** FEM NOUN
cat (*female*)

chatter VERB [28]
to chat (*on the internet*)

★ **chaud** (FEM **chaude**) ADJECTIVE
1 warm
□ des vêtements chauds warm clothes
■ **avoir chaud** to be warm □ J'ai assez chaud. I'm warm enough.
2 hot
□ Il fait chaud aujourd'hui. It's hot today. □ un plat chaud a hot dish □ Attention, c'est chaud! Mind, it's hot! □ J'ai trop chaud! I'm too hot!

★ le **chauffage** MASC NOUN
heating
□ Le chauffage est en panne. The heating isn't working.
■ **le chauffage central** central heating

le **chauffe-eau** (PL les **chauffe-eau**, les **chauffe-eaux**) MASC NOUN
water heater

chauffer VERB [28]
to heat
□ Je vais mettre de l'eau à chauffer pour faire du thé. I'm going to heat some water to make tea.

★ le **chauffeur** MASC NOUN
driver
□ un chauffeur de taxi a taxi driver

le **chaume** MASC NOUN
■ **un toit de chaume** a thatched roof

★ la **chaussée** FEM NOUN
road surface
□ 'Attention! Chaussée déformée' 'Uneven road surface'

chausser VERB [28]
■ **Vous chaussez du combien?** What size shoe do you take?

★ la **chaussette** FEM NOUN
sock

★ le **chausson** MASC NOUN
slipper
■ **un chausson aux pommes** an apple turnover

★ la **chaussure** FEM NOUN
shoe
■ **les chaussures de ski** ski boots

★ **chauve** (FEM **chauve**) ADJECTIVE
bald

la **chauve-souris** (PL les **chauves-souris**) FEM NOUN
bat (*animal*)

★ le **chef** MASC NOUN
1 head
□ le chef de famille the head of the family
■ **le chef de l'État** the Head of State
2 boss
□ Je dois demander la permission à mon chef. I have to get permission from my boss.
■ **un chef d'entreprise** a company director
3 chef
□ la spécialité du chef the chef's speciality
■ **un chef d'orchestre** a conductor

le **chef-d'œuvre** (PL les **chefs-d'œuvre**) MASC NOUN
masterpiece

★ le **chemin** MASC NOUN
1 path
□ un chemin de montagne a mountain path
2 way
□ Quel est le chemin le plus court pour aller à l'aéroport? What's the quickest way to the airport?
■ **en chemin** on the way □ Je mangerai mon sandwich en chemin. I'll eat my sandwich on the way.
■ **le chemin de fer** the railway

★ la **cheminée** FEM NOUN
1 chimney
2 fireplace

★ la **chemise** FEM NOUN
1 shirt
□ une chemise à carreaux a checked shirt
■ **une chemise de nuit** a nightdress
2 folder
□ une chemise en plastique a plastic folder

★ le **chemisier** MASC NOUN
blouse

le **chêne** MASC NOUN
oak
□ une armoire en chêne an oak wardrobe

le **chenil** MASC NOUN
kennels

la **chenille** FEM NOUN
caterpillar

★ le **chèque** MASC NOUN
cheque
■ **les chèques de voyage** traveller's cheques

★ le **chéquier** MASC NOUN
cheque book

★ **cher** (FEM **chère**) ADJECTIVE, ADVERB
1 dear
□ Chère Mélusine ... Dear Mélusine ...
2 expensive
□ C'est trop cher. It's too expensive. □ coûter cher to be expensive

★ **chercher** VERB [28]
1 to look for
□ Je cherche mes clés. I'm looking for my keys.
2 to look up
□ chercher un mot dans le dictionnaire to look up a word in the dictionary
■ **aller chercher** **1** to go to get □ Elle est allée chercher du pain. She's gone to get some bread. **2** to pick up □ J'irai te chercher à la gare. I'll pick you up at the station.

le **chercheur** MASC NOUN
scientist

la **chercheuse** FEM NOUN
scientist

chère FEM ADJECTIVE ▷ *see* **cher**

★ **chéri** (FEM **chérie**) ADJECTIVE
▷ *see also* **chéri** NOUN, **chérie** NOUN
darling
□ ma petite fille chérie my darling daughter

★ le **chéri** MASC NOUN
▷ *see also* **chéri** ADJECTIVE
darling
■ **mon chéri** darling

★ la **chérie** FEM NOUN
▷ *see also* **chéri** ADJECTIVE
darling
■ **ma chérie** darling

★ le **cheval** (PL les **chevaux**) MASC NOUN
horse
■ **un cheval de course** a racehorse
■ **à cheval** on horseback
■ **faire du cheval** to go riding

le **chevalier** MASC NOUN
knight

la **chevalière** FEM NOUN
signet ring

chevalin (FEM **chevaline**) ADJECTIVE
■ **une boucherie chevaline** a horsemeat butcher's

les **chevaux** MASC PL NOUN ▷ *see* **cheval**

le **chevet** MASC NOUN
■ **une table de chevet** a bedside table
■ **une lampe de chevet** a bedside lamp

★ les **cheveux** MASC PL NOUN
hair *sing*
□ Elle a les cheveux courts. She's got short hair.

★ la **cheville** FEM NOUN
ankle
□ Il s'est foulé la cheville. He sprained his ankle.

★ la **chèvre** FEM NOUN
goat
■ **le fromage de chèvre** goat's cheese

le **chevreau** (PL les **chevreaux**) MASC NOUN
kid (*animal, leather*)

le **chèvrefeuille** MASC NOUN
honeysuckle

le **chevreuil** MASC NOUN
1 roe deer
2 venison
□ un rôti de chevreuil roast venison

le **chewing-gum** MASC NOUN
chewing gum

★ **chez** PREPOSITION
■ **chez Pierre 1** at Pierre's house **2** to Pierre's house
■ **chez moi 1** at my house □ Mes amis sont restés chez moi. My friends stayed at my house. **2** to my house □ Allons chez moi. Let's go to my house.
■ **Je rentre chez moi.** I'm going home.
■ **chez le dentiste 1** at the dentist's □ J'ai rendez-vous chez le dentiste demain matin. I've got an appointment at the dentist's tomorrow morning. **2** to the dentist's □ Je vais chez le dentiste. I'm going to the dentist's.

★ **chic** (FEM+PL **chic**) ADJECTIVE
1 smart
□ une tenue chic a smart outfit
2 nice
□ C'est chic de ta part de m'avoir invité. (*informal*) It was nice of you to invite me.

la **chicorée** FEM NOUN
endive

★ le **chien** MASC NOUN
dog
■ **'Attention, chien méchant'** 'Beware of the dog'

★ la **chienne** FEM NOUN
bitch (*dog*)

le **chiffon** MASC NOUN
cloth

chiffonner VERB [28]
to crease
□ Ma robe est toute chiffonnée. My dress is all creased.

★ le **chiffre** MASC NOUN
figure
□ en chiffres ronds in round figures
■ **les chiffres romains** Roman numerals

le **chignon** MASC NOUN
bun (*in hair*)
□ Elle s'est fait un chignon. She put her hair in a bun.

le **Chili** MASC NOUN
Chile

★ la **chimie** FEM NOUN
chemistry
□ un cours de chimie a chemistry lesson

★ **chimique** (FEM **chimique**) ADJECTIVE
chemical
□ une réaction chimique a chemical reaction
■ **les produits chimiques** chemicals

★ la **Chine** FEM NOUN
China

★ **chinois** (FEM **chinoise**) ADJECTIVE, NOUN
Chinese
□ Il apprend le chinois. He's learning Chinese.
■ **un Chinois** a Chinese (*man*)
■ **une Chinoise** a Chinese (*woman*)
■ **les Chinois** the Chinese

le **chiot** MASC NOUN
puppy

★ les **chips** FEM PL NOUN
crisps
□ un paquet de chips a packet of crisps

chirurgical (FEM **chirurgicale**, MASC PL **chirurgicaux**) ADJECTIVE
■ **une intervention chirurgicale** an operation

la **chirurgie** FEM NOUN
surgery
■ **la chirurgie esthétique** plastic surgery

★ le **chirurgien** MASC NOUN
surgeon

le **choc** MASC NOUN
shock
□ Ça m'a fait un sacré choc de le voir comme ça. It gave me a terrible shock to see him in that state.
■ **Elle est encore sous le choc.** She's still in shock.

★ le **chocolat** MASC NOUN
chocolate
■ **un chocolat chaud** a hot chocolate
■ **le chocolat à croquer** dark chocolate
■ **le chocolat au lait** milk chocolate

le **chœur** MASC NOUN
choir

★ **choisir** VERB [38]
to choose

★ le **choix** MASC NOUN
1 choice
■ **avoir le choix** to have the choice
2 selection
□ Il n'y a pas beaucoup de choix dans ce magasin. There's not a very wide selection of things in this shop.

★ le **chômage** MASC NOUN
unemployment
■ **être au chômage** to be unemployed

★ le **chômeur** MASC NOUN
unemployed person
□ Il est chômeur. He's unemployed.

★ la **chômeuse** FEM NOUN
unemployed woman
□ Elle est chômeuse. She's unemployed.

choquer VERB [28]
to shock
□ Cette remarque m'a choqué. I was shocked by that remark.

★ la **chorale** FEM NOUN
choir

★ la **chose** FEM NOUN
thing
□ J'ai des tas de choses à te raconter. I've got loads of things to tell you.
■ **C'est peu de chose.** It's nothing really.

★ le **chou** (PL les **choux**) MASC NOUN
cabbage
■ **les choux de Bruxelles** Brussels sprouts
■ **un chou à la crème** a choux bun

le **chouchou** MASC NOUN (*informal*)
teacher's pet

la **chouchoute** FEM NOUN (*informal*)
teacher's pet

la **choucroute** FEM NOUN
sauerkraut (*with sausages and ham*)

★ la **chouette** FEM NOUN
▷ *see also* **chouette** ADJECTIVE
owl

★ **chouette** (FEM **chouette**) ADJECTIVE (*informal*)
▷ *see also* **chouette** NOUN
brilliant
□ Chouette alors! Brilliant!

★ le **chou-fleur** (PL les **choux-fleurs**) MASC NOUN
cauliflower

★ **chrétien** (FEM **chrétienne**) ADJECTIVE
Christian
□ Il est chrétien. He's a Christian.

le **Christ** MASC NOUN
Christ

chronologique (FEM **chronologique**) ADJECTIVE
chronological

le **chronomètre** MASC NOUN
stopwatch

chronométrer VERB [34]
to time

le **chrysanthème** MASC NOUN
chrysanthemum

DID YOU KNOW...?
Chrysanthemums are strongly associated with funerals in France and it is customary to lay them on graves on All Saints' Day (1 November). Because of this association they are never given as gifts.

chuchoter VERB [28]
to whisper

chut EXCLAMATION
shh!

la **chute** FEM NOUN
fall
■ **faire une chute** to fall
■ **une chute d'eau** a waterfall
■ **la chute des cheveux** hair loss
■ **les chutes de neige** snowfalls

Chypre NOUN
Cyprus

-ci ADVERB
■ **ce livre-ci** this book
■ **ces bottes-ci** these boots

la **cible** FEM NOUN
target

la **ciboulette** FEM NOUN
chives

la **cicatrice** FEM NOUN
scar

se **cicatriser** VERB [28]
to heal up
□ Cette plaie s'est vite cicatrisée. This wound has healed up quickly.

ci-contre ADVERB
opposite
□ la page ci-contre the opposite page

ci-dessous ADVERB
below
□ la photo ci-dessous the picture below

ci-dessus ADVERB
above

★ le **cidre** MASC NOUN
cider

★ le **ciel** MASC NOUN
1 sky
□ un ciel nuageux a cloudy sky
2 heaven
□ être au ciel to be in heaven

le **cierge** MASC NOUN
candle (*in church*)

la **cigale** FEM NOUN
cicada

le **cigare** MASC NOUN
cigar
□ Il fume le cigare. He smokes cigars.

★ la **cigarette** FEM NOUN
cigarette

la **cigogne** FEM NOUN
stork

ci-joint ADVERB
attached
□ Veuillez trouver ci-joint mon curriculum vitae. Please find attached my CV.

le **cil** MASC NOUN
eyelash

le **ciment** MASC NOUN
cement

le **cimetière** MASC NOUN
cemetery

le/la **cinéaste** MASC/FEM NOUN
film-maker

★ le **cinéma** MASC NOUN
cinema

★ **cinq** NUMBER
five
□ Il est cinq heures du matin. It's five in the morning. □ Il a cinq ans. He's five.
■ **le cinq février** the fifth of February

la **cinquantaine** FEM NOUN
about fifty
□ Il y avait une cinquantaine de personnes. There were about fifty people there.
■ **Il a la cinquantaine.** He's in his fifties.

★ **cinquante** NUMBER
fifty
□ Il a cinquante ans. He's fifty.
■ **cinquante et un** fifty-one
■ **cinquante-deux** fifty-two

★ **cinquième** (FEM **cinquième**) ADJECTIVE
▷ *see also* **cinquième** NOUN
fifth
□ au cinquième étage on the fifth floor

★ la **cinquième** FEM NOUN
▷ *see also* **cinquième** ADJECTIVE
year 8
□ Mon frère est en cinquième. My brother's in year 8.

DID YOU KNOW...?
In French secondary schools, years are counted from the **sixième** (youngest) to **première** and **terminale** (oldest).

le **cintre** MASC NOUN
coat hanger

le **cirage** MASC NOUN
shoe polish

circonflexe (FEM **circonflexe**) ADJECTIVE
■ **un accent circonflexe** a circumflex

la **circonstance** FEM NOUN
circumstance
□ dans les circonstances actuelles in the present circumstances

★ la **circulation** FEM NOUN
1 traffic
□ Il y avait beaucoup de circulation. There was a lot of traffic.
2 circulation
□ Elle a des problèmes de circulation. She has bad circulation.

★ **circuler** VERB [28]
to run
□ Il n'y a qu'un bus sur trois qui circule. Only one bus in three is running.

la **cire** FEM NOUN
wax

le **ciré** MASC NOUN
oilskin jacket

cirer VERB [28]
to polish (*shoes, floor*)

★ le **cirque** MASC NOUN
circus

★ les **ciseaux** MASC PL NOUN
■ **une paire de ciseaux** a pair of scissors

le **citadin** MASC NOUN
city dweller

la **citation** FEM NOUN
quotation

★ la **cité** FEM NOUN
estate
□ J'habite dans une cité. I live on an estate.
■ **une cité universitaire** halls of residence
■ **une cité-dortoir** a dormitory town

citer VERB [28]
to quote

le **citoyen** MASC NOUN
citizen

la **citoyenne** FEM NOUN
citizen

la **citoyenneté** FEM NOUN
citizenship

★ le **citron** MASC NOUN
lemon
■ **un citron vert** a lime
■ **un citron pressé** a freshly squeezed lemon juice

la **citronnade** FEM NOUN
still lemonade

la **citrouille** FEM NOUN
pumpkin

le **civet** MASC NOUN
stew
□ du civet de lapin rabbit stew

civil (FEM **civile**) ADJECTIVE
civilian
■ **en civil** in civilian clothes

la **civilisation** FEM NOUN
civilization

★ **civique** (FEM **civique**) ADJECTIVE
■ **l'instruction civique** citizenship

★ **clair** (FEM **claire**) ADJECTIVE, ADVERB
1 light
□ vert clair light green □ C'est une pièce très claire. It's a very light room.
2 clear (*water*)
■ **voir clair** to see clearly
■ **le clair de lune** moonlight

clairement ADVERB
clearly

la **clairière** FEM NOUN
clearing

clandestin (FEM **clandestine**) ADJECTIVE
■ **un passager clandestin** a stowaway

la **claque** FEM NOUN
slap
□ Elle m'a donné une claque. She gave me a slap.

claquer VERB [28]
1 to bang
□ On entend des volets qui claquent. You can hear shutters banging.
2 to slam
□ Elle est partie en claquant la porte. She left, slamming the door behind her.

les **claquettes** FEM PL NOUN
■ **faire des claquettes** to tap-dance

la **clarinette** FEM NOUN
clarinet

★ la **classe** FEM NOUN
1 class
□ C'est la meilleure élève de la classe. She's the best pupil in the class. □ voyager en première classe to travel first class
2 classroom

★ **classer** VERB [28]
to arrange
□ Les livres sont classés par ordre alphabétique. The books are arranged in alphabetical order.

★ le **classeur** MASC NOUN
ring binder

★ **classique** (FEM **classique**) ADJECTIVE
1 classical
□ de la musique classique classical music
2 classic
□ un style classique a classic style

★ le **clavier** MASC NOUN
keyboard (*of computer, typewriter*)

★ la **clé** FEM NOUN
1 key
□ une clé de voiture a car key
2 clef
□ la clé de sol the treble clef □ la clé de fa the bass clef
■ **une clé USB** a USB stick

★ la **clef** FEM NOUN = clé

★ le **client** MASC NOUN
customer

★ la **cliente** FEM NOUN
customer

la **clientèle** FEM NOUN
customers

cligner VERB [28]
■ **cligner des yeux** to blink

le **clignotant** MASC NOUN
indicator
□ Il a mis son clignotant à gauche. He's indicating left.

★ le **climat** MASC NOUN
climate

★ la **climatisation** FEM NOUN
air conditioning

climatisé (FEM **climatisée**) ADJECTIVE
air-conditioned
□ L'hôtel est climatisé. The hotel is air-conditioned.

le **clin d'œil** (PL les **clins d'œil**) MASC NOUN
wink
■ **en un clin d'œil** in a flash

★ la **clinique** FEM NOUN
private hospital

★ **cliquer** VERB [28]
to click
□ cliquer sur une icône to click on an icon

le **clochard** MASC NOUN
tramp

★ la **cloche** FEM NOUN
bell

le **clocher** MASC NOUN
1 church tower
2 steeple

le **clone** MASC NOUN
clone

cloner VERB [28]
to clone

★ le **clou** MASC NOUN
nail
■ **un clou de girofle** a clove

le **clown** MASC NOUN
clown

★ le **club** MASC NOUN
club

★ le **cobaye** MASC NOUN
guinea pig

★ le **coca** MASC NOUN
Coke®

la **cocaïne** FEM NOUN
cocaine

la **coccinelle** FEM NOUN
ladybird

★ **cocher** VERB [28]
to tick
□ Cochez la bonne réponse. Tick the right answer.

★ **cochon** (FEM **cochonne**) ADJECTIVE (*informal*)
▷ *see also* **cochon** NOUN
dirty
□ une histoire cochonne a dirty story

★ le **cochon** MASC NOUN
▷ *see also* **cochon** ADJECTIVE
pig
■ **un cochon d'Inde** a guinea pig

le **cocktail** MASC NOUN
1 cocktail
2 cocktail party

le **coco** MASC NOUN
▪ **une noix de coco** a coconut

cocorico EXCLAMATION
1 cock-a-doodle-doo!
2 three cheers for France!

DID YOU KNOW...?
The symbol of France is the cockerel and so **cocorico!** is sometimes used as an expression of French national pride.

la **cocotte** FEM NOUN
casserole (*pan*)
▪ **une cocotte-minute**® a pressure cooker

★ le **code** MASC NOUN
code
▪ **le code de la route** the highway code
▪ **le code postal** the postcode

★ le **cœur** MASC NOUN
heart
▪ **avoir bon cœur** to be kind-hearted
▪ **la dame de cœur** the queen of hearts
▪ **avoir mal au cœur** to feel sick
▪ **par cœur** by heart □ apprendre quelque chose par cœur to learn something by heart

★ le **coffre** MASC NOUN
1 boot (*of car*)
2 chest (*furniture*)

le **coffre-fort** (PL les **coffres-forts**) MASC NOUN
safe

le **coffret** MASC NOUN
▪ **un coffret à bijoux** a jewellery box

le **cognac** MASC NOUN
brandy

★ se **cogner** VERB [28]
▪ **se cogner à quelque chose** to bang into something □ Je me suis cogné à la table. I banged into the table. □ Je me suis cogné la tête contre la porte du placard. I banged my head on the cupboard door.

coiffé (FEM **coiffée**) ADJECTIVE
▪ **Tu es bien coiffée.** Your hair looks nice.

coiffer VERB [28]
▪ **se coiffer** to do one's hair
▪ **se faire coiffer** to have one's hair done

★ le **coiffeur** MASC NOUN
hairdresser

★ la **coiffeuse** FEM NOUN
hairdresser

★ la **coiffure** FEM NOUN
hairstyle
□ Cette coiffure te va bien. That hairstyle suits you.
▪ **un salon de coiffure** a hairdresser's

★ le **coin** MASC NOUN
corner
□ au coin de la rue on the corner of the street
▪ **Tu habites dans le coin?** Do you live near here?
▪ **Je ne suis pas du coin.** I'm not from here.
▪ **le bistrot du coin** the local pub

BE CAREFUL!
The French word **coin** does not mean **coin**.

coincé (FEM **coincée**) ADJECTIVE
1 stuck
□ La clé est coincée dans la serrure. The key is stuck in the keyhole.
2 stuffy
□ Il est un peu coincé. (*informal*) He's a bit stuffy.

coincer VERB [12]
to jam
□ La porte est coincée. The door's jammed.

la **coïncidence** FEM NOUN
coincidence

le **col** MASC NOUN
1 collar
2 pass (*of mountain*)

★ la **colère** FEM NOUN
anger
▪ **Je suis en colère.** I'm angry.
▪ **se mettre en colère** to get angry

le **colin** MASC NOUN
hake

la **colique** FEM NOUN
diarrhoea

★ le **colis** MASC NOUN
parcel

collaborer VERB [28]
to collaborate

★ **collant** (FEM **collante**) ADJECTIVE
▷ *see also* **collant** NOUN
1 sticky
2 clingy
□ Je le trouve un peu collant. (*informal*) I find him a bit clingy.

★ le **collant** MASC NOUN
▷ *see also* **collant** ADJECTIVE
tights
□ un collant en laine woollen tights

★ la **colle** FEM NOUN
1 glue
□ un tube de colle a tube of glue
2 detention
□ J'ai une heure de colle samedi prochain. I've got an hour's detention next Saturday.
▪ **Je n'en sais rien: tu me poses une colle.** I really don't know: you've got me there.

la **collecte** FEM NOUN
collection (*of money*)
□ On a fait une collecte au profit des victimes. There was a collection for the victims.

French-English

C

★ la **collection** FEM NOUN
collection
□ une collection de timbres a stamp collection

★ **collectionner** VERB [28]
to collect

★ le **collège** MASC NOUN
secondary school

DID YOU KNOW...?
In France, pupils go to a **collège** between the ages of 11 and 15, and then to a **lycée** until the age of 18.

le **collégien** MASC NOUN
schoolboy

la **collégienne** FEM NOUN
schoolgirl

★ le/la **collègue** MASC/FEM NOUN
colleague

★ **coller** VERB [28]
1 to stick
□ Il y a un chewing-gum collé sous la chaise. There's a bit of chewing gum stuck under the chair. □ Ce timbre ne colle plus. This stamp won't stick on.
2 to press
□ J'ai collé mon oreille au mur. I pressed my ear against the wall.

★ le **collier** MASC NOUN
1 necklace
□ un collier de perles a pearl necklace
2 collar (*of dog, cat*)

★ la **colline** FEM NOUN
hill

★ la **collision** FEM NOUN
crash

la **colombe** FEM NOUN
dove

★ la **colonie** FEM NOUN
■ **aller en colonie de vacances** to go to summer camp

la **colonne** FEM NOUN
column
■ **la colonne vertébrale** the spine

le **colorant** MASC NOUN
colouring

le **coloris** MASC NOUN
colour

le **coma** MASC NOUN
coma
□ être dans le coma to be in a coma

le **combat** MASC NOUN
fighting
□ Les combats ont repris ce matin. Fighting started again this morning.
■ **un combat de boxe** a boxing match

le **combattant** MASC NOUN
■ **un ancien combattant** a war veteran

combattre VERB [9]
to fight

★ **combien** ADVERB
1 how much
□ Vous en voulez combien? Un kilo? How much do you want? One kilo? □ C'est combien? How much is that? □ Combien est-ce que ça coûte? How much does it cost? □ Combien ça fait? How much does it come to?
2 how many
□ Tu en veux combien? Deux? How many do you want? Two?
■ **combien de** **1** how much □ Combien de purée est-ce que je vous sers? How much mashed potato shall I give you? **2** how many □ Combien de personnes as-tu invitées? How many people have you invited?
■ **combien de temps** how long □ Combien de temps est-ce que tu seras absente? How long will you be away?
■ **Il y a combien de temps?** How long ago? □ Il est parti il y a combien de temps? How long ago did he leave?
■ **On est le combien aujourd'hui? — On est le vingt.** What's the date today? — It's the 20th.

la **combinaison** FEM NOUN
1 combination
□ J'ai changé la combinaison de mon antivol. I've changed the combination on my bike lock.
2 slip (*petticoat*)
■ **une combinaison de plongée** a wetsuit
■ **une combinaison de ski** a ski suit

le **comble** MASC NOUN
■ **Alors ça, c'est le comble!** That's the last straw!

★ la **comédie** FEM NOUN
comedy
■ **une comédie musicale** a musical

★ le **comédien** MASC NOUN
actor

★ la **comédienne** FEM NOUN
actress

comestible (FEM **comestible**) ADJECTIVE
edible

★ **comique** (FEM **comique**) ADJECTIVE
▷ *see also* **comique** NOUN
comical

★ le/la **comique** MASC/FEM NOUN
▷ *see also* **comique** ADJECTIVE
comedian

★ le **comité** MASC NOUN
committee

le **commandant** MASC NOUN
captain (*of ship, plane*)

★ la **commande** FEM NOUN
order

□ un bon de commande an order form
■ **être aux commandes** to be at the controls

★ **commander** VERB [28]
1 to order
□ J'ai commandé une robe sur Internet. I've ordered a dress on the internet.
2 to give orders
□ C'est moi qui commande ici, pas vous! I give the orders here, not you!

★ **comme** CONJUNCTION, ADVERB
1 like
□ Il est comme son père. He's like his father.
□ Je voudrais un manteau comme celui de la photo. I'd like a coat like the one in the picture.
2 for
□ Qu'est-ce que tu veux comme dessert? What would you like for dessert?
3 as
□ J'ai travaillé comme serveuse cet été. I worked as a waitress this summer. □ Faites comme vous voulez. Do as you like.
■ **comme ça** like this □ Ça se plie comme ça. You fold it like this.
■ **C'était un poisson grand comme ça.** The fish was this big.
■ **comme il faut** properly □ Mets le couvert comme il faut! Set the table properly!
■ **Comme tu as grandi!** How you've grown!
■ **Regarde comme c'est beau!** Look, isn't it lovely!
■ **comme ci comme ça** so-so □ Comment est-ce que tu as trouvé le film? — Comme ci comme ça. What did you think of the film? — So-so.

★ le **commencement** MASC NOUN
beginning

★ **commencer** VERB [12]
to start
□ Les cours commencent à huit heures. Lessons start at 8 o'clock. □ Il a commencé à pleuvoir. It started raining. □ J'ai commencé à réviser pour les examens. I've started revising for the exams.

★ **comment** ADVERB
how
□ Comment arrives-tu à travailler dans ce bruit? How can you possibly work with this noise?
■ **Comment allez-vous?** How are you?
■ **Comment dit-on 'pomme' en anglais?** How do you say 'pomme' in English?
■ **Comment s'appelle-t-il?** What's his name?
■ **Comment?** What did you say?

le **commentaire** MASC NOUN
comment

les **commérages** MASC PL NOUN
gossip *sing*

★ le **commerçant** MASC NOUN
shopkeeper

★ le **commerce** MASC NOUN
1 trade
□ le commerce extérieur foreign trade
■ **le commerce électronique** e-commerce
2 business
□ Il fait des études de commerce. He's studying business.
3 shop
□ tenir un commerce to have a shop
■ **On trouve ça dans le commerce.** You can find it in the shops.

commercial (FEM **commerciale**, MASC PL **commerciaux**) ADJECTIVE
■ **un centre commercial** a shopping centre

★ **commettre** VERB [47]
to commit
□ Il a commis un crime grave. He has committed a serious crime.

le/la **commissaire** MASC/FEM NOUN
police superintendent

★ le **commissariat** MASC NOUN
police station

★ les **commissions** FEM PL NOUN
shopping *sing*
□ J'ai quelques commissions à faire. I've got some shopping to do.

★ la **commode** FEM NOUN
▷ *see also* **commode** ADJECTIVE
chest of drawers

★ **commode** (FEM **commode**) ADJECTIVE
▷ *see also* **commode** NOUN
handy
□ Ce sac est très commode pour les voyages. This bag is very handy for travelling.
■ **Son père n'est pas commode.** His father is a difficult character.

★ **commun** (FEM **commune**) ADJECTIVE
shared
□ une salle de bain commune a shared bathroom
■ **Nous avons des intérêts communs.** We have interests in common.
■ **en commun** in common □ Ils n'ont rien en commun. They've got nothing in common.
■ **les transports en commun** public transport
■ **mettre quelque chose en commun** to share something □ Nous mettons tous nos livres en commun. We share all our books.

la **communauté** FEM NOUN
community

★ la **communication** FEM NOUN
communication
■ **une communication téléphonique** a telephone call

French-English

C

la **communion** FEM NOUN
communion
□ faire sa première communion to make one's first communion

communiquer VERB [28]
to communicate

communiste (FEM **communiste**) ADJECTIVE
communist
□ le Parti communiste the Communist Party

compact (FEM **compacte**) ADJECTIVE
compact
■ **un disque compact** a compact disc

★ la **compagne** FEM NOUN
1 companion
2 partner (*living together*)

★ la **compagnie** FEM NOUN
company
□ J'aime avoir de la compagnie. I like to have company. □ Je viendrai te tenir compagnie. I'll come to keep you company.
■ **une compagnie d'assurances** an insurance company
■ **une compagnie aérienne** an airline

★ le **compagnon** MASC NOUN
1 companion
2 partner (*living together*)

★ la **comparaison** FEM NOUN
comparison
□ en comparaison de in comparison with

★ **comparer** VERB [28]
to compare

★ le **compartiment** MASC NOUN
compartment (*on train*)

le **compas** MASC NOUN
compass (*for drawing circles*)

compatible (FEM **compatible**) ADJECTIVE
compatible

la **compétence** FEM NOUN
1 competence
2 skill
□ les compétences clés pour cet emploi the key skills for this job

compétent (FEM **compétente**) ADJECTIVE
competent

compétitif (FEM **compétitive**) ADJECTIVE
competitive

★ la **compétition** FEM NOUN
competition
■ **avoir l'esprit de compétition** to be competitive

★ **complet** (FEM **complète**) ADJECTIVE
▷ *see also* **complet** NOUN
1 complete
□ les œuvres complètes de Shakespeare the complete works of Shakespeare
2 full
□ L'hôtel est complet. The hotel is full.
■ **'complet'** 'no vacancies'
■ **le pain complet** wholemeal bread

★ le **complet** MASC NOUN
▷ *see also* **complet** ADJECTIVE
suit (*for man*)

★ **complètement** ADVERB
completely
□ J'avais complètement oublié que tu venais. I'd completely forgotten that you were coming.

★ **compléter** VERB [34]
to complete
□ Complétez les phrases suivantes. Complete the following sentences.

complexe (FEM **complexe**) ADJECTIVE
complex

complexé (FEM **complexée**) ADJECTIVE
hung up

la **complication** FEM NOUN
complication

le/la **complice** MASC/FEM NOUN
accomplice

★ le **compliment** MASC NOUN
compliment
■ **faire un compliment** to compliment □ Il m'a fait un compliment sur ma robe. He complimented me on my dress.

★ **compliqué** (FEM **compliquée**) ADJECTIVE
complicated
□ C'est une histoire compliquée. It's a complicated story.

le **complot** MASC NOUN
plot

★ le **comportement** MASC NOUN
behaviour

comporter VERB [28]
1 to consist of
□ Le château comporte trois parties. The castle consists of three parts.
2 to have
□ Ce modèle comporte un écran couleur. This model has a colour screen.
■ **se comporter** to behave □ Il s'est comporté de façon odieuse. He behaved atrociously.

★ **composer** VERB [28]
to compose (*music, text*)
■ **composer un numéro** to dial a number
■ **se composer de** to consist of □ L'uniforme se compose d'une veste, d'un pantalon et d'une cravate. The uniform consists of a jacket, trousers and a tie.

le **compositeur** MASC NOUN
composer

la **composition** FEM NOUN
test
□ Nous avons une composition de français cet après-midi. We've got a French test this afternoon.

la **compositrice** FEM NOUN
composer

★ le **compostage** MASC NOUN
date stamping

★ **composter** VERB [28]
to punch
□ N'oublie pas de composter ton billet avant de monter dans le train. Remember to punch your ticket before you get on the train.

DID YOU KNOW...?
In France, you have to punch your ticket on the platform to validate it before getting onto the train.

la **compote** FEM NOUN
stewed fruit
■ **la compote de prunes** stewed plums

compréhensible (FEM **compréhensible**) ADJECTIVE
understandable

★ **compréhensif** (FEM **compréhensive**) ADJECTIVE
understanding

BE CAREFUL!
compréhensif does not mean **comprehensive**.

la **compréhension** FEM NOUN
1 comprehension
□ la compréhension orale listening comprehension
2 sympathy
□ Elle a fait preuve de beaucoup de compréhension à mon égard. She showed a lot of sympathy for me.

★ **comprendre** VERB [65]
1 to understand
□ Je ne comprends pas ce que vous dites. I don't understand what you're saying.
2 to include
□ Le forfait ne comprend pas la location des skis. The price doesn't include ski hire.

★ le **comprimé** MASC NOUN
tablet
■ **un comprimé d'aspirine** an aspirin

★ **compris** (FEM **comprise**) ADJECTIVE
included
□ Le service n'est pas compris. Service is not included.
■ **y compris** including □ Ils ont tout vendu, y compris leur voiture. They sold everything, including their car.
■ **non compris** excluding □ un menu à vingt euros, vin non compris a set menu for 20 euros, excluding wine
■ **cent euros tout compris** 100 euros all-inclusive

compromettre VERB [47]
to compromise

le **compromis** MASC NOUN
compromise
□ Ils sont parvenus à un compromis. They came to a compromise.

la **comptabilité** FEM NOUN
accounting
□ un cours de comptabilité a course in accounting

★ le/la **comptable** MASC/FEM NOUN
accountant
□ Il est comptable. He's an accountant.

comptant ADVERB
■ **payer comptant** to pay cash

★ le **compte** MASC NOUN
account
□ J'ai déposé le chèque sur mon compte. I've paid the cheque into my account.
■ **Le compte est bon.** That's the right amount.
■ **tenir compte de** 1 to take into account □ Ils ont tenu compte de mon expérience. They took my experience into account. 2 to take notice of □ Il n'a pas tenu compte de mes conseils. He took no notice of my advice.
■ **travailler à son compte** to be self-employed
■ **en fin de compte** all things considered □ Le voyage ne s'est pas mal passé, en fin de compte. The journey wasn't bad, all things considered.

★ **compter** VERB [28]
to count

le **compte rendu** (PL les **comptes rendus**) MASC NOUN
report

le **compteur** MASC NOUN
meter

★ le **comptoir** MASC NOUN
bar
□ au comptoir at the bar

se **concentrer** VERB [28]
to concentrate
□ J'ai du mal à me concentrer. I find it hard to concentrate.

la **conception** FEM NOUN
design

concernant PREPOSITION
regarding
□ Concernant notre nouveau projet, je voudrais ajouter que ... Regarding our new project, I would like to add that ...

concerner VERB [28]
to concern
□ en ce qui me concerne as far as I'm concerned
■ **Je ne me sens pas concerné.** I don't feel it's anything to do with me.

★ le **concert** MASC NOUN
concert

★ le/la **concierge** MASC/FEM NOUN
caretaker

conclure VERB [13]
to conclude

la **conclusion** FEM NOUN
conclusion

★ le **concombre** MASC NOUN
cucumber

concorder VERB [28]
to tally
□ Les dates concordent. The dates tally.

★ le **concours** MASC NOUN
1 competition
□ un concours de chant a singing competition
2 competitive exam (*for a job or a place in a school*)

concret (FEM **concrète**) ADJECTIVE
concrete

conçu VERB
designed
□ Ces appartements sont très mal conçus. These flats are very badly designed.

la **concurrence** FEM NOUN
competition
□ La concurrence est vive sur ce marché. There's a lot of competition in this market.

le **concurrent** MASC NOUN
competitor

la **concurrente** FEM NOUN
competitor

condamner VERB [28]
1 to sentence
□ Il a été condamné à deux ans de prison. He was sentenced to two years in prison.
□ condamner à mort to sentence to death
2 to condemn
□ Le gouvernement a condamné cette décision. The government condemned this decision.

la **condition** FEM NOUN
condition
□ Je le ferai à une condition ... I'll do it, on one condition ...
■ **à condition que** provided that □ Je viendrai à condition qu'il me le demande. I'll come provided he asks me to.
■ **les conditions de travail** working conditions

le **conditionnel** MASC NOUN
conditional tense

★ le **conducteur** MASC NOUN
driver

BE CAREFUL!
The French word **conducteur** does not mean **conductor**.

★ la **conductrice** FEM NOUN
driver

★ **conduire** VERB [23]
to drive
□ Est-ce que tu sais conduire? Can you drive?
□ Je te conduirai chez le docteur. I'll drive you to the doctor's.
■ **se conduire** to behave □ Il s'est mal conduit. He behaved badly.

la **conduite** FEM NOUN
behaviour

★ la **conférence** FEM NOUN
1 lecture
□ donner une conférence to give a lecture
2 conference
□ une conférence internationale an international conference

se **confesser** VERB [28]
to go to confession

les **confettis** MASC PL NOUN
confetti

★ la **confiance** FEM NOUN
1 trust
■ **avoir confiance en quelqu'un** to trust somebody □ Je n'ai pas confiance en lui. I don't trust him.
■ **faire confiance à quelqu'un** to trust somebody □ Tu ne me fais pas confiance? Don't you trust me?
2 confidence
■ **Tu peux avoir confiance. Il sera à l'heure.** You don't need to worry. He'll be on time.
■ **confiance en soi** self-confidence □ Elle manque de confiance en elle. She lacks self-confidence.

confiant (FEM **confiante**) ADJECTIVE
confident

les **confidences** FEM PL NOUN
■ **faire des confidences à quelqu'un** to confide in someone □ Elle me fait quelquefois des confidences. She sometimes confides in me.

confidentiel (FEM **confidentielle**) ADJECTIVE
confidential

confier VERB [19]
■ **se confier à quelqu'un** to confide in somebody □ Elle s'est confiée à sa meilleure amie. She confided in her best friend.

★ **confirmer** VERB [28]
to confirm

★ la **confiserie** FEM NOUN
sweet shop

confisquer VERB [28]
to confiscate

confit (FEM **confite**) ADJECTIVE
■ **des fruits confits** crystallized fruits

★la **confiture** FEM NOUN
jam
□ la confiture de fraises strawberry jam
■ **la confiture d'oranges** marmalade

le **conflit** MASC NOUN
conflict

confondre VERB [69]
to mix up
□ On le confond souvent avec son frère. People often mix him up with his brother.

★le **confort** MASC NOUN
comfort
■ **tout confort** with all mod cons □ un appartement tout confort a flat with all mod cons

★**confortable** (FEM **confortable**) ADJECTIVE
comfortable
□ des chaussures confortables comfortable shoes

confus (FEM **confuse**) ADJECTIVE
1 unclear
□ J'ai trouvé ses explications confuses. I thought his explanation was unclear.
2 embarrassed
□ Il avait l'air confus. He looked embarrassed.

la **confusion** FEM NOUN
1 confusion
2 embarrassment
□ rougir de confusion to go red with embarrassment

★le **congé** MASC NOUN
holiday
□ une semaine de congé a week's holiday
■ **en congé** on holiday □ Je serai en congé la semaine prochaine. I'll be on holiday next week.
■ **un congé de maladie** sick leave □ Il est en congé de maladie. He's on sick leave.

★le **congélateur** MASC NOUN
freezer

★**congeler** VERB [1]
to freeze

la **conjonction** FEM NOUN
conjunction

la **conjonctivite** FEM NOUN
conjunctivitis

la **conjugaison** FEM NOUN
conjugation

★la **connaissance** FEM NOUN
1 knowledge
□ ... pour approfondir vos connaissances ... to increase your knowledge
2 acquaintance
□ Ce n'est pas vraiment une amie, juste une connaissance. She's not really a friend, just an acquaintance.
■ **perdre connaissance** to lose consciousness
■ **faire la connaissance de quelqu'un** to meet somebody □ J'ai fait la connaissance de son frère. I met her brother.

★**connaître** VERB [14]
to know
□ Je ne connais pas du tout cette région. I don't know this area at all. □ Je le connais de vue. I know him by sight.
■ **Ils se sont connus à Nantes.** They first met in Nantes.
■ **s'y connaître en quelque chose** to know about something □ Je ne m'y connais pas beaucoup en musique classique. I don't know much about classical music.

connecté (FEM **connectée**) ADJECTIVE
online (*computer*)

se **connecter** VERB [28]
to log on
□ Je me suis connecté sur Internet il y a dix minutes. I logged onto the internet ten minutes ago.

connu (FEM **connue**) ADJECTIVE
well-known
□ C'est un acteur connu. He's a well-known actor.

conquérir VERB [2]
to conquer

★**consacrer** VERB [28]
to devote
□ Il consacre beaucoup de temps à ses enfants. He devotes a lot of time to his children.
■ **Je suis désolé, je n'ai pas beaucoup de temps à vous consacrer.** I'm afraid I can't spare much time for you.

la **conscience** FEM NOUN
conscience
□ avoir mauvaise conscience to have a guilty conscience
■ **prendre conscience de** to become aware of □ Ils ont fini par prendre conscience de la gravité de la situation. They eventually became aware of the seriousness of the situation.

consciencieux (FEM **consciencieuse**) ADJECTIVE
conscientious

conscient (FEM **consciente**) ADJECTIVE
conscious

consécutif (FEM **consécutive**) ADJECTIVE
consecutive

★le **conseil** MASC NOUN
advice
□ Est-ce que je peux te demander conseil? Can I ask you for some advice?
■ **un conseil** a piece of advice

★**conseiller** VERB [28]
▷ *see also* **conseiller** NOUN

French-English

c

1 to advise
□ Il a été mal conseillé. He has been badly advised.
2 to recommend
□ Il m'a conseillé ce livre. He recommended this book to me.

★ le **conseiller** MASC NOUN
▷ *see also* **conseiller** VERB
1 councillor (*political*)
□ un conseiller municipal a town councillor
2 adviser
□ le conseiller d'orientation the careers adviser

le **consentement** MASC NOUN
consent
□ le consentement des parents the parents' consent

consentir VERB [77]
to agree
□ consentir à quelque chose to agree to something

★ la **conséquence** FEM NOUN
consequence
■ **en conséquence** consequently

conséquent (FEM **conséquente**) ADJECTIVE
■ **par conséquent** consequently

le **conservatoire** MASC NOUN
school of music
□ Elle fait du piano au conservatoire. She's learning the piano at the school of music.

la **conserve** FEM NOUN
tin
□ Je vais ouvrir une conserve. I'll open a tin.
■ **une boîte de conserve** a tin
■ **les conserves** tinned food □ Il n'est pas bon de manger tous les jours des conserves. It's not healthy to eat tinned food every day.
■ **en conserve** tinned □ des petits pois en conserve tinned peas

conserver VERB [28]
to keep
□ J'ai conservé toutes ses lettres. I've kept all her letters.
■ **se conserver** to keep □ Ce pain se conserve plus d'une semaine. This bread will keep for more than a week.

considérable (FEM **considérable**) ADJECTIVE
considerable
□ Il a fait des progrès considérables. He's made considerable progress.

la **considération** FEM NOUN
■ **prendre quelque chose en considération** to take something into consideration

considérer VERB [34]
■ **considérer que** to believe that □ Je considère que le gouvernement devrait investir davantage dans l'éducation. I believe that the government should invest more money in education.

★ la **consigne** FEM NOUN
left-luggage office
■ **une consigne automatique** a left-luggage locker

consistant (FEM **consistante**) ADJECTIVE
substantial
□ un petit déjeuner consistant a substantial breakfast

consister VERB [28]
■ **consister à** to consist of □ Mon travail consiste à répondre au téléphone et à recevoir les clients. My job consists of answering the phone and welcoming the customers.
■ **En quoi consiste votre travail?** What does your job involve?

★ la **console de jeu** FEM NOUN
games console

consoler VERB [28]
to console

le **consommateur** MASC NOUN
1 consumer
2 customer (*in café*)

la **consommation** FEM NOUN
1 consumption
□ la consommation d'électricité electricity consumption
2 drink
□ Le billet d'entrée donne droit à une consommation gratuite. The ticket entitles you to one free drink.

la **consommatrice** FEM NOUN
1 consumer
2 customer (*in café*)

★ **consommer** VERB [28]
1 to use
□ Ces grosses voitures consomment beaucoup d'essence. These big cars use a lot of petrol.
2 to have a drink
□ Est-ce qu'on peut consommer à la terrasse? Can we have drinks outside?

la **consonne** FEM NOUN
consonant

constamment ADVERB
constantly
□ Elle se plaint constamment. She's constantly complaining.

constant (FEM **constante**) ADJECTIVE
constant

★ **constater** VERB [28]
to notice

★ **constipé** (FEM **constipée**) ADJECTIVE
constipated

constitué (FEM **constituée**) ADJECTIVE
■ **être constitué de** to consist of

constituer VERB [28]
to make up
□ les États qui constituent la Fédération russe the states which make up the Russian Federation

la **construction** FEM NOUN
building
□ des matériaux de construction building materials
■ **une maison en construction** a house being built

★ **construire** VERB [23]
to build
□ Ils font construire une maison neuve. They're having a new house built.

le **consulat** MASC NOUN
consulate
□ le consulat de France the French consulate

la **consultation** FEM NOUN
■ **les heures de consultation** surgery hours

★ **consulter** VERB [28]
1 to consult
□ Il vaut toujours mieux consulter un médecin. It's always best to consult a doctor.
2 to see patients
□ Le docteur ne consulte pas le samedi. The doctor doesn't see patients on Saturdays.

le **contact** MASC NOUN
contact
□ les contacts humains human contact
■ **Il a le contact facile.** He's very approachable.
■ **garder le contact avec quelqu'un** to keep in touch with somebody

★ **contacter** VERB [28]
to get in touch with
□ Je te contacterai dès que j'aurai des nouvelles. I'll get in touch with you as soon as I have some news.

contagieux (FEM **contagieuse**) ADJECTIVE
infectious
□ une maladie contagieuse an infectious disease □ Je suis peut-être contagieux. I might have something infectious.

contaminer VERB [28]
to contaminate

le **conte de fées** (PL les **contes de fées**) MASC NOUN
fairy tale

contempler VERB [28]
to gaze at

contemporain (FEM **contemporaine**) ADJECTIVE
contemporary
■ **un auteur contemporain** a modern writer

★ **contenir** VERB [83]
to contain
□ un portefeuille contenant de l'argent a wallet containing money

★ **content** (FEM **contente**) ADJECTIVE
glad
□ Je suis content que tu sois venu. I'm glad you've come.
■ **content de** pleased with □ Elle est contente de mon travail. She is pleased with my work.

contenter VERB [28]
to please
□ Il est difficile à contenter. He's hard to please.
■ **Je me contente de peu.** I can make do with very little.

contesté (FEM **contestée**) ADJECTIVE
controversial
□ Cette décision est très contestée. This is a very controversial decision.

le **continent** MASC NOUN
continent

continu (FEM **continue**) ADJECTIVE
continuous
■ **faire la journée continue** to work without taking a full lunch break

★ **continuellement** ADVERB
constantly

★ **continuer** VERB [28]
to carry on
□ Continuez sans moi! Carry on without me!
□ Il ne veut pas continuer ses études. He doesn't want to carry on studying.
■ **continuer à faire quelque chose** to go on doing something □ Ils ont continué à regarder la télé sans me dire bonjour. They went on watching TV without saying hello to me.
■ **continuer de faire quelque chose** to keep on doing something □ Il continue de fumer malgré son asthme. He keeps on smoking, despite his asthma.

contourner VERB [28]
to go round
□ La route contourne la ville. The road goes round the town.

le **contraceptif** MASC NOUN
contraceptive

la **contraception** FEM NOUN
contraception

le **contractuel** MASC NOUN
traffic warden

la **contractuelle** FEM NOUN
traffic warden

la **contradiction** FEM NOUN
contradiction
■ **par esprit de contradiction** just to be awkward □ Il a refusé de venir par esprit de contradiction. He refused to come, just to be awkward.

★ le **contraire** MASC NOUN
opposite
□ Il a fait le contraire de ce que je lui avais demandé. He did the opposite of what I asked him.
■ **au contraire** on the contrary

contrarier VERB [19]
1 to annoy
□ Il avait l'air contrarié. He looked annoyed.
2 to upset
□ Est-ce que tu serais contrariée si je ne venais pas? Would you be upset if I didn't come?

le **contraste** MASC NOUN
contrast

★ le **contrat** MASC NOUN
contract
□ un contrat de travail an employment contract

la **contravention** FEM NOUN
parking ticket

★ **contre** PREPOSITION
1 against
□ Ne mets pas ton vélo contre le mur. Don't put your bike against the wall. □ Tu es pour ou contre ce projet? Are you for or against this plan?
2 for
□ échanger quelque chose contre quelque chose to swap something for something
■ **par contre** on the other hand

la **contrebande** FEM NOUN
smuggling
■ **des produits de contrebande** smuggled goods

la **contrebasse** FEM NOUN
double bass

contrecœur
■ **à contrecœur** ADVERB reluctantly □ Il est venu à contrecœur. He came reluctantly.

contredire VERB [27]
to contradict
□ Il ne supporte pas d'être contredit. He can't stand being contradicted.

la **contre-indication** FEM NOUN
■ **'Contre-indication en cas d'eczéma'** 'Not to be used by people with eczema'

le **contresens** MASC NOUN
mistranslation

le **contretemps** MASC NOUN
■ **Désolé d'être en retard: j'ai eu un contretemps.** Sorry I'm late: I was held up.

★ **contribuer** VERB [28]
■ **contribuer à** to contribute to □ Est-ce que tu veux contribuer au cadeau pour Marie? Do you want to contribute to Marie's present?

le **contrôle** MASC NOUN
1 control
□ le contrôle des passeports passport control
2 check
□ un contrôle d'identité an identity check
■ **le contrôle des billets** ticket inspection
3 test
□ un contrôle antidopage a drugs test
■ **le contrôle continu** continuous assessment

★ **contrôler** VERB [28]
to check
□ Personne n'a contrôlé mon billet. Nobody checked my ticket.

★ le **contrôleur** MASC NOUN
ticket inspector

★ la **contrôleuse** FEM NOUN
ticket inspector

controversé (FEM **controversée**) ADJECTIVE
controversial

convaincre VERB [86]
1 to persuade
□ Il a essayé de me convaincre de rester. He tried to persuade me to stay.
2 to convince
□ Tu n'as pas l'air convaincu. You don't look convinced.

la **convalescence** FEM NOUN
convalescence

convenable (FEM **convenable**) ADJECTIVE
decent
□ un hôtel convenable a decent hotel
■ **Ce n'est pas convenable.** It's bad manners.

convenir VERB [89]
■ **convenir à** to suit □ Est-ce que cette date te convient? Does this date suit you?
□ J'espère que cela vous conviendra. I hope this will suit you.
■ **convenir de** to agree on □ Nous avons convenu d'une date. We've agreed on a date.

conventionné (FEM **conventionnée**) ADJECTIVE
■ **un médecin conventionné** a Health Service doctor

> **DID YOU KNOW...?**
> All doctors in France charge for treatment, but patients of Health Service doctors get most of their money refunded by the government.

convenu (FEM **convenue**) ADJECTIVE
agreed
□ au moment convenu at the agreed time

★ la **conversation** FEM NOUN
conversation

la **convocation** FEM NOUN
notification

convoquer VERB [28]
▪ **convoquer quelqu'un à une réunion** to invite somebody to a meeting
▪ **Le directeur m'a convoqué dans son bureau.** The headteacher asked me into his office.

cool (FEM+PL **cool**) ADJECTIVE (*informal*)
cool

la **coopération** FEM NOUN
co-operation

coopérer VERB [34]
to co-operate

les **coordonnées** FEM PL NOUN
contact details
□ As-tu ses coordonnées? Do you have his contact details?

★ le **copain** MASC NOUN (*informal*)
1 friend
□ C'est un bon copain. He's a good friend.
2 boyfriend
□ Elle a un copain. She's got a boyfriend.

★ la **copie** FEM NOUN
1 copy
□ Ce tableau n'est qu'une copie. This picture is only a copy.
2 paper
□ Il a des copies à corriger ce week-end. He's got some papers to mark this weekend.

★ **copier** VERB [19]
1 to copy
2 to burn (*CD, DVD*)
▪ **copier-coller** to copy and paste

copieux (FEM **copieuse**) ADJECTIVE
hearty
□ un repas copieux a hearty meal

★ la **copine** FEM NOUN (*informal*)
1 friend
□ Je sors avec une copine ce soir. I'm going out with a friend tonight.
2 girlfriend
□ Il a une copine. He's got a girlfriend.

★ le **coq** MASC NOUN
cockerel

la **coque** FEM NOUN
hull (*of boat*)
▪ **un œuf à la coque** a soft-boiled egg

le **coquelicot** MASC NOUN
poppy

la **coqueluche** FEM NOUN
whooping cough

★ le **coquillage** MASC NOUN
1 shellfish
2 shell
□ Nous avons ramassé des coquillages sur la plage. We picked up some shells on the beach.

la **coquille** FEM NOUN
shell
▪ **une coquille d'œuf** an eggshell
▪ **une coquille Saint-Jacques** a scallop

coquin (FEM **coquine**) ADJECTIVE
cheeky
□ Il m'a regardé d'un air coquin. He gave me a cheeky look.

le **cor** MASC NOUN
horn
□ Je joue du cor. I play the horn.

le **corbeau** (PL les **corbeaux**) MASC NOUN
crow

la **corbeille** FEM NOUN
1 basket
□ une corbeille de fruits a basket of fruit
2 recycle bin (*of a computer*)
▪ **une corbeille à papier** a wastepaper basket

★ la **corde** FEM NOUN
1 rope
2 string (*of violin, tennis racket*)
▪ **une corde à linge** a clothes line
▪ **il pleut des cordes** it's bucketing down

★ la **cordonnerie** FEM NOUN
shoe repair shop

le **cordonnier** MASC NOUN
cobbler

coriace (FEM **coriace**) ADJECTIVE
tough

la **corne** FEM NOUN
horn

la **cornemuse** FEM NOUN
bagpipes
□ jouer de la cornemuse to play the bagpipes

le **cornet** MASC NOUN
▪ **un cornet de frites** a bag of chips
▪ **un cornet de glace** an ice cream cone

le **cornichon** MASC NOUN
gherkin

la **Cornouailles** FEM NOUN
Cornwall

★ le **corps** MASC NOUN
body

★ **correct** (FEM **correcte**) ADJECTIVE
1 correct
□ Ce n'est pas tout à fait correct. That's not quite correct.
2 reasonable
□ un salaire correct a reasonable salary □ Le repas était tout à fait correct. The meal was quite reasonable.

la **correction** FEM NOUN
correction

★ la **correspondance** FEM NOUN
1 correspondence
▪ **un cours par correspondance** a correspondence course

2 connection (*train, plane*)
□ Il y a une correspondance pour Toulouse à dix heures. There's a connection for Toulouse at ten o'clock.

★ le **correspondant** MASC NOUN
penfriend

★ la **correspondante** FEM NOUN
penfriend

★ **correspondre** VERB [69]
to correspond
■ **Faites correspondre les phrases.** Match the sentences together.

le **corridor** MASC NOUN
corridor

★ **corriger** VERB [45]
to mark
□ Vous pouvez corriger mon test? Can you mark my test?

★ le **corsage** MASC NOUN
blouse

★ la **Corse** FEM NOUN
Corsica

★ **corse** (FEM **corse**) ADJECTIVE, NOUN
Corsican
■ **un Corse** a Corsican (*man*)
■ **une Corse** a Corsican (*woman*)

la **corvée** FEM NOUN
chore
□ Quelle corvée! What a chore!

costaud (FEM **costaude**) ADJECTIVE
brawny

★ le **costume** MASC NOUN
1 suit (*man's*)
□ Il porte toujours un costume. He always wears a suit.
2 costume (*theatre*)
□ de superbes costumes superb costumes

★ la **côte** FEM NOUN
1 coastline
□ La route longe la côte. The road follows the coastline.
■ **la Côte d'Azur** the French Riviera
2 hill
□ J'ai grimpé la côte. I went up the hill.
3 rib
□ Il s'est cassé une côte en tombant. He broke a rib when he fell.
4 chop
□ une côte de porc a pork chop
■ **une côte de bœuf** a rib of beef
■ **côte à côte** side by side

★ le **côté** MASC NOUN
side
■ **à côté de** **1** next to □ Le café est à côté du sucre. The coffee's next to the sugar. **2** next door to □ Il habite à côté de chez moi. He lives next door to me.
■ **de l'autre côté** on the other side □ La pharmacie est de l'autre côté de la rue. The chemist's is on the other side of the street.
■ **de chaque côté** on each side □ Il y avait des voitures garées de chaque côté de la rue. There were cars parked on both sides of the street.
■ **De quel côté est-il parti?** Which way did he go?
■ **mettre quelque chose de côté** to save something □ J'ai mis de l'argent de côté. I've saved some money.
■ **d'un côté ... de l'autre côté** on the one hand ... on the other hand

★ la **côtelette** FEM NOUN
chop
□ une côtelette d'agneau a lamb chop

★ la **cotisation** FEM NOUN
1 subscription (*to club, union*)
2 contributions (*to pension, national insurance*)
■ **cotisations sociales** social security contributions

★ le **coton** MASC NOUN
cotton
□ une chemise en coton a cotton shirt
■ **le coton hydrophile** cotton wool

le **Coton-tige**® (PL les **Cotons-tiges**) MASC NOUN
cotton bud

★ le **cou** MASC NOUN
neck

couchant ADJECTIVE
■ **le soleil couchant** the setting sun

★ la **couche** FEM NOUN
1 layer
□ la couche d'ozone the ozone layer
2 coat (*of paint, varnish*)
3 nappy

★ **couché** (FEM **couchée**) ADJECTIVE
1 lying down
□ Il était couché sur le tapis. He was lying on the carpet.
2 in bed
□ Il est déjà couché. He's already in bed.

★ le **coucher** MASC NOUN
▷ *see also* **coucher** VERB
■ **un coucher de soleil** a sunset

★ se **coucher** VERB [28]
▷ *see also* **coucher** NOUN
1 to go to bed
□ Je me suis couché tard hier soir. I went to bed late last night.
2 to set (*sun*)

★ la **couchette** FEM NOUN
1 couchette (*on train*)
2 bunk (*on boat*)

★ le **coude** MASC NOUN
elbow

★ **coudre** VERB [15]
1 to sew
□ J'aime coudre. I like sewing.
2 to sew on
□ Il ne sait même pas coudre un bouton. He can't even sew a button on.

la **couette** FEM NOUN
duvet

les **couettes** FEM PL NOUN
bunches
□ la petite fille avec les couettes the little girl with her hair in bunches

couler VERB [28]
1 to run
□ Ne laissez pas couler les robinets. Don't leave the taps running. □ J'ai le nez qui coule. My nose is running.
2 to flow
□ La rivière coulait lentement. The river was flowing slowly.
3 to leak
□ Mon stylo coule. My pen's leaking.
4 to sink
□ Le bateau a coulé. The boat sank.

★ la **couleur** FEM NOUN
colour
□ De quelle couleur est leur voiture? What colour is their car? □ une pellicule couleur a colour film
■ **Tu as pris des couleurs.** You've got a tan.

la **couleuvre** FEM NOUN
grass snake

les **coulisses** FEM PL NOUN
wings (*in theatre*)
■ **dans les coulisses** behind the scenes

★ le **couloir** MASC NOUN
corridor

★ le **coup** MASC NOUN
1 knock
□ donner un coup à quelque chose to give something a knock
2 blow
■ **Il m'a donné un coup!** He hit me!
■ **un coup de pied** a kick
■ **un coup de poing** a punch
3 shock
□ Ça m'a fait un coup de le voir comme ça! (*informal*) It gave me a shock to see him like that!
■ **un coup de feu** a shot
■ **un coup de fil** (*informal*) a ring □ Je te passerai un coup de fil demain. I'll give you a ring tomorrow.
■ **donner un coup de main à quelqu'un** to give somebody a hand □ Je viendrai te donner un coup de main. I'll come and give you a hand.
■ **un coup d'œil** a quick look □ jeter un coup d'œil to have a quick look
■ **attraper un coup de soleil** to get sunburnt
■ **un coup de téléphone** a phone call
■ **un coup de tonnerre** a clap of thunder
■ **boire un coup** (*informal*) to have a drink
■ **après coup** afterwards □ Après coup j'ai regretté de m'être mis en colère. Afterwards I was sorry I'd got angry.
■ **à tous les coups** (*informal*) every time □ Je me trompe de rue à tous les coups. I get the street wrong every time.
■ **du premier coup** first time □ Il a été reçu au permis du premier coup. He passed his driving test first time.
■ **sur le coup** at first □ Sur le coup je ne l'ai pas reconnu. I didn't recognize him at first.

★ **coupable** (FEM **coupable**) ADJECTIVE
▷ *see also* **coupable** NOUN
guilty

★ le/la **coupable** MASC/FEM NOUN
▷ *see also* **coupable** ADJECTIVE
culprit

la **coupe** FEM NOUN
cup (*sport*)
□ la coupe du monde the World Cup
■ **une coupe de cheveux** a haircut
■ **une coupe de champagne** a glass of champagne

le **coupe-ongle** (PL les **coupe-ongles**) MASC NOUN
nail clippers

★ **couper** VERB [28]
1 to cut
2 to turn off
□ couper le courant to turn off the electricity
3 to take a short-cut
□ On peut couper par la forêt. We could take a short-cut through the woods.
■ **couper l'appétit** to spoil one's appetite
■ **se couper** to cut oneself □ Je me suis coupé le doigt avec une boîte de conserve. I cut my finger on a tin.
■ **couper la parole à quelqu'un** to interrupt somebody

le **couple** MASC NOUN
couple

le **couplet** MASC NOUN
verse
□ le premier couplet the first verse

la **coupure** FEM NOUN
cut
■ **une coupure de courant** a power cut

★ la **cour** FEM NOUN
1 yard
□ la cour de l'école the school yard
2 court
□ la cour de Louis XIV the court of Louis XIV
□ la cour d'assises the criminal court

French-English

C

★ le **courage** MASC NOUN
courage

★ **courageux** (FEM **courageuse**) ADJECTIVE
brave

★ **couramment** ADVERB
1 fluently
□ Elle parle couramment japonais. She speaks Japanese fluently.
2 commonly
□ C'est une expression que l'on emploie couramment. It's a commonly used phrase.

★ **courant** (FEM **courante**) ADJECTIVE
▷ *see also* **courant** NOUN
1 common
□ C'est une erreur courante. It's a common mistake.
2 standard
□ C'est un modèle courant. It's a standard model.

★ le **courant** MASC NOUN
▷ *see also* **courant** ADJECTIVE
1 current (*of river*)
■ **un courant d'air** a draught
2 power
□ une panne de courant a power cut
■ **Je le ferai dans le courant de la semaine.** I'll do it some time during the week.
■ **être au courant de quelque chose** to know about something □ Je n'étais pas au courant de l'accident. I didn't know about the accident.
■ **mettre quelqu'un au courant de quelque chose** to tell somebody about something
■ **Tu es au courant?** Have you heard about it?
■ **se tenir au courant de quelque chose** to keep up with something □ J'essaie de me tenir au courant de l'actualité. I try to keep up with the news.

le **coureur** MASC NOUN
runner
■ **un coureur à pied** a runner
■ **un coureur cycliste** a racing cyclist
■ **un coureur automobile** a racing driver

la **coureuse** FEM NOUN
runner

la **courgette** FEM NOUN
courgette

★ **courir** VERB [16]
to run
□ Elle a traversé la rue en courant. She ran across the street.
■ **courir un risque** to run a risk

la **couronne** FEM NOUN
crown

courons, courez VERB ▷ *see* **courir**

★ le **courriel** MASC NOUN
email

★ le **courrier** MASC NOUN
mail
□ Est-ce qu'il y avait du courrier ce matin? Was there any mail this morning?
■ **N'oublie pas de poster le courrier.** Don't forget to post the letters.
■ **le courrier électronique** email

> **BE CAREFUL!**
> The French word **courrier** does not mean **courier**.

★ le **cours** MASC NOUN
1 lesson
□ un cours d'espagnol a Spanish lesson □ des cours particuliers private lessons
2 course
□ un cours intensif a crash course
3 rate
□ le cours du change the exchange rate
■ **au cours de** during □ Il a été réveillé trois fois au cours de la nuit. He was woken up three times during the night.

★ la **course** FEM NOUN
1 running
□ la course de fond long-distance running
2 race
□ une course hippique a horse race
3 shopping
□ J'ai juste une course à faire. I've just got a bit of shopping to do.
■ **faire les courses** to go shopping □ Elle est partie faire les courses de la semaine. She's gone to do her weekly shopping.

★ **court** (FEM **courte**) ADJECTIVE
▷ *see also* **court** NOUN
short

★ le **court** MASC NOUN
▷ *see also* **court** ADJECTIVE
■ **un court de tennis** a tennis court

couru VERB ▷ *see* **courir**

le **couscous** MASC NOUN
couscous

> **DID YOU KNOW...?**
> **couscous** is a spicy North African dish made with meat, vegetables and steamed semolina.

★ le **cousin** MASC NOUN
cousin

★ la **cousine** FEM NOUN
cousin

★ le **coussin** MASC NOUN
cushion

★ le **coût** MASC NOUN
cost
□ le coût de la vie the cost of living

★ le **couteau** (PL les **couteaux**) MASC NOUN
knife

★ **coûter** VERB [28]
to cost
□ Est-ce que ça coûte cher? Does it cost a lot?
■ **Combien ça coûte?** How much is it?

coûteux (FEM **coûteuse**) ADJECTIVE
expensive

la **coutume** FEM NOUN
custom

★ la **couture** FEM NOUN
1 sewing
□ Je n'aime pas la couture. I don't like sewing.
■ **faire de la couture** to sew
2 seam
□ La couture de mon pantalon s'est défaite. The seam of my trousers has come undone.

le **couturier** MASC NOUN
fashion designer
□ un grand couturier a top designer

la **couturière** FEM NOUN
1 dressmaker
2 designer (*fashion*)

le **couvercle** MASC NOUN
1 lid (*of pan*)
2 top (*of tube, jar, spray can*)

★ **couvert** (FEM **couverte**) ADJECTIVE
▷ *see also* **couvert** NOUN
1 covered
■ **couvert de** covered with □ Cet arbre est couvert de fleurs au printemps. This tree is covered with blossom in spring.
2 overcast (*sky*)

★ **couvert** VERB ▷ *see* **couvrir**

★ le **couvert** MASC NOUN
▷ *see also* **couvert** ADJECTIVE
■ **mettre le couvert** to lay the table

les **couverts** MASC PL NOUN
cutlery *sing*
□ Les couverts sont dans le tiroir de gauche. The cutlery is in the left-hand drawer.

★ la **couverture** FEM NOUN
blanket

le **couvre-lit** MASC NOUN
bedspread

★ **couvrir** VERB [55]
to cover
□ Le chien est revenu couvert de boue. The dog came back covered with mud.
■ **se couvrir** 1 to wrap up □ Couvre-toi bien: il fait très froid dehors. Wrap up well: it's very cold outside. 2 to cloud over □ Le ciel se couvre. The sky's clouding over.

le **covoiturage** MASC NOUN
car sharing

★ le **crabe** MASC NOUN
crab

★ **cracher** VERB [28]
to spit

le **crachin** MASC NOUN
drizzle

la **craie** FEM NOUN
chalk

craindre VERB [17]
to fear
□ Tu n'as rien à craindre. You've got nothing to fear.

la **crainte** FEM NOUN
fear
■ **de crainte de** for fear of □ Il n'ose rien dire de crainte de la vexer. He daren't say anything for fear of upsetting her.

craintif (FEM **craintive**) ADJECTIVE
timid

la **crampe** FEM NOUN
cramp
□ J'ai une crampe au mollet. I've got a cramp in my calf.

le **cran** MASC NOUN
hole (*in belt*)
■ **avoir du cran** (*informal*) to have guts

le **crâne** MASC NOUN
skull

crâner VERB [28] (*informal*)
to show off

le **crapaud** MASC NOUN
toad

craquer VERB [28]
1 to creak
□ Le plancher craque. The floor creaks.
2 to burst
□ Ma fermeture éclair a craqué. My zip's burst.
3 to crack up
□ Je vais finir par craquer! (*informal*) I'm going to crack up at this rate!
■ **Quand j'ai vu cette robe, j'ai craqué!** (*informal*) When I saw that dress, I couldn't resist it!

la **crasse** FEM NOUN
filth

★ la **cravate** FEM NOUN
tie

le **crawl** MASC NOUN
crawl
□ nager le crawl to do the crawl

★ le **crayon** MASC NOUN
pencil
□ un crayon de couleur a coloured pencil
■ **un crayon feutre** a felt-tip pen

la **création** FEM NOUN
creation

la **crèche** FEM NOUN
1 nursery
□ Elle dépose son fils à la crèche à huit heures.

She leaves her son at the nursery at 8 o'clock.
2 nativity scene

le **crédit** MASC NOUN
credit

créer VERB [18]
to create

la **crémaillère** FEM NOUN
■ **pendre la crémaillère** to have a house-warming party

★ la **crème** FEM NOUN
▷ *see also* **crème** NOUN
cream
■ **la crème anglaise** custard
■ **la crème Chantilly** sweetened whipped cream
■ **la crème fouettée** whipped cream
■ **une crème caramel** a crème caramel
■ **une crème au chocolat** a chocolate dessert

★ le **crème** MASC NOUN
▷ *see also* **crème** NOUN
white coffee
□ un grand crème a large white coffee

★ la **crémerie** FEM NOUN
cheese shop

crémeux (FEM **crémeuse**) ADJECTIVE
creamy

★ la **crêpe** FEM NOUN
pancake

★ la **crêperie** FEM NOUN
pancake restaurant

le **crépuscule** MASC NOUN
dusk

le **cresson** MASC NOUN
watercress

la **Crète** FEM NOUN
Crete

★ **creuser** VERB [28]
to dig (*a hole*)
■ **Ça creuse!** That gives you a real appetite!
■ **se creuser la cervelle** (*informal*) to rack one's brains

creux (FEM **creuse**) ADJECTIVE
hollow

★ la **crevaison** FEM NOUN
puncture

★ **crevé** (FEM **crevée**) ADJECTIVE
1 punctured
□ un pneu crevé a puncture
2 knackered
□ Je suis complètement crevé! (*informal*) I'm completely knackered!

crever VERB [43]
1 to burst (*balloon*)
2 to have a puncture (*motorist*)
□ J'ai crevé sur l'autoroute. I had a puncture on the motorway.
■ **Je crève de faim!** (*informal*) I'm starving!
■ **Je crève de froid!** (*informal*) I'm freezing!

★ la **crevette** FEM NOUN
prawn
■ **une crevette rose** a prawn
■ **une crevette grise** a shrimp

★ le **cri** MASC NOUN
1 scream
□ J'ai entendu un cri. I heard a scream.
□ pousser des cris de douleur to scream with pain
2 call
□ Il sait reconnaître les cris des oiseaux. He can identify the calls of birds.
■ **C'est le dernier cri.** It's the latest fashion.
□ Ce haut est du dernier cri. This top is the latest fashion.

criard (FEM **criarde**) ADJECTIVE
garish (*colours*)

le **cric** MASC NOUN
jack (*for car*)

★ **crier** VERB [19]
to shout
■ **crier de douleur** to scream with pain

★ le **crime** MASC NOUN
1 crime
□ un crime de guerre a war crime
2 murder
□ Un crime a été commis ici. There was a murder here.

★ le **criminel** MASC NOUN
1 criminal
□ un criminel de guerre a war criminal
2 murderer

★ la **criminelle** FEM NOUN
1 criminal
2 murderer

le **crin** MASC NOUN
horsehair

la **crinière** FEM NOUN
mane

le **criquet** MASC NOUN
grasshopper

★ la **crise** FEM NOUN
1 crisis
■ **la crise économique** the recession
2 attack
□ une crise d'asthme an asthma attack □ une crise cardiaque a heart attack
■ **une crise de foie** an upset stomach
■ **piquer une crise de nerfs** to go hysterical
■ **avoir une crise de fou rire** to have a fit of the giggles

le **cristal** (PL les **cristaux**) MASC NOUN
crystal
□ un verre en cristal a crystal glass

le **critère** MASC NOUN
criterion

critique (FEM **critique**) ADJECTIVE
▷ *see also* **critique** NOUN
critical

le **critique** MASC NOUN
▷ *see also* **critique** NOUN, ADJECTIVE
critic
□ un critique de cinéma a film critic

la **critique** FEM NOUN
▷ *see also* **critique** NOUN, ADJECTIVE
1 criticism
□ Elle ne supporte pas les critiques. She can't stand being criticized.
2 review
□ Le film a reçu de bonnes critiques. The film's had good reviews.

★**critiquer** VERB [28]
to criticize

la **Croatie** FEM NOUN
Croatia

le **crochet** MASC NOUN
1 hook
2 detour
□ faire un crochet to make a detour
3 crochet
□ un pull au crochet a crocheted sweater

le **crocodile** MASC NOUN
crocodile

★**croire** VERB [20]
to believe
□ Il croit tout ce qu'on lui raconte. He believes everything he's told.
■ **croire que** to think that □ Tu crois qu'il fera meilleur demain? Do you think the weather will be better tomorrow?
■ **croire à quelque chose** to believe in something
■ **croire en Dieu** to believe in God

crois VERB ▷ *see* **croire**

croîs VERB ▷ *see* **croître**

le **croisement** MASC NOUN
crossroads
□ Tournez à gauche au croisement. Turn left at the crossroads.

croiser VERB [28]
■ **J'ai croisé Anne-Laure dans la rue.** I bumped into Anne-Laure in the street.
■ **croiser les bras** to fold one's arms
■ **croiser les jambes** to cross one's legs
■ **se croiser** to pass each other □ Nous nous croisons dans l'escalier tous les matins. We pass each other on the stairs every morning.

★la **croisière** FEM NOUN
cruise

la **croissance** FEM NOUN
growth

★le **croissant** MASC NOUN
croissant
□ un croissant au beurre a butter croissant

croit VERB ▷ *see* **croire**

croître VERB [21]
to grow

★la **croix** FEM NOUN
cross
■ **la Croix-Rouge** the Red Cross

★le **croque-madame** (PL les **croque-madame**) MASC NOUN
toasted ham and cheese sandwich with fried egg on top

★le **croque-monsieur** (PL les **croque-monsieur**) MASC NOUN
toasted ham and cheese sandwich

croquer VERB [28]
to munch
□ croquer une pomme to munch an apple
■ **le chocolat à croquer** dark chocolate

le **croquis** MASC NOUN
sketch

la **crotte** FEM NOUN
■ **une crotte de chien** dog dirt

le **crottin** MASC NOUN
1 manure
□ du crottin de cheval horse manure
2 small goat's cheese

croustillant (FEM **croustillante**) ADJECTIVE
crusty

la **croûte** FEM NOUN
1 crust (*of bread*)
■ **en croûte** in pastry
2 rind (*of cheese*)
3 scab (*on skin*)

le **croûton** MASC NOUN
1 crust (*end of loaf*)
2 crouton
□ des croûtons frottés d'ail garlic croutons

croyons, croyez VERB ▷ *see* **croire**

les **CRS** MASC PL NOUN
French riot police

★**cru** (FEM **crue**) ADJECTIVE
raw
□ la viande crue raw meat
■ **le jambon cru** Parma ham

cru VERB ▷ *see* **croire**

crû VERB ▷ *see* **croître**

la **cruauté** FEM NOUN
cruelty

la **cruche** FEM NOUN
jug

★les **crudités** FEM PL NOUN
assorted raw vegetables

★**cruel** (FEM **cruelle**) ADJECTIVE
cruel

les **crustacés** MASC PL NOUN
shellfish

le **cube** MASC NOUN
cube
▪ **un mètre cube** a cubic metre

la **cueillette** FEM NOUN
picking
□ la cueillette des champignons mushroom picking

★ **cueillir** VERB [22]
to pick (*flowers, fruit*)

★ la **cuiller** FEM NOUN
spoon
▪ **une cuiller à café** a teaspoon
▪ **une cuiller à soupe** a soup spoon

★ la **cuillère** FEM NOUN
spoon
▪ **une cuillère à café** a teaspoon
▪ **une cuillère à soupe** a soup spoon

★ la **cuillerée** FEM NOUN
spoonful

★ le **cuir** MASC NOUN
leather
□ un sac en cuir a leather bag
▪ **le cuir chevelu** the scalp

★ **cuire** VERB [23]
to cook
□ cuire quelque chose à feu vif to cook something on a high heat
▪ **cuire quelque chose au four** to bake something
▪ **cuire quelque chose à la vapeur** to steam something
▪ **faire cuire** to cook □ 'Faire cuire pendant une heure' 'Cook for one hour'
▪ **bien cuit** well done
▪ **trop cuit** overdone

★ la **cuisine** FEM NOUN
1 kitchen
2 cooking
□ la cuisine française French cooking
▪ **faire la cuisine** to cook

cuisiné (FEM **cuisinée**) ADJECTIVE
▪ **un plat cuisiné** a ready-made meal

★ **cuisiner** VERB [28]
to cook
□ J'aime beaucoup cuisiner. I love cooking.

★ le **cuisinier** MASC NOUN
cook

★ la **cuisinière** FEM NOUN
1 cook
2 cooker
□ une cuisinière à gaz a gas cooker

la **cuisse** FEM NOUN
thigh
▪ **une cuisse de poulet** a chicken leg

la **cuisson** FEM NOUN
cooking
□ 'une heure de cuisson' 'cooking time: one hour'

cuit VERB ▷ *see* **cuire**

le **cuivre** MASC NOUN
copper

le **culot** MASC NOUN (*informal*)
cheek
□ Quel culot! What a cheek! □ Il a un sacré culot! He's got a damn cheek!

★ la **culotte** FEM NOUN
knickers

la **culpabilité** FEM NOUN
guilt

le **cultivateur** MASC NOUN
farmer

la **cultivatrice** FEM NOUN
farmer

cultivé (FEM **cultivée**) ADJECTIVE
cultured
□ Il est très cultivé. He's very cultured.

★ **cultiver** VERB [28]
to grow
□ Il cultive la vigne. He grows grapes.
▪ **cultiver la terre** to farm the land

★ la **culture** FEM NOUN
1 farming
□ les cultures intensives intensive farming
2 education
□ une bonne culture générale a good general education
▪ **la culture physique** physical education

le **culturisme** MASC NOUN
body-building

le **curé** MASC NOUN
parish priest

le **cure-dent** MASC NOUN
toothpick

★ **curieux** (FEM **curieuse**) ADJECTIVE
curious

★ la **curiosité** FEM NOUN
curiosity

le **curriculum vitae** MASC NOUN
CV

★ le **curseur** MASC NOUN
cursor

la **cuvette** FEM NOUN
bowl
□ une cuvette en plastique a plastic bowl

le **CV** MASC NOUN (= *curriculum vitae*)
CV

la **cyberattaque** FEM NOUN
cyberattack

★ le **cybercafé** MASC NOUN
internet café

★ le **cybercrime** FEM NOUN
cyber crime

★ le **cyberharcèlement** MASC NOUN
cyber bullying

cyclable (FEM **cyclable**) ADJECTIVE
- **une piste cyclable** a cycle lane

le **cycle** MASC NOUN
cycle

★ le **cyclisme** MASC NOUN
cycling

★ le/la **cycliste** MASC/FEM NOUN
cyclist

le **cyclomoteur** MASC NOUN
moped

le **cyclone** MASC NOUN
hurricane

le **cygne** MASC NOUN
swan

Dd

d' PREPOSITION, ARTICLE ▷ *see* **de**

★ la **dactylo** FEM NOUN

1 typist

□ Elle est dactylo. She's a typist.

2 typing

□ Je prends des cours de dactylo. I'm taking typing lessons.

le **daim** MASC NOUN

suede

□ une veste en daim a suede jacket

★ la **dame** FEM NOUN

1 lady

2 queen (*in cards, chess*)

les **dames** FEM PL NOUN

draughts

★ le **Danemark** MASC NOUN

Denmark

★ le **danger** MASC NOUN

danger

■ **être en danger** to be in danger

■ **'Danger de mort'** 'Extremely dangerous'

★ **dangereux** (FEM **dangereuse**) ADJECTIVE

dangerous

★ **danois** (FEM **danoise**) ADJECTIVE, NOUN

Danish

□ Il parle danois. He speaks Danish.

■ **un Danois** a Dane (*man*)

■ **une Danoise** a Dane (*woman*)

■ **les Danois** the Danish

★ **dans** PREPOSITION

1 in

□ Il est dans sa chambre. He's in his bedroom.

□ dans deux mois in two months' time

2 into

□ Il est entré dans mon bureau. He came into my office.

3 out of

□ On a bu dans des verres en plastique. We drank out of plastic glasses.

la **danse** FEM NOUN

1 dance

□ la danse moderne modern dance □ des danses folkloriques folk dances

■ **la danse classique** ballet

2 dancing

□ des cours de danse dancing lessons

★ **danser** VERB [28]

to dance

le **danseur** MASC NOUN

dancer

la **danseuse** FEM NOUN

dancer

★ la **date** FEM NOUN

date

□ votre date de naissance your date of birth

□ la date limite de vente the sell-by date

■ **un ami de longue date** an old friend

dater VERB [28]

■ **dater de** to date from □ Cette coutume date du Moyen Âge. This custom dates from the Middle Ages.

la **datte** FEM NOUN

date (*fruit*)

le **dauphin** MASC NOUN

dolphin

davantage ADVERB

■ **davantage de** more □ Il faudrait davantage de stages de formation. There should be more training courses.

★ **de** PREPOSITION, ARTICLE

> See also **du (= de + le)** and **des (= de + les)**. **de** changes to **d'** before a vowel and most words beginning with 'h'.

1 of

□ le toit de la maison the roof of the house

□ la voiture de Paul Paul's car □ la voiture de mes parents my parents' car □ la voiture d'Hélène Hélène's car □ deux bouteilles de vin two bottles of wine □ un litre d'essence a litre of petrol

■ **un bébé d'un an** a one-year-old baby

■ **un billet de cinquante euros** a 50-euro note

2 from

□ de Londres à Paris from London to Paris □ Il vient de Londres. He comes from London.

□ une lettre de Victor a letter from Victor

3 by

□ augmenter de dix euros to increase by ten euros

> You use **de** to form expressions with the meaning of 'some' and 'any'.

■ **Je voudrais de l'eau.** I'd like some water.
■ **du pain et de la confiture** bread and jam
■ **Il n'a pas de famille.** He hasn't got any family.
■ **Il n'y a plus de biscuits.** There aren't any more biscuits.

le **dé** MASC NOUN
1 dice
2 thimble

le **dealer** MASC NOUN (*informal*)
drug-pusher

déballer VERB [28]
to unpack

le **débardeur** MASC NOUN
tank top

★**débarquer** VERB [28]
to disembark
□ Nous avons dû débarquer à Marseille. We had to disembark at Marseille.
■ **débarquer chez quelqu'un** (*informal*) to descend on somebody □ Ils ont débarqué chez nous à dix heures du soir. They descended on us at ten o'clock at night.

le **débarras** MASC NOUN
junk room
■ **Bon débarras!** Good riddance!

★**débarrasser** VERB [28]
to clear
□ Tu peux débarrasser la table, s'il te plaît? Can you clear the table please?
■ **se débarrasser de quelque chose** to get rid of something □ Je me suis débarrassé de mon vieux frigo. I got rid of my old fridge.

le **débat** MASC NOUN
debate

se **débattre** VERB [9]
to struggle

débile (FEM **débile**) ADJECTIVE
crazy
□ C'est complètement débile! (*informal*) That's totally crazy!

débordé (FEM **débordée**) ADJECTIVE
■ **être débordé** to be snowed under

déborder VERB [28]
to overflow (*river*)
■ **déborder d'énergie** to be full of energy

le **débouché** MASC NOUN
job prospect
□ Quels débouchés y a-t-il après ces études? What are the job prospects after this course?

déboucher VERB [28]
1 to unblock (*sink, pipe*)
2 to open (*bottle*)
■ **déboucher sur** to lead into □ La rue débouche sur une place. The street leads into a square.

★**debout** ADVERB
1 standing up
□ Il a mangé ses céréales debout. He ate his cereal standing up.
2 upright
□ Mets les livres debout sur l'étagère. Put the books upright on the shelf.
3 up
□ Tu es déjà debout? Are you up already?
■ **Debout!** Get up!

déboutonner VERB [28]
to unbutton

débraillé (FEM **débraillée**) ADJECTIVE
sloppily dressed

débrancher VERB [28]
to unplug

le **débris** MASC NOUN
■ **des débris de verre** bits of glass

débrouillard (FEM **débrouillarde**) ADJECTIVE
streetwise

se **débrouiller** VERB [28]
to manage
□ C'était difficile, mais je ne me suis pas trop mal débrouillé. It was difficult, but I managed OK.
■ **Débrouille-toi tout seul.** Sort things out for yourself.

★le **début** MASC NOUN
beginning
□ au début at the beginning
■ **début mai** in early May

le **débutant** MASC NOUN
beginner

la **débutante** FEM NOUN
beginner

débuter VERB [28]
to start

décaféiné (FEM **décaféinée**) ADJECTIVE
decaffeinated

le **décalage horaire** MASC NOUN
time difference (*between time zones*)
□ Il y a une heure de décalage horaire entre la France et la Grande-Bretagne. There's an hour's time difference between France and Britain.

décalquer VERB [28]
to trace

décapiter VERB [28]
to behead

décapotable (FEM **décapotable**) ADJECTIVE
convertible

décapsuler VERB [28]
■ **décapsuler une bouteille** to take the top off a bottle

★le **décapsuleur** MASC NOUN
bottle-opener

décéder VERB [34, *aux* **être**]
to die
□ Son père est décédé il y a trois ans. His father died three years ago.

★ **décembre** MASC NOUN
December
■ **en décembre** in December

décemment ADVERB
decently

décent (FEM **décente**) ADJECTIVE
decent

la **déception** FEM NOUN
disappointment

décerner VERB [28]
to award

le **décès** MASC NOUN
death

décevant (FEM **décevante**) ADJECTIVE
disappointing
□ Ses résultats sont plutôt décevants. His results are rather disappointing.

★ **décevoir** VERB [67]
to disappoint

> **BE CAREFUL!**
> **décevoir** does not mean **to deceive**.

décharger VERB [45]
to unload

se **déchausser** VERB [28]
to take off one's shoes

★ les **déchets** MASC PL NOUN
waste *sing*
□ les déchets nucléaires nuclear waste □ les déchets toxiques toxic waste

déchiffrer VERB [28]
to decipher

déchirant (FEM **déchirante**) ADJECTIVE
heart-rending

★ **déchirer** VERB [28]
1 to tear (*clothes*)
2 to tear up
□ déchirer une lettre to tear up a letter
3 to tear out
□ déchirer une page d'un livre to tear a page out of a book
■ **se déchirer** to tear □ se déchirer un muscle to tear a muscle

la **déchirure** FEM NOUN
tear (*rip*)
■ **une déchirure musculaire** a torn muscle

décidé (FEM **décidée**) ADJECTIVE
determined
■ **C'est décidé.** It's decided.

décidément ADVERB
certainly
□ Décidément, je n'ai pas de chance aujourd'hui. I'm certainly not having much luck today.

★ **décider** VERB [28]
to decide
■ **décider de faire quelque chose** to decide to do something □ Ils ont décidé de rester. They decided to stay.
■ **se décider** to make up one's mind □ Elle n'arrive pas à se décider. She can't make up her mind.

décisif (FEM **décisive**) ADJECTIVE
decisive

★ la **décision** FEM NOUN
decision

la **déclaration** FEM NOUN
statement
□ Je n'ai aucune déclaration à faire. I have no statement to make.
■ **faire une déclaration de vol** to report something as stolen

★ **déclarer** VERB [28]
to declare
□ déclarer la guerre à un pays to declare war on a country
■ **se déclarer** to break out □ Le feu s'est déclaré dans la cantine. The fire broke out in the canteen.

déclencher VERB [28]
to set off (*alarm, explosion*)
■ **se déclencher** to go off

le **déclic** MASC NOUN
click

décoiffé (FEM **décoiffée**) ADJECTIVE
■ **Elle était toute décoiffée.** Her hair was in a real mess.

le **décollage** MASC NOUN
takeoff (*of plane*)

décollé (FEM **décollée**) ADJECTIVE
■ **avoir les oreilles décollées** to have sticking-out ears

★ **décoller** VERB [28]
1 to unstick
□ décoller une étiquette to unstick a label
■ **se décoller** to come unstuck
2 to take off
□ L'avion a décollé avec dix minutes de retard. The plane took off ten minutes late.

décolleté (FEM **décolletée**) ADJECTIVE
▷ *see also* **décolleté** NOUN
low-cut

le **décolleté** MASC NOUN
▷ *see also* **décolleté** ADJECTIVE
■ **un décolleté plongeant** a plunging neckline

se **décolorer** VERB [28]
to fade
□ Ce T-shirt s'est décoloré au lavage. This T-shirt has faded in the wash.
■ **se faire décolorer les cheveux** to have one's hair bleached

Numbers in brackets refer to verb tables on pages 650 to 658

les **décombres** MASC PL NOUN
rubble *sing*

se **décommander** VERB [28]
to cry off
□ Elle devait venir mais elle s'est décommandée à la dernière minute. She was supposed to be coming, but she cried off at the last minute.

déconcerté (FEM **déconcertée**) ADJECTIVE
disconcerted

décongeler VERB [1]
to thaw

se **déconnecter** VERB [28]
to log out

la **déconnection** FEM NOUN
disconnection

déconseiller VERB [28]
▪ **déconseiller à quelqu'un de faire quelque chose** to advise somebody not to do something □ Je lui ai déconseillé d'y aller. I advised him not to go.
▪ **C'est déconseillé.** It's not recommended.

décontenancé (FEM **décontenancée**) ADJECTIVE
disconcerted

décontracté (FEM **décontractée**) ADJECTIVE
relaxed
▪ **s'habiller décontracté** to dress casually

se **décontracter** VERB [28]
to relax
□ Il est allé faire du footing pour se décontracter. He went jogging to relax.

★ le **décor** MASC NOUN
décor

★ le **décorateur** MASC NOUN
interior decorator

la **décoration** FEM NOUN
decoration

★ la **décoratrice** FEM NOUN
interior decorator

★ **décorer** VERB [28]
to decorate

les **décors** MASC PL NOUN
1 scenery *sing* (*in play*)
2 set (*in film*)

décortiquer VERB [28]
to shell
▪ **des crevettes décortiquées** peeled prawns

découdre VERB [15]
to unpick
▪ **se découdre** to come unstitched

★ **découper** VERB [28]
1 to cut out
□ J'ai découpé cet article dans le journal. I cut this article out of the paper.
2 to carve (*meat*)

décourageant (FEM **décourageante**) ADJECTIVE
discouraging

décourager VERB [45]
to discourage
▪ **se décourager** to get discouraged
▪ **Ne te décourage pas!** Don't give up!

décousu (FEM **décousue**) ADJECTIVE
unstitched
□ L'ourlet est décousu. The hem's come unstitched.

le **découvert** MASC NOUN
overdraft

★ la **découverte** FEM NOUN
discovery

★ **découvrir** VERB [55]
to discover

★ **décrire** VERB [30]
to describe

le **décrochage** MASC NOUN
▪ **le décrochage scolaire** truancy

★ **décrocher** VERB [28]
1 to take down
□ Tu peux m'aider à décrocher les rideaux? Can you help me take down the curtains?
2 to pick up the phone
□ Il a décroché et a composé le numéro. He picked up the phone and dialled the number.
▪ **décrocher le téléphone** to take the phone off the hook

★ **déçu** VERB ▷ *see* **décevoir**
disappointed

dédaigneux (FEM **dédaigneuse**) ADJECTIVE
disdainful
□ d'un air dédaigneux disdainfully

le **dédain** MASC NOUN
disdain
□ avec dédain with disdain

★ **dedans** ADVERB
inside
□ C'est une jolie boîte: qu'est-ce qu'il y a dedans? That's a nice box: what's in it?
▪ **là-dedans** **1** in there □ J'ai trouvé les clés là-dedans. I found the keys in there. **2** in that □ Il y a du vrai là-dedans. There's some truth in that.

dédicacé (FEM **dédicacée**) ADJECTIVE
▪ **un exemplaire dédicacé** a signed copy

dédier VERB [19]
to dedicate

déduire VERB [23]
to take off
□ Tu as déduit les vingt euros que je te devais? Did you take off the twenty euros I owed you?
▪ **J'en déduis qu'il m'a menti.** That means he must have been lying.

défaire VERB [36]
to undo
■ **défaire sa valise** to unpack
■ **se défaire** to come undone

la **défaite** FEM NOUN
defeat

★ le **défaut** MASC NOUN
fault

défavorable (FEM **défavorable**) ADJECTIVE
unfavourable

★ **défavorisé** (FEM **défavorisée**) ADJECTIVE
underprivileged
■ **personnes défavorisées** underprivileged people

défectueux (FEM **défectueuse**) ADJECTIVE
faulty

★ **défendre** VERB [88]
1 to forbid
■ **défendre à quelqu'un de faire quelque chose** to forbid somebody to do something
□ Sa mère lui a défendu de le revoir. Her mother forbade her to see him again.
2 to defend
□ défendre ses idées to defend your ideas
□ défendre quelqu'un to defend somebody

★ **défendu** (FEM **défendue**) ADJECTIVE
forbidden
□ C'est défendu. It's forbidden.

★ la **défense** FEM NOUN
1 defence
■ **prendre la défense de quelqu'un** to back somebody up
■ **'défense de fumer'** 'no smoking'
2 tusk (*of elephant*)

le **défi** MASC NOUN
challenge
■ **d'un air de défi** defiantly
■ **sur un ton de défi** defiantly

défier VERB [19]
1 to challenge
□ Je te défie de trouver un meilleur exemple. I challenge you to find a better example.
2 to dare
□ Il m'a défié d'aller à l'école en pyjama. He dared me to go to school in my pyjamas.

défigurer VERB [28]
to disfigure

le **défilé** MASC NOUN
1 parade
■ **un défilé de mode** a fashion show
2 march

défiler VERB [28]
to march

définir VERB [38]
to define

définitif (FEM **définitive**) ADJECTIVE
final
■ **en définitive** in the end □ En définitive, ils ont décidé de rester. In the end, they decided to stay.

définitivement ADVERB
for good
□ Elle s'est définitivement installée en Écosse en 2004. She settled in Scotland for good in 2004.

déformer VERB [28]
to stretch
□ Ne tire pas sur ton pull, tu vas le déformer. Don't pull at your sweater, you'll stretch it.
■ **se déformer** to stretch □ Ce T-shirt s'est déformé au lavage. This T-shirt has stretched in the wash.

se **défouler** VERB [28]
to unwind
□ Je fais de l'aérobic pour me défouler. I do aerobics to unwind.

dégagé (FEM **dégagée**) ADJECTIVE
■ **d'un air dégagé** casually
■ **sur un ton dégagé** casually

dégager VERB [45]
1 to free
□ Ils ont mis une heure à dégager les victimes. They took an hour to free the victims.
2 to clear
□ des gouttes qui dégagent le nez drops to clear your nose
■ **Ça se dégage.** (*weather*) It's clearing up.

se **dégarnir** VERB [38]
to go bald

les **dégâts** MASC PL NOUN
damage

le **dégel** MASC NOUN
thaw

dégeler VERB [1]
to thaw
□ faire dégeler un poulet congelé to thaw out a frozen chicken

dégivrer VERB [28]
1 to defrost
2 to de-ice

dégonfler VERB [28]
to let down
□ Quelqu'un a dégonflé mes pneus. Somebody let down my tyres.
■ **se dégonfler** (*informal*) to chicken out

dégouliner VERB [28]
to trickle

dégourdi (FEM **dégourdie**) ADJECTIVE
smart (*clever*)
□ Il n'est pas très dégourdi. He's not very smart.

dégourdir VERB [38]
■ **se dégourdir les jambes** to stretch one's legs

le **dégoût** MASC NOUN
disgust
□ une expression de dégoût a disgusted expression
■ **avec dégoût** disgustedly

★ **dégoûtant** (FEM **dégoûtante**) ADJECTIVE
disgusting

dégoûté (FEM **dégoûtée**) ADJECTIVE
disgusted
■ **être dégoûté de tout** to be sick of everything

dégoûter VERB [28]
to disgust
□ Ce genre de comportement me dégoûte. That kind of behaviour disgusts me.
■ **dégoûter quelqu'un de quelque chose** to put somebody off something □ Ça m'a dégoûté de la viande. That put me off meat.

se **dégrader** VERB [28]
to deteriorate

★ le **degré** MASC NOUN
degree
■ **de l'alcool à 90 degrés** surgical spirit

dégringoler VERB [28]
1 to rush down
□ Il a dégringolé l'escalier. He rushed down the stairs.
2 to collapse
■ **Elle a fait dégringoler la pile de livres.** She knocked over the stack of books.

le **déguisement** MASC NOUN
disguise

déguiser VERB [28]
■ **se déguiser en quelque chose** to dress up as something □ Elle s'était déguisée en vampire. She was dressed up as a vampire.

★ la **dégustation** FEM NOUN
tasting

★ **déguster** VERB [28]
1 to taste (*food, wine*)
2 to enjoy

★ **dehors** ADVERB
outside
□ Je t'attends dehors. I'll wait for you outside.
■ **jeter quelqu'un dehors** to throw somebody out
■ **en dehors de** 1 apart from □ En dehors de lui, tout le monde était content. Apart from him, everybody was happy. 2 outside □ en dehors des heures de cours outside school hours

★ **déjà** ADVERB
1 already
□ J'ai déjà fini. I've already finished.
2 before
□ Tu es déjà venu en France? Have you been to France before?

★ **déjeuner** VERB [28]
▷ *see also* **déjeuner** NOUN
to have lunch

★ le **déjeuner** MASC NOUN
▷ *see also* **déjeuner** VERB
lunch

★ le **délai** MASC NOUN
1 extension
□ J'ai demandé un délai d'une semaine. I've asked for a week's extension.
2 time limit
□ être dans les délais to be within the time limit

> **BE CAREFUL!**
> **délai** does not mean **delay**.

délasser VERB [28]
to relax
□ La lecture délasse. Reading's relaxing.
■ **se délasser** to relax □ J'ai pris un bain pour me délasser. I had a bath to relax.

délavé (FEM **délavée**) ADJECTIVE
faded
□ un jean délavé a pair of faded jeans

le **délégué** MASC NOUN
representative
□ les délégués de classe the class representatives

> **DID YOU KNOW...?**
> In French schools, each class elects two representatives or **délégués de classe**.

la **déléguée** FEM NOUN
representative

déléguer VERB [34]
to delegate

délibéré (FEM **délibérée**) ADJECTIVE
deliberate

délicat (FEM **délicate**) ADJECTIVE
1 delicate
□ avoir la peau délicate to have delicate skin
2 tricky
□ une situation délicate a tricky situation
3 tactful
□ Il est toujours très délicat. He's always very tactful.
4 thoughtful
□ C'est une attention délicate de sa part. That was thoughtful on his part.

délicatement ADVERB
1 gently
2 tactfully

le **délice** MASC NOUN
delight
□ Vivre ici est un vrai délice. Living here is a real delight.
■ **Ce gâteau est un vrai délice.** This cake's a real treat.

★ **délicieux** (FEM **délicieuse**) ADJECTIVE
delicious

la **délinquance** FEM NOUN
crime
□ de nouvelles mesures pour combattre la petite délinquance new measures to fight petty crime
■ **la délinquance juvénile** juvenile delinquency

le **délinquant** MASC NOUN
criminal

la **délinquante** FEM NOUN
criminal

délirer VERB [28]
■ **Mais tu délires!** (*informal*) You're crazy!

le **délit** MASC NOUN
criminal offence

délivrer VERB [28]
to set free (*prisoner*)

le **deltaplane** MASC NOUN
hang-glider
■ **faire du deltaplane** to go hang-gliding

★ **demain** ADVERB
tomorrow
□ demain matin tomorrow morning
■ **À demain!** See you tomorrow!

la **demande** FEM NOUN
request
■ **une demande en mariage** an offer of marriage
■ **'demandes d'emploi'** 'situations wanted'

demandé (FEM **demandée**) ADJECTIVE
■ **très demandé** very much in demand

★ **demander** VERB [28]
1 to ask for
□ J'ai demandé la permission. I've asked for permission. □ On a demandé notre chemin à un chauffeur de taxi. We asked a taxi driver the way. □ Je lui ai demandé de m'aider. I asked him to help me.
2 to require
□ un travail qui demande beaucoup de temps a job that requires a lot of time
■ **se demander** to wonder □ Je me demande à quelle heure il va venir. I wonder what time he'll come.

BE CAREFUL!
demander does not mean **to demand**.

le **demandeur d'asile** MASC NOUN
asylum seeker

le **demandeur d'emploi** MASC NOUN
job-seeker

la **demandeuse d'asile** FEM NOUN
asylum seeker

la **demandeuse d'emploi** FEM NOUN
job-seeker

la **démangeaison** FEM NOUN
itching

démanger VERB [45]
to itch
□ Ça me démange. It itches.

le **démaquillant** MASC NOUN
make-up remover

démaquiller VERB [28]
■ **se démaquiller** to remove one's make-up

la **démarche** FEM NOUN
1 walk
□ Il a une drôle de démarche. He's got a funny walk.
2 step
□ faire les démarches nécessaires pour obtenir quelque chose to take the necessary steps to obtain something

★ **démarrer** VERB [28]
to start (*car*)

démêler VERB [28]
to untangle

★ le **déménagement** MASC NOUN
move
□ C'était le jour de notre déménagement. It was the day we moved house.
■ **un camion de déménagement** a removal van

★ **déménager** VERB [45]
to move house

le **déménageur** MASC NOUN
removal man

dément (FEM **démente**) ADJECTIVE
crazy

démentiel (FEM **démentielle**) ADJECTIVE
insane

★ **demeurer** VERB [28]
to live

★ **demi** (FEM **demie**) ADJECTIVE, ADVERB
▷ *see also* **demi** NOUN
half
□ Il a trois ans et demi. He's three and a half.
■ **Il est trois heures et demie.** It's half past three.
■ **Il est midi et demi.** It's half past twelve.
■ **à demi endormi** half-asleep

★ le **demi** MASC NOUN
▷ *see also* **demi** ADJECTIVE, ADVERB
half pint of beer
■ **Un demi, s'il vous plaît!** A beer please!

la **demi-baguette** FEM NOUN
half a baguette

le **demi-cercle** MASC NOUN
semicircle

la **demi-douzaine** FEM NOUN
half-dozen
□ une demi-douzaine d'œufs half a dozen eggs

★ la **demie** FEM NOUN
half-hour
□ Le bus passe à la demie. The bus comes by on the half-hour.

demi-écrémé (FEM **demi-écrémée**) ADJECTIVE
semi-skimmed

la **demi-finale** FEM NOUN
semi-final

★ le **demi-frère** MASC NOUN
half-brother

la **demi-heure** FEM NOUN
half an hour
□ dans une demi-heure in half an hour
□ toutes les demi-heures every half an hour

la **demi-journée** FEM NOUN
half-day
□ On peut louer un parasol à la demi-journée. You can hire a sun umbrella for a half-day.

le **demi-litre** MASC NOUN
half litre
□ un demi-litre de lait half a litre of milk

la **demi-livre** FEM NOUN
half-pound
□ une demi-livre de tomates half a pound of tomatoes

★ la **demi-pension** FEM NOUN
half board
□ Cet hôtel propose des tarifs raisonnables en demi-pension. This hotel has reasonable rates for half board.

★ le/la **demi-pensionnaire** MASC/FEM NOUN
■ **être demi-pensionnaire** to have school lunches

demi-sel (FEM+PL **demi-sel**) ADJECTIVE
■ **du beurre demi-sel** slightly salted butter

★ la **demi-sœur** FEM NOUN
half-sister

la **démission** FEM NOUN
resignation
■ **donner sa démission** to resign

démissionner VERB [28]
to resign

le **demi-tarif** MASC NOUN
1 half-price
□ un billet à demi-tarif a half-price season ticket
2 half-fare
□ voyager à demi-tarif to travel half-fare

le **demi-tour** MASC NOUN
■ **faire demi-tour** to turn back □ La nuit commence à tomber; il est temps de faire demi-tour. It's getting dark; it's time we turned back.

la **démocratie** FEM NOUN
democracy

démocratique (FEM **démocratique**) ADJECTIVE
democratic

★ **démodé** (FEM **démodée**) ADJECTIVE
old-fashioned

la **demoiselle** FEM NOUN
young lady
■ **une demoiselle d'honneur** a bridesmaid

démolir VERB [38]
to demolish

le **démon** MASC NOUN
devil

démonter VERB [28]
1 to take down (*tent*)
2 to take apart (*machine*)

démontrer VERB [28]
to show

dénoncer VERB [12]
to denounce
■ **se dénoncer** to give oneself up □ Il s'est dénoncé à la police. He gave himself up to the police.

le **dénouement** MASC NOUN
outcome

la **densité** FEM NOUN
density

★ la **dent** FEM NOUN
tooth
□ une dent de lait a baby tooth □ une dent de sagesse a wisdom tooth

dentaire (FEM **dentaire**) ADJECTIVE
dental

la **dentelle** FEM NOUN
lace
□ un chemisier en dentelle a lacy blouse

le **dentier** MASC NOUN
denture

★ le **dentifrice** MASC NOUN
toothpaste

★ le/la **dentiste** MASC/FEM NOUN
dentist

le **déodorant** MASC NOUN
deodorant

le **dépannage** MASC NOUN
■ **un service de dépannage** a breakdown service

★ **dépanner** VERB [28]
1 to fix
□ Il a dépanné la voiture en cinq minutes. He fixed the car in five minutes.
2 to help out
□ Il m'a prêté dix euros pour me dépanner. (*informal*) He lent me 10 euros to help me out.

la **dépanneuse** FEM NOUN
breakdown lorry

★ le **départ** MASC NOUN

departure

□ Le départ est à onze heures. The departure is at 11.

■ **Je lui téléphonerai la veille de son départ.** I'll phone him the day before he leaves.

★ le **département** MASC NOUN

1 department

□ le département d'anglais à l'université the English department at the university

2 administrative area

□ le département du Vaucluse the Vaucluse region

> **DID YOU KNOW...?**
> France is divided into 96 **départements**, administrative areas rather like counties.

★ **dépasser** VERB [58]

1 to overtake

□ Il y a une voiture qui essaie de nous dépasser. There's a car trying to overtake us.

2 to pass

□ Nous avons dépassé Dijon. We've passed Dijon.

3 to exceed (*sum, limit*)

dépaysé (FEM **dépaysée**) ADJECTIVE

■ **se sentir un peu dépaysé** to feel a bit lost

se **dépêcher** VERB [28]

to hurry

□ Dépêche-toi! Hurry up!

★ **dépendre** VERB [88]

■ **dépendre de** to depend on □ Ça dépend du temps. It depends on the weather.

■ **dépendre de quelqu'un** to be dependent on somebody

■ **Ça dépend.** It depends.

★ **dépenser** VERB [28]

to spend (*money*)

dépensier (FEM **dépensière**) ADJECTIVE

■ **Il est dépensier.** He's a big spender.

■ **Elle n'est pas dépensière.** She doesn't spend a lot of money.

dépilatoire (FEM **dépilatoire**) ADJECTIVE

■ **une crème dépilatoire** a hair-removing cream

le **dépit** MASC NOUN

■ **en dépit de** in spite of □ Il y est allé en dépit de mes conseils. He went in spite of my advice.

déplacé (FEM **déplacée**) ADJECTIVE

uncalled-for

□ C'était une remarque déplacée. That remark wa[illegible]alled-for.

le **déplacement** MASC NOUN

□ Ça vaut le déplacement. [illegible]orth the trip.

déplacer VERB [12]

1 to move

□ Tu peux m'aider à déplacer la table? Can you help me move the table?

2 to put off

□ déplacer un rendez-vous to put off an appointment

■ **se déplacer** 1 to travel around □ Il se déplace beaucoup pour son travail. He travels around a lot for his work. 2 to get around □ Il a du mal à se déplacer. He has difficulty getting around.

■ **se déplacer une vertèbre** to slip a disc

déplaire VERB [62]

■ **Cela me déplaît.** I dislike this.

déplaisant (FEM **déplaisante**) ADJECTIVE

unpleasant

★ le **dépliant** MASC NOUN

leaflet

déplier VERB [19]

to unfold

★ **déposer** VERB [28]

1 to leave

□ J'ai déposé mon sac à la consigne. I left my bag at the left-luggage office.

2 to put down

□ Déposez le paquet sur la table. Put the parcel down on the table.

■ **déposer quelqu'un** to drop somebody off

dépourvu (FEM **dépourvue**) ADJECTIVE

■ **prendre quelqu'un au dépourvu** to take somebody by surprise □ Sa question m'a pris au dépourvu. His question took me by surprise.

la **dépression** FEM NOUN

depression

■ **faire de la dépression** to be suffering from depression

■ **faire une dépression** to have a breakdown

déprimant (FEM **déprimante**) ADJECTIVE

depressing

★ **déprimer** VERB [28]

to get depressed

□ Il déprime tout le temps. He gets depressed all the time. □ Ce genre de temps me déprime. This kind of weather makes me depressed.

★ **depuis** PREPOSITION, ADVERB

1 since

□ Il habite Paris depuis 2013. He's been living in Paris since 2013. □ Je ne lui ai pas parlé depuis. I haven't spoken to him since.

■ **depuis que** since □ Il a plu tous les jours depuis qu'elle est arrivée. It's rained every day since she arrived.

2 for

□ Il habite Paris depuis cinq ans. He's been living in Paris for five years.

■ **Depuis combien de temps?** How long? □ Depuis combien de temps est-ce que vous le connaissez? How long have you known him?
■ **Depuis quand?** How long? □ Depuis quand est-ce que vous le connaissez? How long have you known him?

le **député** MASC NOUN
Member of Parliament

la **députée** FEM NOUN
Member of Parliament

déraciner VERB [28]
to uproot

le **dérangement** MASC NOUN
■ **en dérangement** out of order □ Le téléphone est en dérangement. The phone's out of order.

★**déranger** VERB [45]
1 to bother
□ Excusez-moi de vous déranger. I'm sorry to bother you.
■ **Ne vous dérangez pas, je vais répondre au téléphone.** You stay there, I'll answer the phone.
2 to mess up
□ Ne dérange pas mes livres, s'il te plaît. Don't mess up my books, please.

déraper VERB [28]
to skid

le/la **dermatologue** MASC/FEM NOUN
dermatologist
□ Elle est dermatologue. She's a dermatologist.

★**dernier** (FEM **dernière**) ADJECTIVE
1 last
□ Il est arrivé dernier. He arrived last. □ la dernière fois the last time
2 latest
□ le dernier film de Spielberg Spielberg's latest film
■ **en dernier** last □ Ajoutez le lait en dernier. Put the milk in last.

dernièrement ADVERB
recently

★**dérouler** VERB [28]
1 to unroll
2 to unwind
■ **se dérouler** to take place □ L'action se déroule dans les années vingt. The action takes place in the 1920s.
■ **Tout s'est déroulé comme prévu.** Everything went as planned.

★**derrière** ADVERB, PREPOSITION
▷ *see also* **derrière** NOUN
behind

★le **derrière** MASC NOUN
▷ *see also* **derrière** ADVERB, PREPOSITION
1 back
□ la porte de derrière the back door
2 backside
□ un coup de pied dans le derrière a kick up the backside

★**des** ARTICLE

des is the contracted form of **de** + **les**.

1 some
□ Tu veux des chips? Would you like some crisps?

des is sometimes not translated.

□ J'ai des cousins en France. I have cousins in France. □ pendant des mois for months
2 any
□ Tu as des frères? Have you got any brothers?
3 of the
□ la fin des vacances the end of the holidays
■ **la voiture des Durand** the Durands' car
■ **Il arrive des États-Unis.** He's arriving from the United States.

★**dès** PREPOSITION
as early as
■ **dès le mois de novembre** from November
■ **dès le début** right from the start
■ **Il vous appellera dès son retour.** He'll call you as soon as he gets back.
■ **dès que** as soon as □ Il m'a reconnu dès qu'il m'a vu. He recognized me as soon as he saw me.

désabusé (FEM **désabusée**) ADJECTIVE
disillusioned

le **désaccord** MASC NOUN
disagreement

★**désagréable** (FEM **désagréable**) ADJECTIVE
unpleasant

désaltérer VERB [34]
■ **L'eau gazeuse désaltère bien.** Sparkling water is very thirst-quenching.
■ **se désaltérer** to have a drink □ Nous sommes allés dans un café pour nous désaltérer. We went into a café to have a drink.

désapprobateur (FEM **désapprobatrice**) ADJECTIVE
disapproving
□ un regard désapprobateur a disapproving look

le **désastre** MASC NOUN
disaster

★le **désavantage** MASC NOUN
disadvantage

désavantager VERB [45]
■ **désavantager quelqu'un** to put somebody at a disadvantage □ Cette nouvelle loi va désavantager les femmes. The new law will put women at a disadvantage.

★**descendre** VERB [24, *aux* **avoir** *or* **être**]
1 to go down
□ Je suis tombé en descendant l'escalier. I fell as I was going down the stairs.

French-English

d

2 to come down
□ Attends en bas; je descends! Wait downstairs; I'm coming down!
3 to get down
□ Vous pouvez descendre ma valise, s'il vous plaît? Can you get my suitcase down, please?
4 to get off
□ Nous descendons à la prochaine station. We're getting off at the next station.

The verb **descendre** uses **être** in the perfect tense when talking about moving downwards. It uses **avoir** in the perfect tense when talking about moving an object down from somewhere else.

la **descente** FEM NOUN
way down
▪ **Je t'attendrai au bas de la descente.** I'll wait for you at the bottom of the hill.
▪ **une descente de police** a police raid

★ la **description** FEM NOUN
description

déséquilibré (FEM **déséquilibrée**) ADJECTIVE
unbalanced

déséquilibrer VERB [28]
▪ **déséquilibrer quelqu'un** to throw somebody off balance □ Le coup de poing l'a déséquilibré. The punch threw him off balance.

★ **désert** (FEM **déserte**) ADJECTIVE
▷ *see also* **désert** NOUN
deserted
□ Le dimanche, le centre commercial est désert. On Sundays, the shopping centre is deserted.
▪ **une île déserte** a desert island

★ le **désert** MASC NOUN
▷ *see also* **désert** ADJECTIVE
desert

déserter VERB [28]
to desert

désertique (FEM **désertique**) ADJECTIVE
desert
□ une région désertique a desert region

désespéré (FEM **désespérée**) ADJECTIVE
desperate

désespérer VERB [34]
to despair
□ Il ne faut pas désespérer. Don't despair.

le **désespoir** MASC NOUN
despair

déshabiller VERB [28]
to undress
▪ **se déshabiller** to get undressed

déshériter VERB [28]
to disinherit
▪ **les déshérités** the underprivileged

déshydraté (FEM **déshydratée**) ADJECTIVE
dehydrated

désigner VERB [28]
to choose
□ On l'a désignée pour remettre le prix. She was chosen to present the prize.
▪ **désigner quelque chose du doigt** to point at something

le **désinfectant** MASC NOUN
disinfectant

désinfecter VERB [28]
to disinfect

désintéressé (FEM **désintéressée**) ADJECTIVE
1 unselfish
□ un acte désintéressé an unselfish action
2 impartial
□ un conseil désintéressé impartial advice

désintéresser VERB [28]
▪ **se désintéresser de quelque chose** to lose interest in something

le **désir** MASC NOUN
1 wish
□ Vos désirs sont des ordres. Your wish is my command.
2 will
□ le désir de réussir the will to succeed
3 desire
□ Ses yeux brillaient de désir. Her eyes were shining with desire.

★ **désirer** VERB [28]
to want
□ Vous désirez? (*in shop*) What would you like?

★ **désobéir** VERB [38]
▪ **désobéir à quelqu'un** to disobey somebody

désobéissant (FEM **désobéissante**) ADJECTIVE
disobedient

désobligeant (FEM **désobligeante**) ADJECTIVE
unpleasant
□ faire une remarque désobligeante to make an unpleasant remark

le **désodorisant** MASC NOUN
air freshener

★ **désolé** (FEM **désolée**) ADJECTIVE
sorry
□ Je suis vraiment désolé. I'm very sorry.
▪ **Désolé!** Sorry!

désopilant (FEM **désopilante**) ADJECTIVE
hilarious

désordonné (FEM **désordonnée**) ADJECTIVE
untidy

le **désordre** MASC NOUN
untidiness

■ **Quel désordre!** What a mess!
■ **en désordre** untidy □ Sa chambre est toujours en désordre. His bedroom is always untidy.

désormais ADVERB
from now on
□ Désormais, je boirai de l'eau. From now on I'll drink water.

desquelles PL PRONOUN

desquelles is the contracted form of **de** + **lesquelles**.

□ des négociations au cours desquelles les patrons ont fait des concessions negotiations during which the employers made concessions

desquels PL PRONOUN

desquels is the contracted form of **de** + **lesquels**.

□ les lacs au bord desquels nous avons campé the lakes on the banks of which we camped

dessécher VERB [34]
to dry out
□ Le soleil dessèche la peau. The sun dries your skin out.

desserrer VERB [28]
to loosen

★ le **dessert** MASC NOUN
pudding
□ Qu'est-ce que vous désirez comme dessert? What would you like for pudding?

★ le **dessin** MASC NOUN
drawing
□ C'est un dessin de ma petite sœur. It's a drawing my little sister did.
■ **un dessin animé** (*film*) a cartoon
■ **un dessin humoristique** (*drawing*) a cartoon

★ le **dessinateur** MASC NOUN
■ **un dessinateur industriel** a draughtsman

★ **dessiner** VERB [28]
to draw

★ **dessous** ADVERB
▷ *see also* **dessous** NOUN
underneath
■ **en dessous** underneath □ Soulève le pot de fleurs, la clé est en dessous. Lift the flowerpot, the key's underneath.
■ **par-dessous** underneath □ Le grillage ne sert à rien, les lapins passent par-dessous. The fence is useless, the rabbits get in underneath.
■ **là-dessous** under there □ Il s'est caché là-dessous. He hid under there.
■ **ci-dessous** below □ Complétez les phrases ci-dessous. Complete the sentences below.
■ **au-dessous de** below □ vingt degrés au-dessous de zéro 20 degrees below zero

★ le **dessous** MASC NOUN
▷ *see also* **dessous** ADVERB
underneath
■ **les voisins du dessous** the downstairs neighbours
■ **les dessous** underwear □ des dessous en soie silk underwear

le **dessous-de-plat** (PL les **dessous-de-plat**) MASC NOUN
tablemat

★ **dessus** ADVERB
▷ *see also* **dessus** NOUN
on top
□ un gâteau avec des bougies dessus a cake with candles on top
■ **par-dessus** over □ Nous avons sauté par-dessus la barrière. We jumped over the gate.
■ **au-dessus** above □ la taille au-dessus the size above □ au-dessus du lit above the bed
■ **là-dessus** **1** on there □ Tu peux écrire là-dessus. You can write on there. **2** with that □ 'Je démissionne!' Là-dessus, il est parti. 'I resign!' With that, he left.
■ **ci-dessus** above □ l'exemple ci-dessus the example above

★ le **dessus** MASC NOUN
▷ *see also* **dessus** ADVERB
top
■ **les voisins du dessus** the upstairs neighbours
■ **avoir le dessus** to have the upper hand

le/la **destinataire** MASC/FEM NOUN
addressee

★ la **destination** FEM NOUN
destination
■ **les passagers à destination de Paris** passengers travelling to Paris

destiné (FEM **destinée**) ADJECTIVE
intended
□ Ce livre est destiné aux enfants. This book is intended for children.
■ **Elle était destinée à faire ce métier.** She was destined to go into that job.

★ la **destruction** FEM NOUN
destruction

le **détachant** MASC NOUN
stain remover

détacher VERB [28]
to undo
■ **se détacher** **1** to come off □ La poignée de la porte s'est détachée. The door handle came off. **2** to break away □ Un wagon s'est détaché du reste du train. A carriage broke away from the rest of the train.

★ le **détail** MASC NOUN
detail
■ **en détail** in detail

le **détective** MASC NOUN
detective
□ un détective privé a private detective

déteindre VERB [60]
to fade (*in wash*)

★**détendre** VERB [88]
to relax
□ La lecture, ça me détend. I find reading relaxing.
■ **se détendre** to relax □ Il est allé prendre un bain pour se détendre. He's gone to have a bath to relax.

la **détente** FEM NOUN
relaxation

le **détenu** MASC NOUN
prisoner

la **détenue** FEM NOUN
prisoner

se **détériorer** VERB [28]
to deteriorate

déterminé (FEM **déterminée**) ADJECTIVE
1 determined
□ C'est un homme déterminé. He's a determined man.
2 specific
□ un but déterminé a specific aim

détestable (FEM **détestable**) ADJECTIVE
horrible

★**détester** VERB [28]
to hate

la **détonation** FEM NOUN
bang
□ J'ai entendu une détonation. I heard a bang.

le **détour** MASC NOUN
detour
■ **Ça vaut le détour.** It's worth the trip.

le **détournement** MASC NOUN
■ **un détournement d'avion** a hijacking

détrempé (FEM **détrempée**) ADJECTIVE
waterlogged

★les **détritus** MASC PL NOUN
litter *sing*

★**détruire** VERB [23]
to destroy

★la **dette** FEM NOUN
debt

le **deuil** MASC NOUN
■ **être en deuil** to be in mourning

★**deux** NUMBER
two
□ Il était deux heures. It was two o'clock.
□ Elle a deux ans. She's two.
■ **deux fois** twice
■ **deux-points** colon
■ **tous les deux** both □ Nous y sommes allées toutes les deux. We both went.
■ **le deux février** the second of February

★**deuxième** (FEM **deuxième**) ADJECTIVE
second
□ au deuxième étage on the second floor

deuxièmement ADVERB
secondly

devais, devait, devaient VERB ▷ *see* devoir

dévaliser VERB [28]
to rob

★**devant** ADVERB, PREPOSITION
▷ *see also* **devant** NOUN
1 in front
□ Il marchait devant. He was walking in front.
2 in front of
□ Il était assis devant moi. He was sitting in front of me.
■ **passer devant** to go past □ Nous sommes passés devant chez toi. We went past your house.

★le **devant** MASC NOUN
▷ *see also* **devant** ADVERB, PREPOSITION
front
□ le devant de la maison the front of the house
■ **les pattes de devant** the front legs

le **développement** MASC NOUN
development
■ **les pays en voie de développement** developing countries
■ **le développement durable** sustainable development

développer VERB [28]
to develop
■ **se développer** to develop

★**devenir** VERB [25, *aux* **être**]
to become

devez VERB ▷ *see* **devoir**

★la **déviation** FEM NOUN
diversion

deviez VERB ▷ *see* **devoir**

★**deviner** VERB [28]
to guess

la **devinette** FEM NOUN
riddle
□ poser une devinette à quelqu'un to ask somebody a riddle

devions VERB ▷ *see* **devoir**

dévisager VERB [45]
■ **dévisager quelqu'un** to stare at somebody

la **devise** FEM NOUN
currency
□ les devises étrangères foreign currency

dévisser VERB [28]
to unscrew

dévoiler VERB [28]
to unveil

★**devoir** VERB [26]

PRESENT TENSE
je dois — nous devons
tu dois — vous devez
il/elle doit — ils/elles doivent
PAST PARTICIPLE
dû

▷ *see also* **devoir** NOUN

1 to have to
□ Je dois partir. I've got to go.
2 must
□ Tu dois être fatigué. You must be tired.
3 to be due to
□ Le nouveau centre commercial doit ouvrir en mai. The new shopping centre is due to open in May.
■ **devoir quelque chose à quelqu'un** to owe somebody something □ Combien est-ce que je vous dois? How much do I owe you?

★le **devoir** MASC NOUN
▷ *see also* **devoir** VERB
1 exercise
■ **les devoirs** homework
■ **un devoir sur table** a written test
2 duty
□ Aller voter fait partie des devoirs du citoyen. Voting is part of one's duty as a citizen.

devons VERB ▷ *see* **devoir**

dévorer VERB [28]
to devour

dévoué (FEM **dévouée**) ADJECTIVE
devoted

devra, devrai, devras, devrez, devrons, devront VERB ▷ *see* **devoir**

le **diabète** MASC NOUN
diabetes

diabétique (FEM **diabétique**) ADJECTIVE
diabetic
□ Je suis diabétique. I'm diabetic.

le **diable** MASC NOUN
devil

le **diabolo** MASC NOUN
fruit cordial and lemonade
■ **un diabolo menthe** a mint cordial and lemonade

diagonal (FEM **diagonale**, MASC PL **diagonaux**) ADJECTIVE
diagonal

la **diagonale** FEM NOUN
diagonal
■ **en diagonale** diagonally

le **diagramme** MASC NOUN
diagram

le **dialecte** MASC NOUN
dialect

★le **dialogue** MASC NOUN
dialogue

le **diamant** MASC NOUN
diamond

le **diamètre** MASC NOUN
diameter

la **diapo** FEM NOUN (*informal*)
slide (*image*)

la **diapositive** FEM NOUN
slide
□ projeter des diapositives to show some slides

★la **diarrhée** FEM NOUN
diarrhoea
□ avoir la diarrhée to have diarrhoea

le **dictateur** MASC NOUN
dictator

la **dictature** FEM NOUN
dictatorship

la **dictée** FEM NOUN
dictation

dicter VERB [28]
to dictate

★le **dictionnaire** MASC NOUN
dictionary

★le **dièse** MASC NOUN
hash (# *sign*)
□ Pour plus d'options, appuyez sur la touche dièse. For more options, press the hash key.

diététique (FEM **diététique**) ADJECTIVE
■ **un magasin diététique** a health food shop

le **dieu** (PL les **dieux**) MASC NOUN
god
■ **Dieu** God □ Mon Dieu! Oh my God!

le **différé** MASC NOUN
■ **une émission en différé** a recording

★la **différence** FEM NOUN
difference
■ **la différence d'âge** the age difference
■ **à la différence de** unlike

★**différent** (FEM **différente**) ADJECTIVE
1 different
□ pour des raisons différentes for different reasons
2 various
□ pour différentes raisons for various reasons
■ **différent de** different from □ Son point de vue est différent du mien. His point of view is different from mine.

★**difficile** (FEM **difficile**) ADJECTIVE
difficult
□ C'est difficile à comprendre. It's difficult to understand.

difficilement ADVERB
■ **faire quelque chose difficilement** to have trouble doing something □ Ma grand-mère se déplace difficilement. My grandmother has trouble getting around.
■ **Je pouvais difficilement refuser.** It was difficult for me to refuse.

★ la **difficulté** FEM NOUN
difficulty
□ avec difficulté with difficulty
■ **élève en difficulté (scolaire)** a student who is struggling

digérer VERB [34]
to digest

le **digestif** MASC NOUN
after-dinner liqueur

digne (FEM **digne**) ADJECTIVE
■ **digne de** worthy of □ digne de confiance trustworthy

la **dignité** FEM NOUN
dignity

le **dilemme** MASC NOUN
dilemma
□ être devant un dilemme to be faced with a dilemma

diluer VERB [28]
to dilute

★ le **dimanche** MASC NOUN
1 Sunday
□ Aujourd'hui, on est dimanche. It's Sunday today.
2 on Sunday
□ Dimanche, nous allons déjeuner chez mes grands-parents. On Sunday we're having lunch at my grandparents'.
■ **le dimanche** on Sundays □ Le dimanche, je fais la grasse matinée. I have a lie-in on Sundays.
■ **tous les dimanches** every Sunday
■ **dimanche dernier** last Sunday
■ **dimanche prochain** next Sunday

★ **diminuer** VERB [28]
to decrease
□ Le chômage a un peu diminué le mois dernier. Unemployment fell slightly last month.

le **diminutif** MASC NOUN
pet name

la **diminution** FEM NOUN
1 reduction
2 decrease

★ la **dinde** FEM NOUN
turkey (*meat*)
□ la dinde de Noël the Christmas turkey

le **dindon** MASC NOUN
turkey (*bird*)

★ le **dîner** MASC NOUN
▷ *see also* **dîner** VERB
dinner (*evening meal*)

★ **dîner** VERB [28]
▷ *see also* **dîner** NOUN
to have dinner (*evening meal*)

dingue (FEM **dingue**) ADJECTIVE (*informal*)
crazy

diplomate (FEM **diplomate**) ADJECTIVE
▷ *see also* **diplomate** NOUN
diplomatic

le/la **diplomate** MASC/FEM NOUN
▷ *see also* **diplomate** ADJECTIVE
diplomat

la **diplomatie** FEM NOUN
diplomacy

★ le **diplôme** MASC NOUN
qualification

diplômé (FEM **diplômée**) ADJECTIVE
qualified

★ **dire** VERB [27]
1 to say
□ Il a dit qu'il ne viendrait pas. He said he wouldn't come.
■ **on dit que ...** they say that ... □ On dit que la nourriture est excellente là-bas. They say that the food is excellent there.
2 to tell
■ **dire quelque chose à quelqu'un** to tell somebody something □ Elle m'a dit la vérité. She told me the truth. □ Il nous a dit de regarder cette émission. He told us to watch this programme.
■ **On dirait qu'il va pleuvoir.** It looks as if it's going to rain.
■ **se dire quelque chose** to think something □ Quand je l'ai vu, je me suis dit qu'il avait vieilli. When I saw him, I thought that he'd aged.
■ **Est-ce que ça se dit?** Can you say that?
■ **Ça ne me dit rien.** 1 That doesn't appeal to me. 2 It doesn't ring a bell.

★ **direct** (FEM **directe**) ADJECTIVE
direct
■ **en direct** live □ une émission en direct a live broadcast

directement ADVERB
straight
□ Il est rentré directement chez lui. He went straight home.

★ le **directeur** MASC NOUN
1 headteacher
□ Il est directeur. He's a headteacher.
2 manager
□ Il est directeur du personnel. He's a personnel manager.

★ la **direction** FEM NOUN
1 management
□ la direction et les ouvriers the management and the workers
2 direction
□ 'toutes directions' 'all directions'

★ la **directrice** FEM NOUN
1 headteacher
□ Elle est directrice. She's a headteacher.

 Numbers in brackets refer to verb tables on pages 650 to 658

2 manager
□ Elle est directrice commerciale. She's a sales manager.

dirent VERB ▷ *see* **dire**

le **dirigeant** MASC NOUN
leader

la **dirigeante** FEM NOUN
leader

★ **diriger** VERB [45]
to manage
□ Il dirige une petite entreprise. He manages a small company.
■ **se diriger vers** to head for □ Il se dirigeait vers la gare. He was heading for the station.

dis VERB ▷ *see* **dire**
■ **Dis-moi la vérité!** Tell me the truth!
■ **dis donc** hey □ Il a drôlement changé, dis donc! Hey, he's really changed! □ Dis donc, tu te souviens de Sam? Hey, do you remember Sam?

disaient, disais, disait VERB ▷ *see* **dire**

★ la **discothèque** FEM NOUN
disco (*club*)

★ le **discours** MASC NOUN
speech

discret (FEM **discrète**) ADJECTIVE
discreet

la **discrimination** FEM NOUN
discrimination
□ la discrimination raciale racial discrimination □ la discrimination sexuelle sex discrimination

la **discussion** FEM NOUN
discussion

discutable (FEM **discutable**) ADJECTIVE
debatable

★ **discuter** VERB [28]
1 to talk
□ Nous avons discuté pendant des heures. We talked for hours.
2 to argue
□ C'est ce que j'ai décidé, alors ne discutez pas! That's what I've decided, so don't argue!

disent, disiez, disions VERB ▷ *see* **dire**

disons VERB ▷ *see* **dire**
let's say
□ C'est à, disons, une demi-heure à pied. It's half an hour's walk, say.

★ **disparaître** VERB [56]
to disappear
■ **faire disparaître quelque chose** 1 to make something disappear □ Il a fait disparaître le lapin dans son chapeau. He made the rabbit disappear in his hat. 2 to get rid of something □ Ils ont fait disparaître tous les documents compromettants. They got rid of all the incriminating documents.

★ la **disparition** FEM NOUN
disappearance
■ **une espèce en voie de disparition** an endangered species

★ **disparu** (FEM **disparue**) ADJECTIVE
■ **être porté disparu** to be reported missing

le **dispensaire** MASC NOUN
community clinic

dispensé (FEM **dispensée**) ADJECTIVE
■ **être dispensé de quelque chose** to be excused something □ Elle est dispensée de gymnastique. She's excused gym.

disperser VERB [28]
to break up
□ La police a dispersé les manifestants. The police broke up the demonstrators.
■ **se disperser** to break up □ Une fois l'ambulance partie, la foule s'est dispersée. Once the ambulance had left, the crowd broke up.

★ **disponible** (FEM **disponible**) ADJECTIVE
available

disposé (FEM **disposée**) ADJECTIVE
■ **être disposé à faire quelque chose** to be willing to do something □ Il était disposé à m'aider. He was willing to help me.

disposer VERB [28]
■ **disposer de quelque chose** to have access to something □ Je dispose d'un ordinateur. I have access to a computer.

la **disposition** FEM NOUN
■ **prendre ses dispositions** to make arrangements □ Est-ce que vous avez pris vos dispositions pour partir en France? Have you made arrangements to go to France?
■ **avoir quelque chose à sa disposition** to have something at one's disposal □ J'ai une voiture à ma disposition pour la semaine. I have a car at my disposal for the week. □ Je tiens ces livres à votre disposition. The books are at your disposal.
■ **Je suis à votre disposition.** I am at your service.

★ la **dispute** FEM NOUN
argument

★ se **disputer** VERB [28]
to argue

le **disquaire** MASC NOUN
record dealer

★ le **disque** MASC NOUN
record
■ **un disque compact** a compact disc
■ **le disque dur** hard disk

disséminé (FEM **disséminée**) ADJECTIVE
scattered

disséquer VERB [34]
to dissect

French-English

d

la **dissertation** FEM NOUN
essay

dissimuler VERB [28]
to conceal

se **dissiper** VERB [28]
to clear
□ Le brouillard va se dissiper dans l'après-midi. The fog will clear during the afternoon.

le **dissolvant** MASC NOUN
nail polish remover

dissoudre VERB [70]
to dissolve
■ **se dissoudre** to dissolve

dissuader VERB [28]
■ **dissuader quelqu'un de faire quelque chose** to dissuade somebody from doing something □ Elle m'a dissuadé d'aller voir ce film. She dissuaded me from going to see the film.

★la **distance** FEM NOUN
distance

la **distillerie** FEM NOUN
distillery

distingué (FEM **distinguée**) ADJECTIVE
distinguished

★**distinguer** VERB [28]
to distinguish

★la **distraction** FEM NOUN
entertainment
□ Il lit beaucoup: c'est sa seule distraction. He reads a lot: it's his only form of entertainment.

distraire VERB [85]
■ **Va voir un film, ça te distraira.** Go and see a film, it'll take your mind off things.

distrait (FEM **distraite**) ADJECTIVE
absent-minded

★**distribuer** VERB [28]
1 to give out
□ Distribue les livres, s'il te plaît. Give out the books, please.
2 to deal (*cards*)

★le **distributeur** MASC NOUN
■ **un distributeur automatique** a vending machine
■ **un distributeur de billets** a cash machine

dit (FEM **dite**) ADJECTIVE
known as
□ Pierre, dit Pierrot Pierre, known as Pierrot

dit VERB ▷ *see* **dire**

dites VERB ▷ *see* **dire**
■ **Dites-moi ce que vous pensez.** Tell me what you think.
■ **dites donc** hey □ Dites donc, vous, là-bas! Hey, you there!

divers (FEM **diverse**) ADJECTIVE
diverse
■ **pour diverses raisons** for various reasons

se **divertir** VERB [38]
to enjoy oneself

divin (FEM **divine**) ADJECTIVE
divine

★**diviser** VERB [28]
to divide
□ Quatre divisé par deux égale deux. 4 divided by 2 equals 2.

★le **divorce** MASC NOUN
divorce

★le **divorcé** MASC NOUN
divorcee

★la **divorcée** FEM NOUN
divorcee

★**divorcer** VERB [12]
to get divorced

★**dix** NUMBER
ten
□ Elle a dix ans. She's ten. □ à dix heures at ten o'clock
■ **le dix février** the tenth of February

★**dix-huit** NUMBER
eighteen
□ Elle a dix-huit ans. She's eighteen. □ à dix-huit heures at 6 p.m.

★**dixième** (FEM **dixième**) ADJECTIVE
tenth
□ au dixième étage on the tenth floor

★**dix-neuf** NUMBER
nineteen
□ Elle a dix-neuf ans. She's nineteen. □ à dix-neuf heures at 7 p.m.

★**dix-sept** NUMBER
seventeen
□ Elle a dix-sept ans. She's seventeen. □ à dix-sept heures at 5 p.m.

★la **dizaine** FEM NOUN
about ten
□ une dizaine de jours about ten days

le **do** MASC NOUN
1 C
□ en do majeur in C major
2 do
□ do, ré, mi ... do, re, mi ...

★le **docteur** MASC NOUN
doctor
□ Elle est docteur. She's a doctor.

le **document** MASC NOUN
document

★le **documentaire** MASC NOUN
documentary

le/la **documentaliste** MASC/FEM NOUN
librarian

★la **documentation** FEM NOUN
documentation

documenter VERB [28]
■ **se documenter sur quelque chose** to gather information on something

dodu (FEM **dodue**) ADJECTIVE
plump

★ le **doigt** MASC NOUN
finger
■ **les doigts de pied** the toes

dois, doit, doivent VERB ▷ *see* **devoir**

le **domaine** MASC NOUN
1 estate
□ Il possède un immense domaine en Normandie. He owns a huge estate in Normandy.
2 field
□ La chimie n'est pas mon domaine. Chemistry's not my field.

★ **domestique** (FEM **domestique**) ADJECTIVE
▷ *see also* **domestique** NOUN
domestic
■ **les animaux domestiques** pets

★ le/la **domestique** MASC/FEM NOUN
▷ *see also* **domestique** ADJECTIVE
servant

★ le **domicile** MASC NOUN
place of residence
■ **à domicile** at home □ Il travaille à domicile. He works at home.

domicilié (FEM **domiciliée**) ADJECTIVE
■ **'domicilié à: ...'** 'address: ...'

dominer VERB [28]
to dominate
■ **se dominer** to control oneself

les **dominos** MASC PL NOUN
dominoes
□ jouer aux dominos to play dominoes

★ le **dommage** MASC NOUN
damage
□ La tempête a causé d'importants dommages. The storm caused a lot of damage.
■ **C'est dommage.** It's a shame. □ C'est dommage que tu ne puisses pas venir. It's a shame you can't come.

dompter VERB [28]
to tame

le **dompteur** MASC NOUN
animal tamer

la **dompteuse** FEM NOUN
animal tamer

le **don** MASC NOUN
1 donation
2 gift
□ avoir un don pour quelque chose to have a gift for something
■ **Elle a le don de m'énerver.** She's got a knack of getting on my nerves.

★ **donc** CONJUNCTION
so

le **dongle** MASC NOUN
dongle

le **donjon** MASC NOUN
keep (*of castle*)

les **données** FEM PL NOUN
data

★ **donner** VERB [28]
1 to give
■ **donner quelque chose à quelqu'un** to give somebody something □ Elle m'a donné son adresse. She gave me her address.
■ **Ça m'a donné faim.** That made me feel hungry.
2 to give away
□ Tu as toujours ta veste en daim? — Non, je l'ai donnée. Have you still got your suede jacket? — No, I gave it away.
■ **donner sur quelque chose** to overlook something □ une fenêtre qui donne sur la mer a window overlooking the sea

★ **dont** PRONOUN
1 of which
□ deux livres, dont l'un est en anglais two books, one of which is in English □ le prix dont il est si fier the prize he's so proud of
2 of whom
□ trois candidats, dont deux parlent italien three candidates, two of whom speak Italian □ la fille dont je t'ai parlé the girl I told you about

doré (FEM **dorée**) ADJECTIVE
golden
□ une étoile dorée a golden star

dorénavant ADVERB
from now on
□ Dorénavant, tu feras attention. From now on, you'll be careful.

dorloter VERB [28]
to pamper

★ **dormir** VERB [29]
1 to sleep
□ Tu as bien dormi? Did you sleep well?
2 to be asleep
□ Tu dors? Are you asleep?

★ le **dortoir** MASC NOUN
dormitory

★ le **dos** MASC NOUN
back
□ dos à dos back to back
■ **faire quelque chose dans le dos de quelqu'un** to do something behind somebody's back □ Elle me critique dans mon dos. She criticizes me behind my back.
■ **de dos** from behind
■ **nager le dos crawlé** to swim backstroke
■ **'voir au dos'** 'see over'

French-English

d

la **dose** FEM NOUN
dose
□ Ne pas dépasser la dose prescrite. Do not exceed the stated dose.

★ le **dossier** MASC NOUN
1 file
□ une pile de dossiers a stack of files
2 report
□ un bon dossier scolaire a good school report
3 feature (*in magazine*)
4 back (*of chair*)

★ la **douane** FEM NOUN
customs

★ le **douanier** MASC NOUN
customs officer

★ le **double** MASC NOUN
■ **le double** twice as much □ Il gagne le double. He earns twice as much.
■ **le double du prix normal** twice the normal price
■ **en double** in duplicate
■ **Garde cette photo, je l'ai en double.** Keep this photo, I've got a copy of it.
■ **le double messieurs** (*tennis*) the men's doubles

le **double-clic** (PL les **double-clics**) MASC NOUN
double-click

double-cliquer VERB [28]
to double-click
□ double-cliquer sur une icône to double-click on an icon

★ **doubler** VERB [28]
1 to double
□ Le prix a doublé en dix ans. The price has doubled in 10 years.
2 to overtake
□ Il est dangereux de doubler sur cette route. It's dangerous to overtake on this road.
■ **un film doublé** a dubbed film

douce FEM ADJECTIVE ▷ *see* **doux**

★ **doucement** ADVERB
1 gently
□ Il a frappé doucement à la porte. He knocked gently at the door.
2 slowly
□ Roulez doucement! Drive slowly! □ Je ne comprends pas, parle plus doucement. I don't understand, speak more slowly.

la **douceur** FEM NOUN
1 softness
□ Cette crème maintient la douceur de votre peau. This cream keeps your skin soft.
2 gentleness
□ parler avec douceur to speak gently
■ **L'avion a atterri en douceur.** The plane made a smooth landing.

★ la **douche** FEM NOUN
shower
■ **les douches** the shower room
■ **prendre une douche** to have a shower

★ se **doucher** VERB [28]
to have a shower

le **doudou** MASC NOUN (*informal*)
1 comfort blanket (*piece of fabric*)
2 cuddly toy (*toy*)

★ **doué** (FEM **douée**) ADJECTIVE
talented
■ **être doué en quelque chose** to be good at something □ Il est doué en maths. He's good at maths.

douillet (FEM **douillette**) ADJECTIVE
1 cosy
□ un anorak douillet a cosy anorak
2 soft
□ Je ne supporte pas la douleur: je suis très douillette. I can't stand pain: I'm a real softie.

★ la **douleur** FEM NOUN
pain

douloureux (FEM **douloureuse**) ADJECTIVE
painful

★ le **doute** MASC NOUN
doubt
■ **sans doute** probably

★ **douter** VERB [28]
to doubt
■ **douter de quelque chose** to have doubts about something □ Je doute de sa sincérité. I have my doubts about his sincerity.
■ **se douter de quelque chose** to suspect something □ Je ne me doutais de rien. I didn't suspect anything.
■ **Je m'en doutais.** I suspected as much.

douteux (FEM **douteuse**) ADJECTIVE
1 dubious
□ une plaisanterie d'un goût douteux a joke in dubious taste
2 suspicious-looking
□ un individu douteux a suspicious-looking person

★ **Douvres** NOUN
Dover

★ **doux** (FEM **douce**, MASC PL **doux**) ADJECTIVE
1 soft
□ un tissu doux soft material □ les drogues douces soft drugs
2 sweet
□ du cidre doux sweet cider
3 mild
□ Il fait doux aujourd'hui. It's mild today.
4 gentle
□ C'est quelqu'un de très doux. He's a very gentle person.
■ **en douce** on the quiet □ Il m'a donné dix euros en douce. He slipped me 10 euros on the quiet.

★ la **douzaine** FEM NOUN
dozen
□ une douzaine d'œufs a dozen eggs
■ **une douzaine de personnes** about twelve people

douze NUMBER
twelve
□ Il a douze ans. He's twelve.
■ **le douze février** the twelfth of February

★ **douzième** (FEM **douzième**) ADJECTIVE
twelfth
□ au douzième étage on the twelfth floor

la **dragée** FEM NOUN
sugared almond

draguer VERB [28] (*informal*)
■ **draguer quelqu'un** to chat somebody up
□ Il est en train de la draguer. He's chatting her up.
■ **se faire draguer** to get chatted up □ Il aime se faire draguer. He likes getting chatted up.

le **dragueur** MASC NOUN (*informal*)
flirt (*person*)

la **dragueuse** FEM NOUN (*informal*)
flirt (*person*)

dramatique (FEM **dramatique**) ADJECTIVE
tragic
□ une situation dramatique a tragic situation
■ **l'art dramatique** drama

le **drame** MASC NOUN
drama (*incident*)
■ **Ça n'est pas un drame si tu ne viens pas.** It's not the end of the world if you don't come.

★ le **drap** MASC NOUN
sheet (*for bed*)

★ le **drapeau** (PL les **drapeaux**) MASC NOUN
flag
□ le drapeau français the French flag □ le drapeau tricolore the French flag

> **DID YOU KNOW...?**
> **le drapeau tricolore** is the French flag: its three colours are blue, white and red.

dressé (FEM **dressée**) ADJECTIVE
trained
□ un chien bien dressé a well-trained dog

★ **dresser** VERB [28]
1 to draw up
□ dresser une liste to draw up a list
2 to train
□ dresser un chien to train a dog
■ **dresser l'oreille** to prick up one's ears
□ Quand elle a dit ça, il a dressé l'oreille. When she said that, he pricked up his ears.

★ la **drogue** FEM NOUN
drug
□ le problème de la drogue the drugs problem
□ la lutte contre la drogue the war against drugs
■ **les drogues douces** soft drugs
■ **les drogues dures** hard drugs

★ le **drogué** MASC NOUN
drug addict

★ la **droguée** FEM NOUN
drug addict

★ **droguer** VERB [28]
■ **droguer quelqu'un** to drug somebody
■ **se droguer** to take drugs

la **droguerie** FEM NOUN
hardware shop

★ **droit** (FEM **droite**) ADJECTIVE, ADVERB
▷ *see also* **droit** NOUN, **droite** NOUN
1 right
□ le bras droit the right arm □ le côté droit the right-hand side
2 straight
□ une ligne droite a straight line □ Tiens-toi droite! Stand up straight!
■ **tout droit** straight on

★ le **droit** MASC NOUN
▷ *see also* **droit** ADJECTIVE, ADVERB
1 right
□ les droits de l'homme human rights
■ **avoir le droit de faire quelque chose** to be allowed to do something □ On n'a pas le droit de fumer à l'école. We're not allowed to smoke at school.
2 law
□ faire son droit to study law □ un étudiant en droit a law student

★ la **droite** FEM NOUN
▷ *see also* **droit** ADJECTIVE, ADVERB
right
□ sur votre droite on your right
■ **à droite** 1 on the right □ la troisième rue à droite the third street on the right 2 to the right □ à droite de la fenêtre to the right of the window
■ **Tournez à droite.** Turn right.
■ **la voie de droite** the right-hand lane
■ **la droite** (*in politics*) the right
■ **Elle est très à droite.** She's very right-wing.

droitier (FEM **droitière**) ADJECTIVE
right-handed
□ Elle est droitière. She's right-handed.

★ **drôle** (FEM **drôle**) ADJECTIVE
funny
□ Ça n'est pas drôle. It's not funny.
■ **un drôle de temps** funny weather

drôlement ADVERB (*informal*)
really
□ C'est drôlement bon. It's really good.

★ le **drone** MASC NOUN
drone

French-English

d

★ **du** ARTICLE

du is the contracted form of **de** + **le**.

1 some
□ Tu veux du fromage? Would you like some cheese?
2 any
□ Tu as du chocolat? Have you got any chocolate?
3 of the
□ la porte du garage the door of the garage
□ la femme du directeur the headmaster's wife

dû (FEM **due**, MASC PL **dus**) ADJECTIVE
▷ *see also* **dû** VERB
■ **dû à** due to □ un retard dû au mauvais temps a delay due to bad weather

dû VERB ▷ *see* **devoir**
▷ *see also* **dû** ADJECTIVE
■ **Nous avons dû nous arrêter.** We had to stop.

le **duc** MASC NOUN
duke

la **duchesse** FEM NOUN
duchess

dupe (FEM **dupe**) ADJECTIVE
■ **Elle me ment mais je ne suis pas dupe.** She lies to me but I'm not taken in by that.

★ **duquel** (MASC PL **desquels**, FEM PL **desquelles**) PRONOUN

duquel is the contracted form of **de** + **lequel**.

□ l'homme duquel il parle the man he is talking about

★ **dur** (FEM **dure**) ADJECTIVE, ADVERB
hard
□ travailler dur to work hard □ être dur avec quelqu'un to be hard on somebody

★ **durant** PREPOSITION
1 during
□ durant la nuit during the night
2 for
□ durant des années for years □ des mois durant for months

★ la **durée** FEM NOUN
length
□ Quelle est la durée des études d'ingénieur? How long does it take to train as an engineer?
■ **pour une durée de quinze jours** for a period of two weeks
■ **de courte durée** short □ un séjour de courte durée a short stay
■ **de longue durée** long □ une absence de longue durée a long absence

durement ADVERB
harshly

★ **durer** VERB [28]
to last

la **dureté** FEM NOUN
harshness
□ traiter quelqu'un avec dureté to treat somebody harshly

le **DVD** MASC NOUN
DVD

★ **dynamique** (FEM **dynamique**) ADJECTIVE
dynamic

dyslexique (FEM **dyslexique**) ADJECTIVE
dyslexic

Ee

★ l'**eau** (PL les **eaux**) FEM NOUN
water
■ **l'eau minérale** mineral water
■ **l'eau plate** still water
■ **tomber à l'eau** to fall through □ Nos projets sont tombés à l'eau. Our plans have fallen through.

ébahi (FEM **ébahie**) ADJECTIVE
amazed

éblouir VERB [38]
to dazzle

l'**éboueur** MASC NOUN
dustman

ébouillanter VERB [28]
to scald

l'**écaille** FEM NOUN
scale (*of fish*)

s'**écailler** VERB [28]
to flake

l'**écart** MASC NOUN
gap
■ **à l'écart de** away from □ Ils se sont assis à l'écart des autres. They sat down away from the others.

écarté (FEM **écartée**) ADJECTIVE
remote
■ **les bras écartés** arms outstretched
■ **les jambes écartées** legs apart

écarter VERB [28]
to open wide (*arms, legs*)
■ **s'écarter** to move □ Ils se sont écartés pour le laisser passer. They moved to let him pass.

l'**échafaudage** MASC NOUN
scaffolding

l'**échalote** FEM NOUN
shallot

★ l'**échange** MASC NOUN
exchange
□ en échange de in exchange for

★ **échanger** VERB [45]
to swap
□ Je t'échange ce jeux contre celui-là. I'll swap you this game for that one.

l'**échantillon** MASC NOUN
sample

échapper VERB [28]
■ **échapper à** to escape from □ Le prisonnier a réussi à échapper à la police. The prisoner managed to escape from the police.
■ **s'échapper** to escape □ Il s'est échappé de prison. He escaped from prison.
■ **l'échapper belle** to have a narrow escape □ Nous l'avons échappé belle. We had a narrow escape.

l'**écharde** FEM NOUN
splinter of wood

★ l'**écharpe** FEM NOUN
scarf

s'**échauffer** VERB [28]
to warm up (*before exercise*)

l'**échec** MASC NOUN
failure

★ les **échecs** MASC PL NOUN
chess *sing*
□ jouer aux échecs to play chess

★ l'**échelle** FEM NOUN
1 ladder
2 scale (*of map*)

échevelé (FEM **échevelée**) ADJECTIVE
dishevelled

l'**écho** MASC NOUN
echo

★ **échouer** VERB [28]
■ **échouer à un examen** to fail an exam

éclabousser VERB [28]
to splash

★ l'**éclair** MASC NOUN
flash of lightning
■ **un éclair au chocolat** a chocolate éclair

l'**éclairage** MASC NOUN
lighting

★ l'**éclaircie** FEM NOUN
bright interval

★ **éclairer** VERB [28]
■ **Cette lampe éclaire bien.** This lamp gives a good light.

l'**éclat** MASC NOUN
1 piece (*of glass*)
□ La vase a volé en éclats. The vase smashed into pieces.
2 brightness (*of sun, colour*)
■ **des éclats de rire** roars of laughter

éclatant (FEM **éclatante**) ADJECTIVE
brilliant
□ des dents d'une blancheur éclatante brilliant white teeth

★ **éclater** VERB [28]
1 to burst (*tyre, balloon*)
■ **éclater de rire** to burst out laughing
■ **éclater en sanglots** to burst into tears
2 to break out
□ La Seconde Guerre mondiale a éclaté en 1939. The Second World War broke out in 1939.

écœurant (FEM **écœurante**) ADJECTIVE
sickly

écœurer VERB [28]
■ **Tous ces mensonges m'écœurent.** All these lies make me sick.

★ l'**école** FEM NOUN
school
□ aller à l'école to go to school □ une école privée a private school □ une école publique a state school □ une école maternelle a nursery school

> **DID YOU KNOW...?**
> The **école maternelle** is a state school for 2–6 year-olds.

l'**écolier** MASC NOUN
schoolboy

l'**écolière** FEM NOUN
schoolgirl

l'**écologie** FEM NOUN
ecology

écologique (FEM **écologique**) ADJECTIVE
ecological
□ une lessive écologique an ecological washing powder

★ l'**économie** FEM NOUN
1 economy
□ l'économie de la France the French economy
2 economics
□ un cours d'économie an economics class

★ les **économies** FEM PL NOUN
savings
■ **faire des économies** to save up □ Je fais des économies pour partir en vacances. I'm saving up for my holidays.

★ **économique** (FEM **économique**) ADJECTIVE
1 economic
□ une crise économique an economic crisis
2 economical
□ Il est plus économique d'acheter une grande boîte de lessive. It's more economical to buy a big box of washing powder. □ Cette petite voiture est économique. This little car is economical.

★ **économiser** VERB [28]
to save

l'**économiseur d'écran** MASC NOUN
screen saver

l'**écorce** FEM NOUN
1 bark (*of tree*)
2 peel (*of orange, lemon*)

s'**écorcher** VERB [28]
■ **Je me suis écorché le genou.** I've grazed my knee.

★ **écossais** (FEM **écossaise**) ADJECTIVE, NOUN
1 Scottish
□ Elle est écossaise. She's Scottish.
■ **un Écossais** a Scot (*man*)
■ **une Écossaise** a Scot (*woman*)
■ **les Écossais** the Scots
2 tartan
□ une jupe écossaise a tartan skirt

★ l'**Écosse** FEM NOUN
Scotland
■ **en Écosse** 1 in Scotland □ Il a passé une semaine en Écosse. He spent a week in Scotland. 2 to Scotland □ Nous allons en Écosse l'été prochain. We're going to Scotland next summer.

★ l'**écotourisme** MASC NOUN
ecotourism

s'**écouler** VERB [28]
1 to flow out (*water*)
2 to pass
□ Le temps s'écoule trop vite. Time passes too quickly.

★ **écouter** VERB [28]
to listen to
□ J'aime écouter de la musique. I like listening to music.
■ **Écoute-moi!** Listen!

l'**écouteur** MASC NOUN
earpiece (*of phone*)

★ l'**écran** MASC NOUN
screen
■ **le petit écran** television
■ **un écran tactile** a touchscreen
■ **l'écran total** sunblock

★ **écraser** VERB [28]
1 to crush
□ Écrasez une gousse d'ail. Crush a clove of garlic.
2 to run over
□ Mon chien s'est fait écraser par une voiture. My dog got run over by a car.
■ **s'écraser** to crash □ L'avion s'est écrasé dans le désert. The plane crashed in the desert.

écrémé (FEM **écrémée**) ADJECTIVE
skimmed
□ le lait écrémé skimmed milk

l'**écrevisse** FEM NOUN
crayfish

★ **écrire** VERB [30]
to write
□ Nous nous écrivons régulièrement. We write to each other regularly.
■ **Ça s'écrit comment?** How do you spell that?

l'**écrit** MASC NOUN
written paper
□ L'écrit d'anglais a lieu la semaine prochaine. The written paper in English is next week.
■ **par écrit** in writing

l'**écriteau** (PL les **écriteaux**) MASC NOUN
notice

l'**écriture** FEM NOUN
writing
□ J'ai du mal à lire son écriture. I can't read his writing.

★ l'**écrivain** MASC NOUN
writer
□ Elle est écrivain. She's a writer.

l'**écrou** MASC NOUN
nut (*metal*)

s'**écrouler** VERB [28]
to collapse

écru (FEM **écrue**) ADJECTIVE
off-white

l'**écureuil** MASC NOUN
squirrel

l'**écurie** FEM NOUN
stable

★ **Édimbourg** NOUN
Edinburgh

éditer VERB [28]
to publish
□ On vient d'éditer un nouveau dictionnaire. A new dictionary has just been published.

l'**éditeur** MASC NOUN
publisher

l'**édition** FEM NOUN
1 edition
□ une édition de poche a paperback edition
2 publishing
□ Il travaille dans l'édition. He works in publishing.

l'**édredon** MASC NOUN
eiderdown

l'**éducateur** MASC NOUN
teacher (*of people with special needs*)

éducatif (FEM **éducative**) ADJECTIVE
educational
□ un jeu éducatif an educational game

★ l'**éducation** FEM NOUN
1 education
□ l'éducation physique physical education
■ **Il n'a pas beaucoup d'éducation.** He's not very well educated.
2 upbringing
□ Il a reçu une éducation très stricte. He had a very strict upbringing.

l'**éducatrice** FEM NOUN
teacher (*of people with special needs*)

éduquer VERB [28]
to educate

★ **effacer** VERB [12]
1 to rub out
2 to delete (*file*)

effarant (FEM **effarante**) ADJECTIVE
amazing
□ Il a mangé une quantité effarante de pain. He ate an amazing amount of bread.

★ **effectivement** ADVERB
indeed
□ Il est effectivement plus rapide de passer par là. It is indeed quicker to go this way.
□ Oui, effectivement. Yes, indeed.

> **BE CAREFUL!**
> **effectivement** does not mean **effectively**.

effectuer VERB [28]
1 to make
□ Ils ont effectué de nombreux changements. They have made a lot of changes.
2 to do
□ On vient d'effectuer des travaux dans le bâtiment. They have just done some work in the building.

effervescent (FEM **effervescente**) ADJECTIVE
effervescent
□ un comprimé effervescent an effervescent tablet

★ l'**effet** MASC NOUN
effect
■ **faire de l'effet** to take effect □ Ce médicament fait rapidement de l'effet. This medicine takes effect quickly.
■ **Ça m'a fait un drôle d'effet de le revoir.** It gave me a strange feeling to see him again.
■ **en effet** yes indeed □ Je ne me sens pas très bien. — En effet, tu as l'air pâle. I don't feel very well. — Yes, you do look pale.

★ **efficace** (FEM **efficace**) ADJECTIVE
1 efficient
□ C'est une femme efficace. She's an efficient woman.
2 effective
□ un médicament efficace an effective medicine

s'**effondrer** VERB [28]
to collapse

s'**efforcer** VERB [12]
■ **s'efforcer de faire quelque chose** to try hard to do something □ Il s'efforce d'être aimable avec la clientèle. He tries hard to be polite to the customers.

l'**effort** MASC NOUN
effort
□ faire un effort to make an effort

★ **effrayant** (FEM **effrayante**) ADJECTIVE
frightening

★ **effrayer** VERB [59]
to frighten

effronté (FEM **effrontée**) ADJECTIVE
cheeky
□ Ce gamin est vraiment effronté. This kid's really cheeky.

★ **effroyable** (FEM **effroyable**) ADJECTIVE
horrifying

★ **égal** (FEM **égale**, MASC PL **égaux**) ADJECTIVE
equal
□ une quantité égale de farine et de sucre an equal quantity of flour and sugar
■ **Ça m'est égal.** **1** I don't mind. □ Tu préfères du riz ou des pâtes? — Ça m'est égal. Would you rather have rice or pasta? — I don't mind. **2** I don't care. □ Fais ce que tu veux, ça m'est égal. Do what you like, I don't care.

★ **également** ADVERB
also

égaler VERB [28]
to equal

★ l'**égalité** FEM NOUN
equality
■ **être à égalité** to be level □ Maintenant les deux joueurs sont à égalité. The two players are now level.

l'**égard** MASC NOUN
■ **à cet égard** in this respect

égarer VERB [28]
to mislay
□ J'ai égaré mes clés. I've mislaid my keys.
■ **s'égarer** to get lost □ Ils se sont égarés dans la forêt. They got lost in the forest.

★ l'**église** FEM NOUN
church
□ aller à l'église to go to church

l'**égoïsme** MASC NOUN
selfishness

★ **égoïste** (FEM **égoïste**) ADJECTIVE
selfish

l'**égout** MASC NOUN
sewer

l'**égratignure** FEM NOUN
scratch

l'**Égypte** FEM NOUN
Egypt

égyptien (FEM **égyptienne**) ADJECTIVE
Egyptian

eh EXCLAMATION
hey!
■ **eh bien** well

l'**élan** MASC NOUN
■ **prendre de l'élan** to gather speed

s'**élancer** VERB [12]
to hurl oneself

élargir VERB [38]
to widen

l'**élastique** MASC NOUN
rubber band

l'**électeur** MASC NOUN
voter (*man*)

★ l'**élection** FEM NOUN
election
□ les élections présidentielles the presidential election

l'**électrice** FEM NOUN
voter (*woman*)

★ l'**électricien** MASC NOUN
electrician

★ l'**électricité** FEM NOUN
electricity
□ une facture d'électricité an electricity bill

★ **électrique** (FEM **électrique**) ADJECTIVE
electric
□ le courant électrique the electric current

★ **électronique** (FEM **électronique**) ADJECTIVE
▷ *see also* **électronique** NOUN
electronic

★ l'**électronique** FEM NOUN
▷ *see also* **électronique** ADJECTIVE
electronics

★ **élégant** (FEM **élégante**) ADJECTIVE
smart

élémentaire (FEM **élémentaire**) ADJECTIVE
elementary

★ l'**éléphant** MASC NOUN
elephant

l'**élevage** MASC NOUN
cattle rearing
□ faire de l'élevage to rear cattle
■ **un élevage de porcs** a pig farm
■ **un élevage de poulets** a chicken farm
■ **les truites d'élevage** farmed trout

élevé (FEM **élevée**) ADJECTIVE
high
□ Le prix est trop élevé. The price is too high.
■ **être bien élevé** to have good manners
■ **être mal élevé** to have bad manners

★ l'**élève** MASC/FEM NOUN
pupil

★ **élever** VERB [43]

1 to bring up

□ Il a été élevé par sa grand-mère. He was brought up by his grandmother.

2 to breed

□ Son oncle élève des chevaux. His uncle breeds horses.

■ **élever la voix** to raise one's voice

■ **s'élever à** to come to □ À combien s'élèvent les dégâts? How much does the damage come to?

l'**éleveur** MASC NOUN

breeder

éliminatoire (FEM **éliminatoire**) ADJECTIVE

■ **une note éliminatoire** a fail mark

■ **une épreuve éliminatoire** (*sport*) a qualifying round

éliminer VERB [28]

to eliminate

élire VERB [44]

to elect

★ **elle** PRONOUN

1 she

□ Elle est ingénieur. She is an engineer.

2 her

□ Vous pouvez avoir confiance en elle. You can trust her.

3 it

□ Prends cette chaise: elle est plus confortable. Take this chair: it's more comfortable.

elle is also used for emphasis.

□ Elle, elle est toujours en retard! Oh her, she's always late!

■ **elle-même** herself □ Elle l'a choisi elle-même. She chose it herself.

★ **elles** PL PRONOUN

they

□ Où sont Anne et Rachel? — Elles sont allées au cinéma. Where are Anne and Rachel? — They've gone to the cinema.

■ **elles-mêmes** themselves

élogieux (FEM **élogieuse**) ADJECTIVE

complimentary

□ Ton professeur a été très élogieux à propos de ton travail. Your teacher was very complimentary about your work.

éloigné (FEM **éloignée**) ADJECTIVE

distant

s'**éloigner** VERB [28]

to go far away

□ Ne vous éloignez pas: le dîner est bientôt prêt! Don't go far away: dinner will soon be ready!

■ **Vous vous éloignez du sujet.** You are getting off the point.

l'**Élysée** MASC NOUN

Élysée Palace

DID YOU KNOW...?
The **Élysée** is the residence of the French president.

l'**e-mail** MASC NOUN

email

★ l'**emballage** MASC NOUN

■ **le papier d'emballage** wrapping paper

★ **emballer** VERB [28]

to wrap

■ **s'emballer** (*informal*) to get excited □ Il s'est emballé pour ce projet. He got really excited about this plan.

★ l'**embarquement** MASC NOUN

boarding

□ 'embarquement immédiat' 'now boarding'

□ L'embarquement des passagers n'a pas encore été annoncé. Passenger boarding has not been announced yet.

l'**embarras** MASC NOUN

embarrassment

□ Votre question me met dans l'embarras. It's difficult for me to answer your question.

■ **Vous n'avez que l'embarras du choix.** The only problem is choosing.

embarrassant (FEM **embarrassante**) ADJECTIVE

embarrassing

embarrasser VERB [28]

to embarrass

□ Cela m'embarrasse de vous demander encore un service. I feel embarrassed to ask you to do something more for me.

embaucher VERB [28]

to take on

□ L'entreprise vient d'embaucher cinquante ouvriers. The firm has just taken on fifty workers.

★ **embêtant** (FEM **embêtante**) ADJECTIVE

annoying

les **embêtements** MASC PL NOUN

trouble *sing*

embêter VERB [28]

to bother

■ **s'embêter** to be bored □ Qu'est-ce qu'on s'embête ici! Isn't it boring here!

★ l'**embouteillage** MASC NOUN

traffic jam

★ **embrasser** VERB [28]

to kiss

□ Ils se sont embrassés. They kissed each other.

s'**embrouiller** VERB [28]

to get confused

□ Il s'embrouille dans ses explications. He gets confused when he explains things.

émerveiller VERB [28]
to dazzle

l'**émeute** FEM NOUN
riot

émigrer VERB [28]
to emigrate

★ l'**émission** FEM NOUN
programme
□ une émission de télévision a TV programme

s'**emmêler** VERB [28]
to get tangled
□ Ma laine s'est emmêlée. My wool has got tangled.

emménager VERB [45]
to move in
□ Nous venons d'emménager dans une nouvelle maison. We've just moved into a new house.

★ **emmener** VERB [43]
to take
□ Ils m'ont emmené au cinéma pour mon anniversaire. They took me to the cinema for my birthday.

l'**émoticon** MASC NOUN
smiley (*computing*)

★ **émotif** (FEM **émotive**) ADJECTIVE
emotional
□ Il est très émotif. He's very emotional.

l'**émotion** FEM NOUN
emotion

émouvoir VERB [31]
to move
□ Sa lettre l'a beaucoup émue. She was deeply moved by his letter.

emparer VERB [28]
■ **s'emparer de** to grab □ Il s'est emparé de ma valise. He grabbed my case.

l'**empêchement** MASC NOUN
■ **Nous avons eu un empêchement de dernière minute.** We were held up at the last minute.

★ **empêcher** VERB [28]
to prevent
□ Le café le soir m'empêche de dormir. Coffee at night keeps me awake.
■ **Il n'a pas pu s'empêcher de rire.** He couldn't help laughing.

l'**empereur** MASC NOUN
emperor

s'**empiffrer** VERB [28] (*informal*)
to stuff one's face
□ Arrête de t'empiffrer! Stop stuffing your face!

empiler VERB [28]
to pile up

empirer VERB [28]
to worsen
□ La situation a encore empiré. The situation got even worse.

★ l'**emplacement** MASC NOUN
site
□ Un panneau indique l'emplacement du château. A sign shows the site of the castle.

★ l'**emploi** MASC NOUN
1 use
□ prêt à l'emploi ready for use
■ **le mode d'emploi** directions for use
2 job
□ la création d'emplois job creation
■ **un emploi du temps** a timetable

★ l'**employé** MASC NOUN
employee
■ **un employé de bureau** an office worker

★ l'**employée** FEM NOUN
employee
■ **une employée de banque** a bank clerk

★ **employer** VERB [53]
1 to use
□ Quelle méthode employez-vous? What method do you use?
2 to employ
□ L'entreprise emploie dix ingénieurs. The firm employs ten engineers.

★ l'**employeur** MASC NOUN
employer

empoisonner VERB [28]
to poison

★ **emporter** VERB [28]
to take
□ N'emportez que le strict nécessaire. Only take the bare minimum.
■ **plats à emporter** take-away meals
■ **s'emporter** to lose one's temper □ Je m'emporte facilement. I'm quick to lose my temper.

l'**empreinte** FEM NOUN
footprint
■ **l'empreinte carbone** carbon footprint
■ **une empreinte digitale** a fingerprint

s'**empresser** VERB [28]
■ **s'empresser de faire quelque chose** to be quick to do something □ Ils se sont empressés de nous annoncer la nouvelle. They were quick to tell us the news.

emprisonner VERB [28]
to imprison

l'**emprunt** MASC NOUN
loan

★ **emprunter** VERB [28]
to borrow
■ **emprunter quelque chose à quelqu'un** to borrow something from somebody □ Je peux t'emprunter dix euros? Can I borrow ten euros from you?

★ **EMT** FEM NOUN (= *éducation manuelle technique*)
technology

ému (FEM **émue**) ADJECTIVE
touched
□ J'ai été très ému par sa gentillesse. I was very touched by her kindness.

★ **en** PREPOSITION, PRONOUN
1 in
□ Il habite en France. He lives in France. □ La mariée est en blanc. The bride is in white. □ Je le verrai en mai. I'll see him in May.
2 to
□ Je vais en France cet été. I'm going to France this summer.
3 by
□ C'est plus rapide en voiture. It's quicker by car.
4 made of
□ C'est en verre. It's made of glass. □ un collier en argent a silver necklace
5 while
□ Il s'est coupé le doigt en ouvrant une boîte de conserve. He cut his finger while opening a tin.
■ **Elle est sortie en courant.** She ran out.

When **en** is used with **avoir** and **il y a**, it is not translated in English.

□ Est-ce que tu as un dictionnaire? — Oui, j'en ai un. Have you got a dictionary? — Yes, I've got one. □ Combien d'élèves y a-t-il dans ta classe? — Il y en a trente. How many pupils are there in your class? — There are 30.

en is also used with verbs and expressions normally followed by **de** to avoid repeating the same word.

□ Si tu as un problème, tu peux m'en parler. If you've got a problem, you can talk to me about it. □ Est-ce que tu peux me rendre ce livre? J'en ai besoin. Can you give me back that book? I need it. □ Il a un beau jardin et il en est très fier. He's got a beautiful garden and is very proud of it.
■ **J'en ai assez.** I've had enough.

★ **encaisser** VERB [28]
to cash (*money*)

enceinte FEM ADJECTIVE
pregnant
□ Elle est enceinte de six mois. She's 6 months pregnant.

★ **enchanté** (FEM **enchantée**) ADJECTIVE
delighted
□ Ma mère est enchantée de sa nouvelle voiture. My mother's delighted with her new car.
■ **Enchanté!** Pleased to meet you!

encombrant (FEM **encombrante**) ADJECTIVE
bulky

encombrer VERB [28]
to clutter

★ **encore** ADVERB
1 still
□ Il est encore au travail. He's still at work. □ Il reste encore deux morceaux de gâteau. There are still two bits of cake left.
2 even
□ C'est encore mieux. That's even better.
3 again
□ Il m'a encore demandé de l'argent. He asked me for money again.
■ **encore une fois** once again
■ **pas encore** not yet □ Je n'ai pas encore fini. I haven't finished yet.

★ **encourager** VERB [45]
to encourage

l'**encre** FEM NOUN
ink

l'**encyclopédie** FEM NOUN
encyclopaedia

l'**endive** FEM NOUN
chicory

★ **endommager** VERB [45]
to damage

★ **endormi** (FEM **endormie**) ADJECTIVE
asleep

endormir VERB [29]
to deaden
□ Cette piqûre sert à endormir le nerf. This injection is to deaden the nerve.
■ **s'endormir** to go to sleep

★ l'**endroit** MASC NOUN
place
□ C'est un endroit très tranquille. It's a very quiet place.
■ **à l'endroit** **1** the right way out **2** the right way up

endurant (FEM **endurante**) ADJECTIVE
tough (*person*)

endurcir VERB [38]
to toughen up
□ Ces exercices servent à endurcir les soldats. These exercises are to toughen up the soldiers.
■ **s'endurcir** to become hardened

endurer VERB [28]
to endure

★ l'**énergie** FEM NOUN
1 energy
□ Je n'ai pas beaucoup d'énergie ce matin. I haven't got much energy this morning.
2 power
□ l'énergie nucléaire nuclear power

■ **avec énergie** vigorously □ Il a protesté avec énergie. He protested vigorously.

★ **énergique** (FEM **énergique**) ADJECTIVE
energetic
■ **des mesures énergiques** strong measures

★ **énerver** VERB [28]
■ **Il m'énerve!** He gets on my nerves!
■ **Ce bruit m'énerve.** This noise gets on my nerves.
■ **s'énerver** to get worked up
■ **Ne t'énerve pas!** Take it easy!

★ l'**enfance** FEM NOUN
childhood
□ Je le connais depuis l'enfance. I've known him since I was a child.

★ l'**enfant** MASC/FEM NOUN
child

l'**enfer** MASC NOUN
hell

★ s'**enfermer** VERB [28]
■ **Il s'est enfermé dans sa chambre.** He shut himself up in his bedroom.

enfiler VERB [28]
1 to put on
□ J'ai rapidement enfilé un pull avant de sortir. I quickly put on a sweater before going out.
2 to thread
□ J'ai du mal à enfiler cette aiguille. I am having difficulty threading this needle.

★ **enfin** ADVERB
at last
□ J'ai enfin réussi à le joindre. I have at last managed to contact him.

enflé (FEM **enflée**) ADJECTIVE
swollen

enfler VERB [28]
to swell

enfoncer VERB [12]
■ **Il marchait, les mains enfoncées dans les poches.** He was walking with his hands thrust into his pockets.
■ **s'enfoncer** to sink □ Les roues de la voiture s'enfonçaient dans la boue. The wheels of the car were sinking into the mud.

s'**enfuir** VERB [39]
to run off

l'**engagement** MASC NOUN
commitment

engager VERB [45]
to take on (*person*)
□ engager quelqu'un to take somebody on

s'**engager** VERB [45]
to commit oneself
□ Le Premier ministre s'est engagé à combattre le chômage. The Prime Minister has committed himself to fighting unemployment.
■ **Il s'est engagé dans l'armée à dix-huit ans.** He joined the army when he was 18.

les **engelures** FEM PL NOUN
chilblains

l'**engin** MASC NOUN
device

> **BE CAREFUL!**
> The French word **engin** does not mean **engine**.

s'**engourdir** VERB [38]
to go numb
□ Mes doigts se sont engourdis avec le froid. My fingers have gone numb with the cold.

engueuler VERB [28] (*informal*)
■ **engueuler quelqu'un** to tell somebody off
□ Tu vas te faire engueuler! You're going to get told off!

l'**énigme** FEM NOUN
riddle

s'**enivrer** VERB [28]
to get drunk

enjamber VERB [28]
to stride over
□ enjamber une barrière to stride over a fence

★ l'**enlèvement** MASC NOUN
kidnapping

★ **enlever** VERB [43]
1 to take off
□ Enlève donc ton manteau! Take off your coat!
2 to kidnap
□ Un groupe terroriste a enlevé la femme de l'ambassadeur. A terrorist group has kidnapped the ambassador's wife.

enneigé (FEM **enneigée**) ADJECTIVE
snowed up
□ Les routes sont encore enneigées. The roads are still snowed up.

★ l'**ennemi** MASC NOUN
enemy

★ l'**ennemie** FEM NOUN
enemy

★ l'**ennui** MASC NOUN
1 boredom
□ C'est à mourir d'ennui. It would make you die of boredom.
2 problem
□ avoir des ennuis to have problems

★ **ennuyer** VERB [53]
to bother
□ J'espère que cela ne vous ennuie pas trop. I hope it doesn't bother you too much.
■ **s'ennuyer** to be bored

★ **ennuyeux** (FEM **ennuyeuse**) ADJECTIVE
1 boring
2 awkward
□ Tu ne peux pas venir plus tôt? C'est bien

ennuyeux. You can't come any earlier? That's rather awkward.

★ **énorme** (FEM **énorme**) ADJECTIVE
huge

★ **énormément** ADVERB
■ **Il a énormément grossi.** He's put on an awful lot of weight.
■ **Il y a énormément de neige.** There's an enormous amount of snow.

★ l'**enquête** FEM NOUN
1 investigation
□ La police a ouvert une enquête. The police have begun an investigation.
2 survey
□ une enquête parmi les étudiants a montré que ... a survey of students has shown that ...

enquêter VERB [28]
to investigate
□ La police enquête actuellement sur le crime. The police are currently investigating the crime.

enrageant (FEM **enrageante**) ADJECTIVE
infuriating

enrager VERB [45]
to be furious
□ J'enrage de n'avoir pas pu profiter de cette occasion. I'm furious I wasn't able to take advantage of this opportunity.

l'**enregistrement** MASC NOUN
recording
■ **l'enregistrement des bagages** baggage check-in

★ **enregistrer** VERB [28]
1 to record
□ Ils viennent d'enregistrer un nouvel album. They've just recorded a new album.
2 to check in
□ Vous pouvez enregistrer plusieurs valises. You can check in several cases.

s'**enrhumer** VERB [28]
to catch a cold
□ Je suis enrhumé. I've got a cold.

s'**enrichir** VERB [38]
to get rich

enrouler VERB [28]
to wind
□ Enroulez le fil autour de la bobine. Wind the thread round the bobbin.

★ l'**enseignant** MASC NOUN
teacher

★ l'**enseignante** FEM NOUN
teacher

★ l'**enseignement** MASC NOUN
1 education
□ les réformes de l'enseignement education reforms
2 teaching
□ l'enseignement des langues étrangères the teaching of foreign languages

★ **enseigner** VERB [28]
to teach
□ Mon père enseigne les maths dans un lycée. My father teaches maths in a secondary school.

★ **ensemble** ADVERB
▷ *see also* **ensemble** NOUN
together
□ tous ensemble all together

★ l'**ensemble** MASC NOUN
▷ *see also* **ensemble** ADVERB
outfit
□ Elle portait un ensemble vert. She was wearing a green outfit.
■ **l'ensemble de** the whole of □ L'ensemble du personnel est en grève. The whole workforce is on strike.
■ **dans l'ensemble** on the whole

★ **ensoleillé** (FEM **ensoleillée**) ADJECTIVE
sunny

★ **ensuite** ADVERB
then
□ Nous sommes allés au cinéma et ensuite au restaurant. We went to the cinema and then to a restaurant.

entamer VERB [28]
to start
□ Qui a entamé le gâteau? Who's started the cake?

s'**entasser** VERB [28]
to cram
□ Ils se sont tous entassés dans ma voiture. They all crammed into my car.

★ **entendre** VERB [88]
1 to hear
□ Je ne t'entends pas. I can't hear you.
■ **J'ai entendu dire qu'il est dangereux de nager ici.** I've heard that it's dangerous to swim here.
2 to mean
□ Qu'est-ce que tu entends par là? What do you mean by that?
■ **s'entendre** to get on □ Il s'entend bien avec sa sœur. He gets on well with his sister.

★ **entendu** (FEM **entendue**) ADJECTIVE
■ **C'est entendu!** Agreed! □ Je passerai te prendre à sept heures, c'est entendu. That's agreed then, I'll pick you up at 7 o'clock.
■ **bien entendu** of course

l'**enterrement** MASC NOUN
funeral (*burial*)

enterrer VERB [28]
to bury

entêté (FEM **entêtée**) ADJECTIVE
stubborn

French-English

e

s'**entêter** VERB [28]
to persist
□ Il s'entête à refuser de voir le médecin. He persists in refusing to go to the doctor.

★ l'**enthousiasme** MASC NOUN
enthusiasm

s'**enthousiasmer** VERB [28]
to get enthusiastic
□ Il s'enthousiasme facilement. He gets very enthusiastic about things.

★ **entier** (FEM **entière**) ADJECTIVE
whole
□ Il a mangé une quiche entière. He ate a whole quiche. □ Je n'ai pas lu le livre en entier. I haven't read the whole book.
■ **le lait entier** full fat milk

entièrement ADVERB
completely

l'**entorse** FEM NOUN
sprain
□ Il s'est fait une entorse à la cheville. He's sprained his ankle.

★ **entourer** VERB [28]
to surround
□ Le jardin est entouré d'un mur de pierres. The garden is surrounded by a stone wall.

★ l'**entracte** MASC NOUN
interval

★ l'**entraînement** MASC NOUN
training

★ **entraîner** VERB [28]
1 to lead
□ Il se laisse facilement entraîner par les autres. He's easily led.
2 to train
□ Il entraîne l'équipe de France depuis cinq ans. He's been training the French team for five years.
3 to involve
□ Un mariage entraîne beaucoup de dépenses. A wedding involves a lot of expense.
■ **s'entraîner** to train □ Il s'entraîne au foot tous les samedis matins. He does football training every Saturday morning.

l'**entraîneur** MASC NOUN
trainer

★ **entre** PREPOSITION
between
□ Il est assis entre son père et son oncle. He's sitting between his father and his uncle.
■ **entre eux** among themselves
■ **l'un d'entre eux** one of them

★ l'**entrecôte** FEM NOUN
rib steak

★ l'**entrée** FEM NOUN
1 entrance
2 starter (*of meal*)
□ Qu'est ce que vous prenez comme entrée? What would you like for the starter?

entreprendre VERB [65]
to start on
□ Elle a entrepris des démarches pour adopter un enfant. She's started on the procedures for adopting a child.

l'**entrepreneur** MASC NOUN
contractor

★ l'**entreprise** FEM NOUN
firm

★ **entrer** VERB [32, *aux* **avoir** *or* **être**]
1 to come in
□ Entrez donc! Come on in!
2 to go in
□ Ils sont tous entrés dans la maison. They all went into the house.
■ **entrer à l'hôpital** to go into hospital
■ **entrer des données** to enter data □ J'ai entré toutes les adresses de mon agenda sur mon ordinateur. I've entered all the addresses in my diary onto my computer.

> The verb **entrer** uses **être** in the perfect tense when talking about going into a place. It uses **avoir** in the perfect tense when it describes keying in information.

entre-temps ADVERB
meanwhile

★ l'**entretien** MASC NOUN
1 maintenance
□ un contrat d'entretien a maintenance contract
2 interview
□ On m'a convoqué à un entretien pour un travail. I've been called for a job interview.

l'**entrevue** FEM NOUN
interview
□ une entrevue avec le ministre an interview with the minister

entrouvert (FEM **entrouverte**) ADJECTIVE
half open
□ La porte était entrouverte. The door was half open.

★ **envahir** VERB [38]
to invade

★ l'**enveloppe** FEM NOUN
envelope

★ **envelopper** VERB [28]
to wrap

★ **envers** PREPOSITION
▷ *see also* **envers** NOUN
towards
□ Il est bien disposé envers elle. He's well disposed towards her. □ son attitude envers moi his attitude towards me

★ l'**envers** MASC NOUN
▷ *see also* **envers** PREPOSITION

■ **à l'envers** inside out □ Je dois repasser ce chemisier à l'envers. I have to iron this blouse inside out.

★ l'**envie** FEM NOUN

■ **avoir envie de faire quelque chose** to feel like doing something □ J'avais envie de pleurer. I felt like crying. □ J'ai envie d'aller aux toilettes. I want to go to the toilet.

■ **Cette glace me fait envie.** I fancy some of that ice cream.

BE CAREFUL!
The French word **envie** does not mean **envy**.

envier VERB [19]
to envy

★ **environ** ADVERB
about
□ C'est à soixante kilomètres environ. It's about 60 kilometres.

★ l'**environnement** MASC NOUN
environment

les **environs** MASC PL NOUN
area *sing*
□ les environs de Nantes the Nantes area □ Il y a beaucoup de choses intéressantes à voir dans les environs. There are a lot of interesting things to see in the area.

■ **aux environs de dix-neuf heures** around 7 p.m.

envisager VERB [45]
to consider
□ Est-ce que vous envisagez de travailler à l'étranger? Are you considering working abroad?

s'**envoler** VERB [28]
1 to fly away
□ Le papillon s'est envolé. The butterfly flew away.
2 to blow away
□ Toutes mes feuilles de cours se sont envolées. All my lecture notes blew away.

★ **envoyer** VERB [33]
to send
□ Ma tante m'a envoyé une carte pour mon anniversaire. My aunt sent me a card for my birthday.

■ **envoyer quelqu'un chercher quelque chose** to send somebody to get something
□ Sa mère l'a envoyé chercher du pain. His mother sent him to get some bread.

■ **envoyer un e-mail à quelqu'un** to send somebody an email

l'**éolienne** FEM NOUN
wind turbine

★ **épais** (FEM **épaisse**) ADJECTIVE
thick

l'**épaisseur** FEM NOUN
thickness

épatant (FEM **épatante**) ADJECTIVE (*informal*)
great
□ C'est un type épatant. He's a great guy.

★ l'**épaule** FEM NOUN
shoulder

l'**épée** FEM NOUN
sword

★ **épeler** VERB [4]
to spell
□ Est-ce que vous pouvez épeler votre nom, s'il vous plaît? Can you spell your name, please?

l'**épice** FEM NOUN
spice

★ **épicé** (FEM **épicée**) ADJECTIVE
spicy
□ un plat épicé a spicy dish

★ l'**épicerie** FEM NOUN
grocer's shop

★ l'**épicier** MASC NOUN
grocer

★ l'**épicière** FEM NOUN
grocer

l'**épidémie** FEM NOUN
epidemic

épiler VERB [28]
■ **s'épiler les jambes** to wax one's legs
■ **s'épiler les sourcils** to pluck one's eyebrows

★ les **épinards** MASC PL NOUN
spinach *sing*

l'**épine** FEM NOUN
thorn

l'**épingle** FEM NOUN
pin
■ **une épingle de sûreté** a safety pin

l'**épisode** MASC NOUN
episode

★ **éplucher** VERB [28]
to peel

★ l'**éponge** FEM NOUN
sponge

★ l'**époque** FEM NOUN
time
□ à cette époque de l'année at this time of year

■ **à l'époque** at that time □ À l'époque, beaucoup de gens n'avaient pas l'eau courante. At that time a lot of people didn't have running water.

★ l'**épouse** FEM NOUN
wife

★ **épouser** VERB [28]
to marry

★ **épouvantable** (FEM **épouvantable**)
ADJECTIVE
awful

★ l'**épouvante** FEM NOUN
terror
▪ **un film d'épouvante** a horror film

épouvanter VERB [28]
to terrify

★ l'**époux** MASC NOUN
husband
▪ **les nouveaux époux** the newly-weds

★ l'**épreuve** FEM NOUN
1 test
□ une épreuve orale an oral test □ une épreuve écrite a written test
2 event (*sport*)

éprouver VERB [28]
to feel
□ Qu'est-ce que vous avez éprouvé à ce moment-là? What did you feel at that moment?

★ l'**EPS** FEM NOUN (= *éducation physique et sportive*)
PE (= *physical education*)

épuisé (FEM **épuisée**) ADJECTIVE
exhausted

★ **épuiser** VERB [28]
to wear out
□ Ce travail m'a complètement épuisé. This job has completely worn me out.
▪ **s'épuiser** to wear oneself out □ Il s'épuise à garder un jardin impeccable. He wears himself out keeping his garden immaculate.

l'**Équateur** MASC NOUN
Ecuador

l'**équateur** MASC NOUN
equator

l'**équation** FEM NOUN
equation

l'**équerre** FEM NOUN
set square

l'**équilibre** MASC NOUN
balance
□ J'ai failli perdre l'équilibre. I nearly lost my balance.

★ **équilibré** (FEM **équilibrée**) ADJECTIVE
well-balanced

l'**équipage** MASC NOUN
crew

★ l'**équipe** FEM NOUN
team

★ **équipé** (FEM **équipée**) ADJECTIVE
▪ **bien équipé** well-equipped

★ l'**équipement** MASC NOUN
equipment

les **équipements** MASC PL NOUN
facilities
□ les équipements sportifs sports facilities

★ l'**équitation** FEM NOUN
riding
□ faire de l'équitation to go riding

l'**équivalent** MASC NOUN
equivalent

★ l'**erreur** FEM NOUN
mistake
▪ **faire erreur** to be mistaken

es VERB ▷ *see* **être**
▪ **Tu es très gentille.** You're very kind.

l'**escabeau** (PL les **escabeaux**) MASC NOUN
stepladder

★ l'**escalade** FEM NOUN
climbing
□ faire de l'escalade to go climbing

escalader VERB [28]
to climb

l'**escale** FEM NOUN
▪ **faire escale** to stop off

★ l'**escalier** MASC NOUN
stairs
□ un escalier roulant an escalator

★ l'**escargot** MASC NOUN
snail

l'**esclavage** MASC NOUN
slavery

l'**esclave** MASC/FEM NOUN
slave

★ l'**escrime** FEM NOUN
fencing

l'**escroc** MASC NOUN
crook

★ l'**espace** MASC NOUN
space
▪ **espace de travail** workspace
▪ **les espaces verts** green spaces

s'**espacer** VERB [12]
to become less frequent
□ Ses visites se sont peu à peu espacées. His visits became less and less frequent.

espadrille FEM NOUN
rope-soled sandal

★ l'**Espagne** FEM NOUN
Spain
▪ **en Espagne** 1 in Spain 2 to Spain

★ **espagnol** (FEM **espagnole**) ADJECTIVE, NOUN
Spanish
□ J'apprends l'espagnol. I'm learning Spanish.
▪ **un Espagnol** a Spaniard (*man*)
▪ **une Espagnole** a Spaniard (*woman*)

★ l'**espèce** FEM NOUN
1 sort
□ Elle portait une espèce de cape en velours. She was wearing a sort of velvet cloak.

2 species
□ une espèce en voie de disparition an endangered species
■ **Espèce d'idiot!** You idiot!

les **espèces** FEM PL NOUN
cash *sing*
□ payer en espèces to pay cash

★ **espérer** VERB [34]
to hope
■ **J'espère bien.** I hope so. □ Tu penses avoir réussi? — Oui, j'espère bien. Do you think you've passed? — Yes, I hope so.

espiègle (FEM **espiègle**) ADJECTIVE
mischievous

l'**espion** MASC NOUN
spy

l'**espionnage** MASC NOUN
spying
■ **un roman d'espionnage** a spy novel

l'**espionne** FEM NOUN
spy

★ l'**espoir** MASC NOUN
hope

★ l'**esprit** MASC NOUN
mind
□ Ça ne m'est pas venu à l'esprit. It didn't cross my mind.
■ **avoir de l'esprit** to be witty □ Il a beaucoup d'esprit. He's very witty.

l'**Esquimau** (PL les **Esquimaux**) MASC NOUN
Eskimo

l'**esquimau**® (PL les **esquimaux**) MASC NOUN
ice lolly

l'**Esquimaude** FEM NOUN
Eskimo

l'**essai** MASC NOUN
attempt
□ Ce n'est pas mal pour un coup d'essai. It's not bad for a first attempt.
■ **prendre quelqu'un à l'essai** to take somebody on for a trial period

★ **essayer** VERB [59]
1 to try
□ Essaie de rentrer de bonne heure. Try to come home early.
2 to try on
□ Essaie ce pull: il devrait bien t'aller. Try this sweater on: it ought to look good on you.

★ l'**essence** FEM NOUN
petrol

★ **essentiel** (FEM **essentielle**) ADJECTIVE
essential
■ **Tu es là: c'est l'essentiel.** You're here: that's the main thing.

s'**essouffler** VERB [28]
to get out of breath

l'**essuie-glace** MASC NOUN
windscreen wiper

★ **essuyer** VERB [53]
to wipe
■ **essuyer la vaisselle** to dry the dishes
■ **s'essuyer** to dry oneself □ Vous pouvez vous essuyer les mains avec cette serviette. You can dry your hands on this towel.

★ **est** VERB ▷ *see* **être**
▷ *see also* **est** ADJECTIVE, NOUN
■ **Elle est merveilleuse.** She's marvellous.

> **est** is pronounced 'ay' when it comes from the verb **être**.

★ **est** (FEM+PL **est**) ADJECTIVE
▷ *see also* **est** VERB, NOUN
1 east
□ la côte est des États-Unis the east coast of the United States
2 eastern
□ dans la partie est du pays in the eastern part of the country

> **est** is pronounced 'ayst' when it means **east** or **eastern**.

★ l'**est** MASC NOUN
▷ *see also* **est** VERB, ADJECTIVE
east
□ Je vis dans l'est de la France. I live in the East of France.
■ **vers l'est** eastwards
■ **à l'est de Paris** east of Paris
■ **l'Europe de l'Est** Eastern Europe
■ **le vent d'est** the east wind

> **est** is pronounced 'ayst' when it means **east** or **eastern**.

★ **est-ce que** ADVERB
■ **Est-ce que c'est cher?** Is it expensive?
■ **Quand est-ce qu'il part?** When is he leaving?

l'**esthéticienne** FEM NOUN
beautician

l'**estime** FEM NOUN
■ **J'ai beaucoup d'estime pour elle.** I think a lot of her.

estimer VERB [28]
■ **estimer quelqu'un** to have great respect for somebody □ Mon père l'estime beaucoup. My father has a lot of respect for him.
■ **estimer que** to consider that □ J'estime que c'est de sa faute. I consider that it's his fault.

l'**estivant** MASC NOUN
holiday-maker

l'**estivante** FEM NOUN
holiday-maker

★ l'**estomac** MASC NOUN
stomach

l'**Estonie** FEM NOUN
Estonia

l'**estrade** FEM NOUN
platform

★ **et** CONJUNCTION
and
□ toi et moi you and me
■ **Et toi, qu'est-ce que tu en penses?** What about you? What do you think?

établir VERB [38]
to establish
■ **s'établir à son compte** to set up in business

★ l'**établissement** MASC NOUN
establishment
■ **un établissement scolaire** a school

★ l'**étage** MASC NOUN
floor
□ au premier étage on the first floor
■ **à l'étage** upstairs

★ l'**étagère** FEM NOUN
shelf

étaient VERB ▷ *see* **être**

l'**étain** MASC NOUN
tin

étais, était VERB ▷ *see* **être**
■ **Il était très jeune.** He was very young.

l'**étalage** MASC NOUN
display

étaler VERB [28]
to spread
□ Il a étalé la carte sur la table. He spread the map on the table.

étanche (FEM **étanche**) ADJECTIVE
1 watertight
□ Le toit n'est pas étanche. The roof isn't watertight.
2 waterproof (*watch*)

l'**étang** MASC NOUN
pond

étant VERB ▷ *see* **être**
■ **Mes revenus étant limités ...** My income being limited ...

★ l'**étape** FEM NOUN
stage
□ une étape importante de la vie an important stage in life
■ **faire étape** to stop off

★ l'**État** MASC NOUN
state (*nation*)
□ un chef d'État a head of state

★ l'**état** MASC NOUN
condition
□ en bon état in good condition □ en mauvais état in poor condition
■ **remettre quelque chose en état** to repair something
■ **le bureau d'état civil** the registry office

★ les **États-Unis** MASC PL NOUN
United States
■ **aux États-Unis** **1** in the United States **2** to the United States

★ **été** VERB ▷ *see* **être**
▷ *see also* **été** NOUN
■ **Il a été licencié.** He's been made redundant.

★ l'**été** MASC NOUN
▷ *see also* **été** VERB
summer
■ **en été** in the summer

★ **éteindre** VERB [60]
1 to switch off
□ Éteins la lumière. Switch the light off.
2 to put out (*cigarette*)

étendre VERB [88]
to spread
□ Elle a étendu une nappe propre sur la table. She spread a clean cloth on the table.
■ **étendre le linge** to hang out the washing
■ **s'étendre** to lie down □ Je vais m'étendre cinq minutes. I'm going to lie down for five minutes.

l'**éternité** FEM NOUN
■ **J'ai attendu une éternité chez le médecin.** I waited for ages at the doctor's.

éternuer VERB [28]
to sneeze

êtes VERB ▷ *see* **être**
■ **Vous êtes en retard.** You're late.

étiez VERB ▷ *see* **être**

étinceler VERB [4]
to sparkle

étions VERB ▷ *see* **être**

l'**étiquette** FEM NOUN
label
□ L'étiquette du pot de confiture s'est décollée. The label has come off the jam pot.

s'**étirer** VERB [28]
to stretch
□ Elle s'est étirée paresseusement. She stretched lazily.

★ l'**étoile** FEM NOUN
star
■ **une étoile de mer** a starfish
■ **une étoile filante** a shooting star
■ **dormir à la belle étoile** to sleep under the stars

★ **étonnant** (FEM **étonnante**) ADJECTIVE
amazing

★ **étonner** VERB [28]
to surprise
□ Cela m'étonnerait que le colis soit arrivé. I'd be surprised if the parcel had arrived.

étouffer VERB [28]
■ **On étouffe ici: ouvre donc les fenêtres.**

It's stifling in here: open the windows.
■ **s'étouffer** to choke □ Ne mange pas si vite: tu vas t'étouffer! Don't eat so fast: you'll choke!

l'**étourderie** FEM NOUN
absent-mindedness
■ **une erreur d'étourderie** a slip

étourdi (FEM **étourdie**) ADJECTIVE
scatterbrained

l'**étourdissement** MASC NOUN
■ **avoir des étourdissements** to feel dizzy

★ **étrange** (FEM **étrange**) ADJECTIVE
strange

★ **étranger** (FEM **étrangère**) ADJECTIVE
▷ *see also* **étranger** NOUN
foreign
□ un pays étranger a foreign country
■ **une personne étrangère** a stranger

★ l'**étranger** MASC NOUN
▷ *see also* **étranger** ADJECTIVE
1 foreigner
2 stranger
■ **à l'étranger** abroad

★ l'**étrangère** FEM NOUN
1 foreigner
2 stranger

étrangler VERB [28]
to strangle
■ **s'étrangler** to choke □ s'étrangler avec quelque chose to choke on something

★ l'**être** MASC NOUN
▷ *see also* **être** VERB
■ **un être humain** a human being

★ **être** VERB [35]

PRESENT TENSE

je suis	nous sommes
tu es	vous êtes
il/elle est	ils/elles sont

PAST PARTICIPLE
été

▷ *see also* **être** NOUN
1 to be
□ Je suis heureux. I'm happy. □ Mon père est instituteur. My father's a primary school teacher. □ Il est dix heures. It's 10 o'clock.
2 to have
□ Il n'est pas encore arrivé. He hasn't arrived yet.

les **étrennes** FEM PL NOUN
■ **Nous avons donné des étrennes à la gardienne.** We gave the caretaker a New Year gift.

★ **étroit** (FEM **étroite**) ADJECTIVE
narrow
■ **être à l'étroit** to be cramped □ Nous sommes un peu à l'étroit dans cet appartement. We're a bit cramped in this flat.

★ l'**étude** FEM NOUN
study
□ une étude de cas a case study
■ **faire des études** to be studying □ Il fait des études de droit. He's studying law.

★ l'**étudiant** MASC NOUN
student

★ l'**étudiante** FEM NOUN
student

★ **étudier** VERB [19]
to study

l'**étui** MASC NOUN
case
□ un étui à lunettes a glasses case

eu VERB ▷ *see* **avoir**
■ **J'ai eu une bonne note.** I got a good mark.

euh EXCLAMATION
er
□ Euh ... je ne m'en souviens pas. Er ... I can't remember.

★ l'**euro** MASC NOUN
euro

★ l'**Europe** FEM NOUN
Europe
■ **en Europe** 1 in Europe 2 to Europe

★ **européen** (FEM **européenne**) ADJECTIVE
European

eux PL PRONOUN
them
□ Je pense souvent à eux. I often think of them.

eux is also used for emphasis.

□ Elle a accepté l'invitation, mais eux, ils ont refusé. She accepted the invitation, but THEY refused.

évacuer VERB [28]
to evacuate

s'**évader** VERB [28]
to escape

l'**évangile** MASC NOUN
gospel

s'**évanouir** VERB [38]
to faint

s'**évaporer** VERB [28]
to evaporate

évasif (FEM **évasive**) ADJECTIVE
evasive

l'**évasion** FEM NOUN
escape
□ Ils ont préparé leur évasion pendant des mois. They spent months planning their escape.

éveillé (FEM **éveillée**) ADJECTIVE
1 awake
□ Il est resté éveillé toute la nuit. He stayed awake all night.

French-English

e

2 bright
□ C'est un enfant très éveillé pour son âge. He's very bright for his age.

s'**éveiller** VERB [28]
to awaken

★ l'**événement** MASC NOUN
event

l'**éventail** MASC NOUN
fan (*hand-held*)
■ **un large éventail de prix** a wide range of prices

l'**éventualité** FEM NOUN
■ **dans l'éventualité d'un retard** in the event of a delay

éventuel (FEM **éventuelle**) ADJECTIVE
possible
□ une solution éventuelle a possible solution
□ les conséquences éventuelles the possible consequences

> **BE CAREFUL!**
> **éventuel** does not mean **eventual**.

éventuellement ADVERB
possibly
□ Nous pourrions éventuellement avoir besoin de vous. We may possibly need you.
□ les difficultés que vous pourriez éventuellement rencontrer the difficulties that you might possibly have

> **BE CAREFUL!**
> **éventuellement** does not mean **eventually**.

l'**évêque** MASC NOUN
bishop

★ **évidemment** ADVERB
1 obviously
□ Les tomates sont évidemment chères en cette saison. Tomatoes are obviously expensive at this time of year.
2 of course
□ Est-ce que je peux utiliser ton téléphone? — Évidemment, tu n'as pas besoin de demander. Can I use your phone? — Of course, you don't need to ask.

l'**évidence** FEM NOUN
■ **C'est une évidence.** It's quite obvious.
■ **de toute évidence** obviously □ De toute évidence, il ne veut pas nous voir. Obviously he doesn't want to see us.
■ **être en évidence** to be clearly visible □ La lettre était en évidence sur la table. The letter was clearly visible on the table.
■ **mettre en évidence** to reveal

★ **évident** (FEM **évidente**) ADJECTIVE
obvious

★ l'**évier** MASC NOUN
sink

★ **éviter** VERB [28]
to avoid

évolué (FEM **évoluée**) ADJECTIVE
advanced

évoluer VERB [28]
to progress
□ La chirurgie esthétique a beaucoup évolué. Cosmetic surgery has progressed a great deal.
■ **Il a beaucoup évolué.** He has come on a great deal.

l'**évolution** FEM NOUN
1 development
□ une évolution rapide rapid development
2 evolution
□ la théorie de l'évolution the theory of evolution

évoquer VERB [28]
to mention
□ Il a évoqué divers problèmes dans son discours. He mentioned various problems in his speech.

★ **exact** (FEM **exacte**) ADJECTIVE
1 right
□ Avez-vous l'heure exacte? Have you got the right time? □ Votre voiture est garée dehors, n'est-ce pas? — C'est exact. Your car's parked outside, isn't it? — That's right.
2 exact
□ Est-ce que vous pouvez m'indiquer le prix exact du billet? Can you tell me the exact price of the ticket?

★ **exactement** ADVERB
exactly
□ C'est exactement ce que je cherchais. That's exactly what I was looking for.

ex aequo (FEM+PL **ex aequo**) ADJECTIVE
■ **Ils sont arrivés ex aequo.** They finished neck and neck.

★ **exagérer** VERB [34]
1 to exaggerate
□ Vous exagérez! You're exaggerating!
2 to go too far
□ Ça fait trois fois que tu arrives en retard: tu exagères! That's three times you've been late: you really go too far sometimes!

★ l'**examen** MASC NOUN
exam
□ Nous allons passer l'examen d'anglais vendredi matin. We're doing our English exam on Friday morning. □ un examen de français a French exam
■ **un examen médical** a medical

examiner VERB [28]
to examine

exaspérant (FEM **exaspérante**) ADJECTIVE
infuriating

exaspérer VERB [34]

Numbers in brackets refer to verb tables on pages 650 to 658

to infuriate

l'**excédent** MASC NOUN

■ **l'excédent de bagages** excess baggage

excéder VERB [34]

to exceed

□ un contrat dont la durée n'excède pas deux ans a contract for a period not exceeding two years

■ **excéder quelqu'un** to drive somebody mad □ Les cris des enfants l'excédaient. The noise of the children was driving her mad.

★**excellent** (FEM **excellente**) ADJECTIVE

excellent

excentrique (FEM **excentrique**) ADJECTIVE

eccentric

excepté PREPOSITION

except

□ Toutes les chaussures excepté les sandales sont en solde. All the shoes except sandals are reduced.

l'**exception** FEM NOUN

exception

■ **à l'exception de** except

★**exceptionnel** (FEM **exceptionnelle**) ADJECTIVE

exceptional

l'**excès** MASC NOUN

■ **faire des excès** to overindulge □ On fait souvent des excès à la période de Noël. People often overindulge around Christmas.

■ **les excès de vitesse** speeding

excessif (FEM **excessive**) ADJECTIVE

excessive

★**excitant** (FEM **excitante**) ADJECTIVE

▷ *see also* **excitant** NOUN

exciting

★l'**excitant** MASC NOUN

▷ *see also* **excitant** ADJECTIVE

stimulant

□ Le thé et le café sont des excitants. Tea and coffee are stimulants.

l'**excitation** FEM NOUN

excitement

exciter VERB [28]

to excite

□ Il était tout excité à l'idée de revoir ses cousins. He was all excited about seeing his cousins again.

■ **s'exciter** (*informal*) to get excited □ Ne t'excite pas trop vite: ça ne va peut-être pas marcher! Don't get excited too soon: it may not work!

l'**exclamation** FEM NOUN

exclamation

★**exclu** (FEM **exclue**) ADJECTIVE

■ **Il n'est pas exclu que ...** It's not impossible that ...

exclusif (FEM **exclusive**) ADJECTIVE

exclusive

★l'**excursion** FEM NOUN

1 trip

□ faire une excursion to go on a trip

2 walk

□ une excursion dans la montagne a walk in the mountains

★l'**excuse** FEM NOUN

1 excuse

□ une bonne excuse a good excuse

2 apology

□ présenter ses excuses to offer one's apologies

■ **un mot d'excuse** a note □ Vous devez apporter un mot d'excuse signé par vos parents. You have to bring a note signed by your parents.

★**excuser** VERB [28]

to excuse

■ **Excusez-moi. 1** Sorry. □ Excusez-moi, je ne vous avais pas vu. Sorry, I didn't see you. **2** Excuse me. □ Excusez-moi, est-ce que vous avez l'heure? Excuse me, have you got the time?

■ **s'excuser** to apologize □ Il s'est excusé de son retard. He apologized for being late.

exécuter VERB [28]

1 to execute

□ Le prisonnier a été exécuté à l'aube. The prisoner was executed at dawn.

2 to perform

□ Le pianiste va maintenant exécuter une valse de Chopin. The pianist is now going to perform a waltz by Chopin.

l'**exemplaire** MASC NOUN

copy

★l'**exemple** MASC NOUN

example

□ donner l'exemple to set an example

■ **par exemple** for example

★s'**exercer** VERB [12]

to practise

★l'**exercice** MASC NOUN

exercise

exhiber VERB [28]

to show off

□ Il aime bien exhiber ses décorations. He likes showing off his medals.

■ **s'exhiber** to expose oneself

l'**exhibitionniste** MASC NOUN

flasher

exigeant (FEM **exigeante**) ADJECTIVE

hard to please

□ Elle est vraiment exigeante. She's really hard to please.

exiger VERB [45]

1 to demand

□ Le propriétaire exige d'être payé immédiatement. The landlord is demanding to be paid immediately.

2 to require

□ Ce travail exige beaucoup de patience. This job requires a lot of patience.

l'**exil** MASC NOUN

exile

★ **exister** VERB [28]

to exist

□ Ça n'existe pas. It doesn't exist.

■ **Ce manteau existe également en rose.** This coat is also available in pink.

exotique (FEM **exotique**) ADJECTIVE

exotic

□ une plante exotique an exotic plant

■ **un yaourt aux fruits exotiques** a tropical fruit yoghurt

expédier VERB [19]

to send

□ expédier un colis to send a parcel

★ l'**expéditeur** MASC NOUN

sender

l'**expédition** FEM NOUN

expedition

■ **l'expédition du courrier** the dispatch of the mail

l'**expéditrice** FEM NOUN

sender

★ l'**expérience** FEM NOUN

1 experience

□ Elle a plusieurs années d'expérience. She's got several years' experience.

2 experiment

□ une expérience de chimie a chemistry experiment

★ **experimenté** (FEM **experimentée**) ADJECTIVE

experienced

□ un plongeur très experimenté a very experienced diver

expérimenter VERB [28]

to test

□ Ces produits de beauté n'ont pas été expérimentés sur des animaux. These cosmetics have not been tested on animals.

l'**expert** MASC NOUN

expert

l'**experte** FEM NOUN

expert

expirer VERB [28]

1 to expire (*document, passport*)

2 to run out (*time allowed*)

3 to breathe out (*person*)

★ l'**explication** FEM NOUN

explanation

■ **une explication de texte** a critical analysis (*of a text*)

★ **expliquer** VERB [28]

to explain

□ Il m'a expliqué comment faire. He explained to me how to do it.

■ **Ça s'explique.** It's understandable.

l'**exploit** MASC NOUN

achievement

l'**exploitation** FEM NOUN

exploitation

□ C'est de l'exploitation. It's exploitation.

■ **une exploitation agricole** a farm

exploiter VERB [28]

to exploit

□ Il se fait exploiter par son patron. He gets exploited by his boss.

explorer VERB [28]

to explore

exploser VERB [28]

to explode

□ La bombe a explosé en pleine rue. The bomb exploded in the middle of the street.

l'**explosif** MASC NOUN

explosive

l'**explosion** FEM NOUN

explosion

l'**exportateur** MASC NOUN

exporter

l'**exportation** FEM NOUN

export

l'**exportatrice** FEM NOUN

exporter

exporter VERB [28]

to export

l'**exposé** MASC NOUN

talk

□ un exposé sur l'environnement a talk on the environment

★ **exposer** VERB [28]

1 to show

□ Il expose ses peintures dans une galerie d'art. He shows his paintings in a private art gallery.

2 to expose

□ N'exposez pas la pellicule à la lumière. Do not expose the film to light.

3 to set out

□ Il nous a exposé les raisons de son départ. He set out the reasons for his departure.

■ **s'exposer au soleil** to stay out in the sun

□ Ne vous exposez pas trop longtemps au soleil. Don't stay out too long in the sun.

★ l'**exposition** FEM NOUN

exhibition

□ une exposition de peinture an exhibition of paintings

★ **exprès** ADVERB

1 on purpose

□ Il l'a fait exprès. He did it on purpose.
2 specially
□ J'ai fait ce gâteau exprès pour toi. I made this cake specially for you.

★ l'**express** MASC NOUN
1 espresso (*coffee*)
2 fast train
□ Il a décidé de prendre l'express de dix heures. He decided to catch the fast train at 10 o'clock.

★ l'**expression** FEM NOUN
1 expression
2 phrase

exprimer VERB [28]
to express
■ **s'exprimer** to express oneself □ Il s'exprime très bien pour un enfant de huit ans. For a child of 8, he expresses himself very well.

exquis (FEM **exquise**) ADJECTIVE
exquisite

★ **extérieur** (FEM **extérieure**) ADJECTIVE
▷ *see also* **extérieur** NOUN
outside

★ l'**extérieur** MASC NOUN
▷ *see also* **extérieur** ADJECTIVE
outside
■ **à l'extérieur** outside □ Les toilettes sont à l'extérieur. The toilet is outside.

l'**externat** MASC NOUN
day school

l'**externe** MASC/FEM NOUN
day pupil

l'**extincteur** MASC NOUN
fire extinguisher

★ **extra** (FEM+PL **extra**) ADJECTIVE
excellent
□ Ce fromage est extra! This cheese is excellent!

extraire VERB [85]
to extract

★ l'**extrait** MASC NOUN
extract

★ **extraordinaire** (FEM **extraordinaire**) ADJECTIVE
extraordinary

extravagant (FEM **extravagante**) ADJECTIVE
extravagant

★ **extrême** (FEM **extrême**) ADJECTIVE
▷ *see also* **extrême** NOUN
extreme
□ l'extrême droite et l'extrême gauche the far right and the far left

★ l'**extrême** MASC NOUN
▷ *see also* **extrême** ADJECTIVE
extreme

extrêmement ADVERB
extremely

l'**Extrême-Orient** MASC NOUN
the Far East

l'**extrémité** FEM NOUN
end
□ La gare est à l'autre extrémité de la ville. The station is at the other end of the town.

Ff

F ABBREVIATION
franc (*currency in Switzerland and many former French colonies*)

le **fa** MASC NOUN
F

la **fabrication** FEM NOUN
manufacture

★**fabriquer** VERB [28]
to make
□ fabriqué en France made in France
■ **Qu'est-ce qu'il fabrique?** (*informal*) What's he up to?

★la **fac** FEM NOUN (*informal*)
university
■ **à la fac** at university

★la **face** FEM NOUN
■ **face à face** face to face
■ **en face de** opposite □ Le bus s'arrête en face de chez moi. The bus stops opposite my house.
■ **faire face à quelque chose** to face something
■ **Pile ou face? — Face.** Heads or tails? — Heads.

facebooker VERB [28]
to Facebook

★**fâché** (FEM **fâchée**) ADJECTIVE
angry
■ **être fâché contre quelqu'un** to be angry with somebody □ Elle est fâchée contre moi. She's angry with me.
■ **être fâché avec quelqu'un** to be on bad terms with somebody □ Elle est fâchée avec sa sœur. She's on bad terms with her sister.

★se **fâcher** VERB [28]
■ **se fâcher contre quelqu'un** to lose one's temper with somebody
■ **se fâcher avec quelqu'un** to fall out with somebody □ Il s'est fâché avec son frère. He's fallen out with his brother.

★**facile** (FEM **facile**) ADJECTIVE
easy
■ **facile à faire** easy to do

facilement ADVERB
easily

la **facilité** FEM NOUN
■ **un logiciel d'une grande facilité d'utilisation** a very user-friendly piece of software
■ **Il a des facilités en langues.** He has a gift for languages.

> **BE CAREFUL!**
> facilité does not mean **facility**.

★la **façon** FEM NOUN
way
□ De quelle façon? In what way?
■ **de toute façon** anyway

★le **facteur** MASC NOUN
postman
□ Il est facteur. He's a postman.

la **factrice** FEM NOUN
postwoman
□ Elle est factrice. She's a postwoman.

la **facture** FEM NOUN
bill
□ une facture de gaz a gas bill

facultatif (FEM **facultative**) ADJECTIVE
optional

★la **faculté** FEM NOUN
faculty
■ **avoir une grande faculté de concentration** to have great powers of concentration

fade (FEM **fade**) ADJECTIVE
tasteless
□ La soupe est un peu fade. The soup is a bit tasteless.

★**faible** (FEM **faible**) ADJECTIVE
weak
□ Je me sens encore faible. I still feel a bit weak.
■ **Il est faible en maths.** He's not very good at maths.

la **faiblesse** FEM NOUN
weakness

la **faïence** FEM NOUN
pottery

faillir VERB [12]
■ **J'ai failli tomber.** I nearly fell down.

la **faillite** FEM NOUN
bankruptcy
■ **une entreprise en faillite** a bankrupt business
■ **faire faillite** to go bankrupt

★ la **faim** FEM NOUN
hunger
▪ **avoir faim** to be hungry

fainéant (FEM **fainéante**) ADJECTIVE
lazy

★ **faire** VERB [36]

PRESENT TENSE	
je fais	nous faisons
tu fais	vous faites
il/elle fait	ils/elles font
PAST PARTICIPLE	
fait	

1 to make
□ Je vais faire un gâteau pour ce soir. I'm going to make a cake for tonight. □ Ils font trop de bruit. They're making too much noise. □ Je voudrais me faire de nouveaux amis. I'd like to make new friends.
2 to do
□ Qu'est-ce que tu fais? What are you doing? □ Il fait de l'italien. He's doing Italian. □ Qui veut faire la vaisselle? Who'll do the dishes?
3 to play
□ Il fait du piano. He plays the piano.
4 to be
□ Qu'est-ce qu'il fait chaud! Isn't it hot! □ Espérons qu'il fera beau demain. Let's hope it'll be nice weather tomorrow.
▪ **Ça ne fait rien.** It doesn't matter.
▪ **Ça fait cinquante-trois euros en tout.** That makes fifty-three euros in all.
▪ **Ça fait trois ans qu'il habite à Paris.** He's lived in Paris for three years.
▪ **faire tomber** to knock over □ Le chat a fait tomber le vase. The cat knocked over the vase.
▪ **faire faire quelque chose** to get something done □ Je dois faire réparer ma voiture. I've got to get my car repaired.
▪ **Je vais me faire couper les cheveux.** I'm going to get my hair cut.
▪ **Ne t'en fais pas!** Don't worry!

fais, faisaient, faisais, faisait VERB
▷ *see* faire

le **faisan** MASC NOUN
pheasant

faisiez, faisions, faisons, fait VERB
▷ *see* faire

le **fait** MASC NOUN
fact
□ Le fait que ... The fact that ...
▪ **un fait divers** a news item
▪ **au fait** by the way □ Au fait, tu as aimé le film d'hier? By the way, did you enjoy the film yesterday?
▪ **en fait** actually □ En fait je n'ai pas beaucoup de temps. I haven't got much time actually.

faites VERB ▷ *see* faire

★ la **falaise** FEM NOUN
cliff

★ **falloir** VERB [37] ▷ *see* **faut, faudra, faudrait**

famé (FEM **famée**) ADJECTIVE
▪ **un quartier mal famé** a rough area

fameux (FEM **fameuse**) ADJECTIVE
▪ **Ce n'est pas fameux.** It's not great.

★ **familial** (FEM **familiale**, MASC PL **familiaux**) ADJECTIVE
family
□ une atmosphère familiale a family atmosphere
▪ **les allocations familiales** child benefit

familier (FEM **familière**) ADJECTIVE
familiar

★ la **famille** FEM NOUN
1 family
□ une famille nombreuse a big family □ Nous passons Noël en famille. We have a family Christmas.
2 relatives
□ Il a de la famille à Paris. He's got relatives in Paris.

la **famine** FEM NOUN
famine

fanatique (FEM **fanatique**) ADJECTIVE
▷ *see also* **fanatique** NOUN
fanatical

le/la **fanatique** MASC/FEM NOUN
▷ *see also* **fanatique** ADJECTIVE
fanatic

la **fanfare** FEM NOUN
brass band

fantaisie (FEM+PL **fantaisie**) ADJECTIVE
▪ **des bijoux fantaisie** costume jewellery

★ **fantastique** (FEM **fantastique**) ADJECTIVE
fantastic

le **fantôme** MASC NOUN
ghost

la **farce** FEM NOUN
1 stuffing (*for chicken, turkey*)
2 practical joke
□ Il aime faire des farces. He likes to play practical jokes.

farci (FEM **farcie**) ADJECTIVE
stuffed
□ des tomates farcies stuffed tomatoes

★ la **farine** FEM NOUN
flour

fascinant (FEM **fascinante**) ADJECTIVE
fascinating

fasciner VERB [28]
to fascinate

le **fascisme** MASC NOUN
fascism

★ = core vocabulary

fasse, fassent, fasses, fassiez, fassions VERB ▷ *see* **faire**
■ **Pourvu qu'il fasse beau demain!** Let's hope it'll be fine tomorrow!

fatal (FEM **fatale**) ADJECTIVE
fatal
■ **C'était fatal.** It was bound to happen.

la **fatalité** FEM NOUN
fate

★ **fatigant** (FEM **fatigante**) ADJECTIVE
tiring

★ la **fatigue** FEM NOUN
tiredness

★ **fatigué** (FEM **fatiguée**) ADJECTIVE
tired

★ se **fatiguer** VERB [28]
to get tired

fauché (FEM **fauchée**) ADJECTIVE (*informal*)
hard up

faudra VERB

faudra is the future tense of **falloir**.

■ **Il faudra qu'on soit plus rapide.** We'll have to be quicker.

faudrait VERB

faudrait is the conditional tense of **falloir**.

■ **Il faudrait qu'on fasse attention.** We ought to be careful.

se **faufiler** VERB [28]
■ **Il s'est faufilé à travers la foule.** He made his way through the crowd.

la **faune** FEM NOUN
wildlife

fausse (FEM **fausse**) ADJECTIVE ▷ *see* **faux**

faut VERB

faut is the present tense of **falloir**.

■ **Il faut faire attention.** You've got to be careful.
■ **Nous n'avons pas le choix, il faut y aller.** We've no choice, we've got to go.
■ **Il faut que je parte.** I've got to go.
■ **Il faut du courage pour faire ce métier.** It takes courage to do that job.
■ **Il me faut de l'argent.** I need money.

★ la **faute** FEM NOUN
1 mistake
□ faire une faute to make a mistake
2 fault
□ Ce n'est pas de ma faute. It's not my fault.
■ **sans faute** without fail □ Je t'appellerai sans faute. I'll phone you without fail.

★ le **fauteuil** MASC NOUN
armchair
■ **un fauteuil roulant** a wheelchair

★ **faux** (FEM **fausse**) ADJECTIVE, ADVERB
▷ *see also* **faux** NOUN
untrue
□ C'est entièrement faux. It's totally untrue.
■ **faire un faux pas** to trip
■ **Il chante faux.** He sings out of tune.

★ le **faux** MASC NOUN
▷ *see also* **faux** ADJECTIVE, ADVERB
fake
□ Ce tableau est un faux. This painting is a fake.

la **faveur** FEM NOUN
favour

★ **favori** (FEM **favorite**) ADJECTIVE
favourite

favoriser VERB [28]
to favour
□ Ce système d'examen favorise ceux qui ont de la mémoire. This exam system favours people with good memories.

★ le **fax** MASC NOUN
fax

faxer VERB [28]
to fax
■ **faxer un document à quelqu'un** to fax somebody a document

la **fée** FEM NOUN
fairy

feignant (FEM **feignante**) ADJECTIVE (*informal*)
lazy

★ les **félicitations** FEM PL NOUN
congratulations

★ **féliciter** VERB [28]
to congratulate

la **femelle** FEM NOUN
female (*animal*)

féminin (FEM **féminine**) ADJECTIVE
1 female
□ les personnages féminins du roman the female characters in the novel
2 feminine
□ Elle est très féminine. She's very feminine.
3 women's
□ Elle joue dans l'équipe féminine de France. She plays in the French women's team.

féministe (FEM **féministe**) ADJECTIVE
feminist

★ la **femme** FEM NOUN
1 woman
2 wife
□ la femme du directeur the headmaster's wife
■ **une femme au foyer** a housewife
■ **une femme de ménage** a cleaner
■ **une femme de chambre** a chambermaid
■ **une femme politique** a politician

se **fendre** VERB [88]
to crack

 Numbers in brackets refer to verb tables on pages 650 to 658

★ la **fenêtre** FEM NOUN
window

le **fenouil** MASC NOUN
fennel

★ la **fente** FEM NOUN
slot

★ le **fer** MASC NOUN
iron
■ **un fer à cheval** a horseshoe
■ **un fer à repasser** an iron

fera, ferai, feras, ferez VERB ▷ *see* **faire**

★ **férié** (FEM **fériée**) ADJECTIVE
■ **un jour férié** a public holiday

feriez, ferions VERB ▷ *see* **faire**

★ **ferme** (FEM **ferme**) ADJECTIVE
▷ *see also* **ferme** NOUN
firm
□ Elle s'est montrée très ferme à mon égard. She was very firm with me.

★ la **ferme** FEM NOUN
▷ *see also* **ferme** ADJECTIVE
farm

★ **fermé** (FEM **fermée**) ADJECTIVE
1 closed
□ La pharmacie est fermée. The chemist's is closed.
2 off
□ Est-ce que le gaz est fermé? Is the gas off?

★ **fermer** VERB [28]
1 to close
□ Ferme la fenêtre. Close the window.
2 to turn off
□ As-tu bien fermé le robinet? Have you turned the tap off?
■ **fermer à clé** to lock □ N'oublie pas de fermer la porte à clé! Don't forget to lock the door!

★ la **fermeture** FEM NOUN
■ **les heures de fermeture** closing times
■ **une fermeture éclair®** a zip

★ le **fermier** MASC NOUN
farmer

★ la **fermière** FEM NOUN
1 farmer (*woman*)
2 farmer's wife

féroce (FEM **féroce**) ADJECTIVE
fierce

ferons, feront VERB ▷ *see* **faire**

les **fesses** FEM PL NOUN
buttocks

le **festival** MASC NOUN
festival

★ les **festivités** FEM PL NOUN
festivities

★ la **fête** FEM NOUN
1 party
□ On organise une petite fête pour son anniversaire. We're having a little party for his birthday.
■ **faire la fête** to party
2 name day
□ C'est sa fête aujourd'hui. It's his name day today.
■ **bonnes fêtes!** happy holidays!
■ **une fête foraine** a funfair
■ **la Fête Nationale** Bastille Day
■ **les fêtes de fin d'année** the festive season
■ **la Fête des Mères** Mother's Day
■ **la Fête du Travail** May Day

DID YOU KNOW...?
La Fête du Travail is on 1 May and traditionally people give each other small bunches of lily of the valley. In many towns and cities, there is no public transport and shops and restaurants close.

■ **la Fête de la Musique**

DID YOU KNOW...?
La Fête de la Musique takes place on 21 June across France and in many other French-speaking countries. The events are free, with all kinds of music by groups and soloists, young and old, amateur and professional. The venues are as varied as the music.

★ **fêter** VERB [28]
to celebrate

★ le **feu** (PL les **feux**) MASC NOUN
1 fire
□ prendre feu to catch fire □ faire du feu to make a fire
■ **Au feu!** Fire!
■ **un feu de joie** a bonfire
2 traffic light
□ un feu rouge a red light □ le feu vert the green light □ Tournez à gauche aux feux. Turn left at the lights.
■ **Avez-vous du feu?** Have you got a light?
3 heat
□ ... mijoter à feu doux ... simmer over a gentle heat
■ **un feu d'artifice** a firework display

le **feuillage** MASC NOUN
leaves

★ la **feuille** FEM NOUN
1 leaf
□ des feuilles mortes fallen leaves
2 sheet
□ une feuille de papier a sheet of paper
■ **une feuille de maladie** a claim form for medical expenses

feuilleté (FEM **feuilletée**) ADJECTIVE
■ **de la pâte feuilletée** flaky pastry

★ **feuilleter** VERB [41]
to leaf through

★ le **feuilleton** MASC NOUN
serial

★ le **feutre** MASC NOUN
felt
■ **un stylo-feutre** a felt-tip pen

la **fève** FEM NOUN
broad bean

★ **février** MASC NOUN
February
■ **en février** in February

fiable (FEM **fiable**) ADJECTIVE
reliable

★ les **fiançailles** FEM PL NOUN
engagement *sing*

★ **fiancé** (FEM **fiancée**) ADJECTIVE
■ **être fiancé à quelqu'un** to be engaged to somebody

se **fiancer** VERB [12]
to get engaged

★ la **ficelle** FEM NOUN
1 string
□ Passe-moi un bout de ficelle. Give me a piece of string.
2 thin baguette (*bread*)

★ la **fiche** FEM NOUN
form
□ Remplissez cette fiche, s'il vous plaît. Fill in this form, please.

se **ficher** VERB [28] (*informal*)
■ **Je m'en fiche!** I don't care!
■ **Quoi, tu n'as fait que ça? Tu te fiches de moi!** You've only done that much? You can't be serious!

★ le **fichier** MASC NOUN
file

fichu (FEM **fichue**) ADJECTIVE (*informal*)
■ **Ce parapluie est fichu.** This umbrella's knackered.

fidèle (FEM **fidèle**) ADJECTIVE
faithful

★ **fier** (FEM **fière**) ADJECTIVE
proud

la **fierté** FEM NOUN
pride

★ la **fièvre** FEM NOUN
fever
■ **avoir de la fièvre** to have a temperature
□ J'ai de la fièvre. I've got a temperature. □ Il a trente-neuf de fièvre. He's got a temperature of 39°C.

★ **fiévreux** (FEM **fiévreuse**) ADJECTIVE
feverish

la **figue** FEM NOUN
fig

★ la **figure** FEM NOUN
1 face
□ Il a reçu le ballon en pleine figure. The ball hit him smack in the face.
2 figure (*illustration*)
□ Voir figure 2.1, page 32. See figure 2.1, page 32.

le **fil** MASC NOUN
thread
□ le fil à coudre sewing thread
■ **le fil de fer** wire
■ **un coup de fil** a phone call

la **file** FEM NOUN
line (*of people, objects*)
■ **une file d'attente** a queue □ se mettre à la file to join the queue
■ **à la file** one after the other
■ **en file indienne** in single file

filer VERB [28]
to speed along
□ Les voitures filent sur l'autoroute. The cars are speeding along the motorway.
■ **File dans ta chambre!** Off to your room with you!

le **filet** MASC NOUN
net

★ la **fille** FEM NOUN
1 girl
□ C'est une école de filles. It's a girls' school.
2 daughter
□ C'est leur fille aînée. She's their oldest daughter.

la **fillette** FEM NOUN
little girl

le **filleul** MASC NOUN
godson

la **filleule** FEM NOUN
goddaughter

★ le **film** MASC NOUN
film
■ **un film policier** a thriller
■ **un film d'aventures** an adventure film
■ **un film d'épouvante** a horror film
■ **le film alimentaire** Clingfilm®

★ le **fils** MASC NOUN
son

★ la **fin** FEM NOUN
▷ *see also* **fin** ADJECTIVE
end
□ à la fin du film at the end of the film □ À la fin, il a réussi à se décider. In the end he managed to make up his mind.
■ **'Fin'** 'The End'
■ **Il sera en vacances fin juin.** He'll be on holiday at the end of June.
■ **en fin de journée** at the end of the day
■ **en fin de compte** when all's said and done
■ **sans fin** endless

★ **fin** (FEM **fine**) ADJECTIVE
▷ *see also* **fin** NOUN
fine
■ **des fines herbes** mixed herbs

la **finale** FEM NOUN
final
□ les quarts de finale the quarter finals

★ **finalement** ADVERB
1 at last
□ Nous sommes finalement arrivés. At last we arrived.
2 after all
□ Finalement, tu avais raison. You were right after all.

fini (FEM **finie**) ADJECTIVE
finished

★ **finir** VERB [38]
to finish
□ Le cours finit à onze heures. The lesson finishes at 11 o'clock. □ Je viens de finir ce livre. I've just finished this book.
■ **Il a fini par se décider.** He made up his mind in the end.

★ **finlandais** (FEM **finlandaise**) ADJECTIVE, NOUN
Finnish
□ Ils parlent finlandais. They speak Finnish.
■ **un Finlandais** a Finn (*man*)
■ **une Finlandaise** a Finn (*woman*)
■ **les Finlandais** the Finns

★ la **Finlande** FEM NOUN
Finland

la **firme** FEM NOUN
firm

fis VERB ▷ *see* **faire**

la **fissure** FEM NOUN
crack

fit VERB ▷ *see* **faire**

★ **fixe** (FEM **fixe**) ADJECTIVE
1 steady
□ Il n'a pas d'emploi fixe. He hasn't got a steady job.
2 set
□ Il mange toujours à heures fixes. He always eats at set times.
■ **un menu à prix fixe** a set menu

★ **fixer** VERB [28]
1 to fix
□ Les volets sont fixés avec des crochets. The shutters are fixed with hooks. □ Nous avons fixé une heure pour nous retrouver. We fixed a time to meet.
2 to stare at
□ Ne fixe pas les gens comme ça! Don't stare at people like that!

★ le **flacon** MASC NOUN
bottle
□ un flacon de parfum a bottle of perfume

le **flageolet** MASC NOUN
small haricot bean

flamand (FEM **flamande**) ADJECTIVE, NOUN
Flemish
□ Il parle flamand chez lui. He speaks Flemish at home.
■ **les Flamands** the Dutch-speaking Belgians

flambé (FEM **flambée**) ADJECTIVE
■ **des bananes flambées** flambéed bananas

la **flamme** FEM NOUN
flame
■ **en flammes** on fire

le **flan** MASC NOUN
baked custard

flâner VERB [28]
to stroll

la **flaque** FEM NOUN
puddle (*of water*)

★ le **flash** (PL les **flashes**) MASC NOUN
flash (*of camera*)
■ **un flash d'information** a newsflash

flatter VERB [28]
to flatter

★ la **flèche** FEM NOUN
arrow

★ les **fléchettes** FEM PL NOUN
darts
□ jouer aux fléchettes to play darts

★ la **fleur** FEM NOUN
flower

fleuri (FEM **fleurie**) ADJECTIVE
1 full of flowers
□ Son jardin était très fleuri. Her garden was full of flowers.
2 flowery
□ un papier peint fleuri flowery wallpaper

fleurir VERB [38]
to flower
□ Cette plante fleurit en automne. This plant flowers in autumn.

★ le/la **fleuriste** MASC/FEM NOUN
florist

★ le **fleuve** MASC NOUN
river

★ le **flic** MASC NOUN (*informal*)
cop

le **flipper** MASC NOUN
pinball machine

flirter VERB [28]
to flirt

le **flocon** MASC NOUN
flake

flotter VERB [28]
to float

flou (FEM **floue**) ADJECTIVE
blurred

le **fluor** MASC NOUN
■ **le dentifrice au fluor** fluoride toothpaste

French-English

f

★ la **flûte** FEM NOUN
flute
□ Je joue de la flûte. I play the flute.
■ **une flûte à bec** a recorder
■ **Flûte!** (*informal*) Heck!

la **foi** FEM NOUN
faith

★ le **foie** MASC NOUN
liver
■ **une crise de foie** a stomach upset

le **foin** MASC NOUN
hay
■ **le rhume des foins** hay fever

★ la **foire** FEM NOUN
fair

★ la **fois** FEM NOUN
time
□ la première fois the first time □ à chaque fois each time □ À chaque fois que je vais à la bibliothèque, j'oublie ma carte. Every time I go to the library, I forget my card. □ Deux fois deux font quatre. 2 times 2 is 4.
■ **une fois** once
■ **deux fois** twice □ deux fois plus de gens twice as many people
■ **une fois que** once □ Tu te sentiras mieux une fois que tu auras mangé. You'll feel better once you've had something to eat.
■ **à la fois** at once □ Je ne peux pas faire deux choses à la fois. I can't do two things at once.

fol MASC ADJECTIVE ▷ *see* **fou**

la **folie** FEM NOUN
madness
□ C'est de la folie pure! It's absolute madness!
■ **faire une folie** to be extravagant

folklorique (FEM **folklorique**) ADJECTIVE
folk
□ de la musique folklorique folk music

★ **folle** FEM ADJECTIVE ▷ *see* **fou**

★ **foncé** (FEM **foncée**) ADJECTIVE
dark
□ bleu foncé dark blue

foncer VERB [12] (*informal*)
■ **Je vais foncer à la boulangerie.** I'm just going to dash to the baker's.

la **fonction** FEM NOUN
function
■ **une voiture de fonction** a company car

★ le/la **fonctionnaire** MASC/FEM NOUN
civil servant

★ **fonctionner** VERB [28]
to work

★ le **fond** MASC NOUN
1 bottom
□ Mon porte-monnaie est au fond de mon sac. My purse is at the bottom of my bag.
2 end
□ Les toilettes sont au fond du couloir. The toilets are at the end of the corridor.
■ **dans le fond** all things considered □ Dans le fond, ce n'est pas si grave. All things considered, it's not that bad.

fonder VERB [28]
to found

★ **fondre** VERB [69]
to melt
□ La tablette de chocolat a fondu dans ma poche. The bar of chocolate melted in my pocket.
■ **fondre en larmes** to burst into tears

fondu (FEM **fondue**) ADJECTIVE
■ **du beurre fondu** melted butter

font VERB ▷ *see* **faire**

★ la **fontaine** FEM NOUN
fountain

★ le **foot** MASC NOUN
football

★ le **football** MASC NOUN
football
□ jouer au football to play football

le **footballeur** MASC NOUN
footballer

le **footing** MASC NOUN
jogging
□ faire du footing to go jogging

forain (FEM **foraine**) ADJECTIVE
▷ *see also* **forain** NOUN
■ **une fête foraine** a funfair

le **forain** MASC NOUN
▷ *see also* **forain** ADJECTIVE
fairground worker

la **force** FEM NOUN
strength
□ Je n'ai pas beaucoup de force dans les bras. I haven't got much strength in my arms.
■ **à force de** by □ Il a grossi à force de manger autant. He got fat by eating so much.
■ **de force** by force □ Ils lui ont enlevé son pistolet de force. They took the gun from him by force.

forcé (FEM **forcée**) ADJECTIVE
forced
□ un sourire forcé a forced smile
■ **C'est forcé.** (*informal*) It's inevitable.

forcément ADVERB
■ **Ça devait forcément arriver.** That was bound to happen.
■ **pas forcément** not necessarily

★ la **forêt** FEM NOUN
forest

le **forfait** MASC NOUN
all-in price
■ **C'est compris dans le forfait.** It's included in the price.

■ **perdre par forfait** to lose by forfeit
■ **un forfait téléphonique a** contract (*mobile phone*)

le **forgeron** MASC NOUN
blacksmith

la **formalité** FEM NOUN
formality
□ Ce n'est qu'une simple formalité. It's just a formality.

le **format** MASC NOUN
size

★la **formation** FEM NOUN
training
□ la formation professionnelle vocational training
■ **la formation continue** continuing education
■ **Il a une formation d'ingénieur.** He is a trained engineer.

★la **forme** FEM NOUN
shape
■ **être en forme** to be in good shape
■ **Je ne suis pas en forme aujourd'hui.** I'm not feeling too good today.
■ **Tu as l'air en forme.** You're looking well.

formellement ADVERB
strictly
□ Il est formellement interdit de fumer dans les couloirs. It is strictly forbidden to smoke in the corridors.

former VERB [28]
1 to form
2 to train

★**formidable** (FEM **formidable**) ADJECTIVE
great

★le **formulaire** MASC NOUN
form

★**fort** (FEM **forte**) ADJECTIVE, ADVERB
1 strong
□ Le café est trop fort. The coffee's too strong.
2 good
□ Il est très fort en espagnol. He's very good at Spanish.
3 loud
□ Est-ce vous pouvez parler plus fort? Can you speak louder?
■ **frapper fort** to hit hard

le **fortifiant** MASC NOUN
tonic (*medicine*)

la **fortune** FEM NOUN
fortune
■ **de fortune** makeshift □ un radeau de fortune a makeshift raft

★le **forum** MASC NOUN
chat room

le **forum de discussion** MASC NOUN
forum (*for discussion*)

le **fossé** MASC NOUN
ditch

★**fou** (FEM **folle**) ADJECTIVE

The masculine singular form **fou** changes to **fol** before a vowel or most words beginning with 'h'.

mad
■ **Il y a un monde fou sur la plage!** (*informal*) There are loads of people on the beach!
■ **attraper le fou rire** to get the giggles

la **foudre** FEM NOUN
lightning
□ Il a été frappé par la foudre. He was struck by lightning.

foudroyant (FEM **foudroyante**) ADJECTIVE
instant
□ un succès foudroyant an instant hit

le **fouet** MASC NOUN
whisk

la **fougère** FEM NOUN
fern

fouiller VERB [28]
to rummage

le **fouillis** MASC NOUN
mess
□ Il y a du fouillis dans sa chambre. His bedroom is a mess.

★le **foulard** MASC NOUN
scarf
□ un foulard en soie a silk scarf

★la **foule** FEM NOUN
crowd
■ **une foule de** masses of □ J'ai une foule de choses à faire ce week-end. I've got masses of things to do this weekend.

se **fouler** VERB [28]
■ **se fouler la cheville** to sprain one's ankle

★le **four** MASC NOUN
oven
□ un four à micro-ondes a microwave oven

★la **fourchette** FEM NOUN
fork

la **fourmi** FEM NOUN
ant
■ **avoir des fourmis dans les jambes** to have pins and needles

le **fourneau** (PL les **fourneaux**) MASC NOUN
stove

fourni (FEM **fournie**) ADJECTIVE
thick (*beard, hair*)

★**fournir** VERB [38]
to supply

le **fournisseur** MASC NOUN
supplier
■ **un fournisseur d'accès à Internet** an internet service provider

French-English

f

les **fournitures** FEM PL NOUN
■ **les fournitures scolaires** school stationery

fourré (FEM **fourrée**) ADJECTIVE
filled
□ un gâteau fourré à la confiture d'abricot a cake filled with apricot jam

fourrer VERB [28] (*informal*)
to put
□ Où as-tu fourré mon sac? Where have you put my bag?

le **fourre-tout** (PL les **fourre-tout**) MASC NOUN
holdall

la **fourrure** FEM NOUN
fur
□ un manteau de fourrure a fur coat

le **foyer** MASC NOUN
home
□ dans la plupart des foyers français in most French homes
■ **un foyer de jeunes** a youth club

la **fracture** FEM NOUN
fracture

★ **fragile** (FEM **fragile**) ADJECTIVE
fragile
□ Attention, c'est fragile! Be careful, it's fragile!

la **fragilité** FEM NOUN
fragility

★ **fraîche** FEM ADJECTIVE ▷ *see* **frais**

la **fraîcheur** FEM NOUN
1 cool
□ la fraîcheur du soir the cool of the evening
2 freshness
□ Je ne suis pas sûre de la fraîcheur du poisson. I'm not sure about the freshness of the fish.

★ **frais** (FEM **fraîche**) ADJECTIVE
▷ *see also* **frais** NOUN
1 fresh
□ des œufs frais fresh eggs □ Cette salade n'est pas très fraîche. This lettuce isn't very fresh.
2 chilly
□ Il fait un peu frais ce soir. It's a bit chilly this evening.
3 cool
□ des boissons fraîches cool drinks
■ **'servir frais'** 'serve chilled'
■ **mettre au frais** to put in a cool place

★ les **frais** MASC PL NOUN
▷ *see also* **frais** ADJECTIVE
expenses

★ la **fraise** FEM NOUN
strawberry
□ une fraise des bois a wild strawberry

★ la **framboise** FEM NOUN
raspberry

★ **franc** (FEM **franche**) ADJECTIVE
▷ *see also* **franc** NOUN
frank

★ le **franc** MASC NOUN
▷ *see also* **franc** ADJECTIVE
franc

DID YOU KNOW...?
The **franc** is the unit of currency in Switzerland and many former French colonies.

★ **français** (FEM **française**) ADJECTIVE, NOUN
French
□ Il parle français couramment. He speaks French fluently.
■ **un Français** a Frenchman
■ **une Française** a Frenchwoman
■ **les Français** the French

★ la **France** FEM NOUN
France
■ **en France** **1** in France □ Je suis né en France. I was born in France. **2** to France □ Je pars en France pour Noël. I'm going to France for Christmas.

franche FEM ADJECTIVE ▷ *see* **franc**

★ **franchement** ADVERB
1 frankly
□ Il m'a parlé franchement. He spoke to me frankly.
2 really
□ C'est franchement mauvais. It's really bad.

★ **franchir** VERB [38]
to get over

la **franchise** FEM NOUN
frankness

francophone (FEM **francophone**) ADJECTIVE
French-speaking

la **frange** FEM NOUN
fringe

la **frangipane** FEM NOUN
almond cream

★ **frapper** VERB [28]
to strike
□ Il l'a frappée au visage. He struck her in the face. □ Son air fatigué m'a frappé. I was struck by how tired she looked.

fredonner VERB [28]
to hum

le **freezer** MASC NOUN
freezing compartment

★ le **frein** MASC NOUN
brake
■ **le frein à main** handbrake

★ **freiner** VERB [28]
to brake

frêle (FEM **frêle**) ADJECTIVE
frail

le **frelon** MASC NOUN
hornet

frémir VERB [38]
shudder
□ Cette idée me fait frémir. The idea makes me shudder.

fréquemment ADVERB
frequently

fréquent (FEM **fréquente**) ADJECTIVE
frequent

fréquenté (FEM **fréquentée**) ADJECTIVE
busy
□ une rue très fréquentée a very busy street
■ **un bar mal fréquenté** a rough pub

★ **fréquenter** VERB [28]
to see (*person*)
□ Je ne le fréquente pas beaucoup. I don't see him often.

★ le **frère** MASC NOUN
brother

le **friand** MASC NOUN
■ **un friand au fromage** a cheese puff

la **friandise** FEM NOUN
sweet

★ le **fric** MASC NOUN (*informal*)
cash

★ le **frigidaire**® MASC NOUN
refrigerator

★ le **frigo** MASC NOUN (*informal*)
fridge

frileux (FEM **frileuse**) ADJECTIVE
■ **être frileux** to feel the cold □ Je suis très frileuse. I really feel the cold.

frimer VERB [28] (*informal*)
to show off

les **fringues** FEM PL NOUN (*informal*)
clothes

fripé (FEM **fripée**) ADJECTIVE
crumpled

frire VERB [80]
■ **faire frire** to fry □ Faites frire les boulettes dans de l'huile très chaude. Fry the meatballs in very hot oil.

★ **frisé** (FEM **frisée**) ADJECTIVE
curly
□ Elle est très frisée. She's got very curly hair.

le **frisson** MASC NOUN
shiver

frissonner VERB [28]
to shiver

frit (FEM **frite**) ADJECTIVE
fried
□ du poisson frit fried fish

frite FEM NOUN
chip
□ Elle mange des frites. She's eating chips.

★ les **frites** FEM PL NOUN
chips

la **friture** FEM NOUN
1 fried food
□ On lui a conseillé d'éviter les fritures. He's been advised to avoid fried food.
2 fried fish
□ Nous allons faire une friture ce soir. We are going to have fried fish tonight.

★ **froid** (FEM **froide**) ADJECTIVE
▷ *see also* **froid** NOUN
cold
□ Ça me laisse froid. It leaves me cold. □ de la viande froide cold meat

★ le **froid** MASC NOUN
▷ *see also* **froid** ADJECTIVE
cold
■ **Il fait froid.** It's cold.
■ **avoir froid** to be cold □ Est-ce que tu as froid? Are you cold?

se **froisser** VERB [28]
1 to crease
□ Ce tissu se froisse très facilement. This material creases very easily.
2 to take offence
□ Paul se froisse très facilement. Paul's very quick to take offence.
■ **se froisser un muscle** to strain a muscle

frôler VERB [28]
1 to brush against
□ Le chat m'a frôlé au passage. The cat brushed against me as it went past.
2 to narrowly avoid
□ Nous avons frôlé la catastrophe. We narrowly avoided disaster.

★ le **fromage** MASC NOUN
cheese

le **froment** MASC NOUN
wheat
■ **une crêpe de froment** a pancake (*made with wheat flour*)

froncer VERB [12]
■ **froncer les sourcils** to frown

le **front** MASC NOUN
forehead

★ la **frontière** FEM NOUN
border

frotter VERB [28]
to rub
□ se frotter les yeux to rub one's eyes
■ **frotter une allumette** to strike a match

★ le **fruit** MASC NOUN
fruit
■ **un fruit** a piece of fruit □ Est-ce que vous

voulez manger un fruit? Would you like some fruit?
■ **les fruits de mer** seafood

fruité (FEM **fruitée**) ADJECTIVE
fruity

frustrer VERB [28]
to frustrate

la **fugue** FEM NOUN
■ **faire une fugue** to run away

★ **fuir** VERB [39]
1 to flee
□ fuir devant un danger to flee from danger
2 to drip
□ Le robinet fuit. The tap's dripping.

★ la **fuite** FEM NOUN
1 leak
□ Il y a une fuite de gaz. There is a gas leak.
2 flight (*escape*)
■ **être en fuite** to be on the run

★ **fumé** (FEM **fumée**) ADJECTIVE
▷ *see also* **fumée** NOUN
smoked
□ du saumon fumé smoked salmon

★ la **fumée** FEM NOUN
▷ *see also* **fumé** ADJECTIVE
smoke

★ **fumer** VERB [28]
to smoke

★ le **fumeur** MASC NOUN
smoker

★ la **fumeuse** FEM NOUN
smoker

le **fur** MASC NOUN
■ **au fur et à mesure** as you go along □ Je vérifie mon travail au fur et à mesure. I check my work as I go along.
■ **au fur et à mesure que** as □ Je réponds à mon courrier au fur et à mesure que je le reçois. I answer my mail as I receive it.

le **furet** MASC NOUN
ferret

la **fureur** FEM NOUN
fury
■ **faire fureur** to be all the rage □ Ce genre de sac fait fureur actuellement. This sort of bag is all the rage at the moment.

★ **furieux** (FEM **furieuse**) ADJECTIVE
furious

le **furoncle** MASC NOUN
boil (*on skin*)

fus VERB ▷ *see* **être**

le **fuseau** (PL les **fuseaux**) MASC NOUN
ski pants

la **fusée** FEM NOUN
rocket

★ le **fusil** MASC NOUN
gun

fut VERB ▷ *see* **être**

futé (FEM **futée**) ADJECTIVE
crafty

★ le **futur** MASC NOUN
future

Gg

★ **gâcher** VERB [28]
to waste
□ Je n'aime pas gâcher la nourriture. I don't like to waste food.

le **gâchis** MASC NOUN
waste

la **gaffe** FEM NOUN
■ **faire une gaffe** to do something stupid
■ **Fais gaffe!** (*informal*) Watch out! □ Fais gaffe: la peinture est encore humide! Watch out: the paint's still wet!

le **gage** MASC NOUN
forfeit (*in a game*)
□ recevoir un gage to pay a forfeit

★ le **gagnant** MASC NOUN
winner

★ la **gagnante** FEM NOUN
winner

★ **gagner** VERB [28]
to win
□ Qui a gagné? Who won?
■ **gagner du temps** to save time
■ **Il gagne bien sa vie.** He makes a good living.

★ **gai** (FEM **gaie**) ADJECTIVE
cheerful
□ Elle est très gaie. She's very cheerful.

la **gaieté** FEM NOUN
cheerfulness

★ la **galerie** FEM NOUN
gallery
□ une galerie de peinture an art gallery
■ **une galerie marchande** a shopping arcade
■ **une galerie de jeux d'arcade** an amusement arcade

le **galet** MASC NOUN
pebble

la **galette** FEM NOUN
1 round flat cake
■ **une galette de blé noir** a buckwheat pancake
2 biscuit
□ des galettes pur beurre shortbread biscuits
■ **la galette des Rois**

DID YOU KNOW...?
A **galette des Rois** is a cake eaten on Twelfth Night (6 January) containing a figurine. The person who finds it is the king (or queen) and gets a paper crown. They then choose someone else to be their queen (or king).

Galles FEM NOUN
■ **le pays de Galles** Wales
■ **le prince de Galles** the Prince of Wales

★ **gallois** (FEM **galloise**) ADJECTIVE, NOUN
Welsh
□ un peintre gallois a Welsh painter
■ **un Gallois** a Welshman
■ **une Galloise** a Welshwoman
■ **les Gallois** the Welsh

le **galop** MASC NOUN
gallop

galoper VERB [28]
to gallop

le **gamin** MASC NOUN (*informal*)
kid

la **gamine** FEM NOUN (*informal*)
kid

la **gamme** FEM NOUN
scale (*in music*)
□ faire des gammes to do scales
■ **une gamme de produits** a range of products

gammée (FEM **gammée**) ADJECTIVE
■ **la croix gammée** the swastika

★ le **gant** MASC NOUN
glove
□ des gants en laine woollen gloves
■ **un gant de toilette** a face cloth

★ le **garage** MASC NOUN
garage

★ le/la **garagiste** MASC/FEM NOUN
1 garage owner
2 mechanic

la **garantie** FEM NOUN
guarantee

garantir VERB [38]
to guarantee

★ le **garçon** MASC NOUN
boy
■ **un vieux garçon** a bachelor

★ le **garde** MASC NOUN
▷ *see also* **garde** NOUN
1 warder (*in prison*)
2 security man
■ **un garde du corps** a bodyguard

★ la **garde** FEM NOUN
▷ *see also* **garde** NOUN
1 guarding
□ Il est chargé de la garde des prisonniers. He's responsible for guarding the prisoners.
2 guard
□ la relève de la garde the changing of the guard
■ **un chien de garde** a guard dog
■ **être de garde** to be on duty □ Mon père est de garde ce soir. My father is on duty tonight. □ La pharmacie de garde ce week-end est ... The duty chemist this weekend is ...
■ **mettre en garde** to warn □ Elle m'a mis en garde contre les pickpockets. She warned me about pickpockets.

le **garde-côte** (PL les **garde-côtes**) MASC NOUN
coastguard

★ **garder** VERB [28]
1 to keep
□ Tu as gardé toutes ses lettres? Have you kept all his letters?
2 to look after
□ Je garde ma nièce samedi après-midi. I'm looking after my niece on Saturday afternoon.
3 to guard
□ Ils ont pris un gros chien pour garder la maison. They got a big dog to guard the house.
■ **garder le lit** to stay in bed
■ **se garder** to keep □ Ces crêpes se gardent bien. These pancakes keep well.

la **garderie** FEM NOUN
nursery

la **garde-robe** FEM NOUN
wardrobe (*clothes*)
□ Elle a une garde-robe bien fournie. She's got an extensive wardrobe.

★ le **gardien** MASC NOUN
1 caretaker
2 attendant (*in a museum*)
■ **un gardien de but** a goalkeeper
■ **un gardien de la paix** a police officer

★ la **gardienne** FEM NOUN
1 caretaker
2 attendant (*in a museum*)

★ la **gare** FEM NOUN
▷ *see also* **gare** EXCLAMATION
station
□ la gare routière the bus station

★ **gare** EXCLAMATION
▷ *see also* **gare** NOUN
■ **Gare aux serpents!** Watch out for snakes!

★ **garer** VERB [28]
to park
■ **se garer** to park □ Où t'es-tu garé? Where are you parked?

garni (FEM **garnie**) ADJECTIVE
■ **un plat garni** a dish served with accompaniments (*vegetables, chips, rice etc*)

le **gars** MASC NOUN (*informal*)
guy

gaspiller VERB [28]
to waste

★ le **gâteau** (PL les **gâteaux**) MASC NOUN
cake
■ **les gâteaux secs** biscuits

★ **gâter** VERB [28]
to spoil
□ Il aime gâter ses petits-enfants. He likes to spoil his grandchildren.
■ **se gâter** to go bad □ Les pommes vont se gâter si on ne les mange pas ce soir. The apples will go bad if we don't eat them tonight.
■ **Le temps va se gâter.** The weather's going to break.

★ **gauche** (FEM **gauche**) ADJECTIVE
▷ *see also* **gauche** NOUN
left
□ le bras gauche the left arm □ le côté gauche the left-hand side

★ la **gauche** FEM NOUN
▷ *see also* **gauche** ADJECTIVE
left
□ sur votre gauche on your left
■ **à gauche 1** on the left □ la deuxième rue à gauche the second street on the left **2** to the left □ à gauche de l'armoire to the left of the cupboard
■ **Tournez à gauche.** Turn left.
■ **la voie de gauche** the left-hand lane
■ **la gauche** (*in politics*) the left
■ **Il est de gauche.** He's left-wing.

gaucher (FEM **gauchère**) ADJECTIVE
left-handed

la **gaufre** FEM NOUN
waffle

la **gaufrette** FEM NOUN
wafer

le **Gaulois** MASC NOUN
Gaul
□ Astérix le Gaulois Asterix the Gaul

gaulois (FEM **gauloise**) ADJECTIVE
Gallic

★ le **gaz** MASC NOUN
gas
■ **les gaz à effet de serre** greenhouse gases

gazeux (FEM **gazeuse**) ADJECTIVE
■ **une boisson gazeuse** a fizzy drink
■ **de l'eau gazeuse** sparkling water

le **gazole** MASC NOUN
diesel (*fuel*)

★ le **gazon** MASC NOUN
lawn

le **géant** MASC NOUN
giant

le **gel** MASC NOUN
frost

la **gelée** FEM NOUN
1 jelly
2 frost

★ **geler** VERB [43]
to freeze
■ **Il a gelé cette nuit.** There was a frost last night.

la **gélule** FEM NOUN
capsule (*containing medicine*)

les **Gémeaux** MASC PL NOUN
Gemini
□ Nicolas est Gémeaux. Nicolas's Gemini.

gémir VERB [38]
to moan

gênant (FEM **gênante**) ADJECTIVE
awkward
□ un silence gênant an awkward silence

la **gencive** FEM NOUN
gum (*in mouth*)

★ le **gendarme** MASC NOUN
policeman

★ la **gendarmerie** FEM NOUN
1 police force
2 police station
□ Vous devriez porter plainte à la gendarmerie. You should go to the police station and report it.

le **gendre** MASC NOUN
son-in-law

gêné (FEM **gênée**) ADJECTIVE
embarrassed

★ **gêner** VERB [28]
1 to bother
□ Je ne voudrais pas vous gêner. I don't want to bother you.
2 to feel awkward
□ Son regard la gênait. The way he was looking at her made her feel awkward.

★ **général** (FEM **générale**, MASC PL **généraux**) ADJECTIVE
▷ *see also* **général** NOUN
general
■ **en général** usually

★ le **général** (PL les **généraux**) MASC NOUN
▷ *see also* **général** ADJECTIVE
general

★ **généralement** ADVERB
generally

le/la **généraliste** MASC/FEM NOUN
GP

la **génération** FEM NOUN
generation

★ **généreux** (FEM **généreuse**) ADJECTIVE
generous

la **générosité** FEM NOUN
generosity

le **genêt** MASC NOUN
broom (*bush*)

la **génétique** FEM NOUN
genetics

génétiquement ADVERB
genetically
□ génétiquement modifié genetically-modified □ les aliments génétiquement modifiés GM foods □ un organisme génétiquement modifié a genetically-modified organism

Genève NOUN
Geneva

★ **génial** (FEM **géniale**, MASC PL **géniaux**) ADJECTIVE (*informal*)
great
□ Le film d'hier soir était génial. The film last night was great.

★ le **genou** (PL les **genoux**) MASC NOUN
knee
□ Elle est à genoux. She's on her knees. □ se mettre à genoux to kneel down

★ le **genre** MASC NOUN
kind
□ C'est un genre de gâteau à la crème. It's a kind of cream cake.

★ les **gens** MASC PL NOUN
people

★ **gentil** (FEM **gentille**) ADJECTIVE
1 nice
□ Nos voisins sont très gentils. Our neighbours are very nice.
2 kind
□ C'était très gentil de votre part. It was very kind of you.

> **BE CAREFUL!**
> **gentil** does not mean **gentle**.

★ la **gentillesse** FEM NOUN
kindness
□ Je l'ai remerciée de sa gentillesse. I thanked her for her kindness.
■ **C'est un homme d'une grande gentillesse.** He is a very nice man.

gentiment ADVERB
1 nicely
□ Demande-le lui gentiment. Ask him nicely.
2 kindly
□ Ils nous ont gentiment proposé de rester dîner. They kindly invited us to stay for dinner.

★ la **géographie** FEM NOUN
geography

la **géolocalisation** FEM NOUN
geolocation

la **géométrie** FEM NOUN
geometry

★ le **gérant** MASC NOUN
manager

★ la **gérante** FEM NOUN
manager

gérer VERB [34]
to manage

germain (FEM **germaine**) ADJECTIVE
■ **un cousin germain** a first cousin

le **geste** MASC NOUN
gesture
□ Il a voulu faire un geste. He wanted to make a gesture.
■ **Ne faites pas un geste!** Don't move!

la **gestion** FEM NOUN
management

le/la **gestionnaire de site** MASC/FEM NOUN
webmaster

la **gifle** FEM NOUN
slap across the face

gifler VERB [28]
to slap across the face

gigantesque (FEM **gigantesque**) ADJECTIVE
gigantic

le **gigot** MASC NOUN
leg of lamb

★ le **gilet** MASC NOUN
1 waistcoat
□ un gilet en cuir a leather waistcoat
2 cardigan
□ un gilet tricoté main a hand-knitted cardigan
■ **un gilet de sauvetage** a life jacket

le **gingembre** MASC NOUN
ginger

la **girafe** FEM NOUN
giraffe

le **gitan** MASC NOUN
gipsy

la **gitane** FEM NOUN
gipsy

★ le **gîte** MASC NOUN
■ **un gîte rural** a holiday house

★ la **glace** FEM NOUN
1 ice
□ L'étang est recouvert de glace. The pond is covered with ice.
2 ice cream
□ une glace à la fraise a strawberry ice cream
3 mirror
□ Il se regarde souvent dans la glace. He often looks at himself in the mirror.

glacé (FEM **glacée**) ADJECTIVE
1 icy
□ un vent glacé an icy wind
2 iced
□ un thé glacé an iced tea

glacial (FEM **glaciale**, MASC PL **glaciaux**) ADJECTIVE
icy

★ le **glaçon** MASC NOUN
ice cube

glissant (FEM **glissante**) ADJECTIVE
slippery

★ **glisser** VERB [28]
1 to slip
□ Il a glissé sur une peau de banane. He slipped on a banana skin.
2 to be slippery
□ Attention, ça glisse! Watch out, it's slippery!

global (FEM **globale**, MASC PL **globaux**) ADJECTIVE
total
□ la somme globale the total amount

les **glucides** MASC PL NOUN
carbohydrates

la **godasse** FEM NOUN (*informal*)
shoe

le **goéland** MASC NOUN
seagull

★ le **golf** MASC NOUN
1 golf
□ Il joue au golf. He plays golf.
2 golf course
□ un golf dix-huit trous an 18-hole golf course

le **golfe** MASC NOUN
gulf
■ **le golfe de Gascogne** the Bay of Biscay

★ la **gomme** FEM NOUN
rubber

gommer VERB [28]
to rub out

gonflé (FEM **gonflée**) ADJECTIVE
1 swollen (*arm, finger, stomach*)
□ Elle a les pieds gonflés. Her feet are swollen.
2 inflated (*ball, tyre*)
□ Le ballon de foot était mal gonflé. The football wasn't properly inflated.
■ **Il est gonflé!** (*informal*) He's got a nerve!

★ **gonfler** VERB [28]
1 to blow up
□ gonfler un ballon to blow up a balloon
2 to pump up
□ gonfler un pneu to pump up a tyre

googler VERB [28]
to google

★ la **gorge** FEM NOUN
1 throat
□ J'ai mal à la gorge. I've got a sore throat.
2 gorge
□ les gorges du Tarn the Tarn gorges

la **gorgée** FEM NOUN
sip
□ une gorgée d'eau a sip of water

le **gorille** MASC NOUN
gorilla

★ le/la **gosse** MASC/FEM NOUN (*informal*)
kid

le **goudron** MASC NOUN
tar

le **gouffre** MASC NOUN
chasm
■ **Cette voiture est un vrai gouffre!** This car eats up money!

la **gourde** FEM NOUN
water bottle

gourmand (FEM **gourmande**) ADJECTIVE
greedy

la **gourmandise** FEM NOUN
greed

la **gousse** FEM NOUN
■ **une gousse d'ail** a clove of garlic

★ le **goût** MASC NOUN
taste
□ Ça n'a pas de goût. It's got no taste. □ Elle a très bon goût. She's got very good taste.

★ **goûter** VERB [28]
▷ *see also* **goûter** NOUN
1 to taste
□ Goûte ce fromage. Taste this cheese.
2 to have a snack (*in the afternoon*)
□ Les enfants goûtent généralement vers quatre heures. The children usually have a snack around 4 o'clock.

★ le **goûter** MASC NOUN
▷ *see also* **goûter** VERB
afternoon snack

★ la **goutte** FEM NOUN
drop

★ le **gouvernement** MASC NOUN
government

gouverner VERB [28]
to govern

la **grâce** FEM NOUN
■ **grâce à** thanks to □ Je suis arrivé à l'heure grâce à toi. I arrived on time thanks to you.

gracieux (FEM **gracieuse**) ADJECTIVE
graceful

les **gradins** MASC PL NOUN
terraces (*in stadium*)

graffiti MASC PL NOUN
graffiti *sing*

★ les **graffitis** MASC PL NOUN
graffiti *sing*

le **grain** MASC NOUN
grain
□ un grain de sable a grain of sand
■ **un grain de beauté** a beauty spot
■ **un grain de café** a coffee bean
■ **un grain de raisin** a grape

la **graine** FEM NOUN
seed

la **graisse** FEM NOUN
fat

la **grammaire** FEM NOUN
grammar

★ le **gramme** MASC NOUN
gram

★ **grand** (FEM **grande**) ADJECTIVE, ADVERB
1 tall
□ Il est grand pour son âge. He's tall for his age.
2 big
□ une grande valise a big suitcase □ C'est sa grande sœur. She's his big sister.
■ **une grande personne** a grown-up
3 long
□ un grand voyage a long journey
■ **les grandes vacances** the summer holidays
4 great
□ C'est un grand ami à moi. He's a great friend of mine.
■ **un grand magasin** a department store
■ **une grande surface** a hypermarket
■ **les grandes écoles** top ranking colleges (*at university level*)
■ **au grand air** out in the open air □ Ça te fera beaucoup de bien d'être au grand air. It'll be very good for you to be out in the open air.
■ **grand ouvert** wide open

★ **grand-chose** PRONOUN
■ **pas grand-chose** not much □ Je n'ai pas acheté grand-chose au marché. I didn't buy much at the market. □ Voici un petit cadeau: ce n'est pas grand-chose. Here's a little present: it's nothing much.

★ la **Grande-Bretagne** FEM NOUN
Britain

la **grandeur** FEM NOUN
size

grandir VERB [38]
to grow
□ Il a beaucoup grandi. He's grown a lot.

★ la **grand-mère** (PL les **grands-mères**) FEM NOUN
grandmother

grand-peine
■ **à grand-peine** ADVERB with great difficulty

★ le **grand-père** (PL les **grands-pères**) MASC NOUN
grandfather

★ les **grands-parents** MASC PL NOUN
grandparents

la **grange** FEM NOUN
barn

la **grappe** FEM NOUN
■ **une grappe de raisin** a bunch of grapes

★ **gras** (FEM **grasse**) ADJECTIVE
1 fatty (*food*)
□ Évitez les aliments gras. Avoid fatty foods.
2 greasy
□ des cheveux gras greasy hair
3 oily
□ une peau grasse oily skin
■ **faire la grasse matinée** to have a lie-in

gratis (FEM+PL **gratis**) ADJECTIVE, ADVERB
free
□ J'ai eu ce stylo gratis. I got this pen free.

★ le **gratte-ciel** (PL les **gratte-ciels**, les **gratte-ciel**) MASC NOUN
skyscraper

gratter VERB [28]
1 to scratch
□ Ne gratte pas tes piqûres de moustiques! Don't scratch your mosquito bites!
2 to be itchy
□ C'est épouvantable comme ça gratte! It's terribly itchy!

★ **gratuit** (FEM **gratuite**) ADJECTIVE
free
□ entrée gratuite entrance free □ J'ai deux places gratuites pour le film. I've got two free tickets for the film.

★ **grave** (FEM **grave**) ADJECTIVE
1 serious
□ une maladie grave a serious illness □ Il avait l'air grave. He was looking serious.
2 deep
□ Il a une voix grave. He's got a deep voice.
■ **Ce n'est pas grave.** It doesn't matter. □ J'ai oublié ma clé. — Ce n'est pas grave, j'ai la mienne. I've forgotten my key. — It doesn't matter, I've got mine.

gravement ADVERB
seriously
□ Il a été gravement blessé. He was seriously injured.

le **graveur** MASC NOUN
■ **un graveur de CD** a CD burner

★ **grec** (FEM **grecque**) ADJECTIVE, NOUN
Greek
□ J'apprends le grec. I'm learning Greek.
■ **un Grec** a Greek (*man*)
■ **une Grecque** a Greek (*woman*)
■ **les Grecs** the Greeks

★ la **Grèce** FEM NOUN
Greece
■ **en Grèce** 1 in Greece 2 to Greece

★ la **grêle** FEM NOUN
hail

grêler VERB [28]
■ **Il grêle.** It's hailing.

grelotter VERB [28]
to shiver

la **grenade** FEM NOUN
1 pomegranate
2 grenade

la **grenadine** FEM NOUN
grenadine

> **DID YOU KNOW...?**
> **grenadine** is a bright pink drink which is very popular with children in France.

★ le **grenier** MASC NOUN
attic

★ la **grenouille** FEM NOUN
frog

★ la **grève** FEM NOUN
1 strike
■ **en grève** on strike □ Ils sont en grève depuis dix jours. They have been on strike for ten days.
■ **faire grève** to be on strike
2 shore
□ Nous nous sommes promenés le long de la grève. We went for a walk along the shore.

le/la **gréviste** MASC/FEM NOUN
striker

grièvement ADVERB
■ **grièvement blessé** seriously injured

la **griffe** FEM NOUN
1 claw
■ **donner un coup de griffe** to scratch □ Le chat m'a donné un coup de griffe. The cat scratched me.
2 label
□ la griffe d'un grand couturier the label of a top designer

griffer VERB [28]
to scratch
□ Le chat m'a griffé. The cat scratched me.

grignoter VERB [28]
to nibble

★ la **grillade** FEM NOUN
grilled food
□ une grillade d'agneau grilled lamb

★ la **grille** FEM NOUN
1 wire fence
□ L'usine est entourée d'une haute grille. The factory is surrounded by a high wire fence.
2 metal gate
□ Le facteur a sonné à la grille du jardin. The postman rang at the garden gate.

3 grid
□ Complétez la grille. Complete the grid.

le **grille-pain** (PL les **grille-pains**) MASC NOUN
toaster

★**griller** VERB [28]
1 to toast
■ **du pain grillé** toast
2 to grill
□ des saucisses grillées grilled sausages

la **grimace** FEM NOUN
■ **faire des grimaces** to make faces

★**grimper** VERB [28]
to climb

grincer VERB [12]
to creak

grincheux (FEM **grincheuse**) ADJECTIVE
grumpy

★la **grippe** FEM NOUN
flu
■ **avoir la grippe** to have flu □ J'ai eu une mauvaise grippe l'hiver dernier. I had a bad bout of flu last winter.
■ **la grippe A** swine flu
■ **la grippe aviaire** bird flu

grippé (FEM **grippée**) ADJECTIVE
■ **être grippé** to have flu

★**gris** (FEM **grise**) ADJECTIVE
grey

le **Groenland** MASC NOUN
Greenland

grogner VERB [28]
1 to growl
□ Le chien a grogné quand je me suis approché de lui. The dog growled when I went near it.
2 to complain
□ Arrête donc de grogner! Stop complaining!

gronder VERB [28]
to tell off
□ Si ma mère l'apprend, elle va me gronder. If my mother finds out, she'll tell me off.
■ **se faire gronder** to get a telling-off □ Tu vas te faire gronder par ton père! You're going to get a telling-off from your father!

★**gros** (FEM **grosse**) ADJECTIVE
1 big
□ une grosse pomme a big apple
2 fat
□ Je suis trop grosse pour porter ça! I'm too fat to wear that!

la **groseille** FEM NOUN
■ **la groseille rouge** redcurrant
■ **la groseille à maquereau** gooseberry

la **grossesse** FEM NOUN
pregnancy

grossier (FEM **grossière**) ADJECTIVE
rude
□ Ne sois pas si grossier! Don't be so rude!
■ **une erreur grossière** a bad mistake

grossir VERB [38]
to put on weight
□ Il a beaucoup grossi. He's put on a lot of weight.

grosso modo ADVERB
roughly
□ Dis-moi grosso modo ce que tu en penses. Tell me roughly what you think of it.

la **grotte** FEM NOUN
cave

★le **groupe** MASC NOUN
group
□ votre groupe sanguin your blood group

grouper VERB [28]
to group
□ On nous a groupés selon notre niveau. We were grouped according to our level.
■ **se grouper** to gather □ Nous nous sommes groupés autour du feu. We gathered round the fire.

le **guépard** MASC NOUN
cheetah

la **guêpe** FEM NOUN
wasp

★**guérir** VERB [38]
to recover
□ Il est maintenant complètement guéri. He's now completely recovered.

la **guérison** FEM NOUN
recovery

★la **guerre** FEM NOUN
war
□ en guerre at war □ une guerre civile a civil war □ la Deuxième Guerre mondiale the Second World War

guetter VERB [28]
to look out for
□ Elle guette l'arrivée du facteur tous les matins. She looks out for the postman every morning.

la **gueule** FEM NOUN
mouth
□ Le chat a ramené une souris dans sa gueule. The cat brought in a mouse in its mouth.
■ **Ta gueule!** (*rude*) Shut your face!
■ **avoir la gueule de bois** (*informal*) to have a hangover

> **gueule** is an impolite way of talking about a person's mouth but it is the correct term for an animal's.

gueuler VERB [28] (*informal*)
to bawl

★ le **guichet** MASC NOUN
counter (*in bank, booking office*)

★ le **guide** MASC NOUN
guide

guider VERB [28]
to guide

le **guidon** MASC NOUN
handlebars

les **guillemets** MASC PL NOUN
inverted commas
□ entre guillemets in inverted commas

la **guirlande** FEM NOUN
tinsel
□ Nous avons décoré le sapin de Noël avec des guirlandes. We decorated the Christmas tree with tinsel.
■ **des guirlandes en papier** paper chains

★ la **guitare** FEM NOUN
guitar
□ Sais-tu jouer de la guitare? Can you play the guitar?

★ la **gym** FEM NOUN (*informal*)
PE

★ le **gymnase** MASC NOUN
gym
□ Le lycée a un nouveau gymnase. The school's got a new gym.

★ la **gymnastique** FEM NOUN
gymnastics
□ Elle fait de la gymnastique. She does gymnastics.
■ **faire sa gymnastique** to do one's exercises

Hh

★ **habile** (FEM **habile**) ADJECTIVE
skilful
□ Il est très habile de ses mains. He is very clever with his hands.

★ **habillé** (FEM **habillée**) ADJECTIVE
1 dressed
□ Il n'est pas encore habillé. He's not dressed yet.
2 smart
□ Cette robe fait très habillé. This dress looks very smart.

s'**habiller** VERB [28]
1 to get dressed
□ Je me suis rapidement habillé. I got dressed quickly.
2 to dress up
□ Est-ce qu'il faut s'habiller pour la réception? Do you have to dress up to go to the party?

★ l'**habitant** MASC NOUN
inhabitant
■ **les habitants du quartier** the local people

★ l'**habitante** FEM NOUN
inhabitant

★ **habiter** VERB [28]
to live
□ Il habite à Montpellier. He lives in Montpellier.

les **habits** MASC PL NOUN
clothes

★ l'**habitude** FEM NOUN
habit
□ une mauvaise habitude a bad habit
■ **avoir l'habitude de quelque chose** to be used to something □ Elle a l'habitude des enfants. She's used to children. □ Je n'ai pas l'habitude de parler en public. I'm not used to speaking in public.
■ **d'habitude** usually
■ **comme d'habitude** as usual

habituel (FEM **habituelle**) ADJECTIVE
usual

s'**habituer** VERB [28]
■ **s'habituer à quelque chose** to get used to something □ Il faudra que tu t'habitues à te lever tôt. You'll have to get used to getting up early.

le **hachis** MASC NOUN
mince
■ **le hachis Parmentier** cottage pie

★ la **haie** FEM NOUN
hedge

la **haine** FEM NOUN
hatred

haïr VERB [40]
to hate

l'**haleine** FEM NOUN
breath
□ avoir mauvaise haleine to have bad breath
□ être hors d'haleine to be out of breath

les **halles** FEM PL NOUN
covered market *sing*

la **halte** FEM NOUN
stop
□ faire halte to make a stop
■ **Halte!** Stop!

l'**haltérophilie** FEM NOUN
weightlifting

★ le **hamburger** MASC NOUN
hamburger

l'**hameçon** MASC NOUN
fish hook

★ le **hamster** MASC NOUN
hamster

la **hanche** FEM NOUN
hip

★ le **handball** MASC NOUN
handball
□ jouer au handball to play handball

le **handicap** MASC NOUN
1 disability (*medical problem*)
2 handicap (*in sport*)

le **handicapé** MASC NOUN
disabled man

la **handicapée** FEM NOUN
disabled woman

★ le **harcèlement** MASC NOUN
1 bullying
2 harassment
□ le harcèlement sexuel sexual harassment

★ **harceler** VERB
to bully

le **hareng** MASC NOUN
herring
■ **un hareng saur** a kipper

★ le **haricot** MASC NOUN
bean
■ **les haricots verts** runner beans
■ **les haricots blancs** haricot beans
■ **C'est la fin des haricots.** (*informal*) It's the last straw.

l'**harmonica** MASC NOUN
mouth organ

la **harpe** FEM NOUN
harp

★ le **hasard** MASC NOUN
coincidence
□ C'était un pur hasard. It was pure coincidence.
■ **au hasard** at random □ Choisis un numéro au hasard. Choose a number at random.
■ **par hasard** by chance □ rencontrer quelqu'un par hasard to meet somebody by chance
■ **à tout hasard** **1** just in case □ Prends un parapluie à tout hasard. Take an umbrella just in case. **2** on the off chance □ Je ne sais pas s'il est chez lui, mais je vais l'appeler à tout hasard. I don't know if he's at home, but I'll phone on the off chance.

★ la **hâte** FEM NOUN
■ **à la hâte** hurriedly □ Elle s'est habillée à la hâte. She got dressed hurriedly.
■ **J'ai hâte de te voir.** I can't wait to see you.

★ la **hausse** FEM NOUN
1 increase
□ la hausse des prix price increase
2 rise
□ On annonce une légère hausse de température. The forecast is for a slight rise in temperature.

★ **hausser** VERB [28]
■ **hausser les épaules** to shrug one's shoulders

★ **haut** (FEM **haute**) ADJECTIVE, ADVERB
▷ *see also* **haut** NOUN
1 high
□ une haute montagne a high mountain
2 aloud
□ penser tout haut to think aloud

★ le **haut** MASC NOUN
▷ *see also* **haut** ADJECTIVE, ADVERB
top
□ un haut à bretelles a strappy top
■ **un mur de trois mètres de haut** a wall 3 metres high
■ **en haut** **1** upstairs □ La salle de bain est en haut. The bathroom is upstairs. **2** at the top □ Le nid est tout en haut de l'arbre. The nest is right at the top of the tree.

★ la **hauteur** FEM NOUN
height

le **haut-parleur** (PL les **haut-parleurs**) MASC NOUN
loudspeaker

★ l'**hebdomadaire** MASC NOUN
weekly (*magazine*)

★ l'**hébergement** MASC NOUN
accommodation

★ **héberger** VERB [45]
to put up
□ Mon cousin a dit qu'il nous hébergerait. My cousin said he would put us up.

★ **hein?** EXCLAMATION
eh?
□ Hein? Qu'est-ce que tu dis? Eh? What did you say?

★ **hélas** ADVERB
unfortunately
□ Hélas, il ne restait plus de billets. Unfortunately there were no tickets left.

l'**hélicoptère** MASC NOUN
helicopter

l'**hémorragie** FEM NOUN
haemorrhage

★ l'**herbe** FEM NOUN
grass
■ **les herbes de Provence** mixed herbs

le **hérisson** MASC NOUN
hedgehog

hériter VERB [28]
to inherit

l'**héritier** MASC NOUN
heir

l'**héritière** FEM NOUN
heiress

hermétique (FEM **hermétique**) ADJECTIVE
airtight

l'**héroïne** FEM NOUN
1 heroine
□ l'héroïne du roman the heroine of the novel
2 heroin (*drug*)

le **héros** MASC NOUN
hero

l'**hésitation** FEM NOUN
hesitation

★ **hésiter** VERB [28]
to hesitate
□ Il n'a pas hésité à nous aider. He didn't hesitate to help us.
■ **J'ai hésité entre le pull vert et le cardigan jaune.** I couldn't decide between the green pullover and the yellow cardigan.
■ **Est-ce que tu viens ce soir? — J'hésite.** Are you coming this evening? — I'm not sure.
■ **sans hésiter** without hesitating

★ l'**heure** FEM NOUN
1 hour
□ Le trajet dure six heures. The journey lasts six hours.
2 time
□ Vous avez l'heure? Have you got the time?
■ **Quelle heure est-il?** What time is it?
■ **À quelle heure?** What time? □ À quelle heure arrivons-nous? What time do we arrive?
■ **deux heures du matin** 2 o'clock in the morning
■ **être à l'heure** to be on time
■ **une heure de français** a period of French

★ **heureusement** ADVERB
luckily
□ Heureusement qu'il n'a pas été blessé. Luckily he wasn't hurt.

★ **heureux** (FEM **heureuse**) ADJECTIVE
happy

★ **heurter** VERB [28]
to hit

l'**hexagone** MASC NOUN
hexagon
■ **l'Hexagone** France

DID YOU KNOW...?
France is often referred to as **l'Hexagone** because of its six-sided shape.

le **hibou** (PL les **hiboux**) MASC NOUN
owl

★ **hier** ADVERB
yesterday
■ **avant-hier** the day before yesterday

★ la **hi-fi** FEM NOUN
stereo
■ **une chaîne hi-fi** a stereo system

hippique (FEM **hippique**) ADJECTIVE
■ **un club hippique** a riding centre
■ **un concours hippique** a horse show

l'**hippopotame** MASC NOUN
hippopotamus

l'**hirondelle** FEM NOUN
swallow (*bird*)

★ l'**histoire** FEM NOUN
1 history
□ un cours d'histoire a history lesson
2 story
□ C'est l'histoire de deux enfants. It's the story of two children.
■ **Ne fais pas d'histoires!** Don't make a fuss!

★ **historique** (FEM **historique**) ADJECTIVE
historic
□ un monument historique a historic monument

★ l'**hiver** MASC NOUN
winter
■ **en hiver** in winter

★ le/la **HLM** MASC/FEM NOUN (= *habitation à loyer modéré*)
council flat
■ **des HLM** council housing

★ le **hockey** MASC NOUN
hockey
■ **le hockey sur glace** ice hockey

★ **hollandais** (FEM **hollandaise**) ADJECTIVE, NOUN
Dutch
□ J'apprends le hollandais. I'm learning Dutch.
■ **un Hollandais** a Dutch man
■ **une Hollandaise** a Dutch woman
■ **les Hollandais** the Dutch

★ la **Hollande** FEM NOUN
Holland
■ **en Hollande** 1 in Holland 2 to Holland

le **homard** MASC NOUN
lobster

homéopathique (FEM **homéopathique**) ADJECTIVE
homeopathic

l'**hommage** MASC NOUN
tribute

★ l'**homme** MASC NOUN
man
■ **un homme d'affaires** a businessman
■ **un homme politique** a politician

★ **homoparental** (FEM **homoparentale**, MASC PL **homoparentaux**) ADJECTIVE
■ **une famille homoparentale** a same-sex-parent family

homosexuel (FEM **homosexuelle**) ADJECTIVE
homosexual

la **Hongrie** FEM NOUN
Hungary

hongrois (FEM **hongroise**) ADJECTIVE, NOUN
Hungarian
□ Il parle le hongrois. He speaks Hungarian.
■ **un Hongrois** a Hungarian (*man*)
■ **une Hongroise** a Hungarian (*woman*)
■ **les Hongrois** the Hungarians

★ **honnête** (FEM **honnête**) ADJECTIVE
honest

l'**honnêteté** FEM NOUN
honesty

l'**honneur** MASC NOUN
honour

★ la **honte** FEM NOUN
shame
■ **avoir honte de quelque chose** to be ashamed of something

★ l'**hôpital** (PL les **hôpitaux**) MASC NOUN
hospital

le **hoquet** MASC NOUN
■ **avoir le hoquet** to have hiccups

French-English

h

★ l'**horaire** MASC NOUN
timetable
■ **les horaires de train** the train timetable

l'**horizon** MASC NOUN
horizon

horizontal (FEM **horizontale**, MASC PL **horizontaux**) ADJECTIVE
horizontal

★ l'**horloge** FEM NOUN
clock

★ l'**horreur** FEM NOUN
horror
□ un film d'horreur a horror film
■ **avoir horreur de** to hate □ J'ai horreur du chou. I hate cabbage.

horrible (FEM **horrible**) ADJECTIVE
horrible

★ **hors** PREPOSITION
■ **hors de** out of □ Elle est hors de danger maintenant. She's out of danger now.
■ **hors taxes** duty-free

le **hors-d'œuvre** (PL les **hors-d'œuvre**) MASC NOUN
starter (*food*)

hospitalier (FEM **hospitalière**) ADJECTIVE
hospitable
□ Ils sont très hospitaliers. They're very hospitable.
■ **les services hospitaliers** hospital services

★ l'**hospitalité** FEM NOUN
hospitality

hostile (FEM **hostile**) ADJECTIVE
hostile

l'**hôte** MASC/FEM NOUN
1 host
□ N'oubliez pas de remercier vos hôtes. Don't forget to thank your hosts.
2 guest
□ Cette ferme accueille des hôtes payants. This farm takes paying guests.

★ l'**hôtel** MASC NOUN
hotel
■ **l'hôtel de ville** the town hall

★ l'**hôtesse** FEM NOUN
hostess
■ **une hôtesse de l'air** a stewardess

la **housse** FEM NOUN
cover
□ une housse de couette a duvet cover □ une housse de téléphone a phone cover

le **houx** MASC NOUN
holly

★ l'**huile** FEM NOUN
oil
■ **l'huile solaire** suntan oil

★ **huit** NUMBER
eight
□ Il est huit heures du matin. It's eight in the morning. □ Il a huit ans. He's eight.
■ **le huit février** the eighth of February
■ **dans huit jours** in a week's time

la **huitaine** FEM NOUN
■ **une huitaine de jours** about a week
□ Nous serons de retour dans une huitaine de jours. We'll be back in about a week.

★ **huitième** (FEM **huitième**) ADJECTIVE
eighth
□ au huitième étage on the eighth floor

★ l'**huître** FEM NOUN
oyster

★ **humain** (FEM **humaine**) ADJECTIVE
▷ *see also* **humain** NOUN
human

★ l'**humain** MASC NOUN
▷ *see also* **humain** ADJECTIVE
human being

★ l'**humeur** FEM NOUN
mood
□ Il est de bonne humeur. He's in a good mood. □ Elle était de mauvaise humeur. She was in a bad mood.

★ **humide** (FEM **humide**) ADJECTIVE
damp
□ L'herbe est humide. The grass is damp.
□ un climat humide a damp climate

★ **humilier** VERB [19]
to humiliate

humoristique (FEM **humoristique**) ADJECTIVE
humorous
■ **des dessins humoristiques** cartoons

★ l'**humour** MASC NOUN
humour
□ Il n'a pas beaucoup d'humour. He hasn't got much of a sense of humour.

hurler VERB [28]
1 to howl
2 to scream

la **hutte** FEM NOUN
hut

hydratant (FEM **hydratante**) ADJECTIVE
■ **une crème hydratante** a moisturizing cream

★ l'**hygiène** FEM NOUN
hygiene

hygiénique (FEM **hygiénique**) ADJECTIVE
hygienic
■ **une serviette hygiénique** a sanitary towel
■ **le papier hygiénique** toilet paper

l'**hymne** MASC NOUN
■ **l'hymne national** the national anthem

l'**hyperlien** MASC NOUN
hyperlink

Numbers in brackets refer to verb tables on pages 650 to 658

★ l'**hypermarché** MASC NOUN
hypermarket

hypermétrope (FEM **hypermétrope**) ADJECTIVE
long-sighted

hypocrite (FEM **hypocrite**) ADJECTIVE
hypocritical
□ Il est hypocrite. He's a hypocrite.

l'**hypothèse** FEM NOUN
hypothesis

Ii

l'**iceberg** MASC NOUN
iceberg

★ **ici** ADVERB
here
□ Les assiettes sont ici. The plates are here.
■ **La mer monte parfois jusqu'ici.** The sea sometimes comes in as far as this.
■ **Jusqu'ici nous n'avons eu aucun problème avec la voiture.** So far we haven't had any problems with the car.

★ l'**icône** FEM NOUN
icon

idéal (FEM **idéale**, MASC PL **idéaux**) ADJECTIVE
ideal
□ C'est l'endroit idéal pour faire un pique-nique. It's an ideal place to have a picnic.

★ l'**idée** FEM NOUN
idea
□ C'est une bonne idée. It's a good idea.

l'**identifiant** MASC NOUN
login (*on a computer*)

★ **identifier** VERB [19]
to identify
□ La police a identifié le meurtrier. The police have identified the murderer.

identique (FEM **identique**) ADJECTIVE
identical
□ Ils ont obtenu des résultats identiques. They obtained identical results.

★ l'**identité** FEM NOUN
identity
■ **une pièce d'identité** a form of identification □ Avez-vous une pièce d'identité? Have you got any form of identification?

★ **idiot** (FEM **idiote**) ADJECTIVE
▷ *see also* **idiot** NOUN, **idiote** NOUN
1 stupid
□ une plaisanterie idiote a stupid joke
2 silly
□ Ne sois pas idiot! Don't be silly!

★ l'**idiot** MASC NOUN
▷ *see also* **idiot** ADJECTIVE
idiot

★ l'**idiote** FEM NOUN
▷ *see also* **idiot** ADJECTIVE
idiot

ignoble (FEM **ignoble**) ADJECTIVE
horrible
□ Il a été ignoble avec elle. He was horrible to her.

ignorant (FEM **ignorante**) ADJECTIVE
ignorant

★ **ignorer** VERB [28]
1 not to know
□ J'ignore son nom. I don't know his name.
2 to ignore
□ Il m'a complètement ignoré. He completely ignored me.

★ **il** PRONOUN
1 he
□ Il est parti ce matin de bonne heure. He left early this morning.
2 it
□ Méfie-toi de ce chien: il mord. Be careful of that dog: it bites. □ Il pleut. It's raining.

★ l'**île** FEM NOUN
island
■ **les îles Anglo-Normandes** the Channel Islands
■ **les îles Britanniques** the British Isles
■ **les îles Féroé** the Faroe Islands

★ **illégal** (FEM **illégale**, MASC PL **illégaux**) ADJECTIVE
illegal

l'**illettrisme** MASC NOUN
illiteracy

illimité (FEM **illimitée**) ADJECTIVE
unlimited

illisible (FEM **illisible**) ADJECTIVE
illegible
□ une écriture illisible illegible handwriting

illuminer VERB [28]
to floodlight
□ Le château est illuminé tous les soirs pendant l'été. The castle is floodlit every night in the summer.

l'**illusion** FEM NOUN
illusion
■ **Tu te fais des illusions!** You're deluding yourself!

★ l'**illustration** FEM NOUN
illustration

★ **illustré** (FEM **illustrée**) ADJECTIVE
▷ *see also* **illustré** NOUN
illustrated

★ l'**illustré** MASC NOUN
▷ *see also* **illustré** ADJECTIVE
comic

illustrer VERB [28]
to illustrate
□ Vous pouvez illustrer votre rédaction avec des exemples. You may illustrate your essay with examples.

★ **ils** PL PRONOUN
they
□ Ils nous ont appelés hier soir. They phoned us last night.

★ l'**image** FEM NOUN
picture
□ Les films donnent une fausse image de l'Amérique. Films give a false picture of America.

l'**imagination** FEM NOUN
imagination
□ Elle a beaucoup d'imagination. She's got a vivid imagination.

★ **imaginer** VERB [28]
to imagine

l'**imam** MASC NOUN
imam

l'**imbécile** MASC/FEM NOUN
idiot

l'**imitation** FEM NOUN
imitation

imiter VERB [28]
to imitate

l'**immatriculation** FEM NOUN
■ **une plaque d'immatriculation** a numberplate (*of car*)

★ l'**immédiat** MASC NOUN
■ **dans l'immédiat** for the moment □ Je n'ai pas besoin de ce livre dans l'immédiat. I don't need this book for the moment.

★ **immédiatement** ADVERB
immediately

immense (FEM **immense**) ADJECTIVE
1 huge
□ une immense fortune a huge fortune
2 tremendous
□ un immense soulagement a tremendous relief

★ l'**immeuble** MASC NOUN
block of flats

l'**immigration** FEM NOUN
immigration

★ l'**immigré** MASC NOUN
immigrant

★ l'**immigrée** FEM NOUN
immigrant

★ **immobile** (FEM **immobile**) ADJECTIVE
motionless

immobilier (FEM **immobilière**) ADJECTIVE
■ **une agence immobilière** an estate agent's

immobiliser VERB [28]
to immobilize

immunisé (FEM **immunisée**) ADJECTIVE
immunized

l'**impact** MASC NOUN
impact

impair (FEM **impaire**) ADJECTIVE
odd
□ un nombre impair an odd number

impardonnable (FEM **impardonnable**) ADJECTIVE
unforgivable

l'**impasse** FEM NOUN
cul-de-sac

l'**impatience** FEM NOUN
impatience

★ **impatient** (FEM **impatiente**) ADJECTIVE
impatient

impeccable (FEM **impeccable**) ADJECTIVE
1 immaculate
□ Elle est toujours impeccable. She's always immaculate.
2 perfect
□ Il a fait un travail impeccable. He's done a perfect job. □ C'est impeccable! That's perfect!

★ l'**imper** MASC NOUN (*informal*)
mac

l'**impératif** MASC NOUN
imperative

l'**impératrice** FEM NOUN
empress

★ l'**imperméable** MASC NOUN
raincoat

impertinent (FEM **impertinente**) ADJECTIVE
cheeky
□ Ne sois pas impertinent! Don't be cheeky!

impitoyable (FEM **impitoyable**) ADJECTIVE
merciless

impliquer VERB [28]
to mean
□ Son silence implique qu'il est d'accord. His silence means he agrees.
■ **être impliqué dans** to be involved in □ Il est impliqué dans un scandale financier. He's involved in a financial scandal.

★ **impoli** (FEM **impolie**) ADJECTIVE
rude

l'**importance** FEM NOUN
importance
■ **C'est sans importance.** It doesn't matter.

★ **important** (FEM **importante**) ADJECTIVE
1 important
□ un rôle important an important role
2 considerable
□ une somme importante a considerable sum

l'**importation** FEM NOUN
import
□ Les importations de pétrole ont baissé. Oil imports have fallen.

★ **importer** VERB [28]
▷ *see also* **n'importe**
1 to import (*goods*)
2 to matter
□ Peu importe. It doesn't matter.

imposant (FEM **imposante**) ADJECTIVE
imposing

imposer VERB [28]
to impose
▪ **La direction leur impose des horaires impossibles.** The managers are making them work ridiculous hours.

★ **impossible** (FEM **impossible**) ADJECTIVE
▷ *see also* **impossible** NOUN
impossible

★ l'**impossible** MASC NOUN
▷ *see also* **impossible** ADJECTIVE
▪ **Nous ferons l'impossible pour finir à temps.** We'll do our utmost to finish on time.

l'**impôt** MASC NOUN
tax

imprécis (FEM **imprécise**) ADJECTIVE
imprecise

★ l'**impression** FEM NOUN
impression
□ Il a fait bonne impression à ma mère. He made a good impression on my mother.

★ **impressionnant** (FEM **impressionnante**) ADJECTIVE
impressive

impressionner VERB [28]
to impress

imprévisible (FEM **imprévisible**) ADJECTIVE
unpredictable

imprévu (FEM **imprévue**) ADJECTIVE
unexpected

★ l'**imprimante** FEM NOUN
printer (*for computer*)

imprimé (FEM **imprimée**) ADJECTIVE
printed
□ un tissu imprimé a printed fabric □ C'est imprimé en grandes lettres. It's printed in large letters.

★ **imprimer** VERB [28]
to print

impropre (FEM **impropre**) ADJECTIVE
▪ **impropre à la consommation** unfit for human consumption

improviser VERB [28]
to improvise

improviste ADVERB
▪ **arriver à l'improviste** to arrive unexpectedly

l'**imprudence** FEM NOUN
carelessness
▪ **Ne fais pas d'imprudences!** Don't do anything silly!

★ **imprudent** (FEM **imprudente**) ADJECTIVE
1 unwise
□ Il serait imprudent de prendre la voiture aujourd'hui. It would be unwise to take the car today.
2 careless
□ un conducteur imprudent a careless driver

impuissant (FEM **impuissante**) ADJECTIVE
helpless
□ Elle se sentait complètement impuissante. She felt completely helpless.

impulsif (FEM **impulsive**) ADJECTIVE
impulsive

inabordable (FEM **inabordable**) ADJECTIVE
prohibitive
□ des prix inabordables prohibitive prices

inaccessible (FEM **inaccessible**) ADJECTIVE
inaccessible
□ Cette plage est inaccessible par la route. This beach is inaccessible by road.

inachevé (FEM **inachevée**) ADJECTIVE
unfinished

★ **inadmissible** (FEM **inadmissible**) ADJECTIVE
intolerable
□ Ce type de comportement est inadmissible! This sort of behaviour is intolerable!

inanimé (FEM **inanimée**) ADJECTIVE
unconscious
□ On l'a retrouvé inanimé sur la route. He was found unconscious on the road.

inaperçu (FEM **inaperçue**) ADJECTIVE
▪ **passer inaperçu** to go unnoticed

inattendu (FEM **inattendue**) ADJECTIVE
unexpected

l'**inattention** FEM NOUN
▪ **une faute d'inattention** a careless mistake

inaugurer VERB [28]
to open (*an exhibition*)

incapable (FEM **incapable**) ADJECTIVE
incapable
□ être incapable de faire quelque chose to be incapable of doing something

★ **incassable** (FEM **incassable**) ADJECTIVE
unbreakable

★ l'**incendie** MASC NOUN
fire
□ un incendie de forêt a forest fire

incertain (FEM **incertaine**) ADJECTIVE
1 uncertain
□ Son avenir est encore incertain. His future is still uncertain.
2 unsettled
□ Le temps est incertain. The weather is unsettled.

★ l'**incident** MASC NOUN
incident

inciter VERB [28]
■ **inciter quelqu'un à faire quelque chose** to encourage somebody to do something
□ J'ai incité mes parents à partir en voyage. I encouraged my parents to go on a trip.

inclure VERB [13]
to enclose
□ Veuillez inclure une enveloppe timbrée libellée à votre adresse. Please enclose a stamped addressed envelope.
■ **jusqu'au dix mars inclus** until 10th March inclusive

incohérent (FEM **incohérente**) ADJECTIVE
incoherent

incollable (FEM **incollable**) ADJECTIVE
■ **être incollable sur quelque chose** (*informal*) to know everything there is to know about something
■ **le riz incollable** non-stick rice

incolore (FEM **incolore**) ADJECTIVE
colourless

incompétent (FEM **incompétente**) ADJECTIVE
incompetent

incompris (FEM **incomprise**) ADJECTIVE
misunderstood

★ l'**inconnu** MASC NOUN
stranger
□ Ne parle pas à des inconnus. Don't speak to strangers.
■ **l'inconnu** the unknown □ la peur de l'inconnu the fear of the unknown

★ l'**inconnue** FEM NOUN
stranger

inconsciemment ADVERB
unconsciously

inconscient (FEM **inconsciente**) ADJECTIVE
1 unconscious
□ Il est resté inconscient quelques minutes. He was unconscious for several minutes.
2 unaware
□ Elle est inconsciente des risques que cela comporte. She is unaware of the risks involved.

incontestable (FEM **incontestable**) ADJECTIVE
indisputable

incontournable (FEM **incontournable**) ADJECTIVE
inevitable
□ l'incontournable petite robe noire the inevitable little black dress

★ l'**inconvénient** MASC NOUN
disadvantage
■ **si vous n'y voyez pas d'inconvénient** if you have no objection

incorrect (FEM **incorrecte**) ADJECTIVE
1 incorrect
□ une réponse incorrecte an incorrect answer
2 rude
□ Il a été incorrect avec la voisine. He was rude to the woman next door.

★ **incroyable** (FEM **incroyable**) ADJECTIVE
incredible

inculper VERB [28]
■ **inculper de** to charge with □ Il a été inculpé de meurtre. He was charged with murder.

★ l'**Inde** FEM NOUN
India

indécis (FEM **indécise**) ADJECTIVE
1 indecisive
□ Il est constamment indécis. He's always indecisive.
2 undecided
□ Je suis encore indécis. I'm still undecided.

indéfiniment ADVERB
indefinitely

indélicat (FEM **indélicate**) ADJECTIVE
tactless

indemne (FEM **indemne**) ADJECTIVE
unharmed
□ Il s'en est sorti indemne. He escaped unharmed.

indemniser VERB [28]
to compensate
□ Les victimes demandent maintenant à être indemnisées. The victims are now demanding compensation.

indépendamment ADVERB
independently
■ **indépendamment de** irrespective of □ Les allocations familiales sont versées indépendamment des revenus. Child benefit is given irrespective of income.

l'**indépendance** FEM NOUN
independence

★ **indépendant** (FEM **indépendante**) ADJECTIVE
independent

l'**index** MASC NOUN
1 index finger
2 index (*in book*)

★ **indicatif** (FEM **indicative**) ADJECTIVE
▷ *see also* **indicatif** NOUN
■ **à titre indicatif** for your information

★ l'**indicatif** MASC NOUN
▷ *see also* **indicatif** ADJECTIVE

1 dialling code
2 indicative (*of verb*)
3 theme tune (*of TV programme*)

les **indications** FEM PL NOUN
instructions
□ Il suffit de suivre les indications. You just have to follow the instructions.

l'**indice** MASC NOUN
clue
□ La police cherche des indices. The police are looking for clues.

★ **indien** (FEM **indienne**) ADJECTIVE, NOUN
Indian
■ **un Indien** an Indian (*man*)
■ **une Indienne** an Indian (*woman*)

l'**indifférence** FEM NOUN
indifference

indifférent (FEM **indifférente**) ADJECTIVE
indifferent

l'**indigène** MASC/FEM NOUN
native

indigeste (FEM **indigeste**) ADJECTIVE
indigestible

l'**indigestion** FEM NOUN
indigestion

indigne (FEM **indigne**) ADJECTIVE
unworthy

indigner VERB [28]
■ **s'indigner de quelque chose** to get indignant about something

indiqué (FEM **indiquée**) ADJECTIVE
advisable
□ Ce n'est pas très indiqué. It's not really advisable.

★ **indiquer** VERB [28]
to point out
□ Il m'a indiqué la mairie. He pointed out the town hall.

indirect (FEM **indirecte**) ADJECTIVE
indirect

indiscipliné (FEM **indisciplinée**) ADJECTIVE
unruly

indiscret (FEM **indiscrète**) ADJECTIVE
indiscreet

★ **indispensable** (FEM **indispensable**) ADJECTIVE
indispensable

indisposé (FEM **indisposée**) ADJECTIVE
indisposed
■ **être indisposée** to be having one's period

★ l'**individu** MASC NOUN
individual

★ **individuel** (FEM **individuelle**) ADJECTIVE
ir
□ une portion individuelle an individual
■ **une chambre individuelle** a single room (*in hotel*)
■ **Vous aurez une chambre individuelle.** You'll have a room of your own.

indolore (FEM **indolore**) ADJECTIVE
painless

l'**Indonésie** FEM NOUN
Indonesia

indulgent (FEM **indulgente**) ADJECTIVE
indulgent
■ **Elle est trop indulgente avec son fils.** She's not firm enough with her son.

★ l'**industrie** FEM NOUN
industry

★ **industriel** (FEM **industrielle**) ADJECTIVE
▷ *see also* **industriel** NOUN
industrial

★ l'**industriel** MASC NOUN
▷ *see also* **industriel** ADJECTIVE
industrialist

inédit (FEM **inédite**) ADJECTIVE
unpublished

inefficace (FEM **inefficace**) ADJECTIVE
1 ineffective (*treatment*)
2 inefficient
□ un service de transports publics inefficace an inefficient public transport system

inégal (FEM **inégale**, MASC PL **inégaux**) ADJECTIVE
1 unequal
□ un combat inégal an unequal struggle
2 uneven
■ **La qualité est inégale.** The quality varies.

inévitable (FEM **inévitable**) ADJECTIVE
unavoidable
■ **C'était inévitable!** That was bound to happen!

inexact (FEM **inexacte**) ADJECTIVE
inaccurate

in extremis ADVERB
■ **Il a réussi à attraper son train in extremis.** He just managed to catch his train.
■ **Ils ont évité un accident in extremis.** They avoided an accident by the skin of their teeth.

l'**infarctus** MASC NOUN
coronary

infatigable (FEM **infatigable**) ADJECTIVE
indefatigable
□ Il est infatigable. He's indefatigable.

infect (FEM **infecte**) ADJECTIVE
revolting (*meal*)

s'**infecter** VERB [28]
to go septic
□ La plaie s'est infectée. The wound has gone septic.

French-English

l'**infection** FEM NOUN
infection

inférieur (FEM **inférieure**) ADJECTIVE
lower
□ les membres inférieurs the lower limbs
□ C'est moins cher, mais de qualité inférieure. It's cheaper but of lower quality.

infernal (FEM **infernale**, MASC PL **infernaux**) ADJECTIVE
terrible
□ Ils faisaient un bruit infernal. They were making a terrible noise.

l'**infini** MASC NOUN
■ **à l'infini** indefinitely □ On pourrait en parler à l'infini. We could discuss this indefinitely.

l'**infinitif** MASC NOUN
infinitive

l'**infirme** MASC/FEM NOUN
disabled person

l'**infirmerie** FEM NOUN
medical room
□ Elle est à l'infirmerie. She's in the medical room.

★ l'**infirmier** MASC NOUN
(male) nurse

★ l'**infirmière** FEM NOUN
(female) nurse

inflammable (FEM **inflammable**) ADJECTIVE
inflammable

l'**influence** FEM NOUN
influence

influencer VERB [12]
to influence

★ l'**informaticien** MASC NOUN
computer scientist

★ l'**informaticienne** FEM NOUN
computer scientist

★ les **informations** FEM PL NOUN
1 news (*on TV*)
□ les informations de vingt heures the 8 o'clock news
2 information
□ Je voudrais quelques informations, s'il vous plaît. I'd like some information, please.
■ **une information** a piece of information

★ l'**informatique** FEM NOUN
computing

★ **informer** VERB [28]
to inform
■ **s'informer** to find out □ Je vais m'informer des heures de fermeture. I'm going to find out when they close.

infuser VERB [28]
1 to brew (*tea*)
2 to infuse (*herbal tea*)

l'**infusion** FEM NOUN
herbal tea

★ l'**ingénieur** MASC/FEM NOUN
engineer

ingrat (FEM **ingrate**) ADJECTIVE
ungrateful

l'**ingrédient** MASC NOUN
ingredient

inhabituel (FEM **inhabituelle**) ADJECTIVE
unusual

l'**inhalateur** MASC NOUN
inhaler

inhumain (FEM **inhumaine**) ADJECTIVE
inhuman

initial (FEM **initiale**, MASC PL **initiaux**) ADJECTIVE
▷ *see also* **initiale** NOUN
initial

l'**initiale** FEM NOUN
▷ *see also* **initial** ADJECTIVE
initial

l'**initiation** FEM NOUN
introduction
□ un stage d'initiation à la planche à voile an introductory course in windsurfing

l'**initiative** FEM NOUN
initiative
□ avoir de l'initiative to have initiative

injecter VERB [28]
to inject

l'**injection** FEM NOUN
injection

l'**injure** FEM NOUN
1 insult
□ Il a pris ça comme une injure. He took this as an insult.
2 abuse
□ lancer des injures à quelqu'un to hurl abuse at somebody

BE CAREFUL!
The French word **injure** does not mean **injury**.

injurier VERB [19]
to insult

injurieux (FEM **injurieuse**) ADJECTIVE
abusive (*language*)

injuste (FEM **injuste**) ADJECTIVE
unfair

★ **innocent** (FEM **innocente**) ADJECTIVE
innocent

innombrable (FEM **innombrable**) ADJECTIVE
innumerable

innover VERB [28]
to break new ground

i

inoccupé (FEM **inoccupée**) ADJECTIVE
empty
□ un appartement inoccupé an empty flat

inoffensif (FEM **inoffensive**) ADJECTIVE
harmless

★ l'**inondation** FEM NOUN
flood

inoubliable (FEM **inoubliable**) ADJECTIVE
unforgettable

inoxydable (FEM **inoxydable**) ADJECTIVE
■ **l'acier inoxydable** stainless steel

★ **inquiet** (FEM **inquiète**) ADJECTIVE
worried

inquiétant (FEM **inquiétante**) ADJECTIVE
worrying

s'**inquiéter** VERB [34]
to worry
□ Ne t'inquiète pas! Don't worry!

l'**inquiétude** FEM NOUN
anxiety

insatisfait (FEM **insatisfaite**) ADJECTIVE
dissatisfied

l'**inscription** FEM NOUN
registration (*for school, course*)

s'**inscrire** VERB [30]
■ **s'inscrire à** 1 to join □ Je me suis inscrit au club de tennis. I've joined the tennis club.
2 to register □ N'attends pas trop pour t'inscrire à la fac. Don't leave it too long to register at the university.

★ l'**insecte** MASC NOUN
insect

insensible (FEM **insensible**) ADJECTIVE
insensitive
□ Il la trouve insensible. He thinks she's insensitive.

l'**insigne** MASC NOUN
badge

insignifiant (FEM **insignifiante**) ADJECTIVE
insignificant

insister VERB [28]
to insist
■ **N'insiste pas!** Don't keep on!

★ l'**insolation** FEM NOUN
sunstroke

insolent (FEM **insolente**) ADJECTIVE
cheeky

insouciant (FEM **insouciante**) ADJECTIVE
carefree

insoutenable (FEM **insoutenable**) ADJECTIVE
unbearable
□ une douleur insoutenable an unbearable pain

inspecter VERB [28]
to inspect

★ l'**inspecteur** MASC NOUN
inspector

l'**inspection** FEM NOUN
inspection

★ l'**inspectrice** FEM NOUN
inspector

inspirer VERB [28]
1 to inspire
■ **s'inspirer de** to take one's inspiration from
□ Le peintre s'est inspiré d'un poème. The painter took his inspiration from a poem.
2 to breathe in
□ Inspirez! Expirez! Breathe in! Breathe out!

instable (FEM **instable**) ADJECTIVE
1 unsteady (*piece of furniture*)
2 unstable (*person*)

les **installations** FEM PL NOUN
facilities
□ Cet appartement est pourvu de toutes les installations modernes. This flat has all modern facilities.

★ **installer** VERB [28]
1 to put up (*shelves*)
2 to install (*gas, telephone*)
■ **s'installer** to settle in □ Nous nous sommes installés dans notre nouvel appartement. We've settled into our new flat.
■ **Installez-vous, je vous en prie.** Have a seat, please.

★ l'**instant** MASC NOUN
moment
□ pour l'instant for the moment
■ **dans un instant** in a moment □ Le dîner sera prêt dans un instant. Dinner will be ready in a moment.

instantané (FEM **instantanée**) ADJECTIVE
instant
□ du café instantané instant coffee

l'**instinct** MASC NOUN
instinct

l'**institut** MASC NOUN
institute

★ l'**instituteur** MASC NOUN
primary school teacher

l'**institution** FEM NOUN
institution

★ l'**institutrice** FEM NOUN
primary school teacher

l'**instruction** FEM NOUN
1 instruction
□ J'ai suivi ses instructions. I followed his instructions.
2 education
□ Il n'a pas beaucoup d'instruction. He's not very well-educated.

s'**instruire** VERB [23]
to educate oneself

★ **instruit** (FEM **instruite**) ADJECTIVE
educated

★ l'**instrument** MASC NOUN
instrument
□ un instrument de musique a musical instrument

insuffisant (FEM **insuffisante**) ADJECTIVE
insufficient
■ **'travail insuffisant'** (*on school report*) 'must try harder'

l'**insuline** FEM NOUN
insulin

insultant (FEM **insultante**) ADJECTIVE
insulting
□ Il s'est montré insultant avec elle. He was insulting to her.

l'**insulte** FEM NOUN
insult

★ **insulter** VERB [28]
to insult

★ **insupportable** (FEM **insupportable**) ADJECTIVE
unbearable

intact (FEM **intacte**) ADJECTIVE
intact

intégral (FEM **intégrale**, MASC PL **intégraux**) ADJECTIVE
■ **le texte intégral** unabridged version
■ **un remboursement intégral** a full refund

l'**intégrisme** MASC NOUN
fundamentalism

l'**intelligence** FEM NOUN
intelligence

★ **intelligent** (FEM **intelligente**) ADJECTIVE
intelligent

intense (FEM **intense**) ADJECTIVE
intense

intensif (FEM **intensive**) ADJECTIVE
intensive
■ **un cours intensif** a crash course

★ l'**intention** FEM NOUN
intention
■ **avoir l'intention de faire quelque chose** to intend to do something □ J'ai l'intention de lui en parler. I intend to speak to him about it.

l'**interdiction** FEM NOUN
■ **'interdiction de stationner'** 'no parking'
■ **'interdiction de fumer'** 'no smoking'

★ **interdire** VERB [27]
to forbid
□ Ses parents lui ont interdit de sortir. His parents have forbidden him to go out.

★ **interdit** (FEM **interdite**) ADJECTIVE
forbidden
□ Il est interdit de fumer dans les couloirs. Smoking in the corridors is forbidden.

★ **intéressant** (FEM **intéressante**) ADJECTIVE
interesting
□ un livre intéressant an interesting book
■ **On lui a fait une offre intéressante.** They made him an attractive offer.
■ **On trouve des CD à des prix très intéressants dans ce magasin.** You can get very cheap CDs in this shop.

★ **intéresser** VERB [28]
to interest
■ **s'intéresser à** to be interested in □ Est-ce que vous vous intéressez à la politique? Are you interested in politics?

★ l'**intérêt** MASC NOUN
interest
■ **avoir intérêt à faire quelque chose** to do well to do something □ Tu as intérêt à accepter. You'd do well to accept.

★ l'**intérieur** MASC NOUN
inside
□ à l'intérieur de la maison inside the house

l'**interlocuteur** MASC NOUN
■ **son interlocuteur** the man he's speaking to

l'**interlocutrice** FEM NOUN
■ **son interlocutrice** the woman he's speaking to

l'**intermédiaire** MASC NOUN
intermediary
■ **par l'intermédiaire de** through □ Je l'ai rencontré par l'intermédiaire de sa sœur. I met him through his sister.

★ l'**internat** MASC NOUN
boarding school

★ **international** (FEM **internationale**, MASC PL **internationaux**) ADJECTIVE
international

l'**internaute** MASC/FEM NOUN
internet user

★ l'**interne** MASC/FEM NOUN
boarder

l'**Internet** MASC NOUN
internet
□ sur Internet on the internet

l'**interphone** MASC NOUN
intercom

★ l'**interprète** MASC/FEM NOUN
interpreter

interpréter VERB [34]
to interpret

interrogatif (FEM **interrogative**) ADJECTIVE
interrogative

l'**interrogation** FEM NOUN
1 question
2 test
□ une interrogation écrite a written test □ une interrogation orale an oral test

French-English

i

l'**interrogatoire** MASC NOUN
questioning
■ **C'est un interrogatoire ou quoi?** Am I being cross-examined?

interroger VERB [45]
to question

interrompre VERB [75]
to interrupt

l'**interrupteur** MASC NOUN
switch

l'**interruption** FEM NOUN
interruption
■ **sans interruption** without stopping □ Il a parlé pendant deux heures sans interruption. He spoke for two hours without stopping.

l'**intervalle** MASC NOUN
interval
■ **dans l'intervalle** in the meantime

★**intervenir** VERB [89, *aux* **être**]
1 to intervene
2 to take action
□ La police est intervenue. The police took action.

l'**intervention** FEM NOUN
intervention
□ une intervention militaire a military intervention
■ **une intervention chirurgicale** an operation (*surgical*)

★l'**interview** FEM NOUN
interview (*on radio, TV*)

l'**intestin** MASC NOUN
intestine

intime (FEM **intime**) ADJECTIVE
intimate
■ **un journal intime** a diary

intimider VERB [28]
to intimidate

l'**intimité** FEM NOUN
■ **dans l'intimité** in private □ Ce que vous faites dans l'intimité ne m'intéresse pas. What you do in private doesn't interest me.
■ **Le mariage a eu lieu dans l'intimité.** The wedding ceremony was private.

intitulé (FEM **intitulée**) ADJECTIVE
entitled

intolérable (FEM **intolérable**) ADJECTIVE
intolerable

l'**intoxication** FEM NOUN
■ **une intoxication alimentaire** food poisoning

l'**Intranet** MASC NOUN
intranet

intransigeant (FEM **intransigeante**) ADJECTIVE
uncompromising

l'**intrigue** FEM NOUN
plot (*of book, film*)

l'**introduction** FEM NOUN
introduction

★**introduire** VERB [23]
to introduce

l'**intuition** FEM NOUN
intuition

inusable (FEM **inusable**) ADJECTIVE
hard-wearing

★**inutile** (FEM **inutile**) ADJECTIVE
useless
■ **Il est inutile d'attendre.** There's no point in waiting.

l'**invalide** MASC/FEM NOUN
person with a disability

l'**invasion** FEM NOUN
invasion

★**inventer** VERB [28]
1 to invent
2 to make up
□ inventer une excuse to make up an excuse

l'**inventeur** MASC NOUN
inventor

l'**invention** FEM NOUN
invention

inverse (FEM **inverse**) ADJECTIVE
▷ *see also* **inverse** NOUN
■ **dans l'ordre inverse** in reverse order
■ **en sens inverse** in the opposite direction

l'**inverse** MASC NOUN
▷ *see also* **inverse** ADJECTIVE
reverse
■ **Tu t'es trompé, c'est l'inverse.** You've got it wrong, it's the other way round.

l'**investissement** MASC NOUN
investment

invisible (FEM **invisible**) ADJECTIVE
invisible

★l'**invitation** FEM NOUN
invitation

l'**invité** MASC NOUN
guest

l'**invitée** FEM NOUN
guest

★**inviter** VERB [28]
to invite

involontaire (FEM **involontaire**) ADJECTIVE
unintentional
□ C'était tout à fait involontaire. It was quite unintentional.

invraisemblable (FEM **invraisemblable**) ADJECTIVE
unlikely
□ une histoire invraisemblable an unlikely story

ira, irai, iraient, irais VERB ▷ *see* **aller**
■ **J'irai demain au supermarché.** I'll go to the supermarket tomorrow.

l'**Irak** MASC NOUN
Iraq

l'**Iran** MASC NOUN
Iran

iras, irez VERB ▷ *see* **aller**

★**irlandais** (FEM **irlandaise**) ADJECTIVE, NOUN
Irish
■ **un Irlandais** an Irishman
■ **une Irlandaise** an Irishwoman
■ **les Irlandais** the Irish

★l'**Irlande** FEM NOUN
Ireland
■ **en Irlande** **1** in Ireland **2** to Ireland
■ **la République d'Irlande** the Irish Republic
■ **l'Irlande du Nord** Northern Ireland

l'**ironie** FEM NOUN
irony

ironique (FEM **ironique**) ADJECTIVE
ironical

irons, iront VERB ▷ *see* **aller**
■ **Nous irons à la plage cet après-midi.** We'll go to the beach this afternoon.

irrationnel (FEM **irrationnelle**) ADJECTIVE
irrational

irréel (FEM **irréelle**) ADJECTIVE
unreal

irrégulier (FEM **irrégulière**) ADJECTIVE
irregular

irrésistible (FEM **irrésistible**) ADJECTIVE
irresistible

irritable (FEM **irritable**) ADJECTIVE
irritable

irriter VERB [28]
to irritate

islamique (FEM **islamique**) ADJECTIVE
Islamic

l'**Islande** FEM NOUN
Iceland

isolé (FEM **isolée**) ADJECTIVE
isolated
□ une ferme isolée an isolated farm

Israël MASC NOUN
Israel

israélien (FEM **israélienne**) ADJECTIVE, NOUN
Israeli
■ **un Israélien** an Israeli (*man*)
■ **une Israélienne** an Israeli (*woman*)
■ **les Israéliens** the Israelis

l'**issue** FEM NOUN
■ **une voie sans issue** a dead end
■ **l'issue de secours** emergency exit

★l'**Italie** FEM NOUN
Italy
■ **en Italie** **1** in Italy **2** to Italy

★**italien** (FEM **italienne**) ADJECTIVE, NOUN
Italian
□ J'apprends l'italien. I'm learning Italian.
■ **un Italien** an Italian (*man*)
■ **une Italienne** an Italian (*woman*)
■ **les Italiens** the Italians

l'**itinéraire** MASC NOUN
route

l'**IUT** MASC NOUN (= *Institut universitaire de technologie*)
institute of technology (*at university level*)

★**ivre** (FEM **ivre**) ADJECTIVE
drunk

l'**ivrogne** MASC/FEM NOUN
drunkard

French-English

i

Jj

★ **j'** PRONOUN ▷ *see* **je**

la **jalousie** FEM NOUN
jealousy

★ **jaloux** (FEM **jalouse**) ADJECTIVE
jealous

★ **jamais** ADVERB
▪ **ne ... jamais** never
□ Ils ne vont jamais au cinéma? They never go to the cinema.
▪ **Il va souvent en vacances? — Non, jamais.** Does he go on holiday often? — No, never.

> Phrases with **jamais** meaning 'ever' are followed by a verb in the subjunctive.

□ C'est la plus belle chose que j'aie jamais vue. It's the most beautiful thing I've ever seen.

★ la **jambe** FEM NOUN
leg

★ le **jambon** MASC NOUN
ham
▪ **le jambon cru** Parma ham

le **jambonneau** (PL les **jambonneaux**) MASC NOUN
knuckle of ham

★ **janvier** MASC NOUN
January
▪ **en janvier** in January

★ le **Japon** MASC NOUN
Japan
▪ **au Japon** **1** in Japan **2** to Japan

★ **japonais** (FEM **japonaise**) ADJECTIVE, NOUN
Japanese
□ Elle parle japonais. She speaks Japanese.
▪ **un Japonais** a Japanese (*man*)
▪ **une Japonaise** a Japanese (*woman*)
▪ **les Japonais** the Japanese

★ le **jardin** MASC NOUN
garden
□ un jardin potager a vegetable garden

★ le **jardinage** MASC NOUN
gardening

★ le **jardinier** MASC NOUN
gardener

★ la **jardinière** FEM NOUN
gardener

★ **jaune** (FEM **jaune**) ADJECTIVE
▷ *see also* **jaune** NOUN
yellow

★ le **jaune** MASC NOUN
▷ *see also* **jaune** ADJECTIVE
yellow
▪ **un jaune d'œuf** an egg yolk

jaunir VERB [38]
to turn yellow

la **jaunisse** FEM NOUN
jaundice

Javel NOUN
▪ **l'eau de Javel** bleach

le **jazz** MASC NOUN
jazz

J.-C. ABBREVIATION= **Jésus-Christ**
▪ **44 avant J.-C.** 44 BC
▪ **115 après J.-C.** 115 AD

★ **je** PRONOUN

> **je** changes to **j'** before a vowel and most words beginning with 'h'.

I
□ Je t'appellerai ce soir. I'll phone you this evening. □ J'arrive! I'm coming! □ J'hésite. I'm not sure.

★ le **jean** MASC NOUN
jeans

la **jeannette** FEM NOUN
Brownie
□ Elle est jeannette. She's a Brownie.

Jésus-Christ MASC NOUN
Jesus Christ

le **jet** MASC NOUN
1 jet (*of water*)
▪ **un jet d'eau** a fountain
2 jet plane

jetable (FEM **jetable**) ADJECTIVE
disposable

la **jetée** FEM NOUN
jetty

★ **jeter** VERB [41]
1 to throw
□ Il a jeté son sac sur le lit. He threw his bag onto the bed.

2 to throw away
□ Ils ne jettent jamais rien. They never throw anything away.
■ **jeter un coup d'œil** to have a look

le **jeton** MASC NOUN
counter (*in board game*)

★ le **jeu** (PL les **jeux**) MASC NOUN
game
□ Les enfants jouaient à un jeu. The children were playing a game.
■ **un jeu d'arcade** an arcade video game
■ **un jeu de cartes** 1 a pack of cards 2 a card game
■ **un jeu de mots** a pun
■ **un jeu de société** a board game
■ **un jeu électronique** an electronic game
■ **les jeux sur ordinateur** computer gaming
■ **les jeux sur téléphone portable** mobile gaming
■ **les jeux vidéo** video games
■ **en jeu** at stake □ Des vies humaines sont en jeu. Human lives are at stake.

★ le **jeudi** MASC NOUN
1 Thursday
□ Aujourd'hui, nous sommes jeudi. It's Thursday today.
2 on Thursday
□ Il arrivera jeudi matin. He's arriving on Thursday morning.
■ **le jeudi** on Thursdays □ Le musée est fermé le jeudi. The museum is closed on Thursdays.
■ **tous les jeudis** every Thursday
■ **jeudi dernier** last Thursday
■ **jeudi prochain** next Thursday

jeun
■ **à jeun** ADVERB on an empty stomach □ à prendre à jeun to be taken on an empty stomach □ Il faut être à jeun pour la prise de sang. You shouldn't have eaten anything before giving a blood sample.

★ **jeune** (FEM **jeune**) ADJECTIVE
▷ *see also* **jeune** NOUN
young
□ un jeune homme a young man □ une jeune femme a young woman
■ **une jeune fille** a girl

★ le/la **jeune** MASC/FEM NOUN
▷ *see also* **jeune** ADJECTIVE
young person
□ les jeunes young people

★ la **jeunesse** FEM NOUN
youth

★ le **job** MASC NOUN (*informal*)
job

★ le **jogging** MASC NOUN
1 jogging
□ Il fait du jogging. He goes jogging.
2 tracksuit
□ un jogging rose a pink tracksuit

★ la **joie** FEM NOUN
joy

joindre VERB [42]
1 to put together
□ On va joindre les deux tables. We're going to put the two tables together.
2 to contact
□ Vous pouvez le joindre chez lui. You can contact him at home.

joint (FEM **jointe**) ADJECTIVE
■ **une pièce jointe** (*in email*) an attachment

★ **joli** (FEM **jolie**) ADJECTIVE
pretty
□ un joli village a pretty village

le **jonc** MASC NOUN
rush

la **jonquille** FEM NOUN
daffodil

la **joue** FEM NOUN
cheek

★ **jouer** VERB [28]
1 to play
□ Viens jouer avec nous. Come and play with us.
■ **jouer de** to play (*instrument*) □ Il joue de la guitare et du piano. He plays the guitar and the piano.
■ **jouer à** to play (*sport, game*) □ Elle joue au tennis. She plays tennis. □ jouer aux cartes to play cards
2 to act
□ Je trouve qu'il joue très bien dans ce film. I think he acts very well in this film.
■ **On joue Hamlet au Théâtre de la Ville.** Hamlet is on at the Théâtre de la Ville.

★ le **jouet** MASC NOUN
toy

★ le **joueur** MASC NOUN
player
■ **un joueur sur ordinateur** a computer gamer
■ **être mauvais joueur** to be a bad loser

★ la **joueuse** FEM NOUN
player

★ le **jour** MASC NOUN
day
□ J'ai passé trois jours chez mes cousins. I stayed with my cousins for three days.
■ **Il fait jour.** It's daylight.
■ **mettre quelque chose à jour** to update something
■ **le jour de l'An** New Year's Day
■ **un jour de congé** a day off
■ **un jour férié** a public holiday
■ **dans huit jours** in a week
■ **dans quinze jours** in a fortnight

★le **journal** (PL les **journaux**) MASC NOUN
1 newspaper
■ **le journal télévisé** the television news
2 diary
□ Elle tient un journal depuis l'âge de douze ans. She has been keeping a diary since she was 12.

journalier (FEM **journalière**) ADJECTIVE
daily

le **journalisme** MASC NOUN
journalism

★le/la **journaliste** MASC/FEM NOUN
journalist
□ Elle est journaliste. She's a journalist.

★la **journée** FEM NOUN
day

★**joyeux** (FEM **joyeuse**) ADJECTIVE
happy
■ **Joyeux anniversaire!** Happy birthday!
■ **Joyeux Noël!** Merry Christmas!

★le **judo** MASC NOUN
judo

★le **juge** MASC NOUN
judge

★**juger** VERB [45]
to judge

★**juif** (FEM **juive**) ADJECTIVE, NOUN
Jewish
□ la cuisine juive Jewish cooking
■ **un Juif** a Jew (*man*)
■ **une Juive** a Jew (*woman*)

★**juillet** MASC NOUN
July
■ **en juillet** in July

★**juin** MASC NOUN
June
■ **en juin** in June

★le **jumeau** (PL les **jumeaux**) MASC NOUN
twin
□ des frères jumeaux twin brothers

★**jumeler** VERB [4]
to twin
□ Saint-Brieuc est jumelée avec Aberystwyth. Saint-Brieuc is twinned with Aberystwyth.

★la **jumelle** FEM NOUN
twin
□ des sœurs jumelles twin sisters

les **jumelles** FEM PL NOUN
binoculars

la **jument** FEM NOUN
mare

la **jungle** FEM NOUN
jungle

★la **jupe** FEM NOUN
skirt

jurer VERB [28]
to swear
□ Je jure que c'est vrai! I swear it's true!

juridique (FEM **juridique**) ADJECTIVE
legal

le **jury** MASC NOUN
jury

★le **jus** MASC NOUN
juice
■ **un jus de fruit** a fruit juice

★**jusqu'à** PREPOSITION
1 as far as
□ Nous avons marché jusqu'au village. We walked as far as the village.
2 until
□ Il fait généralement chaud jusqu'à la mi-août. It's usually hot until mid-August.
■ **jusqu'à ce que** until □ Tu peux rester ici jusqu'à ce qu'il cesse de pleuvoir. You can stay here until it stops raining.
■ **jusqu'à présent** so far

★**jusque** PREPOSITION
as far as
□ Je l'ai raccompagnée jusque chez elle. I went with her as far as her house. □ Jusqu'ici nous n'avons pas eu de problèmes. So far we've had no problems. □ Jusqu'où es-tu allé? How far did you go?

★**juste** (FEM **juste**) ADJECTIVE, ADVERB
1 fair
□ Il est sévère, mais juste. He's strict but fair.
2 tight
□ Cette veste est un peu juste. This jacket is a bit tight.
■ **juste assez** just enough
■ **chanter juste** to sing in tune

justement ADVERB
just
□ C'est justement pour cela qu'il est parti! That's just the reason he left!

la **justesse** FEM NOUN
■ **de justesse** only just □ Il a eu son permis de justesse. He only just passed his driving test.

la **justice** FEM NOUN
justice

justifier VERB [19]
to justify

juteux (FEM **juteuse**) ADJECTIVE
juicy

juvénile (FEM **juvénile**) ADJECTIVE
youthful

 Numbers in brackets refer to verb tables on pages 650 to 658

Kk

kaki (FEM+PL **kaki**) ADJECTIVE
khaki

le **kangourou** MASC NOUN
kangaroo

le **karaté** MASC NOUN
karate

la **kermesse** FEM NOUN
fair

kidnapper VERB [28]
to kidnap

kiffer VERB [28] (*informal*)
to be into
□ Il kiffe le foot. He's into football.

★ le **kilo** MASC NOUN
kilo

★ le **kilogramme** MASC NOUN
kilogram

★ le **kilomètre** MASC NOUN
kilometre

le/la **kiné** MASC/FEM NOUN
physio

le/la **kinésithérapeute** MASC/FEM NOUN
physiotherapist

★ le **kiosque** MASC NOUN
■ **un kiosque à journaux** a news stand

le **kit** MASC NOUN
kit
□ en kit in kit form □ un kit mains libres a hands-free kit □ un kit piéton a hands-free kit

le **klaxon** MASC NOUN
horn (*of car*)

klaxonner VERB [28]
to sound the horn

km ABBREVIATION (= *kilomètre*)
km (= *kilometre*)

km/h ABBREVIATION (= *kilomètres/heure*)
kph (= *kilometres per hour*)

KO (FEM+PL **KO**) ADJECTIVE
knocked out
■ **mettre quelqu'un KO** to knock somebody out □ Il l'a mis KO au troisième round. He knocked him out in the third round.
■ **Je suis complètement KO.** (*informal*) I'm completely knackered.

le **K-way**® MASC NOUN
cagoule

Ll

★ **l'** ARTICLE, PRONOUN ▷ *see* **la, le**

★ **la** ARTICLE, PRONOUN
▷ *see also* **la** NOUN

la changes to **l'** before a vowel and most words beginning with 'h'.

1 the
□ la maison the house □ l'actrice the actress □ l'herbe the grass
2 her
□ Je la connais depuis longtemps. I've known her for a long time. □ C'est une femme intelligente: je l'admire beaucoup. She's an intelligent woman: I admire her very much.
3 it
□ C'est une bonne émission: je la regarde tous les jours. It's a good programme: I watch it every day.
4 one's
■ **se mordre la langue** to bite one's tongue □ Je me suis mordu la langue. I've bitten my tongue.
■ **six euros la douzaine** six euros a dozen

le **la** MASC NOUN
▷ *see also* **la** ARTICLE, PRONOUN
1 A
□ en la bémol in A flat
2 la
□ sol, la, si, do so, la, ti, do

★ **là** ADVERB
1 there
□ Ton livre est là, sur la table. Your book's there, on the table.
2 here
□ Elle n'est pas là. She isn't here.
■ **C'est là que ...** **1** That's where ... □ C'est là que je suis né. That's where I was born. **2** That's when ... □ C'est là que j'ai réalisé que je m'étais trompé. That's when I realized that I had made a mistake.

★ **là-bas** ADVERB
over there
□ Ma maison est là-bas. My house is over there.

★ le **labo** MASC NOUN (*informal*)
lab

★ le **laboratoire** MASC NOUN
laboratory

labourer VERB [28]
to plough

le **labyrinthe** MASC NOUN
maze

★ le **lac** MASC NOUN
lake

lacer VERB [12]
to do up (*shoes*)

le **lacet** MASC NOUN
lace
■ **des chaussures à lacets** lace-up shoes

lâche (FEM **lâche**) ADJECTIVE
▷ *see also* **lâche** NOUN
1 loose
□ Le nœud est trop lâche. The knot's too loose.
2 cowardly
■ **Il est lâche.** He's a coward.

le **lâche** MASC/FEM NOUN
▷ *see also* **lâche** ADJECTIVE
coward

lâcher VERB [28]
1 to let go of
□ Il n'a pas lâché ma main de tout le film. He didn't let go of my hand until the end of the film.
2 to drop
□ Il a été tellement surpris qu'il a lâché son verre. He was so surprised that he dropped his glass.
3 to fail
□ Les freins ont lâché. The brakes failed.

la **lâcheté** FEM NOUN
cowardice

lacrymogène (FEM **lacrymogène**) ADJECTIVE
■ **le gaz lacrymogène** tear gas

la **lacune** FEM NOUN
gap

là-dedans ADVERB
in there
□ Qu'est-ce qu'il y a là-dedans? What's in there?

là-dessous ADVERB
1 under there
□ Mon carnet d'adresses est quelque part

là-dessous. My address book is under there somewhere.
2 behind it
□ Il y a quelque chose de louche là-dessous. There's something fishy behind it.

là-dessus ADVERB
on there

★ **là-haut** ADVERB
up there

★ la **laïcité** FEM NOUN
secularism

★ **laid** (FEM **laide**) ADJECTIVE
ugly

la **laideur** FEM NOUN
ugliness

le **lainage** MASC NOUN
woollen garment

★ la **laine** FEM NOUN
wool
□ un pull en laine a wool jumper
■ **une laine polaire** a fleece (*jacket*)

laïque (FEM **laïque**) ADJECTIVE
■ **une école laïque** a non-denominational state school

la **laisse** FEM NOUN
lead
□ Tenez votre chien en laisse. Keep your dog on a lead.

★ **laisser** VERB [28]
1 to leave
□ J'ai laissé mon parapluie à la maison. I've left my umbrella at home.
2 to let
□ Laisse-le parler. Let him speak.
■ **Il se laisse aller.** He's letting himself go.

le **laisser-aller** MASC NOUN
carelessness

★ le **lait** MASC NOUN
milk
■ **un café au lait** a white coffee

★ la **laitue** FEM NOUN
lettuce

les **lambeaux** MASC PL NOUN
■ **en lambeaux** tattered

la **lame** FEM NOUN
blade
□ une lame de rasoir a razor blade

la **lamelle** FEM NOUN
thin strip

lamentable (FEM **lamentable**) ADJECTIVE
appalling

se **lamenter** VERB [28]
to moan

le **lampadaire** MASC NOUN
standard lamp

★ la **lampe** FEM NOUN
lamp
■ **une lampe de poche** a torch

la **lance** FEM NOUN
spear

le **lancement** MASC NOUN
launch

★ **lancer** VERB [12]
▷ *see also* **lancer** NOUN
1 to throw
□ Lance-moi le ballon! Throw me the ball!
2 to launch
□ Ils viennent de lancer un nouveau modèle. They've just launched a new model.
■ **se lancer dans** to embark on □ Il s'est lancé là-dedans sans bien réfléchir. He embarked on it without thinking properly.

★ le **lancer** MASC NOUN
▷ *see also* **lancer** VERB
■ **le lancer de poids** putting the shot

lancinant (FEM **lancinante**) ADJECTIVE
■ **une douleur lancinante** a shooting pain

le **landau** MASC NOUN
pram

la **lande** FEM NOUN
moor

le **langage** MASC NOUN
language

la **langouste** FEM NOUN
crayfish

★ la **langue** FEM NOUN
1 tongue
□ Il m'a tiré la langue. He stuck out his tongue at me.
2 language
□ une langue étrangère a foreign language
■ **les langues vivantes** modern languages
■ **sa langue maternelle** his mother tongue

la **lanière** FEM NOUN
strap

★ le **lapin** MASC NOUN
rabbit

le **laps** MASC NOUN
■ **un laps de temps** a space of time

la **laque** FEM NOUN
hair spray

laquelle (PL **lesquelles**) FEM PRONOUN
1 which
□ Laquelle de ces photos préfères-tu? Which of these photos do you prefer? □ À laquelle de tes sœurs ressembles-tu? Which of your sisters do you look like?
2 whom
□ la personne à laquelle vous faites référence the person to whom you are referring

laquelle is often not translated in English.

□ la personne à laquelle je pense the person I'm thinking of

le **lard** MASC NOUN
streaky bacon

les **lardons** MASC PL NOUN
chunks of bacon

★ **large** (FEM **large**) ADJECTIVE, ADVERB
▷ *see also* **large** NOUN
wide
■ **voir large** to allow a bit extra □ Achète un autre pain: il vaut mieux voir large. Buy another loaf of bread: it's better to have a bit extra.

★ le **large** MASC NOUN
▷ *see also* **large** ADJECTIVE, ADVERB
■ **cinq mètres de large** 5 m wide
■ **le large** the open sea
■ **au large de** off the coast of □ Le bateau est actuellement au large du Portugal. The boat is off the coast of Portugal at the moment.

> **BE CAREFUL!**
> The French word **large** does not mean **large**.

largement ADVERB
■ **Vous avez largement le temps.** You have plenty of time.
■ **C'est largement suffisant.** That's ample.

la **largeur** FEM NOUN
width

la **larme** FEM NOUN
tear
□ être en larmes to be in tears

la **laryngite** FEM NOUN
laryngitis

le **laser** MASC NOUN
laser
■ **une platine laser** a compact disc player
■ **un disque laser** a compact disc

lasser VERB [28]
■ **se lasser de** to get tired of □ Tu vas te lasser de cette couleur. You're going to get tired of this colour.

★ le **latin** MASC NOUN
Latin

le **laurier** MASC NOUN
laurel tree
□ une feuille de laurier a bay leaf

lavable (FEM **lavable**) ADJECTIVE
washable

★ le **lavabo** MASC NOUN
washbasin

★ le **lavage** MASC NOUN
wash
□ Ce pull a rétréci au lavage. This jumper has shrunk in the wash.

la **lavande** FEM NOUN
lavender

le **lave-linge** (PL les **lave-linges**, les **lave-linge**) MASC NOUN
washing machine

★ **laver** VERB [28]
to wash
■ **se laver** to wash □ se laver les mains to wash one's hands

la **laverie** FEM NOUN
■ **une laverie automatique** a launderette

★ le **lave-vaisselle** (PL les **lave-vaisselles**, les **lave-vaisselle**) MASC NOUN
dishwasher

★ **le** ARTICLE, PRONOUN

> **le** changes to **l'** before a vowel and most words beginning with 'h'.

1 the
□ le livre the book □ l'arbre the tree
□ l'hélicoptère the helicopter
2 him
□ Martin est un vieil ami: je le connais depuis plus de vingt ans. Martin is an old friend: I've known him for over 20 years.
3 it
□ Où est mon stylo? Je ne le trouve plus. Where's my pen? I can't find it. □ Où est le fromage? — Je l'ai mis au frigo. Where's the cheese? — I've put it in the fridge.
4 one's
■ **se laver le visage** to wash one's face
□ Évitez de vous laver le visage avec du savon. Avoid washing your face with soap.
■ **dix euros le kilo** 10 euros a kilo
■ **Il est arrivé le douze mai.** He arrived on 12 May.

lécher VERB [34]
to lick

le **lèche-vitrine** MASC NOUN
■ **faire du lèche-vitrine** to go window-shopping

★ la **leçon** FEM NOUN
lesson

★ le **lecteur** MASC NOUN
1 reader
2 foreign language assistant (*at a university*)
■ **un lecteur de CD** a CD player
■ **un lecteur de DVD** a DVD player
■ **un lecteur MP3** an MP3 player

la **lectrice** FEM NOUN
1 reader
2 foreign language assistant (*at a university*)

★ la **lecture** FEM NOUN
reading

> **BE CAREFUL!**
> The French word **lecture** does not mean **lecture**.

Numbers in brackets refer to verb tables on pages 650 to 658

légal (FEM **légale**, MASC PL **légaux**) ADJECTIVE
legal

la **légende** FEM NOUN
1 legend
2 key (*of map*)
3 caption (*of picture*)

★ **léger** (FEM **légère**) ADJECTIVE
1 light
2 slight
□ un léger retard a slight delay
■ **à la légère** thoughtlessly □ Il a agi à la légère. He acted thoughtlessly.

légèrement ADVERB
1 lightly
□ Habille-toi légèrement: il va faire chaud. Wear light clothes: it's going to be hot.
2 slightly
□ Il est légèrement plus grand que son frère. He's slightly taller than his brother.

★ les **leggings** MASC PL NOUN
leggings

les **législatives** FEM PL NOUN
general election *sing*

★ le **légume** MASC NOUN
vegetable

★ le **lendemain** MASC NOUN
next day
■ **le lendemain de son arrivée** the day after he arrived
■ **le lendemain matin** the next morning

★ **lent** (FEM **lente**) ADJECTIVE
slow

★ **lentement** ADVERB
slowly

la **lenteur** FEM NOUN
slowness

la **lentille** FEM NOUN
1 contact lens
□ Est-ce que tu portes des lentilles? Do you wear contact lenses?
2 lentil
□ un rôti de porc aux lentilles roast pork with lentils

le **léopard** MASC NOUN
leopard

★ le **LEP** MASC NOUN (= *lycée d'enseignement professionnel*)
vocational school

lequel (FEM **laquelle**, MASC PL **lesquels**, FEM PL **lesquelles**) PRONOUN
1 which
□ Lequel de ces films as-tu préféré? Which of the films did you prefer?
2 whom
□ l'homme avec lequel elle a été vue pour la dernière fois the man with whom she was last seen

lequel is often not translated in English.

□ le garçon avec lequel elle est sortie the boy she went out with

les ARTICLE, PRONOUN
1 the
□ les arbres the trees
2 them
□ Elle les a invités à dîner. She invited them to dinner.
3 one's
■ **se brosser les dents** to brush one's teeth
□ Elle s'est brossé les dents. She brushed her teeth.
■ **dix euros les cinq** 10 euros for 5

la **lesbienne** FEM NOUN
lesbian

lesquels (FEM **lesquelles**) PL PRONOUN
1 which
□ Lesquelles de ces photos préfères-tu? Which of the photos do you prefer?
2 whom
□ les personnes avec lesquelles il est associé the people with whom he is in partnership

lesquels is often not translated in English.

□ les gens chez lesquels nous avons dîné the people we had dinner with

★ la **lessive** FEM NOUN
1 washing powder
□ une marque de lessive a brand of washing powder
2 washing
□ Il y a beaucoup de lessive à faire. There's a lot of washing to do.
■ **faire la lessive** to do the washing

leste (FEM **leste**) ADJECTIVE
nimble

la **Lettonie** FEM NOUN
Latvia

★ la **lettre** FEM NOUN
letter
□ écrire une lettre to write a letter
■ **une lettre de motivation** a covering letter (*with CV*)

les **lettres** FEM PL NOUN
arts
□ la faculté de lettres the Faculty of Arts

★ **leur** (FEM **leur**) ADJECTIVE, PRONOUN
1 their
□ leur ami their friend
2 them
□ Je leur ai dit la vérité. I told them the truth.
3 to them
□ Je le leur ai donné. I gave it to them.

■ **le leur** theirs □ mon camion et le leur my truck and theirs □ Ma voiture est rouge, la leur est bleue. My car's red, theirs is blue.

★ **leurs** (FEM **leurs**) PL ADJECTIVE, PL PRONOUN
their
□ leurs amis their friends
■ **les leurs** theirs □ tes livres et les leurs your books and theirs

★ **levé** (FEM **levée**) ADJECTIVE
▷ *see also* **levée** NOUN
■ **être levé** to be up □ Est-ce qu'il est levé? Is he up?

★ la **levée** FEM NOUN
▷ *see also* **levé** ADJECTIVE
collection (*of mail*)
□ Prochaine levée: 17 heures Next collection: 5 p.m.

★ **lever** VERB [43]
▷ *see also* **lever** NOUN
to raise
□ Levez vos verres! Raise your glasses!
■ **Levez la main!** Put your hand up!
■ **lever les yeux** to look up
■ **se lever** **1** to get up □ Il se lève tous les jours à six heures. He gets up at 6 o'clock every day. □ Lève-toi! Get up! **2** to rise □ Le soleil se lève actuellement à cinq heures. At the moment the sun rises at 5 o'clock. **3** to stand up □ Levez-vous! Stand up!

★ le **lever** MASC NOUN
▷ *see also* **lever** VERB
■ **le lever du soleil** sunrise

le **levier** MASC NOUN
lever

★ la **lèvre** FEM NOUN
lip

le **lévrier** MASC NOUN
greyhound

la **levure** FEM NOUN
yeast
■ **la levure chimique** baking powder

le **lexique** MASC NOUN
word list

le **lézard** MASC NOUN
lizard

★ la **liaison** FEM NOUN
affair
□ Ils ont eu une liaison dans leur jeunesse. They had an affair when they were younger.

la **libellule** FEM NOUN
dragonfly

libérer VERB [34]
to free
□ Les otages ont été libérés hier soir. The hostages were freed last night.
■ **se libérer** to find time □ J'essaierai de me libérer cet après-midi. I'll try to find time this afternoon.

★ la **liberté** FEM NOUN
freedom
■ **mettre en liberté** to release □ Il a été mis en liberté au bout d'un an de prison. He was released after a year in prison.

★ le/la **libraire** MASC/FEM NOUN
bookseller

★ la **librairie** FEM NOUN
bookshop

BE CAREFUL!
librairie does not mean **library**.

★ **libre** (FEM **libre**) ADJECTIVE
1 free
□ Tu es libre de faire ce que tu veux. You are free to do as you wish. □ Est-ce que cette place est libre? Is this seat free?
■ **Avez-vous une chambre de libre?** Have you got a free room?
2 clear
□ La route est libre: vous pouvez traverser. The road is clear: you can cross.

★ le **libre-service** (PL les **libres-services**) MASC NOUN
self-service store

la **Libye** FEM NOUN
Libya

★ la **licence** FEM NOUN
1 degree
□ une licence de droit a law degree
2 licence
□ une licence d'exportation an export licence

le **licencié** MASC NOUN
graduate

la **licenciée** FEM NOUN
graduate

★ le **licenciement** MASC NOUN
redundancy

★ **licencier** VERB [19]
to make redundant
□ Ils viennent de licencier sept employés. They've just made 7 employees redundant.

le **liège** MASC NOUN
cork
□ des sets en liège cork mats
■ **un bouchon en liège** a cork (*for bottle*)

★ le **lien** MASC NOUN
1 connection
□ Il n'y aucun lien entre ces deux événements. There's no connection between these two events.
■ **un lien de parenté** a family tie
2 link (*in computing*)

lier VERB [19]
■ **lier conversation avec quelqu'un** to get

into conversation with somebody
■ **se lier avec quelqu'un** to make friends with somebody □ Je ne me lie pas facilement. I don't make friends easily.

le **lierre** MASC NOUN
ivy

★le **lieu** (PL les **lieux**) MASC NOUN
place
□ votre lieu de travail your place of work
■ **avoir lieu** to take place □ La cérémonie a eu lieu dans la salle des fêtes. The ceremony took place in the village hall.
■ **au lieu de** instead of □ J'aimerais une pomme au lieu de la glace. I'd like an apple instead of ice cream.

le **lièvre** MASC NOUN
hare

★la **ligne** FEM NOUN
1 line (*phone, train*)
□ La ligne est mauvaise. It's a bad line.
■ **la ligne de bus numéro six** the number 6 bus
■ **en ligne** (*computing*) online
■ **mettre en ligne** (*computing*) to upload
■ **une ligne fixe** a landline □ Je t'appelle sur ta ligne fixe? Shall I ring you on your landline?
2 figure
□ C'est mauvais pour la ligne. It's bad for your figure.

ligoter VERB [28]
to tie up

la **ligue** FEM NOUN
league

le **lilas** MASC NOUN
lilac

la **limace** FEM NOUN
slug

la **lime** FEM NOUN
■ **une lime à ongles** a nail file

la **limitation** FEM NOUN
■ **la limitation de vitesse** the speed limit

la **limite** FEM NOUN
1 boundary (*of property, football pitch*)
2 limit
□ Est-ce qu'il y a une limite d'âge? Is there an age limit?
■ **À la limite, on pourrait prendre le bus.** At a pinch we could go by bus.
■ **la date limite** the deadline
■ **la date limite de vente** the sell-by date

limiter VERB [28]
to limit
□ Le nombre de billets est limité à deux par personne. The number of tickets is limited to two per person.

★la **limonade** FEM NOUN
lemonade

le **lin** MASC NOUN
linen
□ une veste en lin a linen jacket

★le **linge** MASC NOUN
1 linen
□ le linge sale dirty linen
2 washing
□ laver le linge to do the washing
■ **du linge de corps** underwear

la **lingerie** FEM NOUN
underwear (*women's*)

★le **lion** MASC NOUN
lion
■ **le Lion** Leo □ Louise est Lion. Louise is Leo.

★la **lionne** FEM NOUN
lioness

la **liqueur** FEM NOUN
liqueur

liquide (FEM **liquide**) ADJECTIVE
▷ *see also* **liquide** NOUN
liquid

le **liquide** MASC NOUN
▷ *see also* **liquide** ADJECTIVE
liquid
■ **payer quelque chose en liquide** to pay cash for something

★**lire** VERB [44]
to read
□ Tu as lu 'Madame Bovary'? Have you read 'Madame Bovary'?

lis, lisent, lisez VERB ▷ *see* **lire**
■ **Je lis beaucoup.** I read a lot.

lisible (FEM **lisible**) ADJECTIVE
legible

lisse (FEM **lisse**) ADJECTIVE
smooth

le **lisseur** MASC NOUN
hair straighteners

★la **liste** FEM NOUN
list
■ **faire la liste de** to make a list of □ J'ai fait la liste de tout ce dont j'ai besoin. I've made a list of all the things I need.

★le **lit** MASC NOUN
bed
□ un grand lit a double bed □ lits jumeaux twin beds □ aller au lit to go to bed
■ **faire son lit** to make one's bed □ Il ne fait jamais son lit. He never makes his bed.
■ **un lit de camp** a campbed

★**lit** VERB ▷ *see* **lire**

la **literie** FEM NOUN
bedding

la **litière** FEM NOUN
1 litter (*for cat*)
2 bedding (*of caged pet*)

★ le **litre** MASC NOUN
litre

littéraire (FEM **littéraire**) ADJECTIVE
■ **une œuvre littéraire** a work of literature

★ la **littérature** FEM NOUN
literature

le **littoral** (PL les **littoraux**) MASC NOUN
coast

la **Lituanie** FEM NOUN
Lithuania

la **livraison** FEM NOUN
delivery
■ **la livraison des bagages** baggage reclaim

★ le **livre** MASC NOUN
▷ *see also* **livre** NOUN
book
■ **un livre numérique** an e-book
■ **un livre de poche** a paperback

★ la **livre** FEM NOUN
▷ *see also* **livre** NOUN
pound

DID YOU KNOW...?
The French **livre** is 500 grams.

□ une livre de beurre a pound of butter
■ **la livre sterling** the pound sterling □ Ce jouet coûte trois livres. This toy costs £3.

★ **livrer** VERB [28]
to deliver

le **livret** MASC NOUN
booklet
■ **le livret scolaire** the school report book

le **livreur** MASC NOUN
delivery man

★ **local** (FEM **locale**, MASC PL **locaux**) ADJECTIVE
▷ *see also* **local** NOUN
local

★ le **local** (PL les **locaux**) MASC NOUN
▷ *see also* **local** ADJECTIVE
premises
□ Nous cherchons un local pour les répétitions. We are looking for premises to rehearse in.

★ le/la **locataire** MASC/FEM NOUN
1 tenant
2 lodger
□ Ils ont décidé de prendre un locataire. They have decided to take a lodger.

★ la **location** FEM NOUN
■ **location de voitures** car rental
■ **location de skis** ski hire

BE CAREFUL!
The French word **location** does not mean **location**.

la **locomotive** FEM NOUN
locomotive

la **loge** FEM NOUN
dressing room

★ le **logement** MASC NOUN
1 housing
2 accommodation

★ **loger** VERB [45]
to stay
□ Elle loge chez sa cousine quand elle revient dans la région. She stays with her cousin when she comes back to the area.
■ **trouver à se loger** to find somewhere to live □ J'ai eu du mal à trouver à me loger. I had difficulty finding somewhere to live.

★ le **logiciel** MASC NOUN
software

★ **logique** (FEM **logique**) ADJECTIVE
▷ *see also* **logique** NOUN
logical

★ la **logique** FEM NOUN
▷ *see also* **logique** ADJECTIVE
logic

★ la **loi** FEM NOUN
law

★ **loin** ADVERB
1 far
□ La gare n'est pas très loin d'ici. The station is not very far from here.
2 far off
□ Noël n'est plus tellement loin. Christmas isn't far off now.
3 a long time ago
□ Les vacances paraissent déjà tellement loin! The holidays already seem such a long time ago!
■ **au loin** in the distance □ On aperçoit la mer au loin. You can see the sea in the distance.
■ **de loin** 1 from a long way away □ On voit l'église de loin. You can see the church from a long way away. 2 by far □ C'est de loin l'élève la plus brillante. She is by far the brightest pupil.
■ **C'est plus loin que la gare.** It's further on than the station.

★ **lointain** (FEM **lointaine**) ADJECTIVE
▷ *see also* **lointain** NOUN
distant
□ un pays lointain a distant country □ C'est un lointain parent de ma mère. He's a distant relation of my mother.

★ le **lointain** MASC NOUN
▷ *see also* **lointain** ADJECTIVE
■ **dans le lointain** in the distance

le **loir** MASC NOUN
dormouse
■ **dormir comme un loir** to sleep like a log

★ les **loisirs** MASC PL NOUN
1 free time *sing*

□ Qu'est-ce que vous faites pendant vos loisirs? What do you do in your free time?.

2 hobby

□ Le ski et l'équitation sont des loisirs coûteux. Skiing and riding are expensive hobbies.

le **Londonien** MASC NOUN

Londoner

la **Londonienne** FEM NOUN

Londoner

★ **Londres** NOUN

London

□ le métro de Londres the London underground

■ **à Londres** 1 in London 2 to London

★ **long** (FEM **longue**) ADJECTIVE

▷ *see also* **long** NOUN, **longue** NOUN

long

★ le **long** MASC NOUN

▷ *see also* **long** ADJECTIVE

■ **un bateau de trois mètres de long** a boat 3 m long

■ **tout le long de** all along □ Il y a des chemins de randonnée tout le long de la côte. There are footpaths all along the coast.

■ **marcher de long en large** to walk up and down

longer VERB [45]

■ **La route longe la forêt.** The road runs along the edge of the forest.

■ **Nous avons longé la Seine à pied.** We walked along the Seine.

★ **longtemps** ADVERB

a long time

□ J'ai attendu longtemps chez le dentiste. I waited a long time at the dentist's.

■ **pendant longtemps** for a long time □ On a crû pendant longtemps que la Terre était plate. For a long time people thought the Earth was flat.

■ **mettre longtemps à faire quelque chose** to take a long time to do something □ Il a mis longtemps à répondre à ma lettre. He took a long time to answer my letter.

la **longue** FEM NOUN

▷ *see also* **long** ADJECTIVE

■ **à la longue** in the end □ Elle a fini par agacer tout le monde à la longue. In the end she got on everybody's nerves.

longuement ADVERB

at length

□ Elle m'a longuement parlé de ses projets d'avenir. She talked to me at length about her plans for the future.

la **longueur** FEM NOUN

length

■ **à longueur de journée** all day long □ Elle mâche du chewing-gum à longueur de journée. She chews gum all day long.

le **look** MASC NOUN

look

□ Il a un look d'enfer. He looks so cool.

les **loques** FEM PL NOUN

■ **être en loques** to be torn to bits □ Sa chemise était en loques. His shirt was torn to bits.

lors de PREPOSITION

during

□ Je l'ai rencontré lors de mon stage en entreprise. I met him during my work placement.

★ **lorsque** CONJUNCTION

when

□ J'allais composer ton numéro lorsque tu as appelé. I was about to dial your number when you called.

le **lot** MASC NOUN

prize

■ **le gros lot** the jackpot

★ la **loterie** FEM NOUN

1 lottery

□ la loterie nationale the National Lottery

2 raffle

□ J'ai gagné cet ours en peluche dans une loterie. I won this teddy in a raffle.

la **lotion** FEM NOUN

lotion

□ une bouteille de lotion solaire a bottle of suntan lotion

■ **une lotion après-rasage** aftershave

■ **une lotion démaquillante** cleansing milk

le **lotissement** MASC NOUN

housing estate

le **loto** MASC NOUN

lottery

■ **le loto sportif** the pools

le **loubard** MASC NOUN (*informal*)

lout

louche (FEM **louche**) ADJECTIVE

▷ *see also* **louche** NOUN

fishy

□ une histoire louche a fishy story

la **louche** FEM NOUN

▷ *see also* **louche** ADJECTIVE

ladle

loucher VERB [28]

to squint

★ **louer** VERB [28]

1 to let

□ Ils louent des chambres à des étudiants. They let rooms to students.

■ **'à louer'** 'to let'

2 to rent

□ Je loue un petit appartement au centre-ville. I rent a little flat in the centre of town.

3 to hire
□ Est-ce que vous louez des vélos? Do you hire bikes? □ Nous allons louer une voiture. We're going to hire a car.
4 to praise
□ Les journaux ont loué le courage des pompiers. The newspapers praised the courage of the firefighters.

★le **loup** MASC NOUN
wolf
■ **J'ai une faim de loup!** I'm ravenous!

la **loupe** FEM NOUN
magnifying glass

louper VERB [28] (*informal*)
to miss
□ J'ai loupé mon bus. I've missed my bus.

★**lourd** (FEM **lourde**) ADJECTIVE
▷ *see also* **lourd** ADVERB
heavy
□ Mon sac est très lourd. My bag's very heavy.

★**lourd** ADVERB
▷ *see also* **lourd** ADJECTIVE
close (*weather*)
□ Il fait très lourd aujourd'hui. It's very close today.

la **loutre** FEM NOUN
otter

la **loyauté** FEM NOUN
loyalty

★le **loyer** MASC NOUN
rent

lu VERB ▷ *see* **lire**

la **lucarne** FEM NOUN
skylight

la **luge** FEM NOUN
sledge

lugubre (FEM **lugubre**) ADJECTIVE
gloomy

★**lui** PRONOUN
1 him
□ Il a été très content du cadeau que je lui ai offert. He was very pleased with the present I gave him. □ C'est bien lui! It's definitely him! □ J'ai pensé à lui toute la journée. I thought about him all day long.
2 to him
□ Mon père est d'accord: je lui ai parlé ce matin. My father said yes: I spoke to him this morning.
3 her
□ Elle a été très contente du cadeau que je lui ai offert. She was very pleased with the present I gave her.
4 to her
□ Ma mère est d'accord: je lui ai parlé ce matin. My mother said yes: I spoke to her this morning.
5 it
□ Qu'est-ce que tu donnes à ton chat? — Je lui donne de la viande crue. What do you give your cat? — I give it raw meat.

lui is also used for emphasis.

□ Lui, il est toujours en retard! Oh him, he's always late!
■ **lui-même** himself □ Il a construit son bateau lui-même. He built his boat himself.

★la **lumière** FEM NOUN
light
■ **la lumière du jour** daylight

lumineux (FEM **lumineuse**) ADJECTIVE
■ **une enseigne lumineuse** a neon sign

lunatique (FEM **lunatique**) ADJECTIVE
temperamental
□ Il est plutôt lunatique. He's rather temperamental.

★le **lundi** MASC NOUN
1 Monday
□ Aujourd'hui, nous sommes lundi. It's Monday today.
2 on Monday
□ Ils sont arrivés lundi. They arrived on Monday.
■ **le lundi** on Mondays □ Le lundi, je vais à la piscine. I go swimming on Mondays.
■ **tous les lundis** every Monday
■ **lundi dernier** last Monday
■ **lundi prochain** next Monday
■ **le lundi de Pâques** Easter Monday

★la **lune** FEM NOUN
moon
■ **la lune de miel** honeymoon

★les **lunettes** FEM PL NOUN
glasses
■ **des lunettes de soleil** sunglasses
■ **des lunettes de plongée** swimming goggles

★la **lutte** FEM NOUN
1 fight
□ la lutte contre le racisme the fight against racism
2 wrestling
□ une épreuve de lutte a wrestling bout

★**lutter** VERB [28]
to fight

★le **luxe** MASC NOUN
luxury
■ **de luxe** luxury □ un hôtel de luxe a luxury hotel

★**luxueux** (FEM **luxueuse**) ADJECTIVE
luxurious

★le **lycée** MASC NOUN
secondary school
■ **lycée technique** technical college

DID YOU KNOW...?
In France, pupils go to a **collège** between the ages of 11 and 15, and then to a **lycée** until the age of 18.

★ le **lycéen** MASC NOUN
secondary school pupil

★ la **lycéenne** FEM NOUN
secondary school pupil

Mm

M. ABBREVIATION (= *Monsieur*)
Mr
□ M. Bernard Mr Bernard

★ **m'** PRONOUN ▷ *see* **me**

★ **ma** FEM ADJECTIVE
my
□ ma mère my mother □ ma montre my watch

les **macaronis** MASC PL NOUN
macaroni *sing*

la **Macédoine** FEM NOUN
Macedonia

la **macédoine** FEM NOUN
▪ **la macédoine de fruits** fruit salad
▪ **la macédoine de légumes** mixed vegetables

mâcher VERB [28]
to chew

★ le **machin** MASC NOUN (*informal*)
thingy
□ Passe-moi le machin pour râper les carottes. Pass me the thingy for grating carrots. □ Qu'est-ce que c'est que ce vieux machin? What's this old thing?

machinalement ADVERB
▪ **Elle a regardé sa montre machinalement.** She looked at her watch without thinking.

★ la **machine** FEM NOUN
machine
▪ **une machine à laver** a washing machine
▪ **une machine à écrire** a typewriter
▪ **une machine à coudre** a sewing machine
▪ **une machine à sous** a fruit machine

le **machiste** MASC NOUN
male chauvinist

le **macho** MASC NOUN (*informal*)
male chauvinist pig

la **mâchoire** FEM NOUN
jaw

mâchonner VERB [28]
to chew

★ le **maçon** MASC NOUN
builder

★ **Madame** (PL **Mesdames**) FEM NOUN
1 Mrs
□ Madame Legall Mrs Legall
2 lady
□ Occupez-vous de Madame. Could you look after this lady?
3 Madam
□ Madame, ... Dear Madam, ... (*in letter*)
▪ **Madame! Vous avez oublié votre parapluie!** Excuse me! You've forgotten your umbrella!

★ **Mademoiselle** (PL **Mesdemoiselles**) FEM NOUN
1 Miss
□ Mademoiselle Martin Miss Martin
2 Madam
□ Mademoiselle, ... Dear Madam, ... (*in letter*)

★ le **magasin** MASC NOUN
shop
□ Les magasins ouvrent à huit heures. The shops open at 8 o'clock.
▪ **faire les magasins** to go shopping

★ le **magazine** MASC NOUN
magazine

★ le **magicien** MASC NOUN
magician

★ la **magicienne** FEM NOUN
magician

la **magie** FEM NOUN
magic
□ un tour de magie a magic trick

★ **magique** (FEM **magique**) ADJECTIVE
magic
□ une baguette magique a magic wand

magistral (FEM **magistrale**, MASC PL **magistraux**) ADJECTIVE
▪ **un cours magistral** a lecture (*at university*)

magnétique (FEM **magnétique**) ADJECTIVE
magnetic

★ le **magnétoscope** MASC NOUN
video recorder

★ **magnifique** (FEM **magnifique**) ADJECTIVE
superb

★ **mai** MASC NOUN
May
▪ **en mai** in May

★ **maigre** (FEM **maigre**) ADJECTIVE
1 skinny
□ Ma mère me trouve trop maigre. My mother says I'm too skinny.

2 lean (*meat*)
3 low-fat (*cheese, yoghurt*)

maigrir VERB [38]
to lose weight
□ Il fait un régime pour essayer de maigrir. He's on a diet, to try to lose weight. □ Elle a maigri de deux kilos en un mois. She's lost two kilos in a month.

le **mail** MASC NOUN
email

★ le **maillot de bain** MASC NOUN
1 swimsuit
2 swimming trunks

★ la **main** FEM NOUN
hand
□ Donne-moi la main! Give me your hand!
■ **serrer la main à quelqu'un** to shake hands with somebody
■ **se serrer la main** to shake hands □ Les deux présidents se sont serré la main. The two presidents shook hands.
■ **sous la main** to hand □ Est-ce que tu as son adresse sous la main? Have you got his address to hand?

la **main-d'œuvre** FEM NOUN
workforce
□ la main-d'œuvre de l'usine the workforce of the factory
■ **la main-d'œuvre immigrée** immigrant labour

★ **maintenant** ADVERB
1 now
□ Qu'est-ce que tu veux faire maintenant? What do you want to do now? □ C'est maintenant ou jamais. It's now or never.
2 nowadays
□ Maintenant la plupart des gens font leurs courses au supermarché. Nowadays most people do their shopping at the supermarket.

maintenir VERB [83]
to maintain
□ Il maintient qu'il est innocent. He maintains he is innocent.
■ **se maintenir** to hold □ Espérons que le beau temps va se maintenir pour le week-end! Let's hope the good weather will hold over the weekend!

★ le **maire** MASC NOUN
mayor

★ la **mairie** FEM NOUN
town hall

★ **mais** CONJUNCTION
but
□ C'est cher mais de très bonne qualité. It's expensive, but very good quality.

le **maïs** MASC NOUN
1 maize
2 sweetcorn

★ la **maison** FEM NOUN
▷ *see also* **maison** ADJECTIVE
house
□ C'est la maison de Julie. It's Julie's house.
■ **une maison des jeunes** a youth club
■ **une maison individuelle** a detached house
■ **une maison jumelée** a semi-detached house
■ **une maison mitoyenne** a terraced house
■ **une maison de retraite** a retirement home
■ **à la maison** 1 at home □ Je serai à la maison cet après-midi. I'll be at home this afternoon. 2 home □ Elle est rentrée à la maison. She's gone home.

★ **maison** (FEM+PL **maison**) ADJECTIVE
▷ *see also* **maison** NOUN
home-made
□ Je préfère les tartes maison à celles qu'on achète. I prefer home-made pies to bought ones.

★ le **maître** MASC NOUN
1 teacher (*in primary school*)
2 master (*of dog*)
■ **un maître d'hôtel** a head waiter (*in restaurant*)
■ **un maître nageur** a lifeguard

★ la **maîtresse** FEM NOUN
1 teacher (*in primary school*)
2 mistress
□ Il paraît qu'il a une maîtresse. They say he's got a mistress.

la **maîtrise** FEM NOUN
master's degree
□ Elle a une maîtrise d'anglais. She's got a master's degree in English.
■ **la maîtrise de soi** self-control

maîtriser VERB [28]
■ **se maîtriser** to control oneself □ Il se met facilement en colère et a du mal à se maîtriser. He loses his temper easily and finds it hard to control himself.

majestueux (FEM **majestueuse**) ADJECTIVE
majestic

★ **majeur** (FEM **majeure**) ADJECTIVE
■ **être majeur** to be 18 □ Tu feras ce que tu voudras quand tu seras majeure. You can do what you like once you're 18. □ Elle sera majeure en août. She will be 18 in August.
■ **la majeure partie** most □ la majeure partie de mon salaire most of my salary

la **majorité** FEM NOUN
majority
□ dans la majorité des cas in the majority of cases
■ **la majorité et l'opposition** the government and the opposition

Majorque FEM NOUN
Majorca

la **majuscule** FEM NOUN
capital letter
□ un M majuscule a capital M

★ **mal** (FEM+PL **mal**) ADVERB, ADJECTIVE
▷ *see also* **mal** NOUN
1 badly
□ Ce travail a été mal fait. The work was badly done.
■ **Il a mal compris.** He misunderstood.
2 wrong
□ C'est mal de mentir. It's wrong to tell lies.
■ **aller mal** to be ill □ Son grand-père va très mal. His grandfather is very ill.
■ **pas mal** quite good □ Je te trouve pas mal sur cette photo. I think you look quite good in this photo.

★ le **mal** (PL les **maux**) MASC NOUN
▷ *see also* **mal** ADVERB, ADJECTIVE
1 ache
□ J'ai mal à la tête. I've got a headache. □ J'ai mal aux dents. I've got toothache.
■ **J'ai mal au dos.** My back hurts.
■ **Est-ce que vous avez mal à la gorge?** Have you got a sore throat?
■ **Ça fait mal.** It hurts.
■ **Où est-ce que tu as mal?** Where does it hurt?
■ **faire mal à quelqu'un** to hurt somebody
□ Attention, tu me fais mal! Be careful, you're hurting me!
■ **se faire mal** to hurt oneself □ Je me suis fait mal au bras. I hurt my arm.
■ **se donner du mal pour faire quelque chose** to go to a lot of trouble to do something
□ Il s'est donné beaucoup de mal pour que cette soirée soit réussie. He went to a lot of trouble to make the party a success.
■ **avoir le mal de mer** to be seasick
■ **avoir le mal du pays** to be homesick
2 evil
□ le bien et le mal good and evil
■ **dire du mal de quelqu'un** to speak ill of somebody

★ **malade** (FEM **malade**) ADJECTIVE
▷ *see also* **malade** NOUN
ill
■ **tomber malade** to fall ill

★ le/la **malade** MASC/FEM NOUN
▷ *see also* **malade** ADJECTIVE
patient

★ la **maladie** FEM NOUN
illness

maladif (FEM **maladive**) ADJECTIVE
sickly
□ C'est un enfant maladif. He's a sickly child.

la **maladresse** FEM NOUN
clumsiness

★ **maladroit** (FEM **maladroite**) ADJECTIVE
clumsy

le **malaise** MASC NOUN
■ **avoir un malaise** to feel faint □ Elle a eu un malaise après le déjeuner. She felt faint after lunch.
■ **Son arrivée a créé un malaise parmi les invités.** Her arrival made the guests feel uncomfortable.

★ la **malchance** FEM NOUN
bad luck

mâle (FEM **mâle**) ADJECTIVE
male

la **malédiction** FEM NOUN
curse

mal en point (FEM+PL **mal en point**) ADJECTIVE
■ **Il avait l'air mal en point quand je l'ai vu hier soir.** He didn't look too good when I saw him last night.

le **malentendu** MASC NOUN
misunderstanding

★ le **malfaiteur** MASC NOUN
criminal

mal famé (FEM **mal famée**, MASC PL **mal famés**) ADJECTIVE
■ **un quartier mal famé** a seedy area

malgache (FEM **malgache**) ADJECTIVE
from Madagascar
□ Sa mère est malgache. His mother's from Madagascar.

★ **malgré** PREPOSITION
in spite of
□ Il est toujours généreux malgré ses problèmes d'argent. He's always generous in spite of his financial problems.
■ **malgré tout** all the same □ Il faisait mauvais mais nous sommes sortis malgré tout. The weather was bad but we went out all the same.

le **malheur** MASC NOUN
tragedy
□ Elle a eu beaucoup de malheurs dans sa vie. She's had a lot of tragedy in her life.
■ **faire un malheur** (*informal*) to be a smash hit □ Leur dernier album a fait un malheur. Their latest album was a smash hit.

★ **malheureusement** ADVERB
unfortunately

★ **malheureux** (FEM **malheureuse**) ADJECTIVE
miserable
□ Il a l'air malheureux. He looks miserable.

★ **malhonnête** (FEM **malhonnête**) ADJECTIVE
dishonest

la **malice** FEM NOUN
mischief
□ Son regard était plein de malice. His eyes were full of mischief.

malicieux (FEM **malicieuse**) ADJECTIVE
mischievous

> **BE CAREFUL!**
> **malicieux** does not mean **malicious**.

malin (FEM **maligne**) ADJECTIVE
crafty
■ **C'est malin!** (*informal*) That's clever! □ Ah c'est malin! Nous voilà enfermés à cause de toi! That's clever! You've got us locked in!

la **malle** FEM NOUN
trunk

malsain (FEM **malsaine**) ADJECTIVE
unhealthy

Malte MASC NOUN
Malta

maltraiter VERB [28]
to ill-treat
□ Il maltraite son chien. He ill-treats his dog.
■ **des enfants maltraités** battered children

malveillant (FEM **malveillante**) ADJECTIVE
malicious
□ des rumeurs malveillantes malicious rumours

★ la **maman** FEM NOUN
mum

la **mamie** FEM NOUN
granny

le **mammifère** MASC NOUN
mammal

★ la **manche** FEM NOUN
▷ *see also* **manche** NOUN
1 sleeve (*of clothes*)
2 leg (*of game*)
□ Ils ont gagné la première manche du match. They won the first leg of the match.
■ **la Manche** the Channel

★ le **manche** MASC NOUN
▷ *see also* **manche** NOUN
handle (*of pan*)

la **mandarine** FEM NOUN
mandarin orange

le **manège** MASC NOUN
merry-go-round

la **manette** FEM NOUN
lever

mangeable (FEM **mangeable**) ADJECTIVE
edible
□ C'est à peine mangeable! It's practically inedible!

★ **manger** VERB [45]
to eat

la **mangue** FEM NOUN
mango

maniaque (FEM **maniaque**) ADJECTIVE
fussy

la **manie** FEM NOUN
1 obsession
■ **avoir la manie de** to be obsessive about
□ Il a la manie du rangement. He's obsessive about tidying up.
2 habit
□ J'essaie de respecter ses petites manies. I try to go along with her little ways.

manier VERB [19]
to handle

★ la **manière** FEM NOUN
▷ *see also* **manières** NOUN
way
■ **de manière à** so as to □ Nous sommes partis tôt de manière à éviter la circulation. We left early so as to avoid the traffic.
■ **de toute manière** in any case □ Je n'aurais pas pu venir de toute manière. I couldn't have come in any case.

★ **maniéré** (FEM **maniérée**) ADJECTIVE
affected

★ les **manières** FEM PL NOUN
▷ *see also* **manière** NOUN
1 manners
□ apprendre les bonnes manières to learn good manners
2 fuss
■ **Ne fais pas de manières: prends le dernier morceau!** Don't be shy, take the last bit!

le **manifestant** MASC NOUN
demonstrator

la **manifestante** FEM NOUN
demonstrator

★ la **manifestation** FEM NOUN
demonstration
□ une manifestation pour la paix a peace demonstration

★ **manifester** VERB [28]
to demonstrate

manipuler VERB [28]
1 to handle
□ Ce vase doit être manipulé avec soin. This vase must be handled with care.
2 to manipulate
□ Tous les partis essaient de manipuler l'opinion publique. All the parties are trying to manipulate public opinion.

★ le/la **mannequin** MASC/FEM NOUN
model
□ Elle est mannequin. She's a model.

manœuvrer VERB [28]
to manœuvre

★ le **manque** MASC NOUN

■ **le manque de** lack of □ Le manque de sommeil peut provoquer toutes sortes de troubles. Lack of sleep can cause all sorts of problems.

■ **un drogué en état de manque** a drug addict suffering withdrawal symptoms

manqué (FEM **manquée**) ADJECTIVE

■ **un garçon manqué** a tomboy

★ **manquer** VERB [28]

to miss

□ Tu n'as rien manqué: c'était nul. You didn't miss anything: it was rubbish. □ Il manque des pages à ce livre. There are some pages missing from this book.

■ **Mes parents me manquent.** I miss my parents.

■ **Ma sœur me manque.** I miss my sister.

■ **Il manque encore dix euros.** We are still 10 euros short.

■ **manquer de** to lack □ La quiche manque de sel. The quiche lacks salt.

■ **Je trouve qu'il a manqué de tact.** I don't think he was very tactful.

■ **Il a manqué se tuer.** He nearly got killed.

★ le **manteau** (PL les **manteaux**) MASC NOUN

coat

★ **manuel** (FEM **manuelle**) ADJECTIVE

▷ *see also* **manuel** NOUN

manual

★ le **manuel** MASC NOUN

▷ *see also* **manuel** ADJECTIVE

1 textbook

2 handbook

le **maquereau** (PL les **maquereaux**) MASC NOUN

mackerel

la **maquette** FEM NOUN

model

□ une maquette de bateau a model boat

★ le **maquillage** MASC NOUN

make-up

★ se **maquiller** VERB [28]

to put on one's make-up

□ Je vais me maquiller en vitesse. I'll just quickly put on my make-up.

le **marais** MASC NOUN

marsh

le **marbre** MASC NOUN

marble

□ une statue en marbre a marble statue

★ le **marchand** MASC NOUN

1 shopkeeper

■ **un marchand de journaux** a newsagent

2 stallholder (*in market*)

★ la **marchande** FEM NOUN

1 shopkeeper

■ **une marchande de fruits et de légumes** a greengrocer

2 stallholder (*in market*)

marchander VERB [28]

to haggle

la **marchandise** FEM NOUN

goods

la **marche** FEM NOUN

1 step

□ Fais attention à la marche! Mind the step!

2 walking

□ La marche me fait du bien. Walking does me good.

■ **être en état de marche** to be in working order □ Cette voiture est en parfait état de marche. This car is in perfect running order.

■ **Ne montez jamais dans un train en marche.** Never try to get onto a moving train.

■ **mettre en marche** to start □ Comment est-ce qu'on met la machine à laver en marche? How do you start the washing machine?

■ **la marche arrière** reverse gear

■ **faire marche arrière** to reverse

3 march

□ une marche militaire a military march

★ le **marché** MASC NOUN

market

■ **un marché aux puces** a flea market

■ **le marché noir** the black market

★ **marcher** VERB [28]

1 to walk

□ Elle marche cinq kilomètres par jour. She walks 5 kilometres every day.

2 to run

□ Le métro marche normalement aujourd'hui. The underground is running normally today.

3 to work

□ Est-ce que l'ascenseur marche? Is the lift working?

4 to go well

□ Est-ce que les affaires marchent actuellement? Is business going well at the moment?

■ **Alors les études, ça marche?** (*informal*) How are you getting on at school?

■ **faire marcher quelqu'un** to pull somebody's leg □ Il essaie de te faire marcher. He's pulling your leg.

le **marcheur** MASC NOUN

walker

la **marcheuse** FEM NOUN

walker

★ le **mardi** MASC NOUN

1 Tuesday

□ Aujourd'hui, nous sommes mardi. It's Tuesday today.

2 on Tuesday
□ Ils reviennent mardi. They're coming back on Tuesday.
■ **le mardi** on Tuesdays □ Le mardi, je vais à la gym. I go to the gym on Tuesdays.
■ **tous les mardis** every Tuesday
■ **mardi dernier** last Tuesday
■ **mardi prochain** next Tuesday
■ **Mardi gras** Shrove Tuesday

la **mare** FEM NOUN
pond

le **marécage** MASC NOUN
marsh

★ la **marée** FEM NOUN
tide
□ la marée haute high tide □ la marée basse low tide □ la marée montante the rising tide
□ la marée descendante the ebb tide
■ **une marée noire** an oil slick

la **margarine** FEM NOUN
margarine

la **marge** FEM NOUN
margin

★ le **mari** MASC NOUN
husband
□ son mari her husband

★ le **mariage** MASC NOUN
1 marriage
2 wedding
□ un mariage civil a registry office wedding
□ un mariage religieux a church wedding

★ **marié** (FEM **mariée**) ADJECTIVE
▷ *see also* **marié** NOUN, **mariée** NOUN
married

★ le **marié** MASC NOUN
▷ *see also* **marié** ADJECTIVE
bridegroom
■ **les mariés** the bride and groom

★ la **mariée** FEM NOUN
▷ *see also* **marié** ADJECTIVE
bride

★ se **marier** VERB [19]
to marry
□ Elle s'est mariée avec un ami d'enfance. She married a childhood friend.

★ **marin** (FEM **marine**) ADJECTIVE
▷ *see also* **marin** NOUN, **marine** NOUN, ADJECTIVE
sea
□ l'air marin the sea air
■ **un pull marin** a sailor's jersey

★ le **marin** MASC NOUN
▷ *see also* **marin** ADJECTIVE
sailor

marine (FEM+PL **marine**) ADJECTIVE
▷ *see also* **marine** NOUN, **marin** ADJECTIVE
■ **bleu marine** navy-blue □ un pull bleu marine a navy-blue sweater

la **marine** FEM NOUN
▷ *see also* **marin** ADJECTIVE, **marine** ADJECTIVE
navy
■ **la marine nationale** the French navy

la **marionnette** FEM NOUN
puppet

★ le **marketing** MASC NOUN
marketing

la **marmelade** FEM NOUN
stewed fruit
■ **la marmelade de pommes** stewed apples
■ **la marmelade d'oranges** marmalade

★ la **marmite** FEM NOUN
cooking pot

marmonner VERB [28]
to mumble

★ le **Maroc** MASC NOUN
Morocco

★ **marocain** (FEM **marocaine**) ADJECTIVE, NOUN
Moroccan

la **maroquinerie** FEM NOUN
leather goods shop

marquant (FEM **marquante**) ADJECTIVE
significant
□ un événement marquant a significant event

★ la **marque** FEM NOUN
1 mark
□ des marques de doigts fingermarks
2 make
□ De quelle marque est ton jean? What make are your jeans?
3 brand
□ une grande marque de cognac a well-known brand of cognac
■ **l'image de marque** the public image □ Le ministre tient à son image de marque. The minister cares about his public image.
■ **une marque déposée** a registered trademark
■ **À vos marques! Prêts! Partez!** Ready, steady, go!

★ **marquer** VERB [28]
1 to mark
□ Peux-tu marquer sur la carte où se trouve le village? Can you mark where the village is on the map?
2 to score
□ L'équipe irlandaise a marqué dix points. The Irish team scored ten points.
3 to celebrate
□ On va sortir au restaurant pour marquer ton anniversaire. We'll eat out to celebrate your birthday.

la **marraine** FEM NOUN
godmother

★ **marrant** (FEM **marrante**) ADJECTIVE
(*informal*)
funny

French-English

★ **marre** ADVERB (*informal*)
■ **en avoir marre de quelque chose** to be fed up with something □ J'en ai marre de faire la vaisselle. I'm fed up with doing the dishes.

se **marrer** VERB [28] (*informal*)
to have a good laugh
□ On s'est bien marrés. We had a good laugh.

★ le **marron** MASC NOUN
▷ *see also* **marron** ADJECTIVE
chestnut
□ la crème de marrons chestnut purée

★ **marron** (FEM+PL **marron**) ADJECTIVE
▷ *see also* **marron** NOUN
brown
□ des chaussures marron brown shoes

le **marronnier** MASC NOUN
chestnut tree

★ **mars** MASC NOUN
March
■ **en mars** in March

le **marteau** (PL les **marteaux**) MASC NOUN
hammer

martyriser VERB [28]
to batter
□ des enfants martyrisés battered children

masculin (FEM **masculine**) ADJECTIVE
1 men's
□ la mode masculine men's fashion
2 masculine
□ 'Chat' est un nom masculin. 'Chat' is a masculine noun. □ Elle a une allure assez masculine. She looks rather masculine.

m

le **masque** MASC NOUN
mask

le **massacre** MASC NOUN
massacre

massacrer VERB [28]
to massacre

le **massage** MASC NOUN
massage

la **masse** FEM NOUN
■ **une masse de** (*informal*) masses of □ J'ai une masse de choses à faire. I've got masses of things to do.
■ **produire en masse** to mass-produce □ des meubles produits en masse mass-produced furniture
■ **venir en masse** to come en masse □ Les gens sont venus en masse pour accueillir le président. People came en masse to welcome the president.

masser VERB [28]
to massage
■ **se masser** to gather □ Les manifestants se sont massés devant l'ambassade. The demonstrators gathered in front of the embassy.

massif (FEM **massive**) ADJECTIVE
1 solid (*gold, silver, wood*)
□ un bracelet en or massif a solid gold bracelet
2 massive
□ une dose massive d'antibiotiques a massive dose of antibiotics
3 mass
□ des départs massifs a mass exodus

mat (FEM **mate**) ADJECTIVE
matt
□ blanc mat matt white □ Je voudrais mes photos en mat. I would like my photos matt.
■ **être mat** to be checkmate (*chess*)

★ le **match** MASC NOUN
match
□ un match de football a football match
■ **le match aller** the first leg
■ **le match retour** the second leg
■ **faire match nul** to draw

★ le **matelas** MASC NOUN
mattress
■ **un matelas pneumatique** an air bed

matelassé (FEM **matelassée**) ADJECTIVE
quilted
□ une veste matelassée a quilted jacket

le **matelot** MASC NOUN
sailor

les **matériaux** MASC PL NOUN
materials

★ le **matériel** MASC NOUN
1 equipment
□ du matériel de laboratoire laboratory equipment
2 gear
□ Il a pris tout son matériel de pêche avec lui. He took all his fishing gear with him.

maternel (FEM **maternelle**) ADJECTIVE
▷ *see also* **maternelle** NOUN
motherly
□ Elle est très maternelle. She's very motherly.
■ **ma grand-mère maternelle** my mother's mother
■ **mon oncle maternel** my mother's brother

★ la **maternelle** FEM NOUN
▷ *see also* **maternel** ADJECTIVE
nursery school

DID YOU KNOW...?
The **maternelle** is a state school for 2–6 year-olds.

la **maternité** FEM NOUN
■ **le congé de maternité** maternity leave
□ Notre professeur de musique est en congé de maternité. Our music teacher is on maternity leave.

★ les **mathématiques** FEM PL NOUN
mathematics

★ les **maths** FEM PL NOUN (*informal*)
maths

★ la **matière** FEM NOUN
subject
□ Le latin est une matière facultative. Latin is an optional subject.
■ **sans matières grasses** fat-free
■ **les matières premières** raw materials

★ le **matin** MASC NOUN
morning
□ à trois heures du matin at 3 o'clock in the morning □ du matin au soir from morning till night
■ **Je suis du matin.** I'm at my best in the morning.
■ **de bon matin** early in the morning

matinal (FEM **matinale**, MASC PL **matinaux**) ADJECTIVE
morning
□ Je fais ma gymnastique matinale avant de déjeuner. I do my morning exercises before breakfast.
■ **être matinal** to be up early □ Tu es bien matinal aujourd'hui! You're up early today!

★ la **matinée** FEM NOUN
morning
□ Je t'appellerai demain dans la matinée. I'll call you sometime tomorrow morning. □ en début de matinée early in the morning

le **matou** MASC NOUN
tomcat

maudire VERB [46]
to curse

maudit (FEM **maudite**) ADJECTIVE (*informal*)
blasted
□ Où est passé ce maudit parapluie? Where's that blasted umbrella got to?

★ **maussade** (FEM **maussade**) ADJECTIVE
sullen

★ **mauvais** (FEM **mauvaise**) ADJECTIVE, ADVERB
1 bad
□ une mauvaise note a bad mark □ Tu arrives au mauvais moment. You've come at a bad time.
■ **Il fait mauvais.** The weather's bad.
■ **être mauvais en** to be bad at □ Je suis mauvais en allemand. I'm bad at German.
2 poor
□ J'ai trouvé que le film était mauvais. I thought the film was poor. □ Il est en mauvaise santé. His health is poor.
■ **Tu as mauvaise mine.** You don't look well.
3 wrong
□ Vous avez fait le mauvais numéro. You've dialled the wrong number.
■ **des mauvaises herbes** weeds
■ **sentir mauvais** to smell

les **maux** MASC PL NOUN ▷ *see* **mal** NOUN
■ **des maux de ventre** stomachache
■ **des maux de tête** headache

★ **maximal** (FEM **maximale**, MASC PL **maximaux**) ADJECTIVE
maximum

le **maximum** MASC NOUN
maximum
■ **au maximum** **1** as much as one can
□ Remplis le seau au maximum. Fill the bucket as full as you can. **2** at the very most
□ Ça va vous coûter deux cents euros au maximum. It'll cost you 200 euros at the very most.

★ la **mayonnaise** FEM NOUN
mayonnaise

le **mazout** MASC NOUN
fuel oil

★ **me** PRONOUN

> **me** changes to **m'** before a vowel and most words beginning with 'h'.

1 me
□ Elle me téléphone tous les jours. She phones me every day. □ Il m'attend depuis une heure. He's been waiting for me for an hour.
2 to me
□ Il me parle en allemand. He talks to me in German. □ Elle m'a expliqué la situation. She explained the situation to me.
3 myself
□ Je vais me préparer quelque chose à manger. I'm going to make myself something to eat.

> With reflexive verbs, **me** is often not translated.

□ Je me lève à sept heures tous les matins. I get up at 7 every morning.

le **mec** MASC NOUN (*informal*)
guy

★ le **mécanicien** MASC NOUN
mechanic

la **mécanique** FEM NOUN
1 mechanics
2 mechanism (*of watch, clock*)

le **mécanisme** MASC NOUN
mechanism

méchamment ADVERB
nastily
□ Il lui a répondu méchamment. He answered him nastily.

la **méchanceté** FEM NOUN
nastiness

★ **méchant** (FEM **méchante**) ADJECTIVE
nasty
□ C'est un homme méchant. He's a nasty man. □ Ne sois pas méchant avec ton petit

frère. Don't be nasty to your little brother.
■ **'Attention, chien méchant'** 'Beware of the dog'

la **mèche** FEM NOUN
lock (*of hair*)

★**mécontent** (FEM **mécontente**) ADJECTIVE
■ **mécontent de** unhappy with □ Elle est mécontente de sa coupe de cheveux. She's unhappy with her haircut.

le **mécontentement** MASC NOUN
displeasure
□ Il a exprimé son mécontentement. He expressed his displeasure.

la **médaille** FEM NOUN
medal

★le **médecin** MASC NOUN
doctor
□ aller chez le médecin to go to the doctor

★la **médecine** FEM NOUN
medicine (*subject*)
□ Il fait médecine. He's studying medicine.

les **médias** MASC PL NOUN
media *sing*
■ **étude des médias** media studies

médical (FEM **médicale**, MASC PL **médicaux**) ADJECTIVE
medical
□ la recherche médicale medical research
■ **passer une visite médicale** to have a medical

★le **médicament** MASC NOUN
medicine (*drug*)

médiéval (FEM **médiévale**, MASC PL **médiévaux**) ADJECTIVE
medieval

médiocre (FEM **médiocre**) ADJECTIVE
poor
□ des notes médiocres poor marks

★la **Méditerranée** FEM NOUN
Mediterranean

méditerranéen (FEM **méditerranéenne**) ADJECTIVE
Mediterranean

la **méduse** FEM NOUN
jellyfish

la **méfiance** FEM NOUN
mistrust

méfiant (FEM **méfiante**) ADJECTIVE
mistrustful

se **méfier** VERB [19]
■ **se méfier de quelqu'un** to distrust somebody □ Si j'étais toi, je me méfierais de lui. If I were you, I wouldn't trust him.

le **mégaoctet** MASC NOUN
megabyte

la **mégarde** FEM NOUN
■ **par mégarde** by mistake □ J'ai emporté son livre par mégarde. I took his book by mistake.

le **mégot** MASC NOUN
cigarette end

★**meilleur** (FEM **meilleure**) ADJECTIVE, ADVERB, NOUN
better
□ Ce serait meilleur avec du fromage râpé. It would be better with grated cheese. □ Il paraît que le film est meilleur que le livre. They say that the film is better than the book.
■ **le meilleur** the best □ le meilleur joueur de l'équipe the best player in the team □ Je préfère garder le meilleur pour la fin. I like to keep the best for last. □ C'est elle qui est la meilleure en sport. She's the best at sport.
■ **le meilleur des deux** the better of the two
■ **meilleur marché** cheaper □ La bière est meilleur marché en France. Beer's cheaper in France.

★le **mél** MASC NOUN
email

mélancolique (FEM **mélancolique**) ADJECTIVE
melancholy

le **mélange** MASC NOUN
mixture

★**mélanger** VERB [45]
1 to mix
□ Mélangez le tout. Mix everything together.
2 to muddle up
□ Tu mélanges tout! You're muddling everything up!

la **mêlée** FEM NOUN
scrum

★**mêler** VERB [28]
■ **se mêler** to mix □ Il ne cherche pas à se mêler aux autres. He doesn't try to mix with the others.
■ **Mêle-toi de ce qui te regarde!** (*informal*) Mind your own business!

la **mélodie** FEM NOUN
melody

★le **melon** MASC NOUN
melon

★le **membre** MASC NOUN
1 limb
2 member
□ un membre de la famille a member of the family □ les pays membres de l'Union européenne the member countries of the European Union

★**mème** MASC NOUN
meme

★**même** (FEM **même**) ADJECTIVE, ADVERB, PRONOUN
1 same
□ J'ai le même manteau. I've got the same

coat. □ Tiens, c'est curieux, j'ai le même! That's strange, I've got the same one!
■ **en même temps** at the same time
■ **moi-même** myself □ Je l'ai fait moi-même. I did it myself.
■ **toi-même** yourself □ Est-ce que tu vas faire les travaux toi-même? Are you going to do the work yourself?
■ **eux-mêmes** themselves

2 even
□ Il n'a même pas pleuré. He didn't even cry.
■ **même si** even if □ Je ne ferais jamais ça, même si tu me le demandais. I'd never do that, even if you asked me. □ Même si j'aime les maths, je trouve ça difficile. Although I like maths, I find it difficult.

la **mémé** FEM NOUN (*informal*)
granny

la **mémoire** FEM NOUN
memory

la **menace** FEM NOUN
threat

★ **menacer** VERB [12]
to threaten

★ le **ménage** MASC NOUN
housework
□ faire le ménage to do the housework
■ **une femme de ménage** a cleaning woman

ménager (FEM **ménagère**) ADJECTIVE
■ **les travaux ménagers** housework
■ **les arts ménagers** food technology

★ la **ménagère** FEM NOUN
housewife

le **mendiant** MASC NOUN
beggar

la **mendiante** FEM NOUN
beggar

mendier VERB [19]
to beg

★ **mener** VERB [43]
to lead
□ Cette rue mène directement à la gare. This street leads straight to the station.
■ **Cela ne vous mènera à rien!** That will get you nowhere!

la **méningite** FEM NOUN
meningitis

les **menottes** FEM PL NOUN
handcuffs

★ le **mensonge** MASC NOUN
lie

la **mensualité** FEM NOUN
monthly payment
□ en dix mensualités in ten monthly payments

★ **mensuel** (FEM **mensuelle**) ADJECTIVE
monthly

les **mensurations** FEM PL NOUN
measurements

la **mentalité** FEM NOUN
mentality

le **menteur** MASC NOUN
liar

la **menteuse** FEM NOUN
liar

la **menthe** FEM NOUN
mint

la **mention** FEM NOUN
grade
□ Il a été reçu avec mention bien. He got a grade B pass.

mentionner VERB [28]
to mention

★ **mentir** VERB [77]
to lie
□ Tu mens! You're lying!

★ le **menton** MASC NOUN
chin

★ **menu** (FEM **menue**) ADJECTIVE, ADVERB
▷ *see also* **menu** NOUN

1 slim
□ Elle est menue. She's slim. □ Elle est petite et menue. She's petite.

2 very fine
□ Les oignons doivent être coupés menu. The onions have to be cut up very fine.

★ le **menu** MASC NOUN
▷ *see also* **menu** ADJECTIVE, ADVERB
menu
□ le menu du jour today's menu □ le menu touristique the tourist menu □ le menu d'aide (*on a computer*) the help menu

la **menuiserie** FEM NOUN
woodwork

le **menuisier** MASC NOUN
joiner

le **mépris** MASC NOUN
contempt
□ Il nous a traités avec mépris. He treated us with contempt.

méprisant (FEM **méprisante**) ADJECTIVE
contemptuous

mépriser VERB [28]
to despise

★ la **mer** FEM NOUN

1 sea
□ en mer at sea
■ **au bord de la mer** at the seaside
■ **la mer du Nord** the North Sea

2 tide
□ La mer est basse. The tide is out. □ La mer sera haute à sept heures. It'll be high tide at 7 o'clock.

French-English

la **mercerie** FEM NOUN
1 haberdashery
2 haberdasher's shop

★ **merci** EXCLAMATION
thank you
□ Merci de m'avoir raccompagné. Thank you for taking me home.
■ **merci beaucoup** thank you very much

★ le **mercredi** MASC NOUN
1 Wednesday
□ Aujourd'hui, nous sommes mercredi. It's Wednesday today.
2 on Wednesday
□ Nous comptons partir mercredi. We plan to leave on Wednesday.
■ **le mercredi** on Wednesdays □ Le musée est fermé le mercredi. The museum is shut on Wednesdays.
■ **tous les mercredis** every Wednesday
■ **mercredi dernier** last Wednesday
■ **mercredi prochain** next Wednesday

★ la **mère** FEM NOUN
mother

★ la **merguez** FEM NOUN
spicy sausage

méridional (FEM **méridionale**, MASC PL **méridionaux**) ADJECTIVE
southern
□ Il a un accent méridional. He's got a southern accent.

la **meringue** FEM NOUN
meringue

m

★ **mériter** VERB [28]
to deserve

le **merlan** MASC NOUN
whiting

le **merle** MASC NOUN
blackbird

la **merveille** FEM NOUN
■ **Cet ordinateur est une vraie merveille!** This computer's really wonderful!
■ **à merveille** wonderfully □ Elle se porte à merveille depuis son opération. She's been wonderfully well since the operation.

★ **merveilleux** (FEM **merveilleuse**) ADJECTIVE
marvellous

★ **mes** PL ADJECTIVE
my
□ mes parents my parents

★ **Mesdames** FEM PL NOUN
ladies
□ Bonjour, Mesdames. Good morning, ladies.

Mesdemoiselles FEM PL NOUN
ladies
□ Bonjour, Mesdemoiselles. Good morning, ladies.

mesquin (FEM **mesquine**) ADJECTIVE
mean

★ le **message** MASC NOUN
message
■ **un message SMS** a text message

la **messagerie** FEM NOUN
■ **une messagerie vocale** voice mail
■ **la messagerie électronique** email

★ la **messe** FEM NOUN
mass
□ aller à la messe to go to mass □ la messe de minuit midnight mass

★ **messieurs** MASC PL NOUN
gentlemen
□ Que puis-je faire pour vous, Messieurs? What can I do for you, gentlemen?
■ **Messieurs, ...** (*in letter*) Dear Sirs, ...

★ la **mesure** FEM NOUN
1 measurement
□ J'ai pris les mesures de la fenêtre. I took the measurements of the window.
■ **sur mesure** tailor-made □ un costume sur mesure a tailor-made suit
2 measure
□ L'établissement a pris des mesures pour lutter contre le vandalisme. The school has taken measures to combat vandalism.
■ **au fur et à mesure** as one goes along
□ Quand je cuisine, je préfère faire la vaisselle au fur et à mesure. When I'm cooking, I prefer to wash up as I go along.
■ **être en mesure de faire quelque chose** to be in a position to do something □ Nous ne sommes pas en mesure de vous renseigner. We are not in a position to give you any information.

★ **mesurer** VERB [28]
to measure
□ Mesurez la longueur et la largeur. Measure the length and the width.
■ **Il mesure un mètre quatre-vingts.** He's 1 m 80 tall.

met VERB ▷ *see* **mettre**

★ le **métal** (PL les **métaux**) MASC NOUN
metal

métallique (FEM **métallique**) ADJECTIVE
metallic

★ la **météo** FEM NOUN
weather forecast
□ Que dit la météo pour cet après-midi? What's the weather forecast for this afternoon?

la **méthode** FEM NOUN
1 method
□ des méthodes d'enseignement modernes modern teaching methods
2 tutor
□ une méthode de guitare a guitar tutor

★ le **métier** MASC NOUN
job
□ Tu aimerais faire quel métier plus tard? What job would you like to do when you're older?

★ le **mètre** MASC NOUN
metre
■ **un mètre ruban** a tape measure

★ le **métro** MASC NOUN
underground
□ prendre le métro to go by underground

mets VERB ▷ *see* **mettre**

le **metteur en scène** (PL les **metteurs en scène**) MASC NOUN
director (*of film or play*)

★ **mettre** VERB [47]

PRESENT TENSE	
je mets	nous mettons
tu mets	vous mettez
il/elle met	ils/elles mettent
PAST PARTICIPLE	
mis	

1 to put
□ Où est-ce que tu as mis les clés? Where have you put the keys?
2 to put on
□ Je mets mon manteau et j'arrive. I'll put on my coat and then I'll be ready. □ Il fait froid, je vais mettre le chauffage. It's cold, I'm going to put the heating on.
3 to wear
□ Elle ne met pas souvent de jupe. She doesn't often wear a skirt. □ Je n'ai rien à me mettre! I've got nothing to wear!
4 to take
□ Combien de temps as-tu mis pour aller à Lille? How long did it take you to get to Lille? □ Elle met des heures à se préparer. She takes hours getting ready.
■ **mettre en marche** to start □ Comment met-on la machine à laver en marche? How do you start the washing machine?
■ **Vous pouvez vous mettre là.** You can sit there.
■ **se mettre au lit** to get into bed
■ **se mettre en maillot de bain** to put on one's swimsuit
■ **se mettre à** to start □ Il s'est mis à la peinture à cinquante ans. He started painting when he was 50. □ Il est temps de se mettre au travail. It's time to start work. □ Elle s'est mise à pleurer. She started crying.

★ le **meuble** MASC NOUN
piece of furniture
□ Je me suis cogné contre un meuble. I bumped into a piece of furniture. □ de beaux meubles nice furniture

★ le **meublé** MASC NOUN
1 furnished flat
2 furnished room

meubler VERB [28]
to furnish

★ le **meurtre** MASC NOUN
murder

le **meurtrier** MASC NOUN
murderer

la **meurtrière** FEM NOUN
murderess

Mexico NOUN
Mexico City

le **Mexique** MASC NOUN
Mexico

le **mi** MASC NOUN
1 E
□ mi bémol E flat
2 mi
□ do, ré, mi ... do, re, mi ...

mi- PREFIX
1 half-
□ mi-clos half-shut
2 mid-
□ à la mi-janvier in mid-January

miauler VERB [28]
to mew

la **miche** FEM NOUN
loaf

mi-chemin
■ **à mi-chemin** ADVERB halfway

le **micro** MASC NOUN
microphone

le **microbe** MASC NOUN
germ

★ le **micro-ondes** MASC NOUN
microwave oven

★ le **micro-ordinateur** MASC NOUN
microcomputer

le **microscope** MASC NOUN
microscope

★ le **midi** MASC NOUN
1 midday
□ à midi at midday
■ **midi et demi** half past twelve
2 lunchtime
□ On a bien mangé à midi. We had a good meal at lunchtime.
■ **le Midi** the South of France

la **mie** FEM NOUN
breadcrumbs

★ le **miel** MASC NOUN
honey

mien MASC PRONOUN
■ **le mien** mine □ Ce vélo-là, c'est le mien. That bike's mine.

mienne FEM PRONOUN
■ **la mienne** mine □ Cette valise-là, c'est la mienne. That case is mine.

miennes FEM PL PRONOUN
■ **les miennes** mine □ Tu as tes clés? J'ai oublié les miennes. Have you got your keys? I forgot mine.

miens MASC PL PRONOUN
■ **les miens** mine □ Ces CD-là, ce sont les miens. Those CDs are mine.

la **miette** FEM NOUN
crumb (*of bread, cake*)

★ **mieux** (FEM+PL **mieux**) ADVERB, ADJECTIVE, NOUN
better
□ Je la connais mieux que son frère. I know her better than her brother. □ Elle va mieux. She's better. □ Les cheveux courts lui vont mieux. She looks better with short hair.
■ **Il vaut mieux que tu appelles ta mère.** You'd better phone your mother.
■ **le mieux** the best □ C'est la région que je connais le mieux. It's the region I know best.
■ **faire de son mieux** to do one's best
□ Essaie de faire de ton mieux. Try to do your best.
■ **de mieux en mieux** better and better
■ **au mieux** at best

★ **mignon** (FEM **mignonne**) ADJECTIVE
sweet
□ Qu'est-ce qu'il est mignon! Isn't he sweet!

la **migraine** FEM NOUN
migraine
□ J'ai la migraine. I've got a migraine.

mijoter VERB [28]
to simmer

★ le **milieu** (PL les **milieux**) MASC NOUN
1 middle
■ **au milieu de** in the middle of □ Place le vase au milieu de la table. Put the vase in the middle of the table.
■ **au beau milieu de** in the middle of □ Il est arrivé au beau milieu de la nuit. He arrived in the middle of the night.
2 background
□ le milieu familial the family background □ Il vient d'un milieu modeste. He comes from a modest background.
3 environment
□ le milieu marin the marine environment

★ **militaire** (FEM **militaire**) ADJECTIVE
▷ *see also* **militaire** NOUN
military
□ faire son service militaire to do one's military service

★ le **militaire** MASC NOUN
▷ *see also* **militaire** ADJECTIVE
serviceman
□ Son père est militaire. His father is a serviceman.
■ **un militaire de carrière** a professional soldier

mille NUMBER
a thousand
□ mille euros a thousand euros □ deux mille personnes two thousand people

le **millefeuille** MASC NOUN
vanilla slice

le **millénaire** MASC NOUN
millennium
□ le troisième millénaire the third millennium

le **milliard** MASC NOUN
billion
□ cinq milliards d'euros five billion euros

le/la **milliardaire** MASC/FEM NOUN
billionaire

le **millier** MASC NOUN
thousand
□ des milliers de personnes thousands of people
■ **par milliers** by the thousand

le **milligramme** MASC NOUN
milligram

le **millimètre** MASC NOUN
millimetre

★ le **million** MASC NOUN
million
□ deux millions de personnes two million people

le/la **millionnaire** MASC/FEM NOUN
millionaire

★ **mi-long** (FEM **mi-longue**) ADJECTIVE
medium-length

le/la **mime** MASC/FEM NOUN
mime artist

mimer VERB [28]
to mimic

minable (FEM **minable**) ADJECTIVE
1 shabby
□ un imperméable minable a shabby raincoat
2 pathetic

★ **mince** (FEM **mince**) ADJECTIVE
1 thin
□ une mince tranche de jambon a thin slice of ham
2 slim
□ Il est grand et mince. He's tall and slim.
■ **Mince alors!** (*informal*) Oh bother!

la **minceur** FEM NOUN
1 thinness
□ la minceur des murs the thinness of the walls
2 slimness
□ Elle enviait la minceur de sa sœur. She envied her sister's slimness.

la **mine** FEM NOUN
1 expression

2 look
□ Tu as bonne mine. You look well. □ Il a mauvaise mine. He doesn't look well. □ Elle avait une mine fatiguée. She was looking tired.
3 appearance
□ Il ne faut pas juger les gens d'après leur mine. You shouldn't judge people by their appearance.
4 lead (*of pencil*)
5 mine
□ une mine de charbon a coal mine
■ **faire mine de faire quelque chose** to pretend to do something □ Elle a fait mine de le croire. She pretended to believe him.

minéral (FEM **minérale**, MASC PL **minéraux**) ADJECTIVE
mineral
□ l'eau minérale mineral water

minéralogique (FEM **minéralogique**) ADJECTIVE
■ **une plaque minéralogique** a number plate

★ **mineur** (FEM **mineure**) ADJECTIVE
▷ *see also* **mineur** NOUN, **mineure** NOUN
minor

le **mineur** MASC NOUN
▷ *see also* **mineur** ADJECTIVE
1 boy under 18
■ **les mineurs** the under-18s
2 miner
□ Mon grand-père était mineur. My grandfather was a miner.

★ la **mineure** FEM NOUN
▷ *see also* **mineur** ADJECTIVE
girl under 18

la **minijupe** FEM NOUN
miniskirt

★ **minimal** (FEM **minimale**, MASC PL **minimaux**) ADJECTIVE
minimum

le **minimum** MASC NOUN
minimum
□ Il en fait le minimum. He does the absolute minimum.
■ **au minimum** at the very least

le **ministère** MASC NOUN
ministry
□ le ministère des Affaires étrangères the Foreign Office

★ le **ministre** MASC NOUN
minister
□ le ministre des Affaires étrangères the Foreign Secretary

la **minorité** FEM NOUN
minority

Minorque FEM NOUN
Minorca

★ le **minuit** MASC NOUN
midnight
□ à minuit et quart at a quarter past midnight

minuscule (FEM **minuscule**) ADJECTIVE
▷ *see also* **minuscule** NOUN
tiny

la **minuscule** FEM NOUN
▷ *see also* **minuscule** ADJECTIVE
small letter

★ la **minute** FEM NOUN
minute

minutieux (FEM **minutieuse**) ADJECTIVE
meticulous
■ **C'est un travail minutieux.** It's a fiddly job.

la **mirabelle** FEM NOUN
small yellow plum

le **miracle** MASC NOUN
miracle

★ le **miroir** MASC NOUN
mirror

mis (FEM **mise**) ADJECTIVE
■ **bien mis** well turned out □ Elle est toujours bien mise. She's always well turned out.

mis VERB ▷ *see* **mettre**

miser VERB [28] (*informal*)
to bank on
□ On ne peut pas miser là-dessus. We can't bank on it.

misérable (FEM **misérable**) ADJECTIVE
shabby-looking
□ une femme d'aspect misérable a shabby-looking woman

la **misère** FEM NOUN
extreme poverty
■ **un salaire de misère** starvation wages

le/la **missionnaire** MASC/FEM NOUN
missionary

mit VERB ▷ *see* **mettre**

★ la **mi-temps** FEM NOUN
1 half (*of match*)
□ la première mi-temps the first half □ la deuxième mi-temps the second half
2 half-time
□ Je lui parlerai à la mi-temps. I'll speak to him at half-time.
■ **travailler à mi-temps** to work part-time

la **mitraillette** FEM NOUN
submachine gun

★ le **mi-trimestre** MASC NOUN
half-term

★ **mixte** (FEM **mixte**) ADJECTIVE
■ **une école mixte** a mixed school

★ la **MJC** FEM NOUN (= *maison des jeunes et de la culture*)
youth club and arts centre

Mlle (PL **Mlles**) ABBREVIATION (= *Mademoiselle*)
Miss
□ Mlle Renoir Miss Renoir

Mme (PL **Mmes**) ABBREVIATION (= *Madame*)
Mrs
□ Mme Leroy Mrs Leroy

★ le **mobile** MASC NOUN
1 motive
□ Quel était le mobile du crime? What was the motive for the crime?
2 mobile phone
□ Tu me donnes ton numéro de mobile? Can you give me your mobile number?

le **mobilier** MASC NOUN
furniture

★ la **mobylette**® FEM NOUN
moped

★ **moche** (FEM **moche**) ADJECTIVE (*informal*)
1 awful
□ Cette couleur est vraiment moche. That colour's really awful. □ Je me trouve moche! I think I look awful!
2 rotten
□ Il a la grippe, c'est moche pour lui. He's got flu, that's rotten for him.

★ la **mode** FEM NOUN
▷ *see also* **mode** NOUN
fashion
□ être à la mode to be fashionable

★ le **mode** MASC NOUN
▷ *see also* **mode** NOUN
■ **le mode d'emploi** directions for use
■ **le mode de vie** the way of life

le **modèle** MASC NOUN
1 model
□ Le nouveau modèle sort en septembre. The new model is coming out in September.
2 style (*of clothes*)
□ Est-ce que vous avez le même modèle en plus grand? Have you got the same style in a bigger size?

modéré (FEM **modérée**) ADJECTIVE
moderate

★ **moderne** (FEM **moderne**) ADJECTIVE
modern

moderniser VERB [28]
to modernize

modeste (FEM **modeste**) ADJECTIVE
modest
□ Ne sois pas si modeste! Don't be so modest!

la **modestie** FEM NOUN
modesty

moelleux (FEM **moelleuse**) ADJECTIVE
soft
□ un coussin moelleux a soft cushion

les **mœurs** FEM PL NOUN
social attitudes
■ **l'évolution des mœurs** changing attitudes

★ **moi** PRONOUN
me
□ Coucou, c'est moi! Hello, it's me!
■ **Moi, je pense que tu as tort.** I personally think you're wrong.
■ **à moi** mine □ Ce livre n'est pas à moi. This book isn't mine. □ un ami à moi a friend of mine

moi-même PRONOUN
myself
□ J'ai tricoté ce pull moi-même. I knitted this jumper myself.

★ **moindre** (FEM **moindre**) ADJECTIVE
■ **le moindre** the slightest □ Il ne fait pas le moindre effort. He doesn't make the slightest effort. □ Je n'en ai pas la moindre idée. I haven't the slightest idea.

le **moine** MASC NOUN
monk

le **moineau** (PL les **moineaux**) MASC NOUN
sparrow

★ **moins** ADVERB, PREPOSITION
1 less
□ Ça coûte moins de deux cents euros. It costs less than 200 euros.
2 fewer
□ Il y a moins de gens aujourd'hui. There are fewer people today.
■ **Il est cinq heures moins dix.** It's 10 to 5.
3 minus
□ quatre moins trois 4 minus 3 □ Il a fait moins cinq la nuit dernière. It was minus five last night.
■ **le moins** the least □ C'est le modèle le moins cher. It's the least expensive model. □ Ce sont les plages qui sont les moins polluées. These are the least polluted beaches. □ C'est l'album que j'aime le moins. This is the album I like the least.
■ **de moins en moins** less and less □ Il vient nous voir de moins en moins. He comes to see us less and less often.
■ **Il a trois ans de moins que moi.** He's three years younger than me.
■ **au moins** at least □ Ne te plains pas: au moins il ne pleut pas! Don't complain: at least it's not raining!
■ **à moins que** unless

> **à moins que** is followed by a verb in the subjunctive.

□ Je te retrouverai à dix heures à moins que le train n'ait du retard. I'll meet you at 10 o'clock unless the train's late.

★ le **mois** MASC NOUN
month

le **moisi** MASC NOUN
■ **Ça sent le moisi.** It smells musty.

moisir VERB [38]
to go mouldy
□ Le pain a moisi. The bread's gone mouldy.

la **moisson** FEM NOUN
harvest

moite (FEM **moite**) ADJECTIVE
sweaty
□ J'ai toujours les mains moites. My hands are always sweaty.

★ la **moitié** FEM NOUN
half
□ Il a mangé la moitié du gâteau. He ate half the cake.
■ **la moitié du temps** half the time
■ **à la moitié de** halfway through □ Elle est partie à la moitié du film. She left halfway through the film.
■ **à moitié** half □ Ton verre est encore à moitié plein. Your glass is still half-full. □ Ce sac était à moitié prix. This bag was half-price.
■ **partager moitié moitié** to go halves □ On partage moitié moitié, d'accord? We'll go halves, OK?

la **molaire** FEM NOUN
back tooth

la **Moldavie** FEM NOUN
Moldova

molle FEM ADJECTIVE ▷ *see* **mou**

le **mollet** MASC NOUN
▷ *see also* **mollet** ADJECTIVE
calf (*of leg*)

mollet ADJECTIVE
▷ *see also* **mollet** NOUN
■ **un œuf mollet** a soft-boiled egg

le/la **môme** MASC/FEM NOUN (*informal*)
kid

★ le **moment** MASC NOUN
moment
■ **en ce moment** at the moment □ Nous avons beaucoup de travail en ce moment. We have a lot of work at the moment.
■ **pour le moment** for the moment □ Nous ne pensons pas déménager pour le moment. We're not thinking of moving for the moment.
■ **au moment où** just as □ Il est arrivé au moment où j'allais partir. He turned up just as I was leaving.
■ **à ce moment-là** **1** at that point □ À ce moment-là, on a vu arriver la police. At that point, we saw the police coming. **2** in that case □ À ce moment-là, je devrai partir plus tôt. In that case I'll have to leave earlier.
■ **à tout moment** **1** at any moment □ Elle peut arriver à tout moment. She could arrive at any moment. **2** constantly □ Il nous dérange à tout moment pour des riens. He's constantly bothering us about silly little things.
■ **sur le moment** at the time □ Sur le moment je n'ai rien dit. At the time I didn't say anything.
■ **par moments** at times □ Elle se sent seule par moments. She feels lonely at times.

momentané (FEM **momentanée**) ADJECTIVE
momentary

la **momie** FEM NOUN
mummy (*Egyptian*)

★ **mon** (FEM **ma**, PL **mes**) ADJECTIVE
my
□ mon frère my brother □ mon ami my friend

★ la **monarchie** FEM NOUN
monarchy

le **monastère** MASC NOUN
monastery

★ le **monde** MASC NOUN
world
□ faire le tour du monde to go round the world
■ **Il y a du monde.** There are a lot of people.
■ **beaucoup de monde** a lot of people □ Il y avait beaucoup de monde au concert. There were a lot of people at the concert.
■ **peu de monde** not many people

★ **mondial** (FEM **mondiale**, MASC PL **mondiaux**) ADJECTIVE
1 world
□ la population mondiale the world population
2 world-wide
□ une crise mondiale a world-wide crisis

★ le **moniteur** MASC NOUN
1 instructor
□ un moniteur de voile a sailing instructor
2 monitor
□ le moniteur de mon ordinateur my computer monitor

★ la **monitrice** FEM NOUN
instructor
□ une monitrice de ski a ski instructor

★ la **monnaie** FEM NOUN
■ **une pièce de monnaie** a coin
■ **avoir de la monnaie** to have change
□ Est-ce que tu as de la monnaie? Have you got any change? □ Est-ce que vous avez la monnaie de dix euros? Do you have change for 10 euros?
■ **rendre la monnaie à quelqu'un** to give somebody their change

> **BE CAREFUL!**
> **monnaie** does not mean **money**.

★ **monoparental** (FEM **monoparentale**, MASC PL **monoparentaux**) ADJECTIVE
■ **une famille monoparentale** a one-parent family

French-English

monotone (FEM **monotone**) ADJECTIVE
monotonous

★ **Monsieur** (PL **Messieurs**) MASC NOUN
1 Mr
□ Monsieur Dupont Mr Dupont
2 man
□ Il y a un monsieur qui veut te voir. There's a man to see you.
3 Sir
□ Monsieur, ... Dear Sir, ... (*in letter*)
□ Monsieur! Vous avez oublié votre parapluie! Excuse me! You've forgotten your umbrella!

★ le **monstre** MASC NOUN
▷ *see also* **monstre** ADJECTIVE
monster

★ **monstre** (FEM **monstre**) ADJECTIVE
▷ *see also* **monstre** NOUN
■ **Nous avons un travail monstre.** We've got a terrific amount of work.

le **mont** MASC NOUN
mount
■ **le mont Everest** Mount Everest
■ **le mont Blanc** Mont Blanc

★ la **montagne** FEM NOUN
mountain
□ de hautes montagnes high mountains
□ des vacances à la montagne holidays in the mountains
■ **les montagnes russes** roller coaster

montagneux (FEM **montagneuse**) ADJECTIVE
mountainous
□ une région montagneuse a mountainous area

montant (FEM **montante**) ADJECTIVE
1 rising
□ la marée montante the rising tide
2 high
□ un pull à col montant a high-necked jumper

★ **monter** VERB [48, *aux* **avoir** *or* **être**]
1 to go up
□ Elle a du mal à monter les escaliers. She has difficulty going upstairs. □ Les prix ont encore monté. Prices have gone up again.
2 to assemble
□ Est-ce que ces étagères sont difficiles à monter? Are these shelves difficult to assemble?
■ **monter dans** to get on □ Il est temps de monter dans l'avion. It's time to get on the plane.
■ **monter sur** to stand on □ Monte sur la chaise: tu verras mieux. Stand on the chair: you'll see better.
■ **monter à cheval** to ride

The verb **monter** uses **être** in the perfect tense when you talk about moving upwards. It uses **avoir** in the perfect tense when talking about a person or thing moving up something (for example, up the stairs), describing an increase of something, or talking about putting something together.

★ la **montre** FEM NOUN
watch

★ **montrer** VERB [28]
to show
□ Montre-moi ton nouveau manteau. Show me your new coat.

la **monture** FEM NOUN
frames (*of glasses*)

★ le **monument** MASC NOUN
monument

se **moquer** VERB [28]
■ **se moquer de** 1 to make fun of □ Ils se sont moqués de mes chaussures jaunes. They made fun of my yellow shoes. 2 (*informal*) not to care about □ Il se moque complètement de la mode. He couldn't care less about fashion.

★ la **moquette** FEM NOUN
fitted carpet

moqueur (FEM **moqueuse**) ADJECTIVE
mocking

★ le **moral** MASC NOUN
■ **Elle a le moral.** She's in good spirits.
■ **J'ai le moral à zéro.** I'm feeling really down.

la **morale** FEM NOUN
moral
□ La morale de cette histoire est ... The moral of the story is ...
■ **faire la morale à quelqu'un** to lecture somebody

★ le **morceau** (PL les **morceaux**) MASC NOUN
piece
□ un morceau de pain a piece of bread

★ **mordre** VERB [49]
to bite

mordu (FEM **mordue**) ADJECTIVE
■ **Il est mordu de jazz.** (*informal*) He's crazy about jazz.

la **morgue** FEM NOUN
mortuary

le **morse** MASC NOUN
walrus

la **morsure** FEM NOUN
bite

★ **mort** (FEM **morte**) ADJECTIVE
▷ *see also* **mort** NOUN
dead
□ Nous avons trouvé un oiseau mort. We found a dead bird.
■ **Napoléon est mort en 1821.** Napoleon died in 1821.

m

■ **Il était mort de peur.** He was scared to death.
■ **Je suis morte de fatigue.** I'm dead tired.

★ la **mort** FEM NOUN
▷ *see also* **mort** ADJECTIVE
death

mortel (FEM **mortelle**) ADJECTIVE
1 deadly
□ un poison mortel a deadly poison □ Ces réunions de famille sont mortelles! (*informal*) These family gatherings are deadly!
2 fatal
□ une chute mortelle a fatal fall

la **morue** FEM NOUN
cod

Moscou NOUN
Moscow

★ la **mosquée** FEM NOUN
mosque

★ le **mot** MASC NOUN
1 word
□ mot à mot word for word
■ **des mots croisés** a crossword
■ **un mot de passe** a password
■ **un gros mot** a swearword
2 note
□ Je vais lui écrire un mot pour lui dire qu'on arrive. I'll write her a note to say we're coming.

le **motard** MASC NOUN
1 biker
2 motorcycle cop (*informal*)
□ Il s'est fait arrêter par un motard. He was stopped by a motorcycle cop.

★ le **moteur** MASC NOUN
engine
■ **un bateau à moteur** a motor boat
■ **un moteur de recherche** a search engine

★ le **motif** MASC NOUN
pattern
□ des rideaux avec un motif d'oiseaux curtains with a bird pattern
■ **sans motif** for no reason □ Il s'est fâché sans motif. He got angry for no reason.

motivé (FEM **motivée**) ADJECTIVE
motivated

★ la **moto** FEM NOUN
motorbike

★ le/la **motocycliste** MASC/FEM NOUN
motorcyclist

mou (FEM **molle**) ADJECTIVE
1 soft
□ Mon matelas est trop mou. My mattress is too soft.
2 lethargic
□ Je le trouve un peu mou. I find him a bit lethargic.

★ la **mouche** FEM NOUN
fly
■ **prendre la mouche** to get into a huff

se **moucher** VERB [28]
to blow one's nose

le **moucheron** MASC NOUN
midge

★ le **mouchoir** MASC NOUN
handkerchief
■ **un mouchoir en papier** a tissue

moudre VERB [50]
to grind

la **moue** FEM NOUN
pout
■ **faire la moue** to pout

la **mouette** FEM NOUN
seagull

la **moufle** FEM NOUN
mitt

★ **mouillé** (FEM **mouillée**) ADJECTIVE
wet

mouiller VERB [28]
to get wet
□ J'ai mouillé les manches de mon pull. I got the sleeves of my jumper wet.
■ **se mouiller** to get wet □ Attention, tu vas te mouiller! Careful, you'll get wet!

moulant (FEM **moulante**) ADJECTIVE
figure-hugging
□ une robe moulante a figure-hugging dress

★ la **moule** FEM NOUN
▷ *see also* **moule** NOUN
mussel

★ le **moule** MASC NOUN
▷ *see also* **moule** NOUN
■ **un moule à gâteaux** a cake tin

le **moulin** MASC NOUN
mill

moulu VERB ▷ *see* **moudre**

★ **mourir** VERB [51]
to die
■ **mourir de faim** to starve to death □ Des centaines de personnes sont mortes de faim. Hundreds of people starved to death.
■ **Je meurs de faim!** I'm starving!
■ **mourir de froid** to die of exposure
■ **Je meurs de froid!** I'm freezing!
■ **mourir d'envie de faire quelque chose** to be dying to do something □ Je meurs d'envie d'aller me baigner. I'm dying to go for a swim.

la **mousse** FEM NOUN
1 moss
□ un rocher recouvert de mousse a rock covered with moss
2 froth (*on beer*)
3 lather (*of soap, shampoo*)

4 mousse
□ une mousse au chocolat a chocolate mousse □ une mousse de poisson a fish mousse
■ **la mousse à raser** shaving foam

mousseux (FEM **mousseuse**) ADJECTIVE
■ **un vin mousseux** a sparkling wine

★ la **moustache** FEM NOUN
moustache
■ **les moustaches** (*of a cat*) whiskers

★ le **moustique** MASC NOUN
mosquito

★ la **moutarde** FEM NOUN
mustard

★ le **mouton** MASC NOUN
1 sheep
□ une peau de mouton a sheepskin
2 mutton
□ un gigot de mouton a leg of mutton

★ le **mouvement** MASC NOUN
movement

mouvementé (FEM **mouvementée**) ADJECTIVE
eventful
□ des vacances mouvementées eventful holidays

★ **moyen** (FEM **moyenne**) ADJECTIVE
▷ *see also* **moyen** NOUN, **moyenne** NOUN
1 average
□ Je suis plutôt moyenne en langues. I'm just average at languages.
2 medium
□ Elle est de taille moyenne. She's of medium height.
■ **le Moyen Âge** the Middle Ages

★ le **moyen** MASC NOUN
▷ *see also* **moyen** ADJECTIVE
way
□ Quel est le meilleur moyen de le convaincre? What's the best way of convincing him?
■ **Je n'en ai pas les moyens.** I can't afford it.
■ **Ils n'ont pas les moyens de s'acheter une voiture.** They can't afford to buy a car.
■ **un moyen de transport** a means of transport
■ **par tous les moyens** by every possible means

★ la **moyenne** FEM NOUN
▷ *see also* **moyen** ADJECTIVE
■ **avoir la moyenne** to get a pass mark
□ J'espère avoir la moyenne en maths. I hope to get a pass mark in maths.
■ **en moyenne** on average
■ **la moyenne d'âge** the average age

le **Moyen-Orient** MASC NOUN
Middle East

muet (FEM **muette**) ADJECTIVE
with a speech impairment (*not speaking*)
■ **un film muet** a silent film

le **muguet** MASC NOUN
lily of the valley

multiple (FEM **multiple**) ADJECTIVE
numerous
□ en de multiples occasions on numerous occasions

multiplier VERB [19]
to multiply

multitâche ADJECTIVE
multitasking (*also for computer*)

★ **municipal** (FEM **municipale**, MASC PL **municipaux**) ADJECTIVE
■ **la bibliothèque municipale** the public library

★ la **municipalité** FEM NOUN
town council

munir VERB [38]
■ **munir quelqu'un de** to equip someone with
■ **se munir de** to equip oneself with

les **munitions** FEM PL NOUN
ammunition *sing*

★ le **mur** MASC NOUN
wall

★ **mûr** (FEM **mûre**) ADJECTIVE
▷ *see also* **mûre** NOUN
1 ripe (*fruit*)
2 mature (*person*)

★ la **mûre** FEM NOUN
▷ *see also* **mûr** ADJECTIVE
bramble

mûrir VERB [38]
1 to ripen
□ Les fraises ont mis du temps à mûrir. The strawberries took a while to ripen.
2 to make mature
□ Cette expérience l'a beaucoup mûrie. That experience has made her much more mature.

murmurer VERB [28]
to whisper
□ Il m'a murmuré à l'oreille qu'il allait partir. He whispered in my ear that he was going to go.

la **muscade** FEM NOUN
nutmeg

le **muscat** MASC NOUN
1 muscat grape
2 muscatel (*wine*)
□ un verre de muscat a glass of muscatel

le **muscle** MASC NOUN
muscle

musclé (FEM **musclée**) ADJECTIVE
muscular

★ la **musculation** FEM NOUN
weight training

le **museau** (PL les **museaux**) MASC NOUN
muzzle

★le **musée** MASC NOUN
museum

musical (FEM **musicale**, MASC PL **musicaux**) ADJECTIVE
musical
■ **avoir l'oreille musicale** to be musical

le **music-hall** MASC NOUN
variety
□ une chanteuse de music-hall a variety singer

★le **musicien** MASC NOUN
musician

★la **musicienne** FEM NOUN
musician

★la **musique** FEM NOUN
music

★**musulman** (FEM **musulmane**) ADJECTIVE, NOUN
Muslim
■ **un musulman** a Muslim (*man*)
■ **une musulmane** a Muslim (*woman*)

la **mutation** FEM NOUN
transfer
□ Il a demandé sa mutation à Paris. He asked for a transfer to Paris.

★la **mutuelle** FEM NOUN
private health insurance

myope (FEM **myope**) ADJECTIVE
short-sighted

le **mystère** MASC NOUN
mystery

★**mystérieux** (FEM **mystérieuse**) ADJECTIVE
mysterious

le **mythe** MASC NOUN
myth

Nn

n' PRONOUN ▷ *see* **ne**

la **nage** FEM NOUN

■ **traverser une rivière à la nage** to swim across a river

■ **être en nage** to be sweating profusely

la **nageoire** FEM NOUN

fin

★ **nager** VERB [45]

to swim

le **nageur** MASC NOUN

swimmer

la **nageuse** FEM NOUN

swimmer

naïf (FEM **naïve**) ADJECTIVE

naïve

★ la **naissance** FEM NOUN

birth

■ **votre date de naissance** your date of birth

★ **naître** VERB [52, *aux* **être**]

to be born

■ **Il est né en 2001.** He was born in 2001.

naïve FEM ADJECTIVE ▷ *see* **naïf**

la **nana** FEM NOUN (*informal*)

girl

★ la **nappe** FEM NOUN

tablecloth

la **narine** FEM NOUN

nostril

natal (FEM **natale**) ADJECTIVE

native

□ mon pays natal my native country

★ la **natation** FEM NOUN

swimming

□ La natation est mon sport favori. Swimming's my favourite sport.

■ **faire de la natation** to go swimming

la **nation** FEM NOUN

nation

□ les Nations Unies the United Nations

★ **national** (FEM **nationale**, MASC PL **nationaux**) ADJECTIVE

▷ *see also* **nationale** NOUN

national

■ **la fête nationale espagnole** the national day of Spain

★ la **nationale** FEM NOUN

▷ *see also* **national** ADJECTIVE

main road

□ En vélo, il vaut mieux éviter les nationales. When on a bike it's better to avoid main roads.

★ la **nationalité** FEM NOUN

nationality

la **natte** FEM NOUN

plait

□ Cécile avait des nattes. Cécile had plaits.

★ la **nature** FEM NOUN

▷ *see also* **nature** ADJECTIVE

nature

★ **nature** (FEM **nature**) ADJECTIVE

▷ *see also* **nature** NOUN

plain

□ un yaourt nature a plain yoghurt

★ **naturel** (FEM **naturelle**) ADJECTIVE

natural

naturellement ADVERB

of course

□ Vous viendrez à notre fête? — Naturellement! Are you coming to our party? — Of course! □ Naturellement, il est encore en retard. Of course, he's late again.

le **naufrage** MASC NOUN

shipwreck

★ **nautique** (FEM **nautique**) ADJECTIVE

water

■ **les sports nautiques** water sports

■ **le ski nautique** water-skiing

le **navet** MASC NOUN

turnip

la **navette** FEM NOUN

shuttle

□ la navette entre la gare et l'aéroport the shuttle between the station and the airport

■ **faire la navette** to commute □ Je fais la navette entre Paris et Ivry. I commute between Paris and Ivry.

le **navigateur** MASC NOUN

browser (*on computer*)

la **navigation** FEM NOUN

■ **La navigation est interdite ici.** Boats are not allowed here.

naviguer VERB [28]
to sail

le **navire** MASC NOUN
ship

★ **ne** ADVERB

ne is combined with words such as **pas**, **personne**, **plus**, **rien** and **jamais** to form negative phrases.

□ Je ne peux pas venir. I can't come. □ Ils ne vont jamais en boîte. They never go to discos. □ Je ne connais personne ici. I don't know anyone here.

ne changes to **n'** before a vowel and most words beginning with 'h'.

□ Je n'ai pas d'argent. I haven't got any money. □ Il n'habite plus à Paris. He doesn't live in Paris any more.

ne is sometimes not translated.

□ C'est plus loin que je ne le croyais. It's further than I thought.

★ **né** VERB ▷ *see* **naître**
born
□ Elle est née en 2005. She was born in 2005.

néanmoins ADVERB
nevertheless

★ **nécessaire** (FEM **nécessaire**) ADJECTIVE
necessary
□ Il est nécessaire de réserver. It's necessary to book.

le **nectar** MASC NOUN
■ **le nectar d'abricot** apricot drink

★ **néerlandais** (FEM **néerlandaise**) ADJECTIVE, NOUN
Dutch
□ Manon parle néerlandais. Manon speaks Dutch.
■ **un Néerlandais** a Dutchman
■ **une Néerlandaise** a Dutchwoman
■ **les Néerlandais** the Dutch

★ **négatif** (FEM **négative**) ADJECTIVE
▷ *see also* **négatif** NOUN
negative

★ le **négatif** MASC NOUN
▷ *see also* **négatif** ADJECTIVE
negative (*of photo*)

négligé (FEM **négligée**) ADJECTIVE
scruffy
□ une tenue négligée scruffy clothes

★ **négliger** VERB [45]
to neglect
□ Ces derniers temps il a négligé son travail. He's been neglecting his work recently.

négocier VERB [19]
to negotiate

★ la **neige** FEM NOUN
snow
■ **un bonhomme de neige** a snowman

★ **neiger** VERB [45]
to snow

le **nénuphar** MASC NOUN
water lily

le **néon** MASC NOUN
neon
□ une lampe au néon a neon light □ La cuisine est éclairée au néon. The kitchen has a neon light.

néo-zélandais (FEM **néo-zélandaise**) ADJECTIVE, NOUN
New Zealand
□ Le champion néo-zélandais a gagné la course. The New Zealand champion won the race.
■ **un Néo-Zélandais** a New Zealander (*man*)
■ **une Néo-Zélandaise** a New Zealander (*woman*)

le **nerf** MASC NOUN
nerve
■ **taper sur les nerfs de quelqu'un** to get on somebody's nerves □ Il me tape sur les nerfs. He's getting on my nerves.

★ **nerveux** (FEM **nerveuse**) ADJECTIVE
nervous

la **nervosité** FEM NOUN
nervousness

n'est-ce pas ADVERB

n'est-ce pas is used to check that something is true.

□ Nous sommes le douze aujourd'hui, n'est-ce pas? It's the 12th today, isn't it? □ Ils sont venus l'an dernier, n'est-ce pas? They came last year, didn't they? □ Elle aura dix-huit ans en octobre, n'est-ce pas? She'll be 18 in October, won't she?

le **Net** MASC NOUN
the Net

★ **net** (FEM **nette**) ADJECTIVE, ADVERB
1 clear
□ L'image n'est pas nette. The picture isn't very clear.
2 net
□ Poids net: 500 g. Net weight: 500 g.
3 flatly
□ Il a refusé net de nous aider. He flatly refused to help us.
■ **s'arrêter net** to stop dead

nettement ADVERB
much
□ Ce magasin est nettement plus cher. This shop is much more expensive.

le **nettoyage** MASC NOUN
cleaning
■ **le nettoyage à sec** dry cleaning

★ **nettoyer** VERB [53]
to clean

French-English

★ **neuf** (FEM **neuve**) ADJECTIVE
▷ *see also* **neuf** NUMBER
new
□ des chaussures neuves new shoes

★ **neuf** NUMBER
▷ *see also* **neuf** ADJECTIVE
nine
□ Claire a neuf ans. Claire is nine. □ Il est neuf heures du matin. It's nine in the morning.
■ **le neuf février** the ninth of February

neutre (FEM **neutre**) ADJECTIVE
neutral

neuve FEM ADJECTIVE ▷ *see* **neuf**

neuvième (FEM **neuvième**) ADJECTIVE
ninth
□ au neuvième étage on the ninth floor

★ le **neveu** (PL les **neveux**) MASC NOUN
nephew

★ le **nez** MASC NOUN
nose
■ **se trouver nez à nez avec quelqu'un** to come face to face with somebody

★ **ni** CONJUNCTION
■ **ni ... ni ...** neither ... nor ... □ Je n'aime ni les lentilles ni les épinards. I like neither lentils nor spinach. □ Elles ne sont venues ni l'une ni l'autre. Neither of them came.

la **niche** FEM NOUN
kennel

le **nid** MASC NOUN
nest

★ la **nièce** FEM NOUN
niece

nier VERB [19]
to deny

★ **n'importe** ADVERB
■ **n'importe quel** any old □ N'importe quel stylo fera l'affaire. Any old pen will do.
■ **n'importe qui** anybody □ N'ouvre pas la porte à n'importe qui. Don't open the door to just anybody.
■ **n'importe quoi** anything □ Je ferais n'importe quoi pour elle. I'd do anything for her.
■ **Tu dis n'importe quoi.** You're talking rubbish.
■ **n'importe où** anywhere □ On trouve ces fleurs n'importe où. You can find these flowers anywhere.
■ **Ne laisse pas tes affaires n'importe où.** Don't leave your things lying everywhere.
■ **n'importe quand** any time □ Tu peux venir n'importe quand. You can come any time.
■ **n'importe comment** any old how □ Ces livres sont rangés n'importe comment. These books have been put away any old how.

★ le **niveau** (PL les **niveaux**) MASC NOUN
1 level
□ le niveau de l'eau the water level ■ **Ces deux enfants n'ont pas le même niveau.** These two children aren't at the same level.
2 standard
■ **le niveau de vie** the standard of living
■ **Le niveau est très élevé.** The standard is very high.

noble (FEM **noble**) ADJECTIVE
noble

la **noblesse** FEM NOUN
nobility

★ la **noce** FEM NOUN
wedding
■ **un repas de noces** a wedding reception
■ **leurs noces d'or** their golden wedding anniversary

nocif (FEM **nocive**) ADJECTIVE
harmful
□ une substance nocive a harmful substance

nocturne (FEM **nocturne**) ADJECTIVE
▷ *see also* **nocturne** NOUN
1 nocturnal
□ un oiseau nocturne a nocturnal bird
2 by night
□ Découvrez le Paris nocturne! Discover Paris by night!

la **nocturne** FEM NOUN
▷ *see also* **nocturne** ADJECTIVE
late-night opening
□ Nocturne le vendredi jusqu'à vingt-trois heures. Late-night opening until 11 p.m. on Fridays.

★ le **Noël** MASC NOUN
Christmas
□ Qu'est-ce que tu as eu pour Noël? What did you get for Christmas?
■ **Joyeux Noël!** Merry Christmas!

le **nœud** MASC NOUN
1 knot
□ Il a fait un nœud à la corde. He tied a knot in the rope.
2 bow
□ Janet avait un nœud dans les cheveux. Janet had a bow in her hair.
■ **un nœud papillon** a bow tie

le **Noir** MASC NOUN
black man

★ **noir** (FEM **noire**) ADJECTIVE
▷ *see also* **noir** NOUN
1 black
□ Elle porte une robe noire. She's wearing a black dress. □ Elle est noire. She's black.
2 dark
□ Il fait noir dehors. It's dark outside.

le **noir** MASC NOUN
▷ *see also* **noir** ADJECTIVE
dark
□ J'ai peur du noir. I'm afraid of the dark.
■ **le travail au noir** moonlighting

la **Noire** FEM NOUN
black woman

la **noisette** FEM NOUN
hazelnut

★ la **noix** (PL les **noix**) FEM NOUN
walnut
■ **une noix de coco** a coconut
■ **les noix de cajou** cashew nuts
■ **une noix de beurre** a knob of butter

★ le **nom** MASC NOUN
1 name
□ votre nom your name
■ **mon nom de famille** my surname
■ **son nom de jeune fille** her maiden name
■ **mon nom d'utilisateur** my username
2 noun (*in grammar*)
□ un nom commun a common noun □ un nom propre a proper noun

★ le **nombre** MASC NOUN
number
□ Treize est un nombre impair. Thirteen is an odd number. □ un grand nombre d'amis a large number of friends

★ **nombreux** (FEM **nombreuse**) ADJECTIVE
1 many
□ Il a gagné de nombreux matchs. He's won many matches.
2 large
□ une famille nombreuse a large family
■ **peu nombreux** few □ Nous étions peu nombreux à la réunion. There were few of us at the meeting.

le **nombril** MASC NOUN
navel

nommer VERB [28]
1 to name
□ Il n'a voulu nommer personne. He didn't want to name anybody.
2 to appoint
□ Il a été nommé directeur. He was appointed director.

★ **non** ADVERB
no
□ Tu as vu Amandine? — Non. Have you seen Amandine? — No.
■ **non seulement** not only □ Il est non seulement intelligent, mais aussi très gentil. Not only is he intelligent, he's also very nice.
■ **Moi non plus.** Neither do I. □ Je n'aime pas les hamburgers. — Moi non plus. I don't like hamburgers. — Neither do I. □ Il n'y est pas allé et moi non plus. He didn't go and neither did I.

non alcoolisé (FEM **non alcoolisée**) ADJECTIVE
non-alcoholic
□ les boissons non alcoolisées non-alcoholic drinks

★ le **non-fumeur** MASC NOUN
non-smoker
□ Sébastien est un non-fumeur. Sébastien's a non-smoker.

★ le **nord** MASC NOUN
▷ *see also* **nord** ADJECTIVE
north
□ Ils vivent dans le nord de l'île. They live in the north of the island.
■ **vers le nord** northwards
■ **au nord de Paris** north of Paris
■ **l'Afrique du Nord** North Africa
■ **le vent du nord** the north wind

★ **nord** (FEM+PL **nord**) ADJECTIVE
▷ *see also* **nord** NOUN
1 north
□ la face nord du Mont-Blanc the north face of Mont-Blanc
■ **le pôle Nord** the North Pole
2 northern
□ Nous avons visité la partie nord de l'île. We visited the northern part of the island.

le **nord-est** MASC NOUN
north-east
□ les régions du nord-est north-eastern regions

le **nord-ouest** MASC NOUN
north-west
□ l'Europe du nord-ouest north-west Europe

★ **normal** (FEM **normale**, MASC PL **normaux**) ADJECTIVE
1 normal
□ un bébé normal a normal baby
2 natural
□ C'est tout à fait normal. It's perfectly natural.
■ **Vous trouvez que c'est normal?** Does that seem right to you?

★ **normalement** ADVERB
normally
□ Les aéroports fonctionnent tous normalement. The airports are all working normally.
■ **Normalement, elle doit arriver à huit heures.** She's supposed to arrive at 8 o'clock.
■ **Tu es libre ce week-end? — Oui, normalement.** Are you free this weekend? — Yes, I should be.

normand (FEM **normande**) ADJECTIVE
■ **un village normand** a village in Normandy
■ **la côte normande** the coast of Normandy

★ la **Normandie** FEM NOUN
Normandy

★ la **Norvège** FEM NOUN
Norway

French-English

norvégien (FEM **norvégienne**) ADJECTIVE, NOUN
Norwegian
□ Elle parle norvégien. She speaks Norwegian.
■ **un Norvégien** a Norwegian (*man*)
■ **une Norvégienne** a Norwegian (*woman*)

★ **nos** PL ADJECTIVE
our
□ Où sont nos affaires? Where are our things?

le **notaire** MASC NOUN
solicitor
□ Son père est notaire. His father's a solicitor.

★ la **note** FEM NOUN
1 note
□ J'ai pris des notes pendant la conférence. I took notes at the lecture. □ Il a joué quelques notes au piano. He played a few notes on the piano.
2 mark
□ Vincent a de bonnes notes en maths. Vincent's got good marks in maths.
3 bill
□ Il n'a pas payé sa note. He didn't pay his bill.

★ **noter** VERB [28]
to make a note of
□ Tu as noté leur adresse? Did you make a note of their address?

les **notions** FEM PL NOUN
basics
□ Il faut avoir des notions d'anglais. You have to have some basic English. □ Elle a des notions de comptabilité. She knows the basics of accounting.

n

nôtre PRONOUN
■ **le nôtre** ours □ À qui est ce chien? — C'est le nôtre. Whose dog is it? — It's ours.
■ **la nôtre** ours □ Leur voiture est rouge, la nôtre est bleue. Their car is red, ours is blue.

nôtres PL PRONOUN
■ **les nôtres** ours □ Ces places-là sont les nôtres. Those seats are ours.

nouer VERB [28]
to tie

les **nouilles** FEM PL NOUN
noodles

le **nounours** MASC NOUN
teddy bear

★ **nourrir** VERB [38]
to feed

★ la **nourriture** FEM NOUN
food

★ **nous** PL PRONOUN
1 we
□ Nous avons deux enfants. We have two children.
2 us
□ Viens avec nous. Come with us.
3 ourselves
□ Nous nous sommes bien amusés. We really enjoyed ourselves.

With reflexive verbs, **nous** is often not translated.

□ Nous nous sommes levés très tard. We got up very late.
■ **nous-mêmes** ourselves

★ **nouveau** (FEM **nouvelle**, MASC PL **nouveaux**) ADJECTIVE
▷ *see also* **nouveau** NOUN
new
□ Il me faut un nouveau pantalon. I need some new trousers. □ Elle a une nouvelle voiture. She's got a new car.

The masculine singular form **nouveau** changes to **nouvel** before a vowel and most words beginning with 'h'.

□ le nouvel élève dans ma classe the new boy in my class
■ **le nouvel an** New Year

★ le **nouveau** (PL les **nouveaux**) MASC NOUN
▷ *see also* **nouveau** ADJECTIVE
new pupil
□ Il y a plusieurs nouveaux dans la classe. There are several new pupils in the class.
■ **de nouveau** again □ Il pleut de nouveau. It's raining again.

le **nouveau-né** MASC NOUN
newborn child

la **nouveauté** FEM NOUN
novelty

nouvel, nouvelle ADJECTIVE ▷ *see* **nouveau**

la **nouvelle** FEM NOUN
▷ *see also* **nouveau** ADJECTIVE
1 news
□ Tu connais la nouvelle? Teresa a gagné au loto. Have you heard the news? Teresa won the lottery. □ C'est une bonne nouvelle. That's good news.
2 short story
□ une nouvelle de Balzac a short story by Balzac
■ **les nouvelles** the news □ J'ai écouté les nouvelles à la radio. I listened to the news on the radio.
■ **avoir des nouvelles de quelqu'un** to hear from somebody □ Je n'ai pas eu de nouvelles de lui. I haven't heard from him.

la **Nouvelle-Zélande** FEM NOUN
New Zealand

★ **novembre** MASC NOUN
November
■ **en novembre** in November

le **noyau** (PL les **noyaux**) MASC NOUN
stone (*of fruit*)
□ un noyau d'abricot an apricot stone

★ le **noyer** MASC NOUN
▷ *see also* **noyer** VERB
walnut tree

★ se **noyer** VERB [53]
▷ *see also* **noyer** NOUN
to drown
□ Il s'est noyé dans la rivière. He drowned in the river.

nu (FEM **nue**) ADJECTIVE
1 naked
□ Ils se sont baignés nus. They went for a swim naked. □ tout nus stark naked
2 bare
□ Elle avait les bras nus. Her arms were bare.
□ Les murs étaient nus. The walls were bare.

★ le **nuage** MASC NOUN
cloud
▪ **un nuage de lait** a drop of milk

★ **nuageux** (FEM **nuageuse**) ADJECTIVE
cloudy

★ **nucléaire** (FEM **nucléaire**) ADJECTIVE
nuclear
□ l'énergie nucléaire nuclear power

le/la **nudiste** MASC/FEM NOUN
nudist

★ la **nuit** FEM NOUN
night
□ Ils ont fait du bruit toute la nuit. They were noisy all night.
▪ **Il fait nuit.** It's dark.
▪ **cette nuit** tonight □ Il va rentrer cette nuit. He'll be back tonight.
▪ **Bonne nuit!** Good night!
▪ **de nuit** by night

★ **nul** (FEM **nulle**) ADJECTIVE
rubbish
□ Ce film est nul. (*informal*) This film's rubbish.
▪ **être nul** to be no good □ Je suis nul en maths. I'm no good at maths.
▪ **un match nul** a draw (*in sport*) □ Ils ont fait match nul. It was a draw.
▪ **nulle part** nowhere □ Je ne le vois nulle part. I can't see it anywhere.

numérique (FEM **numérique**) ADJECTIVE
digital
□ un appareil photo numérique a digital camera

★ le **numéro** MASC NOUN
number
□ J'habite au numéro trois. I live at number 3.
▪ **mon numéro de téléphone** my phone number
▪ **le numéro de compte** the account number

nu-pieds (FEM+PL **nu-pieds**) ADJECTIVE, ADVERB
barefoot
□ Il se promenait nu-pieds. He was walking barefoot.

la **nuque** FEM NOUN
nape of the neck

★ le **nylon** MASC NOUN
nylon

French-English

n

Oo

obéir VERB [38]
to obey
■ **obéir à quelqu'un** to obey somebody
□ Elle refuse d'obéir à ses parents. She refuses to obey her parents.

obéissant (FEM **obéissante**) ADJECTIVE
obedient

★ l'**objet** MASC NOUN
object
■ **les objets de valeur** valuables
■ **les objets trouvés** the lost property office

★ **obligatoire** (FEM **obligatoire**) ADJECTIVE
compulsory

★ **obliger** VERB [45]
■ **obliger quelqu'un à faire quelque chose** to force somebody to do something
■ **Je suis bien obligé d'accepter.** I can't really refuse.

obscur (FEM **obscure**) ADJECTIVE
dark

l'**obscurité** FEM NOUN
darkness
□ dans l'obscurité in the dark

l'**obsédé** MASC NOUN
sex maniac
■ **un obsédé sexuel** a sex maniac

obséder VERB [34]
to obsess
□ Il est obsédé par le travail. He's obsessed by work.

l'**observation** FEM NOUN
comment
□ J'ai une ou deux observations à faire. I've got one or two comments to make.

observer VERB [28]
1 to watch
□ Il observait les canards sur le lac. He watched the ducks on the lake.
2 to observe
□ Ils observent le règlement. They observe the rules.

l'**obstacle** MASC NOUN
1 obstacle
□ surmonter un obstacle to overcome an obstacle
2 fence (*in show jumping*)
■ **une course d'obstacles** an obstacle race

obstiné (FEM **obstinée**) ADJECTIVE
stubborn

★ **obtenir** VERB [83]
1 to get
□ Ils ont obtenu cinquante pour cent des voix. They got 50% of the votes.
2 to achieve
□ Nous avons obtenu de bons résultats. We achieved good results.

★ l'**occasion** FEM NOUN
1 opportunity
□ C'est une occasion à ne pas manquer. It's an opportunity not to be missed.
2 occasion
□ à l'occasion de son anniversaire on the occasion of his birthday □ à plusieurs occasions on several occasions
3 bargain
□ Cet ordinateur est une bonne occasion. This computer's a real bargain.
■ **d'occasion** second-hand □ une voiture d'occasion a second-hand car

l'**Occident** MASC NOUN
West
□ en Occident in the West

occidental (FEM **occidentale**, MASC PL **occidentaux**) ADJECTIVE
western
■ **les pays occidentaux** the West

l'**occupation** FEM NOUN
occupation
□ la France sous l'Occupation France during the Occupation

★ **occupé** (FEM **occupée**) ADJECTIVE
1 busy
□ Le directeur est très occupé. The director's very busy.
2 taken
□ Est-ce que cette place est occupée? Is this seat taken?
3 engaged
□ Les toilettes sont occupées. The toilet's engaged. □ La ligne est occupée. The line's engaged.

occuper VERB [28]
to occupy
□ Les enfants ne sont pas faciles à occuper

quand il pleut. Children aren't easy to keep occupied when it rains.

■ **s'occuper de quelque chose 1** to be in charge of something □ Elle s'occupe d'un club de sport. She's in charge of a sports club. **2** to deal with something □ Je vais m'occuper de ce dossier. I'm going to deal with this file.

■ **On s'occupe de vous?** (*in a shop*) Are you being attended to?

l'**océan** MASC NOUN
ocean
□ l'océan Indien the Indian Ocean

★ **octobre** MASC NOUN
October
■ **en octobre** in October

★ l'**odeur** FEM NOUN
smell
□ Il y a une drôle d'odeur ici. There's a funny smell round here.

odieux (FEM **odieuse**) ADJECTIVE
horrible
□ Elle a été odieuse avec nous. She was horrible to us.

l'**œil** (PL les **yeux**) MASC NOUN
eye
□ J'ai quelque chose dans l'œil. I've got something in my eye.
■ **à l'œil** (*informal*) for free □ Il est entré à l'œil. He got in for free.

l'**œillet** MASC NOUN
carnation

★ l'**œuf** MASC NOUN
egg
■ **un œuf à la coque** a soft-boiled egg
■ **un œuf dur** a hard-boiled egg
■ **un œuf au plat** a fried egg
■ **les œufs brouillés** scrambled eggs
■ **un œuf de Pâques** an Easter egg

l'**œuvre** FEM NOUN
work
□ J'étudie une œuvre de Molière. I'm studying one of Molière's works.
■ **une œuvre d'art** a work of art

offert VERB ▷ *see* **offrir**

★ l'**office** MASC NOUN
■ **un office du tourisme** a tourist office

officiel (FEM **officielle**) ADJECTIVE
official

l'**officier** MASC NOUN
officer
□ Il est officier de marine. He's a naval officer.

★ l'**offre** FEM NOUN
offer
□ une offre spéciale a special offer
■ **'offres d'emploi'** 'situations vacant'

★ **offrir** VERB [54]
■ **offrir quelque chose 1** to offer something □ On lui a offert un poste de secrétaire. They offered her a secretarial post. □ Elle lui a offert à boire. She offered him a drink. **2** to give something □ Il lui a offert des roses. He gave her roses.
■ **s'offrir quelque chose** to treat oneself to something □ Je me suis offert un nouveau sac. I treated myself to a new bag.

★ l'**oie** FEM NOUN
goose

★ l'**oignon** MASC NOUN
onion
■ **Ce ne sont pas mes oignons!** (*informal*) It's none of my business!

★ l'**oiseau** (PL les **oiseaux**) MASC NOUN
bird

l'**olive** FEM NOUN
olive
□ l'huile d'olive olive oil

olympique (FEM **olympique**) ADJECTIVE
■ **les Jeux olympiques** the Olympic Games

★ l'**ombre** FEM NOUN
1 shade
□ Je vais me mettre à l'ombre. I'm going to sit in the shade.
2 shadow
■ **l'ombre à paupières** eye shadow

★ l'**omelette** FEM NOUN
omelette

★ l'**omnibus** MASC NOUN
local train

★ **on** PRONOUN
1 we
□ On va à la plage demain. We're going to the beach tomorrow. □ On a pensé que ça te ferait plaisir. We thought you'd be pleased.
2 someone
□ On m'a volé mon sac. Someone has stolen my bag.
■ **On m'a dit d'attendre.** I was told to wait.
■ **On vous demande au téléphone.** There's a phone call for you.
3 you
□ On peut visiter le château en été. You can visit the castle in the summer. □ D'ici on peut voir la côte française. From here you can see the French coast.

★ l'**oncle** MASC NOUN
uncle

★ l'**onde** FEM NOUN
wave (*on radio*)
□ sur les grandes ondes on long wave

★ l'**ongle** MASC NOUN
nail
■ **se couper les ongles** to cut one's nails
□ Elle s'est coupé les ongles. She cut her nails.

ont VERB ▷ *see* **avoir**
■ **Ils ont beaucoup d'argent.** They've got lots of money.

■ **Elles ont passé de bonnes vacances.** They had a good holiday.

l'**ONU** FEM NOUN (= *Organisation des Nations Unies*)
UN (= *United Nations*)

★ **onze** NUMBER
eleven
□ Elle a onze ans. She's eleven. □ à onze heures at eleven o'clock
■ **le onze février** the eleventh of February

★ **onzième** (FEM **onzième**) ADJECTIVE
eleventh
□ au onzième étage on the eleventh floor

★ l'**opéra** MASC NOUN
opera

★ l'**opération** FEM NOUN
operation

opérer VERB [34]
to operate on
□ Elle a été opérée de l'appendicite. She was operated on for appendicitis.
■ **se faire opérer** to have an operation □ Elle s'est fait opérer. She's had an operation.

★ l'**opinion** FEM NOUN
opinion

★ **opposé** (FEM **opposée**) ADJECTIVE
▷ *see also* **opposé** NOUN
opposite
□ Elle est partie dans la direction opposée. She went off in the opposite direction.
■ **être opposé à quelque chose** to be opposed to something

★ l'**opposé** MASC NOUN
▷ *see also* **opposé** ADJECTIVE
the opposite

opposer VERB [28]
■ **opposer quelqu'un à quelqu'un** to pit somebody against somebody □ Ce match oppose les Français aux Allemands. This match pits the French against the Germans.
■ **s'opposer** to conflict □ Ces deux points de vue s'opposent. These two points of view conflict.
■ **s'opposer à quelque chose** to oppose something □ Son père s'oppose à son mariage. Her father's against her marriage.

l'**opposition** FEM NOUN
opposition
■ **par opposition à** as opposed to □ la littérature contemporaine par opposition à la littérature classique modern literature, as opposed to classics
■ **faire opposition à un chèque** to stop a cheque

★ l'**opticien** MASC NOUN
optician
□ Il est opticien. He's an optician.

★ l'**opticienne** FEM NOUN
optician
□ Elle est opticienne. She's an optician.

★ **optimiste** (FEM **optimiste**) ADJECTIVE
optimistic

★ l'**option** FEM NOUN
option
■ **une matière à option** an optional subject

★ l'**or** MASC NOUN
▷ *see also* **or** CONJUNCTION
gold
□ un bracelet en or a gold bracelet

★ **or** CONJUNCTION
▷ *see also* **or** NOUN
and yet
□ Il était sûr de gagner, or il a perdu. He was sure he would win, and yet he lost.

★ l'**orage** MASC NOUN
thunderstorm

★ **orageux** (FEM **orageuse**) ADJECTIVE
stormy

★ **oral** (FEM **orale**, MASC PL **oraux**) ADJECTIVE
▷ *see also* **oral** NOUN
■ **une épreuve orale** an oral exam
■ **à prendre par voie orale** to be taken orally

★ l'**oral** (PL les **oraux**) MASC NOUN
▷ *see also* **oral** ADJECTIVE
oral (*exam*)
□ un oral de français a French oral

★ l'**orange** FEM NOUN
▷ *see also* **orange** ADJECTIVE
orange (*fruit*)

★ **orange** (FEM+PL **orange**) ADJECTIVE
▷ *see also* **orange** NOUN
orange (*in colour*)
□ des fleurs orange orange flowers

★ l'**orchestre** MASC NOUN
1 orchestra
□ un orchestre symphonique a symphony orchestra
2 band
□ un orchestre de jazz a jazz band

l'**ordi** MASC NOUN (*informal*)
computer

★ **ordinaire** (FEM **ordinaire**) ADJECTIVE
▷ *see also* **ordinaire** NOUN
1 ordinary
□ des gens ordinaires ordinary people
2 standard
□ un format ordinaire a standard size

★ l'**ordinaire** MASC NOUN
▷ *see also* **ordinaire** ADJECTIVE
two-star (petrol)
■ **sortir de l'ordinaire** to be out of the ordinary

★ l'**ordinateur** MASC NOUN
computer

■ **un ordinateur de bureau** a desktop computer
■ **un ordinateur portable** a laptop computer

★l'**ordonnance** FEM NOUN
prescription

ordonné (FEM **ordonnée**) ADJECTIVE
tidy

★**ordonner** VERB [28]
■ **ordonner à quelqu'un de faire quelque chose** to order somebody to do something

★l'**ordre** MASC NOUN
order
□ par ordre alphabétique in alphabetical order
■ **dans l'ordre** in order □ dans le bon ordre in the right order
■ **mettre en ordre** to tidy up
■ **jusqu'à nouvel ordre** until further notice

★les **ordures** FEM PL NOUN
rubbish *sing*
■ **jeter quelque chose aux ordures** to throw something in the bin

★l'**oreille** FEM NOUN
ear

★l'**oreiller** MASC NOUN
pillow

les **oreillons** MASC PL NOUN
mumps

l'**organe** MASC NOUN
organ (*in body*)

l'**organisateur** MASC NOUN
organizer

l'**organisation** FEM NOUN
organization

l'**organisatrice** FEM NOUN
organizer

★**organiser** VERB [28]
to organize
■ **s'organiser** to get organized □ Il ne sait pas s'organiser. He can't get himself organized.

l'**organisme** MASC NOUN
body (*organization*)

l'**orgue** MASC NOUN
organ
□ Paul joue de l'orgue. Paul plays the organ.

orgueilleux (FEM **orgueilleuse**) ADJECTIVE
proud

l'**Orient** MASC NOUN
East
□ en Orient in the East

oriental (FEM **orientale**, MASC PL **orientaux**) ADJECTIVE
1 oriental
□ un palais oriental an oriental palace
2 eastern
□ la frontière orientale de la Pologne Poland's eastern border

l'**orientation** FEM NOUN
orientation
■ **avoir le sens de l'orientation** to have a good sense of direction
■ **l'orientation professionnelle** careers advice

originaire (FEM **originaire**) ADJECTIVE
■ **Elle est originaire de Paris.** She's from Paris.

★**original** (FEM **originale**, MASC PL **originaux**) ADJECTIVE
▷ *see also* **original** NOUN
original
□ un film en version originale a film in the original language

★l'**original** (PL les **originaux**) MASC NOUN
▷ *see also* **original** ADJECTIVE
original
□ L'original est au Louvre. The original is in the Louvre.
■ **un vieil original** an old eccentric

l'**origine** FEM NOUN
origin
■ **à l'origine** originally

l'**orphelin** MASC NOUN
orphan

l'**orpheline** FEM NOUN
orphan

l'**orteil** MASC NOUN
toe

l'**orthographe** FEM NOUN
spelling

★l'**os** MASC NOUN
bone
■ **tomber sur un os** (*informal*) to hit a snag

★**oser** VERB [28]
to dare
■ **oser faire quelque chose** to dare to do something

l'**otage** MASC NOUN
hostage

★**ôter** VERB [28]
1 to take off
□ Elle a ôté son manteau. She took off her coat.
2 to take away

★**ou** CONJUNCTION
or
■ **ou ... ou ...** either ... or ...
■ **ou bien** or else □ On pourrait aller au cinéma ou bien rentrer directement. We could go to the cinema or else go straight home.

★**où** PRONOUN, ADVERB
1 where
□ Où est Nick? Where's Nick? □ Où allez-vous? Where are you going? □ Je sais où il est. I know where he is. □ la maison où je suis né the house where I was born □ la ville d'où je viens the town I come from

French-English

O

2 that

□ Le jour où il est parti, tout le monde a pleuré. The day that he left, everyone cried.

■ **Par où allons-nous passer?** Which way are we going to go?

l'**ouate** FEM NOUN

cotton wool

★ **oublier** VERB [19]

1 to forget

□ N'oublie pas de fermer la porte. Don't forget to shut the door.

2 to leave

□ J'ai oublié mon sac chez Sabine. I left my bag at Sabine's.

★ l'**ouest** MASC NOUN

▷ *see also* **ouest** ADJECTIVE

west

□ Elle vit dans l'ouest de l'Angleterre. She lives in the West of England.

■ **à l'ouest de Paris** west of Paris

■ **vers l'ouest** westwards

■ **l'Europe de l'Ouest** Western Europe

■ **le vent d'ouest** the west wind

★ **ouest** (FEM+PL **ouest**) ADJECTIVE

▷ *see also* **ouest** NOUN

1 west

□ la côte ouest de l'Écosse the west coast of Scotland

2 western

□ la partie ouest du pays the western part of the country

ouf EXCLAMATION

phew!

★ **oui** ADVERB

yes

l'**ouragan** MASC NOUN

hurricane

l'**ourlet** MASC NOUN

seam

★ l'**ours** MASC NOUN

bear

■ **un ours en peluche** a teddy bear

★ l'**outil** MASC NOUN

tool

outré (FEM **outrée**) ADJECTIVE

outraged

□ Il a été outré de son insolence. He was outraged at her cheek.

★ **ouvert** (FEM **ouverte**) ADJECTIVE

1 open

□ Le magasin est ouvert. The shop's open.

2 on

□ Il a laissé le robinet ouvert. He left the tap on.

■ **avoir l'esprit ouvert** to be open-minded

★ **ouvert** VERB ▷ *see* **ouvrir**

★ l'**ouverture** FEM NOUN

opening

□ les heures d'ouverture opening hours

★ l'**ouvre-boîte** MASC NOUN

tin opener

★ l'**ouvre-bouteille** MASC NOUN

bottle-opener

★ l'**ouvreuse** FEM NOUN

usherette

★ l'**ouvrier** MASC NOUN

worker

□ Son père est ouvrier dans une usine. His father's a factory worker.

★ l'**ouvrière** FEM NOUN

worker

★ **ouvrir** VERB [55]

to open

□ Ouvrez! Open up! □ Elle a ouvert la porte. She opened the door.

■ **s'ouvrir** to open □ La porte s'est ouverte. The door opened.

ovale (FEM **ovale**) ADJECTIVE

oval

l'**ovni** MASC NOUN (= *objet volant non identifié*)

UFO

l'**oxygène** MASC NOUN

oxygen

l'**ozone** MASC NOUN

ozone

Pp

le **Pacifique** MASC NOUN
Pacific
□ l'océan Pacifique the Pacific Ocean

le/la **pacifiste** MASC/FEM NOUN
pacifist

★ **PACS** MASC NOUN (= *pacte civil de solidarité*)
civil partnership

★ se **pacser** VERB [28]
to become civil partners
□ Ils se sont pacsés au lieu de se marier. They became civil partners instead of getting married.

la **pagaille** FEM NOUN
mess *sing*
□ Quelle pagaille! What a mess!

★ la **page** FEM NOUN
page
□ Tournez la page. Turn the page.
■ **la page d'accueil** (*on internet*) the home page

la **paie** FEM NOUN
wages

★ le **paiement** MASC NOUN
payment

le **paillasson** MASC NOUN
doormat

la **paille** FEM NOUN
straw

★ le **pain** MASC NOUN
1 bread
□ un morceau de pain a piece of bread □ une tranche de pain a slice of bread
2 loaf
□ J'ai acheté un pain. I bought a loaf of bread.
■ **le pain complet** wholemeal bread
■ **le pain d'épice** gingerbread
■ **le pain de mie** sandwich loaf
■ **le pain grillé** toast

DID YOU KNOW...?
Bread is always served with a meal in French restaurants, at no extra cost.

★ **pair** (FEM **paire**) ADJECTIVE
▷ *see also* **paire** NOUN
even
□ un nombre pair an even number
■ **une jeune fille au pair** an au pair

★ la **paire** FEM NOUN
▷ *see also* **pair** ADJECTIVE
pair
□ une paire de chaussures a pair of shoes

★ **paisible** (FEM **paisible**) ADJECTIVE
peaceful
□ un village paisible a peaceful village

★ la **paix** FEM NOUN
peace
■ **faire la paix** **1** to make peace □ Les deux pays ont fait la paix. The two countries have made peace with each other. **2** to make it up □ Laure a fait la paix avec son frère. Laure made it up with her brother.
■ **avoir la paix** to have peace and quiet
□ J'aimerais bien avoir la paix. I'd like to have a bit of peace and quiet.
■ **Fiche-moi la paix!** (*informal*) Leave me alone!

★ le **palais** MASC NOUN
1 palace
□ le palais de Buckingham Buckingham Palace
2 palate (*in mouth*)

★ **pâle** (FEM **pâle**) ADJECTIVE
pale
□ bleu pâle pale blue

la **Palestine** FEM NOUN
Palestine

la **pâleur** FEM NOUN
paleness

le **palier** MASC NOUN
landing
□ Il m'attendait sur le palier. He was waiting for me on the landing.

pâlir VERB [38]
to go pale

la **palme** FEM NOUN
flipper (*for swimming*)

palmé (FEM **palmée**) ADJECTIVE
webbed
□ Les canards ont les pieds palmés. Ducks have webbed feet.

le **palmier** MASC NOUN
palm tree

palpitant (FEM **palpitante**) ADJECTIVE
thrilling
□ un roman palpitant a thrilling novel

★ le **pamplemousse** MASC NOUN
grapefruit

le **panaché** MASC NOUN
shandy

la **pancarte** FEM NOUN
sign
□ Il y a une pancarte dans la vitrine. There's a sign in the window.

la **pandémie** FEM NOUN
pandemic
□ une pandémie de grippe a flu pandemic

pané (FEM **panée**) ADJECTIVE
fried in breadcrumbs
□ du poisson pané fish in breadcrumbs

★ le **panier** MASC NOUN
basket

la **panique** FEM NOUN
panic

paniquer VERB [28]
to panic

★ la **panne** FEM NOUN
breakdown
■ **être en panne** to have broken down
□ L'ascenseur est en panne. The lift's not working.
■ **tomber en panne** to break down □ Nous sommes tombés en panne sur l'autoroute. We broke down on the motorway.
■ **Nous sommes tombés en panne d'essence.** We've run out of petrol.
■ **une panne de courant** a power cut

★ le **panneau** (PL les **panneaux**) MASC NOUN
sign
□ Ce panneau dit que la maison est à vendre. This sign says that the house is for sale.
■ **panneau d'affichage** **1** advertising hoarding **2** (*in station*) arrivals and departures board **3** (*on internet*) bulletin board

le **panorama** MASC NOUN
panorama

★ le **pansement** MASC NOUN
1 dressing (*bandage*)
2 sticking plaster

★ le **pantalon** MASC NOUN
trousers *pl*
□ Son pantalon est trop court. His trousers are too short.
■ **un pantalon de ski** a pair of ski pants

la **panthère** FEM NOUN
panther

★ la **pantoufle** FEM NOUN
slipper

la **PAO** ABBREVIATION (= *publication assistée par ordinateur*)
DTP (= *desktop publishing*)

le **paon** MASC NOUN
peacock

★ le **papa** MASC NOUN
dad

le **pape** MASC NOUN
pope

★ la **papeterie** FEM NOUN
stationer's

le **papi** MASC NOUN (*informal*)
granddad

★ le **papier** MASC NOUN
paper
□ une feuille de papier a sheet of paper
■ **Vos papiers, s'il vous plaît.** Your identity papers, please.
■ **les papiers d'identité** identity papers
■ **le papier à lettres** writing paper
■ **le papier hygiénique** toilet paper
■ **le papier peint** wallpaper

le **papillon** MASC NOUN
butterfly

le **paquebot** MASC NOUN
liner

la **pâquerette** FEM NOUN
daisy

★ **Pâques** MASC NOUN
Easter
□ Je viendrai te voir à Pâques. I'll come and see you at Easter.
■ **les œufs de Pâques** Easter eggs

DID YOU KNOW...?
In France, Easter eggs are said to be brought by the Easter bells or **cloches de Pâques** which fly from Rome and drop them in people's gardens.

★ le **paquet** MASC NOUN
1 packet
□ Je voudrais un paquet de chewing-gums. I'd like a packet of chewing-gum.
2 parcel
□ Sa mère lui a envoyé un paquet. His mother sent him a parcel.

le **paquet-cadeau** (PL les **paquets-cadeaux**) MASC NOUN
gift-wrapped parcel
□ La vendeuse m'a fait un paquet-cadeau. The shop assistant gift-wrapped it for me.

★ **par** PREPOSITION
1 by
□ L'Amérique a été découverte par Christophe Colomb. America was discovered by Christopher Columbus.
■ **deux par deux** two by two □ Les élèves sont entrés deux par deux. The pupils went in two by two.
2 with
□ Son nom commence par un H. His name begins with H.

3 out of
□ Elle regardait par la fenêtre. She was looking out of the window. □ par habitude out of habit

4 via
□ Nous sommes passés par Lyon pour aller à Grenoble. We went via Lyon to Grenoble.

5 through
□ Il faut passer par la douane avant de prendre l'avion. You have to go through customs before boarding the plane.

6 per
□ Prenez trois cachets par jour. Take three tablets per day. □ Le voyage coûte deux mille euros par personne. The trip costs two thousand euros per person.

■ **par ici** 1 this way □ Il faut passer par ici pour y arriver. You have to go this way to get there. 2 round here □ Il y a beaucoup de touristes par ici. There are lots of tourists round here.

■ **par-ci, par-là** here and there

le **parachute** MASC NOUN
parachute

le/la **parachutiste** MASC/FEM NOUN
parachutist

le **paradis** MASC NOUN
heaven

les **parages** MASC PL NOUN
■ **dans les parages** in the area □ Il n'y a pas d'hôtel dans les parages. There are no hotels in the area.

le **paragraphe** MASC NOUN
paragraph

★ **paraître** VERB [56]

1 to seem
□ Ça paraît incroyable. It seems unbelievable.

2 to look
□ Elle paraît plus jeune que son frère. She looks younger than her brother.

■ **il paraît que** it seems that □ Il paraît que c'est la faute de la direction. It seems that it's the management's fault.

★ le **parallèle** MASC NOUN
▷ *see also* **parallèle** NOUN
parallel
□ Il a fait un parallèle entre ces deux événements. He drew a parallel between the two events.

★ la **parallèle** FEM NOUN
▷ *see also* **parallèle** NOUN
parallel line

paralympique ADJECTIVE
Paralympic

paralysé (FEM **paralysée**) ADJECTIVE
paralysed

★ le **parapluie** MASC NOUN
umbrella

★ le **parasol** MASC NOUN
parasol

★ le **parc** MASC NOUN

1 park
□ Le dimanche, Emma va se promener au parc. On Sundays Emma goes for a walk in the park.

■ **un parc d'attractions** an amusement park

■ **un parc éolien** a wind farm

2 grounds
□ Le château est situé au milieu d'un grand parc. The castle is surrounded by extensive grounds.

★ **parce que** CONJUNCTION
because
□ Il n'est pas venu parce qu'il n'avait pas de voiture. He didn't come because he didn't have a car.

★ le **parcmètre** MASC NOUN
parking meter

parcourir VERB [16]

1 to cover
□ Gavin a parcouru cinquante kilomètres à vélo. Gavin covered 50 kilometres on his bike.

2 to glance through
□ J'ai parcouru le journal d'aujourd'hui. I glanced through today's newspaper.

le **parcours** MASC NOUN
journey

★ **par-dessous** ADVERB
underneath
□ Il portait un pull et une chemise par-dessous. He was wearing a jumper with a shirt underneath.

★ le **pardessus** MASC NOUN
overcoat

★ **par-dessus** ADVERB, PREPOSITION

1 on top
□ Elle porte un chemisier et un pull rouge par-dessus. She's wearing a blouse with a red jumper on top.

2 over
□ Elle a sauté par-dessus le mur. She jumped over the wall.

■ **en avoir par-dessus la tête** to have had enough □ J'en ai par-dessus la tête de tous ces problèmes. I've had enough of all these problems.

★ le **pardon** MASC NOUN
▷ *see also* **pardon** EXCLAMATION
forgiveness

★ **pardon** EXCLAMATION
▷ *see also* **pardon** NOUN

1 sorry!
□ Oh, pardon! J'espère que je ne vous ai pas fait mal. Oh, sorry! I hope I didn't hurt you.

■ **demander pardon à quelqu'un** to

pologize to somebody □ Il leur a demandé pardon. He apologized to them.
■ **Je vous demande pardon.** I'm sorry.
2 excuse me!
□ Pardon, madame! Pouvez-vous me dire où se trouve la poste? Excuse me! Could you tell me where the post office is?
3 pardon?
□ Pardon? Je n'ai pas compris ce que vous avez dit. Pardon? I didn't understand what you said.

★ **pardonner** VERB [28]
to forgive
□ Nous lui avons pardonné de nous avoir menti. We forgave him for lying to us.

★ le **pare-brise** (PL les **pare-brise**) MASC NOUN
windscreen

le **pare-chocs** MASC NOUN
bumper

★ **pareil** (FEM **pareille**) ADJECTIVE
1 the same
□ Ces deux maisons ne sont pas pareilles. These two houses aren't the same.
2 like that
□ J'aime bien sa voiture. J'en voudrais une pareille. I like his car. I'd like one like that.
3 such
□ Je refuse d'écouter des bêtises pareilles. I won't listen to such nonsense.
■ **sans pareil** unequalled □ un talent sans pareil an unequalled talent

la **parenthèse** FEM NOUN
bracket
□ entre parenthèses in brackets

★ les **parents** MASC PL NOUN
1 parents (*mother and father*)
2 relatives
□ parents et amis friends and relatives

la **paresse** FEM NOUN
laziness

★ **paresseux** (FEM **paresseuse**) ADJECTIVE
lazy

★ **parfait** (FEM **parfaite**) ADJECTIVE
perfect

parfaitement ADVERB
perfectly
□ Il parle parfaitement l'arabe. He speaks perfect Arabic.

★ **parfois** ADVERB
sometimes

★ le **parfum** MASC NOUN
1 perfume
2 flavour
□ Je voudrais une glace. — Quel parfum veux-tu? I'd like an ice cream. — What flavour would you like?

parfumé (FEM **parfumée**) ADJECTIVE
1 fragrant
□ une rose très parfumée a very fragrant rose
2 flavoured
□ des biscuits parfumés au café coffee-flavoured biscuits

★ la **parfumerie** FEM NOUN
perfume shop

le **pari** MASC NOUN
bet

parier VERB [19]
to bet

★ **Paris** NOUN
Paris
■ **à Paris** **1** in Paris **2** to Paris

★ **parisien** (FEM **parisienne**) ADJECTIVE, NOUN
1 Parisian
□ un célèbre couturier parisien a famous Parisian designer
2 Paris
□ le métro parisien the Paris metro
■ **un Parisien** a Parisian (*man*)
■ **une Parisienne** a Parisian (*woman*)

★ le **parking** MASC NOUN
car park

BE CAREFUL!
The French word **parking** does not mean **parking**.

le **parlement** MASC NOUN
parliament

★ **parler** VERB [28]
1 to speak
□ Vous parlez français? Do you speak French?
2 to talk
□ Nous étions en train de parler quand le directeur est entré. We were talking when the headmaster came in.
■ **parler de quelque chose à quelqu'un** to tell somebody about something □ Il m'a parlé de sa nouvelle voiture. He told me about his new car.

★ **parmi** PREPOSITION
among
□ Ils étaient parmi les meilleurs de la classe. They were among the best pupils in the class.

la **paroi** FEM NOUN
wall

la **paroisse** FEM NOUN
parish

★ la **parole** FEM NOUN
1 speech
□ l'usage de la parole the power of speech
2 word
□ Il m'a donné sa parole. He gave me his word. □ Elle a tenu parole. She kept her word.
■ **les paroles** lyrics □ J'aime les paroles de cette chanson. I like the lyrics of this song.

le **parquet** MASC NOUN
floor (*wooden*)

le **parrain** MASC NOUN
godfather

parrainer VERB [28]
to sponsor
□ Cette entreprise parraine notre équipe de rugby. This firm is sponsoring our rugby team.

pars VERB ▷ *see* **partir**

★ la **part** FEM NOUN
1 share
□ Vous n'avez pas eu votre part. You haven't had your share.
2 piece
□ une part de gâteau a piece of cake
■ **prendre part à quelque chose** to take part in something □ Il va prendre part à la réunion. He's going to take part in the meeting.
■ **de la part de** **1** on behalf of □ Je dois vous remercier de la part de mon frère. I must thank you on behalf of my brother. **2** from □ C'est un cadeau pour toi, de la part de Clémence. It's a present for you, from Clémence.
■ **à part** apart from □ Ils sont tous venus, à part Romain. They all came, apart from Romain.

★ **partager** VERB [45]
1 to share
□ Ils partagent un appartement. They share a flat.
2 to divide
□ Lucie a partagé le gâteau en quatre. Lucie divided the cake into four.

★ le/la **partenaire** MASC/FEM NOUN
partner

le **parti** MASC NOUN
party
□ le Parti socialiste the Socialist Party

le **participant** MASC NOUN
participant

la **participante** FEM NOUN
participant

la **participation** FEM NOUN
participation

le **participe** MASC NOUN
participle
■ **le participe passé** the past participle
■ **le participe présent** the present participle

★ **participer** VERB [28]
■ **participer à quelque chose** **1** to take part in something □ Hugo va participer à la course. Hugo is going to take part in the race. **2** to contribute to something □ Je voudrais participer aux frais. I would like to contribute to the cost.

la **particularité** FEM NOUN
characteristic

la **particule** FEM NOUN
particle
■ **particules fines** fine particulate matter

★ **particulier** (FEM **particulière**) ADJECTIVE
1 private
□ une maison particulière a private house
2 distinctive
□ Ce vin a un arôme particulier. This wine has a distinctive flavour.
3 particular
□ Dans ce cas particulier, je ne peux rien faire. In this particular case, I can't do anything.
■ **en particulier** **1** particularly □ J'aime les fruits, en particulier les fraises. I like fruit, particularly strawberries. **2** in private □ Est-ce que je peux vous parler en particulier? Can I speak to you in private?

particulièrement ADVERB
particularly

★ la **partie** FEM NOUN
1 part
□ Une partie du groupe partira en Italie. Part of the group will go to Italy.
2 game
□ Nous avons fait une partie de tennis. We played a game of tennis. □ une partie de cartes a game of cards
■ **en partie** partly □ Cela explique en partie le problème. That partly explains the problem.
■ **en grande partie** largely □ Son histoire est en grande partie vraie. His story is largely true.
■ **faire partie de** to be part of □ Ce tableau fait partie d'une très belle collection. This picture is part of a very beautiful collection.

partiel (FEM **partielle**) ADJECTIVE
partial

★ **partir** VERB [57, *aux* **être**]
to go
□ Je lui ai téléphoné mais il était déjà parti. I phoned him but he'd already gone.
■ **partir en vacances** to go on holiday
■ **partir de** to leave □ Il est parti de Nice à sept heures. He left Nice at 7.
■ **à partir de** from □ Je serai chez moi à partir de huit heures. I'll be at home from eight o'clock onwards.

la **partition** FEM NOUN
score (*in music*)
□ une partition de piano a piano score

★ **partout** ADVERB
everywhere

paru VERB ▷ *see* **paraître**

la **parution** FEM NOUN
publication
□ Ce roman a eu beaucoup de succès dès sa parution. This novel was very successful from the moment it came out.

French-English

parvenir VERB [89, *aux* **être**]
■ **parvenir à faire quelque chose** to manage to do something □ Elle est finalement parvenue à ouvrir la porte. She finally managed to open the door.
■ **faire parvenir quelque chose à quelqu'un** to send something to somebody □ Je vous ferai parvenir le colis avant lundi. I'll send you the parcel before Monday.

★ **pas** ADVERB
▷ *see also* **pas** NOUN
■ **ne ... pas** not □ Il ne pleut pas. It's not raining. □ Elle n'est pas venue. She didn't come. □ Ils n'ont pas de voiture. They haven't got a car.
■ **Vous viendrez à notre soirée, n'est-ce pas?** You're coming to our party, aren't you?
■ **C'est Harry qui a gagné, n'est-ce pas?** Harry won, didn't he?
■ **pas moi** not me □ Elle veut aller au cinéma, pas moi. She wants to go to the cinema, but I don't.
■ **pas de** no □ pas de problème no problem
■ **pas du tout** not at all □ Je n'aime pas du tout ça. I don't like that at all.
■ **pas mal** not bad □ Ce n'est pas mal pour un début. That's not bad for a first attempt. □ Comment allez-vous? — Pas mal. How are you? — Not bad.
■ **pas mal de** quite a lot of □ Il y avait pas mal de monde au concert. There were quite a lot of people at the concert.

★ le **pas** MASC NOUN
▷ *see also* **pas** ADVERB
1 pace
□ Il marchait d'un pas rapide. He walked at a fast pace.
2 step
□ Faites trois pas en avant. Take three steps forward. □ un pas en arrière a step backwards
3 footstep
□ J'entends des pas dans l'escalier. I can hear footsteps on the stairs.
■ **au pas** at walking pace □ Le cheval est parti au pas. The horse set off at walking pace.
■ **faire les cent pas** to pace up and down □ Il faisait les cent pas dans le couloir. He was pacing up and down the corridor.

★ le **passage** MASC NOUN
passage
□ J'ai traduit un passage de ce livre. I translated a passage from this book.
■ **Il a été éclaboussé au passage de la voiture.** He was soaked by a passing car.
■ **de passage** passing through □ Nous sommes de passage à Toulouse. We're just passing through Toulouse.
■ **un passage à niveau** a level crossing
■ **un passage clouté** a pedestrian crossing
■ **un passage protégé** a pedestrian crossing
■ **un passage souterrain** a subway

★ **passager** (FEM **passagère**) ADJECTIVE
▷ *see also* **passager** NOUN, **passagère** NOUN
temporary

★ le **passager** MASC NOUN
▷ *see also* **passager** ADJECTIVE
passenger
■ **un passager clandestin** a stowaway

★ la **passagère** FEM NOUN
▷ *see also* **passager** ADJECTIVE
passenger

★ le **passant** MASC NOUN
passer-by

★ la **passante** FEM NOUN
passer-by

★ **passé** (FEM **passée**) ADJECTIVE
▷ *see also* **passé** NOUN
1 last
□ Je l'ai vu la semaine passée. I saw him last week.
2 past
□ Il est minuit passé. It's past midnight.

★ le **passé** MASC NOUN
▷ *see also* **passé** ADJECTIVE
1 past
□ dans le passé in the past
2 past tense
□ Mettez ce verbe au passé. Put this verb into the past tense.
■ **le passé composé** the perfect tense
■ **le passé simple** the past historic

★ le **passeport** MASC NOUN
passport

★ **passer** VERB [58, *aux* **avoir** *or* **être**]
1 to cross
□ Nous avons passé la frontière belge. We crossed the Belgian border.
2 to go through
□ Il faut passer la douane en sortant. You have to go through customs on the way out.
3 to spend
□ Elle a passé la journée à ne rien faire. She spent the day doing nothing. □ Ils passent toujours leurs vacances au Danemark. They always spend their holidays in Denmark.
4 to take
□ Mathieu a passé ses examens la semaine dernière. Mathieu took his exams last week.

> **BE CAREFUL!**
> **passer un examen** does not mean **to pass an exam.**

5 to pass
□ Passe-moi le sel, s'il te plaît. Pass me the salt, please.
6 to show
□ On passe 'Le Kid' au cinéma cette semaine. They're showing 'The Kid' at the cinema this week.

P

7 to call in
□ Je passerai chez vous ce soir. I'll call in this evening.
■ **passer à la radio** to be on the radio □ Mon père passe à la radio demain soir. My father's on the radio tomorrow night.
■ **passer à la télévision** to be on the television □ 'Titanic' passe à la télé ce soir. 'Titanic' is on TV tonight.
■ **Ne quittez pas, je vous passe Madame Chevalier.** Hold on please, I'm putting you through to Mrs Chevalier.
■ **passer par** to go through □ Ils sont passés par Paris pour aller à Tours. They went through Paris to get to Tours.
■ **en passant** in passing □ Je lui ai dit en passant que j'allais me marier. I told him in passing that I was getting married.
■ **laisser passer** to let through □ Il m'a laissé passer. He let me through.
■ **se passer 1** to take place □ Cette histoire se passe au Moyen Âge. This story takes place in the Middle Ages. **2** to go □ Comment se sont passés tes examens? How did your exams go? **3** to happen □ Que s'est-il passé? Un accident? What happened? Was there an accident?
■ **Qu'est-ce qui se passe? Pourquoi est-ce qu'elle pleure?** What's the matter? Why is she crying?
■ **se passer de** to do without □ Je me passerai de café ce matin. I'll do without coffee this morning.

The verb **passer** uses **avoir** in the perfect tense when it describes crossing something, going through something, spending time somewhere, taking a test, or passing something to someone else. It uses **être** in the perfect tense when it describes passing through a place, visiting somewhere, showing a film, or being on the TV or radio.

la **passerelle** FEM NOUN
1 footbridge (*over river*)
2 gangway (*onto plane, boat*)

★ le **passe-temps** MASC NOUN
pastime

passif (FEM **passive**) ADJECTIVE
▷ *see also* **passif** NOUN
passive

le **passif** MASC NOUN
▷ *see also* **passif** ADJECTIVE
passive
□ Mettez ce verbe au passif. Put this verb into the passive.

★ la **passion** FEM NOUN
passion

★ **passionnant** (FEM **passionnante**) ADJECTIVE
fascinating

passionné (FEM **passionnée**) ADJECTIVE
keen
□ Lucas est un lecteur passionné. Lucas is a keen reader.
■ **Il est passionné de voile.** He's a sailing fanatic.

passionner VERB [28]
■ **Son travail le passionne.** He's passionate about his work.
■ **se passionner pour quelque chose** to have a passion for something □ Alexis se passionne pour les perroquets. Alexis has a passion for parrots.

la **passoire** FEM NOUN
sieve

la **pastèque** FEM NOUN
watermelon

le **pasteur** MASC NOUN
minister (*priest*)

★ la **pastille** FEM NOUN
cough sweet

la **patate** FEM NOUN (*informal*)
potato
■ **une patate douce** a sweet potato

la **pâte** FEM NOUN
1 pastry
2 dough
3 cake mixture
■ **la pâte à crêpes** pancake batter
■ **la pâte à modeler** Plasticine®
■ **la pâte d'amandes** marzipan

★ le **pâté** MASC NOUN
pâté
□ Nous avons mangé du pâté en entrée. We had pâté as a starter.
■ **un pâté de maisons** a block (*of houses*)

paternel (FEM **paternelle**) ADJECTIVE
■ **ma grand-mère paternelle** my father's mother
■ **mon oncle paternel** my father's brother

★ les **pâtes** FEM PL NOUN
pasta *sing*

la **patience** FEM NOUN
patience

★ **patient** (FEM **patiente**) ADJECTIVE
▷ *see also* **patient** NOUN, **patiente** NOUN
patient

★ le **patient** MASC NOUN
▷ *see also* **patient** ADJECTIVE
patient

★ la **patiente** FEM NOUN
▷ *see also* **patient** ADJECTIVE
patient

patienter VERB [28]
to wait
□ Veuillez patienter un instant, s'il vous plaît. Please wait a moment.

★ le **patin** MASC NOUN
1 skate
□ Nic a enfilé ses patins. Nic put her skates on.
2 skating
□ Ils font du patin tous les mercredis. They go skating every Wednesday.
■ **les patins à glace** ice skates
■ **les patins en ligne** Rollerblades®
■ **les patins à roulettes** roller skates

★ le **patinage** MASC NOUN
skating
■ **le patinage artistique** figure skating

★ **patiner** VERB [28]
to skate

le **patineur** MASC NOUN
skater

la **patineuse** FEM NOUN
skater

★ la **patinoire** FEM NOUN
ice rink

★ la **pâtisserie** FEM NOUN
cake shop
■ **faire de la pâtisserie** to bake □ J'adore faire de la pâtisserie. I love baking.
■ **les pâtisseries** cakes

★ le **pâtissier** MASC NOUN
confectioner

★ la **pâtissière** FEM NOUN
confectioner

la **patrie** FEM NOUN
homeland

★ le **patron** MASC NOUN
1 boss
2 pattern (*for dressmaking*)

★ la **patronne** FEM NOUN
boss
■ **Elle est patronne de café.** She runs a café.

patronner VERB [28]
to sponsor
□ Le festival est patronné par des entreprises locales. The festival is sponsored by local businesses.

la **patrouille** FEM NOUN
patrol

★ la **patte** FEM NOUN
1 paw (*of dog, cat*)
2 leg (*of bird, animal*)

paumer VERB [28] (*informal*)
to lose
□ J'ai paumé mes clés. I've lost my keys.

la **paupière** FEM NOUN
eyelid

★ la **pause** FEM NOUN
1 break
□ Ils font une pause. They're having a break.
□ une pause de midi a lunch break
2 pause
□ Il y a eu une pause dans la conversation. There was a pause in the conversation.

★ **pauvre** (FEM **pauvre**) ADJECTIVE
poor
□ Sa famille est pauvre. His family is poor.
□ Pauvre Vincent! Il n'a pas eu de chance! Poor Vincent! He was unlucky!

★ la **pauvreté** FEM NOUN
poverty

pavé (FEM **pavée**) ADJECTIVE
cobbled
□ Les rues étaient pavées. The streets were cobbled.

le **pavillon** MASC NOUN
house
□ Ils habitent un pavillon de banlieue. They've got a house in the suburbs.

payant (FEM **payante**) ADJECTIVE
paying
□ Ce sont des hôtes payants. They're paying guests.
■ **C'est payant.** You have to pay. □ L'entrée de la boîte est payante. You have to pay to get into the nightclub.

la **paye** FEM NOUN
wages

payé (FEM **payée**) ADJECTIVE
■ **être mal payé** to be badly paid
■ **un travail bien payé** a well-paid job

★ **payer** VERB [59]
1 to pay for
□ Combien as-tu payé ta voiture? How much did you pay for your car?
■ **J'ai payé ce T-shirt vingt euros.** I paid 20 euros for this T-shirt.
2 to pay
□ Elle a été payée aujourd'hui. She got paid today. □ Son métier paye bien. His job pays good money. □ Elle est mal payée. She is badly paid.
■ **faire payer quelque chose à quelqu'un** to charge somebody for something □ Il me l'a fait payer dix euros. He charged me 10 euros for it.
■ **payer quelque chose à quelqu'un** to buy somebody something □ Allez, je vous paye un verre. Come on, I'll buy you a drink.

★ le **pays** MASC NOUN
country
■ **du pays local** □ le vin du pays the local wine

★ le **paysage** MASC NOUN
landscape

★ le **paysan** MASC NOUN
farmer

★ la **paysanne** FEM NOUN
farmer

★ les **Pays-Bas** MASC PL NOUN
Netherlands
■ **aux Pays-Bas** **1** in the Netherlands **2** to the Netherlands

★ le **pays de Galles** MASC NOUN
Wales
■ **au pays de Galles** **1** in Wales □ Daphné habite au pays de Galles. Daphné lives in Wales. **2** to Wales □ Elle part au pays de Galles la semaine prochaine. She is going to Wales next week.

★ le **PC** MASC NOUN
▷ *see also* **PC** ABBREVIATION
PC (= *personal computer*)
□ Il a tapé le rapport sur son PC. He typed the report on his PC.

★ **PC** ABBREVIATION
▷ *see also* **PC** NOUN
(= *Parti communiste*)
Communist Party

le **PDG** MASC NOUN (= *président-directeur général*)
MD (= *managing director*)

★ le **péage** MASC NOUN
1 toll
□ Nous avons payé vingt euros de péage. We paid a toll of 20 euros.
2 tollbooth
□ Sabine s'est arrêtée au péage de l'autoroute. Sabine stopped at the motorway tollbooth.

DID YOU KNOW...?
French motorways charge a toll.

★ la **peau** (PL les **peaux**) FEM NOUN
skin
□ Elle a la peau douce. She's got soft skin.

★ la **pêche** FEM NOUN
1 peach
2 fishing
■ **aller à la pêche** to go fishing
■ **la pêche à la ligne** angling

le **péché** MASC NOUN
sin

★ **pêcher** VERB [28]
1 to fish for
□ Ils sont partis pêcher la truite. They've gone fishing for trout.
2 to catch
□ Léo a pêché deux saumons. Léo caught two salmon.

le **pêcheur** MASC NOUN
fisherman
□ Son père est pêcheur. His father's a fisherman.
■ **un pêcheur à la ligne** an angler

★ **pédagogique** (FEM **pédagogique**) ADJECTIVE
educational

★ la **pédale** FEM NOUN
pedal

★ le **pédalo** MASC NOUN
pedalo

pédestre (FEM **pédestre**) ADJECTIVE
■ **une randonnée pédestre** a ramble

★ le **peigne** MASC NOUN
comb

peigner VERB [28]
to comb
□ Elle peigne sa poupée. She's combing her doll's hair.
■ **se peigner** to comb one's hair □ Il faut que je me peigne. I must comb my hair.

le **peignoir** MASC NOUN
dressing gown
■ **un peignoir de bain** a bathrobe

★ **peindre** VERB [60]
to paint

★ la **peine** FEM NOUN
trouble
■ **avoir de la peine à faire quelque chose** to have trouble doing something □ J'ai eu beaucoup de peine à la convaincre. I had a lot of trouble convincing her.
■ **se donner de la peine** to make a real effort □ Il s'est donné beaucoup de peine pour obtenir ces renseignements. He made a real effort to get this information.
■ **prendre la peine de faire quelque chose** to go to the trouble of doing something □ Il a pris la peine de me rapporter ma valise. He went to the trouble of returning my case to me.
■ **faire de la peine à quelqu'un** to upset somebody □ Ça me fait de la peine de la voir pleurer. It upsets me to see her crying.
■ **ce n'est pas la peine** there's no point □ Ce n'est pas la peine de téléphoner. There's no point in phoning.
■ **à peine** **1** hardly □ J'ai à peine eu le temps de me changer. I hardly had time to get changed. **2** only just □ Elle vient à peine de se lever. She's only just got up.

★ le/la **peintre** MASC/FEM NOUN
painter

★ la **peinture** FEM NOUN
1 painting
□ On expose des peintures d'Aurélie au musée. There's an exhibition of Aurélie's paintings at the museum.
2 paint
□ J'ai acheté de la peinture verte. I bought some green paint.
■ **'peinture fraîche'** 'wet paint'

pêle-mêle ADVERB
higgledy-piggledy

French-English

peler VERB [43]
to peel

la **pelle** FEM NOUN
1 shovel
2 spade

★ la **pellicule** FEM NOUN
film
□ une pellicule couleur a colour film

les **pellicules** FEM PL NOUN
dandruff *sing*

la **pelote** FEM NOUN
ball
□ une pelote de laine a ball of wool

★ la **pelouse** FEM NOUN
lawn

la **peluche** FEM NOUN
■ **un animal en peluche** a soft toy

le **penchant** MASC NOUN
■ **avoir un penchant pour quelque chose** to have a liking for something

★ **pencher** VERB [28]
to tilt
□ Ce tableau penche vers la droite. The picture's tilting to the right.
■ **se pencher** **1** to lean over □ Émilie s'est penchée sur son cahier. Émilie leant over her exercise book. **2** to bend down □ Il s'est penché pour ramasser sa casquette. He bent down to pick his cap up. **3** to lean out □ Annick s'est penchée par la fenêtre. Annick leant out of the window.

★ **pendant** PREPOSITION
during
□ Ça s'est passé pendant l'été. It happened during the summer.
■ **pendant que** while □ Julien a téléphoné pendant que Louise prenait son bain. Julien phoned while Louise was having a bath.

le **pendentif** MASC NOUN
pendant

la **penderie** FEM NOUN
wardrobe (*for hanging clothes*)

pendre VERB [88]
to hang
□ Il a pendu sa veste dans l'armoire. He hung his jacket in the wardrobe.
■ **pendre quelqu'un** to hang somebody
□ L'assassin a été pendu. The murderer was hanged.

★ la **pendule** FEM NOUN
clock

pénétrer VERB [34]
1 to
□ Ils ont pénétré dans la maison en passant par le jardin. They entered the house through
2 to penetrate
□ L'armée a pénétré sur le territoire ennemi. The army penetrated enemy territory.

★ **pénible** (FEM **pénible**) ADJECTIVE
hard
□ Travailler sur un chantier est pénible. Working on a building site is hard.
■ **Il est vraiment pénible.** He's a real nuisance.

péniblement ADVERB
with difficulty

la **péniche** FEM NOUN
barge

le **pénis** MASC NOUN
penis

la **pénombre** FEM NOUN
half-light

la **pensée** FEM NOUN
thought
□ Il était perdu dans ses pensées. He was lost in thought.

★ **penser** VERB [28]
to think
□ Je pense que Yann a eu raison de partir. I think Yann was right to leave.
■ **penser à quelque chose** to think about something □ Je pense à mes vacances. I'm thinking about my holidays. □ Pensez-y. Think about it.
■ **faire penser quelqu'un à quelque chose** to remind someone of something □ Cette photo me fait penser à la Grèce. This photo reminds me of Greece.
■ **faire penser quelqu'un à faire quelque chose** to remind someone to do something □ Fais-moi penser à téléphoner à Claire. Remind me to phone Claire.
■ **penser faire quelque chose** to be planning to do something □ Ils pensent partir en Espagne en juillet. They're planning to go to Spain in July.

★ la **pension** FEM NOUN
1 boarding school
□ Leur fille est en pension. Their daughter is at boarding school.
2 pension
□ Ma grand-mère reçoit sa pension tous les mois. My grandma gets her pension every month.
3 boarding house
■ **la pension complète** full board

★ le/la **pensionnaire** MASC/FEM NOUN
boarder

le **pensionnat** MASC NOUN
boarding school

★ la **pente** FEM NOUN
slope
□ une pente raide a steep slope

P

■ **en pente** sloping □ Le toit de cette maison est en pente. This house has a sloping roof.

★ la **Pentecôte** FEM NOUN
Whitsun

le **pépin** MASC NOUN
1 pip
□ Cette orange est pleine de pépins. This orange is full of pips.
2 problem
□ avoir un pépin (*informal*) to have a slight problem

perçant (FEM **perçante**) ADJECTIVE
1 sharp
□ Il a une vue perçante. He has very sharp eyes.
2 piercing
□ un cri perçant a piercing cry

percer VERB [12]
to pierce
□ Elle s'est fait percer les oreilles. She's had her ears pierced.

★ **percuter** VERB [28]
to smash into

le **perdant** MASC NOUN
loser

la **perdante** FEM NOUN
loser

★ **perdre** VERB [61]
to lose
□ Cécile a perdu ses clés. Cécile's lost her keys.
■ **J'ai perdu mon chemin.** I've lost my way.
■ **perdre un match** to lose a match
■ **perdre du temps** to waste time □ J'ai perdu beaucoup de temps ce matin. I've wasted a lot of time this morning. □ Nous avons perdu notre temps à cette réunion. That meeting was a waste of time.
■ **se perdre** to get lost □ Je me suis perdu en route. I got lost on the way here.

perdu VERB ▷ *see* **perdre**

★ le **père** MASC NOUN
father
■ **le père Noël** Father Christmas

perfectionné (FEM **perfectionnée**) ADJECTIVE
sophisticated

perfectionner VERB [28]
to improve
□ Elle a besoin de perfectionner son anglais. She needs to improve her English.

périmé (FEM **périmée**) ADJECTIVE
out-of-date
□ Mon passeport est périmé. My passport's out of date.
■ **Ces yaourts sont périmés.** These yoghurts are past their use-by date.

la **période** FEM NOUN
period

périodique (FEM **périodique**) ADJECTIVE
periodic

périphérique (FEM **périphérique**) ADJECTIVE
▷ *see also* **périphérique** NOUN
outlying
□ un quartier périphérique an outlying district

le **périphérique** MASC NOUN
▷ *see also* **périphérique** ADJECTIVE
ring road

la **perle** FEM NOUN
pearl

la **permanence** FEM NOUN
■ **assurer une permanence** to operate a basic service □ Ma banque assure une permanence le samedi matin. My bank operates a basic service on Saturday mornings.
■ **être de permanence** to be on duty □ Sophie ne peut pas venir, elle est de permanence ce soir. Sophie can't come, she's on duty tonight.
■ **en permanence** permanently □ Elle se plaint en permanence. She's always complaining.

★ **permanent** (FEM **permanente**) ADJECTIVE
▷ *see also* **permanente** NOUN
1 permanent
□ Il a un poste permanent. He has a permanent job.
2 continuous
□ J'en ai assez de tes critiques permanentes. I've had enough of your constant criticism.

la **permanente** FEM NOUN
▷ *see also* **permanent** ADJECTIVE
perm

★ **permettre** VERB [47]
to allow
■ **permettre à quelqu'un de faire quelque chose** to allow somebody to do something
□ Sa mère lui permet de sortir le soir. His mother allows him to go out at night.

★ le **permis** MASC NOUN
permit
□ Il vous faut un permis pour camper ici. You need a permit to camp here.
■ **le permis de conduire** driving licence
■ **un permis de séjour** a residence permit
■ **un permis de travail** a work permit

★ la **permission** FEM NOUN
permission
□ Qui t'a donné la permission d'entrer? Who gave you permission to come in?
■ **avoir la permission de faire quelque chose** to have permission to do something
□ J'ai la permission d'utiliser son ordinateur.

I've got his permission to use his computer.
▪ **être en permission** to be on leave (*from the army*)

le **Pérou** MASC NOUN
Peru

perpétuel (FEM **perpétuelle**) ADJECTIVE
perpetual

perplexe (FEM **perplexe**) ADJECTIVE
puzzled
□ Ma question l'a laissée perplexe. She was puzzled by my question.

★ le **perroquet** MASC NOUN
parrot

★ la **perruche** FEM NOUN
budgie

la **perruque** FEM NOUN
wig

le **persil** MASC NOUN
parsley
□ un bouquet de persil a bunch of parsley

★ le **personnage** MASC NOUN
1 figure
□ les grands personnages de l'histoire de France the important figures in French history
2 character
□ le personnage principal du film the main character in the film

★ la **personnalité** FEM NOUN
1 personality
□ Ophélie a une forte personnalité. Ophélie has a strong personality.
2 prominent figure
□ Il y avait beaucoup de personnalités politiques à ce dîner. There were lots of prominent political figures at the dinner.

★ la **personne** FEM NOUN
▷ *see also* **personne** PRONOUN
person
□ Il y avait une trentaine de personnes dans la pièce. There were about 30 people in the room. □ une personne âgée an elderly person
▪ **en personne** in person

★ **personne** PRONOUN
▷ *see also* **personne** NOUN
1 nobody
□ Il n'y a personne à la maison. There's nobody at home. □ Personne n'est venu le chercher. Nobody came to fetch him.
2 anybody
□ Elle ne veut voir personne. She doesn't want to see anybody.

★ **personnel** (FEM **personnelle**) ADJECTIVE
▷ *see also* **personnel** NOUN
personal

★ le **personnel** MASC NOUN
▷ *see also* **personnel** ADJECTIVE
staff
□ Il nous faut plus de personnel. We need more staff.
▪ **le service du personnel** the personnel department

personnellement ADVERB
personally
□ Personnellement, je ne suis pas d'accord. Personally, I don't agree.

la **perspective** FEM NOUN
prospect
□ Les perspectives sont bonnes. The prospects are good.
▪ **perspectives d'avenir** prospects □ Il y a des perspectives d'avenir dans ce métier. This job has good prospects.
▪ **en perspective** **1** in prospect □ Il y a des changements en perspective. Changes are in prospect. **2** in perspective □ Il a dessiné la maison en perspective. He drew the house in perspective.

★ **persuader** VERB [28]
to persuade
▪ **persuader quelqu'un de faire quelque chose** to persuade somebody to do something □ Elle m'a persuadé de l'accompagner au cinéma. She persuaded me to go to the cinema with her.

★ la **perte** FEM NOUN
1 loss
□ des pertes d'emploi job losses
2 waste
□ Cette réunion a été une perte de temps. The meeting was a waste of time.

perturber VERB [28]
to disrupt
□ Les manifestations perturbaient la circulation. The demonstrations disrupted the traffic.

le **pèse-personne** MASC NOUN
bathroom scales *pl*

★ **peser** VERB [43]
to weigh
□ Elle pèse cent kilos. She weighs 100 kilos.

★ **pessimiste** (FEM **pessimiste**) ADJECTIVE
pessimistic

le **pétale** MASC NOUN
petal

la **pétanque** FEM NOUN

> **DID YOU KNOW...?**
> **pétanque** is a type of bowls played in France, especially in the south.

le **pétard** MASC NOUN
firecracker

péter VERB [34] (*rude*)
to fart

★ **pétillant** (FEM **pétillante**) ADJECTIVE
sparkling

★ **petit** (FEM **petite**) ADJECTIVE
1 small
□ Sonia habite une petite ville. Sonia lives in a small town.
2 little
□ Elle a une petite maison à la campagne. She has a little house in the country.
■ **petit à petit** bit by bit
■ **un petit ami** a boyfriend
■ **une petite amie** a girlfriend
■ **le petit déjeuner** breakfast □ prendre le petit déjeuner to have breakfast
■ **un petit pain** a bread roll
■ **les petites annonces** the small ads
■ **des petits pois** garden peas
■ **les petits** young (*of animal*) □ la lionne et ses petits the lioness and her young

★ la **petite-fille** (PL les **petites-filles**) FEM NOUN
granddaughter

★ le **petit-fils** (PL les **petits-fils**) MASC NOUN
grandson

★ les **petits-enfants** MASC PL NOUN
grandchildren

★ le **pétrole** MASC NOUN
oil
□ une lampe à pétrole an oil lamp

BE CAREFUL!
pétrole does not mean **petrol**.

★ **peu** ADVERB, NOUN
not much
□ J'ai peu mangé à midi. I didn't eat much for lunch. □ Il voyage peu. He doesn't travel much.
■ **un peu** a bit □ Elle est un peu timide. She's a bit shy. □ un peu de gâteau a bit of cake
■ **un petit peu** a little bit □ un petit peu de crème a little bit of cream
■ **un peu de** a little □ Il a un peu d'argent. He has a little money.
■ **peu de** 1 not many □ Il y a peu de bons films au cinéma. There aren't very many good films on at the cinema. □ Elle a peu d'amis. She hasn't got many friends. 2 not much □ Il a peu d'espoir de réussir. He doesn't have much hope of succeeding. □ Il lui reste peu d'argent. He hasn't got much money left.
■ **à peu près** 1 more or less □ J'ai à peu près fini. I've more or less finished. 2 about □ Le voyage prend à peu près deux heures. The journey takes about two hours.
■ **peu à peu** little by little
■ **peu avant** shortly before
■ **peu après** shortly afterwards
■ **de peu** only just □ Imane a manqué son train de peu. Imane only just missed her train.

★ le **peuple** MASC NOUN
people
□ le peuple français the French people

★ la **peur** FEM NOUN
fear
■ **avoir peur de** to be afraid of □ Il a peur du noir. He's afraid of the dark.
■ **avoir peur de faire quelque chose** to be frightened of doing something □ Elle a peur d'y aller toute seule. She's frightened of going on her own.
■ **faire peur à quelqu'un** to frighten somebody □ Cet homme-là me fait peur. That man frightens me.

peureux (FEM **peureuse**) ADJECTIVE
fearful

peut VERB ▷ *see* **pouvoir**
■ **Il ne peut pas venir.** He can't come.

★ **peut-être** ADVERB
perhaps
□ Je l'ai peut-être oublié à la maison. Perhaps I've left it at home.
■ **peut-être que** perhaps □ Peut-être qu'elles n'ont pas pu téléphoner. Perhaps they weren't able to phone.

peuvent, peux VERB ▷ *see* **pouvoir**
■ **Je ne peux pas le faire.** I can't do it.

p. ex. ABBREVIATION (= *par exemple*)
e.g.

★ le **phare** MASC NOUN
1 lighthouse
□ On voit le phare depuis le pont du bateau. You can see the lighthouse from the ship's deck.
2 headlight
□ Elle a laissé ses phares allumés. She left her headlights on.

★ la **pharmacie** FEM NOUN
chemist's

DID YOU KNOW...?
Chemists' shops in France are identified by a special green cross outside the shop.

★ le **pharmacien** MASC NOUN
pharmacist

★ la **pharmacienne** FEM NOUN
pharmacist

le **phasme** MASC NOUN
stick insect

le **phénomène** MASC NOUN
phenomenon

la **philosophie** FEM NOUN
philosophy

le **phoque** MASC NOUN
seal (*animal*)

★ la **photo** FEM NOUN
photograph
■ **en photo** in photographs □ Je n'ai vu Venise qu'en photo. I've only seen Venice in photographs.
■ **prendre quelqu'un en photo** to take a

photo of somebody □ Claire nous a pris en photo. Claire took a photo of us.
■ **une photo d'identité** a passport photograph

★ la **photocopie** FEM NOUN
photocopy

photocopier VERB [19]
to photocopy

la **photocopieuse** FEM NOUN
photocopier

★ le/la **photographe** MASC/FEM NOUN
photographer

★ la **photographie** FEM NOUN
1 photography
2 photograph

photographier VERB [19]
to photograph

photoshoper VERB [28]
to Photoshop

★ la **phrase** FEM NOUN
sentence

★ **physique** (FEM **physique**) ADJECTIVE
▷ *see also* **physique** NOUN
physical

★ le **physique** MASC NOUN
▷ *see also* **physique** NOUN, ADJECTIVE
■ **Il a un physique agréable.** He's quite good-looking.

★ la **physique** FEM NOUN
▷ *see also* **physique** NOUN, ADJECTIVE
physics
□ Il est professeur de physique. He's a physics teacher.

le/la **pianiste** MASC/FEM NOUN
pianist
□ Elle est pianiste. She's a pianist.

★ le **piano** MASC NOUN
piano

le **pic** MASC NOUN
peak
□ les pics enneigés des Alpes the snowy peaks of the Alps
■ **à pic 1** vertically □ La falaise tombe à pic dans la mer. The cliff drops vertically into the sea. **2** just at the right time □ Tu es arrivé à pic. You arrived just at the right time.

★ la **pièce** FEM NOUN
1 room
□ Mon lit est au centre de la pièce. My bed is in the middle of the room.
■ **un cinq-pièces** a five-roomed flat
2 play
□ On joue une pièce de Shakespeare au théâtre. There's a play by Shakespeare on at the theatre.
3 part
□ Il faut changer une pièce du moteur. There's an engine part which needs changing.
4 coin
□ des pièces d'un euro some one-euro coins
■ **cinquante euros pièce** 50 euros each
□ J'ai acheté ces T-shirts dix euros pièce. I bought these T-shirts for ten euros each.
■ **un maillot une pièce** a one-piece swimsuit
■ **un maillot deux-pièces** a bikini
■ **Avez-vous une pièce d'identité?** Have you got any identification?
■ **une pièce jointe** an email attachment

★ le **pied** MASC NOUN
foot
□ J'ai mal aux pieds. My feet are hurting.
■ **à pied** on foot
■ **avoir pied** to be able to touch the bottom
□ Justine n'aime pas nager là où elle n'a pas pied. Justine doesn't like swimming where she can't touch the bottom.

le **pied-noir** (PL les **pieds-noirs**) MASC NOUN

> **DID YOU KNOW...?**
> A pied-noir is a French person born in Algeria; most of them moved to France during the Algerian war in the 1950s.

□ Sa grand-mère est pied-noir. His grandmother was born in Algeria.

le **piège** MASC NOUN
trap
■ **prendre quelqu'un au piège** to trap somebody

piéger VERB [66]
to trap
■ **un colis piégé** a parcel bomb
■ **une voiture piégée** a car bomb

★ la **pierre** FEM NOUN
stone
■ **une pierre précieuse** a precious stone

★ le **piéton** MASC NOUN
pedestrian

★ la **piétonne** FEM NOUN
pedestrian

piétonnier (FEM **piétonnière**) ADJECTIVE
■ **une rue piétonnière** a pedestrianized street
■ **un quartier piétonnier** a pedestrianized area

la **pieuvre** FEM NOUN
octopus

le **pigeon** MASC NOUN
pigeon

piger VERB [45] (*informal*)
to understand

★ la **pile** FEM NOUN
▷ *see also* **pile** ADVERB
1 pile
□ Il y a une pile de disques sur la table. There's a pile of records on the table.
2 battery

 Numbers in brackets refer to verb tables on pages 650 to 658

□ La pile de ma montre est usée. The battery in my watch has run out.

★ **pile** ADVERB
▷ *see also* **pile** NOUN
■ **à deux heures pile** at two on the dot
■ **jouer à pile ou face** to toss up
■ **Pile ou face?** Heads or tails?

★ le **pilote** MASC NOUN
pilot
■ **un pilote de course** a racing driver
■ **un pilote de ligne** an airline pilot

piloter VERB [28]
to fly (*a plane*)

★ la **pilule** FEM NOUN
pill
■ **prendre la pilule** to be on the pill

le **piment** MASC NOUN
chilli

le **pin** MASC NOUN
pine

le **pinard** MASC NOUN (*informal*)
wine

la **pince** FEM NOUN
1 pliers *pl* (*tool*)
2 pincer (*of crab*)
■ **une pince à épiler** tweezers
■ **une pince à linge** a clothes peg

le **pinceau** (PL les **pinceaux**) MASC NOUN
paintbrush

la **pincée** FEM NOUN
■ **une pincée de sel** a pinch of salt

pincer VERB [12]
to pinch
□ Elle m'a pincé le bras. She pinched my arm.

le **pingouin** MASC NOUN
penguin

★ le **ping-pong** MASC NOUN
table tennis
□ jouer au ping-pong to play table tennis

la **pintade** FEM NOUN
guinea fowl

le **pion** MASC NOUN
1 pawn (*in chess*)
2 piece (*in draughts*)
3 supervisor (*man*)

DID YOU KNOW...?
In French secondary schools, the teachers are not responsible for supervising the pupils outside class. This job is done by people called **pions** or **surveillants**.

la **pionne** FEM NOUN
supervisor (*woman*)

★ la **pipe** FEM NOUN
pipe
□ Mon grand-père fume la pipe. My granddad smokes a pipe.

★ **piquant** (FEM **piquante**) ADJECTIVE
1 prickly
2 spicy

le **pique** MASC NOUN
▷ *see also* **pique** NOUN
spades *pl*
□ l'as de pique the ace of spades

la **pique** FEM NOUN
▷ *see also* **pique** NOUN
cutting remark
□ envoyer des piques à quelqu'un to make cutting remarks to somebody

★ le **pique-nique** MASC NOUN
picnic

★ **piquer** VERB [28]
1 to bite
□ Nous avons été piqués par les moustiques. We were bitten by mosquitoes.
2 to burn
□ Cette sauce me pique la langue. This sauce is burning my tongue.
3 to steal
□ On m'a piqué mon porte-monnaie. (*informal*) I've had my purse stolen.
■ **se piquer** to prick oneself □ Il s'est piqué avec une aiguille. He pricked himself with a needle.

le **piquet** MASC NOUN
1 post
□ Le chien est attaché à un piquet. The dog is tied to a post.
2 peg
□ Il nous manque un des piquets de la tente. One of our tent pegs is missing.

★ la **piqûre** FEM NOUN
1 injection
□ Le médecin lui a fait une piqûre. The doctor gave him an injection.
2 bite
□ une piqûre de moustique a mosquito bite
3 sting
□ une piqûre d'abeille a bee sting

le **pirate** MASC NOUN
pirate
■ **un pirate informatique** a hacker

★ **pire** (FEM **pire**) ADJECTIVE, NOUN
worse
□ C'est encore pire qu'avant. It's even worse than before.
■ **le pire** the worst □ C'est la pire journée que j'aie jamais passée. That's the worst day I've ever had. □ Ce gamin est le pire de la bande. That boy is the worst in the group.
■ **le pire de** the worst of □ Le pire de tout, c'est qu'on s'ennuie tout le temps. The worst of it is that we're always bored.

★ la **piscine** FEM NOUN
swimming pool

pisser VERB [28] (*informal*)
to have a pee

la **pistache** FEM NOUN
pistachio
□ une glace à la pistache a pistachio ice cream

★ la **piste** FEM NOUN
1 lead
□ La police est sur une piste. The police are following a lead.
2 runway
□ L'avion s'est posé sur la piste. The plane landed on the runway.
3 ski run
□ Le skieur a descendu la piste. The skier came down the ski run.
■ **une piste artificielle** a dry ski slope
■ **la piste de danse** the dance floor
■ **une piste cyclable** a cycle lane

le **pistolet** MASC NOUN
pistol

pistonner VERB [28]
■ **Il a été pistonné pour avoir ce travail.** They pulled some strings to get him this job.

la **pitié** FEM NOUN
pity
■ **Il me fait pitié.** I feel sorry for him.
■ **avoir pitié de quelqu'un** to feel sorry for somebody

★ **pittoresque** (FEM **pittoresque**) ADJECTIVE
picturesque

★ la **pizza** FEM NOUN
pizza

★ le **placard** MASC NOUN
cupboard

★ la **place** FEM NOUN
1 place
□ Vincent a eu la troisième place au concours. Vincent got third place in the competition.
2 square
□ la place du village the village square
3 space
□ Il ne reste plus de place pour se garer. There's no more space to park. □ Ça prend de la place. It takes up a lot of room.
4 seat
□ Toutes les places ont été vendues. All the seats have been sold. □ Il y a vingt places assises. There are 20 seats.
■ **remettre quelque chose en place** to put something back in its place
■ **sur place** on the spot
■ **à la place** instead □ Il ne reste plus de tarte; désirez-vous quelque chose d'autre à la place? There's no pie left; would you like something else instead?
■ **à la place de** instead of

placer VERB [12]
1 to seat
□ Nous étions placés à côté du directeur. We were seated next to the manager.
2 to invest
□ Il a placé ses économies en Bourse. He invested his money on the Stock Exchange.

★ le **plafond** MASC NOUN
ceiling

★ la **plage** FEM NOUN
beach

la **plaie** FEM NOUN
wound

★ **plaindre** VERB [17]
■ **plaindre quelqu'un** to feel sorry for somebody □ Je te plains. I feel sorry for you.
■ **se plaindre** to complain □ Il n'arrête pas de se plaindre. He never stops complaining.
■ **se plaindre à quelqu'un** to complain to somebody □ Ils se sont plaints au directeur. They complained to the manager.
■ **se plaindre de quelque chose** to complain about something □ Elle s'est plainte du bruit. She complained about the noise.

la **plaine** FEM NOUN
plain (*level area*)

la **plainte** FEM NOUN
complaint
■ **porter plainte** to lodge a complaint

★ **plaire** VERB [62]
■ **Ce cadeau me plaît beaucoup.** I like this present a lot.
■ **Ce film plaît beaucoup aux jeunes.** The film is very popular with young people.
■ **Ça t'a plu d'aller en Italie?** Did you enjoy going to Italy?
■ **Elle lui plaît.** He fancies her.
■ **s'il te plaît** please
■ **s'il vous plaît** please

plaisanter VERB [28]
to joke

★ la **plaisanterie** FEM NOUN
joke

★ le **plaisir** MASC NOUN
pleasure
■ **faire plaisir à quelqu'un** to please somebody □ J'y suis allé pour lui faire plaisir. I went there to please him. □ Ce cadeau me fait très plaisir. I'm very pleased with this present.

plaît VERB ▷ *see* **plaire**

★ le **plan** MASC NOUN
plan
■ **un plan de la ville** a street map
■ **au premier plan** in the foreground

★ la **planche** FEM NOUN
plank
■ **une planche à repasser** an ironing board
■ **une planche à roulettes** a skateboard
■ **une planche à voile** a sailboard
■ **une planche de surf** a surfboard

★ le **plancher** MASC NOUN
floor

planer VERB [28]
1 to glide
□ L'avion planait dans le ciel. The plane was gliding in the sky.
2 to have one's head in the clouds
■ **Ce garçon plane complètement.** (*informal*) He's not with us at all.

la **planète** FEM NOUN
planet

★ la **plante** FEM NOUN
plant

planter VERB [28]
1 to plant
□ Daphné a planté des tomates. Daphné planted some tomatoes.
2 to hammer in
□ Karim a planté un clou dans le mur. Karim hammered a nail into the wall.
3 to pitch
□ Nathan a planté sa tente au bord du lac. Nathan pitched his tent next to the lake.
■ **Ne reste pas planté là!** Don't just stand there!
■ **se planter** (*informal*) to fail □ Je me suis planté en maths. I failed maths.

la **plaque** FEM NOUN
(metal) plate
■ **une plaque de verglas** a patch of ice
■ **une plaque de chocolat** a bar of chocolate

plaqué (FEM **plaquée**) ADJECTIVE
■ **plaqué or** gold-plated
■ **plaqué argent** silver-plated

plaquer VERB [28] (*informal*)
1 to ditch
□ Elle a plaqué son copain. She ditched her boyfriend.
2 to pack in
□ Il a plaqué son boulot. He packed in his job.

la **plaquette** FEM NOUN
■ **une plaquette de chocolat** a bar of chocolate
■ **une plaquette de beurre** a pack of butter

★ le **plastique** MASC NOUN
plastic

★ **plat** (FEM **plate**) ADJECTIVE
▷ *see also* **plat** NOUN
flat
■ **être à plat ventre** to be lying face down
■ **l'eau plate** still water

★ le **plat** MASC NOUN
▷ *see also* **plat** ADJECTIVE
1 dish
2 course
□ le plat principal the main course
■ **un plat cuisiné** a pre-cooked meal
■ **le plat de résistance** the main course
■ **le plat du jour** the dish of the day

le **platane** MASC NOUN
plane tree

★ le **plateau** (PL les **plateaux**) MASC NOUN
1 tray
■ **un plateau de fromages** a selection of cheeses
2 plateau

★ le **platine** MASC NOUN
▷ *see also* **platine** NOUN
platinum

★ la **platine** FEM NOUN
▷ *see also* **platine** NOUN
turntable (*of record player*)
■ **une platine laser** a CD player

★ le **plâtre** MASC NOUN
plaster
□ une statue en plâtre a statue made of plaster □ avoir un bras dans le plâtre to have an arm in plaster

★ **plein** (FEM **pleine**) ADJECTIVE
▷ *see also* **plein** NOUN
full
■ **à plein temps** full-time □ Elle travaille à plein temps. She works full-time.
■ **plein de** (*informal*) lots of □ un gâteau avec plein de crème a cake with lots of cream
■ **Il y a plein de gens dans la rue.** The street is full of people.
■ **en plein air** in the open air
■ **en pleine nuit** in the middle of the night
■ **en plein jour** in broad daylight

★ le **plein** MASC NOUN
▷ *see also* **plein** ADJECTIVE
■ **faire le plein** to fill up (*petrol tank*) □ Faites le plein, s'il vous plaît. Fill it up, please.

★ **pleurer** VERB [28]
to cry

pleut VERB ▷ *see* **pleuvoir**

★ **pleuvoir** VERB [63]
to rain
□ Il pleut. It's raining.

le **pli** MASC NOUN
1 fold
2 pleat
□ Elle a repassé les plis de sa jupe. She ironed the pleats of her skirt.
3 crease
□ Il y a un pli sur la manche de ta chemise. There's a crease in the sleeve of your shirt.

pliant (FEM **pliante**) ADJECTIVE
folding
□ un lit pliant a folding bed

★ **plier** VERB [19]
1 to fold
□ Elle a plié sa serviette. She folded her towel.
2 to bend
□ Elle a plié le bras. She bent her arm.

le **plomb** MASC NOUN
1 lead
□ Ces jouets sont en plomb. These toys are made of lead.
2 fuse
□ Les plombs ont sauté. The fuses have blown.
■ **l'essence sans plomb** unleaded petrol

★le **plombier** MASC NOUN
plumber
■ **Il est plombier.** He's a plumber.

★la **plongée** FEM NOUN
diving
□ faire de la plongée to go diving

le **plongeoir** MASC NOUN
diving board

le **plongeon** MASC NOUN
dive

★**plonger** VERB [45]
to dive
□ Jean a plongé dans la piscine. Jean dived into the swimming pool.
■ **J'ai plongé ma main dans l'eau.** I plunged my hand into the water.
■ **être plongé dans son travail** to be absorbed in your work
■ **se plonger dans un livre** to get absorbed in a book

plu VERB ▷ *see* **plaire, pleuvoir**

★la **pluie** FEM NOUN
rain
□ sous la pluie in the rain

★la **plume** FEM NOUN
feather
□ une plume d'oiseau a bird's feather
■ **un stylo à plume** a fountain pen

★**plupart**
■ **la plupart** PRONOUN most (of them) □ La plupart ont moins de quinze ans. Most of them are under 15.
■ **la plupart des** most □ La plupart des gens ont vu ce film. Most people have seen this film.
■ **la plupart du temps** most of the time

le **pluriel** MASC NOUN
plural
■ **au pluriel** in the plural

★**plus** ADVERB, PREPOSITION
■ **ne ... plus 1** not ... any more □ Je ne veux plus le voir. I don't want to see him any more. **2** no longer □ Il ne travaille plus ici. He's no longer working here.
■ **Je n'ai plus de pain.** I've got no bread left.
■ **plus ... que** more ... than □ Il est plus intelligent que son frère. He's more intelligent than his brother. □ Il travaille plus que moi. He works more than me. □ Elle est plus grande que moi. She's bigger than me.
■ **C'est le plus grand de la famille.** He's the tallest in his family.
■ **plus ... plus ...** the more ... the more ... □ Plus il gagne d'argent, plus il en veut. The more money he earns, the more he wants.
■ **plus de 1** more □ Il nous faut plus de pain. We need more bread. **2** more than □ Il y avait plus de dix personnes. There were more than 10 people.
■ **de plus** more □ Il nous faut un joueur de plus. We need one more player. □ Le voyage a pris trois heures de plus que prévu. The journey took 3 hours more than planned.
■ **en plus** more □ J'ai apporté quelques gâteaux en plus. I brought a few more cakes.
■ **de plus en plus** more and more □ Il y a de plus en plus de touristes par ici. There are more and more tourists round here. □ Il fait de plus en plus chaud. It's getting hotter and hotter.
■ **un peu plus difficile** a bit more difficult □ Il fait un peu plus froid qu'hier. It's a bit colder than yesterday.
■ **plus ou moins** more or less
■ **Quatre plus deux égalent six.** 4 plus 2 is 6.

★**plusieurs** PL PRONOUN
several
□ Elle a acheté plusieurs chemises. She bought several shirts. □ Il y en a plusieurs. There are several of them.

le **plus-que-parfait** MASC NOUN
pluperfect

★**plutôt** ADVERB
1 quite
□ Elle est plutôt jolie. She's quite pretty.
2 rather
□ L'eau est plutôt froide. The water's rather cold.
3 instead
□ Demande-leur plutôt de venir avec toi. Ask them to come with you instead.
■ **plutôt que** rather than □ Invite Marie plutôt que Juliette. Invite Marie rather than Juliette.

★**pluvieux** (FEM **pluvieuse**) ADJECTIVE
rainy

★le **pneu** MASC NOUN
tyre

la **pneumonie** FEM NOUN
pneumonia

★la **poche** FEM NOUN
pocket
■ **l'argent de poche** pocket money
■ **un livre de poche** a paperback

le **podcast** MASC NOUN
podcast
□ télécharger un podcast to download a podcast

podcaster VERB [28]
to podcast

★ la **poêle** FEM NOUN
frying pan
■ **une poêle à frire** a frying pan

le **poème** MASC NOUN
poem

la **poésie** FEM NOUN
1 poetry
2 poem

le **poète** MASC NOUN
poet

la **poétesse** FEM NOUN
poet

★ le **poids** MASC NOUN
weight
□ vendre quelque chose au poids to sell something by weight
■ **prendre du poids** to put on weight □ Il a pris du poids. He's put on weight.
■ **perdre du poids** to lose weight □ Elle a perdu du poids. She's lost weight.
■ **un poids lourd** a lorry

la **poignée** FEM NOUN
1 handful
□ une poignée de sel a handful of salt
2 handle
□ la poignée de la porte the door handle
■ **une poignée de main** a handshake

★ le **poignet** MASC NOUN
1 wrist
□ Je me suis fait mal au poignet. I've hurt my wrist.
2 cuff (*of shirt*)

le **poil** MASC NOUN
1 hair
□ Il y a des poils de chat partout sur la moquette. There are cat hairs all over the carpet.
2 fur
□ Ton chien a un beau poil. Your dog's got lovely fur.
■ **à poil** (*informal*) stark naked

poilu (FEM **poilue**) ADJECTIVE
hairy

poinçonner VERB [28]
to punch
□ Le contrôleur a poinçonné les billets. The conductor punched the tickets.

★ le **poing** MASC NOUN
fist
■ **un coup de poing** a punch

★ le **point** MASC NOUN
1 point
□ Je ne suis pas d'accord sur ce point. I don't agree with this point. □ Son point faible, c'est qu'elle est trop gentille. Her weak point is she's too nice.
■ **point de vue** point of view
2 full stop
■ **être sur le point de faire quelque chose** to be just about to do something □ J'étais sur le point de te téléphoner. I was just about to phone you.
■ **mettre au point** to finalize
■ **Ce n'est pas encore au point.** It's not finalized yet.
■ **à point** medium □ Comment voulez-vous votre steak? — À point. How would you like your steak? — Medium.
■ **un point d'exclamation** an exclamation mark
■ **un point d'interrogation** a question mark
■ **un point noir** a blackhead

la **pointe** FEM NOUN
point
□ la pointe d'un couteau the point of a knife
■ **être à la pointe du progrès** to be in the forefront of progress
■ **sur la pointe des pieds** on tiptoe
■ **les heures de pointe** peak hours

le **pointillé** MASC NOUN
dotted line

pointu (FEM **pointue**) ADJECTIVE
pointed
□ un chapeau pointu a pointed hat

★ la **pointure** FEM NOUN
size (*of shoes*)
□ Quelle est votre pointure? What size shoes do you take?

le **point-virgule** (PL **points-virgules**) MASC NOUN
semicolon

★ la **poire** FEM NOUN
pear

★ le **poireau** (PL les **poireaux**) MASC NOUN
leek
□ la soupe aux poireaux leek soup

★ le **pois** MASC NOUN
pea
■ **les petits pois** peas
■ **les pois chiches** chickpeas
■ **à pois** spotted □ une robe à pois a spotted dress

le **poison** MASC NOUN
poison

★ le **poisson** MASC NOUN
fish
□ Je n'aime pas le poisson. I don't like fish.
□ Léo a pêché deux poissons. Léo caught two fish.
■ **les Poissons** Pisces □ Justine est Poissons. Justine is Pisces.
■ **Poisson d'avril!** April fool!

DID YOU KNOW...?
Pinning a paper fish to somebody's back is a traditional April fool joke in France.

■ **un poisson rouge** a goldfish

★ la **poissonnerie** FEM NOUN
fish shop

★ le **poissonnier** MASC NOUN
fishmonger

★ la **poitrine** FEM NOUN
1 chest
□ J'ai mal à la poitrine. My chest hurts.
2 bust
□ Quel est votre tour de poitrine? What's your bust size?

★ le **poivre** MASC NOUN
pepper (*spice*)

★ le **poivron** MASC NOUN
pepper (*vegetable*)

★ le **polar** MASC NOUN
thriller

le **pôle** MASC NOUN
pole
■ **le pôle Nord** the North Pole
■ **le pôle Sud** the South Pole

★ **poli** (FEM **polie**) ADJECTIVE
polite

★ la **police** FEM NOUN
police
□ La police recherche le voleur. The police are looking for the thief.
■ **police secours** emergency services □ Ils ont appelé police secours. They phoned the emergency services.
■ **une police d'assurance** an insurance policy

★ **policier** (FEM **policière**) ADJECTIVE
▷ *see also* **policier** NOUN
■ **un roman policier** a detective novel

★ le **policier** MASC NOUN
▷ *see also* **policier** ADJECTIVE
police officer
□ Il est policier. He's a police officer.

la **policière** FEM NOUN
police officer
□ Elle est policière. She's a police officer.

★ la **politesse** FEM NOUN
politeness

★ la **politique** FEM NOUN
politics
□ La politique ne l'intéresse pas du tout. He's not at all interested in politics.

★ **pollué** (FEM **polluée**) ADJECTIVE
polluted

★ **polluer** VERB [28]
to pollute

★ la **pollution** FEM NOUN
pollution

le **polo** MASC NOUN
polo shirt

★ la **Pologne** FEM NOUN
Poland

★ **polonais** (FEM **polonaise**) ADJECTIVE, NOUN
Polish
□ Elle parle polonais. She speaks Polish.
■ **un Polonais** a Pole (*man*)
■ **une Polonaise** a Pole (*woman*)
■ **les Polonais** the Poles

la **Polynésie** FEM NOUN
Polynesia

la **pommade** FEM NOUN
ointment

★ la **pomme** FEM NOUN
apple
■ **les pommes de terre** potatoes
■ **les pommes frites** chips
■ **les pommes vapeur** boiled potatoes
■ **tomber dans les pommes** (*informal*) to faint

la **pompe** FEM NOUN
pump
■ **une pompe à essence** a petrol pump
■ **les pompes funèbres** undertakers

★ le **pompier** MASC NOUN
firefighter

★ le/la **pompiste** MASC/FEM NOUN
petrol pump attendant

ponctuel (FEM **ponctuelle**) ADJECTIVE
1 punctual
□ Elle est toujours très ponctuelle. She's always very punctual.
2 occasional
■ **On a rencontré quelques problèmes ponctuels.** We've had the occasional problem.

pondre VERB [69]
to lay (*eggs*)

le **poney** MASC NOUN
pony

★ le **pont** MASC NOUN
1 bridge
2 deck (*of ship*)
■ **faire le pont** to take a long weekend
□ Nous faisons le pont pour la Pentecôte. We're taking a long weekend for Whitsun.

★ **populaire** (FEM **populaire**) ADJECTIVE
1 popular
□ Ce chanteur est très populaire en France. This singer's very popular in France.
2 working-class
□ un quartier populaire de la ville a working-class area of town

la **population** FEM NOUN
population

Numbers in brackets refer to verb tables on pages 650 to 658

★ le **porc** MASC NOUN
1 pig
□ Ils élèvent des porcs. They breed pigs.
2 pork
□ du rôti de porc roast pork

la **porcelaine** FEM NOUN
china
□ une tasse en porcelaine a china cup

★ le **port** MASC NOUN
1 harbour
2 port

★ **portable** (FEM **portable**) ADJECTIVE
▷ *see also* **portable** NOUN
mobile (*telephone*)
■ **un ordinateur portable** a laptop

★ le **portable** MASC NOUN
▷ *see also* **portable** ADJECTIVE
1 mobile phone
□ Je vais appeler Marie sur mon portable. I'll phone Marie on my mobile.
2 laptop
□ Je vais te montrer sur mon portable. I'll show you on my laptop.

le **portail** MASC NOUN
gate

portatif (FEM **portative**) ADJECTIVE
portable

★ la **porte** FEM NOUN
1 door
□ Ferme la porte, s'il te plaît. Close the door, please.
■ **la porte d'entrée** the front door
2 gate
□ Vol 432 à destination de Paris: porte numéro trois. Flight 432 to Paris: gate 3.
■ **mettre quelqu'un à la porte** to sack somebody

le **porte-bagages** MASC NOUN
luggage rack

★ le **porte-clés** MASC NOUN
key ring

la **portée** FEM NOUN
■ **à portée de main** within arm's reach
■ **hors de portée** out of reach

★ le **portefeuille** MASC NOUN
wallet

le **portemanteau** (PL les **portemanteaux**) MASC NOUN
1 coat hanger
2 coat rack

★ le **porte-monnaie** (PL les **porte-monnaies**) MASC NOUN
purse

★ **porter** VERB [28]
1 to carry
□ Il portait une valise. He was carrying a suitcase.
2 to wear
□ Elle porte une robe bleue. She's wearing a blue dress.
■ **se porter bien** to be well
■ **se porter mal** to be unwell

★ le **porteur** MASC NOUN
porter

★ la **portière** FEM NOUN
door (*of car*)

la **portion** FEM NOUN
portion

le **porto** MASC NOUN
port (*wine*)

le **portrait** MASC NOUN
portrait

★ **portugais** (FEM **portugaise**) ADJECTIVE, NOUN
Portuguese
□ Il parle portugais. He speaks Portuguese.
■ **un Portugais** a Portuguese (*man*)
■ **une Portugaise** a Portuguese (*woman*)
■ **les Portugais** the Portuguese

★ le **Portugal** MASC NOUN
Portugal
■ **au Portugal** 1 in Portugal 2 to Portugal

★ **poser** VERB [28]
1 to put down
□ J'ai posé la cafetière sur la table. I put the coffee pot down on the table.
2 to pose
□ Cela pose un problème. That poses a problem.
■ **poser une question à quelqu'un** to ask somebody a question
■ **se poser** to land □ L'avion s'est posé à huit heures. The plane landed at 8 o'clock.

★ **positif** (FEM **positive**) ADJECTIVE
positive

la **position** FEM NOUN
position

posséder VERB [34]
to own
□ Ils possèdent une jolie maison. They own a lovely house.

la **possibilité** FEM NOUN
possibility

★ **possible** (FEM **possible**) ADJECTIVE
possible
□ Samuel leur a dit que ce n'était pas possible. Samuel told them it wasn't possible.
■ **le plus de gens possible** as many people as possible
■ **le plus tôt possible** as early as possible
■ **le moins d'argent possible** as little money as possible
■ **Il travaille le moins possible.** He works as little as possible.
■ **dès que possible** as soon as possible

French-English

P

■ **faire son possible** to do all one can □ Je ferai tout mon possible. I'll do all I can.

★ la **poste** FEM NOUN
▷ *see also* **poste** NOUN
1 post
□ Je vais l'envoyer par la poste. I'm going to send it by post.
2 post office
□ Je vais à la poste pour acheter des timbres. I'm going to the post office to buy some stamps.
■ **mettre une lettre à la poste** to post a letter

★ le **poste** MASC NOUN
▷ *see also* **poste** NOUN
1 post
□ Bastien a trouvé un poste de professeur. Bastien has found a teaching post.
2 extension (*phone*)
□ Pouvez-vous me passer le poste de M. Salzedo? Can you put me through to Mr Salzedo's extension?
3 set
□ un poste de radio a radio set
■ **un poste de police** a police station

★ **poster** VERB [28]
▷ *see also* **poster** NOUN
to post
□ Je vais poster ce colis. I'm going to post this parcel.

★ le **poster** MASC NOUN
▷ *see also* **poster** VERB
poster
□ un poster de la Grèce a poster of Greece

postérieur (FEM **postérieure**) ADJECTIVE
1 later
□ Ce document est postérieur à 1314. This document is from later than 1314.
2 back
□ la partie postérieure de ma jambe the back of my leg

★ le **pot** MASC NOUN
jar
□ J'ai fait trois pots de confiture. I've made three jars of jam.
■ **prendre un pot** (*informal*) to have a drink
□ On va prendre un pot ce soir. We're going for a drink tonight.
■ **un pot de fleurs** a plant pot

★ **potable** (FEM **potable**) ADJECTIVE
■ **eau potable** drinking water
■ **'eau non potable'** 'not drinking water'

★ le **potage** MASC NOUN
soup

le **potager** MASC NOUN
vegetable garden

le **pot-au-feu** (PL les **pots-au-feu**, les **pot-au-feu**) MASC NOUN
beef stew

le **pot-de-vin** (PL les **pots-de-vin**) MASC NOUN
bribe

le **pote** MASC NOUN (*informal*)
mate
□ Je sors avec mes potes ce soir. I'm going out with my mates tonight.

le **poteau** (PL les **poteaux**) MASC NOUN
post
□ Il s'est appuyé contre un poteau. He leant against a post.
■ **un poteau indicateur** a signpost

potentiel (FEM **potentielle**) ADJECTIVE
potential

★ la **poterie** FEM NOUN
1 pottery
□ Elle fait de la poterie à l'école. She does pottery at school.
2 piece of pottery
□ J'ai acheté deux poteries. I bought two pieces of pottery.

le **potier** MASC NOUN
potter

le **pou** (PL les **poux**) MASC NOUN
louse

★ la **poubelle** FEM NOUN
dustbin

le **pouce** MASC NOUN
1 thumb
□ Je me suis coincé le pouce dans la porte. I trapped my thumb in the door.
2 inch
□ Un pouce fait à peu près deux virgule cinq centimètres. 1 inch equals roughly 2.5 centimetres.
■ **manger sur le pouce** to have a quick snack

★ la **poudre** FEM NOUN
1 powder
2 face powder
■ **la poudre à laver** washing powder
■ **le lait en poudre** powdered milk
■ **le café en poudre** instant coffee

le **poulain** MASC NOUN
foal

★ la **poule** FEM NOUN
hen
■ **quand les poules auront des dents** (*informal*) pigs might fly

★ le **poulet** MASC NOUN
1 chicken
□ J'adore le poulet. I love chicken. □ un poulet rôti a roast chicken
2 cop
□ Il s'est fait attraper par les poulets. (*informal*) He got caught by the cops.

le **pouls** MASC NOUN
pulse
□ Il m'a pris le pouls. He took my pulse.

★ le **poumon** MASC NOUN
lung

★ la **poupée** FEM NOUN
doll

★ **pour** PREPOSITION
for
□ C'est un cadeau pour toi. It's a present for you. □ Qu'est-ce que tu veux pour ton petit déjeuner? What would you like for breakfast?
■ **pour faire quelque chose** to do something □ Je lui ai téléphoné pour l'inviter. I phoned him to invite him.
■ **Pour aller à Strasbourg, s'il vous plaît?** Which way is it to Strasbourg, please?
■ **pour que** so that

pour que is followed by a verb in the subjunctive.

□ Je lui ai prêté mon pull pour qu'elle n'ait pas froid. I lent her my jumper so that she wouldn't be cold.
■ **pour cent** per cent

★ le **pourboire** MASC NOUN
tip
□ Il a donné un pourboire au garçon. He gave the waiter a tip.

★ le **pourcentage** MASC NOUN
percentage

★ **pourquoi** ADVERB, CONJUNCTION
why
□ Pourquoi est-ce qu'il ne vient pas avec nous? Why isn't he coming with us? □ Elle ne m'a pas dit pourquoi. She didn't tell me why.

pourra, pourras, pourrai, pourrez VERB ▷ *see* **pouvoir**

pourri (FEM **pourrie**) ADJECTIVE
rotten

le **pourriel** MASC NOUN
spam (*email*)

pourrir VERB [38]
to go bad
□ Ces poires ont pourri. These pears have gone bad.

pourrons, pourront VERB ▷ *see* **pouvoir**

la **poursuite** FEM NOUN
chase
■ **se lancer à la poursuite de quelqu'un** to chase after somebody

poursuivre VERB [81]
to carry on with
□ Ils ont poursuivi leur travail. They carried on with their work.
■ **se poursuivre** to go on □ Le concert s'est poursuivi très tard. The concert went on very late.

★ **pourtant** ADVERB
yet
□ Il a raté son examen. Pourtant, il n'est pas bête. He failed his exam, yet he's not stupid.
■ **C'est pourtant facile!** But it's easy!

pourvu (FEM **pourvue**) ADJECTIVE
■ **pourvu que ...** let's hope that ...

pourvu que is followed by a verb in the subjunctive.

□ Pourvu qu'il ne pleuve pas! Let's hope it doesn't rain!

★ **pousser** VERB [28]
1 to push
□ Ils ont dû pousser la voiture. They had to push the car.
2 to grow
□ Mes cheveux poussent vite. My hair grows quickly.
■ **pousser un cri** to give a cry
■ **se pousser** to move over □ Pousse-toi, je ne vois rien. Move over, I can't see a thing.

la **poussette** FEM NOUN
pushchair

★ la **poussière** FEM NOUN
1 dust
□ La table est couverte de poussière. The table's covered in dust.
2 speck of dust
□ J'ai une poussière dans l'œil. I've got a speck of dust in my eye.

poussiéreux (FEM **poussiéreuse**) ADJECTIVE
dusty

le **poussin** MASC NOUN
chick

★ **pouvoir** VERB [64]

PRESENT TENSE	
je peux	nous pouvons
tu peux	vous pouvez
il/elle peut	ils/elles peuvent
PAST PARTICIPLE	
pu	

▷ *see also* **pouvoir** NOUN
can
□ Je peux lui téléphoner si tu veux. I can phone her if you want. □ Puis-je venir vous voir samedi? May I come and see you on Saturday? □ Je ne pourrai pas venir samedi. I can't come on Saturday. □ J'ai fait tout ce que j'ai pu. I did all I could.
■ **Je n'en peux plus.** I'm exhausted.
■ **Il se peut que ...** It's possible that ...

il se peut que is followed by a verb in the subjunctive.

□ Il se peut qu'elle ait déménagé. It's possible that she's moved house. □ Il se peut que j'y aille. I might go.

★ le **pouvoir** MASC NOUN
▷ *see also* **pouvoir** VERB
power
□ Le Premier ministre a beaucoup de pouvoir. The Prime Minister has a lot of power.

la **prairie** FEM NOUN
meadow

★ la **pratique** FEM NOUN
▷ *see also* **pratique** ADJECTIVE
practice
□ Je manque de pratique. I'm out of practice.

★ **pratique** (FEM **pratique**) ADJECTIVE
▷ *see also* **pratique** NOUN
practical
□ Ce sac est très pratique. This bag's very practical.

pratiquement ADVERB
virtually
□ J'ai pratiquement fini. I've virtually finished.

pratiquer VERB [28]
to practise
□ Je dois pratiquer mon espagnol. I need to practise my Spanish.
■ **Pratiquez-vous un sport?** Do you do any sport?

★ le **pré** MASC NOUN
meadow

la **précarité** FEM NOUN
precariousness (*of a situation*)
■ **la précarité (de l'emploi)** job insecurity, lack of job security (*in economics*)

la **précaution** FEM NOUN
precaution
□ prendre ses précautions to take precautions
■ **par précaution** as a precaution □ Il a pris une assurance par précaution. He took out insurance as a precaution.
■ **avec précaution** cautiously
■ **'à manipuler avec précaution'** 'handle with care'

précédemment ADVERB
previously

précédent (FEM **précédente**) ADJECTIVE
previous

★ **précieux** (FEM **précieuse**) ADJECTIVE
precious
■ **une pierre précieuse** a precious stone
■ **de précieux conseils** invaluable advice

le **précipice** MASC NOUN
ravine
□ Leur voiture est tombée dans un précipice. Their car fell into a ravine.

précipitamment ADVERB
hurriedly
□ Camille est partie précipitamment. Camille left hurriedly.

la **précipitation** FEM NOUN
haste
□ Il a agi avec précipitation. He acted hastily.

★ se **précipiter** VERB [28]
to rush

★ **précis** (FEM **précise**) ADJECTIVE
precise
■ **à huit heures précises** at exactly eight o'clock

★ **précisément** ADVERB
precisely

préciser VERB [28]
1 to be more specific about
□ Pouvez-vous préciser ce que vous voulez dire? Can you be more specific about what you want to say?
2 to specify
□ Pouvez-vous préciser les raisons de ce changement? Can you specify the reasons for this change?

la **précision** FEM NOUN
1 precision
2 detail
□ Je vais vous donner quelques précisions. I'm going to give you some details.

la **préfecture** FEM NOUN

> **DID YOU KNOW...?**
> A **préfecture** is the headquarters of a **département**, one of the 96 administrative areas of France.

■ **la préfecture de police** the police headquarters

préférable (FEM **préférable**) ADJECTIVE
preferable

★ **préféré** (FEM **préférée**) ADJECTIVE
favourite

★ la **préférence** FEM NOUN
preference
□ Je n'ai pas de préférence. I've no preference.
■ **de préférence** preferably

★ **préférer** VERB [34]
to prefer
□ Je préfère la cuisine de Teresa. I prefer Teresa's cooking. □ Je préfère manger à la cantine. I prefer to eat in the canteen.
■ **Je préférerais du thé.** I'd rather have tea.
■ **préférer quelqu'un à quelqu'un** to prefer somebody to somebody □ Je le préfère à son frère. I prefer him to his brother.

préhistorique (FEM **préhistorique**) ADJECTIVE
prehistoric

le **préjugé** MASC NOUN
prejudice
□ avoir des préjugés contre quelqu'un to be prejudiced against somebody

★ **premier** (FEM **première**) ADJECTIVE
▷ *see also* **première**
first
□ au premier étage on the first floor □ C'est notre premier jour de vacances. It's the first day of our holiday. □ C'est la première fois que

je viens ici. It's the first time I've been here. □ le premier mai the first of May □ Il est arrivé premier. He came first.

■ **le Premier ministre** the Prime Minister

★ la **première** FEM NOUN

▷ *see also* **premier** ADJECTIVE

1 first class

□ Nous avons voyagé en première. We travelled first class.

2 first gear

□ Passe en première pour prendre ce virage. Change into first to go round this bend.

3 lower sixth form

□ Ma sœur est en première. My sister's in the lower sixth.

> **DID YOU KNOW...?**
> In French secondary schools, years are counted from the **sixième** (youngest) to **première** and **terminale** (oldest).

premièrement ADVERB

firstly

★ **prendre** VERB [65]

to take

□ Prends tes affaires et viens avec moi. Take your things and come with me.

■ **prendre quelque chose à quelqu'un** to take something from somebody □ Il m'a pris mon stylo! He's taken my pen!

■ **Nous avons pris le train de huit heures.** We took the eight o'clock train.

■ **Je prends toujours le train pour aller à Paris.** I always go to Paris by train.

■ **passer prendre** to pick up □ Je dois passer prendre Thomas. I have to pick up Thomas.

■ **prendre à gauche** to turn left □ Prenez à gauche en arrivant au rond-point. Turn left at the roundabout.

■ **Il se prend pour Napoléon.** He thinks he's Napoleon.

■ **s'en prendre à quelqu'un** to lay into somebody (*verbally*) □ Il s'en est pris à moi. He laid into me.

■ **s'y prendre** to set about it □ Tu t'y prends mal! You're setting about it the wrong way!

★ le **prénom** MASC NOUN

first name

□ Quel est votre prénom? What's your first name?

préoccupé (FEM **préoccupée**) ADJECTIVE

worried

la **préparation** FEM NOUN

preparation

★ **préparer** VERB [28]

1 to prepare

□ Elle prépare le dîner. She's preparing dinner.

2 to make

□ Je vais préparer le café. I'm going to make the coffee.

3 to prepare for

□ Laure prépare son examen d'économie. Laure's preparing for her economics exam.

■ **se préparer** to get ready □ Ils se préparent à partir. They're getting ready to go.

la **préposition** FEM NOUN

preposition

★ **près** ADVERB

■ **tout près** nearby □ J'habite tout près. I live nearby.

■ **près de 1** near (to) □ Est-ce que c'est près d'ici? Is it near here? **2** next to □ Assieds-toi près de moi. Sit down next to me. **3** nearly □ Il y avait près de cinq cents spectateurs. There were nearly 500 spectators.

■ **de près** closely □ Il a regardé la photo de près. He looked closely at the photo.

■ **à peu de chose près** more or less

la **présence** FEM NOUN

1 presence

□ Sa présence est rassurante. His presence is reassuring.

2 attendance

□ La présence aux cours est obligatoire. Attendance at lessons is compulsory.

★ **présent** (FEM **présente**) ADJECTIVE

▷ *see also* **présent** NOUN

present

★ le **présent** MASC NOUN

▷ *see also* **présent** ADJECTIVE

present tense

■ **à présent** now

la **présentation** FEM NOUN

presentation

■ **faire les présentations** to do the introductions

★ **présenter** VERB [28]

to present

□ Il présentait le spectacle. He presented the show.

■ **présenter quelqu'un à quelqu'un** to introduce somebody to somebody □ Il m'a présenté à sa sœur. He introduced me to his sister.

■ **Marc, je te présente Anaïs.** Marc, this is Anaïs.

■ **se présenter 1** to introduce oneself □ Elle s'est présentée à ses collègues. She introduced herself to her colleagues. **2** to arise □ Si l'occasion se présente, nous irons en Écosse. If the chance arises, we'll go to Scotland. **3** to stand □ Monsieur Legros se présente encore aux élections. Mr Legros is standing for election again.

le **préservatif** MASC NOUN

condom

préserver VERB [28]

to protect

□ préserver du froid to protect from the cold

★ le **président** MASC NOUN

1 president

□ le président des États-Unis the president of the United States

2 chairman

□ le président du conseil d'administration the chairman of the board of directors

■ **le président-directeur général** the chairman and managing director

présider VERB [28]

1 to chair

□ Martin a présidé la réunion. Martin chaired the meeting.

2 to be the guest of honour

□ Il présidait à table. He was the guest of honour at the table.

★ **presque** ADVERB

nearly

□ Il est presque six heures. It's nearly 6 o'clock. □ Nous sommes presque arrivés. We're nearly there.

■ **presque rien** hardly anything □ Elle n'a presque rien mangé. She's hardly eaten anything.

■ **presque pas** hardly at all □ Il ne dort presque pas. He hardly sleeps at all.

■ **presque pas de** hardly any □ Il n'y a presque pas de place. There's hardly any space.

la **presqu'île** FEM NOUN

peninsula

★ la **presse** FEM NOUN

press

□ les représentants de la presse representatives of the press

★ **pressé** (FEM **pressée**) ADJECTIVE

1 in a hurry

□ Je ne peux pas rester, je suis pressé. I can't stay, I'm in a hurry.

2 urgent

□ Ce n'est pas très pressé. It's not very urgent.

■ **une orange pressée** a freshly squeezed orange juice

★ **presser** VERB [28]

1 to squeeze

□ Tu peux me presser un citron? Can you squeeze me a lemon?

2 to be urgent

□ Est-ce que ça presse? Is it urgent?

■ **se presser** to hurry up □ Allez, presse-toi, on va être en retard! Come on, hurry up, we're going to be late!

■ **Rien ne presse.** There's no hurry.

le **pressing** MASC NOUN

dry-cleaner's

★ la **pression** FEM NOUN

1 pressure

■ **faire pression sur quelqu'un** to put pressure on somebody

2 draught beer (*informal*)

★ **prêt** (FEM **prête**) ADJECTIVE

▷ *see also* **prêt** NOUN

ready

□ Le déjeuner est prêt. Lunch is ready. □ Tu es prête? Are you ready?

★ le **prêt** MASC NOUN

▷ *see also* **prêt** ADJECTIVE

loan

le **prêt-à-porter** MASC NOUN

ready-to-wear clothes *pl*

prétendre VERB [88]

■ **prétendre que** to claim that □ Il prétend qu'il ne la connaît pas. He claims he doesn't know her.

> **BE CAREFUL!**
> **prétendre** does not mean **to pretend**.

prétendu (FEM **prétendue**) ADJECTIVE

so-called

□ un prétendu expert a so-called expert

prétentieux (FEM **prétentieuse**) ADJECTIVE

pretentious

★ **prêter** VERB [28]

■ **prêter quelque chose à quelqu'un** to lend something to someone □ Il m'a prêté sa voiture. He lent me his car.

■ **prêter attention à quelque chose** to pay attention to something

le **prétexte** MASC NOUN

excuse

□ Il avait un prétexte pour ne pas venir. He had an excuse for not coming.

■ **sous aucun prétexte** on no account □ Ne le dérangez sous aucun prétexte. On no account must you disturb him.

prétexter VERB [28]

to give as an excuse

□ Elle a prétexté une réunion. She gave a meeting as her excuse. □ Il a prétexté qu'il avait un rendez-vous. He gave the excuse that he had an appointment.

le **prêtre** MASC NOUN

priest

★ la **preuve** FEM NOUN

1 evidence

□ Il y a des preuves contre lui. There's evidence against him.

2 proof

□ Vous n'avez aucune preuve. You haven't got any proof.

■ **faire preuve de courage** to show courage

■ **faire ses preuves** to prove oneself □ Pour être embauché ici, il faut faire ses preuves. To be employed here, you need to prove yourself.

★ **prévenir** VERB [89]

■ **prévenir quelqu'un** to warn somebody

□ Je te préviens, il est de mauvaise humeur. I'm warning you, he's in a bad mood.

la **prévention** FEM NOUN
prevention
■ **des mesures de prévention** preventative measures
■ **la prévention routière** road safety

★ la **prévision** FEM NOUN
■ **les prévisions météorologiques** the weather forecast
■ **en prévision de quelque chose** in anticipation of something

★ **prévoir** VERB [92]
1 to plan
□ Nous prévoyons un pique-nique pour dimanche. We're planning to have a picnic on Sunday.
■ **Le départ est prévu pour dix heures.** The departure's scheduled for 10 o'clock.
2 to allow
□ J'ai prévu assez à manger pour quatre. I allowed enough food for four.
3 to foresee
□ J'avais prévu qu'il serait en retard. I'd foreseen that he'd be late.
■ **Je prévois qu'il me faudra une heure de plus.** I reckon on it taking me another hour.

★ **prier** VERB [19]
to pray to
□ Les Grecs priaient Dionysos. The Greeks prayed to Dionysos.
■ **prier quelqu'un de faire quelque chose** to ask somebody to do something □ Elle l'a prié de sortir. She asked him to leave.
■ **je vous en prie** **1** please do □ Je peux m'asseoir? — Je vous en prie. May I sit down? — Please do. **2** please □ Je vous en prie, ne me laissez pas seule. Please, don't leave me alone. **3** don't mention it □ Merci pour votre aide. — Je vous en prie. Thanks for your help. — Don't mention it.

★ la **prière** FEM NOUN
prayer
□ faire ses prières to say one's prayers
■ **'prière de ne pas fumer'** 'no smoking please'

★ le **primaire** MASC NOUN
primary education
□ Ses enfants sont encore en primaire. His children are still in primary education.
■ **l'école primaire** primary school

la **prime** FEM NOUN
1 bonus
□ Il a eu une prime en récompense de son travail. He received a bonus for his work.
2 free gift
□ J'ai eu ce stylo en prime avec l'agenda. I got this pen as a free gift with the diary.
3 premium
□ une prime d'assurance an insurance premium

la **primevère** FEM NOUN
primrose

le **prince** MASC NOUN
prince
□ le prince Charles Prince Charles

la **princesse** FEM NOUN
princess
□ la princesse Diana Princess Diana

★ **principal** (FEM **principale**, MASC PL **principaux**) ADJECTIVE
▷ *see also* **principal** NOUN
main
□ le rôle principal the main role

★ le **principal** (PL les **principaux**) MASC NOUN
▷ *see also* **principal** ADJECTIVE
1 head teacher
□ le principal du collège the head teacher of the school
2 main thing
□ Personne n'a été blessé; c'est le principal. Nobody was injured; that's the main thing.

le **principe** MASC NOUN
principle
■ **pour le principe** on principle
■ **en principe** **1** as a rule □ Il déjeune en principe à midi et demi. As a rule he has lunch at 12.30. **2** in theory □ En principe Anne doit arriver lundi. In theory, Anne should arrive on Monday.

★ le **printemps** MASC NOUN
spring
■ **au printemps** in spring

★ la **priorité** FEM NOUN
1 priority
□ C'est à faire en priorité. It needs to be done as a priority.
2 right of way
□ Tu n'as pas la priorité. You haven't got right of way.

pris (FEM **prise**) ADJECTIVE
▷ *see also* **prise** NOUN
1 taken
□ Est-ce que cette place est prise? Is this seat taken?
2 busy
□ Je serai très pris la semaine prochaine. I'll be very busy next week.
■ **avoir le nez pris** to have a stuffy nose
■ **être pris de panique** to be panic-stricken

pris VERB ▷ *see* **prendre**

★ la **prise** FEM NOUN
▷ *see also* **pris** ADJECTIVE
1 plug
2 socket
■ **une prise de courant** a power point
■ **une prise multiple** an adaptor
■ **une prise de sang** a blood test

★la **prison** FEM NOUN
prison
□ aller en prison to go to prison □ être en prison to be in prison

★**prisonnier** (FEM **prisonnière**) ADJECTIVE
▷ *see also* **prisonnier** NOUN, **prisonnière** NOUN
captive

★le **prisonnier** MASC NOUN
▷ *see also* **prisonnier** ADJECTIVE
prisoner

★la **prisonnière** FEM NOUN
▷ *see also* **prisonnier** ADJECTIVE
prisoner

prit VERB ▷ *see* **prendre**

★**privé** (FEM **privée**) ADJECTIVE
private
□ la propriété privée private property □ ma vie privée my private life
■ **en privé** in private

priver VERB [28]
■ **priver quelqu'un de quelque chose** to deprive somebody of something □ Le prisonnier a été privé de nourriture. The prisoner was deprived of food.
■ **Tu seras privé de dessert!** You won't get any pudding!

★le **prix** MASC NOUN
1 price
□ Je n'arrive pas à lire le prix de ce livre. I can't see the price of this book.
2 prize
□ Cécile a eu le prix de la meilleure actrice. Cécile got the prize for best actress.
■ **hors de prix** exorbitantly priced □ Les repas sont hors de prix ici! The price of meals here is exorbitant!
■ **à aucun prix** not at any price □ Je n'irai là-bas à aucun prix. I'm not going there, not at any price.
■ **à tout prix** at all costs □ Je veux à tout prix voir ce film. I want to see this film at all costs.

★**probable** (FEM **probable**) ADJECTIVE
likely
□ Il est probable qu'elle viendra. It's likely she'll come.
■ **C'est peu probable.** That's unlikely.

probablement ADVERB
probably

★le **problème** MASC NOUN
problem

le **procédé** MASC NOUN
process

le **procès** MASC NOUN
trial
□ Le procès du meurtrier commence mardi. The murder trial starts on Tuesday.
■ **Il est en procès avec son employeur.** He's involved in a lawsuit with his employer.

★**prochain** (FEM **prochaine**) ADJECTIVE
next
□ Nous descendons au prochain arrêt. We're getting off at the next stop.
■ **la prochaine fois** next time
■ **la semaine prochaine** next week
■ **À la prochaine!** See you!

prochainement ADVERB
soon

★**proche** (FEM **proche**) ADJECTIVE
1 near
□ Les magasins les plus proches étaient à trois kilomètres. The nearest shops were 3 kilometres away. □ dans un proche avenir in the near future
2 close
□ un ami proche a close friend
■ **proche de** near to □ La cathédrale est proche du château. The cathedral is near the castle.
■ **le Proche-Orient** the Middle East

les **proches** MASC PL NOUN
close relatives

proclamer VERB [28]
to proclaim

la **procréation** FEM NOUN
procreation
■ **procréation médicalement assistée, assistance médicale à la procréation** assisted reproduction

procurer VERB [28]
■ **procurer quelque chose à quelqu'un** to get something for somebody □ C'est lui qui m'a procuré ce travail. He got me this job.
■ **se procurer quelque chose** to get something □ Je me suis procuré leur dernier catalogue. I got their latest catalogue.

le **producteur** MASC NOUN
producer

la **production** FEM NOUN
production

la **productrice** FEM NOUN
producer

★**produire** VERB [23]
to produce
■ **se produire** to take place □ Ces changements se sont produits l'an dernier. The changes took place last year.

★le **produit** MASC NOUN
product
□ les produits de beauté beauty products

★le/la **prof** MASC/FEM NOUN (*informal*)
teacher
□ Elle est prof de maths. She's a maths teacher.

 Numbers in brackets refer to verb tables on pages 650 to 658

★ le **professeur** MASC NOUN
1 teacher
□ Guillaume est professeur d'histoire. Guillaume's a history teacher.
2 professor
□ le professeur Dupont Professor Dupont
■ **un professeur de faculté** a university lecturer

★ la **profession** FEM NOUN
profession
□ Quelle est votre profession? What's your profession?
■ **'sans profession'** 'unemployed'

★ **professionnel** (FEM **professionnelle**) ADJECTIVE
professional

le **profil** MASC NOUN
1 profile (*of person*)
□ de profil in profile
2 contours (*of object*)

le **profit** MASC NOUN
profit
□ La société a fait des profits importants. The company made significant profits.
■ **tirer profit de quelque chose** to profit from something
■ **au profit de** in aid of □ un spectacle au profit de l'UNICEF a show in aid of UNICEF

profiter VERB [28]
■ **profiter de quelque chose** to take advantage of something □ Profitez du beau temps pour aller faire du vélo. Take advantage of the good weather and go cycling.
■ **Profitez-en bien!** Make the most of it!

★ **profond** (FEM **profonde**) ADJECTIVE
deep
■ **peu profond** shallow

★ la **profondeur** FEM NOUN
depth

★ le **programme** MASC NOUN
1 programme
□ le programme du festival the festival programme
2 syllabus
□ le programme de maths the maths syllabus
3 program
□ un programme informatique a computer program

programmer VERB [28]
1 to show
□ Ce film est programmé dimanche soir. The film is showing on Sunday evening.
2 to program
□ Mon ordinateur n'est pas programmé pour ça. My computer isn't programmed to do that.

★ le **programmeur** MASC NOUN
programmer
□ Lucas est programmeur. Lucas is a programmer.

★ la **programmeuse** FEM NOUN
programmer
□ Elle est programmeuse. She's a programmer.

★ le **progrès** MASC NOUN
progress
□ faire des progrès to make progress

progresser VERB [28]
to progress

progressif (FEM **progressive**) ADJECTIVE
progressive

★ le **projecteur** MASC NOUN
1 projector
□ Le projecteur est en panne. The projector is broken.
2 spotlight
□ sous les projecteurs under the spotlight

★ le **projet** MASC NOUN
1 plan
□ des projets de vacances holiday plans
2 draft
□ le projet de construction d'un musée the draft for the construction of a museum
■ **un projet de loi** a bill (*in parliament*)

projeter VERB [41]
1 to plan
□ Ils projettent d'acheter une maison. They're planning to buy a house.
2 to cast
□ une ombre projetée sur le mur a shadow cast onto the wall
■ **Elle a été projetée hors de la voiture.** She was thrown out of the car.

prolonger VERB [45]
1 to prolong
□ Je vais prolonger mes vacances en Espagne. I'm going to prolong my holidays in Spain.
2 to extend
□ Je vais prolonger mon abonnement. I'm going to extend my subscription.
■ **se prolonger** to go on □ La réunion s'est prolongée tard. The meeting went on late.

★ la **promenade** FEM NOUN
walk
□ Il y a de belles promenades par ici. There are some nice walks round here.
■ **faire une promenade** to go for a walk
■ **faire une promenade en voiture** to go for a drive
■ **faire une promenade à vélo** to go for a bike ride

★ **promener** VERB [43]
to take for a walk
□ Cordelia promène son chien tous les jours. Cordelia takes her dog for a walk every day.
■ **se promener** to go for a walk □ Léa est partie se promener. Léa has gone for a walk.

la **promesse** FEM NOUN
promise
□ faire une promesse to make a promise
□ tenir sa promesse to keep one's promise

★ **promettre** VERB [47]
to promise
□ On m'a promis une augmentation. They promised me a pay rise. □ Elle m'a promis de me téléphoner. She promised to phone me.

★ la **promotion** FEM NOUN
promotion
□ Il espère avoir bientôt une promotion. He's hoping to get a promotion soon.
■ **être en promotion** to be on special offer
□ Les côtes de porc sont en promotion. Pork chops are on special offer.

le **pronom** MASC NOUN
pronoun

★ **prononcer** VERB [12]
1 to pronounce
□ Le russe est difficile à prononcer. Russian is difficult to pronounce.
2 to deliver
□ prononcer un discours to deliver a speech
■ **se prononcer** to be pronounced □ Le 'e' final ne se prononce pas. The final 'e' isn't pronounced.

la **prononciation** FEM NOUN
pronunciation

la **propagande** FEM NOUN
propaganda

se **propager** VERB [45]
to spread
□ Le feu s'est propagé rapidement. The fire spread quickly.

la **proportion** FEM NOUN
proportion

le **propos** MASC NOUN
■ **à propos** by the way □ À propos, quand est-ce que tu viens? By the way, when are you coming?
■ **à propos de quelque chose** about something □ C'est à propos de la soirée de vendredi. It's about the party on Friday.

★ **proposer** VERB [28]
■ **proposer quelque chose à quelqu'un**
1 to suggest something to somebody □ Nous lui avons proposé une promenade en bateau. We suggested going on a boat ride to him.
2 to offer somebody something □ Ils m'ont proposé des chocolats. They offered me some chocolates.

★ la **proposition** FEM NOUN
offer
□ J'accepte ta proposition avec plaisir. I'll be pleased to accept your offer.

★ **propre** (FEM **propre**) ADJECTIVE
▷ *see also* **propre** NOUN
1 clean
□ Ce mouchoir n'est pas propre. This handkerchief isn't clean.
2 own
□ Valentin l'a fabriqué de ses propres mains. Valentin made it with his own hands.
■ **propre à** characteristic of □ C'est une coutume propre au Berry. It's a custom you find in the Berry region.

BE CAREFUL!
The French word **propre** does not mean **proper**.

★ le **propre** MASC NOUN
▷ *see also* **propre** ADJECTIVE
■ **recopier quelque chose au propre** to make a fair copy of something

proprement ADVERB
properly
□ Mange proprement! Eat properly!
■ **le village proprement dit** the village itself
■ **à proprement parler** strictly speaking

la **propreté** FEM NOUN
cleanliness

★ le **propriétaire** MASC NOUN
▷ *see also* **propriétaire** NOUN
1 owner
2 landlord

★ la **propriétaire** FEM NOUN
▷ *see also* **propriétaire** NOUN
1 owner
2 landlady

la **propriété** FEM NOUN
property
□ la propriété privée private property

le **prospectus** MASC NOUN
leaflet

prospère (FEM **prospère**) ADJECTIVE
prosperous

la **prostituée** FEM NOUN
prostitute

protecteur (FEM **protectrice**) ADJECTIVE
1 protective
□ un vernis protecteur a protective varnish
2 patronizing
□ un ton protecteur a patronizing tone

★ la **protection** FEM NOUN
protection

★ **protéger** VERB [66]
to protect

la **protéine** FEM NOUN
protein

protestant (FEM **protestante**) ADJECTIVE
Protestant
□ une église protestante a Protestant church
■ **Il est protestant.** He's a Protestant.

la **protestation** FEM NOUN
protest

★ **protester** VERB [28]
to protest
□ Ils protestent contre leurs conditions de travail. They're protesting about their working conditions.

★ **prouver** VERB [28]
to prove

★ la **provenance** FEM NOUN
origin
■ **un avion en provenance de Berlin** a plane arriving from Berlin

provenir VERB [89, *aux* être]
■ **provenir de** 1 to come from □ Ces tomates proviennent d'Espagne. These tomatoes come from Spain. 2 to be the result of □ Cela provient d'un manque d'organisation. This is the result of a lack of organization.

le **proverbe** MASC NOUN
proverb

★ la **province** FEM NOUN
province
■ **en province** in the provinces □ Ils habitent en province. They live in the provinces.

★ le **proviseur** MASC NOUN
headteacher (*of state secondary school*)
□ Elle est proviseur. She's a headteacher.

★ la **provision** FEM NOUN
supply
□ une provision de pommes de terre a supply of potatoes

★ les **provisions** FEM PL NOUN
food
□ Nous n'avons plus beaucoup de provisions. We haven't got much food left.

★ **provisoire** (FEM **provisoire**) ADJECTIVE
temporary
□ un emploi provisoire a temporary job

provoquer VERB [28]
1 to provoke
□ Il l'a provoquée en la traitant d'imbécile. He provoked her by calling her stupid.
2 to cause
□ Cet accident a provoqué la mort de quarante personnes. The accident caused the death of 40 people.

★ la **proximité** FEM NOUN
proximity
■ **à proximité** nearby □ Sabine habite à proximité. Sabine lives nearby.

prudemment ADVERB
1 carefully
□ Conduisez prudemment! Drive carefully!
2 wisely
□ Prudemment, il a fait des économies. Wisely, he saved some money.
3 cautiously
□ Le gouvernement a réagi prudemment. The government reacted cautiously.

la **prudence** FEM NOUN
caution
■ **avec prudence** carefully □ Ils ont conduit avec prudence. They drove carefully.

prudent (FEM **prudente**) ADJECTIVE
1 careful
□ Soyez prudents! Be careful!
2 wise
□ Laisse ton passeport à la maison, c'est plus prudent. It would be wiser to leave your passport at home.

★ la **prune** FEM NOUN
plum

le **pruneau** (PL les **pruneaux**) MASC NOUN
prune

le/la **psychiatre** MASC/FEM NOUN
psychiatrist

la **psychologie** FEM NOUN
psychology

psychologique (FEM **psychologique**) ADJECTIVE
psychological

le/la **psychologue** MASC/FEM NOUN
psychologist

pu VERB ▷ *see* **pouvoir**
■ **Je n'ai pas pu venir.** I couldn't come.

la **pub** FEM NOUN (*informal*)
1 advertising
□ Il y a trop de pub à la télé. There's too much advertising on TV.
2 adverts
□ Le film a été coupé par la pub. The film was interrupted by adverts.

★ **public** (FEM **publique**) ADJECTIVE
▷ *see also* **public** NOUN
public
□ un jardin public a public park
■ **une école publique** a state school

★ le **public** MASC NOUN
▷ *see also* **public** ADJECTIVE
1 public
□ Ce parc est ouvert au public. The park's open to the public.
2 audience
□ Le public a applaudi le chanteur. The audience applauded the singer.
■ **en public** in public □ Je déteste parler en public. I hate speaking in public.

publicitaire (FEM **publicitaire**) ADJECTIVE
■ **une agence publicitaire** an advertising agency
■ **un film publicitaire** a publicity film

★ la **publicité** FEM NOUN
1 advertising

□ Marine travaille dans la publicité. Marine works in advertising.

2 advert

□ Il y a trop de publicités dans ce journal. There are too many adverts in this newspaper.

■ **faire de la publicité pour quelque chose** to publicize something

publier VERB [19]

to publish

□ Cédric vient de publier son nouveau roman. Cédric has just published his new novel.

publique FEM ADJECTIVE ▷ *see* **public**

la **puce** FEM NOUN

1 flea

□ Ce chien a des puces. This dog has fleas.

2 chip

□ une puce électronique a microchip

■ **une carte à puce** a smart card

les **puces** FEM PL NOUN

flea market *sing*

puer VERB [28]

to stink

□ Ça pue le tabac ici! It stinks of tobacco round here!

puéril (FEM **puérile**) ADJECTIVE

childish

★ **puis** VERB ▷ *see* **pouvoir**

▷ *see also* **puis** ADVERB

■ **Puis-je venir vous voir samedi?** May I come and see you on Saturday?

★ **puis** ADVERB

▷ *see also* **puis** VERB

then

□ Faites dorer le poulet, puis ajoutez le vin blanc. Fry the chicken till golden, then add white wine.

★ **puisque** CONJUNCTION

since

□ Puisque c'est si cher, nous irons manger ailleurs. Since it's so expensive, we'll eat elsewhere.

★ la **puissance** FEM NOUN

power

puissant (FEM **puissante**) ADJECTIVE

powerful

le **puits** MASC NOUN

well

□ Il a un puits dans son jardin. He's got a well in his garden.

★ le **pull** MASC NOUN

jumper

le **pull-over** MASC NOUN

jumper

le **pulvérisateur** MASC NOUN

spray

□ un pulvérisateur de parfum a perfume spray

pulvériser VERB [28]

1 to pulverize

□ L'explosion a pulvérisé le bâtiment. The explosion pulverized the building.

2 to spray

□ Il a pulvérisé de l'insecticide sur ses plantes. He sprayed insecticide on his plants.

la **punaise** FEM NOUN

drawing pin

★ **punir** VERB [38]

to punish

□ Il a été puni pour avoir menti. He was punished for lying.

la **punition** FEM NOUN

punishment

★ le **pupitre** MASC NOUN

desk (*for pupil*)

pur (FEM **pure**) ADJECTIVE

1 pure

□ L'eau de cette source est très pure. The water from this spring is very pure.

2 neat (*undiluted*)

□ du whisky pur neat whisky □ de l'eau de Javel pure concentrated bleach

■ **C'est de la folie pure.** It's sheer madness.

★ la **purée** FEM NOUN

mashed potatoes

■ **la purée de marrons** chestnut purée

le **puzzle** MASC NOUN

jigsaw puzzle

le **P.-V.** MASC NOUN (= *procès-verbal*)

parking ticket

★ le **pyjama** MASC NOUN

pyjamas *pl*

la **pyramide** FEM NOUN

pyramid

★ les **Pyrénées** FEM PL NOUN

Pyrenees

■ **dans les Pyrénées** in the Pyrenees

Qq

le **QI** MASC NOUN (= *quotient intellectuel*)
IQ

★ le **quai** MASC NOUN
1 quay
□ être à quai to be alongside the quay
2 platform
□ Le train partira du quai numéro quatre. The train will leave from platform 4.

★ **qualifié** (FEM **qualifiée**) ADJECTIVE
qualified

qualifier VERB [19]
■ **se qualifier** to qualify □ Maxime s'est qualifié pour la demi-finale. Maxime has qualified for the semifinal.

★ la **qualité** FEM NOUN
quality
□ Ces outils sont de très bonne qualité. These are very good quality tools.

★ **quand** CONJUNCTION, ADVERB
when
□ Quand est-ce que tu pars en vacances? When are you going on holiday? □ Quand je serai riche, j'achèterai une belle maison. When I'm rich, I'll buy a nice house.
■ **quand même** all the same □ Je ne voulais pas de dessert, mais j'en ai mangé quand même. I didn't want any dessert, but I had some all the same.

quant à PREPOSITION
regarding
□ Quant au problème de chauffage ... Regarding the problem with the heating ...
□ Quant à moi, je n'arriverai qu'à dix heures. As for me, I won't be arriving till 10 o'clock.

★ la **quantité** FEM NOUN
amount
■ **des quantités de** a great deal of

la **quarantaine** FEM NOUN
about forty
□ une quarantaine de personnes about forty people
■ **Elle a la quarantaine.** She's in her forties.

★ **quarante** NUMBER
forty
□ Elle a quarante ans. She's forty.
■ **quarante et un** forty-one
■ **quarante-deux** forty-two

★ le **quart** MASC NOUN
quarter
■ **le quart de** a quarter of □ Elle a mangé le quart du gâteau. She ate a quarter of the cake.
■ **trois quarts** three quarters
■ **un quart d'heure** a quarter of an hour
■ **deux heures et quart** a quarter past two
■ **dix heures moins le quart** a quarter to ten
■ **Un quart d'eau minérale, s'il vous plaît.** A small bottle of mineral water, please.

★ le **quartier** MASC NOUN
1 area (*of town*)
□ un quartier tranquille a quiet area
■ **un cinéma de quartier** a local cinema
2 piece
□ un quartier d'orange a piece of orange

le **quartz** MASC NOUN
■ **une montre à quartz** a quartz watch

quasi ADVERB
nearly
□ La quasi-totalité des récoltes a été détruite. Nearly all of the crop was destroyed.

quasiment ADVERB
nearly
□ Le film est quasiment fini. The film's nearly finished.
■ **quasiment jamais** hardly ever □ Ils ne vont quasiment jamais en boîte. They hardly ever go clubbing.

★ **quatorze** NUMBER
fourteen
□ Mon frère a quatorze ans. My brother's fourteen. □ à quatorze heures at 2 p.m.
■ **le quatorze février** the fourteenth of February

★ **quatre** NUMBER
four
□ Il est quatre heures du matin. It's four in the morning. □ Il a quatre ans. He's four.
■ **le quatre février** the fourth of February
■ **faire les quatre cents coups** to be a bit wild □ Todd a fait les quatre cents coups dans sa jeunesse. Todd was a bit wild in his youth.

★ **quatre-vingts** NUMBER
eighty

> **quatre-vingts** is spelt with an **-s** when it is followed by a noun, but not when it is followed by another number.

★ = core vocabulary

□ quatre-vingts euros eighty euros □ Elle a quatre-vingt-deux ans. She's eighty-two.
■ **quatre-vingt-dix** ninety
■ **quatre-vingt-onze** ninety-one
■ **quatre-vingt-quinze** ninety-five
■ **quatre-vingt-dix-huit** ninety-eight

★ **quatrième** (FEM **quatrième**) ADJECTIVE
▷ *see also* **quatrième** NOUN
fourth
□ au quatrième étage on the fourth floor

★ la **quatrième** FEM NOUN
▷ *see also* **quatrième** ADJECTIVE
year 9
□ Mon frère est en quatrième. My brother's in year 9.

> **DID YOU KNOW...?**
> In French secondary schools, years are counted from the **sixième** (youngest) to **première** and **terminale** (oldest).

★ **que** CONJUNCTION, PRONOUN, ADVERB
1 that
□ Il sait que tu es là. He knows that you're here. □ la dame que j'ai rencontrée hier the lady that I met yesterday □ Le gâteau qu'elle a fait est délicieux. The cake she's made is delicious.
■ **Je veux que tu viennes.** I want you to come.
2 what
□ Que fais-tu? What are you doing? □ Que vas-tu lui dire? What are you going to tell him?
■ **Qu'est-ce que ...?** What ...? □ Qu'est-ce que tu fais? What are you doing? □ Qu'est-ce que c'est? What's that?
■ **plus ... que** more ... than □ C'est plus difficile que je ne le pensais. It's more difficult than I thought. □ Il est plus grand que moi. He's bigger than me.
■ **aussi ... que** as ... as □ Elle est aussi jolie que sa sœur. She's as pretty as her sister. □ Le train est aussi cher que l'avion. The train is as expensive as the plane.
■ **ne ... que** only □ Il ne boit que de l'eau. He only drinks water. □ Je ne l'ai vu qu'une fois. I've only seen him once.
■ **Qu'il est bête!** He's so silly!

★ **quel** (FEM **quelle**) ADJECTIVE
1 who
□ Quel est ton chanteur préféré? Who's your favourite singer?
2 what
□ Quelle est ta couleur préférée? What's your favourite colour? □ Quelle heure est-il? What time is it? □ Quelle bonne surprise! What a nice surprise! □ Quel dommage! What a pity!
3 which
□ Quel groupe préfères-tu? Which band do you like best?
■ **quel que soit** **1** whoever □ quel que soit le coupable whoever is guilty **2** whatever □ quel que soit votre avis whatever your opinion

★ **quelle** FEM ADJECTIVE ▷ *see* **quel**

★ **quelque** (FEM **quelque**) ADJECTIVE, ADVERB
1 some
□ Il a quelques amis à Paris. He has some friends in Paris. □ J'ai acheté quelques disques. I bought some records.
2 a few
□ Il reste quelques bouteilles. There are a few bottles left.
3 few
□ Ils ont fini les quelques bouteilles qui restaient. They finished the few bottles that were left.
■ **quelque chose** **1** something □ J'ai quelque chose pour toi. I've got something for you. □ Je voudrais quelque chose de moins cher. I'd like something cheaper. **2** anything □ Avez-vous quelque chose à déclarer? Have you got anything to declare? □ Tu as pensé à quelque chose d'autre? Did you think of anything else?
■ **quelque part** **1** somewhere □ J'ai oublié mon sac quelque part. I've left my bag somewhere. **2** anywhere □ Vous allez quelque part ce week-end? Are you going anywhere this weekend?

★ **quelquefois** ADVERB
sometimes

★ **quelques-uns** (FEM **quelques-unes**) PL PRONOUN
some
□ As-tu vu ses films? J'en ai vu quelques-uns. Have you seen his films? I've seen some of them.

★ **quelqu'un** PRONOUN
1 somebody
□ Quelqu'un t'a appelé. Somebody phoned you. □ Il y a quelqu'un à la porte. There's somebody at the door.
2 anybody
□ Est-ce que quelqu'un a vu mon parapluie? Has anybody seen my umbrella? □ Il y a quelqu'un? Is there anybody there?

la **querelle** FEM NOUN
quarrel

qu'est-ce que ▷ *see* **que**

qu'est-ce qui ▷ *see* **qui**

★ la **question** FEM NOUN
1 question
□ Je t'ai posé une question. I asked you a question.
2 matter
□ Ils se sont disputés pour des questions d'argent. They argued over money matters.
■ **Il n'en est pas question.** There's no

question of it. □ Il n'est pas question que je paye. There's no question of me paying.
■ **De quoi est-il question?** What's it about? □ Il est question de l'organisation du concert. It's about the organization of the concert.
■ **hors de question** out of the question □ Il est hors de question que nous restions ici. It's out of the question that we stay here.

le **questionnaire** MASC NOUN
questionnaire

questionner VERB [28]
to question

★ la **queue** FEM NOUN
1 tail
□ Le chien a agité la queue. The dog wagged its tail.
■ **faire la queue** to queue
■ **une queue de cheval** a ponytail
2 rear
□ en queue du train at the rear of the train
3 bottom
□ en queue de liste at the bottom of the list
4 stalk (*of fruit, leaf*)
□ la queue d'une cerise a cherry stalk

★ **qui** PRONOUN
1 who
□ Qui a téléphoné? Who phoned? □ Einstein, qui était un génie ... Einstein, who was a genius ...
2 whom
■ **C'est la personne à qui j'ai parlé hier.** It's the person who I spoke to yesterday.
3 that
□ Donne-moi la veste qui est sur la chaise. Give me the jacket that's on the chair.
■ **Qui est-ce qui ...?** Who ...? □ Qui est-ce qui t'emmène au spectacle? Who's taking you to the show?
■ **Qui est-ce que ...?** Who ...? □ Qui est-ce que tu as vu à cette soirée? Who did you see at the party?
■ **Qu'est-ce qui ...?** What ...? □ Qu'est-ce qui est sur la table? What's on the table?
□ Qu'est-ce qui te prend? What's the matter with you?
■ **À qui est ce sac?** Whose bag is this?
■ **À qui parlais-tu?** Who were you talking to?

la **quille** FEM NOUN
■ **un jeu de quilles** skittles

★ la **quincaillerie** FEM NOUN
ironmonger's (shop)

le **quinquennat** MASC NOUN

> **DID YOU KNOW...?**
> **le quinquennat** is the five-year term of office of the French President.

★ la **quinzaine** FEM NOUN
about fifteen
□ Il y avait une quinzaine de personnes. There were about fifteen people there.
■ **une quinzaine de jours** a fortnight

★ **quinze** NUMBER
fifteen
□ Anaïs a quinze ans. Anaïs is fifteen. □ à quinze heures at 3 p.m.
■ **le quinze février** the fifteenth of February
■ **dans quinze jours** in a fortnight's time

★ la **quittance** FEM NOUN
1 receipt
2 bill

★ **quitter** VERB [28]
to leave
□ J'ai quitté la maison à huit heures. I left the house at 8 o'clock.
■ **se quitter** to part □ Les deux amis se sont quittés devant le café. The two friends parted in front of the café.
■ **Ne quittez pas.** (*on telephone*) Hold the line. □ Ne quittez pas, je vous passe Monsieur Divan. Hold the line, I'll put you through to Monsieur Divan.

★ **quoi** PRONOUN
what
□ À quoi penses-tu? What are you thinking about? □ C'est quoi, ce truc? What's this thing?
■ **Quoi de neuf?** What's new?
■ **As-tu de quoi écrire?** Have you got anything to write with?
■ **Je n'ai pas de quoi acheter une voiture.** I can't afford to buy a car.
■ **Quoi qu'il arrive.** Whatever happens.
■ **Il n'y a pas de quoi.** Don't mention it.
■ **Il n'y a pas de quoi s'énerver.** There's no reason for getting worked up.
■ **En quoi puis-je vous aider?** How may I help you?

quoique CONJUNCTION
even though

> **quoique** is followed by a verb in the subjunctive.

□ Il va l'acheter quoique ce soit cher. He's going to buy it even though it's expensive.

★ **quotidien** (FEM **quotidienne**) ADJECTIVE
▷ *see also* **quotidien** NOUN
daily
□ Il est parti faire sa promenade quotidienne. He's gone for his daily walk.
■ **la vie quotidienne** everyday life

★ le **quotidien** MASC NOUN
▷ *see also* **quotidien** ADJECTIVE
daily paper
□ Le Monde est un quotidien. Le Monde is a daily paper.

French-English

Rr

le **rab** MASC NOUN (*informal*)
seconds (*of meal*)
□ Il y a du rab? Are there any seconds?

le **rabais** MASC NOUN
reduction (*in price*)
■ **au rabais** at a discount

★ la **racaille** FEM NOUN
riff-raff

raccompagner VERB [28]
to take home
□ Tu peux me raccompagner? Can you take me home?

le **raccourci** MASC NOUN
shortcut

★ **raccrocher** VERB [28]
to hang up (*telephone*)

la **race** FEM NOUN
1 race
□ la race humaine the human race
2 breed
□ De quelle race est ton chat? What breed is your cat?
■ **de race** pedigree □ un chien de race a pedigree dog

racheter VERB [1]
1 to buy another
□ J'ai racheté un portefeuille. I've bought another wallet. □ racheter du lait to buy more milk
2 to buy
□ Il m'a racheté ma moto. He bought my bike from me.

la **racine** FEM NOUN
root

★ le **racisme** MASC NOUN
racism

raciste (FEM **raciste**) ADJECTIVE
racist

★ **raconter** VERB [28]
■ **raconter quelque chose à quelqu'un** to tell somebody about something □ Raconte-moi ce qui s'est passé. Tell me what happened. □ Raconte-moi une histoire. Tell me a story.
■ **Qu'est-ce que tu racontes?** What are you talking about?

le **radar** MASC NOUN
radar

★ le **radiateur** MASC NOUN
radiator
■ **un radiateur électrique** an electric heater

radin (FEM **radine**) ADJECTIVE (*informal*)
stingy

★ la **radio** FEM NOUN
1 radio
□ à la radio on the radio
■ **une radio numérique** a digital radio
2 X-ray
■ **passer une radio** to have an X-ray □ Elle a passé une radio des poumons. She had a chest X-ray.

le **radio-réveil** (PL les **radios-réveils**) MASC NOUN
clock radio

le **radis** MASC NOUN
radish

raffoler VERB [28]
■ **raffoler de** to be crazy about □ Elle raffole de la tarte aux pommes. She really loves apple tart.

rafraîchir VERB [38]
to cool down
■ **se rafraîchir** **1** to get cooler □ Le temps se rafraîchit. The weather's getting cooler. **2** to freshen up □ Il a pris une douche pour se rafraîchir. He had a shower to freshen up.

rafraîchissant (FEM **rafraîchissante**) ADJECTIVE
refreshing

la **rage** FEM NOUN
rabies
■ **une rage de dents** raging toothache

le **ragoût** MASC NOUN
stew

★ **raide** (FEM **raide**) ADJECTIVE
1 steep
□ Cette pente est raide. This is a steep slope.
2 straight
□ Laure a les cheveux raides. Laure has straight hair.
3 stiff
□ Son bras est encore raide. His arm's still stiff.

r

4 flat broke
□ Je suis raide ce mois-ci. (*informal*) I'm flat broke this month.

la **raie** FEM NOUN
1 skate (*fish*)
2 parting (*in hair*)

le **rail** MASC NOUN
rail
□ par rail by rail

★ le **raisin** MASC NOUN
grapes
□ le raisin blanc green grapes
■ **des raisins secs** raisins

★ la **raison** FEM NOUN
reason
□ sans raison for no reason □ Raison de plus pour y aller. All the more reason for going.
■ **Ce n'est pas une raison.** That's no excuse.
■ **avoir raison** to be right □ Tu as raison. You're right.
■ **en raison de** because of □ en raison d'une grève because of a strike

raisonnable (FEM **raisonnable**) ADJECTIVE
sensible
□ Elle est très raisonnable pour son âge. She's very sensible for her age.

le **raisonnement** MASC NOUN
reasoning
□ J'ai du mal à suivre son raisonnement. I have difficulty following his reasoning.

rajouter VERB [28]
to add

★ **ralentir** VERB [38]
to slow down

râler VERB [28] (*informal*)
to moan

le **ramassage** MASC NOUN
■ **le ramassage scolaire** the school bus service

★ **ramasser** VERB [28]
1 to pick up
□ Il a ramassé son crayon. He picked up his pencil.
2 to take in
□ Il a ramassé les copies. He took in the exam papers.

la **rame** FEM NOUN
1 oar (*of boat*)
2 train (*on the underground*)

le **rameau** (PL les **rameaux**) MASC NOUN
branch
■ **le dimanche des Rameaux** Palm Sunday

ramener VERB [43]
1 to bring back
□ J'ai ramené mes copains à la maison pour regarder le match. I brought my friends back to my place to watch the match.
2 to take home
□ Tu me ramènes? Will you take me home?

★ **ramer** VERB [28]
to row
□ C'est Sébastien qui ramait. Sébastien was rowing.

la **rampe** FEM NOUN
banister

la **rancune** FEM NOUN
■ **garder rancune à quelqu'un** to bear somebody a grudge
■ **Sans rancune!** No hard feelings!

rancunier (FEM **rancunière**) ADJECTIVE
vindictive

★ la **randonnée** FEM NOUN
■ **une randonnée à vélo** a bike ride
■ **une randonnée pédestre** a ramble
■ **faire de la randonnée** to go hiking

le **randonneur** MASC NOUN
hiker

la **randonneuse** FEM NOUN
hiker

★ le **rang** MASC NOUN
row (*line*)
□ au premier rang in the front row □ se mettre en rangs to get into rows

la **rangée** FEM NOUN
row (*line*)
□ une rangée de chaises a row of chairs

★ **ranger** VERB [45]
1 to put away
□ J'ai rangé tes affaires. I've put your things away.
2 to tidy up
□ Va ranger ta chambre. Go and tidy up your room.

le **rap** MASC NOUN
rap
□ C'est un chanteur de rap très connu. He's a well-known rapper.

râper VERB [28]
to grate
□ le fromage râpé grated cheese

★ **rapide** (FEM **rapide**) ADJECTIVE
1 fast
□ Cette voiture est très rapide. This is a very fast car.
2 quick
□ J'ai jeté un coup d'œil rapide sur ton travail. I had a quick glance at your work.

★ **rapidement** ADVERB
quickly

★ le **rappel** MASC NOUN
1 booster (*vaccination*)
2 curtain call

★ **rappeler** VERB [4]
to call back

French-English

r

★ = core vocabulary

□ Je te rappelle dans cinq minutes. I'll call you back in 5 minutes.
■ **rappeler quelque chose à quelqu'un** to remind somebody of something □ Cette odeur me rappelle mon enfance. This smell reminds me of my childhood.
■ **rappeler à quelqu'un de faire quelque chose** to remind somebody to do something □ Rappelle-moi d'acheter des billets. Remind me to get tickets.
■ **se rappeler** to remember □ Il s'est rappelé qu'il avait une course à faire. He remembered he had some shopping to do.

le **rapport** MASC NOUN
▷ *see also* **rapports**
1 report
□ Il a écrit un rapport. He wrote a report.
2 connection
□ Je ne vois pas le rapport. I can't see the connection.
■ **par rapport à** in comparison with

★ **rapporter** VERB [28]
to bring back
□ Je leur ai rapporté un cadeau. I brought them back a present.

le **rapporteur** MASC NOUN
telltale

la **rapporteuse** FEM NOUN
telltale

★ les **rapports** MASC PL NOUN
▷ *see also* **rapport** NOUN
relations
□ Leurs rapports avec leurs voisins se sont améliorés. Their relations with their neighbours have improved.
■ **les rapports sexuels** sexual intercourse

rapprocher VERB [28]
1 to bring together
□ Cet accident a rapproché les deux frères. The accident brought the two brothers together.
2 to bring closer
□ Il a rapproché le fauteuil de la télé. He brought the armchair closer to the TV.
■ **se rapprocher** to come closer
□ Rapproche-toi, tu verras mieux. Come closer, you'll see better.

la **raquette** FEM NOUN
1 racket (*tennis*)
2 bat (*table tennis*)

★ **rare** (FEM **rare**) ADJECTIVE
rare
□ une plante rare a rare plant

★ **rarement** ADVERB
rarely

ras (FEM **rase**) ADJECTIVE, ADVERB
short
□ un chien à poil ras a short-haired dog
■ **à ras bords** to the brim □ Il a rempli son verre à ras bords. He filled his glass to the brim.
■ **en avoir ras le bol de quelque chose** (*informal*) to be fed up with something
■ **un pull ras du cou** a crew-neck jumper

★ **raser** VERB [28]
to shave off
□ Anthony a rasé sa barbe. Anthony has shaved off his beard.
■ **se raser** to shave

★ le **rasoir** MASC NOUN
▷ *see also* **rasoir** ADJECTIVE
razor

★ **rasoir** (FEM+PL **rasoir**) ADJECTIVE (*informal*)
▷ *see also* **rasoir** NOUN
dead boring

rassembler VERB [28]
to assemble
□ Il a rassemblé les enfants dans la cour. He assembled the children in the playground.
■ **se rassembler** to gather together □ Les passagers se sont rassemblés près du car. The passengers gathered near the coach.

★ **rassurer** VERB [28]
to reassure
■ **Je suis rassuré.** I don't need to worry any more.
■ **se rassurer** to be reassured
■ **Rassure-toi!** Don't worry!

le **rat** MASC NOUN
rat

raté (FEM **ratée**) ADJECTIVE
failed
□ une tentative ratée a failed attempt

le **râteau** (PL les **râteaux**) MASC NOUN
rake

★ **rater** VERB [28]
1 to miss
□ Marion a raté son train. Marion missed her train.
2 to fail
□ J'ai raté mon examen de maths. I failed my maths exam.
■ **Elle a raté sa pizza.** Her pizza didn't turn out right.

la **RATP** FEM NOUN
Paris transport authority

rattacher VERB [28]
to tie up again
□ rattacher ses lacets to retie one's laces

rattraper VERB [28]
1 to recapture
□ La police a rattrapé le voleur. The police recaptured the thief.
2 to catch up with
□ Je vais rattraper Cécile. I'll catch up with Cécile.
3 to make up for
□ Il faut rattraper le temps perdu. We must

make up for lost time.

■ **se rattraper** to make up for it □ Quand il ne mange pas à midi il se rattrape au dîner. When he doesn't have lunch he makes up for it at dinnertime.

la **rature** FEM NOUN
correction
□ un texte sans ratures a text with no corrections

★ **ravi** (FEM **ravie**) ADJECTIVE
■ **être ravi** to be delighted □ Ils étaient ravis de nous voir. They were delighted to see us.
□ Je suis ravi que vous puissiez venir. I'm delighted that you can come.

se **raviser** VERB [28]
to change your mind
□ Il allait accepter, mais il s'est ravisé. He was going to accept, but he changed his mind.

ravissant (FEM **ravissante**) ADJECTIVE
lovely

★ **rayé** (FEM **rayée**) ADJECTIVE
striped
□ une chemise rayée a striped shirt

rayer VERB [59]
1 to scratch
□ Il a rayé la peinture de sa voiture. He scratched the paintwork of his car.
2 to cross off
□ Son nom a été rayé de la liste. His name has been crossed off the list.

★ le **rayon** MASC NOUN
1 ray
□ un rayon de soleil a ray of sunshine
2 radius
□ le rayon d'un cercle the radius of a circle
3 shelf
□ les rayons d'une bibliothèque the shelves of a bookcase
4 department
□ le rayon hi-fi vidéo the hi-fi and video department
■ **les rayons X** X-rays

la **rayure** FEM NOUN
stripe

le **ré** MASC NOUN
1 D
□ en ré majeur in D major
2 re
□ do, ré, mi ... do, re, mi ...

★ la **réaction** FEM NOUN
reaction

réagir VERB [38]
to react

le **réalisateur** MASC NOUN
director (*of film*)
□ Spielberg est réalisateur. Spielberg is a film director.

la **réalisatrice** FEM NOUN
director (*of film*)
□ Elle est réalisatrice. She's a film director.

★ **réaliser** VERB [28]
1 to carry out
□ Ils ont réalisé leur projet. They carried out their plan.
2 to fulfil
□ Il a réalisé son rêve. He has fulfilled his dream.
3 to realize
□ Tu réalises ce que tu dis? Do you realize what you're saying?
4 to make
□ réaliser un film to make a film
■ **se réaliser** to come true □ Mon rêve s'est réalisé. My dream has come true.

réaliste (FEM **réaliste**) ADJECTIVE
realistic

la **réalité** FEM NOUN
reality
■ **en réalité** in fact
■ **dans la réalité** in reality
■ **réalité augmentée** augmented reality

le **rebelle** MASC NOUN
rebel

rebondir VERB [38]
to bounce

le **rebord** MASC NOUN
edge
□ le rebord du lavabo the edge of the washbasin
■ **le rebord de la fenêtre** the window ledge

recaler VERB [28] (*informal*)
■ **J'ai été recalé en maths.** I failed maths.

★ **récemment** ADVERB
recently

★ **récent** (FEM **récente**) ADJECTIVE
recent

★ le **récepteur** MASC NOUN
receiver

★ la **réception** FEM NOUN
reception desk

★ le/la **réceptionniste** MASC/FEM NOUN
receptionist
□ Elle est réceptionniste. She's a receptionist.

★ la **recette** FEM NOUN
recipe

★ **recevoir** VERB [67]
1 to receive
□ J'ai reçu une lettre. I received a letter.
2 to see
□ Il a déjà reçu trois clients. He has already seen three clients.
3 to have round
□ Je reçois des amis à dîner. I'm having friends round for dinner.

■ **être reçu à un examen** to pass an exam

le **rechange** MASC NOUN
■ **de rechange** spare (*battery*, *bulb*)
■ **des vêtements de rechange** a change of clothes

la **recharge** FEM NOUN
refill

le **réchaud** MASC NOUN
stove

le **réchauffement** MASC NOUN
warming
■ **le réchauffement climatique** global warming

réchauffer VERB [28]
1 to reheat
□ Je vais réchauffer les légumes. I'll reheat the vegetables.
2 to warm up
□ Un bon café va te réchauffer. A nice cup of coffee will warm you up.
■ **se réchauffer** to warm oneself □ Je vais me réchauffer près du feu. I'll go and warm myself by the fire.

la **recherche** FEM NOUN
research
□ Je voudrais faire de la recherche. I'd like to do some research.
■ **être à la recherche de quelque chose** to be looking for something □ Je suis à la recherche d'un emploi. I'm looking for a job.
■ **les recherches** search □ La police a interrompu les recherches. The police called off the search.

★ **recherché** (FEM **recherchée**) ADJECTIVE
much sought-after

rechercher VERB [28]
to look for
□ La police recherche l'assassin. The police are looking for the killer.

la **rechute** FEM NOUN
relapse

le **récipient** MASC NOUN
container

★ le **récit** MASC NOUN
story

réciter VERB [28]
to recite

la **réclamation** FEM NOUN
complaint
□ J'ai une réclamation à faire. I want to make a complaint.
■ **les réclamations** the complaints department

★ la **réclame** FEM NOUN
advert
□ une réclame de lessive an advert for washing powder
■ **en réclame** on special offer □ Le saumon était en réclame au supermarché. Salmon was on special offer at the supermarket.

réclamer VERB [28]
1 to demand
□ Nous réclamons la semaine de trente heures. We demand a 30-hour week.
2 to complain
□ Elles sont toujours en train de réclamer. They're always complaining about something.

reçois VERB ▷ *see* **recevoir**

la **récolte** FEM NOUN
harvest

récolter VERB [28]
1 to harvest
□ Ils ont récolté le blé. They harvested the wheat.
2 to collect
□ Ils ont récolté deux cents euros. They collected 200 euros.
3 to get
□ Il a récolté une amende. (*informal*) He got a fine.

le **recommandé** MASC NOUN
registered mail
■ **en recommandé** by registered mail
■ **Je voudrais envoyer ce paquet en recommandé.** I'd like to send this parcel registered.

★ **recommander** VERB [28]
to recommend
□ Je vous recommande ce restaurant. I recommend this restaurant.

recommencer VERB [12]
1 to start again
□ Il a recommencé à pleuvoir. It's started raining again.
2 to do again
□ S'il n'est pas puni, il va recommencer. If he's not punished he'll do it again.

★ la **récompense** FEM NOUN
reward

récompenser VERB [28]
to reward
□ Il m'a récompensée de mes efforts. He rewarded me for my efforts.

réconcilier VERB [19]
■ **se réconcilier avec quelqu'un** to make it up with somebody □ Il s'est réconcilié avec sa sœur. He has made it up with his sister.

★ **reconnaissant** (FEM **reconnaissante**) ADJECTIVE
grateful

★ **reconnaître** VERB [14]
1 to recognize
□ Je ne l'ai pas reconnu. I didn't recognize him.

2 to admit
□ Je reconnais que j'ai eu tort. I admit I was wrong.

reconstruire VERB [23]
to rebuild

le **record** MASC NOUN
record
□ battre un record to break a record

recouvrir VERB [55]
to cover
□ La neige recouvre le sol. The ground is covered in snow.

★ la **récréation** FEM NOUN
break
□ Les élèves sont en récréation. The pupils are having their break.
■ **la cour de récréation** the playground (*of school*)

le **rectangle** MASC NOUN
rectangle

rectangulaire (FEM **rectangulaire**) ADJECTIVE
rectangular

rectifier VERB [19]
to correct

★ le **reçu** MASC NOUN
▷ *see also* **reçu** VERB
receipt

★ **reçu** VERB ▷ *see* **recevoir**
▷ *see also* **reçu** NOUN
■ **J'ai reçu un colis ce matin.** I received a parcel this morning.
■ **être reçu à un examen** to pass an exam

★ **reculer** VERB [28]
1 to step back
□ Il a reculé pour la laisser entrer. He stepped back to let her in.
2 to reverse
□ J'ai reculé pour laisser passer le camion. I reversed to let the lorry past.
3 to postpone
□ Ils ont reculé la date du spectacle. They postponed the show.

reculons
■ **à reculons** ADVERB backwards □ Elle est entrée à reculons. She came in backwards.

récupérer VERB [34]
1 to get back
□ Je vais récupérer ma voiture au garage. I'm going to get my car back from the garage.
2 to make up
□ J'ai des heures à récupérer. I've got time to make up.
3 to recover
□ J'ai besoin de récupérer. I need to recover.

★ **recyclage** MASC NOUN
recycling
■ **un centre de recyclage** a recycling centre
■ **faire le recyclage** to recycle

★ **recycler** VERB [28]
to recycle
■ **se recycler** to retrain □ Il a décidé de se recycler en informatique. He decided to retrain in IT.

la **rédaction** FEM NOUN
essay

redemander VERB [28]
1 to ask again for
□ Je vais lui redemander son adresse. I'll ask him for his address again.
2 to ask for more
□ Je vais redemander des carottes. I'm going to ask for more carrots.

redescendre VERB [24, *aux* **avoir** *or* **être**]
to go back down
□ Il est redescendu au premier étage. He went back down to the first floor. □ Elle a redescendu l'escalier. She went back down the stairs.

> The verb **redescendre** uses **être** in the perfect tense when talking about moving downwards. It uses **avoir** in the perfect tense when talking about a person or thing moving down something (for example, down the stairs).

rédiger VERB [45]
to write (*an essay*)

★ **redoubler** VERB [28]
to repeat a year
□ Il a raté son examen et doit redoubler. He's failed his exam and will have to repeat the year.

★ la **réduction** FEM NOUN
1 reduction
□ une réduction du nombre des touristes a reduction in the number of tourists
2 discount
□ une réduction de vingt euros a 20 euro discount

★ **réduire** VERB [23]
to cut
□ Ils ont réduit leurs prix. They've cut their prices. □ Il a réduit de moitié ses dépenses. He has cut his spending by half.

★ **réel** (FEM **réelle**) ADJECTIVE
real

réellement ADVERB
really

refaire VERB [36]
1 to do again
□ Je dois refaire ce rapport. I've got to do this report again.
2 to take up again
□ Je voudrais refaire de la gym. I'd like to take up gymnastics again.

French-English

le **réfectoire** MASC NOUN
refectory

la **référence** FEM NOUN
reference
▪ **faire référence à quelque chose** to refer to something
▪ **Ce n'est pas une référence!** That's no recommendation!

réfléchi (FEM **réfléchie**) ADJECTIVE
reflexive (*verb*)
▪ **C'est tout réfléchi.** My mind's made up.

★ **réfléchir** VERB [38]
to think
□ Il est en train de réfléchir. He's thinking.
▪ **réfléchir à quelque chose** to think about something □ Je vais réfléchir à ta proposition. I'll think about your suggestion.

le **reflet** MASC NOUN
reflection
□ les reflets du soleil sur la mer the reflection of the sun on the sea

refléter VERB [34]
to reflect

le **réflexe** MASC NOUN
reflex
□ avoir de bons réflexes to have good reflexes

la **réflexion** FEM NOUN
1 thought
□ Elle est en pleine réflexion. She's deep in thought.
2 remark
□ faire des réflexions désagréables to make nasty remarks
▪ **réflexion faite** on reflection

le **refrain** MASC NOUN
chorus (*of song*)

le **réfrigérateur** MASC NOUN
refrigerator

refroidir VERB [38]
to cool
□ Laissez le gâteau refroidir. Leave the cake to cool.
▪ **se refroidir** to get colder □ Le temps se refroidit. It's getting colder.

se **réfugier** VERB [19]
to take shelter
□ Je me suis réfugié sous un arbre. I took shelter under a tree.

le **refus** MASC NOUN
refusal
▪ **Ce n'est pas de refus.** I wouldn't say no.
□ Voulez-vous une bière? — Ce n'est pas de refus. Would you like a beer? — I wouldn't say no.

★ **refuser** VERB [28]
to refuse
□ Il a refusé de payer sa part. He refused to pay his share. □ On lui a refusé une augmentation. He was refused a pay rise.
▪ **Je refuse qu'on me parle ainsi!** I won't let anybody talk to me like that!

se **régaler** VERB [28]
▪ **Merci beaucoup: je me suis régalé!** Thank you very much: it was absolutely delicious!

le **regard** MASC NOUN
look
□ Il lui a jeté un regard méfiant. He gave him a mistrustful look. □ On voyait à son regard qu'elle était contrariée. You could tell from the look in her eyes that she was upset.
▪ **Tous les regards se sont tournés vers lui.** All eyes turned towards him.

★ **regarder** VERB [28]
1 to look at
□ Il regardait ses photos de vacances. He was looking at his holiday photos. □ Regarde! J'ai presque fini. Look! I've nearly finished.
2 to watch
□ Je regarde la télévision. I'm watching television. □ Regarde où tu mets les pieds! Watch where you put your feet!
3 to concern
□ Ça ne nous regarde pas. It doesn't concern us.
▪ **ne pas regarder à la dépense** to spare no expense

★ le **régime** MASC NOUN
1 régime (*of a country*)
2 diet
□ un régime sans sel a salt-free diet □ se mettre au régime to go on a diet □ suivre un régime to be on a diet
▪ **un régime de bananes** a bunch of bananas

★ la **région** FEM NOUN
region

régional (FEM **régionale**, MASC PL **régionaux**) ADJECTIVE
regional

le **registre** MASC NOUN
register

★ la **règle** FEM NOUN
1 ruler
□ Il a souligné son nom avec une règle. He underlined his name with a ruler.
2 rule
□ C'est la règle. That's the rule. □ en règle générale as a general rule
▪ **être en règle** to be in order □ Mes papiers sont en règle. My papers are in order.
▪ **les règles** period (*menstruation*)

★ le **règlement** MASC NOUN
rules
□ Le règlement est affiché à l'entrée. The rules are up on the wall by the entrance.

r

★ **régler** VERB [34]

1 to adjust
□ Il faut que je règle mon rétroviseur. I'll have to adjust my rear-view mirror.

2 to tune
□ J'ai réglé ma radio sur 476 FM. I tuned my radio to 476 FM.

3 to set
□ J'ai réglé le thermostat à vingt degrés. I've set the thermostat to 20 degrees.

4 to solve
□ Le problème est réglé. The problem's solved.

5 to settle
□ Elle a réglé sa facture. She's settled her bill.
□ J'ai réglé Justin pour l'essence. I've settled up with Justin for the petrol.

la **réglisse** FEM NOUN
liquorice

le **règne** MASC NOUN
reign
□ sous le règne d'Henri IV in the reign of Henry IV

régner VERB [34]
to reign

le **regret** MASC NOUN
regret
■ **à regret** reluctantly

★ **regretter** VERB [28]

1 to regret
□ Elle regrette ce qu'elle a dit. She regrets saying what she did.
■ **Je regrette.** I'm sorry. □ Je regrette, je ne peux pas vous aider. I'm sorry, I can't help you.

2 to miss
□ Je regrette mon ancien travail. I miss my old job.

regrouper VERB [28]
to group together
□ Nous avons regroupé les enfants suivant leur âge. We grouped the children together according to age.
■ **se regrouper** to gather together □ Les agriculteurs se sont regroupés pour constituer un syndicat. The farmers joined together to form a union.

★ **régulier** (FEM **régulière**) ADJECTIVE

1 regular
□ des livraisons régulières regular deliveries
□ des bus réguliers a regular bus service

2 steady
□ à un rythme régulier at a steady rate

3 scheduled
□ des vols réguliers pour Marseille scheduled flights to Marseille

régulièrement ADVERB
regularly

le **rein** MASC NOUN
kidney
■ **les reins** back (*of body*) □ J'ai mal aux reins. My back hurts.

★ la **reine** FEM NOUN
queen

★ **rejoindre** VERB [42]
to go back to
□ J'ai rejoint mes amis. I went back to my friends.
■ **Je te rejoins au café.** I'll see you at the café.
■ **se rejoindre** to meet up □ Elles se sont rejointes une heure après. They met up an hour later.

relâcher VERB [28]
to release (*prisoner, animal*)
■ **se relâcher** to get slack □ Il se relâche dans son travail. He is slacking in his work.

le **relais** MASC NOUN
relay race
□ le relais quatre fois cent mètres the 4 x 100 metre relay
■ **prendre le relais** to take over

la **relation** FEM NOUN
relationship
■ **les relations franco-britanniques** Anglo-French relations

se **relaxer** VERB [28]
to relax

se **relayer** VERB [59]
■ **se relayer pour faire quelque chose** to take it in turns to do something

le **relevé** MASC NOUN
■ **un relevé de compte** a bank statement

relever VERB [43]

1 to collect
□ Je relève les copies dans cinq minutes. I'll collect the papers in five minutes.

2 to react to
□ Je n'ai pas relevé sa réflexion. I didn't react to his remark.
■ **relever la tête** to look up
■ **se relever** to get up □ Il est tombé mais s'est relevé aussitôt. He fell, but got up immediately.

la **religieuse** FEM NOUN

1 nun

2 choux cream bun
□ des religieuses au chocolat choux buns with chocolate cream and icing

★ **religieux** (FEM **religieuse**) ADJECTIVE
religious

★ la **religion** FEM NOUN
religion

relire VERB [44]

1 to read over
□ Il a relu sa copie avant de la rendre. He read

his exam paper over before handing it in.

2 to read again
□ Je voudrais relire ce roman. I'd like to read this novel again.

remarquable (FEM **remarquable**)
ADJECTIVE
remarkable

la **remarque** FEM NOUN
1 remark
□ Il a fait une remarque désagréable. He made a nasty remark.
2 comment
□ Avez-vous des remarques à faire? Have you any comments to make?

★ **remarquer** VERB [28]
to notice
□ J'ai remarqué qu'elle avait l'air triste. I noticed she was looking sad.
■ **faire remarquer quelque chose à quelqu'un** to point something out to somebody □ Je lui ai fait remarquer que c'était un peu cher. I pointed out to him that it was rather expensive.
■ **Remarquez, il n'est pas si bête que ça.** Mind you, he's not as stupid as all that.
■ **se remarquer** to be noticeable □ David ne s'est pas rasé ce matin. Ça se remarque. It's obvious David didn't shave this morning.
■ **se faire remarquer** to call attention to oneself

★ le **remboursement** MASC NOUN
refund

★ **rembourser** VERB [28]
to pay back
□ Il m'a remboursé l'argent qu'il me devait. He paid me back the money he owed me.
■ **se faire rembourser** to get your money back
■ **'satisfait ou remboursé'** 'satisfaction or your money back'

★ le **remède** MASC NOUN
1 medicine
2 cure

★ **remercier** VERB [19]
to thank
□ Je te remercie pour ton cadeau. Thank you for your present.
■ **remercier quelqu'un d'avoir fait quelque chose** to thank somebody for doing something □ Je vous remercie de m'avoir invité. Thank you for inviting me.

★ **remettre** VERB [47]
1 to put back on
□ Il a remis son pull. He put his sweater back on.
2 to put back
□ Il a remis sa veste dans l'armoire. He put his jacket back in the wardrobe.
3 to put off
□ J'ai dû remettre mon rendez-vous. I've had to put my appointment off.
■ **se remettre** to recover (*from illness*)
□ Mélusine s'est bien remise de son opération. Mélusine has fully recovered from her operation.

le **remonte-pente** MASC NOUN
ski-lift

remonter VERB [48, *aux* **avoir** *or* **être**]
1 to go back up
□ Il est remonté au premier étage. He has gone back up to the first floor.
2 to go up
□ Ils ont remonté la pente. They went up the hill.
3 to buck up
□ Cette nouvelle m'a un peu remontée. The news bucked me up a bit.
■ **remonter le moral à quelqu'un** to cheer somebody up

> The verb **remonter** uses **être** in the perfect tense when talking about moving upwards. It uses **avoir** in the perfect tense when talking about a person or thing moving up something (for example, up the hill), or when talking about cheering someone up.

le **remords** MASC NOUN
■ **avoir des remords** to feel remorse

la **remorque** FEM NOUN
trailer (*of car*)

les **remparts** MASC PL NOUN
city walls

le **remplaçant** MASC NOUN
supply teacher

la **remplaçante** FEM NOUN
supply teacher

★ **remplacer** VERB [12]
to replace
□ Il faut remplacer cette ampoule. We need to replace this bulb. □ Il remplace le prof de maths. He's replacing the maths teacher.
■ **remplacer par** to replace with

rempli (FEM **remplie**) ADJECTIVE
busy
□ une journée bien remplie a very busy day
■ **rempli de** full of □ La salle était remplie de monde. The room was full of people.

★ **remplir** VERB [38]
1 to fill up
□ Elle a rempli son verre de vin. She filled up her glass with wine.
2 to fill in
□ Tu as rempli ton formulaire? Have you filled in your form?
■ **se remplir** to fill up □ La salle s'est remplie de monde. The room filled up with people.

remporter VERB [28]
to win (*a competition, a prize*)

remuer VERB [28]
1 to move
□ Elle a remué le bras. She moved her arm.
2 to stir
□ Remuez la sauce pendant deux minutes. Stir the sauce for two minutes.
■ **se remuer** (*informal*) to get a move on □ Rien n'est prêt et les invités arrivent dans une heure, il faut se remuer! Nothing is ready and the guests arrive in an hour, we'd better get a move on!

★ le **renard** MASC NOUN
fox

★ la **rencontre** FEM NOUN
■ **faire la rencontre de quelqu'un** to meet somebody □ J'ai fait la rencontre de personnes intéressantes ce soir. I met some interesting people this evening.
■ **aller à la rencontre de quelqu'un** to go and meet somebody □ Je viendrai à ta rencontre. I'll come and meet you.

★ **rencontrer** VERB [28]
to meet
■ **se rencontrer** to meet □ Ils se sont rencontrés il y a deux ans. They met two years ago.

★ le **rendez-vous** MASC NOUN
1 appointment
□ J'ai rendez-vous chez le coiffeur. I've got an appointment at the hairdresser's. □ prendre rendez-vous avec quelqu'un to make an appointment with somebody
2 date
□ Tu sors ce soir? — Oui, j'ai un rendez-vous. Are you going out tonight? — Yes, I've got a date.
■ **donner rendez-vous à quelqu'un** to arrange to meet somebody

★ **rendre** VERB [7]
1 to give back
□ J'ai rendu ses CD à Lucie. I've given Lucie her CDs back.
2 to take back
□ J'ai rendu mes livres à la bibliothèque. I've taken my books back to the library.
■ **rendre quelqu'un célèbre** to make somebody famous
■ **se rendre** to give oneself up □ Le meurtrier s'est rendu à la police. The murderer gave himself up to the police.
■ **se rendre compte de quelque chose** to realize something

le **renfermé** MASC NOUN
■ **sentir le renfermé** to smell stuffy

renifler VERB [28]
to sniff

le **renne** MASC NOUN
reindeer

renommé (FEM **renommée**) ADJECTIVE
renowned
□ La Bretagne est renommée pour ses plages. Brittany is renowned for its beaches.

★ **renoncer** VERB [12]
■ **renoncer à** to give up □ Ils ont renoncé à leur projet. They've given up their plan.
■ **renoncer à faire quelque chose** to give up the idea of doing something

★ **renouvelable** (FEM **renouvelable**) ADJECTIVE
renewable
□ une énergie renouvelable a renewable energy source

renouveler VERB [4]
to renew (*passport, contract*)
■ **se renouveler** to happen again □ J'espère que ça ne se renouvellera pas. I hope that won't happen again.

★ le **renseignement** MASC NOUN
piece of information
□ Il me manque un renseignement. There's one piece of information I still need.
■ **les renseignements** 1 information □ Il m'a donné des renseignements. He gave me some information. 2 information desk
3 directory enquiries

★ **renseigner** VERB [28]
■ **renseigner quelqu'un sur quelque chose** to give somebody information about something
■ **Est-ce que je peux vous renseigner?** Can I help you?
■ **se renseigner** to find out □ Je vais me renseigner pour voir s'il n'y a pas un vol direct. I'm going to find out if there's a direct flight.

rentable (FEM **rentable**) ADJECTIVE
profitable

★ la **rentrée** FEM NOUN
■ **la rentrée (des classes)** the start of the new school year

★ **rentrer** VERB [68, *aux* **avoir** *or* **être**]
1 to come in
□ Rentre, tu vas prendre froid. Come in, you'll catch cold.
2 to go in
□ Elle est rentrée dans le magasin. She went into the shop.
3 to get home
□ Je suis rentré à sept heures hier soir. I got home at 7 o'clock last night.
4 to put away
□ Tu as rentré la voiture? Have you put the car away?
■ **rentrer dans** to crash into □ Sa voiture est rentrée dans un arbre. He crashed into a tree.

■ **rentrer dans l'ordre** to get back to normal

The verb **rentrer** uses **être** in the perfect tense when talking about returning somewhere. It uses **avoir** in the perfect tense when when talking about putting an object away.

la **renverse** FEM NOUN
■ **tomber à la renverse** to fall backwards

★ **renverser** VERB [28]
1 to knock over
□ J'ai renversé mon verre. I knocked my glass over.
2 to knock down
□ Elle a été renversée par une voiture. She was knocked down by a car.
3 to spill
□ Il a renversé de l'eau partout. He has spilt water everywhere.
■ **se renverser** (*glass, vase*) to fall over

★ **renvoyer** VERB [33]
1 to send back
□ Je t'ai renvoyé ton courrier. I've sent your mail back to you.
2 to dismiss
□ On a renvoyé deux employés. Two employees have been dismissed.

répandu (FEM **répandue**) ADJECTIVE
common
□ C'est un préjugé très répandu. It's a very common prejudice.
■ **du vin répandu sur la table** wine spilt on the table
■ **des papiers répandus sur le sol** papers scattered over the floor

★ le **réparateur** MASC NOUN
repairman

★ la **réparation** FEM NOUN
repair

★ **réparer** VERB [28]
to repair

repartir VERB [57, *aux* **être**]
to set off again
□ Il s'est arrêté pour déjeuner avant de repartir. He stopped for lunch before setting off again. □ Il était là tout à l'heure, mais il est reparti. He was here a moment ago, but he's gone again.
■ **repartir à zéro** to start again from scratch

★ le **repas** MASC NOUN
meal
■ **le repas de midi** lunch
■ **le repas du soir** dinner

★ le **repassage** MASC NOUN
ironing
□ Je déteste le repassage. I hate ironing.

★ **repasser** VERB [28, *aux* **avoir** *or* **être**]
1 to come back
□ Je repasserai demain. I'll come back tomorrow.
2 to go back
□ Je dois repasser au magasin. I've got to go back to the shop.
3 to iron
□ J'ai repassé ma chemise. I've ironed my shirt.
4 to resit
□ Elle doit repasser son examen. She's got to resit her exam.

The verb **repasser** uses **être** in the perfect tense when talking about going back somewhere. It uses **avoir** in the perfect tense when talking about tasks like doing ironing or taking a resit.

repérer VERB [34]
to spot
□ J'ai repéré deux fautes. I spotted two mistakes.
■ **se repérer** to find one's way around □ J'ai du mal à me repérer de nuit. I have difficulty finding my way around when it's dark.

le **répertoire** MASC NOUN
directory

★ **répéter** VERB [34]
1 to repeat
□ Elle répète toujours la même chose. She keeps repeating the same thing.
2 to rehearse
□ Les acteurs répètent une scène. The actors are rehearsing a scene.
■ **se répéter** to happen again □ J'espère que cela ne se répétera pas! I hope this won't happen again!

la **répétition** FEM NOUN
1 repetition
□ Il y a beaucoup de répétitions dans ce texte. There's a lot of repetition in this text.
■ **des grèves à répétition** repeated strikes
2 rehearsal
□ Ils ont une répétition cet après-midi. They've got a rehearsal this afternoon.
■ **la répétition générale** the dress rehearsal

★ le **répondeur** MASC NOUN
answering machine

★ **répondre** VERB [69]
to answer
□ répondre à quelqu'un to answer somebody

★ la **réponse** FEM NOUN
answer
□ C'est la bonne réponse. That's the right answer.

le **reportage** MASC NOUN
1 report
□ J'ai vu ce reportage aux informations. I saw that report on the news.

2 story
□ J'ai lu ce reportage dans 'La Gazette'. I read that story in 'La Gazette'.

le **reporter** MASC NOUN
reporter
□ Mathis est reporter. Mathis is a reporter.

le **repos** MASC NOUN
rest

★ **reposer** VERB [28]
to put back down
□ Elle a reposé son verre sur la table. She put her glass back down on the table.
■ **se reposer** to have a rest □ Tu pourras te reposer demain. You'll be able to have a rest tomorrow.
■ **se reposer sur quelqu'un** to rely on somebody

repousser VERB [28]
1 to grow again
□ Ses cheveux ont repoussé. Her hair has grown again.
2 to postpone
□ Le voyage est repoussé. The trip's been postponed.

★ **reprendre** VERB [65]
1 to take back
□ Il a repris son livre. He's taken his book back.
2 to go back to
□ Elle a repris le travail. She went back to work.
3 to start again
□ La réunion reprendra à deux heures. The meeting will start again at 2 o'clock.
■ **reprendre du pain** to take more bread
■ **reprendre la route** to set off again
■ **reprendre son souffle** to get one's breath back

★ le **représentant** MASC NOUN
rep
□ Il est représentant chez HarperCollins. He's a rep for HarperCollins.

★ la **représentante** FEM NOUN
rep
□ Elle est représentante. She's a sales rep.

la **représentation** FEM NOUN
performance
□ la dernière représentation d'une pièce the final performance of a play

représenter VERB [28]
to show
□ Le tableau représente un enfant et un chat. The picture shows a child with a cat.
■ **se représenter** to arise again □ Cette occasion ne se représentera pas. This opportunity won't arise again.

le **reproche** MASC NOUN
■ **faire des reproches à quelqu'un** to reproach somebody

reprocher VERB [28]
■ **reprocher quelque chose à quelqu'un** to reproach somebody for something □ Il m'a reproché mon retard. He reproached me for being late.
■ **Qu'est-ce que tu lui reproches?** What have you got against him?

la **reproduction** FEM NOUN
reproduction

reproduire VERB [23]
to reproduce
■ **se reproduire** to happen again □ Je te promets que ça ne se reproduira pas! I promise it won't happen again!

républicain (FEM **républicaine**) ADJECTIVE
republican

★ la **république** FEM NOUN
republic
□ la République française the French Republic

répugnant (FEM **répugnante**) ADJECTIVE
repulsive

la **réputation** FEM NOUN
reputation

le **requin** MASC NOUN
shark

le **RER** MASC NOUN
Greater Paris high-speed train service

★ le **réseau** (PL les **réseaux**) MASC NOUN
network
■ **les réseaux sociaux** social networks

le **réseautage** MASC NOUN
networking
□ un site de réseautage a social networking site

★ la **réservation** FEM NOUN
reservation

la **réserve** FEM NOUN
stock
□ avoir quelque chose en réserve to have a stock of something
■ **mettre quelque chose en réserve** to put something aside

réservé (FEM **réservée**) ADJECTIVE
1 reserved
□ Cette table est réservée. This table's reserved.
2 shy
□ Mon frère est réservé. My brother is shy.

★ **réserver** VERB [28]
1 to reserve
□ Je voudrais réserver une table. I'd like to reserve a table.
2 to book
□ Nous avons réservé une chambre. We've booked a room.
3 to save
□ Je t'ai réservé une part de gâteau. I've saved you a piece of cake.

le **réservoir** MASC NOUN
petrol tank

la **résidence** FEM NOUN
block of flats
■ **une résidence secondaire** a second home

résistant (FEM **résistante**) ADJECTIVE
1 hard-wearing
□ Ce tissu est résistant. This fabric is hard-wearing.
2 robust
□ Il est très résistant. He's very robust.

résister VERB [28]
to resist

résolu (FEM **résolue**) ADJECTIVE
■ **Le problème est résolu.** The problem's solved.

résoudre VERB [70]
to solve

le **respect** MASC NOUN
respect

★ **respecter** VERB [28]
to respect

la **respiration** FEM NOUN
breathing

★ **respirer** VERB [28]
to breathe

★ la **responsabilité** FEM NOUN
responsibility

★ **responsable** (FEM **responsable**) ADJECTIVE
▷ *see also* **responsable** NOUN
responsible
□ être responsable de quelque chose to be responsible for something

★ le/la **responsable** MASC/FEM NOUN
▷ *see also* **responsable** ADJECTIVE
1 person in charge
□ Je voudrais parler au responsable. I'd like to speak to the person in charge.
2 person responsible
□ Il faut punir les responsables. The people responsible must be punished.

★ **ressembler** VERB [28]
■ **ressembler à** **1** to look like □ Elle ne ressemble pas à sa sœur. She doesn't look like her sister. **2** to be like □ Ça ressemble à un conte de fées. It's like a fairy tale.
■ **se ressembler** **1** to look alike □ Les deux frères ne se ressemblent pas. The two brothers don't look alike. **2** to be alike □ Ces deux pays ne se ressemblent pas. These two countries aren't alike.

le **ressort** MASC NOUN
spring (*metal*)
□ Le ressort est cassé. The spring is broken.

ressortir VERB [79, *aux* **être**]
to go out again

★ le **restaurant** MASC NOUN
restaurant

★ le **reste** MASC NOUN
rest
■ **un reste de poulet** some left-over chicken
■ **les restes** the left-overs

★ **rester** VERB [71, *aux* **être**]
1 to stay
□ Je reste à la maison ce week-end. I'm staying at home this weekend.
2 to be left
□ Il reste du pain. There's some bread left. □ Il me reste assez de temps. I still have enough time.
■ **Il ne me reste plus qu'à ...** I've just got to ... □ Il ne me reste plus qu'à ranger mes affaires. I've just got to put my things away.
■ **Restons-en là.** Let's leave it at that.

★ le **résultat** MASC NOUN
result
□ le résultat des examens the exam results

★ le **résumé** MASC NOUN
summary

résumer VERB [28]
to summarize

> **BE CAREFUL!**
> **résumer** does not mean **to resume**.

se **rétablir** VERB [38]
to get well

★ le **retard** MASC NOUN
delay
□ un retard de livraison a delay in delivery
■ **avoir du retard** to be late
■ **être en retard de deux heures** to be two hours late
■ **prendre du retard** to be delayed

retarder VERB [28]
1 to be slow
□ Ma montre retarde. My watch is slow.
2 to put back
□ Je dois retarder la pendule d'une heure. I've got to put the clock back an hour.
■ **être retardé** to be delayed □ J'ai été retardé par un coup de téléphone. I was held up by a phone call.

★ **retenir** VERB [83]
1 to remember
□ Tu as retenu leur adresse? Do you remember their address?
2 to book
□ J'ai retenu une chambre à l'hôtel. I've booked a room at the hotel.
■ **retenir son souffle** to hold one's breath

retenu (FEM **retenue**) ADJECTIVE
▷ *see also* **retenue** NOUN
1 reserved
□ Cette place est retenue. This seat is reserved.

2 held up
□ J'ai été retenu par un coup de téléphone. I was held up by a phone call.

★ la **retenue** FEM NOUN
▷ *see also* **retenu** ADJECTIVE
detention
□ Antoine est en retenue. Antoine's in detention.

★ **retirer** VERB [28]
1 to withdraw
□ Elle a retiré de l'argent. She withdrew some money.
2 to take off
□ Il a retiré son pull. He took off his sweater.

★ le **retour** MASC NOUN
return
■ **être de retour** to be back □ Je serai de retour la semaine prochaine. I'll be back next week.

★ **retourner** VERB [72, *aux* **avoir** *or* **être**]
1 to go back
□ Est-ce que tu es retourné à Londres? Have you been back to London?
2 to turn over
□ Elle a retourné la crêpe. She turned the pancake over. □ Il a retourné la poubelle. He turned the bin upside down.
■ **se retourner** 1 to turn round □ Jade s'est retournée. Jade turned round. 2 to turn over □ La voiture s'est retournée. The car turned over.

The verb **retourner** uses **être** in the perfect tense when talking about going back somewhere. It uses **avoir** in the perfect tense when talking about turning an object over.

★ la **retraite** FEM NOUN
■ **être à la retraite** to be retired
■ **prendre sa retraite** to retire

retraité (FEM **retraitée**) ADJECTIVE
▷ *see also* **retraité** NOUN, **retraitée** NOUN
retired
□ Mon oncle est maintenant retraité. My uncle's now retired.

le **retraité** MASC NOUN
▷ *see also* **retraité** ADJECTIVE
pensioner

la **retraitée** FEM NOUN
▷ *see also* **retraité** ADJECTIVE
pensioner

rétrécir VERB [38]
to shrink
□ Son pull a rétréci au lavage. Her sweater shrank in the wash.
■ **se rétrécir** to get narrower □ La rue se rétrécit. The street gets narrower.

★ **retrouver** VERB [28]
1 to find
□ J'ai retrouvé mon portefeuille. I've found my wallet.
2 to meet up with
□ Je te retrouve au café à trois heures. I'll meet you at the café at 3 o'clock.
■ **se retrouver** 1 to meet up □ Ils se sont retrouvés devant le cinéma. They met up in front of the cinema. 2 to find one's way around □ Je n'arrive pas à me retrouver. I can't find my way around.

★ le **rétroviseur** MASC NOUN
rear-view mirror

le **retweet** MASC NOUN
retweet

retweeter VERB [28]
to retweet

★ la **réunion** FEM NOUN
meeting

se **réunir** VERB [38]
to meet
□ Ils se sont réunis à cinq heures. They met at 5 o'clock.

réussi (FEM **réussie**) ADJECTIVE
successful
□ une soirée très réussie a very successful party
■ **être réussi** to be a success □ Le repas était très réussi. The meal was a success.

★ **réussir** VERB [38]
to be successful
□ Tous ses enfants ont très bien réussi. All her children are very successful.
■ **réussir à faire quelque chose** to succeed in doing something
■ **réussir à un examen** to pass an exam

la **réussite** FEM NOUN
success

la **revanche** FEM NOUN
return match
■ **prendre sa revanche** to get one's own back □ Il a pris sa revanche en refusant de lui prêter son vélo. He got his own back by refusing to lend him his bike.
■ **en revanche** on the other hand □ C'est cher mais en revanche c'est de la bonne qualité. It is expensive but on the other hand it's good quality.

★ le **rêve** MASC NOUN
dream
■ **de rêve** fantastic □ des vacances de rêve fantastic holidays

★ le **réveil** MASC NOUN
alarm clock
■ **mettre le réveil à huit heures** to set the alarm for eight o'clock

le **réveille-matin** (PL les **réveille-matins**, les **réveille-matin**) MASC NOUN
alarm clock

★ **réveiller** VERB [28]
to wake up
□ réveiller quelqu'un to wake somebody up
■ **se réveiller** to wake up

le **réveillon** MASC NOUN
■ **le réveillon du Premier de l'an** New Year's Eve celebrations
■ **le réveillon de Noël** Christmas Eve celebrations

réveillonner VERB [28]
1 to celebrate New Year's Eve
2 to celebrate Christmas Eve

★ **revenir** VERB [73, *aux* être]
to come back
□ Reviens vite! Come back soon! □ Son nom m'est revenu cinq minutes après. His name came back to me five minutes later.
■ **Ça revient au même.** It comes to the same thing.
■ **Ça revient cher.** It costs a lot.
■ **Je n'en reviens pas!** I can't get over it!
■ **revenir sur ses pas** to retrace one's steps

le **revenu** MASC NOUN
income

★ **rêver** VERB [28]
to dream
■ **rêver de quelque chose** to dream of something □ J'ai rêvé de mes vacances cette nuit. I dreamt about my holidays last night.

le **réverbère** MASC NOUN
street lamp

le **revers** MASC NOUN
1 backhand
□ Murray a un excellent revers. Murray has an excellent backhand.
2 lapel (*of jacket*)
■ **le revers de la médaille** the other side of the coin

revient VERB ▷ *see* **revenir**

★ **réviser** VERB [28]
1 to revise
□ Je dois réviser mon anglais. I've got to revise my English.
2 to service
□ Je dois faire réviser ma voiture. I must get my car serviced.

la **révision** FEM NOUN
revision

★ **revoir** VERB [92]
1 to see again
□ J'ai revu Sophie hier soir. I saw Sophie again last night.
2 to revise
□ Il est en train de revoir sa géographie. He's revising his geography.
■ **au revoir** goodbye

la **révolution** FEM NOUN
revolution
□ la Révolution française the French Revolution

★ le **revolver** MASC NOUN
revolver

★ la **revue** FEM NOUN
magazine

★ le **rez-de-chaussée** MASC NOUN
ground floor
□ au rez-de-chaussée on the ground floor

★ le **Rhin** MASC NOUN
Rhine

le **rhinocéros** MASC NOUN
rhinoceros

★ le **Rhône** MASC NOUN
Rhone

la **rhubarbe** FEM NOUN
rhubarb

le **rhum** MASC NOUN
rum

★ le **rhume** MASC NOUN
cold
□ J'ai attrapé un rhume. I've caught a cold.
■ **un rhume de cerveau** a head cold
■ **le rhume des foins** hay fever

ri VERB ▷ *see* **rire**
■ **Nous avons bien ri.** We had a good laugh.

★ **riche** (FEM **riche**) ADJECTIVE
1 well-off
□ Sa famille est très riche. His family's very well-off.
2 rich
□ riche en vitamines rich in vitamins

★ le **rideau** (PL les **rideaux**) MASC NOUN
curtain
□ tirer les rideaux to draw the curtains

★ **ridicule** (FEM **ridicule**) ADJECTIVE
ridiculous
□ Je trouve ça complètement ridicule. I think that's absolutely ridiculous.

★ **rien** PRONOUN
▷ *see also* **rien** NOUN
1 nothing
□ Qu'est-ce que tu as acheté? — Rien. What have you bought? — Nothing. □ Ça n'a rien à voir. It has nothing to do with it.
■ **rien d'intéressant** nothing interesting
■ **rien d'autre** nothing else
■ **rien du tout** nothing at all
2 anything
□ Il n'a rien dit. He didn't say anything.
■ **rien que** 1 just □ rien que pour lui faire plaisir just to please him □ Rien que la voiture coûte un million. The car alone costs a million.
2 nothing but □ rien que la vérité nothing but the truth
■ **De rien!** Not at all! □ Merci beaucoup! — De rien! Thank you very much! — Not at all!

★ le **rien** MASC NOUN

▷ *see also* **rien** PRONOUN

■ **Il se met en colère pour un rien.** He loses his temper over the slightest thing.

■ **en un rien de temps** in no time at all

rigoler VERB [28] (*informal*)

1 to laugh

□ Elle a rigolé en le voyant tomber. She laughed when she saw him fall.

2 to have fun

□ On a bien rigolé hier soir. We had good fun last night.

3 to be joking

□ Ne te fâche pas, je rigolais. Don't get upset, I was only joking.

■ **pour rigoler** for a laugh

★ **rigolo** (FEM **rigolote**) ADJECTIVE (*informal*)

funny

rincer VERB [12]

to rinse

★ **rire** VERB [74]

▷ *see also* **rire** NOUN

to laugh

□ Ce film m'a vraiment fait rire. That film really made me laugh. □ Nous avons bien ri. We had a good laugh.

■ **pour rire** for a laugh

★ le **rire** MASC NOUN

▷ *see also* **rire** VERB

laughter

□ Il a un rire bruyant. He has a loud laugh.

★ le **risque** MASC NOUN

1 risk

□ prendre des risques to take risks □ à tes risques et périls at your own risk

2 danger

□ Il n'y a pas de risque qu'il l'apprenne. There's no danger of him finding out.

risqué (FEM **risquée**) ADJECTIVE

risky

★ **risquer** VERB [28]

to risk

■ **Ça ne risque rien.** It's quite safe.

■ **Il risque de se tuer.** He could get himself killed.

■ **C'est ce qui risque de se passer.** That's what might well happen.

le **rivage** MASC NOUN

shore

★ la **rivière** FEM NOUN

river

★ le **riz** MASC NOUN

rice

la **RN** FEM NOUN (= *route nationale*)

A road

★ la **robe** FEM NOUN

dress

■ **une robe de soirée** an evening dress

■ **une robe de mariée** a wedding dress

■ **une robe de chambre** a dressing gown

★ le **robinet** MASC NOUN

tap

le **robot** MASC NOUN

robot

la **roche** FEM NOUN

rock (*stone*)

★ le **rocher** MASC NOUN

rock

★ le **rock** MASC NOUN

rock (*music*)

□ un chanteur de rock a rock singer

rôder VERB [28]

to loiter

□ Il y a un homme louche qui rôde autour de l'école. There's a suspicious man loitering around the school.

les **rognons** MASC PL NOUN

kidneys (*in cooking*)

★ le **roi** MASC NOUN

king

■ **le jour des Rois** Twelfth Night

★ le **rôle** MASC NOUN

role

les **rollers** MASC PL NOUN

Rollerblades®

romain (FEM **romaine**) ADJECTIVE

Roman

□ des ruines romaines Roman remains

★ le **roman** MASC NOUN

novel

■ **un roman policier** a detective story

■ **un roman d'espionnage** a spy story

★ le **romancier** MASC NOUN

novelist

★ la **romancière** FEM NOUN

novelist

★ **romantique** (FEM **romantique**) ADJECTIVE

romantic

rompre VERB [75]

1 to split up

□ Paul et Justine ont rompu. Paul and Justine have split up.

2 to break off

□ Ils ont rompu leurs fiançailles. They've broken off their engagement.

les **ronces** FEM PL NOUN

brambles

ronchonner VERB [28] (*informal*)

to grouse

★ **rond** (FEM **ronde**) ADJECTIVE

▷ *see also* **rond** NOUN

1 round

□ La Terre est ronde. The earth is round.

■ **ouvrir des yeux ronds** to stare in amazement

2 chubby
□ Il a les joues rondes. He has chubby cheeks.
3 drunk
□ Il est complètement rond. (*informal*) He's completely drunk.

★ le **rond** MASC NOUN
▷ *see also* **rond** ADJECTIVE
circle
□ Elle a dessiné un rond sur le sable. She drew a circle in the sand.
■ **en rond** in a circle □ Ils se sont assis en rond. They sat down in a circle.
■ **tourner en rond** to go round in circles
■ **Je n'ai plus un rond.** (*informal*) I haven't a penny left.

la **rondelle** FEM NOUN
slice
□ une rondelle de citron a slice of lemon

★ le **rond-point** (PL les **ronds-points**) MASC NOUN
roundabout
□ La voiture s'est arrêtée au rond-point. The car stopped at the roundabout.

ronfler VERB [28]
to snore

le **rosbif** MASC NOUN
roast beef

★ la **rose** FEM NOUN
▷ *see also* **rose** ADJECTIVE
rose

★ **rose** (FEM **rose**) ADJECTIVE
▷ *see also* **rose** NOUN
pink

★ le **rosé** MASC NOUN
rosé (wine)
□ Je prendrai un verre de rosé. I'll have a glass of rosé.

le **rosier** MASC NOUN
rosebush

★ le **rôti** MASC NOUN
roast meat
■ **un rôti de bœuf** a joint of beef

★ **rôtir** VERB [38]
to roast
□ faire rôtir quelque chose to roast something

★ la **roue** FEM NOUN
wheel
□ une roue de secours a spare wheel

★ **rouge** (FEM **rouge**) ADJECTIVE
▷ *see also* **rouge** NOUN
red

★ le **rouge** MASC NOUN
▷ *see also* **rouge** ADJECTIVE
1 red
□ Le rouge est ma couleur préférée. Red is my favourite colour.
2 red wine
□ un verre de rouge a glass of red wine
■ **passer au rouge 1** to change to red □ Le feu est passé au rouge. The light changed to red. **2** to go through a red light □ Pierre est passé au rouge. Pierre went through a red light.
■ **un rouge à lèvres** a lipstick

la **rougeole** FEM NOUN
measles

rougir VERB [38]
1 to blush
□ Il a rougi en me voyant. He blushed when he saw me.
2 to flush
□ Il a rougi de colère. He flushed with anger.

la **rouille** FEM NOUN
rust

rouillé (FEM **rouillée**) ADJECTIVE
rusty

rouiller VERB [28]
to go rusty

roulant (FEM **roulante**) ADJECTIVE
■ **un fauteuil roulant** a wheelchair
■ **une table roulante** a trolley

le **rouleau** (PL les **rouleaux**) MASC NOUN
roll
□ un rouleau de papier peint a roll of wallpaper
■ **un rouleau à pâtisserie** a rolling pin

★ **rouler** VERB [28]
1 to go
□ Le train roulait à 250 km/h. The train was going at 250 km an hour.
2 to drive
□ Il a roulé sans s'arrêter. He drove without stopping.
3 to roll
□ Pauline a roulé une cigarette. Pauline rolled a cigarette.
4 to roll up
□ Il a roulé le tapis. He rolled the carpet up.
5 to con
□ Ils se sont fait rouler. (*informal*) They were conned.
■ **Alors, ça roule?** (*informal*) How's it going?

la **Roumanie** FEM NOUN
Romania

le **rouquin** MASC NOUN (*informal*)
redhead

la **rouquine** FEM NOUN (*informal*)
redhead

rousse FEM ADJECTIVE ▷ *see* **roux**

★ la **rousse** FEM NOUN
▷ *see also* **rousse** ADJECTIVE
redhead

★ la **route** FEM NOUN
1 road

□ au bord de la route at the roadside
■ **une route nationale** an A road
2 way
□ Je ne connais pas la route. I don't know the way.
■ **Il y a trois heures de route.** It's a 3-hour journey.
■ **en route** on the way □ Ils se sont arrêtés en route. They stopped on the way.
■ **mettre en route** to start up □ Il a mis le moteur en route. He started the engine up.
■ **se mettre en route** to set off □ Il s'est mis en route à cinq heures. He set off at 5 o'clock.

★ le **routier** MASC NOUN
1 lorry driver
□ Son père est routier. His father's a lorry driver.
2 transport café
□ Nous avons mangé dans un routier. We ate in a transport café.

la **routine** FEM NOUN
routine

★ **roux** (FEM **rousse**) ADJECTIVE
▷ *see also* **roux** NOUN
1 red
□ Harry a les cheveux roux. Harry has red hair.
2 red-haired
□ Gaëlle est rousse. Gaëlle's red-haired.

★ le **roux** MASC NOUN
▷ *see also* **roux** ADJECTIVE
redhead

royal (FEM **royale**, MASC PL **royaux**) ADJECTIVE
royal

le **royaume** MASC NOUN
kingdom
■ **le Royaume-Uni** the United Kingdom

le **RSA** MASC NOUN
Income Support
□ Il touche le RSA. He's on Income Support.

★ le **ruban** MASC NOUN
ribbon
■ **le ruban adhésif** adhesive tape

la **rubéole** FEM NOUN
German measles

la **ruche** FEM NOUN
hive

rudement ADVERB (*informal*)
terribly
□ C'était rudement bon. It was terribly good.

★ la **rue** FEM NOUN
street

la **ruelle** FEM NOUN
alley

★ le **rugby** MASC NOUN
rugby
□ Yann joue au rugby. Yann plays rugby.

rugueux (FEM **rugueuse**) ADJECTIVE
rough

la **ruine** FEM NOUN
ruin
□ les ruines de la cathédrale the ruins of the cathedral

ruiner VERB [28]
to ruin

★ le **ruisseau** (PL les **ruisseaux**) MASC NOUN
stream

la **rumeur** FEM NOUN
rumour

la **rupture** FEM NOUN
break-up

la **ruse** FEM NOUN
trickery
■ **une ruse** a trick

rusé (FEM **rusée**) ADJECTIVE
cunning

★ **russe** (FEM **russe**) ADJECTIVE, NOUN
Russian
□ Il parle russe. He speaks Russian.
■ **un Russe** a Russian (*man*)
■ **une Russe** a Russian (*woman*)
■ **les Russes** the Russians

★ la **Russie** FEM NOUN
Russia

le **rythme** MASC NOUN
1 rhythm
■ **J'aime le rythme de cette musique.** I like the beat of this music.
2 pace
□ Il marche à un bon rythme. He walks at a good pace.

Ss

★ **s'** PRONOUN ▷ *see* **se**

★ **sa** FEM ADJECTIVE

1 his

□ Paul est allé voir sa grand-mère. Paul's gone to see his grandmother.

2 her

□ Elle a embrassé sa mère. She kissed her mother.

★ le **sable** MASC NOUN

sand

■ **des sables mouvants** quicksand

le **sablé** MASC NOUN

shortbread biscuit

le **sabot** MASC NOUN

1 clog

2 hoof (*of horse*)

★ le **sac** MASC NOUN

bag

■ **un sac de voyage** a travel bag

■ **un sac de couchage** a sleeping bag

■ **un sac à main** a handbag

■ **un sac en plastique** a plastic bag

■ **voyager sac au dos** to go backpacking

le **sachet** MASC NOUN

sachet (*of sugar, coffee*)

■ **du potage en sachet** packet soup

■ **un sachet de thé** a tea bag

la **sacoche** FEM NOUN

bag

■ **une sacoche de bicyclette** a saddlebag

sacré (FEM **sacrée**) ADJECTIVE

sacred

★ **sage** (FEM **sage**) ADJECTIVE

1 good (*well-behaved*)

□ Sois sage. Be good.

2 wise (*sensible*)

□ Il serait plus sage d'attendre. It would be wiser to wait.

la **sagesse** FEM NOUN

wisdom

□ Il a eu la sagesse de ne pas y aller. He wisely didn't go.

■ **une dent de sagesse** a wisdom tooth

le **Sagittaire** MASC NOUN

Sagittarius

□ Il est Sagittaire. He is Sagittarius.

★ **saignant** (FEM **saignante**) ADJECTIVE

rare (*meat*)

★ **saigner** VERB [28]

to bleed

■ **saigner du nez** to have a nosebleed

★ **sain** (FEM **saine**) ADJECTIVE

healthy

■ **sain et sauf** safe and sound

★ **saint** (FEM **sainte**) ADJECTIVE

▷ *see also* **saint** NOUN, **sainte** NOUN

holy

□ la semaine sainte Holy Week □ le Saint-Esprit the Holy Spirit

■ **la Sainte Vierge** the Blessed Virgin

■ **le vendredi saint** Good Friday

■ **la Saint-Sylvestre** New Year's Eve

■ **la Saint-Valentin** Valentine's day

le **saint** MASC NOUN

▷ *see also* **saint** ADJECTIVE

saint

la **sainte** FEM NOUN

▷ *see also* **saint** ADJECTIVE

saint

sais VERB ▷ *see* **savoir**

■ **Je ne sais pas.** I don't know.

★ **saisir** VERB [38]

to take hold of

■ **saisir l'occasion de faire quelque chose** to seize the opportunity to do something

★ la **saison** FEM NOUN

season

□ Ce n'est pas la saison des fraises. Strawberries are out of season. □ un temps de saison seasonable weather

■ **la saison des vendanges** harvest time

sait VERB ▷ *see* **savoir**

■ **Il sait que ...** He knows that ...

■ **On ne sait jamais!** You never know!

★ la **salade** FEM NOUN

1 lettuce

2 salad

□ une salade composée a mixed salad □ une salade de fruits a fruit salad

le **saladier** MASC NOUN

salad bowl

★ le **salaire** MASC NOUN

salary

le **salami** MASC NOUN
salami

★ le **salarié** MASC NOUN
salaried employee

★ la **salariée** FEM NOUN
salaried employee

★ **sale** (FEM **sale**) ADJECTIVE
dirty

★ **salé** (FEM **salée**) ADJECTIVE
1 salty
□ La soupe est trop salée. The soup's too salty.
2 salted
□ du beurre salé salted butter
3 savoury
□ des biscuits salés savoury biscuits

★ **saler** VERB [28]
to put salt in
□ J'ai oublié de saler la soupe. I forgot to put salt in the soup.

la **saleté** FEM NOUN
dirt
□ J'ai horreur de la saleté. I hate dirt. □ Il y a une saleté sur ta chemise. There's some dirt on your shirt.
■ **faire des saletés** to make a mess

★ **salir** VERB [38]
■ **salir quelque chose** to get something dirty
■ **se salir** to get oneself dirty □ Mets un tablier, sinon tu vas te salir. Put on an apron or you'll get yourself dirty.

★ la **salle** FEM NOUN
1 room
2 audience
□ Toute la salle l'a applaudi. The whole audience applauded him.
3 ward (*in hospital*)
□ Il est à la salle douze. He's in Ward 12.
■ **la salle à manger** the dining room
■ **la salle de séjour** the living room
■ **la salle de bains** the bathroom
■ **la salle d'attente** the waiting room
■ **une salle de classe** a classroom
■ **la salle des professeurs** the staffroom
■ **la salle informatique** the computer room
■ **une salle de concert** a concert hall
■ **la salle d'embarquement** the departure lounge

★ le **salon** MASC NOUN
lounge
■ **un salon de thé** a tearoom
■ **un salon de coiffure** a hair salon
■ **un salon de beauté** a beauty salon
■ **un salon de discussion** a chatroom

la **salopette** FEM NOUN
1 dungarees
2 overalls

★ **saluer** VERB [28]
■ **saluer quelqu'un** 1 to say hello to somebody □ Je l'ai croisé dans la rue et il m'a salué. I met him in the street and he said hello. 2 to say goodbye to somebody □ Il nous a salués et il est parti. He said goodbye and left.

★ **salut** EXCLAMATION (*informal*)
hi!

★ la **salutation** FEM NOUN
greeting

★ le **samedi** MASC NOUN
1 Saturday
□ Aujourd'hui, nous sommes samedi. It's Saturday today.
2 on Saturday
□ Nous sommes allés au cinéma samedi. We went to the cinema on Saturday.
■ **le samedi** on Saturdays □ Le magasin ferme à dix-huit heures le samedi. The shop closes at 6 p.m. on Saturdays.
■ **tous les samedis** every Saturday
■ **samedi dernier** last Saturday
■ **samedi prochain** next Saturday

★ le **SAMU** MASC NOUN
ambulance service

★ la **sandale** FEM NOUN
sandal

★ le **sandwich** MASC NOUN
sandwich

★ le **sang** MASC NOUN
blood
■ **en sang** covered in blood

le **sang-froid** MASC NOUN
■ **garder son sang-froid** to keep calm
■ **perdre son sang-froid** to lose one's cool
■ **faire quelque chose de sang-froid** to do something in cold blood

le **sanglier** MASC NOUN
wild boar

le **sanglot** MASC NOUN
■ **éclater en sanglots** to burst into tears

★ **sans** PREPOSITION
without
□ Elle est venue sans son frère. She came without her brother.
■ **un pull sans manches** a sleeveless sweater

le/la **sans-abri** (PL les **sans-abris**, les **sans-abri**) MASC/FEM NOUN
homeless person
□ les sans-abri(s) the homeless

sans-gêne (FEM **sans-gêne**) ADJECTIVE
inconsiderate

★ la **santé** FEM NOUN
health
□ en bonne santé in good health
■ **Santé!** Cheers!

French-English

saoudien (FEM **saoudienne**) ADJECTIVE, NOUN
Saudi Arabian
▪ **un Saoudien** a Saudi Arabian (*man*)
▪ **une Saoudienne** a Saudi Arabian (*woman*)

★ le **sapeur-pompier** (PL les **sapeurs-pompiers**) MASC NOUN
firefighter
▪ **les sapeurs-pompiers** the fire brigade

le **sapin** MASC NOUN
fir tree
▪ **un sapin de Noël** a Christmas tree

la **Sardaigne** FEM NOUN
Sardinia

★ la **sardine** FEM NOUN
sardine

★ le **satellite** MASC NOUN
satellite
□ la télévision par satellite satellite TV

satisfaire VERB [36]
to satisfy

satisfaisant (FEM **satisfaisante**) ADJECTIVE
satisfactory

★ **satisfait** (FEM **satisfaite**) ADJECTIVE
satisfied
□ être satisfait de quelque chose to be satisfied with something

★ la **sauce** FEM NOUN
1 sauce
2 gravy

★ la **saucisse** FEM NOUN
sausage

★ le **saucisson** MASC NOUN
salami

★ **sauf** PREPOSITION
except
□ Tout le monde est venu sauf lui. Everyone came except him.
▪ **sauf si** unless □ On ira se promener, sauf s'il fait mauvais. We'll go for a walk, unless the weather's bad.
▪ **sauf que** except that □ Tout s'est bien passé, sauf que nous sommes arrivés en retard. Everything went OK, except that we arrived late.

★ le **saumon** MASC NOUN
salmon

saur MASC ADJECTIVE
▪ **un hareng saur** a kipper

le **saut** MASC NOUN
jump
▪ **le saut en longueur** the long jump
▪ **le saut en hauteur** the high jump
▪ **le saut à la perche** the pole vault
▪ **le saut à l'élastique** bungee jumping
▪ **un saut périlleux** a somersault

★ **sauter** VERB [28]
to jump
□ Nous avons sauté par-dessus la barrière. We jumped over the gate.
▪ **sauter à la corde** to skip (*with a rope*)
▪ **faire sauter quelque chose** to blow something up □ Ils ont fait sauter le pont. They blew up the bridge.

la **sauterelle** FEM NOUN
grasshopper

★ **sauvage** (FEM **sauvage**) ADJECTIVE
1 wild
□ les animaux sauvages wild animals □ faire du camping sauvage to camp in the wild
▪ **une région sauvage** an unspoiled area
2 shy
□ Il est sauvage. He's shy.

★ **sauvegarder** VERB [28]
to save (*file on computer*)

★ **sauver** VERB [28]
to save
▪ **se sauver 1** to run away □ Il s'est sauvé à toutes jambes. He ran away as fast as he could. **2** (*informal*) to be off □ Allez, je me sauve! Right, I'm off.

le **sauvetage** MASC NOUN
rescue

le **sauveur** MASC NOUN
saviour

savais, savait VERB ▷ *see* **savoir**
▪ **Je ne savais pas qu'il devait venir.** I didn't know he was going to come.

le **savant** MASC NOUN
scientist

la **savante** FEM NOUN
scientist

savent VERB ▷ *see* **savoir**
▪ **Ils ne savent pas ce qu'ils veulent.** They don't know what they want.

la **saveur** FEM NOUN
flavour

savez VERB ▷ *see* **savoir**
▪ **Est-ce que vous savez où elle habite?** Do you know where she lives?

★ **savoir** VERB [76]
to know
□ Je ne sais pas où il est allé. I don't know where he's gone. □ Nous ne savons pas s'il est bien arrivé. We don't know if he's arrived safely. □ Tu savais que Canberra était la capitale de l'Australie? Did you know that Canberra was the capital of Australia? □ Il ne sait pas ce qu'il va faire ce week-end. He doesn't know what he's going to do this weekend.
▪ **Tu sais nager?** Can you swim?

★ le **savon** MASC NOUN
soap

S

la **savonnette** FEM NOUN
bar of soap

savons VERB ▷ *see* savoir

★ **savoureux** (FEM **savoureuse**) ADJECTIVE
tasty

le **saxo** MASC NOUN (*informal*)
sax

le **scandale** MASC NOUN
scandal
■ **faire scandale** to cause a scandal ◻ Ce film a fait scandale. The film caused a scandal.

scandaleux (FEM **scandaleuse**) ADJECTIVE
outrageous

le/la **Scandinave** MASC/FEM NOUN
Scandinavian

scandinave (FEM **scandinave**) ADJECTIVE
Scandinavian

la **Scandinavie** FEM NOUN
Scandinavia

le **scarabée** MASC NOUN
beetle

★ la **scène** FEM NOUN
scene
◻ une scène d'amour a love scene ◻ la scène du crime the scene of the crime ◻ Il m'a fait une scène. He made a scene.
■ **une scène de ménage** a domestic row

sceptique (FEM **sceptique**) ADJECTIVE
sceptical

le **schéma** MASC NOUN
diagram

schématique (FEM **schématique**) ADJECTIVE
■ **l'explication schématique d'une théorie** the broad outline of a theory
■ **Cette interprétation est un peu trop schématique.** This interpretation is a bit oversimplified.

la **scie** FEM NOUN
saw
■ **une scie à métaux** a hacksaw

★ la **science** FEM NOUN
science
■ **Elle est forte en sciences.** She is good at science.
■ **les sciences physiques** physics
■ **les sciences naturelles** biology
■ **les sciences économiques** economics
■ **sciences po** (*informal*) politics ◻ Mon frère fait sciences po à Paris. My brother is studying politics in Paris.

★ la **science-fiction** FEM NOUN
science fiction

★ **scientifique** (FEM **scientifique**) ADJECTIVE
▷ *see also* **scientifique** NOUN
scientific

★ le/la **scientifique** MASC/FEM NOUN
▷ *see also* **scientifique** ADJECTIVE
1 scientist
2 science student

scier VERB [19]
to saw

★ **scolaire** (FEM **scolaire**) ADJECTIVE
school
◻ l'année scolaire the school year ◻ les vacances scolaires the school holidays ◻ mon livret scolaire my school report

le **Scorpion** MASC NOUN
Scorpio
◻ Océane est Scorpion. Océane is Scorpio.

le **Scotch®** MASC NOUN
adhesive tape

scotché (FEM **scotchée**) ADJECTIVE (*informal*)
◻ Il reste des heures scotché devant la télévision. He spends hours glued to the television.
■ **je suis resté scotché** I was flabbergasted (*astounded*)

le **scrupule** MASC NOUN
scruple

sculpter VERB [28]
to sculpt

★ le **sculpteur** MASC NOUN
sculptor

★ la **sculpture** FEM NOUN
sculpture

★ le/la **SDF** MASC/FEM NOUN (= *sans domicile fixe*)
homeless person
■ **les SDF** the homeless

★ **se** PRONOUN

> se changes to s' before a vowel and most words beginning with 'h'.

1 himself
◻ Il se regarde dans la glace. He's looking at himself in the mirror.
2 herself
◻ Elle se regarde dans la glace. She's looking at herself in the mirror.
3 itself
◻ Le chien s'est fait mal. The dog hurt itself.
4 oneself
◻ se regarder dans une glace to look at oneself in a mirror
5 themselves
◻ Ils se sont regardés dans la glace. They looked at themselves in the mirror.
6 each other
◻ Ils s'aiment. They love each other.

> With reflexive verbs, **se** is often not translated.

◻ Il s'est cassé le bras. He broke his arm.

French-English

★ la **séance** FEM NOUN
1 session
□ une séance de rééducation **a physiotherapy session**
2 showing (*at the cinema*)
□ La prochaine séance est à dix-neuf heures. **The next showing is at 7 p.m.**

★ le **seau** (PL les **seaux**) MASC NOUN
bucket

★ **sec** (FEM **sèche**) ADJECTIVE
1 dry
□ Mon jean n'est pas encore sec. **My jeans aren't dry yet.**
2 dried
□ des figues sèches **dried figs**

le **sèche-cheveux** (PL les **sèche-cheveux**) MASC NOUN
hair dryer

le **sèche-linge** (PL les **sèche-linges**, PL les **sèche-linge**) MASC NOUN
tumble dryer

★ **sécher** VERB [34]
1 to dry
2 to be stumped
□ J'ai complètement séché à l'interrogation de maths. (*informal*) **I was completely stumped in the maths test.**
■ **se sécher** to dry oneself □ Sèche-toi avec cette serviette. **Dry yourself with this towel.**

★ la **sécheresse** FEM NOUN
drought
□ une terrible sécheresse **a terrible drought**

le **séchoir** MASC NOUN
dryer

★ **second** (FEM **seconde**) ADJECTIVE
▷ *see also* **second** NOUN
second
□ Il est arrivé second. **He came second.**

★ le **second** MASC NOUN
▷ *see also* **second** ADJECTIVE
second floor
□ Elle habite au second. **She lives on the second floor.**

★ **secondaire** (FEM **secondaire**) ADJECTIVE
secondary
□ l'enseignement secondaire **secondary education**
■ **des effets secondaires** side effects

★ la **seconde** FEM NOUN
▷ *see also* **second** ADJECTIVE
1 second
□ Attends une seconde! **Wait a second!**
2 year 11
□ Ma sœur est en seconde. **My sister's in year 11.**

DID YOU KNOW...?
In French secondary schools, years are counted from the **sixième** (youngest) to **première** and **terminale** (oldest).

3 second class
□ voyager en seconde **to travel second-class**

★ **secouer** VERB [28]
to shake
□ secouer la tête **to shake one's head**

★ **secourir** VERB [16]
to rescue

le **secourisme** MASC NOUN
first aid
□ J'ai un brevet de secourisme. **I've got a first aid qualification.**

★ le **secours** MASC NOUN
help
□ Il est allé chercher du secours. **He went to get help.** □ Au secours! **Help!**
■ **les premiers secours** first aid
■ **une sortie de secours** an emergency exit
■ **la roue de secours** the spare wheel

★ **secret** (FEM **secrète**) ADJECTIVE
▷ *see also* **secret** NOUN
secret

★ le **secret** MASC NOUN
▷ *see also* **secret** ADJECTIVE
secret

★ le **secrétaire** MASC NOUN
▷ *see also* **secrétaire** NOUN
1 secretary
2 writing desk

★ la **secrétaire** FEM NOUN
▷ *see also* **secrétaire** NOUN
secretary

le **secrétariat** MASC NOUN
secretary's office

le **secteur** MASC NOUN
sector
□ le secteur public **the public sector** □ le secteur privé **the private sector**

★ la **section** FEM NOUN
department (*of school*)

la **sécu** FEM NOUN (*informal*)
Social Security

★ la **sécurité** FEM NOUN
1 safety
■ **être en sécurité** to be safe □ On ne se sent pas en sécurité dans ce quartier. **You don't feel safe in this neighbourhood.**
■ **la sécurité routière** road safety
■ **une ceinture de sécurité** a seatbelt
2 security
□ par mesure de sécurité **as a security measure**
■ **la sécurité sociale** Social Security
■ **la sécurité de l'emploi** job security

séduisant (FEM **séduisante**) ADJECTIVE
attractive

S

le **seigle** MASC NOUN
rye
□ un pain de seigle a loaf of rye bread

le **seigneur** MASC NOUN
lord
■ **le Seigneur** the Lord

le **sein** MASC NOUN
breast
■ **au sein de** within □ Chaque pays est autonome au sein de l'Europe. Each country is independent within Europe.

★ **seize** NUMBER
sixteen
□ Elle a seize ans. She's sixteen. □ à seize heures at 4 p.m.
■ **le seize février** the sixteenth of February

★ **seizième** (FEM **seizième**) ADJECTIVE
sixteenth

★ le **séjour** MASC NOUN
stay
□ J'ai fait un séjour d'une semaine en Italie. I stayed in Italy for a week.

★ le **sel** MASC NOUN
salt

sélectionner VERB [28]
to select

★ le **self** MASC NOUN (*informal*)
self-service restaurant

★ **selfie** MASC NOUN
selfie
■ **une perche à selfie** a selfie stick

le **self-service** MASC NOUN
self-service restaurant

la **selle** FEM NOUN
saddle

★ **selon** PREPOSITION
according to
□ selon lui according to him □ selon mon humeur according to what mood I'm in □ Ils sont répartis selon leur âge. They're divided up according to age.

★ la **semaine** FEM NOUN
week
□ la semaine prochaine next week
■ **en semaine** on weekdays

★ **semblable** (FEM **semblable**) ADJECTIVE
similar

le **semblant** MASC NOUN
■ **faire semblant de faire quelque chose** to pretend to do something □ Il fait semblant de dormir. He's pretending to be asleep.

★ **sembler** VERB [28]
to seem
□ Le temps semble s'améliorer. The weather seems to be improving. □ Il me semble inutile de s'en inquiéter. It seems pointless to me to worry about it.

la **semelle** FEM NOUN
1 sole
2 insole

la **semoule** FEM NOUN
semolina

★ le **sens** MASC NOUN
1 sense
□ avoir le sens de l'humour to have a sense of humour □ Je n'ai pas le sens de l'orientation. I've got no sense of direction. □ avoir le sens du rythme to have a sense of rhythm □ Ça n'a pas de sens. It doesn't make sense.
■ **le bon sens** common sense
2 direction
□ Tu tournes la poignée dans le mauvais sens. You're turning the handle in the wrong direction.
■ **sens dessus dessous** upside down
■ **un sens interdit** a one-way street □ J'ai failli prendre un sens interdit. I nearly went the wrong way down a one-way street.
■ **un sens unique** a one-way street

la **sensation** FEM NOUN
feeling

★ **sensationnel** (FEM **sensationnelle**) ADJECTIVE
sensational

sensé (FEM **sensée**) ADJECTIVE
sensible

★ **sensible** (FEM **sensible**) ADJECTIVE
1 sensitive
□ Elle est très sensible. She's very sensitive.
■ **Ce film est déconseillé aux personnes sensibles.** This film contains scenes which some viewers may find disturbing.
2 visible
□ une amélioration sensible a visible improvement

> **BE CAREFUL!**
> The French word **sensible** does not mean **sensible**.

sensiblement ADVERB
1 visibly
□ Elle a sensiblement progressé. She's made visible progress.
2 approximately
□ Elles sont sensiblement de la même taille. They are approximately the same height.

la **sentence** FEM NOUN
sentence (*judgement*)

★ le **sentier** MASC NOUN
path

★ le **sentiment** MASC NOUN
feeling

sentimental (FEM **sentimentale**, MASC PL **sentimentaux**) ADJECTIVE
sentimental

★ **sentir** VERB [77]

1 to smell
□ Ça sent bon. That smells good. □ Ça sent mauvais. It smells bad.

2 to smell of
□ Ça sent les frites ici. It smells of chips in here.

3 to taste
□ Tu sens l'ail dans le rôti? Can you taste the garlic in the roast?

4 to feel
□ Ça t'a fait mal? — Non, je n'ai rien senti. Did it hurt? — No, I didn't feel a thing. □ Je ne me sens pas bien. I don't feel well.
■ **Il ne peut pas la sentir.** (*informal*) He can't stand her.

★ **séparé** (FEM **séparée**) ADJECTIVE
separated
□ Mes parents sont séparés. My parents are separated.

séparément ADVERB
separately

★ **séparer** VERB [28]
to separate
□ Séparez le blanc du jaune. Separate the yolk from the white.
■ **se séparer** to separate □ Mes parents se sont séparés l'année dernière. My parents separated last year.

★ **sept** NUMBER
seven
□ Il est arrivé à sept heures. He arrived at seven o'clock. □ Elle a sept ans. She's seven.
■ **le sept février** the seventh of February

★ **septembre** MASC NOUN
September
■ **en septembre** in September

★ **septième** (FEM **septième**) ADJECTIVE
seventh
□ au septième étage on the seventh floor

sera, serai, seras, serez VERB ▷ *see* **être**
■ **Je serai de retour à dix heures.** I'll be back at 10 o'clock.

★ la **série** FEM NOUN
series

sérieusement ADVERB
seriously

★ **sérieux** (FEM **sérieuse**) ADJECTIVE
▷ *see also* **sérieux** NOUN

1 serious
□ Il plaisantait? — Non, il était sérieux. Was he joking? — No, he was serious.

2 responsible
□ C'est un employé très sérieux. He's a very responsible employee.

★ le **sérieux** MASC NOUN
▷ *see also* **sérieux** ADJECTIVE
■ **garder son sérieux** to keep a straight face
□ J'ai eu du mal à garder mon sérieux. I had trouble keeping a straight face.
■ **prendre quelque chose au sérieux** to take something seriously
■ **prendre quelqu'un au sérieux** to take somebody seriously
■ **Il manque un peu de sérieux.** He's not very responsible.

la **seringue** FEM NOUN
syringe

séronégatif (FEM **séronégative**) ADJECTIVE
HIV-negative

serons, seront VERB ▷ *see* **être**

séropositif (FEM **séropositive**) ADJECTIVE
HIV-positive

★ le **serpent** MASC NOUN
snake

la **serre** FEM NOUN
greenhouse
■ **l'effet de serre** the greenhouse effect

serré (FEM **serrée**) ADJECTIVE

1 tight
□ Mon pantalon est trop serré. My trousers are too tight.

2 close-fought
□ Ça a été un match serré. It was a close-fought game.

★ **serrer** VERB [28]
■ **Ce pantalon me serre trop.** These trousers are too tight for me.
■ **serrer la main à quelqu'un** to shake hands with somebody
■ **se serrer** to squeeze up □ Serrez-vous un peu pour que je puisse m'asseoir. Squeeze up a bit so I can sit down.
■ **serrer quelqu'un dans ses bras** to hug somebody
■ **'Serrer à droite'** 'Keep right'

★ la **serrure** FEM NOUN
lock

sers, sert VERB ▷ *see* **servir**

★ le **serveur** MASC NOUN
1 waiter (*in café*)
2 server (*computer*)

★ la **serveuse** FEM NOUN
waitress

serviable (FEM **serviable**) ADJECTIVE
helpful

★ le **service** MASC NOUN

1 service (*in restaurant*)
□ Le service est compris. Service is included.
■ **être de service** to be on duty
■ **hors service** out of order
■ **faire le service** to serve (*at table*) □ Tu peux faire le service s'il te plaît? Could you serve please?

2 favour
□ rendre service à quelqu'un to do somebody a favour □ Est-ce que je peux te demander un service? Can I ask you a favour?
3 serve (*sport*)
□ Il a un bon service. He's got a good serve.
■ **le service militaire** military service
■ **les services sociaux** the social services
■ **les services secrets** the secret service

★ la **serviette** FEM NOUN
1 towel
□ une serviette de bain a bath towel
■ **une serviette hygiénique** a sanitary towel
2 serviette (*napkin*)
3 briefcase

★ **servir** VERB [78]
to serve
□ On vous sert? Are you being served?
■ **À toi de servir.** (*tennis*) It's your serve.
■ **se servir** to help oneself □ Servez-vous. Help yourself.
■ **se servir de** to use □ Tu te sers souvent de ton vélo? Do you use your bike a lot?
■ **servir à quelqu'un** to be of use to somebody □ Ça m'a beaucoup servi. I found it very useful.
■ **À quoi ça sert?** What's it for?
■ **Ça ne sert à rien.** It's no use. □ Ça ne sert à rien d'insister. It's no use insisting.

★ **ses** PL ADJECTIVE
1 his
□ Il est parti voir ses grands-parents. He's gone to see his grandparents.
2 her
□ Delphine a oublié ses baskets. Delphine's forgotten her trainers.
3 its
□ la ville et ses alentours the town and its surroundings

le **set** MASC NOUN
1 tablemat (*on table*)
2 set (*in tennis*)

le **seuil** MASC NOUN
doorstep

★ **seul** (FEM **seule**) ADJECTIVE, ADVERB
1 alone
□ vivre seul to live alone
2 by oneself
□ Elle est venue seule. She came by herself.
■ **faire quelque chose tout seul** to do something by oneself □ Elle a fait ça toute seule? Did she do it by herself?
■ **se sentir seul** to feel lonely
■ **un seul livre** one book only □ Vous avez droit à un seul livre. You're entitled to one book only.
■ **Il reste une seule nectarine.** There's only one nectarine left.
■ **le seul livre que ...** the only book that ...
□ C'est le seul Agatha Christie que je n'aie pas lu. That's the only Agatha Christie I haven't read.
■ **le seul** the only one □ C'est la seule que je ne connaisse pas. She's the only one I don't know.

★ **seulement** ADVERB
only
■ **non seulement ... mais** not only ... but
□ Non seulement il a plu, mais en plus il a fait froid. Not only did it rain, but it was cold as well.

★ **sévère** (FEM **sévère**) ADJECTIVE
strict
□ Mon prof de maths est très sévère. My maths teacher is very strict.

★ le **sexe** MASC NOUN
sex

sexuel (FEM **sexuelle**) ADJECTIVE
sexual
□ l'éducation sexuelle sex education

★ le **shampooing** MASC NOUN
shampoo
■ **se faire un shampooing** to wash one's hair

★ le **short** MASC NOUN
shorts
□ Il était en short. He was wearing shorts.

★ **si** CONJUNCTION, ADVERB
▷ *see also* **si** NOUN
1 if
□ si tu veux if you like □ Je me demande si elle va venir. I wonder if she'll come. □ si seulement if only
2 so
□ Elle est si gentille. She's so kind. □ Tout s'est passé si vite. Everything happened so fast.
3 yes
□ Tu n'es pas allé à l'école habillé comme ça? — Si. You didn't go to school dressed like that? — Yes I did.

★ le **si** MASC NOUN
▷ *see also* **si** CONJUNCTION, ADVERB
1 B
□ en si bémol in B flat
2 ti
□ la, si, do la, ti, do

la **Sicile** FEM NOUN
Sicily

★ le **sida** MASC NOUN
AIDS
□ Il a le sida. He's got AIDS.

★ le **siècle** MASC NOUN
century
□ le vingtième siècle the twentieth century

★ le **siège** MASC NOUN
1 seat (*in vehicle*)
2 head office

sien MASC PRONOUN
■ **le sien** 1 his □ C'est le vélo de Paul? — Oui, c'est le sien. Is this Paul's bike? — Yes, it's his. 2 hers □ C'est le vélo d'Isabelle? — Oui, c'est le sien. Is this Isabelle's bike? — Yes, it's hers.

sienne FEM PRONOUN
■ **la sienne** 1 his □ C'est la montre de Paul? — Oui, c'est la sienne. Is this Paul's watch? — Yes, it's his. 2 hers □ C'est la montre d'Isabelle? — Oui, c'est la sienne. Is this Isabelle's watch? — Yes, it's hers.

siennes FEM PL PRONOUN
■ **les siennes** 1 his □ Ce sont les chaussures de Julien? — Oui, ce sont les siennes. Are these Julien's shoes? — Yes, they're his.
2 hers □ Ce sont les lunettes de Marine? — Oui, ce sont les siennes. Are these Marine's glasses? — Yes, they're hers.

siens MASC PL PRONOUN
■ **les siens** 1 his □ Ce sont les sandwichs de Pierre? — Oui, ce sont les siens. Are these Pierre's sandwiches? — Yes, they're his.
2 hers □ Ce sont les sandwichs de Justine? — Oui, ce sont les siens. Are these Justine's sandwiches? — Yes, they're hers.

la **sieste** FEM NOUN
nap
□ faire la sieste to have a nap

★ **siffler** VERB [28]
to whistle

le **sifflet** MASC NOUN
whistle

le **sigle** MASC NOUN
acronym

★ le **signal** (PL les **signaux**) MASC NOUN
signal

★ la **signature** FEM NOUN
signature

★ le **signe** MASC NOUN
sign
■ **faire un signe de la main** to wave
■ **faire signe à quelqu'un d'entrer** to beckon to somebody to come in
■ **les signes du zodiaque** the signs of the zodiac

★ **signer** VERB [28]
to sign

le **signet** MASC NOUN
bookmark

la **signification** FEM NOUN
meaning

signifier VERB [19]
to mean
□ Que signifie ce mot? What does this word mean?

★ le **silence** MASC NOUN
silence
■ **Silence!** Be quiet!

★ **silencieux** (FEM **silencieuse**) ADJECTIVE
1 silent
□ Elle est restée silencieuse. She remained silent.
2 quiet
□ C'est très silencieux ici. It's very quiet here.

la **silhouette** FEM NOUN
figure
□ J'ai vu une silhouette dans le brouillard. I saw a figure in the mist.

similaire (FEM **similaire**) ADJECTIVE
similar

★ le **simple** MASC NOUN
▷ *see also* **simple** ADJECTIVE
singles (*tennis*)
□ le simple messieurs the men's singles □ le simple dames the ladies' singles

★ **simple** (FEM **simple**) ADJECTIVE
▷ *see also* **simple** NOUN
simple

simplement ADVERB
simply
□ C'est tout simplement inadmissible. It's quite simply unacceptable.

simuler VERB [28]
to simulate

simultané (FEM **simultanée**) ADJECTIVE
simultaneous

sincère (FEM **sincère**) ADJECTIVE
sincere

sincèrement ADVERB
sincerely

la **sincérité** FEM NOUN
sincerity

★ le **singe** MASC NOUN
monkey

le **singulier** MASC NOUN
singular
□ au féminin singulier in the feminine singular

sinistre (FEM **sinistre**) ADJECTIVE
sinister

sinon CONJUNCTION
otherwise
□ Dépêche-toi, sinon je pars sans toi. Hurry up, otherwise I'll leave without you.

la **sinusite** FEM NOUN
sinusitis
□ avoir de la sinusite to have sinusitis

la **sirène** FEM NOUN
mermaid
■ **la sirène d'alarme** the fire alarm

★ le **sirop** MASC NOUN
syrup
■ **le sirop contre la toux** cough mixture

★ le **site** MASC NOUN
setting
□ un site très sauvage a totally unspoiled setting
■ **un site pittoresque** a beauty spot
■ **un site touristique** a tourist attraction
■ **un site archéologique** an archaeological site
■ **un site web** a website

sitôt ADVERB
■ **sitôt dit, sitôt fait** no sooner said than done
■ **pas de sitôt** not for a long time □ On ne le reverra pas de sitôt. We won't see him again for a long time.

★ la **situation** FEM NOUN
1 situation
■ **la situation de famille** marital status
2 job
□ Il a une belle situation. He's got a good job.

se **situer** VERB [28]
to be situated
□ Versailles se situe à l'ouest de Paris. Versailles is situated to the west of Paris.
■ **bien situé** well situated

★ **six** NUMBER
six
□ Il est rentré à six heures. He got back at six o'clock. □ Il a six ans. He's six.
■ **le six février** the sixth of February

★ **sixième** (FEM **sixième**) ADJECTIVE
▷ *see also* **sixième** NOUN
sixth
□ au sixième étage on the sixth floor

★ la **sixième** FEM NOUN
▷ *see also* **sixième** ADJECTIVE
year 7
□ Mon frère est en sixième. My brother's in year 7.

DID YOU KNOW...?
In French secondary schools, years are counted from the **sixième** (youngest) to **première** and **terminale** (oldest).

★ le **skate** MASC NOUN
skateboarding
■ **faire du skate** to skateboard

★ le **ski** MASC NOUN
1 ski
□ J'ai loué des skis. I hired skis.
2 skiing
□ J'adore le ski. I love skiing. □ faire du ski to go skiing
■ **le ski de fond** cross-country skiing
■ **le ski nautique** water-skiing
■ **le ski de piste** downhill skiing
■ **le ski de randonnée** cross-country skiing

★ **skier** VERB [19]
to ski

le **skieur** MASC NOUN
skier

la **skieuse** FEM NOUN
skier

skyper VERB [28]
to Skype
□ Pour skyper, il faut une webcam et un micro. To Skype, you need a webcam and a microphone.

★ le **slip** MASC NOUN
pants
■ **un slip de bain** swimming trunks

la **Slovaquie** FEM NOUN
Slovakia

la **Slovénie** FEM NOUN
Slovenia

le **SMIC** MASC NOUN
guaranteed minimum wage
□ Il touche le SMIC. He's on the legal minimum wage.

le **smoking** MASC NOUN
dinner suit

le **SMS** MASC NOUN
text message

★ la **SNCF** FEM NOUN (= *Société nationale des chemins de fer français*)
French railways

snob (FEM **snob**) ADJECTIVE
snobbish

sobre (FEM **sobre**) ADJECTIVE
1 sober
2 plain
□ C'est une veste très sobre. It's a very plain jacket.

★ **social** (FEM **sociale**, MASC PL **sociaux**) ADJECTIVE
social

le/la **socialiste** MASC/FEM NOUN
socialist

★ la **société** FEM NOUN
1 society
2 company
□ une société financière a finance company

la **sociologie** FEM NOUN
sociology

la **socquette** FEM NOUN
ankle sock

la **sœur** FEM NOUN
sister
■ **une bonne sœur** (*informal*) a nun

soi PRONOUN
oneself
□ avoir confiance en soi to have confidence in

oneself
■ **rester chez soi** to stay at home
■ **Ça va de soi.** It goes without saying.

soi-disant (FEM **soi-disante**) ADVERB, ADJECTIVE
supposedly
□ Il était soi-disant parti à Paris. He had supposedly left for Paris.
■ **un soi-disant poète** a so-called poet

★ la **soie** FEM NOUN
silk

★ la **soif** FEM NOUN
thirst
■ **avoir soif** to be thirsty

★ **soigner** VERB [28]
to look after (*ill person, animal*)
□ Soigne-toi bien ce week-end! Take good care of yourself this weekend!

soigneux (FEM **soigneuse**) ADJECTIVE
careful
□ Tu devrais être plus soigneux avec tes livres. You should be more careful with your books.

soi-même PRONOUN
oneself
□ Il vaut mieux le faire soi-même. It's better to do it oneself.

★ le **soin** MASC NOUN
care
■ **prendre soin de quelque chose** to take care of something □ Prends bien soin de ce livre. Take good care of this book.

les **soins** MASC PL NOUN
treatment *sing*
■ **les premiers soins** first aid
■ **'aux bons soins de Madame Martin'** (*on letter*) 'c/o Mrs Martin'

★ le **soir** MASC NOUN
evening
□ ce soir this evening
■ **à sept heures du soir** at 7 p.m.
■ **demain soir** tomorrow night
■ **hier soir** last night

★ la **soirée** FEM NOUN
evening
□ en tenue de soirée in evening dress

sois VERB ▷ *see* **être**
■ **Sois tranquille!** Don't worry!

soit CONJUNCTION
■ **soit ..., soit ...** either ... or ... □ soit lundi, soit mardi either Monday or Tuesday

la **soixantaine** FEM NOUN
about sixty
□ une soixantaine de personnes about sixty people
■ **Elle a la soixantaine.** She's in her sixties.

★ **soixante** NUMBER
sixty
□ Il a soixante ans. He's sixty. □ soixante et un sixty-one □ soixante-deux sixty-two
■ **soixante et onze** seventy-one
■ **soixante-dix** seventy
■ **soixante-quinze** seventy-five

le **soja** MASC NOUN
soya
■ **des germes de soja** beansprouts

★ le **sol** MASC NOUN
1 floor
□ un sol carrelé a tiled floor
■ **à même le sol** on the floor
2 soil
□ sur le sol français on French soil
3 G
□ sol dièse G sharp
4 so
□ do, ré, mi, fa, sol ... do, re, mi, fa, so ...

solaire (FEM **solaire**) ADJECTIVE
solar
□ le système solaire the solar system
■ **la crème solaire** sun cream

★ le **soldat** MASC NOUN
soldier

★ le **solde** MASC NOUN
■ **être en solde** to be reduced □ Les chemisiers sont en solde. The blouses are reduced.
■ **les soldes** the sales □ faire les soldes to go round the sales □ les soldes de janvier the January sales

soldé (FEM **soldée**) ADJECTIVE
■ **être soldé** to be reduced □ un article soldé à dix euros an item reduced to 10 euros

la **sole** FEM NOUN
sole (*fish*)

★ le **soleil** MASC NOUN
sun
□ au soleil in the sun
■ **Il y a du soleil.** It's sunny.

le **solfège** MASC NOUN
musical theory
□ un cours de solfège a music theory lesson
■ **Il joue du violon sans connaître le solfège.** He plays the violin but he can't read music.

solidaire (FEM **solidaire**) ADJECTIVE
■ **être solidaire de quelqu'un** to back somebody up

★ **solide** (FEM **solide**) ADJECTIVE
1 strong (*person*)
2 solid (*object*)

solitaire (FEM **solitaire**) ADJECTIVE
▷ *see also* **solitaire** NOUN
solitary

le/la **solitaire** MASC/FEM NOUN
▷ *see also* **solitaire** ADJECTIVE
loner

la **solitude** FEM NOUN
loneliness

la **solution** FEM NOUN
solution
■ **une solution de facilité** an easy way out

★ **sombre** (FEM **sombre**) ADJECTIVE
dark

le **sommaire** MASC NOUN
summary

★ la **somme** FEM NOUN
▷ *see also* **somme** NOUN
sum

★ le **somme** MASC NOUN
▷ *see also* **somme** NOUN
nap
□ faire un somme to take a nap

★ le **sommeil** MASC NOUN
sleep
■ **avoir sommeil** to be sleepy

sommes VERB ▷ *see* **être**
■ **Nous sommes en vacances.** We're on holiday.

★ le **sommet** MASC NOUN
summit

le **somnifère** MASC NOUN
sleeping pill

somptueux (FEM **somptueuse**) ADJECTIVE
sumptuous

★ **son** (FEM **sa**, PL **ses**) ADJECTIVE
▷ *see also* **son** NOUN
1 his
□ son père his father □ Il a perdu son portefeuille. He's lost his wallet.
2 her
□ son père her father □ Elle a perdu son sac. She's lost her bag.

★ le **son** MASC NOUN
▷ *see also* **son** ADJECTIVE
1 sound
□ Le son n'est pas très bon. The sound's not very good. □ baisser le son to turn the sound down
2 bran
■ **le pain de son** brown bread

★ le **sondage** MASC NOUN
survey
■ **un sondage d'opinion** an opinion poll

★ **sonner** VERB [28]
to ring
□ On a sonné. Somebody rang the doorbell.
□ Le téléphone a sonné. The phone rang.

la **sonnerie** FEM NOUN
1 bell (*electric*)
■ **La sonnerie du téléphone l'a réveillé.** He was woken by the phone ringing.
2 ringtone (*on mobile phone*)
□ J'ai téléchargé une nouvelle sonnerie sur mon portable. I've downloaded a new ringtone onto my mobile.

la **sonnette** FEM NOUN
bell
□ la sonnette d'alarme the alarm bell

la **sono** FEM NOUN (*informal*)
PA system

sont VERB ▷ *see* **être**
■ **Ils sont en vacances.** They're on holiday.

sophistiqué (FEM **sophistiquée**) ADJECTIVE
sophisticated

le **sorcier** MASC NOUN
wizard

la **sorcière** FEM NOUN
witch

le **sort** MASC NOUN
1 spell
□ jeter un sort à quelqu'un to cast a spell on somebody
■ **un mauvais sort** a curse
2 fate
□ abandonner quelqu'un à son triste sort to leave somebody to their fate
■ **tirer au sort** to draw lots

★ la **sorte** FEM NOUN
sort
□ C'est une sorte de gâteau. It's a sort of cake.
□ toutes sortes de choses all sorts of things

★ la **sortie** FEM NOUN
way out
□ Où est la sortie? Where's the way out?
■ **la sortie de secours** the emergency exit
■ **Attends-moi à la sortie de l'école.** Meet me after school.

★ **sortir** VERB [79, *aux* **avoir** *or* **être**]
1 to go out
□ Il est sorti sans rien dire. He went out without saying a word. □ Il est sorti acheter un journal. He's gone out to buy a newspaper.
□ J'aime sortir. I like going out.
2 to come out
□ Elle sort de l'hôpital demain. She's coming out of hospital tomorrow. □ Je l'ai rencontré en sortant de la pharmacie. I met him coming out of the chemist's. □ Ce modèle vient juste de sortir. This model has just come out.
3 to take out
□ Elle a sorti son porte-monnaie de son sac. She took her purse out of her handbag. □ Je vais sortir la voiture du garage. I'll get the car out of the garage.
■ **sortir avec quelqu'un** to be going out with somebody □ Tu sors avec lui? Are you going out with him?
■ **s'en sortir** to manage □ Ne t'en fais pas, tu t'en sortiras. Don't worry, you'll manage OK.

The verb **sortir** uses **être** in the perfect tense when talking about going out somewhere. It uses **avoir** when talking about taking an object out of something.

la **sottise** FEM NOUN
■ **Ne fais pas de sottises.** Don't do anything silly.
■ **Ne dis pas de sottises.** Don't talk nonsense.

le **sou** MASC NOUN
■ **une machine à sous** a fruit machine
■ **Je n'ai pas un sou sur moi.** I haven't got a penny on me.
■ **être près de ses sous** (*informal*) to be tight-fisted

★ le **souci** MASC NOUN
worry
■ **se faire du souci** to worry
■ **pas de souci** (*informal*) no worries

soucieux (FEM **soucieuse**) ADJECTIVE
worried
□ Tu as l'air soucieux. You look worried.

★ la **soucoupe** FEM NOUN
saucer
■ **une soucoupe volante** a flying saucer

★ **soudain** (FEM **soudaine**) ADJECTIVE, ADVERB
1 sudden
□ une douleur soudaine a sudden pain
2 suddenly
□ Soudain, il s'est fâché. Suddenly, he got angry.

le **souffle** MASC NOUN
breath
■ **à bout de souffle** out of breath

le **soufflé** MASC NOUN
soufflé
□ un soufflé au fromage a cheese soufflé

★ **souffler** VERB [28]
1 to blow
□ Le vent soufflait fort. The wind was blowing hard.
2 to blow out
□ Souffle les bougies! Blow out the candles!

la **souffrance** FEM NOUN
suffering

souffrant (FEM **souffrante**) ADJECTIVE
unwell

★ **souffrir** VERB [54]
to be in pain
□ Il souffre beaucoup. He's in a lot of pain.

le **souhait** MASC NOUN
wish
□ faire un souhait to make a wish □ Tous nos souhaits de réussite. All our best wishes for your success. □ les souhaits de bonne année New Year's wishes
■ **Atchoum! — À tes souhaits!** Atchoo! — Bless you!

★ **souhaiter** VERB [28]
to wish
□ Il souhaite aller à l'université. He wishes to go to university. □ Nous vous souhaitons une bonne année. We wish you a happy New Year.

soûl (FEM **soûle**) ADJECTIVE (*informal*)
drunk

★ **soulager** VERB [45]
to relieve

★ **soulever** VERB [43]
1 to lift
□ Je n'arrive pas à soulever cette valise. I can't lift this suitcase.
2 to raise
□ Il faudra soulever la question lors de la réunion. We'll have to raise the matter at the meeting.

★ le **soulier** MASC NOUN
shoe

★ **souligner** VERB [28]
to underline

★ le **soupçon** MASC NOUN
suspicion
■ **un soupçon de** a dash of □ Ajoutez un soupçon de rhum. Add a dash of rum.

★ **soupçonner** VERB [28]
to suspect

★ la **soupe** FEM NOUN
soup

★ **souper** VERB [28]
to have supper

le **soupir** MASC NOUN
sigh

soupirer VERB [28]
to sigh

★ **souple** (FEM **souple**) ADJECTIVE
1 supple (*person*)
2 flexible (*system*)

la **source** FEM NOUN
spring
□ l'eau de source spring water

le **sourcil** MASC NOUN
eyebrow

★ **sourd** (FEM **sourde**) ADJECTIVE
deaf

souriant (FEM **souriante**) ADJECTIVE
cheerful

★ le **sourire** MASC NOUN
▷ *see also* **sourire** VERB
smile

★ **sourire** VERB [74]
▷ *see also* **sourire** NOUN
to smile
□ sourire à quelqu'un to smile at somebody

★ la **souris** FEM NOUN
mouse

sournois (FEM **sournoise**) ADJECTIVE
sly

★ **sous** PREPOSITION
under
■ **sous terre** underground
■ **sous la pluie** in the rain

sous-entendu (FEM **sous-entendue**) ADJECTIVE
▷ *see also* **sous-entendu** NOUN
implied

le **sous-entendu** MASC NOUN
▷ *see also* **sous-entendu** ADJECTIVE
insinuation

sous-marin (FEM **sous-marine**) ADJECTIVE
▷ *see also* **sous-marin** NOUN
underwater

le **sous-marin** MASC NOUN
▷ *see also* **sous-marin** ADJECTIVE
submarine

★ le **sous-sol** MASC NOUN
basement

★ le **sous-titre** MASC NOUN
subtitle

★ **sous-titré** (FEM **sous-titrée**) ADJECTIVE
with subtitles

la **soustraction** FEM NOUN
subtraction

★ les **sous-vêtements** MASC PL NOUN
underwear *sing*

★ **soutenir** VERB [83]
to support
□ Il m'a toujours soutenu contre elle. He's always supported me against her.
■ **soutenir que** to maintain that □ Elle soutenait que c'était impossible. She maintained that it was impossible.
■ **soutenir l'allure** to keep up □ Il marchait trop vite et je n'arrivais pas à soutenir l'allure. He was walking too fast and I couldn't keep up.

★ **souterrain** (FEM **souterraine**) ADJECTIVE
▷ *see also* **souterrain** NOUN
underground

★ le **souterrain** MASC NOUN
▷ *see also* **souterrain** ADJECTIVE
underground passage

le **soutien** MASC NOUN
support

★ le **soutien-gorge** (PL les **soutiens-gorge**) MASC NOUN
bra

★ le **souvenir** MASC NOUN
▷ *see also* **souvenir** VERB
1 memory
□ garder un bon souvenir de quelque chose to have happy memories of something
2 souvenir
■ **Garde ce livre en souvenir de moi.** Keep the book: it'll remind you of me.

★ se **souvenir** VERB [83]
▷ *see also* **souvenir** NOUN
■ **se souvenir de quelque chose** to remember something □ Je ne me souviens pas de son adresse. I can't remember his address.
■ **se souvenir que** to remember that □ Je me souviens qu'il neigeait. I remember it was snowing.

★ **souvent** ADVERB
often

soyez, soyons VERB ▷ *see* **être**
■ **Soyons clairs!** Let's be clear about this!

la **SPA** FEM NOUN (= *Société protectrice des animaux*)
RSPCA

★ **spacieux** (FEM **spacieuse**) ADJECTIVE
spacious

★ les **spaghettis** MASC PL NOUN
spaghetti *sing*

★ le **sparadrap** MASC NOUN
sticking plaster

le **speaker** MASC NOUN
announcer

la **speakerine** FEM NOUN
announcer

★ **spécial** (FEM **spéciale**, MASC PL **spéciaux**) ADJECTIVE
1 special
□ Qu'est-ce que tu fais ce week-end? — Rien de spécial. What are you doing this weekend? — Nothing special.
■ **les effets spéciaux** special effects
2 peculiar
□ Elle a des goûts un peu spéciaux. She has rather peculiar tastes.

spécialement ADVERB
1 specially
□ Il est venu spécialement pour te parler. He came specially to speak to you.
2 particularly
□ Ce n'est pas spécialement difficile. It's not particularly difficult.

se **spécialiser** VERB [28]
■ **se spécialiser dans quelque chose** to specialize in something □ Je me suis spécialisé en histoire contemporaine. I specialized in modern history.

le/la **spécialiste** MASC/FEM NOUN
specialist

★ la **spécialité** FEM NOUN
speciality

spécifier VERB [19]
to specify

★ le **spectacle** MASC NOUN
show

spectaculaire (FEM **spectaculaire**) ADJECTIVE
spectacular

★ le **spectateur** MASC NOUN
1 member of the audience
2 spectator

★ la **spectatrice** FEM NOUN
1 member of the audience
2 spectator

la **spéléologie** FEM NOUN
potholing

spirituel (FEM **spirituelle**) ADJECTIVE
1 spiritual
2 witty

★ **splendide** (FEM **splendide**) ADJECTIVE
magnificent

spontané (FEM **spontanée**) ADJECTIVE
spontaneous

★ le **sport** MASC NOUN
▷ *see also* **sport** ADJECTIVE
sport
□ faire du sport to do sport
■ **les sports d'hiver** winter sports

★ **sport** (FEM+PL **sport**) ADJECTIVE
▷ *see also* **sport** NOUN
casual
□ une veste sport a casual jacket

★ **sportif** (FEM **sportive**) ADJECTIVE
▷ *see also* **sportif** NOUN
1 sporty
□ Elle est très sportive. She's very sporty.
2 sports
□ un club sportif a sports club

★ le **sportif** MASC NOUN
▷ *see also* **sportif** ADJECTIVE
sportsman

★ la **sportive** FEM NOUN
sportswoman

le **spot** MASC NOUN
spotlight
■ **un spot publicitaire** a commercial break

le **square** MASC NOUN
public gardens

le **squelette** MASC NOUN
skeleton

stable (FEM **stable**) ADJECTIVE
stable
■ **un emploi stable** a steady job

★ le **stade** MASC NOUN
stadium

★ le **stage** MASC NOUN
1 training course
□ faire un stage de formation professionnelle to go on a vocational training course
2 work experience
□ Caroline a fait un stage chez Collins. Caroline did work experience at Collins.
■ **faire un stage en entreprise** to do a work placement

> **BE CAREFUL!**
> The French word **stage** does not mean **stage**.

★ le/la **stagiaire** MASC/FEM NOUN
▷ *see also* **stagiaire** ADJECTIVE
trainee

stagiaire (FEM **stagiaire**) ADJECTIVE
▷ *see also* **stagiaire** ADJECTIVE
trainee
□ un professeur stagiaire a trainee teacher

le **stand** MASC NOUN
1 stand (*at exhibition*)
2 stall (*at fair*)

le/la **standardiste** MASC/FEM NOUN
operator

★ la **station** FEM NOUN
■ **une station de métro** an underground station
■ **une station de taxis** a taxi rank
■ **une station de ski** a ski resort

★ le **stationnement** MASC NOUN
parking
■ **'stationnement interdit'** 'no parking'

★ **stationner** VERB [28]
to park

★ la **station-service** (PL les **stations-service**) FEM NOUN
service station

la **statistique** FEM NOUN
statistic

le **statut** MASC NOUN
status

★ le **steak** MASC NOUN
steak
■ **un steak frites** steak and chips
■ **un steak haché** a hamburger

la **sténo** FEM NOUN
shorthand
□ un cours de sténo a shorthand course

la **sténodactylo** FEM NOUN
shorthand typist

stérile (FEM **stérile**) ADJECTIVE
sterile

stimulant (FEM **stimulante**) ADJECTIVE
stimulating

stimuler VERB [28]
to stimulate

le **stop** MASC NOUN
stop sign
■ **faire du stop** to hitchhike

stopper VERB [28]
to stop

le **store** MASC NOUN
1 blind (*on window*)
2 awning

BE CAREFUL!
The French word **store** does not mean **store**.

le **strapontin** MASC NOUN
foldaway seat

la **stratégie** FEM NOUN
strategy

stratégique (FEM **stratégique**) ADJECTIVE
strategic

stressant (FEM **stressante**) ADJECTIVE
stressful

stressé (FEM **stressée**) ADJECTIVE
stressed out

★ **strict** (FEM **stricte**) ADJECTIVE
1 strict (*person*)
□ Ma prof de français est très stricte. My French teacher's very strict.
2 severe (*clothes*)
□ une tenue très stricte a very severe outfit
■ **le strict minimum** the bare minimum

la **strophe** FEM NOUN
stanza

studieux (FEM **studieuse**) ADJECTIVE
studious

★ le **studio** MASC NOUN
1 studio flat
2 studio
□ un studio de télévision a television studio

stupéfait (FEM **stupéfaite**) ADJECTIVE
astonished

les **stupéfiants** MASC PL NOUN
narcotics

stupéfier VERB [19]
to astonish
□ Sa réponse m'a stupéfié. I was astonished by his answer.

★ **stupide** (FEM **stupide**) ADJECTIVE
stupid

★ le **style** MASC NOUN
style

le/la **styliste** MASC/FEM NOUN
designer

★ le **stylo** MASC NOUN
pen
■ **un stylo plume** a fountain pen
■ **un stylo bille** a ballpoint pen
■ **un stylo-feutre** a felt-tip pen

su VERB ▷ *see* **savoir**
■ **Si j'avais su ...** If I'd known ...

subir VERB [38]
to suffer (*defeat*)
■ **subir une opération** to have an operation

subit (FEM **subite**) ADJECTIVE
sudden

subitement ADVERB
suddenly

subjectif (FEM **subjective**) ADJECTIVE
subjective

le **subjonctif** MASC NOUN
subjunctive

substituer VERB [28]
to substitute
□ substituer un mot à un autre to substitute one word for another

subtil (FEM **subtile**) ADJECTIVE
subtle

la **subvention** FEM NOUN
subsidy

subventionner VERB [28]
to subsidize

★ le **succès** MASC NOUN
success
■ **avoir du succès** to be successful

le **successeur** MASC NOUN
successor

la **succursale** FEM NOUN
branch (*of company*)

sucer VERB [12]
to suck

la **sucette** FEM NOUN
lollipop

★ le **sucre** MASC NOUN
sugar
■ **un sucre** a sugar lump □ Je prends deux sucres dans mon café. I take two lumps of sugar in my coffee.
■ **du sucre en morceaux** lump sugar
■ **un sucre d'orge** a barley sugar
■ **du sucre en poudre** caster sugar
■ **du sucre glace** icing sugar

★ **sucré** (FEM **sucrée**) ADJECTIVE
1 sweet
□ Ce gâteau est un peu trop sucré. This cake is a bit too sweet.
2 sweetened
□ du lait concentré sucré sweetened condensed milk

les **sucreries** FEM PL NOUN
sweet things

le **sucrier** MASC NOUN
sugar bowl

★ le **sud** MASC NOUN
▷ *see also* **sud** ADJECTIVE
south
□ Ils vivent dans le sud de la France. They live in the South of France.
■ **vers le sud** southwards
■ **au sud de Paris** south of Paris
■ **l'Amérique du Sud** South America
■ **le vent du sud** the south wind

French-English

★ **sud** (FEM+PL **sud**) ADJECTIVE
▷ *see also* **sud** NOUN
1 south
□ la côte sud de l'Espagne the south coast of Spain
■ **le pôle Sud** the South Pole
2 southern
□ Nous avons visité la partie sud du pays. We visited the southern part of the country.

sud-africain (FEM **sud-africaine**) ADJECTIVE
South African

sud-américain (FEM **sud-américaine**) ADJECTIVE
South American

le **sud-est** MASC NOUN
south-east
□ au sud-est in the south-east

le **sud-ouest** MASC NOUN
south-west
□ au sud-ouest in the south-west

★ la **Suède** FEM NOUN
Sweden

★ **suédois** (FEM **suédoise**) ADJECTIVE, NOUN
Swedish
□ Ils parlent suédois. They speak Swedish.
■ **un Suédois** a Swede (*man*)
■ **une Suédoise** a Swede (*woman*)
■ **les Suédois** the Swedes

suer VERB [28]
to sweat

la **sueur** FEM NOUN
sweat
■ **en sueur** sweating

★ **suffire** VERB [80]
to be enough
□ Tiens, voilà dix euros. Ça te suffit? Here's 10 euros. Is that enough for you?
■ **Ça suffit!** That's enough!

★ **suffisamment** ADVERB
enough
□ Ça n'est pas suffisamment grand. It's not big enough. □ Il n'y a pas suffisamment de chaises. There aren't enough chairs.

suffisant (FEM **suffisante**) ADJECTIVE
1 sufficient
□ Ça n'est pas une raison suffisante. That's not sufficient reason.
2 smug
□ Il est un peu trop suffisant. He's rather smug.

suffoquer VERB [28]
to suffocate

★ **suggérer** VERB [34]
to suggest

se **suicider** VERB [28]
to commit suicide

suis VERB ▷ *see* **être, suivre**
■ **Je suis écossais.** I'm Scottish.
■ **Suis-moi.** Follow me.

★ la **Suisse** FEM NOUN
▷ *see also* **suisse** ADJECTIVE, NOUN
Switzerland
□ la Suisse allemande German-speaking Switzerland □ la Suisse romande French-speaking Switzerland

★ **suisse** (FEM **suisse**) ADJECTIVE, NOUN
▷ *see also* **Suisse** NOUN
Swiss
□ le franc suisse the Swiss franc
■ **un Suisse** a Swiss man
■ **une Suisse** a Swiss woman
■ **les Suisses** the Swiss

la **suite** FEM NOUN
1 rest
□ Je vous raconterai la suite de l'histoire demain. I'll tell you the rest of the story tomorrow.
2 sequel (*to book, film*)
■ **tout de suite** straightaway □ J'y vais tout de suite. I'll go straightaway.
■ **de suite** in succession □ Il a commis la même erreur trois fois de suite. He made the same mistake three times in succession.
■ **par la suite** subsequently □ Il s'est avéré par la suite qu'il était coupable. He subsequently turned out to be guilty.

★ **suivant** (FEM **suivante**) ADJECTIVE
following
□ le jour suivant the following day □ l'exercice suivant the following exercise
■ **Au suivant!** Next!

★ **suivre** VERB [81]
1 to follow
□ Il m'a suivie jusque chez moi. He followed me home. □ Vous me suivez ou est-ce que je parle trop vite? Are you following me or am I speaking too fast?
2 to do
□ Je suis un cours d'anglais à la fac. I'm doing an English course at college.
3 to keep up
□ Il n'arrive pas à suivre en maths. He can't keep up in maths. □ J'aime suivre l'actualité. I like to keep up with the news.
■ **'à suivre'** 'to be continued'
■ **suivre un régime** to be on a diet

★ le **sujet** MASC NOUN
▷ *see also* **sujet** ADJECTIVE
subject
■ **au sujet de** about □ C'est à quel sujet? — C'est au sujet de l'annonce parue dans 'Le Monde' d'aujourd'hui. What's it about? — It's about the advertisement in today's 'Le Monde'.

S

■ **un sujet de conversation** a topic of conversation
■ **un sujet d'examen** an examination question
■ **un sujet de plaisanterie** something to joke about

★ **sujet** (FEM **sujette**) ADJECTIVE
▷ *see also* **sujet** NOUN
■ **être sujet à** to be prone to □ Il est sujet à des crises de panique. He is prone to panic attacks.

★ **super** (FEM+PL **super**) ADJECTIVE
▷ *see also* **super** NOUN
great

★ le **super** MASC NOUN
▷ *see also* **super** ADJECTIVE
super (*petrol*)

superficiel (FEM **superficielle**) ADJECTIVE
superficial

superflu (FEM **superflue**) ADJECTIVE
superfluous

★ **supérieur** (FEM **supérieure**) ADJECTIVE
▷ *see also* **supérieur** NOUN
1 upper
□ la lèvre supérieure the upper lip
2 superior
□ qualité supérieure superior quality □ Il a toujours l'air tellement supérieur! He always looks so superior!
■ **supérieur à** greater than □ Choisissez un nombre supérieur à cent. Choose a number greater than 100.

★ le **supérieur** MASC NOUN
▷ *see also* **supérieur** ADJECTIVE
superior
□ mon supérieur hiérarchique my immediate superior

★ la **supérieure** FEM NOUN
▷ *see also* **supérieur** ADJECTIVE
superior

★ le **supermarché** MASC NOUN
supermarket

★ **superposé** (FEM **superposée**) ADJECTIVE
■ **des lits superposés** bunk beds

superstitieux (FEM **superstitieuse**) ADJECTIVE
superstitious

★ le **supplément** MASC NOUN
■ **payer un supplément** to pay an additional charge
■ **Le vin est en supplément.** Wine is extra.
■ **un supplément de travail** extra work

★ **supplémentaire** (FEM **supplémentaire**) ADJECTIVE
additional
□ Voici quelques exercices supplémentaires. Here are some additional exercises.
■ **faire des heures supplémentaires** to do overtime

le **supplice** MASC NOUN
torture
□ C'était un supplice. It was torture.

supplier VERB [19]
■ **supplier quelqu'un de faire quelque chose** to beg somebody to do something □ Je t'en supplie! I'm begging you!

supportable (FEM **supportable**) ADJECTIVE
bearable

★ **supporter** VERB [28]
to stand (*tolerate*)
□ Je ne supporte pas l'hypocrisie. I can't stand hypocrisy. □ Elle ne supporte pas qu'on la critique. She can't stand being criticized. □ Je ne peux pas la supporter. I can't stand her. □ Je supporte mal la chaleur. I can't stand hot weather.

> **BE CAREFUL!**
> **supporter** does not mean **to support**.

★ **supposer** VERB [28]
to suppose

supprimer VERB [28]
1 to cut
□ Deux mille emplois ont été supprimés. Two thousand jobs have been cut.
2 to cancel
□ Le train de Londres a été supprimé. The train to London has been cancelled.
3 to get rid of
□ Ils ont supprimé les témoins gênants. They got rid of the awkward witnesses.

★ **sur** PREPOSITION
1 on
□ Pose-le sur la table. Put it down on the table. □ Vous verrez l'hôpital sur votre droite. You'll see the hospital on your right. □ une conférence sur Balzac a lecture on Balzac
2 in
□ une personne sur dix 1 person in 10
3 out of
□ J'ai eu onze sur vingt en maths. I got 11 out of 20 in maths.
4 by
□ quatre mètres sur deux 4 metres by 2

★ **sûr** (FEM **sûre**) ADJECTIVE
1 sure
□ Tu es sûr? Are you sure?
■ **sûr et certain** absolutely certain
2 reliable
□ C'est quelqu'un de très sûr. He's a very reliable person.
3 safe
□ Ce quartier n'est pas très sûr la nuit. This neighbourhood isn't very safe at night.
■ **sûr de soi** self-confident □ Elle est très sûre d'elle. She's very self-confident.

sûrement ADVERB
certainly
□ Sûrement pas! Certainly not! □ Il est sûrement déjà parti. He'll certainly already have left.

la **sûreté** FEM NOUN
■ **mettre quelque chose en sûreté** to put something in a safe place

le **surf** MASC NOUN
surfing

la **surface** FEM NOUN
surface
■ **les grandes surfaces** the supermarkets

★ **surfer** VERB [28]
to go surfing
■ **surfer sur le Net** to surf the Net

surgelé (FEM **surgelée**) ADJECTIVE
frozen
□ des frites surgelées frozen chips

les **surgelés** MASC PL NOUN
frozen food *sing*

surhumain (FEM **surhumaine**) ADJECTIVE
superhuman

sur-le-champ ADVERB
immediately

le **surlendemain** MASC NOUN
■ **le surlendemain de son arrivée** two days after he arrived
■ **le surlendemain dans la matinée** two days later, in the morning

se **surmener** VERB [43]
to work too hard
□ Ne te surmène pas trop pendant le week-end. Don't work too hard over the weekend.

surmonter VERB [48]
to overcome
□ Il nous reste de nombreux obstacles à surmonter. We still have many obstacles to overcome.

surnaturel (FEM **surnaturelle**) ADJECTIVE
supernatural

le **surnom** MASC NOUN
nickname

surnommer VERB [28]
to nickname
□ On l'a surnommé 'Kiki'. We nicknamed him 'Kiki'.

★ **surpeuplé** (FEM **surpeuplée**) ADJECTIVE
overpopulated

surprenant (FEM **surprenante**) ADJECTIVE
surprising

★ **surprendre** VERB [65]
to surprise
□ Ça me surprendrait beaucoup qu'il arrive à l'heure. I'd be very surprised if he arrived on time.
■ **surprendre quelqu'un en train de faire quelque chose** to catch somebody doing something □ Je l'ai surpris en train de fouiller dans mon placard. I caught him rummaging in my cupboard.

★ **surpris** (FEM **surprise**) ADJECTIVE
▷ *see also* **surprise** NOUN
surprised
□ Il était surpris de me voir. He was surprised to see me.

★ la **surprise** FEM NOUN
▷ *see also* **surpris** ADJECTIVE
surprise
□ faire une surprise à quelqu'un to give somebody a surprise

sursauter VERB [28]
to jump
□ J'ai sursauté en entendant mon nom. I jumped when I heard my name.

★ **surtout** ADVERB
1 especially
□ Il est assez timide, surtout avec les filles. He's rather shy, especially with girls.
2 crucially
□ Ce canapé est joli et surtout, il n'est pas salissant. This sofa is pretty and, crucially, it doesn't show the dirt.
■ **Surtout, ne répète pas ce que je t'ai dit!** Whatever you do, don't repeat what I told you!

★ le **surveillant** MASC NOUN
supervisor (*man*)

DID YOU KNOW...?
In French secondary schools, the teachers are not responsible for supervising the pupils outside class. This job is done by people called **surveillants** or **pions**.

★ la **surveillante** FEM NOUN
supervisor (*woman*)

★ **surveiller** VERB [28]
1 to keep an eye on
□ Tu peux surveiller mes bagages? Can you keep an eye on my luggage?
2 to keep a watch on
■ **La police a surveillé la maison pendant une semaine.** The police kept the house under surveillance for a week.
3 to supervise
□ Nous sommes toujours surveillés pendant la récréation. We're always supervised during break.
■ **surveiller un examen** to invigilate an exam
■ **surveiller sa ligne** to watch one's figure

★ le **survêtement** MASC NOUN
tracksuit
□ un haut de survêtement a tracksuit top
□ un pantalon de survêtement tracksuit bottoms

la **survie** FEM NOUN
survival

le **survivant** MASC NOUN
survivor

la **survivante** FEM NOUN
survivor

survivre VERB [91]
to survive
□ survivre à un accident to survive an accident

survoler VERB [28]
to fly over

sus ADVERB
■ **en sus** in addition

susceptible (FEM **susceptible**) ADJECTIVE
touchy

suspect (FEM **suspecte**) ADJECTIVE
suspicious
□ dans des circonstances suspectes under suspicious circumstances

suspecter VERB [28]
to suspect

le **suspense** MASC NOUN
suspense
■ **un film à suspense** a thriller

la **suture** FEM NOUN
■ **un point de suture** a stitch

svelte (FEM **svelte**) ADJECTIVE
slender

SVP ABBREVIATION (= *s'il vous plaît*)
please

★ le **sweat** MASC NOUN
sweatshirt

la **syllabe** FEM NOUN
syllable

★ le **symbole** MASC NOUN
symbol

symbolique (FEM **symbolique**) ADJECTIVE
symbolic

symboliser VERB [28]
to symbolize

symétrique (FEM **symétrique**) ADJECTIVE
symmetrical

★ **sympa** (FEM+PL **sympa**) ADJECTIVE (*informal*)
nice
□ Elle est très sympa. She's a really nice person.

★ la **sympathie** FEM NOUN
■ **J'ai beaucoup de sympathie pour lui.** I like him a lot.

★ **sympathique** (FEM **sympathique**)
ADJECTIVE
nice
□ Ce sont des gens très sympathiques. They're very nice people.

> **BE CAREFUL!**
> **sympathique** does not mean **sympathetic**.

sympathiser VERB [28]
to get on well
□ Nous avons immédiatement sympathisé avec nos voisins. We got on well with our neighbours straight away.

★ le **symptôme** MASC NOUN
symptom

la **synagogue** FEM NOUN
synagogue

★ le **syndicat** MASC NOUN
trade union
■ **le syndicat d'initiative** the tourist information office

synonyme (FEM **synonyme**) ADJECTIVE
▷ *see also* **synonyme** NOUN
synonymous
□ être synonyme de to be synonymous with

le **synonyme** MASC NOUN
▷ *see also* **synonyme** ADJECTIVE
synonym

synthétique (FEM **synthétique**) ADJECTIVE
synthetic

la **Syrie** FEM NOUN
Syria

syrien (FEM **syrienne**) ADJECTIVE, NOUN
Syrian

systématique (FEM **systématique**)
ADJECTIVE
systematic

le **système** MASC NOUN
system

Tt

★ **t'** PRONOUN ▷ *see* **te**

★ **ta** FEM ADJECTIVE
your
□ J'ai vu ta sœur hier. I saw your sister yesterday.

★ le **tabac** MASC NOUN
1 tobacco
□ le tabac blond light tobacco □ le tabac brun dark tobacco
2 smoking
□ Le tabac est mauvais pour la santé. Smoking is bad for you.

★ la **table** FEM NOUN
table
■ **mettre la table** to lay the table
■ **se mettre à table** to sit down to eat
■ **À table!** Dinner's ready!
■ **une table de nuit** a bedside table
■ **'table des matières'** 'contents'

★ le **tableau** (PL les **tableaux**) MASC NOUN
painting
□ un tableau de Monet a painting by Monet
■ **le tableau d'affichage** the notice board
■ **le tableau noir** the blackboard

la **tablette** FEM NOUN
tablet (*computer*)
■ **une tablette de chocolat** a bar of chocolate

le **tableur** MASC NOUN
spreadsheet

★ le **tablier** MASC NOUN
apron

le **tabouret** MASC NOUN
stool

★ la **tache** FEM NOUN
mark (*stain*)
■ **des taches de rousseur** freckles

★ la **tâche** FEM NOUN
task

tacher VERB [28]
to leave a stain

tâcher VERB [28]
■ **tâcher de faire quelque chose** to try to do something □ Tâche d'être à l'heure! Try to be on time!

le **tact** MASC NOUN
tact
■ **avoir du tact** to be tactful

tactile ADJECTIVE
■ **écran tactile** touch-sensitive display (*for computer*)

la **tactique** FEM NOUN
tactics
■ **changer de tactique** to try something different

la **taie** FEM NOUN
■ **une taie d'oreiller** a pillowcase

★ la **taille** FEM NOUN
1 waist
□ Elle a la taille fine. She has a slim waist.
2 height
□ un homme de taille moyenne a man of average height
3 size
□ Avez-vous ma taille? Have you got my size?

★ le **taille-crayon** MASC NOUN
pencil sharpener

le **tailleur** MASC NOUN
1 tailor
2 suit (*lady's*)
■ **Il est assis en tailleur.** He's sitting cross-legged.

★ se **taire** VERB [82]
to stop talking
■ **Taisez-vous!** Be quiet!

★ le **talon** MASC NOUN
heel

le **tambour** MASC NOUN
drum

★ la **Tamise** FEM NOUN
Thames

le **tampon** MASC NOUN
pad
□ un tampon à récurer a scouring pad
■ **un tampon hygiénique** a tampon

tamponneuse FEM ADJECTIVE
■ **les autos tamponneuses** dodgems

tandis que CONJUNCTION
while
□ Il a toujours de bonnes notes, tandis que les miennes sont mauvaises. He always gets good

marks, while mine are poor.

★ **tant** ADVERB
so much
□ Je l'aime tant! I love him so much!
■ **tant de** **1** so much □ tant de nourriture so much food **2** so many □ tant de livres so many books
■ **tant que** **1** until □ Tu ne sortiras pas tant que tu n'auras pas fini tes devoirs. You're not going out until you've finished your homework. **2** while □ Profites-en tant que tu peux. Make the most of it while you can.
■ **tant mieux** so much the better
■ **tant pis** never mind

★ la **tante** FEM NOUN
aunt

tantôt ADVERB
sometimes
□ Nous venons tantôt à pied, tantôt en bus. Sometimes we walk, sometimes we come by bus.

le **tapage** MASC NOUN
1 racket
□ Ils ont fait du tapage toute la nuit. They made a racket all night long.
2 fuss
□ On a fait beaucoup de tapage autour de cette affaire. There was a lot of fuss about that business.

★ **taper** VERB [28]
to beat down
□ Le soleil tape. The sun's really beating down.
■ **taper quelqu'un** to hit somebody
□ Maman, il m'a tapé! Mum, he hit me!
■ **taper sur quelque chose** to bang on something
■ **taper des pieds** to stamp one's feet
■ **taper des mains** to clap one's hands
■ **taper à l'ordinateur** to type □ Tu sais taper à l'ordinateur? Can you type? □ Je vais taper cette lettre. I'm going to type this letter.

★ le **tapis** MASC NOUN
carpet
■ **le tapis roulant** **1** (*for people*) the Travelator® **2** (*in factory*) the conveyor belt **3** (*at baggage reclaim*) the carousel

tapisser VERB [28]
to paper

la **tapisserie** FEM NOUN
1 wallpaper
□ Tu aimes la tapisserie de ma chambre? Do you like the wallpaper in my bedroom?
2 tapestry

taquiner VERB [28]
to tease

★ **tard** ADVERB
late
□ Il est tard. It's late.
■ **plus tard** later on
■ **au plus tard** at the latest

tardif (FEM **tardive**) ADJECTIVE
late
□ un petit déjeuner tardif a late breakfast

★ le **tarif** MASC NOUN
■ **le tarif des consommations** (*in café*) the price list
■ **une communication à tarif réduit** an off-peak phone call
■ **un billet de train à tarif réduit** a concessionary train ticket
■ **un billet de train à plein tarif** a full-price train ticket
■ **Est-ce que vous faites un tarif de groupe?** Is there a reduction for groups?

★ la **tarte** FEM NOUN
tart

★ la **tartine** FEM NOUN
slice of bread
□ une tartine de confiture a slice of bread and jam

tartiner VERB [28]
to spread
■ **le fromage à tartiner** cheese spread

★ le **tas** MASC NOUN
heap
□ un tas de charbon a heap of coal
■ **un tas de** (*informal*) loads of □ J'ai lu un tas de livres pendant les vacances. I read loads of books in the holidays.

★ la **tasse** FEM NOUN
cup

le **tatouage** MASC NOUN
tattoo

★ le **taureau** (PL les **taureaux**) MASC NOUN
bull
■ **le Taureau** Taurus □ Ils sont tous les deux Taureau. They're both Taurus.

★ le **taux** MASC NOUN
rate
□ le taux de change the exchange rate

★ la **taxe** FEM NOUN
tax
■ **la boutique hors taxes** the duty-free shop

★ le **taxi** MASC NOUN
taxi

tchater, tchatter VERB [28]
to chat (*on the internet*)
to talk online

tchèque (FEM **tchèque**) ADJECTIVE, NOUN
Czech
■ **la République tchèque** the Czech Republic
■ **un Tchèque** a Czech (*man*)
■ **une Tchèque** a Czech (*woman*)
■ **les Tchèques** the Czechs

★ **te** PRONOUN

> **te** changes to **t'** before a vowel and most words beginning with 'h'.

1 you
□ Je te vois. I can see you. □ Il t'a vu? Did he see you?
2 to you
□ Est-ce qu'il te parle en français? Does he talk to you in French? □ Elle t'a parlé? Did she speak to you?
3 yourself
□ Tu vas te rendre malade. You'll make yourself sick.

> With reflexive verbs, **te** is often not translated.

□ Comment tu t'appelles? What's your name?

★ le **technicien** MASC NOUN
technician

★ la **technicienne** FEM NOUN
technician

★ **technique** (FEM **technique**) ADJECTIVE
▷ *see also* **technique** NOUN
technical

★ la **technique** FEM NOUN
▷ *see also* **technique** ADJECTIVE
technique

la **techno** FEM NOUN
techno music

★ la **technologie** FEM NOUN
technology

le **teint** MASC NOUN
complexion
□ Elle a le teint clair. She's got a fair complexion.

la **teinte** FEM NOUN
shade (*colour*)

le **teinturier** MASC NOUN
dry cleaner's
□ Je vais porter ce manteau chez le teinturier. I'm going to take this coat to the dry cleaner's.

★ **tel** (FEM **telle**) ADJECTIVE
■ **Il a un tel enthousiasme!** He's got such enthusiasm!
■ **rien de tel** nothing like □ Il n'y a rien de tel qu'une bonne nuit de sommeil. There's nothing like a good night's sleep.
■ **J'ai tout laissé tel quel.** I left everything as it was.
■ **tel que** such as

★ la **télé** FEM NOUN
telly
□ à la télé on telly
■ **la télé réalité** reality TV

le **téléchargement** MASC NOUN
download

★ **télécharger** VERB [45]
1 to download (*receive*)
2 to upload (*send*)

la **télécommande** FEM NOUN
remote control

la **téléconférence** FEM NOUN
video conference

★ la **télécopie** FEM NOUN
fax

★ le **télégramme** MASC NOUN
telegram

le **télépéage** MASC NOUN
motorway toll payment system

> **DID YOU KNOW...?**
> Certain lanes at motorway tolls are reserved for drivers who have a sensor inside their car which allows them to pay monthly rather than on the spot. These lanes are marked with a yellow T and should be avoided by tourists.

★ le **téléphérique** MASC NOUN
cable car

★ le **téléphone** MASC NOUN
telephone
□ Elle est au téléphone. She's on the phone.
■ **un téléphone portable** a mobile phone

★ **téléphoner** VERB [28]
to phone
□ Je vais téléphoner à Claire. I'll phone Claire.
□ Je peux téléphoner? Can I make a phone call?

la **téléréalité** FEM NOUN
reality TV

le **télésiège** MASC NOUN
chairlift

le **téléski** MASC NOUN
ski-tow

★ le **téléspectateur** MASC NOUN
viewer (*TV*)

★ la **téléspectatrice** FEM NOUN
viewer (*TV*)

★ le **téléviseur** MASC NOUN
television set

★ la **télévision** FEM NOUN
television
□ à la télévision on television
■ **la télévision numérique** digital TV

telle FEM ADJECTIVE
▷ *see also* **tel**
■ **Je n'ai jamais eu une telle peur.** I've never had such a fright.
■ **telle que** such as

★ **tellement** ADVERB
1 so
□ Benjamin est tellement gentil. Benjamin's so nice. □ Il travaille tellement. He works so hard.

2 so much
□ Il a tellement mangé que ... He ate so much that ...
3 so many
□ Il y avait tellement de monde. There were so many people.

telles FEM PL ADJECTIVE
such
□ Je n'ai jamais entendu de telles bêtises! I've never heard such nonsense!

tels MASC PL ADJECTIVE
such
□ Nous n'avons pas de tels orages chez nous. We don't have such storms back home.

★ le **témoignage** MASC NOUN
testimony

témoigner VERB [28]
to testify

★ le **témoin** MASC NOUN
witness

★ la **température** FEM NOUN
temperature
□ avoir de la température to have a temperature

★ la **tempête** FEM NOUN
storm

le **temple** MASC NOUN
1 church (*Protestant*)
2 temple (*Hindu, Sikh, Buddhist*)

★ **temporaire** (FEM **temporaire**) ADJECTIVE
temporary

★ le **temps** MASC NOUN
1 weather
□ Quel temps fait-il? What's the weather like?
2 time
□ Je n'ai pas le temps. I haven't got time. □ Prends ton temps. Take your time. □ Il est temps de partir. It's time to go.
■ **juste à temps** just in time
■ **de temps en temps** from time to time
■ **en même temps** at the same time
■ **à temps** in time □ Il est arrivé à temps pour le match. He arrived in time for the match.
■ **à plein temps** full time □ Elle travaille à plein temps. She works full time.
■ **à temps complet** full time
■ **à temps partiel** part time □ le travail à temps partiel part-time work
■ **dans le temps** at one time □ Dans le temps, on pouvait circuler en vélo sans danger. At one time, it was safe to go around by bike.
3 tense (*of verb*)

tenais, tenait VERB ▷ *see* **tenir**

la **tendance** FEM NOUN
■ **avoir tendance à faire quelque chose** to tend to do something □ Il a tendance à exagérer. He tends to exaggerate.

tendre (FEM **tendre**) ADJECTIVE
▷ *see also* **tendre** VERB
tender

tendre VERB [88]
▷ *see also* **tendre** ADJECTIVE
to stretch out
□ Ils ont tendu une corde entre deux arbres. They stretched out a rope between two trees.
■ **tendre quelque chose à quelqu'un** to hold something out to somebody □ Il lui a tendu les clés. He held out the keys to her.
■ **tendre la main** to hold out one's hand
■ **tendre le bras** to reach out
■ **tendre un piège à quelqu'un** to set a trap for someone

tendrement ADVERB
tenderly

la **tendresse** FEM NOUN
tenderness

tendu (FEM **tendue**) ADJECTIVE
tense
□ Il était très tendu aujourd'hui. He was very tense today.

★ **tenir** VERB [83]
to hold
□ Tu peux tenir la lampe, s'il te plaît? Can you hold the torch, please? □ Il tenait un enfant par la main. He was holding a child by the hand.
■ **Tenez votre chien en laisse.** Keep your dog on the lead.
■ **tenir à quelqu'un** to be attached to somebody □ Il tient beaucoup à elle. He's very attached to her.
■ **tenir à faire quelque chose** to be determined to do something □ Elle tient à y aller. She's determined to go.
■ **tenir de quelqu'un** to take after somebody □ Il tient de son père. He takes after his father.
■ **Tiens, voilà un stylo.** Here's a pen.
■ **Tiens, c'est Corentin là-bas!** Look, that's Corentin over there!
■ **Tiens?** Really?
■ **se tenir** **1** to stand □ Il se tenait près de la porte. He was standing by the door. **2** to be held □ La foire va se tenir place du marché. The fair will be held in the market place.
■ **se tenir droit** **1** to stand up straight □ Tiens-toi droit! Stand up straight! **2** to sit up straight □ Arrête de manger le nez dans ton assiette, tiens-toi droit. Don't slouch while you're eating, sit up straight.
■ **Tiens-toi bien!** Behave yourself!

★ le **tennis** MASC NOUN
1 tennis
□ Elle joue au tennis. She plays tennis.
■ **le tennis de table** table tennis
2 tennis court
□ Il est au tennis. He's at the tennis court.
■ **les tennis** trainers

tentant (FEM **tentante**) ADJECTIVE
tempting

la **tentation** FEM NOUN
temptation

la **tentative** FEM NOUN
attempt

★ la **tente** FEM NOUN
tent

tenter VERB [28]
to tempt
□ J'ai été tenté de tout abandonner. I was tempted to give up. □ Ça ne me tente vraiment pas d'aller à la piscine. I really don't fancy going to the swimming pool.
■ **tenter de faire quelque chose** to try to do something □ Il a tenté plusieurs fois de s'évader. He tried several times to escape.

tenu VERB ▷ *see* **tenir**

★ la **tenue** FEM NOUN
clothes
■ **en tenue de soirée** in evening dress

le **terme** MASC NOUN
■ **à court terme** short-term
■ **à long terme** long-term

★ la **terminale** FEM NOUN
upper sixth
□ Je suis en terminale. I'm in the upper sixth.

> **DID YOU KNOW...?**
> In French secondary schools, years are counted from the **sixième** (youngest) to **première** and **terminale** (oldest).

★ **terminer** VERB [28]
to finish
■ **se terminer** to end □ Les vacances se terminent demain. The holidays end tomorrow.

le **terminus** MASC NOUN
terminus

★ le **terrain** MASC NOUN
land
□ Il veut acheter un terrain en Normandie. He wants to buy some land in Normandy.
■ **un terrain de camping** a campsite
■ **un terrain de football** a football pitch
■ **un terrain de golf** a golf course
■ **un terrain de jeu** a playground
■ **un terrain de sport** a sports ground
■ **un terrain vague** a piece of waste ground

★ la **terrasse** FEM NOUN
terrace
■ **Si on s'asseyait en terrasse?** (*at café*) Shall we sit outside?

★ la **terre** FEM NOUN
earth
■ **la Terre** the Earth
■ **Elle s'est assise par terre.** She sat on the floor.
■ **Il est tombé par terre.** He fell down.
■ **la terre cuite** terracotta □ un pot en terre cuite a terracotta pot
■ **la terre glaise** clay

★ **terrible** (FEM **terrible**) ADJECTIVE
terrible
□ Quelque chose de terrible est arrivé. Something terrible has happened.
■ **pas terrible** (*informal*) nothing special □ Ce film n'est pas terrible. The film's nothing special.

★ la **terrine** FEM NOUN
pâté

le **territoire** MASC NOUN
territory

terrorisé (FEM **terrorisée**) ADJECTIVE
terrified

le **terrorisme** MASC NOUN
terrorism

le/la **terroriste** MASC/FEM NOUN
terrorist

★ **tes** PL ADJECTIVE
your
□ J'aime bien tes baskets. I like your trainers.

le **test** MASC NOUN
test

le **testament** MASC NOUN
will
□ Il est mort sans testament. He died without leaving a will.

tester VERB [28]
to test

le **tétanos** MASC NOUN
tetanus

le **têtard** MASC NOUN
tadpole

★ la **tête** FEM NOUN
head
□ de la tête aux pieds from head to foot
■ **se laver la tête** to wash one's hair
■ **la tête la première** headfirst
■ **tenir tête à quelqu'un** to stand up to somebody
■ **faire la tête** to sulk
■ **en avoir par-dessus la tête** to be fed up

★ **têtu** (FEM **têtue**) ADJECTIVE
stubborn

★ le **texte** MASC NOUN
text (*written work*)

le **Texto**® MASC NOUN
text message

★ le **TGV** MASC NOUN (= *train à grande vitesse*)
high-speed train

★ le **thé** MASC NOUN
tea
□ Je vous offre un thé? Would you like a cup of tea? □ un thé au lait a white tea

★ le **théâtre** MASC NOUN
theatre
■ **faire du théâtre** to act □ Est-ce que tu as déjà fait du théâtre? Have you ever acted?

★ la **théière** FEM NOUN
teapot

★ le **thème** MASC NOUN
1 subject
□ Quel est le thème de l'émission? What's the programme about?
2 prose (*translation into the foreign language*)

la **théorie** FEM NOUN
theory

le **thermomètre** MASC NOUN
thermometer

★ le **thon** MASC NOUN
tuna

la **thune** FEM NOUN (*informal*)
dosh

le **tibia** MASC NOUN
1 shinbone
□ une fracture du tibia a broken shinbone
2 shin
□ Il m'a donné un coup de pied dans le tibia. He kicked me in the shin.

les **TIC** FEM PL NOUN (= *technologies de l'information et de la communication*)
ICT *sing*

le **tic** MASC NOUN
nervous twitch

★ le **ticket** MASC NOUN
ticket
□ un ticket de métro an underground ticket
■ **le ticket de caisse** the till receipt

★ **tiède** (FEM **tiède**) ADJECTIVE
1 warm (*water, air*)
2 lukewarm (*food, drink*)

tien MASC PRONOUN
■ **le tien** yours □ J'ai oublié mon stylo. Tu peux me prêter le tien? I've forgotten my pen. Can you lend me yours?

tienne FEM PRONOUN
■ **la tienne** yours □ Ce n'est pas ma raquette, c'est la tienne. It's not my racket, it's yours.
■ **À la tienne!** Cheers!

tiennes FEM PL PRONOUN
■ **les tiennes** yours □ J'ai pris mes baskets, mais j'ai oublié les tiennes. I've brought my trainers, but I've forgotten yours.

tiens MASC PL PRONOUN
■ **les tiens** yours □ Je ne trouve pas mes feutres. Je peux utiliser les tiens? I can't find my felt pens. Can I use yours?

tiens, tient VERB ▷ *see* **tenir**

★ le **tiers** MASC NOUN
third
□ Un tiers de la classe était pour. A third of the class were in favour.
■ **le tiers-monde** the Third World

la **tige** FEM NOUN
stem

★ le **tigre** MASC NOUN
tiger

le **tilleul** MASC NOUN
lime tea

★ le **timbre** MASC NOUN
stamp

★ le **timbre-poste** MASC NOUN
postage stamp

★ **timide** (FEM **timide**) ADJECTIVE
shy

timidement ADVERB
shyly

la **timidité** FEM NOUN
shyness

le **tir** MASC NOUN
shooting
■ **le tir à l'arc** archery

le **tirage** MASC NOUN
■ **par tirage au sort** by drawing lots □ Les prix seront attribués par tirage au sort. The prizes will be awarded by drawing lots.

★ le **tire-bouchon** MASC NOUN
corkscrew

la **tirelire** FEM NOUN
money box

★ **tirer** VERB [28]
1 to pull
□ Elle a tiré un mouchoir de son sac. She pulled a handkerchief out of her bag. □ Il m'a tiré les cheveux. He pulled my hair. □ 'Tirer' 'Pull'
2 to draw
□ tirer les rideaux to draw the curtains □ tirer un trait to draw a line □ tirer des conclusions to draw conclusions
■ **tirer au sort** to draw lots
3 to fire
□ Il a tiré plusieurs coups de feu. He fired several shots. □ Il a tiré sur les policiers. He fired at the police.
■ **Tu t'en tires bien.** You're doing well.

le **tiret** MASC NOUN
dash (*hyphen*)
■ **tiret du 8** underscore
■ **tiret du 6** dash

★ le **tiroir** MASC NOUN
drawer

la **tisane** FEM NOUN
herbal tea

tisser VERB [28]
to weave

★ le **tissu** MASC NOUN
material
■ **un sac en tissu** a cloth bag

★ le **titre** MASC NOUN
title
■ **les gros titres** the headlines
■ **un titre de transport** a travel ticket

tituber VERB [28]
to stagger

la **TNT** FEM NOUN (= *télévision numérique terrestre*)
digital television

★ le **toast** MASC NOUN
1 piece of toast
2 toast
□ porter un toast à quelqu'un to drink a toast to somebody

le **toboggan** MASC NOUN
slide

★ **toi** PRONOUN
you
□ Ça va? — Oui, et toi? How are you? — Fine, and you? □ J'ai faim, pas toi? I'm hungry, aren't you?
■ **Assieds-toi.** Sit down.
■ **C'est à toi de jouer.** It's your turn to play.
■ **Est-ce que ce stylo est à toi?** Is this pen yours?

la **toile** FEM NOUN
■ **un pantalon de toile** cotton trousers
■ **un sac de toile** a canvas bag
■ **une toile cirée** an oilcloth
■ **une toile d'araignée** a cobweb
■ **la Toile** the internet

★ la **toilette** FEM NOUN
1 wash
□ faire sa toilette to have a wash
2 outfit
□ une toilette élégante an elegant outfit

★ les **toilettes** FEM PL NOUN
toilet *sing*

toi-même PRONOUN
yourself
□ Tu as fait ça toi-même? Did you do it yourself?

★ le **toit** MASC NOUN
roof
■ **un toit ouvrant** a sunroof

tolérant (FEM **tolérante**) ADJECTIVE
tolerant

tolérer VERB [34]
to tolerate

★ la **tomate** FEM NOUN
tomato

la **tombe** FEM NOUN
grave

le **tombeau** (PL les **tombeaux**) MASC NOUN
tomb

la **tombée** FEM NOUN
■ **à la tombée de la nuit** at nightfall

★ **tomber** VERB [84, *aux* **être**]
to fall
□ Attention, tu vas tomber! Be careful, you'll fall!
■ **laisser tomber** 1 to drop □ Elle a laissé tomber son stylo. She dropped her pen. 2 to give up □ Il a laissé tomber le piano. He gave up the piano. 3 to let down □ Il ne laisse jamais tomber ses amis. He never lets his friends down.
■ **tomber amoureux de quelqu'un** to fall in love with somebody
■ **tomber sur quelqu'un** to bump into somebody □ Je suis tombé sur lui en sortant de chez Pierre. I bumped into him coming out of Pierre's place.
■ **Ça tombe bien.** That's lucky.
■ **Il tombe de sommeil.** He's asleep on his feet.

★ **ton** (FEM **ta**, PL **tes**) ADJECTIVE
▷ *see also* **ton** NOUN
your
□ C'est ton stylo? Is this your pen?

★ le **ton** MASC NOUN
▷ *see also* **ton** ADJECTIVE
1 tone of voice
□ Ne me parle pas sur ce ton. Don't speak to me in that tone of voice.
2 colour
□ J'adore les tons pastel. I love pastel colours.

★ la **tonalité** FEM NOUN
dialling tone

★ la **tondeuse** FEM NOUN
lawnmower

★ **tondre** VERB [69]
to mow

tonique (FEM **tonique**) ADJECTIVE
fortifying

la **tonne** FEM NOUN
tonne

le **tonneau** (PL les **tonneaux**) MASC NOUN
barrel

★ le **tonnerre** MASC NOUN
thunder

le **tonus** MASC NOUN
■ **avoir du tonus** to be energetic

★ le **torchon** MASC NOUN
tea towel

tordre VERB [49]
■ **se tordre la cheville** to twist one's ankle

tordu (FEM **tordue**) ADJECTIVE
1 bent
□ Ce clou est un peu tordu. This nail's a bit bent.

2 crazy
□ une histoire complètement tordue a crazy story

le **torrent** MASC NOUN
mountain stream

le **torse** MASC NOUN
chest
□ Il était torse nu. He was bare-chested.

★ le **tort** MASC NOUN
■ **avoir tort** to be wrong
■ **donner tort à quelqu'un** to lay the blame on somebody

le **torticolis** MASC NOUN
stiff neck
□ J'ai un torticolis. I've got a stiff neck.

★ la **tortue** FEM NOUN
tortoise

la **torture** FEM NOUN
torture

torturer VERB [28]
to torture

★ **tôt** ADVERB
early
■ **au plus tôt** at the earliest
■ **tôt ou tard** sooner or later

★ **total** (FEM **totale**, MASC PL **totaux**) ADJECTIVE
▷ *see also* **total** NOUN
total

★ le **total** (PL les **totaux**) MASC NOUN
▷ *see also* **total** ADJECTIVE
total
□ faire le total to work out the total
■ **au total** in total

totalement ADVERB
totally

la **totalité** FEM NOUN
■ **la totalité des profs** all the teachers
■ **la totalité du personnel** the entire staff

touchant (FEM **touchante**) ADJECTIVE
touching

★ la **touche** FEM NOUN
key (*keyboard, phone*)

★ **toucher** VERB [28]
1 to touch
□ Ne touche pas à mes livres! Don't touch my books!
■ **Nos deux jardins se touchent.** Our gardens are next to each other.
2 to feel
□ Ce pull a l'air doux. Je peux toucher? That sweater looks soft. Can I feel it?
3 to hit
□ La balle l'a touché en pleine poitrine. The bullet hit him right in the chest.
4 to affect
□ Ces nouvelles réformes ne nous touchent pas. The new reforms don't affect us.
5 to receive
□ Il a touché une grosse somme d'argent. He received a large sum of money.

★ **toujours** ADVERB
1 always
□ Il est toujours très gentil. He's always very nice.
■ **pour toujours** forever
2 still
□ Quand on est revenus, Pierre était toujours là. When we got back Pierre was still there.

le **toupet** MASC NOUN (*informal*)
■ **avoir du toupet** to have a nerve

★ la **tour** FEM NOUN
▷ *see also* **tour** NOUN
1 tower
□ la Tour Eiffel the Eiffel Tower
2 tower block
□ Il y a beaucoup de tours dans ce quartier. There are a lot of tower blocks in this area.

★ le **tour** MASC NOUN
▷ *see also* **tour** NOUN
turn
□ C'est ton tour de jouer. It's your turn to play.
■ **faire un tour** to go for a walk □ Allons faire un tour dans le parc. Let's go for a walk in the park.
■ **faire un tour en voiture** to go for a drive
■ **faire un tour à vélo** to go for a ride □ Tu veux aller faire un tour à vélo? Do you want to go for a bike ride?
■ **faire le tour du monde** to travel round the world
■ **à tour de rôle** alternately

le **tourbillon** MASC NOUN
whirlpool

★ le **tourisme** MASC NOUN
tourism

★ le/la **touriste** MASC/FEM NOUN
tourist

★ **touristique** (FEM **touristique**) ADJECTIVE
tourist

se **tourmenter** VERB [28]
to fret
□ Ne te tourmente pas, ça s'arrangera. Don't fret about it, it'll be all right.

le **tournant** MASC NOUN
1 bend
□ Il y a beaucoup de tournants dangereux sur cette route. There are a lot of dangerous bends on this road.
2 turning point
□ Ça a été un tournant dans sa vie. It was a turning point in his life.

★ la **tournée** FEM NOUN
1 round
□ Le facteur commence sa tournée à sept heures du matin. The postman starts his

round at 7 o'clock in the morning. □ Allez, qu'est-ce que vous voulez boire? C'est ma tournée. Right, what are you drinking? It's my round.

2 tour

□ Il est en tournée aux États-Unis. He's on tour in the United States.

★ **tourner** VERB [28]

1 to turn

□ Tournez à droite au prochain feu. Turn right at the lights. □ Tourne-toi un peu plus vers moi, et souris! Turn towards me a bit more, and smile!

2 to go sour

□ Le lait a tourné. The milk's gone sour.

■ **mal tourner** to go wrong □ Ça a mal tourné. It all went wrong.

■ **tourner le dos à quelqu'un** to have one's back to somebody

■ **tourner un film** to make a film

le **tournesol** MASC NOUN

sunflower

le **tournevis** MASC NOUN

screwdriver

★ le **tournoi** MASC NOUN

tournament

la **tourte** FEM NOUN

pie

□ une tourte aux poireaux a leek pie

tous PL ADJECTIVE, PL PRONOUN ▷ *see* **tout**

★ la **Toussaint** FEM NOUN

All Saints' Day

★ **tousser** VERB [28]

to cough

★ **tout** (FEM **toute**, MASC PL **tous**) ADJECTIVE, ADVERB, PRONOUN

1 all

□ tout le lait all the milk □ toute la nuit all night □ tous les livres all the books □ toutes les filles all the girls □ toute la journée all day □ tout le temps all the time □ C'est tout. That's all. □ Je les connais tous. I know them all. □ Nous y sommes toutes allées. We all went. □ Ça fait combien en tout? How much is that all together?

■ **Il est tout seul.** He's all alone.

■ **pas du tout** not at all

■ **tout de même** all the same

2 every

□ tous les jours every day □ tous les deux jours every two days

■ **tout le monde** everybody

■ **tous les deux** both □ Nous y sommes allés tous les deux. We both went.

■ **tous les trois** all three □ Je les ai invités tous les trois. I invited all three of them.

3 everything

□ Il a tout organisé. He organized everything.

4 very

□ Elle habite tout près. She lives very close.

■ **tout en haut** right at the top

■ **tout droit** straight ahead

■ **tout d'abord** first of all

■ **tout à coup** suddenly

■ **tout à fait** absolutely

■ **tout à l'heure** **1** just now □ Je l'ai vu tout à l'heure. I saw him just now. **2** in a moment □ Je finirai ça tout à l'heure. I'll finish it in a moment.

■ **À tout à l'heure!** See you later!

■ **tout de suite** straight away

■ **Il a fait son travail tout en chantant.** He sang as he worked.

toutefois ADVERB

however

toutes FEM PL ADJECTIVE, FEM PL PRONOUN ▷ *see* **tout**

★ la **toux** FEM NOUN

cough

★ le/la **toxicomane** MASC/FEM NOUN

drug addict

la **toxicomanie** FEM NOUN

drug addiction

le **TP** MASC NOUN (= *travaux pratiques*)

practical class

■ **J'ai un TP de biologie à deux heures.** I've got a biology practical at two o'clock.

le **trac** MASC NOUN

■ **avoir le trac** to be feeling nervous

tracasser VERB [28]

to worry

□ La santé de mon père me tracasse. My dad's health worries me.

■ **se tracasser** to worry □ Arrête de te tracasser pour rien! Stop worrying about nothing!

la **trace** FEM NOUN

1 trace

□ Le voleur n'a pas laissé de traces. The thief left no traces.

2 mark

□ des traces de doigts finger marks

■ **des traces de pas** footprints

tracer VERB [12]

to draw

□ tracer un trait to draw a line

★ le **tracteur** MASC NOUN

tractor

la **tradition** FEM NOUN

tradition

traditionnel (FEM **traditionnelle**) ADJECTIVE

traditional

★ le **traducteur** MASC NOUN

translator

la **traduction** FEM NOUN
translation

★ la **traductrice** FEM NOUN
translator

★ **traduire** VERB [23]
to translate

le **trafic** MASC NOUN
traffic
▪ **le trafic de drogue** drug trafficking

le **trafiquant** MASC NOUN
▪ **un trafiquant de drogue** a drug trafficker

tragique (FEM **tragique**) ADJECTIVE
tragic

trahir VERB [38]
to betray

la **trahison** FEM NOUN
betrayal

★ le **train** MASC NOUN
train
▪ **un train électrique** a train set
▪ **Il est en train de manger.** He's eating.

le **traîneau** (PL les **traîneaux**) MASC NOUN
sledge

traîner VERB [28]
1 to wander around
□ J'ai vu des jeunes qui traînaient en ville. I saw some young people wandering around town.
2 to hang about
□ Dépêche-toi, ne traîne pas! Hurry up, don't hang about!
3 to drag on
□ La réunion a traîné jusqu'à midi. The meeting dragged on till 12 o'clock.
▪ **traîner des pieds** to drag one's feet
▪ **laisser traîner quelque chose** to leave something lying around □ Ne laisse pas traîner tes affaires. Don't leave your things lying around.

le **train-train** MASC NOUN
humdrum routine

traire VERB [85]
to milk

le **trait** MASC NOUN
1 line
□ Tracez un trait. Draw a line.
2 feature
□ Elle a les traits fins. She has delicate features.
▪ **boire quelque chose d'un trait** to drink something down in one gulp
▪ **un trait d'union** a hyphen

★ le **traitement** MASC NOUN
treatment

traiter VERB [28]
to treat
□ Elle le traite comme un chien. She treats him like a dog.
▪ **Il m'a traité d'imbécile.** He called me an idiot.
▪ **traiter de** to be about □ Cet article traite des sans-abri. This article is about the homeless.

le **traiteur** MASC NOUN
caterer

★ le **trajet** MASC NOUN
1 journey
□ Il n'a pas arrêté de parler pendant tout le trajet. He talked for the whole journey. □ J'ai une heure de trajet pour aller au travail. My journey to work takes an hour.
2 route
□ C'est le trajet le plus court. It's the shortest route.

le **tramway** MASC NOUN
tram

tranchant (FEM **tranchante**) ADJECTIVE
sharp (*knife*)

★ la **tranche** FEM NOUN
slice

★ **tranquille** (FEM **tranquille**) ADJECTIVE
quiet
□ Cette rue est très tranquille. This is a very quiet street.
▪ **Sois tranquille, il ne va rien lui arriver.** Don't worry, nothing will happen to him.
▪ **Tiens-toi tranquille!** Be quiet!
▪ **Laisse-moi tranquille.** Leave me alone.
▪ **Laisse ça tranquille.** Leave it alone.

tranquillement ADVERB
quietly
□ Nous étions tranquillement installés dans le salon. We were just sitting quietly in the living room.
▪ **Je peux travailler tranquillement cinq minutes?** Can I have five minutes to myself to work in peace?

la **tranquillité** FEM NOUN
peace and quiet

transférer VERB [34]
to transfer

★ **transformer** VERB [28]
1 to transform
□ Son séjour en France l'a transformé. His stay in France has transformed him.
2 to convert
□ Ils ont transformé la grange en garage. They've converted the barn into a garage.
▪ **se transformer en** to turn into □ La chenille se transforme en papillon. The caterpillar turns into a butterfly.

la **transfusion** FEM NOUN
▪ **une transfusion sanguine** a blood transfusion

transiger VERB [45]
to compromise

French-English

t

French-English

transmettre VERB [47]
■ **transmettre quelque chose à quelqu'un** to pass something on to somebody

transpercer VERB [12]
to go through
□ La pluie a transpercé mes vêtements. The rain went through my clothes.

la **transpiration** FEM NOUN
perspiration

transpirer VERB [28]
to perspire

★ le **transport** MASC NOUN
transport
■ **les transports en commun** public transport

★ **transporter** VERB [28]
1 to carry
□ Le train transportait des marchandises. The train was carrying freight.
2 to move
□ Je ne sais pas comment je vais transporter mes affaires. I don't know how I'm going to move my stuff.

traumatiser VERB [28]
to traumatize

★ le **travail** (PL les **travaux**) MASC NOUN
1 work
□ J'ai beaucoup de travail. I've got a lot of work.
2 job
□ Il a un travail intéressant. He's got an interesting job.
■ **Il est sans travail depuis un an.** He has been out of work for a year.
■ **le travail au noir** moonlighting

★ **travailler** VERB [28]
to work

★ **travailleur** (FEM **travailleuse**) ADJECTIVE
▷ *see also* **travailleur** NOUN, **travailleuse** NOUN
hard-working

★ le **travailleur** MASC NOUN
▷ *see also* **travailleur** ADJECTIVE
worker

★ la **travailleuse** FEM NOUN
▷ *see also* **travailleur** ADJECTIVE
worker

les **travaillistes** MASC PL NOUN
the Labour Party *sing*

les **travaux** MASC PL NOUN
1 work *sing*
□ des travaux de construction building work
2 roadworks
□ Il y a beaucoup de bruit à cause des travaux dans la rue. There's a lot of noise from the roadworks.
■ **être en travaux** to be undergoing alterations
■ **les travaux dirigés** supervised practical work
■ **les travaux manuels** handicrafts
■ **les travaux ménagers** housework
■ **les travaux pratiques** practical work

★ le **travers** MASC NOUN
■ **en travers de** across □ Il y avait un arbre en travers de la route. There was a tree lying across the road.
■ **de travers** crooked □ Son chapeau était de travers. His hat was crooked.
■ **comprendre de travers** to misunderstand
■ **Elle comprend toujours tout de travers.** She always gets the wrong idea.
■ **J'ai avalé de travers.** Something went down the wrong way.
■ **à travers** through □ Cette vitre est tellement sale qu'on ne voit rien à travers. This window is so dirty you can't see anything through it.

★ la **traversée** FEM NOUN
crossing

★ **traverser** VERB [28]
1 to cross
□ Traversez la rue. Cross the street.
2 to go through
□ Nous avons traversé la France pour aller en Espagne. We went through France on the way to Spain. □ La pluie a traversé mon manteau. The rain went through my coat.

le **traversin** MASC NOUN
bolster

trébucher VERB [28]
to trip up

le **trèfle** MASC NOUN
1 clover
2 clubs (*at cards*)
□ le roi de trèfle the king of clubs

★ **treize** NUMBER
thirteen
□ Il a treize ans. He's thirteen. □ à treize heures at 1 p.m.
■ **le treize février** the thirteenth of February

★ **treizième** (FEM **treizième**) ADJECTIVE
thirteenth

le **tréma** MASC NOUN
diaeresis

★ le **tremblement de terre** MASC NOUN
earthquake

★ **trembler** VERB [28]
to shake
□ trembler de peur to shake with fear
■ **trembler de froid** to shiver

trempé (FEM **trempée**) ADJECTIVE
soaking wet
■ **trempé jusqu'aux os** soaked to the skin

★ **tremper** VERB [28]
to soak

t

■ **tremper sa main dans l'eau** to dip one's hand in the water

le **tremplin** MASC NOUN
springboard

la **trentaine** FEM NOUN
about thirty
□ une trentaine de personnes about thirty people
■ **Il a la trentaine.** He's in his thirties.

★ **trente** NUMBER
thirty
□ Elle a trente ans. She's thirty.
■ **le trente janvier** the thirtieth of January
■ **trente et un** thirty-one
■ **trente-deux** thirty-two

★ **trentième** (FEM **trentième**) ADJECTIVE
thirtieth

★ **très** ADVERB
very
□ J'ai très faim. I'm very hungry.

★ le **trésor** MASC NOUN
treasure

la **tresse** FEM NOUN
plait

le **triangle** MASC NOUN
triangle

la **tribu** FEM NOUN
tribe

le **tribunal** (PL les **tribunaux**) MASC NOUN
court

★ **tricher** VERB [28]
to cheat

tricolore (FEM **tricolore**) ADJECTIVE
three-coloured
■ **le drapeau tricolore** the French flag

DID YOU KNOW...?
le drapeau tricolore is the French flag which is blue, white and red.

★ le **tricot** MASC NOUN
1 knitting
□ On fait du tricot à l'école. We do knitting at school.
2 sweater
□ Mets un tricot, il fait froid. Put a sweater on, it's cold.

★ **tricoter** VERB [28]
to knit

trier VERB [19]
to sort out
□ Je vais trier mes papiers avant les vacances. I'm going to sort out my papers before the holidays.

★ le **trimestre** MASC NOUN
term

trinquer VERB [28]
to clink glasses

le **triomphe** MASC NOUN
triumph

triompher VERB [28]
to triumph

les **tripes** FEM PL NOUN
tripe

le **triple** MASC NOUN
■ **Ça m'a coûté le triple.** It cost me three times as much.
■ **Il gagne le triple de mon salaire.** He earns three times my salary.

tripler VERB [28]
to treble

les **triplés** MASC PL NOUN
triplets

★ **triste** (FEM **triste**) ADJECTIVE
sad

la **tristesse** FEM NOUN
sadness

le **trognon** MASC NOUN
core
□ un trognon de pomme an apple core

★ **trois** NUMBER
three
□ à trois heures du matin at three in the morning □ Elle a trois ans. She's three. □ trois fois three times
■ **le trois février** the third of February

★ **troisième** (FEM **troisième**) ADJECTIVE
▷ *see also* **troisième** NOUN
third
□ au troisième étage on the third floor

★ la **troisième** FEM NOUN
▷ *see also* **troisième** ADJECTIVE
year 10
□ Mon frère est en troisième. My brother's in year 10.

DID YOU KNOW...?
In French secondary schools, years are counted from the **sixième** (youngest) to **première** and **terminale** (oldest).

les **trois-quarts** MASC PL NOUN
three-quarters
□ les trois-quarts de la classe three-quarters of the class

le **trombone** MASC NOUN
1 trombone
□ Il joue du trombone. He plays the trombone.
2 paper clip

la **trompe** FEM NOUN
trunk
□ la trompe d'un éléphant an elephant's trunk

★ **tromper** VERB [28]
to deceive
■ **se tromper** to make a mistake □ Tout le monde peut se tromper. Anyone can make a mistake.

■ **se tromper de jour** to get the wrong day
■ **Vous vous êtes trompé de numéro.** You've got the wrong number.

★ la **trompette** FEM NOUN
trumpet
□ Il joue de la trompette. He plays the trumpet.
■ **Il a le nez en trompette.** He's got a turned-up nose.

le **tronc** MASC NOUN
trunk
□ un tronc d'arbre a tree trunk

★ **trop** ADVERB
1 too
□ Il conduit trop vite. He drives too fast.
2 too much
□ J'ai trop mangé. I've eaten too much.
■ **trop de** 1 too much □ J'ai acheté trop de pain. I bought too much bread. □ trois euros de trop 3 euros too much 2 too many □ J'ai apporté trop de vêtements. I've brought too many clothes.
■ **trois personnes de trop** 3 people too many

le **tropique** MASC NOUN
tropic

★ le **trottoir** MASC NOUN
pavement

★ le **trou** MASC NOUN
hole
■ **J'ai eu un trou de mémoire.** My mind went blank.

trouble (FEM **trouble**) ADJECTIVE, ADVERB
cloudy
□ L'eau est trouble. The water's cloudy.
■ **Sans mes lunettes je vois trouble.** Without my glasses I can't see properly.

les **troubles** MASC PL NOUN
■ **une période de troubles politiques** a period of political instability

trouer VERB [28]
to make a hole in
□ Il a troué la moquette avec sa cigarette. He made a hole in the carpet with his cigarette.

la **trouille** FEM NOUN
■ **avoir la trouille** (*informal*) to be scared to death

la **troupe** FEM NOUN
troop
■ **une troupe de théâtre** a theatre company

le **troupeau** (PL les **troupeaux**) MASC NOUN
■ **un troupeau de moutons** a flock of sheep
■ **un troupeau de vaches** a herd of cows

★ la **trousse** FEM NOUN
pencil case
■ **une trousse de secours** a first-aid kit
■ **une trousse de toilette** a toilet bag

★ **trouver** VERB [28]
1 to find
□ Je ne trouve pas mes lunettes. I can't find my glasses.
2 to think
□ Je trouve que c'est bête. I think it's stupid.
■ **se trouver** to be □ Où se trouve la poste? Where is the post office? □ Nice se trouve dans le sud de la France. Nice is in the South of France.
■ **se trouver mal** to pass out

★ le **truc** MASC NOUN (*informal*)
1 thing
□ un truc en plastique a plastic thing □ J'ai plein de trucs à faire ce week-end. I've got loads of things to do this weekend.
2 trick
□ Je vais te montrer un truc qui réussit à tous les coups. I'll show you a trick that never fails.

★ la **truite** FEM NOUN
trout

★ le **T-shirt** MASC NOUN
T-shirt

TSVP ABBREVIATION (= *tournez s'il vous plaît*)
PTO (= *please turn over*)

★ **tu** PRONOUN

> **tu** is used when speaking to one person your own age or younger.

you
□ Est-ce que tu as un animal familier? Have you got a pet?

le **tuba** MASC NOUN
1 tuba
□ Je joue du tuba. I play the tuba.
2 snorkel

★ le **tube** MASC NOUN
1 tube
□ un tube de dentifrice a tube of toothpaste
■ **un tube de rouge à lèvres** a lipstick
2 hit
□ Ça va être le tube de l'été. It's going to be this summer's hit.

★ **tuer** VERB [28]
to kill
■ **se tuer** to get killed □ Il s'est tué dans un accident de voiture. He got killed in a car accident.

tue-tête
■ **à tue-tête** ADVERB at the top of one's voice
□ crier à tue-tête to shout at the top of one's voice □ Il chantait à tue-tête. He was singing at the top of his voice.

la **tuile** FEM NOUN
tile
□ un toit en tuiles a tiled roof

la **tunique** FEM NOUN
tunic

★la **Tunisie** FEM NOUN
Tunisia

★**tunisien** (FEM **tunisienne**) ADJECTIVE, NOUN
Tunisian

★le **tunnel** MASC NOUN
tunnel
■ **le tunnel sous la Manche** the Channel Tunnel

turbulent (FEM **turbulente**) ADJECTIVE
boisterous

turc (FEM **turque**) ADJECTIVE, NOUN
Turkish
□ Il parle turc. He speaks Turkish.
■ **un Turc** a Turk (*man*)
■ **une Turque** a Turk (*woman*)

la **Turquie** FEM NOUN
Turkey

★**tutoyer** VERB [53]
■ **tutoyer quelqu'un** to address somebody as 'tu'
■ **On se tutoie?** Shall we use 'tu' with each other?

DID YOU KNOW...?
tutoyer quelqu'un means to use **tu** when speaking to someone, rather than **vous**.
Use **tu** only when speaking to one person you know well or who is your own age or younger; use **vous** to everyone else. If in doubt use **vous**.

le **tuyau** (PL les **tuyaux**) MASC NOUN
1 pipe
■ **un tuyau d'arrosage** a hosepipe
2 tip
□ Il m'a donné un bon tuyau. (*informal*) He gave me a handy tip.

★la **TVA** FEM NOUN (= *taxe sur la valeur ajoutée*)
VAT

le **tweet** MASC NOUN
tweet

tweeter VERB [28]
to tweet

le **tympan** MASC NOUN
eardrum

★le **type** MASC NOUN (*informal*)
guy
□ C'est un type formidable. He's a great guy.

★**typique** (FEM **typique**) ADJECTIVE
typical

le **tyran** MASC NOUN
tyrant
□ C'est un vrai tyran. He's a real tyrant.

le/la **tzigane** MASC/FEM NOUN
gipsy

Uu

l'**UE** FEM NOUN (= *Union européenne*)
the EU (= *European Union*)

★ **un** (FEM **une**) ARTICLE, MASC PRONOUN, MASC ADJECTIVE

1 a
□ un garçon a boy

2 an
□ un œuf an egg

3 one
□ l'un des meilleurs one of the best □ un citron et deux oranges one lemon and two oranges □ Combien de timbres? — Un. How many stamps? — One. □ Elle a un an. She's one year old.

■ **l'un ..., l'autre ...** one ..., the other ... □ L'un est grand, l'autre est petit. One is tall, the other is short.

■ **les uns ..., les autres ...** some ..., others ... □ Les uns marchaient, les autres couraient. Some were walking, others were running.

■ **l'un ou l'autre** either of them □ Prends l'un ou l'autre, ça m'est égal. Take either of them, I don't mind.

■ **un par un** one by one □ Ils entraient un par un. They went in one by one.

unanime (FEM **unanime**) ADJECTIVE
unanimous

l'**unanimité** FEM NOUN
■ **à l'unanimité** unanimously

★ **une** ARTICLE, FEM PRONOUN, FEM ADJECTIVE

1 a
□ une fille a girl

2 an
□ une pomme an apple

3 one
□ une pomme et deux bananes one apple and two bananas □ Combien de cartes postales? — Une. How many postcards? — One. □ à une heure du matin at one in the morning □ l'une des meilleures one of the best

■ **l'une ..., l'autre ...** one ..., the other ... □ L'une est grande, l'autre est petite. One is tall, the other is short.

■ **les unes..., les autres...** some ..., others ... □ Les unes marchaient, les autres couraient. Some were walking, others were running.

■ **l'une ou l'autre** either of them □ Prends l'une ou l'autre, ça m'est égal. Take either of them, I don't mind.

■ **une par une** one by one □ Elles entraient une par une. They went in one by one.

★ **uni** (FEM **unie**) ADJECTIVE

1 plain
□ un tissu uni a plain fabric

2 close-knit
□ une famille unie a close-knit family

★ l'**uniforme** MASC NOUN
uniform

l'**union** FEM NOUN
union
■ **l'Union européenne** the European Union

★ **unique** (FEM **unique**) ADJECTIVE
unique
□ Tout individu a des empreintes uniques. Everyone's fingerprints are unique. □ C'est une occasion unique. It's a unique opportunity.

■ **Il est fils unique.** He's an only child.

■ **Elle est fille unique.** She's an only child.

uniquement ADVERB
only

★ l'**unité** FEM NOUN

1 unity
□ l'unité européenne European unity

2 unit
□ une unité de mesure a unit of measurement

l'**univers** MASC NOUN
universe

universitaire (FEM **universitaire**) ADJECTIVE
university
□ un diplôme universitaire a university degree

■ **faire des études universitaires** to study at university

★ l'**université** FEM NOUN
university
□ aller à l'université to go to university

★ l'**urgence** FEM NOUN
■ **C'est une urgence.** It's urgent.

■ **Il n'y a pas urgence.** It's not urgent.

■ **le service des urgences** the accident and emergency department

■ **Il a été transporté d'urgence à l'hôpital.** He was rushed to hospital.

■ **Téléphonez d'urgence.** Phone as soon as possible.

★ **urgent** (FEM **urgente**) ADJECTIVE
urgent

l'**urine** FEM NOUN
urine

les **USA** MASC PL NOUN
USA
■ **aux USA** **1** in the USA **2** to the USA

l'**usage** MASC NOUN
use
□ à usage interne **for internal use** □ à usage externe **for external use only**
■ **hors d'usage** out of action □ Cet appareil est hors d'usage. **That machine's out of action.**

usagé (FEM **usagée**) ADJECTIVE
1 old
□ un manteau usagé **an old coat**
2 used
□ une seringue usagée **a used syringe**

l'**usager** MASC NOUN
user
□ les usagers de la route **road users**

★ **usé** (FEM **usée**) ADJECTIVE
worn
□ Mon jean est un peu usé. **My jeans are a bit worn.**

★ s'**user** VERB [28]
to wear out
□ Mes baskets se sont usées en quinze jours. **My trainers wore out in two weeks.**

★ l'**usine** FEM NOUN
factory
□ une usine de sardines **a sardine factory**

l'**ustensile** MASC NOUN
■ **un ustensile de cuisine** a kitchen utensil

usuel (FEM **usuelle**) ADJECTIVE
everyday
□ la langue usuelle **everyday language**

★ **utile** (FEM **utile**) ADJECTIVE
useful

l'**utilisation** FEM NOUN
use
□ L'utilisation des calculatrices est interdite. **It is forbidden to use calculators.**

★ **utiliser** VERB [28]
to use

l'**utilité** FEM NOUN
use
□ Cet objet n'est pas d'une grande utilité. **This object isn't much use.**

Vv

va VERB ▷ *see* **aller**

★ les **vacances** FEM PL NOUN
holidays
□ aller en vacances to go on holiday □ être en vacances to be on holiday
■ **les vacances de Noël** the Christmas holidays
■ **les vacances de Pâques** the Easter holidays
■ **les grandes vacances** the summer holidays

le **vacancier** MASC NOUN
holiday-maker

la **vacancière** FEM NOUN
holiday-maker

le **vacarme** MASC NOUN
racket
□ Qu'est-ce que c'est que ce vacarme? What's all this racket?

le **vaccin** MASC NOUN
vaccination

la **vaccination** FEM NOUN
vaccination
□ La vaccination est obligatoire. Vaccination is compulsory.

vacciner VERB [28]
to vaccinate
□ se faire vacciner contre la rubéole to be vaccinated against German measles

★ la **vache** FEM NOUN
▷ *see also* **vache** ADJECTIVE
cow

★ **vache** (FEM **vache**) ADJECTIVE (*informal*)
▷ *see also* **vache** NOUN
mean
□ C'est vraiment vache, ce qu'il a dit. What he said was really mean. □ Il est vache. He's a mean sod.

vachement ADVERB (*informal*)
really
□ Viens te baigner, l'eau est vachement chaude. Come in the water, it's really warm.

le **vagabond** MASC NOUN
tramp

le **vagin** MASC NOUN
vagina

★ la **vague** FEM NOUN
▷ *see also* **vague** ADJECTIVE
wave (*in sea*)
■ **une vague de chaleur** a heat wave

vague (FEM **vague**) ADJECTIVE
▷ *see also* **vague** NOUN
vague
□ J'ai un vague souvenir de lui. I vaguely remember him.

vain (FEM **vaine**) ADJECTIVE
■ **en vain** in vain

vaincre VERB [86]
1 to defeat
□ L'armée a été vaincue. The army was defeated.
2 to overcome
□ Il a réussi à vaincre sa timidité. He managed to overcome his shyness.

le **vainqueur** MASC NOUN
winner

vais VERB ▷ *see* **aller**
■ **Je vais écrire à mes cousins.** I'm going to write to my cousins.

le **vaisseau** (PL les **vaisseaux**) MASC NOUN
■ **un vaisseau spatial** a spaceship
■ **un vaisseau sanguin** a blood vessel

★ la **vaisselle** FEM NOUN
1 washing-up
□ Je vais faire la vaisselle. I'll do the washing-up.
2 dishes
□ Tu peux ranger la vaisselle s'il te plaît? Can you put the dishes away please?

★ **valable** (FEM **valable**) ADJECTIVE
valid
□ Ce billet d'avion est valable un an. This plane ticket is valid for one year.

le **valet** MASC NOUN
jack (*in card games*)
□ le valet de carreau the jack of diamonds

★ la **valeur** FEM NOUN
value
□ sans valeur of no value
■ **des objets de valeur** valuables □ Ne laissez pas d'objets de valeur dans votre chambre. Don't leave any valuables in your room.

valider VERB [28]
to stamp
□ Vous devez faire valider votre billet avant votre départ. You must get your ticket stamped before you leave.

★ la **valise** FEM NOUN
suitcase
■ **faire sa valise** to pack

★ la **vallée** FEM NOUN
valley

★ **valoir** VERB [87]
to be worth
□ Ça vaut combien? How much is it worth?
□ Cette voiture vaut très cher. This car's worth a lot of money.
■ **Ça vaut mieux.** That would be better. □ Il vaut mieux ne rien dire. It would be better to say nothing.
■ **valoir la peine** to be worth it □ Ça vaudrait la peine d'essayer. It would be worth a try.

le **vampire** MASC NOUN
vampire

★ le **vandalisme** MASC NOUN
vandalism

★ la **vanille** FEM NOUN
vanilla
□ une glace à la vanille a vanilla ice cream

la **vanité** FEM NOUN
vanity

vaniteux (FEM **vaniteuse**) ADJECTIVE
conceited

se **vanter** VERB [28]
to boast

★ la **vapeur** FEM NOUN
steam
□ des légumes cuits à la vapeur steamed vegetables

la **varappe** FEM NOUN
rock climbing
□ faire de la varappe to go rock climbing

★ **variable** (FEM **variable**) ADJECTIVE
changeable (*weather*)

la **varicelle** FEM NOUN
chickenpox
□ Elle a la varicelle. She's got chickenpox.

★ **varié** (FEM **variée**) ADJECTIVE
varied
□ Son travail est très varié. His job is very varied.

★ **varier** VERB [19]
to vary
■ **Le menu varie tous les jours.** The menu changes every day.

la **variété** FEM NOUN
variety
□ Il n'y a pas beaucoup de variété. There isn't much variety.
■ **une émission de variétés** a television variety show

vas VERB ▷ *see* **aller**

★ le **vase** MASC NOUN
▷ *see also* **vase** NOUN
vase

★ la **vase** FEM NOUN
▷ *see also* **vase** NOUN
mud

vaste (FEM **vaste**) ADJECTIVE
vast

vaudrait, vaut VERB ▷ *see* **valoir**

le **vautour** MASC NOUN
vulture

★ le **veau** (PL les **veaux**) MASC NOUN
1 calf (*animal*)
2 veal (*meat*)

vécu VERB ▷ *see* **vivre**
■ **Il a vécu à Paris pendant dix ans.** He lived in Paris for ten years.

★ la **vedette** FEM NOUN
1 star
□ une vedette de cinéma a film star
2 motor boat
■ **une vedette de police** a police launch

végétal (FEM **végétale**, MASC PL **végétaux**) ADJECTIVE
vegetable
□ l'huile végétale vegetable oil

★ **végétalien** (FEM **végétalienne**) ADJECTIVE
vegan
□ Je suis végétalien. I'm a vegan.

★ **végétarien** (FEM **végétarienne**) ADJECTIVE
vegetarian
□ Je suis végétarien. I'm a vegetarian.

la **végétation** FEM NOUN
vegetation

★ le **véhicule** MASC NOUN
vehicle

★ la **veille** FEM NOUN
the day before
□ la veille de son départ the day before he left
□ la veille au soir the previous evening
■ **la veille de Noël** Christmas Eve
■ **la veille du jour de l'An** New Year's Eve

veiller VERB [28]
to stay up
■ **veiller sur quelqu'un** to watch over somebody

le **veinard** MASC NOUN (*informal*)
lucky devil

la **veinarde** FEM NOUN (*informal*)
lucky devil

la **veinarde** FEM NOUN (*informal*)
lucky devil

★ la **veine** FEM NOUN
vein
■ **avoir de la veine** (*informal*) to be lucky

le/la **véliplanchiste** MASC/FEM NOUN
windsurfer

★ le **vélo** MASC NOUN
bike
□ faire du vélo to go cycling
■ **un vélo tout-terrain** a mountain bike

★ le **vélomoteur** MASC NOUN
moped

le **velours** MASC NOUN
velvet
□ une robe en velours a velvet dress
■ **le velours côtelé** corduroy □ un pantalon en velours côtelé corduroy trousers

les **vendanges** FEM PL NOUN
grape harvest *sing*
□ On fait les vendanges en septembre. The grape harvest is in September.

★ le **vendeur** MASC NOUN
shop assistant

★ la **vendeuse** FEM NOUN
shop assistant

★ **vendre** VERB [88]
to sell
■ **vendre quelque chose à quelqu'un** to sell somebody something □ Il m'a vendu son vélo. He sold me his bike.
■ **'à vendre'** 'for sale'

★ le **vendredi** MASC NOUN
1 Friday
□ Aujourd'hui, nous sommes vendredi. It's Friday today.
2 on Friday
□ Il est venu vendredi. He came on Friday.
■ **le vendredi** on Fridays □ Je joue au foot le vendredi. I play football on Fridays.
■ **tous les vendredis** every Friday
■ **vendredi dernier** last Friday
■ **vendredi prochain** next Friday
■ **le Vendredi saint** Good Friday

vénéneux (FEM **vénéneuse**) ADJECTIVE
poisonous (*plant*)
□ un champignon vénéneux a poisonous mushroom

la **vengeance** FEM NOUN
revenge

se **venger** VERB [45]
to get revenge

venimeux (FEM **venimeuse**) ADJECTIVE
poisonous (*animal*)
□ un serpent venimeux a poisonous snake

le **venin** MASC NOUN
poison

★ **venir** VERB [89, *aux* être]
to come
□ Il viendra demain. He'll come tomorrow. □ Il est venu nous voir. He came to see us.
■ **venir de** to have just □ Je viens de le voir. I've just seen him. □ Je viens de lui téléphoner. I've just phoned him.
■ **faire venir quelqu'un** to call somebody out □ faire venir le médecin to call the doctor out

★ le **vent** MASC NOUN
wind
□ Il y a du vent. It's windy.

★ la **vente** FEM NOUN
sale
■ **en vente** on sale □ Ce modèle est en vente dans les grands magasins. This model is on sale in the department stores.
■ **la vente par téléphone** telesales
■ **une vente aux enchères** an auction

le **ventilateur** MASC NOUN
fan (*for cooling*)

★ le **ventre** MASC NOUN
stomach
□ avoir mal au ventre to have stomachache

venu VERB ▷ *see* **venir**

le **ver** MASC NOUN
worm
■ **un ver de terre** an earthworm

le **verbe** MASC NOUN
verb

le **verdict** MASC NOUN
verdict

le **verger** MASC NOUN
orchard

verglacé (FEM **verglacée**) ADJECTIVE
icy
□ La route était verglacée. The road was icy.

★ le **verglas** MASC NOUN
black ice

véridique (FEM **véridique**) ADJECTIVE
truthful

la **vérification** FEM NOUN
check
□ une vérification d'identité an identity check

★ **vérifier** VERB [19]
to check

véritable (FEM **véritable**) ADJECTIVE
real
□ C'était un véritable cauchemar. It was a real nightmare.
■ **en cuir véritable** made of real leather

★ la **vérité** FEM NOUN
truth
□ dire la vérité to tell the truth

verni (FEM **vernie**) ADJECTIVE
varnished
■ **des chaussures vernies** patent leather shoes

vernir VERB [38]
to varnish

le **vernis** MASC NOUN
varnish
□ le vernis à ongles nail varnish

verra, verrai, verras VERB ▷ *see* voir
■ **on verra ...** we'll see ...

★ le **verre** MASC NOUN
1 glass
□ une table en verre a glass table □ un verre d'eau a glass of water
■ **boire un verre** to have a drink
2 lens (*of spectacles*)
□ des verres de contact contact lenses

verrez, verrons, verront VERB ▷ *see* voir

le **verrou** MASC NOUN
bolt (*on door*)

verrouiller VERB [28]
to bolt
□ N'oublie pas de verrouiller la porte du garage. Don't forget to bolt the garage door.

la **verrue** FEM NOUN
wart

★ le **vers** MASC NOUN
▷ *see also* vers PREPOSITION
line (*of poetry*)
□ au troisième vers in the third line

★ **vers** PREPOSITION
▷ *see also* vers NOUN
1 towards
□ Il allait vers la gare. He was going towards the station.
2 at about
□ Il est rentré chez lui vers cinq heures. He went home at about 5 o'clock.

verse
■ **à verse** ADVERB □ Il pleut à verse. It's pouring with rain.

le **Verseau** MASC NOUN
Aquarius
□ Georges est Verseau. Georges is Aquarius.

le **versement** MASC NOUN
instalment
□ en cinq versements in 5 instalments

★ **verser** VERB [28]
to pour
□ Est-ce que tu peux me verser un verre d'eau? Could you pour me a glass of water?

★ la **version** FEM NOUN
1 version
2 translation (*from the foreign language*)
■ **un film en version originale** a film in the original language

le **verso** MASC NOUN
back (*of sheet of paper*)
■ **voir au verso** see overleaf

★ **vert** (FEM **verte**) ADJECTIVE
▷ *see also* vert NOUN
1 green
2 green (*ecological*)

le **vert** MASC NOUN
▷ *see also* vert ADJECTIVE
green
■ **les Verts** the Greens (*in politics*)

la **vertèbre** FEM NOUN
vertebra

vertical (FEM **verticale**, MASC PL **verticaux**) ADJECTIVE
vertical

le **vertige** MASC NOUN
vertigo
□ avoir le vertige to have vertigo

la **verveine** FEM NOUN
verbena tea

la **vessie** FEM NOUN
bladder

★ la **veste** FEM NOUN
jacket

★ le **vestiaire** MASC NOUN
1 cloakroom (*in theatre, museum*)
2 changing room (*at sports ground*)

★ le **vestibule** MASC NOUN
hall

★ le **vêtement** MASC NOUN
garment
■ **les vêtements** clothes

★ le/la **vétérinaire** MASC/FEM NOUN
vet
□ Elle est vétérinaire. She's a vet.

★ le **veuf** MASC NOUN
widower
□ Il est veuf. He's a widower.

veuille, veuillez, veuillons, veulent, veut VERB ▷ *see* vouloir
■ **Veuillez fermer la porte en sortant.** Please shut the door when you go out.

★ la **veuve** FEM NOUN
widow
□ Elle est veuve. She's a widow.

veux VERB ▷ *see* vouloir

vexer VERB [28]
■ **vexer quelqu'un** to hurt somebody's feelings
■ **se vexer** to be offended

★ la **viande** FEM NOUN
meat
■ **la viande hachée** mince

vibrer VERB [28]
to vibrate

le **vice** MASC NOUN
vice

vicieux (FEM **vicieuse**) ADJECTIVE
lecherous
■ **Il est un peu vicieux.** He's a bit of a lecher.

French-English

★ la **victime** FEM NOUN
victim

la **victoire** FEM NOUN
victory

★ **vide** (FEM **vide**) ADJECTIVE
▷ *see also* **vide** NOUN
empty

★ le **vide** MASC NOUN
▷ *see also* **vide** ADJECTIVE
vacuum
□ emballé sous vide vacuum-packed
■ **avoir peur du vide** to be afraid of heights

★ la **vidéo** FEM NOUN
▷ *see also* **vidéo** ADJECTIVE
video

★ **vidéo** (FEM+PL **vidéo**) ADJECTIVE
▷ *see also* **vidéo** NOUN
video
□ un jeu vidéo a video game □ une caméra vidéo a video camera

le **vidéoclip** MASC NOUN
music video

le **vidéoclub** MASC NOUN
video shop

la **vidéosurveillance** FEM NOUN
CCTV

★ **vider** VERB [28]
to empty

★ la **vie** FEM NOUN
life
■ **être en vie** to be alive

★ **vieil** MASC ADJECTIVE

vieil is used in place of **vieux** when the noun begins with a vowel sound.

old
□ un vieil arbre an old tree □ un vieil homme an old man

★ le **vieillard** MASC NOUN
old man

★ **vieille** FEM ADJECTIVE ▷ *see* **vieux**

★ la **vieille** FEM NOUN
▷ *see also* **vieux** ADJECTIVE
old woman
■ **Eh bien, ma vieille ...** (*informal*) Well, my dear ...

la **vieillesse** FEM NOUN
old age

vieillir VERB [38]
to age
□ Il a beaucoup vieilli. He's aged a lot.

viendrai, vienne, viens VERB ▷ *see* venir
■ **Je viendrai dès que possible.** I'll come as soon as possible.
■ **Je voudrais que tu viennes.** I'd like you to come.
■ **Viens ici!** Come here!

la **Vierge** FEM NOUN
▷ *see also* **vierge** ADJECTIVE
Virgo
□ Axel est Vierge. Axel is Virgo.
■ **la Vierge** the Virgin Mary

vierge (FEM **vierge**) ADJECTIVE
▷ *see also* **Vierge** NOUN
1 virgin
□ Il est vierge. He's a virgin.
2 blank
□ un CD vierge a blank CD

le **Viêt-Nam** MASC NOUN
Vietnam

vietnamien (FEM **vietnamienne**) ADJECTIVE, NOUN
Vietnamese
■ **un Vietnamien** a Vietnamese (*man*)
■ **une Vietnamienne** a Vietnamese (*woman*)
■ **les Vietnamiens** the Vietnamese

★ **vieux** (FEM **vieille**) ADJECTIVE
▷ *see also* **vieux** NOUN

The masculine singular form **vieux** changes to **vieil** before a vowel or most words beginning with 'h'.

old
□ Il fait plus vieux que son âge. He looks older than he is. □ une vieille dame an old lady

★ le **vieux** MASC NOUN
▷ *see also* **vieux** ADJECTIVE
old man
■ **Eh bien, mon vieux ...** (*informal*) Well, my old mate ...
■ **les vieux** old people

vieux jeu (FEM+PL **vieux jeu**) ADJECTIVE
old-fashioned
□ Il est un peu vieux jeu. He's a bit old-fashioned.

★ **vif** (FEM **vive**) ADJECTIVE
1 sharp (*mentally*)
□ Il est très vif. He's very sharp.
■ **avoir l'esprit vif** to be quick-witted
2 crisp
□ L'air est plus vif à la campagne qu'en ville. The air is crisper in the country than in the town.
3 bright (*colour*)
□ un bleu vif a bright blue
■ **à vive allure** at a brisk pace
■ **de vive voix** in person
■ **Je te le dirai de vive voix.** I'll tell you about it when I see you.

la **vigne** FEM NOUN
vine
■ **des champs de vigne** vineyards

★ le **vigneron** MASC NOUN
wine grower

★ le **vignoble** MASC NOUN
vineyard

★ **vilain** (FEM **vilaine**) ADJECTIVE
1 naughty
□ C'est très vilain de dire des mensonges. It's very naughty to tell lies.
2 ugly
□ Il n'est pas vilain. He's not bad-looking.

la **villa** FEM NOUN
villa
□ une villa en multipropriété a time-share villa

★ le **village** MASC NOUN
village

le **villageois** MASC NOUN
villager

la **villageoise** FEM NOUN
villager

★ la **ville** FEM NOUN
town
□ Je vais en ville. I'm going into town.
■ **une grande ville** a city

★ le **vin** MASC NOUN
wine
□ le vin blanc white wine □ le vin rouge red wine □ le vin de pays the local wine □ le vin ordinaire table wine

★ le **vinaigre** MASC NOUN
vinegar

la **vinaigrette** FEM NOUN
French dressing

★ **vingt** NUMBER
twenty
□ Elle a vingt ans. She's twenty. □ à vingt heures at 8 p.m.
■ **le vingt février** the twentieth of February
■ **vingt et un** twenty-one
■ **vingt-deux** twenty-two

★ la **vingtaine** FEM NOUN
about twenty
□ une vingtaine de personnes about twenty people
■ **Il a une vingtaine d'années.** He's about twenty.

★ **vingtième** (FEM **vingtième**) ADJECTIVE
twentieth

le **viol** MASC NOUN
rape

violemment ADVERB
violently

★ la **violence** FEM NOUN
violence
■ **violence conjugale** domestic violence

violent (FEM **violente**) ADJECTIVE
violent

violer VERB [28]
to rape

★ **violet** (FEM **violette**) ADJECTIVE
purple

la **violette** FEM NOUN
violet (*flower*)

★ le **violon** MASC NOUN
violin
□ Je joue du violon. I play the violin.

le **violoncelle** MASC NOUN
cello
□ Elle joue du violoncelle. She plays the cello.

le/la **violoniste** MASC/FEM NOUN
violinist

la **vipère** FEM NOUN
viper

★ le **virage** MASC NOUN
bend
□ une route pleine de virages dangereux a road full of dangerous bends

viral (FEM **virale**, MASC PL **viraux**) MASC ADJECTIVE
viral
■ **une vidéo virale** a viral video

la **virgule** FEM NOUN
1 comma
2 decimal point
□ trois virgule cinq three point five

le **virus** MASC NOUN
virus

vis VERB ▷ *see* **vivre**
▷ *see also* **vis** NOUN
■ **Je vis en Écosse.** I live in Scotland.

la **vis** FEM NOUN
▷ *see also* **vis** VERB
screw

le **visa** MASC NOUN
visa

★ le **visage** MASC NOUN
face
□ Elle a le visage rond. She's got a round face.

vis-à-vis de PREPOSITION
with regard to
□ Ce n'est pas très juste vis-à-vis de lui. It's not very fair to him.

viser VERB [28]
to aim at
□ Il faut viser la cible. You have to aim at the target.

★ la **visibilité** FEM NOUN
visibility

visible (FEM **visible**) ADJECTIVE
visible

la **visière** FEM NOUN
peak (*of cap*)

★ la **visite** FEM NOUN
visit
■ **rendre visite à quelqu'un** to visit

French-English

V

somebody □ Je vais rendre visite à mon grand-père. I'm going to visit my grandfather.
■ **avoir de la visite** to have visitors □ Nous avons de la visite aujourd'hui. We've got visitors today.
■ **une visite guidée** a guided tour
■ **une visite médicale** a medical examination

★ **visiter** VERB [28]
to visit

★ le **visiteur** MASC NOUN
visitor

★ la **visiteuse** FEM NOUN
visitor

le **vison** MASC NOUN
mink (*fur*)
□ un manteau en vison a mink coat

vit VERB ▷ *see* **vivre**

vital (FEM **vitale**, MASC PL **vitaux**) ADJECTIVE
vital
□ C'est une question vitale. It's of vital importance.

★ la **vitamine** FEM NOUN
vitamin

★ **vite** ADVERB
1 quick
□ Vite, ils arrivent! Quick, they're coming! □ Je peux aller dire au revoir à Claire? — Oui, mais fais vite! Can I go and say goodbye to Claire? — Yes, but be quick! □ Prenons la voiture, ça ira plus vite. Let's take the car, it'll be quicker.
■ **Le temps passe vite.** Time flies.
2 fast
□ Il roule trop vite. He drives too fast.
3 soon
□ Il va vite oublier. He'll soon forget.
■ **Il a vite compris.** He understood immediately.

★ la **vitesse** FEM NOUN
1 speed
□ à toute vitesse at top speed □ Nous sommes rentrés à toute vitesse. We rushed back home.
2 gear

★ le **viticulteur** MASC NOUN
wine grower
□ Mon oncle est viticulteur. My uncle is a wine grower.

le **vitrail** (PL les **vitraux**) MASC NOUN
stained-glass window

la **vitre** FEM NOUN
window
□ Il a cassé une vitre. He broke a window.

★ la **vitrine** FEM NOUN
shop window

vivant (FEM **vivante**) ADJECTIVE
1 living
□ les êtres vivants living creatures
■ **les expériences sur les animaux vivants** experiments on live animals
2 lively
□ Elle est très vivante. She's very lively.

★ **vive** FEM ADJECTIVE ▷ *see* **vif**

★ **vive** EXCLAMATION
■ **Vive le roi!** Long live the king!

vivement EXCLAMATION
■ **Vivement les vacances!** Roll on the holidays!

★ **vivre** VERB [91]
to live
□ J'aimerais vivre à l'étranger. I'd like to live abroad. □ Et ton grand-père? Il vit encore? What about your grandfather? Is he still alive?

vlan EXCLAMATION
wham!

la **VO** FEM NOUN
■ **un film en VO** a film in the original language

★ le **vocabulaire** MASC NOUN
vocabulary

la **vocation** FEM NOUN
vocation

★ le **vœu** (PL les **vœux**) MASC NOUN
wish
□ faire un vœu to make a wish □ Meilleurs vœux de bonne année! Best wishes for the New Year!

la **vogue** FEM NOUN
fashion
■ **C'est très en vogue en ce moment.** It's very fashionable at the moment.

★ **voici** PREPOSITION
1 this is
□ Voici mon frère et voilà ma sœur. This is my brother and that's my sister.
2 here is
□ Tu as perdu ton stylo? Tiens, en voici un autre. Have you lost your pen? Here's another one.
■ **Le voici!** Here he is! □ Tu veux tes clés? Tiens, les voici! You want your keys? Here you are!

★ la **voie** FEM NOUN
lane
□ une route à trois voies a 3-lane road
■ **par voie orale** orally □ à prendre par voie orale to be taken orally
■ **la voie ferrée** the railway track

★ **voilà** PREPOSITION
1 there is
□ Tiens! Voilà Paul. Look! There's Paul. □ Tu as perdu ton stylo? Tiens, en voilà un autre. Have you lost your pen? There's another one.
■ **Les voilà!** There they are!

2 that is
□ Voilà ma sœur. That's my sister.

★ la **voile** FEM NOUN
▷ *see also* **voile** NOUN
1 sail
2 sailing
□ faire de la voile to go sailing
■ **un bateau à voiles** a sailing boat

★ le **voile** MASC NOUN
▷ *see also* **voile** NOUN
veil
□ un voile de mariée a wedding veil

le **voilier** MASC NOUN
sailing boat

★ **voir** VERB [92]

PRESENT TENSE	
je vois	nous voyons
tu vois	vous voyez
il/elle voit	ils/elles voient
PAST PARTICIPLE	
vu	

to see
□ Venez me voir quand vous serez à Paris. Come and see me when you're in Paris. □ Je ne vois pas pourquoi il a fait ça. I can't see why he did that.
■ **faire voir quelque chose à quelqu'un** to show somebody something □ Il m'a fait voir sa maison. He showed me his house.
■ **se voir** to be obvious □ Ça fait des années qu'elle n'a pas joué au tennis — Oui, ça se voit! She hasn't played tennis for years — Yes, that's obvious! □ Est-ce que cette tache se voit? Does that stain show?
■ **avoir quelque chose à voir avec** to have something to do with □ Ça n'a rien à voir avec lui, c'est entre toi et moi. It's nothing to do with him, it's between you and me.
■ **Je ne peux vraiment pas la voir.** (*informal*) I really can't stand her.

★ le **voisin** MASC NOUN
neighbour

le **voisinage** MASC NOUN
■ **dans le voisinage** in the vicinity

★ la **voisine** FEM NOUN
neighbour

★ la **voiture** FEM NOUN
car
□ une voiture de sport a sports car

★ la **voix** (PL les **voix**) FEM NOUN
1 voice
□ à voix basse in a low voice
■ **à haute voix** aloud
2 vote
□ Il a obtenu cinquante pour cent des voix. He got 50% of the votes.

★ le **vol** MASC NOUN
1 flight
■ **à vol d'oiseau** as the crow flies
■ **le vol à voile** gliding
2 theft
□ un vol à main armée an armed robbery

la **volaille** FEM NOUN
poultry

★ le **volant** MASC NOUN
1 steering wheel
2 shuttlecock

le **volcan** MASC NOUN
volcano

la **volée** FEM NOUN
volley (*in tennis*)
■ **rattraper une balle à la volée** to catch a ball in mid-air

★ **voler** VERB [28]
1 to fly
□ J'aimerais savoir voler. I'd like to be able to fly.
2 to steal
□ On a volé mon appareil photo. My camera's been stolen.
■ **voler quelque chose à quelqu'un** to steal something from somebody □ Ça n'est pas son stylo, il me l'a volé. That's not his pen, he stole it from me.
■ **voler quelqu'un** to rob somebody

★ le **volet** MASC NOUN
shutter

★ le **voleur** MASC NOUN
thief
■ **Au voleur !** Stop thief!

★ la **voleuse** FEM NOUN
thief

★ le **volley** MASC NOUN
volleyball
□ jouer au volley to play volleyball

le/la **volontaire** MASC/FEM NOUN
volunteer

la **volonté** FEM NOUN
willpower
□ Il a beaucoup de volonté. He's got a lot of willpower.
■ **la bonne volonté** goodwill
■ **la mauvaise volonté** lack of goodwill

★ **volontiers** ADVERB
1 gladly
□ Je l'aiderais volontiers s'il me le demandait. I'd gladly help him if he asked me.
2 please
□ Voulez-vous boire quelque chose? — Volontiers! Would you like something to drink? — Yes, please!

le **volume** MASC NOUN
volume
□ un dictionnaire en deux volumes a two-volume dictionary

volumineux (FEM **volumineuse**) ADJECTIVE
bulky

★**vomir** VERB [38]
to vomit
□ Il a vomi toute la nuit. He was vomiting all night.

vont VERB ▷ *see* **aller**

★**vos** PL ADJECTIVE
your
□ Rangez vos jouets, les enfants! Children, put your toys away! □ Merci pour vos fleurs, M. Durand. Thanks for your flowers, Mr Durand.

le **vote** MASC NOUN
vote

voter VERB [28]
to vote

★**votre** (FEM **votre**, PL **vos**) ADJECTIVE
your
□ C'est votre manteau? Is this your coat?

vôtre PRONOUN
■ **le vôtre** yours □ J'aime bien notre prof de maths, mais le vôtre est plus patient. I like our maths teacher, but yours is more patient. □ À qui est cette écharpe? C'est la vôtre? Whose is this scarf? Is it yours?
■ **À la vôtre!** Cheers!

vôtres PL PRONOUN
■ **les vôtres** yours □ J'ai oublié mes lunettes de soleil. Vous avez les vôtres? I've forgotten my sunglasses. Have you got yours?

voudra, voudrai, voudrais, voudras, voudrez, voudrons, voudront VERB ▷ *see* **vouloir**
■ **Je voudrais ...** I'd like ... □ Je voudrais deux litres de lait, s'il vous plaît. I'd like two litres of milk, please. □ Je voudrais aller au concert. I'd like to go to the concert.

★**vouloir** VERB [93]

PRESENT TENSE	
je veux	nous voulons
tu veux	vous voulez
il/elle veut	ils/elles veulent
PAST PARTICIPLE	
voulu	

to want
□ Elle veut un vélo pour Noël. She wants a bike for Christmas. □ Je ne veux pas de dessert. I don't want any pudding. □ Il ne veut pas venir. He doesn't want to come. □ On va au cinéma? — Si tu veux. Shall we go to the cinema? — If you want.
■ **Je veux bien.** I'll be happy to. □ Je veux bien le faire à ta place si ça t'arrange. I'd be happy to do it for you if you prefer.
■ **Voulez-vous une tasse de thé? — Je veux bien.** Would you like a cup of tea? — Yes, please.
■ **sans le vouloir** without meaning to □ Je l'ai vexé sans le vouloir. I upset him without meaning to.
■ **en vouloir à quelqu'un** to be angry with somebody □ Il m'en veut de ne pas l'avoir invité. He's angry with me for not inviting him.
■ **vouloir dire** to mean □ Qu'est-ce que ça veut dire? What does that mean?

voulu VERB ▷ *see* **vouloir**

★**vous** SING, PL PRONOUN

> **vous** is used when speaking to several people, or to one person you don't know well.

1 you
□ Vous aimez la pizza? Do you like pizza?
2 to you
□ Je vous écrirai bientôt. I'll write to you soon.
3 yourself
□ Vous vous êtes fait mal? Have you hurt yourself?

> With reflexive verbs, **vous** is often not translated.

□ Est-ce que vous vous intéressez à la politique? Are you interested in politics?
■ **vous-même** yourself □ Vous l'avez fait vous-même? Did you do it yourself?

vouvoyer VERB [53]
■ **vouvoyer quelqu'un** to address somebody as 'vous' □ Est-ce que je dois vouvoyer ta sœur? Should I use 'vous' with your sister?

> **DID YOU KNOW...?**
> **vouvoyer quelqu'un** means to use **vous** when speaking to someone, rather than **tu**. Use **tu** only when speaking to one person you know well or who is your own age or younger; use **vous** to everyone else. If in doubt use **vous**.

★le **voyage** MASC NOUN
journey
□ Avez-vous fait bon voyage? Did you have a good journey?
■ **Bon voyage!** Have a good trip!

★**voyager** VERB [45]
to travel

★le **voyageur** MASC NOUN
passenger

★la **voyageuse** FEM NOUN
passenger

voyaient, voyais, voyait VERB ▷ *see* **voir**

la **voyelle** FEM NOUN
vowel

voyez, voyiez, voyions VERB ▷ *see* **voir**

voyons VERB ▷ *see* **voir**
1 let's see
□ Voyons ce qu'on peut faire. Let's see what we can do.

2 come on
□ Voyons, sois raisonnable! Come on, be reasonable!

★ le **voyou** MASC NOUN
hooligan

vrac
■ **en vrac** ADVERB loose □ du thé en vrac loose tea

★ **vrai** (FEM **vraie**) ADJECTIVE
true
□ une histoire vraie a true story □ C'est vrai? Is that true?
■ **à vrai dire** to tell the truth

★ **vraiment** ADVERB
really

vraisemblable (FEM **vraisemblable**) ADJECTIVE
likely
□ C'est peu vraisemblable. That's not very likely.
■ **une excuse vraisemblable** a convincing excuse

★ le **VTT** MASC NOUN (= *vélo tout-terrain*)
mountain bike

vu VERB ▷ *see* **voir**
□ J'ai vu ce film au cinéma. I saw this film at the cinema.
■ **être bien vu** (*person*) to be popular □ Est-ce qu'il est bien vu à l'école? Is he popular at school?
■ **C'est mal vu de fumer ici.** They don't like people smoking here.

★ la **vue** FEM NOUN
1 eyesight
□ J'ai une mauvaise vue. I've got bad eyesight.
2 view
□ Il y a une belle vue d'ici. There's a lovely view from here.
■ **à vue d'œil** visibly □ Elle grandit à vue d'œil. Every time you see her, she's got taller.

vulgaire (FEM **vulgaire**) ADJECTIVE
vulgar
□ Ne dis pas ça, c'est très vulgaire. Don't say that, it's very vulgar.

Ww

★ le **wagon** MASC NOUN
railway carriage

★ le **wagon-lit** (PL les **wagons-lits**) MASC NOUN
sleeper (*on train*)

★ le **wagon-restaurant** (PL les **wagons-restaurants**) MASC NOUN
restaurant car

wallon (FEM **wallonne**) ADJECTIVE, NOUN
Walloon (*French-speaking Belgian*)
■ **les Wallons** the French-speaking Belgians

la **Wallonie** FEM NOUN
French-speaking Belgium

les **W.-C.** MASC PL NOUN
toilet *sing*

le **Web** MASC NOUN
Web

la **webcam** FEM NOUN
webcam

le **webmaster** MASC NOUN
webmaster

le **webzine** MASC NOUN
webzine

★ le **week-end** MASC NOUN
weekend

★ le **western** MASC NOUN
western (*film*)

le **whisky** (PL les **whiskies**) MASC NOUN
whisky

le **wifi** MASC NOUN
Wi-Fi

xénophobe (FEM **xénophobe**) ADJECTIVE
prejudiced against foreigners

la **xénophobie** FEM NOUN
prejudice against foreigners

le **xylophone** MASC NOUN
xylophone
□ Elle joue du xylophone. She plays the xylophone.

★**y** PRONOUN
there
▫ Nous y sommes allés l'été dernier. We went there last summer. ▫ Regarde dans le tiroir: je pense que les clés y sont. Look in the drawer: I think the keys are in there.

y replaces phrases with **à** in constructions like the ones below:

▪ **Je pensais à l'examen. — Mais arrête d'y penser!** I was thinking about the exam. — Well, stop thinking about it!
▪ **Je ne m'attendais pas à ça. — Moi, je m'y attendais.** I wasn't expecting that. — I was expecting it.

★le **yaourt** MASC NOUN
yoghurt
▫ un yaourt nature a plain yoghurt ▫ un yaourt aux fruits a fruit yoghurt

★les **yeux** (SING **œil**) MASC PL NOUN
eyes
▫ Elle a les yeux bleus. She's got blue eyes.

★le **yoga** MASC NOUN
yoga

le **yoghourt** MASC NOUN
yoghurt

la **Yougoslavie** FEM NOUN
Yugoslavia
▪ **l'ex-Yougoslavie** the former Yugoslavia

youpi EXCLAMATION
yippee!

le **yoyo** MASC NOUN
yo-yo

Zz

zapper VERB [28]
to channel hop

le **zèbre** MASC NOUN
zebra

★ le **zéro** MASC NOUN
zero
■ **Ils ont gagné trois à zéro.** They won three-nil.

zézayer VERB [59]
to lisp
■ **Il zézaie.** He's got a lisp.

le **zigzag** MASC NOUN
■ **faire des zigzags** to zigzag

★ la **zone** FEM NOUN
zone
■ **une zone industrielle** an industrial estate
■ **une zone piétonne** a pedestrian precinct

★ le **zoo** MASC NOUN
zoo

zoologique (FEM **zoologique**) ADJECTIVE
zoological
□ un jardin zoologique zoological gardens

★ **zut** EXCLAMATION
oh heck!

French in Action

At home

Où habites-tu?	Where do you live?
J'habite ...	**I live ...**
dans un village	in a village
dans une petite ville	in a small town
dans le centre-ville	in the town centre
dans la banlieue de Londres	in the suburbs of London
à la campagne	in the countryside
au bord de la mer	at the seaside
à 100 km de Manchester	100 km from Manchester
au nord de Birmingham	north of Birmingham
dans une maison individuelle	in a detached house
dans une maison jumelée	in a semi-detached house
dans une maison à deux étages	in a two-storey house
dans un immeuble	in a block of flats
dans un lotissement	on a housing estate
J'habite dans un appartement ...	**I live in a flat ...**
au rez-de-chaussée	on the ground floor
au premier étage	on the first floor
au deuxième étage	on the second floor
au dernier étage	on the top floor
J'habite ...	**I live ...**
dans une maison moderne	in a modern house
dans une maison neuve	in a new house
dans une vieille maison	in an old house

À la maison	At home
Au rez-de-chaussée, il y a ...	**On the ground floor there is ...**
la cuisine	the kitchen
la salle de séjour	the living room
la salle à manger	the dining room
le salon	the lounge
À l'étage, il y a ...	**Upstairs there is ...**
ma chambre	my bedroom
la chambre de mon frère	my brother's bedroom
la chambre de mes parents	my parents' room
la chambre d'amis	the spare bedroom
la salle de bains	the bathroom
un bureau	a study
un jardin	a garden
un court de tennis	a tennis court
un voisin	a neighbour
les voisins d'à côté	the next-door neighbours

De la maison au collège	From home to school
Le collège est assez loin de chez moi.	School is quite a long way from my house.
J'habite à cinq minutes à pied du collège.	I live five minutes' walk from school.
Mon père m'emmène au collège en voiture.	My dad takes me to school in the car.
Je vais au collège en bus.	I go to school by bus.

Phrases utiles	Useful phrases
Chez moi, c'est tout petit.	My house is very small.
Ma chambre est bien rangée.	My room is tidy.
Je partage ma chambre avec mon frère.	I share my bedroom with my brother.
Mon meilleur copain habite dans la même rue que moi.	My best friend lives in the same street as me.
Il y a un court de tennis à côté de chez moi.	There's a tennis court next to my house.
Chez moi, il n'y a pas de salle à manger.	Our house doesn't have a dining room.
Nous déménageons le mois prochain.	We're moving next month.
Nous habitons ici depuis 5 ans.	We've been living here for 5 years.
Je n'aime pas mon quartier.	I don't like the area where I live.
C'est un quartier très calme.	It's a very quiet area.
Les transports en commun dans la ville sont excellents.	The public transport in the town is excellent.
Il n'y a pas grand-chose à faire dans mon quartier.	There's not much to do in my area.
Mon nouveau quartier est beaucoup plus agréable que l'ancien.	My new area is much better than the old one.
Notre parc est le plus grand de la ville.	Our park is the biggest in town.

Quelques endroits importants	Some important places
un cinéma	a cinema
un théâtre	a theatre
un musée	a museum
un parc	a park
un restaurant	a restaurant
un café	a café
un cybercafé	an internet café
un distributeur de billets	a cash machine
l'office de tourisme	the tourist office
une cathédrale	a cathedral
une église	a church
une mosquée	a mosque
une synagogue	a synagogue
les magasins	the shops
un centre commercial	a shopping centre
la mairie	the town hall
le marché	the market
une banque	a bank
la piscine	the swimming pool
le centre sportif	the sports centre
le stade de foot	the football stadium
la patinoire	the ice rink
le skate-parc	the skate park
le parc d'attractions	the amusement park
la bibliothèque	the library

Les choses à voir et à faire	Things to see and do
visiter un musée	go to a museum
visiter la cathédrale	visit the cathedral
visiter la vieille ville	do a tour of the old quarter
se promener le long du fleuve	walk along the river
monter en haut de la tour	go up the tower
aller au théâtre	go to the theatre
faire du tourisme	go sightseeing
Visiter la ville	**Visiting the town**
Les endroits les plus importants à visiter sont dans le centre.	The most important sights are in the centre.
C'est intéressant de visiter le musée.	It's interesting to visit the museum.
N'oubliez pas de visiter la vieille ville.	Don't forget to go to the old quarter.

Les moyens de transport	Means of transport
un bus	a bus
un car	a coach
le métro	the underground
le tramway	the tram
le train	the train
la gare	the station
la gare routière	the bus station
une ligne de métro	an underground line
changer de ligne	to change lines

Les directions	Directions
en face de	opposite
à côté de	next to
près de	near
entre ... et ...	between ... and ...
derrière	behind
devant	in front of
Où se trouve la gare routière?	Where's the bus station?
Je cherche l'office de tourisme.	I'm looking for the tourist office.
Allez jusqu'au bout de la rue.	Go right to the end of the street.
Tournez à droite.	Turn right.
Traversez le pont.	Cross the bridge.
Prenez la première rue à gauche.	Take the first street on the left.
C'est sur votre droite.	It's on your right.
C'est en face du cinéma.	It's opposite the cinema.
C'est à côté de la poste.	It's next to the post office.
L'arrêt de bus est près de l'école.	The bus stop is near the school.

Ville ou campagne?	Town or country?
La ville c'est bien parce qu'il y a beaucoup de magasins.	Cities are good because there are lots of shops.
Ce qui est bien à la campagne, c'est le calme.	The good thing about the countryside is that it's quiet.
Je n'aime pas habiter en ville, il y a trop de pollution.	I don't like living in town, there's too much pollution.
Il n'y a rien à faire à la campagne.	There's nothing to do in the country.

Describing someone

La personnalité	Personality
Il/Elle est ...	**He/She is ...**
drôle	funny
sympa	nice
gentil/gentille	nice, friendly
froid/froide	unfriendly
timide	shy
réservé/réservée	quiet
énervant/énervante	annoying
généreux/généreuse	generous
bavard/bavarde	talkative
intelligent/intelligente	intelligent
doué/douée	clever
bête	stupid, silly
radin/radine	stingy
bizarre	strange
sportif/sportive	sporty
mûr/mûre	mature
responsable	responsible
ordonné/ordonnée	tidy
désordonné/désordonnée	untidy

Les caractéristiques	Characteristics
Il/Elle est ...	**He/She is ...**
grand/grande	tall
petit/petite	small
mince	slim
gros/grosse	fat
beau/belle	good-looking
jeune	young
vieux/vieille	old
Il a une trentaine d'années.	He's about thirty.
Elle est grande, mince et assez jolie.	She's tall, slim and quite good-looking.
Ma sœur est plus grande que moi.	My sister is taller than me.
L'un de ses frères est gros, mais l'autre est mince.	One of his brothers is fat but the other one is slim.
Elle ressemble à sa sœur.	She looks like her sister.

C'est quoi, un bon ami?	What makes a good friend
Il/Elle me comprend.	He/She understands me.
Il/Elle me soutient.	He/She supports me.
Il/Elle m'aide.	He/She helps me.
Il/Elle me respecte.	He/She respects me.
Il/Elle ne me met pas la pression.	He/She doesn't put pressure on me.
Il/Elle ne me ment pas.	He/She doesn't lie to me.
Il/Elle ne me critique pas.	He/She doesn't criticise me.
Andrea est ma meilleure amie parce qu'elle est toujours là pour m'aider.	Andrea is my best friend because she is always there to help me.
Mes amis me soutiennent toujours quand j'ai des problèmes.	My friends have always supported me in difficult times.
Je m'entends bien avec mes parents parce qu'en général, ils respectent mes décisions.	I get on with my parents as generally they respect my decisions.
Ma sœur aînée m'aide à faire mes devoirs si je ne les comprends pas.	My elder sister helps me with homework if I don't understand it.
Rafa est mon ami parce qu'avant tout, il me comprend.	Rafa is my friend because, above all, he understands me.
Ma grand-mère m'écoute quand j'ai des problèmes.	My grandmother listens to me when I have problems.
Un bon ami ne ment jamais.	A good friend never lies.

Describing someone

Les couleurs	Colours
jaune (*pl* jaunes)	yellow
orange (*masc, fem, pl*)	orange
rouge (*pl* rouges)	red
rose (*pl* roses)	pink
violet/violette (*pl* violets/violettes)	purple
bleu/bleue (*pl* bleus/bleues)	blue
vert/verte (*pl* verts/vertes)	green
marron (*masc, fem, pl*)	brown
gris/grise (*pl* gris/grises)	grey
noir/noire (*pl* noirs/noires)	black
blanc/blanche (*pl* blancs/blanches)	white
bordeaux (*masc, fem, pl*)	maroon
bleu marine (*masc, fem, pl*)	navy (blue)
turquoise (*masc, fem, pl*)	turquoise
beige (*pl* beiges)	beige
crème (*masc, fem, pl*)	cream
pour les yeux:	**for eyes:**
noisette (*masc, fem, pl*)	hazel
pour les cheveux:	**for hair:**
blond/blonde (*pl* blonds/blondes)	blonde
châtain (*masc, fem, pl*)	brown
châtain clair (*masc, fem, pl*)	light brown
brun/brune (*pl* bruns/brunes)	dark brown
roux/rousse (*pl* roux/rousses)	red

Les vêtements	Clothes
un pull	a jumper
un pantalon	trousers
un chemisier	a blouse
un T-shirt	a T-shirt
un manteau	a coat
un blouson	a jacket
un gilet	a cardigan
un jean	jeans
un sweat à capuche	a hoodie
une robe	a dress
une jupe	a skirt
une cravate	a tie
une veste	a jacket
une chemise	a shirt
des leggings	leggings
des chaussures	shoes
des baskets	trainers
des bottes	boots
des tongs	flip-flops
une tenue habillée	formal clothes
une tenue décontractée	casual clothes
une tenue élégante	smart clothes
des vêtements de sport	sports clothes
des vêtements confortables	comfortable clothes

Quand j'étais ...	When I was ...
Quand elle était petite, elle était très sympa.	When she was a child she was very friendly.
Quand il était petit, il avait les cheveux longs.	When he was a child he had long hair.
À l'âge de 20 ans, mon père avait une moustache.	When my father was 20 he had a moustache.
Il était très timide quand il avait 15 ans. Maintenant, il est plus extraverti.	He was very shy at 15. Now he is more extrovert.
Avant, j'étais assez petit, mais j'ai grandi.	I used to be quite short but I have grown now.

Phrases utiles	Useful phrases
J'ai les yeux noisette.	I've got hazel eyes.
Il a les cheveux châtain et courts.	He's got short brown hair.
Elle est rousse.	She's got red hair.
Il est chauve.	He's bald.
Elle a les cheveux blonds, longs et frisés.	She's got long curly blonde hair.
Il a une moustache/Il est barbu.	He's got a moustache/a beard.
Il porte des lunettes.	He wears glasses.
Ils portent toujours des couleurs vives.	They always wear bright colours.
Ces baskets sont très cool.	These trainers are really cool.
Elle porte un T-shirt bleu clair.	She's wearing a light blue T-shirt.
Il porte un costume gris foncé.	He's wearing a dark grey suit.
Je déteste les tenues formelles.	I hate formal clothes.
Je préfère des leggings parce qu'ils sont confortables.	I prefer leggings because they're comfortable.
A l'école, il faut porter un blazer.	At school, you have to wear a blazer.

School and my plans for the future

Les matières	Subjects
la langue	languages (French/ English etc)
la littérature	literature
la physique	physics
la chimie	chemistry
les maths	maths
la biologie	biology
le théâtre	drama
la danse	dance
la musique	music
les arts plastiques	art
la technologie	design and technology
l'informatique	computing
la géographie	geography
l'histoire	history
l'EPS (= éducation physique et sportive)	PE
C'est ...	**It's ...**
Je le/la trouve ...	**I find it ...**
difficile	difficult
facile	easy
ennuyeux/ennuyeuse	boring
intéressant/ intéressante	interesting
pratique	practical
utile	useful
L'informatique est pratique et le français est utile, mais je trouve la chimie difficile.	Computing is practical and French is useful, but I find chemistry difficult.
Ma matière préférée, ce sont les maths parce que cela ne m'ennuie pas du tout.	My favourite subject is maths because it is not boring at all.
Bien que je déteste les maths, je trouve les statistiques très intéressantes.	Even though I hate maths, I find statistics interesting.
Je ne peux pas supporter le cours de littérature parce que le professeur est très strict et me donne aussi de mauvaises notes.	I can't stand going to literature classes because the teacher is very strict and also gives me bad marks.

Mon collège/ lycée	My (secondary) school
Mon collège/lycée a ...	**My school has ...**
une salle de classe	a classroom
des toilettes	toilets
une cantine	a dinner hall/canteen
une cour de récréation	a playground
une bibliothèque	a library
un gymnase	a gymnasium
un laboratoire	a lab
une salle où se réunissent les élèves le matin	an assembly hall
un théâtre	a theatre
une salle de musique	a music room
une salle d'informatique	an IT room
une salle des professeurs	a staffroom
un bureau d'accueil	a reception
un bureau	an office

La journée au collège/lycée	The school day
Ma journée préférée, c'est le ... parce que j'ai cours/nous avons cours ...	My favourite day is ... because I study/we study ...
le matin	in the morning
l'après-midi	in the afternoon
après la récréation	after break
Le mardi, j'ai cours de maths, d'informatique et aussi de français.	On Tuesdays I have maths, computing and also French.
Le lundi, mon premier cours est la biologie.	I have biology first period on Monday.
Le vendredi, je fais deux heures d'EPS.	On Fridays I do two hours of PE.
Quelle est ta journée préférée?	What's your favourite day?

School and my plans for the future

Les instruments de musique	Musical instruments
Je joue ...	**I play the ...**
du violon	violin
du piano	piano
de la guitare	guitar
de la flûte	flute
Je sais jouer du piano.	I can play the piano.
Je joue du violon depuis l'âge de huit ans.	I've been playing the violin since I was eight.
Je joue dans l'orchestre du collège.	I play in the school orchestra.
Je voudrais apprendre à jouer de la guitare.	I'd like to learn to play the guitar.

Les choses à faire	Things to do
faire ses devoirs	do homework
passer un examen	do an exam
avoir de bonnes/mauvaises notes	get good/bad marks
faire une activité	do an activity
résoudre un problème de maths	do a maths problem
faire un exposé sur ...	do a project about ...
prendre des notes	take notes
répondre aux questions	answer the questions
faire des exercices	do exercises

Mes projets	My plans
Je voudrais faire des études ...	**I'd like to study ...**
de médecine	medicine
d'ingénieur	engineering
de droit	law
de sociologie	sociology
de psychologie	psychology
de langues	languages
d'architecture	architecture
d'informatique	computer science
Je voudrais ...	**I'd like to ...**
gagner beaucoup d'argent	earn lots of money
travailler dans un magasin	work in a shop
travailler dans une banque	work in a bank
travailler dans le tourisme	work in tourism
faire un apprentissage	do an apprenticeship
faire un diplôme	get a qualification

Les examens	Exams
un examen	an exam
un examen blanc	a mock exam
les résultats	the results
Cette année, je prépare le GCSE.	I'm doing my GCSEs this year.
Je vais passer mon premier examen blanc lundi prochain.	I'm doing my first mock exam next Monday.
J'espère réussir à mes examens.	I hope I'll pass my exams.
Je crois que j'ai raté mon examen de maths.	I think I've failed my maths exam.
J'aurai les résultats au mois d'août.	I'll get the results in August.
J'ai bien réussi à mes examens.	I've done well in my exams.
Il faut que je révise mes maths.	I need to revise my maths.
Je dois repasser mon GCSE d'anglais.	I need to resit my English GCSE.

Les ambitions	Ambitions
J'ai l'intention d'aller à l'université.	I'm planning to go to university.
Après, j'aimerais bien aller à l'étranger.	Afterwards I'd like to go abroad.
Je voudrais voyager avant d'aller à l'université.	I'd like to go travelling before university.
Je ne sais pas encore ce que je veux faire.	I don't know yet what I want to do.
Je ferai peut-être des études de maths.	Maybe I'll study maths.

Jobs and hobbies

Les professions	Professions
Je voudrais être ...	**I'd like to be ...**
avocat/avocate	a solicitor
prof	a teacher
dentiste	a dentist
chanteur/chanteuse	a singer
coiffeur/coiffeuse	a hairdresser
journaliste	a journalist
acteur/actrice	an actor
footballeur professionnel	a professional footballer
musicien/musicienne	a musician
homme/femme politique	a politician
Je pense que c'est ...	**I think it's ...**
bien payé	well paid
mal payé	badly paid

Les sports	Sports
Je joue ...	**I play ...**
au foot	football
au basket	basketball
au netball	netball
au rugby	rugby
au tennis	tennis
au ping-pong	table tennis
Je fais ...	**I ...**
du kayak	canoe
de la gymnastique	do gymnastics
de la natation	swim
de l'équitation	go horse riding
de l'athlétisme	do athletics
de la randonnée	hiking
Cet été, je vais faire un stage de foot.	I'm going to do a football course this summer.
Je n'ai jamais fait de ski.	I've never been skiing.
Je m'entraîne au foot deux fois par semaine.	I do football training twice a week.
J'ai participé à une compétition d'athlétisme.	I took part in an athletics competition.

Le travail	Work
un CV	a CV
une demande d'emploi	a job application
poser sa candidature à un poste	to apply for a job
un entretien	an interview
l'expérience professionnelle	work experience
un emploi à temps partiel/à plein temps	a full-/part-time job
un emploi en CDD/en CDI	a temporary/permanent job
les heures de travail	working hours
un emploi	a job
un poste	a job/position
le patron/la patronne	the boss
l'employé/l'employée	the employee
l'apprenti/l'apprentie	the apprentice
la formation	training
l'expérience	experience
le salaire	salary
travailler	to work
être sans emploi	to be unemployed
être à la retraite	to be retired
faire un apprentissage	to do an apprenticeship
faire un stage	to do work experience
être payé/payée	to get paid
Je travaille ...	**I work ...**
au supermarché le samedi	at the supermarket on Saturdays
dans un magasin de vêtements	in a clothes shop
Je fais du baby-sitting.	I do baby-sitting.
Je distribue les journaux.	I deliver papers.
Je gagne 7,50 euros de l'heure.	I earn 7.50 euros an hour.
C'est fatigant comme travail.	It's a tiring job.
Je n'ai jamais travaillé.	I've never had a job.
Je vais chercher un boulot pour cet été.	I'm going to look for a job for this summer.
Mes parents ne me donnent pas d'argent de poche.	My parents don't give me pocket money.

Mes hobbys	My hobbies
J'aime lire des romans.	I like reading novels.
J'adore écouter de la musique dans ma chambre.	I love listening to music in my room.
J'aime bien aller en ville avec mes copines.	I love going into town with my friends.
Je suis passionné/passionnée de sport.	I'm mad about sports.
Faire du skate, c'est très cool.	Skateboarding is really cool.
Je déteste les activités en plein air.	I hate outdoor activities.
Je passe beaucoup de temps sur ma console.	I spend a lot of time on my games console.
Je préfère sortir avec mes copains.	I'd rather go out with my friends.
Je ne sais pas cuisiner.	I can't cook.

Les repas	Meals
le petit déjeuner	breakfast
le déjeuner	lunch
le goûter	afternoon snack
le dîner	dinner
J'adore ...	**I love ...**
le chocolat	chocolate
la salade	salad
les fraises	strawberries
J'aime ...	**I like ...**
le poisson	fish
la viande	meat
le fromage	cheese
les œufs	eggs
les bonbons	sweets
les légumes	vegetables
Je n'aime pas ...	**I don't like ...**
le jus d'orange	orange juice
l'eau gazeuse	sparkling water
l'eau plate	still water
les bananes	bananas
Je déteste ...	**I hate ...**
les épinards	spinach
Les légumes sont très bons pour la santé.	Vegetables are very good for you.
Je ne mange pas de porc.	I don't eat pork.
Je mange beaucoup de fruits.	I eat a lot of fruit.
J'évite les boissons gazeuses.	I avoid fizzy drinks.
Je suis végétarien/végétarienne.	I'm a vegetarian.
Je suis allergique aux cacahuètes.	I'm allergic to peanuts.
Bon appétit.	Enjoy your meal.
C'est très bon.	It's very tasty.
C'est délicieux.	It's delicious.

Des conseils	Some advice
Si tu veux améliorer ton mode de vie,	If you want to improve your lifestyle,
tu devrais ...	you should ...
tu dois ...	you have to ...
il est recommandé de ...	it's advisable to ...
faire de l'exercice deux fois par semaine.	exercise twice a week.
manger beaucoup de fruits.	have lots of fruit.
boire moins de café.	drink less coffee.
éviter les cochonneries.	avoid junk food.

Comment je me sens	How I'm feeling
J'ai mal au ...	**I have a sore ...**
ventre	stomach
dos	back
genou	knee
pied	foot
cou	neck
J'ai mal à la ...	**I have a sore ...**
tête	head
gorge	throat
jambe	leg
J'ai mal aux dents.	I've got toothache.
J'ai mal aux oreilles.	I've got earache.
J'ai mal aux yeux.	My eyes are hurting.
J'ai la grippe.	I've got flu.
J'ai envie de vomir.	I feel sick.
Je suis enrhumé.	I've got a cold.
Je suis fatigué.	I'm tired.
Je suis malade.	I'm ill.
Je me suis cassé la jambe.	I broke my leg.
Il s'est coupé le doigt.	He cut his finger.
J'ai ...	**I'm ...**
froid	cold
chaud	hot
peur	scared
soif	thirsty
faim	hungry

Une vie saine	Staying healthy
Qu'est-ce que tu fais pour rester en forme?	What do you do to keep fit?
Je fais beaucoup de sport.	I do a lot of sport.
Je ne fume pas.	I don't smoke.
Je me couche de bonne heure.	I go to bed early.
Je vais au collège à pied.	I walk to school.
Vous devez manger des produits frais tous les jours.	You should eat fresh food every day.
Je dois boire plus d'eau.	I should drink more water.
Je n'en bois pas assez.	I don't drink enough.
C'est bon pour la santé.	It's good for your health.
L'alcool est mauvais pour la santé.	Alcohol is bad for your health.
Il mène une vie saine.	He has a healthy lifestyle.
Je ne bois pas d'alcool et je ne fume pas.	I don't drink or smoke.

Relationships and feelings

Les relations	Relationships
Je m'entends très/ assez bien avec ma sœur.	I get on very/quite well with my sister.
Je ne m'entends pas du tout avec mon frère.	I don't get on at all with my brother.
Je ne la supporte pas.	I can't stand her.
Mon meilleur copain s'appelle Tamir.	My best friend is called Tamir.
J'ai trois meilleures copines.	I've got three best friends.
Nous sommes inséparables.	We're always together.
Je me suis disputée avec Rachida.	I've had a quarrel with Rachida.
On ne se parle plus avec Nathan.	I'm not talking to Nathan any more.

Les émotions	Emotions
être ...	**to be ...**
triste	sad
content/contente	pleased
heureux/heureuse	happy
fâché/fâchée	angry
amoureux/amoureuse	in love
vexé/vexée	hurt
déprimé/déprimée	depressed
agité/agitée	nervous
de bonne/mauvaise humeur	in a good/bad mood
Je suis amoureuse de Fabien.	I'm in love with Fabien.
Bruno et moi, on s'est séparés.	Bruno and I have split up.
Je suis contente que tu viennes.	I'm pleased you're coming.
Je suis triste de partir.	I'm sad to be leaving.
Je m'ennuie, on s'en va?	I'm bored, shall we go?
J'espère que tu n'es pas trop fâché.	I hope you're not too angry.
Elle était vexée de ne pas avoir été invitée.	She was hurt that she wasn't invited.

Les membres de la famille	Members of the family
mon père	my father, my dad
ma mère	my mother, my mum
mes parents	my parents
mon beau-père	my stepfather
ma belle-mère	my stepmother
mon frère	my brother
ma sœur	my sister
mon demi-frère	my half-brother
ma demi-sœur	my half-sister
mon beau-frère	my stepbrother
ma belle- sœur	my stepsister
mon oncle	my uncle
ma tante	my aunt
mon cousin	my cousin (male)
ma cousine	my cousin (female)
mon grand-père	my grandfather
ma grand-mère	my grandmother
mes grands-parents	my grandparents
mon arrière-grand-père	my great-grandfather
mon arrière-grand-mère	my great-grandmother
mon grand frère	my big brother
ma petite sœur	my little sister

Phrases utiles	Useful phrases
Voici ma sœur Sandrine.	This is my sister, Sandrine.
Elle va se marier l'été prochain.	She's getting married next summer.
J'ai une sœur jumelle.	I have a twin sister.
J'ai un demi-frère.	I have a half-brother.
Je suis fils unique.	I'm an only child. (boy)
Je suis fille unique.	I'm an only child. (girl)
Mes parents sont séparés/divorcés.	My parents are separated/divorced.
Mon grand-père est mort l'année dernière.	My grandfather died last year.
Ma mère s'est remariée.	My mother has got married again.
Elle est mère célibataire.	She's a single mother.
Il est père célibataire.	He's a single father.
Ils ne sont pas mariés.	They are not married.
Ils sont pacsés.	They are in a civil partnership.

Greetings, meeting people and expressing opinions

Salutations et présentations	Greetings and introductions
Bonjour	Hello/Good morning/ Good afternoon
Bonsoir	Good evening
Bonne nuit	Good night
À plus tard	See you later.
À bientôt	See you soon.
À demain	See you tomorrow.
À lundi/à la semaine prochaine	See you on Monday/ next week.
Au revoir	Goodbye/Bye!
Passez une bonne journée.	Have a good day!
Je vous présente ma mère.	Let me introduce you to my mother.
Tu connais Sara?	Have you met Sara?
Je vous présente Alberto.	This is Alberto.
Enchanté/enchantée	Nice to meet you.
Ravi/ravie de faire votre connaissance.	Pleased to meet you.

Les opinions	Opinions
Génial!	Great!
C'est affreux!	That's dreadful!
Quelle horreur!	That's terrible!
C'est super!	That's great!
Cool!	Cool!
Comme c'est effrayant!	How scary!
Que c'est ennuyeux!	How boring!
Dommage!	What a shame!
Comme c'est gênant!	How embarrasing!
Je pense que ...	I think that ...
Je crois que ...	I think/I believe that ...
Il me semble que ...	I think that ...
Je pense que c'est une bonne idée.	I think it's a good idea.
À mon avis ...	In my opinion/view ...
Pour moi ...	For me ...

Pour rencontrer quelqu'un	Arranging to meet someone
Aimerais-tu ...	**Would you like to ...**
Tu veux ...	**Do you want to ...**
aller au cinéma?	go to the cinema?
faire du patin à glace?	go skating?
jouer au foot?	play football?
venir chez moi?	come to my house?
Désolé/désolée, je dois ...	**I'm sorry, I have to ...**
faire mes devoirs.	do my homework.
faire le ménage.	do housework.
ranger ma chambre.	tidy my room.
aider mes parents.	help my parents.
aller promener le chien.	take the dog for a walk.
Je ne peux pas parce que ...	**I can't because ...**
je suis chez mes grands-parents.	I'm visiting my grandparents.
je suis absent/absente ce week-end.	I'm away this weekend.
je n'ai pas le droit de sortir.	I'm grounded.
je n'ai pas d'argent.	I don't have any money.
Si on se retrouvait ...	**Shall we meet ...**
en face du cinéma?	opposite the cinema?
à l'arrêt de bus?	at the bus stop?
C'est OK pour moi/c'est d'accord.	It's OK for me.
C'est bien.	That's fine.
D'accord.	Alright.
Ça me semble bien.	Sounds good to me.

Phrases utiles	Useful phrases
Qu'est-ce qu'on fait ce week-end?	What shall we do this weekend?
Je ne peux pas venir samedi, mais dimanche après-midi, ça me va.	I can't come on Saturday but Sunday afternoon is OK for me.
Nous allons au théâtre ce soir. Tu veux venir avec nous?	We are going to the theatre this evening. Would you like to come with us?
Je préfere rester à la maison aujourd'hui.	I'd rather not go out today.
Tu veux venir chez moi cet après-midi?	Why don't you drop by my house this afternoon?
C'est dommage. J'ai des choses à faire.	What a shame! I've got things to do.
Pas question! Je déteste le sport.	No way! I hate sports.

Communications: letters and emails

Un mail	An email

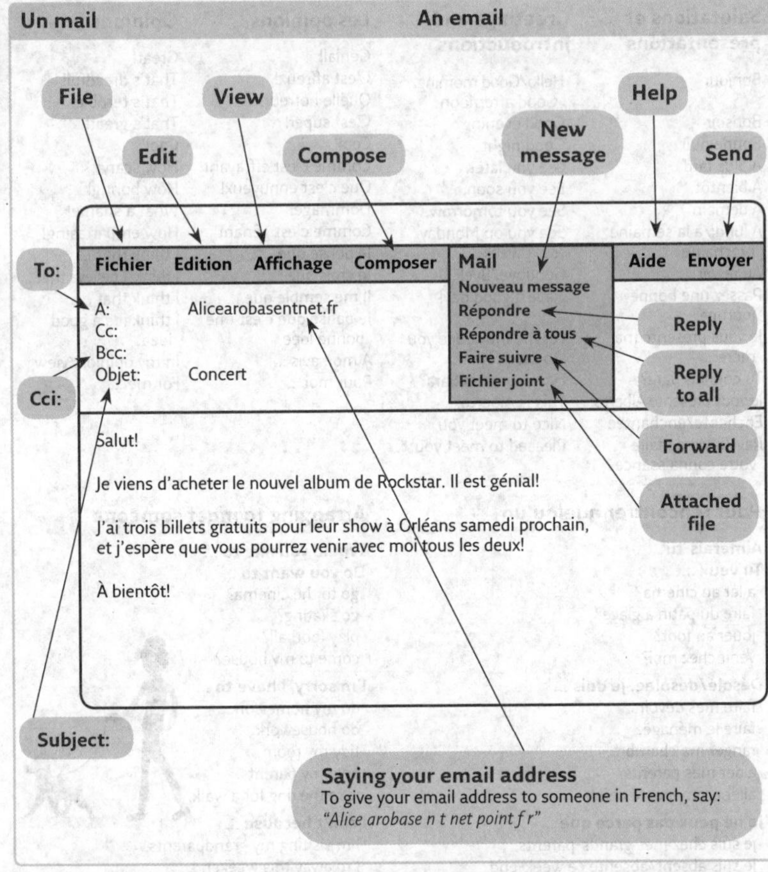

Saying your email address

To give your email address to someone in French, say:

"Alice arobase n t net point f r"

Lettres et mails	Letters and emails
une lettre	a letter
une carte postale	a postcard
un mail/un e-mail	an email
Bonjour	Hello
Cher/chère ...	Dear ...
Cher Monsieur ...	Dear Mr ...
Chère Madame ...	Dear Mrs ...
Merci de votre lettre.	Thank you for your letter.
Écris-moi bientôt!	Write soon!
Embrasse ... pour moi.	Give my love to ...
Samuel vous adresse ses amitiés.	Samuel sends his best wishes.
Amitiés	Love
Bisous	Hugs and kisses
Amicalement	Best wishes
Cordialement	Kind regards
J'espère avoir bientôt de tes nouvelles.	Looking forward to hearing from you
Désolé/désolée de ne pas avoir écrit plus tôt.	I'm sorry I didn't write earlier.
à l'attention de	for the attention of
expéditeur/expéditrice	sent by

Communications: on the phone and online

Au téléphone et sur Internet	On the phone and the internet
le téléphone	telephone
le portable	mobile
le fixe	landline
l'indicatif régional	area code
le faux numéro	wrong number
un texto/SMS	a text
une appli	an app
un post	a post
le nom d'utilisateur	username
le mot de passe	password
le wifi	Wi-Fi
le signal	signal
la connexion	connection
les données	data
les médias sociaux	social media
les réseaux sociaux	social networks
un blog	a blog
un vlog	a vlog
en ligne	online
composer le numéro	to dial the number
répondre au téléphone	to answer the phone
appuyer sur la touche	to press the key
raccrocher	to hang up
connecter	to connect
un message vocal	a voice mail
la messagerie vocale	voice mail
envoyer un SMS	to send a text
transférer un message	to forward a message
tweeter	to tweet
discuter avec quelqu'un sur Skype®	to Skype® someone
télécharger	to download
chatter	to chat

Au téléphone et sur Internet	On the phone and the internet
Le soir, je chatte avec mes copains.	I chat to my friends in the evenings.
Tu es sur Twitter®?	Are you on Twitter®?
J'ai mis les photos de mes vacances sur Facebook®.	I put my holiday photos on Facebook®.
Tu peux télécharger une appli pour ça.	You can download an app for that.
Tu as le wifi?	Do you have Wi-Fi?
J'ai cherché son nom sur Google®.	I googled his/her name.

Avantages et inconvénients	Advantages and disadvantages
Internet est ...	**The internet is ...**
utile	useful
pratique	handy/practical
rapide	fast
mais d'un autre côté, cela ...	**but on the other hand it is ...**
entraîne une dépendance	addictive
Les nouvelles technologies sont ...	**New technology is ...**
faciles	easy
populaires	popular
nécessaires	necessary
mais elles peuvent être ...	**but they are also ...**
dangereuses	dangerous

Phrases utiles	Useful phrases
Allô! J'aimerais parler à Valérie.	Hello! Could I speak to Valérie?
Pourrais-je parler à ...?	Can I speak to ...?
Est-ce que vous pourriez me passer ...?	Could you put me through to ...?
Je voudrais parler à ...	I would like to speak to ...
Allô?	Hello!
Je vous le passe.	I'll put you through to him.
Un instant.	One moment please.
Ne quittez pas.	Hold the line, please.
Je vais vous le/la chercher.	I'll get him/her for you.
Je suis désolé, j'ai fait un faux numéro.	I'm sorry, I dialled the wrong number.
Pourriez-vous lui demander de me rappeler?	Would you ask him/her to call me back?
Pourriez-vous rappeler plus tard?	Could you call later?
Je rappellerai dans une demi-heure.	I'll call back in half an hour.
Il n'y a pas de réseau ici.	There's no signal here.
Je n'ai plus de crédit.	I've run out of credit.
La ligne est très mauvaise.	It's a very bad line.
Je ne te capte plus!	You're breaking up!
Envoie-moi un texto.	Send me a text.
Je partage avec mes amis les vidéos que j'aime.	I share videos that I like with my friends.
Il vient de poster une nouvelle vidéo.	He's just posted a new video.
On n'a pas droit au portable au lycée.	We're not allowed mobile phones in school.
Mets ton portable en silencieux.	Put your mobile on silent.
Il faut éteindre les portables.	You have to switch your mobiles off.

My world

Le temps	The weather
Il fait froid.	It's cold.
Il fait chaud.	It's hot.
Il fait beau.	It's a nice day.
Il y a du vent.	It's windy.
Il y a du soleil.	It's sunny.
Il pleut/il neige.	It's raining/snowing.
Il fait 30 degrés.	It's 30 degrees.
Il gèle.	It's frosty.
Il y a du brouillard.	It's foggy.
Il fait beau/ne fait pas beau aujourd'hui.	The weather is nice/ bad today.

Les problèmes dans le monde qui m'entoure	Problems in my world
Je m'inquiète au sujet de ...	**I'm worried about ...**
la pollution	pollution
la pauvreté	poverty
le chômage	unemployment
la violence	violence
les sans-abri	the homeless
le réchauffement climatique	global warming
le changement climatique	climate change
la désertification	desertification
la déforestation	deforestation
les inondations	floods
les incendies	fires
les guerres	wars
la migration	migration
le travail des enfants	child labour
les espèces en voie de disparition	endangered species
les pesticides	pesticides
l'inégalité	inequality
la manque de solidarité	lack of solidarity
Qu'est-ce qu'on peut faire?	**What can we do?**
On peut ...	We/one can ...
On devrait ...	We/one should ...
Il est important de ...	It's important to ...

Campagnes et bonnes causes	Campaigns and good causes
Nous devons ...	**We have to ...**
recycler le verre/les boîtes de conserve/ le papier.	recycle glass/tins/ paper.
éteindre les lumières/ les appareils la nuit.	switch off the light/ devices at night.
ne pas gaspiller l'énergie.	not waste energy.
économiser l'eau.	save water.
protéger l'environnement.	protect the environment.
prendre les transports en commun.	use public transport.
utiliser moins souvent la voiture.	use the car less.
réduire l'empreinte carbone.	reduce the carbon footprint.
utiliser des énergies renouvelables.	use renewable energy.
ne pas utiliser de sacs en plastique.	avoid using plastic bags.
acheter des produits issus du commerce équitable.	buy fairtrade products.
faire du bénévolat.	do voluntary work.
devenir travailleur humanitaire.	become an aid worker.
collaborer avec une ONG.	collaborate with an NGO.
apporter son aide dans un refuge.	help at a refuge.
donner de l'argent à des associations caritatives.	donate to a charity.
collecter des fonds.	fundraise.
faire une collecte de vêtements d'occasion.	collect secondhand clothes.
faire campagne.	campaign.
protester (contre) ...	protest (against) ...
manifester (contre) ...	demonstrate (against) ...

Phrases utiles	Useful phrases
D'habitude, il ne fait pas trop froid en avril.	It's not usually too cold in April.
L'hiver, je fais du footing le matin.	In the winter I go running in the morning.
S'il pleut, nous irons visiter un musée, mais s'il fait beau, nous irons au parc.	If it rains we'll go to a museum but if it's a nice day we'll go to the park.
Il vaut mieux ne pas jouer au tennis s'il fait trop chaud.	It is better not to play tennis if it's too hot.
Nous allons organiser une tombola afin de collecter des fonds pour la recherche sur le cancer.	We are going to organize a raffle to raise funds for cancer research.
À mon avis, les problèmes principaux dans le monde sont les guerres et la pollution maritime.	In my point of view, the main world problems are wars and also sea pollution.
Dans ma ville, il y a beaucoup de chômage.	In my town, there is a lot of unemployment.

Dates, festivals and holidays

Les jours de la semaine	Days of the week
lundi	Monday
mardi	Tuesday
mercredi	Wednesday
jeudi	Thursday
vendredi	Friday
samedi	Saturday
dimanche	Sunday
lundi	on Monday
le lundi	on Mondays
tous les lundis	every Monday
mardi dernier	last Tuesday
vendredi prochain	next Friday
samedi dans une semaine	a week on Saturday

Les mois de l'an	Months of the year
janvier	January
février	February
mars	March
avril	April
mai	May
juin	June
juillet	July
août	August
septembre	September
octobre	October
novembre	November
décembre	December
Quelle est la date aujourd'hui?	What date is it today?
Nous sommes le 16 juin	It's the 16th of June.
Quelle est la date de ton anniversaire?	What date is your birthday?
C'est le 22 mai.	It's the 22nd of May.

Les fêtes	Festivals
Noël (*masc*)	Christmas
le jour de Noël	Christmas Day
la veille de Noël	Christmas Eve
le réveillon de Noël	Christmas Eve
le lendemain de Noël	Boxing Day
la Saint-Sylvestre	New Year's Eve
le Nouvel An	New Year's Day
le Nouvel An chinois	Chinese New Year
la Saint-Valentin	Valentine's Day
mardi gras	Pancake Day
le premier avril	April Fools' Day
Pâques (*fem pl*)	Easter
la fête des Mères	Mother's Day
la fête des Pères	Father's Day
la Toussaint	All Saints' Day
le 11 novembre	Remembrance Day
l'Aïd	Eid
Hanoukka (*fem*)	Hanukkah
Joyeux Noël!	Happy Christmas!
Poisson d'avril!	April fool!
fêter le Nouvel An	to celebrate New Year
Qu'est-ce que tu fais pour le réveillon?	What are you doing on New Year's Eve?

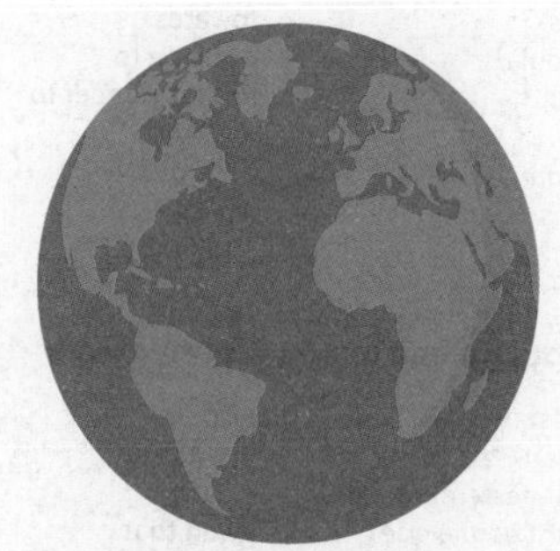

Les vacances	Holidays
les grandes vacances	the summer holidays
les vacances de la Toussaint	the autumn half-term
les vacances de Noël	the Christmas holidays
les vacances de février	the spring half-term
les vacances de Pâques	the Easter holidays
la mer	the seaside
la montagne	the mountains
Qu'est-ce que tu vas faire pendant les vacances?	What are you going to do in the holidays?
Cet été, nous partons une semaine en Italie.	We're going to Italy for a week this summer.
Nous ne partons pas en vacances cette année.	We're not going on holiday this year.
J'aimerais bien aller aux sports d'hiver cette année.	I'd like to go skiing this year.
L'été prochain, nous allons louer un gîte en Bretagne.	Next summer we're going to rent a house in Brittany.
Je déteste le camping.	I hate camping.

Building phrases

Comparaisons	Comparisons
assez	quite
trop	too/too much
plus (que)	more (than)
plus grand/petit (que)	bigger/smaller (than)
la majorité	the majority
mieux (que)	better (than)
moins grand/petit (que)	not as big/small (as)
moins (que)	less (than)
comme	like
pareil (que)	the same (as)
semblable (à)	similar (to)
pire(que)	worse (than)
peu	little/few
un peu	a little/a few
aussi ... que ...	as ... as ...
autant... que ...	as much/many ... as ...

Conjonctions	Conjunctions
malgré	despite
donc	so/therefore
même (si)	even (if)
bien que	although
parce que/puisque	as/because/since
à cause de	because of
quand	when
tandis que	whereas
ou	or
mais	but
c'est pour ça que	that's why
bon/eh bien, ...	well, ...
si	if
cependant	however
peut-être	perhaps/maybe
aussi	also
et	and

Prépositions	Prepositions
à	at/to
avec	with
de	from/of
dans/sur	in/on
vers	towards
jusqu'à	until/up to
pour	for/to/in order to
par	for/by
selon	according to
sans	without

Questions	Questions
où?	where?
comment?	how?
quel/quelle/quels/quelles?	which?
quand?	when?
combien?	how much?
d'où?	where ... from?
pourquoi?	why?
quel jour/ quelle date/ quelle heure?	which (day/date/ time)?
qui?	who?

Mots de liaison	Connectives
aussi	also
à part/sauf	apart from
manifestement	clearly
étant donné que	given that
c'est-à-dire	so/that is to say
d'un côté, ... d'un autre côté, ...	on the one hand ... on the other ...
sans aucun doute	without doubt
où	where ... to
quand	when
où	where
que/qui	that/which/who

Négations	Negatives
ne ... jamais	never
ni ... ni ...	neither ... nor ...
ne ... rien	nothing
ne ... personne	nobody/no one
aucun	none
sauf	except
non plus	neither
ne ... plus	no longer

Some examples in context

Ma ville est petite. → La ville **où** j'habite depuis 12 ans est petite, **et en plus**, elle **n'**est **pas** vivante **parce qu'**il n'y a pas d'activités pour les jeunes. **C'est pénible!**

Je m'entends bien avec ma mère. → Je m'entends très bien avec ma mère **parce que**, **bien que** nous soyons **assez** différentes, elle me soutient toujours.

Il est important de ne pas gaspiller l'énergie. → **À mon avis, pour** protéger l'environnement **autant que possible**, il est important de recycler et de **ne rien** gaspiller.

Aa

★**a** ARTICLE

Use **un** for masculine nouns, **une** for feminine nouns.

un *masc*

□ a book un livre □ a year ago il y a un an

une *fem*

□ an apple une pomme

You do not translate 'a' when you want to describe somebody's job in French.

□ He's a butcher. Il est boucher. □ She's a doctor. Elle est médecin.

▪ **once a week** une fois par semaine

▪ **10 km an hour** dix kilomètres à l'heure

▪ **£4 a kilo** quatre livres le kilo

▪ **a hundred pounds** cent livres

AA NOUN (= *Automobile Association*)

la société de dépannage *fem*

aback ADVERB

▪ **I was taken aback by his reaction.** Sa réaction m'a décontenancé.

★to **abandon** VERB

abandonner [28]

abbey NOUN

l'abbaye *fem*

abbreviation NOUN

l'abréviation *fem*

★**ability** NOUN

▪ **to have the ability to do something** être [35] capable de faire quelque chose

★**able** ADJECTIVE

▪ **to be able to do something** être [35] capable de faire quelque chose

to **abolish** VERB

abolir [38]

abortion NOUN

l'avortement *masc*

▪ **She had an abortion.** Elle s'est fait avorter.

★**about** PREPOSITION, ADVERB

1 à propos de (*concerning*)

□ He emailed me about the exams. Il m'a envoyé un e-mail à propos des examens.

2 environ (*approximately*)

□ It takes about 10 hours. Ça prend dix heures environ.

▪ **about a hundred pounds** une centaine de livres

▪ **at about 11 o'clock** vers onze heures

3 dans (*around*)

□ to walk about the town se promener dans la ville

4 sur

□ a book about London un livre sur Londres

▪ **to be about to do something** être [35] sur le point de faire quelque chose □ I was about to go out. J'étais sur le point de sortir.

▪ **to talk about something** parler [28] de quelque chose

▪ **What's it about?** De quoi s'agit-il?

▪ **How about going to the cinema?** Et si nous allions au cinéma?

★**above** PREPOSITION, ADVERB

1 au-dessus de (*higher than*)

□ He put his hands above his head. Il a mis ses mains au-dessus de sa tête.

▪ **the flat above** l'appartement du dessus

▪ **mentioned above** mentionné ci-dessus

▪ **above all** par-dessus tout

2 plus de (*more than*)

□ above 40 degrees plus de quarante degrés

★**abroad** ADVERB

à l'étranger

□ to go abroad partir à l'étranger

abrupt ADJECTIVE

brusque (FEM brusque)

□ He was a bit abrupt with me. Il s'est montré un peu brusque avec moi.

abruptly ADVERB

brusquement

□ He got up abruptly. Il s'est levé brusquement.

★**absence** NOUN

l'absence *fem*

★**absent** ADJECTIVE

absent (FEM absente)

absent-minded ADJECTIVE

distrait (FEM distraite)

□ She's a bit absent-minded. Elle est un peu distraite.

★**absolutely** ADVERB

1 tout à fait (*completely*)

□ Jia's absolutely right. Jia a tout à fait raison.

2 absolument

□ Do you think it's a good idea? — Absolutely!

★ = core vocabulary

Tu trouves que c'est une bonne idée? — Absolument!

absorbed ADJECTIVE
■ **to be absorbed in something** être [35] absorbé par quelque chose
■ **to be absorbed in a book** être [35] plongé dans un livre

absurd ADJECTIVE
absurde (FEM absurde)
□ That's absurd! C'est absurde!

★ **abuse** NOUN
▷ *see also* **abuse** VERB
l'abus *masc* (*misuse*)
■ **to shout abuse at somebody** insulter [28] quelqu'un
■ **the issue of child abuse** la question des enfants maltraités
■ **the problem of drug abuse** le problème de la drogue

★ to **abuse** VERB
▷ *see also* **abuse** NOUN
1 maltraiter [28]
□ abused children les enfants maltraités *masc pl*
■ **to be abused** être [35] maltraité (*child, woman*)
2 injurier [19] (*insult*)
■ **to abuse drugs** se droguer [28]

abusive ADJECTIVE
insultant (FEM insultante) (*insulting*)
□ abusive behaviour un comportement insultant
■ **When I refused, he became abusive.** Quand j'ai refusé, il s'est mis à m'injurier.
■ **children with abusive parents** les enfants maltraités par leurs parents

★ **academic** ADJECTIVE
universitaire (FEM universitaire)
□ the academic year l'année universitaire *fem*

academy NOUN
le collège *masc*
□ a military academy un collège militaire

to **accelerate** VERB
accélérer [34]

accelerator NOUN
l'accélérateur *masc*

★ **accent** NOUN
l'accent *masc*
□ He's got a French accent. Il a l'accent français.

★ to **accept** VERB
accepter [28]

★ **acceptable** ADJECTIVE
acceptable (FEM acceptable)

★ **access** NOUN
1 l'accès *masc*
□ He has access to my phone. Il a accès à mon téléphone.
2 le droit de visite *masc*
□ Her ex-husband has access to the children. Son ex-mari a le droit de visite.

accessible ADJECTIVE
accessible (FEM accessible)

accessory NOUN
l'accessoire *masc*
□ fashion accessories les accessoires de mode

★ **accident** NOUN
l'accident *masc*
□ to have an accident avoir un accident
■ **by accident 1** (*by mistake*) accidentellement □ I broke the glass by accident. J'ai cassé le verre accidentellement.
2 (*by chance*) par hasard □ She met him by accident. Elle l'a rencontré par hasard.

accidental ADJECTIVE
accidentel (FEM accidentelle)

to **accommodate** VERB
accueillir [22]
□ The sports hall can accommodate 150 people. Le gymnase peut accueillir cent cinquante personnes.

★ **accommodation** NOUN
le logement *masc*

to **accompany** VERB
accompagner [28]

accord NOUN
■ **of his own accord** de son plein gré □ He left of his own accord. Il est parti de son plein gré.

accordingly ADVERB
en conséquence

★ **according to** PREPOSITION
selon
□ According to him, everyone had gone. Selon lui, tout le monde était parti.

accordion NOUN
l'accordéon *masc*

★ **account** NOUN
1 le compte *masc*
□ a bank account un compte en banque
■ **to do the accounts** tenir [83] la comptabilité
2 le compte rendu *masc* (PL les comptes rendus) (*report*)
□ He gave a detailed account of what happened. Il a donné un compte rendu détaillé des événements.
■ **to take something into account** tenir [83] compte de quelque chose
■ **on account of** à cause de □ We couldn't go out on account of the bad weather. Nous n'avons pas pu sortir à cause du mauvais temps.

to **account for** VERB
expliquer [28]

□ She had to account for her absence. Elle a dû expliquer son absence.

accountable ADJECTIVE
■ **to be accountable to someone for something** être [35] responsable de quelque chose devant quelqu'un

accountancy NOUN
la comptabilité *fem*

accountant NOUN
le/la comptable *masc/fem*
□ She's an accountant. Elle est comptable.

accuracy NOUN
l'exactitude *fem*

★ **accurate** ADJECTIVE
précis (FEM précise)
□ accurate information les renseignements précis *masc pl*

accurately ADVERB
avec précision

accusation NOUN
l'accusation *fem*

★ to **accuse** VERB
■ **to accuse somebody of something** accuser [28] quelqu'un de quelque chose
□ The police are accusing her of murder. La police l'accuse de meurtre.

ace NOUN
l'as *masc*
□ the ace of hearts l'as de cœur

★ **ache** NOUN
▷ *see also* **ache** VERB
la douleur *fem*

★ to **ache** VERB
▷ *see also* **ache** NOUN
■ **My leg's aching.** J'ai mal à la jambe.

★ to **achieve** VERB
1 atteindre [60] (*an aim*)
2 remporter [28] (*victory*)

★ **achievement** NOUN
l'exploit *masc*
□ That was quite an achievement. C'était un véritable exploit.

★ **acid** NOUN
l'acide *masc*

acid rain NOUN
les pluies acides *fem pl*

acne NOUN
l'acné *fem*

★ **acre** NOUN
le demi-hectare *masc*

DID YOU KNOW...?
In France, land is measured in hectares. One acre is about 0.4 hectares.

acrobat NOUN
l'acrobate *masc/fem*
□ He's an acrobat. Il est acrobate.

★ **across** PREPOSITION, ADVERB
de l'autre côté de
□ the shop across the road la boutique de l'autre côté de la rue
■ **to walk across the road** traverser [28] la rue
■ **to run across the road** traverser [28] la rue en courant
■ **across from** (*opposite*) en face de □ He sat down across from her. Il s'est assis en face d'elle.

★ to **act** VERB
▷ *see also* **act** NOUN
1 jouer [28] (*in play, film*)
□ He acts really well. Il joue vraiment bien.
□ She's acting the part of Juliet. Elle joue le rôle de Juliette.
2 agir [38] (*take action*)
□ The police acted quickly. La police a agi rapidement.
■ **She acts as his interpreter.** Elle lui sert d'interprète.

★ **act** NOUN
▷ *see also* **act** VERB
l'acte *masc* (*in play*)
□ in the first act au premier acte

★ **action** NOUN
l'action *fem*
□ The film was full of action. Il y avait beaucoup d'action dans le film.
■ **to take firm action against** prendre [65] des mesures énergiques contre

★ **active** ADJECTIVE
actif (FEM active)
□ He's a very active person. Il est très actif.
■ **an active volcano** un volcan en activité

★ **activity** NOUN
l'activité *fem*
□ outdoor activities les activités de plein air

★ **actor** NOUN
l'acteur *masc*
□ Brad Pitt is a well-known actor. Brad Pitt est un acteur connu.

★ **actress** NOUN
l'actrice *fem*
□ Jennifer Lawrence is a well-known actress. Jennifer Lawrence est une actrice connue.

★ **actual** ADJECTIVE
réel (FEM réelle)
□ The film is based on actual events. Le film repose sur des faits réels.
■ **What's the actual amount?** Quel est le montant exact?

BE CAREFUL!
Do not translate **actual** by the French word **actuel**.

★**actually** ADVERB
1 vraiment (*really*)
□ Did it actually happen? Est-ce que c'est vraiment arrivé?
2 en fait (*in fact*)
□ Actually, I don't know him at all. En fait, je ne le connais pas du tout.

BE CAREFUL!
Do not translate **actually** by the French word **actuellement**.

acupuncture NOUN
l'acuponcture *fem*

AD ABBREVIATION
ap. J.-C. (= *après Jésus-Christ*)
□ in 800 AD en huit cents après Jésus-Christ

★**ad** NOUN
1 l'annonce *fem* (*in paper*)
2 la pub *fem* (*on TV, radio*)

to **adapt** VERB
adapter [28]
□ His novel was adapted for television. Son roman a été adapté pour la télévision.
■ **to adapt to something** (*get used to*) s'adapter [28] à quelque chose □ He adapted to his new school very quickly. Il s'est adapté très vite à sa nouvelle école.

adaptor NOUN
l'adaptateur *masc*

★to **add** VERB
ajouter [28]
□ Add two eggs to the mixture. Ajoutez deux œufs au mélange.

to **add up** VERB
additionner [28]
□ Add the figures up. Additionnez les chiffres.

addict NOUN
le drogué *masc*
la droguée *fem* (*drug addict*)
■ **Jean-Pierre's a football addict.** Jean-Pierre est un mordu de football.

addicted ADJECTIVE
■ **to be addicted to** être [35] dépendant de
□ She's addicted to heroin. Elle est héroïnomane.
■ **She's addicted to YouTube.** Elle est fan de YouTube.

★**addition** NOUN
■ **in addition** en plus □ He's broken his leg and, in addition, he's caught a cold. Il s'est cassé la jambe et en plus, il a attrapé un rhume.
■ **in addition to** en plus de □ There's a swimming pool in addition to the gym. Il y a une piscine en plus de la salle de gym.

★**address** NOUN
l'adresse *fem*
□ What's your address? Quelle est votre adresse?

★**adjective** NOUN
l'adjectif *masc*

to **adjust** VERB
régler [34]
□ You can adjust the height of the chair. Tu peux régler la hauteur de la chaise.
■ **to adjust to something** (*get used to*) s'adapter [28] à quelque chose □ He adjusted to his new school very quickly. Il s'est adapté très vite à sa nouvelle école.

adjustable ADJECTIVE
réglable (FEM réglable)

★**administration** NOUN
l'administration *fem*

admiral NOUN
l'amiral *masc*

★to **admire** VERB
admirer [28]

admission NOUN
l'entrée *fem*
■ **'admission free'** 'entrée gratuite'

★to **admit** VERB
1 admettre [47] (*agree*)
□ I must admit that ... Je dois admettre que ...
2 reconnaître [14] (*confess*)
□ He admitted that he'd done it. Il a reconnu qu'il l'avait fait.

admittance NOUN
■ **'no admittance'** 'accès interdit'

adolescence NOUN
l'adolescence *fem*

adolescent NOUN
l'adolescent *masc*
l'adolescente *fem*

★to **adopt** VERB
adopter [28]
□ Taylor was adopted. Taylor a été adopté.

★**adopted** ADJECTIVE
adoptif (FEM adoptive)
□ an adopted son un fils adoptif

adoption NOUN
l'adoption *fem*

to **adore** VERB
adorer [28]

Adriatic Sea NOUN
la mer Adriatique *fem*

★**adult** NOUN
l'adulte *masc/fem*
■ **adult education** l'enseignement pour adultes *masc*

★to **advance** VERB
▷ *see also* **advance** NOUN
1 avancer [12] (*move forward*)
□ The enemy is advancing. L'ennemi avance.
2 progresser [28] (*progress*)
□ Technology has advanced a lot. La technologie a beaucoup progressé.

★ **advance** NOUN
▷ *see also* **advance** VERB
■ **in advance** à l'avance □ They bought the tickets in advance. Ils ont acheté les billets à l'avance.

advance booking NOUN
■ **Advance booking is essential.** Il est indispensable de réserver.

★ **advanced** ADJECTIVE
avancé (FEM avancée)

★ **advantage** NOUN
l'avantage *masc*
□ Going to university has many advantages. Aller à l'université présente de nombreux avantages.
■ **to take advantage of something** profiter [28] de quelque chose □ He took advantage of the good weather to go for a walk. Il a profité du beau temps pour faire une promenade.
■ **to take advantage of somebody** exploiter [28] quelqu'un □ She takes advantage of her younger brother. Elle exploite son frère cadet.

★ **adventure** NOUN
l'aventure *fem*

adverb NOUN
l'adverbe *masc*

advert, advertisement NOUN
1 la publicité *fem* (*on TV*)
2 l'annonce *fem* (*in newspaper*)

★ to **advertise** VERB
faire [36] de la publicité pour
□ They're advertising their new smartphone. Ils font de la publicité pour leur nouveau smartphone.
■ **Jobs are advertised on the website.** Le site Internet publie des offres d'emploi.

advertising NOUN
la publicité *fem*

★ **advice** NOUN
les conseils *masc pl*
□ to give somebody advice donner des conseils à quelqu'un
■ **a piece of advice** un conseil □ He gave me a good piece of advice. Il m'a donné un bon conseil.

★ to **advise** VERB
conseiller [28]
□ He advised me to wait. Il m'a conseillé d'attendre. □ He advised me not to go there. Il m'a conseillé de ne pas y aller.

aerial NOUN
l'antenne *fem*

★ **aerobics** NOUN
l'aérobic *fem*
□ I'm going to aerobics tonight. Je vais au cours d'aérobic ce soir.

★ **aeroplane** NOUN
l'avion *masc*

aerosol NOUN
la bombe *fem*

★ **affair** NOUN
1 l'aventure *fem* (*romantic*)
□ to have an affair with somebody avoir une aventure avec quelqu'un
2 l'affaire *fem* (*event*)
□ the contaminated blood affair l'affaire du sang contaminé

★ to **affect** VERB
affecter [1]

affectionate ADJECTIVE
affectueux (FEM affectueuse)

★ to **afford** VERB
avoir [8] les moyens de
□ I can't afford to buy a new pair of jeans. Je n'ai pas les moyens d'acheter un nouveau jean. □ We can't afford to go on holiday. Nous n'avons pas les moyens de partir en vacances.

★ **afraid** ADJECTIVE
■ **to be afraid of something** avoir [8] peur de quelque chose □ I'm afraid of spiders. J'ai peur des araignées.
■ **I'm afraid I can't come.** Je crains de ne pouvoir venir.
■ **I'm afraid so.** Hélas oui.
■ **I'm afraid not.** Hélas non.

★ **Africa** NOUN
l'Afrique *fem*
■ **in Africa** en Afrique

African NOUN
▷ *see also* **African** ADJECTIVE
l'Africain *masc*
l'Africaine *fem*

African ADJECTIVE
▷ *see also* **African** NOUN
africain (FEM africaine)

★ **after** PREPOSITION, ADVERB, CONJUNCTION
après
□ after dinner après le dîner □ He ran after me. Il a couru après moi. □ soon after peu après
■ **after I'd had a rest** après m'être reposé
■ **after having asked** après avoir demandé
■ **after all** après tout □ After all, nobody can make us go. Après tout, personne ne peut nous obliger à y aller.

★ **afternoon** NOUN
l'après-midi *masc/fem*
□ 3 o'clock in the afternoon trois heures de l'après-midi □ this afternoon cet après-midi
□ on Saturday afternoon samedi après-midi

afters NOUN
le dessert *masc*

aftershave NOUN
l'après-rasage *masc*

★ **afterwards** ADVERB
après

English-French

a

★ = core vocabulary

□ She left not long afterwards. Elle est partie peu de temps après.

★**again** ADVERB

1 de nouveau (*once more*)

□ They're friends again. Ils sont de nouveau amis.

2 encore une fois (*one more time*)

□ Can you tell me again? Tu peux me le dire encore une fois?

■ **not ... again** ne ... plus □ I won't go there again. Je n'y retournerai plus.

■ **Do it again!** Refais-le!

■ **again and again** à plusieurs reprises

★**against** PREPOSITION

contre

□ He leant against the wall. Il s'est appuyé contre le mur. □ I'm against drugs. Je suis contre les drogues.

★**age** NOUN

l'âge *masc*

□ at the age of 16 à l'âge de seize ans □ an age limit une limite d'âge

■ **I haven't been to the cinema for ages.** Ça fait une éternité que je ne suis pas allé au cinéma.

★**aged** ADJECTIVE

■ **aged 10** âgé de dix ans

★**agenda** NOUN

l'ordre du jour *masc*

□ on the agenda à l'ordre du jour □ the agenda for today's activities l'ordre du jour des activités organisées aujourd'hui

BE CAREFUL!
Do not translate **agenda** by the French word **agenda**.

★**agent** NOUN

l'agent *masc*

□ an estate agent un agent immobilier □ a travel agent un agent de voyage

★**aggressive** ADJECTIVE

agressif (FEM agressive)

★**ago** ADVERB

■ **two days ago** il y a deux jours

■ **two years ago** il y a deux ans

■ **not long ago** il n'y a pas longtemps

■ **How long ago did it happen?** Il y a combien de temps que c'est arrivé?

agony NOUN

■ **to be in agony** souffrir [54] le martyre □ He was in agony. Il souffrait le martyre.

★to **agree** VERB

■ **to agree with** être [35] d'accord avec □ I agree with Erin. Je suis d'accord avec Erin.

■ **to agree to do something** accepter [28] de faire quelque chose □ He agreed to go and pick her up. Il a accepté d'aller la chercher.

■ **to agree that ...** admettre [47] que ... □ I agree that it's difficult. J'admets que c'est difficile.

■ **Garlic doesn't agree with me.** Je ne supporte pas l'ail.

agreed ADJECTIVE

convenu (FEM convenue)

□ at the agreed time au moment convenu

★**agreement** NOUN

l'accord *masc*

■ **to be in agreement** être [35] d'accord

□ Everybody was in agreement with Tomasz. Tout le monde était d'accord avec Tomasz.

agricultural ADJECTIVE

agricole (FEM agricole)

★**agriculture** NOUN

l'agriculture *fem*

★**ahead** ADVERB

devant

□ She looked straight ahead. Elle regardait droit devant elle.

■ **ahead of time** en avance

■ **to plan ahead** organiser [28] à l'avance

■ **The French are 5 points ahead.** Les Français ont cinq points d'avance.

■ **Go ahead!** Allez-y!

★**aid** NOUN

■ **in aid of charity** au profit d'associations caritatives

★**AIDS** NOUN

le sida *masc*

★to **aim** VERB

▷ *see also* **aim** NOUN

■ **to aim at** braquer [28] sur □ He aimed his gun at the target. Il a braqué son revolver sur la cible.

■ **The film is aimed at children.** Le film est destiné aux enfants.

■ **to aim to do something** avoir [8] l'intention de faire quelque chose □ Sami aimed to leave at 5 o'clock. Sami avait l'intention de partir à cinq heures.

★**aim** NOUN

▷ *see also* **aim** VERB

l'objectif *masc*

□ The aim of the festival is to raise money. L'objectif du festival est de collecter des fonds.

★**air** NOUN

l'air *masc*

□ to get some fresh air prendre l'air

■ **by air** en avion □ I prefer to travel by air. Je préfère voyager en avion.

★**air-conditioned** ADJECTIVE

climatisé (FEM climatisée)

air conditioning NOUN

la climatisation *fem*

Air Force NOUN

l'armée de l'air *fem*

air hostess NOUN
l'hôtesse de l'air *fem*
□ She's an air hostess. Elle est hôtesse de l'air.

★**airline** NOUN
la compagnie aérienne *fem*

★**airmail** NOUN
■ **by airmail** par avion

airplane NOUN (US)
l'avion *masc*

★**airport** NOUN
l'aéroport *masc*

aisle NOUN
l'allée centrale *fem*

★**alarm** NOUN
l'alarme *fem* (*warning*)
■ **a fire alarm** une alarme à incendie

alarm clock NOUN
le réveil *masc*

★**album** NOUN
l'album *masc*

★**alcohol** NOUN
l'alcool *masc*

alcoholic NOUN
▷ *see also* **alcoholic** ADJECTIVE
l'alcoolique *masc/fem*
□ He's an alcoholic. C'est un alcoolique.

alcoholic ADJECTIVE
▷ *see also* **alcoholic** NOUN
alcoolisé (FEM alcoolisée)
□ alcoholic drinks des boissons alcoolisées

alert ADJECTIVE
1 vif (FEM vive) (*bright*)
□ a very alert baby un bébé très vif
2 vigilant (FEM vigilante) (*paying attention*)
□ We must stay alert. Nous devons rester vigilants.

★**A levels** PL NOUN
le baccalauréat *masc sing*

DID YOU KNOW...?
The **baccalauréat** (or **bac** for short) is taken at the age of 17 or 18. Students have to sit one of a variety of set subject combinations, rather than being able to choose any combination of subjects they want. If you pass you have the right to a place at university.

Algeria NOUN
l'Algérie *fem*
■ **in Algeria** en Algérie

alien NOUN
l'extra-terrestre *masc/fem* (*from outer space*)

alike ADVERB
■ **to look alike** se ressembler [28] □ The two sisters look alike. Les deux sœurs se ressemblent.

★**alive** ADJECTIVE
vivant (FEM vivante)

★**all** ADJECTIVE, PRONOUN, ADVERB
tout (FEM toute, MASC PL tous)
□ all the time tout le temps □ I ate all of it. J'ai tout mangé. □ all day toute la journée □ all the books tous les livres □ all the girls toutes les filles
■ **All of us went.** Nous y sommes tous allés.
■ **after all** après tout □ After all, nobody can make us go. Après tout, personne ne peut nous obliger à y aller.
■ **all alone** tout seul □ She's all alone. Elle est toute seule.
■ **not at all** pas du tout □ I'm not tired at all. Je ne suis pas du tout fatigué.
■ **The score is 5 all.** Le score est de cinq partout.

★**allergic** ADJECTIVE
allergique (FEM allergique)
■ **to be allergic to something** être [35] allergique à quelque chose □ I'm allergic to cat hair. Je suis allergique aux poils de chat.

allergy NOUN
le allergie *fem*

alley NOUN
la ruelle *fem*

★to **allow** VERB
■ **to be allowed to do something** être [35] autorisé à faire quelque chose □ He's not allowed to go out at night. Il n'est pas autorisé à sortir le soir.
■ **to allow somebody to do something** permettre [47] à quelqu'un de faire quelque chose □ His mum allowed him to go bowling. Sa mère lui a permis d'aller au bowling.

★**all right** ADVERB
1 bien (*okay*)
□ Everything turned out all right. Tout s'est bien terminé.
■ **Are you all right?** Ça va?
2 pas mal (*not bad*)
□ The film was all right. Le film n'était pas mal.
3 d'accord (*when agreeing*)
□ We'll talk about it later. — All right. On en reparlera plus tard. — D'accord.
■ **Is that all right with you?** Tu es d'accord?

all-round ADJECTIVE
général (FEM générale)
■ **a good all-round performance** de bons résultats à tous les niveaux

almond NOUN
l'amande *fem*

★**almost** ADVERB
presque
□ I've almost finished. J'ai presque fini.

★**alone** ADJECTIVE, ADVERB
seul (FEM seule)
□ She lives alone. Elle habite seule.

English-French

a

■ **to leave somebody alone** laisser [28] quelqu'un tranquille □ Leave her alone! Laisse-la tranquille!

■ **to leave something alone** ne pas toucher [28] à quelque chose □ Leave my things alone! Ne touche pas à mes affaires!

★ **along** PREPOSITION, ADVERB
le long de
□ Adam was walking along the beach. Adam se promenait le long de la plage.
■ **all along** depuis le début □ He was lying to me all along. Il m'a menti depuis le début.

★ **aloud** ADVERB
à haute voix
□ He read the poem aloud. Il a lu le poème à haute voix.

★ **alphabet** NOUN
l'alphabet *masc*

★ **Alps** PL NOUN
les Alpes *fem pl*

★ **already** ADVERB
déjà
□ Olivia had already gone. Olivia était déjà partie.

★ **also** ADVERB
aussi

altar NOUN
l'autel *masc*

to **alter** VERB
changer [45]

alternate ADJECTIVE
■ **on alternate days** tous les deux jours

★ **alternative** NOUN
▷ *see also* **alternative** ADJECTIVE
le choix *masc*
□ You have no alternative. Tu n'a pas le choix.
■ **Fruit is a healthy alternative to chocolate.** Les fruits sont plus sains que le chocolat.
■ **There are several alternatives.** Il y a plusieurs possibilités.

★ **alternative** ADJECTIVE
▷ *see also* **alternative** NOUN
autre (FEM autre)
□ They made alternative plans. Ils ont pris d'autres dispositions.
■ **an alternative solution** une solution de rechange
■ **alternative medicine** la médecine douce

alternatively ADVERB
■ **Alternatively, we could just stay at home.** On pourrait aussi rester à la maison.

★ **although** CONJUNCTION
bien que

> **bien que** has to be followed by a verb in the subjunctive.

□ Although she is tired, she's going out tonight. Bien qu'elle soit fatiguée, elle sort ce soir.

altogether ADVERB
1 en tout (*in total*)
□ You owe me £20 altogether. Tu me dois vingt livres en tout.
2 tout à fait (*completely*)
□ I'm not altogether happy with your work. Je ne suis pas tout à fait satisfait de votre travail.

aluminium (US **aluminum**) NOUN
l'aluminium *masc*

★ **always** ADVERB
toujours
□ He's always moaning. Il est toujours en train de ronchonner.

am VERB ▷ *see* **be**

★ **a.m.** ABBREVIATION
du matin
□ at 4 a.m. à quatre heures du matin

amateur NOUN
l'amateur *masc*
l'amatrice *fem*

to **amaze** VERB
■ **to be amazed** être [35] stupéfait □ I was amazed that I managed to do it. J'étais stupéfait d'avoir réussi.

amazed ADJECTIVE
stupéfait (FEM stupéfaite)

★ **amazing** ADJECTIVE
1 stupéfiant (FEM stupéfiante) (*surprising*)
□ That's amazing news! C'est une nouvelle stupéfiante!
2 exceptionnel (FEM exceptionnelle) (*excellent*)
□ Emily's an amazing cook. Emily est une cuisinière exceptionnelle.

ambassador NOUN
l'ambassadeur *masc*
l'ambassadrice *fem*

amber ADJECTIVE
■ **an amber light** un feu orange

★ **ambition** NOUN
l'ambition *fem*

ambitious ADJECTIVE
ambitieux (FEM ambitieuse)
□ She's very ambitious. Elle est très ambitieuse.

★ **ambulance** NOUN
l'ambulance *fem*

amenities PL NOUN
les aménagements *masc pl*
■ **The hotel has very good amenities.** L'hôtel est très bien aménagé.

★ **America** NOUN
l'Amérique *fem*
■ **in America** en Amérique
■ **to America** en Amérique

American NOUN
▷ *see also* **American** ADJECTIVE
l'Américain *masc*
l'Américaine *fem*
■ **the Americans** les Américains

American ADJECTIVE
▷ *see also* **American** NOUN
américain (FEM américaine)
□ He's American. Il est américain. □ She's American. Elle est américaine.

★**among, amongst** PREPOSITION
parmi
□ There were six children among them. Il y avait six enfants parmi eux.
■ **We were among friends.** Nous étions entre amis.
■ **among other things** entre autres

★**amount** NOUN
1 la somme *fem*
□ a large amount of money une grosse somme d'argent
2 la quantité *fem*
□ a huge amount of rice une énorme quantité de riz

amp NOUN
1 l'ampère *masc* (*of electricity*)
2 l'ampli *masc* (*for hi-fi*)

amplifier NOUN
l'amplificateur *masc* (*for hi-fi*)

to **amuse** VERB
amuser [28]
□ He was very amused by the story. L'histoire l'a beaucoup amusé.

amusement arcade NOUN
la salle de jeux électroniques *fem*

an ARTICLE ▷ *see* **a**

to **analyse** VERB
analyser [28]

analysis NOUN
l'analyse *fem*

to **analyze** VERB (US)
analyser [28]

ancestor NOUN
l'ancêtre *masc/fem*

anchor NOUN
l'ancre *fem*

ancient ADJECTIVE
1 antique (FEM antique) (*civilization*)
□ ancient Greece la Grèce antique
2 ancien (FEM ancienne) (*custom, building*)
□ an ancient monument un monument ancien

★**and** CONJUNCTION
et
□ you and me toi et moi □ 2 and 2 are 4 deux et deux font quatre
■ **Please try and come!** Essaie de venir!
■ **He talked and talked.** Il n'a pas arrêté de parler.
■ **better and better** de mieux en mieux

★**angel** NOUN
l'ange *masc*

★**anger** NOUN
la colère *fem*

★**angle** NOUN
l'angle *masc*

angler NOUN
le pêcheur à la ligne *masc*
la pêcheuse à la ligne *fem*

angling NOUN
la pêche à la ligne *fem*

★**angry** ADJECTIVE
en colère
□ Dad looks very angry. Papa a l'air très en colère.
■ **to be angry with somebody** être [35] furieux contre quelqu'un □ Mum's really angry with you. Maman est vraiment furieuse contre toi.
■ **to get angry** se fâcher [28]

★**animal** NOUN
l'animal *masc* (PL les animaux)

ankle NOUN
la cheville *fem*

★**anniversary** NOUN
l'anniversaire *masc*
□ a wedding anniversary un anniversaire de mariage

★to **announce** VERB
annoncer [12]

announcement NOUN
l'annonce *fem*

to **annoy** VERB
agacer [12]
□ He's really annoying me. Il m'agace vraiment.
■ **to get annoyed** se fâcher [28] □ Don't get so annoyed! Ne vous fâchez pas!

★**annoying** ADJECTIVE
agaçant (FEM agaçante)
□ It's really annoying. C'est vraiment agaçant.

★**annual** ADJECTIVE
annuel (FEM annuelle)
□ an annual music festival un festival de musique annuel

anorak NOUN
l'anorak *masc*

anorexic ADJECTIVE
anorexique (FEM anorexique)

★**another** ADJECTIVE
un autre (FEM une autre)
□ Would you like another piece of cake? Tu veux un autre morceau de gâteau?

□ Have you got another skirt? Tu as une autre jupe?

★ to **answer** VERB

▷ *see also* **answer** NOUN

répondre [69] à

□ Can you answer my question? Peux-tu répondre à ma question? □ to answer the phone répondre au téléphone

■ **to answer the door** aller [3E] ouvrir □ Can you answer the door please? Tu peux aller ouvrir s'il te plaît?

★ **answer** NOUN

▷ *see also* **answer** VERB

1 la réponse *fem* (*to question*)

2 la solution *fem* (*to problem*)

answering machine NOUN

le répondeur *masc*

ant NOUN

la fourmi *fem*

Antarctic NOUN

l'Antarctique *fem*

anthem NOUN

■ **the national anthem** l'hymne national *masc*

antibiotic NOUN

l'antibiotique *masc*

antidepressant NOUN

l'antidépresseur *masc*

★ **antique** NOUN

le meuble ancien *masc* (*furniture*)

antique shop NOUN

le magasin d'antiquités *masc*

antiseptic NOUN

l'antiseptique *masc*

★ **any** ADJECTIVE, PRONOUN, ADVERB

> Use **du**, **de la** or **des** to translate 'any' according to the gender of the French noun that follows it. **du** and **de la** become **de l'** before a vowel and most words beginning with 'h'.

1 du

□ Have you got any bread? Avez-vous du pain?

de la

□ Have you got any lemonade? Avez-vous de la limonade?

de l'

□ Have you got any water? Avez-vous de l'eau?

des

□ Have you got any crisps? Avez-vous des chips?

> If you want to say you haven't got any of something, use **de** whatever the gender of the following noun is. **de** becomes **d'** before a vowel and most words beginning with 'h'.

2 de

□ I haven't got any books. Je n'ai pas de livres.

d'

□ I haven't got any money. Je n'ai pas d'argent.

3 en

> Use **en** where there is no noun after 'any'.

□ Sorry, I haven't got any. Désolé, je n'en ai pas.

■ **any more** 1 (*additional*) encore de

□ Would you like any more coffee? Est-ce que tu veux encore du café? 2 (*no longer*) ne ... plus □ I don't love him any more. Je ne l'aime plus.

★ **anybody** PRONOUN

1 quelqu'un (*in question*)

□ Has anybody got a pen? Est-ce que quelqu'un a un stylo?

2 n'importe qui (*no matter who*)

□ Anybody can learn to swim. N'importe qui peut apprendre à nager.

3 ne ... personne

> Use **ne ... personne** in a negative sentence. **ne** comes before the verb, **personne** after it.

□ I can't see anybody. Je ne vois personne.

anyhow ADVERB

de toute façon

□ He doesn't want to go out and anyhow he's not allowed. Il ne veut pas sortir et de toute façon il n'y est pas autorisé.

★ **anyone** PRONOUN

1 quelqu'un (*in question*)

□ Has anyone got a pen? Est-ce que quelqu'un a un stylo?

2 n'importe qui (*no matter who*)

□ Anyone can learn to swim. N'importe qui peut apprendre à nager.

3 ne ... personne

> Use **ne ... personne** in a negative sentence. **ne** comes before the verb, **personne** after it.

□ I can't see anyone. Je ne vois personne.

★ **anything** PRONOUN

1 quelque chose (*in question*)

□ Do you have anything to drink? Tu as quelque chose à boire?

2 n'importe quoi (*no matter what*)

□ Anything could happen. Il pourrait arriver n'importe quoi.

3 ne ... rien

> Use **ne ... rien** in a negative sentence. **ne** comes before the verb, **rien** after it.

□ I can't hear anything. Je n'entends rien.

★ **anyway** ADVERB

de toute façon

□ He doesn't want to go out and anyway he's not allowed. Il ne veut pas sortir et de toute façon il n'y est pas autorisé.

★ **anywhere** ADVERB

1 quelque part (*in question*)

□ Have you seen my coat anywhere? Est-ce que tu as vu mon manteau quelque part?

2 n'importe où (*no matter where*)

□ You can buy stamps almost anywhere. On peut acheter des timbres presque n'importe où.

3 ne ... nulle part

Use **ne ... nulle part** in a negative sentence. **ne** comes before the verb, **nulle part** after it.

□ I can't find it anywhere. Je ne le trouve nulle part.

★ **apart** ADVERB

■ **The two towns are 10 kilometres apart.** Les deux villes sont à dix kilomètres l'une de l'autre.

■ **apart from** à part □ Apart from that, everything's fine. À part ça, tout va bien.

★ **apartment** NOUN

l'appartement *masc*

★ to **apologize** VERB

s'excuser [28]

□ He apologized for being late. Il s'est excusé de son retard.

■ **I apologize!** Je vous prie de m'excuser.

apology NOUN

les excuses *fem pl*

★ **apostrophe** NOUN

l'apostrophe *fem*

app NOUN (= *application*)

l'appli *fem*

□ a mobile app une appli pour portable

apparatus NOUN

1 le matériel *masc* (*in lab*)

2 les agrès *masc pl* (*in gym*)

apparent ADJECTIVE

apparent (FEM apparente)

★ **apparently** ADVERB

apparemment

to **appeal** VERB

▷ *see also* **appeal** NOUN

lancer [12] un appel

□ They appealed for help. Ils ont lancé un appel au secours.

■ **Greece doesn't appeal to me.** Ça ne me tente pas d'aller en Grèce.

■ **Does that appeal to you?** Ça te tente?

appeal NOUN

▷ *see also* **appeal** VERB

l'appel *masc*

□ They have launched an appeal. Ils ont lancé un appel.

★ to **appear** VERB

1 apparaître [56E] (*come into view*)

□ The bus appeared around the corner. Le bus est apparu au coin de la rue.

■ **to appear on TV** passer [58E] à la télé

2 paraître [56] (*seem*)

□ She appeared to be asleep. Elle paraissait dormir.

★ **appearance** NOUN

l'apparence *fem* (*looks*)

□ She takes great care over her appearance. Elle prend grand soin de son apparence.

appendicitis NOUN

l'appendicite *fem*

appetite NOUN

l'appétit *masc*

to **applaud** VERB

applaudir [38]

applause NOUN

les applaudissements *masc pl*

★ **apple** NOUN

la pomme *fem*

■ **an apple tree** un pommier

applicant NOUN

le candidat *masc*

la candidate *fem*

□ There were a hundred applicants for the job. Il y avait cent candidats pour le poste.

★ **application** NOUN

■ **a job application** une candidature

application form NOUN

1 le dossier de candidature *masc* (*for job*)

2 le dossier d'inscription *masc* (*for university*)

★ to **apply** VERB

■ **to apply for a job** poser [28] sa candidature à un poste

■ **to apply to** (*be relevant*) s'appliquer [28] à

□ This rule doesn't apply to us. Ce règlement ne s'applique pas à nous.

★ **appointment** NOUN

le rendez-vous *masc*

□ I've got a dental appointment. J'ai rendez-vous chez le dentiste.

★ to **appreciate** VERB

être [35] reconnaissant de

□ I really appreciate your help. Je vous suis extrêmement reconnaissant de votre aide.

apprentice NOUN

l'apprenti *masc*

l'apprentie *fem*

★ to **approach** VERB

1 s'approcher [28] de (*get nearer to*)

□ He approached the house. Il s'est approché de la maison.

2 aborder [28] (*tackle*)

□ to approach a problem aborder un problème

★**appropriate** ADJECTIVE
appropriée (FEM appropriée)
□ Those shoes aren't very appropriate for school. Ces chaussures ne sont pas très appropriées pour aller à l'école.

approval NOUN
l'approbation *fem*

★to **approve** VERB
■ **to approve of** approuver [28] □ I don't approve of his choice. Je n'approuve pas son choix.
■ **They didn't approve of his girlfriend.** Sa copine ne leur a pas plu.

approximate ADJECTIVE
approximatif (FEM approximative)

apricot NOUN
l'abricot *masc*

★**April** NOUN
avril *masc*
■ **in April** en avril
■ **April Fools' Day** le premier avril

DID YOU KNOW...?
Pinning a paper fish to somebody's back is a traditional April Fool joke in France.

apron NOUN
le tablier *masc*

Aquarius NOUN
le Verseau *masc*
□ I'm Aquarius. Je suis Verseau.

Arab NOUN
▷ *see also* **Arab** ADJECTIVE
l'Arabe *masc/fem*

Arab ADJECTIVE
▷ *see also* **Arab** NOUN
arabe (FEM arabe)
□ the Arab countries les pays arabes

Arabic NOUN
l'arabe *masc*

arch NOUN
l'arc *masc*

archaeologist NOUN
l'archéologue *masc/fem*
□ He's an archaeologist. Il est archéologue.

archaeology NOUN
l'archéologie *fem*

archbishop NOUN
l'archevêque *masc/fem*

archeologist NOUN (US)
l'archéologue *masc/fem*
□ He's an archeologist. Il est archéologue.

archeology NOUN (US)
l'archéologie *fem*

architect NOUN
l'architecte *masc/fem*
□ She's an architect. Elle est architecte.

architecture NOUN
l'architecture *fem*

Arctic NOUN
l'Arctique *masc*

are VERB ▷ *see* **be**

★**area** NOUN
1 la région *fem*
□ She lives in the Paris area. Elle habite dans la région parisienne.
2 le quartier *masc*
□ My favourite area of Paris is Montmartre. Montmartre est le quartier de Paris que je préfère.
3 la superficie *fem*
□ The field has an area of 1500m². Le champ a une superficie de mille cinq cents mètres carrés.

Argentina NOUN
l'Argentine *fem*
■ **in Argentina** en Argentine

Argentinian ADJECTIVE
argentin (FEM argentine)

★to **argue** VERB
se disputer [28]
□ They never stop arguing. Ils n'arrêtent pas de se disputer.

★**argument** NOUN
■ **to have an argument** se disputer [28]
□ They had an argument. Ils se sont disputés.

Aries NOUN
le Bélier *masc*
□ I'm Aries. Je suis Bélier.

★**arm** NOUN
le bras *masc*

armchair NOUN
le fauteuil *masc*

armour (US **armor**) NOUN
l'armure *fem*

★**army** NOUN
l'armée *fem*

★**around** PREPOSITION, ADVERB
1 autour de
□ She wore a scarf around her neck. Elle portait une écharpe autour du cou.
2 environ (*approximately*)
□ It costs around £100. Cela coûte environ cent livres.
3 vers (*date, time*)
□ Let's meet at around 8 p.m. Retrouvons-nous vers vingt heures.
■ **around here** **1** (*nearby*) près d'ici □ Is there a chemist's around here? Est-ce qu'il y a une pharmacie près d'ici? **2** (*in this area*) dans les parages □ He lives around here. Il habite dans les parages.

★to **arrange** VERB
■ **to arrange to do something** prévoir [92]

de faire quelque chose □ They arranged to go out together on Friday. Ils ont prévu de sortir ensemble vendredi.

■ **to arrange a meeting** convenir [89] d'un rendez-vous □ Can we arrange a meeting? Pouvons-nous convenir d'un rendez-vous?

■ **to arrange a party** organiser [28] une fête

arrangement NOUN
l'arrangement *masc* (*plan*)
■ **They made arrangements to go out on Friday night.** Ils ont organisé une sortie vendredi soir.

★ to **arrest** VERB
▷ *see also* **arrest** NOUN
arrêter [28]
□ The police have arrested 5 people. La police a arrêté cinq personnes.

★ **arrest** NOUN
▷ *see also* **arrest** VERB
l'arrestation *fem*
■ **to be under arrest** être [35] en état d'arrestation □ You're under arrest! Vous êtes en état d'arrestation!

arrival NOUN
l'arrivée *fem*

★ to **arrive** VERB
arriver [5E]
□ I arrived at 5 o'clock. Je suis arrivé à cinq heures.

arrow NOUN
la flèche *fem*

★ **art** NOUN
l'art *masc*

artery NOUN
l'artère *fem*

art gallery NOUN
la galerie d'art *fem*

★ **article** NOUN
l'article *masc*
□ a newspaper article un article de journal

artificial ADJECTIVE
artificiel (FEM artificielle)

★ **artist** NOUN
l'artiste *masc/fem*
□ She's an artist. C'est une artiste.

artistic ADJECTIVE
artistique (FEM artistique)

★ **as** CONJUNCTION, ADVERB
1 au moment où (*while*)
□ He came in as I was leaving. Il est arrivé au moment où je partais.
2 puisque (*since*)
□ As it's Sunday, you can have a lie-in. Tu peux faire la grasse matinée, puisque c'est dimanche.

■ **as ... as** aussi ... que □ Pierre's as tall as Michel. Pierre est aussi grand que Michel.

■ **twice as ... as** deux fois plus ... que □ Her coat cost twice as much as mine. Son manteau a coûté deux fois plus cher que le mien.

■ **as much ... as** autant ... que □ I haven't got as much money as you. Je n'ai pas autant d'argent que toi.

■ **as soon as possible** dès que possible □ I'll do it as soon as possible. Je le ferai dès que possible.

■ **as from tomorrow** à partir de demain □ As from tomorrow, the shop will be closed on Sundays. À partir de demain, le magasin sera fermé le dimanche.

■ **as though** comme si □ She acted as though she hadn't seen me. Elle a fait comme si elle ne m'avait pas vu.

■ **as if** comme si

■ **He works as a waiter in the holidays.** Il travaille comme serveur pendant les vacances.

asap ABBREVIATION (= *as soon as possible*)
dès que possible

ashamed ADJECTIVE
■ **to be ashamed** avoir [8] honte □ You should be ashamed of yourself! Tu devrais avoir honte!

ashtray NOUN
le cendrier *masc*

★ **Asia** NOUN
l'Asie *fem*
■ **in Asia** en Asie

Asian NOUN
▷ *see also* **Asian** ADJECTIVE
l'Asiatique *masc/fem*

Asian ADJECTIVE
▷ *see also* **Asian** NOUN
asiatique (FEM asiatique)
■ **He's Asian.** C'est un Asiatique.
■ **She's Asian.** C'est une Asiatique.

★ to **ask** VERB
1 demander [28] (*inquire, request*)
□ 'Have you finished?' she asked. 'Tu as fini?' a-t-elle demandé.

■ **to ask somebody something** demander [28] quelque chose à quelqu'un □ He asked her how old she was. Il lui a demandé quel âge elle avait.

■ **to ask for something** demander [28] quelque chose □ He asked for a cup of tea. Il a demandé une tasse de thé.

■ **to ask somebody to do something** demander [28] à quelqu'un de faire quelque chose □ She asked him to do the shopping. Elle lui a demandé de faire les courses.

■ **to ask about something** se renseigner [28] sur quelque chose □ I asked about train times to Leeds. Je me suis renseigné sur les horaires des trains pour Leeds.

English-French

a

■ **to ask somebody a question** poser [28] une question à quelqu'un

2 inviter [28]

□ Have you asked Omar to the party? Est-ce que tu as invité Omar à la fête?

■ **He asked her out.** (*on a date*) Il lui a demandé de sortir avec lui.

★**asleep** ADJECTIVE

■ **to be asleep** dormir [29] □ He's asleep. Il dort.

■ **to fall asleep** s'endormir [29] □ I fell asleep in front of the TV. Je me suis endormi devant la télé.

asparagus NOUN

les asperges *fem pl*

★**aspect** NOUN

l'aspect *masc*

aspirin NOUN

l'aspirine *fem*

assembly NOUN

DID YOU KNOW...?
There is no assembly in French schools.

asset NOUN

l'atout *masc*

□ Her knowledge of maths will be an asset in the exam. Ses connaissances en maths seront un atout à l'examen.

assignment NOUN

le devoir *masc* (*in school*)

assistance NOUN

l'aide *fem*

★**assistant** NOUN

1 le vendeur *masc*
la vendeuse *fem* (*in shop*)

2 l'assistant *masc*
l'assistante *fem* (*helper*)

association NOUN

l'association *fem*

assortment NOUN

l'assortiment *masc*

to **assume** VERB

supposer [28]

□ I assume she won't be coming. Je suppose qu'elle ne viendra pas.

to **assure** VERB

assurer [28]

□ He assured me he was coming. Il m'a assuré qu'il viendrait.

★**asthma** NOUN

l'asthme *masc*

□ I've got asthma. J'ai de l'asthme.

to **astonish** VERB

étonner [28]

astonished ADJECTIVE

étonné (FEM étonnée)

astonishing ADJECTIVE

étonnant (FEM étonnante)

astrology NOUN

l'astrologie *fem*

astronaut NOUN

l'astronaute *masc/fem*

astronomy NOUN

l'astronomie *fem*

asylum seeker NOUN

le demandeur d'asile *masc*
la demandeuse d'asile *fem*

★**at** PREPOSITION

▷ *see also* **at** NOUN

à + **le** becomes **au**, **à** + **les** becomes **aux**.

à

□ at 4 o'clock à quatre heures □ at Christmas à Noël □ at 50 km/h à cinquante km/h □ at home à la maison □ two at a time deux à la fois □ at school à l'école

au

□ at the office au bureau

aux

□ at the toilet aux toilettes

■ **at night** la nuit

■ **What are you doing at the weekend?** Qu'est-ce que tu fais ce week-end?

★**at** NOUN

▷ *see also* **at** PREPOSITION

l'arobase *fem* (*@ symbol*)

ate VERB ▷ *see* **eat**

Athens NOUN

Athènes

■ **in Athens** à Athènes

★**athlete** NOUN

l'athlète *masc/fem*

athletic ADJECTIVE

athlétique (FEM athlétique)

athletics NOUN

l'athlétisme *masc*

□ I love athletics. J'adore l'athlétisme.

★**Atlantic** NOUN

l'océan Atlantique *masc*

★**atlas** NOUN

l'atlas *masc*

atmosphere NOUN

l'atmosphère *fem*

atom NOUN

l'atome *masc*

atomic ADJECTIVE

atomique (FEM atomique)

★to **attach** VERB

fixer [28]

□ He attached a rope to the car. Il a fixé une corde à la voiture.

■ **Please find attached ...** Veuillez trouver ci-joint ...

attached ADJECTIVE
■ **to be attached to** être [35] attaché à
□ He's very attached to his family. Il est très attaché à sa famille.

attachment NOUN
la pièce jointe *fem* (*email*)

★ to **attack** VERB
▷ *see also* **attack** NOUN
attaquer [28]
□ The dog attacked her. Le chien l'a attaquée.

★ **attack** NOUN
▷ *see also* **attack** VERB
l'attaque *fem*

★ **attempt** NOUN
▷ *see also* **attempt** VERB
la tentative *fem*
□ She gave up after several attempts. Elle y a renoncé après plusieurs tentatives.

★ to **attempt** VERB
▷ *see also* **attempt** NOUN
■ **to attempt to do something** essayer [59] de faire quelque chose □ I attempted to write a song. J'ai essayé d'écrire une chanson.

★ to **attend** VERB
assister [28] à
□ to attend a match assister à un match

> BE CAREFUL!
> Do not translate **to attend** by the French word **attendre**.

★ **attention** NOUN
■ **to pay attention to** faire [36] attention à
□ He didn't pay attention to what I was saying. Il ne faisait pas attention à ce que je disais.

attic NOUN
le grenier *masc*

attitude NOUN
l'attitude *fem* (*way of thinking*)
□ I really don't like your attitude! Je n'aime pas du tout ton attitude!

attorney NOUN (US)
l'avocat *masc*
l'avocate *fem*

to **attract** VERB
attirer [28]
□ Disneyland attracts lots of tourists. Disneyland attire de nombreux touristes.

attraction NOUN
l'attraction *fem*
□ a tourist attraction une attraction touristique

★ **attractive** ADJECTIVE
séduisant (FEM séduisante)
□ She's very attractive. Elle est très séduisante.

aubergine NOUN
l'aubergine *fem*

auction NOUN
la vente aux enchères *fem*

★ **audience** NOUN
les spectateurs *masc pl* (*in theatre*)

audition NOUN
l'audition *fem*

★ **August** NOUN
août *masc*
■ **in August** en août

★ **aunt, aunty** NOUN
la tante *fem*
□ my aunt ma tante

★ **au pair** NOUN
la jeune fille au pair *fem*
□ She's an au pair. Elle est jeune fille au pair.

★ **Australia** NOUN
l'Australie *fem*
■ **in Australia** en Australie
■ **to Australia** en Australie

Australian NOUN
▷ *see also* **Australian** ADJECTIVE
l'Australien *masc*
l'Australienne *fem*
■ **the Australians** les Australiens

Australian ADJECTIVE
▷ *see also* **Australian** NOUN
australien (FEM australienne)
□ He's Australian. Il est australien.

★ **Austria** NOUN
l'Autriche *fem*
■ **in Austria** en Autriche

Austrian NOUN
▷ *see also* **Austrian** ADJECTIVE
l'Autrichien *masc*
l'Autrichienne *fem*
■ **the Austrians** les Autrichiens

Austrian ADJECTIVE
▷ *see also* **Austrian** NOUN
autrichien (FEM autrichienne)
□ She's Austrian. Elle est autrichienne.

★ **author** NOUN
l'auteur *masc*
□ She's a famous author. C'est un auteur connu.

autobiography NOUN
l'autobiographie *fem*

autograph NOUN
l'autographe *masc*

★ **automatic** ADJECTIVE
automatique (FEM automatique)
□ an automatic door une porte automatique

automatically ADVERB
automatiquement

★ **autumn** NOUN
l'automne *masc*
■ **in autumn** en automne

availability NOUN
la disponibilité *fem*

★**available** ADJECTIVE
disponible (FEM disponible)
□ The album is available on the internet. L'album est disponible sur Internet. □ Is Mr Cooke available today? Est-ce que Monsieur Cooke est disponible aujourd'hui?

avalanche NOUN
l'avalanche *fem*

avatar NOUN
l'avatar *masc*

avenue NOUN
l'avenue *fem*

★**average** NOUN
▷ *see also* **average** ADJECTIVE
la moyenne *fem*
□ on average en moyenne

★**average** ADJECTIVE
▷ *see also* **average** NOUN
moyen (FEM moyenne)
□ the average price le prix moyen

avocado NOUN
l'avocat *masc*

★to **avoid** VERB
éviter [28]
□ He avoids her when she's in a bad mood. Il l'évite lorsqu'elle est de mauvaise humeur.
■ **to avoid doing something** éviter [28] de faire quelque chose □ Avoid going out on your own at night. Évite de sortir seul le soir.

awake ADJECTIVE
■ **to be awake** être [35] réveillé □ Is she awake? Elle est réveillée?
■ **He was still awake.** Il ne dormait pas encore.

award NOUN
le prix *masc*
□ He's won an award. Il a remporté un prix.
□ the award for the best actor le prix du meilleur acteur

aware ADJECTIVE
■ **to be aware of something** être [35] conscient de quelque chose

★**away** ADJECTIVE, ADVERB
absent (FEM absente) (*not here*)
□ André's away today. André est absent aujourd'hui.
■ **He's away for a week.** Il est parti pour une semaine.
■ **The town's 2 kilometres away.** La ville est à deux kilomètres d'ici.
■ **The coast is 2 hours away by car.** La côte est à deux heures de route.
■ **Go away!** Va-t'en!
■ **to put something away** ranger [45] quelque chose □ He put this sports kit away in the cupboard. Il a rangé ses affaires de sport dans le placard.

away match NOUN
le match à l'extérieur *masc*

★**awful** ADJECTIVE
affreux (FEM affreuse)
□ That's awful! C'est affreux!
■ **an awful lot of ...** énormément de ...

awfully ADVERB
■ **I'm awfully sorry.** Je suis vraiment désolé.

awkward ADJECTIVE
1 délicat (FEM délicate) (*difficult to deal with*)
□ an awkward situation une situation délicate
2 gênant (FEM gênante) (*embarrassing*)
□ an awkward question une question gênante
■ **It's a bit awkward for me to come and see you.** Ce n'est pas très pratique pour moi de venir vous voir.

axe NOUN
la hache *fem*

Bb

BA NOUN
la licence *fem*
■ **a BA in French** une licence de français

★ **baby** NOUN
le bébé *masc*

baby carriage NOUN (US)
le landau *masc*

★ to **babysit** VERB
faire [36] du baby-sitting

babysitter NOUN
le/la baby-sitter *masc/fem*

babysitting NOUN
le baby-sitting *masc*

bachelor NOUN
le célibataire *masc*
□ He's a bachelor. Il est célibataire.

★ **back** NOUN
▷ *see also* **back** ADJECTIVE, ADVERB, VERB
1 le dos *masc* (*of person, horse, book*)
2 l'arrière *masc* (*of car, house*)
□ in the back à l'arrière
3 le verso *masc* (*of page*)
□ on the back au verso
4 le fond *masc* (*of room, garden*)
□ at the back au fond

★ **back** ADJECTIVE, ADVERB
▷ *see also* **back** NOUN, VERB
arrière (FEM+PL arrière)
□ the back seat le siège arrière □ the back wheel of my bike la roue arrière de mon vélo
■ **the back door** la porte de derrière
■ **to get back** rentrer [68E] □ What time did you get back? À quelle heure est-ce que tu es rentré?
■ **We went there by bus and walked back.** Nous y sommes allés en bus et nous sommes rentrés à pied.
■ **He's not back yet.** Il n'est pas encore rentré.
■ **to call somebody back** rappeler [4] quelqu'un □ I'll call back later. Je rappellerai plus tard.

★ to **back** VERB
▷ *see also* **back** NOUN, ADJECTIVE, ADVERB
soutenir [83] (*support*)
□ We're backing our school team. Nous soutenons l'équipe de notre école.

to **back out** VERB
se désister [28]
□ They backed out at the last minute. Ils se sont désistés au dernier moment.

to **back up** VERB
■ **to back somebody up** soutenir [83] quelqu'un

backache NOUN
le mal au dos *masc*
□ to have backache avoir mal au dos

backbone NOUN
la colonne vertébrale *fem*

to **backfire** VERB
échouer [28] (*go wrong*)

★ **background** NOUN
1 l'arrière-plan *masc* (*of picture*)
□ a house in the background une maison à l'arrière-plan
■ **background noise** les bruits de fond *masc pl*
2 le milieu *masc* (PL les milieux)
□ his family background son milieu familial

backhand NOUN
le revers *masc*

backing NOUN
le soutien *masc* (*support*)

backpack NOUN
le sac à dos *masc*

backpacker NOUN
1 le routard *masc*
la routarde *fem* (*globe-trotter*)
2 le randonneur *masc*
la randonneuse *fem* (*hill-walker*)

backpacking NOUN
■ **to go backpacking** voyager [45] sac au dos

back pain NOUN
le mal au dos *masc*
□ to have back pain avoir mal au dos

backside NOUN
le derrière *masc*

backstroke NOUN
le dos crawlé *masc*

backup NOUN
le soutien *masc* (*support*)
■ **a backup file** une sauvegarde

English-French

b

★ **backwards** ADVERB
en arrière
□ to take a step backwards faire un pas en arrière
■ **to fall backwards** tomber [84E] à la renverse

back yard NOUN
la cour *fem*

★ **bacon** NOUN
1 le lard *masc* (*French type*)
2 le bacon *masc* (*British type*)
□ bacon and eggs des œufs au bacon

★ **bad** ADJECTIVE
1 mauvais (FEM mauvaise)
□ a bad film un mauvais film □ the bad weather le mauvais temps □ to be in a bad mood être de mauvaise humeur

WORD POWER
You can use a number of other words instead of **bad** to mean 'terrible':
awful affreux
□ an awful day une journée affreuse
dreadful terrible
□ a dreadful mistake une terrible erreur
rubbish nul
□ a rubbish team une équipe nulle
terrible épouvantable
□ a terrible book un livre épouvantable

■ **to be bad at something** être [35] mauvais en quelque chose □ I'm really bad at maths. Je suis vraiment mauvais en maths.
2 grave (FEM grave) (*serious*)
□ a bad accident un accident grave
3 vilain (FEM vilaine) (*naughty*)
□ You bad boy! Vilain!
■ **to go bad** (*food*) se gâter [28]
■ **I feel bad about it.** Ça m'ennuie.
■ **not bad** pas mal □ That's not bad at all. Ce n'est pas mal du tout.

badge NOUN
le badge *masc*

★ **badly** ADVERB
mal
□ badly paid mal payé
■ **badly wounded** grièvement blessé
■ **He badly needs a rest.** Il a sérieusement besoin de se reposer.

badminton NOUN
le badminton *masc*
□ to play badminton jouer au badminton

bad-tempered ADJECTIVE
■ **to be bad-tempered** 1 (*by nature*) avoir [8] mauvais caractère □ He's a really bad-tempered person. Il a vraiment mauvais caractère. 2 (*temporarily*) être [35] de mauvaise humeur □ He was really bad-tempered yesterday. Il était vraiment de mauvaise humeur hier.

baffled ADJECTIVE
déconcerté (FEM déconcertée)

★ **bag** NOUN
le sac *masc*

baggage NOUN
les bagages *masc pl*

baggage reclaim NOUN
la livraison des bagages *fem*

baggy ADJECTIVE
ample (FEM ample)

bagpipes PL NOUN
la cornemuse *fem sing*
□ Ed plays the bagpipes. Ed joue de la cornemuse.

★ to **bake** VERB
■ **to bake a cake** faire [36] un gâteau

baked ADJECTIVE
cuit au four (FEM cuite au four)
□ baked potatoes les pommes de terre cuites au four *fem pl*
■ **baked beans** les haricots blancs en sauce *masc pl*

★ **baker** NOUN
le boulanger *masc*
la boulangère *fem*
□ He's a baker. Il est boulanger.

bakery NOUN
la boulangerie *fem*

baking ADJECTIVE
■ **It's baking in here!** Il fait une chaleur torride ici!

★ **balance** NOUN
l'équilibre *masc*
□ to lose one's balance perdre l'équilibre

balanced ADJECTIVE
équilibré (FEM équilibrée)

★ **balcony** NOUN
le balcon *masc*

bald ADJECTIVE
chauve (FEM chauve)

★ **ball** NOUN
1 la balle *fem* (*tennis, golf, cricket*)
2 le ballon *masc* (*football, rugby*)

ballet NOUN
le ballet *masc*
□ We went to a ballet. Nous sommes allés voir un ballet.
■ **ballet lessons** les cours de ballet *masc pl*

ballet dancer NOUN
le danseur classique *masc*
la danseuse classique *fem*

ballet shoes PL NOUN
les chaussons de ballet *masc pl*

★ **balloon** NOUN
le ballon *masc* (*for parties*)
■ **a hot-air balloon** une montgolfière

 Numbers in brackets refer to verb tables on pages 650 to 658

ballpoint pen NOUN
le stylo à bille *masc*
ballroom dancing NOUN
la danse de salon *fem*
★ **ban** NOUN
▷ *see also* **ban** VERB
l'interdiction *fem*
★ to **ban** VERB
▷ *see also* **ban** NOUN
interdire [27]
★ **banana** NOUN
la banane *fem*
□ a banana skin une peau de banane
★ **band** NOUN
1 le groupe *masc* (*rock band*)
2 la fanfare *fem* (*brass band*)
bandage NOUN
▷ *see also* **bandage** VERB
le bandage *masc*
to **bandage** VERB
▷ *see also* **bandage** NOUN
mettre [47] un bandage à
□ The nurse bandaged his arm. L'infirmière lui a mis un bandage au bras.
Band-Aid® NOUN (US)
le pansement adhésif *masc*
bandit NOUN
le bandit *masc*
bang NOUN
▷ *see also* **bang** VERB
1 la détonation *fem*
□ I heard a loud bang. J'ai entendu une forte détonation.
2 le coup *masc*
□ a bang on the head un coup sur la tête
■ **Bang!** Pan!
to **bang** VERB
▷ *see also* **bang** NOUN
se cogner [28] (*part of body*)
□ I banged my head. Je me suis cogné la tête.
■ **to bang the door** claquer [28] la porte
■ **to bang on the door** cogner [28] à la porte
banger NOUN
1 le tacot *masc* (*old car*)
□ His car's an old banger. Sa voiture est un vieux tacot.
2 la saucisse *fem* (*sausage*)
□ bangers and mash les saucisses à la purée
Bangladesh NOUN
le Bangladesh *masc*
■ **from Bangladesh** du Bangladesh
★ **bank** NOUN
1 la banque *fem* (*financial*)
2 le bord *masc* (*of river, lake*)
bank account NOUN
le compte en banque *masc*
★ **banker** NOUN
le banquier *masc*
bank holiday NOUN
le jour férié *masc*
banknote NOUN
le billet de banque *masc*
banned ADJECTIVE
interdit (FEM interdite)
★ **bar** NOUN
1 le bar *masc* (*pub*)
2 le comptoir *masc* (*counter*)
■ **a bar of chocolate** une tablette de chocolat
■ **a bar of soap** une savonnette
barbaric ADJECTIVE
barbare (FEM barbare)
★ **barbecue** NOUN
le barbecue *masc*
barber NOUN
le coiffeur pour hommes *masc*
★ **bare** ADJECTIVE
nu (FEM nue)
barefoot ADJECTIVE, ADVERB
nu-pieds (FEM+PL nu-pieds)
□ The children go around barefoot. Les enfants se promènent nu-pieds.
■ **to be barefoot** avoir [8] les pieds nus □ She was barefoot. Elle avait les pieds nus.
barely ADVERB
à peine
□ I could barely hear what she was saying. J'entendais à peine ce qu'elle disait.
★ **bargain** NOUN
l'affaire *fem*
□ It was a bargain! C'était une affaire!
barge NOUN
la péniche *fem*
to **bark** VERB
aboyer [53]
barmaid NOUN
la barmaid *fem*
□ She's a barmaid. Elle est barmaid.
barman NOUN
le barman *masc*
□ He's a barman. Il est barman.
barn NOUN
la grange *fem*
barrel NOUN
le tonneau *masc* (PL les tonneaux)
barrier NOUN
la barrière *fem*
bartender NOUN (US)
le barman *masc*
□ He's a bartender. Il est barman.
base NOUN
la base *fem*

★ **baseball** NOUN
le base-ball *masc*
■ **a baseball cap** une casquette de base-ball

based ADJECTIVE
■ **based on** fondé sur

★ **basement** NOUN
le sous-sol *masc*

to **bash** VERB
▷ *see also* **bash** NOUN
■ **to bash something** taper [28] sur quelque chose

bash NOUN
▷ *see also* **bash** VERB
■ **I'll have a bash.** Je vais essayer.

basic ADJECTIVE
1 de base
□ It's a basic model. C'est un modèle de base.
2 rudimentaire (FEM rudimentaire)
□ The youth hostel is pretty basic. L'auberge de jeunesse est plutôt rudimentaire.

★ **basically** ADVERB
tout simplement
□ Basically, I just don't like him. Tout simplement, je ne l'aime pas.

basics PL NOUN
les rudiments *masc pl*

basil NOUN
le basilic *masc*

basin NOUN
le lavabo *masc* (*washbasin*)

basis NOUN
■ **on a daily basis** quotidiennement
■ **on a regular basis** régulièrement

★ **basket** NOUN
le panier *masc*

> **BE CAREFUL!**
> Do not translate **basket** by the French word **basket**.

★ **basketball** NOUN
le basket *masc*

bass NOUN
1 la basse *fem* (*guitar, singer*)
□ He plays the bass. Il joue de la basse. □ He's a bass. Il est basse.
■ **a bass guitar** une guitare basse
■ **a double bass** une contrebasse
2 les graves *masc pl* (*on hi-fi*)

bass drum NOUN
la grosse caisse *fem*

bassoon NOUN
le basson *masc*
□ I play the bassoon. Je joue du basson.

★ **bat** NOUN
1 la batte *fem* (*for cricket, rounders*)
2 la raquette *fem* (*for table tennis*)
3 la chauve-souris *fem* (PL les chauves-souris) (*animal*)

★ **bath** NOUN
1 le bain *masc*
□ to have a bath prendre un bain
■ **a hot bath** un bain chaud
2 la baignoire *fem* (*bathtub*)
□ There's a spider in the bath. Il y a une araignée dans la baignoire.

to **bathe** VERB
se baigner [28]

bathing suit NOUN (US)
le maillot de bain *masc*

★ **bathroom** NOUN
la salle de bains *fem*

baths PL NOUN
la piscine *fem sing*

bath towel NOUN
la serviette de bain *fem*

batter NOUN
la pâte à frire *fem*

battery NOUN
1 la pile *fem* (*for torch, toy*)
2 la batterie *fem* (*of car*)

★ **battle** NOUN
la bataille *fem*
□ the Battle of Hastings la bataille de Hastings
■ **It was a battle, but we managed in the end.** Il a fallu se battre, mais on a fini par y arriver.

battleship NOUN
le cuirassé *masc*

bay NOUN
la baie *fem*

BC ABBREVIATION (= *before Christ*)
av. J.-C. (= *avant Jésus-Christ*)
□ in 200 BC en deux cents avant Jésus-Christ

★ to **be** VERB
être [35]
□ I'm tired. Je suis fatigué. □ You're late. Tu es en retard. □ She's English. Elle est anglaise. □ Edinburgh is in Scotland. Édimbourg est en Écosse. □ It's 4 o'clock. Il est quatre heures. □ We are all happy. Nous sommes tous heureux. □ They are in Paris at the moment. Ils sont à Paris en ce moment. □ I've been ill. J'ai été malade.
■ **It's the 28th of October today.** Nous sommes le vingt-huit octobre.
■ **Have you been to Greece before?** Est-ce que tu es déjà allé en Grèce?
■ **I've never been to Paris.** Je ne suis jamais allé à Paris.
■ **to be killed** être [35] tué

> When you are saying what somebody's occupation is in French, you do not translate 'a'.

□ She's a doctor. Elle est médecin. □ He's a student. Il est étudiant.

With certain adjectives, such as 'cold', 'hot', 'hungry' and 'thirsty', use **avoir** instead of **être**.

■ **I'm cold.** J'ai froid.
■ **I'm hungry.** J'ai faim.

When saying how old somebody is, use **avoir** not **être**.

■ **I'm fourteen.** J'ai quatorze ans.
■ **How old are you?** Quel âge as-tu?

When referring to the weather, use **faire**.

■ **It's cold.** Il fait froid.
■ **It's a nice day.** Il fait beau.
■ **It's too hot.** Il fait trop chaud.

★**beach** NOUN
la plage *fem*

bead NOUN
la perle *fem*

beak NOUN
le bec *masc*

beam NOUN
le rayon *masc*

beans NOUN
1 les haricots *masc pl*
2 les haricots blancs à la sauce tomate *masc pl* (*baked beans*)
■ **broad beans** les fèves *fem pl*
■ **green beans** les haricots verts *masc pl*
■ **kidney beans** les haricots rouges *masc pl*

★**bear** NOUN
▷ *see also* **bear** VERB
l'ours *masc*

★to **bear** VERB
▷ *see also* **bear** NOUN
■ **I can't bear it!** C'est insupportable!

beard NOUN
la barbe *fem*
■ **He's got a beard.** Il est barbu.
■ **a man with a beard** un barbu

bearded ADJECTIVE
barbu (FEM barbue)

★**beat** NOUN
▷ *see also* **beat** VERB
le rythme *masc*

★to **beat** VERB
▷ *see also* **beat** NOUN
battre [9]
□ We beat them 3-0. On les a battus trois à zéro.
■ **Beat it!** Fiche le camp! (*informal*)
■ **to beat somebody up** (*informal*) tabasser [28] quelqu'un

★**beautiful** ADJECTIVE
beau (FEM belle, MASC PL beaux)

beau changes to **bel** before a vowel and most words beginning with 'h'.

beautifully ADVERB
admirablement

★**beauty** NOUN
la beauté *fem*

beauty spot NOUN
le site pittoresque *masc*

became VERB ▷ *see* **become**

★**because** CONJUNCTION
parce que
□ I did it because ... Je l'ai fait parce que ...
■ **because of** à cause de □ because of the weather à cause du temps

★to **become** VERB
devenir [25E]
□ He became a famous writer. Il est devenu un grand écrivain.

★**bed** NOUN
le lit *masc*
□ in bed au lit
■ **to go to bed** aller [3E] se coucher
■ **to go to bed with somebody** coucher [28] avec quelqu'un

bed and breakfast NOUN
la chambre d'hôte *fem*
□ We stayed in a bed and breakfast. Nous avons logé dans une chambre d'hôte.
■ **How much is it for bed and breakfast?** C'est combien pour la chambre et le petit déjeuner?

bedclothes PL NOUN
les draps et les couvertures *masc pl*

bedding NOUN
la literie *fem*

★**bedroom** NOUN
la chambre *fem*

bedsit NOUN
la chambre meublée *fem*

bedspread NOUN
le dessus-de-lit *masc* (PL les dessus-de-lit)

★**bedtime** NOUN
■ **Ten o'clock is my usual bedtime.** Je me couche généralement à dix heures.
■ **Bedtime!** Au lit!

bee NOUN
l'abeille *fem*

★**beef** NOUN
le bœuf *masc*
■ **roast beef** le rosbif

★**beefburger** NOUN
le hamburger *masc*

been VERB ▷ *see* **be**

★**beer** NOUN
la bière *fem*

beetle NOUN
le scarabée *masc*

beetroot NOUN
la betterave rouge *fem*

★ **before** PREPOSITION, CONJUNCTION, ADVERB
1 avant
□ before Tuesday avant mardi
2 avant de
□ before going avant de partir □ Before opening the packet, read the instructions. Avant d'ouvrir le paquet, lisez le mode d'emploi. □ I'll phone before I leave. J'appellerai avant de partir.
3 déjà (*already*)
□ I've seen this film before. J'ai déjà vu ce film. □ Have you been rock climbing before? Vous avez déjà fait de la varappe?
■ **the day before** la veille
■ **the week before** la semaine précédente

beforehand ADVERB
à l'avance

to **beg** VERB
1 mendier [19] (*for money*)
2 supplier [19]
□ He begged me to stop. Il m'a supplié d'arrêter.

began VERB ▷ *see* **begin**

beggar NOUN
le mendiant *masc*
la mendiante *fem*

★ to **begin** VERB
commencer [12]
■ **to begin doing something** commencer [12] à faire quelque chose

beginner NOUN
le débutant *masc*
la débutante *fem*
□ I'm just a beginner. Je ne suis qu'un débutant.

★ **beginning** NOUN
le début *masc*
□ at the beginning au début

begun VERB ▷ *see* **begin**

★ **behalf** NOUN
■ **on behalf of somebody** pour quelqu'un

★ to **behave** VERB
se comporter [28]
□ He behaved like an idiot. Il s'est comporté comme un idiot. □ She behaved very badly. Elle s'est très mal comportée.
■ **to behave oneself** être [35] sage □ Did the children behave themselves? Est-ce que les enfants ont été sages?
■ **Behave!** Sois sage!

★ **behaviour** (US **behavior**) NOUN
le comportement *masc*

★ **behind** PREPOSITION, ADVERB
▷ *see also* **behind** NOUN
derrière
□ behind the television derrière la télévision
■ **to be behind** (*late*) avoir [8] du retard □ I'm behind with my revision. J'ai du retard dans mes révisions.

★ **behind** NOUN
▷ *see also* **behind** PREPOSITION, ADVERB
le derrière *masc*

beige ADJECTIVE
beige (FEM beige)

★ **Belgian** NOUN
▷ *see also* **Belgian** ADJECTIVE
le/la Belge *masc/fem*
■ **the Belgians** les Belges

★ **Belgian** ADJECTIVE
▷ *see also* **Belgian** NOUN
belge (FEM belge)
□ Belgian chocolate le chocolat belge □ She's Belgian. Elle est belge.

★ **Belgium** NOUN
la Belgique *fem*
■ **in Belgium** en Belgique

★ to **believe** VERB
croire [20]
□ I don't believe you. Je ne te crois pas.
■ **to believe in something** croire [20] à quelque chose □ Do you believe in ghosts? Tu crois aux fantômes?
■ **to believe in God** croire [20] en Dieu

★ **bell** NOUN
1 la sonnette *fem* (*doorbell*)
■ **to ring the bell** sonner [28] à la porte
2 la cloche *fem* (*in church*)
3 la sonnerie *fem* (*in school*)
4 la clochette *fem*
□ Our cat has a bell on its collar. Notre chat a une clochette sur son collier.

belly NOUN
le ventre *masc*

★ to **belong** VERB
■ **to belong to somebody** être [35] à quelqu'un □ Who does it belong to? C'est à qui? □ That belongs to me. C'est à moi.
■ **Do you belong to any clubs?** Est-ce que tu es membre d'un club?
■ **Where does this belong?** Où est-ce que ça va?

belongings PL NOUN
les affaires *fem pl*

★ **below** PREPOSITION, ADVERB
1 au-dessous de
□ below the castle au-dessous du château
2 en dessous
□ on the floor below à l'étage en dessous
■ **10 degrees below freezing** moins dix

★ **belt** NOUN
la ceinture *fem*

beltway NOUN (US)
le périphérique *masc*

bench NOUN
1 le banc *masc* (*seat*)
2 l'établi *masc* (*for woodwork*)

benchmark NOUN
l'référence *fem*

★ **bend** NOUN
▷ *see also* **bend** VERB
1 le virage *masc* (*in road*)
2 le coude *masc* (*in river*)

★ to **bend** VERB
▷ *see also* **bend** NOUN
1 courber [28] (*back*)
2 plier [19] (*leg, arm*)
□ I can't bend my arm. Je n'arrive pas à plier le bras.
■ **'do not bend'** 'ne pas plier'
3 tordre [49] (*object*)
□ You've bent it. Tu l'as tordu.
4 se tordre [49]
□ It bends easily. Ça se tord facilement.

to **bend down** VERB
se baisser [28]

to **bend over** VERB
se pencher [28]

★ **beneath** PREPOSITION
sous

★ **benefit** NOUN
▷ *see also* **benefit** VERB
l'avantage *masc* (*advantage*)
■ **She's on benefits.** Elle touche les allocations chômage.

★ to **benefit** VERB
▷ *see also* **benefit** NOUN
■ **He'll benefit from the change.** Le changement lui fera du bien.

bent VERB ▷ *see* **bend**

bent ADJECTIVE
tordu (FEM tordue)
□ a bent fork une fourchette tordue

beret NOUN
le béret *masc*

berserk ADJECTIVE
■ **to go berserk** devenir [25E] fou furieux
□ She went berserk. Elle est devenue folle furieuse.

berth NOUN
la couchette *fem*

★ **beside** PREPOSITION
à côté de
□ beside the television à côté de la télévision
■ **He was beside himself.** Il était hors de lui.
■ **That's beside the point.** Cela n'a rien à voir.

besides ADVERB
en plus
□ Besides, it's too expensive. En plus, c'est trop cher.

★ **best** ADJECTIVE, ADVERB
1 meilleur (FEM meilleure)
□ He's the best player in the team. Il est le meilleur joueur de l'équipe. □ Layla's the best at maths. Layla est la meilleure en maths.
2 le mieux
□ Emma sings best. C'est Emma qui chante le mieux. □ That's the best I can do. Je ne peux pas faire mieux.
■ **to do one's best** faire [36] de son mieux
□ It's not perfect, but I did my best. Ça n'est pas parfait, mais j'ai fait de mon mieux.
■ **to make the best of it** s'en contenter [28]
□ We'll have to make the best of it. Il va falloir nous en contenter.

best man NOUN
le garçon d'honneur *masc*

bet NOUN
▷ *see also* **bet** VERB
le pari *masc*
□ to make a bet faire un pari

to **bet** VERB
▷ *see also* **bet** NOUN
parier [19]
□ I bet you he won't come. Je te parie qu'il ne viendra pas. □ I bet he forgot. Je parie qu'il a oublié.

to **betray** VERB
trahir [38]

★ **better** ADJECTIVE, ADVERB
1 meilleur (FEM meilleure)
□ This one's better than that one. Celui-ci est meilleur que celui-là. □ a better way to do it une meilleure façon de le faire
2 mieux
□ That's better! C'est mieux comme ça.
■ **better still** encore mieux □ Go and see her tomorrow, or better still, go today. Va la voir demain, ou encore mieux, vas-y aujourd'hui.
■ **the sooner the better** le plus tôt sera le mieux □ Phone her, the sooner the better. Appelle-la, le plus tôt sera le mieux.
■ **to get better 1** (*improve*) s'améliorer [28]
□ I hope the weather gets better soon. J'espère que le temps va s'améliorer bientôt.
□ My French is getting better. Mon français s'améliore. **2** (*from illness*) se remettre [47]
□ I hope you get better soon. J'espère que tu vas vite te remettre.
■ **to feel better** se sentir [77] mieux □ Are you feeling better now? Tu te sens mieux maintenant?
■ **You'd better do it straight away.** Vous feriez mieux de le faire immédiatement.

■ **I'd better go home.** Je ferais mieux de rentrer.

betting shop NOUN
le bureau de paris *masc*

★**between** PREPOSITION
entre
□ Stroud is between Oxford and Bristol. Stroud est entre Oxford et Bristol. □ between 15 and 20 minutes entre quinze et vingt minutes

bewildered ADJECTIVE
■ **He looked bewildered.** Il avait l'air perplexe.

★**beyond** PREPOSITION
au-delà de
□ There was a lake beyond the mountain. Il y avait un lac au-delà de la montagne.
■ **beyond belief** incroyable
■ **beyond repair** irréparable

biased ADJECTIVE
partial (FEM partiale)

★**Bible** NOUN
la Bible *fem*

★**bicycle** NOUN
le vélo *masc*

★**big** ADJECTIVE
1 grand (FEM grande)
□ a big house une grande maison □ my big brother mon grand frère □ her big sister sa grande sœur

> **WORD POWER**
> You can use a number of other words instead of **big** to mean 'large':
> **enormous** énorme
> □ an enormous cake un gâteau énorme
> **gigantic** gigantesque
> □ a gigantic house une maison gigantesque
> **huge** immense
> □ a huge garden un jardin immense
> **massive** énorme
> □ a massive TV une télé énorme

■ **He's a big guy.** C'est un grand gaillard.
2 gros (FEM grosse) (*car, animal, book, parcel*)
□ a big car une grosse voiture

bigheaded ADJECTIVE
■ **to be bigheaded** avoir [8] la grosse tête

★**bike** NOUN
le vélo *masc*
□ by bike en vélo

bikini NOUN
le bikini *masc*

bilingual ADJECTIVE
bilingue (FEM bilingue)

★**bill** NOUN
1 l'addition *fem* (*in restaurant*)
□ Can we have the bill, please? L'addition, s'il vous plaît.
2 la facture *fem* (*for gas, electricity*)
3 le billet *masc* (US)
□ a five-dollar bill un billet de cinq dollars

★**billion** NOUN
le milliard *masc*

bin NOUN
la poubelle *fem*

bingo NOUN
le bingo *masc*

binoculars PL NOUN
les jumelles *fem pl*
■ **a pair of binoculars** des jumelles

biochemistry NOUN
la biochimie *fem*

biofuel NOUN
le biocarburant *masc*

biography NOUN
la biographie *fem*

★**biology** NOUN
la biologie *fem*

★**bird** NOUN
l'oiseau *masc* (PL les oiseaux)

bird flu NOUN
la grippe aviaire *fem*

birdwatching NOUN
■ **My hobby's birdwatching.** Mon passe-temps favori est d'observer les oiseaux.
■ **to go birdwatching** aller [3E] observer les oiseaux

Biro® NOUN
le bic® *masc*

★**birth** NOUN
la naissance *fem*
□ date of birth la date de naissance

birth certificate NOUN
l'acte de naissance *masc*

birth control NOUN
la contraception *fem*

★**birthday** NOUN
l'anniversaire *masc*
□ When's your birthday? Quelle est la date de ton anniversaire?
■ **a birthday cake** un gâteau d'anniversaire
■ **a birthday card** une carte d'anniversaire
■ **I'm going to have a birthday party.** Je vais faire une fête pour mon anniversaire.

★**biscuit** NOUN
le gâteau sec *masc* (PL les gâteaux secs)

bishop NOUN
l'évêque *masc/fem*

★**bit** VERB ▷ *see* **bite**

★**bit** NOUN
le morceau *masc* (PL les morceaux)
□ Would you like another bit? Est-ce que tu en veux un autre morceau?
■ **a bit of 1** (*piece of*) un morceau de □ a bit of cake un morceau de gâteau **2** (*a little*) un

peu de □ a bit of music un peu de musique
■ **It's a bit of a nuisance.** C'est ennuyeux.
■ **a bit** un peu □ He's a bit mad. Il est un peu fou. □ a bit too hot un peu trop chaud □ Wait a bit! Attends un peu! □ Do you play football? — A bit. Tu joues au football? — Un peu.
■ **to fall to bits** se désintégrer [34]
■ **to take something to bits** démonter [28] quelque chose
■ **bit by bit** petit à petit

bitch NOUN
la chienne *fem* (*female dog*)

★ to **bite** VERB
▷ *see also* **bite** NOUN
1 mordre [49] (*person, dog*)
2 piquer [28] (*insect*)
□ I got bitten by mosquitoes. Je me suis fait piquer par des moustiques.
■ **to bite one's nails** se ronger [45] les ongles

★ **bite** NOUN
▷ *see also* **bite** VERB
1 la piqûre *fem* (*insect bite*)
2 la morsure *fem* (*animal bite*)
■ **to have a bite to eat** manger [45] un morceau

bitten VERB ▷ *see* **bite**

★ **bitter** ADJECTIVE
▷ *see also* **bitter** NOUN
1 amer (FEM amère)
2 glacial (FEM glaciale, MASC PL glaciaux) (*weather, wind*)
□ It's bitter today. Il fait un froid glacial aujourd'hui.

★ **bitter** NOUN
▷ *see also* **bitter** ADJECTIVE
la bière brune *fem*

★ **black** ADJECTIVE
noir (FEM noire)
□ a black jacket une veste noire

blackberry NOUN
la mûre *fem*

blackbird NOUN
le merle *masc*

blackboard NOUN
le tableau noir *masc* (PL les tableaux noirs)

black coffee NOUN
le café *masc*

blackcurrant NOUN
le cassis *masc*

blackmail NOUN
▷ *see also* **blackmail** VERB
le chantage *masc*
□ That's blackmail! C'est du chantage!

to **blackmail** VERB
▷ *see also* **blackmail** NOUN
■ **to blackmail somebody** faire [36] chanter quelqu'un □ He blackmailed her. Il l'a fait chanter.

blackout NOUN
la panne d'électricité *fem* (*power cut*)
■ **to have a blackout** (*faint*) s'évanouir [38]

black pudding NOUN
le boudin *masc*

blade NOUN
la lame *fem*

to **blame** VERB
■ **Don't blame me!** Ça n'est pas ma faute!
■ **I blame the police.** À mon avis, c'est la faute de la police.
■ **He blamed it on my sister.** Il a dit que c'était la faute de ma sœur.

blank ADJECTIVE
▷ *see also* **blank** NOUN
1 blanc (FEM blanche) (*paper*)
2 vierge (FEM vierge) (*form*)
■ **My mind went blank.** J'ai eu un trou.

blank NOUN
▷ *see also* **blank** ADJECTIVE
le blanc *masc*
□ Fill in the blanks. Remplissez les blancs.

blank cheque NOUN
le chèque en blanc *masc*

★ **blanket** NOUN
la couverture *fem*

blast NOUN
■ **a bomb blast** une explosion

blatant ADJECTIVE
flagrant (FEM flagrante)

blaze NOUN
l'incendie *masc*

blazer NOUN
le blazer *masc*

bleach NOUN
l'eau de Javel *fem*

bleached ADJECTIVE
décoloré (FEM décolorée)
□ bleached hair les cheveux décolorés

bleak ADJECTIVE
désolé (FEM désolée) (*place*)
■ **The future looks bleak.** L'avenir semble peu prometteur.

to **bleed** VERB
saigner [28]
□ My nose is bleeding. Je saigne du nez.

bleeper NOUN
le bip *masc*

blender NOUN
le mixer *masc*

to **bless** VERB
bénir [38] (*religiously*)
■ **Bless you!** (*after sneezing*) À tes souhaits!

English-French

b

BE CAREFUL!
Do not translate **to bless** by the French word **blesser**.

blew VERB ▷ *see* **blow**

★ **blind** ADJECTIVE
▷ *see also* **blind** NOUN
aveugle (FEM aveugle)

★ **blind** NOUN
▷ *see also* **blind** ADJECTIVE
le store *masc* (*for window*)

blindfold NOUN
▷ *see also* **blindfold** VERB
le bandeau *masc* (PL les bandeaux)

to **blindfold** VERB
▷ *see also* **blindfold** NOUN
■ **to blindfold somebody** bander [28] les yeux à quelqu'un

to **blink** VERB
cligner [28] des yeux

bliss NOUN
■ **It was bliss!** C'était merveilleux!

blister NOUN
l'ampoule *fem*

blizzard NOUN
la tempête de neige *fem*

blob NOUN
la goutte *fem*
□ a blob of glue une goutte de colle

★ **block** NOUN
▷ *see also* **block** VERB
l'immeuble *masc*
□ He lives in our block. Il habite dans notre immeuble.
■ **a block of flats** un immeuble

★ to **block** VERB
▷ *see also* **block** NOUN
bloquer [28]

blockage NOUN
l'obstruction *fem*

blog NOUN
▷ *see also* **blog** VERB
le blog *masc*
□ She has her own blog. Elle a son blog.

to **blog** VERB
▷ *see also* **blog** NOUN
bloguer [28]
■ **He has been blogging about his school.** Il parle de son école sur son blog.

blogger NOUN
le bloggeur *masc*
la bloggeuse *fem*

blogpost NOUN
le post de blog *masc*

bloke NOUN
le mec *masc* (*informal*)

★ **blonde** ADJECTIVE
blond (FEM blonde)
□ She's got blonde hair. Elle a les cheveux blonds.

★ **blood** NOUN
le sang *masc*

blood pressure NOUN
■ **to have high blood pressure** faire [36] de la tension

blood sports NOUN
les sports sanguinaires *masc pl*

blood test NOUN
la prise de sang *fem*

★ **blouse** NOUN
le chemisier *masc*

★ **blow** NOUN
▷ *see also* **blow** VERB
le coup *masc*

★ to **blow** VERB
▷ *see also* **blow** NOUN
souffler [28] (*wind, person*)
■ **to blow one's nose** se moucher [28]
■ **to blow a whistle** siffler [28]
■ **to blow out a candle** éteindre [60] une bougie

to **blow up** VERB
1 faire [36] sauter
□ The police station was blown up yesterday. On a fait sauter le commissariat hier.
2 gonfler [28]
□ to blow up a balloon gonfler un ballon
■ **The house blew up.** La maison a sauté.

blow-dry NOUN
le brushing *masc*
■ **A cut and blow-dry, please.** Une coupe brushing, s'il vous plaît.

blown VERB ▷ *see* **blow**

★ **blue** ADJECTIVE
bleu (FEM bleue)
□ a blue dress une robe bleue
■ **It came out of the blue.** C'était complètement inattendu.

blues PL NOUN
le blues *masc sing*

to **bluff** VERB
▷ *see also* **bluff** NOUN
bluffer [28]

bluff NOUN
▷ *see also* **bluff** VERB
le bluff *masc*
□ It's just a bluff. C'est du bluff.

blunder NOUN
la gaffe *fem*

blunt ADJECTIVE
1 brusque (FEM brusque) (*person*)
2 émoussé (FEM émoussée) (*knife*)

to **blush** VERB
rougir [38]

★**board** NOUN
1 la planche *fem* (*wooden*)
2 le tableau *masc* (PL les tableaux) (*blackboard*)
□ on the board au tableau
3 le panneau *masc* (PL les panneaux) (*noticeboard*)
4 le jeu *masc* (PL les jeux) (*for board games*)
5 l'échiquier *masc* (*for chess*)
■ **on board** à bord
■ **full board** pension complète

boarder NOUN
l'interne *masc/fem*

board game NOUN
le jeu de société *masc* (PL les jeux de société)

boarding card NOUN
la carte d'embarquement *fem*

boarding school NOUN
le pensionnat *masc*
■ **I go to boarding school.** Je suis interne.

to **boast** VERB
se vanter [28]
□ Stop boasting! Arrête de te vanter!
■ **to boast about something** se vanter [28] de quelque chose

★**boat** NOUN
le bateau *masc* (PL les bateaux)

★**body** NOUN
le corps *masc*

bodybuilding NOUN
le culturisme *masc*

bodyguard NOUN
le garde du corps *masc*

bog NOUN
la tourbière *fem* (*marsh*)

★**boil** NOUN
▷ *see also* **boil** VERB
le furoncle *masc*

★to **boil** VERB
▷ *see also* **boil** NOUN
1 faire [36] bouillir
□ to boil some water faire bouillir de l'eau
■ **to boil an egg** faire [36] cuire un œuf
2 bouillir [11]
□ The water's boiling. L'eau bout. □ The water's boiled. L'eau a bouilli.

to **boil over** VERB
déborder [28]

boiled ADJECTIVE
à l'eau
□ boiled potatoes des pommes de terre à l'eau
■ **a boiled egg** un œuf à la coque

boiling ADJECTIVE
■ **It's boiling in here!** Il fait une chaleur torride ici!
■ **boiling hot** torride □ a boiling hot day une journée torride

bolt NOUN
1 le verrou *masc* (*on door*)
2 le boulon *masc* (*with nut*)

★**bomb** NOUN
▷ *see also* **bomb** VERB
la bombe *fem*

★to **bomb** VERB
▷ *see also* **bomb** NOUN
bombarder [28]

bomber NOUN
le bombardier *masc*

bombing NOUN
l'attentat à la bombe *masc*

bond NOUN
le lien *masc*

★**bone** NOUN
1 l'os *masc* (*of human, animal*)
2 l'arête *fem* (*of fish*)

bone dry ADJECTIVE
complètement sec (FEM complètement sèche)

bonfire NOUN
le feu *masc* (PL les feux)

> **DID YOU KNOW...?**
> The French do not celebrate Bonfire Night, though they have fireworks on the 14th July, which is Bastille Day.

bonnet NOUN
le capot *masc* (*of car*)

bonus NOUN
1 la prime *fem* (*extra payment*)
2 le plus *masc* (*added advantage*)

★**book** NOUN
▷ *see also* **book** VERB
le livre *masc*

★to **book** VERB
▷ *see also* **book** NOUN
réserver [28]
□ We haven't booked. Nous n'avons pas réservé.

bookcase NOUN
la bibliothèque *fem*

booklet NOUN
la brochure *fem*

bookmark NOUN
le signet *masc* (*computing*)

bookshelf NOUN
l'étagère à livres *fem*

★**bookshop** NOUN
la librairie *fem*

to **boost** VERB
stimuler [28]
□ to boost the economy stimuler l'économie
■ **The win boosted the team's morale.** La victoire a remonté le moral de l'équipe.

★ **boot** NOUN
1 le coffre *masc* (*of car*)
2 la botte *fem* (*fashion boot*)
3 la chaussure de marche *fem* (*for hiking*)
■ **football boots** des chaussures de foot

booze NOUN
l'alcool *masc*

★ **border** NOUN
la frontière *fem*

bore VERB ▷ *see* **bear**

★ **bored** ADJECTIVE
■ **to be bored** s'ennuyer [53] □ I was bored. Je m'ennuyais.
■ **to get bored** s'ennuyer [53]

boredom NOUN
l'ennui *masc*

★ **boring** ADJECTIVE
ennuyeux (FEM ennuyeuse)

★ **born** ADJECTIVE
■ **to be born** naître [52E] □ I was born in 2000. Je suis né en deux mille.

★ to **borrow** VERB
emprunter [28]
□ Can I borrow your tablet? Je peux emprunter ta tablette?
■ **to borrow something from somebody** emprunter [28] quelque chose à quelqu'un
□ I borrowed some money from a friend. J'ai emprunté de l'argent à un ami.

Bosnia NOUN
la Bosnie *fem*

Bosnian ADJECTIVE
bosniaque (FEM bosniaque)

★ **boss** NOUN
le patron *masc*
la patronne *fem*

to **boss around** VERB
■ **to boss somebody around** donner [28] des ordres à quelqu'un

bossy ADJECTIVE
autoritaire (FEM autoritaire)

★ **both** ADJECTIVE, PRONOUN
tous les deux *masc pl*
toutes les deux *fem pl*
□ We both went. Nous y sommes allés tous les deux. □ Emma and Zahara both went. Emma et Zahara y sont allées toutes les deux.
□ Both of your answers are wrong. Vos réponses sont toutes les deux mauvaises.
□ Both of them have left. Ils sont partis tous les deux. □ Both of us went. Nous y sommes allés tous les deux. □ Both Ava and Harry are against it. Ava et Harry sont tous les deux contre.
■ **He speaks both German and Italian.** Il parle allemand et italien.

★ to **bother** VERB
1 tracasser [28] (*worry*)
□ What's bothering you? Qu'est-ce qui te tracasse?
2 déranger [45] (*disturb*)
□ I'm sorry to bother you. Je suis désolé de vous déranger.
■ **no bother** aucun problème
■ **Don't bother!** Ça n'est pas la peine!
■ **to bother to do something** prendre [65] la peine de faire quelque chose □ He didn't bother to tell me about it. Il n'a pas pris la peine de m'en parler.

★ **bottle** NOUN
la bouteille *fem*

bottle bank NOUN
le conteneur à verre *masc*

bottle-opener NOUN
l'ouvre-bouteille *masc*

★ **bottom** NOUN
▷ *see also* **bottom** ADJECTIVE
1 le fond *masc* (*of container, bag, sea*)
2 le derrière *masc* (*buttocks*)
3 le bas *masc* (*of page, list*)

★ **bottom** ADJECTIVE
▷ *see also* **bottom** NOUN
inférieur (FEM inférieure)
□ the bottom shelf l'étagère inférieure
■ **the bottom sheet** le drap de dessous

bought VERB ▷ *see* **buy**

to **bounce** VERB
rebondir [38]

bouncer NOUN
le videur *masc*

bound ADJECTIVE
■ **He's bound to fail.** Il va sûrement échouer.

boundary NOUN
la frontière *fem*

bow NOUN
▷ *see also* **bow** VERB
1 le nœud *masc* (*knot*)
□ to tie a bow faire un nœud
2 l'arc *masc*
□ a bow and arrows un arc et des flèches

to **bow** VERB
▷ *see also* **bow** NOUN
faire [36] une révérence

bowels PL NOUN
les intestins *masc pl*

★ **bowl** NOUN
▷ *see also* **bowl** VERB
le bol *masc* (*for soup, cereal*)

★ to **bowl** VERB
▷ *see also* **bowl** NOUN
lancer [12] la balle (*in cricket*)

bowler NOUN
le lanceur *masc* (*in cricket*)

bowling NOUN
le bowling *masc*
■ **to go bowling** jouer [28] au bowling
■ **a bowling alley** un bowling

bowls NOUN
les boules *fem pl*
□ to play bowls jouer aux boules

bow tie NOUN
le nœud papillon *masc*

★**box** NOUN
la boîte *fem*
□ a box of matches une boîte d'allumettes
■ **a cardboard box** un carton

boxer NOUN
le boxeur *masc*

boxer shorts PL NOUN
le caleçon *masc sing*

boxing NOUN
la boxe *fem*

Boxing Day NOUN
le lendemain de Noël *masc*
□ on Boxing Day le lendemain de Noël

★**boy** NOUN
le garçon *masc*

★**boyfriend** NOUN
le copain *masc*
□ Have you got a boyfriend? Est-ce que tu as un copain?

bra NOUN
le soutien-gorge *masc* (PL les soutiens-gorge)

brace NOUN
l'appareil *masc* (*on teeth*)
□ She wears a brace. Elle a un appareil.

bracelet NOUN
le bracelet *masc*

braces PL NOUN
l'appareil *masc sing* (*on teeth*)
□ She wears braces. Elle a un appareil.

brackets PL NOUN
■ **in brackets** entre parenthèses

★**brain** NOUN
le cerveau *masc* (PL les cerveaux)

brainy ADJECTIVE
intelligent (FEM intelligente)

brake NOUN
▷ *see also* **brake** VERB
le frein *masc*

to **brake** VERB
▷ *see also* **brake** NOUN
freiner [28]

★**branch** NOUN
1 la branche *fem* (*of tree*)
2 l'agence *fem* (*of bank*)

brand NOUN
la marque *fem*
□ a well-known brand of trainers une marque de baskets bien connue

brand name NOUN
la marque *fem*

brand-new ADJECTIVE
tout neuf (FEM toute neuve)

brandy NOUN
le cognac *masc*

brass NOUN
le cuivre *masc*
■ **the brass section** les cuivres

brass band NOUN
la fanfare *fem*

brat NOUN
■ **He's a spoiled brat.** C'est un enfant gâté.

★**brave** ADJECTIVE
courageux (FEM courageuse)

Brazil NOUN
le Brésil *masc*
■ **in Brazil** au Brésil

★**bread** NOUN
le pain *masc*
□ brown bread le pain complet □ white bread le pain blanc
■ **bread and butter** les tartines de pain beurrées *fem pl*

★**break** NOUN
▷ *see also* **break** VERB
1 la pause *fem* (*rest*)
□ to take a break faire une pause
2 la récréation *fem* (*at school*)
□ during morning break pendant la récréation du matin
■ **the Christmas break** les vacances de Noël
■ **Give me a break!** Laisse-moi tranquille!

★to **break** VERB
▷ *see also* **break** NOUN
1 casser [28]
□ Careful, you'll break something! Attention, tu vas casser quelque chose!
2 se casser [28] (*get broken*)
□ Careful, it'll break! Attention, ça va se casser!
■ **to break one's leg** se casser [28] la jambe
□ I broke my leg. Je me suis cassé la jambe.
■ **to break a promise** rompre [75] une promesse
■ **to break a record** battre [9] un record
■ **to break the law** violer [28] la loi

to **break down** VERB
tomber [84E] en panne
□ The car broke down. La voiture est tombée en panne.

to **break in** VERB
entrer [32E] par effraction

to **break off** VERB
1 casser [28]
□ He broke off a piece of chocolate. Il a cassé un bout de chocolat.

2 se casser [28]
□ The branch broke off in the storm. La branche s'est cassée pendant l'orage.

to **break open** VERB
forcer [12] (*door, cupboard*)

to **break out** VERB
1 se déclarer [28] (*fire*)
2 éclater [28] (*war*)
3 s'évader [28] (*prisoner*)
■ **to break out in a rash** être [35] couvert de boutons

to **break up** VERB
1 se disperser [28] (*crowd*)
2 se terminer [28] (*meeting, party*)
3 se séparer [28] (*couple*)
■ **to break up a fight** mettre [47] fin à une bagarre
■ **We break up next Wednesday.** Nos vacances commencent mercredi.

breakdown NOUN
1 la panne *fem* (*in vehicle*)
□ to have a breakdown tomber en panne
2 la dépression *fem* (*mental*)
□ to have a breakdown faire une dépression

breakdown van NOUN
la dépanneuse *fem*

★ **breakfast** NOUN
le petit déjeuner *masc*
□ What would you like for breakfast? Qu'est-ce que vous voulez pour le petit déjeuner?

break-in NOUN
le cambriolage *masc*

breast NOUN
le sein *masc* (*of woman*)
■ **chicken breast** le blanc de poulet

to **breast-feed** VERB
allaiter [28]

breaststroke NOUN
la brasse *fem*

★ **breath** NOUN
l'haleine *fem*
□ to have bad breath avoir mauvaise haleine
■ **to be out of breath** être [35] essoufflé
■ **to get one's breath back** reprendre [65] son souffle

★ to **breathe** VERB
respirer [28]

to **breathe in** VERB
inspirer [28]

to **breathe out** VERB
expirer [28]

to **breed** VERB
▷ *see also* **breed** NOUN
se reproduire [23] (*reproduce*)
■ **to breed dogs** faire [36] de l'élevage de chiens

breed NOUN
▷ *see also* **breed** VERB
la race *fem*

breeze NOUN
la brise *fem*

brewery NOUN
la brasserie *fem*

to **bribe** VERB
soudoyer [53]

brick NOUN
la brique *fem*
□ a brick wall un mur en brique

bricklayer NOUN
le maçon *masc*

bride NOUN
la mariée *fem*

bridegroom NOUN
le marié *masc*

bridesmaid NOUN
la demoiselle d'honneur *fem*

★ **bridge** NOUN
1 le pont *masc*
□ a suspension bridge un pont suspendu
2 le bridge *masc*
□ to play bridge jouer au bridge

brief ADJECTIVE
bref (FEM brève)

briefcase NOUN
la serviette *fem*

briefly ADVERB
brièvement

briefs PL NOUN
le slip *masc sing*
■ **a pair of briefs** un slip

★ **bright** ADJECTIVE
1 vif (FEM vive) (*colour, light*)
□ a bright colour une couleur vive
■ **bright blue** bleu vif □ a bright blue car une voiture bleu vif
2 intelligent (FEM intelligente)
□ He's not very bright. Il n'est pas très intelligent.

★ **brilliant** ADJECTIVE
1 génial (FEM géniale, MASC PL géniaux) (*wonderful*)
□ Brilliant! Génial!
2 brillant (FEM brillante) (*clever*)
□ a brilliant scientist un savant brillant

★ to **bring** VERB
1 apporter [28]
□ I always bring my lunch with me. J'apporte toujours mon déjeuner. □ You never bring me a present. Tu ne m'apportes jamais de cadeau. □ She brought me some beautiful flowers. Elle m'a apporté de jolies fleurs. □ Bring warm clothes. Apportez des vêtements chauds. □ Could you bring me my trainers? Tu peux m'apporter mes baskets?

Numbers in brackets refer to verb tables on pages 650 to 658

2 amener [43] (*person*)
□ Can I bring a friend? Est-ce que je peux amener un ami?

to **bring back** VERB
rapporter [28]

to **bring forward** VERB
avancer [12]
□ The rugby match was brought forward. On a avancé le match de rugby.

to **bring up** VERB
élever [43]
□ She brought up 5 children on her own. Elle a élevé cinq enfants toute seule.

★ **Britain** NOUN
la Grande-Bretagne *fem*
■ **in Britain** en Grande-Bretagne
■ **to Britain** en Grande-Bretagne
■ **I'm from Britain.** Je suis britannique.
■ **Great Britain** la Grande-Bretagne

★ **British** ADJECTIVE
britannique (FEM britannique)
■ **the British** les Britanniques *masc pl*
■ **the British Isles** les îles Britanniques *fem pl*

★ **Brittany** NOUN
la Bretagne *fem*
■ **in Brittany** en Bretagne
■ **to Brittany** en Bretagne
■ **She's from Brittany.** Elle est bretonne.

broad ADJECTIVE
large (FEM large) (*wide*)
■ **in broad daylight** en plein jour
■ **broad beans** les fèves *fem pl*

broadband NOUN
l'ADSL *masc*
□ Do you have fast broadband? Tu as une connexion haut débit?

broadcast NOUN
▷ *see also* **broadcast** VERB
l'émission *fem*

to **broadcast** VERB
▷ *see also* **broadcast** NOUN
diffuser [28]
□ The concert was broadcast yesterday. Le concert a été diffusé hier.
■ **to broadcast live** retransmettre [47] en direct

broad-minded ADJECTIVE
large d'esprit (FEM large d'esprit)

★ **broccoli** NOUN
les brocolis *masc pl*

brochure NOUN
la brochure *fem*

to **broil** VERB (US)
■ **to broil something** faire [36] griller quelque chose

broke VERB ▷ *see* **break**

broke ADJECTIVE
■ **to be broke** (*without money*) être [35] fauché

broken ADJECTIVE
cassé (FEM cassée)
□ It's broken. C'est cassé. □ a broken leg une jambe cassée □ He's got a broken arm. Il a le bras cassé.

bronchitis NOUN
la bronchite *fem*

bronze NOUN
le bronze *masc*
□ the bronze medal la médaille de bronze

brooch NOUN
la broche *fem*

broom NOUN
le balai *masc*

★ **brother** NOUN
le frère *masc*
□ my brother mon frère □ my big brother mon grand frère

brother-in-law NOUN
le beau-frère *masc* (PL les beaux-frères)

brought VERB ▷ *see* **bring**

★ **brown** ADJECTIVE
1 marron (FEM+PL marron) (*clothes*)
2 brun (FEM brune) (*hair*)
3 bronzé (FEM bronzée) (*tanned*)
■ **brown bread** le pain complet

Brownie NOUN
la jeannette *fem*

to **browse** VERB
parcourir [16] le Net (*on internet*)

browser NOUN
le navigateur *masc* (*for internet*)

bruise NOUN
le bleu *masc*

★ **brush** NOUN
▷ *see also* **brush** VERB
1 la brosse *fem*
2 le pinceau *masc* (PL les pinceaux) (*paintbrush*)

★ to **brush** VERB
▷ *see also* **brush** NOUN
brosser [28]
■ **to brush one's hair** se brosser [28] les cheveux □ I brushed my hair. Je me suis brossé les cheveux.
■ **to brush one's teeth** se brosser [28] les dents □ I brush my teeth every night. Je me brosse les dents tous les soirs.

★ **Brussels** NOUN
Bruxelles
■ **in Brussels** à Bruxelles
■ **to Brussels** à Bruxelles

Brussels sprouts PL NOUN
les choux de Bruxelles *masc pl*

English–French

b

brutal ADJECTIVE
brutal (FEM brutale, MASC PL brutaux)

BSc NOUN (= *Bachelor of Science*)
la licence *fem*
■ **a BSc in Mathematics** une licence de mathématiques

bubble NOUN
la bulle *fem*

bubble bath NOUN
le bain moussant *masc*

bubble gum NOUN
le chewing-gum *masc*

bucket NOUN
le seau *masc* (PL les seaux)

buckle NOUN
la boucle *fem* (*on belt, watch, shoe*)

Buddhism NOUN
le bouddhisme *masc*

Buddhist ADJECTIVE
bouddhiste (FEM bouddhiste)

buddy NOUN (US)
le copain *masc*
la copine *fem*

★ **budget** NOUN
le budget *masc*

budgie NOUN
la perruche *fem*

buffet NOUN
le buffet *masc*

buffet car NOUN
la voiture-bar *fem*

bug NOUN
1 l'insecte *masc* (*insect*)
2 le microbe *masc* (*infection*)
□ There's a bug going round. Il y a un microbe qui traîne.
■ **a stomach bug** une gastroentérite
3 le bug *masc* (*in computer*)

bugged ADJECTIVE
sur écoute
□ The room was bugged. La pièce était sur écoute.

★ to **build** VERB
construire [23]
□ He's building a garage. Il construit un garage.

to **build up** VERB
s'accumuler [28] (*increase*)

builder NOUN
1 l'entrepreneur *masc* (*owner of firm*)
2 le maçon *masc* (*worker*)

★ **building** NOUN
le bâtiment *masc*
■ **a building site** un chantier

built VERB ▷ *see* **build**

bulb NOUN
l'ampoule *fem* (*electric*)

Bulgaria NOUN
la Bulgarie *fem*

bull NOUN
le taureau *masc* (PL les taureaux)

bullet NOUN
la balle *fem*

bulletin board NOUN
la messagerie électronique *fem* (*computer*)

bullfighting NOUN
la tauromachie *fem*

bully NOUN
▷ *see also* **bully** VERB
la brute *fem*
□ He's a big bully. C'est une brute.

to **bully** VERB
▷ *see also* **bully** NOUN
tyranniser [28]

bum NOUN
le derrière *masc* (*bottom*)

bum bag NOUN
la banane *fem*

bump NOUN
▷ *see also* **bump into** VERB
1 la bosse *fem* (*lump*)
2 l'accrochage *masc* (*minor accident*)
□ We had a bump. Nous avons eu un accrochage.

to **bump into** VERB
▷ *see also* **bump** NOUN
■ **to bump into something** rentrer [68E] dans quelque chose □ I bumped into the table in the dark. Je suis rentrée dans la table dans le noir.
■ **to bump into somebody** 1 (*literally*) rentrer [68E] dans quelqu'un □ He stopped suddenly and I bumped into him. Il s'est arrêté subitement et je lui suis rentré dedans.
2 (*meet by chance*) rencontrer [28] par hasard □ I bumped into Nadiya in the supermarket. J'ai rencontré Nadiya par hasard au supermarché.

bumper NOUN
le pare-chocs *masc* (PL les pare-chocs)

bumpy ADJECTIVE
cahoteux (FEM cahoteuse)

bun NOUN
le petit pain au lait *masc*

★ **bunch** NOUN
■ **a bunch of flowers** un bouquet de fleurs
■ **a bunch of grapes** une grappe de raisin
■ **a bunch of keys** un trousseau de clés

bunches PL NOUN
les couettes *fem pl*
□ She has her hair in bunches. Elle a des couettes.

bungalow NOUN
le bungalow *masc*

bunk NOUN
la couchette *fem*
■ **bunk beds** les lits superposés *masc pl*

★ **burger** NOUN
le hamburger *masc*

burglar NOUN
le cambrioleur *masc*
la cambrioleuse *fem*

to **burglarize** VERB (US)
cambrioler [28]

burglary NOUN
le cambriolage *masc*

to **burgle** VERB
cambrioler [28]
□ Her house was burgled. Sa maison a été cambriolée.

★ **burn** NOUN
▷ *see also* **burn** VERB
la brûlure *fem*

★ to **burn** VERB
▷ *see also* **burn** NOUN
1 brûler [28] (*rubbish, documents*)
2 faire [36] brûler (*food*)
□ I burned the cake. J'ai fait brûler le gâteau.
3 graver [28] (*CD, DVD*)
■ **to burn oneself** se brûler [28] □ I burned myself on the oven door. Je me suis brûlé sur la porte du four.
■ **I've burned my hand.** Je me suis brûlé la main.

to **burn down** VERB
brûler [28]
□ The factory burned down. L'usine a brûlé.

to **burst** VERB
éclater [28]
□ The balloon burst. Le ballon a éclaté.
■ **to burst a balloon** faire [36] éclater un ballon
■ **to burst out laughing** éclater [28] de rire
■ **to burst into flames** prendre [65] feu
■ **to burst into tears** fondre [69] en larmes

★ to **bury** VERB
enterrer [28]

★ **bus** NOUN
l'autobus *masc*
□ the bus driver le conducteur d'autobus □ a bus stop un arrêt d'autobus
■ **the school bus** le car scolaire
■ **a bus pass** une carte d'abonnement pour le bus
■ **a bus station** une gare routière
■ **a bus ticket** un ticket de bus

bush NOUN
le buisson *masc*

★ **business** NOUN
1 l'entreprise *fem* (*firm*)
□ He's got his own business. Il a sa propre entreprise.
2 les affaires *fem pl* (*commerce*)
□ He's away on business. Il est en voyage d'affaires.
■ **a business trip** un voyage d'affaires
■ **It's none of my business.** Ça ne me regarde pas.

★ **businessman** NOUN
l'homme d'affaires *masc*

★ **businesswoman** NOUN
la femme d'affaires *fem*

busker NOUN
le musicien de rue *masc*
la musicienne de rue *fem*

bust NOUN
la poitrine *fem* (*chest*)

★ **busy** ADJECTIVE
1 occupé (FEM occupée) (*person, phone line*)
2 chargé (FEM chargée) (*day, schedule*)
3 très fréquenté (FEM très fréquentée) (*shop, street*)

busy signal NOUN (US)
la tonalité 'occupé' *fem*

★ **but** CONJUNCTION
mais
□ I'd like to come, but I'm busy. J'aimerais venir mais je suis occupé.

★ **butcher** NOUN
le boucher *masc*
□ He's a butcher. Il est boucher.

★ **butcher's** NOUN
la boucherie *fem*

★ **butter** NOUN
le beurre *masc*

butterfly NOUN
le papillon *masc*

buttocks PL NOUN
les fesses *fem pl*

★ **button** NOUN
le bouton *masc*

★ to **buy** VERB
▷ *see also* **buy** NOUN
acheter [1]
□ I bought him an ice cream. Je lui ai acheté une glace.
■ **to buy something from somebody** acheter [1] quelque chose à quelqu'un □ I bought a watch from him. Je lui ai acheté une montre.

★ **buy** NOUN
▷ *see also* **buy** VERB
■ **It was a good buy.** C'était une bonne affaire.

★ **by** PREPOSITION
1 par
□ The thieves were caught by the police. Les voleurs ont été arrêtés par la police.

2 de
□ a painting by Picasso un tableau de Picasso □ a book by Philip Pullman un livre de Philip Pullman

3 en
□ by car en voiture □ by train en train □ by bus en autobus

4 à côté de (*close to*)
□ Where's the bank? — It's by the post office. Où est la banque? — Elle est à côté de la poste.

5 avant (*not later than*)
□ We have to be there by 4 o'clock. Nous devons y être avant quatre heures.

■ **by the time ...** quand ... □ By the time I got there it was too late. Quand je suis arrivé il était déjà trop tard. □ It'll be ready by the time you get back. Ça sera prêt quand vous reviendrez.

■ **That's fine by me.** Ça me va.

■ **all by himself** tout seul

■ **all by herself** toute seule

■ **I did it all by myself.** Je l'ai fait tout seul.

■ **by the way** au fait

★ **bye** EXCLAMATION
salut!

bypass NOUN
la route de contournement *fem*

Cc

cab NOUN
le taxi *masc*

★**cabbage** NOUN
le chou *masc* (PL les choux)

cabin NOUN
la cabine *fem* (*on ship*)

cabinet NOUN
■ **a bathroom cabinet** une armoire de salle de bain

★**cable** NOUN
le câble *masc*

cable car NOUN
le téléphérique *masc*

cable television NOUN
la télévision par câble *fem*

cactus NOUN
le cactus *masc*

cadet NOUN
■ **a police cadet** un élève policier
■ **a cadet officer** un élève officier

★**café** NOUN
le café *masc*

DID YOU KNOW...?
Cafés in France sell both alcoholic and non-alcoholic drinks.

cafeteria NOUN
la cafétéria *fem*

cage NOUN
la cage *fem*

cagoule NOUN
le K-way® *masc*

★**cake** NOUN
le gâteau *masc* (PL les gâteaux)

to **calculate** VERB
calculer [28]

calculation NOUN
le calcul *masc*

★**calculator** NOUN
la machine à calculer *fem*

calendar NOUN
le calendrier *masc*

★**calf** NOUN
1 le veau *masc* (PL les veaux) (*of cow*)
2 le mollet *masc* (*of leg*)

★**call** NOUN
▷ *see also* **call** VERB
l'appel *masc* (*by phone*)
□ Thanks for your call. Merci de votre appel.
■ **a phone call** un coup de téléphone
■ **to be on call** (*doctor*) être [35] de permanence □ He's on call this evening. Il est de permanence ce soir.

★to **call** VERB
▷ *see also* **call** NOUN
appeler [4]
□ I'll tell him you called. Je lui dirai que vous avez appelé. □ This is the number to call. C'est le numéro à appeler. □ We called the police. Nous avons appelé la police. □ Everyone calls him Jimmy. Tout le monde l'appelle Jimmy.
■ **to be called** s'appeler [4] □ He's called Fluffy. Il s'appelle Fluffy. □ What's she called? Elle s'appelle comment?
■ **to call somebody names** insulter [28] quelqu'un
■ **He called me an idiot.** Il m'a traité d'idiot.

to **call back** VERB
rappeler [4] (*phone again*)
□ I'll call back at 6 o'clock. Je rappellerai à six heures.

to **call for** VERB
passer [58ᴱ] prendre
□ I'll call for you at 2.30. Je passerai te prendre à deux heures et demie.

to **call off** VERB
annuler [28]
□ The match was called off. Le match a été annulé.

call box NOUN
la cabine téléphonique *fem*

call centre NOUN
le centre d'appels *masc*

★**calm** ADJECTIVE
calme (FEM calme)

to **calm down** VERB
se calmer [28]
□ Calm down! Calme-toi!

Calor gas® NOUN
le butane *masc*

calorie NOUN
la calorie *fem*

★ = core vocabulary

calves PL NOUN ▷ *see* **calf**

Cambodia NOUN
le Cambodge *masc*
■ **in Cambodia** au Cambodge

camcorder NOUN
le caméscope *masc*

came VERB ▷ *see* **come**

camel NOUN
le chameau *masc* (PL les chameaux)

★ **camera** NOUN
1 l'appareil photo *masc* (PL les appareils photo) (*for photos*)
2 la caméra *fem* (*for filming, TV*)

cameraman NOUN
le caméraman *masc*

camera phone NOUN
le téléphone appareil photo *masc*

★ to **camp** VERB
▷ *see also* **camp** NOUN
camper [28]

★ **camp** NOUN
▷ *see also* **camp** VERB
le camp *masc*
■ **a camp bed** un lit de camp

★ **campaign** NOUN
la campagne *fem*

camper NOUN
1 le campeur *masc*
la campeuse *fem* (*person*)
2 le camping-car *masc* (*van*)

★ **camping** NOUN
le camping *masc*
■ **to go camping** faire [36] du camping □ We went camping in Cornwall. Nous avons fait du camping en Cornouailles.

camping gas NOUN
le butane *masc*

★ **campsite** NOUN
le camping *masc*

campus NOUN
le campus *masc*

★ **can** VERB
▷ *see also* **can** NOUN
1 pouvoir [64] (*be able to, be allowed to*)
□ I can call her. Je peux l'appeler. □ You can come with me. Vous pouvez venir avec moi. □ He can help you. Il peut t'aider. □ I can't come. Je ne peux pas venir. □ Can I help you? Est-ce que je peux vous aider? □ Can I use your phone? Est-ce que je peux me servir de votre téléphone? □ You could hire a bike. Tu pourrais louer un vélo. □ I couldn't sleep because of the noise. Je ne pouvais pas dormir à cause du bruit.

'can' is sometimes not translated.

□ I can't hear you. Je ne t'entends pas. □ I can't remember. Je ne m'en souviens pas. □ Can you speak French? Parlez-vous français?
2 savoir [76] (*have learnt how to*)
□ I can swim. Je sais nager. □ He can't drive. Il ne sait pas conduire.
■ **That can't be true!** Ce n'est pas possible!
■ **You could be right.** Vous avez peut-être raison.

★ **can** NOUN
▷ *see also* **can** VERB
1 la boîte *fem* (*tin*)
□ a can of sweetcorn une boîte de maïs
■ **a can of beer** une cannette de bière
2 le bidon *masc* (*container*)
□ a can of petrol un bidon d'essence

★ **Canada** NOUN
le Canada *masc*
■ **in Canada** au Canada
■ **to Canada** au Canada

★ **Canadian** NOUN
▷ *see also* **Canadian** ADJECTIVE
le Canadien *masc*
la Canadienne *fem*

★ **Canadian** ADJECTIVE
▷ *see also* **Canadian** NOUN
canadien (FEM canadienne)

canal NOUN
le canal *masc* (PL les canaux)

Canaries PL NOUN
■ **the Canaries** les îles Canaries *fem pl*

canary NOUN
le canari *masc*

★ to **cancel** VERB
annuler [28]
□ The match was cancelled. Le match a été annulé.

cancellation NOUN
l'annulation *fem*

★ **cancer** NOUN
1 le cancer *masc*
□ He's got cancer. Il a le cancer.
2 le Cancer *masc*
□ I'm Cancer. Je suis Cancer.

★ **candidate** NOUN
le candidat *masc*
la candidate *fem*

candle NOUN
la bougie *fem*

candy NOUN (US)
les bonbons *masc pl*
■ **a candy** un bonbon

candyfloss NOUN
la barbe à papa *fem*

cannabis NOUN
le cannabis *masc*

canned ADJECTIVE
en conserve (*food*)

cannot VERB ▷ *see* **can**

canoe NOUN
le canoë *masc*

canoeing NOUN
■ **to go canoeing** faire [36] du canoë □ We went canoeing. Nous avons fait du canoë.

can-opener NOUN
l'ouvre-boîte *masc*

can't VERB ▷ *see* **can**

canteen NOUN
la cantine *fem*

to **canter** VERB
aller [3E] au petit galop

canvas NOUN
la toile *fem*

★**cap** NOUN
1 la casquette *fem* (*hat*)
2 le bouchon *masc* (*of bottle, tube*)

★**capable** ADJECTIVE
capable (FEM capable)

capacity NOUN
la capacité *fem*

★**capital** NOUN
1 la capitale *fem*
□ Cardiff is the capital of Wales. Cardiff est la capitale du pays de Galles.
2 la majuscule *fem* (*letter*)
□ Write your address in capitals. Écris ton adresse en majuscules.

capitalism NOUN
le capitalisme *masc*

capital punishment NOUN
la peine capitale *fem*

Capricorn NOUN
le Capricorne *masc*
□ I'm Capricorn. Je suis Capricorne.

to **capsize** VERB
chavirer [28]

★**captain** NOUN
le capitaine *masc*
□ She's captain of the hockey team. Elle est capitaine de l'équipe de hockey.

★**caption** NOUN
la légende *fem*

to **capture** VERB
capturer [28]

★**car** NOUN
la voiture *fem*
■ **to go by car** aller [3E] en voiture □ We went by car. Nous y sommes allés en voiture.
■ **a car crash** un accident de voiture

caramel NOUN
le caramel *masc*

★**caravan** NOUN
la caravane *fem*
□ a caravan site un camping pour caravanes

carbohydrate NOUN
le glucide *masc*

carbon footprint NOUN
l'empreinte carbone *fem*
□ We need to reduce our carbon footprint. Nous devons réduire notre empreinte carbone.

★**card** NOUN
la carte *fem*
■ **a card game** un jeu de cartes

★**cardboard** NOUN
le carton *masc*
■ **a cardboard box** un carton

cardigan NOUN
le cardigan *masc*

★**care** NOUN
▷ *see also* **care** VERB
le soin *masc*
□ with care avec soin
■ **to take care of** s'occuper [28] de □ I take care of the children on Saturdays. Le samedi, je m'occupe des enfants.
■ **Take care! 1** (*Be careful!*) Fais attention!
2 (*Look after yourself!*) Prends bien soin de toi!

★to **care** VERB
▷ *see also* **care** NOUN
■ **to care about** se soucier [19] de □ They don't really care about global warming. Ils ne se soucient pas trop du réchauffement climatique.
■ **I don't care!** Ça m'est égal! □ She doesn't care. Ça lui est égal.
■ **to care for somebody** (*patients, old people*) s'occuper [28] de quelqu'un

★**career** NOUN
la carrière *fem*
■ **a careers adviser** un conseiller d'orientation

★**careful** ADJECTIVE
■ **Be careful!** Fais attention!

carefully ADVERB
1 soigneusement
□ She carefully avoided talking about it. Elle évitait soigneusement d'en parler.
2 prudemment (*safely*)
□ Drive carefully! Conduisez prudemment!
■ **Think carefully!** Réfléchis bien!

careless ADJECTIVE
1 peu soigné (FEM peu soignée) (*work*)
■ **a careless mistake** une faute d'inattention
2 peu soigneux (FEM peu soigneuse) (*person*)
□ She's very careless. Elle est bien peu soigneuse.
3 imprudent (FEM imprudente)
□ a careless driver un conducteur imprudent

★**caretaker** NOUN
le gardien *masc*
la gardienne *fem*

car-ferry NOUN
le ferry *masc*

cargo NOUN
la cargaison *fem*

car hire NOUN
la location de voitures *fem*

Caribbean NOUN
▷ *see also* **Caribbean** ADJECTIVE
1 les Caraïbes *fem pl* (*islands*)
□ We're going to the Caribbean. Nous allons aux Caraïbes.
■ **He's from the Caribbean.** Il est antillais.
2 la mer des Caraïbes *fem* (*sea*)

Caribbean ADJECTIVE
▷ *see also* **Caribbean** NOUN
antillais (FEM antillaise)
□ Caribbean food la cuisine antillaise

caring ADJECTIVE
■ **She's a very caring teacher.** C'est un professeur qui se préoccupe du bien-être de ses élèves.
■ **She has very caring parents.** Ses parents sont très affectueux.

carnation NOUN
l'œillet *masc*

carnival NOUN
le carnaval *masc*

carol NOUN
■ **a Christmas carol** un chant de Noël

★ **car park** NOUN
le parking *masc*

carpenter NOUN
le charpentier *masc*
□ He's a carpenter. Il est charpentier.

carpentry NOUN
la menuiserie *fem*

★ **carpet** NOUN
1 le tapis *masc*
□ a Persian carpet un tapis persan
2 la moquette *fem* (*fitted*)

car phone NOUN
le téléphone de voiture *masc*

car rental NOUN (US)
la location de voitures *fem*

carriage NOUN
la voiture *fem*

carrier bag NOUN
le sac en plastique *masc*

★ **carrot** NOUN
la carotte *fem*

★ to **carry** VERB
1 porter [28]
□ I'll carry your bag. Je vais porter ton sac.
2 transporter [28]
□ a plane carrying 100 passengers un avion transportant cent passagers

to **carry on** VERB
continuer [28]
□ Carry on! Continue! □ She carried on talking. Elle a continué à parler.

to **carry out** VERB
exécuter [28] (*orders*)

cart NOUN
la charrette *fem*

carton NOUN
la brique *fem* (*of milk, juice*)

★ **cartoon** NOUN
1 le dessin animé *masc* (*film*)
2 le dessin humoristique *masc* (*in newspaper*)
■ **a strip cartoon** une bande dessinée

cartridge NOUN
la cartouche *fem*

to **carve** VERB
découper [28] (*meat*)

★ **case** NOUN
1 la valise *fem*
□ I've packed my case. J'ai fait ma valise.
2 le cas *masc* (PL les cas)
□ in some cases dans certains cas
■ **in that case** dans ce cas □ I don't want it. — In that case, I'll take it. Je n'en veux pas. — Dans ce cas, je le prends.
■ **in case** au cas où □ in case it rains au cas où il pleuvrait
■ **just in case** à tout hasard □ Take some money, just in case. Prends de l'argent à tout hasard.

★ **cash** NOUN
l'argent *masc*
□ I'm a bit short of cash. Je suis un peu à court d'argent.
■ **in cash** en liquide □ £2000 in cash deux mille livres en liquide
■ **to pay cash** payer [59] comptant
■ **a cash card** une carte de retrait
■ **the cash desk** la caisse
■ **a cash machine** un distributeur de billets
■ **a cash register** une caisse

cashew NOUN
la noix de cajou *fem* (PL les noix de cajou)

cashier NOUN
le caissier *masc*
la caissière *fem*

cashmere NOUN
le cachemire *masc*
□ a cashmere sweater un pull en cachemire

casino NOUN
le casino *masc*

casserole NOUN
le ragoût *masc*
□ I'm going to make a casserole. Je vais faire un ragoût.
■ **a casserole dish** une cocotte

cast NOUN
les acteurs *masc pl*
□ the cast of Star Wars les acteurs de la série La Guerre des étoiles.

★ **castle** NOUN
le château *masc* (PL les châteaux)

casual ADJECTIVE
1 décontracté (FEM décontractée)
□ casual clothes les vêtements décontractés
2 désinvolte (FEM désinvolte)
□ a casual attitude une attitude désinvolte
3 en passant
□ It was just a casual remark. C'était juste une remarque en passant.

casually ADVERB
■ **to dress casually** s'habiller [28] de façon décontractée

★ **casualty** NOUN
les urgences *fem pl* (*in hospital*)

★ **cat** NOUN
le chat *masc*
la chatte *fem* (*female*)
□ Have you got a cat? Est-ce que tu as un chat?

catalogue NOUN
le catalogue *masc*

catalytic converter NOUN
le catalyseur *masc*

catarrh NOUN
le rhume chronique *masc*

catastrophe NOUN
la catastrophe *fem*

★ to **catch** VERB
1 attraper [28]
□ to catch a thief attraper un voleur □ My cat catches birds. Mon chat attrape des oiseaux.
■ **to catch a cold** attraper [28] un rhume
2 surprendre [65]
■ **to catch somebody doing something** surprendre [65] quelqu'un en train de faire quelque chose
□ She caught him playing computer games in class. Elle l'a surpris en train de jouer à des jeux vidéo en classe.
3 saisir [38] (*hear*)
□ I didn't catch his name. Je n'ai pas saisi son nom.
4 prendre [65] (*bus, train*)
□ We caught the last bus. On a pris le dernier bus.

to **catch up** VERB
rattraper [28] son retard
□ I was off yesterday so I've got to catch up. J'étais absent hier, donc je dois rattraper mon retard.

catching ADJECTIVE
contagieux (FEM contagieuse)
□ It's not catching. Ce n'est pas contagieux.

catering NOUN
la restauration *fem*

cathedral NOUN
la cathédrale *fem*

Catholic ADJECTIVE
▷ *see also* **Catholic** NOUN
catholique (FEM catholique)

Catholic NOUN
▷ *see also* **Catholic** ADJECTIVE
le/la catholique *masc/fem*
□ I'm a Catholic. Je suis catholique.

cattle PL NOUN
le bétail *masc sing*

caught VERB ▷ *see* **catch**

★ **cauliflower** NOUN
le chou-fleur *masc* (PL les choux-fleurs)

★ **cause** NOUN
▷ *see also* **cause** VERB
la cause *fem*

★ to **cause** VERB
▷ *see also* **cause** NOUN
provoquer [28]
□ to cause an accident provoquer un accident

cautious ADJECTIVE
prudent (FEM prudente)

cautiously ADVERB
avec précaution
□ She cautiously opened the door. Elle a ouvert la porte avec précaution.

★ **cave** NOUN
la grotte *fem*

CCTV NOUN (= *closed-circuit television*)
la vidéosurveillance *fem*

CCTV camera NOUN
la caméra de vidéosurveillance *fem*

★ **CD** NOUN
le CD *masc* (PL les CD)

CD burner NOUN
le graveur de CD *masc*

★ **CD player** NOUN
la platine laser *fem*

★ **CD-ROM** NOUN
le CD-ROM *masc* (PL les CD-ROM)

★ **ceasefire** NOUN
le cessez-le-feu *masc* (PL les cessez-le-feu)

★ **ceiling** NOUN
le plafond *masc*

★ to **celebrate** VERB
fêter [28] (*birthday*)

celebrity NOUN
la célébrité *fem*

celery NOUN
le céleri *masc*

★ **cell** NOUN
la cellule *fem*

★**cellar** NOUN
la cave *fem*
□ a wine cellar une cave à vins

cello NOUN
le violoncelle *masc*
□ I play the cello. Je joue du violoncelle.

cell phone NOUN (US)
le téléphone portable *masc*

cement NOUN
le ciment *masc*

cemetery NOUN
le cimetière *masc*

★**cent** NOUN
le cent *masc*
□ twenty cents vingt cents

centenary NOUN
le centenaire *masc*

center NOUN (US)
le centre *masc*

★**centigrade** ADJECTIVE
centigrade (FEM centigrade)
□ 20 degrees centigrade vingt degrés centigrade

★**centimetre** (US **centimeter**) NOUN
le centimètre *masc*

★**central** ADJECTIVE
central (FEM centrale, MASC PL centraux)

★**central heating** NOUN
le chauffage central *masc*

★**centre** NOUN
le centre *masc*
□ a sports centre un centre sportif

★**century** NOUN
le siècle *masc*
□ the 20th century le vingtième siècle □ the 21st century le vingt et unième siècle

★**cereal** NOUN
les céréales *fem pl*
□ I have cereal for breakfast. Je prends des céréales au petit déjeuner.

★**ceremony** NOUN
la cérémonie *fem*

★**certain** ADJECTIVE
certain (FEM certaine)
□ a certain person une certaine personne
□ I'm absolutely certain it was him. Je suis absolument certain que c'était lui.
■ **I don't know for certain.** Je n'en suis pas certain.
■ **to make certain** s'assurer [28] □ I made certain the door was locked. Je me suis assuré que la porte était fermée à clé.

★**certainly** ADVERB
vraiment
□ I certainly expected something better. Je m'attendais vraiment à quelque chose de mieux.
■ **Certainly not!** Certainement pas!
■ **So it was a surprise? — It certainly was!** C'était donc une surprise? — Ça oui alors

CFCs PL NOUN
les CFC *masc pl*

★**chain** NOUN
la chaîne *fem*

★**chair** NOUN
1 la chaise *fem*
□ a table and 4 chairs une table et quatre chaises
2 le fauteuil *masc* (*armchair*)

chairlift NOUN
le télésiège *masc*

★**chairman** NOUN
le président *masc*

chairperson NOUN
le président *masc*
la présidente *fem*

★**chairwoman** NOUN
la présidente *fem*

chalet NOUN
le chalet *masc*

chalk NOUN
la craie *fem*

★**challenge** NOUN
▷ *see also* **challenge** VERB
le défi *masc*

★to **challenge** VERB
▷ *see also* **challenge** NOUN
■ **She challenged me to a race.** Elle m'a proposé de faire la course avec elle.

challenging ADJECTIVE
stimulant (FEM stimulante)
□ a challenging exam un examen

champagne NOUN
le champagne *masc*

★**champion** NOUN
le champion *masc*
la championne *fem*

★**championship** NOUN
le championnat *masc*

★**chance** NOUN
1 la chance *fem*
□ Do you think I've got any chance? Tu crois que j'ai une chance? □ Their chances of winning are very good. Ils ont de fortes chances de gagner.
■ **No chance!** Pas question!
2 l'occasion *fem*
□ I'd like to have a chance to travel. J'aimerais avoir l'occasion de voyager.
■ **I'll text you when I get the chance.** Je t'enverrai un SMS quand j'aurai un moment.
■ **by chance** par hasard □ We met by chance. Nous nous sommes rencontrés par hasard.
■ **to take a chance** prendre [65] un risque
□ I'm taking no chances! Je ne veux prendre aucun risque!

Chancellor of the Exchequer NOUN
le chancelier de l'Échiquier *masc*

★ to **change** VERB
▷ *see also* **change** NOUN
1 changer [45]
◻ The town has changed a lot. La ville a beaucoup changé. ◻ I'd like to change £50. Je voudrais changer cinquante livres.
2 changer [45] de

Use **changer de** when you change one thing for another.

◻ You have to change trains in Paris. Il faut changer de train à Paris. ◻ I'm going to change my shoes. Je vais changer de chaussures. ◻ He wants to change his job. Il veut changer d'emploi.
▪ **to change one's mind** changer [45] d'avis ◻ I've changed my mind. J'ai changé d'avis.
▪ **to change gear** changer [45] de vitesse
3 se changer [45]
◻ She changed to go to the party. Elle s'est changée pour aller à la fête.
▪ **to get changed** se changer [45] ◻ I'm going to get changed. Je vais me changer.
4 échanger [45] (*swap*)
◻ Can I change this jumper? It's too small. Est-ce que je peux échanger ce pull? Il est trop petit.

★ **change** NOUN
▷ *see also* **change** VERB
1 le changement *masc*
◻ There's been a change of plan. Il y a eu un changement de programme.
2 la monnaie *fem* (*money*)
◻ I haven't got any change. Je n'ai pas de monnaie.
▪ **a change of clothes** des vêtements de rechange
▪ **for a change** pour changer ◻ Let's go ice skating for a change. Si on faisait du patin à glace pour changer?

changeable ADJECTIVE
variable (FEM variable)

changing room NOUN
1 la cabine d'essayage *fem* (*in shop*)
2 le vestiaire *masc* (*for sport*)

★ **channel** NOUN
la chaîne *fem* (*TV*)
◻ There's football on the other channel. Il y a du football sur l'autre chaîne.
▪ **the Channel** la Manche
▪ **the Channel Islands** les îles Anglo-Normandes *fem pl*
▪ **the Channel Tunnel** le tunnel sous la Manche

★ **chaos** NOUN
le chaos *masc*

chapel NOUN
la chapelle *fem* (*part of church*)

★ **chapter** NOUN
le chapitre *masc*

★ **character** NOUN
1 le caractère *masc*
▪ **She's quite a character.** C'est un drôle de numéro.
2 le personnage *masc* (*in play, film*)
◻ the main character in the book le personnage principal du livre

characteristic NOUN
la caractéristique *fem*

charcoal NOUN
le charbon de bois *masc*

★ **charge** NOUN
▷ *see also* **charge** VERB
les frais *masc pl*
◻ Is there a charge for delivery? Est-ce qu'il y a des frais de livraison?
▪ **an extra charge** un supplément
▪ **free of charge** gratuit
▪ **to be in charge** être [35] responsable
◻ Mrs Munday was in charge of the group. Madame Munday était responsable du groupe.

★ to **charge** VERB
▷ *see also* **charge** NOUN
1 prendre [65] (*money*)
◻ How much did he charge you? Combien est-ce qu'il vous a pris? ◻ They charge £10 an hour. Ils prennent dix livres de l'heure.
2 inculper [28] (*with crime*)
◻ The police have charged him with murder. La police l'a inculpé de meurtre.

★ **charity** NOUN
l'association caritative *fem*
◻ He gave the money to charity. Il a donné l'argent à une association caritative.

charm NOUN
le charme *masc*
◻ He's got a lot of charm. Il a beaucoup de charme.

charming ADJECTIVE
charmant (FEM charmante)

★ **chart** NOUN
le tableau *masc* (PL les tableaux)
◻ The chart shows the rise in the number of students taking A-levels. Le tableau indique la progression du nombre de lycéens qui passent le bac.
▪ **the charts** le hit-parade ◻ This album is number one in the charts. Cet album est numéro un au hit-parade.

charter flight NOUN
le charter *masc*

★ to **chase** VERB
▷ *see also* **chase** NOUN
pourchasser [28]

★**chase** NOUN
▷ *see also* **chase** VERB
la poursuite *fem*
□ a car chase une poursuite en voiture

★**chat** NOUN
▷ *see also* **chat** VERB
■ **to have a chat** bavarder [28]

★to **chat** VERB
▷ *see also* **chat** NOUN
bavarder [28]
■ **to chat somebody up** draguer [28] quelqu'un (*informal*) □ He likes to chat up the girls. Il aime bien draguer les filles.
■ **She likes chatting online.** Elle aime chatter sur Internet.

chatroom NOUN
le forum de discussion *masc*

chat show NOUN
le talk-show *masc*

★**cheap** ADJECTIVE
pas cher (FEM pas chère)
□ a cheap T-shirt un T-shirt pas cher

cheaper ADJECTIVE
moins cher (FEM moins chère)
□ It's cheaper by bus. C'est moins cher en bus.

to **cheat** VERB
▷ *see also* **cheat** NOUN
tricher [28]
□ You're cheating! Tu triches!

cheat NOUN
▷ *see also* **cheat** VERB
le tricheur *masc*
la tricheuse *fem*

★**check** NOUN
▷ *see also* **check** VERB
1 le contrôle *masc*
□ a security check un contrôle de sécurité
2 le chèque *masc* (US)
□ to write a check faire un chèque
3 l'addition *fem* (US)
□ Can we have the check, please? L'addition, s'il vous plaît.

★to **check** VERB
▷ *see also* **check** NOUN
vérifier [19]
□ I'll check the time of the train. Je vais vérifier l'heure du train. □ Check that you haven't made any mistakes. Vérifiez que vous n'avez pas fait de fautes.

to **check in** VERB
1 se présenter [28] à l'enregistrement (*at airport*)
□ Where do we check in? Où est-ce qu'on doit se présenter à l'enregistrement?
■ **They checked in online.** Ils se sont enregistré sur Internet.
2 se présenter [28] à la réception (*in hotel*)
■ **I'd like to check in.** Je voudrais prendre ma chambre.

to **check out** VERB
régler [34] la note (*from hotel*)
□ Can I check out, please? Je peux régler la note, s'il vous plaît?

checked ADJECTIVE
à carreaux (*fabric*)

check-in NOUN
l'enregistrement *masc*

checking account NOUN (US)
le compte courant *masc* (PL les comptes courants)

checkout NOUN
la caisse *fem*

check-up NOUN
l'examen de routine *masc*

cheek NOUN
1 la joue *fem*
□ He kissed her on the cheek. Il l'a embrassée sur la joue.
2 le culot *masc*
□ What a cheek! Quel culot!

★**cheeky** ADJECTIVE
effronté (FEM effrontée)
□ Don't be cheeky! Ne sois pas effronté!
■ **a cheeky smile** un sourire malicieux

★**cheer** NOUN
▷ *see also* **cheer** VERB
les hourras *masc pl*
■ **to give a cheer** pousser [28] des hourras
■ **Cheers! 1** (*good health*) À la vôtre!
2 (*thanks*) Merci!

★to **cheer** VERB
▷ *see also* **cheer** NOUN
applaudir [38]
■ **to cheer somebody up** remonter [48] le moral à quelqu'un □ I was trying to cheer him up. J'essayais de lui remonter le moral.
■ **Cheer up!** Ne te laisse pas abattre!

★**cheerful** ADJECTIVE
gai (FEM gaie)

cheerio EXCLAMATION
salut!

★**cheese** NOUN
le fromage *masc*

★**chef** NOUN
le chef *masc*

★**chemical** NOUN
le produit chimique *masc*

★**chemist** NOUN
1 le pharmacien *masc*
la pharmacienne *fem* (*dispenser*)
2 la pharmacie *fem* (*shop*)
□ You get it from the chemist. C'est vendu en pharmacie.

DID YOU KNOW...?
Chemists' shops in France are identified by a special green cross outside the shop.

3 le/la chimiste *masc/fem (scientist)*

★**chemistry** NOUN
la chimie *fem*
□ the chemistry lab le laboratoire de chimie

cheque NOUN
le chèque *masc*
□ to write a cheque faire un chèque □ to pay by cheque payer par chèque

chequebook NOUN
le carnet de chèques *masc*

★**cherry** NOUN
la cerise *fem*

chess NOUN
les échecs *masc pl*
□ to play chess jouer aux échecs

chessboard NOUN
l'échiquier *masc*

★**chest** NOUN
la poitrine *fem (of person)*
□ his chest measurement son tour de poitrine
■ **a chest of drawers** une commode

chestnut NOUN
le marron *masc*
□ We have turkey with chestnuts. Nous mangeons de la dinde aux marrons.

to **chew** VERB
mâcher [28]

chewing gum NOUN
le chewing-gum *masc*

chick NOUN
le poussin *masc*
□ a hen and her chicks une poule et ses poussins

★**chicken** NOUN
le poulet *masc*

chickenpox NOUN
la varicelle *fem*

chickpeas PL NOUN
les pois chiches *masc pl*

★**chief** NOUN
▷ *see also* **chief** ADJECTIVE
le chef *masc*
□ the chief of security le chef de la sécurité

★**chief** ADJECTIVE
▷ *see also* **chief** NOUN
principal (FEM principale)
□ My chief problem was that I didn't understand the question. Mon problème principal, c'était que je n'avais pas compris la question.

★**child** NOUN
l'enfant *masc/fem*
□ all the children tous les enfants

childish ADJECTIVE
puéril (FEM puérile)

child minder NOUN
la nourrice *fem*

★**children** PL NOUN ▷ *see* **child**

Chile NOUN
le Chili *masc*
■ **in Chile** au Chili

to **chill** VERB
mettre [47] au frais
□ Put the juice in the fridge to chill. Mets le jus de fruits au frais dans le réfrigérateur.

chilli NOUN
le piment *masc*

chilly ADJECTIVE
froid (FEM froide)

chimney NOUN
la cheminée *fem*

chin NOUN
le menton *masc*

★**China** NOUN
la Chine *fem*
■ **in China** en Chine

china NOUN
la porcelaine *fem*
□ a china plate une assiette en porcelaine

Chinese NOUN
▷ *see also* **Chinese** ADJECTIVE
le chinois *masc (language)*
■ **the Chinese** les Chinois

Chinese ADJECTIVE
▷ *see also* **Chinese** NOUN
chinois (FEM chinoise)
□ a Chinese restaurant un restaurant chinois
■ **a Chinese man** un Chinois
■ **a Chinese woman** une Chinoise

★**chip** NOUN
1 la frite *fem (food)*
□ We bought some chips. Nous avons acheté des frites.
2 la puce *fem (in computer)*

chiropodist NOUN
le/la pédicure *masc/fem*
□ He's a chiropodist. Il est pédicure.

chives PL NOUN
la ciboulette *fem sing*

★**chocolate** NOUN
le chocolat *masc*
□ a chocolate cake un gâteau au chocolat
■ **hot chocolate** le chocolat chaud

★**choice** NOUN
le choix *masc*
□ I had no choice. Je n'avais pas le choix.

choir NOUN
la chorale *fem*
□ I sing in the school choir. Je chante dans la chorale de l'école.

English-French

C

★ to **choke** VERB
s'étrangler [28]
◻ He choked on a fishbone. Il s'est étranglé avec une arête de poisson.

★ to **choose** VERB
choisir [38]
◻ It's difficult to choose. C'est difficile de choisir.

★ to **chop** VERB
▷ *see also* **chop** NOUN
émincer [12]
◻ Chop the onions. Émincez les oignons.

★ **chop** NOUN
▷ *see also* **chop** VERB
la côte *fem*
◻ a pork chop une côte de porc

chopsticks PL NOUN
les baguettes *fem pl*

chose, chosen VERB ▷ *see* **choose**

Christ NOUN
le Christ *masc*
◻ the birth of Christ la naissance du Christ

christening NOUN
le baptême *masc*

Christian NOUN
▷ *see also* **Christian** ADJECTIVE
le chrétien *masc*
la chrétienne *fem*

Christian ADJECTIVE
▷ *see also* **Christian** NOUN
chrétien (FEM chrétienne)

Christian name NOUN
le prénom *masc*

★ **Christmas** NOUN
Noël *masc*
◻ Happy Christmas! Joyeux Noël!
▪ **Christmas Day** le jour de Noël
▪ **Christmas Eve** la veille de Noël
▪ **a Christmas tree** un arbre de Noël
▪ **a Christmas card** une carte de Noël

> DID YOU KNOW...?
> The French more often send greetings cards (**une carte de vœux**) with best wishes for the New Year rather than for Christmas.

▪ **Christmas dinner** le repas de Noël

> DID YOU KNOW...?
> Most French people have their Christmas meal (**réveillon de Noël**) on the evening of Christmas Eve, though some have a **repas de Noël** on Christmas Day. The French usually have a Yule log (**une bûche de Noël**) for pudding at the Christmas meal.

chubby ADJECTIVE
potelé (FEM potelée)
◻ a chubby baby un bébé potelé

chunk NOUN
le gros morceau *masc* (PL les gros morceaux)
◻ Cut the meat into chunks. Coupez la viande en gros morceaux.

★ **church** NOUN
l'église *fem*
◻ I don't go to church every Sunday. Je ne vais pas à l'église tous les dimanches.
▪ **the Church of England** l'Église anglicane

cider NOUN
le cidre *masc*

cigar NOUN
le cigare *masc*

★ **cigarette** NOUN
la cigarette *fem*

cigarette lighter NOUN
le briquet *masc*

★ **cinema** NOUN
le cinéma *masc*
◻ I'm going to the cinema this evening. Je vais au cinéma ce soir.

cinnamon NOUN
la cannelle *fem*

★ **circle** NOUN
le cercle *masc*

circular ADJECTIVE
circulaire (FEM circulaire)

circulation NOUN
1 la circulation *fem* (*of blood*)
2 le tirage *masc* (*of newspaper*)

circumflex NOUN
l'accent circonflexe *masc*

circumstances PL NOUN
les circonstances *fem pl*

circus NOUN
le cirque *masc*

★ **citizen** NOUN
le citoyen *masc*
la citoyenne *fem*
◻ a French citizen un citoyen français

citizenship NOUN
la citoyenneté *fem*

★ **city** NOUN
la ville *fem*
▪ **the city centre** le centre-ville ◻ It's in the city centre. C'est au centre-ville.

city technology college NOUN
le collège technique *masc*

civilization NOUN
la civilisation *fem*

civil servant NOUN
le/la fonctionnaire *masc/fem*

civil war NOUN
la guerre civile *fem*

★ to **claim** VERB
1 prétendre [88]

□ He claims to have found the money. Il prétend avoir trouvé l'argent.

2 percevoir [28] (*receive*)

□ She's claiming housing benefit. Elle perçoit des allocations logement.

■ **She can't claim housing benefit.** Elle n'a pas droit à l'allocation logement.

to **clap** VERB

applaudir [38] (*applaud*)

■ **to clap one's hands** frapper [28] dans ses mains □ My dog sits when I clap my hands. Mon chien s'assoit quand je frappe dans mes mains.

clarinet NOUN

la clarinette *fem*

□ I play the clarinet. Je joue de la clarinette.

to **clash** VERB

1 jurer [28] (*colours*)

□ These two colours clash. Ces deux couleurs jurent.

2 tomber [84E] en même temps (*events*)

□ The concert clashes with Ella's party. Le concert tombe en même temps que la soirée d'Ella.

clasp NOUN

le fermoir *masc* (*of necklace*)

★**class** NOUN

1 la classe *fem* (*group*)

□ We're in the same class. Nous sommes dans la même classe.

2 le cours *masc* (*lesson*)

□ I go to dancing classes. Je vais à des cours de danse.

classic ADJECTIVE

▷ *see also* **classic** NOUN

classique (FEM classique)

□ a classic example un cas classique

classic NOUN

▷ *see also* **classic** ADJECTIVE

le classique *masc* (*book, film*)

classical ADJECTIVE

classique (FEM classique)

□ I like classical music. J'aime la musique classique.

classmate NOUN

le/la camarade de classe *masc/fem*

classroom NOUN

la classe *fem*

classroom assistant NOUN

l'aide-éducateur *masc*

l'aide-éducatrice *fem*

claw NOUN

1 la griffe *fem* (*of cat, dog*)

2 la serre *fem* (*of bird*)

3 la pince *fem* (*of crab, lobster*)

★**clean** ADJECTIVE

▷ *see also* **clean** VERB

propre (FEM propre)

□ a clean shirt une chemise propre

★to **clean** VERB

▷ *see also* **clean** ADJECTIVE

nettoyer [53]

cleaner NOUN

la femme de ménage *fem*

l'agent d'entretien *masc* (*woman, man*)

cleaner's NOUN

la teinturerie *fem*

cleaning lady NOUN

la femme de ménage *fem*

cleansing lotion NOUN

la lotion démaquillante *fem*

★**clear** ADJECTIVE

▷ *see also* **clear** VERB

1 clair (FEM claire)

□ a clear explanation une explication claire

□ It's clear you don't believe me. Il est clair que tu ne me crois pas.

2 libre (FEM libre) (*road, way*)

□ The road's clear now. La route est libre maintenant.

★to **clear** VERB

▷ *see also* **clear** ADJECTIVE

1 dégager [45]

□ The police are clearing the road after the accident. La police dégage la route après l'accident.

2 se dissiper [28] (*fog, mist*)

□ The mist cleared. La brume s'est dissipée.

■ **to be cleared of a crime** être [35] reconnu non coupable d'un crime □ She was cleared of murder. Elle a été reconnue non coupable du meurtre.

■ **to clear the table** débarrasser [28] la table □ I'll clear the table. Je vais débarrasser la table.

to **clear up** VERB

ranger [45]

□ Who's going to clear all this up? Qui va ranger tout ça?

■ **I think it's going to clear up.** (*weather*) Je pense que le temps va se lever.

clearly ADVERB

1 clairement

□ She explained it very clearly. Elle l'a expliqué très clairement.

2 nettement

□ You could clearly make out the French coast. On distinguait nettement la côte française.

3 distinctement

□ to speak clearly parler distinctement

clementine NOUN

la clémentine *fem*

★**clever** ADJECTIVE

1 intelligent (FEM intelligente)

English-French

C

□ She's very clever. Elle est très intelligente.

2 astucieux (FEM astucieuse) (*ingenious*)

□ a clever system un système astucieux

■ **What a clever idea!** Quelle bonne idée!

click NOUN

▷ *see also* **click** VERB

1 le petit bruit *masc* (*of door, camera*)

2 le clic *masc* (*with mouse*)

to **click** VERB

▷ *see also* **click** NOUN

cliquer [28] (*with mouse*)

□ to click on an icon cliquer sur une icône

★ **client** NOUN

le client *masc*

la cliente *fem*

cliff NOUN

la falaise *fem*

★ **climate** NOUN

le climat *masc*

climate change NOUN

le changement climatique *masc*

□ We need to combat climate change. Nous devons lutter contre le changement climatique.

★ to **climb** VERB

1 escalader [28]

□ We're going to climb Snowdon. Nous allons escalader le Snowdon.

2 monter [48] (*stairs*)

climber NOUN

le grimpeur *masc*

la grimpeuse *fem*

climbing NOUN

l'escalade *fem*

■ **to go climbing** faire [36] de l'escalade

□ We're going climbing in Scotland. Nous allons faire de l'escalade en Écosse.

Clingfilm® NOUN

le film alimentaire *masc*

clinic NOUN

le centre médical *masc* (PL les centres médicaux)

clip NOUN

1 la barrette *fem* (*for hair*)

2 le court extrait *masc* (*film*)

□ some clips from Disney's latest film quelques courts extraits du dernier film Disney

clippers PL NOUN

■ **nail clippers** le coupe-ongle *sing*

cloakroom NOUN

1 le vestiaire *masc* (*for coats*)

2 les toilettes *fem pl* (*toilet*)

★ **clock** NOUN

1 l'horloge *fem*

□ the church clock l'horloge de l'église

2 la pendule *fem* (*smaller*)

■ **an alarm clock** un réveil

■ **a clock-radio** un radio-réveil

clockwork NOUN

■ **Everything went like clockwork.** Tout a marché comme sur des roulettes.

clog NOUN

le sabot *masc*

clone NOUN

▷ *see also* **clone** VERB

le clone *masc* (*animal, plant*)

to **clone** VERB

▷ *see also* **clone** NOUN

cloner [28]

□ a cloned sheep un mouton cloné

★ **close** ADJECTIVE, ADVERB

▷ *see also* **close** VERB

1 près (FEM+PL près) (*near*)

□ The shops are very close. Les magasins sont tout près.

■ **close to** près de □ The youth hostel is close to the station. L'auberge de jeunesse est près de la gare.

■ **Come closer.** Rapproche-toi.

2 proche (FEM proche) (*in relationship*)

□ We're just inviting close relations. Nous n'invitons que les parents proches. □ She's a close friend of mine. C'est une proche amie.

□ I'm very close to my sister. Je suis très proche de ma sœur.

3 très serré (FEM très serrée) (*contest*)

□ It's going to be very close. Ça va être très très serré.

4 lourd (FEM lourde) (*weather*)

□ It's close this afternoon. Il fait lourd cet après-midi.

★ to **close** VERB

▷ *see also* **close** ADJECTIVE, ADVERB

1 fermer [28]

□ What time does the pool close? La piscine ferme à quelle heure? □ The shops close at 5.30. Les magasins ferment à cinq heures et demie. □ Please close the door. Fermez la porte, s'il vous plaît.

2 se fermer [28]

□ The doors close automatically. Les portes se ferment automatiquement.

★ **closed** ADJECTIVE

fermé (FEM fermée)

□ The bank's closed. La banque est fermée.

closely ADVERB

de près (*look, examine*)

cloth NOUN

le tissu *masc* (*material*)

■ **a cloth** un chiffon □ Wipe it with a damp cloth. Nettoyez-le avec un chiffon humide.

★ **clothes** PL NOUN

les vêtements *masc pl*

□ new clothes des vêtements neufs

■ **a clothes line** un fil à linge
■ **a clothes peg** une pince à linge

★**cloud** NOUN
▷ *see also* **cloud** ADJECTIVE
1 le nuage *masc*
2 le cloud *masc*
□ My photos are stored in the cloud. Mes photos sont stockées dans le cloud.

cloud ADJECTIVE
▷ *see also* **cloud** NOUN
■ **cloud computing** l'informatique dans le cloud
■ **cloud applications** les applications dans le cloud

cloudy ADJECTIVE
nuageux (FEM nuageuse)

clove NOUN
■ **a clove of garlic** une gousse d'ail

clown NOUN
le clown *masc*

★**club** NOUN
le club *masc*
□ a golf club un club de golf
■ **the youth club** la maison des jeunes
■ **clubs** (*in cards*) le trèfle *sing* □ the ace of clubs l'as de trèfle

to **club together** VERB
se cotiser [28]
□ We clubbed together to buy her a present. Nous nous sommes cotisés pour lui acheter un cadeau.

clubbing NOUN
■ **to go clubbing** sortir [79E] en boîte

clue NOUN
l'indice *masc*
□ an important clue un indice important
■ **I haven't got a clue.** Je n'en ai pas la moindre idée.

clumsy ADJECTIVE
maladroit (FEM maladroite)

clutch NOUN
la pédale d'embrayage *fem* (*of car*)

clutter NOUN
le désordre *masc*
□ There's too much clutter in here. Il y a trop de désordre ici.

★**coach** NOUN
1 le car *masc*
□ We went there by coach. Nous y sommes allés en car.
■ **the coach station** la gare routière
■ **a coach trip** une excursion en car
2 l'entraîneur *masc* (*trainer*)
□ the French coach l'entraîneur de l'équipe de France

★**coal** NOUN
le charbon *masc*
■ **a coal mine** une mine de charbon
■ **a coal miner** un mineur

coarse ADJECTIVE
1 rugueux (FEM rugueuse) (*surface, fabric*)
□ The bag was made of coarse cloth. Le sac était fait d'un tissu rugueux.
2 grossier (FEM grossière) (*vulgar*)
□ coarse language un langage grossier

★**coast** NOUN
la côte *fem*
□ It's on the west coast of Scotland. C'est sur la côte ouest de l'Écosse.

coastguard NOUN
le garde-côte *masc* (PL les garde-côtes)

★**coat** NOUN
le manteau *masc* (PL les manteaux)
□ a warm coat un manteau chaud
■ **a coat of paint** une couche de peinture

coat hanger NOUN
le cintre *masc*

cobweb NOUN
la toile d'araignée *fem*

cock NOUN
le coq *masc* (*cockerel*)

cockerel NOUN
le coq *masc*

cockney NOUN
le cockney *masc*
□ I'm a cockney. Je suis cockney.

cocoa NOUN
le cacao *masc*
□ a cup of cocoa une tasse de cacao

coconut NOUN
la noix de coco *fem*

cod NOUN
le cabillaud *masc*

★**code** NOUN
▷ *see also* **code** VERB
le code *masc*

to **code** VERB
▷ *see also* **code** NOUN
coder [28]

★**coffee** NOUN
le café *masc*
■ **a white coffee** un café au lait
■ **A cup of coffee, please.** Un café, s'il vous plaît.

coffeepot NOUN
la cafetière *fem*

coffee table NOUN
la table basse *fem*

coffin NOUN
le cercueil *masc*

coin NOUN
la pièce de monnaie *fem*
■ **a 2 euro coin** une pièce de deux euros

BE CAREFUL!
Do not translate **coin** by the French word coin.

coincidence NOUN
la coïncidence *fem*

★ **Coke®** NOUN
le coca *masc*
□ a can of Coke® une cannette de coca

colander NOUN
la passoire *fem*

★ **cold** ADJECTIVE
▷ *see also* **cold** NOUN
froid (FEM froide)
□ The water's cold. L'eau est froide.
■ **It's cold today.** Il fait froid aujourd'hui.
■ **to be cold** (*person*) avoir [8] froid □ I'm cold. J'ai froid. □ Are you cold? Est-ce que tu as froid?

★ **cold** NOUN
▷ *see also* **cold** ADJECTIVE
1 le froid *masc*
□ I can't stand the cold. Je ne supporte pas le froid.
2 le rhume *masc*
□ to catch a cold attraper un rhume
■ **to have a cold** avoir [8] un rhume □ I've got a bad cold. J'ai un gros rhume.
■ **a cold sore** un bouton de fièvre

coleslaw NOUN
la salade de chou cru à la mayonnaise *fem*

★ to **collapse** VERB
s'effondrer [28]
□ He collapsed. Il s'est effondré.

collar NOUN
1 le col *masc* (*of coat, shirt*)
2 le collier *masc* (*for animal*)

collarbone NOUN
la clavicule *fem*
□ I broke my collarbone. Je me suis cassé la clavicule.

★ **colleague** NOUN
le/la collègue *masc/fem*

★ to **collect** VERB
1 ramasser [28]
□ The teacher collected the exercise books. Le professeur a ramassé les cahiers. □ They collect the rubbish on Fridays. Ils ramassent les ordures le vendredi.
2 collectionner [28]
□ I collect comics. Je collectionne les BD.
3 aller [3E] chercher
□ Their dad collects them from school. Leur père va les chercher à l'école.
4 faire [36] une collecte
□ They're collecting for charity. Ils font une collecte pour une association caritative.

collect call NOUN (US)
la communication en PCV *fem*

★ **collection** NOUN
1 la collection *fem*
□ my jewellery collection ma collection de bijoux
2 la collecte *fem*
□ a collection for charity une collecte pour une association caritative
3 la levée *fem* (*of mail*)
□ Next collection: 5p.m. Prochaine levée: 17 heures

collector NOUN
le collectionneur *masc*
la collectionneuse *fem*

★ **college** NOUN
le collège *masc*
□ a technical college un collège d'enseignement technique

to **collide** VERB
entrer [32E] en collision

colliery NOUN
la houillère *fem*

collision NOUN
la collision *fem*

colon NOUN
les deux-points *masc pl* (*punctuation mark*)

colonel NOUN
le colonel *masc*

★ **colour** (US **color**) NOUN
la couleur *fem*
□ What colour is it? C'est de quelle couleur?
■ **a colour film** (*for camera*) une pellicule en couleur

colourful (US **colorful**) ADJECTIVE
coloré (FEM colorée)

colouring (US **coloring**) NOUN
le colorant *masc* (*for food*)

★ **comb** NOUN
▷ *see also* **comb** VERB
le peigne *masc*

to **comb** VERB
▷ *see also* **comb** NOUN
■ **to comb one's hair** se peigner [28] □ You haven't combed your hair. Tu ne t'es pas peigné.

★ **combination** NOUN
la combinaison *fem*

★ to **combine** VERB
1 allier [19]
□ The film combines humour with suspense. Le film allie l'humour au suspense.
2 concilier [19]
□ It's difficult to combine playing sport with studying for exams. Il est difficile de concilier la pratique du sport et la révision des examens.

★ to **come** VERB

1 venir [89E]

◻ I come when I can. Je viens quand je peux. ◻ You never come with us. Tu ne viens jamais avec nous. ◻ He always comes to see us. Il vient toujours nous voir. ◻ Can I come too? Est-ce que je peux venir aussi? ◻ Some friends came to see us. Quelques amis sont venus nous voir. ◻ I'll come with you. Je viens avec toi.

2 arriver [5E] (*arrive*)

◻ I'm coming! J'arrive! ◻ They came late. Ils sont arrivés en retard. ◻ The letter came this morning. La lettre est arrivée ce matin.

▪ **Where do you come from?** Tu viens d'où?

▪ **Come on!** Allez!

to **come back** VERB

revenir [73E]

◻ Come back! Reviens!

to **come down** VERB

1 descendre [24E] (*person, lift*)

2 baisser [28] (*prices*)

to **come in** VERB

entrer [32E]

◻ Come in! Entrez!

to **come out** VERB

sortir [79E]

◻ I tripped as we came out of the cinema. J'ai trébuché quand nous sommes sortis du cinéma. ◻ The film has just come out in the UK. Le film vient de sortir au Royaume-Uni.

▪ **None of my photos came out.** Mes photos n'ont rien donné.

to **come round** VERB

reprendre [65] connaissance (*after faint, operation*)

to **come up** VERB

monter [48E]

◻ Come up here! Monte!

▪ **to come up to somebody** **1** s'approcher [28] de quelqu'un ◻ She came up to me and kissed me. Elle s'est approchée de moi et m'a embrassé. **2** (*to speak to them*) aborder [28] quelqu'un ◻ A man came up to me and said ... Un homme m'a abordé et m'a dit ...

comedian NOUN

le comique *masc*

★ **comedy** NOUN

la comédie *fem*

★ **comfortable** ADJECTIVE

1 confortable (FEM confortable) (*bed, chair*)

2 à l'aise (*person*)

◻ I'm very comfortable, thanks. Je suis parfaitement à l'aise, merci.

comic NOUN

l'illustré *masc* (*magazine*)

comic strip NOUN

la bande dessinée *fem*

coming ADJECTIVE

prochain (FEM prochaine)

◻ in the coming months au cours des prochains mois

comma NOUN

la virgule *fem*

★ **command** NOUN

l'ordre *masc*

★ **comment** NOUN

▷ *see also* **comment** VERB

le commentaire *masc*

◻ He made no comment. Il n'a fait aucun commentaire.

▪ **No comment!** Je n'ai rien à dire!

★ to **comment** VERB

▷ *see also* **comment** NOUN

▪ **to comment on something** faire [36] des commentaires sur quelque chose

commentary NOUN

le reportage en direct *masc* (*on TV, radio*)

commentator NOUN

le commentateur sportif *masc*

la commentatrice sportive *fem*

★ **commercial** NOUN

le spot publicitaire *masc*

★ to **commit** VERB

▪ **to commit a crime** commettre [47] un crime

▪ **to commit oneself** s'engager [45] ◻ I don't want to commit myself. Je ne veux pas m'engager.

▪ **to commit suicide** se suicider [28] ◻ He committed suicide. Il s'est suicidé.

★ **committee** NOUN

le comité *masc*

★ **common** ADJECTIVE

▷ *see also* **common** NOUN

courant (FEM courante)

◻ 'Smith' is a very common surname. 'Smith' est un nom de famille très courant.

▪ **in common** en commun ◻ We've got a lot in common. Nous avons beaucoup de choses en commun.

★ **common** NOUN

▷ *see also* **common** ADJECTIVE

le terrain communal *masc*

◻ The boys play football on the common. Les garçons jouent au football sur le terrain communal.

Commons PL NOUN

▪ **the House of Commons** la Chambre des communes

common sense NOUN

le bon sens *masc*

◻ Use your common sense! Sers-toi de ton bon sens!

★ to **communicate** VERB
communiquer [28]

★ **communication** NOUN
la communication *fem*

communion NOUN
la communion *fem*
□ my First Communion ma première communion

communism NOUN
le communisme *masc*

★ **communist** NOUN
▷ *see also* **communist** ADJECTIVE
le/la communiste *masc/fem*

communist ADJECTIVE
▷ *see also* **communist** NOUN
communiste (FEM communiste)
▪ **the Communist Party** le Parti communiste

★ **community** NOUN
la communauté *fem*

to **commute** VERB
faire [36] la navette
□ She commutes between Brighton and London. Elle fait la navette entre Brighton et Londres.

compact disc NOUN
le disque compact *masc*
▪ **a compact disc player** une platine laser

companion NOUN
le compagnon *masc*
la compagne *fem*

★ **company** NOUN
1 la société *fem*
□ He works for a big company. Il travaille pour une grosse société.
2 la compagnie *fem*
□ an insurance company une compagnie d'assurance □ a theatre company une compagnie théâtrale
▪ **to keep somebody company** tenir [83] compagnie à quelqu'un □ I'll keep you company. Je vais te tenir compagnie.

comparatively ADVERB
relativement

★ to **compare** VERB
comparer [28]
□ People always compare him with his brother. On le compare toujours à son frère.
▪ **compared with** en comparaison de
□ Oxford is small compared with London. Oxford est une petite ville en comparaison de Londres.

★ **comparison** NOUN
la comparaison *fem*

compartment NOUN
le compartiment *masc*

compass NOUN
la boussole *fem*

compensation NOUN
l'indemnité *fem*
□ They got £2000 compensation. Ils ont reçu une indemnité de deux mille livres.

compere NOUN
l'animateur *masc*
l'animatrice *fem*

★ to **compete** VERB
participer [28]
□ I'm competing in the marathon. Je participe au marathon.
▪ **to compete for something** se disputer [28] quelque chose □ There are 50 students competing for 6 places. Ils sont cinquante étudiants à se disputer six places.

competent ADJECTIVE
compétent (FEM compétente)

★ **competition** NOUN
le concours *masc*
□ a singing competition un concours de chant

★ **competitive** ADJECTIVE
compétitif (FEM compétitive)
□ a very competitive price un prix très compétitif
▪ **to be competitive** (*person*) avoir [8] l'esprit de compétition □ He's a very competitive person. Il a vraiment l'esprit de compétition.

★ **competitor** NOUN
le concurrent *masc*
la concurrente *fem*

★ to **complain** VERB
se plaindre [17]
□ I'm going to complain to the manager. Je vais me plaindre au directeur. □ We complained about the noise. Nous nous sommes plaints du bruit.

★ **complaint** NOUN
la plainte *fem*
□ There were lots of complaints about the food. Il y a eu beaucoup de plaintes à propos de la nourriture.
▪ **to make a complaint** faire [36] une réclamation □ I'd like to make a complaint. J'ai une réclamation à faire.

★ **complete** ADJECTIVE
complet (FEM complète)

★ **completely** ADVERB
complètement

complexion NOUN
le teint *masc*

★ **complicated** ADJECTIVE
compliqué (FEM compliquée)

compliment NOUN
▷ *see also* **compliment** VERB
le compliment *masc*

to **compliment** VERB
▷ *see also* **compliment** NOUN

complimenter [28]
□ They complimented me on my French. Ils m'ont complimenté sur mon français.

complimentary ADJECTIVE
1 élogieux (FEM élogieuse) (*flattering*)
□ He was very complimentary about my haircut. Il a été très élogieux à propos de ma coupe de cheveux.
2 gratuit (FEM gratuite) (*free*)
□ I've got two complimentary tickets for tonight. J'ai deux places gratuites pour ce soir.

composer NOUN
le compositeur *masc*
la compositrice *fem*

comprehension NOUN
1 la compréhension *fem* (*understanding*)
2 l'exercice de compréhension *masc* (*school exercise*)

comprehensive ADJECTIVE
complet (FEM complète)
□ a comprehensive guide un guide complet

> **BE CAREFUL!**
> Do not translate **comprehensive** by the French word **compréhensif**.

comprehensive school NOUN
1 le collège *masc*
2 le lycée *masc*

> **DID YOU KNOW...?**
> In France, pupils go to a **collège** between the ages of 11 and 15, and then to a **lycée** until the age of 18.

★ **compromise** NOUN
▷ *see also* **compromise** VERB
le compromis *masc*
□ We reached a compromise. Nous sommes parvenus à un compromis.

★ to **compromise** VERB
▷ *see also* **compromise** NOUN
■ **Let's compromise.** Essayons de trouver un compromis.

compulsory ADJECTIVE
obligatoire (FEM obligatoire)

★ **computer** NOUN
l'ordinateur *masc*

★ **computer game** NOUN
le jeu vidéo *masc* (PL les jeux vidéo)

computer programmer NOUN
le programmeur *masc*
la programmeuse *fem*
□ She's a computer programmer. Elle est programmeuse.

computer room NOUN
la salle informatique *fem*

computer science NOUN
l'informatique *fem*

computing NOUN
l'informatique *fem*

★ to **concentrate** VERB
se concentrer [28]
□ I couldn't concentrate. Je n'arrivais pas à me concentrer.

concentration NOUN
la concentration *fem*

concern NOUN
l'inquiétude *fem* (*preoccupation*)
□ They expressed concern about her health. Ils ont exprimé leur inquiétude concernant sa santé.

concerned ADJECTIVE
■ **to be concerned** s'inquiéter [34] □ His mother is concerned about him. Sa mère s'inquiète à son sujet.
■ **as far as I'm concerned** en ce qui me concerne

concerning PREPOSITION
concernant
□ Your teacher will give you information concerning the new timetable. Votre professeur vous donnera les informations concernant le nouvel emploi du temps.

★ **concert** NOUN
le concert *masc*

concrete NOUN
le béton *masc*

to **condemn** VERB
condamner [28]
□ The university has condemned the decision. L'université a condamné la décision.

★ **condition** NOUN
1 la condition *fem*
□ I'll do it, on one condition. Je veux bien le faire, à une condition.
2 l'état *masc*
□ in bad condition en mauvais état □ in good condition en bon état

conditional NOUN
le conditionnel *masc*

conditioner NOUN
le baume démêlant *masc* (*for hair*)

condom NOUN
le préservatif *masc*

to **conduct** VERB
diriger [45] (*orchestra*)

conductor NOUN
le chef d'orchestre *masc*

> **BE CAREFUL!**
> Do not translate **conductor** by the French word **conducteur**.

cone NOUN
le cornet *masc*
□ an ice-cream cone un cornet de glace

conference NOUN
la conférence *fem*

English-French

C

English-French

c

to **confess** VERB
avouer [28]
□ He finally confessed. Il a fini par avouer.
□ He confessed to the murder. Il a avoué avoir commis le meurtre.

confession NOUN
la confession *fem*

confetti NOUN
les confettis *masc pl*

★ **confidence** NOUN
1 la confiance *fem*
□ I've got confidence in you. J'ai confiance en toi.
2 l'assurance *fem*
□ She lacks confidence. Elle manque d'assurance.

confident ADJECTIVE
sûr (FEM sûre)
□ I'm confident everything will be okay. Je suis sûr que tout ira bien.
■ **She's seems quite confident.** Elle a l'air sûre d'elle.

confidential ADJECTIVE
confidentiel (FEM confidentielle)

★ to **confirm** VERB
confirmer [28] (*booking*)

confirmation NOUN
la confirmation *fem*

conflict NOUN
le conflit *masc*

to **confuse** VERB
■ **to confuse somebody** embrouiller [28] les idées de quelqu'un □ Don't confuse me! Ne m'embrouille pas les idées!

confused ADJECTIVE
désorienté (FEM désorientée)

confusing ADJECTIVE
■ **The road signs are confusing.** Les panneaux de signalisation ne sont pas clairs.

confusion NOUN
la confusion *fem*

to **congratulate** VERB
féliciter [28]
□ My aunt congratulated me on my results. Ma tante m'a félicité pour mes résultats.

★ **congratulations** PL NOUN
les félicitations *fem pl*
□ Congratulations on winning the match! Félicitations pour votre victoire lors du match!

conjunction NOUN
la conjonction *fem*

conjurer NOUN
le prestidigitateur *masc*

★ **connection** NOUN
1 le rapport *masc*
□ There's no connection between the two events. Il n'y a aucun rapport entre les deux événements.
2 le contact *masc* (*electrical*)
□ There's a loose connection. Il y a un mauvais contact.
3 la correspondance *fem* (*of trains, planes*)
□ We missed our connection. Nous avons raté la correspondance.

to **conquer** VERB
conquérir [2]

conscience NOUN
la conscience *fem*

★ **conscious** ADJECTIVE
conscient (FEM consciente)

consciousness NOUN
la connaissance *fem*
■ **to lose consciousness** perdre [61] connaissance □ I lost consciousness. J'ai perdu connaissance.

★ **consequence** NOUN
la conséquence *fem*
□ What are the consequences for the environment? Quelles sont les conséquences pour l'environnement?
■ **as a consequence** en conséquence

consequently ADVERB
par conséquent

conservation NOUN
la protection *fem*

Conservative NOUN
le conservateur *masc*
la conservatrice *fem*
■ **to vote Conservative** voter [28] conservateur
■ **the Conservatives** les conservateurs

★ **conservative** ADJECTIVE
conservateur (FEM conservatrice)
■ **the Conservative Party** le Parti conservateur

conservatory NOUN
le jardin d'hiver *masc*

★ to **consider** VERB
1 considérer [34]
□ He considers it a waste of time. Il considère que c'est une perte de temps.
2 envisager [45]
□ We considered cancelling our holiday. Nous avons envisagé d'annuler nos vacances.
■ **I'm considering the idea.** J'y songe.

considerate ADJECTIVE
délicat (FEM délicate)

considering PREPOSITION
1 étant donné
□ Considering we were there for a month ... Étant donné que nous étions là pour un mois ...
2 tout compte fait
□ I got a good mark, considering. J'ai eu une bonne note, tout compte fait.

to **consist** VERB
■ **to consist of** être [35] composé de □ The band consists of a singer and a guitarist. Le groupe est composé d'un chanteur et d'un guitariste.

consonant NOUN
la consonne *fem*

★ **constant** ADJECTIVE
constant (FEM constante)

constantly ADVERB
constamment

constipated ADJECTIVE
constipé (FEM constipée)

to **construct** VERB
construire [23]

construction NOUN
la construction *fem*

★ to **consult** VERB
consulter [28]

★ **consumer** NOUN
le consommateur *masc*
la consommatrice *fem*

★ **contact** NOUN
▷ *see also* **contact** VERB
le contact *masc*
□ I'm in contact with her. Je suis en contact avec elle.
■ **your contact details** vos coordonnées
■ **a contact number** un numéro de téléphone

★ to **contact** VERB
▷ *see also* **contact** NOUN
joindre [42]
□ Where can we contact you? Où pouvons-nous vous joindre?

contact lenses PL NOUN
les verres de contact *masc pl*

contactless ADJECTIVE
sans contact

★ to **contain** VERB
contenir [83]

container NOUN
le récipient *masc*

contempt NOUN
le mépris *masc*

contents PL NOUN
1 le contenu *masc sing* (*of container*)
2 la table des matières *fem sing* (*of book*)

★ **contest** NOUN
le concours *masc*

contestant NOUN
le concurrent *masc*
la concurrente *fem*

★ **context** NOUN
le contexte *masc*

★ **continent** NOUN
le continent *masc*
□ How many continents are there? Combien y a-t-il de continents?

continental breakfast NOUN
le petit déjeuner à la française *masc*

★ to **continue** VERB
1 continuer [28]
□ She continued talking to her friend. Elle a continué à parler à son amie.
2 reprendre [65] (*after interruption*)
□ We continued working after lunch. Nous avons repris le travail après le déjeuner.

continuous ADJECTIVE
continu (FEM continue)
■ **continuous assessment** le contrôle continu

contraceptive NOUN
le contraceptif *masc*

★ **contract** NOUN
le contrat *masc*

to **contradict** VERB
contredire [27]

contrary NOUN
le contraire *masc*
■ **on the contrary** au contraire

★ **contrast** NOUN
le contraste *masc*

★ to **contribute** VERB
1 contribuer [28] (*to success, achievement*)
□ The treaty will contribute to world peace. Le traité va contribuer à la paix dans le monde.
2 participer [28] (*share in*)
□ He didn't contribute to the discussion. Il n'a pas participé à la discussion.
3 donner [28] (*give*)
□ She contributed £10. Elle a donné dix livres.

★ **contribution** NOUN
1 la contribution *fem*
2 la cotisation *fem* (*to pension, national insurance*)

★ **control** NOUN
▷ *see also* **control** VERB
le contrôle *masc*
■ **to lose control** (*of vehicle*) perdre [61] le contrôle □ He lost control of the car. Il a perdu le contrôle de son véhicule.
■ **the controls** les commandes *fem pl* (*of machine*)
■ **to be in control** être [35] maître de la situation
■ **to keep control** (*of people*) se faire [36] obéir □ He can't keep control of the class. Il ne se fait pas obéir de la classe.
■ **out of control** (*child, class*) déchaîné

★ to **control** VERB
▷ *see also* **control** NOUN
1 diriger [45] (*country, organization*)
2 se faire [36] obéir de
□ He can't control the class. Il ne se fait pas obéir de la classe.

3 maîtriser [28]
□ I couldn't control the horse. Je ne suis pas arrivé à maîtriser le cheval.
■ **to control oneself** se contrôler [28]

★ **controversial** ADJECTIVE
controversé (FEM controversée)
□ a controversial book un livre controversé

convenient ADJECTIVE
bien situé (FEM bien située) (*place*)
□ Our house is convenient for the school. Notre maison est bien située par rapport à l'école.
■ **It's not a convenient time for me.** C'est une heure qui ne m'arrange pas.
■ **Would Monday be convenient for you?** Est-ce que lundi vous conviendrait?

conventional ADJECTIVE
conventionnel (FEM conventionnelle)

convent school NOUN
le couvent *masc*
□ She goes to convent school. Elle va au couvent.

★ **conversation** NOUN
la conversation *fem*
□ a French conversation class un cours de conversation française

to **convert** VERB
transformer [28]
□ We've converted the loft into a spare room. Nous avons transformé le grenier en chambre d'amis.

to **convict** VERB
reconnaître [14] coupable
□ He was convicted of the murder. Il a été reconnu coupable du meurtre.

★ to **convince** VERB
persuader [28]
□ I'm not convinced. Je n'en suis pas persuadé.

★ to **cook** VERB
▷ *see also* **cook** NOUN
1 faire [36] la cuisine
□ I can't cook. Je ne sais pas faire la cuisine.
2 préparer [28]
□ She's cooking lunch. Elle est en train de préparer le déjeuner.
3 faire [36] cuire
□ Cook the pasta for 10 minutes. Faites cuire les pâtes pendant dix minutes.
■ **to be cooked** être [35] cuit □ When the potatoes are cooked ... Lorsque les pommes de terre sont cuites ...

★ **cook** NOUN
▷ *see also* **cook** VERB
le cuisinier *masc*
la cuisinière *fem*
□ Matthew's an excellent cook. Matthew est un excellent cuisinier.

cookbook NOUN
le livre de cuisine *masc*

★ **cooker** NOUN
la cuisinière *fem*
□ a gas cooker une cuisinière à gaz

cookery NOUN
la cuisine *fem*

cookie NOUN (US)
le gâteau sec *masc* (PL les gâteaux secs)

cooking NOUN
la cuisine *fem*
□ I like cooking. J'aime bien faire la cuisine.

★ **cool** ADJECTIVE
1 frais (FEM fraîche)
□ a cool place un endroit frais
2 cool (FEM+PL cool) (*great*)
□ That's really cool! C'est vraiment cool!

cooperation NOUN
la coopération *fem*

cop NOUN
le flic *masc* (*informal*)

co-parent VERB
élever [43] en coparentalité

to **cope** VERB
se débrouiller [28]
□ It was hard, but we coped. C'était dur, mais nous nous sommes débrouillés.
■ **to cope with** faire [36] face à □ She's got a lot of problems to cope with. Elle doit faire face à de nombreux problèmes.

copper NOUN
1 le cuivre *masc*
□ a copper bracelet un bracelet en cuivre
2 le flic *masc* (*informal: police officer*)

★ **copy** NOUN
▷ *see also* **copy** VERB
1 la copie *fem* (*of letter, document*)
2 l'exemplaire *masc* (*of book*)

★ to **copy** VERB
▷ *see also* **copy** NOUN
copier [19]
□ The teacher accused him of copying. Le professeur l'a accusé d'avoir copié.
■ **to copy and paste** copier-coller [28]

core NOUN
le trognon *masc* (*of fruit*)
□ an apple core un trognon de pomme

cork NOUN
1 le bouchon *masc* (*of bottle*)
2 le liège *masc* (*material*)
□ a cork notice board un panneau d'affichage en liège

corkscrew NOUN
le tire-bouchon *masc*

corn NOUN
1 le blé *masc* (*wheat*)
2 le maïs *masc* (*sweetcorn*)
■ **corn on the cob** l'épi de maïs *masc*

★ **corner** NOUN
1 le coin *masc*
□ in a corner of the room dans un coin de la pièce
■ **the shop on the corner** la boutique au coin de la rue
■ **He lives just round the corner.** Il habite tout près d'ici.
2 le corner *masc* (*in football*)

cornet NOUN
1 le cornet à pistons *masc*
□ He plays the cornet. Il joue du cornet à pistons.
2 le cornet *masc* (*ice cream*)

cornflakes PL NOUN
les corn-flakes *masc pl*

cornstarch NOUN (US)
la farine de maïs *fem*

Cornwall NOUN
la Cornouailles *fem*
■ **in Cornwall** en Cornouailles

corporal NOUN
le caporal *masc*

corporal punishment NOUN
le châtiment corporel *masc*

corpse NOUN
le cadavre *masc*

★ **correct** ADJECTIVE
▷ *see also* **correct** VERB
exact (FEM exacte)
□ That's correct. C'est exact.
■ **the correct choice** le bon choix
■ **the correct answer** la bonne réponse

★ to **correct** VERB
▷ *see also* **correct** ADJECTIVE
corriger [45]

correction NOUN
la correction *fem*

correctly ADVERB
correctement

correspondent NOUN
le correspondant *masc*
la correspondante *fem*
□ our foreign correspondent notre correspondant à l'étranger

corridor NOUN
le couloir *masc*

corruption NOUN
la corruption *fem*

Corsica NOUN
la Corse *fem*
■ **in Corsica** en Corse

cosmetics PL NOUN
les produits de beauté *masc pl*

cosmetic surgery NOUN
la chirurgie esthétique *fem*

★ to **cost** VERB
▷ *see also* **cost** NOUN
coûter [28]
□ His sweatshirt cost £50. Son sweat-shirt a coûté 50 livres. □ How much does it cost? Combien est-ce que ça coûte? □ It costs too much. Ça coûte trop cher.

★ **cost** NOUN
▷ *see also* **cost** VERB
le coût *masc*
■ **the cost of living** le coût de la vie
■ **at all costs** à tout prix

costume NOUN
le costume *masc*

cosy ADJECTIVE
douillet (FEM douillette)

cot NOUN
le lit d'enfant *masc*

★ **cottage** NOUN
le cottage *masc*

cottage cheese NOUN
le cottage cheese *masc*

★ **cotton** NOUN
le coton *masc*
□ a cotton shirt une chemise en coton
■ **cotton wool** le coton hydrophile

couch NOUN
le canapé *masc*

couchette NOUN
la couchette *fem*

★ to **cough** VERB
▷ *see also* **cough** NOUN
tousser [28]

★ **cough** NOUN
▷ *see also* **cough** VERB
la toux *fem*
□ a bad cough une mauvaise toux
■ **I've got a cough.** Je tousse.
■ **a cough sweet** une pastille

★ **could** VERB ▷ *see* **can**

★ **council** NOUN
le conseil *masc*

DID YOU KNOW...?
The nearest French equivalent of a local council would be a **conseil municipal**, which administers a **commune**.

■ **He's on the council.** Il fait partie du conseil municipal.
■ **a council estate** une cité HLM
■ **a council house** une HLM

DID YOU KNOW...?
HLM stands for **habitation à loyer modéré** which means 'low-rent home'.

councillor NOUN
■ **She's a local councillor.** Elle fait partie du conseil municipal.

★ to **count** VERB
compter [28]

to **count on** VERB
compter [28] sur
□ You can count on me. Tu peux compter sur moi.

★**counter** NOUN
1 le comptoir *masc* (*in shop*)
2 le guichet *masc* (*in post office, bank*)
3 le jeton *masc* (*in game*)

★**country** NOUN
1 le pays *masc*
□ the border between the two countries la frontière entre les deux pays
2 la campagne *fem*
□ I live in the country. J'habite à la campagne.
■ **country dancing** la danse folklorique

★**countryside** NOUN
la campagne *fem*

★**county** NOUN
le comté *masc*

DID YOU KNOW...?
The nearest French equivalent of a county would be a **département**.

■ **the county council**

DID YOU KNOW...?
The nearest French equivalent of a county council would be a **conseil général**, which administers a **département**.

★**couple** NOUN
le couple *masc*
□ the couple who live next door le couple qui habite à côté
■ **a couple** deux □ a couple of hours deux heures
■ **Could you wait a couple of minutes?** Pourriez-vous attendre quelques minutes?

★**courage** NOUN
le courage *masc*

courgette NOUN
la courgette *fem*

courier NOUN
1 l'accompagnateur *masc*
l'accompagnatrice *fem* (*for tourists*)
2 le coursier *masc* (*delivery service*)
□ They sent it by courier. Ils l'ont envoyé par coursier.

BE CAREFUL!
Do not translate **courier** by the French word **courrier**.

★**course** NOUN
1 le cours *masc*
□ a French course un cours de français □ to go on a course suivre un cours
2 le plat *masc*
□ the main course le plat principal
■ **the first course** l'entrée *fem*
3 le terrain *masc*
□ a golf course un terrain de golf
■ **of course** bien sûr □ Do you love me? — Of course I do! Tu m'aimes? — Bien sûr que oui!

★**court** NOUN
1 le tribunal *masc* (PL les tribunaux) (*of law*)
□ He was in court yesterday. Il est passé devant le tribunal hier.
2 le court *masc* (*tennis*)
□ There are tennis and squash courts. Il y a des courts de tennis et de squash.

courtyard NOUN
la cour *fem*

★**cousin** NOUN
le cousin *masc*
la cousine *fem*

★**cover** NOUN
▷ *see also* **cover** VERB
1 la couverture *fem* (*of book*)
2 la housse *fem* (*of duvet*)

★to **cover** VERB
▷ *see also* **cover** NOUN
couvrir [55]
□ My face was covered with mosquito bites. J'avais le visage couvert de piqûres de moustique.
■ **to cover up a scandal** étouffer [28] un scandale

★**cow** NOUN
la vache *fem*

coward NOUN
le lâche *masc*
□ She's a coward. Elle est lâche.

cowardly ADJECTIVE
lâche (FEM lâche)

crab NOUN
le crabe *masc*

★**crack** NOUN
▷ *see also* **crack** VERB
1 la fissure *fem* (*in wall*)
2 la fêlure *fem* (*in cup, window*)
■ **I'll have a crack at it.** Je vais tenter le coup.

★to **crack** VERB
▷ *see also* **crack** NOUN
casser [28] (*nut, egg*)
■ **to crack a joke** sortir [79] une blague

to **crack down** VERB
être [35] ferme
□ The police are cracking down on drink-drivers. La police va être ferme avec les automobilistes en état d'ébriété.

cracked ADJECTIVE
fêlé (FEM fêlée) (*cup, window*)

cracker NOUN
1 le cracker *masc* (*biscuit*)
2 la papillote *fem* (*Christmas cracker*)

DID YOU KNOW...?
Papillotes are different from crackers in Britain. They consist of a sweet with a joke and a banger wrapped around it, covered in foil. You unwrap the **papillote** and then pull the banger.

cradle NOUN
le berceau *masc* (PL les berceaux)

craft NOUN
les travaux manuels *masc pl*
□ We do craft at school. Nous avons des cours de travaux manuels à l'école.
■ **a craft centre** un centre artisanal

craftsman NOUN
l'artisan *masc*

to **cram** VERB
1 entasser [28]
□ We crammed our stuff into the boot. Nous avons entassé nos affaires dans le coffre.
2 bachoter [28] (*for exams*)

crammed ADJECTIVE
■ **crammed with** bourré de □ Her bag was crammed with books. Son sac était bourré de livres.

crane NOUN
la grue *fem* (*machine*)

★ to **crash** VERB
▷ *see also* **crash** NOUN
avoir [8] un accident
□ He's crashed his car. Il a eu un accident de voiture.
■ **The plane crashed.** L'avion s'est écrasé.

★ **crash** NOUN
▷ *see also* **crash** VERB
1 la collision *fem* (*of car*)
2 l'accident *masc* (*of plane*)
■ **a crash helmet** un casque
■ **a crash course** un cours intensif

to **crawl** VERB
▷ *see also* **crawl** NOUN
marcher [28] à quatre pattes (*baby*)

crawl NOUN
▷ *see also* **crawl** VERB
le crawl *masc*
□ to do the crawl nager le crawl

★ **crazy** ADJECTIVE
fou (FEM folle)

fou changes to **fol** before a vowel and most words beginning with 'h'.

★ **cream** ADJECTIVE
▷ *see also* **cream** NOUN
crème (FEM+PL crème) (*colour*)

★ **cream** NOUN
▷ *see also* **cream** ADJECTIVE
la crème *fem*
□ strawberries and cream les fraises à la crème
■ **a cream cake** un gâteau à la crème
■ **cream cheese** le fromage à la crème
■ **sun cream** la crème solaire

crease NOUN
le pli *masc*

creased ADJECTIVE
froissé (FEM froissée)

★ to **create** VERB
créer [18]

creation NOUN
la création *fem*

★ **creative** ADJECTIVE
créatif (FEM créative)

creature NOUN
la créature *fem*

crèche NOUN
la crèche *fem*

★ **credit** NOUN
le crédit *masc*
□ on credit à crédit
■ **I've no credit left on my phone.** Je n'ai plus de crédit sur mon portable.

credit card NOUN
la carte de crédit *fem*

creeps PL NOUN
■ **It gives me the creeps.** Ça me donne la chair de poule.

to **creep up** VERB
■ **to creep up on somebody** s'approcher [28] de quelqu'un à pas de loup

crept VERB ▷ *see* **creep up**

cress NOUN
le cresson *masc*

crew NOUN
1 l'équipage *masc* (*of ship, plane*)
2 l'équipe *fem*
□ a film crew une équipe de tournage

crew cut NOUN
les cheveux en brosse *masc pl*

★ **cricket** NOUN
1 le cricket *masc*
□ I play cricket. Je joue au cricket.
■ **a cricket bat** une batte de cricket
2 le grillon *masc* (*insect*)

★ **crime** NOUN
1 le délit *masc*
□ Murder is a crime. Le meurtre est un délit.
2 la criminalité *fem* (*lawlessness*)
□ Crime is rising. La criminalité augmente.

★ **criminal** NOUN
▷ *see also* **criminal** ADJECTIVE
le criminel *masc*
la criminelle *fem*

★ **criminal** ADJECTIVE
▷ *see also* **criminal** NOUN
criminel (FEM criminelle)
□ It's criminal! C'est criminel!

■ **It's a criminal offence.** C'est un crime puni par la loi.
■ **to have a criminal record** avoir [8] un casier judiciaire

★ **crisis** NOUN
la crise *fem*

crisp ADJECTIVE
croquant (FEM croquante) (*food*)

★ **crisps** PL NOUN
les chips *fem pl*
□ a packet of crisps un paquet de chips

criterion NOUN
le critère *masc*

★ **critic** NOUN
le critique *masc*

critical ADJECTIVE
critique (FEM critique)
■ **a critical remark** une critique

★ **criticism** NOUN
la critique *fem*

★ to **criticize** VERB
critiquer [28]

Croatia NOUN
la Croatie *fem*
■ **in Croatia** en Croatie

to **crochet** VERB
crocheter [1]

crocodile NOUN
le crocodile *masc*

crook NOUN
l'escroc *masc* (*criminal*)

★ **crop** NOUN
la récolte *fem*
□ a good crop of apples une bonne récolte de pommes

★ **cross** NOUN
▷ *see also* **cross** ADJECTIVE, VERB
la croix *fem*

★ **cross** ADJECTIVE
▷ *see also* **cross** NOUN, VERB
fâché (FEM fâchée)
□ to be cross about something être fâché à propos de quelque chose

★ to **cross** VERB
▷ *see also* **cross** ADJECTIVE, NOUN
traverser [28] (*street, bridge*)

to **cross out** VERB
barrer [28]

to **cross over** VERB
traverser [28]

cross-country NOUN
le cross *masc* (*race*)
■ **cross-country skiing** le ski de fond

★ **crossing** NOUN
1 la traversée *fem* (*by boat*)
□ the crossing from Dover to Calais la traversée de Douvres à Calais
2 le passage clouté *masc* (*for pedestrians*)

★ **crossroads** NOUN
le carrefour *masc*

crossword NOUN
les mots croisés *masc pl*
□ I like doing crosswords. J'aime faire les mots croisés.

to **crouch down** VERB
s'accroupir [38]

crow NOUN
le corbeau *masc* (PL les corbeaux)

★ **crowd** NOUN
la foule *fem*
■ **the crowd** (*at sports match*) les spectateurs

crowded ADJECTIVE
bondé (FEM bondée)

crowdfunding NOUN
la crowdfunding *masc*

★ **crown** NOUN
la couronne *fem*

crucifix NOUN
le crucifix *masc*

crude ADJECTIVE
grossier (FEM grossière) (*vulgar*)

cruel ADJECTIVE
cruel (FEM cruelle)

cruise NOUN
la croisière *fem*
□ to go on a cruise faire une croisière

crumb NOUN
la miette *fem*

to **crush** VERB
écraser [28]

crutch NOUN
la béquille *fem*

★ **cry** NOUN
▷ *see also* **cry** VERB
le cri *masc*
□ He gave a cry of surprise. Il a poussé un cri de surprise.
■ **Go on, have a good cry!** Vas-y, pleure un bon coup!

★ to **cry** VERB
▷ *see also* **cry** NOUN
pleurer [28]
□ The baby's crying. Le bébé pleure.

crystal NOUN
le cristal *masc* (PL les cristaux)

CTC NOUN (= *city technology college*)
le collège technique *masc*

cub NOUN
1 le petit *masc* (*animal*)
2 le louveteau *masc* (PL les louveteaux) (*scout*)

cube NOUN
le cube *masc*

cubic ADJECTIVE
■ **a cubic metre** un mètre cube

English-French

C

★**cucumber** NOUN
le concombre *masc*

cuddle NOUN
▷ *see also* **cuddle** VERB
le câlin *masc*
□ Come and give me a cuddle. Viens me faire un câlin.

cuddle VERB
▷ *see also* **cuddle** NOUN
■ **to cuddle something** faire [36] un câlin à quelque chose □ Emma cuddled her teddy bear. Emma a fait un câlin à son nounours.

cue NOUN
la queue de billard *fem* (*for snooker, pool*)

culottes PL NOUN
la jupe-culotte *fem sing*

★**culture** NOUN
la culture *fem*

cunning ADJECTIVE
1 rusé (FEM rusée) (*person*)
2 astucieux (FEM astucieuse) (*plan, idea*)

★**cup** NOUN
1 la tasse *fem*
□ a china cup une tasse en porcelaine
■ **a cup of coffee** un café
2 la coupe *fem* (*trophy*)

★**cupboard** NOUN
le placard *masc*

to **cure** VERB
▷ *see also* **cure** NOUN
guérir [38]

cure NOUN
▷ *see also* **cure** VERB
le remède *masc*

★**curious** ADJECTIVE
curieux (FEM curieuse)

curl NOUN
la boucle *fem* (*in hair*)

curly ADJECTIVE
1 bouclé (FEM bouclée) (*loosely curled*)
2 frisé (FEM frisée) (*tightly curled*)

currant NOUN
le raisin sec *masc* (*dried fruit*)

★**currency** NOUN
la devise *fem*
□ foreign currency les devises étrangères

current NOUN
▷ *see also* **current** ADJECTIVE
le courant *masc*
□ The current is very strong. Le courant est très fort.

current ADJECTIVE
▷ *see also* **current** NOUN
actuel (FEM actuelle)
□ the current situation la situation actuelle

current account NOUN
le compte courant *masc*

current affairs PL NOUN
l'actualité *fem*

curriculum NOUN
le programme *masc*

curriculum vitae NOUN
le curriculum vitae *masc*

curry NOUN
le curry *masc*

curse NOUN
la malédiction *fem* (*spell*)

★**curtain** NOUN
le rideau *masc* (PL les rideaux)
□ to draw the curtains tirer les rideaux

cushion NOUN
le coussin *masc*

custard NOUN
la crème anglaise *fem* (*for pouring*)

custody NOUN
la garde *fem* (*of child*)

custom NOUN
la coutume *fem, masc*
□ It's an old custom. C'est une ancienne coutume.

★**customer** NOUN
le client *masc*
la cliente *fem*

customs PL NOUN
la douane *fem sing*

customs officer NOUN
le douanier *masc*
la douanière *fem*

★**cut** NOUN
▷ *see also* **cut** VERB
1 la coupure *fem*
□ He's got a cut on his forehead. Il a une coupure au front.
2 la coupe *fem*
□ a cut and blow-dry une coupe brushing
3 la réduction *fem* (*in price, spending*)

★to **cut** VERB
▷ *see also* **cut** NOUN
1 couper [28]
□ I'll cut some bread. Je vais couper du pain.
■ **to cut oneself** se couper [28] □ I cut my foot on a piece of glass. Je me suis coupé au pied avec un morceau de verre.
2 réduire [23] (*price, spending*)

to **cut down** VERB
abattre [9] (*tree*)

to **cut off** VERB
couper [28]
□ The electricity was cut off. L'électricité a été coupée.

to **cut up** VERB
hacher [28] (*vegetables, meat*)

cutback NOUN
la réduction *fem*
□ staff cutbacks des réductions de personnel

cute ADJECTIVE
mignon (FEM mignonne)

cutlery NOUN
les couverts *masc pl*

cutting NOUN
la coupure de presse *fem* (*from newspaper*)

★ **CV** NOUN
le C.V. *masc*

cyberbully NOUN
le personne *fem* coupable de cyberharcèlement

cyberbullying NOUN
le cyberharcèlement *masc*

cybercafé NOUN
le cybercafé *masc*

★ to **cycle** VERB
▷ *see also* **cycle** NOUN
faire [36] de la bicyclette
■ **I cycle to school.** Je vais à l'école à bicyclette.

★ **cycle** NOUN
▷ *see also* **cycle** VERB
la bicyclette *fem*
■ **a cycle ride** une promenade à bicyclette
■ **a cycle lane** une piste cyclable

cycling NOUN
le cyclisme *masc*

cyclist NOUN
le/la cycliste *masc/fem*

cylinder NOUN
le cylindre *masc*

Cyprus NOUN
Chypre
■ **in Cyprus** à Chypre
■ **to Cyprus** à Chypre

Czech NOUN
▷ *see also* **Czech** ADJECTIVE
1 le/la Tchèque *masc/fem* (*person*)
2 le tchèque *masc* (*language*)

Czech ADJECTIVE
▷ *see also* **Czech** NOUN
tchèque (FEM tchèque)
■ **the Czech Republic** la République tchèque

Dd

★ **dad** NOUN
1 le père *masc*
□ **my dad** mon père □ **her dad** son père
2 le papa *masc*

Use **papa** only when you are talking to your father or using it as his name; otherwise use **père**.

■ **Dad!** Papa! □ **I'll ask Dad.** Je vais demander à papa.

daddy NOUN
le papa *masc*
□ **Say hello to your daddy!** Dis bonjour à ton papa! □ **Hello Daddy!** Bonjour Papa!

daffodil NOUN
la jonquille *fem*

daft ADJECTIVE
idiot (FEM idiote)

★ **daily** ADJECTIVE, ADVERB
1 quotidien (FEM quotidienne)
□ **It's part of my daily routine.** Ça fait partie de mes occupations quotidiennes.
2 tous les jours
□ **The pool is open daily.** La piscine est ouverte tous les jours.

dairy NOUN
la crémerie *fem* (*shop*)

dairy products PL NOUN
les produits laitiers *masc pl*

daisy NOUN
la pâquerette *fem*

dam NOUN
le barrage *masc*

★ **damage** NOUN
▷ *see also* **damage** VERB
les dégâts *masc pl*
□ **The storm did a lot of damage.** La tempête a fait beaucoup de dégâts.

★ to **damage** VERB
▷ *see also* **damage** NOUN
endommager [45]

damp ADJECTIVE
humide (FEM humide)

★ **dance** NOUN
▷ *see also* **dance** VERB
1 la danse *fem*
□ **The last dance was a waltz.** La dernière danse était une valse.
2 le bal *masc*
□ **Are you going to the dance tonight?** Tu vas au bal ce soir?

★ to **dance** VERB
▷ *see also* **dance** NOUN
danser [28]
■ **to go dancing** aller [3E] danser □ **Let's go dancing!** Si on allait danser?

dancer NOUN
le danseur *masc*
la danseuse *fem*

dandruff NOUN
les pellicules *fem pl*

Dane NOUN
le Danois *masc*
la Danoise *fem*

★ **danger** NOUN
le danger *masc*
■ **in danger** en danger □ **His life is in danger.** Sa vie est en danger.
■ **to be in danger of** risquer [28] de □ **We were in danger of missing the plane.** Nous risquions de rater l'avion.

★ **dangerous** ADJECTIVE
dangereux (FEM dangereuse)

★ **Danish** ADJECTIVE
▷ *see also* **Danish** NOUN
danois (FEM danoise)

★ **Danish** NOUN
▷ *see also* **Danish** ADJECTIVE
le danois *masc* (*language*)

to **dare** VERB
oser [28]
■ **to dare to do something** oser [28] faire quelque chose □ **I didn't dare to tell my parents.** Je n'ai pas osé le dire à mes parents.
■ **I dare say it'll be okay.** Je suppose que ça va aller.

daring ADJECTIVE
audacieux (FEM audacieuse)

★ **dark** ADJECTIVE
▷ *see also* **dark** NOUN
1 sombre (FEM sombre) (*room*)
□ **It's dark.** (*inside*) Il fait sombre.
■ **It's dark outside.** Il fait nuit dehors.
■ **It's getting dark.** La nuit tombe.

2 foncé (FEM foncée) (*colour*)
□ She's got dark hair. Elle a les cheveux foncés. □ a dark green sweater un pull vert foncé

★**dark** NOUN
▷ *see also* **dark** ADJECTIVE
le noir *masc*
□ I'm afraid of the dark. J'ai peur du noir.
■ **after dark** après la tombée de la nuit

darkness NOUN
l'obscurité *fem*
□ The room was in darkness. La chambre était dans l'obscurité.

darling NOUN
le chéri *masc*
la chérie *fem*
□ Thank you, darling! Merci, chéri!

dart NOUN
la fléchette *fem*
□ to play darts jouer aux fléchettes

to **dash** VERB
▷ *see also* **dash** NOUN
se précipiter [28]
□ Everyone dashed to the window. Tout le monde s'est précipité vers la fenêtre.
■ **I must dash!** Il faut que je me sauve!

dash NOUN
▷ *see also* **dash** VERB
le tiret *masc* (*punctuation mark*)

★**data** PL NOUN
les données *fem pl*

database NOUN
la base de données *fem* (*on computer*)

★**date** NOUN
1 la date *fem*
□ my date of birth ma date de naissance
■ **What's the date today?** Quel jour sommes-nous?
■ **to have a date with somebody** sortir [79E] avec quelqu'un □ She's got a date with Ethan tonight. Elle sort avec Ethan ce soir.
■ **out of date 1** (*passport*) périmé **2** (*technology*) dépassé **3** (*clothes*) démodé
2 la datte *fem* (*fruit*)

★**daughter** NOUN
la fille *fem*

daughter-in-law NOUN
la belle-fille *fem* (PL les belles-filles)

dawn NOUN
l'aube *fem*
□ at dawn à l'aube

★**day** NOUN

> Use **jour** to refer to the whole 24-hour period. **journée** only refers to the time when you are awake.

1 le jour *masc*
□ We stayed in Nice for three days. Nous sommes restés trois jours à Nice.
■ **every day** tous les jours
2 la journée *fem*
□ during the day dans la journée □ I stayed at home all day. Je suis resté à la maison toute la journée.
■ **the day before** la veille □ the day before my birthday la veille de mon anniversaire
■ **the day after** le lendemain
■ **the day after tomorrow** après-demain
□ We're leaving the day after tomorrow. Nous partons après-demain.
■ **the day before yesterday** avant-hier □ He arrived the day before yesterday. Il est arrivé avant-hier.

★**dead** ADJECTIVE, ADVERB
1 mort (FEM morte)
□ He was already dead when the doctor came. Il était déjà mort quand le docteur est arrivé.
■ **He was shot dead.** Il a été abattu.
2 absolument (*totally*)
□ You're dead right! Tu as absolument raison!
■ **dead on time** à l'heure pile □ The train arrived dead on time. Le train est arrivé à l'heure pile.

dead end NOUN
l'impasse *fem*

★**deadline** NOUN
la date limite *fem*
□ The deadline for entries is May 2nd. La date limite d'inscription est le deux mai.

★**deaf** ADJECTIVE
sourd (FEM sourde)

deafening ADJECTIVE
assourdissant (FEM assourdissante)

★**deal** NOUN
▷ *see also* **deal** VERB
le marché *masc*
■ **It's a deal!** Marché conclu!
■ **a great deal** beaucoup □ a great deal of money beaucoup d'argent

★to **deal** VERB
▷ *see also* **deal** NOUN
donner [28] (*cards*)
□ It's your turn to deal. C'est à toi de donner.
■ **to deal with something** s'occuper [28] de quelque chose □ He promised to deal with it immediately. Il a promis de s'en occuper immédiatement.

dealer NOUN
1 le marchand *masc*
la marchande *fem*
2 le dealer *masc* (*of drugs*)

dealt VERB ▷ *see* **deal**

★**dear** ADJECTIVE
1 cher (FEM chère)
□ Dear Mrs Duval Chère Madame Duval

■ **Dear Sir/Madam** (*in a letter*) Madame, Monsieur
2 coûteux (FEM coûteuse) (*expensive*)

★**death** NOUN
la mort *fem*
□ after his death après sa mort
■ **I was bored to death.** Je me suis ennuyé à mourir.

debate NOUN
▷ *see also* **debate** VERB
le débat *masc*

to **debate** VERB
▷ *see also* **debate** NOUN
débattre [9]

debt NOUN
la dette *fem*
□ He's got a lot of debts. Il a beaucoup de dettes.
■ **to be in debt** avoir [8] des dettes

★**decade** NOUN
la décennie *fem*

decaffeinated ADJECTIVE
décaféiné (FEM décaféinée)

to **decay** VERB
se délabrer [28] (*building*)
□ a decaying mansion un manoir qui se délabre

to **deceive** VERB
tromper [28]

BE CAREFUL!
Do not translate **to deceive** by the French word **décevoir**.

★**December** NOUN
décembre *masc*
■ **in December** en décembre

decent ADJECTIVE
convenable (FEM convenable)
□ a decent education une éducation convenable

★to **decide** VERB
1 décider [28]
□ I decided to write to her. J'ai décidé de lui écrire. □ I decided not to go. J'ai décidé de ne pas y aller.
2 se décider [28]
□ I can't decide. Je n'arrive pas à me décider. □ Haven't you decided yet? Tu ne t'es pas encore décidé?
■ **to decide on something** se mettre [47] d'accord sur quelque chose □ They haven't decided on a name yet. Ils ne se sont pas encore mis d'accord sur un nom.

decimal ADJECTIVE
décimal (FEM décimale)
□ the decimal system le système décimal

★**decision** NOUN
la décision *fem*
■ **to make a decision** prendre [65] une décision

decisive ADJECTIVE
décidé (FEM décidée) (*person*)

★**deck** NOUN
1 le pont *masc* (*of ship*)
■ **on deck** sur le pont
2 le jeu *masc* (PL les jeux) (*of cards*)

deckchair NOUN
la chaise longue *fem*

to **declare** VERB
déclarer [28]

★to **decorate** VERB
1 décorer [28]
□ I decorated the cake with pink icing. J'ai décoré le gâteau avec un glaçage rose.
2 peindre [60] (*paint*)
3 tapisser [28] (*wallpaper*)

decrease NOUN
▷ *see also* **decrease** VERB
la diminution *fem*
□ a decrease in the number of unemployed une diminution du nombre de chômeurs

to **decrease** VERB
▷ *see also* **decrease** NOUN
diminuer [28]

dedicated ADJECTIVE
dévoué (FEM dévouée)
□ a very dedicated teacher un professeur très dévoué
■ **dedicated to** **1** consacré à □ a museum dedicated to Napoleon un musée consacré à Napoléon **2** dédicacé à □ The book is dedicated to Emma. Le livre est dédicacé à Emma.

dedication NOUN
1 le dévouement *masc* (*commitment*)
2 la dédicace *fem* (*in book, on radio*)

to **deduct** VERB
déduire [23]

★**deep** ADJECTIVE
1 profond (FEM profonde) (*water, hole, cut*)
□ Is it deep? Est-ce que c'est profond?
■ **How deep is the lake?** Quelle est la profondeur du lac?
■ **a hole 4 metres deep** un trou de quatre mètres de profondeur
2 épais (FEM épaisse) (*layer*)
□ a deep layer of snow une épaisse couche de neige □ The snow was really deep. Il y avait une épaisse couche de neige.
■ **He's got a deep voice.** Il a la voix grave.
■ **to take a deep breath** respirer [28] à fond

deeply ADVERB
profondément (*depressed*)

deer NOUN
1 le cerf *masc* (*red deer*)
2 le daim *masc* (*fallow deer*)
3 le chevreuil *masc* (*roe deer*)

★ **defeat** NOUN

▷ *see also* **defeat** VERB

la défaite *fem*

★ to **defeat** VERB

▷ *see also* **defeat** NOUN

battre [9]

defect NOUN

le défaut *masc*

★ **defence** NOUN

la défense *fem*

★ to **defend** VERB

défendre [88]

defender NOUN

le défenseur *masc*

to **define** VERB

définir [38]

definite ADJECTIVE

1 précis (FEM précise)

□ I haven't got any definite plans. Je n'ai pas de projets précis.

2 net (FEM nette)

□ It's a definite improvement. Cela constitue une nette amélioration.

3 sûr (FEM sûre)

□ We might go to Spain, but it's not definite. Nous irons peut-être en Espagne, mais ce n'est pas sûr.

■ **He was definite about it.** Il a été catégorique.

★ **definitely** ADVERB

vraiment

□ He's definitely the best player. C'est vraiment lui le meilleur joueur.

■ **He's the best player. — Definitely!** C'est le meilleur joueur. — C'est sûr!

■ **I definitely think he'll come.** Je suis sûr qu'il va venir.

definition NOUN

la définition *fem*

defriend VERB

supprimer [28] de sa liste d'amis

□ Her brother has defriended her on Facebook. Son frère l'a supprimée de sa liste d'amis sur Facebook.

★ **degree** NOUN

1 le degré *masc*

□ a temperature of 30 degrees une température de trente degrés

2 la licence *fem*

□ a degree in English une licence d'anglais

★ to **delay** VERB

▷ *see also* **delay** NOUN

1 retarder [28]

□ We decided to delay our departure. Nous avons décidé de retarder notre départ.

2 tarder [28]

□ Don't delay! Ne tarde pas!

■ **to be delayed** être [35] retardé □ Our flight was delayed. Notre vol a été retardé.

★ **delay** NOUN

▷ *see also* **delay** VERB

le retard *masc*

□ There will be delays to trains on the London-Brighton line. Il y aura des retards sur la ligne Londres-Brighton.

> **BE CAREFUL!**
> Do not translate **delay** by the French word **délai**.

to **delete** VERB

effacer [12] (*on computer, tape*)

deliberate ADJECTIVE

délibéré (FEM délibérée)

deliberately ADVERB

exprès

□ She did it deliberately. Elle l'a fait exprès.

delicate ADJECTIVE

délicat (FEM délicate)

delicatessen NOUN

l'épicerie fine *fem*

delicious ADJECTIVE

délicieux (FEM délicieuse)

delight NOUN

■ **to her delight** à sa plus grande joie

★ **delighted** ADJECTIVE

ravi (FEM ravie)

□ He'll be delighted to see you. Il sera ravi de vous voir.

delightful ADJECTIVE

délicieux (FEM délicieuse) (*meal, evening*)

★ to **deliver** VERB

1 livrer [28]

□ I deliver newspapers. Je livre les journaux.

2 distribuer [28] (*mail*)

delivery NOUN

la livraison *fem*

★ to **demand** VERB

▷ *see also* **demand** NOUN

exiger [45]

> **BE CAREFUL!**
> Do not translate **to demand** by the French word **demander**.

★ **demand** NOUN

▷ *see also* **demand** VERB

la demande *fem* (*for product*)

demanding ADJECTIVE

1 astreignant (FEM astreignante)

□ It's a very demanding job. C'est un travail très astreignant.

2 exigeant (FEM exigeante)

□ a very demanding child un enfant très exigeant.

demo NOUN
la manif *fem* (*protest*)

★ **democracy** NOUN
la démocratie *fem*

★ **democratic** ADJECTIVE
démocratique (FEM démocratique)

to **demolish** VERB
démolir [38]

★ to **demonstrate** VERB
1 faire [36] une démonstration de (*show*)
□ She demonstrated the technique. Elle a fait une démonstration de la technique.
2 manifester [28] (*protest*)
□ to demonstrate against something manifester contre quelque chose

★ **demonstration** NOUN
1 la démonstration *fem* (*of method, technique*)
2 la manifestation *fem* (*protest*)

demonstrator NOUN
le manifestant *masc*
la manifestante *fem* (*protester*)

denim NOUN
le jean *masc*
□ a denim jacket une veste en jean

denims PL NOUN
le jean *masc sing* (*jeans*)

★ **Denmark** NOUN
le Danemark *masc*
■ **in Denmark** au Danemark
■ **to Denmark** au Danemark

dense ADJECTIVE
1 dense (FEM dense) (*crowd, fog*)
2 épais (FEM épaisse) (*smoke*)
■ **He's so dense!** Il est vraiment bouché!

dent NOUN
▷ *see also* **dent** VERB
la bosse *fem*

to **dent** VERB
▷ *see also* **dent** NOUN
cabosser [28]

dental ADJECTIVE
dentaire (FEM dentaire)
■ **dental floss** le fil dentaire

★ **dentist** NOUN
le/la dentiste *masc/fem*
□ Catherine is a dentist. Catherine est dentiste.

to **deny** VERB
nier [19]
□ She denied everything. Elle a tout nié.

deodorant NOUN
le déodorant *masc*

to **depart** VERB
partir [57E]

★ **department** NOUN
1 le rayon *masc* (*in shop*)
□ the shoe department le rayon chaussures
2 le département *masc* (*in university, school*)
□ the English department le département d'anglais

department store NOUN
le grand magasin *masc*

★ **departure** NOUN
le départ *masc*

departure lounge NOUN
le hall des départs *masc*

★ to **depend** VERB
■ **to depend on** dépendre [88] de □ The price depends on which model it is. Le prix dépend du modèle.
■ **depending on the weather** selon le temps
■ **It depends.** Ça dépend.

to **deport** VERB
expulser [28]

★ **deposit** NOUN
1 les arrhes *fem pl* (*part payment*)
□ You have to pay a deposit when you book. Il faut verser des arrhes lors de la réservation.
2 la caution *fem* (*when hiring something*)
□ You get the deposit back when you return the bike. On vous remboursera la caution quand vous ramènerez le vélo.
3 la consigne *fem* (*on bottle*)

depressed ADJECTIVE
déprimé (FEM déprimée)
□ I'm feeling depressed. Je suis déprimé.

depressing ADJECTIVE
déprimant (FEM déprimante)

★ **depth** NOUN
la profondeur *fem*

deputy head NOUN
le directeur adjoint *masc*
la directrice adjointe *fem*

to **descend** VERB
descendre [24E]

★ to **describe** VERB
décrire [30]

★ **description** NOUN
la description *fem*

★ **desert** NOUN
le désert *masc*

desert island NOUN
l'île déserte *fem*

★ to **deserve** VERB
mériter [28]

★ **design** NOUN
▷ *see also* **design** VERB
1 la conception *fem*
□ It's a completely new design. C'est une conception entièrement nouvelle.
2 le motif *masc*
□ a geometric design un motif géométrique
■ **fashion design** le stylisme

★ to **design** VERB
▷ *see also* **design** NOUN
dessiner [28] (*clothes, furniture*)

★ **designer** NOUN
le/la styliste *masc/fem* (*of clothes*)
■ **designer clothes** les vêtements griffés

desire NOUN
▷ *see also* **desire** VERB
le désir *masc*

to **desire** VERB
▷ *see also* **desire** NOUN
désirer [28]

★ **desk** NOUN
1 le bureau *masc* (PL les bureaux) (*in office*)
2 le pupitre *masc* (*for pupil*)
3 la réception *fem* (*in hotel*)
4 le comptoir *masc* (*at airport*)

desktop NOUN
l'ordinateur de bureau *masc* (PL les ordinateurs de bureau) (*computer*)

despair NOUN
le désespoir *masc*
■ **I was in despair.** J'étais désespéré.

★ **desperate** ADJECTIVE
désespéré (FEM désespérée)
□ **a desperate situation** une situation désespérée
■ **to get desperate** désespérer [34] □ **I was getting desperate.** Je commençais à désespérer.

desperately ADVERB
1 terriblement
□ **We're desperately worried.** Nous sommes terriblement inquiets.
2 désespérément
□ **He was desperately trying to persuade her.** Il essayait désespérément de la persuader.

to **despise** VERB
mépriser [28]

★ **despite** PREPOSITION
malgré

dessert NOUN
le dessert *masc*
□ **for dessert** comme dessert

destination NOUN
la destination *fem*

★ to **destroy** VERB
détruire [23]

destruction NOUN
la destruction *fem*

detached house NOUN
la maison individuelle *fem*

★ **detail** NOUN
le détail *masc*
□ **in detail** en détail

detailed ADJECTIVE
détaillé (FEM détaillée)

★ **detective** NOUN
l'inspecteur de police *masc*
■ **a private detective** un détective privé
■ **a detective story** un roman policier

★ **detention** NOUN
■ **to get a detention** être [35] consigné

detergent NOUN
1 le détergent *masc*
2 la lessive *fem* (US)

determined ADJECTIVE
déterminé (FEM déterminée)
■ **to be determined to do something** être [35] déterminé à faire quelque chose □ **She's determined to succeed.** Elle est déterminée à réussir.

detour NOUN
le détour *masc*

devaluation NOUN
la dévaluation *fem*

devastated ADJECTIVE
anéanti (FEM anéantie)
□ **I was devastated.** J'étais anéanti.

devastating ADJECTIVE
1 accablant (FEM accablante) (*upsetting*)
2 dévastateur (FEM dévastatrice) (*flood, storm*)

★ to **develop** VERB
1 développer [28]
□ **The teacher helped them develop their writing skills.** L'enseignant les a aidés à développer leur aptitude à l'écriture.
2 se développer [28]
□ **Girls often develop faster.** Les filles souvent se développent plus vite.
■ **to develop into** se transformer [28] en
□ **The argument developed into a fight.** La dispute s'est transformée en bagarre.
■ **a developing country** un pays en voie de développement

development NOUN
le développement *masc*
□ **the latest developments** les derniers développements

device NOUN
l'appareil *masc*

devil NOUN
le diable *masc*
□ **Poor devil!** Pauvre diable!

to **devise** VERB
concevoir [67]

devoted ADJECTIVE
dévoué (FEM dévouée)
□ **He's completely devoted to her.** Il lui est très dévoué.

diabetes NOUN
le diabète *masc*

diabetic NOUN
le/la diabétique *masc/fem*
□ **I'm a diabetic.** Je suis diabétique.

diagonal ADJECTIVE
diagonal (FEM diagonale, MASC PL diagonaux)

diagram NOUN
le diagramme *masc*

to **dial** VERB
composer [28] (*number*)

dialling tone NOUN
la tonalité *fem*

★ **dialogue** NOUN
le dialogue *masc*

diamond NOUN
le diamant *masc*
□ a diamond ring une bague en diamant
■ **diamonds** (*in cards*) le carreau *sing* □ the ace of diamonds l'as de carreau

diaper NOUN (US)
la couche *fem*

diarrhoea NOUN
la diarrhée *fem*
□ I've got diarrhoea. J'ai la diarrhée.

★ **diary** NOUN
1 l'agenda *masc*
□ She put the date of the school concert in her diary. Elle a noté la date du concert de l'école dans son agenda.
2 le journal *masc* (PL les journaux)
□ I keep a diary. Je tiens un journal.

dice NOUN
le dé *masc*

dictation NOUN
la dictée *fem*

★ **dictionary** NOUN
le dictionnaire *masc*

did VERB ▷ *see* **do**

★ to **die** VERB
mourir [51]
□ He died last year. Il est mort l'année dernière.
■ **to be dying to do something** mourir [51] d'envie de faire quelque chose □ I'm dying to see you. Je meurs d'envie de te voir.

diesel NOUN
1 le gazole *masc* (*fuel*)
□ 30 litres of diesel trente litres de gazole
2 la voiture diesel *fem* (*car*)
□ My car's a diesel. J'ai une voiture diesel.

★ **diet** NOUN
▷ *see also* **diet** VERB
1 l'alimentation *fem*
□ a healthy diet une alimentation saine
2 le régime *masc* (*for slimming*)
□ I'm on a diet. Je suis au régime.

★ to **diet** VERB
▷ *see also* **diet** NOUN
faire [36] un régime
□ I've been dieting for two months. Je fais un régime depuis deux mois.

★ **difference** NOUN
la différence *fem*
□ There's not much difference in age between us. Il n'y a pas une grande différence d'âge entre nous.
■ **It makes no difference.** Ça revient au même.

★ **different** ADJECTIVE
différent (FEM différente)
□ We are very different. Nous sommes très différents. □ Paris is different from London. Paris est différent de Londres.

★ **difficult** ADJECTIVE
difficile (FEM difficile)
□ It's difficult to choose. C'est difficile de choisir.

★ **difficulty** NOUN
la difficulté *fem*
□ without difficulty sans difficulté
■ **to have difficulty doing something** avoir [8] du mal à faire quelque chose

★ to **dig** VERB
1 creuser [28] (*hole*)
2 bêcher [28] (*garden*)
■ **to dig something up** déterrer [28] quelque chose

digestion NOUN
la digestion *fem*

digger NOUN
la pelleteuse *fem* (*machine*)

digital television NOUN
la télévision numérique *fem*

dim ADJECTIVE
1 faible (FEM faible) (*light*)
2 limité (FEM limitée) (*stupid*)

dimension NOUN
la dimension *fem*

to **diminish** VERB
diminuer [28]

din NOUN
le vacarme *masc*

diner NOUN (US)
le snack *masc*

dinghy NOUN
■ **a rubber dinghy** un canot pneumatique
■ **a sailing dinghy** un dériveur

dining car NOUN
le wagon-restaurant *masc* (PL les wagons-restaurants)

dining room NOUN
la salle à manger *fem*

★ **dinner** NOUN
1 le déjeuner *masc* (*at midday*)
2 le dîner *masc* (*in the evening*)

dinner jacket NOUN
le smoking *masc*

dinner lady NOUN
la dame de service *fem*

dinner party NOUN
le dîner *masc*

dinner time NOUN
1 l'heure du déjeuner *fem* (*midday*)
2 l'heure du dîner *fem* (*in the evening*)

dinosaur NOUN
le dinosaure *masc*

dip NOUN
▷ *see also* **dip** VERB
■ **to go for a dip** aller [3E] se baigner

to **dip** VERB
▷ *see also* **dip** NOUN
tremper [28]
□ He dipped a biscuit into his tea. Il a trempé un biscuit dans son thé.

diploma NOUN
le diplôme *masc*
□ a diploma in social work un diplôme d'assistante sociale

diplomat NOUN
le/la diplomate *masc/fem*

diplomatic ADJECTIVE
diplomatique (FEM diplomatique)

★**direct** ADJECTIVE, ADVERB
▷ *see also* **direct** VERB
direct (FEM directe)
□ the most direct route le chemin le plus direct □ You can't fly to Nice direct from Cork. Il n'y a pas de vols directs de Cork à Nice.

★to **direct** VERB
▷ *see also* **direct** ADJECTIVE, ADVERB
1 réaliser [28] (*film, programme*)
2 mettre [47] en scène (*play, show*)

★**direction** NOUN
la direction *fem*
□ We're going in the wrong direction. Nous allons dans la mauvaise direction.
■ **to ask somebody for directions** demander [28] son chemin à quelqu'un

★**director** NOUN
1 le directeur *masc*
la directrice *fem* (*of company*)
2 le metteur en scène *masc* (*of play*)
3 le réalisateur *masc*
la réalisatrice *fem* (*of film, programme*)

directory NOUN
1 l'annuaire *masc* (*phone book*)
2 le répertoire *masc* (*computing*)

dirt NOUN
la saleté *fem*

★**dirty** ADJECTIVE
sale (FEM sale)
■ **to get dirty** se salir [38]
■ **to get something dirty** salir [38] quelque chose

disabled ADJECTIVE
handicapé (FEM handicapée)
■ **disabled people** les handicapés

disadvantage NOUN
le désavantage *masc*

to **disagree** VERB
■ **We always disagree.** Nous ne sommes jamais d'accord.
■ **I disagree!** Je ne suis pas d'accord!
■ **He disagrees with me.** Il n'est pas d'accord avec moi.

disagreement NOUN
le désaccord *masc*

★to **disappear** VERB
disparaître [56]

disappearance NOUN
la disparition *fem*

★**disappointed** ADJECTIVE
déçu (FEM déçue)

disappointing ADJECTIVE
décevant (FEM décevante)

disappointment NOUN
la déception *fem*

★**disaster** NOUN
le désastre *masc*

disastrous ADJECTIVE
désastreux (FEM désastreuse)

disc NOUN
le disque *masc*

★**discipline** NOUN
la discipline *fem*

disco NOUN
la soirée disco *fem*
□ There's a disco at the school tonight. Il y a une soirée disco à l'école ce soir.

to **disconnect** VERB
1 débrancher [28] (*electrical equipment*)
2 couper [28] (*telephone, water supply*)

★**discount** NOUN
la réduction *fem*
□ a discount for students une réduction pour les étudiants

to **discourage** VERB
décourager [45]
■ **to get discouraged** se décourager [45]
□ Don't get discouraged! Ne te décourage pas!

★to **discover** VERB
découvrir [55]

discrimination NOUN
la discrimination *fem*
□ racial discrimination la discrimination raciale

★to **discuss** VERB
1 discuter [28] de
□ I'll discuss it with my parents. Je vais en discuter avec mes parents.

2 discuter [28] sur (*topic*)
□ We discussed the problem of pollution. Nous avons discuté sur le problème de la pollution.

★ **discussion** NOUN
la discussion *fem*

disease NOUN
la maladie *fem*

disgraceful ADJECTIVE
scandaleux (FEM scandaleuse)

to **disguise** VERB
déguiser [28]
□ He was disguised as a police officer. Il était déguisé en policier.

disgusted ADJECTIVE
dégoûté (FEM dégoûtée)
□ I was absolutely disgusted. J'étais complètement dégoûté.

disgusting ADJECTIVE
1 dégoûtant (FEM dégoûtante) (*food, smell*)
□ It looks disgusting. Ça a l'air dégoûtant.
2 honteux (FEM honteuse) (*disgraceful*)
□ That's disgusting! C'est honteux!

★ **dish** NOUN
le plat *masc*
□ a china dish un plat en porcelaine □ a vegetarian dish un plat végétarien
■ **to do the dishes** faire [36] la vaisselle □ He never does the dishes. Il ne fait jamais la vaisselle.

dishonest ADJECTIVE
malhonnête (FEM malhonnête)

dish soap NOUN (US)
le produit à vaisselle *masc*

dish towel NOUN (US)
le torchon *masc*

dishwasher NOUN
le lave-vaisselle *masc* (PL les lave-vaisselle)

disinfectant NOUN
le désinfectant *masc*

disk NOUN
le disque *masc*
■ **the hard disk** le disque dur

diskette NOUN
la disquette *fem*

to **dislike** VERB
▷ *see also* **dislike** NOUN
ne pas aimer [28]
□ I really dislike cabbage. Je n'aime vraiment pas le chou.

dislike NOUN
▷ *see also* **dislike** VERB
■ **my likes and dislikes** ce que j'aime et ce que je n'aime pas

dismal ADJECTIVE
lugubre (FEM lugubre)

to **dismiss** VERB
renvoyer [33] (*employee*)

disobedient ADJECTIVE
désobéissant (FEM désobéissante)

display NOUN
▷ *see also* **display** VERB
l'étalage *masc*
□ There was a lovely display of fruit in the window. Il y avait un superbe étalage de fruits en vitrine.
■ **to be on display** être [35] exposé □ Her best paintings were on display. Ses meilleurs tableaux étaient exposés.
■ **a firework display** un feu d'artifice

to **display** VERB
▷ *see also* **display** NOUN
1 montrer [28]
□ She proudly displayed her medal. Elle a montré sa médaille avec fierté.
2 exposer [28] (*in shop window*)

disposable ADJECTIVE
jetable (FEM jetable)

to **disqualify** VERB
disqualifier [19]
■ **to be disqualified** être [35] disqualifié
□ He was disqualified. Il a été disqualifié.

to **disrupt** VERB
perturber [28]
□ Protesters disrupted the meeting. Des manifestants ont perturbé la réunion. □ Train services are being disrupted by the strike. Les horaires de train sont perturbés par la grève.

dissatisfied ADJECTIVE
■ **We were dissatisfied with the service.** Nous n'étions pas satisfaits du service.

to **dissolve** VERB
dissoudre [70]

★ **distance** NOUN
la distance *fem*
□ a distance of 40 kilometres une distance de quarante kilomètres
■ **It's within walking distance.** On peut y aller à pied.
■ **in the distance** au loin

distant ADJECTIVE
lointain (FEM lointaine)
□ in the distant future dans un avenir lointain

distillery NOUN
la distillerie *fem*
□ a whisky distillery une distillerie de whisky

distinction NOUN
1 la distinction *fem*
□ to make a distinction between ... faire la distinction entre ...
2 la mention très bien *fem*
□ I got a distinction in my piano exam. J'ai eu la mention très bien à mon examen de piano.

distinctive ADJECTIVE
distinctif (FEM distinctive)

to **distract** VERB
distraire [85]

to **distribute** VERB
distribuer [28]

★ **district** NOUN
1 le quartier *masc* (*of town*)
2 la région *fem* (*of country*)

to **disturb** VERB
déranger [45]
□ **I'm sorry to disturb you.** Je suis désolé de vous déranger.

ditch NOUN
▷ *see also* **ditch** VERB
le fossé *masc*

to **ditch** VERB
▷ *see also* **ditch** NOUN
plaquer [28] (*informal*)
□ **She's just ditched her boyfriend.** Elle vient de plaquer son copain.

dive NOUN
▷ *see also* **dive** VERB
le plongeon *masc*

to **dive** VERB
▷ *see also* **dive** NOUN
plonger [45]

diver NOUN
le plongeur *masc*
la plongeuse *fem*

diversion NOUN
la déviation *fem* (*for traffic*)

★ to **divide** VERB
1 diviser [28]
□ **Divide the cake in half.** Divisez le gâteau en deux. □ **12 divided by 3 is 4.** Douze divisé par trois égale quatre.
2 se diviser [28]
□ **We divided into two groups.** Nous nous sommes divisés en deux groupes.

diving NOUN
la plongée *fem*
■ **a diving board** un plongeoir

division NOUN
la division *fem*

divorce NOUN
le divorce *masc*

★ **divorced** ADJECTIVE
divorcé (FEM divorcée)
□ **My parents are divorced.** Mes parents sont divorcés.

★ **DIY** NOUN
le bricolage *masc*
□ **to do DIY** faire du bricolage □ **a DIY shop** un magasin de bricolage

dizzy ADJECTIVE
■ **to feel dizzy** avoir [8] la tête qui tourne □ **I feel dizzy.** J'ai la tête qui tourne.

DJ NOUN
le disc-jockey *masc*

★ to **do** VERB
1 faire [36]
□ **What are you doing this evening?** Qu'est-ce que tu fais ce soir? □ **I do a lot of cycling.** Je fais beaucoup de vélo. □ **I haven't done my homework.** Je n'ai pas fait mes devoirs. □ **She did it by herself.** Elle l'a fait toute seule. □ **I'll do my best.** Je ferai de mon mieux.
■ **to do well** marcher [28] bien □ **She's doing well at school.** Ses études marchent bien.
2 aller [3E] (*be enough*)
□ **It's not very good, but it'll do.** Ce n'est pas très bon, mais ça ira.
■ **That'll do, thanks.** Ça ira, merci.

> In English 'do' is used to make questions. In French questions are made either with **est-ce que** or by reversing the order of verb and subject.

□ **Do you like French food?** Est-ce que vous aimez la cuisine française? □ **Where does he live?** Où est-ce qu'il habite? □ **Do you speak English?** Parlez-vous anglais? □ **What do you do in your free time?** Qu'est-ce que vous faites pendant vos loisirs? □ **Where did you go for your holidays?** Où es-tu allé pendant tes vacances?

> Use **ne ... pas** in negative sentences for 'don't'.

□ **I don't understand.** Je ne comprends pas. □ **Why didn't you come?** Pourquoi n'êtes-vous pas venus?

> 'do' is not translated when it is used in place of another verb.

□ **I hate maths. — So do I.** Je déteste les maths. — Moi aussi. □ **I didn't like the film. — Neither did I.** Je n'ai pas aimé le film. — Moi non plus. □ **Do you like horses? — No I don't.** Est-ce que tu aimes les chevaux? — Non.

> Use **n'est-ce pas** to check information.

□ **You go swimming on Fridays, don't you?** Tu fais de la natation le vendredi, n'est-ce pas? □ **The bus stops at the youth hostel, doesn't it?** Le bus s'arrête à l'auberge de jeunesse, n'est-ce pas?
■ **How do you do?** Enchanté!

to **do up** VERB
1 lacer [12] (*shoes*)
□ **Do up your shoes!** Lace tes chaussures!
2 retaper [28] (*renovate*)
□ **They're doing up my grandparents' house.** Ils retapent la maison de mes grands-parents.
3 boutonner [28] (*shirt, cardigan*)
■ **Do up your zip!** (*on trousers*) Ferme ta braguette!

to **do without** VERB
se passer [58] de
◻ I couldn't do without my computer. Je ne pourrais pas me passer de mon ordinateur.

dock NOUN
le dock *masc* (*for ships*)

★ **doctor** NOUN
le médecin *masc*
◻ She's a doctor. Elle est médecin. ◻ I'd like to be a doctor. Je voudrais être médecin.

document NOUN
le document *masc*

documentary NOUN
le documentaire *masc*

to **dodge** VERB
échapper [28] à (*attacker*)

dodgems PL NOUN
les autos tamponneuses *fem pl*
◻ to go on the dodgems aller faire un tour d'autos tamponneuses

★ **does** VERB ▷ *see* **do**

★ **doesn't** = **does not**

★ **dog** NOUN
le chien *masc*
la chienne *fem*
◻ Have you got a dog? Est-ce que tu as un chien?

do-it-yourself NOUN
le bricolage *masc*

dole NOUN
les allocations chômage *fem pl*
■ **to be on the dole** toucher [28] le chômage
◻ A lot of people are on the dole. Beaucoup de gens touchent le chômage.
■ **to go on the dole** s'inscrire [30] au chômage

doll NOUN
la poupée *fem*

★ **dollar** NOUN
le dollar *masc*

dolphin NOUN
le dauphin *masc*

★ **domestic** ADJECTIVE
■ **a domestic flight** un vol intérieur

dominoes PL NOUN
■ **to have a game of dominoes** faire [36] une partie de dominos

to **donate** VERB
donner [28]

★ **done** VERB ▷ *see* **do**

dongle NOUN
le dongle *masc*

donkey NOUN
l'âne *masc*

donor NOUN
1 le donateur *masc*
la donatrice *fem* (*to charity*)
2 le donneur *masc*
la donneuse *fem* (*of blood, organ for transplant*)

★ **don't** = **do not**

★ **door** NOUN
1 la porte *fem*
◻ the first door on the right la première porte à droite
2 la portière *fem* (*of car, train*)

doorbell NOUN
la sonnette *fem*
■ **to ring the doorbell** sonner [28]
■ **Suddenly the doorbell rang.** Soudain, on a sonné.

doorman NOUN
le portier *masc*

doorstep NOUN
le pas de la porte *masc*

dormitory NOUN
le dortoir *masc*

dose NOUN
la dose *fem*

dosh NOUN
le fric *masc* (*informal: money*)

dot NOUN
le point *masc* (*on letter 'i', in email address*)
■ **on the dot** à l'heure pile ◻ He arrived at 9 o'clock on the dot. Il est arrivé à neuf heures pile.

★ **double** ADJECTIVE, ADVERB
▷ *see also* **double** VERB
double (FEM double)
◻ a double helping une double portion
■ **to cost double** coûter [28] le double
◻ First-class tickets cost double. Les billets de première classe coûtent le double.
■ **a double bed** un grand lit
■ **a double room** une chambre pour deux personnes
■ **a double-decker bus** un autobus à impériale

★ to **double** VERB
▷ *see also* **double** ADJECTIVE, ADVERB
doubler [28]
◻ The number of attacks has doubled. Le nombre d'agressions a doublé.

double bass NOUN
la contrebasse *fem*
◻ I play the double bass. Je joue de la contrebasse.

to **double-click** VERB
double-cliquer [28]
◻ to double-click on an icon double-cliquer sur une icône

double glazing NOUN
le double vitrage *masc*

doubles PL NOUN
le double *masc sing* (*in tennis*)

□ to play mixed doubles jouer en double mixte

★ **doubt** NOUN

▷ *see also* **doubt** VERB

le doute *masc*

□ I have my doubts. J'ai des doutes.

★ to **doubt** VERB

▷ *see also* **doubt** NOUN

douter [28] de

■ **I doubt it.** J'en doute.

■ **to doubt that** douter [28] que

douter que has to be followed by a verb in the subjunctive.

□ I doubt he'll agree. Je doute qu'il soit d'accord.

doubtful ADJECTIVE

■ **to be doubtful about doing something** hésiter [28] à faire quelque chose □ I'm doubtful about going by myself. J'hésite à y aller tout seul.

■ **It's doubtful.** Ce n'est pas sûr.

■ **You sound doubtful.** Tu n'as pas l'air sûr.

dough NOUN

la pâte *fem*

doughnut NOUN

le beignet *masc*

□ a jam doughnut un beignet à la confiture

Dover NOUN

Douvres

□ We went from Dover to Boulogne. Nous sommes allés de Douvres à Boulogne.

■ **in Dover** à Douvres

★ **down** ADVERB, ADJECTIVE, PREPOSITION

1 en bas (*below*)

□ His office is down on the first floor. Son bureau est en bas, au premier étage. □ It's down there. C'est là-bas.

2 à terre (*to the ground*)

□ He threw down his racket. Il a jeté sa raquette à terre.

■ **They live just down the road.** Ils habitent tout à côté.

■ **to come down** descendre [24E] □ Come down here! Descends!

■ **to go down** descendre [24E] □ The rabbit went down the hole. Le lapin est descendu dans le terrier.

■ **to sit down** s'asseoir [6] □ Sit down! Asseyez-vous!

■ **to feel down** avoir [8] le cafard □ I'm feeling a bit down. J'ai un peu le cafard.

■ **The computer's down.** L'ordinateur est en panne.

★ to **download** VERB

▷ *see also* **download** NOUN

télécharger [45]

□ to download a file télécharger un fichier

★ **download** NOUN

▷ *see also* **download** VERB

le téléchargement *masc*

□ a free download un téléchargement gratuit

downpour NOUN

la pluie torrentielle *fem*

□ a sudden downpour une pluie soudaine et torrentielle

★ **downstairs** ADVERB, ADJECTIVE

1 au rez-de-chaussée

□ The bathroom's downstairs. La salle de bain est au rez-de-chaussée.

2 du rez-de-chaussée

□ the downstairs bathroom la salle de bain du rez-de-chaussée

■ **the people downstairs** les voisins du dessous

downtown ADJECTIVE (US)

dans le centre

to **doze** VERB

sommeiller [28]

to **doze off** VERB

s'assoupir [38]

★ **dozen** NOUN

la douzaine *fem*

□ two dozen deux douzaines □ a dozen eggs une douzaine d'œufs

■ **I've told you that dozens of times.** Je t'ai dit ça des centaines de fois.

drab ADJECTIVE

terne (FEM terne) (*clothes*)

★ **draft** NOUN (US)

le courant d'air *masc*

to **drag** VERB

▷ *see also* **drag** NOUN

traîner [28] (*thing, person*)

■ **'drag and drop'** 'glisser déposer'

drag NOUN

▷ *see also* **drag** VERB

■ **It's a real drag!** (*informal*) C'est la barbe!

■ **in drag** travesti □ He was in drag. Il était travesti.

dragon NOUN

le dragon *masc*

★ **drain** NOUN

▷ *see also* **drain** VERB

l'égout *masc*

□ The drains are blocked. Les égouts sont bouchés.

★ to **drain** VERB

▷ *see also* **drain** NOUN

égoutter [28] (*vegetables, pasta*)

draining board NOUN

l'égouttoir *masc*

drainpipe NOUN

le tuyau d'écoulement *masc*

★ **drama** NOUN

l'art dramatique *masc*

□ Drama is my favourite subject. L'art dramatique est ma matière préférée.

■ **drama school** l'école d'art dramatique
□ I'd like to go to drama school. J'aimerais entrer dans une école d'art dramatique.
■ **Greek drama** le théâtre grec

★ **dramatic** ADJECTIVE
spectaculaire (FEM spectaculaire)
□ It was really dramatic! C'était vraiment spectaculaire! □ a dramatic improvement une amélioration spectaculaire
■ **dramatic news** une nouvelle extraordinaire

drank VERB ▷ *see* **drink**

drapes PL NOUN (US)
les rideaux *masc pl*

drastic ADJECTIVE
radical (FEM radicale, MASC PL radicaux) (*change*)
■ **to take drastic action** prendre [65] des mesures énergiques

draught NOUN
le courant d'air *masc*

draughts NOUN
les dames *fem pl*
□ to play draughts jouer aux dames

★ to **draw** VERB
▷ *see also* **draw** NOUN
1 dessiner [28]
□ He's good at drawing. Il dessine bien.
■ **to draw a picture** faire [36] un dessin
■ **to draw a picture of somebody** faire [36] le portrait de quelqu'un
■ **to draw a line** tirer [28] un trait
2 faire [36] match nul (*sport*)
□ We drew 2-2. Nous avons fait match nul deux à deux.
■ **to draw the curtains** tirer [28] les rideaux
■ **to draw lots** tirer [28] au sort

★ **draw** NOUN
▷ *see also* **draw** VERB
1 le match nul *masc* (*sport*)
□ The game ended in a draw. La partie s'est soldée par un match nul.
2 le tirage au sort *masc* (*in lottery*)
□ The draw takes place on Saturday. Le tirage au sort a lieu samedi.

drawback NOUN
l'inconvénient *masc*

drawer NOUN
le tiroir *masc*

★ **drawing** NOUN
le dessin *masc*

drawing pin NOUN
la punaise *fem*

drawn VERB ▷ *see* **draw**

dreadful ADJECTIVE
1 terrible (FEM terrible)
□ a dreadful mistake une terrible erreur
2 affreux (FEM affreuse)
□ The weather was dreadful. Il a fait un temps affreux.
■ **I feel dreadful.** Je ne me sens vraiment pas bien.
■ **You look dreadful.** (*ill*) Tu as une mine affreuse.

★ to **dream** VERB
▷ *see also* **dream** NOUN
rêver [28]
□ I dreamed I was playing basketball. J'ai rêvé que je jouais au basket.

★ **dream** NOUN
▷ *see also* **dream** VERB
le rêve *masc*
□ It was just a dream. Ce n'était qu'un rêve.
■ **a bad dream** un cauchemar

to **drench** VERB
■ **to get drenched** se faire [36] tremper
□ We got drenched. Nous nous sommes fait tremper.

★ **dress** NOUN
▷ *see also* **dress** VERB
la robe *fem*

★ to **dress** VERB
▷ *see also* **dress** NOUN
s'habiller [28]
□ I got up, dressed, and went downstairs. Je me suis levé, je me suis habillé et je suis descendu.
■ **to dress somebody** habiller [28] quelqu'un
□ She dressed the children. Elle a habillé les enfants.
■ **to get dressed** s'habiller [28] □ I got dressed quickly. Je me suis habillé rapidement.

to **dress up** VERB
se déguiser [28]
□ I dressed up as a ghost. Je me suis déguisé en fantôme.

★ **dressed** ADJECTIVE
habillé (FEM habillée)
□ I'm not dressed yet. Je ne suis pas encore habillé. □ How was she dressed? Comment est-ce qu'elle était habillée?
■ **She was dressed in a green jumper and jeans.** Elle portait un pull vert et un jean.

dresser NOUN
le vaisselier *masc* (*furniture*)

dressing gown NOUN
la robe de chambre *fem*

dressing table NOUN
la coiffeuse *fem*

drew VERB ▷ *see* **draw**

dried VERB ▷ *see* **dry**

drier NOUN
le séchoir *masc*

drift NOUN
▷ *see also* **drift** VERB
■ **a snow drift** une congère

English–French

d

to drift VERB
▷ *see also* **drift** NOUN
1 aller [3E] à la dérive (*boat*)
2 s'amonceler [4] (*snow*)

drill NOUN
▷ *see also* **drill** VERB
la perceuse *fem*

to drill VERB
▷ *see also* **drill** NOUN
percer [12]

★ **to drink** VERB
▷ *see also* **drink** NOUN
boire [10]
□ What would you like to drink? Qu'est-ce que vous voulez boire? □ She drank three cups of tea. Elle a bu trois tasses de thé. □ He'd been drinking. Il avait bu.
■ **I don't drink.** Je ne bois pas d'alcool.

★ **drink** NOUN
▷ *see also* **drink** VERB
la boisson *fem*
□ a cold drink une boisson fraîche □ a hot drink une boisson chaude
■ **They've gone out for a drink.** Ils sont allés prendre un verre.
■ **to have a drink** prendre [65] un verre

drinking water NOUN
l'eau potable *fem*

★ **drive** NOUN
▷ *see also* **drive** VERB
1 le tour en voiture *masc*
■ **to go for a drive** aller [3E] faire un tour en voiture □ We went for a drive in the country. Nous sommes allés faire un tour à la campagne.
■ **We've got a long drive tomorrow.** Nous avons une longue route à faire demain.
2 l'allée *fem* (*of house*)
□ He parked his car in the drive. Il a garé sa voiture dans l'allée.

★ **to drive** VERB
▷ *see also* **drive** NOUN
1 conduire [23] (*a car*)
□ She's learning to drive. Elle apprend à conduire. □ Can you drive? Tu sais conduire?
2 aller [3E] en voiture (*go by car*)
□ I'd rather drive than take the train. Je préfère conduire que de prendre le train.
3 emmener [43] en voiture
□ My mother drives me to school. Ma mère m'emmène à l'école en voiture.
■ **to drive somebody home** raccompagner [28] quelqu'un □ He offered to drive me home. Il m'a proposé de me raccompagner.
■ **to drive somebody mad** rendre [7] quelqu'un fou □ He drives her mad. Il la rend folle.

★ **driver** NOUN
1 le conducteur *masc*
la conductrice *fem*
□ She's an excellent driver. C'est une excellente conductrice.
2 le chauffeur *masc* (*of taxi, bus*)
□ He's a bus driver. Il est chauffeur d'autobus.

driver's license NOUN (US)
le permis de conduire *masc*

driving instructor NOUN
le moniteur d'auto-école *masc*
□ He's a driving instructor. Il est moniteur d'auto-école.

driving lesson NOUN
la leçon de conduite *fem*

driving licence NOUN
le permis de conduire *masc*

driving test NOUN
■ **to take one's driving test** passer [58] son permis de conduire □ He's taking his driving test tomorrow. Il passe son permis de conduire demain.
■ **She's just passed her driving test.** Elle vient d'avoir son permis.

drizzle NOUN
la bruine *fem*

★ **drop** NOUN
▷ *see also* **drop** VERB
la goutte *fem*
□ a drop of water une goutte d'eau

★ **to drop** VERB
▷ *see also* **drop** NOUN
1 laisser [28] tomber
□ I dropped the glass and it broke. J'ai laissé tomber le verre et il s'est cassé. □ I'm going to drop chemistry. Je vais laisser tomber la chimie.
2 déposer [28]
□ Could you drop me at the station? Pouvez-vous me déposer à la gare?

drought NOUN
la sécheresse *fem*

drove VERB ▷ *see* **drive**

to drown VERB
se noyer [53]
□ A boy drowned here yesterday. Un jeune garçon s'est noyé ici hier.

★ **drug** NOUN
1 le médicament *masc* (*medicine*)
□ They need food and drugs. Ils ont besoin de nourriture et de médicaments.
2 la drogue *fem* (*illegal*)
□ hard drugs les drogues dures □ soft drugs les drogues douces
■ **to take drugs** se droguer [28]
■ **a drug addict** un drogué □ She's a drug addict. C'est une droguée.
■ **a drug dealer** un dealer
■ **a drug smuggler** un trafiquant de drogue

■ **the drugs squad** la brigade antidrogue
■ **the problem of drug abuse** le problème de la drogue

drugstore NOUN (US)
le drugstore *masc*

★ **drum** NOUN
le tambour *masc*
□ an African drum un tambour africain
■ **a drum kit** une batterie
■ **drums** la batterie *sing* □ I play drums. Je joue de la batterie.

drummer NOUN
le batteur *masc*
la batteuse *fem* (*in rock group*)

drunk ADJECTIVE
▷ *see also* **drunk** NOUN
ivre (FEM ivre)
□ He was drunk. Il était ivre.

drunk NOUN
▷ *see also* **drunk** ADJECTIVE
l'ivrogne *masc/fem*
□ The streets were full of drunks. Les rues étaient pleines d'ivrognes.

★ **dry** ADJECTIVE
▷ *see also* **dry** VERB
1 sec (FEM sèche)
□ The paint isn't dry yet. La peinture n'est pas encore sèche.
2 sans pluie (*weather*)
□ a long dry period une longue période sans pluie

★ to **dry** VERB
▷ *see also* **dry** ADJECTIVE
1 sécher [34]
□ The washing will dry quickly in the sun. Le linge va sécher vite au soleil. □ some dried flowers des fleurs séchées
■ **to dry one's hair** se sécher [34] les cheveux
□ I haven't dried my hair yet. Je ne me suis pas encore séché les cheveux.
2 faire [36] sécher (*clothes*)
□ There's nowhere to dry clothes here. Il n'y a pas d'endroit où faire sécher les vêtements ici.
■ **to dry the dishes** essuyer [53] la vaisselle

dry-cleaner's NOUN
la teinturerie *fem*

dryer NOUN
le séchoir *masc* (*for clothes*)
■ **a tumble dryer** un séchoir à linge
■ **a hair dryer** un sèche-cheveux

DTP NOUN (= *desktop publishing*)
la PAO *fem* (= *publication assistée par ordinateur*)

dubbed ADJECTIVE
doublé (FEM doublée)
□ The film was dubbed into French. Le film était doublé en français.

dubious ADJECTIVE
réticent (FEM réticente)
□ My parents were a bit dubious about it. Mes parents étaient un peu réticents à ce sujet.

★ **duck** NOUN
le canard *masc*

★ **due** ADJECTIVE, ADVERB
■ **to be due to do something** devoir [26] faire quelque chose □ He's due to arrive tomorrow. Il doit arriver demain.
■ **The plane's due in half an hour.** L'avion doit arriver dans une demi-heure.
■ **When's the baby due?** Le bébé est prévu pour quand?
■ **due to** à cause de □ The trip was cancelled due to bad weather. Le voyage a été annulé à cause du mauvais temps.

dug VERB ▷ *see* **dig**

dull ADJECTIVE
1 ennuyeux (FEM ennuyeuse)
□ He's nice, but a bit dull. Il est sympathique, mais un peu ennuyeux.
2 maussade (FEM maussade) (*weather, day*)
□ It was dull this morning. Le temps était maussade ce matin.

dumb ADJECTIVE
bête (FEM bête)
□ That was a really dumb thing I did! C'était vraiment bête de ma part!

dummy NOUN
la tétine *fem* (*for baby*)

★ **dump** NOUN
▷ *see also* **dump** VERB
■ **It's a real dump!** C'est un endroit minable!
■ **a rubbish dump** une décharge

to **dump** VERB
▷ *see also* **dump** NOUN
1 déposer [28] (*waste*)
□ 'no dumping' 'défense de déposer des ordures'
2 plaquer [28] (*informal*)
□ He's just dumped his girlfriend. Il vient de plaquer sa copine.

dungarees PL NOUN
la salopette *fem sing*

dungeon NOUN
le cachot *masc*

duration NOUN
la durée *fem*

★ **during** PREPOSITION
pendant
□ during the day pendant la journée

dusk NOUN
le crépuscule *masc*
□ at dusk au crépuscule

★ **dust** NOUN
▷ *see also* **dust** VERB
la poussière *fem*

★ to **dust** VERB
▷ *see also* **dust** NOUN
épousseter [41]
□ I dusted the shelves. J'ai épousseté les étagères.
■ **I hate dusting!** Je déteste faire les poussières!

★ **dustbin** NOUN
la poubelle *fem*

dustman NOUN
l'éboueur *masc*
□ He's a dustman. Il est éboueur.

dusty ADJECTIVE
poussiéreux (FEM poussiéreuse)

★ **Dutch** NOUN
▷ *see also* **Dutch** ADJECTIVE
le hollandais *masc* (*language*)
■ **the Dutch** les Hollandais

★ **Dutch** ADJECTIVE
▷ *see also* **Dutch** NOUN
hollandais (FEM hollandaise)
□ She's Dutch. Elle est hollandaise.

Dutchman NOUN
le Hollandais *masc*

Dutchwoman NOUN
la Hollandaise *fem*

★ **duty** NOUN
le devoir *masc*
□ It was his duty to tell the police. C'était son devoir de prévenir la police.
■ **to be on duty** **1** (*police officer*) être [35] de service **2** (*doctor, nurse*) être [35] de garde

duty-free ADJECTIVE
hors taxes
■ **the duty-free shop** la boutique hors taxes

★ **duvet** NOUN
la couette *fem*

★ **DVD** NOUN
le DVD *masc* (PL les DVD)
□ I've got that film on DVD. J'ai ce film en DVD.

★ **DVD player** NOUN
le lecteur de DVD *masc*

dying VERB ▷ *see* **die**

dynamic ADJECTIVE
dynamique (FEM dynamique)

dyslexia NOUN
la dyslexie *fem*

dyspraxia NOUN
la dyspraxie *fem*

dyspraxic ADJECTIVE
le dyspraxique

Ee

★ **each** ADJECTIVE, PRONOUN

1 chaque (FEM chaque)
□ **each day** chaque jour □ **Each house in our street has its own garden.** Chaque maison dans notre rue a son propre jardin.

2 chacun (FEM chacune)
□ **The girls each have their own bedroom.** Les filles ont chacune leur chambre. □ **They have 10 points each.** Ils ont dix points chacun. □ **The postcards cost £1 each.** Les cartes postales coûtent une livre chacune. □ **He gave each of us £10.** Il nous a donné dix livres à chacun.

Use a reflexive verb to translate 'each other'.

■ **They hate each other.** Ils se détestent.
■ **We wrote to each other.** Nous nous sommes écrit.
■ **They don't know each other.** Ils ne se connaissent pas.

eager ADJECTIVE
■ **to be eager to do something** être [35] impatient de faire quelque chose

★ **ear** NOUN
l'oreille *fem*

earache NOUN
■ **to have earache** avoir [8] mal aux oreilles

★ **earlier** ADVERB

1 tout à l'heure
□ **I saw him earlier.** Je l'ai vu tout à l'heure.

2 plus tôt (*in the morning*)
□ **I ought to get up earlier.** Je devrais me lever plus tôt.

★ **early** ADVERB, ADJECTIVE

1 tôt (*early in the day*)
□ **I have to get up early.** Je dois me lever tôt.
■ **to have an early night** se coucher [28] tôt

2 en avance (*ahead of time*)
□ **I came early to get a good seat.** Je suis venu en avance pour avoir une bonne place.

★ to **earn** VERB
gagner [28]
□ **She earns £10 an hour.** Elle gagne dix livres de l'heure.

★ **earnings** PL NOUN
le salaire *masc sing*

earphones PL NOUN
les écouteurs *pl noun*

earring NOUN
la boucle d'oreille *fem*

★ **earth** NOUN
la terre *fem*

earthquake NOUN
le tremblement de terre *masc*

★ **easily** ADVERB
facilement

★ **east** ADJECTIVE, ADVERB
▷ *see also* **east** NOUN

1 est (FEM+PL est)
□ **the east coast** la côte est
■ **an east wind** un vent d'est
■ **east of** à l'est de □ **It's east of London.** C'est à l'est de Londres.

2 vers l'est
□ **We were travelling east.** Nous allions vers l'est.

★ **east** NOUN
▷ *see also* **east** ADJECTIVE, ADVERB
l'est *masc*
□ **in the east** dans l'est

eastbound ADJECTIVE
■ **The car was eastbound on the M25.** La voiture se trouvait sur la M25 en direction de l'est.
■ **Eastbound traffic is moving very slowly.** La circulation vers l'est avance très lentement.

Easter NOUN
Pâques *fem*
□ **at Easter** à Pâques □ **We went to my grandparents' for Easter.** Nous sommes allés chez mes grands-parents à Pâques.

Easter egg NOUN
l'œuf de Pâques *masc*

DID YOU KNOW...?
In France, Easter eggs are said to be brought by the Easter bells or **cloches de Pâques** which fly from Rome and drop them in people's gardens.

★ **eastern** ADJECTIVE
■ **the eastern part of the island** la partie est de l'île
■ **Eastern Europe** l'Europe de l'Est

★ **easy** ADJECTIVE
facile (FEM facile)

easy chair NOUN
le fauteuil *masc*

easy-going ADJECTIVE
facile à vivre (FEM facile à vivre)
□ She's very easy-going. Elle est très facile à vivre.

★ to **eat** VERB
manger [45]
▪ **Would you like something to eat?** Est-ce que tu veux manger quelque chose?

e-book NOUN
le livre numérique *masc*

EC NOUN (= *European Community*)
la CE *fem* (= *Communauté européenne*)

e-card NOUN
la carte de vœux électronique *fem*

eccentric ADJECTIVE
excentrique (FEM excentrique)

★ **echo** NOUN
l'écho *masc*

eco-friendly ADJECTIVE
respectueux de l'environnement (FEM respectueuse de l'environnement)

ecological ADJECTIVE
écologique (FEM écologique)

ecology NOUN
l'écologie *fem*

e-commerce NOUN
le commerce électronique *masc*

★ **economic** ADJECTIVE
rentable (FEM rentable) (*profitable*)

economical ADJECTIVE
1 économe (FEM économe) (*person*)
2 économique (FEM économique) (*method, car*)

★ **economics** NOUN
l'économie *fem*
□ He's studying economics. Il étudie les sciences économiques.

to **economize** VERB
faire [36] des économies
□ to economize on something faire des économies sur quelque chose

★ **economy** NOUN
l'économie *fem*

ecstasy NOUN
l'ecstasy *fem* (*drug*)
▪ **to be in ecstasy** s'extasier [19]

eczema NOUN
l'eczéma *masc*

★ **edge** NOUN
le bord *masc*

edgy ADJECTIVE
tendu (FEM tendue)

Edinburgh NOUN
Édimbourg

★ **editor** NOUN
le rédacteur en chef *masc*
la rédactrice en chef *fem* (*of newspaper*)

educated ADJECTIVE
cultivé (FEM cultivée)

★ **education** NOUN
1 l'éducation *fem*
□ There should be more investment in education. On devrait investir plus dans l'éducation.
2 l'enseignement *masc* (*teaching*)
□ She works in education. Elle travaille dans l'enseignement.

★ **educational** ADJECTIVE
éducatif (FEM éducative) (*experience, toy*)
□ It was very educational. C'était très éducatif.

★ **effect** NOUN
l'effet *masc*
□ special effects les effets spéciaux

★ **effective** ADJECTIVE
efficace (FEM efficace)

effectively ADVERB
efficacement

> **BE CAREFUL!**
> Do not translate **effectively** by the French word **effectivement**.

★ **efficient** ADJECTIVE
efficace (FEM efficace)

★ **effort** NOUN
l'effort *masc*

e.g. ABBREVIATION
p. ex. (= *par exemple*)

★ **egg** NOUN
l'œuf *masc*
□ a hard-boiled egg un œuf dur □ a soft-boiled egg un œuf à la coque □ a fried egg un œuf sur le plat
▪ **scrambled eggs** les œufs brouillés

egg cup NOUN
le coquetier *masc*

eggplant NOUN (US)
l'aubergine *fem*

Egypt NOUN
l'Égypte *fem*
▪ **in Egypt** en Égypte

Eiffel Tower NOUN
la tour Eiffel *fem*

★ **eight** NUMBER
huit
□ She's eight. Elle a huit ans.

★ **eighteen** NUMBER
dix-huit
□ She's eighteen. Elle a dix-huit ans.

★ **eighteenth** ADJECTIVE
dix-huitième (FEM dix-huitième)
□ her eighteenth birthday son dix-huitième anniversaire □ the eighteenth floor le dix-huitième étage
■ **the eighteenth of August** le dix-huit août

★ **eighth** ADJECTIVE
huitième (FEM huitième)
□ the eighth floor le huitième étage
■ **the eighth of August** le huit août

★ **eighty** NUMBER
quatre-vingts

★ **Eire** NOUN
la République d'Irlande *fem*
■ **in Eire** en République d'Irlande

★ **either** ADVERB, CONJUNCTION, PRONOUN
non plus
□ I don't like milk, and I don't like eggs either. Je n'aime pas le lait, et je n'aime pas les œufs non plus. □ I've never been to Spain. — I haven't either. Je ne suis jamais allé en Espagne. — Moi non plus.
■ **either ... or ...** soit ... soit ... □ You can have either ice cream or yoghurt. Tu peux prendre soit une glace soit un yaourt.
■ **either of them** l'un ou l'autre □ Take either of them. Prends l'un ou l'autre.
■ **I don't like either of them.** Je n'aime ni l'un ni l'autre.

elastic NOUN
l'élastique *masc*

elastic band NOUN
l'élastique *masc*

elbow NOUN
le coude *masc*

★ **elder** ADJECTIVE
aîné (FEM aînée)
□ my elder sister ma sœur aînée

★ **elderly** ADJECTIVE
âgé (FEM âgée)

★ **eldest** ADJECTIVE
aîné (FEM aînée)
□ my eldest sister ma sœur aînée □ He's the eldest. C'est l'aîné.

to **elect** VERB
élire [44]

★ **election** NOUN
l'élection *fem*

★ **electric** ADJECTIVE
électrique (FEM électrique)
□ an electric fire un radiateur électrique □ an electric guitar une guitare électrique
■ **an electric blanket** une couverture chauffante
■ **an electric shock** une décharge

electrical ADJECTIVE
électrique (FEM électrique)
■ **an electrical engineer** un ingénieur électricien

electrician NOUN
l'électricien *masc*
□ He's an electrician. Il est électricien.

★ **electricity** NOUN
l'électricité *fem*

★ **electronic** ADJECTIVE
électronique (FEM électronique)

electronics NOUN
l'électronique *fem*
□ My hobby is electronics. Ma passion, c'est l'électronique.

★ **elegant** ADJECTIVE
élégant (FEM élégante)

elementary school NOUN (US)
l'école primaire *fem*

★ **elephant** NOUN
l'éléphant *masc*

elevator NOUN (US)
l'ascenseur *masc*

★ **eleven** NUMBER
onze
□ She's eleven. Elle a onze ans.

★ **eleventh** ADJECTIVE
onzième (FEM onzième)
□ the eleventh floor le onzième étage □ the eleventh of August le onze août

★ **else** ADVERB
d'autre
□ somebody else quelqu'un d'autre □ nobody else personne d'autre □ nothing else rien d'autre
■ **something else** autre chose
■ **anything else** autre chose □ Would you like anything else? Désirez-vous autre chose?
■ **I don't want anything else.** Je ne veux rien d'autre.
■ **somewhere else** ailleurs
■ **anywhere else** autre part

★ **email** NOUN
▷ *see also* **email** VERB
le e-mail *masc*
le mail *masc*
■ **email address** adresse e-mail *fem* □ My email address is: ... Mon adresse e-mail, c'est: ...

★ to **email** VERB
▷ *see also* **email** NOUN
■ **to email somebody** envoyer [33] un mail à quelqu'un
□ Email me your essay. Envoyez-moi par mail votre rédaction d'anglais.

embankment NOUN
le talus *masc*

★ **embarrassed** ADJECTIVE
gêné (FEM gênée)

□ I was really embarrassed. J'étais vraiment gêné.

embarrassing ADJECTIVE
gênant (FEM gênante)
□ It was so embarrassing. C'était tellement gênant.

★ **embassy** NOUN
l'ambassade *fem*
□ the British Embassy l'ambassade de Grande-Bretagne □ the French Embassy l'ambassade de France

to **embroider** VERB
broder [28]

embroidery NOUN
la broderie *fem*
□ I do embroidery. Je fais de la broderie.

★ **emergency** NOUN
l'urgence *fem*
□ This is an emergency! C'est une urgence!
■ **in an emergency** en cas d'urgence
■ **an emergency exit** une sortie de secours
■ **an emergency landing** un atterrissage forcé
■ **the emergency services** les services d'urgence *masc pl*

to **emigrate** VERB
émigrer [28]

emoji NOUN
le emoji *masc*

emotion NOUN
l'émotion *fem*

★ **emotional** ADJECTIVE
émotif (FEM émotive) (*person*)

emperor NOUN
l'empereur *masc*

★ to **emphasize** VERB
■ **to emphasize something** insister [28] sur quelque chose
■ **to emphasize that ...** souligner [28] que ...

empire NOUN
l'empire *masc*

★ to **employ** VERB
employer [53]
□ The factory employs 600 people. L'usine emploie six cents personnes.

★ **employee** NOUN
l'employé *masc*
l'employée *fem*

★ **employer** NOUN
l'employeur *masc*

★ **employment** NOUN
l'emploi *masc*

★ **empty** ADJECTIVE
▷ *see also* **empty** VERB
vide (FEM vide)

★ to **empty** VERB
▷ *see also* **empty** ADJECTIVE
vider [28]
■ **to empty something out** vider [28] quelque chose

★ to **encourage** VERB
encourager [45]
■ **to encourage somebody to do something** encourager [45] quelqu'un à faire quelque chose

encouragement NOUN
l'encouragement *masc*

encyclopedia NOUN
l'encyclopédie *fem*

★ **end** NOUN
▷ *see also* **end** VERB
1 la fin *fem*
□ the end of the film la fin du film □ the end of the holidays la fin des vacances
■ **in the end** en fin de compte □ In the end I decided to stay at home. En fin de compte j'ai décidé de rester à la maison.
■ **It turned out all right in the end.** Ça s'est bien terminé.
2 le bout *masc*
□ at the end of the street au bout de la rue □ at the other end of the table à l'autre bout de la table
■ **for hours on end** des heures entières

★ to **end** VERB
▷ *see also* **end** NOUN
finir [38]
□ What time does the film end? À quelle heure est-ce que le film finit?
■ **to end up doing something** finir [38] par faire quelque chose □ I ended up walking home. J'ai fini par rentrer chez moi à pied.

ending NOUN
la fin *fem*
□ It was an exciting film, especially the ending. C'était un film passionnant, surtout la fin.

endless ADJECTIVE
interminable (FEM interminable)
□ The journey seemed endless. Le voyage a paru interminable.

★ **enemy** NOUN
l'ennemi *masc*
l'ennemie *fem*

energetic ADJECTIVE
énergique (FEM énergique) (*person*)

★ **energy** NOUN
l'énergie *fem*

★ **engaged** ADJECTIVE
1 occupé (FEM occupée) (*busy, in use*)
□ I phoned, but it was engaged. J'ai téléphoné, mais c'était occupé.
2 fiancé (FEM fiancée) (*to be married*)
□ She's engaged to Jacob. Elle est fiancée à Jacob.
■ **to get engaged** se fiancer [12]

engaged tone NOUN
la tonalité 'occupé' *fem*

engagement NOUN
les fiançailles *fem pl*
□ an engagement ring une bague de fiançailles

★ **engine** NOUN
le moteur *masc*

BE CAREFUL!
Do not translate **engine** by the French word **engin**.

★ **engineer** NOUN
l'ingénieur *masc*
□ He's an engineer. Il est ingénieur.

★ **engineering** NOUN
l'ingénierie *fem*

★ **England** NOUN
l'Angleterre *fem*
■ **in England** en Angleterre
■ **to England** en Angleterre
■ **I'm from England.** Je suis anglais.

★ **English** NOUN
▷ *see also* **English** ADJECTIVE
l'anglais *masc* (*language*)
□ Do you speak English? Est-ce que vous parlez anglais?
■ **the English** les Anglais

★ **English** ADJECTIVE
▷ *see also* **English** NOUN
anglais (FEM anglaise)
□ I'm English. Je suis anglais.
■ **English people** les Anglais

★ **Englishman** NOUN
l'Anglais *masc*

★ **Englishwoman** NOUN
l'Anglaise *fem*

★ to **enjoy** VERB
aimer [28]
□ Did you enjoy the film? Est-ce que vous avez aimé le film?
■ **to enjoy oneself** s'amuser [28] □ I really enjoyed myself. Je me suis vraiment bien amusé. □ Did you enjoy yourselves at the party? Est-ce vous vous êtes bien amusés à la fête?

enjoyable ADJECTIVE
agréable (FEM agréable)

enlargement NOUN
l'agrandissement *masc* (*of photo*)

★ **enormous** ADJECTIVE
énorme (FEM énorme)

★ **enough** PRONOUN, ADJECTIVE
assez de
□ enough time assez de temps □ I didn't have enough money. Je n'avais pas assez d'argent.
□ Have you got enough? Tu en as assez? □ I've had enough! J'en ai assez!
■ **big enough** suffisamment grand
■ **warm enough** suffisamment chaud
■ **That's enough.** Ça suffit.

to **enquire** VERB
■ **to enquire about something** se renseigner [28] sur quelque chose □ I am going to enquire about train times. Je vais me renseigner sur les horaires de trains.

enquiry NOUN
■ **to make enquiries (about something)** se renseigner [28] (sur quelque chose)
□ 'enquiries' 'renseignements'

★ to **enter** VERB
entrer [32[E]]
■ **to enter a room** entrer [32[E]] dans une pièce
■ **to enter a competition** s'inscrire [30] à une compétition

★ to **entertain** VERB
recevoir [67] (*guests*)

entertainer NOUN
l'artiste de variétés *masc/fem*

entertaining ADJECTIVE
amusant (FEM amusante)

★ **enthusiasm** NOUN
l'enthousiasme *masc*

enthusiast NOUN
■ **a maths enthusiast** un passionné de maths
■ **She's a DIY enthusiast.** C'est une passionnée de bricolage.

enthusiastic ADJECTIVE
enthousiaste (FEM enthousiaste)

entire ADJECTIVE
entier (FEM entière)
□ the entire world le monde entier

entirely ADVERB
entièrement

★ **entrance** NOUN
l'entrée *fem*
■ **an entrance exam** un concours d'entrée
■ **entrance fee** le prix d'entrée

★ **entry** NOUN
l'entrée *fem*
■ **'no entry'** **1** (*on door*) 'défense d'entrer' **2** (*on road sign*) 'sens interdit'
■ **an entry form** une feuille d'inscription

entry phone NOUN
l'interphone *masc*

envelope NOUN
l'enveloppe *fem*

envious ADJECTIVE
envieux (FEM envieuse)

★ **environment** NOUN
l'environnement *masc*

★ **environmental** ADJECTIVE
écologique (FEM écologique)

environment-friendly ADJECTIVE
écologique (FEM écologique)

envy NOUN
▷ *see also* **envy** VERB
l'envie *fem*

to **envy** VERB
▷ *see also* **envy** NOUN
envier [19]
□ **I don't envy you!** Je ne t'envie pas!

epileptic ADJECTIVE
épileptique (FEM épileptique)

episode NOUN
l'épisode *masc* (*of TV programme, story*)

★ **equal** ADJECTIVE
▷ *see also* **equal** VERB
égal (FEM égale, MASC PL égaux)

★ to **equal** VERB
▷ *see also* **equal** ADJECTIVE
égaler [28]

equality NOUN
l'égalité *fem*

to **equalize** VERB
égaliser [28] (*in sport*)

equator NOUN
l'équateur *masc*

★ **equipment** NOUN
l'équipement *masc*
□ **fishing equipment** l'équipement de pêche
□ **skiing equipment** l'équipement de ski

equipped ADJECTIVE
■ **equipped with** équipé de
■ **to be well equipped** être [35] bien équipé

★ **equivalent** NOUN
l'équivalent *masc*
■ **equivalent to** équivalent à

e-reader NOUN
liseuse *fem*

★ **error** NOUN
l'erreur *fem*

escalator NOUN
l'escalier roulant *masc*

★ **escape** NOUN
▷ *see also* **escape** VERB
l'évasion *fem* (*from prison*)

★ to **escape** VERB
▷ *see also* **escape** NOUN
s'échapper [28]
□ **A lion has escaped.** Un lion s'est échappé.
■ **to escape from prison** s'évader [28] de prison

escort NOUN
l'escorte *fem*
□ **a police escort** une escorte de police

★ **especially** ADVERB
surtout
□ **It's very hot there, especially in the summer.** Il fait très chaud là-bas, surtout en été.

essay NOUN
la dissertation *fem*
□ **a history essay** une dissertation d'histoire

★ **essential** ADJECTIVE
essentiel (FEM essentielle)
□ **It's essential to bring warm clothes.** Il est essentiel d'apporter des vêtements chauds.

estate NOUN
la cité *fem* (*housing estate*)
□ **I live on an estate.** J'habite dans une cité.

estate agent NOUN
l'agent immobilier *masc*

estate car NOUN
le break *masc*

★ to **estimate** VERB
estimer [28]
□ **They estimated it would take three weeks.** Ils ont estimé que cela prendrait trois semaines.

★ **etc** ABBREVIATION (= *et cetera*)
etc.

Ethiopia NOUN
l'Éthiopie *fem*
■ **in Ethiopia** en Éthiopie

★ **ethnic** ADJECTIVE
1 ethnique (FEM ethnique) (*racial*)
□ **an ethnic minority** une minorité ethnique
2 folklorique (FEM folklorique) (*clothes, music*)

e-ticket NOUN
le billet électronique *masc*

EU NOUN (= *European Union*)
l'Union européenne *fem*

★ **euro** NOUN
l'euro *masc*
□ **50 euros** 50 euros

★ **Europe** NOUN
l'Europe *fem*
■ **in Europe** en Europe
■ **to Europe** en Europe

★ **European** NOUN
▷ *see also* **European** ADJECTIVE
l'Européen *masc*
l'Européenne *fem* (*person*)

★ **European** ADJECTIVE
▷ *see also* **European** NOUN
européen (FEM européenne)

to **evacuate** VERB
évacuer [28]

eve NOUN
■ **Christmas Eve** la veille de Noël
■ **New Year's Eve** la Saint-Sylvestre

★ **even** ADVERB
▷ *see also* **even** ADJECTIVE
même
□ **I like all animals, even snakes.** J'aime tous les animaux, même les serpents.
■ **even if** même si □ **I'd never do that, even if**

you asked me. Je ne ferais jamais ça, même si tu me le demandais.
■ **not even** même pas □ He never stops working, not even at the weekend. Il n'arrête jamais de travailler, même pas le week-end.
■ **even though** bien que

bien que has to be followed by a verb in the subjunctive.

□ He wants to go out, even though it's raining. Il veut sortir bien qu'il pleuve.
■ **even more** encore plus □ I liked Boulogne even more than Paris. J'ai encore plus aimé Boulogne que Paris.

★ **even** ADJECTIVE
▷ *see also* **even** ADVERB
régulier (FEM régulière)
□ an even layer of snow une couche régulière de neige
■ **an even number** un nombre pair
■ **to get even with somebody** prendre [65] sa revanche sur quelqu'un □ He wanted to get even with her. Il voulait prendre sa revanche sur elle.

★ **evening** NOUN
le soir *masc*
□ in the evening le soir □ yesterday evening hier soir □ tomorrow evening demain soir
■ **all evening** toute la soirée
■ **Good evening!** Bonsoir!

evening class NOUN
le cours du soir *masc* (PL les cours du soir)

★ **event** NOUN
l'événement *masc*
■ **a sporting event** une épreuve sportive

eventful ADJECTIVE
mouvementé (FEM mouvementée)

eventual ADJECTIVE
final (FEM finale)

BE CAREFUL!
Do not translate **eventual** by the French word **éventuel**.

★ **eventually** ADVERB
finalement

BE CAREFUL!
Do not translate **eventually** by the French word **éventuellement**.

★ **ever** ADVERB
■ **Have you ever been to Germany?** Est-ce que tu es déjà allé en Allemagne?
■ **Have you ever seen her?** Vous l'avez déjà vue?
■ **I haven't ever done that.** Je ne l'ai jamais fait.
■ **the best I've ever seen** le meilleur que j'aie jamais vu
■ **for the first time ever** pour la première fois
■ **ever since** depuis que □ ever since I met him depuis que je l'ai rencontré
■ **ever since then** depuis ce moment-là

★ **every** ADJECTIVE
chaque (FEM chaque)
□ every pupil chaque élève
■ **every time** chaque fois □ Every time I see him he's depressed. Chaque fois que je le vois il est déprimé.
■ **every day** tous les jours
■ **every week** toutes les semaines
■ **every now and then** de temps en temps

★ **everybody** PRONOUN
tout le monde
□ Everybody had a good time. Tout le monde s'est bien amusé. □ Everybody makes mistakes. Tout le monde peut se tromper.

★ **everyone** PRONOUN
tout le monde
□ Everyone opened their presents. Tout le monde a ouvert ses cadeaux. □ Everyone should have a hobby. Tout le monde devrait avoir un passe-temps.

★ **everything** PRONOUN
tout
□ You've thought of everything! Tu as pensé à tout!
■ **Have you remembered everything?** Est-ce que tu n'as rien oublié?
■ **Money isn't everything.** L'argent ne fait pas le bonheur.

★ **everywhere** ADVERB
partout
□ I looked everywhere, but I couldn't find it. J'ai regardé partout, mais je n'ai pas pu le trouver. □ There were policemen everywhere. Il y avait des policiers partout.

evil ADJECTIVE
mauvais (FEM mauvaise)

ex- PREFIX
ex-
□ his ex-wife son ex-femme

★ **exact** ADJECTIVE
exact (FEM exacte)

★ **exactly** ADVERB
exactement
□ exactly the same exactement le même
□ Not exactly. Pas exactement.
■ **It's exactly 10 o'clock.** Il est dix heures précises.

to **exaggerate** VERB
exagérer [34]

exaggeration NOUN
l'exagération *fem*

★ **exam** NOUN
l'examen *masc*
□ a French exam un examen de français □ the exam results les résultats des examens *masc pl*

English-French

e

examination NOUN
l'examen *masc*

to **examine** VERB
examiner [28]
□ He examined her passport. Il a examiné son passeport. □ The doctor examined him. Le docteur l'a examiné.

examiner NOUN
l'examinateur *masc*
l'examinatrice *fem*

★ **example** NOUN
l'exemple *masc*
■ **for example** par exemple

★ **excellent** ADJECTIVE
excellent (FEM excellente)
□ Her results were excellent. Elle a eu d'excellents résultats.
■ **It was excellent fun.** C'était vraiment super.

★ **except** PREPOSITION
sauf
□ everyone except me tout le monde sauf moi
■ **except for** sauf
■ **except that** sauf que □ The holiday was great, except that it rained. Les vacances étaient super, sauf qu'il a plu.

exception NOUN
l'exception *fem*
■ **to make an exception** faire [36] une exception

exceptional ADJECTIVE
exceptionnel (FEM exceptionnelle)

excess baggage NOUN
l'excédent de bagages *masc*

★ to **exchange** VERB
échanger [45]
□ I exchanged the book for a game. J'ai échangé le livre contre un jeu.

★ **exchange rate** NOUN
le taux de change *masc*

★ **excited** ADJECTIVE
excité (FEM excitée)

★ **exciting** ADJECTIVE
passionnant (FEM passionnante)

exclamation mark NOUN
le point d'exclamation *masc*

★ **excuse** NOUN
▷ *see also* **excuse** VERB
l'excuse *fem*

★ to **excuse** VERB
▷ *see also* **excuse** NOUN
■ **Excuse me!** Pardon!

to **execute** VERB
exécuter [28]

execution NOUN
l'exécution *fem*

executive NOUN
le cadre *masc* (*in business*)
□ He's an executive. Il est cadre.

★ **exercise** NOUN
l'exercice *masc*
■ **an exercise bike** un vélo d'appartement
■ **an exercise book** un cahier

★ **exhausted** ADJECTIVE
épuisé (FEM épuisée)

exhaust fumes PL NOUN
les gaz d'échappement *masc pl*

exhaust pipe NOUN
le tuyau d'échappement *masc*

★ **exhibition** NOUN
l'exposition *fem*

ex-husband NOUN
l'ex-mari *masc*

to **exist** VERB
exister [28]

★ **exit** NOUN
la sortie *fem*

exotic ADJECTIVE
exotique (FEM exotique)

★ to **expect** VERB
1 attendre [7]
□ I'm expecting him for dinner. Je l'attends pour dîner. □ She's expecting a baby. Elle attend un enfant.
2 s'attendre [7] à
□ I was expecting the worst. Je m'attendais au pire.
3 supposer [28]
□ I expect it's a mistake. Je suppose qu'il s'agit d'une erreur.

expedition NOUN
l'expédition *fem*

to **expel** VERB
■ **to get expelled** (*from school*) se faire [36] renvoyer

expenses PL NOUN
les frais *masc pl*

★ **expensive** ADJECTIVE
cher (FEM chère)

★ **experience** NOUN
l'expérience *fem*

experienced ADJECTIVE
expérimenté (FEM expérimentée)

experiment NOUN
l'expérience *fem*

★ **expert** NOUN
le/la spécialiste *masc/fem*
□ He's a computer expert. C'est un spécialiste en informatique.
■ **He's an expert cook.** Il cuisine très bien.

to **expire** VERB
expirer [28]

★ to **explain** VERB
expliquer [28]

explanation NOUN
l'explication *fem*

★ to **explode** VERB
exploser [28]

to **exploit** VERB
exploiter [28]

exploitation NOUN
l'exploitation *fem*

to **explore** VERB
explorer [28] (*place*)

explorer NOUN
l'explorateur *masc*
l'exploratrice *fem*

★ **explosion** NOUN
l'explosion *fem*

explosive ADJECTIVE
▷ *see also* **explosive** NOUN
explosif (FEM explosive)

explosive NOUN
▷ *see also* **explosive** ADJECTIVE
l'explosif *masc*

★ to **express** VERB
exprimer [28]
■ **to express oneself** s'exprimer [28] □ It's hard to express oneself in French. C'est dur de s'exprimer en français.

★ **expression** NOUN
l'expression *fem*
□ It's an English expression. C'est une expression anglaise.

expressway NOUN (US)
l'autoroute urbaine *fem*

extension NOUN
1 l'annexe *fem* (*of building*)
2 le poste *masc* (*telephone*)
■ **Extension 3137, please.** Poste trente et un trente-sept, s'il vous plaît.

In France, phone numbers are broken into groups of two digits where possible.

extensive ADJECTIVE
1 vaste (FEM vaste) (*knowledge, range*)
□ The castle is set in extensive grounds. Le château est situé au cœur d'un vaste domaine.
2 considérable (FEM considérable) (*damage, alterations*)
□ The earthquake caused extensive damage. Le tremblement de terre a causé des dommages considérables.

extensively ADVERB
■ **He has travelled extensively in Europe.** Il a beaucoup voyagé en Europe.
■ **The building was extensively renovated last year.** Le bâtiment a eu d'importantes rénovations l'année dernière.

★ **extent** NOUN
■ **to some extent** dans une certaine mesure

exterior ADJECTIVE
extérieur (FEM extérieure)

extinct ADJECTIVE
■ **to become extinct** disparaître [56]
■ **to be extinct** avoir [8] disparu □ The species is almost extinct. Cette espèce a presque disparu.

extinguisher NOUN
l'extincteur *masc* (*fire extinguisher*)

extortionate ADJECTIVE
exorbitant (FEM exorbitante)

★ **extra** ADJECTIVE, ADVERB
supplémentaire (FEM supplémentaire)
□ an extra blanket une couverture supplémentaire
■ **to pay extra** payer [59] un supplément
■ **Breakfast is extra.** Il y a un supplément pour le petit déjeuner.
■ **It costs extra.** Il y a un supplément.

★ **extraordinary** ADJECTIVE
extraordinaire (FEM extraordinaire)

extravagant ADJECTIVE
dépensier (FEM dépensière) (*person*)

★ **extreme** ADJECTIVE
extrême (FEM extrême)

★ **extremely** ADVERB
extrêmement

extremist NOUN
l'extrémiste *masc/fem*

★ **eye** NOUN
l'œil *masc* (PL les yeux)
□ I've got green eyes. J'ai les yeux verts.
■ **to keep an eye on something** surveiller [28] quelque chose

eyebrow NOUN
le sourcil *masc*

eyelash NOUN
le cil *masc*

eyelid NOUN
la paupière *fem*

eyeliner NOUN
l'eye-liner *masc*

eye shadow NOUN
l'ombre à paupières *fem*

eyesight NOUN
la vue *fem*

Ff

fabric NOUN
le tissu *masc*

fabulous ADJECTIVE
fabuleux (FEM fabuleuse)
□ The show was fabulous. Le spectacle était fabuleux.

★ **face** NOUN
▷ *see also* **face** VERB
1 le visage *masc* (*of person*)
2 le cadran *masc* (*of clock*)
3 la paroi *fem* (*of cliff*)
■ **on the face of it** à première vue
■ **in the face of these difficulties** face à ces difficultés
■ **face to face** face à face

★ to **face** VERB
▷ *see also* **face** NOUN
faire [36] face à (*place, problem*)
■ **to face up to something** faire [36] face à quelque chose □ You must face up to your responsibilities. Vous devez faire face à vos responsabilités.

Facebook® NOUN
Facebook® *masc*

to **facebook** VERB
facebooker [28]

face cloth NOUN
le gant de toilette *masc*

> DID YOU KNOW...?
> The French traditionally wash with a towelling glove rather than a flannel.

facilities PL NOUN
l'équipement *masc sing*
□ This school has excellent facilities. Cette école dispose d'un excellent équipement.
■ **toilet facilities** les toilettes *fem pl*
■ **cooking facilities** la cuisine équipée *sing*

★ **fact** NOUN
le fait *masc*
■ **in fact** en fait

★ **factory** NOUN
l'usine *fem*

to **fade** VERB
1 passer [58] (*colour*)
□ The colour has faded in the sun. La couleur a passé au soleil.
■ **My jeans have faded.** Mon jean est délavé.
2 baisser [28]
□ The light was fading fast. La lumière baissait rapidement.
3 diminuer [28]
□ The noise gradually faded. Le bruit a diminué peu à peu.

fag NOUN
la clope *fem* (*cigarette*)

★ to **fail** VERB
▷ *see also* **fail** NOUN
1 rater [28]
□ I failed the history exam. J'ai raté l'examen d'histoire.
2 échouer [28]
□ In our class, no one failed. Dans notre classe, personne n'a échoué.
3 lâcher [28]
□ My brakes failed. Mes freins ont lâché.
■ **to fail to do something** ne pas faire [36] quelque chose □ She failed to return her library books. Elle n'a pas rendu ses livres à la bibliothèque.

★ **fail** NOUN
▷ *see also* **fail** VERB
■ **without fail** sans faute

★ **failure** NOUN
1 l'échec *masc*
□ feelings of failure un sentiment d'échec *sing*
2 le raté *masc*
la ratée *fem*
□ He's a failure. C'est un raté.
3 la défaillance *fem*
□ a mechanical failure une défaillance mécanique

faint ADJECTIVE
▷ *see also* **faint** VERB
faible (FEM faible)
□ His voice was very faint. Sa voix était très faible.
■ **to feel faint** se trouver [28] mal

to **faint** VERB
▷ *see also* **faint** ADJECTIVE
s'évanouir [38]
□ All of a sudden she fainted. Tout à coup elle s'est évanouie.

★ **fair** ADJECTIVE
▷ *see also* **fair** NOUN
1 juste (FEM juste)
□ That's not fair. Ce n'est pas juste.
2 blond (FEM blonde) (*hair*)
□ He's got fair hair. Il a les cheveux blonds.
3 clair (FEM claire) (*skin*)
□ people with fair skin les gens qui ont la peau claire
4 beau (FEM belle) (*weather*)
□ The weather was fair. Il faisait beau.
5 assez bon (FEM assez bonne) (*good enough*)
□ I have a fair chance of winning. J'ai d'assez bonnes chances de gagner.
6 considérable (FEM considérable) (*sizeable*)
□ That's a fair distance. Ça représente une distance considérable.

★ **fair** NOUN
▷ *see also* **fair** ADJECTIVE
la foire *fem*
□ They went to the fair. Ils sont allés à la foire.
■ **a trade fair** une foire commerciale

fairground NOUN
le champ de foire *masc*

fair-haired ADJECTIVE
■ **My mother is fair-haired.** Ma mère a les cheveux blonds.

★ **fairly** ADVERB
1 équitablement
□ The cake was divided fairly. Le gâteau a été partagé équitablement.
2 assez (*quite*)
□ That's fairly good. C'est assez bien.

fairness NOUN
la justice *fem*

fairy NOUN
la fée *fem*

fairy tale NOUN
le conte de fées *masc*

★ **faith** NOUN
1 la foi *fem*
□ the Catholic faith la foi catholique
2 la confiance *fem*
□ People have lost faith in the government. Les gens ont perdu confiance dans le gouvernement.

faithful ADJECTIVE
fidèle (FEM fidèle)

faithfully ADVERB
■ **Yours faithfully ...** (*in letter*) Veuillez agréer mes salutations distinguées ...

fake NOUN
▷ *see also* **fake** ADJECTIVE
le faux *masc*
□ The painting was a fake. Le tableau était un faux.

fake ADJECTIVE
▷ *see also* **fake** NOUN
faux (FEM fausse)
□ She wore fake fur. Elle portait une fausse fourrure.

★ **fall** NOUN
▷ *see also* **fall** VERB
1 la chute *fem*
□ a fall of snow une chute de neige □ She had a nasty fall. Elle a fait une mauvaise chute.
■ **Niagara Falls** les chutes du Niagara
2 l'automne *masc* (US: *autumn*)

★ to **fall** VERB
▷ *see also* **fall** NOUN
1 tomber [84[E]]
□ He tripped and fell. Il a trébuché et il est tombé.
2 baisser [28]
□ Prices are falling. Les prix baissent.

to **fall down** VERB
1 tomber [84[E]] (*person*)
□ She's fallen down. Elle est tombée.
2 s'écrouler [28] (*building*)
□ The house is slowly falling down. La maison est en train de s'écrouler.

to **fall for** VERB
1 se laisser [28] prendre à
□ They fell for it. Ils s'y sont laissé prendre.
2 tomber [84[E]] amoureux de
□ She's falling for him. Elle est en train de tomber amoureuse de lui.

to **fall off** VERB
tomber [84[E]] de
□ The book fell off the shelf. Le livre est tombé de l'étagère.

to **fall out** VERB
■ **to fall out with somebody** se fâcher [28] avec quelqu'un □ Sarah's fallen out with her boyfriend. Sarah s'est fâchée avec son copain.

to **fall through** VERB
tomber [84[E]] à l'eau
□ Our plans have fallen through. Nos projets sont tombés à l'eau.

fallen VERB ▷ *see* **fall**

★ **false** ADJECTIVE
faux (FEM fausse)
■ **a false alarm** une fausse alerte
■ **false teeth** les fausses dents

fame NOUN
la renommée *fem*

★ **familiar** ADJECTIVE
familier (FEM familière)
□ a familiar face un visage familier
■ **to be familiar with something** bien connaître [14] quelque chose □ I'm familiar with his work. Je connais bien ses œuvres.

English-French

f

★ **family** NOUN
la famille *fem*
■ **the Cooke family** la famille Cooke

famine NOUN
la famine *fem*

★ **famous** ADJECTIVE
célèbre (FEM célèbre)

★ **fan** NOUN
1 l'éventail *masc* (*hand-held*)
2 le ventilateur *masc* (*electric*)
3 le/la fan *masc/fem* (*of person, band*)
□ I'm a fan of Ed Sheeran. Je suis une fan d'Ed Sheeran.
4 le/la supporter *masc/fem* (*of sport*)
□ football fans les supporters de football

fanatic NOUN
le/la fanatique *masc/fem*

to **fancy** VERB
■ **to fancy something** avoir [8] envie de quelque chose □ I fancy an ice cream. J'ai envie d'une glace.
■ **to fancy doing something** avoir [8] envie de faire quelque chose
■ **He fancies her.** Elle lui plaît.

fancy dress NOUN
le déguisement *masc*
□ He was wearing fancy dress. Il portait un déguisement.
■ **a fancy-dress ball** un bal costumé

★ **fantastic** ADJECTIVE
fantastique (FEM fantastique)

★ **far** ADJECTIVE, ADVERB
loin
□ Is it far? Est-ce que c'est loin?
■ **far from** loin de □ It's not far from Manchester. Ce n'est pas loin de Manchester.
□ It's far from easy. C'est loin d'être facile.
■ **How far is it?** C'est à quelle distance?
■ **How far is it to Geneva?** Combien y a-t-il jusqu'à Genève?
■ **How far have you got?** (*with a task*) Où en êtes-vous?
■ **at the far end** à l'autre bout □ at the far end of the room à l'autre bout de la pièce
■ **far better** beaucoup mieux
■ **as far as I know** pour autant que je sache

★ **fare** NOUN
1 le prix du billet *masc* (*on trains, buses*)
2 le prix de la course *masc* (*in taxi*)
■ **half fare** le demi-tarif
■ **full fare** le plein tarif

Far East NOUN
l'Extrême-Orient *masc*
■ **in the Far East** en Extrême-Orient

★ **farm** NOUN
la ferme *fem*

★ **farmer** NOUN
l'agriculteur *masc*
l'agricultrice *fem*
□ He's a farmer. Il est agriculteur.
■ **a farmers' market** un marché fermier

farmhouse NOUN
la ferme *fem*

farming NOUN
l'agriculture *fem*
■ **dairy farming** l'industrie laitière

fascinating ADJECTIVE
fascinant (FEM fascinante)

★ **fashion** NOUN
la mode *fem*
□ a fashion show un défilé de mode
■ **in fashion** à la mode

fashionable ADJECTIVE
à la mode
□ Aisha wears very fashionable clothes. Aisha porte des vêtements très à la mode. □ a fashionable restaurant un restaurant à la mode

★ **fast** ADJECTIVE, ADVERB
1 vite
□ He can run fast. Il sait courir vite.
2 rapide (FEM rapide)
□ a fast car une voiture rapide
■ **That clock's fast.** Cette pendule avance.
■ **He's fast asleep.** Il est profondément endormi.

★ **fat** ADJECTIVE
▷ *see also* **fat** NOUN
gros (FEM grosse)

> **WORD POWER**
> You can use a number of other words instead of **fat**:
> **chubby** potelé
> □ a chubby baby un bébé potelé
> **overweight** trop gros
> □ an overweight child un enfant trop gros
> **plump** dodu
> □ a plump woman une femme dodue

★ **fat** NOUN
▷ *see also* **fat** ADJECTIVE
1 le gras *masc* (*on meat, in food*)
□ It's very high in fat. C'est très gras.
2 les matières grasses *fem pl* (*for cooking*)
□ Don't use too much fat when you cook. En cuisinant, n'utilisez pas trop de matières grasses.

fatal ADJECTIVE
1 mortel (FEM mortelle) (*causing death*)
□ a fatal accident un accident mortel
2 fatal (FEM fatale) (*disastrous*)
□ He made a fatal mistake. Il a fait une erreur fatale.

★ **father** NOUN
le père *masc*
□ my father mon père

 Numbers in brackets refer to verb tables on pages 650 to 658

father-in-law NOUN
le beau-père *masc* (PL les beaux-pères)

faucet NOUN (US)
le robinet *masc*

★ **fault** NOUN
1 la faute *fem* (*mistake*)
□ It's my fault. C'est de ma faute.
2 le défaut *masc* (*defect*)
□ There's a fault in this material. Ce tissu a un défaut.
■ **a mechanical fault** une défaillance mécanique

faulty ADJECTIVE
défectueux (FEM défectueuse)
□ This machine is faulty. Cette machine est défectueuse.

★ **favour** (US **favor**) NOUN
le service *masc*
■ **to do somebody a favour** rendre [7] service à quelqu'un □ Could you do me a favour? Tu peux me rendre service?
■ **to be in favour of something** être [35] pour quelque chose □ I'm in favour of recycling. Je suis pour le recyclage.

★ **favourite** (US **favorite**) ADJECTIVE
▷ *see also* **favourite** NOUN
favori (FEM favorite)
□ Blue's my favourite colour. Le bleu est ma couleur favorite.

★ **favourite** (US **favorite**) NOUN
▷ *see also* **favourite** ADJECTIVE
le favori *masc*
la favorite *fem*
□ Liverpool are favourites to win the Cup. L'équipe de Liverpool est favorite pour la coupe.

★ **fear** NOUN
▷ *see also* **fear** VERB
la peur *fem*

★ to **fear** VERB
▷ *see also* **fear** NOUN
craindre [17]
□ You have nothing to fear. Vous n'avez rien à craindre.

feather NOUN
la plume *fem*

★ **feature** NOUN
la caractéristique *fem* (*of person, object*)
□ an important feature une caractéristique essentielle

★ **February** NOUN
février *masc*
■ **in February** en février

fed VERB ▷ *see* **feed**

fed up ADJECTIVE
■ **to be fed up with something** en avoir [8] marre de quelque chose □ I'm fed up with waiting for him. J'en ai marre de l'attendre.

★ to **feed** VERB
donner [28] à manger à
□ Have you fed the cat? Est-ce que tu as donné à manger au chat?
■ **He worked hard to feed his family.** Il travaillait dur pour nourrir sa famille.

★ to **feel** VERB
1 se sentir [77]
□ I don't feel well. Je ne me sens pas bien. □ I feel a bit lonely. Je me sens un peu seul.
2 sentir [77]
□ I didn't feel much pain. Je n'ai presque rien senti.
3 toucher [28]
□ The doctor felt his forehead. Le docteur lui a touché le front.
■ **I was feeling hungry.** J'avais faim.
■ **I was feeling cold, so I went inside.** J'avais froid, alors je suis rentré.
■ **I feel like ...** (*want*) J'ai envie de ... □ Do you feel like an ice cream? Tu as envie d'une glace?

★ **feeling** NOUN
1 la sensation *fem* (*physical*)
□ a burning feeling une sensation de brûlure
2 le sentiment *masc* (*emotional*)
□ a feeling of satisfaction un sentiment de satisfaction

feet PL NOUN ▷ *see* **foot**

fell VERB ▷ *see* **fall**

felt VERB ▷ *see* **feel**

felt-tip pen NOUN
le stylo-feutre *masc*

★ **female** ADJECTIVE
▷ *see also* **female** NOUN
1 femelle (FEM femelle)
□ a female animal un animal femelle
2 féminin (FEM féminine)
□ the female sex le sexe féminin

★ **female** NOUN
▷ *see also* **female** ADJECTIVE
la femelle *fem* (*animal*)

feminine ADJECTIVE
féminin (FEM féminine)

feminist NOUN
le/la féministe *masc/fem*

★ **fence** NOUN
la barrière *fem*

fern NOUN
la fougère *fem*

ferret NOUN
le furet *masc*

ferry NOUN
le ferry *masc*
■ **the ferry crossing** la traversée en ferry
■ **the ferry terminal** le terminal pour ferries

fertile ADJECTIVE
fertile (FEM fertile)

English-French

f

fertilizer NOUN
l'engrais *masc*

★ **festival** NOUN
le festival *masc*
▫ a rock festival un festival de rock

to **fetch** VERB
1 aller [3E] chercher
▫ Fetch the bucket. Va chercher le seau.
2 se vendre [88] (*sell for*)
▫ His painting fetched £5000. Son tableau s'est vendu cinq mille livres.

fever NOUN
la fièvre *fem* (*temperature*)

★ **few** ADJECTIVE, PRONOUN
peu de (*not many*)
▫ few books peu de livres
▪ **a few 1** quelques ▫ a few hours quelques heures **2** quelques-uns ▫ How many apples do you want? — A few. Tu veux combien de pommes? — Quelques-unes.
▪ **quite a few people** pas mal de monde

fewer ADJECTIVE
moins de
▫ There are fewer people than there were yesterday. Il y a moins de monde qu'hier.
▫ There are fewer pupils in this class. Il y a moins d'élèves dans cette classe.

★ **fiancé** NOUN
le fiancé *masc*
▫ He's my fiancé. C'est mon fiancé.

★ **fiancée** NOUN
la fiancée *fem*
▫ She's my fiancée. C'est ma fiancée.

fiction NOUN
les romans *masc pl* (*novels*)

★ **field** NOUN
1 le champ *masc* (*in countryside*)
▫ a field of wheat un champ de blé
2 le terrain *masc* (*for sport*)
▫ a football field un terrain de football
3 le domaine *masc* (*subject*)
▫ He's an expert in his field. C'est un expert dans son domaine.

★ **fierce** ADJECTIVE
1 féroce (FEM féroce)
▫ The dog looked very fierce. Le chien avait l'air très féroce.
2 violent (FEM violente)
▫ The wind was very fierce. Le vent était très violent. ▫ a fierce attack une attaque violente

★ **fifteen** NUMBER
quinze
▫ I'm fifteen. J'ai quinze ans.

★ **fifteenth** ADJECTIVE
quinzième (FEM quinzième)
▫ the fifteenth floor le quinzième étage
▪ **the fifteenth of August** le quinze août

★ **fifth** ADJECTIVE
cinquième (FEM cinquième)
▫ the fifth floor le cinquième étage
▪ **the fifth of August** le cinq août

★ **fifty** NUMBER
cinquante
▫ He's fifty. Il a cinquante ans.

fifty-fifty ADJECTIVE, ADVERB
moitié-moitié
▫ They split the prize money fifty-fifty. Ils ont partagé l'argent du prix moitié-moitié.
▪ **a fifty-fifty chance** une chance sur deux

★ **fight** NOUN
▷ *see also* **fight** VERB
1 la bagarre *fem*
▫ There was a fight in the playground. Il y a eu une bagarre dans la cour de récréation.
2 la lutte *fem*
▫ the fight against cancer la lutte contre le cancer

★ to **fight** VERB
▷ *see also* **fight** NOUN
1 se battre [9]
▫ They were fighting. Ils se battaient.
▫ Women are fighting for equal rights. Les femmes se battent pour obtenir l'égalité des droits.
2 lutter [28] contre
▫ This organization fights against racism. Cette organisation lutte contre le racisme.

fighting NOUN
les bagarres *fem pl*
▫ Fighting broke out on the football pitch. Des bagarres ont éclaté sur le terrain de foot.

★ **figure** NOUN
1 le chiffre *masc* (*number*)
▫ Can you give me the exact figures? Pouvez-vous me donner les chiffres exacts?
2 la silhouette *fem* (*outline of person*)
▫ Yasmin saw the figure of a man on the bridge. Yasmin a vu la silhouette d'un homme sur le pont.
▪ **She's got a good figure.** Elle est bien faite.
▪ **I have to watch my figure.** Je dois faire attention à ma ligne.
3 le personnage *masc* (*personality*)
▫ She's an important political figure. C'est un personnage politique important.

to **figure out** VERB
1 calculer [28]
▫ I'll try to figure out how much it'll cost. Je vais essayer de calculer combien ça va coûter.
2 voir [92]
▫ I couldn't figure out what it meant. Je n'arrivais pas à voir ce que ça voulait dire.
3 cerner [28]
▫ I can't figure him out at all. Je n'arrive pas du tout à le cerner.

★ **file** NOUN
▷ *see also* **file** VERB
1 le dossier *masc* (*document*)
□ Have we got a file on the suspect? Est-ce que nous avons un dossier sur le suspect?
2 la chemise *fem* (*folder*)
□ She keeps all her notes in a cardboard file. Elle garde toutes ses notes dans une chemise en carton.
3 le classeur *masc* (*ring binder*)
4 le fichier *masc* (*on computer*)
5 la lime *fem* (*for nails, metal*)

★ to **file** VERB
▷ *see also* **file** NOUN
1 classer [28] (*papers*)
2 limer [28] (*nails, metal*)
□ to file one's nails se limer les ongles

★ to **fill** VERB
remplir [38]
□ She filled the glass with water. Elle a rempli le verre d'eau.

to **fill in** VERB
1 remplir [38]
□ Can you fill this form in please? Est-ce que vous pouvez remplir ce formulaire s'il vous plaît?
2 boucher [28]
□ He filled the hole in with soil. Il a bouché le trou avec de la terre.

to **fill up** VERB
remplir [38]
□ He filled the cup up to the brim. Il a rempli la tasse à ras bords.

★ **film** NOUN
1 le film *masc* (*movie*)
2 la pellicule *fem* (*for camera*)

film star NOUN
la vedette de cinéma *fem*
□ He's a film star. C'est une vedette de cinéma.

filthy ADJECTIVE
dégoûtant (FEM dégoûtante)

★ **final** ADJECTIVE
▷ *see also* **final** NOUN
1 dernier (FEM dernière) (*last*)
□ our final farewells nos derniers adieux
2 définitif (FEM définitive) (*definite*)
□ a final decision une décision définitive
■ **I'm not going and that's final.** Je n'y vais pas, un point c'est tout.

★ **final** NOUN
▷ *see also* **final** ADJECTIVE
la finale *fem*
□ Andy Murray is in the final. Andy Murray va disputer la finale.

★ **finally** ADVERB
1 enfin (*lastly*)
□ Finally, I would like to say ... Enfin, je voudrais dire ...
2 finalement (*eventually*)
□ She finally chose the red shoes. Elle a finalement choisi les chaussures rouges.

★ to **find** VERB
1 trouver [28]
□ I can't find the exit. Je ne trouve pas la sortie.
2 retrouver [28] (*something lost*)
□ Did you find your pen? Est-ce que tu as retrouvé ton crayon?

to **find out** VERB
découvrir [55]
□ I'm determined to find out the truth. Je suis décidé à découvrir la vérité.
■ **to find out about 1** (*make enquiries*) se renseigner [28] sur □ Try to find out about the exam. Essaye de te renseigner sur l'examen. **2** (*by chance*) apprendre [65] □ I found out about what he said. J'ai appris ce qu'il avait dit.

★ **fine** ADJECTIVE, ADVERB
▷ *see also* **fine** NOUN
1 excellent (FEM excellente) (*very good*)
□ He's a fine musician. C'est un excellent musicien.
■ **to be fine** aller [3E] bien □ How are you? — I'm fine. Comment ça va? — Ça va bien.
■ **I feel fine.** Je me sens bien.
■ **The weather is fine today.** Il fait beau aujourd'hui.
2 fin (FEM fine) (*not coarse*)
□ She's got very fine hair. Elle a les cheveux très fins.

★ **fine** NOUN
▷ *see also* **fine** ADJECTIVE, ADVERB
1 l'amende *fem*
□ She got a £50 fine. Elle a eu une amende de cinquante livres.
2 la contravention *fem* (*for traffic offence*)
□ My dad got a fine for speeding. Mon père a eu une contravention pour excès de vitesse.

★ **finger** NOUN
le doigt *masc*
■ **my little finger** mon petit doigt

fingernail NOUN
l'ongle *masc*

★ **finish** NOUN
▷ *see also* **finish** VERB
l'arrivée *fem* (*of race*)
□ We saw the finish of the London Marathon. Nous avons vu l'arrivée du marathon de Londres.

★ to **finish** VERB
▷ *see also* **finish** NOUN
1 finir [38]
□ I've finished! J'ai fini!
■ **to finish doing something** finir [38] de faire quelque chose

English-French

f

2 terminer [28]
□ I've finished the book. J'ai terminé ce livre.
□ The film has finished. Le film est terminé.

★ **Finland** NOUN
la Finlande *fem*
■ **in Finland** en Finlande
■ **to Finland** en Finlande

Finn NOUN
le Finlandais *masc*
la Finlandaise *fem*

★ **Finnish** NOUN
▷ *see also* **Finnish** ADJECTIVE
le finnois *masc* (*language*)

★ **Finnish** ADJECTIVE
▷ *see also* **Finnish** NOUN
finlandais (FEM finlandaise)

★ **fire** NOUN
▷ *see also* **fire** VERB
1 le feu *masc* (PL les feux)
□ He made a fire in the woods. Il a fait du feu dans les bois.
■ **to be on fire** être [35] en feu
2 l'incendie *masc* (*accidental*)
□ The house was destroyed by fire. La maison a été détruite par un incendie.
3 le radiateur *masc* (*heater*)
□ Turn the fire on. Allume le radiateur.
■ **the fire brigade** les pompiers *masc pl*
■ **a fire alarm** une alarme à incendie
■ **a fire engine** une voiture de pompiers
■ **a fire escape** un escalier de secours
■ **a fire extinguisher** un extincteur
■ **a fire station** une caserne de pompiers

★ to **fire** VERB
▷ *see also* **fire** NOUN
tirer [28] (*shoot*)
□ She fired twice. Elle a tiré deux fois.
■ **to fire at somebody** tirer [28] sur quelqu'un
■ **to fire a gun** tirer [28] un coup de feu
■ **to fire somebody** mettre [47] quelqu'un à la porte □ He was fired from his job. Il a été mis à la porte.

fire exit NOUN
la sortie de secours *fem*

firefighter NOUN
le pompier *masc*
□ She's a firefighter. Elle est pompier.

fireplace NOUN
la cheminée *fem*

fireworks PL NOUN
le feu d'artifice *masc sing*
□ Are you going to see the fireworks? Est-ce que tu vas voir le feu d'artifice?

★ **firm** ADJECTIVE
▷ *see also* **firm** NOUN
ferme (FEM ferme)
□ **to be firm with somebody** se montrer ferme avec quelqu'un

★ **firm** NOUN
▷ *see also* **firm** ADJECTIVE
l'entreprise *fem*
□ He works for a large firm in Newcastle. Il travaille pour une grande entreprise à Newcastle.

★ **first** ADJECTIVE, ADVERB
▷ *see also* **first** NOUN
1 premier (FEM première)
□ **the first of September** le premier septembre
□ **the first time** la première fois
■ **to come first** (*in exam, race*) arriver [5E] premier □ Rachel came first. Rachel est arrivée première.
2 d'abord
□ I want to get a job, but first I have to graduate. Je veux trouver du travail, mais d'abord je dois finir mes études.
■ **first of all** tout d'abord

★ **first** NOUN
▷ *see also* **first** ADJECTIVE, ADVERB
le premier *masc*
la première *fem*
□ She was the first to arrive. Elle est arrivée la première.
■ **at first** au début

first aid NOUN
les premiers secours *masc pl*
■ **a first aid kit** une trousse de secours

first-class ADJECTIVE, ADVERB
1 de première classe
□ She has booked a first-class ticket. Elle a réservé un billet de première classe.
■ **to travel first class** voyager [45] en première
2 excellent (FEM excellente)
□ a first-class meal un excellent repas
■ **a first-class stamp**

DID YOU KNOW...?
In France, there is no first-class or second-class postage. However letters cost more to send than postcards, so you have to remember to say what you are sending when buying stamps.

firstly ADVERB
premièrement
□ Firstly, let's see what the book is about. Premièrement, voyons de quoi parle ce livre.

fir tree NOUN
le sapin *masc*

★ **fish** NOUN
▷ *see also* **fish** VERB
le poisson *masc*
□ I caught three fish. J'ai pêché trois poissons.
□ I don't like fish. Je n'aime pas le poisson.
■ **a fish tank** un aquarium

★ to **fish** VERB
▷ *see also* **fish** NOUN
pêcher [28]
■ **to go fishing** aller [3E] à la pêche □ We went fishing in the River Dee. Nous sommes allés à la pêche sur la Dee.

fisherman NOUN
le pêcheur *masc*
□ He's a fisherman. Il est pêcheur.

fish fingers PL NOUN
les bâtonnets de poisson *masc pl*

★ **fishing** NOUN
la pêche *fem*
□ My hobby is fishing. La pêche est mon passe-temps favori.

fishing boat NOUN
le bateau de pêche *masc*

fishing rod NOUN
la canne à pêche *fem*

fishing tackle NOUN
le matériel de pêche *masc*

fish sticks PL NOUN (US)
les bâtonnets de poisson *masc pl*

fist NOUN
le poing *masc*

★ **fit** ADJECTIVE
▷ *see also* **fit** VERB, NOUN
en forme (*in condition*)
□ He likes to stay fit. Il aime se maintenir en forme.
■ **to keep fit** se maintenir [83] en forme
□ She does zumba to keep fit. Elle fait de la zumba pour se maintenir en forme.

★ **fit** NOUN
▷ *see also* **fit** ADJECTIVE, VERB
■ **to have a fit** **1** (*epileptic*) avoir [8] une crise d'épilepsie **2** (*be angry*) piquer [28] une crise de nerfs □ My mum will have a fit when she sees the carpet! Ma mère va piquer une crise de nerfs quand elle va voir la moquette!

★ to **fit** VERB
▷ *see also* **fit** ADJECTIVE, NOUN
1 être [35] la bonne taille (*be the right size*)
□ Does it fit? Est-ce que c'est la bonne taille?

> In French you usually specify whether something is too big, small, tight etc.

■ **These trousers don't fit me.** **1** (*too big*) Ce pantalon est trop grand pour moi. **2** (*too small*) Ce pantalon est trop petit pour moi.
■ **My clothes won't all fit in my backpack.** Mes vêtements ne rentreront pas tous dans mon sac à dos.
2 installer [28] (*fix up*)
□ He fitted an alarm in his car. Il a installé une alarme dans sa voiture.
3 poser [28] (*attach*)
□ She fitted a lock on her bedroom door. Elle a posé un cadenas sur la porte de sa chambre.

to **fit in** VERB
s'intégrer [28] (*person*)
□ She fitted in well at her new school. Elle s'est bien intégrée dans sa nouvelle école.
■ **We fitted in a visit to the Eiffel Tower.** On a trouvé le temps de visiter la tour Eiffel.

fitness NOUN
la forme physique *fem*

fitting room NOUN
la cabine d'essayage *fem*

★ **five** NUMBER
cinq
□ He's five. Il a cinq ans.

★ to **fix** VERB
1 réparer [28] (*mend*)
□ Can you fix my bike? Est-ce que tu peux réparer mon vélo?
2 fixer [28] (*decide*)
□ Let's fix a date for the party. Fixons une date pour la soirée. □ They fixed a price for the laptop. Ils ont fixé un prix pour l'ordinateur portable.
3 préparer [28]
□ Dylan's dad fixed some food for us. Le père de Dylan nous a préparé à manger.

★ **fixed** ADJECTIVE
fixe (FEM fixe)
□ at a fixed time à une heure fixe □ at a fixed price à un prix fixe □ a fixed-price menu un menu à prix fixe
■ **My parents have very fixed ideas.** Mes parents ont des idées très arrêtées.

fizzy ADJECTIVE
gazeux (FEM gazeuse)
□ I don't like fizzy drinks. Je n'aime pas les boissons gazeuses.

flabby ADJECTIVE
flasque (FEM flasque)

★ **flag** NOUN
le drapeau *masc* (PL les drapeaux)

flame NOUN
la flamme *fem*

flamingo NOUN
le flamant rose *masc*

flan NOUN
1 la quiche *fem* (*savoury*)
□ a cheese and onion flan une quiche au fromage et aux oignons
2 la tarte *fem* (*sweet*)
□ a raspberry flan une tarte aux framboises

flannel NOUN
le gant de toilette *masc* (*for face*)

> **DID YOU KNOW...?**
> The French traditionally wash with a towelling glove rather than a flannel.

to **flap** VERB
battre [9] de

English-French

◻ The bird flapped its wings. L'oiseau battait des ailes.

★ **flash** NOUN
▷ *see also* **flash** VERB
le flash *masc* (PL les flashes)
◻ Did the flash go off? Le flash s'est déclenché?
■ **a flash of lightning** un éclair
■ **in a flash** en un clin d'œil

★ to **flash** VERB
▷ *see also* **flash** NOUN
1 clignoter [28]
◻ The light on the police car was flashing. Le gyrophare de la voiture de police clignotait.
2 projeter [41]
◻ They flashed a torch in his face. Ils lui ont projeté la lumière d'une torche en plein visage.
■ **She flashed her headlights.** Elle a fait un appel de phares.

f

flask NOUN
le thermos *masc* (*vacuum flask*)

★ **flat** ADJECTIVE
▷ *see also* **flat** NOUN
1 plat (FEM plate)
◻ a flat roof un toit plat ◻ flat shoes des chaussures plates
2 crevé (FEM crevée) (*tyre*)
◻ I've got a flat tyre. J'ai un pneu crevé.

★ **flat** NOUN
▷ *see also* **flat** ADJECTIVE
l'appartement *masc*
◻ She lives in a flat. Elle habite un appartement.

to **flatter** VERB
flatter [28]

flattered ADJECTIVE
flatté (FEM flattée)

★ **flavour** (US **flavor**) NOUN
1 le goût *masc* (*taste*)
◻ It has a very strong flavour. Ça a un goût très fort.
2 le parfum *masc* (*variety*)
◻ Which flavour of ice cream would you like? Quel parfum de glace est-ce que tu veux?

flavouring (US **flavoring**) NOUN
le parfum *masc*

flew VERB ▷ *see* **fly**

★ **flexible** ADJECTIVE
flexible (FEM flexible)
◻ flexible working hours les horaires flexibles

to **flick** VERB
appuyer [53] sur
◻ She flicked the switch to turn the light on. Elle a appuyé sur le bouton pour allumer la lumière.
■ **to flick through a book** feuilleter [41] un livre

to **flicker** VERB
trembloter [28]
◻ The light flickered. La lumière a tremblоté.

★ **flight** NOUN
le vol *masc*
◻ What time is the flight to Paris? À quelle heure est le vol pour Paris?
■ **a flight of stairs** un escalier

flight attendant NOUN
1 l'hôtesse de l'air *fem* (*woman*)
2 le steward *masc* (*man*)

to **fling** VERB
jeter [41]
◻ He flung the book onto the floor. Il a jeté le livre par terre.

flippers NOUN
les palmes *fem pl*

★ to **float** VERB
flotter [28]
◻ A leaf was floating on the water. Une feuille flottait sur l'eau.

flock NOUN
■ **a flock of sheep** un troupeau de moutons
■ **a flock of birds** un vol d'oiseaux

★ **flood** NOUN
▷ *see also* **flood** VERB
1 l'inondation *fem*
◻ We had a flood in the kitchen. On a eu une inondation dans la cuisine.
2 le flot *masc*
◻ He received a flood of emails. Il a reçu un flot de mails.

★ to **flood** VERB
▷ *see also* **flood** NOUN
inonder [28]
◻ The river has flooded the village. La rivière a inondé le village.

flooding NOUN
les inondations *fem pl*

★ **floor** NOUN
1 le sol *masc*
◻ a tiled floor un sol carrelé
■ **on the floor** par terre
2 l'étage *masc* (*storey*)
◻ the first floor le premier étage
■ **the ground floor** le rez-de-chaussée
■ **on the third floor** au troisième étage

flop NOUN
le fiasco *masc*
◻ The film was a flop. Le film a été un fiasco.

florist NOUN
le/la fleuriste *masc/fem*

flour NOUN
la farine *fem*

Numbers in brackets refer to verb tables on pages 650 to 658

★ to **flow** VERB
1 couler [28] (*river*)
2 s'écouler [28] (*flow out*)
◻ Water was flowing from the pipe. De l'eau s'écoulait du tuyau.

★ **flower** NOUN
▷ *see also* **flower** VERB
la fleur *fem*

★ to **flower** VERB
▷ *see also* **flower** NOUN
fleurir [38]

flown VERB ▷ *see* **fly**

flu NOUN
la grippe *fem*
◻ She's got flu. Elle a la grippe.

fluent ADJECTIVE
■ **He speaks fluent French.** Il parle couramment le français.

flung VERB ▷ *see* **fling**

flush NOUN
▷ *see also* **flush** VERB
la chasse d'eau *fem* (*of toilet*)

to **flush** VERB
▷ *see also* **flush** NOUN
■ **to flush the toilet** tirer [28] la chasse

flute NOUN
la flûte *fem*
◻ I play the flute. Je joue de la flûte.

★ **fly** NOUN
▷ *see also* **fly** VERB
la mouche *fem* (*insect*)

★ to **fly** VERB
▷ *see also* **fly** NOUN
1 voler [28]
◻ The plane flew through the night. L'avion a volé toute la nuit.
2 aller [3E] en avion (*passenger*)
◻ He flew from Paris to New York. Il est allé de Paris à New York en avion.

to **fly away** VERB
s'envoler [28]
◻ The bird flew away. L'oiseau s'est envolé.

foal NOUN
le poulain *masc*

★ **focus** NOUN
▷ *see also* **focus** VERB
■ **to be out of focus** être [35] flou ◻ The house is out of focus in this photo. La maison est floue sur cette photo.

★ to **focus** VERB
▷ *see also* **focus** NOUN
mettre [47] au point
◻ Try to focus the binoculars. Essaye de mettre les jumelles au point.
■ **to focus on something 1** (*with camera, telescope*) régler [34] la mise au point sur quelque chose ◻ The cameraman focused on the bird. Le caméraman a réglé la mise au point sur l'oiseau. **2** (*concentrate*) se concentrer [28] sur quelque chose ◻ Let's focus on the plot of the play. Concentrons-nous sur l'intrigue de la pièce.

★ **fog** NOUN
le brouillard *masc*

★ **foggy** ADJECTIVE
■ **It's foggy.** Il y a du brouillard.
■ **a foggy day** un jour de brouillard

foil NOUN
le papier d'aluminium *masc* (*kitchen foil*)
◻ She wrapped the meat in foil. Elle a enveloppé la viande dans du papier d'aluminium.

★ **fold** NOUN
▷ *see also* **fold** VERB
le pli *masc*

★ to **fold** VERB
▷ *see also* **fold** NOUN
plier [19]
◻ He folded the newspaper in half. Il a plié le journal en deux.
■ **to fold something up** plier [19] quelque chose
■ **to fold one's arms** croiser [28] ses bras
◻ She folded her arms. Elle a croisé les bras.

folder NOUN
1 la chemise *fem*
◻ She kept all her notes in a folder. Elle gardait toutes ses notes dans une chemise.
2 le classeur *masc* (*ring binder*)

folding ADJECTIVE
■ **a folding chair** une chaise pliante
■ **a folding bed** un lit pliant

★ to **follow** VERB
suivre [81]
◻ She followed him. Elle l'a suivi. ◻ You go first and I'll follow. Va devant, je te suis.
■ **to follow somebody on Twitter** suivre [81] quelqu'un sur Twitter

follower NOUN
le follower *masc* (*on Twitter*)
◻ How do I get more followers on Twitter? Comment puis-je avoir plus de followers sur Twitter?

★ **following** ADJECTIVE
suivant (FEM suivante)
◻ the following day le jour suivant

fond ADJECTIVE
■ **to be fond of somebody** aimer [28] beaucoup quelqu'un ◻ I'm very fond of her. Je l'aime beaucoup.

★ **food** NOUN
la nourriture *fem*
■ **We need to buy some food.** Nous devons acheter à manger.
■ **cat/dog food** la nourriture pour chat/chien

English-French

f

English-French

food processor NOUN
le robot *masc*

★ **fool** NOUN
l'idiot *masc*
l'idiote *fem*

★ **foot** NOUN
1 le pied *masc* (*of person*)
□ My feet are aching. J'ai mal aux pieds.
■ **on foot** à pied
2 la patte *fem* (*of animal*)
□ The rabbit's foot was injured. Le lapin était blessé à la patte.
3 le pied *masc* (*12 inches*)

> **DID YOU KNOW...?**
> In France, measurements are in metres and centimetres rather than feet and inches. A foot is about 30 centimetres.

■ **Hassan is 6 foot tall.** Hassan mesure un mètre quatre-vingts.
■ **That mountain is 5000 feet high.** Cette montagne fait mille six cents mètres de haut.

f

★ **football** NOUN
1 le football *masc* (*game*)
□ I like playing football. J'aime jouer au football.
2 le ballon *masc* (*ball*)
□ Paul threw the football over the fence. Paul a envoyé le ballon par dessus la clôture.

★ **footballer** NOUN
le footballeur *masc*
la footballeuse *fem*

football player NOUN
le joueur de football *masc*
la joueuse de football *fem*
□ He's a famous football player. C'est un joueur de football célèbre.

footie NOUN
le foot *masc* (*informal*)

footpath NOUN
le sentier *masc*
□ Chloe followed the footpath through the forest. Chloe a suivi le sentier à travers la forêt.

footprint NOUN
la trace de pas *fem*
□ He saw some footprints in the sand. Il a vu des traces de pas sur le sable.

footstep NOUN
le pas *masc*
□ I can hear footsteps on the stairs. J'entends des pas dans l'escalier.

★ **for** PREPOSITION

> There are several ways of translating 'for'. Scan the examples to find one that is similar to what you want to say.

1 pour
□ a present for me un cadeau pour moi □ the train for York le train pour York □ He works for the government. Il travaille pour le gouvernement. □ I'll do it for you. Je vais le faire pour toi. □ Can you do it for tomorrow? Est-ce que vous pouvez le faire pour demain? □ Are you for or against the idea? Êtes-vous pour ou contre cette idée? □ Oxford is famous for its university. Oxford est célèbre pour son université.

> When referring to periods of time, use **pendant** for the future and completed actions in the past, and **depuis** (with the French verb in the present tense) for something that started in the past and is still going on.

2 pendant
□ He worked in France for two years. Il a travaillé en France pendant deux ans. □ She will be away for a month. Elle sera absente pendant un mois. □ There are roadworks for three kilometres. Il y a des travaux pendant trois kilomètres.
3 depuis
□ He's been learning French for two years. Il apprend le français depuis deux ans. □ She's been away for a month. Elle est absente depuis un mois.

> When talking about amounts of money, you do not translate 'for'.

□ I sold it for £5. Je l'ai vendu cinq livres. □ He paid fifty pence for his ticket. Il a payé son billet cinquante pence.
■ **What's the French for 'house'?** Comment dit-on 'house' en français?
■ **It's time for lunch.** C'est l'heure du déjeuner.
■ **What for?** Pour quoi faire? □ Give me some money! — What for? Donne-moi de l'argent! — Pour quoi faire?
■ **What's it for?** Ça sert à quoi?
■ **for sale** à vendre
■ **The factory's for sale.** L'usine est en vente.

to **forbid** VERB
défendre [88]
■ **to forbid somebody to do something** défendre [88] à quelqu'un de faire quelque chose □ I forbid you to go out tonight! Je te défends de sortir ce soir.

forbidden ADJECTIVE
défendu (FEM défendue)
□ Smoking is strictly forbidden. Il est strictement défendu de fumer.

★ **force** NOUN
▷ *see also* **force** VERB
la force *fem*
□ the force of the explosion la force de l'explosion
■ **in force** en vigueur □ No-smoking rules are

now in force. Un règlement qui interdit de fumer est maintenant en vigueur.

★ to **force** VERB
▷ *see also* **force** NOUN
forcer [12]
◻ They forced him to open the safe. Ils l'ont forcé à ouvrir le coffre-fort.

★ **forecast** NOUN
■ **the weather forecast** la météo

foreground NOUN
le premier plan *masc*
◻ in the foreground au premier plan

forehead NOUN
le front *masc*

★ **foreign** ADJECTIVE
étranger (FEM étrangère)

★ **foreigner** NOUN
l'étranger *masc*
l'étrangère *fem*

to **foresee** VERB
prévoir [92]
◻ He had foreseen the problem. Il avait prévu ce problème.

★ **forest** NOUN
la forêt *fem*

forever ADVERB
1 pour toujours
◻ He's gone forever. Il est parti pour toujours.
2 toujours (*always*)
◻ She's forever complaining. Elle est toujours en train de se plaindre.

forgave VERB ▷ *see* **forgive**

to **forge** VERB
contrefaire [36]
◻ She tried to forge his signature. Elle a essayé de contrefaire sa signature.

forged ADJECTIVE
faux (FEM fausse)
◻ forged banknotes des faux billets

★ to **forget** VERB
oublier [19]
◻ I've forgotten his name. J'ai oublié son nom.
◻ I'm sorry, I completely forgot! Je suis désolé, j'ai complètement oublié!

★ to **forgive** VERB
■ **to forgive somebody** pardonner [28] à quelqu'un ◻ I forgive you. Je te pardonne.
■ **to forgive somebody for doing something** pardonner [28] à quelqu'un d'avoir fait quelque chose ◻ She forgave him for forgetting her birthday. Elle lui a pardonné d'avoir oublié son anniversaire.

forgot, forgotten VERB ▷ *see* **forget**

fork NOUN
1 la fourchette *fem* (*for eating*)
2 la fourche *fem* (*for gardening*)
3 la bifurcation *fem* (*in road*)

★ **form** NOUN
1 le formulaire *masc* (*paper*)
◻ to fill in a form remplir un formulaire
2 la forme *fem* (*type*)
◻ I'm against hunting in any form. Je suis contre la chasse sous toutes ses formes.
■ **in top form** en pleine forme

★ **formal** ADJECTIVE
1 officiel (FEM officielle) (*occasion*)
◻ a formal dinner un dîner officiel
2 guindé (FEM guindée) (*person*)
3 soutenu (FEM soutenue) (*language*)
◻ In English, 'residence' is a formal term. En anglais, 'residence' est un terme soutenu.
■ **formal clothes** une tenue habillée
■ **He's got no formal education.** Il n'a pas fait beaucoup d'études.

★ **former** ADJECTIVE
ancien (FEM ancienne)
◻ a former pupil un ancien élève ◻ the former Prime Minister l'ancien Premier ministre

formerly ADVERB
autrefois

fort NOUN
le fort *masc*

★ **forth** ADVERB
■ **to go back and forth** aller [3E] et venir [89E]
■ **and so forth** et ainsi de suite

fortnight NOUN
■ **a fortnight** quinze jours ◻ I'm going on holiday for a fortnight. Je pars en vacances pendant quinze jours.

fortunate ADJECTIVE
■ **to be fortunate** avoir [8] de la chance ◻ He was extremely fortunate to survive. Il a eu énormément de chance de survivre.
■ **It's fortunate that I remembered the map.** C'est une chance que j'aie pris la carte.

fortunately ADVERB
heureusement
◻ Fortunately, it didn't rain. Heureusement, il n'a pas plu.

★ **fortune** NOUN
la fortune *fem*
◻ Kate earns a fortune! Kate gagne une fortune!
■ **to tell somebody's fortune** dire [27] la bonne aventure à quelqu'un

★ **forty** NUMBER
quarante
◻ He's forty. Il a quarante ans.

★ **forward** ADVERB
▷ *see also* **forward** VERB
■ **to move forward** avancer [12]

★ to **forward** VERB
▷ *see also* **forward** ADVERB
faire [36] suivre

English-French

f

□ Can you forward the email she sent you? Est-ce que tu peux me faire suivre le mail qu'elle t'a envoyé?

forward slash NOUN
la barre oblique *fem*

to **foster** VERB
■ **She has fostered more than fifteen children.** Plus de quinze enfants ont été placés chez elle.

foster child NOUN
l'enfant adoptif *masc*
l'enfant adoptive *fem*

fought VERB ▷ *see* **fight**

foul ADJECTIVE
▷ *see also* **foul** NOUN
infect (FEM infecte)
□ The weather was foul. Le temps était infect.
□ What a foul smell! Quelle odeur infecte!

foul NOUN
▷ *see also* **foul** ADJECTIVE
la faute *fem*
□ Ferguson committed a foul. Ferguson a fait une faute.

found VERB ▷ *see* **find**

to **found** VERB
fonder [28]
□ Baden Powell founded the Scout Movement. Baden Powell a fondé le mouvement scout.

foundations PL NOUN
les fondations *fem pl*

★ **fountain** NOUN
la fontaine *fem*

fountain pen NOUN
le stylo à encre *masc*

★ **four** NUMBER
quatre
□ She's four. Elle a quatre ans.

★ **fourteen** NUMBER
quatorze
□ I'm fourteen. J'ai quatorze ans.

★ **fourteenth** ADJECTIVE
quatorzième (FEM quatorzième)
□ the fourteenth floor le quatorzième étage
■ **the fourteenth of August** le quatorze août

★ **fourth** ADJECTIVE
quatrième (FEM quatrième)
□ the fourth floor le quatrième étage
■ **the fourth of July** le quatre juillet

★ **fox** NOUN
le renard *masc*

fragile ADJECTIVE
fragile (FEM fragile)

★ **frame** NOUN
le cadre *masc* (*for picture*)

★ **France** NOUN
la France *fem*
■ **in France** en France
■ **to France** en France
■ **He's from France.** Il est français.

frantic ADJECTIVE
■ **I was going frantic.** J'étais dans tous mes états.
■ **to be frantic with worry** être [35] fou d'inquiétude

fraud NOUN
1 la fraude *fem* (*crime*)
□ He was jailed for fraud. On l'a mis en prison pour fraude.
2 l'imposteur *masc* (*person*)
□ He's not a real doctor, he's a fraud. Ce n'est pas un vrai médecin, c'est un imposteur.

freckles PL NOUN
les taches de rousseur *fem pl*

★ **free** ADJECTIVE
▷ *see also* **free** VERB
1 gratuit (FEM gratuite) (*free of charge*)
□ a free brochure une brochure gratuite
2 libre (FEM libre) (*not busy, not taken*)
□ Is this seat free? Est-ce que cette place est libre? □ Are you free after school? Tu es libre après l'école?

★ to **free** VERB
▷ *see also* **free** ADJECTIVE
libérer [34]

★ **freedom** NOUN
la liberté *fem*

freeway NOUN (US)
l'autoroute *fem*

★ to **freeze** VERB
1 geler [43]
□ The water had frozen. L'eau avait gelé.
2 congeler [1] (*food*)
□ She froze the rest of the raspberries. Elle a congelé le reste des framboises.

★ **freezer** NOUN
le congélateur *masc*

★ **freezing** ADJECTIVE
■ **It's freezing!** Il fait un froid de canard! (*informal*)
■ **I'm freezing!** Je suis gelé! (*informal*)
■ **3 degrees below freezing** moins trois

freight NOUN
la cargaison *fem* (*goods*)
■ **a freight train** un train de marchandises

★ **French** NOUN
▷ *see also* **French** ADJECTIVE
le français *masc* (*language*)
□ Do you speak French? Est-ce que tu parles français?
■ **the French** (*people*) les Français

★ **French** ADJECTIVE

▷ *see also* **French** NOUN
français (FEM française)
☐ He's French. Il est français. ☐ She's French. Elle est française.

French beans PL NOUN
les haricots verts *masc pl*

French fries PL NOUN
les frites *fem pl*

French horn NOUN
le cor (d'harmonie) *masc*
☐ I play the French horn. Je joue du cor.

French kiss NOUN
le baiser profond *masc*

French loaf NOUN
la baguette *fem*

★ **Frenchman** NOUN
le Français *masc*

French windows PL NOUN
la porte-fenêtre *fem sing* (PL les portes-fenêtres)

★ **Frenchwoman** NOUN
la Française *fem*

★ **frequent** ADJECTIVE
fréquent (FEM fréquente)
☐ frequent showers des averses fréquentes
■ **There are frequent buses to the town centre.** Il y a beaucoup de bus pour le centre ville.

★ **fresh** ADJECTIVE
frais (FEM fraîche)
■ **I need some fresh air.** J'ai besoin de prendre l'air.

to **freshen up** VERB
faire [36] un brin de toilette
☐ I'd like to go and freshen up. Je voudrais faire un brin de toilette.

to **fret** VERB
se tracasser [28]
☐ Theo was fretting about his exams. Theo se tracassait au sujet de ses examens.

★ **Friday** NOUN
le vendredi *masc*
☐ on Friday vendredi ☐ on Fridays le vendredi ☐ every Friday tous les vendredis ☐ last Friday vendredi dernier ☐ next Friday vendredi prochain

★ **fridge** NOUN
le frigo *masc*
■ **a fridge magnet** un aimant pour frigo

fried ADJECTIVE
frit (FEM frite)
☐ fried vegetables des légumes frits
■ **a fried egg** un œuf sur le plat

★ **friend** NOUN
▷ *see also* **friend** VERB
l'ami *masc*
l'amie *fem*

to **friend** VERB
▷ *see also* **friend** NOUN
ajouter [28] comme ami
☐ I've friended her on Facebook. Je l'ai ajoutée comme amie sur Facebook.

★ **friendly** ADJECTIVE
1 gentil (FEM gentille)
☐ She's really friendly. Elle est vraiment gentille.
2 accueillant (FEM accueillante)
☐ Liverpool is a very friendly city. Liverpool est une ville très accueillante.

★ **friendship** NOUN
l'amitié *fem*

fright NOUN
la peur *fem*
☐ I got a terrible fright! Ça m'a fait une peur terrible!

to **frighten** VERB
faire [36] peur à
☐ Horror films frighten him. Les films d'horreur lui font peur.

★ **frightened** ADJECTIVE
■ **to be frightened** avoir [8] peur ☐ I'm frightened! J'ai peur!
■ **to be frightened of something** avoir [8] peur de quelque chose ☐ Anna's frightened of spiders. Anna a peur des araignées.

frightening ADJECTIVE
effrayant (FEM effrayante)

fringe NOUN
la frange *fem (of hair)*
☐ She's got a fringe. Elle a une frange.

Frisbee® NOUN
le Frisbee® *masc*
☐ to play Frisbee jouer au Frisbee

fro ADVERB
■ **to go to and fro** aller [3E] et venir [89E]

★ **frog** NOUN
la grenouille *fem*
■ **frogs' legs** les cuisses de grenouille

★ **from** PREPOSITION
de
☐ Where do you come from? D'où venez-vous? ☐ I come from Perth. Je viens de Perth. ☐ a letter from my sister une lettre de ma sœur ☐ The hotel is one kilometre from the beach. L'hôtel est à un kilomètre de la plage.
■ **from ... to ...** de ... à ... ☐ He flew from Birmingham to Paris. Il a pris l'avion de Birmingham à Paris. ☐ from 1 o'clock to 2 d'une heure à deux heures ☐ The price was reduced from £10 to £5. Ils ont réduit le prix de dix livres à cinq.
■ **from ... onwards** à partir de ... ☐ We'll be at home from 7 o'clock onwards. Nous serons chez nous à partir de sept heures.

English-French

★ **front** NOUN
▷ *see also* **front** ADJECTIVE
le devant *masc*
◻ the front of the house le devant de la maison
■ **in front** devant ◻ a house with a car in front une maison avec une voiture devant ◻ the car in front la voiture de devant
■ **in front of** devant ◻ in front of the house devant la maison ◻ the car in front of us la voiture devant nous
■ **in the front** (*of car*) à l'avant ◻ I was sitting in the front. J'étais assis à l'avant.
■ **at the front of the train** à l'avant du train

★ **front** ADJECTIVE
▷ *see also* **front** NOUN
1 de devant
◻ the front row la rangée de devant
2 avant
◻ the front seats of the car les sièges avant de la voiture
■ **the front door** la porte d'entrée

frontier NOUN
la frontière *fem*

★ **frost** NOUN
le gel *masc*

frosting NOUN (US)
le glaçage *masc* (*on cake*)

★ **frosty** ADJECTIVE
■ **It's frosty today.** Il gèle aujourd'hui.

to **frown** VERB
froncer [12] les sourcils
◻ He frowned. Il a froncé les sourcils.

froze, frozen VERB ▷ *see* **freeze**

★ **frozen** ADJECTIVE
surgelé (FEM surgelée) (*food*)
◻ frozen chips des frites surgelées

★ **fruit** NOUN
le fruit *masc*
■ **fruit juice** le jus de fruits
■ **a fruit salad** une salade de fruits

fruit machine NOUN
la machine à sous *fem*

frustrated ADJECTIVE
frustré (FEM frustrée)

★ to **fry** VERB
faire [36] frire
◻ Fry the onions for 5 minutes. Faites frire les oignons pendant cinq minutes.

frying pan NOUN
la poêle *fem*

★ **fuel** NOUN
le carburant *masc* (*for car, aeroplane*)
◻ to run out of fuel avoir une panne de carburant

to **fulfil** VERB
réaliser [28]
◻ Josh fulfilled his dream to visit China. Josh a réalisé son rêve de visiter la Chine.

★ **full** ADJECTIVE, ADVERB
1 plein (FEM pleine)
◻ The tank's full. Le réservoir est plein.
2 complet (FEM complète)
◻ He asked for full details about the job. Il a demandé des renseignements complets sur le poste.
■ **your full name** vos nom et prénoms ◻ My full name is Oliver Luke Marr. Mes noms et prénoms sont Oliver Luke Marr.
■ **I'm full.** (*after meal*) J'ai bien mangé.
■ **at full speed** à toute vitesse ◻ He drove at full speed. Il conduisait à toute vitesse.
■ **There was a full moon.** C'était la pleine lune.

full stop NOUN
le point *masc*

full-time ADJECTIVE, ADVERB
à plein temps
◻ She's got a full-time job. Elle a un travail à plein temps. ◻ She works full-time. Elle travaille à plein temps.

fully ADVERB
complètement
◻ He hasn't fully recovered from his illness. Il n'est pas complètement remis de sa maladie.

fumes PL NOUN
les fumées *fem pl*
◻ There was a smell of fumes from the factory. On sentait les fumées s'échappant de l'usine.
■ **exhaust fumes** les gaz d'échappement *masc pl*

★ **fun** ADJECTIVE
▷ *see also* **fun** NOUN
marrant (FEM marrante)
◻ She's a fun person. Elle est marrante.

★ **fun** NOUN
▷ *see also* **fun** ADJECTIVE
■ **to have fun** s'amuser [28] ◻ We had great fun playing in the snow. Nous nous sommes bien amusés à jouer dans la neige.
■ **for fun** pour rire ◻ He entered the competition just for fun. Il a participé à la compétition juste pour rire.
■ **to make fun of somebody** se moquer [28] de quelqu'un ◻ They made fun of him. Ils se sont moqués de lui.
■ **It's fun!** C'est chouette!
■ **Have fun!** Amuse-toi bien!

funds PL NOUN
les fonds *masc pl*
◻ to raise funds collecter des fonds

funeral NOUN
l'enterrement *masc*

funfair NOUN
la fête foraine *fem*

★ **funny** ADJECTIVE
1 drôle (FEM drôle) (*amusing*)
□ It was really funny. C'était vraiment drôle.
2 bizarre (FEM bizarre) (*strange*)
□ There's something funny about him. Il est un peu bizarre.

fur NOUN
1 la fourrure *fem*
□ a fur coat un manteau de fourrure
2 le poil *masc*
□ the dog's fur le poil du chien

furious ADJECTIVE
furieux (FEM furieuse)
□ Dad was furious with me. Papa était furieux contre moi.

★ **furniture** NOUN
les meubles *masc pl*
□ a piece of furniture un meuble

★ **further** ADVERB, ADJECTIVE
plus loin
□ London is further from Manchester than Leeds is. Londres est plus loin de Manchester que Leeds.
■ **How much further is it?** C'est encore loin?

further education NOUN
l'enseignement postscolaire *masc*

fuse NOUN
le fusible *masc*
□ The fuse has blown. Le fusible a sauté.

fuss NOUN
l'agitation *fem*
□ What's all the fuss about? Qu'est-ce que c'est que toute cette agitation?
■ **to make a fuss** faire [36] des histoires
□ He's always making a fuss about nothing. Il fait toujours des histoires pour rien.

fussy ADJECTIVE
difficile (FEM difficile)
□ She is very fussy about her food. Elle est très difficile sur la nourriture.

★ **future** NOUN
1 l'avenir *masc*
□ What are your plans for the future? Quels sont vos projets pour l'avenir?
■ **in future** à l'avenir □ Be more careful in future. Sois plus prudent à l'avenir.
2 le futur *masc* (*in grammar*)
□ Put this sentence into the future. Mettez cette phrase au futur.

Gg

to **gain** VERB
- **to gain weight** prendre [65] du poids
- **to gain speed** prendre [65] de la vitesse

gallery NOUN
le musée *masc*
□ an art gallery un musée d'art

to **gamble** VERB
jouer [28]
□ He gambled £100 on the horse race. Il a joué cent livres à la course de chevaux.

gambler NOUN
le joueur *masc*

gambling NOUN
le jeu *masc*
□ He likes gambling. Il aime le jeu.

★**game** NOUN
1 le jeu *masc* (PL les jeux)
□ The children were playing a game. Les enfants jouaient à un jeu.
2 le match *masc* (*sport*)
□ a game of football un match de football
- **a game of cards** une partie de cartes

gamer NOUN
1 le joueur sur ordinateur *masc*
la joueuse sur ordinateur *fem* (*on computer*)
2 le joueur sur téléphone portable *masc*
la joueuse sur téléphone portable *fem* (*on mobile phone*)

games console NOUN
la console de jeux *fem*

gaming NOUN
1 les jeux sur ordinateur *masc pl* (*on computer*)
2 les jeux sur téléphone portable *masc pl* (*on mobile phone*)

★**gang** NOUN
la bande *fem*

gangster NOUN
le gangster *masc*

gap NOUN
1 le trou *masc*
□ There's a gap in the hedge. Il y a un trou dans la haie.
2 l'intervalle *masc*
□ a gap of four years un intervalle de quatre ans

gap year NOUN
l'année sabbatique avant d'aller à l'université
□ My sister's in Australia on her gap year. Ma sœur prend une année sabbatique en Australie avant d'aller à l'université.

garage NOUN
le garage *masc*

garbage NOUN
les ordures *fem pl*

★**garden** NOUN
le jardin *masc*

gardener NOUN
le jardinier *masc*
□ He's a gardener. Il est jardinier.

gardening NOUN
le jardinage *masc*
□ My gran loves gardening. Ma grand-mère aime le jardinage.

gardens PL NOUN
le jardin public *masc sing*

garlic NOUN
l'ail *masc*

garment NOUN
le vêtement *masc*

★**gas** NOUN
1 le gaz *masc*
- **a gas cooker** une cuisinière à gaz
- **a gas cylinder** une bouteille de gaz
- **a gas fire** un radiateur à gaz
- **a gas leak** une fuite de gaz

2 l'essence *fem* (US: *petrol*)

gasoline NOUN (US)
l'essence *fem*

★**gate** NOUN
1 le portail *masc* (*of garden*)
2 la barrière *fem* (*of field*)
3 la porte *fem* (*at airport*)

gateau NOUN
le gâteau à la crème *masc*

to **gather** VERB
se rassembler [28] (*assemble*)
□ People gathered in front of Buckingham Palace. Les gens se sont rassemblés devant Buckingham Palace.
- **to gather speed** prendre [65] de la vitesse

□ The train gathered speed. Le train a pris de la vitesse.

gave VERB ▷ *see* **give**

gay ADJECTIVE
homosexuel (FEM homosexuelle)

to **gaze** VERB
■ **to gaze at something** fixer [28] quelque chose du regard □ **He gazed at her.** Il l'a fixée du regard.

★ **GCSE** NOUN
le brevet des collèges *masc*

DID YOU KNOW...?
Exams in France are different from exams in Britain. **le brevet des collèges** is an exam you take at the end of fourth year in secondary school.

gear NOUN
1 la vitesse *fem* (*in car*)
□ **in first gear** en première vitesse □ **to change gear** changer de vitesse
2 le matériel *masc*
□ **camping gear** le matériel de camping
■ **your sports gear** (*clothes*) tes affaires de sport

gear lever NOUN
le levier de vitesse *masc*

gearshift NOUN (US)
le levier de vitesse *masc*

geese PL NOUN ▷ *see* **goose**

gel NOUN
le gel *masc*
■ **hair gel** le gel pour les cheveux

gem NOUN
la pierre précieuse *fem*

Gemini NOUN
les Gémeaux *masc pl*
□ **I'm Gemini.** Je suis Gémeaux.

gender NOUN
1 le sexe *masc* (*of person*)
2 le genre *masc* (*of noun*)

gene NOUN
le gène *masc*

★ **general** NOUN
▷ *see also* **general** ADJECTIVE
le général *masc* (PL les généraux)

★ **general** ADJECTIVE
▷ *see also* **general** NOUN
général (FEM générale, MASC PL généraux)
■ **in general** en général

general election NOUN
les élections législatives *fem pl*

general knowledge NOUN
les connaissances générales *fem pl*

★ **generally** ADVERB
généralement
□ **I generally go shopping on Saturday.** Généralement, je fais mes courses le samedi.

★ **generation** NOUN
la génération *fem*
□ **the younger generation** la nouvelle génération

generator NOUN
le générateur *masc*

★ **generous** ADJECTIVE
généreux (FEM généreuse)
□ **That's very generous of you.** C'est très généreux de votre part.

genetic ADJECTIVE
génétique (FEM génétique)

genetically-modified ADJECTIVE
génétiquement modifié (FEM génétiquement modifiée)

genetics NOUN
la génétique *fem*

Geneva NOUN
Genève
■ **in Geneva** à Genève
■ **to Geneva** à Genève
■ **Lake Geneva** le lac Léman

genius NOUN
le génie *masc*
□ **She's a genius!** C'est un génie!

★ **gentle** ADJECTIVE
doux (FEM douce)

BE CAREFUL!
Do not translate **gentle** by the French word **gentille**.

★ **gentleman** NOUN
le monsieur *masc* (PL les messieurs)
□ **Good morning, gentlemen.** Bonjour messieurs.

gently ADVERB
doucement

gents NOUN
les toilettes pour hommes *fem pl*
□ **Can you tell me where the gents is, please?** Pouvez-vous me dire où sont les toilettes, s'il vous plaît?
■ **'gents'** (*on sign*) 'messieurs'

★ **genuine** ADJECTIVE
1 véritable (FEM véritable) (*real*)
□ **These are genuine diamonds.** Ce sont de véritables diamants.
2 sincère (FEM sincère) (*sincere*)
□ **She's a very genuine person.** C'est quelqu'un de très sincère.

geography NOUN
la géographie *fem*

gerbil NOUN
la gerbille *fem*

germ NOUN
le microbe *masc*

★**German** NOUN
▷ *see also* **German** ADJECTIVE
1 l'Allemand *masc*
l'Allemande *fem* (*person*)
2 l'allemand (*language*)
□ Do you speak German? Parlez-vous allemand?

★**German** ADJECTIVE
▷ *see also* **German** NOUN
allemand (FEM allemande)

German measles NOUN
la rubéole *fem*

★**Germany** NOUN
l'Allemagne *fem*
■ **in Germany** en Allemagne
■ **to Germany** en Allemagne

gesture NOUN
le geste *masc*

★to **get** VERB

There are several ways of translating 'get'. Scan the examples to find one that is similar to what you want to say.

1 avoir [8] (*have, receive*)
□ I got lots of presents. J'ai eu beaucoup de cadeaux. □ He got first prize. Il a eu le premier prix. □ He got good exam results. Il a eu de bons résultats aux examens. □ How many have you got? Combien en avez-vous?
2 aller [3E] chercher (*fetch*)
□ Quick, get help! Allez vite chercher de l'aide!
3 attraper [28] (*catch*)
□ They've got the thief. Ils ont attrapé le voleur.
4 prendre [65] (*train, bus*)
□ I'm getting the bus into town. Je prends le bus pour aller en ville.
5 comprendre [65] (*understand*)
□ I don't get it. Je ne comprends pas.
6 aller [3E] (*go*)
□ How do you get to the castle? Comment est-ce qu'on va au château?
7 arriver [5E] (*arrive*)
□ He should get here soon. Il devrait arriver bientôt.
8 devenir [25E] (*become*)
□ to get old devenir vieux
■ **to get something done** faire [36] faire quelque chose □ to get one's hair cut se faire couper les cheveux
■ **to get something for somebody** trouver [28] quelque chose pour quelqu'un □ The librarian got the book for me. Le bibliothécaire m'a trouvé le livre.
■ **to have got to do something** devoir [26] faire quelque chose □ I've got to tell him. Je dois le lui dire.

to **get away** VERB
s'échapper [28]
□ One of the burglars got away. L'un des cambrioleurs s'est échappé.

to **get back** VERB
1 rentrer [68E]
□ What time did you get back? Tu es rentré à quelle heure?
2 récupérer [34]
□ He got his money back. Il a récupéré son argent.

to **get in** VERB
rentrer [68E]
□ What time did you get in last night? Tu es rentré à quelle heure hier soir?

to **get into** VERB
monter [48E] dans
□ Marek got into the car. Marek est monté dans la voiture.

to **get off** VERB
descendre [24E] de (*vehicle, bike*)
□ Ella got off the train. Ella est descendue du train.

to **get on** VERB
1 monter [48E] dans (*vehicle*)
□ Mohammed got on the bus. Mohammed est monté dans le bus.
2 enfourcher [28] (*bike*)
□ Jessica got on her bike. Jessica a enfourché son vélo.
■ **to get on with somebody** s'entendre [88] avec quelqu'un □ He doesn't get on with his parents. Il ne s'entend pas avec ses parents. □ We got on really well. Nous nous sommes très bien entendus.

to **get out** VERB
sortir [79E]
□ Brodie got out of the car. Brodie est sorti de la voiture. □ Get out! Sortez!
■ **to get something out** sortir [79] quelque chose □ She got the map out. Elle a sorti la carte.

to **get over** VERB
se remettre [47]
□ She never got over his death. Elle ne s'est jamais remise de sa mort.

to **get together** VERB
se retrouver [28]
□ Could we get together this evening? Pourrait-on se retrouver ce soir?

to **get up** VERB
se lever [43]
□ What time do you get up? Tu te lèves à quelle heure?

ghost NOUN
le fantôme *masc*

★**giant** ADJECTIVE
▷ *see also* **giant** NOUN
énorme (FEM énorme)
□ They ate a giant meal. Ils ont mangé un énorme repas.

★ **giant** NOUN
▷ *see also* **giant** ADJECTIVE
le géant *masc*
la géante *fem*

★ **gift** NOUN
1 le cadeau *masc* (PL les cadeaux) (*present*)
2 le don *masc* (*talent*)
■ **to have a gift for something** être [35] doué pour quelque chose ◻ Lucas has a gift for painting. Lucas est doué pour la peinture.

gifted ADJECTIVE
doué (FEM douée)
◻ Maryam is a gifted dancer. Maryam est douée pour la danse.

gift shop NOUN
la boutique de cadeaux *fem*

gig NOUN
1 le show *masc* (*performance*)
2 le giga *masc* (*gigabyte*)

gigantic ADJECTIVE
gigantesque (FEM gigantesque)

gin NOUN
le gin *masc*

ginger NOUN
▷ *see also* **ginger** ADJECTIVE
le gingembre *masc*
◻ Add a teaspoon of ginger. Ajoutez une cuillère à café de gingembre.

ginger ADJECTIVE
▷ *see also* **ginger** NOUN
roux (FEM rousse)
◻ Robbie has ginger hair. Robbie a les cheveux roux.

★ **giraffe** NOUN
la girafe *fem*

★ **girl** NOUN
1 la fille *fem*
◻ They've got a girl and two boys. Ils ont une fille et deux garçons.
2 la petite fille *fem* (*young*)
◻ a five-year-old girl une petite fille de cinq ans
3 la jeune fille *fem* (*older*)
◻ a sixteen-year-old girl une jeune fille de seize ans ◻ an English girl une jeune Anglaise

★ **girlfriend** NOUN
1 la copine *fem* (*lover*)
◻ Jake's girlfriend is called Erin. La copine de Jake s'appelle Erin.
2 l'amie *fem* (*friend*)
◻ She often went out with her girlfriends. Elle sortait souvent avec ses amies.

★ to **give** VERB
donner [28]
◻ I give you what I can. Je te donne ce que je peux. ◻ You give good advice. Tu donnes de bons conseils. ◻ He gives me money when I need it. Il me donne de l'argent quand j'en ai besoin.
■ **to give something to somebody** donner [28] quelque chose à quelqu'un ◻ He gave me £10. Il m'a donné dix livres.
■ **to give something back to somebody** rendre [7] quelque chose à quelqu'un ◻ I gave the book back to him. Je lui ai rendu le livre.
■ **to give way** céder [34] la priorité (*in traffic*)

to **give in** VERB
céder [34]
◻ His mum gave in and let him go out. Sa mère a cédé et l'a laissé sortir.

to **give out** VERB
distribuer [28]
◻ He gave out the exam papers. Il a distribué les sujets d'examen.

to **give up** VERB
laisser [28] tomber
◻ I couldn't do it, so I gave up. Je n'arrivais pas à le faire, alors j'ai laissé tomber.
■ **to give up doing something** arrêter [28] de faire quelque chose ◻ He gave up smoking. Il a arrêté de fumer.
■ **to give oneself up** se rendre [7] ◻ The thief gave himself up. Le voleur s'est rendu.

★ **glad** ADJECTIVE
content (FEM contente)
◻ She's glad she's done it. Elle est contente de l'avoir fait.

glamorous ADJECTIVE
1 glamour (FEM+PL glamour) (*person*)
◻ She's very glamorous. Elle est très glamour.
2 prestigieux (FEM prestigieuse) (*job*)
■ **to have a glamorous lifestyle** vivre [91] comme une star

to **glance** VERB
▷ *see also* **glance** NOUN
■ **to glance at something** jeter [41] un coup d'œil à quelque chose ◻ Aaron glanced at his watch. Aaron a jeté un coup d'œil à sa montre.

glance NOUN
▷ *see also* **glance** VERB
le coup d'œil *masc*
◻ at first glance au premier coup d'œil

to **glare** VERB
■ **to glare at somebody** lancer [12] un regard furieux à quelqu'un ◻ He glared at me. Il m'a lancé un regard furieux.

glaring ADJECTIVE
■ **a glaring mistake** une erreur qui saute aux yeux

★ **glass** NOUN
le verre *masc*
◻ a glass of milk un verre de lait

glasses PL NOUN
les lunettes *fem pl*
◻ Jean-Pierre wears glasses. Jean-Pierre porte des lunettes.

glider NOUN
le planeur *masc*

gliding NOUN
le vol à voile *masc*
□ My hobby is gliding. Je fais du vol à voile.

★**global** ADJECTIVE
mondial (FEM mondiale, MASC PL mondiaux)
■ **on a global scale** à l'échelle mondiale

global warming NOUN
le réchauffement climatique *masc*

globe NOUN
le globe *masc*

gloomy ADJECTIVE
1 morose (FEM morose)
□ She looked gloomy when she heard the news. Elle avait l'air morose quand elle a entendu les nouvelles.
2 lugubre (FEM lugubre)
□ He lives in a small gloomy flat. Il habite un petit appartement lugubre.

glorious ADJECTIVE
magnifique (FEM magnifique)

glove NOUN
le gant *masc*

glove compartment NOUN
la boîte à gants *fem*

glue NOUN
▷ *see also* **glue** VERB
la colle *fem*

to **glue** VERB
▷ *see also* **glue** NOUN
coller [28]

GM ADJECTIVE (= *genetically modified*)
génétiquement modifié (FEM génétiquement modifiée)
□ GM foods les aliments génétiquement modifiés *masc pl*
■ **GM-free** sans OGM

GMO ABBREVIATION (= *genetically-modified organism*)
l'OGM *masc* (= *l'organisme génétiquement modifié*)

★**go** NOUN
▷ *see also* **go** VERB
■ **to have a go at doing something** essayer [59] de faire quelque chose □ He had a go at making a cake. Il a essayé de faire un gâteau.
■ **Whose go is it?** À qui le tour?

★to **go** VERB
▷ *see also* **go** NOUN
1 aller [3E]
□ I'm going to the cinema tonight. Je vais au cinéma ce soir.
2 partir [57E] (*leave*)
□ Where's Jin? — He's gone. Où est Jin? — Il est parti.
3 s'en aller [3] (*go away*)
□ I'm going now. Je m'en vais.
4 marcher [28] (*vehicle*)
□ My car won't go. Ma voiture ne marche pas.
■ **to go home** rentrer [68E] à la maison □ I go home at about 4 o'clock. Je rentre à la maison vers quatre heures.
■ **to go for a walk** aller [3E] se promener □ Shall we go for a walk? Si on allait se promener?
■ **How did it go?** Comment est-ce que ça s'est passé?
■ **I'm going to do it tomorrow.** Je vais le faire demain.
■ **It's going to be difficult.** Ça va être difficile.

to **go after** VERB
suivre [81]
□ Quick, go after them! Vite, suivez-les!

to **go ahead** VERB
■ **The meeting with your parents will go ahead as planned.** La réunion avec vos parents aura bien lieu comme prévu.
■ **We'll go ahead with your plan.** Nous allons mettre votre projet à exécution.
■ **Go ahead!** Vas-y!

to **go away** VERB
s'en aller [3]
□ Go away! Allez-vous-en!

to **go back** VERB

> Use **retourner** in most cases, unless you are entering a building (usually your home) when you would use **rentrer**.

1 retourner [72E]
□ We went back to the same place. Nous sommes retournés au même endroit.
2 rentrer [68E]
□ After the film he went back home. Il est rentré chez lui après le film.

to **go by** VERB
passer [58E]
□ A group of tourists went by. Un groupe de touristes est passé.

to **go down** VERB
1 descendre [24E] (*person*)
□ to go down the stairs descendre l'escalier

> The verb **descendre** uses **avoir** in the perfect tense instead of **être** when talking about a person or thing moving down something (for example, down the stairs).

2 baisser [28] (*decrease*)
□ The price of computers has gone down. Le prix des ordinateurs a baissé.
3 se dégonfler [28] (*deflate*)
□ My airbed kept going down. Mon matelas pneumatique se dégonflait constamment.
■ **My brother's gone down with flu.** Mon frère a attrapé la grippe.

to **go for** VERB
attaquer [28] (*attack*)
□ Suddenly the dog went for me. Soudain, le chien m'a attaqué.
■ **Go for it!** (*go on!*) Vas-y, fonce!

to **go in** VERB
entrer [32E]
□ He knocked on the door and went in. Il a frappé à la porte et il est entré.

to **go off** VERB
1 exploser [28] (*bomb*)
□ The bomb went off. La bombe a explosé.
2 se déclencher [28] (*alarm, gun*)
□ The fire alarm went off. L'alarme à incendie s'est déclenchée.
3 sonner [28] (*alarm clock*)
□ My alarm clock goes off at seven every morning. Mon réveil sonne à sept heures tous les matins.
4 tourner [28] (*food*)
□ The milk's gone off. Le lait a tourné.
5 partir [57E] (*go away*)
□ He went off in a huff. Il est parti de mauvaise humeur.

to **go on** VERB
1 se passer [58] (*happen*)
□ What's going on? Qu'est-ce qui se passe?
2 continuer [28] (*carry on*)
□ The concert went on until 11 o'clock at night. Le concert a continué jusqu'à onze heures du soir.
■ **to go on doing something** continuer [28] à faire quelque chose □ He went on reading. Il a continué à lire.
■ **to go on at somebody** être [35] sur le dos de quelqu'un □ My parents always go on at me. Mes parents sont toujours sur mon dos.
■ **Go on!** Allez! □ Go on, tell me what the problem is! Allez, dis-moi quel est le problème!

to **go out** VERB
1 sortir [79E] (*person*)
□ Are you going out tonight? Tu sors ce soir?
■ **to go out with somebody** sortir [79E] avec quelqu'un □ Are you going out with him? Est-ce que tu sors avec lui?
2 s'éteindre [60] (*light, fire, candle*)
□ Suddenly the lights went out. Soudain, les lumières se sont éteintes.

to **go past** VERB
■ **to go past something** passer [58E] devant quelque chose □ He went past the shop. Il est passé devant la boutique.

to **go round** VERB
■ **to go round a corner** prendre [65] un tournant
■ **to go round to somebody's house** aller [3E] chez quelqu'un
■ **to go round a museum** visiter [28] un musée
■ **to go round the shops** faire [36] les boutiques
■ **There's a bug going round.** Il y a un microbe qui circule.

to **go through** VERB
traverser [28]
□ We went through Paris to get to Rennes. Nous avons traversé Paris pour aller à Rennes.

to **go up** VERB
1 monter [48E] (*person*)
□ to go up the stairs monter l'escalier

> The verb **monter** uses **avoir** in the perfect tense instead of **être** when talking about a person or thing moving up something (for example, up the stairs).

2 augmenter [28] (*increase*)
□ The price has gone up. Le prix a augmenté.
■ **to go up in flames** s'embraser [28] □ The whole factory went up in flames. L'usine toute entière s'est embrasée.

to **go with** VERB
aller [3E] avec
□ Does this T-shirt go with this skirt? Est-ce que ce tee-shirt va avec cette jupe?

★**goal** NOUN
le but *masc*
□ to score a goal marquer un but □ His goal is to become the world champion. Son but est de devenir champion du monde.

goalkeeper NOUN
le gardien de but *masc*

goat NOUN
la chèvre *fem*
■ **goat's cheese** le fromage de chèvre

★**god** NOUN
le dieu *masc* (PL les dieux)
□ I believe in God. Je crois en Dieu.

goddaughter NOUN
la filleule *fem*

godfather NOUN
le parrain *masc*

godmother NOUN
la marraine *fem*

godson NOUN
le filleul *masc*

goggles PL NOUN
1 les lunettes de protection *fem pl* (*of welder, mechanic etc*)
2 les lunettes de plongée *fem pl* (*of swimmer*)

★**gold** NOUN
l'or *masc*
□ They found some gold. Ils ont trouvé de l'or.
□ a gold necklace un collier en or

goldfish NOUN
le poisson rouge *masc*

□ I've got five goldfish. J'ai cinq poissons rouges.

gold-plated ADJECTIVE
plaqué or (FEM plaquée or)

★ **golf** NOUN
le golf *masc*
□ My dad plays golf. Mon père joue au golf.
■ **a golf club** un club de golf

golf course NOUN
le terrain de golf *masc*

★ **gone** VERB ▷ *see* **go**

★ **good** ADJECTIVE
1 bon (FEM bonne)
□ It's a very good film. C'est un très bon film.
□ Vegetables are good for you. Les légumes sont bons pour la santé.
■ **to be good at something** être [35] bon en quelque chose □ Samir's very good at maths. Samir est très bon en maths.

WORD POWER
You can use a number of other words instead of **good** to mean 'great':
excellent excellent
□ an excellent book un livre excellent
fantastic fantastique
□ fantastic weather un temps fantastique
great génial
□ a great film un film génial
super formidable
□ a super idea une idée formidable

2 gentil (FEM gentille) (*kind*)
□ They were very good to me. Ils ont été très gentils avec moi. □ That's very good of you. C'est très gentil de votre part.
3 sage (FEM sage) (*not naughty*)
□ Be good! Sois sage!
■ **for good** pour de bon □ One day he left for good. Un jour il est parti pour de bon.
■ **Good morning!** Bonjour!
■ **Good afternoon!** Bonjour!
■ **Good evening!** Bonsoir!
■ **Good night!** Bonne nuit!
■ **It's no good complaining.** Cela ne sert à rien de se plaindre.

goodbye EXCLAMATION
au revoir!

Good Friday NOUN
le Vendredi saint *masc*

good-looking ADJECTIVE
beau (FEM belle, MASC PL beaux)
□ He's very good-looking. Il est très beau.

beau changes to **bel** before a vowel and most words beginning with 'h'.

□ a good-looking man un bel homme

good-natured ADJECTIVE
facile à vivre (FEM facile à vivre) (*person*)

★ **goods** PL NOUN
les marchandises *fem pl* (*in shop*)
■ **a goods train** un train de marchandises

to **google** VERB
googler [28]

goose NOUN
l'oie *fem*

gooseberry NOUN
la groseille à maquereau *fem*

gorgeous ADJECTIVE
1 superbe (FEM superbe)
□ She's gorgeous! Elle est superbe!
2 splendide (FEM splendide)
□ The weather was gorgeous. Il a fait un temps splendide.

gorilla NOUN
le gorille *masc*

gospel NOUN
le gospel *masc* (*music*)

gossip NOUN
▷ *see also* **gossip** VERB
1 les cancans *masc pl* (*rumours*)
□ Tell me the gossip! Raconte-moi les cancans!
2 la commère *fem* (*woman*)
□ She's such a gossip! C'est une vraie commère!
3 le bavard *masc* (*man*)
□ What a gossip! Quel bavard!

to **gossip** VERB
▷ *see also* **gossip** NOUN
1 bavarder [28] (*chat*)
□ They were always gossiping. Elles étaient tout le temps en train de bavarder.
2 faire [36] des commérages (*about somebody*)
□ They gossiped about her. Elles faisaient des commérages à son sujet.

★ **got** VERB ▷ *see* **get**

gotten VERB (US) ▷ *see* **get**

★ **government** NOUN
le gouvernement *masc*

★ **GP** NOUN
le médecin généraliste *masc*

GPS NOUN
le GPS *masc*

★ to **grab** VERB
saisir [38]

graceful ADJECTIVE
élégant (FEM élégante)

★ **grade** NOUN
la note *fem* (*at school*)
□ He got good grades in his exams. Il a eu de bonnes notes à ses examens.

grade school NOUN (US)
l'école primaire *fem*

gradual ADJECTIVE
progressif (FEM progressive)

★ **gradually** ADVERB

peu à peu
□ We gradually got used to it. Nous nous y sommes habitués peu à peu.

★ **graduate** NOUN
1 le diplômé *masc*
la diplômée *fem (from university)*
2 le bachelier *masc*
la bachelière *fem (from US high school)*

graffiti PL NOUN
les graffiti *masc pl*

grain NOUN
le grain *masc*

gram NOUN
le gramme *masc*

grammar NOUN
la grammaire *fem*

grammar school NOUN
1 le collège *masc*
2 le lycée *masc*

DID YOU KNOW...?
In France, pupils go to a **collège** between the ages of 11 and 15, and then to a **lycée** until the age of 18. French schools are mostly non-selective.

grammatical ADJECTIVE
grammatical (FEM grammaticale, MASC PL grammaticaux)

gramme NOUN
le gramme *masc*
□ 500 grammes of cheese cinq cents grammes de fromage

grand ADJECTIVE
somptueux (FEM somptueuse)
□ Samantha lives in a very grand house. Samantha habite une maison somptueuse.

★ **grandchild** NOUN
le petit-fils *masc*
la petite-fille *fem*
■ **my grandchildren** mes petits-enfants *masc pl*

granddad NOUN
le papi *masc*
□ my granddad mon papi

★ **granddaughter** NOUN
la petite-fille *fem* (PL les petites-filles)

★ **grandfather** NOUN
le grand-père *masc* (PL les grands-pères)
□ my grandfather mon grand-père

grandma NOUN
la mamie *fem*
□ my grandma ma mamie

★ **grandmother** NOUN
la grand-mère *fem* (PL les grands-mères)
□ my grandmother ma grand-mère

grandpa NOUN
le papi *masc*
□ my grandpa mon papi

★ **grandparents** PL NOUN
les grands-parents *masc pl*
□ my grandparents mes grands-parents

★ **grandson** NOUN
le petit-fils *masc* (PL les petits-fils)

granny NOUN
la mamie *fem*
□ my granny ma mamie

grant NOUN
la bourse *fem*

★ **grape** NOUN
le raisin *masc*

grapefruit NOUN
le pamplemousse *masc*

graph NOUN
le graphique *masc*

graphics PL NOUN
1 les images de synthèse *fem pl (computer generated)*
2 le graphisme *masc pl (graphic design)*
□ I designed the graphics, she wrote the text. J'ai fait le graphisme, elle a écrit le texte.
■ **He wants to study computer graphics.** Il veut faire des études d'infographie.

to **grasp** VERB
saisir [38]

★ **grass** NOUN
l'herbe *fem*
□ The grass is long. L'herbe est haute.
■ **to cut the grass** tondre [69] le gazon

grasshopper NOUN
la sauterelle *fem*

to **grate** VERB
râper [28]
□ to grate some cheese râper du fromage

grateful ADJECTIVE
reconnaissant (FEM reconnaissante)

grave NOUN
la tombe *fem*

gravel NOUN
le gravier *masc*

graveyard NOUN
le cimetière *masc*

gravy NOUN
la sauce au jus de viande *fem*

grease NOUN
le lubrifiant *masc*

greasy ADJECTIVE
gras (FEM grasse)
□ He has greasy hair. Il a les cheveux gras.
□ The food was very greasy. La nourriture était très grasse.

★ **great** ADJECTIVE
1 génial (FEM géniale, MASC PL géniaux)
□ That's great! C'est génial!

WORD POWER
You can use a number of other words instead of **great** to mean 'good':
amazing extraordinaire
□ an amazing view une vue extraordinaire
fabulous formidable
□ a fabulous idea une idée formidable
terrific super
□ a terrific party une super fête
wonderful formidable
□ a wonderful opportunity une occasion formidable

2 grand (FEM grande)
□ a great mansion un grand manoir

★**Great Britain** NOUN
la Grande-Bretagne *fem*
■ **in Great Britain** en Grande-Bretagne
■ **to Great Britain** en Grande-Bretagne
■ **I'm from Great Britain.** Je suis britannique.

great-grandfather NOUN
l'arrière-grand-père *masc* (PL les arrière-grands-pères)

great-grandmother NOUN
l'arrière-grand-mère *fem* (PL les arrière-grands-mères)

★**Greece** NOUN
la Grèce *fem*
■ **in Greece** en Grèce
■ **to Greece** en Grèce

greedy ADJECTIVE
1 gourmand (FEM gourmande) *(for food)*
□ I want some more cake. — Don't be so greedy! Je veux encore du gâteau. — Ne sois pas si gourmand!
2 avide (FEM avide) *(for money)*

Greek NOUN
▷ *see also* **Greek** ADJECTIVE
1 le Grec *masc*
la Grecque *fem (person)*
2 le grec *masc (language)*

Greek ADJECTIVE
▷ *see also* **Greek** NOUN
grec (FEM grecque)
□ Dionysis is Greek. Dionysis est grec. □ She's Greek. Elle est grecque.

★**green** ADJECTIVE
▷ *see also* **green** NOUN
1 vert (FEM verte)
□ a green car une voiture verte □ a green light un feu vert □ a green salad une salade verte
2 écologiste (FEM écologiste) *(movement, candidate)*
□ the Green Party le parti écologiste
■ **green beans** les haricots verts *masc pl*

★**green** NOUN
▷ *see also* **green** ADJECTIVE
le vert *masc*
□ a dark green un vert foncé
■ **greens** *(vegetables)* les légumes verts *masc pl*
■ **the Greens** *(party)* les Verts *masc pl*

★**greengrocer's** NOUN
le marchand de fruits et légumes *masc*

greenhouse NOUN
la serre *fem*
■ **the greenhouse effect** l'effet de serre *masc*
■ **greenhouse gases** les gaz à effet de serre *masc pl*

Greenland NOUN
le Groenland *masc*

to **greet** VERB
accueillir [22]
□ He greeted me with a kiss. Il m'a accueillie en me faisant la bise.

greeting NOUN
■ **Greetings from Bangor!** Bonjour de Bangor!
■ **'Season's greetings'** 'Meilleurs vœux pour les fêtes de fin d'année'

greetings card NOUN
la carte de vœux *fem*

grew VERB ▷ *see* **grow**

★**grey** ADJECTIVE
gris (FEM grise)
□ She's got grey hair. Elle a les cheveux gris.
■ **He's going grey.** Il grisonne.

grey-haired ADJECTIVE
grisonnant (FEM grisonnante)

grid NOUN
1 la grille *fem (in road)*
2 le réseau *masc* (PL les réseaux) *(of electricity)*

grief NOUN
le chagrin *masc*

grill NOUN
▷ *see also* **grill** VERB
le gril *masc (of cooker)*

to **grill** VERB
▷ *see also* **grill** NOUN
■ **to grill something** faire [36] griller quelque chose

grim ADJECTIVE
sinistre (FEM sinistre)

to **grin** VERB
▷ *see also* **grin** NOUN
sourire [74]
□ Aziz grinned at me. Aziz m'a souri.

grin NOUN
▷ *see also* **grin** VERB
le large sourire *masc*

to **grind** VERB
moudre [50] *(coffee, pepper)*

to **grip** VERB
saisir [38]

gripping ADJECTIVE
palpitant (FEM palpitante) (*exciting*)

grit NOUN
le gravillon *masc*

to **groan** VERB
▷ *see also* **groan** NOUN
gémir [38]
□ He groaned with pain. Il a gémi sous l'effet de la douleur.

groan NOUN
▷ *see also* **groan** VERB
le gémissement *masc* (*of pain*)

grocer NOUN
l'épicier *masc*
□ He's a grocer. Il est épicier.

groceries PL NOUN
les provisions *fem pl*

grocer's NOUN
l'épicerie *fem*

grocer's shop NOUN
l'épicerie *fem*

grocery store NOUN (US)
l'épicerie *fem*

groom NOUN
le marié *masc* (*bridegroom*)
□ the groom and his best man le marié et son témoin

to **grope** VERB
■ **to grope for something** chercher [28] quelque chose à tâtons □ He groped for the light switch. Il a cherché à tâtons l'interrupteur.

gross ADJECTIVE
dégoûtant (FEM dégoûtante) (*revolting*)
□ It was really gross! C'était vraiment dégoûtant!

grossly ADVERB
largement
□ We're grossly underpaid. Nous sommes largement sous-payés.

★**ground** VERB ▷ *see* **grind**

★**ground** NOUN
▷ *see also* **ground** ADJECTIVE
1 le sol *masc* (*earth*)
□ The ground's wet. Le sol est mouillé.
2 le terrain *masc* (*for sport*)
□ a football ground un terrain de football
3 la raison *fem* (*reason*)
□ We've got grounds for complaint. Nous avons des raisons de nous plaindre.
■ **on the ground** par terre □ We sat on the ground. Nous nous sommes assis par terre.

★**ground** ADJECTIVE
▷ *see also* **ground** NOUN
■ **ground coffee** le café moulu

ground floor NOUN
le rez-de-chaussée *masc*
■ **on the ground floor** au rez-de-chaussée

★**group** NOUN
le groupe *masc*

★to **grow** VERB
1 pousser [28] (*plant*)
□ Grass grows quickly. L'herbe pousse vite.
2 grandir [38] (*person, animal*)
□ Haven't you grown! Comme tu as grandi!
3 augmenter [28] (*increase*)
□ The number of pupils who go to university has grown. Le nombre d'élèves qui accèdent à l'université a augmenté.
4 faire [36] pousser (*cultivate*)
□ My dad grows potatoes. Mon père fait pousser des pommes de terre.
■ **to grow a beard** se laisser [28] pousser la barbe
■ **He's grown out of his jacket.** Sa veste est devenue trop petite pour lui.

to **grow up** VERB
grandir [38]
■ **Oh, grow up!** Ne fais pas l'enfant!

to **growl** VERB
grogner [28]

grown VERB ▷ *see* **grow**

growth NOUN
la croissance *fem*
□ economic growth la croissance économique

grub NOUN
la bouffe *fem* (*informal*)

grudge NOUN
la rancune *fem*
■ **to bear a grudge against somebody** garder [28] rancune à quelqu'un

gruesome ADJECTIVE
horrible (FEM horrible)

guarantee NOUN
▷ *see also* **guarantee** VERB
la garantie *fem*
■ **a five-year guarantee** une garantie de cinq ans

to **guarantee** VERB
▷ *see also* **guarantee** NOUN
garantir [38]
□ I can't guarantee he'll come. Je ne peux pas garantir qu'il viendra.

★to **guard** VERB
▷ *see also* **guard** NOUN
garder [28]
□ They guarded the palace. Ils gardaient le palais.
■ **to guard against something** protéger [66] contre quelque chose

★**guard** NOUN
▷ *see also* **guard** VERB
le chef de train *masc* (*of train*)
■ **a security guard** un vigile
■ **a guard dog** un chien de garde

★ to **guess** VERB
▷ *see also* **guess** NOUN
deviner [28]
□ Guess what this is! Devine ce que c'est!
▪ **to guess wrong** se tromper [28] □ Daniel guessed wrong. Daniel s'est trompé.

★ **guess** NOUN
▷ *see also* **guess** VERB
la supposition *fem*
□ It's just a guess. C'est une simple supposition.
▪ **Have a guess!** Devine!

★ **guest** NOUN
1 l'invité *masc*
l'invitée *fem*
□ We have guests staying with us. Nous avons des invités.
2 le client *masc*
la cliente *fem* (*of hotel*)

guesthouse NOUN
le petit hôtel *masc*

★ **guide** NOUN
1 le guide *masc* (*book, person*)
□ We bought a guide to Paris. Nous avons acheté un guide sur Paris. □ The guide showed us round the castle. Le guide nous a fait visiter le château.
2 l'éclaireuse *fem* (*girl guide*)
▪ **the Guides** les Éclaireuses

guidebook NOUN
le guide *masc*

guide dog NOUN
le chien d'aveugle *masc*

★ **guilty** ADJECTIVE
coupable (FEM coupable)
□ to feel guilty se sentir coupable □ She was found guilty. Elle a été reconnue coupable.

★ **guinea pig** NOUN
le cobaye *masc*

★ **guitar** NOUN
la guitare *fem*
□ I play the guitar. Je joue de la guitare.

gum NOUN
le chewing-gum *masc* (*sweet*)
▪ **gums** (*in mouth*) les gencives *fem pl*

★ **gun** NOUN
1 le revolver *masc* (*small*)
2 le fusil *masc* (*rifle*)

gunpoint NOUN
▪ **at gunpoint** sous la menace d'une arme

gust NOUN
▪ **a gust of wind** une rafale de vent

★ **guy** NOUN
le type *masc*
□ Who's that guy? C'est qui ce type? □ He's a nice guy. C'est un type sympa.

★ **gym** NOUN
la gym *fem*
□ I go to the gym every day. Je vais tous les jours à la gym.

gymnast NOUN
le/la gymnaste *masc/fem*
□ She's a gymnast. Elle est gymnaste.

gymnastics NOUN
la gymnastique *fem*
□ to do gymnastics faire de la gymnastique

gypsy NOUN
le Tzigane *masc*
la Tzigane *fem*

Hh

★ **habit** NOUN
l'habitude *fem*
▫ a bad habit une mauvaise habitude

to **hack** VERB
■ **to hack into a system** s'introduire [23] dans un système

hacker NOUN
le/la pirate informatique *masc/fem*

had VERB ▷ *see* **have**

haddock NOUN
l'églefin *masc*

hadn't = **had not**

hail NOUN
▷ *see also* **hail** VERB
la grêle *fem*

to **hail** VERB
▷ *see also* **hail** NOUN
grêler [28]
▫ It's hailing. Il grêle.

★ **hair** NOUN
1 les cheveux *masc pl*
▫ She's got long hair. Elle a les cheveux longs.
▫ He's got black hair. Il a les cheveux noirs.
▫ He's losing his hair. Il perd ses cheveux.
■ **to brush one's hair** se brosser [28] les cheveux ▫ I'm brushing my hair. Je me brosse les cheveux.
■ **to wash one's hair** se laver [28] les cheveux ▫ I need to wash my hair. Il faut que je me lave les cheveux.
■ **to have one's hair cut** se faire [36] couper les cheveux ▫ I've just had my hair cut. Je viens de me faire couper les cheveux.
■ **a hair** 1 (*from head*) un cheveu 2 (*from body*) un poil
2 le pelage *masc* (*fur of animal*)

hairbrush NOUN
la brosse à cheveux *fem*

haircut NOUN
la coupe *fem*
■ **to have a haircut** se faire [36] couper les cheveux ▫ I've just had a haircut. Je viens de me faire couper les cheveux.

★ **hairdresser** NOUN
le coiffeur *masc*
la coiffeuse *fem*
▫ He's a hairdresser. Il est coiffeur.

★ **hairdresser's** NOUN
le coiffeur *masc*
▫ at the hairdresser's chez le coiffeur

hair dryer NOUN
le sèche-cheveux *masc* (PL les sèche-cheveux)

hair gel NOUN
le gel pour les cheveux *masc*

hairgrip NOUN
la pince à cheveux *fem*

hair spray NOUN
la laque *fem*

hair straighteners PL NOUN
le lisseur *masc*

hairstyle NOUN
la coiffure *fem*

hairy ADJECTIVE
poilu (FEM poilue)
▫ He's got hairy legs. Il a les jambes poilues.

★ **half** NOUN
▷ *see also* **half** ADJECTIVE, ADVERB
1 la moitié *fem*
▫ half of the cake la moitié du gâteau
2 le billet demi-tarif *masc* (*ticket*)
▫ A half to York, please. Un billet demi-tarif pour York, s'il vous plaît.
■ **two and a half** deux et demi
■ **half an hour** une demi-heure
■ **half past ten** dix heures et demie
■ **half a kilo** cinq cents grammes
■ **to cut something in half** couper [28] quelque chose en deux

★ **half** ADJECTIVE, ADVERB
▷ *see also* **half** NOUN
1 demi (FEM demie)
▫ a half chicken un demi-poulet
2 à moitié
▫ He was half asleep. Il était à moitié endormi.

half-brother NOUN
le demi-frère *masc* (PL les demi-frères)

half-hour NOUN
la demi-heure *fem*

half-price ADJECTIVE, ADVERB
■ **at half-price** à moitié prix

half-sister NOUN
la demi-sœur *fem* (PL les demi-sœurs)

half-term NOUN
les petites vacances *fem pl*

DID YOU KNOW...?
There are two half-term holidays in France: **les vacances de la Toussaint** (in October/ November) and **les vacances de février** (in February).

half-time NOUN
la mi-temps *fem*

halfway ADVERB
1 à mi-chemin
□ halfway between Oxford and Swindon à mi-chemin entre Oxford et Swindon
2 à la moitié
□ halfway through the chapter à la moitié du chapitre

★ **hall** NOUN
1 l'entrée *fem* (*in house*)
2 la salle *fem*
□ the village hall la salle des fêtes

Hallowe'en NOUN
la veille de la Toussaint *fem*

DID YOU KNOW...?
The French do not traditionally celebrate Hallowe'en (although it is starting to become more popular). The next day, All Saints' Day (November 1st), is a public holiday, and is the day when people often visit family graves.

hallway NOUN
le vestibule *masc*

halt NOUN
■ **to come to a halt** s'arrêter [28] □ The train came to a halt at the station. Le train s'est arrêté dans la gare.

★ **ham** NOUN
le jambon *masc*
□ a ham sandwich un sandwich au jambon

★ **hamburger** NOUN
le hamburger *masc*

hammer NOUN
le marteau *masc* (PL les marteaux)

★ **hamster** NOUN
le hamster *masc*

★ **hand** NOUN
▷ *see also* **hand** VERB
1 la main *fem* (*of person*)
■ **to give somebody a hand** donner [28] un coup de main à quelqu'un □ Can you give me a hand? Tu peux me donner un coup de main?
■ **on the one hand ..., on the other hand ...** d'une part ..., d'autre part ...
2 l'aiguille *fem* (*of clock*)

★ to **hand** VERB
▷ *see also* **hand** NOUN
passer [58]
□ He handed me the book. Il m'a passé le livre.
■ **to hand something in** rendre [7] quelque chose □ He handed his exam paper in. Il a rendu sa copie d'examen.
■ **to hand something out** distribuer [28] quelque chose □ The teacher handed out the books. Le professeur a distribué les livres.
■ **to hand something over** remettre [47] quelque chose □ She handed the keys over to me. Elle m'a remis les clés.

★ **handbag** NOUN
le sac à main *masc*

handball NOUN
le handball *masc* (*game*)
■ **to play handball** jouer [28] au handball

handbook NOUN
le manuel *masc*

handcuffs PL NOUN
les menottes *fem pl*

★ **handkerchief** NOUN
le mouchoir *masc*

★ **handle** NOUN
▷ *see also* **handle** VERB
1 la poignée *fem* (*of door*)
2 l'anse *fem* (*of cup*)
3 le manche *masc* (*of knife*)
4 la queue *fem* (*of saucepan*)

★ to **handle** VERB
▷ *see also* **handle** NOUN
■ **He handled it well.** Il s'en est bien tiré.
■ **Phoebe's mum handled the travel arrangements.** La mère de Phoebe s'est occupée de l'organisation du voyage.
■ **She's good at handling children.** Elle sait bien s'y prendre avec les enfants.

handlebars PL NOUN
le guidon *masc sing*

handmade ADJECTIVE
fait à la main (FEM faite à la main)

hands-free kit NOUN
le kit mains libres *masc* (*for phone*)

★ **handsome** ADJECTIVE
beau (FEM belle, MASC PL beaux)
□ He's handsome. Il est beau.

beau changes to **bel** after a vowel and most words beginning with 'h'.

□ a handsome man un bel homme

handwriting NOUN
l'écriture *fem*

handy ADJECTIVE
1 pratique (FEM pratique)
□ This knife's very handy. Ce couteau est très pratique.
2 sous la main
□ Have you got a pen handy? Est-ce que tu as un stylo sous la main?

★ to **hang** VERB
1 accrocher [28]
□ Riley hung the painting on the wall. Riley a accroché le tableau au mur.
2 pendre [88]
□ They hanged the criminal. Ils ont pendu le criminel.

to **hang around** VERB
traîner [28]
□ On Saturdays we hang around in the park. Le samedi nous traînons dans le parc.

to **hang on** VERB
patienter [28]
□ Hang on a minute please. Patientez une minute s'il vous plaît.

to **hang up** VERB
1 accrocher [28] (*clothes*)
□ Hang your jacket up on the hook. Accrochez votre veste au portemanteau.
2 raccrocher [28] (*phone*)
□ Don't hang up! Ne raccroche pas!
■ **to hang up on someone** raccrocher [28] au nez de quelqu'un □ He always hangs up on me. Il me raccroche toujours au nez.

hanger NOUN
le cintre *masc* (*coat hanger*)

hang-gliding NOUN
le deltaplane *masc*
■ **to go hang-gliding** faire [36] du deltaplane

hangover NOUN
la gueule de bois *fem*
□ He's got a terrible hangover. Il a une gueule de bois terrible.

Hanukkah NOUN
Hanoukka *fem*

to **happen** VERB
se passer [58]
□ What's happened? Qu'est-ce qui s'est passé?
■ **as it happens** justement □ As it happens, I don't want to go. Justement, je ne veux pas y aller.

happily ADVERB
1 joyeusement
□ 'I passed!' he said happily. 'Je suis reçu!' dit-il joyeusement.
2 heureusement (*fortunately*)
□ Happily, everything went well. Heureusement, tout s'est bien passé.

happiness NOUN
le bonheur *masc*

★ **happy** ADJECTIVE
heureux (FEM heureuse)
□ Rafi looks happy. Rafi a l'air heureux.
■ **I'm very happy with your work.** Je suis très satisfait de ton travail.
■ **Happy birthday!** Bon anniversaire!

> **WORD POWER**
> You can use a number of other words instead of **happy** to mean 'glad':
> **cheerful** gai
> □ a cheerful song une chanson gaie
> **delighted** ravi
> □ a delighted smile un sourire ravi
> **glad** content
> □ to be glad être content
> **satisfied** satisfait
> □ a satisfied customer un client satisfait

harassment NOUN
le harcèlement *masc*
□ police harassment le harcèlement policier

★ **harbour** (US **harbor**) NOUN
le port *masc*

★ **hard** ADJECTIVE, ADVERB
1 dur (FEM dure)
□ This cheese is very hard. Ce fromage est très dur. □ He's worked very hard. Il a travaillé très dur.
2 difficile (FEM difficile)
□ This question's too hard for me. Cette question est trop difficile pour moi.

hard disk NOUN
le disque dur *masc* (*of computer*)

★ **hardly** ADVERB
■ **I've hardly got any money.** Je n'ai presque pas d'argent.
■ **I hardly know you.** Je te connais à peine.
■ **hardly ever** presque jamais

hard up ADJECTIVE
fauché (FEM fauchée)

hardware NOUN
le hardware *masc* (*computing*)

hare NOUN
le lièvre *masc*

★ to **harm** VERB
■ **to harm somebody** faire [36] du mal à quelqu'un □ I didn't mean to harm you. Je ne voulais pas te faire de mal.
■ **to harm something** nuire [23] à quelque chose □ Chemicals harm the environment. Les produits chimiques nuisent à l'environnement.

harmful ADJECTIVE
nocif (FEM nocive)
□ harmful chemicals des produits chimiques nocifs

harmless ADJECTIVE
inoffensif (FEM inoffensive)
□ Most spiders are harmless. La plupart des araignées sont inoffensives.

harsh ADJECTIVE
dur (FEM dure)

has VERB ▷ *see* **have**

English-French

h

English-French

h

hashtag NOUN
le hashtag *masc*

hasn't = **has not**

★ **hat** NOUN
le chapeau *masc* (PL les chapeaux)

★ to **hate** VERB
détester [28]
□ I hate maths. Je déteste les maths.

hatred NOUN
la haine *fem*

haunted ADJECTIVE
hanté (FEM hantée)
□ a haunted house une maison hantée

★ to **have** VERB
1 avoir [8]
□ I have a cold. J'ai un rhume. □ You have a beautiful smile. Tu as un beau sourire. □ She has two brothers. Elle a deux frères. □ Have you got a sister? Tu as une sœur? □ He's got blue eyes. Il a les yeux bleus. □ He's done it, hasn't he? Il l'a fait, non? □ Have you got any money? — No, I haven't! Est-ce que tu as de l'argent? — Non, je n'en ai pas!
2 être [35]

> The perfect tense of some verbs is formed with **être**.

□ They have arrived. Ils sont arrivés. □ Has he gone? Est-ce qu'il est parti?
3 prendre [65]
□ He had his breakfast. Il a pris son petit déjeuner. □ to have a shower prendre une douche
■ **to have got to do something** devoir [26] faire quelque chose □ She's got to do it. Elle doit le faire.
■ **to have a party** faire [36] une fête
■ **to have one's hair cut** se faire [36] couper les cheveux

haven't = **have not**

hay NOUN
le foin *masc*

hay fever NOUN
le rhume des foins *masc*
□ Do you get hay fever? Est-ce que vous êtes sujet au rhume des foins?

hazelnut NOUN
la noisette *fem*

★ **he** PRONOUN
il
□ He loves dogs. Il aime les chiens.

★ **head** NOUN
▷ *see also* **head** VERB
1 la tête *fem* (*of person*)
□ I have a sore head. J'ai mal à la tête.
2 le directeur *masc*
la directrice *fem* (*of private or primary school*)
3 le proviseur *masc* (*of state secondary school*)
4 le chef *masc* (*leader*)
□ a head of state un chef d'État
■ **Heads or tails? — Heads.** Pile ou face? — Face.

★ to **head** VERB
▷ *see also* **head** NOUN
■ **to head for something** se diriger [45] vers quelque chose □ They headed for the church. Ils se sont dirigés vers l'église.

★ **headache** NOUN
■ **I've got a headache.** J'ai mal à la tête.

headlight NOUN
le phare *masc*

★ **headline** NOUN
le titre *masc*

headmaster NOUN
1 le directeur *masc* (*of private or primary school*)
2 le proviseur *masc* (*of state secondary school*)

headmistress NOUN
1 la directrice *fem* (*of private or primary school*)
2 le proviseur *masc* (*of state secondary school*)

headphones PL NOUN
les écouteurs *masc pl*

★ **headquarters** PL NOUN
le siège *masc sing* (*of organization*)

headteacher NOUN
1 le directeur *masc*
la directrice *fem* (*of private or primary school*)
2 le proviseur *masc* (*of state secondary school*)
□ She's a headteacher. Elle est proviseur.

★ to **heal** VERB
cicatriser [28]
□ The wound soon healed. La blessure a vite cicatrisé.

★ **health** NOUN
la santé *fem*

★ **healthy** ADJECTIVE
1 en bonne santé (*person*)
□ My grandparents are still very healthy. Mes grands-parents sont toujours en très bonne santé.
2 sain (FEM saine) (*climate, food*)
□ a healthy diet une alimentation saine

heap NOUN
le tas *masc*
□ a rubbish heap un tas d'ordures

★ to **hear** VERB
1 entendre [88]
□ He heard the dog bark. Il a entendu le chien aboyer. □ She can't hear very well. Elle entend mal. □ I heard that she was ill. J'ai entendu dire qu'elle était malade.
■ **to hear about something** entendre [88] parler de quelque chose
2 apprendre [65] (*news*)
□ Did you hear the good news? Est-ce que tu as appris la bonne nouvelle?

■ **to hear from somebody** avoir [8] des nouvelles de quelqu'un □ I haven't heard from him recently. Je n'ai pas eu de ses nouvelles récemment.

★ **heart** NOUN
le cœur *masc*
□ My heart's beating very fast. J'ai le cœur qui bat très fort.
■ **to learn something by heart** apprendre [65] quelque chose par cœur
■ **hearts** (*in cards*) le cœur *sing* □ the ace of hearts l'as de cœur

heart attack NOUN
la crise cardiaque *fem*

heartbroken ADJECTIVE
■ **to be heartbroken** avoir [8] le cœur brisé

★ **heat** NOUN
▷ *see also* **heat** VERB
la chaleur *fem*

★ to **heat** VERB
▷ *see also* **heat** NOUN
faire [36] chauffer
□ Heat gently for 5 minutes. Faire chauffer à feu doux pendant cinq minutes.

to **heat up** VERB
1 faire [36] réchauffer (*cooked food*)
□ He heated the soup up. Il a fait réchauffer la soupe.
2 chauffer [28] (*water, oven*)
□ The water is heating up. L'eau chauffe.

heater NOUN
le radiateur *masc*
□ an electric heater un radiateur électrique

heather NOUN
la bruyère *fem*

heating NOUN
le chauffage *masc*

heaven NOUN
le paradis *masc*

heavily ADVERB
lourdement
□ The car was heavily loaded. La voiture était lourdement chargée.
■ **He drinks heavily.** C'est un gros buveur.

★ **heavy** ADJECTIVE
1 lourd (FEM lourde)
□ This bag's very heavy. Ce sac est très lourd.
■ **heavy rain** une grosse averse
2 chargé (FEM chargée) (*busy*)
□ I've got a very heavy week ahead. Je vais avoir une semaine très chargée.
■ **to be a heavy drinker** être [35] un gros buveur

he'd = **he would, he had**

hedge NOUN
la haie *fem*

hedgehog NOUN
le hérisson *masc*

heel NOUN
le talon *masc*

★ **height** NOUN
1 la taille *fem* (*of person*)
2 la hauteur *fem* (*of object*)
3 l'altitude *fem* (*of mountain*)

heir NOUN
l'héritier *masc*

heiress NOUN
l'héritière *fem*

held VERB ▷ *see* **hold**

★ **helicopter** NOUN
l'hélicoptère *masc*

★ **hell** NOUN
l'enfer *masc*

he'll = **he will, he shall**

★ **hello** EXCLAMATION
bonjour!

helmet NOUN
le casque *masc*

★ to **help** VERB
▷ *see also* **help** NOUN
aider [28]
□ Can you help me? Est-ce que vous pouvez m'aider?
■ **Help!** Au secours!
■ **Help yourself!** Servez-vous!
■ **He can't help it.** Il n'y peut rien.

★ **help** NOUN
▷ *see also* **help** VERB
l'aide *fem*
□ Do you need any help? Vous avez besoin d'aide?

help desk NOUN
le service d'assistance *masc*
■ **an IT help desk** un service d'assistance informatique

helpful ADJECTIVE
serviable (FEM serviable)
□ He was very helpful. Il a été très serviable.

helpline NOUN
le service d'assistance téléphonique *masc*
■ **a customer helpline** un service clients
□ Why don't you call the customer helpline? Pourquoi n'appelles-tu pas le service clients?

hen NOUN
la poule *fem*

★ **her** ADJECTIVE
▷ *see also* **her** PRONOUN
son *masc*
□ her father son père
sa *fem*
□ her mother sa mère
ses *pl*
□ her parents ses parents

sa becomes son before a vowel sound.

English-French

h

■ **her friend** **1** (*male*) son ami **2** (*female*) son amie

Do not use **son/sa/ses** with parts of the body.

□ She's going to wash her hair. Elle va se laver les cheveux. □ She's cleaning her teeth. Elle se brosse les dents. □ She's hurt her foot. Elle s'est fait mal au pied.

★ **her** PRONOUN

▷ *see also* **her** ADJECTIVE

1 la

□ I can see her. Je la vois. □ Look at her! Regarde-la!

l'

la becomes **l'** before a vowel sound.

□ I saw her. Je l'ai vue.

2 lui

Use **lui** when 'her' means 'to her'.

□ I gave her a book. Je lui ai donné un livre. □ I told her the truth. Je lui ai dit la vérité.

3 elle

Use **elle** after prepositions.

□ I'm going with her. Je vais avec elle. □ He sat next to her. Il s'est assis à côté d'elle.

elle is also used in comparisons.

□ I'm older than her. Je suis plus âgé qu'elle.

herb NOUN

l'herbe *fem*

■ **herbs** les fines herbes *fem pl* □ What herbs do you use in this sauce? Quelles fines herbes utilise-t-on pour cette sauce?

★ **here** ADVERB

ici

□ I live here. J'habite ici.

■ **here is ...** voici ... □ Here's Elise. Voici Elise. □ Here he is! Le voici!

■ **here are ...** voici ... □ Here are the books. Voici les livres.

heritage NOUN

le patrimoine *masc*

★ **hero** NOUN

le héros *masc*

□ He's a real hero! C'est un véritable héros!

heroin NOUN

l'héroïne *fem*

□ Heroin is a hard drug. L'héroïne est une drogue dure.

■ **a heroin addict** un héroïnomane □ She's a heroin addict. C'est une héroïnomane.

heroine NOUN

l'héroïne *fem*

□ the heroine of the novel l'héroïne du roman

★ **hers** PRONOUN

le sien + *masc noun*

□ Is this her coat? — No, hers is black. C'est son manteau? — Non, le sien est noir.

la sienne + *fem noun*

□ Is this her car? — No, hers is white. C'est sa voiture? — Non, la sienne est blanche.

les siens + *masc pl noun*

□ my parents and hers mes parents et les siens

les siennes + *fem pl noun*

□ my shoes and hers mes chaussures et les siennes

■ **Is this hers?** C'est à elle?

■ **This book is hers.** Ce livre est à elle.

■ **Whose is this? — It's hers.** C'est à qui? — À elle.

★ **herself** PRONOUN

1 se

□ She's hurt herself. Elle s'est blessée.

2 elle (*after preposition*)

□ She talked mainly about herself. Elle a surtout parlé d'elle.

3 elle-même

□ She did it herself. Elle l'a fait elle-même.

■ **by herself** toute seule □ She doesn't like travelling by herself. Elle n'aime pas voyager toute seule.

he's = **he is**, **he has**

to **hesitate** VERB

hésiter [28]

heterosexual ADJECTIVE

hétérosexuel (FEM hétérosexuelle)

★ **hi** EXCLAMATION

salut!

hiccups PL NOUN

■ **to have hiccups** avoir [8] le hoquet

★ to **hide** VERB

se cacher [28]

□ He hid behind a bush. Il s'est caché derrière un buisson.

■ **to hide something** cacher [28] quelque chose □ Lucy hid the present. Lucy a caché le cadeau.

hide-and-seek NOUN

■ **to play hide-and-seek** jouer [28] à cache-cache

hideous ADJECTIVE

hideux (FEM hideuse)

hi-fi NOUN

la chaîne hi-fi *fem* (PL les chaînes hi-fi)

★ **high** ADJECTIVE, ADVERB

1 haut (FEM haute)

□ It's too high. C'est trop haut.

■ **How high is the wall?** Quelle est la hauteur du mur?

■ **The wall's 2 metres high.** Le mur fait deux mètres de haut.

2 élevé (FEM élevée)

□ a high price un prix élevé □ a high temperature une température élevée

■ **at high speed** à grande vitesse

■ **It's very high in fat.** C'est très gras. ■ **She's got a very high voice.** Elle a la voix très aiguë.

★ **higher education** NOUN
l'enseignement supérieur *masc*

high-heeled ADJECTIVE
à hauts talons
□ high-heeled shoes des chaussures à hauts talons

high jump NOUN
le saut en hauteur *masc* (*sport*)

★ **highlight** NOUN
▷ *see also* **highlight** VERB
le clou *masc*
□ the highlight of the evening le clou de la soirée

★ to **highlight** VERB
▷ *see also* **highlight** NOUN
1 souligner [28] (*underline*)
2 surligner [28] (*with highlighter pen*)

highlighter NOUN
le surligneur *masc*

high-rise NOUN
la tour *fem*
□ I live in a high-rise. J'habite dans une tour.

high school NOUN
1 le collège *masc*
2 le lycée *masc*

> DID YOU KNOW...?
> In France, pupils go to a **collège** between the ages of 11 and 15, then to a **lycée** until the age of 18.

to **hijack** VERB
détourner [28]

hijacker NOUN
le pirate de l'air *masc*

hike NOUN
la randonnée *fem*

hiking NOUN
■ **to go hiking** faire [36] une randonnée

hilarious ADJECTIVE
hilarant (FEM hilarante)
□ It was hilarious! C'était hilarant!

★ **hill** NOUN
la colline *fem*
□ She walked up the hill. Elle a gravi la colline.

hill-walking NOUN
la randonnée de basse montagne *fem*
□ to go hill-walking faire de la randonnée de basse montagne

★ **him** PRONOUN
1 le
□ I can see him. Je le vois. □ Look at him! Regarde-le!
l'

> **le** becomes l' before a vowel sound.

□ I saw him. Je l'ai vu.
2 lui

> Use **lui** when 'him' means 'to him', and after prepositions.

□ I gave him a book. Je lui ai donné un livre. □ I told him the truth. Je lui ai dit la vérité. □ I'm going with him. Je vais avec lui. □ She sat next to him. Elle s'est assise à côté de lui.

> **lui** is also used in comparisons.

□ I'm older than him. Je suis plus âgé que lui.

★ **himself** PRONOUN
1 se
□ He's hurt himself. Il s'est blessé.
2 lui
□ He talked mainly about himself. Il a surtout parlé de lui.
3 lui-même
□ He did it himself. Il l'a fait lui-même.
■ **by himself** tout seul □ He was travelling by himself. Il voyageait tout seul.

Hindu ADJECTIVE
hindou (FEM hindoue)
□ a Hindu temple un temple hindou

★ **hint** NOUN
▷ *see also* **hint** VERB
l'allusion *fem*
■ **to drop a hint** faire [36] une allusion

★ to **hint** VERB
▷ *see also* **hint** NOUN
laisser [28] entendre
□ He hinted that something was going on. Il a laissé entendre qu'il se passait quelque chose.
■ **What are you hinting at?** Qu'est-ce que vous voulez dire par là ?

★ **hip** NOUN
la hanche *fem*

hippie NOUN
le/la hippie *masc/fem*

hippo NOUN
l'hippopotame *masc*

★ to **hire** VERB
▷ *see also* **hire** NOUN
1 louer [28]
□ to hire a car louer une voiture
2 engager [45] (*person*)
□ They hired a cleaner. Ils ont engagé une femme de ménage.

★ **hire** NOUN
▷ *see also* **hire** VERB
la location *fem*
■ **car hire** location de voitures
■ **for hire** à louer

hire car NOUN
la voiture de location *fem*

★ **his** ADJECTIVE
▷ *see also* **his** PRONOUN

son *masc*
□ his father son père
sa *fem*
□ his mother sa mère
ses *pl*
□ his parents ses parents

sa becomes **son** before a vowel sound.

■ **his friend** **1** (*male*) son ami **2** (*female*) son amie

Do not use **son/sa/ses** with parts of the body.

□ He's going to wash his hair. Il va se laver les cheveux. □ He's cleaning his teeth. Il se brosse les dents. □ He's hurt his foot. Il s'est fait mal au pied.

★ **his** PRONOUN
▷ *see also* **his** ADJECTIVE
le sien *masc*
□ Is this his coat? — No, his is black. C'est son manteau? — Non, le sien est noir.
la sienne *fem*
□ Is this his car? — No, his is white. C'est sa voiture? — Non, la sienne est blanche.
les siens *masc pl*
□ my parents and his mes parents et les siens
les siennes *fem pl*
□ my shoes and his mes chaussures et les siennes
■ **Is this his?** C'est à lui?
■ **This book is his.** Ce livre est à lui.
■ **Whose is this? — It's his.** C'est à qui? — À lui.

★ **history** NOUN
l'histoire *fem*

★ to **hit** VERB
▷ *see also* **hit** NOUN
1 frapper [28]
□ Andrew hit him. Andrew l'a frappé.
2 renverser [28]
□ He was hit by a car. Il a été renversé par une voiture.
3 toucher [28]
□ The arrow hit the target. La flèche a touché la cible.

★ **hit** NOUN
▷ *see also* **hit** VERB
1 le tube *masc* (*song*)
□ Beyoncé's latest hit le dernier tube de Beyoncé
2 le succès *masc* (*success*)
□ The film was a massive hit. Le film a eu un immense succès.

hitch NOUN
le contretemps *masc*
□ There's been a slight hitch. Il y a eu un léger contretemps.

to **hitchhike** VERB
faire [36] de l'auto-stop

hitchhiker NOUN
l'auto-stoppeur *masc*
l'auto-stoppeuse *fem*

hitchhiking NOUN
l'auto-stop *masc*
□ Hitchhiking can be dangerous. Il peut être dangereux de faire de l'auto-stop.

hit man NOUN
le tueur à gages *masc*

HIV-negative ADJECTIVE
séronégatif (FEM séronégative)

HIV-positive ADJECTIVE
séropositif (FEM séropositive)

hobby NOUN
le passe-temps favori *masc*
□ What are your hobbies? Quels sont tes passe-temps favoris?

hockey NOUN
le hockey *masc*
□ I play hockey. Je joue au hockey.

★ to **hold** VERB
1 tenir [83] (*hold on to*)
□ She held the baby. Elle tenait le bébé.
2 contenir [83] (*contain*)
□ This bottle holds one litre. Cette bouteille contient un litre.
■ **to hold a meeting** avoir [8] une réunion
■ **Hold it!** (*wait*) Attends!
■ **to get hold of something** (*obtain*) trouver [28] quelque chose □ I couldn't get hold of it. Je n'ai pas réussi à en trouver.

to **hold on** VERB
1 tenir [83] bon (*keep hold*)
□ Hold on! I'll help you get down. Tiens bon! Je vais t'aider à descendre.
■ **to hold on to something** se cramponner [28] à quelque chose □ He held on to the chair. Il se cramponnait à la chaise.
2 attendre [7] (*wait*)
□ Hold on, I'm coming! Attends, je viens!
■ **Hold on!** (*on telephone*) Ne quittez pas!

to **hold up** VERB
■ **to hold up one's hand** lever [43] la main
□ Pierre held up his hand. Pierre a levé la main.
■ **to hold somebody up** (*delay*) retenir [83] quelqu'un □ I was held up at the office. J'ai été retenu au bureau.
■ **to hold up a bank** (*rob*) braquer [28] une banque (*informal*)

hold-up NOUN
1 le hold-up *masc* (*at bank*)
2 le retard *masc* (*delay*)
3 le bouchon *masc* (*traffic jam*)

★ **hole** NOUN
le trou *masc*

★ **holiday** NOUN
1 les vacances *fem pl*
▫ Did you have a good holiday? Tu as passé de bonnes vacances? ▫ our holidays in Italy nos vacances en Italie
▪ **on holiday** en vacances ▫ to go on holiday partir en vacances ▫ We are on holiday. Nous sommes en vacances.
▪ **the school holidays** les vacances scolaires
2 le jour férié *masc* (*public holiday*)
▫ Next Wednesday is a holiday. Mercredi prochain est un jour férié.
3 le jour de congé *masc* (*day off*)
▫ He took a day's holiday. Il a pris un jour de congé.
▪ **a holiday camp** un camp de vacances

holiday home NOUN
la maison de vacances *fem*

★ **Holland** NOUN
la Hollande *fem*
▪ **in Holland** en Hollande
▪ **to Holland** en Hollande

hollow ADJECTIVE
creux (FEM creuse)

holly NOUN
le houx *masc*
▫ a sprig of holly un brin de houx

★ **holy** ADJECTIVE
saint (FEM sainte)

★ **home** NOUN
▹ *see also* **home** ADVERB
la maison *fem*
▪ **at home** à la maison
▪ **Make yourself at home.** Faites comme chez vous.
▪ **My aunt's at home from 5 p.m.** Ma tante est chez elle à partir de cinq heures.

★ **home** ADVERB
▹ *see also* **home** NOUN
à la maison
▫ I'll be home at 5 o'clock. Je serai à la maison à cinq heures.
▪ **to get home** rentrer [68E] ▫ What time did he get home? Il est rentré à quelle heure?

home address NOUN
l'adresse *fem*
▫ What's your home address? Quelle est votre adresse?

homeland NOUN
la patrie *fem*

★ **homeless** ADJECTIVE
sans abri
▪ **the homeless** les sans-abri

home match NOUN
le match à domicile *masc*

homeopathy NOUN
l'homéopathie *fem*

★ **home page** NOUN
la page d'accueil *fem*

homesick ADJECTIVE
▪ **to be homesick** avoir [8] le mal du pays

★ **homework** NOUN
les devoirs *masc pl*
▫ Have you done your homework? Est-ce que tu as fait tes devoirs? ▫ my geography homework mes devoirs de géographie

homosexual ADJECTIVE
▹ *see also* **homosexual** NOUN
homosexuel (FEM homosexuelle)

homosexual NOUN
▹ *see also* **homosexual** ADJECTIVE
l'homosexuel *masc*
l'homosexuelle *fem*

★ **honest** ADJECTIVE
1 honnête (FEM honnête) (*trustworthy*)
▫ She's a very honest person. Elle est très honnête.
2 franc (FEM franche) (*sincere*)
▫ He was very honest with her. Il a été très franc avec elle.

honestly ADVERB
franchement
▫ I honestly don't know. Franchement, je n'en sais rien.

honesty NOUN
l'honnêteté *fem*

honey NOUN
le miel *masc*

honeymoon NOUN
la lune de miel *fem*

★ **honour** (US **honor**) NOUN
l'honneur *masc*

hood NOUN
1 la capuche *fem* (*on coat*)
2 le capot *masc* (US: *of car*)

★ **hook** NOUN
le crochet *masc*
▫ He hung the painting on the hook. Il a suspendu le tableau au crochet.
▪ **to take the phone off the hook** décrocher [28] le téléphone
▪ **a fish hook** un hameçon

hooligan NOUN
le voyou *masc* (PL les voyoux)

hooray EXCLAMATION
hourra!

Hoover® NOUN
l'aspirateur *masc*

to **hoover** VERB
passer [58] l'aspirateur
▫ to hoover the lounge passer l'aspirateur dans le salon

★ to **hope** VERB
▹ *see also* **hope** NOUN

espérer [34]
□ I hope he comes. J'espère qu'il va venir.
□ I'm hoping for good marks in the exam. J'espère avoir de bonnes notes à l'examen.
■ **I hope so.** Je l'espère.
■ **I hope not.** J'espère que non.

★ **hope** NOUN
▷ *see also* **hope** VERB
l'espoir *masc*
■ **to give up hope** perdre [61] espoir □ Don't give up hope! Ne perds pas espoir!

hopeful ADJECTIVE
1 plein d'espoir (FEM pleine d'espoir)
□ I'm hopeful. Je suis plein d'espoir.
■ **He's hopeful of winning.** Il a bon espoir de gagner.
2 prometteur (FEM prometteuse) (*situation*)
□ The future looks hopeful. L'avenir semble prometteur.

hopefully ADVERB
avec un peu de chance
□ Hopefully he'll make it in time. Avec un peu de chance, il arrivera à temps.

hopeless ADJECTIVE
nul (FEM nulle)
□ I'm hopeless at maths. Je suis nul en maths.

horizon NOUN
l'horizon *masc*

horizontal ADJECTIVE
horizontal (FEM horizontale, MASC PL horizontaux)

horn NOUN
1 le klaxon *masc*
□ He sounded his horn. Il a klaxonné.
2 le cor *masc*
□ I play the horn. Je joue du cor.

horoscope NOUN
l'horoscope *masc*

★ **horrible** ADJECTIVE
horrible (FEM horrible)
□ What a horrible dress! Quelle robe horrible!

horrifying ADJECTIVE
effrayant (FEM effrayante)

★ **horror** NOUN
l'horreur *fem*

horror film NOUN
le film d'horreur *masc*

★ **horse** NOUN
le cheval *masc* (PL les chevaux)

horse-racing NOUN
les courses de chevaux *fem pl*

horseshoe NOUN
le fer à cheval *masc*

hose NOUN
le tuyau *masc* (PL les tuyaux)
□ a garden hose un tuyau d'arrosage

hosepipe NOUN
le tuyau d'arrosage *masc*

★ **hospital** NOUN
l'hôpital *masc* (PL les hôpitaux)
□ Take me to the hospital! Emmenez-moi à l'hôpital! □ in hospital à l'hôpital

hospitality NOUN
l'hospitalité *fem*

host NOUN
l'hôte *masc*
l'hôtesse *fem*
□ Don't forget to thank your hosts. N'oublie pas de remercier tes hôtes.

★ **hostage** NOUN
l'otage *masc*
■ **to take somebody hostage** prendre [65] quelqu'un en otage

hostel NOUN
le foyer *masc* (*for refugees, homeless people*)
■ **a youth hostel** une auberge de jeunesse

hostile ADJECTIVE
hostile (FEM hostile)

★ **hot** ADJECTIVE
1 chaud (FEM chaude) (*warm*)
□ a hot bath un bain chaud □ a hot country un pays chaud

> When you are talking about a person being hot, you use **avoir chaud**.

□ I'm hot. J'ai chaud. □ I'm too hot. J'ai trop chaud.

> When you mean that the weather is hot, you use **faire chaud**.

□ It's hot. Il fait chaud. □ It's very hot today. Il fait très chaud aujourd'hui.
2 épicé (FEM épicée) (*spicy*)
□ a very hot curry un curry très épicé

hot dog NOUN
le hot-dog *masc*

★ **hotel** NOUN
l'hôtel *masc*
□ We stayed in a hotel. Nous avons logé à l'hôtel.

★ **hour** NOUN
l'heure *fem*
□ She always takes hours to get ready. Elle passe toujours des heures à se préparer.
■ **a quarter of an hour** un quart d'heure
■ **half an hour** une demi-heure
■ **two and a half hours** deux heures et demie

hourly ADJECTIVE, ADVERB
toutes les heures
□ There are hourly buses. Il y a des bus toutes les heures.
■ **to be paid hourly** être [35] payé à l'heure

★ **house** NOUN
la maison *fem*
□ Our house is at the end of the road. Notre maison est au bout de la rue.
■ **at his house** chez lui
■ **We stayed at their house.** Nous avons séjourné chez eux.

housewife NOUN
la femme au foyer *fem*
□ She's a housewife. Elle est femme au foyer.

housework NOUN
le ménage *masc*
■ **to do the housework** faire [36] le ménage

hovercraft NOUN
l'aéroglisseur *masc*

★ **how** ADVERB
comment
□ How are you? Comment allez-vous?
■ **How many?** Combien?
■ **How many ...?** Combien de ...? □ How many pupils are there in the class? Combien d'élèves y a-t-il dans la classe?
■ **How much?** Combien?
■ **How much ...?** Combien de ...? □ How much sugar do you want? Combien de sucres voulez-vous?
■ **How old are you?** Quel âge as-tu?
■ **How far is it to Edinburgh?** Combien y a-t-il de kilomètres d'ici à Édimbourg?
■ **How long have you been here?** Depuis combien de temps êtes-vous là?
■ **How do you say 'apple' in French?** Comment dit-on 'apple' en français?

★ **however** CONJUNCTION
pourtant
□ This, however, isn't true. Pourtant, ce n'est pas vrai.

to **howl** VERB
hurler [28]

HTML NOUN
le langage HTML *masc*
□ an HTML document un document en langage HTML

to **hug** VERB
▷ *see also* **hug** NOUN
serrer [28] dans ses bras
□ He hugged her. Il l'a serrée dans ses bras.

hug NOUN
▷ *see also* **hug** VERB
■ **to give somebody a hug** serrer [28] quelqu'un dans ses bras □ She gave them a hug. Elle les a serrés dans ses bras.

★ **huge** ADJECTIVE
immense (FEM immense)

to **hum** VERB
fredonner [28]

★ **human** ADJECTIVE
humain (FEM humaine)
□ the human body le corps humain

human being NOUN
l'être humain *masc*

humble ADJECTIVE
humble (FEM humble)

★ **humour** (US **humor**) NOUN
l'humour *masc*
■ **to have a sense of humour** avoir [8] le sens de l'humour

★ **hundred** NUMBER
■ **a hundred** cent □ a hundred euros cent euros
■ **five hundred** cinq cents
■ **five hundred and one** cinq cent un
■ **hundreds of people** des centaines de personnes

hung VERB ▷ *see* **hang**

Hungarian NOUN
▷ *see also* **Hungarian** ADJECTIVE
1 le Hongrois *masc*
la Hongroise *fem* (*person*)
2 le hongrois *masc* (*language*)

Hungarian ADJECTIVE
▷ *see also* **Hungarian** NOUN
hongrois (FEM hongroise)
□ She's Hungarian. Elle est hongroise.

Hungary NOUN
la Hongrie *fem*
■ **in Hungary** en Hongrie
■ **to Hungary** en Hongrie

hunger NOUN
la faim *fem*

hungry ADJECTIVE
■ **to be hungry** avoir [8] faim □ I'm hungry. J'ai faim.

to **hunt** VERB
1 chasser [28] (*animal*)
□ It's illegal to hunt foxes. Il est interdit de chasser le renard.
■ **to go hunting** aller [3E] à la chasse
2 pourchasser [28] (*criminal*)
□ The police are hunting the killer. La police pourchasse le criminel.
■ **to hunt for something** (*search*) chercher [28] quelque chose partout □ I hunted everywhere for that book. J'ai cherché ce livre partout.

hunting NOUN
la chasse *fem*
□ I'm against hunting. Je suis contre la chasse.
■ **fox-hunting** la chasse au renard

hurdle NOUN
l'obstacle *masc*

hurricane NOUN
l'ouragan *masc*

to **hurry** VERB
▷ *see also* **hurry** NOUN
se dépêcher [28]

English-French

h

★ = core vocabulary

□ Amber hurried back home. Amber s'est dépêchée de rentrer chez elle.
■ **Hurry up!** Dépêche-toi!

hurry NOUN
▷ *see also* **hurry** VERB
■ **to be in a hurry** être [35] pressé
■ **to do something in a hurry** faire [36] quelque chose en vitesse
■ **There's no hurry.** Rien ne presse.

★ to **hurt** VERB
▷ *see also* **hurt** ADJECTIVE
■ **to hurt somebody** **1** (*physically*) faire [36] mal à quelqu'un □ You're hurting me! Tu me fais mal! **2** (*emotionally*) blesser [28] quelqu'un □ His remarks really hurt me. Ses remarques m'ont vraiment blessé.
■ **to hurt oneself** se faire [36] mal □ I fell over and hurt myself. Je me suis fait mal en tombant.
■ **That hurts.** Ça fait mal. □ It hurts to have a tooth out. Ça fait mal de se faire arracher une dent.
■ **My leg hurts.** J'ai mal à la jambe.

★ **hurt** ADJECTIVE
▷ *see also* **hurt** VERB
blessé (FEM blessée)
□ Is he badly hurt? Est-ce qu'il est grièvement blessé? □ He was hurt in the leg. Il a été blessé à la jambe. □ I was hurt by what he said. J'ai été blessé par ce qu'il a dit.
■ **Luckily, nobody got hurt.** Heureusement, il n'y a pas eu de blessés.

★ **husband** NOUN
le mari *masc*

hut NOUN
la hutte *fem*

hybrid ADJECTIVE
hybride
□ a hybrid car une voiture hybride

hymn NOUN
le cantique *masc*

hypermarket NOUN
l'hypermarché *masc*

hyphen NOUN
le trait d'union *masc*

I i

★ **I** PRONOUN

1 je

□ I speak French. Je parle français.

je changes to j' before a vowel and most words beginning with 'h'.

j'

□ I love cats. J'aime les chats.

2 moi

□ Lily and I Lily et moi

★ **ice** NOUN

1 la glace *fem*

□ There was ice on the lake. Il y avait de la glace sur le lac.

2 le verglas *masc* (*on road*)

iceberg NOUN

l'iceberg *masc*

icebox NOUN (US)

le frigo *masc*

★ **ice cream** NOUN

la glace *fem*

□ vanilla ice cream la glace à la vanille

ice cube NOUN

le glaçon *masc*

ice hockey NOUN

le hockey sur glace *masc*

Iceland NOUN

l'Islande *fem*

■ **in Iceland** en Islande

■ **to Iceland** en Islande

ice lolly NOUN

la glace à l'eau *fem*

ice rink NOUN

la patinoire *fem*

ice-skating NOUN

le patinage sur glace *masc*

■ **to go ice-skating** faire [36] du patin à glace

icing NOUN

le glaçage *masc* (*on cake*)

■ **icing sugar** le sucre glace

icon NOUN

l'icône *fem*

ICT NOUN

l'informatique *fem*

icy ADJECTIVE

glacial (FEM glaciale, MASC PL glaciaux)

□ There was an icy wind. Il y avait un vent glacial.

■ **The roads are icy.** Il y a du verglas sur les routes.

I'd = **I had, I would**

★ **idea** NOUN

l'idée *fem*

□ Good idea! Bonne idée!

★ **ideal** ADJECTIVE

idéal (FEM idéale, MASC PL idéaux)

identical ADJECTIVE

identique (FEM identique)

identification NOUN

l'identification *fem*

★ to **identify** VERB

identifier [19]

identity card NOUN

la carte d'identité *fem*

idiot NOUN

l'idiot *masc*

l'idiote *fem*

idiotic ADJECTIVE

stupide (FEM stupide)

idle ADJECTIVE

fainéant (FEM fainéante) (*lazy*)

i.e. ABBREVIATION

c.-à-d. (= *c'est-à-dire*)

★ **if** CONJUNCTION

si

□ You can have it if you like. Tu peux le prendre si tu veux.

s'

si changes to s' before il and ils.

□ Do you know if he's there? Savez-vous s'il est là?

■ **if only** si seulement □ If only I had more money! Si seulement j'avais plus d'argent!

■ **if not** sinon □ Are you coming? If not, I'll go with Zhu. Est-ce que tu viens? Sinon, j'irai avec Zhu.

ignorant ADJECTIVE

ignorant (FEM ignorante)

★ to **ignore** VERB

■ **to ignore something** ne tenir [83] aucun compte de quelque chose □ She ignored my advice. Elle n'a tenu aucun compte de mes conseils.

■ **to ignore somebody** ignorer [28] quelqu'un □ She saw me, but she ignored me. Elle m'a vu, mais elle m'a ignoré.
■ **Just ignore him!** Ne fais pas attention à lui!

★ **ill** ADJECTIVE
malade (FEM malade) (*sick*)
■ **to be taken ill** tomber [84E] malade □ She was taken ill while on holiday. Elle est tombée malade pendant qu'elle était en vacances.

I'll = I will

★ **illegal** ADJECTIVE
illégal (FEM illégale, MASC PL illégaux)

illegible ADJECTIVE
illisible (FEM illisible)

★ **illness** NOUN
la maladie *fem*

to **ill-treat** VERB
maltraiter [28]

illusion NOUN
l'illusion *fem*

★ **illustration** NOUN
l'illustration *fem*

★ **image** NOUN
l'image *fem*
□ She wants to change her image. Elle veut changer son image.

★ **imagination** NOUN
l'imagination *fem*

★ to **imagine** VERB
imaginer [28]
□ You can imagine how I felt! Tu peux imaginer ce que j'ai ressenti! □ Is he angry? — I imagine so. Est-ce qu'il est en colère? — J'imagine que oui.

to **imitate** VERB
imiter [28]

imitation NOUN
l'imitation *fem*

★ **immediate** ADJECTIVE
immédiat (FEM immédiate)

★ **immediately** ADVERB
immédiatement
□ I'll do it immediately. Je vais le faire immédiatement.

★ **immigrant** NOUN
l'immigré *masc*
l'immigrée *fem*

immigration NOUN
l'immigration *fem*

immoral ADJECTIVE
immoral (FEM immorale, MASC PL immoraux)

impartial ADJECTIVE
impartial (FEM impartiale, MASC PL impartiaux)

impatience NOUN
l'impatience *fem*

impatient ADJECTIVE
impatient (FEM impatiente)
■ **to get impatient** s'impatienter [28]
□ People are getting impatient. Les gens commencent à s'impatienter.

impatiently ADVERB
avec impatience
□ We waited impatiently. Nous avons attendu avec impatience.

impersonal ADJECTIVE
impersonnel (FEM impersonnelle)

★ **importance** NOUN
l'importance *fem*

★ **important** ADJECTIVE
important (FEM importante)

★ **impossible** ADJECTIVE
impossible (FEM impossible)

to **impress** VERB
impressionner [28]
□ She's trying to impress you. Elle essaie de t'impressionner.

impressed ADJECTIVE
impressionné (FEM impressionnée)
□ I'm very impressed! Je suis très impressionné!

impression NOUN
l'impression *fem*
□ I was under the impression that ... J'avais l'impression que ...

impressive ADJECTIVE
impressionnant (FEM impressionnante)

★ to **improve** VERB
1 améliorer [28] (*make better*)
□ They have improved the sports facilities. Ils ont amélioré les installations sportives.
2 s'améliorer [28] (*get better*)
□ The weather is improving. Le temps s'améliore. □ My French has improved. Mon français s'est amélioré.

★ **improvement** NOUN
1 l'amélioration *fem* (*of condition*)
□ It's a great improvement. C'est une nette amélioration.
2 le progrès *masc* (*of learner*)
□ There's been an improvement in his physics. Il a fait des progrès en physique.

★ **in** PREPOSITION, ADVERB

> There are several ways of translating 'in'. Scan the examples to find one that is similar to what you want to say. For other expressions with 'in', see the verbs 'go', 'come', 'get', 'give' etc.

1 dans
□ in the house dans la maison □ in my bag dans mon sac □ in the sixties dans les années

soixante □ I'll see you in three weeks. Je te verrai dans trois semaines.

2 à

□ in the country à la campagne □ in school à l'école □ in hospital à l'hôpital □ in Cardiff à Cardiff □ in spring au printemps □ in the sun au soleil □ in the shade à l'ombre □ in a loud voice à voix haute □ the boy in the blue shirt le garçon à la chemise bleue □ It was written in pencil. C'était écrit au crayon.

3 en

□ in French en français □ in summer en été □ in May en mai □ in 2019 en deux mille dix-neuf □ I did it in three hours. Je l'ai fait en trois heures. □ in town en ville □ in prison en prison □ in tears en larmes □ in good condition en bon état

When 'in' refers to a country which is feminine, use **en**; when the country is masculine, use **au**; when the country is plural, use **aux**.

□ in France en France □ in Portugal au Portugal □ in the United States aux États-Unis

4 de

□ the best pupil in the class le meilleur élève de la classe □ the best team in the world la meilleure équipe du monde □ the tallest person in the family le plus grand de la famille □ at 4 o'clock in the afternoon à quatre heures de l'après-midi □ at 6 in the morning à six heures du matin

■ **in the afternoon** l'après-midi

■ **You look good in that dress.** Tu es jolie avec cette robe.

■ **in time** à temps □ We arrived in time for dinner. Nous sommes arrivés à temps pour le dîner.

■ **in here** ici □ It's hot in here. Il fait chaud ici.

■ **in the rain** sous la pluie

■ **one person in ten** une personne sur dix

■ **to be in** (*at home, work*) être [35] là □ He wasn't in. Il n'était pas là.

■ **to ask somebody in** inviter [28] quelqu'un à entrer

inaccurate ADJECTIVE

inexact (FEM inexacte)

inadequate ADJECTIVE

inadéquat (FEM inadéquate) (*measures, resources*)

■ **I felt completely inadequate.** Je ne me sentais absolument pas à la hauteur.

inbox NOUN

la boîte de réception *fem*

incentive NOUN

■ **There is no incentive to work.** Il n'y a rien qui incite à travailler.

★ **inch** NOUN

le pouce *masc*

DID YOU KNOW...?

In France, measurements are in metres and centimetres rather than feet and inches. An inch is about 2.5 centimetres.

■ **6 inches** quinze centimètres

★ **incident** NOUN

l'incident *masc*

inclined ADJECTIVE

■ **to be inclined to do something** avoir [8] tendance à faire quelque chose □ He's inclined to be lazy. Il a tendance à être paresseux. □ I'm inclined to agree. J'aurais tendance à être d'accord.

★ to **include** VERB

comprendre [65]

□ Service is not included. Le service n'est pas compris.

★ **including** PREPOSITION

compris

□ It will be 200 euros, including tax. Ça coûtera deux cents euros, toutes taxes comprises.

inclusive ADJECTIVE

inclus (FEM incluse)

□ from Monday to Thursday inclusive de lundi à jeudi inclus

■ **inclusive of tax** taxes comprises

income NOUN

le revenu *masc*

income tax NOUN

l'impôt sur le revenu *masc*

incompetent ADJECTIVE

incompétent (FEM incompétente)

incomplete ADJECTIVE

incomplet (FEM incomplète)

inconsistent ADJECTIVE

incohérent (FEM incohérente)

inconvenience NOUN

■ **I don't want to cause any inconvenience.** Je ne veux pas vous déranger.

inconvenient ADJECTIVE

■ **That's very inconvenient for me.** Ça ne m'arrange pas du tout.

incorrect ADJECTIVE

incorrect (FEM incorrecte)

★ **increase** NOUN

▷ *see also* **increase** VERB

l'augmentation *fem*

□ an increase in road accidents une augmentation des accidents de la route

★ to **increase** VERB

▷ *see also* **increase** NOUN

augmenter [28]

★ **incredible** ADJECTIVE

incroyable (FEM incroyable)

indecisive ADJECTIVE

indécis (FEM indécise) (*person*)

★ **indeed** ADVERB
vraiment
□ It's very hard indeed. C'est vraiment très difficile.
■ **Know what I mean? — Indeed I do.** Tu vois ce que je veux dire? — Oui, tout à fait.
■ **Thank you very much indeed!** Merci beaucoup!

★ **independence** NOUN
l'indépendance *fem*

★ **independent** ADJECTIVE
indépendant (FEM indépendante)
■ **an independent school** une école privée

★ **index** NOUN
l'index *masc* (*in book*)

index finger NOUN
l'index *masc*

★ **India** NOUN
l'Inde *fem*
■ **in India** en Inde
■ **to India** en Inde

Indian NOUN
▷ *see also* **Indian** ADJECTIVE
l'Indien *masc*
l'Indienne *fem* (*person*)
■ **an American Indian** un Indien d'Amérique

Indian ADJECTIVE
▷ *see also* **Indian** NOUN
indien (FEM indienne)

★ to **indicate** VERB
indiquer [28]

indicator NOUN
le clignotant *masc* (*on car*)
□ Put your indicator on. Mets ton clignotant.

indigestion NOUN
l'indigestion *fem*
■ **I've got indigestion.** J'ai une indigestion.

★ **individual** ADJECTIVE
individuel (FEM individuelle)

indoor ADJECTIVE
■ **an indoor swimming pool** une piscine couverte

indoors ADVERB
à l'intérieur
□ They're indoors. Ils sont à l'intérieur.
■ **to go indoors** rentrer [68E] □ We'd better go indoors. Nous ferions mieux de rentrer.

industrial ADJECTIVE
industriel (FEM industrielle)

industrial estate NOUN
la zone industrielle *fem*

industry NOUN
l'industrie *fem*
□ the tourist industry l'industrie du tourisme
□ the oil industry l'industrie pétrolière □ I'd like to work in industry. J'aimerais travailler dans l'industrie.

inefficient ADJECTIVE
inefficace (FEM inefficace)

inevitable ADJECTIVE
inévitable (FEM inévitable)

inexpensive ADJECTIVE
bon marché (FEM+PL bon marché)
□ an inexpensive hotel un hôtel bon marché
□ inexpensive holidays des vacances bon marché

inexperienced ADJECTIVE
inexpérimenté (FEM inexpérimentée)

infant school NOUN
■ **He's just started at infant school.** Il vient d'entrer au cours préparatoire.

DID YOU KNOW...?
CP (cours préparatoire) is the equivalent of first-year infants, and **CE1 (cours élémentaire première année)** the equivalent of second-year infants.

★ **infection** NOUN
l'infection *fem*
□ an ear infection une infection de l'oreille
■ **a throat infection** une angine

infectious ADJECTIVE
contagieux (FEM contagieuse)
□ It's not infectious. Ce n'est pas contagieux.

infinitive NOUN
l'infinitif *masc*

infirmary NOUN
l'hôpital *masc* (PL les hôpitaux)

inflatable ADJECTIVE
gonflable (FEM gonflable) (*mattress, dinghy*)

★ **inflation** NOUN
l'inflation *fem*

influence NOUN
▷ *see also* **influence** VERB
l'influence *fem*
□ He's a bad influence on her. Il a mauvaise influence sur elle.

to **influence** VERB
▷ *see also* **influence** NOUN
influencer [12]

influenza NOUN
la grippe *fem*

★ to **inform** VERB
informer [28]
■ **to inform somebody of something** informer [28] quelqu'un de quelque chose
□ Nobody informed me that the class had been cancelled. Personne ne m'a informé de l'annulation du cours.

informal ADJECTIVE
1 décontracté (FEM décontractée) (*person, party*)
2 familier (FEM familière) (*colloquial*)
□ informal language le langage familier
■ **an informal visit** une visite non officielle

★ **information** NOUN
les renseignements *masc pl*
□ important information les renseignements importants
■ **a piece of information** un renseignement
■ **Could you give me some information about trains to Paris?** Pourriez-vous me renseigner sur les trains pour Paris?

information office NOUN
le bureau des renseignements *masc* (PL les bureaux des renseignements)

information technology NOUN
l'informatique *fem*

infuriating ADJECTIVE
exaspérant (FEM exaspérante)

ingenious ADJECTIVE
ingénieux (FEM ingénieuse)

★ **ingredient** NOUN
l'ingrédient *masc*

inhabitant NOUN
l'habitant *masc*
l'habitante *fem*

inhaler NOUN
l'inhalateur
□ I mustn't forget my inhaler. Il ne faut pas que j'oublie mon inhalateur.

to **inherit** VERB
hériter [28] de
□ She inherited her father's house. Elle a hérité de la maison de son père.

initials PL NOUN
les initiales *fem pl*
□ Her initials are CDT. Ses initiales sont CDT.

initiative NOUN
l'initiative *fem*

to **inject** VERB
injecter [28] (*drug*)

injection NOUN
la piqûre *fem*

to **injure** VERB
blesser [28]

★ **injured** ADJECTIVE
blessé (FEM blessée)

★ **injury** NOUN
la blessure *fem*

> **BE CAREFUL!**
> Do not translate **injury** by the French word **injure**.

injury time NOUN
les arrêts de jeu *masc pl*

injustice NOUN
l'injustice *fem*

ink NOUN
l'encre *fem*

in-laws PL NOUN
les beaux-parents *masc pl*

inn NOUN
l'auberge *fem*

inner ADJECTIVE
intérieur (FEM intérieure)
■ **the inner city** les quartiers déshérités du centre ville

inner tube NOUN
la chambre à air *fem*

★ **innocent** ADJECTIVE
innocent (FEM innocente)

inquest NOUN
l'enquête *fem*

to **inquire** VERB
■ **to inquire about something** se renseigner [28] sur quelque chose □ I'm going to inquire about train times. Je vais me renseigner sur les horaires des trains.

inquiries office NOUN
le bureau des renseignements *masc* (PL les bureaux des renseignements)

★ **inquiry** NOUN
■ **to make inquiries about something** faire [36] des demandes de renseignement
□ 'inquiries' 'renseignements'

inquisitive ADJECTIVE
curieux (FEM curieuse)

insane ADJECTIVE
fou (FEM folle)

> **fou** changes to **fol** before a vowel and most words beginning with 'h'.

inscription NOUN
l'inscription *fem*

insect NOUN
l'insecte *masc*

insect repellent NOUN
l'insectifuge *masc*

insensitive ADJECTIVE
indélicat (FEM indélicate)
□ That was a bit insensitive of you. C'était un peu indélicat de ta part.

★ **inside** NOUN
▷ *see also* **inside** ADVERB, PREPOSITION
l'intérieur *masc*

★ **inside** ADVERB, PREPOSITION
▷ *see also* **inside** NOUN
à l'intérieur
□ They're inside. Ils sont à l'intérieur. □ inside the house à l'intérieur de la maison
■ **to go inside** rentrer [68E]
■ **Come inside!** Rentrez!

insincere ADJECTIVE
peu sincère (FEM peu sincère)

★ to **insist** VERB
insister [28]
□ I didn't want to, but he insisted. Je ne voulais pas, mais il a insisté.
■ **to insist on doing something** insister [28]

pour faire quelque chose □ She insisted on paying. Elle a insisté pour payer.
■ **He insisted he was innocent.** Il affirmait qu'il était innocent.

★ **inspector** NOUN
l'inspecteur *masc* (*police*)
□ Inspector Jill Brown l'inspecteur Jill Brown
■ **ticket inspector** le contrôleur (*on trains*)

instalment NOUN
1 le versement *masc* (*payment*)
□ to pay in instalments payer en plusieurs versements
2 l'épisode *masc* (*episode*)

★ **instance** NOUN
■ **for instance** par exemple

★ **instant** ADJECTIVE
immédiat (FEM immédiate)
□ It was an instant success. Ça a été un succès immédiat.
■ **instant coffee** le café instantané

instantly ADVERB
tout de suite

★ **instead** ADVERB
■ **instead of 1** (*followed by noun*) à la place de □ He went instead of Finn. Il y est allé à la place de Finn. **2** (*followed by verb*) au lieu de □ We played tennis instead of going swimming. Nous avons joué au tennis au lieu d'aller nager.
■ **The pool was closed, so we played tennis instead.** La piscine était fermée, alors nous avons joué au tennis.

instinct NOUN
l'instinct *masc*

★ **institute** NOUN
l'institut *masc*

★ **institution** NOUN
l'institution *fem*

to **instruct** VERB
■ **to instruct somebody to do something** donner [28] l'ordre à quelqu'un de faire quelque chose □ She instructed us to wait outside. Elle nous a donné l'ordre d'attendre dehors.

★ **instructions** PL NOUN
1 les instructions *fem pl*
□ Follow the instructions carefully. Suivez soigneusement les instructions.
2 le mode d'emploi *masc sing* (*booklet*)
□ Where are the instructions? Où est le mode d'emploi?

instructor NOUN
le moniteur *masc*
la monitrice *fem*
□ a skiing instructor un moniteur de ski □ a driving instructor un moniteur d'auto-école

★ **instrument** NOUN
l'instrument *masc*
□ Do you play an instrument? Est-ce que tu joues d'un instrument?

insufficient ADJECTIVE
insuffisant (FEM insuffisante)

insulin NOUN
l'insuline *fem*

insult NOUN
▷ *see also* **insult** VERB
l'insulte *fem*

to **insult** VERB
▷ *see also* **insult** NOUN
insulter [28]

★ **insurance** NOUN
l'assurance *fem*
□ his car insurance son assurance automobile
■ **an insurance policy** une police d'assurance

★ **intelligent** ADJECTIVE
intelligent (FEM intelligente)

★ to **intend** VERB
■ **to intend to do something** avoir [8] l'intention de faire quelque chose □ I intend to do geography at university. J'ai l'intention d'étudier la géographie à l'université.

★ **intense** ADJECTIVE
intense (FEM intense)

intensive ADJECTIVE
intensif (FEM intensive)

intention NOUN
l'intention *fem*

intercom NOUN
l'interphone *masc*

★ **interest** NOUN
▷ *see also* **interest** VERB
l'intérêt *masc*
□ to show an interest in something manifester de l'intérêt pour quelque chose
■ **What interests do you have?** Quels sont tes centres d'intérêt?
■ **My main interest is music.** Ce qui m'intéresse le plus c'est la musique.

★ to **interest** VERB
▷ *see also* **interest** NOUN
intéresser [28]
□ It doesn't interest me. Ça ne m'intéresse pas.
■ **to be interested in something** s'intéresser [28] à quelque chose □ I'm not interested in politics. Je ne m'intéresse pas à la politique.

★ **interesting** ADJECTIVE
intéressant (FEM intéressante)

interior NOUN
l'intérieur *masc*

interior designer NOUN
l'architecte d'intérieur *masc/fem*

intermediate ADJECTIVE
moyen (FEM moyenne) (*course, level*)

internal ADJECTIVE
interne (FEM interne)

★**international** ADJECTIVE
international (FEM internationale, MASC PL internationaux)

★**internet** NOUN
l'Internet *masc*
□ on the internet sur Internet

internet user NOUN
l'internaute *masc/fem*

to **interpret** VERB
faire [36] l'interprète
□ Jack interpreted into English for his friend. Jack a fait l'interprète en anglais pour son ami.

interpreter NOUN
l'interprète *masc/fem*

to **interrupt** VERB
interrompre [75]

interruption NOUN
l'interruption *fem*

interval NOUN
l'entracte *masc* (*in play, concert*)

★**interview** NOUN
▷ *see also* **interview** VERB
1 l'interview *fem* (*on TV, radio*)
2 l'entretien *masc* (*for job*)

★to **interview** VERB
▷ *see also* **interview** NOUN
interviewer [28] (*on TV, radio*)
□ I was interviewed on the radio. J'ai été interviewé à la radio.

interviewer NOUN
l'interviewer *masc* (*on TV, radio*)

intimate ADJECTIVE
intime (FEM intime)

★**into** PREPOSITION
1 dans
□ He got into the car. Il est monté dans la voiture.
2 en
□ I'm going into town. Je vais en ville.
□ Translate it into French. Traduisez ça en français. □ Divide into two groups. Répartissez-vous en deux groupes.

★to **introduce** VERB
présenter [28]
□ I'd like to introduce Michelle Davies. Je vous présente Michelle Davies. □ He introduced me to his parents. Il m'a présenté à ses parents.

introduction NOUN
l'introduction *fem* (*in book*)

intruder NOUN
l'intrus *masc*
l'intruse *fem*

intuition NOUN
l'intuition *fem*

to **invade** VERB
envahir [38]

invalid NOUN
le/la malade *masc/fem*

to **invent** VERB
inventer [28]

invention NOUN
l'invention *fem*

inventor NOUN
l'inventeur *masc*
l'inventrice *fem*

investigation NOUN
l'enquête *fem* (*police*)

investment NOUN
l'investissement *masc*
□ They bought the house as an investment. Ils ont acheté la maison comme investissement.

invigilator NOUN
le surveillant *masc*
la surveillante *fem*

invisible ADJECTIVE
invisible (FEM invisible)

★**invitation** NOUN
l'invitation *fem*

★to **invite** VERB
inviter [28]
□ He's not invited. Il n'est pas invité. □ To invite somebody to a party. Inviter quelqu'un à une fête.

★to **involve** VERB
nécessiter [28]
□ His job involves a lot of travelling. Son travail nécessite de nombreux déplacements.
■ **to be involved in something** (*crime*) être [35] impliqué dans quelque chose
■ **to be involved with somebody** (*in relationship*) avoir [8] une relation avec quelqu'un

iPad® NOUN
l'iPad® *masc*

iPhone® NOUN
l'iPhone® *masc*

iPod® NOUN
l'iPod® *masc*

IQ NOUN (= *intelligence quotient*)
le Q.I. *masc* (= *quotient intellectuel*)

Iran NOUN
l'Iran *masc*
■ **in Iran** en Iran

Iranian NOUN
▷ *see also* **Iranian** ADJECTIVE
l'Iranien *masc*
l'Iranienne *fem*

★ = core vocabulary

■ **the Iranians** les Iraniens

Iranian ADJECTIVE
▷ *see also* **Iranian** NOUN
iranien (FEM iranienne)

Iraq NOUN
l'Irak *masc*
■ **in Iraq** en Irak

Iraqi NOUN
▷ *see also* **Iraqi** ADJECTIVE
l'Irakien *masc*
l'Irakienne *fem*

Iraqi ADJECTIVE
▷ *see also* **Iraqi** NOUN
irakien (FEM irakienne)

★ **Ireland** NOUN
l'Irlande *fem*
■ **in Ireland** en Irlande
■ **to Ireland** en Irlande
■ **I'm from Ireland.** Je suis irlandais.

★ **Irish** NOUN
▷ *see also* **Irish** ADJECTIVE
l'irlandais *masc* (*language*)
■ **the Irish** (*people*) les Irlandais

★ **Irish** ADJECTIVE
▷ *see also* **Irish** NOUN
irlandais (FEM irlandaise)
□ Irish music la musique irlandaise

★ **Irishman** NOUN
l'Irlandais *masc*

★ **Irishwoman** NOUN
l'Irlandaise *fem*

★ **iron** NOUN
▷ *see also* **iron** VERB
1 le fer *masc* (*metal*)
2 le fer à repasser *masc* (*for clothes*)

★ to **iron** VERB
▷ *see also* **iron** NOUN
repasser [28]

ironic ADJECTIVE
ironique (FEM ironique)

ironing NOUN
le repassage *masc*
□ to do the ironing faire le repassage

ironing board NOUN
la planche à repasser *fem*

ironmonger's NOUN
la quincaillerie *fem*

ironmonger's shop NOUN
la quincaillerie *fem*

irrelevant ADJECTIVE
hors de propos
□ That's irrelevant. C'est hors de propos.

irresponsible ADJECTIVE
irresponsable (FEM irresponsable)
□ That was irresponsible of him. C'était irresponsable de sa part.

irritating ADJECTIVE
irritant (FEM irritante)

is VERB ▷ *see* **be**

Islam NOUN
l'Islam *masc*

Islamic ADJECTIVE
islamique (FEM islamique)
□ Islamic law la loi islamique
■ **Islamic fundamentalists** les intégristes musulmans

★ **island** NOUN
l'île *fem*

isle NOUN
■ **the Isle of Man** l'île de Man *fem*
■ **the Isle of Wight** l'île de Wight *fem*

isolated ADJECTIVE
isolé (FEM isolée)

ISP NOUN (= *internet service provider*)
le fournisseur d'accès à Internet *masc*

Israel NOUN
Israël *masc*
■ **in Israel** en Israël

Israeli ADJECTIVE
▷ *see also* **Israeli** NOUN
israélien (FEM israélienne)

Israeli NOUN
▷ *see also* **Israeli** ADJECTIVE
l'Israélien *masc*
l'Israélienne *fem*

issue NOUN
▷ *see also* **issue** VERB
1 la question *fem* (*matter*)
□ a controversial issue une question controversée
2 le numéro *masc* (*of magazine*)

to **issue** VERB
▷ *see also* **issue** NOUN
distribuer [28] (*equipment, supplies*)

★ **it** PRONOUN

Remember to check if 'it' stands for a masculine or feminine noun.

1 il
□ Where's my book? — It's on the table. Où est mon livre? — Il est sur la table.
elle
□ When does the library close? — It closes at 8. La bibliothèque ferme à quelle heure? — Elle ferme à vingt heures.

Use **le** or **la** when 'it' is the object of the sentence. **le** and **la** change to **l'** before a vowel and most words beginning with 'h'.

2 le
□ There's a croissant left. Do you want it? Il reste un croissant. Tu le veux?
la

□ I don't want this apple. Take it. Je ne veux pas de cette pomme. Prends-la.
l'
□ It's a good film. Did you see it? C'est un bon film. L'as-tu vu? □ He's got a new car. — Yes, I saw it. Il a une nouvelle voiture. — Oui, je l'ai vue.
■ **It's raining.** Il pleut.
■ **It's 6 o'clock.** Il est six heures.
■ **It's Friday tomorrow.** Demain c'est vendredi.
■ **Who is it? — It's me.** Qui est-ce? — C'est moi.
■ **It's expensive.** C'est cher.

Italian NOUN
▷ *see also* **Italian** ADJECTIVE
1 l'Italien *masc*
l'Italienne *fem* (*person*)
2 l'italien *masc* (*language*)

Italian ADJECTIVE
▷ *see also* **Italian** NOUN
italien (FEM italienne)

★ **Italy** NOUN
l'Italie *fem*
■ **in Italy** en Italie
■ **to Italy** en Italie

to **itch** VERB
■ **It itches.** Ça me démange.
■ **My head's itching.** J'ai des démangeaisons à la tête.

itchy ADJECTIVE
■ **My arm is itchy.** J'ai des fourmis dans le bras.

it'd = **it had, it would**

★ **item** NOUN
l'article *masc* (*object*)

itinerary NOUN
l'itinéraire *masc*

it'll = **it will**

★ **its** ADJECTIVE

Remember to check if 'its' refers to a masculine, feminine or plural noun.

son *masc*
□ What's its name? Quel est son nom?
sa *fem*
□ Every thing in its place. Chaque chose à sa place.
ses *pl*
□ The dog is losing its hair. Le chien perd ses poils.

it's = **it is, it has**

★ **itself** PRONOUN
se

se changes to **s'** before a vowel and most words beginning with 'h'.

s'
□ The heating switches itself off. Le chauffage s'arrête automatiquement.

I've = **I have**

Jj

jab NOUN
la piqûre *fem* (*injection*)

jack NOUN
1 le cric *masc* (*for car*)
2 le valet *masc* (*playing card*)

★**jacket** NOUN
la veste *fem*
▪ **jacket potatoes** les pommes de terre en robe des champs

jackpot NOUN
le gros lot *masc*
□ to win the jackpot gagner le gros lot

★**jail** NOUN
▷ *see also* **jail** VERB
la prison *fem*
▪ **to go to jail** aller [3E] en prison

★to **jail** VERB
▷ *see also* **jail** NOUN
emprisonner [28]

jam NOUN
la confiture *fem*
□ strawberry jam la confiture de fraises
▪ **a traffic jam** un embouteillage

jam jar NOUN
le pot à confiture *masc*

jammed ADJECTIVE
coincé (FEM coincée)
□ The window's jammed. La fenêtre est coincée.

jam-packed ADJECTIVE
bondé (FEM bondée)
□ The shopping centre was jam-packed. Le centre commercial était bondé.

janitor NOUN
le/la concierge *masc/fem*
□ He's a janitor. Il est concierge.

★**January** NOUN
janvier *masc*
▪ **in January** en janvier

★**Japan** NOUN
le Japon *masc*
▪ **in Japan** au Japon
▪ **from Japan** du Japon

Japanese NOUN
▷ *see also* **Japanese** ADJECTIVE
1 le Japonais *masc*
la Japonaise *fem* (*person*)
▪ **the Japanese** les Japonais
2 le japonais *masc* (*language*)

Japanese ADJECTIVE
▷ *see also* **Japanese** NOUN
japonais (FEM japonaise)

jar NOUN
le bocal *masc* (PL les bocaux)
□ an empty jar un bocal vide
▪ **a jar of honey** un pot de miel

jaundice NOUN
la jaunisse *fem*

javelin NOUN
le javelot *masc*

jaw NOUN
la mâchoire *fem*

★**jazz** NOUN
le jazz *masc*

★**jealous** ADJECTIVE
jaloux (FEM jalouse)

★**jeans** PL NOUN
le jean *masc sing*

Jehovah's Witness NOUN
le témoin de Jéhovah *masc*
□ She's a Jehovah's Witness. Elle est témoin de Jéhovah.

Jello® NOUN (US)
la gelée *fem*

jelly NOUN
la gelée *fem*

jellyfish NOUN
la méduse *fem*

★**jersey** NOUN
le pull-over *masc* (*pullover*)

Jesus NOUN
Jésus *masc*

jet NOUN
le jet *masc* (*plane*)

jetlag NOUN
▪ **to be suffering from jetlag** être [35] sous le coup du décalage horaire

jetty NOUN
la jetée *fem*

Jew NOUN
le Juif *masc*
la Juive *fem*

jewel NOUN
le bijou *masc* (PL les bijoux)

jeweller (US **jeweler**) NOUN
le bijoutier *masc*
la bijoutière *fem*
□ He's a jeweller. Il est bijoutier.

jeweller's shop (US **jeweler's shop**) NOUN
la bijouterie *fem*

jewellery (US **jewelry**) NOUN
les bijoux *masc pl*

Jewish ADJECTIVE
juif (FEM juive)

jigsaw NOUN
le puzzle *masc*

★**job** NOUN
1 l'emploi *masc*
□ He's lost his job. Il a perdu son emploi.
■ **I've got a Saturday job.** Je travaille le samedi.
2 le travail *masc* (PL les travaux) (*chore, task*)
□ That was a difficult job. C'était un travail difficile.

job centre NOUN
l'agence pour l'emploi *fem*

jobless ADJECTIVE
sans emploi

jockey NOUN
le jockey *masc*

to **jog** VERB
faire [36] du jogging

jogging NOUN
le jogging *masc*
■ **to go jogging** faire [36] du jogging

john NOUN (US)
les toilettes *fem pl*

★to **join** VERB
1 s'inscrire [30] à (*become member of*)
□ I'm going to join the ski club. Je vais m'inscrire au club de ski.
2 se joindre [42] à
□ Do you mind if I join you? Puis-je me joindre à vous?

joiner NOUN
le menuisier *masc*
□ He's a joiner. Il est menuisier.

★**joint** NOUN
1 l'articulation *fem* (*in body*)
2 le rôti *masc* (*of meat*)

★**joke** NOUN
▷ *see also* **joke** VERB
la plaisanterie *fem*
□ to tell a joke raconter une plaisanterie

★to **joke** VERB
▷ *see also* **joke** NOUN
plaisanter [28]
□ I'm only joking. Je plaisante.

jolly ADJECTIVE
jovial (FEM joviale, MASC PL joviaux)

Jordan NOUN
la Jordanie *fem* (*country*)
■ **in Jordan** en Jordanie

to **jot down** VERB
noter [28]

jotter NOUN
le bloc-notes *masc* (PL les blocs-notes) (*pad*)

journalism NOUN
le journalisme *masc*

★**journalist** NOUN
le/la journaliste *masc/fem*
□ She's a journalist. Elle est journaliste.

★**journey** NOUN
1 le voyage *masc*
□ I don't like long journeys. Je n'aime pas les longs voyages.
■ **to go on a journey** faire [36] un voyage
2 le trajet *masc* (*to school, work*)
□ The journey to school takes about half an hour. Il y a une demi-heure de trajet pour aller à l'école.
■ **a bus journey** un trajet en autobus

★**joy** NOUN
la joie *fem*

joystick NOUN
la manette de jeu *fem* (*for computer game*)

★**judge** NOUN
▷ *see also* **judge** VERB
le juge *masc*
□ She's a judge. Elle est juge.

★to **judge** VERB
▷ *see also* **judge** NOUN
juger [45]

judo NOUN
le judo *masc*
□ My hobby is judo. Je fais du judo.

jug NOUN
le pot *masc*

juggler NOUN
le jongleur *masc*
la jongleuse *fem*

★**juice** NOUN
le jus *masc*
□ orange juice le jus d'orange

★**July** NOUN
juillet *masc*
■ **in July** en juillet

DID YOU KNOW...?
The fourteenth of July (**la fête nationale**) is the French national holiday. There's a firework display and military parade in Paris.

jumble sale NOUN
la vente de charité *fem*

★ to **jump** VERB
sauter [28]
□ to jump over something sauter par-dessus quelque chose □ to jump out of the window sauter par la fenêtre □ to jump off the roof sauter du toit

★ **jumper** NOUN
le pull-over *masc* (*pullover*)

junction NOUN
le carrefour *masc* (*of roads*)

★ **June** NOUN
juin *masc*
■ **in June** en juin

jungle NOUN
la jungle *fem*

junior NOUN
■ **the juniors** (*in school*) les élèves des petites classes

junior school NOUN
l'école primaire *fem*

junk NOUN
le bric-à-brac *masc* (*old things*)
□ The attic's full of junk. Le grenier est rempli de bric-à-brac.
■ **You eat too much junk food.** Tu manges trop de cochonneries.
■ **a junk shop** un magasin de brocante

★ **jury** NOUN
le jury *masc*

★ **just** ADVERB
juste
□ just after Christmas juste après Noël □ We had just enough money. Nous avions juste assez d'argent. □ just in time juste à temps
■ **just here** ici
■ **I'm rather busy just now.** Je suis assez occupé en ce moment.
■ **I did it just now.** Je viens de le faire.
■ **He's just arrived.** Il vient d'arriver.
■ **I'm just coming!** J'arrive!
■ **It's just a suggestion.** Ce n'est qu'une suggestion.

★ **justice** NOUN
la justice *fem*

★ to **justify** VERB
justifier [19]

Kk

kangaroo NOUN
le kangourou *masc*

karaoke NOUN
le karaoké *masc*

karate NOUN
le karaté *masc*

kebab NOUN
1 la brochette *fem* (*shish kebab*)
2 le doner kebab *masc* (*doner kebab*)

★ **keen** ADJECTIVE
enthousiaste (FEM enthousiaste)
◻ He doesn't seem very keen. Il n'a pas l'air très enthousiaste.
■ **She's a keen student.** C'est une étudiante assidue.
■ **to be keen on something** aimer [28] quelque chose ◻ I'm keen on maths. J'aime les maths. ◻ I'm not very keen on maths. Je n'aime pas trop les maths.
■ **to be keen on somebody** (*fancy them*) être [35] très attiré par quelqu'un ◻ He's keen on her. Il est très attiré par elle.
■ **to be keen on doing something** avoir [8] très envie de faire quelque chose ◻ I'm not very keen on going. Je n'ai pas très envie d'y aller.

★ to **keep** VERB
1 garder [28] (*retain*)
◻ You can keep it. Tu peux le garder.
2 rester [71E] (*remain*)
◻ Keep still! Reste tranquille!
■ **Keep quiet!** Tais-toi!
■ **I keep forgetting my keys.** J'oublie tout le temps mes clés.

to **keep on** VERB
■ **to keep on doing something** **1** (*continue*) continuer [28] à faire quelque chose ◻ He kept on reading. Il a continué à lire.
2 (*repeatedly*) ne pas arrêter [28] de faire quelque chose ◻ The car keeps on breaking down. La voiture n'arrête pas de tomber en panne.

to **keep out** VERB
■ **'keep out'** 'défense d'entrer'

to **keep up** VERB
se maintenir [83] à la hauteur de quelqu'un ◻ Matthew walks so fast I can't keep up. Matthew marche tellement vite que je n'arrive pas à me maintenir à sa hauteur.
■ **I can't keep up with the rest of the class.** Je n'arrive pas à suivre le reste de la classe.

keep-fit NOUN
la gymnastique d'entretien *fem*
■ **I go to keep-fit classes.** Je vais à des cours de gymnastique.

kennel NOUN
la niche *fem*

kept VERB ▷ *see* **keep**

kerosene NOUN (US)
le pétrole *masc*

kettle NOUN
la bouilloire *fem*

★ **key** NOUN
la clé *fem*

keyboard NOUN
le clavier *masc*
◻ ... with Matt Bellamy on keyboards ... avec Matt Bellamy aux claviers

keyring NOUN
le porte-clés *masc* (PL les porte-clés)

★ **kick** NOUN
▷ *see also* **kick** VERB
le coup de pied *masc*

★ to **kick** VERB
▷ *see also* **kick** NOUN
■ **to kick somebody** donner [28] un coup de pied à quelqu'un ◻ He kicked me. Il m'a donné un coup de pied. ◻ He kicked the ball hard. Il a donné un bon coup de pied dans le ballon.

to **kick off** VERB
donner [28] le coup d'envoi (*in football*)

kick-off NOUN
le coup d'envoi *masc*
◻ Kick-off is at 10 o'clock. Le coup d'envoi sera donné à dix heures.

★ **kid** NOUN
▷ *see also* **kid** VERB
le/la gosse *masc/fem* (*child*)

★ to **kid** VERB
▷ *see also* **kid** NOUN

★ = core vocabulary

plaisanter [28]
□ I'm just kidding. Je plaisante.

to **kidnap** VERB
kidnapper [28]

kidney NOUN
1 le rein *masc* (*human*)
□ He's got kidney trouble. Il a des problèmes de reins.
2 le rognon *masc* (*to eat*)
□ I don't like kidneys. Je n'aime pas les rognons.
■ **kidney beans** les haricots rouges *masc pl*

★ to **kill** VERB
tuer [28]
□ He was killed in a car accident. Il a été tué dans un accident de voiture.
■ **Luckily, nobody was killed.** Il n'y a heureusement pas eu de victimes.
■ **Six people were killed in the accident.** L'accident a fait six morts.
■ **to kill oneself** se suicider [28] □ He killed himself. Il s'est suicidé.

★ **killer** NOUN
1 le meurtrier *masc*
la meurtrière *fem* (*murderer*)
□ The police are searching for the killer. La police recherche le meurtrier.
2 le tueur *masc*
la tueuse *fem* (*assassin*)
□ a hired killer un tueur à gages
■ **Meningitis can be a killer.** La méningite peut être mortelle.

★ **kilo** NOUN
le kilo *masc*
□ 10 euros a kilo dix euros le kilo

★ **kilometre** (US **kilometer**) NOUN
le kilomètre *masc*

kilt NOUN
le kilt *masc*

★ **kind** ADJECTIVE
▷ *see also* **kind** NOUN
gentil (FEM gentille)
■ **to be kind to somebody** être [35] gentil avec quelqu'un
■ **Thank you for being so kind.** Merci pour votre gentillesse.

★ **kind** NOUN
▷ *see also* **kind** ADJECTIVE
la sorte *fem*
□ It's a kind of sausage. C'est une sorte de saucisse.

kindergarten NOUN
l'école maternelle *fem*

kindly ADVERB
gentiment
□ 'Don't worry,' she said kindly. 'Ne t'en fais pas', m'a-t-elle dit gentiment.

kindness NOUN
la gentillesse *fem*

★ **king** NOUN
le roi *masc*

kingdom NOUN
le royaume *masc*

kiosk NOUN
la cabine téléphonique *fem* (*phone box*)

kipper NOUN
le hareng fumé *masc*

★ **kiss** NOUN
▷ *see also* **kiss** VERB
le baiser *masc*
□ a passionate kiss un baiser passionné

DID YOU KNOW...?
Between friends and family members, the normal French way of saying hello and goodbye is with two kisses, usually one on each cheek, but sometimes three or even four depending on the region. Boys shake hands with their friends or kiss them on the cheek when they arrive at school in the morning.

★ to **kiss** VERB
▷ *see also* **kiss** NOUN
1 embrasser [28]
□ He kissed her passionately. Il l'a embrassée passionnément.
2 s'embrasser [28]
□ They kissed. Ils se sont embrassés.

kit NOUN
1 les affaires *fem pl* (*clothes for sport*)
□ I've forgotten my gym kit. J'ai oublié mes affaires de gym.
2 la trousse *fem*
□ a tool kit une trousse à outils □ a first aid kit une trousse de secours □ a puncture repair kit une trousse de réparations
■ **a drum kit** une batterie
■ **a sewing kit** un nécessaire à couture

★ **kitchen** NOUN
la cuisine *fem*
□ a fitted kitchen une cuisine aménagée
■ **the kitchen units** les éléments de cuisine
■ **a kitchen knife** un couteau de cuisine

kite NOUN
le cerf-volant *masc* (PL les cerfs-volants)

kitten NOUN
le chaton *masc*

★ **knee** NOUN
le genou *masc* (PL les genoux)
□ He was on his knees. Il était à genoux.

★ to **kneel** VERB
s'agenouiller [28]

to **kneel down** VERB
s'agenouiller [28]

knew VERB ▷ *see* **know**

★ **knickers** PL NOUN
la culotte *fem sing*
■ **a pair of knickers** une culotte

★ **knife** NOUN
le couteau *masc* (PL les couteaux)
■ **a kitchen knife** un couteau de cuisine
■ **a penknife** un canif

to **knit** VERB
tricoter [28]

knitting NOUN
le tricot *masc*
□ I like knitting. J'aime faire du tricot.

knives PL NOUN ▷ *see* **knife**

knob NOUN
le bouton *masc* (*on door, radio, TV, radiator*)

★ to **knock** VERB
▷ *see also* **knock** NOUN
frapper [28]
□ Someone's knocking at the door. Quelqu'un frappe à la porte.

★ **knock** NOUN
▷ *see also* **knock** VERB
le coup *masc*

to **knock down** VERB
renverser [28]
□ She was knocked down by a car. Elle a été renversée par une voiture.

to **knock out** VERB
1 éliminer [28] (*defeat*)
□ They were knocked out early in the tournament. Ils ont été éliminés au début du tournoi.
2 assommer [28] (*stun*)
□ They knocked out the security guard. Ils ont assommé le vigile.

knot NOUN
le nœud *masc*
■ **to tie a knot in something** faire [36] un nœud à quelque chose

★ to **know** VERB

> Use **savoir** for knowing facts, **connaître** for knowing people and places.

1 savoir [76]
□ It's a long way. — Yes, I know. C'est loin. — Oui, je sais. □ You know what you have to do. Tu sais ce que tu dois faire. □ She knows where we live. Elle sait où nous habitons. □ I don't know. Je ne sais pas. □ I don't know what to do. Je ne sais pas quoi faire. □ I don't know how to do it. Je ne sais pas comment faire.
2 connaître [14]
□ I know her. Je la connais. □ I know Bordeaux well. Je connais bien Bordeaux.
■ **I don't know any German.** Je ne parle pas du tout allemand.
■ **to know that ...** savoir [76] que ... □ I know that you like chocolate. Je sais que tu aimes le chocolat. □ I didn't know that your dad was a police officer. Je ne savais pas que ton père était policier.
■ **to know about something** **1** (*be aware of*) être [35] au courant de quelque chose □ Do you know about the training session this afternoon? Tu es au courant de la séance d'entraînement cet après-midi? **2** (*be knowledgeable about*) s'y connaître [14] en quelque chose □ He knows a lot about cars. Il s'y connaît en voitures. □ I don't know much about computers. Je ne m'y connais pas bien en informatique.
■ **to get to know somebody** apprendre [65] à connaître quelqu'un
■ **How should I know?** (*I don't know!*) Comment veux-tu que je le sache?
■ **You never know!** On ne sait jamais!

know-all NOUN
le/la je-sais-tout *masc/fem*
□ He's such a know-all! C'est Monsieur je-sais-tout!

know-how NOUN
le savoir-faire *masc*

★ **knowledge** NOUN
la connaissance *fem*

knowledgeable ADJECTIVE
■ **to be knowledgeable about something** s'y connaître [14] en quelque chose □ She's very knowledgeable about martial arts. Elle s'y connaît bien en arts martiaux.

known VERB ▷ *see* **know**

Koran NOUN
le Coran *masc*

Korea NOUN
la Corée *fem*
■ **in Korea** en Corée

kosher ADJECTIVE
kascher (FEM+PL kascher)

lab NOUN (= *laboratory*)
le labo *masc*
■ **a lab technician** un laborantin

★ **label** NOUN
l'étiquette *fem*

labor NOUN (US)
■ **to be in labor** être [35] en train d'accoucher
■ **the labor market** le marché du travail
■ **a labor union** un syndicat

★ **laboratory** NOUN
le laboratoire *masc*

Labour NOUN
les travaillistes *masc pl*
□ My parents vote Labour. Mes parents votent pour les travaillistes.
■ **the Labour Party** le parti travailliste

labour NOUN
■ **to be in labour** être [35] en train d'accoucher
■ **the labour market** le marché du travail

labourer NOUN
le manœuvre *masc*
■ **a farm labourer** un ouvrier agricole

lace NOUN
1 le lacet *masc* (*of shoe*)
2 la dentelle *fem*
□ a lace collar un col en dentelle

★ **lack** NOUN
le manque *masc*
□ He got the job despite his lack of experience. Il a obtenu le poste en dépit de son manque d'expérience.
■ **There was no lack of volunteers.** Les volontaires ne manquaient pas.

lacquer NOUN
la laque *fem*

lad NOUN
le gars *masc*

ladder NOUN
l'échelle *fem*

★ **lady** NOUN
la dame *fem*
■ **a young lady** une jeune fille
■ **Ladies and gentlemen ...** Mesdames, Messieurs ...
■ **the ladies** les toilettes pour dames *fem pl*

ladybird NOUN
la coccinelle *fem*

to **lag behind** VERB
rester [71[E]] en arrière

lager NOUN
la bière blonde *fem*

laid VERB ▷ *see* **lay**

laid-back ADJECTIVE
relaxe (FEM relaxe)

lain VERB ▷ *see* **lie**

★ **lake** NOUN
le lac *masc*
■ **Lake Geneva** le lac Léman

lamb NOUN
l'agneau *masc* (PL les agneaux)
■ **a lamb chop** une côtelette d'agneau

lame ADJECTIVE
boiteux (FEM boiteuse)
□ My pony is lame. Mon poney boite.

lamp NOUN
la lampe *fem*

lamppost NOUN
le réverbère *masc*

lampshade NOUN
l'abat-jour *masc* (PL les abat-jour)

★ **land** NOUN
▷ *see also* **land** VERB
la terre *fem*
■ **a piece of land** un terrain

★ to **land** VERB
▷ *see also* **land** NOUN
atterrir [38] (*plane, passenger*)

landing NOUN
1 l'atterrissage *masc* (*of plane*)
2 le palier *masc* (*of staircase*)

landlady NOUN
la propriétaire *fem*

landline NOUN
la ligne fixe *fem*
□ Shall I call you on the landline? Je t'appelle sur ta ligne fixe?

landlord NOUN
le propriétaire *masc*

landmark NOUN
le point de repère *masc* (*for finding your way*)
■ **Big Ben is one of London's most famous**

landmarks. Big Ben est l'un des sites les plus célèbres du paysage londonien.

landowner NOUN
le propriétaire terrien *masc*

★ **landscape** NOUN
le paysage *masc*

★ **lane** NOUN
1 le chemin *masc* (*in country*)
2 la voie *fem* (*on motorway*)

★ **language** NOUN
la langue *fem*
□ French isn't a difficult language. Le français n'est pas une langue difficile.
■ **to use bad language** dire [27] des grossièretés

language laboratory NOUN
le laboratoire de langues *masc*

lanky ADJECTIVE
dégingandé (FEM dégingandée)
□ a lanky boy un garçon dégingandé

★ **lap** NOUN
le tour de piste *masc* (*sport*)
□ I ran ten laps. J'ai fait dix tours de piste en courant.
■ **on my lap** sur mes genoux

★ **laptop** NOUN
le portable *masc* (*computer*)

larder NOUN
le garde-manger *masc* (PL les garde-manger)

★ **large** ADJECTIVE
1 grand (FEM grande)
□ a large house une grande maison
2 gros (FEM grosse) (*person, animal*)
□ a large dog un gros chien

> **BE CAREFUL!**
> Do not translate **large** by the French word **large**.

★ **largely** ADVERB
en grande partie
□ It's largely your own fault. C'est en grande partie de ta faute.

laser NOUN
le laser *masc*

lass NOUN
la jeune fille *fem*

★ **last** ADJECTIVE, ADVERB
▷ *see also* **last** VERB
1 dernier (FEM dernière)
□ last Friday vendredi dernier □ last week la semaine dernière □ last summer l'été dernier
2 en dernier
□ He arrived last. Il est arrivé en dernier.
3 pour la dernière fois
□ I've lost my bag. — When did you see it last? J'ai perdu mon sac. — Quand est-ce que tu l'as vu pour la dernière fois? □ When I last saw him, he was wearing a blue shirt. La dernière fois que je l'ai vu, il portait une chemise bleue.
■ **the last time** la dernière fois □ the last time I saw her la dernière fois que je l'ai vue □ That's the last time I take your advice! C'est la dernière fois que je suis tes conseils!
■ **last night** **1** (*evening*) hier soir □ I got home at midnight last night. Je suis rentré à minuit hier soir. **2** (*sleeping hours*) la nuit dernière □ I couldn't sleep last night. J'ai eu du mal à dormir la nuit dernière.
■ **at last** enfin

★ to **last** VERB
▷ *see also* **last** ADJECTIVE, ADVERB
durer [28]
□ The concert lasts two hours. Le concert dure deux heures.

lastly ADVERB
finalement
□ Lastly, what time do you arrive? Finalement, à quelle heure arrives-tu?

★ **late** ADJECTIVE, ADVERB
1 en retard
□ Hurry up or you'll be late! Dépêche-toi, sinon tu vas être en retard! □ I'm often late for school. J'arrive souvent en retard à l'école.
■ **to arrive late** arriver [5^E] en retard □ She arrived late. Elle est arrivée en retard.
2 tard
□ I went to bed late. Je me suis couché tard.
■ **in the late afternoon** en fin d'après-midi
■ **in late May** fin mai

lately ADVERB
ces derniers temps
□ I haven't seen him lately. Je ne l'ai pas vu ces derniers temps.

★ **later** ADVERB
plus tard
□ I'll do it later. Je ferai ça plus tard.
■ **See you later!** À tout à l'heure!

★ **latest** ADJECTIVE
dernier (FEM dernière)
□ their latest album leur dernier album
■ **at the latest** au plus tard □ by 10 o'clock at the latest à dix heures au plus tard

★ **Latin** NOUN
le latin *masc*
□ I do Latin. Je fais du latin.

Latin America NOUN
l'Amérique latine *fem*
■ **in Latin America** en Amérique latine

Latin American ADJECTIVE
latino-américain (FEM latino-américaine)

latter NOUN
le second *masc*
la seconde *fem*
■ **the former ..., the latter ...** le premier ..., le second ... □ The former lives in the US, the latter in Australia. Le premier habite aux États-Unis, le second en Australie.

■ **The latter is the more expensive of the two games consoles.** Cette dernière console de jeu est la plus coûteuse des deux.

★ **laugh** NOUN
▷ *see also* **laugh** VERB
le rire *masc*
■ **It was a good laugh.** (*it was fun*) On s'est bien amusés.

★ to **laugh** VERB
▷ *see also* **laugh** NOUN
rire [74]
■ **to laugh at something** se moquer [28] de quelque chose □ They laughed at her. Ils se sont moqués d'elle.

★ to **launch** VERB
lancer [12] (*product, rocket, boat*)
□ They're going to launch a new model. Ils vont lancer un nouveau modèle.

Launderette® NOUN
la laverie *fem*

Laundromat® NOUN (US)
la laverie *fem*

laundry NOUN
le linge *masc* (*clothes*)

lavatory NOUN
les toilettes *fem pl*

lavender NOUN
la lavande *fem*

★ **law** NOUN
1 la loi *fem*
□ The laws are very strict. Les lois sont très sévères.
■ **It's against the law.** C'est illégal.
2 le droit *masc* (*subject*)
□ My sister's studying law. Ma sœur fait des études de droit.

lawn NOUN
la pelouse *fem*

lawnmower NOUN
la tondeuse à gazon *fem*

law school NOUN (US)
la faculté de droit *fem*

★ **lawyer** NOUN
l'avocat *masc*
l'avocate *fem*
□ My mother's a lawyer. Ma mère est avocate.

★ to **lay** VERB
'lay' is also a form of the verb 'lie'.
mettre [47]
□ She laid the baby in her cot. Elle a mis le bébé dans son lit. □ He laid the table. Il a mis la table.
■ **to lay something on** **1** (*provide*) organiser [28] quelque chose □ They laid on extra buses. Ils ont organisé un service de bus supplémentaire. **2** (*prepare*) préparer [28] quelque chose □ They laid on a special meal. Ils ont préparé un repas soigné.

to **lay off** VERB
licencier [19]
□ My father's been laid off. Mon père a été licencié.

lay-by NOUN
l'aire de stationnement *fem*

★ **layer** NOUN
la couche *fem*
□ the ozone layer la couche d'ozone

layout NOUN
la disposition *fem* (*of house, buildings*)
□ No one likes the new layout of the classroom. Personne n'aime la nouvelle disposition de la salle de classe.

lazy ADJECTIVE
paresseux (FEM paresseuse)

★ **lead** NOUN
▷ *see also* **lead** VERB
This word has two pronunciations. Make sure you choose the right translation.
1 le fil *masc* (*cable*)
2 la laisse *fem* (*for dog*)
■ **to be in the lead** être [35] en tête □ Our team is in the lead. Notre équipe est en tête.
3 le plomb *masc* (*metal*)

★ to **lead** VERB
▷ *see also* **lead** NOUN
mener [43]
□ the road that leads to the airport la route qui mène à l'aéroport
■ **to lead the way** montrer [28] le chemin
■ **to lead somebody away** emmener [43] quelqu'un □ The police led the man away. La police a emmené l'homme.

★ **leader** NOUN
1 le chef *masc* (*of expedition, gang*)
2 le dirigeant *masc*
la dirigeante *fem* (*of political party*)

lead singer NOUN
le chanteur principal *masc*
la chanteuse principale *fem*

★ **leaf** NOUN
la feuille *fem*

leaflet NOUN
la brochure *fem*

★ **league** NOUN
le championnat *masc*
□ They are at the top of the league. Ils sont en tête du championnat.
■ **the Premier League** la première division

★ **leak** NOUN
▷ *see also* **leak** VERB
la fuite *fem*
□ a gas leak une fuite de gaz

★ to **leak** VERB
▷ *see also* **leak** NOUN
fuir [39] (*pipe, water, gas*)

★ to **lean** VERB
se pencher [28]
■ **to be leaning against something** être [35] appuyé contre quelque chose □ The ladder was leaning against the wall. L'échelle était appuyée contre le mur.
■ **to lean something against a wall** appuyer [53] quelque chose contre un mur □ He leant his bike against the wall. Il a appuyé son vélo contre le mur.

to **lean forward** VERB
se pencher [28] en avant

to **lean on** VERB
■ **to lean on something** s'appuyer [53] contre quelque chose □ He leant on the wall. Il s'est appuyé contre le mur.

to **lean out** VERB
se pencher [28] au dehors
■ **She leant out of the window.** Elle s'est penchée par la fenêtre.

to **lean over** VERB
se pencher [28]
□ Don't lean over too far. Ne te penche pas trop loin.

to **leap** VERB
sauter [28]
□ They leapt over the stream. Ils ont sauté pour traverser la rivière.
■ **He leapt out of his chair when his team scored.** Il s'est levé d'un bond lorsque son équipe a marqué.

leap year NOUN
l'année bissextile *fem*

★ to **learn** VERB
apprendre [65]
□ I'm learning to ski. J'apprends à skier.

learner NOUN
■ **She's a quick learner.** Elle apprend vite.
■ **French learners** (*people learning French*) ceux qui apprennent le français

learner driver NOUN
le conducteur débutant *masc*
la conductrice débutante *fem*

learnt VERB ▷ *see* **learn**

★ **least** ADVERB, ADJECTIVE, PRONOUN
■ **the least 1** (*followed by noun*) le moins de □ It takes the least time. C'est ce qui prend le moins de temps. **2** (*after a verb*) le moins □ Maths is the subject I like the least. Les maths sont la matière que j'aime le moins.

When 'least' is followed by an adjective, the translation depends on whether the noun referred to is masculine, feminine or plural.

■ **the least ... 1** le moins ... □ the least expensive hotel l'hôtel le moins cher **2** la moins ... □ the least expensive seat la place la moins chère **3** les moins ... □ the least expensive hotels les hôtels les moins chers □ the least expensive seats les places les moins chères
■ **It's the least I can do.** C'est le moins que je puisse faire.
■ **at least 1** au moins □ It'll cost at least £200. Ça va coûter au moins deux cents livres. **2** du moins □ ... but at least nobody was hurt. ... mais du moins personne n'a été blessé. □ It's totally unfair – at least, that's my opinion. C'est vraiment injuste – du moins c'est ce que je pense.

★ **leather** NOUN
le cuir *masc*
□ a black leather jacket un blouson en cuir noir

★ **leave** NOUN
▷ *see also* **leave** VERB
1 le congé *masc* (*from job*)
2 la permission *fem* (*from army*)
□ My brother is on leave for a week. Mon frère est en permission pendant une semaine.

★ to **leave** VERB
▷ *see also* **leave** NOUN
1 laisser [28] (*deliberately*)
□ Don't leave your camera in the car. Ne laisse pas ton appareil photo dans la voiture.
2 oublier [19] (*by mistake*)
□ I've left my book at home. J'ai oublié mon livre à la maison. □ Make sure you haven't left anything behind. Vérifiez bien que vous n'avez rien oublié.
3 partir [57E] (*go*)
□ The bus leaves at 8. Le car part à huit heures. □ She's just left. Elle vient de partir.
4 quitter [28] (*go away from*)
□ We leave Cambridge at six o'clock. Nous quittons Cambridge à six heures. □ My sister left home last year. Ma sœur a quitté la maison l'an dernier.
■ **to leave somebody alone** laisser [28] quelqu'un tranquille □ Leave me alone! Laisse-moi tranquille!

to **leave out** VERB
mettre [47] à l'écart
□ As the new girl, I felt really left out. En tant que nouvelle, je me suis vraiment sentie à l'écart.

leaves PL NOUN ▷ *see* **leaf**

Lebanon NOUN
le Liban *masc*
■ **in Lebanon** au Liban

★ **lecture** NOUN
▷ *see also* **lecture** VERB
1 la conférence *fem* (*public*)
2 le cours magistral *masc* (PL les cours magistraux) (*at university*)

BE CAREFUL!
Do not translate **lecture** by the French word **lecture.**

★ to **lecture** VERB
▷ *see also* **lecture** NOUN
1 enseigner [28]
□ She lectures at the university. Elle enseigne à l'université.
2 faire [36] la morale
□ He's always lecturing us. Il n'arrête pas de nous faire la morale.

lecturer NOUN
le professeur d'université *masc*
□ She's a lecturer. Elle est professeur d'université.

led VERB ▷ *see* **lead**

leek NOUN
le poireau *masc* (PL les poireaux)

★ **left** VERB ▷ *see* **leave**

★ **left** ADJECTIVE, ADVERB
▷ *see also* **left** NOUN
1 gauche (FEM gauche) (*not right*)
□ my left hand ma main gauche □ on the left side of the road sur le côté gauche de la route
2 à gauche
□ Turn left at the traffic lights. Tournez à gauche aux prochains feux.
■ **I haven't got any money left.** Il ne me reste plus d'argent.

★ **left** NOUN
▷ *see also* **left** ADJECTIVE, ADVERB
la gauche *fem*
■ **on the left** à gauche □ Remember to drive on the left. N'oubliez pas de conduire à gauche.

left-hand ADJECTIVE
■ **the left-hand side** la gauche □ It's on the left-hand side. C'est à gauche.

left-handed ADJECTIVE
gaucher (FEM gauchère)

left-luggage locker NOUN
la consigne automatique *fem*

left-luggage office NOUN
la consigne *fem*

★ **leg** NOUN
la jambe *fem*
□ She's broken her leg. Elle s'est cassé la jambe.
■ **a chicken leg** une cuisse de poulet
■ **a leg of lamb** un gigot d'agneau

★ **legal** ADJECTIVE
légal (FEM légale, MASC PL légaux)

leggings PL NOUN
les leggings *masc pl*

leisure NOUN
les loisirs *masc pl*
□ What do you do in your leisure time? Qu'est-ce que tu fais pendant tes loisirs?

leisure centre NOUN
le centre de loisirs *masc*

lemon NOUN
le citron *masc*

lemonade NOUN
la limonade *fem*

★ to **lend** VERB
prêter [28]
□ I can lend you some money. Je peux te prêter de l'argent.

★ **length** NOUN
la longueur *fem*
■ **It's about a metre in length.** Ça fait environ un mètre de long.

★ **lens** NOUN
1 la lentille *fem* (*contact lens*)
2 le verre *masc* (*of spectacles*)
3 l'objectif *masc* (*of camera*)

Lent NOUN
le carême *masc*

lent VERB ▷ *see* **lend**

lentil NOUN
la lentille *fem*

Leo NOUN
le Lion *masc*
□ I'm Leo. Je suis Lion.

leotard NOUN
le justaucorps *masc*

lesbian NOUN
la lesbienne *fem*

★ **less** PRONOUN, ADVERB, ADJECTIVE
1 moins
□ He's less intelligent than her. Il est moins intelligent qu'elle. □ A bit less, please. Un peu moins, s'il vous plaît.
2 moins de
□ I've got less time for hobbies now. J'ai moins de temps pour les loisirs maintenant.
■ **less than** 1 (*with amounts*) moins de □ It's less than a kilometre from here. C'est à moins d'un kilomètre d'ici. □ It costs less than 100 euros. Ça coûte moins de cent euros. □ less than half moins de la moitié 2 (*in comparisons*) moins que □ He spent less than me. Il a dépensé moins que moi. □ I've got less than you. J'en ai moins que toi. □ It cost less than we thought. Ça a coûté moins cher que nous ne le pensions.

★ **lesson** NOUN
1 la leçon *fem*
□ a history lesson une leçon d'histoire
□ 'Lesson Sixteen' (*in textbook*) 'Leçon seize'
2 le cours *masc* (*class*)
□ The lessons last forty minutes each. Chaque cours dure quarante minutes.

★ to **let** VERB
1 laisser [28] (*allow*)
■ **to let somebody do something** laisser

[28] quelqu'un faire quelque chose □ Let me have a look. Laisse-moi voir. □ My parents won't let me stay out that late. Mes parents ne me laissent pas sortir aussi tard.

■ **to let somebody know** faire [36] savoir à quelqu'un □ I'll let you know as soon as possible. Je vous le ferai savoir dès que possible.

■ **to let somebody go** lâcher [28] quelqu'un □ Let me go! Lâche-moi!

To make suggestions using 'let's', you can ask questions beginning with **si on**.

□ Let's go to the cinema! Si on allait au cinéma?

■ **Let's go!** Allons-y!

2 louer [28] (*hire out*)

■ **'to let'** 'à louer'

to **let down** VERB

décevoir [67]

□ I won't let you down. Je ne vous décevrai pas.

to **let in** VERB

laisser [28] entrer

□ They wouldn't let me in because I was under 18. Ils ne m'ont pas laissé entrer parce que j'avais moins de dix-huit ans.

★ **letter** NOUN

la lettre *fem*

letterbox NOUN

la boîte à lettres *fem*

lettuce NOUN

la salade *fem*

leukaemia NOUN

la leucémie *fem*

★ **level** ADJECTIVE

▷ *see also* **level** NOUN

plan (FEM plane)

□ A snooker table must be perfectly level. Un billard doit être parfaitement plan.

★ **level** NOUN

▷ *see also* **level** ADJECTIVE

le niveau *masc* (PL les niveaux)

□ The level of the river is rising. Le niveau de la rivière monte.

■ **A levels** le baccalauréat

DID YOU KNOW...?

The French **baccalauréat** (or **bac** for short) is taken at the age of 17 or 18. Students have to sit one of a variety of set subject combinations, rather than being able to choose any combination of subjects they want. If you pass you have the right to a place at university.

level crossing NOUN

le passage à niveau *masc*

lever NOUN

le levier *masc*

liable ADJECTIVE

■ **He's liable to lose his temper.** Il se met facilement en colère.

liar NOUN

le menteur *masc*

la menteuse *fem*

★ **liberal** ADJECTIVE

libéral (FEM libérale, MASC PL libéraux) (*opinions*)

■ **the Liberal Democrats** le parti libéral-démocrate

liberation NOUN

la libération *fem*

Libra NOUN

la Balance *fem*

□ I'm Libra. Je suis Balance.

librarian NOUN

le/la bibliothécaire *masc/fem*

□ She's a librarian. Elle est bibliothécaire.

★ **library** NOUN

la bibliothèque *fem*

BE CAREFUL!

Do not translate **library** by the French word **librairie**.

Libya NOUN

la Libye *fem*

■ **in Libya** en Libye

★ **licence** (US **license**) NOUN

le permis *masc*

■ **a driving licence** un permis de conduire

to **lick** VERB

lécher [34]

lid NOUN

le couvercle *masc*

★ to **lie** VERB

▷ *see also* **lie** NOUN

mentir [77] (*not tell the truth*)

□ I know she's lying. Je sais qu'elle ment.

■ **to lie down** s'allonger [45]

■ **to be lying down** être [35] allongé □ He was lying down on the sofa. Il était allongé sur le canapé.

■ **to lie on the beach** être [35] allongé sur la plage

★ **lie** NOUN

▷ *see also* **lie** VERB

le mensonge *masc*

■ **to tell a lie** mentir [77]

■ **That's a lie!** Ce n'est pas vrai!

lie-in NOUN

■ **to have a lie-in** faire [36] la grasse matinée

□ I have a lie-in on Sundays. Je fais la grasse matinée le dimanche.

lieutenant NOUN

le lieutenant *masc*

★ **life** NOUN
la vie *fem*

lifebelt NOUN
la bouée de sauvetage *fem*

lifeboat NOUN
le canot de sauvetage *masc*

lifeguard NOUN
le maître nageur *masc*

life jacket NOUN
le gilet de sauvetage *masc*

life-saving NOUN
le sauvetage *masc*
□ I've done a course in life-saving. J'ai pris des cours de sauvetage.

lifestyle NOUN
le style de vie *masc*

★ to **lift** VERB
▷ *see also* **lift** NOUN
soulever [43]
□ It's too heavy, I can't lift it. C'est trop lourd, je ne peux pas le soulever.

★ **lift** NOUN
▷ *see also* **lift** VERB
l'ascenseur *masc*
□ The lift isn't working. L'ascenseur est en panne.
■ **He gave me a lift to the cinema.** Il m'a emmené au cinéma en voiture.
■ **Would you like a lift?** Est-ce que je peux vous déposer quelque part?

★ **light** ADJECTIVE
▷ *see also* **light** NOUN, VERB
1 léger (FEM légère) (*not heavy*)
□ a light jacket une veste légère □ a light meal un repas léger
2 clair (FEM claire) (*colour*)
□ a light blue coat un manteau bleu clair

★ **light** NOUN
▷ *see also* **light** ADJECTIVE, VERB
1 la lumière *fem*
□ to switch on the light allumer la lumière
□ to switch off the light éteindre la lumière
2 la lampe *fem*
□ There's a light by my bed. Il y a une lampe près de mon lit.
■ **the traffic lights** les feux *masc pl*

★ to **light** VERB
▷ *see also* **light** ADJECTIVE, NOUN
allumer [28] (*candle, cigarette, fire*)

light bulb NOUN
l'ampoule *fem*

lighthouse NOUN
le phare *masc*

★ **lightning** NOUN
les éclairs *masc pl*
■ **a flash of lightning** un éclair

★ to **like** VERB
▷ *see also* **like** PREPOSITION
1 aimer [28]
□ I don't like mustard. Je n'aime pas la moutarde. □ I like riding. J'aime monter à cheval.

Note that **aimer** also means to love, so make sure you use **aimer bien** for just liking somebody.

2 aimer [28] bien
□ I like Kieran, but I don't want to go out with him. J'aime bien Kieran, mais je ne veux pas sortir avec lui.
■ **I'd like ...** Je voudrais ... □ I'd like an orange juice, please. Je voudrais un jus d'orange, s'il vous plaît. □ Would you like some coffee? Voulez-vous du café?
■ **I'd like to ...** J'aimerais ... □ I'd like to go to Russia one day. J'aimerais aller en Russie un jour. □ I'd like to wash my hands. J'aimerais me laver les mains.
■ **Would you like to go for a walk?** Tu veux aller faire une promenade?
■ **... if you like** ... si tu veux

★ **like** PREPOSITION
▷ *see also* **like** VERB
comme
□ It's fine like that. C'est bien comme ça. □ Do it like this. Fais-le comme ça. □ a city like Chicago une ville comme Chicago □ It's a bit like salmon. C'est un peu comme du saumon.
■ **What's the weather like?** Quel temps fait-il?
■ **to look like somebody** ressembler [28] à quelqu'un □ You look like my brother. Tu ressembles à mon frère.

★ **likely** ADJECTIVE
probable (FEM probable)
□ That's not very likely. C'est peu probable.
■ **She's likely to come.** Elle viendra probablement.
■ **She's not likely to come.** Elle ne viendra probablement pas.

Lilo® NOUN
le matelas pneumatique *masc*

lily of the valley NOUN
le muguet *masc*

DID YOU KNOW...?
On May 1st French people celebrate May Day by giving each other small bunches of lily of the valley.

lime NOUN
le citron vert *masc* (*fruit*)

★ **limit** NOUN
la limite *fem*
□ The speed limit is 70 mph. La vitesse est limitée à cent dix kilomètres à l'heure.

limousine NOUN
la limousine *fem*

to **limp** VERB
boiter [28]

★ **line** NOUN
1 la ligne *fem*
▫ a straight line une ligne droite
2 le trait *masc* (*to divide, cancel*)
▫ Draw a line under each answer. Tirez un trait après chaque réponse.
3 la voie *fem* (*railway track*)
▪ **It's a very bad line.** La ligne est très mauvaise.

linen NOUN
le lin *masc*
▫ a linen jacket une veste en lin

liner NOUN
le paquebot *masc* (*ship*)

linguist NOUN
▪ **to be a good linguist** être [35] doué pour les langues ▫ She's a good linguist. Elle est douée pour les langues.

lining NOUN
la doublure *fem* (*of jacket, skirt etc*)

★ **link** NOUN
▷ *see also* **link** VERB
1 le rapport *masc*
▫ the link between smoking and cancer le rapport entre le tabagisme et le cancer
2 le lien *masc* (*computing*)

★ to **link** VERB
▷ *see also* **link** NOUN
relier [19]

lino NOUN
le linoléum *masc*

★ **lion** NOUN
le lion *masc*

lioness NOUN
la lionne *fem*

★ **lip** NOUN
la lèvre *fem*

to **lip-read** VERB
lire [44] sur les lèvres

lip salve NOUN
la pommade pour les lèvres *fem*

lipstick NOUN
le rouge à lèvres *masc*

liqueur NOUN
la liqueur *fem*

liquid NOUN
le liquide *masc*

liquidizer NOUN
le mixer *masc*

★ **list** NOUN
▷ *see also* **list** VERB
la liste *fem*

★ to **list** VERB
▷ *see also* **list** NOUN
faire [36] une liste de
▫ List your hobbies and say which is your favourite. Fais une liste de tes hobbies et dis quel est ton préféré.

★ to **listen** VERB
écouter [28]
▫ Listen to this! Écoutez ceci! ▫ Listen to me! Écoutez-moi!

listener NOUN
l'auditeur *masc*
l'auditrice *fem*

lit VERB ▷ *see* **light**

liter NOUN (US)
le litre *masc*

literally ADVERB
vraiment (*completely*)
▫ It was literally impossible to find a seat. Il était vraiment impossible de trouver une place.
▪ **to translate literally** faire [36] une traduction littérale

★ **literature** NOUN
la littérature *fem*
▫ I'm studying English Literature. J'étudie la littérature anglaise.

litre NOUN
le litre *masc*

litter NOUN
les ordures *fem pl*

litter bin NOUN
la poubelle *fem*

★ **little** ADJECTIVE
petit (FEM petite)
▫ a little girl une petite fille

> **WORD POWER**
> You can use a number of other words instead of **little** to mean 'small':
> **miniature** miniature
> ▫ a miniature version une version miniature
> **minute** infime
> ▫ a minute chance une chance infime
> **tiny** minuscule
> ▫ a tiny garden un jardin minuscule

▪ **a little** un peu ▫ How much would you like? — Just a little. Combien en voulez-vous? — Juste un peu.
▪ **very little** très peu ▫ We've got very little time. Nous avons très peu de temps.
▪ **little by little** petit à petit

★ **live** ADJECTIVE
▷ *see also* **live** VERB
1 vivant (FEM vivante) (*animal*)
2 en direct (*broadcast*)
▪ **There's live music on Fridays.** Il y a des musiciens qui jouent le vendredi.

English-French

★ to **live** VERB
▷ *see also* **live** ADJECTIVE
1 vivre [91]
□ I live with my grandmother. Je vis avec ma grand-mère.
2 habiter [28] (*reside*)
□ Where do you live? Où est-ce que tu habites? □ I live in Edinburgh. J'habite à Édimbourg.

to **live together** VERB
1 partager [45] un appartement (*as flatmates*)
□ She and her sister are living together in London. Elle partage un appartement à Londres avec sa soeur.
2 vivre [91] ensemble
□ My parents aren't living together any more. Mes parents ne vivent plus ensemble.
■ **They're not married, they're living together.** Ils ne sont pas mariés, ils vivent en concubinage.

lively ADJECTIVE
animé (FEM animée)
□ It was a lively party. C'était une soirée animée.
■ **She's got a lively personality.** Elle est pleine de vitalité.

liver NOUN
le foie *masc*

lives PL NOUN ▷ *see* **life**

livestream NOUN
▷ *see also* **livestream** VERB
la diffusion en direct sur Internet *fem*

to **livestream** VERB
▷ *see also* **livestream** NOUN
diffuser en direct sur Internet

living NOUN
■ **to make a living** gagner [28] sa vie
■ **What does she do for a living?** Qu'est-ce qu'elle fait dans la vie?

living room NOUN
la salle de séjour *fem*

lizard NOUN
le lézard *masc*

★ **load** NOUN
▷ *see also* **load** VERB
■ **loads of** un tas de □ loads of people un tas de gens □ loads of money un tas d'argent
■ **You're talking a load of rubbish!** Tu ne dis que des bêtises!

★ to **load** VERB
▷ *see also* **load** NOUN
charger [45]
□ a trolley loaded with luggage un chariot chargé de bagages

loaf NOUN
le pain *masc*
■ **a loaf of bread** un pain

★ **loan** NOUN
▷ *see also* **loan** VERB
le prêt *masc*

★ to **loan** VERB
▷ *see also* **loan** NOUN
prêter [28]

to **loathe** VERB
détester [28]
□ I loathe her. Je la déteste.

loaves PL NOUN ▷ *see* **loaf**

lobster NOUN
le homard *masc*

★ **local** ADJECTIVE
local (FEM locale, MASC PL locaux)
□ the local paper le journal local

location NOUN
l'endroit *masc*
□ a hotel set in a beautiful location un hôtel situé dans un endroit magnifique

> **BE CAREFUL!**
> Do not translate **location** by the French word **location**.

loch NOUN
le loch *masc*

★ **lock** NOUN
▷ *see also* **lock** VERB
la serrure *fem*
□ The lock is broken. La serrure est cassée.

★ to **lock** VERB
▷ *see also* **lock** NOUN
fermer [28] à clé
□ Make sure you lock your door. N'oubliez pas de fermer votre porte à clé.

to **lock out** VERB
■ **The door slammed and I was locked out.** La porte a claqué et je me suis retrouvé à la porte.

locker NOUN
le casier *masc*
■ **the locker room** le vestiaire
■ **the left-luggage lockers** la consigne automatique *sing*

locket NOUN
le médaillon *masc*

lodger NOUN
le/la locataire *masc/fem*

loft NOUN
le grenier *masc*

★ **log** NOUN
la bûche *fem* (*of wood*)

to **log in** VERB
se connecter [28]

to **log off** VERB
se déconnecter [28]

to **log on** VERB
se connecter [28]

to **log out** VERB
se déconnecter [28]

logical ADJECTIVE
logique (FEM logique)

lollipop NOUN
la sucette *fem*

lolly NOUN
la glace à l'eau *fem* (*ice lolly*)

★ **London** NOUN
Londres
▪ **in London** à Londres
▪ **to London** à Londres
▪ **I'm from London.** Je suis de Londres.

★ **Londoner** NOUN
le Londonien *masc*
la Londonienne *fem*

loneliness NOUN
la solitude *fem*

lonely ADJECTIVE
seul (FEM seule)
▪ **to feel lonely** se sentir [77] seul ▫ She feels a bit lonely. Elle se sent un peu seule.

★ **long** ADJECTIVE, ADVERB
▷ *see also* **long** VERB
long (FEM longue)
▫ She's got long hair. Elle a les cheveux longs.
▪ **The room is 6 metres long.** La pièce fait six mètres de long.
▪ **how long?** (*time*) combien de temps?
▫ How long did you stay there? Combien de temps êtes-vous resté là-bas? ▫ How long have you been here? Depuis combien de temps êtes-vous ici? ▫ How long is the flight? Combien de temps dure le vol?
▪ **I've been waiting a long time.** J'attends depuis longtemps.
▪ **It takes a long time.** Ça prend du temps.
▪ **as long as** si ▫ I'll come as long as it's not too expensive. Je viendrai si ce n'est pas trop cher.

★ to **long** VERB
▷ *see also* **long** ADJECTIVE, ADVERB
▪ **to long to do something** attendre [7] avec impatience de faire quelque chose ▫ I'm longing to see my boyfriend again. J'attends avec impatience de revoir mon copain.

long-distance ADJECTIVE
▪ **a long-distance call** une communication interurbaine

longer ADVERB
▷ *see also* **long** ADJECTIVE, ADVERB
▪ **They're no longer going out together.** Ils ne sortent plus ensemble.
▪ **I can't stand it any longer.** Je ne peux plus le supporter.

long jump NOUN
le saut en longueur *masc*

loo NOUN
les toilettes *fem pl*
▫ Where's the loo? Où sont les toilettes?

★ **look** NOUN
▷ *see also* **look** VERB
▪ **to have a look** regarder [28] ▫ Have a look at this! Regardez ceci!
▪ **I don't like the look of it.** Ça ne me dit rien.

★ to **look** VERB
▷ *see also* **look** NOUN
1 regarder [28]
▫ Look! Regardez!
▪ **to look at something** regarder [28] quelque chose ▫ Look at the picture. Regardez cette image.
2 avoir [8] l'air (*seem*)
▫ She looks surprised. Elle a l'air surprise.
▫ That cake looks nice. Ce gâteau a l'air bon.
▫ It looks fine. Ça a l'air bien.
▪ **to look like somebody** ressembler [28] à quelqu'un ▫ He looks like his brother. Il ressemble à son frère.
▪ **What does she look like?** Comment est-elle physiquement?
▪ **to look forward to something** attendre [7] quelque chose avec impatience ▫ I'm looking forward to the holidays. J'attends les vacances avec impatience.
▪ **Looking forward to hearing from you ...** J'espère avoir bientôt de tes nouvelles ... (*at the end of email, letter*)
▪ **Look out!** Attention!

to **look after** VERB
s'occuper [28] de
▫ I look after my little sister. Je m'occupe de ma petite sœur.

to **look for** VERB
chercher [28]
▫ I'm looking for my passport. Je cherche mon passeport.

to **look round** VERB
1 se retourner [72] (*look behind*)
▫ I shouted and he looked round. J'ai crié et il s'est retourné.
2 jeter [41] un coup d'œil (*have a look*)
▫ I'm just looking round. Je jette simplement un coup d'œil.
▪ **to look round a museum** visiter [28] un musée
▪ **I like looking round the shops.** J'aime faire les boutiques.

to **look up** VERB
chercher [28] (*word, name*)
▫ Look the word up in the dictionary. Cherchez le mot dans le dictionnaire.

★ **loose** ADJECTIVE
ample (FEM ample) (*clothes*)
▪ **loose change** la petite monnaie

English-French

l

lord NOUN
le seigneur *masc* (*feudal*)
■ **the House of Lords** la Chambre des lords

lorry NOUN
le camion *masc*

lorry driver NOUN
le routier *masc*
□ He's a lorry driver. Il est routier.

★to **lose** VERB
perdre [61]
□ I've lost my purse. J'ai perdu mon porte-monnaie.
■ **to get lost** se perdre [61] □ I was afraid of getting lost. J'avais peur de me perdre.

loser NOUN
1 le perdant *masc*
la perdante *fem*
■ **to be a bad loser** être [35] mauvais perdant
2 le loser *masc* (*pathetic person*)
□ He's such a loser! C'est un vrai loser!

★**loss** NOUN
la perte *fem*

lost VERB ▷ *see* **lose**

★**lost** ADJECTIVE
perdu (FEM perdue)

lost-and-found NOUN (US)
les objets trouvés *masc pl*

lost property office NOUN
les objets trouvés *masc pl*

★**lot** NOUN
■ **a lot** beaucoup
■ **a lot of** beaucoup de □ We saw a lot of interesting things. Nous avons vu beaucoup de choses intéressantes.
■ **lots of** un tas de □ She's got lots of money. Elle a un tas d'argent. □ He's got lots of friends. Il a un tas d'amis.
■ **What did you do at the weekend? — Not a lot.** Qu'as-tu fait ce week-end? — Pas grand-chose.
■ **Do you like football? — Not a lot.** Tu aimes le football? — Pas tellement.
■ **That's the lot.** C'est tout.

lottery NOUN
la loterie *fem*
□ to win the lottery gagner à la loterie

★**loud** ADJECTIVE
fort (FEM forte)
□ The television is too loud. La télévision est trop forte.

loudly ADVERB
fort

loudspeaker NOUN
le haut-parleur *masc*

lounge NOUN
le salon *masc*

lousy ADJECTIVE
infect (FEM infecte)
□ The food in the canteen is lousy. La nourriture de la cantine est infecte.
■ **I feel lousy.** Je suis mal fichu. (*informal*)

★**love** NOUN
▷ *see also* **love** VERB
l'amour *masc*
■ **to be in love** être [35] amoureux □ She's in love with Ryan. Elle est amoureuse de Ryan.
■ **Give your brother my love.** Embrasse ton frère pour moi.
■ **Love, Mum.** Bisous, Maman.

★to **love** VERB
▷ *see also* **love** NOUN
1 aimer [28] (*be in love with*)
□ I love you. Je t'aime.
2 aimer [28] beaucoup (*like a lot*)
□ Everybody loves her. Tout le monde l'aime beaucoup. □ I'd love to come. J'aimerais beaucoup venir.
3 adorer [28] (*things*)
□ I love chocolate. J'adore le chocolat. □ I love skiing. J'adore le ski.

★**lovely** ADJECTIVE
charmant (FEM charmante)
□ What a lovely surprise! Quelle charmante surprise! □ She's a lovely person. Elle est charmante.
■ **It's a lovely day.** Il fait très beau aujourd'hui.
■ **Is your meal OK? — Yes, it's lovely.** Est-ce que c'est bon? — Oui, c'est délicieux.
■ **They've got a lovely house.** Ils ont une très belle maison.
■ **Have a lovely time!** Amusez-vous bien!

lover NOUN
1 l'amant *masc*
la maîtresse *fem* (*in relationship*)
2 l'amateur *masc* (*fan*)
□ a music lover un amateur de musique

★**low** ADJECTIVE, ADVERB
bas (FEM basse) (*price, level*)
□ That plane is flying very low. Cet avion vole très bas.
■ **the low season** la basse saison □ in the low season en basse saison

lower ADJECTIVE
▷ *see also* **lower** VERB
inférieur (FEM inférieure)
□ on the lower floor a l'étage inférieur

to **lower** VERB
▷ *see also* **lower** ADJECTIVE
baisser [28]

low-fat ADJECTIVE
allégé (FEM allégée)
□ a low-fat yoghurt un yaourt allégé

loyalty NOUN
la fidélité *fem*
loyalty card NOUN
la carte de fidélité *fem*
L-plates PL NOUN
les plaques de conducteur débutant *fem pl*
★ **luck** NOUN
la chance *fem*
□ She hasn't had much luck. Elle n'a pas eu beaucoup de chance.
▪ **Good luck!** Bonne chance!
▪ **Bad luck!** Pas de chance!
luckily ADVERB
heureusement
★ **lucky** ADJECTIVE
▪ **to be lucky** **1** (*be fortunate*) avoir [8] de la chance □ Lucky you! Tu as de la chance! □ He's lucky, he's got a job. Il a de la chance, il a un emploi. □ He wasn't hurt. — That was lucky! Il n'a pas été blessé. — C'est une chance! **2** (*bring luck*) porter [28] bonheur □ Black cats are lucky in Britain. Les chats noirs portent bonheur en Grande-Bretagne.
▪ **a lucky horseshoe** un fer à cheval porte-bonheur
luggage NOUN
les bagages *masc pl*
lukewarm ADJECTIVE
tiède (FEM tiède) (*water, food*)
▪ **The response was lukewarm.** La réponse a été peu enthousiaste.
lump NOUN
1 le morceau *masc* (PL les morceaux)
□ a lump of butter un morceau de beurre
2 la bosse *fem* (*swelling*)
□ He's got a lump on his forehead. Il a une bosse sur le front.
★ **lunch** NOUN
le déjeuner *masc*
▪ **to have lunch** déjeuner [28] □ We have lunch at 12.30. Nous déjeunons à midi et demi.
luncheon voucher NOUN
le ticket-restaurant *masc*
lung NOUN
le poumon *masc*
□ lung cancer le cancer du poumon
luscious ADJECTIVE
délicieux (FEM délicieuse)
lush ADJECTIVE
luxuriant (FEM luxuriante)
lust NOUN
le désir *masc*
Luxembourg NOUN
1 le Luxembourg *masc* (*country*)
▪ **in Luxembourg** au Luxembourg
▪ **to Luxembourg** au Luxembourg
2 Luxembourg (*city*)
▪ **in Luxembourg** à Luxembourg
luxurious ADJECTIVE
luxueux (FEM luxueuse)
★ **luxury** NOUN
le luxe *masc*
□ It was luxury! C'était le luxe!
▪ **a luxury hotel** un hôtel de luxe
lying VERB ▷ *see* **lie**
lyrics PL NOUN
les paroles *fem pl* (*of song*)

Mm

mac NOUN
l'imper *masc*

macaroni NOUN
les macaronis *masc pl*

★ **machine** NOUN
la machine *fem*

machine gun NOUN
la mitrailleuse *fem*

machinery NOUN
les machines *fem pl*

mackerel NOUN
le maquereau *masc* (PL les maquereaux)

★ **mad** ADJECTIVE
1 fou (FEM folle) (*insane*)
□ You're mad! Tu es fou!

fou changes to **fol** before a vowel and most words beginning with 'h'.

2 furieux (FEM furieuse) (*angry*)
□ She'll be mad when she finds out. Elle sera furieuse quand elle va s'en apercevoir.
■ **to be mad about** **1** (*sport, activity*) être [35] dingue de □ He's mad about basketball. Il est dingue de basket. **2** (*person, animal*) adorer [28] □ She's mad about horses. Elle adore les chevaux.

madam NOUN
madame *fem*
□ Would you like to order, Madam? Désirez-vous commander, Madame?

made VERB ▷ *see* **make**

madly ADVERB
■ **They're madly in love.** Ils sont éperdument amoureux.

madman NOUN
le fou *masc*

madness NOUN
la folie *fem*
□ It's absolute madness. C'est de la pure folie.

★ **magazine** NOUN
le magazine *masc*

maggot NOUN
l'asticot *masc*

magic ADJECTIVE
▷ *see also* **magic** NOUN
1 magique (FEM magique) (*magical*)
□ a magic wand une baguette magique
2 super (FEM+PL super) (*brilliant*)
□ It was magic! C'était super!

★ **magic** NOUN
▷ *see also* **magic** ADJECTIVE
la magie *fem*
■ **a magic trick** un tour de magie
■ **My hobby is magic.** Je fais des tours de magie.

magician NOUN
le prestidigitateur *masc* (*conjurer*)

magnet NOUN
l'aimant *masc*

magnificent ADJECTIVE
1 magnifique (FEM magnifique) (*beautiful*)
□ a magnificent view une vue magnifique
2 superbe (FEM superbe) (*outstanding*)
□ It was a magnificent effort. Ils ont fait un superbe effort.

magnifying glass NOUN
la loupe *fem*

maid NOUN
la domestique *fem* (*servant*)

maiden name NOUN
le nom de jeune fille *masc*

★ **mail** NOUN
▷ *see also* **mail** VERB
1 le courrier *masc*
□ Here's your mail. Voici ton courrier.
2 les mails *masc pl* (*emails*)
□ Can I check my mail on your laptop? Je peux consulter mes mails sur ton ordinateur portable?
■ **by mail** par la poste

★ to **mail** VERB
▷ *see also* **mail** NOUN
■ **to mail something** (*email*) envoyer [33] quelque chose par mail □ I'll mail you my address. Je t'enverrai mon adresse par mail.

mailbox NOUN (US)
la boîte à lettres *fem*

mailing list NOUN
la liste d'adresses *fem*

mailman NOUN (US)
le facteur *masc*

★ **main** ADJECTIVE
principal (FEM principale, MASC PL principaux)

□ the main problem le principal problème
■ **the main thing is to ...** l'essentiel est de ...

★ **mainly** ADVERB
principalement

main road NOUN
la grande route *fem*
□ I don't like cycling on main roads. Je n'aime pas faire du vélo sur les grandes routes.

★ to **maintain** VERB
entretenir [83] (*machine, building*)

maintenance NOUN
l'entretien *masc* (*of machine, building*)

maize NOUN
le maïs *masc*

majesty NOUN
la majesté *fem*
■ **Your Majesty** Votre Majesté

★ **major** ADJECTIVE
majeur (FEM majeure)
□ a major problem un problème majeur
■ **in C major** en do majeur
■ **a major operation** une opération d'envergure

Majorca NOUN
Majorque *fem*
□ We went to Majorca in August. Nous sommes allés à Majorque en août.

★ **majority** NOUN
la majorité *fem*

★ **make** NOUN
▷ *see also* **make** VERB
la marque *fem*
□ What make is that car? De quelle marque est cette voiture?

★ to **make** VERB
▷ *see also* **make** NOUN
1 faire [36]
□ I'm going to make a cake. Je vais faire un gâteau. □ He made it himself. Il l'a fait lui-même. □ I make my bed every morning. Je fais mon lit tous les matins. □ 2 and 2 make 4. Deux et deux font quatre.
2 fabriquer [28] (*manufacture*)
□ made in France fabriqué en France
3 gagner [28] (*earn*)
□ He makes a lot of money. Il gagne beaucoup d'argent.
■ **to make somebody do something** obliger [45] quelqu'un à faire quelque chose □ My mother makes me do my homework. Ma mère m'oblige à faire mes devoirs.
■ **to make lunch** préparer [28] le repas
□ She's making lunch. Elle prépare le repas.
■ **to make a phone call** donner [28] un coup de téléphone □ I'd like to make a phone call. J'aimerais donner un coup de téléphone.
■ **to make fun of somebody** se moquer [28] de quelqu'un □ They made fun of him. Ils se sont moqués de lui.
■ **What time do you make it?** Quelle heure avez-vous?

to **make out** VERB
1 déchiffrer [28] (*read*)
□ I can't make out the address on the label. Je n'arrive pas à déchiffrer l'adresse sur l'étiquette.
2 comprendre [65] (*understand*)
□ I can't make her out at all. Je n'arrive pas du tout à la comprendre.
3 prétendre [88] (*claim, pretend*)
□ They're making out it was my fault. Ils prétendent que c'était ma faute.

to **make up** VERB
1 inventer [28] (*invent*)
□ He made up the whole story. Il a inventé cette histoire de toutes pièces.
2 se réconcilier [19] (*after argument*)
□ They had a quarrel, but soon made up. Ils se sont disputés, mais se sont vite réconciliés.

makeover NOUN
le relookage *masc*
■ **She had a complete makeover.** Elle est relookée des pieds à la tête.

★ **maker** NOUN
1 le fabriquant *masc*
□ Europe's biggest car maker le plus grand fabriquant de voitures d'Europe
2 la machine *fem*
□ a bread maker une machine à pain □ a pasta maker une machine à pâtes
■ **an ice-cream maker** une sorbetière
■ **a film maker** un cinéaste

★ **make-up** NOUN
le maquillage *masc*

Malaysia NOUN
la Malaisie *fem*
■ **in Malaysia** en Malaisie

★ **male** ADJECTIVE
1 mâle (FEM mâle) (*animals, plants*)
□ a male kitten un chaton mâle
2 masculin (FEM masculine) (*person, on official forms*)
□ Sex: male. Sexe : masculin.
■ **Most football players are male.** La plupart des joueurs de football sont des hommes.
■ **a male nurse** un infirmier

malicious ADJECTIVE
malveillant (FEM malveillante)
□ a malicious rumour une rumeur malveillante

BE CAREFUL!
Do not translate **malicious** by the French word **malicieux**.

mall NOUN
le centre commercial *masc*

English-French

Malta NOUN
Malte
■ **in Malta** à Malte
■ **to Malta** à Malte

mammoth NOUN
▷ *see also* **mammoth** ADJECTIVE
le mammouth *masc*

mammoth ADJECTIVE
▷ *see also* **mammoth** NOUN
monstre (FEM monstre)
□ a mammoth task un travail monstre

★ **man** NOUN
l'homme *masc*
□ an old man un vieil homme

★ to **manage** VERB
1 diriger [45] (*be in charge of*)
□ She manages a big store. Elle dirige un grand magasin. □ He manages our football team. Il dirige notre équipe de foot.
2 se débrouiller [28] (*get by*)
□ We haven't got much money, but we manage. Nous n'avons pas beaucoup d'argent, mais nous nous débrouillons. □ It's okay, I can manage. Ça va, je me débrouille.
■ **Can you manage okay?** Tu y arrives?
■ **to manage to do something** réussir [38] à faire quelque chose □ Luckily I managed to pass the exam. J'ai heureusement réussi à avoir mon examen.
■ **I can't manage all that.** (*food*) C'est trop pour moi.

manageable ADJECTIVE
faisable (FEM faisable) (*task*)

★ **management** NOUN
1 la gestion *fem* (*organization*)
□ He's responsible for the management of the sports centre. Il est responsable de la gestion du centre sportif.
2 la direction *fem* (*people in charge*)
■ **'under new management'** 'changement de direction'

★ **manager** NOUN
1 le directeur *masc*
la directrice *fem* (*of company*)
2 le gérant *masc*
la gérante *fem* (*of shop, restaurant*)
3 le manager *masc* (*of team, performer*)

★ **manageress** NOUN
la gérante *fem*

mandarin NOUN
la mandarine *fem* (*fruit*)

mango NOUN
la mangue *fem*

mania NOUN
la manie *fem*

maniac NOUN
le fou *masc*
la folle *fem*
□ He drives like a maniac. Il conduit comme un fou.

to **manipulate** VERB
manipuler [28]

mankind NOUN
l'humanité *fem*

man-made ADJECTIVE
synthétique (FEM synthétique) (*fibre*)

★ **manner** NOUN
la façon *fem*
□ She was behaving in an odd manner. Elle se comportait de façon étrange.
■ **He has a confident manner.** Il a de l'assurance.

manners PL NOUN
les manières *fem pl*
□ good manners les bonnes manières □ Her manners are appalling. Elle a de très mauvaises manières.
■ **It's bad manners to speak with your mouth full.** Ce n'est pas poli de parler la bouche pleine.

manpower NOUN
la main-d'œuvre *fem*

mansion NOUN
le manoir *masc*

mantelpiece NOUN
la cheminée *fem*

manual NOUN
le manuel *masc*

★ to **manufacture** VERB
fabriquer [28]

★ **manufacturer** NOUN
le fabricant *masc*
la fabricante *fem*

manure NOUN
le fumier *masc*

manuscript NOUN
le manuscrit *masc*

★ **many** ADJECTIVE, PRONOUN
beaucoup de
□ The country has many natural resources. Le pays a beaucoup de ressources naturelles. □ He hasn't got many friends. Il n'a pas beaucoup d'amis. □ Were there many people at the concert? Est-ce qu'il y avait beaucoup de gens au concert?
■ **very many** beaucoup de □ I haven't got very many summer clothes. Je n'ai pas beaucoup de vêtements d'été.
■ **Not many.** Pas beaucoup.
■ **How many?** Combien? □ How many do you want? Combien en veux-tu?
■ **how many ...?** combien de ...? □ How many euros do you get for £100? Combien d'euros a-t-on pour cent livres?
■ **too many** trop □ That's too many. C'est trop.

m

■ **too many ...** trop de ... □ She makes too many mistakes. Elle fait trop d'erreurs.
■ **so many** autant □ I didn't know there would be so many. Je ne pensais pas qu'il y en aurait autant.
■ **so many ...** autant de ... □ I've never seen so many policemen. Je n'ai jamais vu autant de policiers.

★ **map** NOUN
1 la carte *fem* (*of country, area*)
2 le plan *masc* (*of town*)

marathon NOUN
le marathon *masc*
□ the London marathon le marathon de Londres

marble NOUN
le marbre *masc*
□ a marble statue une statue en marbre
■ **to play marbles** jouer [28] aux billes

★ **March** NOUN
mars *masc*
■ **in March** en mars

★ **march** NOUN
▷ *see also* **march** VERB
la manifestation *fem* (*demonstration*)

★ to **march** VERB
▷ *see also* **march** NOUN
1 marcher [28] au pas (*soldiers*)
2 défiler [28] (*protesters*)

mare NOUN
la jument *fem*

margarine NOUN
la margarine *fem*

margin NOUN
la marge *fem*
□ Write notes in the margin. Écrivez vos notes dans la marge.

marijuana NOUN
la marijuana *fem*

marina NOUN
la marina *fem*

marital status NOUN
la situation de famille *fem*

★ **mark** NOUN
▷ *see also* **mark** VERB
1 la note *fem* (*in school*)
□ I get good marks for maths. J'ai de bonnes notes en maths.
2 la tache *fem* (*stain*)
□ You've got a mark on your skirt. Tu as une tache sur ta jupe.

★ to **mark** VERB
▷ *see also* **mark** NOUN
corriger [45]
□ The teacher hasn't marked my homework yet. Le professeur n'a pas encore corrigé mon devoir.

★ **market** NOUN
le marché *masc*

★ **marketing** NOUN
le marketing *masc*

marketplace NOUN
la place du marché *fem*

marmalade NOUN
la confiture d'oranges *fem*

maroon ADJECTIVE
bordeaux (FEM+PL bordeaux) (*colour*)

★ **marriage** NOUN
le mariage *masc*

★ **married** ADJECTIVE
marié (FEM mariée)
□ They are not married. Ils ne sont pas mariés.
□ They have been married for 15 years. Ils sont mariés depuis quinze ans. □ a married couple un couple marié

marrow NOUN
la courge *fem* (*vegetable*)
■ **bone marrow** la moelle

★ to **marry** VERB
épouser [28]
□ He wants to marry her. Il veut l'épouser.
■ **to get married** se marier [19] □ My sister's getting married in June. Ma sœur se marie en juin.

marvellous (US **marvelous**) ADJECTIVE
1 excellent (FEM excellente)
□ She's a marvellous cook. C'est une excellente cuisinière.
2 superbe (FEM superbe)
□ The weather was marvellous. Il a fait un temps superbe.

marzipan NOUN
la pâte d'amandes *fem*

mascara NOUN
le mascara *masc*

masculine ADJECTIVE
masculin (FEM masculine)

mashed potatoes PL NOUN
la purée *fem sing*
□ chicken with mashed potatoes du poulet avec de la purée

★ **mask** NOUN
le masque *masc*

masked ADJECTIVE
masqué (FEM masquée)

★ **mass** NOUN
1 la multitude *fem*
□ a mass of books and papers une multitude de livres et de papiers
2 la messe *fem* (*in church*)
□ We go to mass on Sunday. Nous allons à la messe le dimanche.
■ **the mass media** les médias

massage NOUN
le massage *masc*

★ **massive** ADJECTIVE
énorme (FEM énorme)

★ to **master** VERB
maîtriser [28]

masterpiece NOUN
le chef-d'œuvre *masc* (PL les chefs-d'œuvre)

mat NOUN
le paillasson *masc* (*doormat*)
■ **a table mat** un set de table
■ **a beach mat** un tapis de plage

★ **match** NOUN
▷ *see also* **match** VERB
1 l'allumette *fem*
□ a box of matches une boîte d'allumettes
2 le match *masc* (*sport*)
□ a football match un match de foot

★ to **match** VERB
▷ *see also* **match** NOUN
être [35] assorti à
□ The jacket matches the trousers. La veste est assortie au pantalon.
■ **These colours don't match.** Ces couleurs ne vont pas ensemble.

matching ADJECTIVE
assorti (FEM assortie)
□ My bedroom has matching wallpaper and curtains. Ma chambre a du papier peint et des rideaux assortis.

★ **mate** NOUN
le pote *masc* (*informal*)
□ On Friday night I go out with my mates. Vendredi soir, je sors avec mes potes.

★ **material** NOUN
1 le tissu *masc* (*cloth*)
2 la documentation *fem* (*information, data*)
□ I'm collecting material for my project. Je rassemble une documentation pour mon dossier.
■ **raw materials** les matières premières *fem pl*

mathematics NOUN
les mathématiques *fem pl*

maths NOUN
les maths *fem pl*

matron NOUN
l'infirmière-chef *fem* (PL les infirmières-chefs) (*in hospital*)

★ **matter** NOUN
▷ *see also* **matter** VERB
la question *fem*
□ It's a matter of life and death. C'est une question de vie ou de mort.
■ **What's the matter?** Qu'est-ce qui ne va pas?
■ **as a matter of fact** en fait

★ to **matter** VERB
▷ *see also* **matter** NOUN
■ **it doesn't matter** **1** (*I don't mind*) ça ne fait rien □ I can't give you the money today. — It doesn't matter. Je ne peux pas te donner l'argent aujourd'hui. — Ça ne fait rien. **2** (*it makes no difference*) ça n'a pas d'importance □ It doesn't matter if you're late. Ça n'a pas d'importance si tu es en retard.
■ **It matters a lot to me.** C'est très important pour moi.

mattress NOUN
le matelas *masc*

mature ADJECTIVE
mûr (FEM mûre)
□ She's quite mature for her age. Elle est très mûre pour son âge.

★ **maximum** NOUN
▷ *see also* **maximum** ADJECTIVE
le maximum *masc*

★ **maximum** ADJECTIVE
▷ *see also* **maximum** NOUN
maximum (FEM+PL maximum)
□ The maximum speed is 100 km/h. La vitesse maximum autorisée est de cent kilomètres à l'heure.
■ **the maximum amount** le maximum

★ **May** NOUN
mai *masc*
■ **in May** en mai
■ **May Day** le Premier Mai

★ **may** VERB
■ **He may come.** Il va peut-être venir. □ It may rain. Il va peut-être pleuvoir.
■ **May I sit down?** Est-ce que je peux m'asseoir?

★ **maybe** ADVERB
peut-être
□ maybe not peut-être pas □ a bit boring, maybe peut-être un peu ennuyeux □ Maybe she's at home. Elle est peut-être chez elle.
□ Maybe he'll change his mind. Il va peut-être changer d'avis.

mayonnaise NOUN
la mayonnaise *fem*

★ **mayor** NOUN
le maire *masc*

maze NOUN
le labyrinthe *masc*

★ **me** PRONOUN
1 me
□ Could you lend me your ruler? Est-ce que tu peux me prêter ton ta règle?
m'

me becomes m' before a vowel sound.

□ Can you tell me the way to the station? Est-ce que vous pouvez m'indiquer le chemin de la gare? □ Can you help me? Est-ce que tu peux m'aider? □ He heard me. Il m'a entendu.

2 moi

moi is used in exclamations.

□ Me too! Moi aussi! □ Excuse me! Excusez-moi! □ Look at me! Regarde-moi! □ Wait for me! Attends-moi! □ Come with me! Suivez-moi!

moi is also used after prepositions and in comparisons.

□ You're after me. Tu es après moi. □ Is it for me? C'est pour moi? □ She's older than me. Elle est plus âgée que moi.

★ **meal** NOUN
le repas *masc*

mealtime NOUN
■ **at mealtimes** aux heures des repas

★ to **mean** VERB
▷ *see also* **mean** ADJECTIVE, **means** NOUN
vouloir [93] dire
□ What does 'complet' mean? Qu'est-ce que 'complet' veut dire? □ I don't know what it means. Je ne sais pas ce que ça veut dire.
□ What do you mean? Qu'est que vous voulez dire? □ That's not what I meant. Ce n'est pas ce que je voulais dire.
■ **Which one do you mean?** Duquel veux-tu parler?
■ **Do you really mean it?** Tu es sérieux?
■ **to mean to do something** avoir [8] l'intention de faire quelque chose □ I didn't mean to offend you. Je n'avais pas l'intention de vous blesser.

★ **mean** ADJECTIVE
▷ *see also* **mean** VERB, **means** NOUN
1 radin (FEM radine) (*with money*)
□ He's too mean to buy Christmas presents. Il est trop radin pour acheter des cadeaux de Noël.
2 méchant (FEM méchante) (*unkind*)
□ You're being mean to me. Tu es méchant avec moi.
■ **That's a really mean thing to say!** Ce n'est vraiment pas gentil de dire ça!

★ **meaning** NOUN
le sens *masc*

★ **means** NOUN
▷ *see also* **mean** VERB, ADJECTIVE
le moyen *masc*
□ He'll do it by any possible means. Il le fera par tous les moyens. □ a means of transport un moyen de transport
■ **by means of** au moyen de □ He got in by means of a stolen key. Il est entré au moyen d'une clé volée.
■ **by all means** bien sûr □ Can I come? — By all means! Est-ce que je peux venir? — Bien sûr!

meant VERB ▷ *see* **mean**

★ **meanwhile** ADVERB
pendant ce temps

measles NOUN
la rougeole *fem*

★ to **measure** VERB
1 mesurer [28]
□ I measured the page. J'ai mesuré la page.
2 faire [36]
□ The room measures 3 metres by 4. La pièce fait trois mètres sur quatre.

measurements PL NOUN
1 les dimensions *fem pl* (*of object*)
□ What are the measurements of the room? Quelles sont les dimensions de la pièce?
2 les mensurations *fem pl* (*of body*)
□ What are your measurements? Quelles sont tes mensurations?
■ **my waist measurement** mon tour de taille
■ **What's your neck measurement?** Quel est votre tour de cou?

★ **meat** NOUN
la viande *fem*
□ I don't eat meat. Je ne mange pas de viande.

Mecca NOUN
La Mecque

mechanic NOUN
le mécanicien *masc*
□ He's a mechanic. Il est mécanicien.

mechanical ADJECTIVE
mécanique (FEM mécanique)

★ **medal** NOUN
la médaille *fem*
■ **the gold medal** la médaille d'or

medallion NOUN
le médaillon *masc*

★ **media** PL NOUN
les médias *masc pl*

median strip NOUN (US)
le terre-plein central *masc*

★ **medical** ADJECTIVE
▷ *see also* **medical** NOUN
médical (FEM médicale, MASC PL médicaux)
□ medical treatment les soins médicaux
■ **medical insurance** l'assurance maladie
■ **to have medical problems** avoir [8] des problèmes de santé
■ **She's a medical student.** Elle est étudiante en médecine.

★ **medical** NOUN
▷ *see also* **medical** ADJECTIVE
■ **to have a medical** passer [58] une visite médicale

★ **medicine** NOUN
1 la médecine *fem* (*subject*)
□ I want to study medicine. Je veux faire médecine.

■ **alternative medicine** la médecine douce

2 le médicament *masc* (*medication*)

□ I need some medicine. J'ai besoin d'un médicament.

Mediterranean ADJECTIVE

méditerranéen (FEM méditerranéenne)

■ **the Mediterranean** la Méditerranée

★ **medium** ADJECTIVE

moyen (FEM moyenne)

□ a man of medium height un homme de taille moyenne

medium-sized ADJECTIVE

de taille moyenne

□ a medium-sized town une ville de taille moyenne

★ to **meet** VERB

1 rencontrer [28] (*by chance*)

□ I met Ali in the street. J'ai rencontré Ali dans la rue. □ Have you met him before? Tu l'as déjà rencontré?

2 se rencontrer [28]

□ We met by chance in the shopping centre. Nous nous sommes rencontrés par hasard dans le centre commercial.

3 retrouver [28] (*by arrangement*)

□ I'm going to meet my friends. Je vais retrouver mes amis.

4 se retrouver [28]

□ Let's meet in front of the tourist office. Retrouvons-nous devant l'office de tourisme.

■ **I like meeting new people.** J'aime faire de nouvelles connaissances.

5 aller [3E] chercher (*pick up*)

□ I'll meet you at the station. J'irai te chercher à la gare.

to **meet up** VERB

se retrouver [28]

□ What time shall we meet up? On se retrouve à quelle heure?

★ **meeting** NOUN

1 la réunion *fem* (*for work*)

□ a business meeting une réunion d'affaires

2 la rencontre *fem* (*socially*)

□ their first meeting leur première rencontre

meg NOUN (= *megabyte*)

le mégaoctet *masc*

mega ADJECTIVE

■ **He's mega rich.** Il est hyper-riche. (*informal*)

melody NOUN

la mélodie *fem*

melon NOUN

le melon *masc*

to **melt** VERB

fondre [69]

□ The snow is melting. La neige est en train de fondre.

★ **member** NOUN

le/la membre *masc/fem*

■ **a Member of Parliament** un député

★ **membership** NOUN

l'adhésion *fem* (*of club*)

□ to apply for membership faire une demande d'adhésion

membership card NOUN

la carte de membre *fem*

meme NOUN

le mème *masc*

memento NOUN

le souvenir *masc*

memorial NOUN

le monument *masc*

□ a war memorial un monument aux morts

to **memorize** VERB

apprendre [65] par cœur

★ **memory** NOUN

1 la mémoire *fem* (*also for computer*)

□ I haven't got a good memory. Je n'ai pas une bonne mémoire.

2 le souvenir *masc* (*recollection*)

□ That brings back memories. Cela me rappelle des souvenirs.

memory card NOUN

la carte mémoire *fem*

memory stick NOUN

la clé USB *fem* (*for computer*)

men PL NOUN ▷ *see* **man**

to **mend** VERB

réparer [28]

meningitis NOUN

la méningite *fem*

★ **mental** ADJECTIVE

mental (FEM mentale, MASC PL mentaux)

□ a mental illness une maladie mentale

mentality NOUN

la mentalité *fem*

★ to **mention** VERB

mentionner [28]

■ **Thank you! — Don't mention it!** Merci! — Il n'y a pas de quoi!

mentor NOUN

▷ *see also* **mentor** VERB

le mentor *masc*

mentor VERB

▷ *see also* **mentor** NOUN

le servir [78] de mentor à

menu NOUN

le menu *masc*

□ Could I have the menu please? Est-ce que je pourrais avoir le menu s'il vous plaît?

★ **merchant** NOUN

le marchand *masc*

la marchande *fem*

□ a wine merchant un marchand de vin

mercy NOUN
la pitié *fem*

mere ADJECTIVE
■ **a mere five per cent** à peine cinq pour cent
■ **It's a mere formality.** C'est une simple formalité.
■ **the merest hint of criticism** la moindre petite critique

meringue NOUN
la meringue *fem*

merry ADJECTIVE
■ **Merry Christmas!** Joyeux Noël!

merry-go-round NOUN
le manège *masc*

★ **mess** NOUN
le fouillis *masc*
□ My bedroom's usually in a mess. Il y a généralement du fouillis dans ma chambre.

to **mess about** VERB
■ **to mess about with something** (*interfere with*) tripoter [28] quelque chose □ Stop messing about with my computer! Arrête de tripoter mon ordinateur!
■ **Don't mess about with my things!** Ne touche pas à mes affaires!

to **mess up** VERB
■ **to mess something up** mettre [47] la pagaille dans quelque chose □ My little brother has messed up my drawings. Mon petit frère a mis la pagaille dans mes dessins.

★ **message** NOUN
▷ *see also* **message** VERB
le message *masc*

★ to **message** VERB
▷ *see also* **message** NOUN
envoyer [33] un message
□ She messaged me on Facebook. Elle m'a envoyé un message sur Facebook.

messenger NOUN
le messager *masc*

messy ADJECTIVE
1 salissant (FEM salissante) (*dirty*)
□ a messy job un travail salissant
2 en désordre (*untidy*)
□ Your desk is really messy. Ton bureau est vraiment en désordre.
3 désordonné (FEM désordonnée) (*person*)
□ She's so messy! Elle est tellement désordonnée!
■ **My writing is terribly messy.** J'ai une écriture de cochon.

met VERB ▷ *see* **meet**

★ **metal** NOUN
le métal *masc* (PL les métaux)

meter NOUN
1 le compteur *masc* (*for gas, electricity, taxi*)
2 le parcmètre *masc* (*parking meter*)
3 le mètre *masc* (US: *unit of measurement*)

★ **method** NOUN
la méthode *fem*

★ **metre** NOUN
le mètre *masc*

metric ADJECTIVE
métrique (FEM métrique)

Mexico NOUN
le Mexique *masc*
■ **in Mexico** au Mexique
■ **to Mexico** au Mexique

to **miaow** VERB
miauler [28]

mice PL NOUN ▷ *see* **mouse**

microblog NOUN
le microblog *masc*

microblogging site NOUN
le site de microblogging *masc*

microchip NOUN
la puce *fem*

microphone NOUN
le microphone *masc*

microscope NOUN
le microscope *masc*

microwave oven NOUN
le four à micro-ondes *masc*

mid ADJECTIVE
■ **in mid May** à la mi-mai

midday NOUN
midi *masc*
■ **at midday** à midi

★ **middle** NOUN
le milieu *masc*
□ in the middle of the road au milieu de la route □ in the middle of the night au milieu de la nuit □ the middle seat la place du milieu

middle-aged ADJECTIVE
d'un certain âge
□ a middle-aged man un homme d'un certain âge
■ **to be middle-aged** avoir [8] la cinquantaine
■ **She's middle-aged.** Elle a la cinquantaine.

Middle Ages PL NOUN
■ **the Middle Ages** le Moyen Âge *sing*

middle-class ADJECTIVE
de la classe moyenne
□ a middle-class family une famille de la classe moyenne

Middle East NOUN
le Moyen-Orient *masc*
■ **in the Middle East** au Moyen-Orient

middle name NOUN
le deuxième nom *masc*

midge NOUN
le moucheron *masc*

★**midnight** NOUN
minuit *masc*
■ **at midnight** à minuit

midwife NOUN
la sage-femme *fem* (PL les sages-femmes)
□ She's a midwife. Elle est sage-femme.

★**might** VERB
□ He might come later. Il va peut-être venir plus tard. □ We might go to Spain next year. Nous irons peut-être en Espagne l'an prochain. □ She might not have understood. Elle n'a peut-être pas compris.

migraine NOUN
la migraine *fem*
□ I've got a migraine. J'ai la migraine.

mike NOUN
le micro *masc*

★**mild** ADJECTIVE
doux (FEM douce)
□ The winters are quite mild. Les hivers sont assez doux.

★**mile** NOUN
le mille *masc*
□ It's 5 miles from here. C'est à huit kilomètres d'ici.

> **DID YOU KNOW...?**
> In France, distances are expressed in kilometres. A mile is about 1.6 kilometres.

■ **We walked miles!** Nous avons fait des kilomètres à pied!

★**military** ADJECTIVE
militaire (FEM militaire)

★**milk** NOUN
▷ *see also* **milk** VERB
le lait *masc*
□ tea with milk du thé au lait

★to **milk** VERB
▷ *see also* **milk** NOUN
traire [85]

milk chocolate NOUN
le chocolat au lait *masc*

milk shake NOUN
le milk-shake *masc*

mill NOUN
le moulin *masc* (*for grain*)

millennium NOUN
le millénaire *masc*
□ the third millennium le troisième millénaire

millimetre (US **millimeter**) NOUN
le millimètre *masc*

★**million** NOUN
le million *masc*

millionaire NOUN
le/la millionnaire *masc/fem*

to **mimic** VERB
imiter [28]

mince NOUN
la viande hachée *fem*

mince pie NOUN
la tartelette de Noël *fem*

★to **mind** VERB
▷ *see also* **mind** NOUN
1 garder [28]
□ Could you mind the baby this afternoon? Est-ce que tu pourrais garder le bébé cet après-midi?
2 surveiller [28] (*keep an eye on*)
□ Could you mind my bags for a few minutes? Est-ce que vous pourriez surveiller mes bagages pendant quelques minutes?
■ **Do you mind if I open the window?** Est-ce que je pourrais ouvrir la fenêtre?
■ **I don't mind.** Ça ne me dérange pas. □ I don't mind the noise. Le bruit ne me dérange pas.
■ **Never mind!** Ça ne fait rien!
■ **Mind that bike!** Attention au vélo!
■ **Mind the step!** Attention à la marche!

★**mind** NOUN
▷ *see also* **mind** VERB
■ **to make up one's mind** se décider [28] □ I haven't made up my mind yet. Je ne me suis pas encore décidé.
■ **to change one's mind** changer [45] d'avis □ He's changed his mind. Il a changé d'avis.
■ **Are you out of your mind?** Tu as perdu la tête?

mindfulness NOUN
la pleine conscience *fem*

★**mine** PRONOUN
▷ *see also* **mine** NOUN
le mien + *masc noun*
□ Is this your coat? — No, mine's black. C'est ton manteau? — Non, le mien est noir.
la mienne + *fem noun*
□ Is this your car? — No, mine's green. C'est ta voiture? — Non, la mienne est verte.
les miens + *masc pl noun*
□ her parents and mine ses parents et les miens
les miennes + *fem pl noun*
□ Your hands are dirty, mine are clean. Tes mains sont sales, les miennes sont propres.
■ **It's mine.** C'est à moi. □ This book is mine. Ce livre est à moi. □ Whose is this? — It's mine. C'est à qui? — À moi.

mine NOUN
▷ *see also* **mine** PRONOUN
la mine *fem*
□ a coal mine une mine de charbon □ a land mine une mine terrestre

miner NOUN
le mineur *masc*

mineral water NOUN
l'eau minérale *fem*

miniature ADJECTIVE
▷ *see also* **miniature** NOUN
miniature (FEM miniature)
◻ a miniature version une version miniature

miniature NOUN
▷ *see also* **miniature** ADJECTIVE
la miniature *fem*

minibus NOUN
le minibus *masc*

minicab NOUN
le taxi *masc*

DID YOU KNOW...?
In France, the distinction between black taxis and minicabs does not exist.

★ **minimum** NOUN
▷ *see also* **minimum** ADJECTIVE
le minimum *masc*

★ **minimum** ADJECTIVE
▷ *see also* **minimum** NOUN
minimum (FEM+PL minimum)
◻ The minimum age for driving is 17. L'âge minimum pour conduire est dix-sept ans.
▪ **the minimum amount** le minimum

miniskirt NOUN
la mini-jupe *fem*

★ **minister** NOUN
1 le ministre *masc* (*in government*)
2 le pasteur *masc* (*of church*)

ministry NOUN
le ministère *masc* (*in government*)
◻ The Ministry of Defence Le ministère de la Défense

★ **minor** ADJECTIVE
mineur (FEM mineure)
◻ a minor problem un problème mineur
▪ **in D minor** en ré mineur
▪ **a minor operation** une opération bénigne

minority NOUN
la minorité *fem*

mint NOUN
1 la menthe *fem* (*plant*)
◻ mint sauce la sauce à la menthe
2 le bonbon à la menthe *masc* (*sweet*)

minus PREPOSITION
moins
◻ 16 minus 3 is 13. Seize moins trois égale treize. ◻ It's minus two degrees outside. Il fait moins deux dehors. ◻ I got a B minus. J'ai eu un B moins.

★ **minute** NOUN
▷ *see also* **minute** ADJECTIVE
la minute *fem*
◻ Wait a minute! Attends une minute!

★ **minute** ADJECTIVE
▷ *see also* **minute** NOUN
minuscule (FEM minuscule)
◻ Her flat is minute. Son appartement est minuscule.

miracle NOUN
le miracle *masc*

★ **mirror** NOUN
1 la glace *fem* (*on wall*)
2 le rétroviseur *masc* (*in car*)

to **misbehave** VERB
se conduire [23] mal

miscellaneous ADJECTIVE
divers (FEM diverse)

mischief NOUN
les bêtises *fem pl*
◻ My little sister's always up to mischief. Ma petite sœur fait constamment des bêtises.

mischievous ADJECTIVE
coquin (FEM coquine)

miser NOUN
l'avare *masc/fem*

miserable ADJECTIVE
1 malheureux (FEM malheureuse) (*person*)
◻ You're looking miserable. Tu as l'air malheureux.
2 épouvantable (FEM épouvantable) (*weather*)
◻ The weather was miserable. Il faisait un temps épouvantable.
▪ **to feel miserable** ne pas avoir [8] le moral
◻ I'm feeling miserable. Je n'ai pas le moral.

misery NOUN
1 la tristesse *fem* (*unhappiness*)
◻ All that money brought nothing but misery. Tout cet argent n'a apporté que de la tristesse.
2 le pleurnicheur *masc*
la pleurnicheuse *fem* (*unhappy person*)
◻ She's a real misery. C'est une vraie pleurnicheuse.

misfortune NOUN
le malheur *masc*

mishap NOUN
la mésaventure *fem*

to **misjudge** VERB
mal juger [45] (*person*)
◻ I've misjudged her. Je l'ai mal jugée.
▪ **He misjudged the bend.** Il a mal pris le virage.

to **mislay** VERB
égarer [28]
◻ I've mislaid my passport. J'ai égaré mon passeport.

misleading ADJECTIVE
trompeur (FEM trompeuse)

Miss NOUN
1 Mademoiselle (PL Mesdemoiselles)
2 Mlle (PL Mlles) (*in address*)

★ to **miss** VERB
1 rater [28]

□ Hurry or you'll miss the bus. Dépêche-toi ou tu vas rater le bus. □ He missed the target. Il a raté la cible.

2 manquer [28]

□ to miss an opportunity manquer une occasion

■ **I miss you.** Tu me manques. □ I'm missing my family. Ma famille me manque. □ I miss him. Il me manque. □ I miss them. Ils me manquent.

★ **missing** ADJECTIVE

manquant (FEM manquante)

□ the missing part la pièce manquante

■ **to be missing** avoir [8] disparu □ My rucksack is missing. Mon sac à dos a disparu. □ Two members of the group are missing. Deux membres du groupe ont disparu.

missionary NOUN

le/la missionnaire *masc/fem*

mist NOUN

la brume *fem*

★ **mistake** NOUN

▷ *see also* **mistake** VERB

1 la faute *fem* (*slip*)

□ a spelling mistake une faute d'orthographe

■ **to make a mistake** **1** (*in writing, speaking*) faire [36] une faute **2** (*get mixed up*) se tromper [28] □ I'm sorry, I made a mistake. Je suis désolé, je me suis trompé.

2 l'erreur *fem* (*misjudgement*)

□ It was a mistake to come. J'ai fait une erreur en venant.

■ **by mistake** par erreur □ I took his bag by mistake. J'ai pris son sac par erreur.

★ to **mistake** VERB

▷ *see also* **mistake** NOUN

■ **He mistook me for my sister.** Il m'a prise pour ma sœur.

mistaken ADJECTIVE

■ **to be mistaken** se tromper [28] □ If you think I'm coming with you, you're mistaken. Si tu penses que je vais venir avec toi, tu te trompes.

mistakenly ADVERB

à tort

mistletoe NOUN

le gui *masc*

mistook VERB ▷ *see* **mistake**

misty ADJECTIVE

brumeux (FEM brumeuse)

□ a misty morning un matin brumeux

to **misunderstand** VERB

mal comprendre [65]

□ Sorry, I misunderstood you. Je suis désolé, je t'avais mal compris.

misunderstanding NOUN

le malentendu *masc*

misunderstood VERB ▷ *see* **misunderstand**

★ **mix** NOUN

▷ *see also* **mix** VERB

le mélange *masc*

□ It's a mix of science fiction and comedy. C'est un mélange de science-fiction et de comédie.

■ **a cake mix** une préparation pour gâteau

★ to **mix** VERB

▷ *see also* **mix** NOUN

1 mélanger [45]

□ Mix the flour with the sugar. Mélangez la farine au sucre.

2 combiner [28]

□ He's mixing business with pleasure. Il combine les affaires et le plaisir.

■ **to mix with somebody** (*associate*) fréquenter [28] quelqu'un

■ **He doesn't mix much.** Il se tient à l'écart.

to **mix up** VERB

confondre [69] (*people*)

□ He always mixes me up with my sister. Il me confond toujours avec ma sœur.

■ **The travel agent mixed up the bookings.** L'agence de voyage s'est embrouillée dans les réservations.

■ **I'm getting mixed up.** Je ne m'y retrouve plus.

★ **mixed** ADJECTIVE

■ **a mixed salad** une salade composée

■ **a mixed school** une école mixte

■ **a mixed grill** un assortiment de grillades

mixer NOUN

le mixeur *masc*

■ **She's a good mixer.** Elle est très sociable.

★ **mixture** NOUN

le mélange *masc*

□ a mixture of spices un mélange d'épices

■ **cough mixture** le sirop pour la toux

mix-up NOUN

la confusion *fem*

MMS NOUN

le MMS *masc*

to **moan** VERB

râler [28]

□ She's always moaning. Elle est toujours en train de râler.

★ **mobile** NOUN

le portable *masc* (*phone*)

mobile home NOUN

le mobile home *masc*

★ **mobile phone** NOUN

le portable *masc*

■ **a mobile-phone mast** une antenne-relais

to **mock** VERB

▷ *see also* **mock** ADJECTIVE

ridiculiser [28]

mock ADJECTIVE
▷ *see also* **mock** VERB
▪ **a mock exam** un examen blanc

★ **model** NOUN
▷ *see also* **model** ADJECTIVE
1 le modèle *masc* (*type*)
□ His TV is the latest model. Sa télé est le tout dernier modèle.
2 la maquette *fem* (*mock-up*)
□ a model of the castle une maquette du château
3 le mannequin *masc* (*fashion*)
□ She's a famous model. C'est un mannequin célèbre.

★ **model** ADJECTIVE
▷ *see also* **model** NOUN
▪ **a model plane** un modèle réduit d'avion
▪ **a model railway** un modèle réduit de voie ferrée
▪ **He's a model pupil.** C'est un élève modèle.

★ to **model** VERB
▷ *see also* **model** NOUN
▪ **She was modelling a Victoria Beckham outfit.** Elle présentait une tenue de la collection Victoria Beckham.

modem NOUN
le modem *masc*

★ **moderate** ADJECTIVE
modéré (FEM modérée)
□ His views are quite moderate. Ses opinions sont assez modérées.
▪ **a moderate amount of** un peu de
▪ **a moderate price** un prix raisonnable

★ **modern** ADJECTIVE
moderne (FEM moderne)

to **modernize** VERB
moderniser [28]

★ **modest** ADJECTIVE
modeste (FEM modeste)

to **modify** VERB
modifier [19]

moist ADJECTIVE
humide (FEM humide) (*skin, soil*)
□ Make sure the soil is moist. Assurez-vous que la terre est humide.

moisture NOUN
l'humidité *fem*

moisturizer NOUN
1 la crème hydratante *fem* (*cream*)
2 le lait hydratant *masc* (*lotion*)

moldy ADJECTIVE (US)
moisi (FEM moisie)

mole NOUN
1 la taupe *fem* (*animal*)
2 le grain de beauté *masc* (*on skin*)

★ **moment** NOUN
l'instant *masc*
□ Could you wait a moment? Pouvez-vous attendre un instant? □ in a moment dans un instant □ Just a moment! Un instant!
▪ **at the moment** en ce moment
▪ **any moment now** d'un moment à l'autre
□ They'll be arriving any moment now. Ils vont arriver d'un moment à l'autre.

momentous ADJECTIVE
capital (FEM capitale) (*event*)

Monaco NOUN
Monaco
▪ **in Monaco** à Monaco

monarch NOUN
le monarque *masc*

monarchy NOUN
la monarchie *fem*

monastery NOUN
le monastère *masc*

★ **Monday** NOUN
le lundi *masc*
□ on Monday lundi □ on Mondays le lundi
□ every Monday tous les lundis □ last Monday lundi dernier □ next Monday lundi prochain

to **monetize** VERB
monétiser [28]

★ **money** NOUN
l'argent *masc*
□ I need to change some money. J'ai besoin de changer de l'argent.
▪ **to make money** gagner [28] de l'argent

> **BE CAREFUL!**
> Do not translate **money** by the French word **monnaie**.

mongrel NOUN
le bâtard *masc*
□ My dog's a mongrel. Mon chien est un bâtard.

★ **monitor** NOUN
le moniteur *masc* (*of computer*)

monk NOUN
le moine *masc*

★ **monkey** NOUN
le singe *masc*

monotonous ADJECTIVE
monotone (FEM monotone)

monster NOUN
le monstre *masc*

★ **month** NOUN
le mois *masc*
□ this month ce mois-ci □ next month le mois prochain □ last month le mois dernier □ every month tous les mois □ at the end of the month à la fin du mois

★ **monthly** ADJECTIVE
mensuel (FEM mensuelle)

monument NOUN
le monument *masc*

★ **mood** NOUN
l'humeur *fem*
■ **to be in a bad mood** être [35] de mauvaise humeur
■ **to be in a good mood** être [35] de bonne humeur

moody ADJECTIVE
1 lunatique (FEM lunatique) (*temperamental*)
2 maussade (FEM maussade) (*in a bad mood*)

★ **moon** NOUN
la lune *fem*
□ There's a full moon tonight. Il y a pleine lune ce soir.
■ **to be over the moon** (*happy*) être [35] aux anges

moor NOUN
▷ *see also* **moor** VERB
la lande *fem*

to **moor** VERB
▷ *see also* **moor** NOUN
amarrer [28] (*boat*)

mop NOUN
le balai laveur *masc* (*for floor*)

moped NOUN
le cyclomoteur *masc*

moral ADJECTIVE
▷ *see also* **moral** NOUN
moral (FEM morale, MASC PL moraux)

★ **moral** NOUN
▷ *see also* **moral** ADJECTIVE
la morale *fem*
□ the moral of the story la morale de l'histoire
■ **morals** la moralité

morale NOUN
le moral *masc*
□ Their morale is very low. Leur moral est très bas.

★ **more** ADJECTIVE, PRONOUN, ADVERB

When comparing one amount with another, you usually use **plus**.

1 plus
□ The cost of living is more expensive in Britain. Le coût de la vie est plus élevé en Grande-Bretagne. □ Could you speak more slowly? Est-ce que vous pourriez parler plus lentement? □ a bit more un peu plus □ There isn't any more. Il n'y en a plus.
■ **more ... than** plus ... que □ He's more intelligent than me. Il est plus intelligent que moi. □ She practises more than I do. Elle s'entraîne plus que moi. □ More girls than boys do French. Il y a plus de filles que de garçons qui font du français.
2 plus de (*followed by noun*)
□ There are more girls in the class. Il y a plus de filles dans la classe. □ I get more homework than you do. J'ai plus de devoirs que toi. □ I spent more than 500 euros. J'ai dépensé plus de cinq cents euros.

When referring to an additional amount, more than there is already, you usually use **encore**.

3 encore
□ Is there any more? Est-ce qu'il y en a encore? □ Would you like some more? Vous en voulez encore? □ It'll take a few more days. Ça prendra encore quelques jours.
4 encore de (*followed by noun*)
□ Could I have some more chips? Est-ce que je pourrais avoir encore des frites? □ Do you want some more tea? Voulez-vous encore du thé?
■ **more or less** plus ou moins
■ **more than ever** plus que jamais

moreover ADVERB
en outre

★ **morning** NOUN
le matin *masc*
□ this morning ce matin □ tomorrow morning demain matin □ every morning tous les matins
■ **in the morning** le matin □ at 7 o'clock in the morning à sept heures du matin

Morocco NOUN
le Maroc *masc*
■ **in Morocco** au Maroc

Moscow NOUN
Moscou
■ **in Moscow** à Moscou

mosque NOUN
la mosquée *fem*

mosquito NOUN
le moustique *masc*
■ **a mosquito bite** une piqûre de moustique

★ **most** ADVERB, ADJECTIVE, PRONOUN

Use **la plupart de** when 'most (of)' is followed by a plural noun and **la majeure partie (de)** when 'most (of)' is followed by a singular noun.

1 la plupart de
□ most of my friends la plupart de mes amis □ most people la plupart des gens □ Most cats are affectionate. La plupart des chats sont affectueux.
■ **most of them** la plupart d'entre eux
■ **most of the time** la plupart du temps
2 la majeure partie de
□ most of the work la majeure partie du travail □ most of the class la majeure partie de la classe □ most of the night la majeure partie de la nuit
■ **the most** le plus □ He's the one who talks the most. C'est lui qui parle le plus.

When 'most' is followed by an adjective, the translation depends on whether the noun referred to is masculine, feminine or plural.

■ **the most ...** **1** les plus ... ▫ the most expensive restaurants les restaurants les plus chers ▫ the most expensive seats les places les plus chères **2** le plus ... ▫ the most expensive restaurant le restaurant le plus cher **3** la plus ... ▫ the most expensive seat la place la plus chère
■ **to make the most of something** profiter [28] au maximum de quelque chose
■ **at the most** au maximum ▫ Two hours at the most. Deux heures au maximum.

★ **mostly** ADVERB
■ **The teachers are mostly quite nice.** La plupart des professeurs sont assez gentils.

MOT NOUN
le contrôle technique *masc*
▫ Her car failed its MOT. Sa voiture n'a pas obtenu le certificat du contrôle technique.

motel NOUN
le motel *masc*

moth NOUN
le papillon de nuit *masc*

★ **mother** NOUN
la mère *fem*
▫ my mother ma mère
■ **mother tongue** la langue maternelle

mother-in-law NOUN
la belle-mère *fem* (PL les belles-mères)

Mother's Day NOUN
la fête des Mères *fem*

DID YOU KNOW...?
Mother's Day is usually on the last Sunday of May in France.

motionless ADJECTIVE
immobile (FEM immobile)

motivated ADJECTIVE
motivé (FEM motivée)
▫ He is highly motivated. Il est très motivé.

motivation NOUN
la motivation *fem*

motive NOUN
le mobile *masc*
▫ the motive for the killing le mobile du crime

★ **motor** NOUN
le moteur *masc*
▫ The boat has a motor. Le bateau a un moteur.

motorbike NOUN
la moto *fem*

motorboat NOUN
le bateau à moteur *masc* (PL les bateaux à moteur)

motorcycle NOUN
le vélomoteur *masc*

motorcyclist NOUN
le motard *masc*
la motarde *fem*

motorist NOUN
l'automobiliste *masc/fem*

motor mechanic NOUN
le mécanicien garagiste *masc*

motor racing NOUN
la course automobile *fem*

motorway NOUN
l'autoroute *fem*
▫ on the motorway sur l'autoroute

mouldy ADJECTIVE
moisi (FEM moisie)

to **mount** VERB
1 monter [48]
▫ They're mounting a publicity campaign. Ils montent une campagne publicitaire.
2 augmenter [28]
▫ Tension is mounting. La tension augmente.

to **mount up** VERB
1 s'accumuler [28]
▫ The bills are mounting up. Les factures s'accumulent.
2 augmenter [28]
▫ My savings are mounting up gradually. Mes économies augmentent progressivement.

★ **mountain** NOUN
la montagne *fem*
■ **a mountain bike** un VTT (= *vélo tout-terrain*)

mountaineer NOUN
l'alpiniste *masc/fem*

mountaineering NOUN
l'alpinisme *masc*
▫ I go mountaineering. Je fais de l'alpinisme.

mountainous ADJECTIVE
montagneux (FEM montagneuse)

★ **mouse** NOUN
la souris *fem* (*also for computer*)

mouse mat NOUN
le tapis de souris *masc*

mousse NOUN
1 la mousse *fem* (*food*)
▫ chocolate mousse la mousse au chocolat
2 la mousse coiffante *fem* (*for hair*)

moustache NOUN
la moustache *fem*
▫ He's got a moustache. Il a une moustache.
■ **a man with a moustache** un moustachu

★ **mouth** NOUN
la bouche *fem*

mouthful NOUN
la bouchée *fem*

mouthwash NOUN
le bain de bouche *masc*

★ **move** NOUN
▷ *see also* **move** VERB
1 le tour *masc*
□ It's your move. C'est ton tour.
2 le déménagement *masc*
□ Our move from Oxford to Luton ... Notre déménagement d'Oxford à Luton ...
■ **to get a move on** se remuer [28] □ Get a move on! Remue-toi!

★ to **move** VERB
▷ *see also* **move** NOUN
1 bouger [45]
□ Don't move! Ne bouge pas! □ Could you move your stuff please? Est-ce que tu peux bouger tes affaires s'il te plaît?
2 avancer [12]
□ The taxi was moving very slowly. Le taxi avançait très lentement.
3 émouvoir [31]
□ I was very moved by the film. J'ai été très émue par ce film.
■ **to move house** déménager [45] □ We're moving house in July. Nous allons déménager en juillet.

to **move forward** VERB
avancer [12]

to **move in** VERB
emménager [45]
□ They're moving in next week. Ils emménagent la semaine prochaine.

to **move over** VERB
se pousser [28]
□ Could you move over a bit? Est-ce que vous pouvez vous pousser un peu?

★ **movement** NOUN
le mouvement *masc*

movie NOUN
le film *masc*
■ **the movies** le cinéma □ Let's go to the movies! Si on allait au cinéma?

moving ADJECTIVE
1 en marche (*not stationary*)
□ a moving bus un bus en marche
2 touchant (FEM touchante) (*touching*)
□ a moving story une histoire touchante

to **mow** VERB
tondre [69]
□ to mow the lawn tondre le gazon

mower NOUN
la tondeuse à gazon *fem*

mown VERB ▷ *see* **mow**

★ **MP** NOUN
le député *masc*
□ She's an MP. Elle est député.

MP3 player NOUN
le baladeur numérique *masc*
□ I need a new MP3 player. Il me faut un nouveau baladeur numérique.

mph ABBREVIATION (= *miles per hour*)
km/h (= *kilomètres-heure*)
□ to drive at 50 mph rouler à 80 km/h

> **DID YOU KNOW...?**
> In France, speed is expressed in kilometres per hour. 50 mph is about 80 km/h.

★ **Mr** NOUN
1 Monsieur (PL Messieurs)
2 M. (PL MM.) (*in address*)

★ **Mrs** NOUN
1 Madame (PL Mesdames)
2 Mme (PL Mmes) (*in address*)

MS NOUN (= *multiple sclerosis*)
la sclérose en plaques *fem*
□ She's got MS. Elle a la sclérose en plaques.

★ **Ms** NOUN
1 Madame (PL Mesdames)
2 Mme (PL Mmes) (*in address*)

> **DID YOU KNOW...?**
> There isn't a direct equivalent of 'Ms' in French. If you are writing to somebody and don't know whether she is married, use **Madame**.

★ **much** ADJECTIVE, ADVERB, PRONOUN
1 beaucoup (*with verb*)
□ Do you go out much? Tu sors beaucoup? □ I don't like sport much. Je n'aime pas beaucoup le sport. □ I feel much better now. Je me sens beaucoup mieux maintenant.
2 beaucoup de (*with noun*)
□ I haven't got much money. Je n'ai pas beaucoup d'argent. □ I don't want much rice. Je ne veux pas beaucoup de riz.
■ **very much** 1 (*with verb*) beaucoup □ I enjoyed the film very much. J'ai beaucoup apprécié le film. □ Thank you very much. Merci beaucoup. 2 (*followed by noun*) beaucoup de □ I haven't got very much money. Je n'ai pas beaucoup d'argent.
■ **not much** 1 pas beaucoup □ Have you got a lot of luggage? — No, not much. As-tu beaucoup de bagages? — Non, pas beaucoup. 2 pas grand-chose □ What's on TV? — Not much. Qu'est-ce qu'il y a à la télé? — Pas grand-chose. □ What did you think of it? — Not much. Qu'est-ce que tu en as pensé? — Pas grand-chose.
■ **How much?** Combien? □ How much do you want? Tu en veux combien? □ How much time have you got? Tu as combien de temps? □ How much is it? (*cost*) Combien est-ce que ça coûte?
■ **too much** trop □ That's too much! C'est trop! □ It costs too much. Ça coûte trop cher.

□ They give us too much homework. Ils nous donnent trop de devoirs.
■ **so much** autant □ I didn't think it would cost so much. Je ne pensais pas que ça coûterait autant. □ I've never seen so much traffic. Je n'ai jamais vu autant de circulation.

mud NOUN
la boue *fem*

muddle NOUN
le désordre *masc*
□ The photos are in a muddle. Les photos sont en désordre.

to **muddle up** VERB
confondre [69] (*people*)
□ He muddles me up with my sister. Il me confond avec ma sœur.
■ **to get muddled up** s'embrouiller [28]
□ I'm getting muddled up. Je m'embrouille.

muddy ADJECTIVE
boueux (FEM boueuse)

muesli NOUN
le muesli *masc*

muffler NOUN (US)
le silencieux *masc*

mug NOUN
▷ *see also* **mug** VERB
la grande tasse *fem*
□ Do you want a cup or a mug? Est-ce que vous voulez une tasse normale ou une grande tasse?

to **mug** VERB
▷ *see also* **mug** NOUN
agresser [28]
□ He was mugged in the city centre. Il s'est fait agresser au centre-ville.

mugger NOUN
l'agresseur *masc*

mugging NOUN
l'agression *fem*

muggy ADJECTIVE
lourd (FEM lourde)
□ It's muggy today. Il fait lourd aujourd'hui.

multiple choice test NOUN
le QCM *masc* (= *le questionnaire à choix multiples*)

multiple sclerosis NOUN
la sclérose en plaques *fem*
□ She's got multiple sclerosis. Elle a la sclérose en plaques.

multiplication NOUN
la multiplication *fem*

to **multiply** VERB
multiplier [19]
□ to multiply 6 by 3 multiplier six par trois

multi-storey car park NOUN
le parking à plusieurs étages *masc*

★ **mum** NOUN

You use **mère** in most cases, except when you are talking to your mother or using it as her name, then you would use **maman**.

1 la mère *fem*
□ my mum ma mère □ her mum sa mère
2 la maman *fem*
□ Mum! Maman! □ I'll ask Mum. Je vais demander à maman.

mummy NOUN
1 la maman *fem* (*mum*)
□ Mummy says I can go. Maman dit que je peux y aller.
2 la momie *fem* (*Egyptian*)

mumps NOUN
les oreillons *masc pl*

★ **murder** NOUN
▷ *see also* **murder** VERB
le meurtre *masc*

★ to **murder** VERB
▷ *see also* **murder** NOUN
assassiner [28]
□ He was murdered. Il a été assassiné.

murderer NOUN
l'assassin *masc*

★ **muscle** NOUN
le muscle *masc*

muscular ADJECTIVE
musclé (FEM musclée)

★ **museum** NOUN
le musée *masc*

★ **mushroom** NOUN
le champignon *masc*
□ a mushroom omelette une omelette aux champignons

★ **music** NOUN
la musique *fem*

★ **musical** ADJECTIVE
▷ *see also* **musical** NOUN
doué pour la musique (FEM douée pour la musique)
□ I'm not musical. Je ne suis pas doué pour la musique.
■ **a musical instrument** un instrument de musique

★ **musical** NOUN
▷ *see also* **musical** ADJECTIVE
la comédie musicale *fem*

music centre NOUN
la chaîne stéréo *fem* (PL les chaînes stéréo)

★ **musician** NOUN
le musicien *masc*
la musicienne *fem*

Muslim NOUN
le musulman *masc*
la musulmane *fem*
□ He's a Muslim. Il est musulman.

English-French

m

mussel NOUN
la moule *fem*

★ **must** VERB

> When 'must' means that you assume or suppose something, use **devoir**; when it means it's necessary to do something, eg 'I must buy some presents', use **il faut que** ..., which comes from the verb **falloir** and is followed by a verb in the subjunctive.

1 devoir [26] (*I suppose*)
□ You must be tired. Tu dois être fatigué. □ They must have plenty of money. Ils doivent avoir beaucoup d'argent. □ There must be some problem. Il doit y avoir un problème.
2 il faut que
□ I must buy some presents. Il faut que j'achète des cadeaux. □ I really must go now. Il faut que j'y aille.
■ **You mustn't forget to send her a card.** N'oublie surtout pas de lui envoyer une carte.
■ **You must come and see us.** (*invitation*) Venez donc nous voir.

mustard NOUN
la moutarde *fem*

mustn't VERB = **must not**

to **mutter** VERB
marmonner [28]

mutton NOUN
le mouton *masc*

★ **my** ADJECTIVE
mon *masc*
□ my father mon père
ma *fem*
□ my aunt ma tante
mes *pl*
□ my parents mes parents

> **ma** becomes **mon** before a vowel sound.

■ **my friend 1** (*male*) mon ami **2** (*female*) mon amie

> Do not use **mon/ma/mes** with parts of the body.

□ I want to wash my hair. Je voudrais me laver les cheveux. □ I'm going to clean my teeth. Je vais me brosser les dents. □ I've hurt my foot. Je me suis fait mal au pied.

★ **myself** PRONOUN
1 me
□ I've hurt myself. Je me suis fait mal. □ I really enjoyed myself. Je me suis vraiment bien amusé. □ ... when I look at myself in the mirror. ... quand je me regarde dans la glace.
2 moi
□ I don't like talking about myself. Je n'aime pas parler de moi.
3 moi-même
□ I made it myself. Je l'ai fait moi-même.
■ **by myself** tout seul □ I don't like travelling by myself. Je n'aime pas voyager tout seul.

mysterious ADJECTIVE
mystérieux (FEM mystérieuse)

★ **mystery** NOUN
le mystère *masc*
■ **a murder mystery** (*novel*) un roman policier

myth NOUN
1 le mythe *masc* (*legend*)
□ a Greek myth un mythe grec
2 l'idée reçue *fem* (*untrue idea*)
□ That's a myth. C'est une idée reçue.

mythology NOUN
la mythologie *fem*

Numbers in brackets refer to verb tables on pages 650 to 658

Nn

to **nag** VERB
harceler [43] (*scold*)
□ She's always nagging me. Elle me harcèle constamment.

nail NOUN
1 l'ongle *masc* (*on finger, toe*)
□ Don't bite your nails! Ne te ronge pas les ongles!
2 le clou *masc* (*made of metal*)

nailbrush NOUN
la brosse à ongles *fem*

nailfile NOUN
la lime à ongles *fem*

nail scissors PL NOUN
les ciseaux à ongles *masc pl*

nail varnish NOUN
le vernis à ongles *masc*
■ **nail varnish remover** le dissolvant

naked ADJECTIVE
nu (FEM nue)

★ **name** NOUN
le nom *masc*
■ **What's your name?** Comment vous appelez-vous?

nanny NOUN
la garde d'enfants *fem*
□ She's a nanny. C'est une garde d'enfants.

nap NOUN
le petit somme *masc*
■ **to have a nap** faire [36] un petit somme

napkin NOUN
la serviette *fem*

nappy NOUN
la couche *fem*

★ **narrow** ADJECTIVE
étroit (FEM étroite)

narrow-minded ADJECTIVE
borné (FEM bornée)

nasty ADJECTIVE
1 mauvais (FEM mauvaise) (*bad*)
□ a nasty cold un mauvais rhume □ a nasty smell une mauvaise odeur
2 méchant (FEM méchante) (*unfriendly*)
□ He gave me a nasty look. Il m'a regardé d'un air méchant.

★ **nation** NOUN
la nation *fem*

★ **national** ADJECTIVE
national (FEM nationale, MASC PL nationaux)
□ He's the national champion. C'est le champion national.
■ **the national elections** les élections législatives

national anthem NOUN
l'hymne national *masc*

National Health Service NOUN
la Sécurité sociale *fem*

> **DID YOU KNOW...?**
> In France you have to pay for medical treatment when you receive it, and then claim it back from the **Sécurité sociale**.

nationalism NOUN
le nationalisme *masc*
□ Scottish nationalism le nationalisme écossais

nationalist NOUN
le/la nationaliste *masc/fem*

nationality NOUN
la nationalité *fem*

National Lottery NOUN
la Loterie nationale *fem*

national park NOUN
le parc national *masc* (PL les parcs nationaux)

★ **native** ADJECTIVE
natal (FEM natale)
□ my native country mon pays natal
■ **native language** la langue maternelle
□ English is not their native language. L'anglais n'est pas leur langue maternelle.

★ **natural** ADJECTIVE
naturel (FEM naturelle)

naturalist NOUN
le naturaliste *masc*

★ **naturally** ADVERB
naturellement
□ Naturally, we were very disappointed. Nous avons naturellement été très déçus.

★ **nature** NOUN
la nature *fem*

English-French

naughty ADJECTIVE
vilain (FEM vilaine)
□ Naughty girl! Vilaine! □ Don't be naughty! Ne fais pas le vilain!

★ **navy** NOUN
la marine *fem*
□ He's in the navy. Il est dans la marine.

navy-blue ADJECTIVE
bleu marine (FEM+PL bleu marine)
□ a navy-blue skirt une jupe bleu marine

Nazi NOUN
le Nazi *masc*
la Nazie *fem*
□ the Nazis les Nazis

★ **near** ADJECTIVE
▷ *see also* **near** PREPOSITION, ADVERB
proche (FEM proche)
□ It's fairly near. C'est assez proche.
■ **It's near enough to walk.** On peut facilement y aller à pied.
■ **the nearest** le plus proche □ Where's the nearest service station? Où est la station-service la plus proche? □ The nearest shops were three kilometres away. Les magasins les plus proches étaient à trois kilomètres.

★ **near** PREPOSITION, ADVERB
▷ *see also* **near** ADJECTIVE
près de
□ I live near Liverpool. J'habite près de Liverpool. □ near my house près de chez moi
■ **near here** près d'ici □ Is there a bank near here? Est-ce qu'il y a une banque près d'ici?
■ **near to** près de □ It's very near to the school. C'est tout près de l'école.

n

★ **nearby** ADVERB
▷ *see also* **nearby** ADJECTIVE
à proximité
□ There's a supermarket nearby. Il y a un supermarché à proximité.

★ **nearby** ADJECTIVE
▷ *see also* **nearby** ADVERB
1 proche (FEM proche) (*close*)
□ a nearby garage un garage proche
2 voisin (FEM voisine) (*neighbouring*)
□ We went to the nearby village of Torrance. Nous sommes allés à Torrance, le village voisin.

★ **nearly** ADVERB
presque
□ Dinner's nearly ready. Le dîner est presque prêt. □ I'm nearly 15. J'ai presque quinze ans.
■ **I nearly missed the train.** J'ai failli rater le train.

★ **neat** ADJECTIVE
soigné (FEM soignée)
□ She has very neat writing. Elle a une écriture très soignée.

neatly ADVERB
soigneusement
□ neatly folded soigneusement plié
■ **neatly dressed** impeccable

★ **necessarily** ADVERB
■ **not necessarily** pas forcément

★ **necessary** ADJECTIVE
nécessaire (FEM nécessaire)

necessity NOUN
la chose nécessaire *fem*
□ A car is a necessity, not a luxury. Une voiture est une chose nécessaire et non pas un luxe.

★ **neck** NOUN
1 le cou *masc* (*of body*)
■ **a stiff neck** un torticolis
2 l'encolure *fem* (*of garment*)
□ a V-neck sweater un pull avec une encolure en V

necklace NOUN
le collier *masc*

★ to **need** VERB
▷ *see also* **need** NOUN
avoir [8] besoin de
□ I need a bigger size. J'ai besoin d'une plus grande taille.
■ **to need to do something** avoir [8] besoin de faire quelque chose □ I need to change some money. J'ai besoin de changer de l'argent.

★ **need** NOUN
▷ *see also* **need** VERB
■ **There's no need to book.** Il n'est pas nécessaire de réserver.

needle NOUN
l'aiguille *fem*

★ **negative** NOUN
▷ *see also* **negative** ADJECTIVE
le négatif *masc* (*photo*)

★ **negative** ADJECTIVE
▷ *see also* **negative** NOUN
négatif (FEM négative)
□ He's got a very negative attitude. Il a une attitude très négative.

neglected ADJECTIVE
mal tenu (FEM mal tenue) (*untidy*)
□ The garden is neglected. Le jardin est mal tenu.

negligee NOUN
le déshabillé *masc*

★ to **negotiate** VERB
négocier [19]

negotiations PL NOUN
les négociations *fem pl*

★ **neighbour** (US **neighbor**) NOUN
le voisin *masc*
la voisine *fem*
□ the neighbours' garden le jardin des voisins

neighbourhood (US **neighborhood**) NOUN
le quartier *masc*

★**neither** PRONOUN, CONJUNCTION, ADVERB
aucun des deux
□ Neither of them is coming. Aucun des deux ne vient. □ Carrots or peas? — Neither, thanks. Des carottes ou des petits pois? — Aucun des deux merci.
aucune des deux
□ neither team aucune des deux équipes
■ **neither ... nor ...** ni ... ni ... □ Neither Sarah nor Tamsin is coming to the party. Ni Sarah ni Tamsin ne viennent à la soirée.
■ **Neither do I.** Moi non plus. □ I don't like him. — Neither do I! Je ne l'aime pas. — Moi non plus!
■ **Neither have I.** Moi non plus. □ I've never been to Spain. — Neither have I. Je ne suis jamais allé en Espagne. — Moi non plus.

neon NOUN
le néon *masc*
□ a neon light une lampe au néon

★**nephew** NOUN
le neveu *masc* (PL les neveux)
□ my nephew mon neveu

★**nerve** NOUN
1 le nerf *masc*
□ She sometimes gets on my nerves. Elle me tape quelquefois sur les nerfs.
2 le toupet *masc* (*cheek*)
□ He's got a nerve! Il a du toupet!

nerve-racking ADJECTIVE
angoissant (FEM angoissante)

★**nervous** ADJECTIVE
tendu (FEM tendue) (*tense*)
□ I bite my nails when I'm nervous. Je me ronge les ongles quand je suis tendu.
■ **to be nervous about something**
appréhender [28] de faire quelque chose
□ I'm a bit nervous about flying to the States by myself. J'appréhende un peu d'aller toute seule en avion aux États-Unis.

nest NOUN
le nid *masc*

★**Net** NOUN
le Net *masc*
□ to surf the Net surfer sur le Net

★**net** NOUN
le filet *masc*
□ a fishing net un filet de pêche

netball NOUN
■ **Netball is a bit like basketball.** Le netball ressemble un peu au basket.

★**Netherlands** PL NOUN
les Pays-Bas *masc*
■ **in the Netherlands** aux Pays-Bas

★**network** NOUN
1 le réseau *masc* (PL les réseaux)
2 l'opérateur *masc* (*for mobile phone*)
□ Which network are you on? Tu es avec quel opérateur?

neurotic ADJECTIVE
névrosé (FEM névrosée)

★**never** ADVERB
1 jamais
□ Have you ever been to Germany? — No, never. Est-ce que tu es déjà allé en Allemagne? — Non, jamais. □ When are you going to phone him? — Never! Quand est-ce que tu vas l'appeler? — Jamais!
2 ne ... jamais

> Add **ne** if the sentence contains a verb.

□ I never write letters. Je n'écris jamais. □ I have never been camping. Je n'ai jamais fait de camping. □ Never leave valuables in your locker. Ne laissez jamais d'objets de valeur dans votre casier.
■ **Never again!** Plus jamais!
■ **Never mind.** Ça ne fait rien.

★**new** ADJECTIVE
1 nouveau (FEM nouvelle, MASC PL nouveaux)
□ her new boyfriend son nouveau copain □ I need a new dress. J'ai besoin d'une nouvelle robe.

> **nouveau** changes to **nouvel** before a vowel and most words beginning with 'h'.

□ the new hotel le nouvel hôtel
2 neuf (FEM neuve) (*brand new*)
□ They've got a new car. Ils ont une voiture neuve.

newborn ADJECTIVE
■ **a newborn baby** un nouveau-né

newcomer NOUN
le nouveau venu *masc* (MASC PL les nouveaux venus)
la nouvelle venue *fem*

★**news** NOUN
1 les nouvelles *fem pl*
□ good news de bonnes nouvelles □ I've had some bad news. J'ai reçu de mauvaises nouvelles. □ It was nice to have your news. J'ai été content d'avoir de tes nouvelles.
2 la nouvelle *fem* (*single piece of news*)
□ That's wonderful news! Quelle bonne nouvelle!
3 le journal télévisé *masc* (*on TV*)
□ I watch the news every evening. Je regarde le journal télévisé tous les soirs.
4 les informations *fem pl* (*on radio*)
□ I listen to the news every morning. J'écoute les informations tous les matins.

★**newsagent** NOUN
le marchand de journaux *masc*
la marchande de journaux *fem*

English-French

★ **newspaper** NOUN
le journal *masc* (PL les journaux)
□ I deliver newspapers. Je distribue des journaux.

newsreader NOUN
le présentateur *masc*
la présentatrice *fem*

★ **New Year** NOUN
le Nouvel An *masc*
□ to celebrate New Year fêter le Nouvel An
■ **Happy New Year!** Bonne Année!
■ **New Year's Day** le Premier de l'an
■ **New Year's Eve** la Saint-Sylvestre

New Zealand NOUN
la Nouvelle-Zélande *fem*
■ **in New Zealand** en Nouvelle-Zélande

New Zealander NOUN
le Néo-Zélandais *masc*
la Néo-Zélandaise *fem*

★ **next** ADJECTIVE, ADVERB, PREPOSITION
1 prochain (FEM prochaine) (*in time*)
□ next Saturday samedi prochain □ next year l'année prochaine □ next summer l'été prochain
2 suivant (FEM suivante) (*in sequence*)
□ the next train le train suivant □ Next please! Au suivant!
3 ensuite (*afterwards*)
□ What shall I do next? Qu'est-ce que je fais ensuite? □ What happened next? Qu'est-ce qui s'est passé ensuite?
■ **next to** à côté de □ next to the bank à côté de la banque
■ **the next day** le lendemain □ The next day we visited Versailles. Le lendemain nous avons visité Versailles.
■ **the next time** la prochaine fois □ the next time you see her la prochaine fois que tu la verras
■ **next door** à côté □ They live next door. Ils habitent à côté. □ the people next door les gens d'à côté
■ **the next room** la pièce d'à côté

NHS NOUN
la Sécurité sociale *fem*

DID YOU KNOW...?
In France, you have to pay for medical treatment when you receive it, and then claim it back from the **Sécurité sociale**.

★ **nice** ADJECTIVE
1 gentil (FEM gentille) (*kind*)
□ Your parents are very nice. Tes parents sont très gentils. □ It was nice of you to remember my birthday. C'était gentil de ta part de te souvenir de mon anniversaire.
■ **to be nice to somebody** être [35] gentil avec quelqu'un
2 joli (FEM jolie) (*pretty*)
□ That's a nice dress! Qu'est-ce qu'elle est jolie, cette robe! □ Aix is a nice town. Aix est une jolie ville.

WORD POWER
You can use a number of other words instead of **nice** to mean 'pretty':
attractive séduisant
□ an attractive girl une fille séduisante
beautiful beau
□ a beautiful painting un beau tableau
lovely charmant
□ a lovely surprise une charmante surprise
pretty joli
□ a pretty dress une jolie robe

3 bon (FEM bonne) (*food*)
□ It's very nice. C'est très bon. □ a nice cup of coffee une bonne tasse de café
■ **Have a nice time!** Amuse-toi bien!
■ **nice weather** le beau temps
■ **It's a nice day.** Il fait beau.

nickname NOUN
le surnom *masc*

★ **niece** NOUN
la nièce *fem*
□ my niece ma nièce

Nigeria NOUN
le Nigéria *masc*
■ **in Nigeria** au Nigéria

★ **night** NOUN
1 la nuit *fem*
□ I want a single room for two nights. Je veux une chambre à un lit pour deux nuits.
■ **My mother works nights.** Ma mère travaille de nuit.
■ **at night** la nuit
■ **Goodnight!** Bonne nuit!
2 le soir *masc* (*evening*)
□ last night hier soir

night club NOUN
la boîte de nuit *fem*

nightdress NOUN
la chemise de nuit *fem*

nightie NOUN
la chemise de nuit *fem*

nightlife NOUN
■ **There's plenty of nightlife.** Il y a plein de choses à faire le soir.

★ **nightmare** NOUN
le cauchemar *masc*
□ It was a real nightmare! Ça a été un vrai cauchemar!
■ **to have a nightmare** faire [36] un cauchemar

nightshirt NOUN
la chemise de nuit *fem*

 Numbers in brackets refer to verb tables on pages 650 to 658

nil NOUN
le zéro *masc*
□ We won one-nil. Nous avons gagné un à zéro.

★ **nine** NUMBER
neuf
□ She's nine. Elle a neuf ans.

★ **nineteen** NUMBER
dix-neuf
□ She's nineteen. Elle a dix-neuf ans.

★ **nineteenth** ADJECTIVE
dix-neuvième (FEM dix-neuvième)
□ her nineteenth birthday son dix-neuvième anniversaire □ the nineteenth floor le dix-neuvième étage
■ **the nineteenth of August** le dix-neuf août

★ **ninety** NUMBER
quatre-vingt-dix

★ **ninth** ADJECTIVE
neuvième (FEM neuvième)
□ the ninth floor le neuvième étage
■ **the ninth of August** le neuf août

★ **no** ADVERB, ADJECTIVE
1 non
□ Are you coming? — No. Est-ce que vous venez? — Non. □ Would you like some more? — No thank you. Vous en voulez encore? — Non merci.
2 pas de (*not any*)
□ There's no hot water. Il n'y a pas d'eau chaude. □ There are no trains on Sundays. Il n'y a pas de trains le dimanche. □ No problem. Pas de problème.
■ **I've got no idea.** Je n'en ai aucune idée.
■ **No way!** Pas question!
■ **'no smoking'** 'défense de fumer'

★ **nobody** PRONOUN
1 personne
□ Who's going with you? — Nobody. Qui t'accompagne? — Personne.
2 ne ... personne
Add **ne** if the sentence contains a verb.
□ There was nobody in the office. Il n'y avait personne au bureau.
■ **Nobody likes him.** Personne ne l'aime.

★ to **nod** VERB
acquiescer [12] d'un signe de tête (*in agreement*)
■ **to nod at somebody** (*as greeting*) saluer [28] quelqu'un d'un signe de tête

★ **noise** NOUN
le bruit *masc*
□ Please make less noise. Faites moins de bruit s'il vous plaît.

noisy ADJECTIVE
bruyant (FEM bruyante)

to **nominate** VERB
1 nommer [28] (*appoint*)
□ She was nominated as director. Elle a été nommée directrice.
2 proposer [28] (*propose*)
□ I nominate Kyle Alexander as team captain. Je propose Kyle Alexander comme capitaine de l'équipe.
■ **He was nominated for an Oscar.** Il a été nominé pour un Oscar.

★ **none** PRONOUN
1 aucun
□ What sports do you do? — None. Qu'est-ce que tu fais comme sport? — Je n'en fais aucun.
aucune
□ How many sisters have you got? — None. Tu as combien de sœurs? — Aucune.
2 aucun ... ne
Add **ne** if the sentence contains a verb.
□ None of my friends wanted to come. Aucun de mes amis n'a voulu venir.
■ **There's none left.** Il n'y en a plus.
■ **There are none left.** Il n'y en a plus.

nonsense NOUN
les bêtises *fem pl*
□ She talks a lot of nonsense. Elle dit beaucoup de bêtises. □ Nonsense! Ne dis pas de bêtises!

non-smoker NOUN
le non-fumeur *masc*
□ He's a non-smoker. Il est non-fumeur.

non-stop ADJECTIVE, ADVERB
1 direct (FEM directe)
□ a non-stop flight un vol direct □ We flew non-stop. Nous avons pris un vol direct.
2 sans arrêt
□ He talks non-stop. Il parle sans arrêt.

noodles PL NOUN
les nouilles *fem pl*

noon NOUN
midi *masc*
□ at noon à midi □ before noon avant midi

★ **no one** PRONOUN
1 personne
□ Who's going with you? — No one. Qui t'accompagne? — Personne.
2 ne ... personne
Add **ne** if the sentence contains a verb.
□ There was no one in the office. Il n'y avait personne au bureau.
■ **No one likes Harry.** Personne n'aime Harry.

★ **nor** CONJUNCTION
■ **neither ... nor** ni ... ni □ neither the cinema nor the swimming pool ni le cinéma, ni la piscine

English–French

■ **Nor do I.** Moi non plus. ◻ I didn't like the film. — Nor did I. Je n'ai pas aimé le film. — Moi non plus.

■ **Nor have I.** Moi non plus. ◻ I haven't seen him. — Nor have I. Je ne l'ai pas vu. — Moi non plus.

★ **normal** ADJECTIVE

1 habituel (FEM habituelle) (*usual*)
◻ at the normal time à l'heure habituelle

2 normal (FEM normale, MASC PL normaux) (*standard*)
◻ a normal car une voiture normale

★ **normally** ADVERB

1 généralement (*usually*)
◻ I normally arrive at nine o'clock. J'arrive généralement à neuf heures.

2 normalement (*as normal*)
◻ In spite of the strike, the airports are working normally. Malgré la grève, les aéroports fonctionnent normalement.

Normandy NOUN
la Normandie *fem*
■ **in Normandy** en Normandie
■ **to Normandy** en Normandie

★ **north** ADJECTIVE, ADVERB
▷ *see also* **north** NOUN

1 nord (FEM+PL nord)
◻ the north coast la côte nord
■ **a north wind** un vent du nord

2 vers le nord
◻ We were travelling north. Nous allions vers le nord.
■ **north of** au nord de ◻ It's north of London. C'est au nord de Londres.

★ **north** NOUN
▷ *see also* **north** ADJECTIVE, ADVERB
le nord *masc*
◻ in the north dans le nord

North America NOUN
l'Amérique du Nord *fem*

northbound ADJECTIVE
■ **The truck was northbound on the M5.** Le camion se trouvait sur la M5 en direction du nord.
■ **Northbound traffic is moving very slowly.** La circulation vers le nord avance très lentement.

northeast NOUN
le nord-est *masc*
◻ in the northeast au nord-est

★ **northern** ADJECTIVE
■ **the northern part of the island** la partie nord de l'île
■ **Northern Europe** l'Europe du Nord

★ **Northern Ireland** NOUN
l'Irlande du Nord *fem*
■ **in Northern Ireland** en Irlande du Nord
■ **to Northern Ireland** en Irlande du Nord
■ **I'm from Northern Ireland.** Je viens d'Irlande du Nord.

North Pole NOUN
le pôle Nord *masc*

North Sea NOUN
la mer du Nord *fem*

northwest NOUN
le nord-ouest *masc*
◻ in the northwest au nord-ouest

★ **Norway** NOUN
la Norvège *fem*
■ **in Norway** en Norvège

★ **Norwegian** NOUN
▷ *see also* **Norwegian** ADJECTIVE

1 le Norvégien *masc*
la Norvégienne *fem* (*person*)

2 le norvégien *masc* (*language*)

★ **Norwegian** ADJECTIVE
▷ *see also* **Norwegian** NOUN
norvégien (FEM norvégienne)

★ **nose** NOUN
le nez *masc* (PL les nez)

nosebleed NOUN
■ **to have a nosebleed** saigner [28] du nez
◻ I often get nosebleeds. Je saigne souvent du nez.

nosy ADJECTIVE
fouineur (FEM fouineuse)

★ **not** ADVERB

1 pas
◻ Are you coming or not? Est-ce que tu viens ou pas?
■ **not really** pas vraiment
■ **not at all** pas du tout
■ **not yet** pas encore ◻ Have you finished? — Not yet. As-tu fini? — Pas encore.

2 ne ... pas

> Add **ne** if the sentence contains a verb.

◻ I'm not sure. Je ne suis pas sûr. ◻ It's not raining. Il ne pleut pas. ◻ You shouldn't do that. Tu ne devrais pas faire ça. ◻ They haven't arrived yet. Ils ne sont pas encore arrivés.

3 non
◻ I hope not. J'espère que non. ◻ Can you lend me £10? — I'm afraid not. Est-ce que tu peux me prêter dix livres? — Non, désolé.

★ **note** NOUN

1 la note *fem*
◻ to take notes prendre des notes

2 le mot *masc* (*letter*)
◻ I'll write her a note. Je vais lui écrire un mot.

3 le billet *masc* (*banknote*)
◻ a £5 note un billet de cinq livres

to **note down** VERB
noter [28]

n

Numbers in brackets refer to verb tables on pages 650 to 658

notebook NOUN
le carnet *masc*

notepad NOUN
le bloc-notes *masc* (PL les blocs-notes)

notepaper NOUN
le papier à lettres *masc*

★ **nothing** NOUN
1 rien
□ What's wrong? — Nothing. Qu'est-ce qui ne va pas? — Rien. □ nothing special rien de particulier
2 ne … rien

Add **ne** if the sentence contains a verb.

□ He does nothing. Il ne fait rien. □ He ate nothing for breakfast. Il n'a rien mangé au petit déjeuner.
■ **Nothing is open on Sundays.** Rien n'est ouvert le dimanche.

★ **notice** NOUN
▷ *see also* **notice** VERB
le panneau *masc* (PL les panneaux) (*sign*)
■ **to put up a notice** mettre [47] un panneau
■ **a warning notice** un avertissement
■ **Don't take any notice of him!** Ne fais pas attention à lui!

★ to **notice** VERB
▷ *see also* **notice** NOUN
remarquer [28]

notice board NOUN
le panneau d'affichage *masc* (PL les panneaux d'affichage)

nought NOUN
le zéro *masc*

noun NOUN
le nom *masc*

★ **novel** NOUN
le roman *masc*

novelist NOUN
le romancier *masc*
la romancière *fem*

★ **November** NOUN
novembre *masc*
■ **in November** en novembre

★ **now** ADVERB, CONJUNCTION
maintenant
□ What are you doing now? Qu'est-ce que tu fais maintenant?
■ **just now** en ce moment □ I'm rather busy just now. Je suis très occupé en ce moment.
■ **I did it just now.** Je viens de le faire.
■ **He should be there by now.** Il doit être arrivé à l'heure qu'il est.
■ **It should be ready by now.** Ça devrait être déjà prêt.
■ **now and then** de temps en temps

nowhere ADVERB
nulle part
□ nowhere else nulle part ailleurs

★ **nuclear** ADJECTIVE
nucléaire (FEM nucléaire)
□ nuclear power l'énergie nucléaire □ a nuclear power station une centrale nucléaire

nude ADJECTIVE
▷ *see also* **nude** NOUN
nu (FEM nue)

nude NOUN
▷ *see also* **nude** ADJECTIVE
■ **in the nude** nu

nudist NOUN
le/la nudiste *masc/fem*

nuisance NOUN
■ **It's a nuisance.** C'est très embêtant.
■ **Sorry to be a nuisance.** Désolé de vous déranger.

numb ADJECTIVE
engourdi (FEM engourdie)
□ My leg's gone numb. J'ai la jambe engourdie.
■ **numb with cold** engourdi par le froid

★ **number** NOUN
1 le nombre *masc* (*total amount*)
□ a large number of people un grand nombre de gens
2 le numéro *masc* (*of house, telephone, bank account*)
□ They live at number 5. Ils habitent au numéro cinq. □ What's your phone number? Quel est votre numéro de téléphone? □ You've got the wrong number. Vous vous êtes trompé de numéro.
3 le chiffre *masc* (*figure, digit*)
□ I can't read the second number. Je n'arrive pas à lire le deuxième chiffre.

number plate NOUN
la plaque d'immatriculation *fem*

nun NOUN
la religieuse *fem*
□ She's a nun. Elle est religieuse.

★ **nurse** NOUN
l'infirmier *masc*
l'infirmière *fem*
□ She's a nurse. Elle est infirmière.

nursery NOUN
1 la crèche *fem* (*for children*)
2 la pépinière *fem* (*for plants*)

nursery school NOUN
l'école maternelle *fem*

DID YOU KNOW…?
The **école maternelle** is a state school for 2-6 year-olds.

nursery slope NOUN
la piste pour débutants *fem*

nut NOUN
1 la cacahuète *fem* (*peanut*)
2 la noisette *fem* (*hazelnut*)
3 la noix *fem* (PL les noix) (*walnut*)
4 l'écrou *masc* (*made of metal*)

nutmeg NOUN
la noix de muscade *fem*

nutritious ADJECTIVE
nourrissant (FEM nourrissante)

nuts ADJECTIVE
■ **He's nuts.** Il est dingue.

nylon NOUN
le nylon *masc*

Oo

oak NOUN
le chêne *masc*
□ an oak table une table en chêne

oar NOUN
l'aviron *masc*

oats NOUN
l'avoine *fem*

obedient ADJECTIVE
obéissant (FEM obéissante)

to **obey** VERB
■ **to obey the rules** respecter [28] le règlement

★ **object** NOUN
l'objet *masc*
□ a familiar object un objet familier

objection NOUN
l'objection *fem*

★ **objective** NOUN
l'objectif *masc*

oblong ADJECTIVE
rectangulaire (FEM rectangulaire)

oboe NOUN
le hautbois *masc*
□ I play the oboe. Je joue du hautbois.

obscene ADJECTIVE
obscène (FEM obscène)

observant ADJECTIVE
observateur (FEM observatrice)

to **observe** VERB
observer [28]

obsessed ADJECTIVE
obsédé (FEM obsédée)
□ He's obsessed with trains. Il est obsédé par les trains.

obsession NOUN
l'obsession *fem*
□ It's getting to be an obsession with you. Ça devient une obsession chez toi.
■ **Football's an obsession of mine.** Le football est une de mes passions.

obsolete ADJECTIVE
dépassé (FEM dépassée)

obstacle NOUN
l'obstacle *masc*

obstinate ADJECTIVE
obstiné (FEM obstinée)

to **obstruct** VERB
bloquer [28]
□ A lorry was obstructing the traffic. Un camion bloquait la circulation.

to **obtain** VERB
obtenir [83]

★ **obvious** ADJECTIVE
évident (FEM évidente)

★ **obviously** ADVERB
1 évidemment (*of course*)
□ Do you want to pass the exam? — Obviously! Tu veux être reçu à l'examen? — Évidemment!
■ **Obviously not!** Bien sûr que non!
2 manifestement (*visibly*)
□ She was obviously exhausted. Elle était manifestement épuisée.

★ **occasion** NOUN
l'occasion *fem*
□ a special occasion une occasion spéciale
■ **on several occasions** à plusieurs reprises

occasionally ADVERB
de temps en temps

occupation NOUN
la profession *fem*

to **occupy** VERB
occuper [28]
□ That seat is occupied. Cette place est occupée.

to **occur** VERB
avoir [8] lieu (*happen*)
□ The accident occurred yesterday. L'accident a eu lieu hier.
■ **It suddenly occurred to me that ...** Il m'est soudain venu à l'esprit que ...

OCD NOUN (= *obsessive compulsive disorder*)
la TOC *masc*

★ **ocean** NOUN
l'océan *masc*

★ **o'clock** ADVERB
■ **at four o'clock** à quatre heures
■ **It's five o'clock.** Il est cinq heures.

★ **October** NOUN
octobre *masc*
■ **in October** en octobre

octopus NOUN
la pieuvre *fem*

★**odd** ADJECTIVE
1 bizarre (FEM bizarre)
□ That's odd! C'est bizarre!
2 impair (FEM impaire)
□ an odd number un chiffre impair

★**of** PREPOSITION
1 de
□ some photos of my holiday des photos de mes vacances □ a boy of ten un garçon de dix ans

de changes to **d'** before a vowel and most words beginning with 'h'.

d'
□ a kilo of oranges un kilo d'oranges

de + le changes to **du**, and **de + les** changes to **des**.

du
□ the end of the film la fin du film
des
□ the end of the holidays la fin des vacances
2 en (*with quantity, amount*)
□ He's got four sisters. I've met two of them. Il a quatre sœurs. J'en ai rencontré deux. □ Can I have half of that? Je peux en avoir la moitié?
■ **three of us** trois d'entre nous
■ **a friend of mine** un de mes amis
■ **the 14th of September** le quatorze septembre
■ **That's very kind of you.** C'est très gentil de votre part.
■ **It's made of wood.** C'est en bois.

★**off** ADVERB, PREPOSITION, ADJECTIVE

For other expressions with 'off', see the verbs 'get', 'take', 'turn' etc.

1 éteint (FEM éteinte) (*heater, light, TV*)
□ All the lights are off. Toutes les lumières sont éteintes.
2 fermé (FEM fermée) (*tap, gas*)
□ Are you sure the tap is off? Tu es sûr que le robinet est fermé?
3 annulé (FEM annulée) (*cancelled*)
□ The match is off. Le match est annulé.
■ **to be off sick** être [35] malade
■ **a day off** un jour de congé □ to take a day off work prendre un jour de congé
■ **She's off school today.** Elle n'est pas à l'école aujourd'hui.
■ **I must be off now.** Je dois m'en aller maintenant.
■ **I'm off.** Je m'en vais.

offence (US **offense**) NOUN
le délit *masc* (*crime*)

offensive ADJECTIVE
choquant (FEM choquante)

★**offer** NOUN
▷ *see also* **offer** VERB
la proposition *fem*
□ a good offer une proposition intéressante
■ **'on special offer'** 'en promotion'

★to **offer** VERB
▷ *see also* **offer** NOUN
proposer [28]
□ He offered to help me. Il m'a proposé de m'aider. □ I offered to go with them. Je leur ai proposé de les accompagner.

★**office** NOUN
le bureau *masc* (PL les bureaux)
□ She works in an office. Elle travaille dans un bureau.

★**officer** NOUN
l'officier *masc*

★**official** ADJECTIVE
officiel (FEM officielle)

off-licence NOUN
le marchand de vins et spiritueux *masc*

off-peak ADVERB
hors saison (*off-season*)
□ It's cheaper to go on holiday off-peak. C'est moins cher de partir en vacances hors saison.
■ **an off-peak gym membership** un abonnement à une salle de sport en heures creuses

offside ADJECTIVE
hors jeu (*in football*)

★**often** ADVERB
souvent
□ It often rains. Il pleut souvent. □ How often do you go to the gym? Tu vas souvent à la gym? □ I'd like to go skiing more often. J'aimerais aller skier plus souvent.

★**oil** NOUN
▷ *see also* **oil** VERB
1 l'huile *fem* (*for lubrication, cooking*)
■ **an oil painting** une peinture à l'huile
2 le pétrole *masc* (*crude oil*)
□ North Sea oil le pétrole de la mer du Nord

★to **oil** VERB
▷ *see also* **oil** NOUN
graisser [28]

oil rig NOUN
la plateforme pétrolière *fem*
□ He works on an oil rig. Il travaille sur une plateforme pétrolière.

oil slick NOUN
la marée noire *fem*

oil well NOUN
le puits de pétrole *masc* (PL les puits de pétrole)

ointment NOUN
la pommade *fem*

Numbers in brackets refer to verb tables on pages 650 to 658

★ **okay** EXCLAMATION, ADJECTIVE
d'accord (*agreed*)
□ Could you call back later? — Okay! Tu peux rappeler plus tard? — D'accord! □ I'll meet you at six o'clock, okay? Je te retrouve à six heures, d'accord? □ Is that okay? C'est d'accord?
■ **I'll do it tomorrow, if that's okay with you.** Je le ferai demain, si tu es d'accord.
■ **Are you okay?** Ça va?
■ **How was your holiday? — It was okay.** C'était comment tes vacances? — Pas mal.
■ **What's your teacher like? — He's okay.** Il est comment ton prof? — Il est sympa. (*informal*)

★ **old** ADJECTIVE
1 vieux (FEM vieille, MASC PL vieux)
□ an old dog un vieux chien □ an old house une vieille maison

vieux changes to **vieil** before a vowel and most words beginning with 'h'.

vieil
□ an old man un vieil homme
âgé (FEM âgée)

When talking about people it is more polite to use **âgé** instead of **vieux**.

□ old people les personnes âgées
2 ancien (FEM ancienne) (*former*)
□ my old English teacher mon ancien professeur d'anglais
■ **How old are you?** Quel âge as-tu?
■ **He's ten years old.** Il a dix ans.
■ **my older brother** mon frère aîné □ my older sister ma sœur aînée
■ **She's two years older than me.** Elle a deux ans de plus que moi.
■ **I'm the oldest in the family.** Je suis l'aîné de la famille.

old age pensioner NOUN
le retraité *masc*
la retraitée *fem*
□ She's an old age pensioner. Elle est retraitée.

old-fashioned ADJECTIVE
1 démodé (FEM démodée)
□ She wears old-fashioned clothes. Elle porte des vêtements démodés.
2 vieux jeu (FEM+PL vieux jeu) (*person*)
□ My parents are rather old-fashioned. Mes parents sont plutôt vieux jeu.

olive NOUN
l'olive *fem*

olive oil NOUN
l'huile d'olive *fem*

olive tree NOUN
l'olivier *masc*

Olympic® ADJECTIVE
olympique (FEM olympique)
■ **the Olympics®** les Jeux olympiques *masc pl*

omelette NOUN
l'omelette *fem*

★ **on** PREPOSITION, ADVERB
▷ *see also* **on** ADJECTIVE

There are several ways of translating 'on'. Scan the examples to find one that is similar to what you want to say. For other expressions with 'on', see the verbs 'go', 'put', 'turn' etc.

1 sur
□ on the table sur la table □ on an island sur une île
2 à
□ on the left à gauche □ on the 2nd floor au deuxième étage □ I go to school on my bike. Je vais à l'école à vélo.

With days and dates 'on' is not translated.

□ on Friday vendredi □ on Fridays le vendredi □ on Christmas Day le jour de Noël □ on June 20th le vingt juin □ on my birthday le jour de mon anniversaire
■ **on TV** à la télé □ What's on TV? Qu'est-ce qu'il y a à la télé?
■ **on the radio** à la radio □ I heard it on the radio. Je l'ai entendu à la radio.
■ **on the bus 1** (*by bus*) en bus □ I go into town on the bus. Je vais en ville en bus.
2 (*inside bus*) dans le bus □ There were no empty seats on the bus. Il n'y avait pas de places libres dans le bus.
■ **on holiday** en vacances □ They're on holiday. Ils sont en vacances.
■ **on strike** en grève

★ **on** ADJECTIVE
▷ *see also* **on** PREPOSITION, ADVERB
1 allumé (FEM allumée) (*heater, light, TV*)
□ I think I left the light on. Je crois que j'ai laissé la lumière allumée.
2 ouvert (FEM ouverte) (*tap, gas*)
□ Leave the tap on. Laisse le robinet ouvert.
3 en marche (*machine*)
□ Is the dishwasher on? Est-ce que le lave-vaisselle est en marche?
■ **What's on at the cinema?** Qu'est-ce qui passe au cinéma?

★ **once** ADVERB
une fois
□ once a week une fois par semaine □ once more encore une fois □ I've been to France once before. J'ai déjà été une fois en France.
■ **Once upon a time ...** Il était une fois ...
■ **at once** tout de suite
■ **once in a while** de temps en temps

★ **one** NUMBER, PRONOUN

Use **un** for masculine nouns and **une** for feminine nouns.

1 un
□ one day un jour □ Do you need a pencil? — No thanks, I've got one. Est-ce que tu as besoin d'un crayon? — Non merci, j'en ai un.
une
□ one minute une minute □ I've got one brother and one sister. J'ai un frère et une sœur.
2 on (*impersonal*)
□ One never knows. On ne sait jamais.
▪ **this one** 1 celui-ci *masc* □ Which foot is hurting? — This one. Quel pied te fait mal? — Celui-ci. 2 celle-ci *fem* □ Which is the best photo? — This one. Quelle est la meilleure photo? — Celle-ci.
▪ **that one** 1 celui-là *masc* □ Which bag is yours? — That one. Lequel est ton sac? — Celui-là. 2 celle-là *fem* □ Which seat do you want? — That one. Quelle place voulez-vous? — Celle-là.

oneself PRONOUN
1 se
□ to hurt oneself se faire mal
2 soi-même
□ It's quicker to do it oneself. C'est plus rapide de le faire soi-même.

one-way ADJECTIVE
▪ **a one-way street** une impasse

★ **onion** NOUN
l'oignon *masc*
□ onion soup la soupe à l'oignon

★ **online** ADJECTIVE, ADVERB
en ligne
▪ **to go online** se connecter [28] à Internet

★ **only** ADVERB, ADJECTIVE, CONJUNCTION
1 seul (FEM seule)
□ Monday is the only day I'm free. Le lundi est le seul jour où je suis libre. □ French is the only subject I like. Le français est la seule matière que j'aime.
2 seulement
□ How much was it? — Only 10 euros. Combien c'était? — Seulement dix euros.
3 ne ... que
□ We only want to stay for one night. Nous ne voulons rester qu'une nuit. □ These books are only 3 euros. Ces livres ne coûtent que trois euros.
4 mais
□ I'd like the same jumper, only in black. Je voudrais le même pull, mais en noir.
▪ **an only child** un enfant unique

onwards ADVERB
à partir de
□ from July onwards à partir de juillet

★ **open** ADJECTIVE
▷ *see also* **open** VERB
ouvert (FEM ouverte)
□ The baker's is open on Sunday morning. La boulangerie est ouverte le dimanche matin.
▪ **in the open air** en plein air

★ to **open** VERB
▷ *see also* **open** ADJECTIVE
1 ouvrir [55]
□ Can I open the window? Est-ce que je peux ouvrir la fenêtre? □ What time do the shops open? Les magasins ouvrent à quelle heure?
2 s'ouvrir [55]
□ The door opens automatically. La porte s'ouvre automatiquement. □ The door opened and in came the teacher. La porte s'est ouverte et le professeur est entré.

opening hours PL NOUN
les heures d'ouverture *fem pl*

opera NOUN
l'opéra *masc*

★ to **operate** VERB
1 fonctionner [28]
□ The lights operate on a timer. Les lumières fonctionnent avec une minuterie.
2 faire [36] fonctionner
□ How do you operate the remote control? Comment fait-on fonctionner la télécommande?
3 opérer [34] (*perform surgery*)
▪ **to operate on someone** opérer [34] quelqu'un

★ **operation** NOUN
l'opération *fem*
□ a major operation une grave opération
▪ **to have an operation** se faire [36] opérer
□ I have never had an operation. Je ne me suis jamais fait opérer.

operator NOUN
le/la standardiste *masc/fem* (*on telephone*)

★ **opinion** NOUN
l'avis *masc*
□ in my opinion à mon avis □ He asked me my opinion. Il m'a demandé mon avis.
▪ **What's your opinion?** Qu'est-ce que vous en pensez?

opinion poll NOUN
le sondage *masc*

★ **opponent** NOUN
l'adversaire *masc/fem*

★ **opportunity** NOUN
l'occasion *fem*
▪ **to have the opportunity to do something** avoir [8] l'occasion de faire quelque chose □ I've never had the opportunity to go abroad. Je n'ai jamais eu l'occasion d'aller à l'étranger.

opposed ADJECTIVE
▪ **I've always been opposed to eating meat.** J'ai toujours été contre la consommation de viande.
▪ **as opposed to** par opposition à

opposing ADJECTIVE
opposé (FEM opposée) *(team)*

★**opposite** ADJECTIVE, ADVERB, PREPOSITION
1 opposé (FEM opposée)
□ It's in the opposite direction. C'est dans la direction opposée.
2 en face
□ They live opposite. Ils habitent en face.
3 en face de
□ the girl sitting opposite me la fille assise en face de moi
■ **the opposite sex** l'autre sexe

★**opposition** NOUN
l'opposition *fem*

optician NOUN
l'opticien *masc*
l'opticienne *fem*
□ She's an optician. Elle est opticienne.

optimist NOUN
l'optimiste *masc/fem*

★**optimistic** ADJECTIVE
optimiste (FEM optimiste)

★**option** NOUN
1 le choix *masc (choice)*
□ I've got no option. Je n'ai pas le choix.
2 la matière à option *fem (optional subject)*
□ I'm doing geology as my option. La géologie est ma matière à option.

optional ADJECTIVE
facultatif (FEM facultative)

★**or** CONJUNCTION
1 ou
□ Would you like tea or coffee? Est-ce que tu veux du thé ou du café?

Use **ni ... ni** in negative sentences.

□ I don't eat meat or fish. Je ne mange ni viande, ni poisson.
2 sinon *(otherwise)*
□ Hurry up or you'll miss the bus. Dépêche-toi, sinon tu vas rater le bus.
■ **Give me the money, or else!** Donne-moi l'argent, sinon tu vas le regretter!

oral ADJECTIVE
▷ *see also* **oral** NOUN
oral (FEM orale, MASC PL oraux)
■ **an oral exam** un oral

oral NOUN
▷ *see also* **oral** ADJECTIVE
l'oral *masc* (PL les oraux)
□ I've got my French oral soon. Je vais bientôt passer mon oral de français.

★**orange** NOUN
▷ *see also* **orange** ADJECTIVE
l'orange *fem*
■ **an orange juice** un jus d'orange

★**orange** ADJECTIVE
▷ *see also* **orange** NOUN
orange (FEM+PL orange)

orchard NOUN
le verger *masc*

orchestra NOUN
l'orchestre *masc*
□ I play in the school orchestra. Je joue dans l'orchestre de l'école.

★**order** NOUN
▷ *see also* **order** VERB
1 l'ordre *masc (sequence)*
□ in alphabetical order dans l'ordre alphabétique
2 la commande *fem (instruction)*
□ The waiter took our order. Le garçon a pris notre commande.
■ **in order to** pour □ He does it in order to earn money. Il le fait pour gagner de l'argent.
■ **'out of order'** 'en panne'

★to **order** VERB
▷ *see also* **order** NOUN
commander [28]
□ We ordered steak and chips. Nous avons commandé un steak frites. □ Are you ready to order? Vous êtes prêt à commander?
■ **to order somebody about** donner [28] des ordres à quelqu'un □ She liked to order him about. Elle aimait lui donner des ordres.

★**ordinary** ADJECTIVE
1 ordinaire (FEM ordinaire)
□ an ordinary day une journée ordinaire
2 comme les autres *(people)*
□ an ordinary family une famille comme les autres □ He's just an ordinary guy. C'est un type comme les autres.

organ NOUN
l'orgue *masc (instrument)*
□ I play the organ. Je joue de l'orgue.

organic ADJECTIVE
biologique (FEM biologique) *(vegetables, fruit)*

★**organization** NOUN
l'organisation *fem*

★to **organize** VERB
organiser [28]

origin NOUN
l'origine *fem*

★**original** ADJECTIVE
original (FEM originale, MASC PL originaux)
□ It's a very original idea. C'est une idée très originale.
■ **Our original plan was to go camping.**
À l'origine nous avions l'intention de faire du camping.

★**originally** ADVERB
à l'origine

Orkney NOUN
les Orcades *fem pl*
■ **in Orkney** dans les Orcades

ornament NOUN
le bibelot *masc*

orphan NOUN
l'orphelin *masc*
l'orpheline *fem*

ostrich NOUN
l'autruche *fem*

★ **other** ADJECTIVE, PRONOUN
autre (FEM autre)
□ Have you got these jeans in other colours? Est-ce que vous avez ce jean dans d'autres couleurs? □ on the other side of the street de l'autre côté de la rue □ the other day l'autre jour
■ **the other one** l'autre □ This one? — No, the other one. Celui-ci? — Non, l'autre.
■ **the others** les autres □ The others are going but I'm not. Les autres y vont mais pas moi.

★ **otherwise** ADVERB, CONJUNCTION
1 sinon (*if not*)
□ Note down the number, otherwise you'll forget it. Note le numéro, sinon tu vas l'oublier. □ Put some sunscreen on, you'll burn otherwise. Mets de la crème solaire, sinon tu vas attraper des coups de soleil.
2 à part ça (*in other ways*)
□ I'm tired, but otherwise I'm fine. Je suis fatigué, mais à part ça, ça va.

★ **ought** VERB

To translate 'ought to' use the conditional tense of **devoir**.

□ I ought to phone my parents. Je devrais appeler mes parents. □ You ought not to do that. Tu ne devrais pas faire ça. □ He ought to win. Il devrait gagner.

ounce NOUN
l'once *fem*

DID YOU KNOW...?
In France, measurements are in grams and kilograms. One ounce is about 30 grams.

□ 8 ounces of cheese 250 grammes de fromage

★ **our** ADJECTIVE
notre (FEM notre, PL nos)
□ Our house is quite big. Notre maison est plutôt grande. □ Our neighbours are very nice. Nos voisins sont très gentils.

★ **ours** PRONOUN
le nôtre + *masc noun*
□ Your garden is very big, ours is much smaller. Votre jardin est très grand, le nôtre est beaucoup plus petit.
la nôtre + *fem noun*
□ Your school is very different from ours. Votre école est très différente de la nôtre.
les nôtres + *pl noun*
□ Our teachers are strict. — Ours are too. Nos professeurs sont sévères. — Les nôtres aussi.
■ **Is this ours?** C'est à nous? □ This car is ours. Cette voiture est à nous. □ Whose is this? — It's ours. C'est à qui? — À nous.

★ **ourselves** PRONOUN
1 nous
□ We really enjoyed ourselves. Nous nous sommes vraiment bien amusés.
2 nous-mêmes
□ We built our garage ourselves. Nous avons construit notre garage nous-mêmes.

★ **out** ADVERB, ADJECTIVE

There are several ways of translating 'out'. Scan the examples to find one that is similar to what you want to say. For other expressions with 'out', see the verbs 'go', 'put', 'turn' etc.

1 dehors (*outside*)
□ It's cold out. Il fait froid dehors.
2 éteint (FEM éteinte) (*light, fire*)
□ All the lights are out. Toutes les lumières sont éteintes.
■ **She's out.** Elle est sortie.
■ **She's out shopping.** Elle est sortie faire des courses.
■ **She's out for the afternoon.** Elle ne sera pas là de tout l'après-midi.
■ **out there** dehors □ It's cold out there. Il fait froid dehors.
■ **to go out** sortir [79E] □ I'm going out tonight. Je sors ce soir.
■ **to go out with somebody** sortir [79E] avec quelqu'un □ I've been going out with him for two months. Je sors avec lui depuis deux mois.
■ **out of 1** dans □ to drink out of a glass boire dans un verre **2** sur □ in 9 cases out of 10 dans neuf cas sur dix **3** en dehors de □ He lives out of town. Il habite en dehors de la ville.
■ **3 km out of town** à trois kilomètres de la ville
■ **out of curiosity** par curiosité
■ **out of work** sans emploi
■ **That is out of the question.** C'est hors de question.
■ **You're out!** (*in game*) Tu es éliminé!
■ **'way out'** 'sortie'

outbreak NOUN
1 l'épidémie *fem* (*of disease*)
□ a flu outbreak une épidémie de grippe
2 le début *masc*
□ the outbreak of war le début de la guerre

★ **outcome** NOUN
l'issue *fem*
□ What was the outcome of the negotiations? Quelle a été l'issue des négociations?

outdoor ADJECTIVE
en plein air

□ an outdoor swimming pool une piscine en plein air

■ **outdoor activities** les activités de plein air

outdoors ADVERB
au grand air

outfit NOUN
la tenue *fem*
□ She bought a new outfit for the wedding. Elle a acheté une nouvelle tenue pour le mariage.
■ **a cowboy outfit** une panoplie de cowboy

outgoing ADJECTIVE
extraverti (FEM extravertie)
□ She's very outgoing. Elle est très extravertie.

outing NOUN
la sortie *fem*
□ to go on an outing faire une sortie

★ **outline** NOUN
1 les grandes lignes *fem pl* (*summary*)
□ This is an outline of the plan. Voici les grandes lignes du projet.
2 les contours *masc pl* (*shape*)
□ We could see the outline of the mountain in the mist. Nous distinguions les contours de la montagne dans la brume.

outlook NOUN
1 l'attitude *fem* (*attitude*)
□ my outlook on life mon attitude face à la vie
2 les perspectives *fem pl* (*prospects*)
□ the economic outlook les perspectives économiques
■ **The outlook is poor.** Les choses s'annoncent mal.

outrageous ADJECTIVE
1 scandaleux (FEM scandaleuse) (*behaviour*)
2 exorbitant (FEM exorbitante) (*price*)

outset NOUN
le début *masc*
□ at the outset dès le début

★ **outside** NOUN
▷ *see also* **outside** ADJECTIVE, ADVERB, PREPOSITION
l'extérieur *masc*

outside ADJECTIVE, ADVERB, PREPOSITION
▷ *see also* **outside** NOUN
1 extérieur (FEM extérieure)
□ the outside walls les murs extérieurs
2 dehors
□ It's very cold outside. Il fait très froid dehors.
3 en dehors de
□ outside the school en dehors de l'école
□ outside school hours en dehors des heures de cours

outskirts PL NOUN
la banlieue *fem*
□ on the outskirts of the town dans les banlieues de la ville

★ **outstanding** ADJECTIVE
remarquable (FEM remarquable)

oval ADJECTIVE
ovale (FEM ovale)

oven NOUN
le four *masc*

★ **over** PREPOSITION, ADVERB, ADJECTIVE

> When there is movement over something, use **par-dessus**; when something is located above something, use **au-dessus de**.

1 par-dessus
□ The ball went over the wall. Le ballon est passé par-dessus le mur.
2 au-dessus de
□ There's a mirror over the washbasin. Il y a une glace au-dessus du lavabo.
3 plus de (*more than*)
□ It's over twenty kilos. Ça pèse plus de vingt kilos. □ The temperature was over thirty degrees. Il faisait une température de plus de trente degrés.
4 pendant (*during*)
□ over the holidays pendant les vacances
□ over Christmas pendant les fêtes de Noël
5 terminé (FEM terminée) (*finished*)
□ I'll be happy when the exams are over. Je serai content quand les examens seront terminés.
■ **over here** ici
■ **over there** là-bas
■ **all over Scotland** dans toute l'Écosse
■ **The baker's is over the road.** La boulangerie est de l'autre côté de la rue.
■ **I spilled orange juice over my shirt.** J'ai renversé du jus d'orange sur ma chemise.

★ **overall** ADVERB
dans l'ensemble (*generally*)
□ My results were quite good overall. Mes résultats étaient assez bons dans l'ensemble.

overalls PL NOUN
les bleus de travail *masc pl*

overcast ADJECTIVE
couvert (FEM couverte)
□ The sky was overcast. Le ciel était couvert.

to **overcharge** VERB
■ **He overcharged me.** Il m'a fait payer trop cher.
■ **They overcharged us for the meal.** Ils nous ont fait payer de trop pour le repas.

overcoat NOUN
le pardessus *masc*

overdone ADJECTIVE
trop cuit (FEM trop cuite) (*food*)

overdraft NOUN
le découvert *masc*
■ **to have an overdraft** être [35] à découvert

to **overestimate** VERB
surestimer [28]

to **overlook** VERB
1 donner [28] sur *(have view of)*
□ The hotel overlooked the beach. L'hôtel donnait sur la plage.
2 négliger [45] *(forget about)*
□ He had overlooked one important problem. Il avait négligé un problème important.

★ **overseas** ADVERB
à l'étranger
□ I'd like to work overseas. J'aimerais travailler à l'étranger.

oversight NOUN
l'oubli *masc*

to **oversleep** VERB
se réveiller [28] en retard
□ I overslept this morning. Je me suis réveillé en retard ce matin.

to **overtake** VERB
dépasser [58]

overtime NOUN
les heures supplémentaires *fem pl*
□ to work overtime faire des heures supplémentaires

overtook VERB ▷ *see* **overtake**

overweight ADJECTIVE
trop gros (FEM trop grosse)

★ to **owe** VERB
devoir [26]
■ **to owe somebody something** devoir [26] quelque chose à quelqu'un □ I owe you 50 euros. Je te dois cinquante euros

owing to PREPOSITION
en raison de
□ owing to bad weather en raison du mauvais temps

owl NOUN
le hibou *masc* (PL les hiboux)

★ **own** ADJECTIVE
▷ *see also* **own** VERB
propre (FEM propre)
□ I've got my own bathroom. J'ai ma propre salle de bain.
■ **I'd like a room of my own.** J'aimerais avoir une chambre à moi.
■ **on his own** tout seul □ on her own toute seule □ on our own tout seuls

★ to **own** VERB
▷ *see also* **own** ADJECTIVE
posséder [34]

to **own up** VERB
avouer [28]
■ **to own up to something** admettre [47] quelque chose

★ **owner** NOUN
le/la propriétaire *masc/fem*

oxygen NOUN
l'oxygène *masc*

oyster NOUN
l'huître *fem*

ozone NOUN
l'ozone *fem*

ozone layer NOUN
la couche d'ozone *fem*

Pp

PA NOUN
le/la secrétaire de direction *masc/fem* (*personal assistant*)
□ She's a PA. Elle est secrétaire de direction.
■ **the PA system** (*public address*) la sono

pace NOUN
l'allure *fem* (*speed*)
□ He was walking at a brisk pace. Il marchait à vive allure.

Pacific NOUN
le Pacifique *masc*

pacifier NOUN (US)
la tétine *fem*

★ to **pack** VERB
▷ *see also* **pack** NOUN
faire [36] ses bagages
□ I'll help you pack. Je vais t'aider à faire tes bagages.
■ **I've already packed my case.** J'ai déjà fait ma valise.
■ **Pack it in!** (*stop it*) Laisse tomber!

★ **pack** NOUN
▷ *see also* **pack** VERB
1 le paquet *masc* (*packet*)
□ a pack of chewing gum un paquet de chewing-gum
2 le pack *masc* (*of yoghurts, cans*)
□ a six-pack un pack de six
■ **a pack of cards** un jeu de cartes

★ **package** NOUN
le paquet *masc*
■ **a package holiday** un voyage organisé

packed ADJECTIVE
bondé (FEM bondée)
□ The cinema was packed. Le cinéma était bondé.

packed lunch NOUN
le repas froid *masc*
□ I take a packed lunch to school. J'apporte un repas froid à l'école.

DID YOU KNOW...?
French schoolchildren do not take packed lunches to school. They either eat at the canteen or go home.

packet NOUN
le paquet *masc*
□ a packet of biscuits un paquet de biscuits

pad NOUN
le bloc-notes *masc* (PL les blocs-notes) (*notepad*)

to **paddle** VERB
▷ *see also* **paddle** NOUN
1 pagayer [59] (*canoe*)
2 faire [36] trempette (*in water*)

paddle NOUN
▷ *see also* **paddle** VERB
la pagaie *fem* (*for canoe*)
■ **to go for a paddle** faire [36] trempette

padlock NOUN
le cadenas *masc*

★ **page** NOUN
la page *fem* (*of book*)

pager NOUN
le récepteur d'appel *masc*

paid VERB ▷ *see* **pay**

paid ADJECTIVE
1 rémunéré (FEM rémunérée) (*work*)
2 payé (FEM payée)
□ 3 weeks' paid holiday trois semaines de congés payés

pail NOUN
le seau *masc* (PL les seaux)

★ **pain** NOUN
la douleur *fem*
□ a terrible pain une douleur insupportable
■ **I've got a pain in my stomach.** J'ai mal à l'estomac.
■ **to be in pain** souffrir [54] □ She's in a lot of pain. Elle souffre beaucoup.
■ **He's a real pain.** Il est vraiment pénible.

★ **painful** ADJECTIVE
douloureux (FEM douloureuse)
□ to suffer from painful periods souffrir de règles douloureuses
■ **Is it painful?** Ça te fait mal?

painkiller NOUN
l'analgésique *masc*

★ **paint** NOUN
▷ *see also* **paint** VERB
la peinture *fem*

★ to **paint** VERB
▷ *see also* **paint** NOUN

peindre [60]
□ to paint something green peindre quelque chose en vert

paintbrush NOUN
le pinceau *masc* (PL les pinceaux)

painter NOUN
le/la peintre *masc/fem*

★ **painting** NOUN
1 la peinture *fem*
□ My hobby is painting. Je fais de la peinture.
2 le tableau *masc* (PL les tableaux) (*picture*)
□ a painting by Picasso un tableau de Picasso

★ **pair** NOUN
la paire *fem*
□ a pair of shoes une paire de chaussures □ a pair of scissors une paire de ciseaux
■ **a pair of trousers** un pantalon
■ **a pair of jeans** un jean
■ **a pair of pants** 1 (*briefs*) un slip 2 (*boxer shorts*) un caleçon 3 (US: *trousers*) un pantalon
■ **in pairs** deux par deux □ We work in pairs. On travaille deux par deux.

pajamas PL NOUN (US)
le pyjama *masc sing*
□ my pajamas mon pyjama □ a pair of pajamas un pyjama
■ **a pajama top** un haut de pyjama

Pakistan NOUN
le Pakistan *masc*
■ **in Pakistan** au Pakistan
■ **to Pakistan** au Pakistan
■ **He's from Pakistan.** Il est pakistanais.

Pakistani NOUN
▷ *see also* **Pakistani** ADJECTIVE
le Pakistanais *masc*
la Pakistanaise *fem*

Pakistani ADJECTIVE
▷ *see also* **Pakistani** NOUN
pakistanais (FEM pakistanaise)

pal NOUN
le copain *masc*
la copine *fem*

★ **palace** NOUN
le palais *masc*

★ **pale** ADJECTIVE
pâle (FEM pâle)
□ a pale blue shirt une chemise bleu pâle

Palestine NOUN
la Palestine *fem*
■ **in Palestine** en Palestine

Palestinian NOUN
▷ *see also* **Palestinian** ADJECTIVE
le Palestinien *masc*
la Palestinienne *fem*

Palestinian ADJECTIVE
▷ *see also* **Palestinian** NOUN
palestinien (FEM palestinienne)

palm NOUN
la paume *fem* (*of hand*)
■ **a palm tree** un palmier

pamphlet NOUN
la brochure *fem*

★ **pan** NOUN
1 la casserole *fem* (*saucepan*)
2 la poêle *fem* (*frying pan*)

pancake NOUN
la crêpe *fem*
■ **Pancake Day** mardi gras

DID YOU KNOW...?
Pancake Day is celebrated in France as well. Children dress up and eat **crêpes**.

pandemic NOUN
la pandémie *fem*
□ a flu pandemic une pandémie de grippe

★ **panic** NOUN
▷ *see also* **panic** VERB
la panique *fem*

★ to **panic** VERB
▷ *see also* **panic** NOUN
s'affoler [28]
■ **Don't panic!** Pas de panique!

panther NOUN
la panthère *fem*

panties PL NOUN
le slip *masc sing*

pantomime NOUN
le spectacle de Noël pour enfants *masc*

DID YOU KNOW...?
Pantomimes don't exist in France.

pants PL NOUN
1 le slip *masc sing* (*briefs*)
□ a pair of pants un slip
2 le caleçon *masc sing* (*boxer shorts*)
□ a pair of pants un caleçon
3 le pantalon *masc sing* (*trousers*: US)
□ a pair of pants un pantalon

pantyhose PL NOUN (US)
le collant *masc sing*

★ **paper** NOUN
1 le papier *masc*
□ a piece of paper un morceau de papier
■ **a paper towel** une serviette en papier
■ **an exam paper** une épreuve écrite
2 le journal *masc* (PL les journaux) (*newspaper*)
□ I saw an advert in the paper. J'ai vu une annonce dans le journal.

paperback NOUN
le livre de poche *masc*

paper boy NOUN
le livreur de journaux *masc*

paper clip NOUN
le trombone *masc*

paper girl NOUN
la livreuse de journaux *fem*
paper round NOUN
la tournée de distribution de journaux *fem*
paperweight NOUN
le presse-papiers *masc*
paperwork NOUN
la paperasse *fem*
□ He had a lot of paperwork to do. Il avait beaucoup de paperasse à faire.
parachute NOUN
le parachute *masc*
parade NOUN
le défilé *masc*
paradise NOUN
le paradis *masc*
paragraph NOUN
le paragraphe *masc*
parallel ADJECTIVE
parallèle (FEM parallèle)
paralysed ADJECTIVE
paralysé (FEM paralysée)
paramedic NOUN
l'auxiliaire médical *masc*
l'auxiliaire médicale *fem*
parcel NOUN
le colis *masc*
pardon NOUN
■ **Pardon?** Pardon?
★ **parent** NOUN
1 le père *masc* (*father*)
2 la mère *fem* (*mother*)
■ **my parents** mes parents *masc pl*
★ **Paris** NOUN
Paris *masc*
■ **in Paris** à Paris
■ **to Paris** à Paris
■ **She's from Paris.** Elle est parisienne.
★ **Parisian** NOUN
▷ *see also* **Parisian** ADJECTIVE
le Parisien *masc*
la Parisienne *fem*
★ **Parisian** ADJECTIVE
▷ *see also* **Parisian** NOUN
parisien (FEM parisienne)
★ **park** NOUN
▷ *see also* **park** VERB
le parc *masc*
■ **a national park** un parc national
■ **a theme park** un parc à thème
■ **a car park** un parking
★ to **park** VERB
▷ *see also* **park** NOUN
1 garer [28]
□ Where can I park my car? Où est-ce que je peux garer ma voiture?
2 se garer [28]
□ We couldn't find anywhere to park. Nous avons eu du mal à nous garer.
parking NOUN
le stationnement *masc*
□ 'no parking' 'stationnement interdit'

BE CAREFUL!
Do not translate **parking** by the French word **parking**.

parking lot NOUN (US)
le parking *masc*
parking meter NOUN
le parcmètre *masc*
parking ticket NOUN
le P.-V. *masc*
★ **parliament** NOUN
le parlement *masc*
parrot NOUN
le perroquet *masc*
parsley NOUN
le persil *masc*
★ **part** NOUN
1 la partie *fem* (*section*)
□ The first part of the film was boring. La première partie du film était ennuyeuse.
2 la pièce *fem* (*component*)
□ spare parts les pièces de rechange
3 le rôle *masc* (*in play, film*)
■ **to take part in something** participer [28] à quelque chose □ A lot of people took part in the demonstration. Beaucoup de gens ont participé à la manifestation.
to **part with** VERB
■ **to part with something** se défaire [36] de quelque chose
particular ADJECTIVE
particulier (FEM particulière)
□ Are you looking for anything particular? Est-ce que vous voulez quelque chose de particulier?
■ **nothing in particular** rien de particulier
particularly ADVERB
particulièrement
parting NOUN
la raie *fem* (*in hair*)
★ **partly** ADVERB
en partie
★ **partner** NOUN
1 le/la partenaire *masc/fem* (*in game*)
2 l'associé *masc*
l'associée *fem* (*in business*)
3 le cavalier *masc*
la cavalière *fem* (*in dance*)
4 le compagnon *masc*
la compagne *fem* (*in relationship*)
part-time ADJECTIVE, ADVERB
à temps partiel

□ a part-time job un travail à temps partiel
□ She works part-time. Elle travaille à temps partiel.

★ **party** NOUN
1 la fête *fem*
□ a birthday party une fête d'anniversaire □ a Christmas party une fête de Noël □ a New Year party une fête du Nouvel An
2 la soirée *fem* (*more formal*)
□ I'm going to a party on Saturday. Je vais à une soirée samedi.
3 le parti *masc* (*political*)
□ the Conservative Party le Parti conservateur
4 le groupe *masc* (*group*)
□ a party of tourists un groupe de touristes

★ **pass** NOUN
▷ *see also* **pass** VERB
1 le col *masc* (*in mountains*)
□ The pass was blocked with snow. Le col était enneigé.
2 la passe *fem* (*in football*)
■ **to get a pass** (*in exam*) être [35] reçu □ She got a pass in her piano exam. Elle a été reçue à son examen de piano. □ I got six passes. J'ai été reçu dans six matières.
■ **a bus pass** une carte de bus

★ to **pass** VERB
▷ *see also* **pass** NOUN
1 être [35] reçu (*exam*)
□ Did you pass? Tu as été reçu?
■ **to pass an exam** être [35] reçu à un examen □ I hope I'll pass the exam. J'espère que je serai reçu à l'examen.

BE CAREFUL!
Do not translate **to pass an exam** by the French expression **passer un examen.**

2 passer [58]
□ Could you pass me the salt, please? Est-ce que vous pourriez me passer le sel, s'il vous plaît? □ The time has passed quickly. Le temps a passé rapidement.
3 passer [58E] devant
□ I pass his house on my way to school. Je passe devant chez lui en allant à l'école.

to **pass out** VERB
s'évanouir [38] (*faint*)

passage NOUN
1 le passage *masc* (*piece of writing*)
□ Read the passage carefully. Lisez attentivement le passage.
2 le couloir *masc* (*corridor*)

★ **passenger** NOUN
le passager *masc*
la passagère *fem*

passion NOUN
la passion *fem*

passive ADJECTIVE
passif (FEM passive)
■ **passive smoking** le tabagisme passif

Passover NOUN
la Pâque juive *fem*
□ at Passover à la Pâque juive

passport NOUN
le passeport *masc*
□ passport control le contrôle des passeports

★ **password** NOUN
le mot de passe *masc*

★ **past** ADVERB, PREPOSITION
▷ *see also* **past** NOUN
après (*beyond*)
□ It's on the right, just past the station. C'est sur la droite, juste après la gare.
■ **to go past** 1 passer [58E] □ The bus went past without stopping. Le bus est passé sans s'arrêter. 2 passer [58E] devant □ The bus goes past our house. Le bus passe devant notre maison.
■ **It's half past ten.** Il est dix heures et demie.
■ **It's quarter past nine.** Il est neuf heures et quart.
■ **It's ten past eight.** Il est huit heures dix.
■ **It's past midnight.** Il est minuit passé.

★ **past** NOUN
▷ *see also* **past** ADVERB, PREPOSITION
le passé *masc*
□ She lives in the past. Elle vit dans le passé.
■ **in the past** (*previously*) autrefois □ This was common in the past. C'était courant autrefois.

★ **pasta** NOUN
les pâtes *fem pl*
□ Pasta is easy to cook. Les pâtes sont faciles à préparer.

paste NOUN
la colle *fem* (*glue*)

pasteurized ADJECTIVE
pasteurisé (FEM pasteurisée)

pastime NOUN
le passe-temps *masc* (PL les passe-temps)
□ Her favourite pastime is knitting. Son passe-temps favori est le tricot.

pastry NOUN
la pâte *fem*
■ **pastries** les pâtisseries *fem pl*

patch NOUN
1 la pièce *fem*
□ a patch of material une pièce de tissu
2 la rustine *fem* (*for flat tyre*)
■ **He's got a bald patch.** Il a le crâne dégarni.

patched ADJECTIVE
rapiécé (FEM rapiécée)
□ a pair of patched jeans un jean rapiécé

★ **pâté** NOUN
le pâté *masc*

★ **path** NOUN
1 le chemin *masc* (*footpath*)
2 l'allée *fem* (*in garden, park*)

pathetic ADJECTIVE
lamentable (FEM lamentable)
□ Our team was pathetic. Notre équipe a été lamentable.

patience NOUN
1 la patience *fem*
□ He hasn't got much patience. Il n'a pas beaucoup de patience.
2 la réussite *fem* (*card game*)
□ to play patience faire une réussite

★ **patient** NOUN
▷ *see also* **patient** ADJECTIVE
le patient *masc*
la patiente *fem*

★ **patient** ADJECTIVE
▷ *see also* **patient** NOUN
patient (FEM patiente)

patio NOUN
le patio *masc*

patriotic ADJECTIVE
patriote (FEM patriote)

patrol NOUN
la patrouille *fem*

patrol car NOUN
la voiture de police *fem*

★ **pattern** NOUN
le motif *masc*
□ a geometric pattern un motif géométrique
■ **a sewing pattern** un patron

★ **pause** NOUN
la pause *fem*

pavement NOUN
le trottoir *masc*

pavilion NOUN
le pavillon *masc*

paw NOUN
la patte *fem*

★ **pay** NOUN
▷ *see also* **pay** VERB
le salaire *masc*

★ to **pay** VERB
▷ *see also* **pay** NOUN
1 payer [59]
□ They pay me more on Sundays. Je suis payé davantage le dimanche.
2 régler [34]
□ to pay by cheque régler par chèque □ to pay by credit card régler par carte de crédit
■ **to pay for something** payer [59] quelque chose □ I paid for my ticket. J'ai payé mon billet. □ I paid 50 euros for it. Je l'ai payé cinquante euros.
■ **to pay extra for something** payer [59] un supplément pour quelque chose □ You have to pay extra for breakfast. Il faut payer un supplément pour le petit déjeuner.
■ **to pay attention** faire [36] attention
□ Don't pay any attention to him! Ne fais pas attention à lui!
■ **to pay somebody a visit** rendre [7] visite à quelqu'un □ Meena paid us a visit last night. Meena nous a rendu visite hier soir.
■ **to pay somebody back** rembourser [28] quelqu'un □ I'll pay you back tomorrow. Je te rembourserai demain.

★ **payment** NOUN
le paiement *masc*

payphone NOUN
le téléphone public *masc*

★ **PC** NOUN (= *personal computer*)
le PC *masc*
□ She typed the report on her PC. Elle a tapé le rapport sur son PC.

PE NOUN
l'EPS *fem*
□ We do PE twice a week. Nous avons EPS deux fois par semaine.

★ **pea** NOUN
le petit pois *masc*

★ **peace** NOUN
1 la paix *fem* (*after war*)
2 le calme *masc* (*quietness*)

★ **peaceful** ADJECTIVE
1 paisible (FEM paisible) (*calm*)
□ a peaceful afternoon un après-midi paisible
2 pacifique (FEM pacifique) (*not violent*)
□ a peaceful protest une manifestation pacifique

★ **peach** NOUN
la pêche *fem*

peacock NOUN
le paon *masc*

peak NOUN
la cime *fem* (*of mountain*)
■ **in peak season** en haute saison
■ **It's more expensive during peak travel times.** C'est plus cher en haute saison.

★ **peanut** NOUN
la cacahuète *fem*
□ a packet of peanuts un paquet de cacahuètes

peanut butter NOUN
le beurre de cacahuètes *masc*
□ a peanut-butter sandwich un sandwich au beurre de cacahuètes

★ **pear** NOUN
la poire *fem*

pearl NOUN
la perle *fem*

pebble NOUN
le galet *masc*
□ a pebble beach une plage de galets

peckish ADJECTIVE
■ **to feel a bit peckish** avoir [8] un petit creux

peculiar ADJECTIVE
bizarre (FEM bizarre)
□ He's a peculiar person. Il est bizarre. □ It tastes peculiar. Ça a un goût bizarre.

pedal NOUN
la pédale *fem*

★ **pedestrian** NOUN
le piéton *masc*
la piétonne *fem*

pedestrian crossing NOUN
le passage pour piétons *masc*

pedestrianized ADJECTIVE
■ **a pedestrianized street** une rue piétonne

pedestrian precinct NOUN
la zone piétonnière *fem*

pedigree ADJECTIVE
de race (*animal*)
□ a pedigree dog un chien de race □ a pedigree labrador un labrador de pure race

pee NOUN
■ **to have a pee** faire [36] pipi

peek NOUN
■ **to have a peek at something** jeter [41] un coup d'œil à quelque chose
■ **No peeking!** On ne regarde pas!

peel NOUN
▷ *see also* **peel** VERB
l'écorce *fem* (*of orange*)

to **peel** VERB
▷ *see also* **peel** NOUN
1 éplucher [28]
□ Shall I peel the potatoes? J'épluche les pommes de terre?
2 peler [43]
□ My nose is peeling. Mon nez pèle.

★ **peg** NOUN
1 le portemanteau *masc* (PL les portemanteaux) (*for coats*)
2 la pince à linge *fem* (*clothes peg*)
3 le piquet *masc* (*tent peg*)

Pekinese NOUN
le pékinois *masc*

pelican crossing NOUN
le passage pour piétons *masc*

pellet NOUN
le plomb *masc* (*for gun*)

pelvis NOUN
le bassin *masc*

★ **pen** NOUN
le stylo *masc*

to **penalize** VERB
pénaliser [28]

★ **penalty** NOUN
1 la peine *fem* (*punishment*)
■ **the death penalty** la peine de mort
2 le penalty *masc* (*in football*)
3 la pénalité *fem* (*in rugby*)
■ **a penalty shoot-out** les tirs au but

pence PL NOUN
les pence *masc pl*

★ **pencil** NOUN
le crayon *masc*
■ **in pencil** au crayon

pencil case NOUN
la trousse *fem*

pencil sharpener NOUN
le taille-crayon *masc* (PL les taille-crayons)

pendant NOUN
le pendentif *masc*

penfriend NOUN
le correspondant *masc*
la correspondante *fem*

penguin NOUN
le pingouin *masc*

penicillin NOUN
la pénicilline *fem*

penis NOUN
le pénis *masc*

penitentiary NOUN (US)
la prison *fem*

penknife NOUN
le canif *masc*

★ **penny** NOUN
le penny *masc* (PL les pence)

★ **pension** NOUN
la retraite *fem*

pensioner NOUN
le retraité *masc*
la retraitée *fem*

pentathlon NOUN
le pentathlon *masc*

★ **people** PL NOUN
1 les gens *masc pl*
□ The people were nice. Les gens étaient sympathiques. □ a lot of people beaucoup de gens
2 les personnes *fem pl* (*individuals*)
□ six people six personnes □ several people plusieurs personnes
■ **How many people are there in your family?** Vous êtes combien dans votre famille?
■ **French people** les Français
■ **People say that ...** On dit que ...

★ **pepper** NOUN
1 le poivre *masc* (*spice*)
□ Pass the pepper, please. Passez-moi le poivre, s'il vous plaît.
2 le poivron *masc* (*vegetable*)
□ a green pepper un poivron vert

peppermill NOUN
le moulin à poivre *masc*

peppermint NOUN
la pastille de menthe *fem* (*sweet*)
■ **peppermint chewing gum** le chewing-gum à la menthe

★**per** PREPOSITION
par
□ per day par jour □ per week par semaine
■ **30 miles per hour** trente miles à l'heure

★**per cent** ADVERB
pour cent
□ fifty per cent cinquante pour cent

★**percentage** NOUN
le pourcentage *masc*

percolator NOUN
la cafetière électrique *fem*

percussion NOUN
la percussion *fem*
□ I play percussion. Je joue des percussions.

★**perfect** ADJECTIVE
parfait (FEM parfaite)
□ Chantal speaks perfect English. Chantal parle un anglais parfait.

★**perfectly** ADVERB
parfaitement

★to **perform** VERB
jouer [28] (*act, play*)

★**performance** NOUN
1 le spectacle *masc* (*show*)
□ The performance lasts two hours. Le spectacle dure deux heures.
2 l'interprétation *fem* (*acting*)
□ his performance as Hamlet son interprétation d'Hamlet
3 la performance *fem* (*results*)
□ the team's poor performance la médiocre performance de l'équipe

perfume NOUN
le parfum *masc*

★**perhaps** ADVERB
peut-être
□ a bit boring, perhaps peut-être un peu ennuyeux □ Perhaps he's ill. Il est peut-être malade.
■ **perhaps not** peut-être pas

★**period** NOUN
1 la période *fem*
□ for a limited period pour une période limitée
2 l'époque *fem* (*in history*)
□ the Victorian period l'époque victorienne
3 les règles *fem pl* (*menstruation*)
□ I'm having my period. J'ai mes règles.
4 le cours *masc* (*lesson time*)
□ Each period lasts forty minutes. Chaque cours dure quarante minutes.

★**permanent** ADJECTIVE
permanent (FEM permanente)

★**permission** NOUN
la permission *fem*
□ Could I have permission to leave early? Pourrais-je avoir la permission de partir plus tôt?

★**permit** NOUN
le permis *masc*
□ a fishing permit un permis de pêche

to **persecute** VERB
persécuter [28]

Persian ADJECTIVE
■ **a Persian cat** un chat persan

persistent ADJECTIVE
tenace (FEM tenace) (*person*)

★**person** NOUN
la personne *fem*
□ She's a very nice person. C'est une personne très sympathique.
■ **in person** en personne

★**personal** ADJECTIVE
personnel (FEM personnelle)

★**personality** NOUN
la personnalité *fem*

★**personally** ADVERB
personnellement
□ I don't know him personally. Je ne le connais pas personnellement. □ Personally I don't agree. Personnellement, je ne suis pas d'accord.

personnel NOUN
le personnel *masc*

perspiration NOUN
la transpiration *fem*

★to **persuade** VERB
persuader [28]
■ **to persuade somebody to do something** persuader [28] quelqu'un de faire quelque chose □ She persuaded me to go with her. Elle m'a persuadé de l'accompagner.

pessimist NOUN
le/la pessimiste *masc/fem*
□ I'm a pessimist. Je suis un(e) pessimiste.

pessimistic ADJECTIVE
pessimiste (FEM pessimiste)

pest NOUN
le/la casse-pieds *masc/fem* (*person*)
□ He's a real pest! C'est un vrai casse-pieds!

to **pester** VERB
importuner [28]

★**pet** NOUN
l'animal familier *masc*
□ Have you got a pet? Est-ce que tu as un animal familier?
■ **She's the teacher's pet.** C'est la chouchoute de la maîtresse.

petition NOUN
la pétition *fem*

petrified ADJECTIVE
pétrifié (FEM pétrifiée)

★ **petrol** NOUN
l'essence *fem*
■ **unleaded petrol** l'essence sans plomb

> **BE CAREFUL!**
> Do not translate **petrol** by the French word **pétrole**.

petrol station NOUN
la station-service *fem* (PL les stations-service)

petrol tank NOUN
le réservoir d'essence *masc*

phantom NOUN
le fantôme *masc*

pharmacy NOUN
la pharmacie *fem*

> **DID YOU KNOW...?**
> Pharmacies in France are identified by a special green cross outside the shop.

pheasant NOUN
le faisan *masc*

★ **philosophy** NOUN
la philosophie *fem*

phobia NOUN
la phobie *fem*

★ **phone** NOUN
▷ *see also* **phone** VERB
le téléphone *masc*
□ Where's the phone? Où est le téléphone?
□ Is there a phone here? Est-ce qu'il y a un téléphone ici?
■ **by phone** par téléphone
■ **to be on the phone** être [35] au téléphone
□ She's on the phone at the moment. Elle est au téléphone en ce moment.
■ **Can I use your phone, please?** Est-ce que je peux utiliser votre téléphone, s'il vous plaît?

★ to **phone** VERB
▷ *see also* **phone** NOUN
appeler [4]
□ I'll phone the station. Je vais appeler la gare.

phone bill NOUN
la facture de téléphone *fem*

phone book NOUN
l'annuaire *masc*

★ **phone box** NOUN
la cabine téléphonique *fem*

★ **phone call** NOUN
l'appel *masc*
□ There's a phone call for you. Il y a un appel pour vous.
■ **to make a phone call** téléphoner [28]
□ Can I make a phone call? Est-ce que peux téléphoner?

phonecard NOUN
la carte téléphonique *fem*

★ **phone number** NOUN
le numéro de téléphone *masc*

★ **photo** NOUN
la photo *fem*
■ **to take a photo** prendre [65] une photo
■ **to take a photo of somebody** prendre [65] quelqu'un en photo

photocopier NOUN
la photocopieuse *fem*

photocopy NOUN
▷ *see also* **photocopy** VERB
la photocopie *fem*

to **photocopy** VERB
▷ *see also* **photocopy** NOUN
photocopier [19]

★ **photograph** NOUN
▷ *see also* **photograph** VERB
la photo *fem*
■ **to take a photograph** prendre [65] une photo
■ **to take a photograph of somebody** prendre [65] quelqu'un en photo

★ to **photograph** VERB
▷ *see also* **photograph** NOUN
photographier [19]

★ **photographer** NOUN
le/la photographe *masc/fem*
□ She's a photographer. Elle est photographe.

photography NOUN
la photo *fem*
□ My hobby is photography. Je fais de la photo.

Photoshop® NOUN
▷ *see also* **Photoshop** VERB
Photoshop® *masc*

to **Photoshop** VERB
▷ *see also* **Photoshop** NOUN
photoshoper [28]

★ **phrase** NOUN
l'expression *fem*

phrase book NOUN
le guide de conversation *masc*

★ **physical** ADJECTIVE
▷ *see also* **physical** NOUN
physique (FEM physique)

★ **physical** NOUN (US)
▷ *see also* **physical** ADJECTIVE
l'examen médical *masc*

physicist NOUN
le physicien *masc*
la physicienne *fem*
□ He's a physicist. Il est physicien.

★ **physics** NOUN
la physique *fem*
□ She teaches physics. Elle enseigne la physique.

physiotherapist NOUN
le/la kinésithérapeute *masc/fem*

physiotherapy NOUN
la kinésithérapie *fem*

pianist NOUN
le/la pianiste *masc/fem*

★ **piano** NOUN
le piano *masc*
□ I play the piano. Je joue du piano. □ I have piano lessons. Je prends des leçons de piano.

★ **pick** NOUN
▷ *see also* **pick** VERB
■ **Take your pick!** Faites votre choix!

★ to **pick** VERB
▷ *see also* **pick** NOUN
1 choisir [38] (*choose*)
□ I picked the biggest piece. J'ai choisi le plus gros morceau.
2 sélectionner [28] (*for team*)
□ I've been picked for the team. J'ai été sélectionné pour faire partie de l'équipe.
3 cueillir [22] (*fruit, flowers*)

to **pick on** VERB
harceler [43]
□ She's always picking on me. Elle me harcèle constamment.

to **pick out** VERB
choisir [38]
□ I like them all — it's difficult to pick one out. Ils me plaisent tous — c'est difficile d'en choisir un.

to **pick up** VERB
1 venir [89E] chercher (*collect*)
□ We'll come to the airport to pick you up. Nous viendrons vous chercher à l'aéroport.
2 ramasser [28] (*from floor*)
□ Could you help me pick up the toys? Tu peux m'aider à ramasser les jouets?
3 apprendre [65] (*learn*)
□ I picked up some Spanish during my holiday. J'ai appris quelques mots d'espagnol pendant mes vacances.

pickpocket NOUN
le/la pickpocket *masc/fem*

picnic NOUN
le pique-nique *masc*
■ **to have a picnic** pique-niquer [28] □ We had a picnic on the beach. Nous avons pique-niqué sur la plage.

★ **picture** NOUN
1 l'illustration *fem*
□ Children's books have lots of pictures. Il y a beaucoup d'illustrations dans les livres pour enfants.
2 la photo *fem*
□ My picture was in the paper. Ma photo était dans le journal.
3 le tableau *masc* (PL les tableaux) (*painting*)
□ a famous picture un tableau célèbre
■ **to paint a picture of something** peindre [60] quelque chose
4 le dessin *masc* (*drawing*)
■ **to draw a picture of something** dessiner [28] quelque chose

picture messaging NOUN
l'envoi de photos par MMS *masc*

picturesque ADJECTIVE
pittoresque (FEM pittoresque)

★ **pie** NOUN
la tourte *fem*
□ an apple pie une tourte aux pommes

★ **piece** NOUN
le morceau *masc* (PL les morceaux)
□ A small piece, please. Un petit morceau, s'il vous plaît.
■ **a piece of furniture** un meuble
■ **a piece of advice** un conseil

pier NOUN
la jetée *fem*

to **pierce** VERB
percer [12]
□ She's going to have her ears pierced. Elle va se faire percer les oreilles.

pierced ADJECTIVE
percé (FEM percée)
□ I've got pierced ears. J'ai les oreilles percées.

piercing NOUN
le piercing *masc*
□ She has several piercings. Elle a plusieurs piercings.

★ **pig** NOUN
le cochon *masc*

pigeon NOUN
le pigeon *masc*

piggyback NOUN
■ **to give somebody a piggyback** porter [28] quelqu'un sur son dos □ I can't give you a piggyback, you're too heavy. Je ne peux pas te porter sur mon dos, tu es trop lourd.

piggy bank NOUN
la tirelire *fem*

pigtail NOUN
la natte *fem*

★ **pile** NOUN
1 le tas *masc* (*untidy heap*)
2 la pile *fem* (*tidy stack*)

pile-up NOUN
le carambolage *masc*

★ **pill** NOUN
la pilule *fem*
■ **to be on the pill** prendre [65] la pilule

pillar NOUN
le pilier *masc*

pillar box NOUN
la boîte aux lettres *fem*

English-French

pillow NOUN
l'oreiller *masc*

★**pilot** NOUN
le pilote *masc*
□ He's a pilot. Il est pilote.

pimple NOUN
le bouton *masc*

PIN NOUN (= *personal identification number*)
le code confidentiel *masc*
▪ **chip and PIN** la CB

★**pin** NOUN
l'épingle *fem*
▪ **I've got pins and needles.** J'ai des fourmis dans les jambes.

pinafore NOUN
le tablier *masc*

pinball NOUN
le flipper *masc*
□ to play pinball jouer au flipper
▪ **a pinball machine** un flipper

to **pinch** VERB
1 pincer [12]
□ He pinched me! Il m'a pincé!
2 piquer [28] (*informal: steal*)
□ Who's pinched my pen? Qui est-ce qui m'a piqué mon stylo?

pine NOUN
le pin *masc*
□ a pine table une table en pin

★**pineapple** NOUN
l'ananas *masc*

★**pink** ADJECTIVE
rose (FEM rose)

pint NOUN
la pinte *fem*

DID YOU KNOW...?
In France, measurements are in litres and centilitres. A pint is about 0.6 litres.

▪ **a pint of milk** un demi-litre de lait
▪ **to have a pint** boire [10] une bière □ He's gone out for a pint. Il est parti boire une bière.

★**pipe** NOUN
1 la conduite *fem* (*for water, gas*)
□ The pipes froze. Les conduites d'eau ont gelé.
2 la pipe *fem* (*for smoking*)
□ He smokes a pipe. Il fume la pipe.
▪ **the pipes** (*bagpipes*) la cornemuse □ He plays the pipes. Il joue de la cornemuse.

pirate NOUN
le pirate *masc*

Pisces NOUN
les Poissons *masc*
□ I'm Pisces. Je suis Poissons.

pistol NOUN
le pistolet *masc*

★**pitch** NOUN
▷ *see also* **pitch** VERB
le terrain *masc*
□ a football pitch un terrain de football

★to **pitch** VERB
▷ *see also* **pitch** NOUN
dresser [28] (*tent*)
□ We pitched our tent near the beach. Nous avons dressé notre tente près de la plage.

pity NOUN
▷ *see also* **pity** VERB
la pitié *fem*
▪ **What a pity!** Quel dommage!

to **pity** VERB
▷ *see also* **pity** NOUN
plaindre [17]

★**pizza** NOUN
la pizza *fem*

★**place** NOUN
▷ *see also* **place** VERB
1 l'endroit *masc* (*location*)
□ It's a quiet place. C'est un endroit tranquille.
□ There are a lot of interesting places to visit. Il y a beaucoup d'endroits intéressants à visiter.
2 la place *fem* (*space*)
□ a parking place une place de parking □ a university place une place à l'université
▪ **to change places** changer [45] de place
□ Lara, change places with Delphine! Lara, change de place avec Delphine!
▪ **to take place** avoir [8] lieu
▪ **at your place** chez toi □ Shall we meet at your place? On se retrouve chez toi?
▪ **to my place** chez moi □ Do you want to come round to my place? Tu veux venir chez moi?

★to **place** VERB
▷ *see also* **place** NOUN
1 poser [28]
□ He placed his hand on hers. Il a posé la main sur la sienne.
2 classer [28] (*in competition, contest*)

placement NOUN
le stage *masc*
▪ **to do a work placement** faire [36] un stage en entreprise

plaid ADJECTIVE
écossais (FEM écossaise)
□ a plaid shirt une chemise écossaise

★**plain** NOUN
▷ *see also* **plain** ADJECTIVE, ADVERB
la plaine *fem*

★**plain** ADJECTIVE, ADVERB
▷ *see also* **plain** NOUN
1 uni (FEM unie) (*not patterned*)
□ a plain carpet un tapis uni
2 simple (FEM simple) (*not fancy*)

P

□ a plain white blouse un chemisier blanc simple

plain chocolate NOUN
le chocolat à croquer *masc*

plait NOUN
la natte *fem*
□ She wears her hair in a plait. Elle a une natte.

★ **plan** NOUN
▷ *see also* **plan** VERB
1 le projet *masc*
□ What are your plans for the holidays? Quels sont tes projets pour les vacances? □ to make plans faire des projets
■ **Everything went according to plan.** Tout s'est passé comme prévu.
2 le plan *masc* (*map*)
□ a plan of the campsite un plan du terrain de camping
■ **my essay plan** le plan de ma dissertation

★ to **plan** VERB
▷ *see also* **plan** NOUN
1 préparer [28] (*make plans for*)
□ We're planning a trip to Canada. Nous préparons un voyage au Canada.
2 planifier [19] (*make schedule for*)
□ Plan your revision carefully. Planifiez vos révisions avec soin.
■ **to plan to do something** avoir [8] l'intention de faire quelque chose □ I'm planning to get a job in the holidays. J'ai l'intention de trouver un job pour les vacances.

★ **plane** NOUN
l'avion *masc*
□ by plane en avion

★ **planet** NOUN
la planète *fem*

★ **planning** NOUN
la préparation *fem*
□ The trip needs careful planning. Le voyage nécessite une préparation méticuleuse.
■ **family planning** le planning familial

★ **plant** NOUN
▷ *see also* **plant** VERB
1 la plante *fem*
□ to water the plants arroser les plantes
2 l'usine *fem* (*factory*)

★ to **plant** VERB
▷ *see also* **plant** NOUN
planter [28]

plant pot NOUN
le pot de fleurs *masc*

plaque NOUN
la plaque *fem* (*on wall*)

plaster NOUN
1 le pansement adhésif *masc* (*sticking plaster*)
□ Have you got a plaster, by any chance? Vous n'auriez pas un pansement adhésif, par hasard?
2 le plâtre *masc* (*for fracture*)
□ Her leg's in plaster. Elle a la jambe dans le plâtre.

★ **plastic** NOUN
▷ *see also* **plastic** ADJECTIVE
le plastique *masc*
□ It's made of plastic. C'est en plastique.

★ **plastic** ADJECTIVE
▷ *see also* **plastic** NOUN
en plastique
□ a plastic bag un sac en plastique

★ **plate** NOUN
l'assiette *fem* (*for food*)

★ **platform** NOUN
1 le quai *masc* (*at station*)
□ on platform 7 sur le quai numéro sept
2 l'estrade *fem* (*for performers*)

★ **play** NOUN
▷ *see also* **play** VERB
la pièce *fem*
□ a play by Shakespeare une pièce de Shakespeare
■ **to put on a play** monter [48] une pièce

★ to **play** VERB
▷ *see also* **play** NOUN
1 jouer [28]
□ He's playing with his friends. Il joue avec ses amis. □ What sort of music do they play? Quel genre de musique jouent-ils?
2 jouer [28] contre (*against person, team*)
□ France will play Scotland next month. La France jouera contre l'Écosse le mois prochain.
3 jouer [28] à (*sport, game*)
□ I play hockey. Je joue au hockey. □ Can you play pool? Tu sais jouer au billard américain?
4 jouer [28] de (*instrument*)
□ I play the guitar. Je joue de la guitare.
5 écouter [28] (*CD, music*)
□ She's always playing that song. Elle écoute tout le temps cette chanson.

to **play down** VERB
dédramatiser [28]
□ He tried to play down his illness. Il a essayé de dédramatiser sa maladie.

★ **player** NOUN
1 le joueur *masc*
la joueuse *fem* (*of sport*)
□ a football player un joueur de football
2 le musicien *masc*
la musicienne *fem* (*of instrument*)
■ **a piano player** un pianiste
■ **a saxophone player** un saxophoniste

playful ADJECTIVE
espiègle (FEM espiègle)

★ **playground** NOUN
1 la cour de récréation *fem* (*at school*)
2 l'aire de jeux *fem* (*in park*)

playgroup NOUN
la garderie *fem*

playing card NOUN
la carte à jouer *fem*

playing field NOUN
le terrain de sport *masc*

★ **playtime** NOUN
la récréation *fem*

playwright NOUN
le dramaturge *masc*

★ **pleasant** ADJECTIVE
agréable (FEM agréable)

★ **please** EXCLAMATION
1 s'il vous plaît (*polite form*)
□ Two coffees, please. Deux cafés, s'il vous plaît.
2 s'il te plaît (*familiar form*)
□ Please come with me. Viens avec moi, s'il te plaît.

★ **pleased** ADJECTIVE
content (FEM contente)
□ My mum's not going to be very pleased. Ma mère ne va pas être contente du tout. □ It's beautiful: she'll be pleased with it. C'est beau: elle va être contente.
■ **Pleased to meet you!** Enchanté!

★ **pleasure** NOUN
le plaisir *masc*
□ I read for pleasure. Je lis pour le plaisir.

★ **plenty** NOUN
largement assez
□ I've got plenty. J'en ai largement assez.
□ That's plenty, thanks. Ça suffit largement, merci.
■ **plenty of 1** (*a lot*) beaucoup de □ I've got plenty of things to do. J'ai beaucoup de choses à faire. **2** (*enough*) largement assez de □ I've got plenty of money. J'ai largement assez d'argent. □ We've got plenty of time. Nous avons largement le temps.

pliers PL NOUN
la pince *fem sing*
■ **a pair of pliers** une pince

★ **plot** NOUN
▷ *see also* **plot** VERB
1 l'intrigue *fem* (*of story, play*)
2 la conspiration *fem* (*against somebody*)
□ a plot against the president une conspiration contre le président
3 le carré *masc* (*of land*)
□ a vegetable plot un carré de légumes

★ to **plot** VERB
▷ *see also* **plot** NOUN
comploter [28]
□ They were plotting to kill him. Ils complotaient son assassinat.

plough NOUN
▷ *see also* **plough** VERB
la charrue *fem*

to **plough** VERB
▷ *see also* **plough** NOUN
labourer [28]

plug NOUN
1 la prise de courant *fem* (*electrical*)
□ The plug is faulty. La prise est défectueuse.
2 le bouchon *masc* (*for sink*)

to **plug in** VERB
brancher [28]
□ Is it plugged in? Est-ce que c'est branché?

plum NOUN
la prune *fem*
□ plum jam la confiture de prunes

plumber NOUN
le plombier *masc*
□ He's a plumber. Il est plombier.

plump ADJECTIVE
dodu (FEM dodue)

to **plunge** VERB
plonger [45]

plural NOUN
le pluriel *masc*

★ **plus** PREPOSITION, ADJECTIVE
plus
□ 4 plus 3 equals 7. Quatre plus trois égalent sept. □ three children plus a dog trois enfants plus un chien

p.m. ABBREVIATION
■ **at 8 p.m.** à huit heures du soir
■ **at 2 p.m.** à quatorze heures

> **DID YOU KNOW...?**
> In France, times are often given using the 24-hour clock.

pneumonia NOUN
la pneumonie *fem*

poached ADJECTIVE
■ **a poached egg** un œuf poché

★ **pocket** NOUN
la poche *fem*
■ **pocket money** l'argent de poche *masc*
□ £8 a week pocket money huit livres d'argent de poche par semaine

pocket calculator NOUN
la calculette *fem*

podcast NOUN
le podcast *masc*
■ **to download a podcast** télécharger [45] un podcast

★ **poem** NOUN
le poème *masc*

★ **poet** NOUN
le poète *masc*
la poétesse *fem*

★ **poetry** NOUN
la poésie *fem*

★ **point** NOUN
▷ *see also* **point** VERB
1 le point *masc* (*spot, score*)
□ a point on the horizon un point à l'horizon
□ They scored 5 points. Ils ont marqué cinq points.
2 la remarque *fem* (*comment*)
□ He made some interesting points. Il a fait quelques remarques intéressantes.
3 la pointe *fem* (*tip*)
□ a pencil with a sharp point un crayon à la pointe aiguisée
4 le moment *masc* (*in time*)
□ At that point, we decided to leave. À ce moment-là, nous avons décidé de partir.
■ **a point of view** un point de vue
■ **to get the point** comprendre [65] □ Sorry, I don't get the point. Désolé, je ne comprends pas.
■ **That's a good point!** C'est vrai!
■ **There's no point.** Cela ne sert à rien.
□ There's no point in waiting. Cela ne sert à rien d'attendre.
■ **What's the point?** À quoi bon? □ What's the point of leaving so early? À quoi bon partir si tôt?
■ **Physics isn't my strong point.** La physique n'est pas mon fort.
■ **two point five (2.5)** deux virgule cinq (2,5)

DID YOU KNOW...?
In decimal numbers, the French use a comma instead of a point.

★ to **point** VERB
▷ *see also* **point** NOUN
montrer [28] du doigt
□ Don't point! Ne montre pas du doigt!
■ **to point at somebody** montrer [28] quelqu'un du doigt □ She pointed at Maryam. Elle a montré Maryam du doigt.
■ **to point a gun at somebody** braquer [28] un revolver sur quelqu'un

to **point out** VERB
1 montrer [28] (*show*)
□ The guide pointed out Notre-Dame to us. Le guide nous a montré Notre-Dame.
2 signaler [28] (*mention*)
□ I should point out that ... Je dois vous signaler que ...

pointless ADJECTIVE
inutile (FEM inutile)
□ It's pointless to argue. Il est inutile de discuter.

poison NOUN
▷ *see also* **poison** VERB
le poison *masc*

to **poison** VERB
▷ *see also* **poison** NOUN
empoisonner [28]

poisonous ADJECTIVE
1 venimeux (FEM venimeuse) (*snake*)
2 vénéneux (FEM vénéneuse) (*plant, mushroom*)
3 toxique (FEM toxique) (*gas*)

to **poke** VERB
■ **He poked the ground with his stick.** Il tapotait le sol avec sa canne.
■ **She poked me in the ribs.** Elle m'a enfoncé le doigt dans les côtes.

poker NOUN
le poker *masc*
□ I play poker. Je joue au poker.

★ **Poland** NOUN
la Pologne *fem*
■ **in Poland** en Pologne
■ **to Poland** en Pologne

polar bear NOUN
l'ours blanc *masc*

Pole NOUN
le Polonais *masc*
la Polonaise *fem*

pole NOUN
le poteau *masc* (PL les poteaux)
□ a telegraph pole un poteau télégraphique
■ **a tent pole** un montant de tente
■ **a ski pole** un bâton de ski
■ **the North Pole** le pôle Nord
■ **the South Pole** le pôle Sud

pole vault NOUN
le saut à la perche *masc*

★ **police** PL NOUN
la police *fem*
□ We called the police. Nous avons appelé la police.
■ **a police car** une voiture de police
■ **a police station** un commissariat de police

DID YOU KNOW...?
There are several different types of police force in France. The **police nationale** are in charge of national security and public order in general, while the **police municipale** mainly deal with traffic and minor crimes. The **gendarmerie nationale** look after rural policing and border patrols. The **CRS** are involved in crowd and riot control.

★ **policeman** NOUN
le policier *masc*
□ He's a policeman. Il est policier.

★ **police officer** NOUN
le policier *masc*
la policière *fem*

★ **policewoman** NOUN
la policière *fem*
□ She's a policewoman. Elle est policière.

polio NOUN
la polio *fem*

★**Polish** NOUN
▷ *see also* **Polish** ADJECTIVE
le polonais *masc* (*language*)

★**Polish** ADJECTIVE
▷ *see also* **Polish** NOUN
polonais (FEM polonaise)

polish NOUN
▷ *see also* **polish** VERB
1 le cirage *masc* (*for shoes*)
2 la cire *fem* (*for furniture*)

to **polish** VERB
▷ *see also* **polish** NOUN
1 cirer [28] (*shoes, furniture*)
2 faire [36] briller (*glass*)

polite ADJECTIVE
poli (FEM polie)

politely ADVERB
poliment

politeness NOUN
la politesse *fem*

★**political** ADJECTIVE
politique (FEM politique)

★**politician** NOUN
1 l'homme politique *masc*
2 la femme politique *fem*

★**politics** PL NOUN
la politique *fem sing*
□ I'm not interested in politics. La politique ne m'intéresse pas.

poll NOUN
le sondage *masc*
□ A recent poll revealed that ... Un sondage récent a révélé que ...

pollen NOUN
le pollen *masc*

to **pollute** VERB
polluer [28]

polluted ADJECTIVE
pollué (FEM polluée)

★**pollution** NOUN
la pollution *fem*

polo-necked sweater NOUN
le pull à col roulé *masc*

polo shirt NOUN
le polo *masc*

polythene bag NOUN
le sac en plastique *masc*

pond NOUN
1 l'étang *masc* (*big*)
2 la mare *fem* (*smaller*)
3 le bassin *masc* (*in garden*)
□ We've got a pond in our garden. Nous avons un bassin dans notre jardin.

pony NOUN
le poney *masc*

ponytail NOUN
la queue de cheval *fem*
□ He's got a ponytail. Il a une queue de cheval.

pony trekking NOUN
■ **to go pony trekking** faire [36] une randonnée à dos de poney

poodle NOUN
le caniche *masc*

★**pool** NOUN
1 la flaque *fem* (*puddle*)
2 l'étang *masc* (*pond*)
3 la piscine *fem* (*for swimming*)
4 le billard américain *masc* (*game*)
□ Shall we have a game of pool? Si on jouait au billard américain?

★**poor** ADJECTIVE
1 pauvre (FEM pauvre)
□ a poor family une famille pauvre □ Poor David, he's very unlucky! Le pauvre David, il n'a vraiment pas de chance!
■ **the poor** les pauvres *masc*
2 médiocre (FEM médiocre) (*bad*)
□ a poor mark une note médiocre

poorly ADJECTIVE
souffrant (FEM souffrante)
□ She's poorly. Elle est souffrante.

★**pop** ADJECTIVE
pop (FEM+PL pop)
□ pop music la musique pop □ a pop star une pop star □ a pop group un groupe pop □ a pop song une chanson pop

to **pop in** VERB
passer [58E]
□ I just popped in to say hello. Je suis juste passé dire bonjour. □ I need to pop in to the supermarket for some milk. Je dois passer au supermarché pour chercher du lait.

to **pop out** VERB
sortir [79E]
□ He's just popped out to the supermarket. Il vient de sortir pour aller au supermarché.

to **pop round** VERB
passer [58E]
□ I'm just popping round to my aunt's. Je vais juste passer chez ma tante.

popcorn NOUN
le pop-corn *masc*

poppy NOUN
le coquelicot *masc*

Popsicle® NOUN (US)
la glace à l'eau *fem*

★**popular** ADJECTIVE
populaire (FEM populaire)
□ She's a very popular girl. C'est une fille très

populaire. □ This is a very popular style. C'est un style très populaire.

★ **population** NOUN
la population *fem*

porch NOUN
le porche *masc*

pork NOUN
le porc *masc*
□ a pork chop une côtelette de porc □ I don't eat pork. Je ne mange pas de porc.

pornography NOUN
la pornographie *fem*

porridge NOUN
le porridge *masc*

★ **port** NOUN
1 le port *masc* (*harbour*)
2 le porto *masc* (*wine*)
□ a glass of port un verre de porto

portable ADJECTIVE
portable (FEM portable)

porter NOUN
1 le portier *masc* (*in hotel*)
2 le porteur *masc* (*at station*)

portion NOUN
la portion *fem*
□ a large portion of chips une grosse portion de frites

portrait NOUN
le portrait *masc*

★ **Portugal** NOUN
le Portugal *masc*
■ **in Portugal** au Portugal
■ **We went to Portugal.** Nous sommes allés au Portugal.

★ **Portuguese** NOUN
▷ *see also* **Portuguese** ADJECTIVE
1 le Portugais *masc*
la Portugaise *fem* (*person*)
2 le portugais *masc* (*language*)

★ **Portuguese** ADJECTIVE
▷ *see also* **Portuguese** NOUN
portugais (FEM portugaise)

posh ADJECTIVE
chic (FEM+PL chic)
□ a posh hotel un hôtel chic

★ **position** NOUN
la position *fem*
□ an uncomfortable position une position inconfortable

★ **positive** ADJECTIVE
1 positif (FEM positive) (*good*)
□ a positive attitude une attitude positive
2 certain (FEM certaine) (*sure*)
□ I'm positive. J'en suis certain.

to **possess** VERB
posséder [34]

possession NOUN
■ **Have you got all your possessions?** Est-ce que tu as toutes tes affaires?

★ **possibility** NOUN
■ **It's a possibility.** C'est possible.

★ **possible** ADJECTIVE
possible (FEM possible)
□ as soon as possible aussitôt que possible

★ **possibly** ADVERB
peut-être (*perhaps*)
□ Are you coming to the party? — Possibly. Est-ce que tu viens à la soirée? — Peut-être.
■ **... if you possibly can.** ... si cela vous est possible.
■ **I can't possibly come.** Je ne peux vraiment pas venir.

★ **post** NOUN
▷ *see also* **post** VERB
1 le courrier *masc* (*letters*)
□ Is there any post for me? Est-ce qu'il y a du courrier pour moi?
2 le poteau *masc* (PL les poteaux) (*pole*)
□ The ball hit the post. Le ballon a heurté le poteau.
3 le post *masc* (*on forum, blog*)

★ to **post** VERB
▷ *see also* **post** NOUN
poster [28] (*also online*)
□ I've got some cards to post. J'ai quelques cartes à poster. □ She posted it on my wall. Elle l'a posté sur mon mur.

postage NOUN
l'affranchissement *masc*

postbox NOUN
la boîte aux lettres *fem*

> **DID YOU KNOW...?**
> French postboxes are yellow.

★ **postcard** NOUN
la carte postale *fem*

postcode NOUN
le code postal *masc*

★ **poster** NOUN
1 le poster *masc*
□ I've got posters on my bedroom walls. J'ai des posters sur les murs de ma chambre.
2 l'affiche *fem* (*advertising*)
□ There are posters all over town. Il y a des affiches dans toute la ville.

★ **postman** NOUN
le facteur *masc*
□ He's a postman. Il est facteur.

postmark NOUN
le cachet de la poste *masc*

★ **post office** NOUN
la poste *fem*
□ Where's the post office, please? Où est la

poste, s'il vous plaît? □ She works for the post office. Elle travaille à la poste.

to **postpone** VERB
remettre [47] à plus tard
□ The match has been postponed. Le match a été remis à plus tard.

★ **postwoman** NOUN
la factrice *fem*
□ She's a postwoman. Elle est factrice.

★ **pot** NOUN
1 le pot *masc*
□ a pot of jam un pot de confiture
▪ **the pots and pans** les casseroles
2 la théière *fem* (*teapot*)
3 la cafetière *fem* (*coffeepot*)

★ **potato** NOUN
la pomme de terre *fem*
□ potato salad la salade de pommes de terre
▪ **mashed potatoes** la purée
▪ **boiled potatoes** les pommes vapeur
▪ **a baked potato** une pomme de terre en robe des champs

★ **potential** NOUN
▷ *see also* **potential** ADJECTIVE
▪ **He has great potential.** Il a de l'avenir.

★ **potential** ADJECTIVE
▷ *see also* **potential** NOUN
possible (FEM possible)
□ a potential problem un problème possible

pothole NOUN
le nid de poule *masc* (*in road*)

pot plant NOUN
la plante en pot *fem*

pottery NOUN
la poterie *fem*

★ **pound** NOUN
▷ *see also* **pound** VERB
la livre *fem* (*weight, money*)
□ How many euros do you get to the pound? Combien d'euros a-t-on pour une livre? □ a pound coin une pièce d'une livre

DID YOU KNOW...?
In France, measurements are in grams and kilograms. One pound is about 450 grams.

□ a pound of carrots un demi-kilo de carottes

★ to **pound** VERB
▷ *see also* **pound** NOUN
battre [9]
□ My heart was pounding. J'avais le cœur qui battait.

★ to **pour** VERB
1 verser [28] (*liquid*)
□ She poured some water into the pan. Elle a versé de l'eau dans la casserole.
▪ **She poured him a drink.** Elle lui a servi à boire.
▪ **Shall I pour you a cup of tea?** Je vous sers une tasse de thé?
2 pleuvoir [63] à verse (*rain*)
□ It's pouring. Il pleut à verse.
▪ **in the pouring rain** sous une pluie torrentielle

★ **poverty** NOUN
la pauvreté *fem*

powder NOUN
la poudre *fem*

★ **power** NOUN
1 le courant *masc* (*electricity*)
□ The power's off. Le courant est coupé.
▪ **a power cut** une coupure de courant
▪ **a power point** une prise de courant
▪ **a power station** une centrale électrique
2 l'énergie *fem* (*energy*)
□ nuclear power l'énergie nucléaire □ solar power l'énergie solaire
3 le pouvoir *masc* (*authority*)
□ to be in power être au pouvoir

★ **powerful** ADJECTIVE
puissant (FEM puissante)

★ **practical** ADJECTIVE
pratique (FEM pratique)
□ a practical suggestion un conseil pratique
▪ **She's very practical.** Elle a l'esprit pratique.

practically ADVERB
pratiquement
□ It's practically impossible. C'est pratiquement impossible.

★ **practice** NOUN
l'entraînement *masc* (*for sport*)
□ football practice l'entraînement de foot
▪ **I've got to do my clarinet practice.** Je dois travailler ma clarinette.
▪ **It's normal practice in our school.** C'est ce qui se fait dans notre école.
▪ **in practice** en pratique
▪ **a medical practice** un cabinet médical

★ to **practise** (US **practice**) VERB
1 s'exercer [12] (*music, hobby*)
□ I ought to practise more. Je devrais m'exercer davantage.
2 travailler [28] (*instrument*)
□ I practise the flute every evening. Je travaille ma flûte tous les soirs.
3 pratiquer [28] (*language*)
□ I practised my French when we were on holiday. J'ai pratiqué mon français pendant les vacances.
4 s'entraîner [28] (*sport*)
□ The team practises on Thursdays. L'équipe s'entraîne le jeudi. □ I don't practise enough. Je ne m'entraîne pas assez.

Numbers in brackets refer to verb tables on pages 650 to 658

practising ADJECTIVE
pratiquant (FEM pratiquante)
□ She's a practising Catholic. Elle est catholique pratiquante.

★ to **praise** VERB
faire [36] l'éloge de
□ Everyone praises her cooking. Tout le monde fait l'éloge de sa cuisine. □ The teachers praised our work. Les professeurs ont fait l'éloge de notre travail.

pram NOUN
le landau *masc*

prawn NOUN
la crevette *fem*

prawn cocktail NOUN
le cocktail de crevettes *masc*

to **pray** VERB
prier [19]
□ to pray for something prier pour quelque chose

prayer NOUN
la prière *fem*

precaution NOUN
la précaution *fem*
■ **to take precautions** prendre [65] ses précautions

preceding ADJECTIVE
précédent (FEM précédente)

precinct NOUN
■ **a shopping precinct** un centre commercial
■ **a pedestrian precinct** une zone piétonnière

precious ADJECTIVE
précieux (FEM précieuse)

precise ADJECTIVE
précis (FEM précise)
□ at that precise moment à cet instant précis

★ **precisely** ADVERB
précisément
□ Precisely! Précisément!
■ **at 10 a.m. precisely** à dix heures précises

to **predict** VERB
prédire [27]

predictable ADJECTIVE
prévisible (FEM prévisible)

prefect NOUN

> **DID YOU KNOW...?**
> French schools do not have prefects. You could explain what a prefect is using the example given.

■ **My sister's a prefect.** Ma sœur est en dernière année et est chargée de maintenir la discipline.

★ to **prefer** VERB
préférer [34]
□ Which would you prefer? Lequel préfères-tu? □ I prefer biology to chemistry. Je préfère les SVT à la chimie.

preference NOUN
la préférence *fem*

★ **pregnant** ADJECTIVE
enceinte
□ She's six months pregnant. Elle est enceinte de six mois.

prehistoric ADJECTIVE
préhistorique (FEM préhistorique)

prejudice NOUN
1 le préjugé *masc*
□ That's just a prejudice. C'est un préjugé.
2 les préjugés *masc pl*
□ There's a lot of racial prejudice. Il y a beaucoup de préjugés raciaux.

prejudiced ADJECTIVE
■ **to be prejudiced against somebody** avoir [8] des préjugés contre quelqu'un

premature ADJECTIVE
prématuré (FEM prématurée)
■ **a premature baby** un prématuré

Premier League NOUN
la première division *fem*
□ in the Premier League en première division

premises PL NOUN
les locaux *masc pl*
□ They're moving to new premises. Ils vont occuper de nouveaux locaux.

premonition NOUN
la prémonition *fem*

preoccupied ADJECTIVE
préoccupé (FEM préoccupée)

prep NOUN
les devoirs *masc pl* (*homework*)
□ history prep les devoirs d'histoire

preparation NOUN
la préparation *fem*

★ to **prepare** VERB
préparer [28]
□ She has to prepare lessons in the evening. Elle doit préparer ses cours le soir.
■ **to prepare for something** se préparer [28] pour quelque chose □ We're preparing for our skiing holiday. Nous nous préparons pour nos vacances à la neige.

★ **prepared** ADJECTIVE
■ **to be prepared to do something** être [35] prêt à faire quelque chose □ I'm prepared to help you. Je suis prêt à t'aider.

prep school NOUN
l'école primaire privée *fem*

Presbyterian NOUN
▷ *see also* **Presbyterian** ADJECTIVE
le presbytérien *masc*
la presbytérienne *fem*

Presbyterian ADJECTIVE
▷ *see also* **Presbyterian** NOUN
presbytérien (FEM presbytérienne)

to **prescribe** VERB
prescrire [30]

prescription NOUN
l'ordonnance *fem*
□ You can't get it without a prescription. On ne peut pas se le procurer sans ordonnance.

presence NOUN
la présence *fem*
■ **presence of mind** présence d'esprit

★ **present** ADJECTIVE
▷ *see also* **present** NOUN, VERB
1 présent (FEM présente) (*in attendance*)
□ He wasn't present at the school assembly. Il n'était pas présent à l'assemblée de l'école.
2 actuel (FEM actuelle) (*current*)
□ the present situation la situation actuelle
■ **the present tense** le présent

★ **present** NOUN
▷ *see also* **present** ADJECTIVE, VERB
1 le cadeau *masc* (PL les cadeaux) (*gift*)
□ I'm going to buy presents. Je vais acheter des cadeaux.
■ **to give somebody a present** offrir [54] un cadeau à quelqu'un
2 le présent *masc* (*time*)
□ up to the present jusqu'à présent
■ **for the present** pour l'instant
■ **at present** en ce moment

★ to **present** VERB
▷ *see also* **present** ADJECTIVE, NOUN
■ **to present somebody with something** (*prize, medal*) remettre [47] quelque chose à quelqu'un

presenter NOUN
le présentateur *masc*
la présentatrice *fem* (*on TV*)

presently ADVERB
1 bientôt (*soon*)
□ You'll feel better presently. Tu vas bientôt te sentir mieux.
2 actuellement (*at present*)
□ They're presently on tour. Ils sont actuellement en tournée.

★ **president** NOUN
le président *masc*
la présidente *fem*

★ **press** NOUN
▷ *see also* **press** VERB
la presse *fem*
■ **a press conference** une conférence de presse

★ to **press** VERB
▷ *see also* **press** NOUN
1 appuyer [53]
□ Don't press too hard! N'appuie pas trop fort!
2 appuyer [53] sur
□ He pressed the start button. Il a appuyé sur le bouton de démarrage.

pressed ADJECTIVE
■ **We are pressed for time.** Le temps nous manque.

press-up NOUN
■ **to do press-ups** faire [36] des pompes □ I do twenty press-ups every morning. Je fais vingt pompes tous les matins.

★ **pressure** NOUN
▷ *see also* **pressure** VERB
la pression *fem*
□ He's under a lot of pressure at work. Il est sous pression au travail.
■ **a pressure group** un groupe de pression

★ to **pressure** VERB
▷ *see also* **pressure** NOUN
faire [36] pression sur
□ My parents are pressuring me. Mes parents font pression sur moi.

to **pressurize** VERB
■ **to pressurize somebody to do something** faire [36] pression sur quelqu'un pour qu'il fasse quelque chose □ My parents are pressurizing me to stay on at school. Mes parents font pression sur moi pour que je reste à l'école.

prestige NOUN
le prestige *masc*

prestigious ADJECTIVE
prestigieux (FEM prestigieuse)

presumably ADVERB
vraisemblablement

to **presume** VERB
supposer [28]
□ I presume so. Je suppose que oui.

★ to **pretend** VERB
■ **to pretend to do something** faire [36] semblant de faire quelque chose □ He pretended to be asleep. Il faisait semblant de dormir.

> **BE CAREFUL!**
> Do not translate **to pretend** by the French word **prétendre**.

★ **pretty** ADJECTIVE, ADVERB
1 joli (FEM jolie)
□ She's very pretty. Elle est très jolie.
2 plutôt (*rather*)
□ That film was pretty bad. Ce film était plutôt mauvais.
■ **The weather was pretty awful.** Il faisait un temps minable.
■ **It's pretty much the same.** C'est pratiquement la même chose.

 Numbers in brackets refer to verb tables on pages 650 to 658

★ to **prevent** VERB
empêcher [28]
▪ **to prevent somebody from doing something** empêcher [28] quelqu'un de faire quelque chose ▫ They tried to prevent us from staying out late. Ils ont essayé de nous empêcher de rentrer tard.

★ **previous** ADJECTIVE
précédent (FEM précédente)

previously ADVERB
auparavant

prey NOUN
la proie *fem*
▫ a bird of prey un oiseau de proie

★ **price** NOUN
le prix *masc*

price list NOUN
la liste des prix *fem*

to **prick** VERB
piquer [28]
▫ I've pricked my finger. Je me suis piqué le doigt.

★ **pride** NOUN
la fierté *fem*

★ **priest** NOUN
le prêtre *masc*
▫ He's a priest. Il est prêtre.

primarily ADVERB
principalement

★ **primary** ADJECTIVE
principal (FEM principale, MASC PL principaux)

primary school NOUN
l'école primaire *fem*
▫ She's still at primary school. Elle est encore à l'école primaire.

DID YOU KNOW...?
In France, children start primary school at the age of six. The first year is **CP**, followed by **CE1** and **CE2**. The last two years are **CM1** and **CM2**.

prime minister NOUN
le Premier ministre *masc*

primitive ADJECTIVE
primitif (FEM primitive)

★ **prince** NOUN
le prince *masc*
▫ the Prince of Wales le prince de Galles

★ **princess** NOUN
la princesse *fem*
▫ Princess Anne la princesse Anne

★ **principal** ADJECTIVE
▷ *see also* **principal** NOUN
principal (FEM principale, MASC PL principaux)

★ **principal** NOUN
▷ *see also* **principal** ADJECTIVE
le principal *masc* (PL les principaux) (*of college*)

principle NOUN
le principe *masc*
▪ **on principle** par principe

★ **print** NOUN
1 les caractères *masc pl* (*letters*)
▫ in small print en petits caractères
2 l'empreinte digitale *fem* (*fingerprint*)
3 la gravure *fem* (*picture*)
▫ a framed print une gravure encadrée

printer NOUN
l'imprimante *fem* (*machine*)

printout NOUN
le tirage *masc*

★ **priority** NOUN
la priorité *fem*

★ **prison** NOUN
la prison *fem*
▪ **in prison** en prison

★ **prisoner** NOUN
le prisonnier *masc*
la prisonnière *fem*

prison officer NOUN
le gardien de prison *masc*
la gardienne de prison *fem*

privacy NOUN
l'intimité *fem*

★ **private** ADJECTIVE
privé (FEM privée)
▫ a private school une école privée
▪ **'private property'** 'propriété privée'
▪ **'private'** (*on envelope*) 'personnel'
▪ **a private bathroom** une salle de bain individuelle
▪ **I have private lessons.** Je prends des cours particuliers.

★ to **privatize** VERB
privatiser [28]

privilege NOUN
le privilège *masc*

★ **prize** NOUN
le prix *masc*
▫ to win a prize gagner un prix

prize-giving NOUN
la distribution des prix *fem*

prizewinner NOUN
le gagnant *masc*
la gagnante *fem*

pro NOUN
▪ **the pros and cons** le pour et le contre
▫ We weighed up the pros and cons. Nous avons pesé le pour et le contre.

probability NOUN
la probabilité *fem*

probable ADJECTIVE
probable (FEM probable)

★ **probably** ADVERB
probablement
□ probably not probablement pas

★ **problem** NOUN
le problème *masc*
□ No problem! Pas de problème!

proceeds PL NOUN
la recette *fem sing*

★ **process** NOUN
le processus *masc*
□ the peace process le processus de paix
■ **to be in the process of doing something** être [35] en train de faire quelque chose
□ We're in the process of painting the kitchen. Nous sommes en train de peindre la cuisine.

procession NOUN
la procession *fem* (*religious*)

★ to **produce** VERB
1 produire [23] (*manufacture*)
2 monter [48] (*play, show*)

★ **producer** NOUN
le metteur en scène *masc* (*of play, show*)

★ **product** NOUN
le produit *masc*

★ **production** NOUN
1 la production *fem*
□ The latest smartphone has just gone into production. On vient de lancer la production du tout dernier smartphone.
2 la mise en scène *fem* (*play, show*)
□ a production of 'Hamlet' une mise en scène de 'Hamlet'

profession NOUN
la profession *fem*

★ **professional** NOUN
▷ *see also* **professional** ADJECTIVE
le professionnel *masc*
la professionnelle *fem*

★ **professional** ADJECTIVE
▷ *see also* **professional** NOUN
professionnel (FEM professionnelle) (*player*)
□ a professional musician un musicien professionnel
■ **a very professional piece of work** un vrai travail de professionnel

professionally ADVERB
■ **She sings professionally.** C'est une chanteuse professionnelle.

★ **professor** NOUN
le professeur d'université *masc*
■ **He's the French professor.** Il est titulaire de la chaire de français.

★ **profit** NOUN
le bénéfice *masc*

profitable ADJECTIVE
rentable (FEM rentable)

★ **program** NOUN
▷ *see also* **program** VERB
le programme *masc*
□ a computer program un programme informatique
■ **a TV program** (US) une émission de télévision

★ to **program** VERB
▷ *see also* **program** NOUN
programmer [28] (*computer*)

★ **programme** NOUN
1 l'émission *fem* (*on TV, radio*)
2 le programme *masc* (*of events*)

programmer NOUN
le programmeur *masc*
la programmeuse *fem*
□ She's a programmer. Elle est programmeuse.

programming NOUN
la programmation *fem*

★ **progress** NOUN
le progrès *masc*
□ You're making progress! Vous faites des progrès!

to **prohibit** VERB
interdire [27]
□ Smoking is prohibited. Il est interdit de fumer.

★ **project** NOUN
1 le projet *masc* (*plan*)
□ a development project un projet de développement
2 le dossier *masc* (*research*)
□ I'm doing a project on education in France. Je prépare un dossier sur l'éducation en France.

projector NOUN
le projecteur *masc*

promenade NOUN
le front de mer *masc*

★ **promise** NOUN
▷ *see also* **promise** VERB
la promesse *fem*
□ He made me a promise. Il m'a fait une promesse.
■ **That's a promise!** C'est promis!

★ to **promise** VERB
▷ *see also* **promise** NOUN
promettre [47]
□ She promised to write. Elle a promis d'écrire. □ I'll text you, I promise! Je t'enverrai un SMS, c'est promis!

promising ADJECTIVE
■ **a promising player** un joueur prometteur

★ to **promote** VERB
■ **to be promoted** être [35] promu □ She

was promoted after six months. Elle a été promue au bout de six mois.

★ **promotion** NOUN
la promotion *fem*

★ **prompt** ADJECTIVE, ADVERB
rapide (FEM rapide)
□ a prompt reply une réponse rapide
■ **at eight o'clock prompt** à huit heures précises

promptly ADVERB
■ **We left promptly at seven.** Nous sommes partis à sept heures précises.

pronoun NOUN
le pronom *masc*

to **pronounce** VERB
prononcer [12]
□ How do you pronounce that word? Comment est-ce qu'on prononce ce mot?

pronunciation NOUN
la prononciation *fem*

★ **proof** NOUN
la preuve *fem*

★ **proper** ADJECTIVE
1 vrai (FEM vraie) (*genuine*)
□ proper French bread du vrai pain français
□ We didn't have a proper lunch, just sandwiches. Nous n'avons pas pris de vrai repas, juste des sandwichs.
■ **It's difficult to get a proper job.** Il est difficile de trouver un travail correct.
2 adéquat (FEM adéquate)
□ You have to have the proper equipment. Il faut avoir l'équipement adéquat. □ We need proper training. Il nous faut une formation adéquate.
■ **If you had come at the proper time ...** Si tu étais venu à l'heure dite ...

BE CAREFUL!
Do not translate **proper** by the French word **propre**.

★ **properly** ADVERB
1 comme il faut (*correctly*)
□ You're not doing it properly. Tu ne t'y prends pas comme il faut.
2 convenablement (*appropriately*)
□ Dress properly for your interview. Habille-toi convenablement pour ton entretien.

★ **property** NOUN
la propriété *fem*
■ **'private property'** 'propriété privée'
■ **stolen property** les objets volés

proportional ADJECTIVE
proportionnel (FEM proportionnelle)
□ proportional representation la représentation proportionnelle

★ **proposal** NOUN
la proposition *fem* (*suggestion*)

★ to **propose** VERB
proposer [28]
□ I propose a new plan. Je propose un changement de programme.
■ **to propose to do something** avoir [8] l'intention de faire quelque chose □ What do you propose to do? Qu'est-ce que tu as l'intention de faire?
■ **to propose to somebody** (*for marriage*) demander [28] quelqu'un en mariage □ He proposed to her at the restaurant. Il l'a demandée en mariage au restaurant.

to **prosecute** VERB
poursuivre [81] en justice
□ They were prosecuted for murder. Ils ont été poursuivis en justice pour meurtre.
■ **'Trespassers will be prosecuted'** 'Défense d'entrer sous peine de poursuites'

prospect NOUN
la perspective *fem*
□ It'll improve my career prospects. Ça va améliorer mes perspectives d'avenir.

prospectus NOUN
le prospectus *masc*

★ to **protect** VERB
protéger [66]

protection NOUN
la protection *fem*

protein NOUN
la protéine *fem*

★ **protest** NOUN
▷ *see also* **protest** VERB
la protestation *fem*
□ He ignored their protests. Il a ignoré leurs protestations.
■ **a protest march** une manifestation

★ to **protest** VERB
▷ *see also* **protest** NOUN
protester [28]

Protestant NOUN
▷ *see also* **Protestant** ADJECTIVE
le protestant *masc*
la protestante *fem*
□ I'm a Protestant. Je suis protestant.

Protestant ADJECTIVE
▷ *see also* **Protestant** NOUN
protestant (FEM protestante)
□ a Protestant church une église protestante

protester NOUN
le manifestant *masc*
la manifestante *fem*

★ **proud** ADJECTIVE
fier (FEM fière)
□ Her parents are proud of her. Ses parents sont fiers d'elle.

★ to **prove** VERB
prouver [28]
□ The police couldn't prove it. La police n'a pas pu le prouver.

proverb NOUN
le proverbe *masc*

★ to **provide** VERB
fournir [38]
■ **to provide somebody with something** fournir [38] quelque chose à quelqu'un
□ They provided us with maps. Ils nous ont fourni des cartes.

to **provide for** VERB
subvenir [89] aux besoins de
□ He can't provide for his family any more. Il ne peut plus subvenir aux besoins de sa famille.

provided CONJUNCTION
à condition que

à condition que has to be followed by the subjunctive.

□ He'll play in the next match provided he's fit. Il jouera dans le prochain match, à condition qu'il soit en forme.

provisional ADJECTIVE
provisoire (FEM provisoire)

prowler NOUN
le rôdeur *masc*
la rôdeuse *fem*

prune NOUN
le pruneau *masc* (PL les pruneaux)

to **pry** VERB
■ **He's always prying into other people's affairs.** Il met toujours son nez dans les affaires des autres.

pseudonym NOUN
le pseudonyme *masc*

psychiatrist NOUN
le/la psychiatre *masc/fem*
□ She's a psychiatrist. Elle est psychiatre.

psychoanalyst NOUN
le/la psychanalyste *masc/fem*

★ **psychological** ADJECTIVE
psychologique (FEM psychologique)

psychologist NOUN
le/la psychologue *masc/fem*
□ He's a psychologist. Il est psychologue.

psychology NOUN
la psychologie *fem*

PTO ABBREVIATION (= *please turn over*)
TSVP (= *tournez, s'il vous plaît*)

★ **pub** NOUN
le pub *masc*

★ **public** NOUN
▷ *see also* **public** ADJECTIVE
le public *masc*
□ open to the public ouvert au public
■ **in public** en public

★ **public** ADJECTIVE
▷ *see also* **public** NOUN
public (FEM publique)
■ **a public holiday** un jour férié
■ **public opinion** l'opinion publique *fem*
■ **the public address system** la sono *fem*

publican NOUN
le patron de pub *masc*
la patronne de pub *fem*
■ **My uncle's a publican.** Mon oncle tient un pub.

★ **publicity** NOUN
la publicité *fem*

public school NOUN
l'école privée *fem*

public transport NOUN
les transports en commun *masc pl*

★ to **publish** VERB
publier [19]

★ **publisher** NOUN
l'éditeur *masc*

pudding NOUN
le dessert *masc*
□ What's for pudding? Qu'est-ce qu'il y a comme dessert?
■ **rice pudding** le riz au lait
■ **black pudding** le boudin noir

puddle NOUN
la flaque *fem*

puff pastry NOUN
la pâte feuilletée *fem*

★ to **pull** VERB
tirer [28]
□ Pull! Tirez!
■ **He pulled the trigger.** Il a appuyé sur la gâchette.
■ **to pull a muscle** se froisser [28] un muscle
□ I pulled a muscle when I was training. Je me suis froissé un muscle à l'entraînement.
■ **You're pulling my leg!** Tu me fais marcher!

to **pull down** VERB
démolir [38]

to **pull out** VERB
1 arracher [28] (*tooth, weed*)
2 déboîter [28] (*car*)
□ The car pulled out to overtake. La voiture a déboîté pour doubler.
3 se retirer [28] (*withdraw*)
□ She pulled out of the tournament. Elle s'est retirée du tournoi.

to **pull through** VERB
s'en sortir [79]
□ They think he'll pull through. Ils pensent qu'il va s'en sortir.

to **pull up** VERB
s'arrêter [28] (*car*)
□ A black car pulled up beside me. Une voiture noire s'est arrêtée à côté de moi.

pullover NOUN
le pull-over *masc*

pulse NOUN
le pouls *masc*
□ The nurse took his pulse. L'infirmière a pris son pouls.

pulses PL NOUN
les légumes secs *masc pl*

★ **pump** NOUN
▷ *see also* **pump** VERB
1 la pompe *fem*
□ a bicycle pump une pompe à vélo □ a petrol pump une pompe à essence
2 le chausson de gym *masc* (*shoe*)

★ to **pump** VERB
▷ *see also* **pump** NOUN
pomper [28]

to **pump up** VERB
gonfler [28] (*tyre*)

pumpkin NOUN
le potiron *masc*

★ **punch** NOUN
▷ *see also* **punch** VERB
1 le coup de poing *masc* (*blow*)
□ He gave me a punch. Il m'a donné un coup de poing.
2 le punch *masc* (*drink*)

★ to **punch** VERB
▷ *see also* **punch** NOUN
1 donner [28] un coup de poing à (*hit*)
□ He punched me! Il m'a donné un coup de poing!
2 composter [28] (*in ticket machine*)
□ Punch your ticket before you get on the train. Compostez votre billet avant de monter dans le train.
3 poinçonner [28] (*by hand*)
□ He forgot to punch my ticket. Il a oublié de poinçonner mon billet.

DID YOU KNOW...?
In France, you have to punch your ticket before you get on the train. If you don't, you could be fined.

punch-up NOUN
la bagarre *fem* (*informal*)

punctual ADJECTIVE
ponctuel (FEM ponctuelle)

punctuation NOUN
la ponctuation *fem*

puncture NOUN
la crevaison *fem*
□ I had to mend a puncture. J'ai dû réparer une crevaison.
■ **to have a puncture** crever [43] □ I had a puncture on the motorway. J'ai crevé sur l'autoroute.

to **punish** VERB
punir [38]
■ **to punish somebody for something** punir [38] quelqu'un pour quelque chose
■ **to punish somebody for doing something** punir [38] quelqu'un d'avoir fait quelque chose

punishment NOUN
la punition *fem*

★ **pupil** NOUN
l'élève *masc/fem*

puppet NOUN
la marionnette *fem*

puppy NOUN
le chiot *masc*

to **purchase** VERB
acheter [1]

★ **pure** ADJECTIVE
pur (FEM pure)
□ pure orange juice du pur jus d'orange
□ He's doing pure maths. Il fait des maths pures.

★ **purple** ADJECTIVE
violet (FEM violette)

★ **purpose** NOUN
le but *masc*
□ What is the purpose of these changes? Quel est le but de ces changements? □ his purpose in life son but dans la vie
■ **on purpose** exprès □ He did it on purpose. Il l'a fait exprès.

to **purr** VERB
ronronner [28]

purse NOUN
1 le porte-monnaie *masc* (PL les porte-monnaie)
2 le sac à main *masc* (US: *handbag*)

to **pursue** VERB
poursuivre [81]

pursuit NOUN
l'activité *fem*
□ outdoor pursuits les activités de plein air

★ **push** NOUN
▷ *see also* **push** VERB
■ **to give somebody a push** pousser [28] quelqu'un □ He gave me a push. Il m'a poussé.

★ to **push** VERB
▷ *see also* **push** NOUN
1 pousser [28]
□ Don't push! Arrêtez de pousser!
2 appuyer [53] sur (*button*)
■ **to push somebody to do something** pousser [28] quelqu'un à faire quelque chose

□ My parents are pushing me to go to university. Mes parents me poussent à entrer à l'université.

to **push around** VERB
bousculer [28]
□ He likes pushing people around. Il aime bien bousculer les gens.

to **push through** VERB
se frayer [59] un passage
□ The paramedics pushed through the crowd. Les secouristes se sont frayé un passage dans la foule.
▪ **I pushed my way through.** Je me suis frayé un passage.

pushchair NOUN
la poussette *fem*

push-up NOUN
▪ **to do push-ups** faire [36] des pompes □ I do twenty push-ups every morning. Je fais vingt pompes tous les matins.

★ to **put** VERB
1 mettre [47] (*place*)
□ Where shall I put my things? Où est-ce que je peux mettre mes affaires? □ She's putting the baby to bed. Elle met le bébé au lit.
2 écrire [30] (*write*)
□ Don't forget to put your name on the paper. N'oubliez pas d'écrire votre nom sur la feuille.

to **put aside** VERB
mettre [47] de côté
□ Can you put this aside for me till tomorrow? Est-ce que vous pouvez mettre ça de côté pour moi jusqu'à demain?

to **put away** VERB
ranger [45]
□ Can you put away the dishes, please? Tu peux ranger la vaisselle, s'il te plaît?

P

to **put back** VERB
remettre [47] en place (*replace*)
□ Put it back when you've finished with it. Remets-le en place une fois que tu auras fini.

to **put down** VERB
1 poser [28]
□ I'll put these bags down for a minute. Je vais poser ces sacs une minute.
2 noter [28] (*in writing*)
□ I've put down a few ideas. J'ai noté quelques idées.
▪ **to have an animal put down** faire [36] piquer un animal □ We had to have our old dog put down. Nous avons dû faire piquer notre vieux chien.

to **put forward** VERB
1 avancer [12] (*clock*)
□ Don't forget to put the clocks forward. N'oubliez pas d'avancer les pendules d'une heure.
2 proposer [28] (*idea, argument*)
□ to put forward a suggestion proposer une suggestion

to **put in** VERB
installer [28] (*install*)
□ We're going to get central heating put in. Nous allons faire installer le chauffage central.
▪ **He has put in a lot of work on this project.** Il a fourni beaucoup de travail pour ce projet.

to **put off** VERB
1 éteindre [60] (*switch off*)
□ Shall I put the light off? Est-ce que j'éteins la lumière?
2 remettre [47] à plus tard (*postpone*)
□ I keep putting it off. Je n'arrête pas de remettre ça à plus tard.
3 déranger [45] (*distract*)
□ Stop putting me off! Arrête de me déranger!
4 décourager [45] (*discourage*)
□ He's not easily put off. Il ne se laisse pas facilement décourager.

to **put on** VERB
1 mettre [47] (*clothes, lipstick, album*)
□ I'll put my coat on. Je vais mettre mon manteau.
2 allumer [28] (*light, heater, TV*)
□ Shall I put the heater on? J'allume le chauffage?
3 monter [48] (*play, show*)
□ We're putting on 'Bugsy Malone'. Nous sommes en train de monter 'Bugsy Malone'.
4 mettre [47] à cuire
□ I'll put the potatoes on. Je vais mettre les pommes de terre à cuire.
▪ **to put on weight** grossir [38] □ He's put on a lot of weight. Il a beaucoup grossi.

to **put out** VERB
éteindre [60] (*light, cigarette, fire*)
□ It took them five hours to put out the fire. Ils ont mis cinq heures à éteindre l'incendie.

to **put through** VERB
passer [58]
□ Can you put me through to the manager? Est-ce que vous pouvez me passer le directeur?
▪ **I'm putting you through.** Je vous passe la communication.

to **put up** VERB
1 mettre [47] (*pin up*)
□ I'll put the poster up on my wall. Je vais mettre le poster sur mon mur.
2 monter [48] (*tent*)
□ We put up our tent in a field. Nous avons monté la tente dans un champ.
3 augmenter [28] (*price*)
□ They've put up the price. Ils ont augmenté le prix.

4 héberger [45] (*accommodate*)
□ My friend will put me up for the night. Mon ami va m'héberger pour la nuit.
■ **to put one's hand up** lever [43] la main
□ If you have any questions, put up your hand. Si vous avez une question, levez la main.
■ **to put up with something** supporter [28] quelque chose □ I'm not going to put up with it any longer. Je ne vais pas supporter ça plus longtemps.

puzzle NOUN
le puzzle *masc* (*jigsaw*)

puzzled ADJECTIVE
perplexe (FEM perplexe)
□ You look puzzled! Tu as l'air perplexe!

puzzling ADJECTIVE
déconcertant (FEM déconcertante)

pyjamas PL NOUN
le pyjama *masc sing*
□ my pyjamas mon pyjama □ a pair of pyjamas un pyjama
■ **a pyjama top** un haut de pyjama

pyramid NOUN
la pyramide *fem*

Pyrenees PL NOUN
les Pyrénées *fem pl*
■ **in the Pyrenees** dans les Pyrénées
■ **We went to the Pyrenees.** Nous sommes allés dans les Pyrénées.

Qq

quaint ADJECTIVE
pittoresque (FEM pittoresque) (*house, village*)

qualification NOUN
le diplôme *masc*
□ to leave school without any qualifications quitter l'école sans aucun diplôme
■ **vocational qualifications** des qualifications professionnelles

★**qualified** ADJECTIVE
1 qualifié (FEM qualifiée) (*trained*)
□ a qualified driving instructor un moniteur d'auto-école qualifié
2 diplômé (FEM diplômée) (*nurse, teacher*)
□ a qualified nurse une infirmière diplômée

★to **qualify** VERB
1 obtenir [83] son diplôme (*for job*)
□ She qualified as a teacher last year. Elle a obtenu son diplôme de professeur l'année dernière.
2 se qualifier [19] (*in competition*)
□ Our team didn't qualify. Notre équipe ne s'est pas qualifiée.

★**quality** NOUN
la qualité *fem*
□ a good quality of life une bonne qualité de vie □ good-quality ingredients des ingrédients de bonne qualité □ She's got lots of good qualities. Elle a beaucoup de qualités.

★**quantity** NOUN
la quantité *fem*

quarrel NOUN
▷ *see also* **quarrel** VERB
la dispute *fem*

to **quarrel** VERB
▷ *see also* **quarrel** NOUN
se disputer [28]

quarry NOUN
la carrière *fem* (*for stone*)

★**quarter** NOUN
le quart *masc*
■ **three quarters** trois quarts
■ **a quarter of an hour** un quart d'heure
□ three quarters of an hour trois quarts d'heure
■ **a quarter past ten** dix heures et quart
■ **a quarter to eleven** onze heures moins le quart

quarter final NOUN
le quart de finale *masc*

quartet NOUN
le quatuor *masc*
□ a string quartet un quatuor à cordes

quay NOUN
le quai *masc*

queasy ADJECTIVE
■ **to feel queasy** avoir [8] mal au cœur □ I'm feeling queasy. J'ai mal au cœur.

★**queen** NOUN
1 la reine *fem*
□ Queen Elizabeth la reine Élisabeth
2 la dame *fem* (*playing card*)
□ the queen of hearts la dame de cœur
■ **the Queen Mother** la reine mère

query NOUN
▷ *see also* **query** VERB
la question *fem*

to **query** VERB
▷ *see also* **query** NOUN
mettre [47] en question
□ No one queried my decision. Personne n'a mis en question ma décision.

★**question** NOUN
▷ *see also* **question** VERB
la question *fem*
□ Can I ask a question? Est-ce que je peux poser une question? □ That's a difficult question. C'est une question difficile.
■ **It's out of the question.** C'est hors de question.

★to **question** VERB
▷ *see also* **question** NOUN
interroger [45]
□ He was questioned by the police. Il a été interrogé par la police.

question mark NOUN
le point d'interrogation *masc*

questionnaire NOUN
le questionnaire *masc*

queue NOUN
▷ *see also* **queue** VERB
la queue *fem*

to **queue** VERB
▷ *see also* **queue** NOUN

faire [36] la queue
■ **to queue for something** faire [36] la queue pour avoir quelque chose □ We had to queue for tickets. Nous avons dû faire la queue pour avoir les billets.

★ **quick** ADJECTIVE, ADVERB
rapide (FEM rapide)
□ a quick lunch un déjeuner rapide □ It's quicker by train. C'est plus rapide en train.
■ **Be quick!** Dépêche-toi!
■ **She's a quick learner.** Elle apprend vite.
■ **Quick, phone the police!** Téléphonez vite à la police!

★ **quickly** ADVERB
vite
□ It was all over very quickly. Ça s'est passé très vite.

★ **quiet** ADJECTIVE
1 silencieux (FEM silencieuse) (*not talkative or noisy*)
□ You're very quiet today. Tu es bien silencieux aujourd'hui. □ The engine's very quiet. Le moteur est très silencieux.
2 tranquille (FEM tranquille) (*peaceful*)
□ a quiet little town une petite ville tranquille
□ a quiet weekend un week-end tranquille
■ **Be quiet!** Tais-toi!
■ **Quiet!** Silence!

★ **quietly** ADVERB
1 doucement (*speak*)
□ 'She's dead,' he said quietly. 'Elle est morte' dit-il doucement.
2 silencieusement (*move*)
■ **He quietly opened the door.** Il a ouvert la porte sans faire de bruit.

quilt NOUN
la couette *fem* (*duvet*)

★ to **quit** VERB
quitter [28] (*place, premises, job*)
□ She's decided to quit her job. Elle a décidé de quitter son emploi.
■ **I quit!** J'abandonne!

★ **quite** ADVERB
1 assez (*rather*)
□ It's quite warm today. Il fait assez bon aujourd'hui. □ I quite liked the play, but ... J'ai trouvé la pièce assez bonne, mais ...
2 tout à fait (*entirely*)
□ I'm not quite sure. Je n'en suis pas tout à fait sûr. □ It's not quite the same. Ce n'est pas tout à fait la même chose.
■ **quite good** pas mal
■ **I've been there quite a lot.** J'y suis allé pas mal de fois.
■ **quite a lot of money** pas mal d'argent
■ **It costs quite a lot to go abroad.** Ça coûte assez cher d'aller à l'étranger.
■ **It's quite a long way.** C'est assez loin.
■ **It was quite a shock.** Ça a été un sacré choc.
■ **There were quite a few people there.** Il y avait pas mal de gens.

quiz NOUN
le jeu-concours *masc*

quota NOUN
le quota *masc*

quotation NOUN
la citation *fem*
□ a quotation from Shakespeare une citation de Shakespeare

★ **quote** NOUN
▷ *see also* **quote** VERB
la citation *fem*
□ a Shakespeare quote une citation de Shakespeare
■ **quotes** (*quotation marks*) les guillemets *masc pl* □ in quotes entre guillemets

★ to **quote** VERB
▷ *see also* **quote** NOUN
citer [28]
□ He's always quoting Shakespeare. Il n'arrête pas de citer Shakespeare.

Rr

rabbi NOUN
le rabbin *masc*

★ **rabbit** NOUN
le lapin *masc*
▪ **a rabbit hutch** un clapier

rabies NOUN
la rage *fem*
▪ **a dog with rabies** un chien enragé

★ **race** NOUN
▷ *see also* **race** VERB
1 la course *fem* (*sport*)
□ a cycle race une course cycliste
2 la race *fem* (*species*)
□ the human race la race humaine
▪ **race relations** les relations interraciales *fem pl*

★ to **race** VERB
▷ *see also* **race** NOUN
1 courir [16]
□ We raced to catch the bus. Nous avons couru pour attraper le bus.
2 faire [36] la course (*have a race*)
▪ **I'll race you!** On fait la course!

racecourse NOUN
le champ de courses *masc*

racehorse NOUN
le cheval de course *masc* (PL les chevaux de course)

racer NOUN
le vélo de course *masc* (*bike*)

racetrack NOUN
la piste *fem*

racial ADJECTIVE
racial (FEM raciale, MASC PL raciaux)
□ racial discrimination la discrimination raciale

racing car NOUN
la voiture de course *fem*

racing driver NOUN
le pilote de course *masc*

racism NOUN
le racisme *masc*

racist ADJECTIVE
▷ *see also* **racist** NOUN
raciste (FEM raciste)

racist NOUN
▷ *see also* **racist** ADJECTIVE
le/la raciste *masc/fem*

rack NOUN
le porte-bagages *masc* (PL les porte-bagages) (*for luggage*)

racket NOUN
1 la raquette *fem* (*for sport*)
□ my tennis racket ma raquette de tennis
2 le boucan *masc* (*noise*)
□ They're making a terrible racket. Ils font un boucan de tous les diables. (*informal*)

racquet NOUN
la raquette *fem*

radar NOUN
le radar *masc*

radiation NOUN
la radiation *fem*

radiator NOUN
le radiateur *masc*

★ **radio** NOUN
la radio *fem*
▪ **on the radio** à la radio
▪ **a radio station** une station de radio

radioactive ADJECTIVE
radioactif (FEM radioactive)

radio-controlled ADJECTIVE
téléguidé (FEM téléguidée) (*model plane, car*)

radish NOUN
le radis *masc*

RAF NOUN (= *Royal Air Force*)
la R.A.F. *fem*
□ He's in the RAF. Il est dans la R.A.F.

raffle NOUN
la tombola *fem*
□ a raffle ticket un billet de tombola

raft NOUN
le radeau *masc* (PL les radeaux)

rag NOUN
le chiffon *masc*
□ a piece of rag un chiffon
▪ **dressed in rags** en haillons

★ **rage** NOUN
la rage *fem*
□ mad with rage fou de rage

■ **to be in a rage** être [35] furieux □ She was in a rage. Elle était furieuse.

raid NOUN
▷ *see also* **raid** VERB
1 le hold-up *masc* (PL les hold-up) (*burglary*)
□ There was a bank raid near my house. Il y a eu un hold-up dans une banque près de chez moi.
2 la descente *fem*
□ a police raid une descente de police

to **raid** VERB
▷ *see also* **raid** NOUN
faire [36] une descente dans (*police*)
□ The police raided the club. La police a fait une descente dans le club.

★ **rail** NOUN
1 la rampe *fem* (*on stairs*)
2 la balustrade *fem* (*on bridge, balcony*)
□ Don't lean over the rail! Ne vous penchez pas sur la balustrade!
3 le rail *masc* (*on railway line*)
■ **by rail** en train

railcard NOUN
la carte de chemin de fer *fem*
□ a young person's railcard une carte de chemin de fer tarif jeune

railroad NOUN (US)
le chemin de fer *masc*
■ **a railroad line** une ligne de chemin de fer
■ **a railroad station** une gare

★ **railway** NOUN
le chemin de fer *masc*
□ the privatization of the railways la privatisation des chemins de fer
■ **a railway line** une ligne de chemin de fer
■ **a railway station** une gare

★ **rain** NOUN
▷ *see also* **rain** VERB
la pluie *fem*
□ in the rain sous la pluie

★ to **rain** VERB
▷ *see also* **rain** NOUN
pleuvoir [63]
□ It rains a lot here. Il pleut beaucoup par ici.
■ **It's raining.** Il pleut.

rainbow NOUN
l'arc-en-ciel *masc* (PL les arcs-en-ciel)

raincoat NOUN
l'imperméable *masc*

rainforest NOUN
la forêt tropicale humide *fem*

★ **rainy** ADJECTIVE
pluvieux (FEM pluvieuse)

★ to **raise** VERB
1 lever [43] (*lift*)
□ He raised his hand. Il a levé la main.
2 améliorer [28] (*improve*)
□ They want to raise standards in schools. Ils veulent améliorer le niveau dans les écoles.
■ **to raise money** collecter [28] des fonds
□ The school is raising money for a new gym. L'école collecte des fonds pour un nouveau gymnase.

raisin NOUN
le raisin sec *masc*

rake NOUN
le râteau *masc* (PL les râteaux)

rally NOUN
1 le rassemblement *masc* (*of people*)
2 le rallye *masc* (*sport*)
□ a rally driver un pilote de rallye
3 l'échange *masc* (*in tennis*)

ram NOUN
▷ *see also* **ram** VERB
le bélier *masc* (*sheep*)

to **ram** VERB
▷ *see also* **ram** NOUN
emboutir [2] (*vehicle*)
□ The thieves rammed a police car. Les voleurs ont embouti une voiture de police.

Ramadan NOUN
le ramadan *masc*

ramble NOUN
la randonnée *fem*
□ to go for a ramble faire une randonnée

rambler NOUN
le randonneur *masc*
la randonneuse *fem*

ramp NOUN
la rampe d'accès *fem* (*for wheelchairs*)

ran VERB ▷ *see* **run**

ranch NOUN
le ranch *masc*

random ADJECTIVE
■ **a random selection** une sélection effectuée au hasard
■ **at random** au hasard □ We picked the number at random. Nous avons pris le numéro au hasard.

rang VERB ▷ *see* **ring**

★ **range** NOUN
▷ *see also* **range** VERB
le choix *masc*
□ a wide range of colours un grand choix de coloris
■ **a range of subjects** diverses matières
□ We study a range of subjects. Nous étudions diverses matières.
■ **a mountain range** une chaîne de montagnes

★ to **range** VERB
▷ *see also* **range** NOUN
■ **to range from ... to** se situer [28] entre ... et □ Temperatures in summer range

from 20 to 35 degrees. Les températures estivales se situent entre vingt et trente-cinq degrés.
■ **Tickets range from £2 to £20.** Les billets coûtent entre deux et vingt livres.

rank NOUN
▷ *see also* **rank** VERB
■ **a taxi rank** une station de taxis

to **rank** VERB
▷ *see also* **rank** NOUN
■ **He's ranked third in the United States.** Il est classé troisième aux États-Unis.

ransom NOUN
la rançon *fem*

rap NOUN
le rap *masc* (*music*)

rape NOUN
▷ *see also* **rape** VERB
le viol *masc*

to **rape** VERB
▷ *see also* **rape** NOUN
violer [28]

rapids PL NOUN
les rapides *masc pl*

rapist NOUN
le violeur *masc*

★ **rare** ADJECTIVE
1 rare (FEM rare) (*unusual*)
□ a rare plant une plante rare
2 saignant (FEM saignante) (*steak*)

rash NOUN
l'éruption de boutons *fem*
□ I've got a rash on my chest. J'ai une éruption de boutons sur la poitrine.

rasher NOUN
la tranche *fem*
□ an egg and two rashers of bacon un œuf et deux tranches de bacon

★ **raspberry** NOUN
la framboise *fem*
□ raspberry jam la confiture de framboises

rat NOUN
le rat *masc*

★ **rate** NOUN
▷ *see also* **rate** VERB
1 le tarif *masc* (*price*)
□ There are reduced rates for students. Il y a des tarifs réduits pour les étudiants.
2 le taux *masc* (*level*)
□ the divorce rate le taux de divorce □ a high rate of interest un taux d'intérêt élevé

★ to **rate** VERB
▷ *see also* **rate** NOUN
considérer [34] comme
■ **He is rated the best.** Il est considéré comme le meilleur.
■ **How do you rate him?** Qu'est-ce que vous pensez de lui?

★ **rather** ADVERB
plutôt
□ I was rather disappointed. J'étais plutôt déçu. □ £20! That's rather a lot! Vingt livres! C'est plutôt cher!
■ **rather a lot of** pas mal de □ I've got rather a lot of homework to do. J'ai pas mal de devoirs à faire.
■ **rather than** plutôt que □ We decided to camp, rather than stay at a hotel. Nous avons décidé de camper plutôt que d'aller à l'hôtel.
■ **I'd rather ...** J'aimerais mieux ... □ I'd rather stay in tonight. J'aimerais mieux rester à la maison ce soir. □ I'd rather have an apple than a banana. J'aimerais mieux une pomme qu'une banane.

rattle NOUN
le hochet *masc* (*for baby*)

rattlesnake NOUN
le serpent à sonnette *masc*

to **rave** VERB
s'extasier [19]
□ They raved about the film. Ils se sont extasiés sur le film.

raven NOUN
le corbeau *masc* (PL les corbeaux)

ravenous ADJECTIVE
■ **to be ravenous** avoir [8] une faim de loup
□ I'm ravenous! J'ai une faim de loup!

raving ADJECTIVE
■ **raving mad** fou à lier □ She's raving mad! Elle est folle à lier.

★ **raw** ADJECTIVE
cru (FEM crue) (*food*)
■ **raw materials** les matières premières *fem pl*

razor NOUN
le rasoir *masc*
□ some disposable razors des rasoirs jetables
■ **a razor blade** une lame de rasoir

RE NOUN
l'éducation religieuse *fem*

★ **reach** NOUN
▷ *see also* **reach** VERB
■ **out of reach** hors de portée □ The light switch was out of reach. L'interrupteur était hors de portée.
■ **within easy reach of** à proximité de □ The campsite is within easy reach of the bus station. Le camping se trouve à proximité de la gare routière.

★ to **reach** VERB
▷ *see also* **reach** NOUN
1 arriver [5E] à
□ We reached the hotel at 7 p.m. Nous sommes arrivés à l'hôtel à sept heures du soir.
■ **We hope to reach the final.** Nous espérons aller en finale.

2 parvenir [89E] à (*decision*)
□ Eventually they reached a decision. Ils sont finalement parvenus à une décision.
■ **He reached for his phone.** Il a tendu la main pour prendre son téléphone.

★ to **react** VERB
réagir [38]

★ **reaction** NOUN
la réaction *fem*

reactor NOUN
le réacteur *masc*
□ a nuclear reactor un réacteur nucléaire

★ to **read** VERB
lire [44]
□ I don't read much. Je ne lis pas beaucoup.
□ Have you read 'The Hunger Games'? Est-ce que tu as lu 'Hunger Games'? □ Read the text out loud. Lis le texte à haute voix.

to **read out** VERB
lire [44]
□ He read out the article to me. Il m'a lu l'article.
■ **to read out the results** annoncer [12] les résultats

★ **reader** NOUN
le lecteur *masc*
la lectrice *fem* (*person*)

readily ADVERB
volontiers
□ She readily agreed. Elle a accepté volontiers.

★ **reading** NOUN
la lecture *fem*
□ Reading is one of my hobbies. La lecture est l'un de mes passe-temps.

★ **ready** ADJECTIVE
prêt (FEM prête)
□ She's nearly ready. Elle est presque prête.
□ He's always ready to help. Il est toujours prêt à rendre service.
■ **a ready meal** un plat cuisiné
■ **to get ready** se préparer [28] □ She's getting ready to go out. Elle est en train de se préparer pour sortir.
■ **to get something ready** préparer [28] quelque chose □ He's getting the dinner ready. Il est en train de préparer le dîner.

★ **real** ADJECTIVE
1 vrai (FEM vraie)
□ He wasn't a real policeman. Ce n'était pas un vrai policier. □ Her real name is Cordelia. Son vrai nom est Cordelia.
2 véritable (FEM véritable)
□ It's real leather. C'est du cuir véritable. □ It was a real nightmare. C'était un véritable cauchemar.
■ **in real life** dans la réalité

realistic ADJECTIVE
réaliste (FEM réaliste)

★ **reality** NOUN
la réalité *fem*

reality TV NOUN
la téléréalité *fem*
□ a reality TV show une émission de téléréalité

★ to **realize** VERB
■ **to realize that ...** se rendre [7] compte que ... □ We realized that something was wrong. Nous nous sommes rendu compte que quelque chose n'allait pas.

★ **really** ADVERB
vraiment
□ She's really nice. Elle est vraiment sympathique. □ Do you want to go? — Not really. Tu veux y aller? — Pas vraiment.
■ **I'm learning German. — Really?** J'apprends l'allemand. — Ah bon?
■ **Do you really think so?** Tu es sûr?

realtor NOUN (US)
l'agent immobilier *masc*

rear ADJECTIVE
▷ *see also* **rear** NOUN
arrière (FEM+PL arrière)
□ a rear wheel une roue arrière

rear NOUN
▷ *see also* **rear** ADJECTIVE
l'arrière *masc*
□ at the rear of the train à l'arrière du train

★ **reason** NOUN
la raison *fem*
□ There's no reason to think that ... Il n'y a aucune raison de penser que ... □ for security reasons pour des raisons de sécurité
■ **That was the main reason I went.** C'est surtout pour ça que j'y suis allé.

★ **reasonable** ADJECTIVE
1 raisonnable (FEM raisonnable) (*sensible*)
□ Be reasonable! Sois raisonnable!
2 correct (FEM correcte) (*not bad*)
□ He wrote a reasonable essay. Sa dissertation était correcte.

reasonably ADVERB
raisonnablement
□ The team played reasonably well. L'équipe a joué raisonnablement bien.
■ **reasonably priced jeans** un jean à un prix raisonnable

to **reassure** VERB
rassurer [28]

reassuring ADJECTIVE
rassurant (FEM rassurante)

rebellious ADJECTIVE
rebelle (FEM rebelle)

★ **receipt** NOUN
le reçu *masc*

★ to **receive** VERB
recevoir [67]

English-French

r

receiver NOUN
le combiné *masc* (*of phone*)
■ **to pick up the receiver** décrocher [28]

★**recent** ADJECTIVE
récent (FEM récente)

★**recently** ADVERB
ces derniers temps
□ I've been doing a lot of training recently. Je me suis beaucoup entraîné ces derniers temps.

reception NOUN
la réception *fem*
□ Please leave your key at reception. Merci de laisser votre clé à la réception. □ The reception will be at a big hotel. La réception aura lieu dans un grand hôtel.

receptionist NOUN
le/la réceptionniste *masc/fem*

★**recession** NOUN
la récession *fem*

★**recipe** NOUN
la recette *fem*

★to **reckon** VERB
penser [28]
□ What do you reckon? Qu'est-ce que tu en penses?

reclining ADJECTIVE
■ **a reclining seat** un siège inclinable

recognizable ADJECTIVE
reconnaissable (FEM reconnaissable)

★to **recognize** VERB
reconnaître [14]
□ You'll recognize me by my red hair. Vous me reconnaîtrez à mes cheveux roux.

★to **recommend** VERB
conseiller [28]
□ What do you recommend? Qu'est-ce que vous me conseillez?

to **reconsider** VERB
reconsidérer [34]

★**record** NOUN
▷ *see also* **record** VERB
1 le record *masc* (*sport*)
□ the world record le record du monde
■ **in record time** en un temps record □ She finished the job in record time. Elle a terminé le travail en un temps record.
2 le disque *masc* (*recording*)
□ my favourite record mon disque préféré
■ **a criminal record** un casier judiciaire
□ He's got a criminal record. Il a un casier judiciaire.
■ **records** (*of police, hospital*) les archives *fem pl* □ I'll check in the records. Je vais vérifier dans les archives.
■ **There is no record of your booking.** Il n'y a aucune trace de votre réservation.

★to **record** VERB
▷ *see also* **record** NOUN
enregistrer [28] (*on film*)
□ They've just recorded their new album. Ils viennent d'enregistrer leur nouveau disque.

recorded delivery NOUN
■ **to send something recorded delivery** envoyer [33] quelque chose en recommandé

recorder NOUN
la flûte à bec *fem* (*instrument*)
□ She plays the recorder. Elle joue de la flûte à bec.

★**recording** NOUN
l'enregistrement *masc*

record player NOUN
le tourne-disque *masc*

★to **recover** VERB
se remettre [47]
□ He's recovering from a knee injury. Il se remet d'une blessure au genou.

★**recovery** NOUN
le rétablissement *masc*
■ **Best wishes for a speedy recovery!** Meilleurs vœux de prompt rétablissement!

rectangle NOUN
le rectangle *masc*

rectangular ADJECTIVE
rectangulaire (FEM rectangulaire)

to **recycle** VERB
recycler [28]

recycling NOUN
le recyclage *masc*

★**red** ADJECTIVE
1 rouge (FEM rouge)
□ a red rose une rose rouge □ red meat la viande rouge
■ **a red light** (*traffic light*) un feu rouge □ to go through a red light brûler un feu rouge
2 roux (FEM rousse) (*hair*)
□ Sam's got red hair. Sam a les cheveux roux.

Red Cross NOUN
la Croix-Rouge *fem*

redcurrant NOUN
la groseille *fem*

to **redecorate** VERB
1 retapisser [28] (*with wallpaper*)
2 refaire [36] les peintures (*with paint*)

red-haired ADJECTIVE
roux (FEM rousse)

red-handed ADJECTIVE
■ **to catch somebody red-handed** prendre [65] quelqu'un la main dans le sac □ He was caught red-handed. Il a été pris la main dans le sac.

redhead NOUN
le roux *masc*
la rousse *fem*

to **redo** VERB
refaire [36]

★ to **reduce** VERB
réduire [23]
□ at a reduced price à prix réduit

★ **reduction** NOUN
la réduction *fem*
□ a 5% reduction une réduction de cinq pour cent

redundancy NOUN
le licenciement *masc*
□ There were fifty redundancies. Il y a eu cinquante licenciements.
■ **his redundancy payment** ses indemnités de licenciement

redundant ADJECTIVE
■ **to be made redundant** être [35] licencié
□ He was made redundant yesterday. Il a été licencié hier.

red wine NOUN
le vin rouge *masc*

reed NOUN
le roseau *masc* (PL les roseaux) (*plant*)

reel NOUN
la bobine *fem* (*of thread*)

★ to **refer** VERB
■ **to refer to** faire [36] allusion à □ What are you referring to? À quoi faites-vous allusion?

referee NOUN
l'arbitre *masc*

★ **reference** NOUN
1 l'allusion *fem*
□ He made no reference to the murder. Il n'a fait aucune allusion au meurtre.
2 les références *fem pl* (*for job application*)
□ Would you please give me a reference? Pouvez-vous me fournir des références?
■ **a reference book** un ouvrage de référence

to **refill** VERB
remplir [38] à nouveau
□ He refilled my glass. Il a rempli mon verre à nouveau.

refinery NOUN
la raffinerie *fem*

to **reflect** VERB
refléter [34] (*light, image*)

reflection NOUN
le reflet *masc* (*in mirror*)

reflex NOUN
le réflexe *masc*

reflexive ADJECTIVE
réfléchi (FEM réfléchie)
□ a reflexive verb un verbe réfléchi

refresher course NOUN
le cours de remise à niveau *masc*

refreshing ADJECTIVE
rafraîchissant (FEM rafraîchissante)

refreshments PL NOUN
les rafraîchissements *masc pl*

refrigerator NOUN
le réfrigérateur *masc*

to **refuel** VERB
se ravitailler [28] en carburant
□ The plane stops in Boston to refuel. L'avion s'arrête à Boston pour se ravitailler en carburant.

refuge NOUN
le refuge *masc*

★ **refugee** NOUN
le réfugié *masc*
la réfugiée *fem*

refund NOUN
▷ *see also* **refund** VERB
le remboursement *masc*

to **refund** VERB
▷ *see also* **refund** NOUN
rembourser [28]

refusal NOUN
le refus *masc*

★ to **refuse** VERB
▷ *see also* **refuse** NOUN
refuser [28]

★ **refuse** NOUN
▷ *see also* **refuse** VERB
les ordures *fem pl*
■ **refuse collection** le ramassage des ordures

to **regain** VERB
■ **to regain consciousness** reprendre [65] connaissance

regard NOUN
▷ *see also* **regard** VERB
■ **Give my regards to Alice.** Transmettez mon bon souvenir à Alice.
■ **Louis sends his regards.** Vous avez le bonjour de Louis.
■ **'kind regards'** 'bien cordialement'

to **regard** VERB
▷ *see also* **regard** NOUN
■ **to regard something as** considérer [34] quelque chose comme
■ **as regards ...** concernant ...

regarding PREPOSITION
relatif à (FEM relative à)
□ the laws regarding the export of animals les lois relatives à l'exportation des animaux
■ **Regarding John, ...** Quant à John, ...

regardless ADVERB
■ **regardless of the weather** peu importe le temps
■ **regardless of the consequences** peu importent les conséquences

regiment NOUN
le régiment *masc*

English-French

★ **region** NOUN
la région *fem*

regional ADJECTIVE
régional (FEM régionale, MASC PL régionaux)

★ **register** NOUN
▷ *see also* **register** VERB
le registre d'absences *masc* (*in school*)

★ to **register** VERB
▷ *see also* **register** NOUN
s'inscrire [30] (*at school, college*)

registered ADJECTIVE
▪ **a registered letter** une lettre recommandée

registration NOUN
1 l'appel *masc* (*roll call*)
2 le numéro d'immatriculation *masc* (*of car*)

★ **regret** NOUN
▷ *see also* **regret** VERB
le regret *masc*
▪ **I've got no regrets.** Je ne regrette rien.

★ to **regret** VERB
▷ *see also* **regret** NOUN
regretter [28]
□ Give me the money or you'll regret it! Donne-moi l'argent, sinon tu vas le regretter!
▪ **to regret doing something** regretter [28] d'avoir fait quelque chose □ I regret saying that. Je regrette d'avoir dit ça.

★ **regular** ADJECTIVE
1 régulier (FEM régulière)
□ at regular intervals à intervalles réguliers
□ a regular verb un verbe régulier
▪ **to take regular exercise** faire [36] régulièrement de l'exercice
2 normal (FEM normale, MASC PL normaux) (*average*)
□ a regular portion of fries une portion de frites normale

regularly ADVERB
régulièrement

regulation NOUN
le règlement *masc*

rehearsal NOUN
la répétition *fem*

to **rehearse** VERB
répéter [34]

rein NOUN
la rêne *fem*
□ the reins les rênes

★ **reindeer** NOUN
le renne *masc*

to **reject** VERB
rejeter [41] (*idea, suggestion*)
□ We rejected that idea straight away. Nous avons immédiatement rejeté cette idée.
▪ **I applied but they rejected me.** J'ai posé ma candidature mais ils l'ont rejetée.

relapse NOUN
la rechute *fem*
□ to have a relapse faire une rechute

★ **related** ADJECTIVE
apparenté (FEM apparentée) (*people*)
□ We're related. Nous sommes apparentés.
▪ **The two events were not related.** Il n'y avait aucun rapport entre les deux événements.

★ **relation** NOUN
1 le parent *masc*
la parente *fem* (*person*)
□ He's a distant relation. C'est un parent éloigné. □ my close relations mes parents proches
▪ **my relations** ma famille
▪ **I've got relations in Spain.** J'ai de la famille en Espagne.
2 le rapport *masc* (*connection*)
□ It has no relation to reality. Cela n'a aucun rapport avec la réalité.
▪ **in relation to** par rapport à

★ **relationship** NOUN
les relations *fem pl*
□ We have a good relationship. Nous avons de bonnes relations.
▪ **I'm not in a relationship at the moment.** Je ne sors avec personne en ce moment.

★ **relative** NOUN
le parent *masc*
la parente *fem*
□ my close relatives mes proches parents
▪ **all her relatives** toute sa famille

★ **relatively** ADVERB
relativement

★ to **relax** VERB
se détendre [88]
□ I relax by listening to music. Je me détends en écoutant de la musique.
▪ **Relax! Everything's fine.** Ne t'en fais pas! Tout va bien.

relaxation NOUN
la détente *fem*
□ I don't have much time for relaxation. Je n'ai pas beaucoup de moments de détente.

relaxed ADJECTIVE
détendu (FEM détendue)

relaxing ADJECTIVE
reposant (FEM reposante)
▪ **I find cooking relaxing.** Cela me détend de faire la cuisine.

relay NOUN
▪ **a relay race** une course de relais

★ to **release** VERB
▷ *see also* **release** NOUN
1 libérer [34] (*prisoner*)
2 divulguer [28] (*report, news*)
3 sortir [79] (*film, album*)

r

★ **release** NOUN
▷ *see also* **release** VERB
la libération *fem* (*from prison*)
□ the release of the prisoners la libération des prisonniers
■ **the band's latest release** le dernier disque du groupe

relegated ADJECTIVE
relégué (FEM reléguée) (*sport*)

relevant ADJECTIVE
approprié (FEM appropriée) (*documents*)
■ **That's not relevant.** Ça n'a aucun rapport.
■ **to be relevant to something** être [35] en rapport avec quelque chose □ Education should be relevant to real life. L'enseignement devrait être en rapport avec la réalité.

★ **reliable** ADJECTIVE
fiable (FEM fiable)
□ a reliable car une voiture fiable □ He's not very reliable. Il n'est pas très fiable.

★ **relief** NOUN
le soulagement *masc*
□ That's a relief! Quel soulagement!

to **relieve** VERB
soulager [45]
□ This injection will relieve the pain. Cette piqûre va soulager la douleur.

relieved ADJECTIVE
soulagé (FEM soulagée)
□ I was relieved to hear ... J'ai été soulagé d'apprendre ...

★ **religion** NOUN
la religion *fem*
□ What religion are you? Quelle est votre religion?

★ **religious** ADJECTIVE
1 religieux (FEM religieuse)
□ my religious beliefs mes croyances religieuses
2 croyant (FEM croyante)
□ I'm not religious. Je ne suis pas croyant.

★ **reluctant** ADJECTIVE
réticent (FEM réticente)
■ **to be reluctant to do something** être [35] peu disposé à faire quelque chose □ They were reluctant to help us. Ils étaient peu disposés à nous aider.

reluctantly ADVERB
à contrecœur
□ She reluctantly accepted. Elle a accepté à contrecœur.

to **rely on** VERB
compter [28] sur
□ I'm relying on you. Je compte sur toi.

★ to **remain** VERB
rester [71E]
■ **to remain silent** garder [28] le silence

★ **remaining** ADJECTIVE
le reste de
□ the remaining ingredients le reste des ingrédients

remains PL NOUN
les restes *masc pl*
□ the remains of the picnic les restes du pique-nique □ human remains des restes humains
■ **Roman remains** les vestiges romains

remake NOUN
le remake *masc* (*of film*)

★ **remark** NOUN
la remarque *fem*

★ **remarkable** ADJECTIVE
remarquable (FEM remarquable)

remarkably ADVERB
remarquablement

to **remarry** VERB
se remarier [19]
□ She remarried three years ago. Elle s'est remariée il y a trois ans.

remedy NOUN
le remède *masc*
□ a good remedy for a sore throat un bon remède contre le mal de gorge

★ to **remember** VERB
se souvenir [83] de
□ I can't remember his name. Je ne me souviens pas de son nom. □ I don't remember. Je ne m'en souviens pas.

> In French you often say 'don't forget' instead of 'remember'.

□ Remember your passport! N'oublie pas ton passeport! □ Remember to write your name on the form. N'oubliez pas d'écrire votre nom sur le formulaire.

Remembrance Day NOUN
le jour de l'Armistice *masc*
□ on Remembrance Day le jour de l'Armistice

★ to **remind** VERB
rappeler [4]
□ It reminds me of Scotland. Cela me rappelle l'Écosse. □ I'll remind you tomorrow. Je te le rappellerai demain. □ Remind me to speak to Mariusz. Rappelle-moi de parler à Mariusz.

remorse NOUN
le remords *masc*
□ He showed no remorse. Il n'a manifesté aucun remords.

★ **remote** ADJECTIVE
isolé (FEM isolée)
□ a remote village un village isolé

remote control NOUN
la télécommande *fem*

remotely ADVERB
■ **I'm not remotely interested.** Je ne suis

absolument pas intéressé.
■ **Do you think it would be remotely possible?** Pensez-vous que cela serait éventuellement possible?

removable ADJECTIVE
amovible (FEM amovible)

removal NOUN
le déménagement *masc* (*from house*)
■ **a removal van** un camion de déménagement

★to **remove** VERB
1 enlever [43]
□ Can you remove your laptop from my seat? Est-ce que vous pouvez enlever votre ordinateur portable de mon siège?
2 faire [36] partir (*stain*)
□ Did you remove the stain? Est-ce que tu as fait partir la tache?

rendezvous NOUN
le rendez-vous *masc* (PL les rendez-vous)

★to **renew** VERB
renouveler [4] (*passport, licence*)

renewable ADJECTIVE
renouvelable (FEM renouvelable) (*energy, resource*)

to **renovate** VERB
rénover [28]
□ The leisure centre has been renovated. Le centre de loisirs a été rénové.

renowned ADJECTIVE
renommé (FEM renommée)

★**rent** NOUN
▷ *see also* **rent** VERB
le loyer *masc*

★to **rent** VERB
▷ *see also* **rent** NOUN
louer [28]
□ We rented a car. Nous avons loué une voiture.

rental NOUN
la location *fem*
□ Car rental is included in the price. Le prix comprend la location d'une voiture.

rental car NOUN
la voiture de location *fem*

to **reorganize** VERB
réorganiser [28]

rep NOUN (= *representative*)
le représentant *masc*
la représentante *fem*

repaid VERB ▷ *see* **repay**

to **repair** VERB
▷ *see also* **repair** NOUN
réparer [28]
■ **to get something repaired** faire [36] réparer quelque chose □ I got the washing machine repaired. J'ai fait réparer la machine à laver.

★**repair** NOUN
▷ *see also* **repair** VERB
la réparation *fem*

to **repay** VERB
rembourser [28] (*money*)

repayment NOUN
le remboursement *masc*

★to **repeat** VERB
▷ *see also* **repeat** NOUN
répéter [34]

★**repeat** NOUN
▷ *see also* **repeat** VERB
la rediffusion *fem*
□ There are too many repeats on TV. Il y a trop de rediffusions à la télé.

repeatedly ADVERB
à plusieurs reprises

repellent NOUN
■ **insect repellent** l'insectifuge *masc*

repetitive ADJECTIVE
répétitif (FEM répétitive) (*movement, work*)

★to **replace** VERB
remplacer [12]

replay NOUN
▷ *see also* **replay** VERB
■ **There will be a replay on Friday.** Le match sera rejoué vendredi.

to **replay** VERB
▷ *see also* **replay** NOUN
rejouer [28] (*match*)

replica NOUN
la réplique *fem*

★**reply** NOUN
▷ *see also* **reply** VERB
la réponse *fem*

★to **reply** VERB
▷ *see also* **reply** NOUN
répondre [69]

★**report** NOUN
▷ *see also* **report** VERB
1 le compte rendu *masc* (PL les comptes rendus) (*of event*)
2 le reportage *masc* (*news report*)
□ a report in the paper un reportage dans le journal
3 le bulletin scolaire *masc* (*at school*)
□ I got a good report this term. J'ai un bon bulletin scolaire ce trimestre.

★to **report** VERB
▷ *see also* **report** NOUN
1 signaler [28]
□ I reported the theft to the police. J'ai signalé le vol au commissariat.
2 se présenter [28]
□ Report to the caretaker when you arrive. Présentez-vous chez le gardien à votre arrivée.

★ **reporter** NOUN
le reporter *masc*
□ I'd like to be a reporter. J'aimerais être reporter.

★ to **represent** VERB
représenter [28]

★ **representative** ADJECTIVE
représentatif (FEM représentative)

reproduction NOUN
la reproduction *fem*

reptile NOUN
le reptile *masc*

★ **republic** NOUN
la république *fem*

repulsive ADJECTIVE
repoussant (FEM repoussante)

reputable ADJECTIVE
de bonne réputation

★ **reputation** NOUN
la réputation *fem*

★ **request** NOUN
▷ *see also* **request** VERB
la demande *fem*

★ to **request** VERB
▷ *see also* **request** NOUN
demander [28]

★ to **require** VERB
exiger [45]
□ The job requires good IT skills. Cet emploi exige une bonne connaissance de l'informatique.
■ **What qualifications are required?** Quels sont les diplômes requis?

★ **requirement** NOUN
la condition requise *fem*
□ What are the requirements for this apprenticeship? Quelles sont les conditions requises pour cet apprentissage?
■ **entry requirements** (*for university*) les critères d'entrée

★ to **rescue** VERB
▷ *see also* **rescue** NOUN
sauver [28]

★ **rescue** NOUN
▷ *see also* **rescue** VERB
1 le sauvetage *masc*
□ a rescue operation une opération de sauvetage
■ **a mountain rescue team** une équipe de sauvetage en montagne
2 le secours *masc*
□ the rescue services les services de secours
■ **to come to somebody's rescue** venir [89E] au secours de quelqu'un □ He came to my rescue. Il est venu à mon secours.

★ **research** NOUN
1 la recherche *fem* (*experimental*)
□ He's doing research. Il fait de la recherche.
2 les recherches *fem pl* (*theoretical*)
□ She's doing some research in the library. Elle fait des recherches à la bibliothèque.

resemblance NOUN
la ressemblance *fem*

to **resent** VERB
être [35] contrarié par
□ I really resented your criticism. J'ai été vraiment contrarié par tes critiques.

resentful ADJECTIVE
plein de ressentiment (FEM pleine de ressentiment)
■ **to feel resentful towards somebody** en vouloir [93] à quelqu'un

reservation NOUN
la réservation *fem* (*booking*)
□ I've got a reservation for two nights. J'ai une réservation pour deux nuits. □ I'd like to make a reservation for this evening. J'aimerais faire une réservation pour ce soir.

★ **reserve** NOUN
▷ *see also* **reserve** VERB
1 la réserve *fem* (*place*)
□ a nature reserve une réserve naturelle
2 le remplaçant *masc*
la remplaçante *fem* (*person*)
□ I was reserve in the game last Saturday. J'étais remplaçant dans le match de samedi dernier.

★ to **reserve** VERB
▷ *see also* **reserve** NOUN
réserver [28]
□ I'd like to reserve a table for tomorrow evening. J'aimerais réserver une table pour demain soir.

reserved ADJECTIVE
réservé (FEM réservée)
□ a reserved seat une place réservée □ He's quite reserved. Il est assez réservé.

reservoir NOUN
le réservoir *masc*

★ **resident** NOUN
le résident *masc*
la résidente *fem*

residential ADJECTIVE
résidentiel (FEM résidentielle)
□ a residential area un quartier résidentiel

★ to **resign** VERB
donner [28] sa démission

to **resit** VERB
repasser [28]
□ I'm resitting the exam in December. Je vais repasser l'examen en décembre.

★ **resolution** NOUN
la résolution *fem*
■ **Have you made any New Year's**

English-French

r

English-French

resolutions? Tu as pris de bonnes résolutions pour l'année nouvelle?

★ **resort** NOUN
la station balnéaire *fem* (*at seaside*)
□ It's a resort on the Costa del Sol. C'est une station balnéaire sur la Costa del Sol.
■ **a ski resort** une station de ski
■ **as a last resort** en dernier recours

★ **resource** NOUN
la ressource *fem*

★ **respect** NOUN
▷ *see also* **respect** VERB
le respect *masc*

★ to **respect** VERB
▷ *see also* **respect** NOUN
respecter [28]

respectable ADJECTIVE
1 respectable (FEM respectable)
2 correct (FEM correcte) (*standard, marks*)

respectively ADVERB
respectivement

★ **responsibility** NOUN
la responsabilité *fem*

★ **responsible** ADJECTIVE
1 responsable (FEM responsable) (*in charge*)
■ **to be responsible for something** être [35] responsable de quelque chose □ He's responsible for booking the tickets. Il est responsable de la réservation des billets.
■ **It's a responsible job.** C'est un poste à responsabilités.
2 sérieux (FEM sérieuse) (*mature*)
□ You should be more responsible. Tu devrais être un peu plus sérieux.

★ **rest** NOUN
▷ *see also* **rest** VERB
1 le repos *masc* (*relaxation*)
□ five minutes' rest cinq minutes de repos
■ **to have a rest** se reposer [28] □ We stopped to have a rest. Nous nous sommes arrêtés pour nous reposer.
2 le reste *masc* (*remainder*)
□ I'll do the rest. Je ferai le reste. □ the rest of the money le reste de l'argent
■ **the rest of them** les autres □ The rest of them went swimming. Les autres sont allés nager.

★ to **rest** VERB
▷ *see also* **rest** NOUN
1 se reposer [28] (*relax*)
□ She's resting in her room. Elle se repose dans sa chambre.
2 ménager [45] (*not overstrain*)
□ He has to rest his knee. Il doit ménager son genou.
3 appuyer [53] (*lean*)
□ I rested my bike against the window. J'ai appuyé mon vélo contre la fenêtre.

★ **restaurant** NOUN
le restaurant *masc*
□ We don't often go to restaurants. Nous n'allons pas souvent au restaurant.

restful ADJECTIVE
reposant (FEM reposante)

restless ADJECTIVE
agité (FEM agitée)

restoration NOUN
la restauration *fem*

to **restore** VERB
restaurer [28] (*building, picture*)

to **restrict** VERB
limiter [28]

rest room NOUN (US)
les toilettes *fem pl*

★ **result** NOUN
▷ *see also* **result** VERB
le résultat *masc*
□ my exam results mes résultats d'examen
□ What was the result? — One-nil. Quel a été le résultat? — Un à zéro.

★ to **result** VERB
▷ *see also* **result** NOUN
■ **to result in** occasionner [28] □ Many road accidents result in head injuries. De nombreux accidents de la route occasionnent des blessures à la tête.

to **resume** VERB
reprendre [65]
□ They've resumed work. Ils ont repris le travail.

> **BE CAREFUL!**
> Do not translate **to resume** by the French word **résumer**.

résumé NOUN (US)
le curriculum vitae *masc*

★ to **retire** VERB
prendre [65] sa retraite
□ He retired last year. Il a pris sa retraite l'an dernier.

retired ADJECTIVE
retraité (FEM retraitée)
□ She's retired. Elle est retraitée.
■ **a retired teacher** un professeur à la retraite

★ **retirement** NOUN
la retraite *fem*

to **retrace** VERB
■ **to retrace one's steps** revenir [73E] sur ses pas □ I retraced my steps. Je suis revenu sur mes pas.

★ **return** NOUN
▷ *see also* **return** VERB
1 le retour *masc*
□ after our return à notre retour

r

■ **the return journey** le voyage de retour
■ **a return match** un match retour
2 l'aller-retour *masc* (*ticket*)
□ A return to Avignon, please. Un aller-retour pour Avignon, s'il vous plaît.
■ **in return** en échange □ ... and I help her in return ... et je l'aide en échange
■ **in return for** en échange de
■ **Many happy returns!** Bon anniversaire!

★ to **return** VERB
▷ *see also* **return** NOUN
1 revenir [73E] (*come back*)
□ I've just returned from holiday. Je viens de revenir de vacances.
■ **to return home** rentrer [68E] à la maison
2 retourner [72E] (*go back*)
□ He returned to China the following year. Il est retourné en Chine l'année suivante.
3 rendre [7] (*give back*)
□ She borrows my things and doesn't return them. Elle m'emprunte mes affaires et ne me les rend pas.

retweet NOUN
▷ *see also* **retweet** VERB
le retweet *masc*

to **retweet** VERB
▷ *see also* **retweet** NOUN
retweeter [28]

reunion NOUN
la réunion *fem*

to **reuse** VERB
réutiliser [28]

to **reveal** VERB
révéler [34]

revenge NOUN
la vengeance *fem*
□ in revenge par vengeance
■ **to take revenge** se venger [45] □ They planned to take revenge on him. Ils voulaient se venger de lui.

★ to **reverse** VERB
▷ *see also* **reverse** ADJECTIVE
faire [36] marche arrière (*car*)
□ He reversed without looking. Il a fait marche arrière sans regarder.

★ **reverse** ADJECTIVE
▷ *see also* **reverse** VERB
inverse (FEM inverse)
□ in reverse order dans l'ordre inverse
■ **in reverse gear** en marche arrière

★ **review** NOUN
la critique *fem* (*of book, film, programme*)
□ The book had good reviews. Ce livre a eu de bonnes critiques.

to **revise** VERB
réviser [28]
□ I haven't started revising yet. Je n'ai pas encore commencé à réviser.
■ **I've revised my opinion.** J'ai changé d'opinion.

revision NOUN
les révisions *fem pl*
□ Have you done a lot of revision? Est-ce que tu as fait beaucoup de révisions?

to **revive** VERB
ranimer [28]
□ The nurses tried to revive him. Les infirmières ont essayé de le ranimer.

revolting ADJECTIVE
dégoûtant (FEM dégoûtante)

★ **revolution** NOUN
la révolution *fem*
■ **the French Revolution** la Révolution française

revolutionary ADJECTIVE
révolutionnaire (FEM révolutionnaire)

revolver NOUN
le revolver *masc*

★ **reward** NOUN
la récompense *fem*

rewarding ADJECTIVE
gratifiant (FEM gratifiante)
□ a rewarding job un travail gratifiant

rheumatism NOUN
le rhumatisme *masc*

Rhine NOUN
le Rhin *masc*

rhinoceros NOUN
le rhinocéros *masc*

Rhone NOUN
le Rhône *masc*

rhubarb NOUN
la rhubarbe *fem*
□ a rhubarb tart une tarte à la rhubarbe

★ **rhythm** NOUN
le rythme *masc*

rib NOUN
la côte *fem*

ribbon NOUN
le ruban *masc*

★ **rice** NOUN
le riz *masc*
■ **rice pudding** le riz au lait

★ **rich** ADJECTIVE
riche (FEM riche)
■ **the rich** les riches *masc pl*

★ to **rid** VERB
■ **to get rid of** se débarrasser [28] de □ I want to get rid of some old clothes. Je veux me débarrasser de vieux vêtements.

ridden VERB ▷ *see* **ride**

★ **ride** NOUN
▷ *see also* **ride** VERB
■ **to go for a ride 1** (*on horse*) monter [48E] à

English-French

cheval **2** (*on bike*) faire [36] un tour en vélo
□ We went for a bike ride. Nous sommes allés faire un tour en vélo.
■ **It's a short bus ride to the town centre.** Ce n'est pas loin du centre-ville en bus.

★ to **ride** VERB
▷ *see also* **ride** NOUN
monter [48E] à cheval (*on horse*)
□ I'm learning to ride. J'apprends à monter à cheval.
■ **to ride a bike** faire [36] du vélo □ Can you ride a bike? Tu sais faire du vélo?

★ **rider** NOUN
1 le cavalier *masc*
la cavalière *fem* (*on horse*)
□ She's a good rider. C'est une bonne cavalière.
2 le/la cycliste *masc/fem* (*on bike*)

ridiculous ADJECTIVE
ridicule (FEM ridicule)
□ Don't be ridiculous! Ne sois pas ridicule!

riding NOUN
l'équitation *fem*
■ **to go riding** faire [36] de l'équitation
■ **a riding school** une école d'équitation

rifle NOUN
le fusil *masc*

rig NOUN
■ **an oil rig** une plateforme pétrolière

★ **right** ADJECTIVE, ADVERB
▷ *see also* **right** NOUN

There are several ways of translating 'right'. Scan the examples to find one that is similar to what you want to say.

1 bon (FEM bonne) (*factually correct, suitable*)
□ the right answer la bonne réponse □ It isn't the right size. Ce n'est pas la bonne taille.
□ We're on the right train. Nous sommes dans le bon train.
■ **Is this the right road for Arles?** Est-ce que c'est bien la route pour aller à Arles?
2 correctement (*correctly*)
□ Am I pronouncing it right? Est-ce que je prononce ça correctement?
■ **to be right 1** (*person*) avoir [8] raison
□ You were right! Tu avais raison!
2 (*statement, opinion*) être [35] vrai □ That's right! C'est vrai!
3 juste (FEM juste) (*accurate*)
□ Do you have the right time? Est-ce que vous avez l'heure juste?
4 bien (*morally correct*)
□ It's not right to behave like that. Ce n'est pas bien d'agir comme ça.
■ **I think you did the right thing.** Je pense que tu as bien fait.
5 droit (FEM droite) (*not left*)
□ my right hand ma main droite
6 à droite (*turn, look*)
□ Turn right at the traffic lights. Tournez à droite aux prochains feux.
■ **Right! Let's get started.** Bon! On commence.
■ **right away** tout de suite □ I'll do it right away. Je vais le faire tout de suite.

★ **right** NOUN
▷ *see also* **right** ADJECTIVE, ADVERB
1 le droit *masc*
■ **You've got no right to do that.** Vous n'avez pas le droit de faire ça.
2 la droite *fem* (*not left*)
■ **on the right** à droite □ Remember to drive on the right. N'oubliez pas de conduire à droite.
■ **right of way** la priorité □ It was our right of way. Nous avions la priorité.

right-hand ADJECTIVE
■ **the right-hand side** la droite □ It's on the right-hand side. C'est à droite.

right-handed ADJECTIVE
droitier (FEM droitière)

rightly ADVERB
avec raison
□ She rightly decided not to go. Elle a décidé, avec raison, de ne pas y aller.
■ **if I remember rightly** si je me souviens bien

rim NOUN
la monture *fem*
□ glasses with wire rims des lunettes avec une monture métallique

★ **ring** NOUN
▷ *see also* **ring** VERB
1 l'anneau *masc* (PL les anneaux)
□ a gold ring un anneau en or
2 la bague *fem* (*with stones*)
□ a diamond ring une bague de diamants
■ **a wedding ring** une alliance
3 le cercle *masc* (*circle*)
□ to stand in a ring se mettre en cercle
4 le coup de sonnette *masc* (*of bell*)
□ I was woken by a ring at the door. J'ai été réveillé par un coup de sonnette.
■ **to give somebody a ring** appeler [4] quelqu'un □ I'll give you a ring this evening. Je t'appellerai ce soir.

★ to **ring** VERB
▷ *see also* **ring** NOUN
1 téléphoner [28]
□ Your mother rang this morning. Ta mère a téléphoné ce matin.
■ **to ring somebody** appeler [4] quelqu'un
□ I'll ring you tomorrow morning. Je t'appellerai demain matin.
2 sonner [28]
□ The phone's ringing. Le téléphone sonne.
■ **to ring the bell** (*doorbell*) sonner [28] à la

r

porte □ I rang the bell three times. J'ai sonné trois fois à la porte.

to **ring back** VERB
rappeler [4]
□ I'll ring back later. Je rappellerai plus tard.

to **ring up** VERB
■ **to ring somebody up** donner [28] un coup de fil à quelqu'un

ring binder NOUN
le classeur *masc*

ring road NOUN
1 la rocade *fem* (*ordinary road*)
2 le périphérique *masc* (*motorway*)

★ **ringtone** NOUN
la sonnerie *fem*

rink NOUN
1 la patinoire *fem* (*for ice-skating*)
2 la piste *fem* (*for roller-skating*)

to **rinse** VERB
rincer [12]

★ **riot** NOUN
▷ *see also* **riot** VERB
l'émeute *fem*

★ to **riot** VERB
▷ *see also* **riot** NOUN
faire [36] une émeute

to **rip** VERB
1 déchirer [28]
□ I've ripped my jeans. J'ai déchiré mon jean.
2 se déchirer [28]
□ My skirt's ripped. Ma jupe s'est déchirée.

to **rip off** VERB
arnaquer [28]
□ The hotel ripped us off. L'hôtel nous a arnaqués.

to **rip up** VERB
déchirer [28]
□ He read the note and then ripped it up. Il a lu le mot, puis l'a déchiré.

ripe ADJECTIVE
mûr (FEM mûre)

rip-off NOUN
■ **It's a rip-off!** C'est de l'arnaque! (*informal*)

★ **rise** NOUN
▷ *see also* **rise** VERB
1 la hausse *fem* (*in prices, temperature*)
□ a sudden rise in temperature une hausse subite de température
2 l'augmentation *fem* (*pay rise*)

★ to **rise** VERB
▷ *see also* **rise** NOUN
1 augmenter [28] (*increase*)
□ Prices are rising. Les prix augmentent.
2 se lever [43]
□ The sun rises early in June. Le soleil se lève tôt en juin.

riser NOUN
■ **to be an early riser** être [35] matinal

★ **risk** NOUN
▷ *see also* **risk** VERB
le risque *masc*
■ **to take risks** prendre [65] des risques
■ **It's at your own risk.** C'est à vos risques et périls.

★ to **risk** VERB
▷ *see also* **risk** NOUN
risquer [28]
□ You risk getting a fine. Vous risquez de recevoir une amende.
■ **I wouldn't risk it if I were you.** À votre place, je ne prendrais pas ce risque.

risky ADJECTIVE
risqué (FEM risquée)

★ **rival** NOUN
▷ *see also* **rival** ADJECTIVE
le rival *masc* (PL les rivaux)
la rivale *fem*

★ **rival** ADJECTIVE
▷ *see also* **rival** NOUN
1 rival (FEM rivale, MASC PL rivaux)
□ a rival gang une bande rivale
2 concurrent (FEM concurrente)
□ a rival company une société concurrente

rivalry NOUN
la rivalité *fem* (*between towns, schools*)

★ **river** NOUN
1 la rivière *fem*
□ The river runs alongside the canal. La rivière longe le canal.
2 le fleuve *masc* (*major*)
□ the rivers of France les fleuves de France
■ **the river Seine** la Seine

Riviera NOUN
■ **the French Riviera** la Côte d'Azur
■ **the Italian Riviera** la Riviera italienne

★ **road** NOUN
1 la route *fem*
□ There's a lot of traffic on the roads. Il y a beaucoup de circulation sur les routes.
2 la rue *fem* (*street*)
□ They live across the road. Ils habitent de l'autre côté de la rue.

road map NOUN
la carte routière *fem*

road rage NOUN
l'agressivité au volant *fem*

road sign NOUN
le panneau de signalisation *masc* (PL les panneaux de signalisation)

roadworks PL NOUN
les travaux *masc pl*

roast ADJECTIVE
rôti (FEM rôtie)

□ roast chicken le poulet rôti □ roast potatoes les pommes de terre rôties
■ **roast pork** le rôti de porc
■ **roast beef** le rôti de bœuf

to **rob** VERB
■ **to rob somebody** voler [28] quelqu'un □ I've been robbed. On m'a volé.
■ **to rob somebody of something** voler [28] quelque chose à quelqu'un □ He was robbed of his wallet. On lui a volé son portefeuille.
■ **to rob a bank** dévaliser [28] une banque

robber NOUN
le voleur *masc*
la voleuse *fem*
■ **a bank robber** un braqueur de banques

robbery NOUN
le vol *masc*
■ **a bank robbery** un hold-up
■ **armed robbery** le vol à main armée

robin NOUN
le rouge-gorge *masc*

robot NOUN
le robot *masc*

★ **rock** NOUN
▷ *see also* **rock** VERB
1 la roche *fem* (*substance*)
□ They tunnelled through the rock. Ils ont creusé un tunnel dans la roche.
2 le rocher *masc* (*boulder*)
□ I sat on a rock. Je me suis assis sur un rocher.
3 la pierre *fem* (*stone*)
□ The crowd started to throw rocks. La foule s'est mise à lancer des pierres.
4 le rock *masc* (*music*)
□ a rock concert un concert de rock □ He's a rock star. C'est une rock star.
■ **rock and roll** le rock'n'roll

★ to **rock** VERB
▷ *see also* **rock** NOUN
ébranler [28]
□ The explosion rocked the building. L'explosion a ébranlé le bâtiment.

rockery NOUN
la rocaille *fem*

★ **rocket** NOUN
la fusée *fem* (*firework, spacecraft*)

rocking chair NOUN
le rocking-chair *masc*

rocking horse NOUN
le cheval à bascule *masc* (PL les chevaux à bascule)

rod NOUN
la canne à pêche *fem* (*for fishing*)

rode VERB ▷ *see* **ride**

★ **role** NOUN
le rôle *masc*

role play NOUN
le jeu de rôle *masc* (PL les jeux de rôles)
□ to do a role play faire un jeu de rôle

★ **roll** NOUN
▷ *see also* **roll** VERB
1 le rouleau *masc* (PL les rouleaux)
□ a roll of tape un rouleau de ruban adhésif
□ a toilet roll un rouleau de papier hygiénique
2 le petit pain *masc* (*bread*)

★ to **roll** VERB
▷ *see also* **roll** NOUN
rouler [28]
■ **to roll out the pastry** abaisser [28] la pâte

roll call NOUN
l'appel *masc*

roller NOUN
le rouleau *masc* (PL les rouleaux)

Rollerblade® NOUN
le roller *masc*
□ a pair of Rollerblades une paire de rollers

rollercoaster NOUN
les montagnes russes *fem pl*

roller skates PL NOUN
les patins à roulettes *masc pl*

roller-skating NOUN
le patin à roulettes *masc*
■ **to go roller-skating** faire [36] du patin à roulettes

rolling pin NOUN
le rouleau à pâtisserie *masc*

Roman ADJECTIVE, NOUN
romain (FEM romaine) (*ancient*)
□ a Roman villa une villa romaine □ the Roman empire l'Empire romain
■ **the Romans** les Romains

Roman Catholic NOUN
le/la catholique *masc/fem*
□ He's a Roman Catholic. Il est catholique.

romance NOUN
1 l'amour *masc* (*love*)
□ There's no romance between them. Il n'y a pas d'histoire d'amour entre eux.
2 le charme *masc* (*glamour*)
□ the romance of Paris le charme de Paris
■ **a holiday romance** une idylle de vacances

Romania NOUN
la Roumanie *fem*
■ **in Romania** en Roumanie

Romanian NOUN
▷ *see also* **Romanian** ADJECTIVE
1 le Roumain *masc*
la Roumaine *fem* (*person*)
2 le roumain *masc* (*language*)

Romanian ADJECTIVE
▷ *see also* **Romanian** NOUN
roumain (FEM roumaine)

★ **romantic** ADJECTIVE
romantique (FEM romantique)

r

★ **roof** NOUN
le toit *masc*
roof rack NOUN
la galerie *fem*
★ **room** NOUN
1 la pièce *fem*
□ the biggest room in the house la plus grande pièce de la maison
2 la chambre *fem* (*bedroom*)
□ She's in her room. Elle est dans sa chambre.
■ **a single room** une chambre pour une personne
■ **a double room** une chambre pour deux personnes
3 la salle *fem* (*in school*)
□ the music room la salle de musique
4 la place *fem* (*space*)
□ There's no room for that box. Il n'y a pas de place pour cette boîte.
roommate NOUN
le/la camarade de chambre *masc/fem*
★ **root** NOUN
la racine *fem*
to **root around** VERB
fouiller [28]
□ She started rooting around in her handbag. Elle a commencé à fouiller dans son sac à main.
rope NOUN
la corde *fem*
to **rope in** VERB
enrôler [28]
□ I was roped in to help with the school concert. J'ai été enrôlé pour aider à l'organisation du concert de l'école.
★ **rose** VERB ▷ *see* **rise**
★ **rose** NOUN
la rose *fem* (*flower*)
to **rot** VERB
pourrir [38]
rotten ADJECTIVE
pourri (FEM pourrie) (*decayed*)
□ a rotten apple une pomme pourrie
■ **rotten weather** un temps pourri
■ **That's a rotten thing to do.** Ce n'est vraiment pas gentil.
■ **to feel rotten** être [35] mal fichu (*informal*)
★ **rough** ADJECTIVE
1 rêche (FEM rêche) (*surface*)
□ My hands are rough. J'ai les mains rêches.
2 violent (FEM violente) (*game*)
□ Rugby's a rough sport. Le rugby est un sport violent.
3 difficile (FEM difficile) (*place*)
□ It's a rough area. C'est un quartier difficile.
4 houleux (FEM houleuse) (*water*)
□ The sea was rough. La mer était houleuse.
5 approximatif (FEM approximative)
□ I've got a rough idea. J'en ai une idée approximative.
■ **to feel rough** ne pas être [35] dans son assiette □ I feel rough. Je ne suis pas dans mon assiette.
roughly ADVERB
à peu près
□ It weighs roughly 20 kilos. Ça pèse à peu près vingt kilos.
★ **round** ADJECTIVE, ADVERB, PREPOSITION
▷ *see also* **round** NOUN
1 rond (FEM ronde)
□ a round table une table ronde
2 autour de (*around*)
□ We were sitting round the table. Nous étions assis autour de la table. □ She wore a scarf round her neck. Elle portait une écharpe autour du cou.
■ **It's just round the corner.** (*very near*) C'est tout près.
■ **to go round to somebody's house** aller [3E] chez quelqu'un □ I went round to my friend's house. Je suis allé chez mon ami.
■ **to have a look round** faire [36] un tour
□ We're going to have a look round. Nous allons faire un tour.
■ **to go round a museum** visiter [28] un musée
■ **round here** près d'ici □ Is there a bakery round here? Est-ce qu'il y a une boulangerie près d'ici?
■ **He lives round here.** Il habite dans les parages.
■ **all year round** toute l'année
■ **round about** (*roughly*) environ □ It costs round about £100. Cela coûte environ cent livres. □ round about 8 o'clock à huit heures environ
★ **round** NOUN
▷ *see also* **round** ADJECTIVE, ADVERB, PREPOSITION
1 la manche *fem* (*of tournament*)
2 le round *masc* (*of boxing match*)
■ **a round of golf** une partie de golf
■ **a round of drinks** une tournée □ He bought a round of drinks. Il a offert une tournée.
to **round off** VERB
terminer [28]
□ They rounded off the holiday with a helicopter trip. Ils ont terminé leurs vacances par une excursion en hélicoptère.
to **round up** VERB
1 rassembler [28] (*sheep, cattle, suspects*)
2 arrondir [38] (*figure*)
roundabout NOUN
1 le rond-point *masc* (PL les ronds-points) (*at junction*)
2 le manège *masc* (*at funfair*)

English-French

r

rounders NOUN
■ **Rounders is a bit like baseball.** Le 'rounders' ressemble un peu au base-ball.

DID YOU KNOW...?
Rounders is not played in France.

round trip NOUN (US)
l'aller-retour *masc*
■ **a round-trip ticket** un billet aller-retour

★ **route** NOUN
1 l'itinéraire *masc*
□ We're planning our route. Nous préparons notre itinéraire.
2 le parcours *masc* (*of bus*)

★ **routine** NOUN
■ **my daily routine** mes occupations quotidiennes

★ **row** NOUN
This word has two pronunciations. Make sure you choose the right translation.
1 la rangée *fem*
□ a row of houses une rangée de maisons
2 le rang *masc* (*of seats*)
□ Our seats are in the front row. Nos places se trouvent au premier rang.
■ **five times in a row** cinq fois d'affilée
3 le vacarme *masc* (*noise*)
□ What's that terrible row? Qu'est-ce que c'est que ce vacarme?
4 la dispute *fem* (*quarrel*)
■ **to have a row** se disputer [28] □ They've had a row. Ils se sont disputés.

★ to **row** VERB
1 ramer [28]
□ We took turns to row. Nous avons ramé à tour de rôle.
2 faire [36] de l'aviron (*as sport*)

rowboat NOUN (US)
le bateau à rames *masc*

rowing NOUN
l'aviron *masc* (*sport*)
□ My hobby is rowing. Je fais de l'aviron.
■ **a rowing boat** un bateau à rames

★ **royal** ADJECTIVE
royal (FEM royale, MASC PL royaux)
■ **the royal family** la famille royale

to **rub** VERB
1 frotter [28] (*stain*)
2 se frotter [28] (*part of body*)
□ Don't rub your eyes! Ne te frotte pas les yeux!
■ **to rub something out** effacer [12] quelque chose

rubber NOUN
1 le caoutchouc *masc*
□ rubber soles des semelles en caoutchouc
2 la gomme *fem* (*eraser*)
□ Can I borrow your rubber? Je peux emprunter ta gomme?
■ **a rubber band** un élastique

★ **rubbish** NOUN
▷ *see also* **rubbish** ADJECTIVE
1 les ordures *fem pl* (*refuse*)
□ When do they collect the rubbish? Quand est-ce qu'ils ramassent les ordures?
2 la camelote *fem* (*junk*)
□ They sell a lot of rubbish at the market. Ils vendent beaucoup de camelote au marché.
3 les bêtises *fem pl* (*nonsense*)
□ Don't talk rubbish! Ne dis pas de bêtises!
■ **That's a load of rubbish!** C'est vraiment n'importe quoi! (*informal*)
■ **a rubbish bin** une poubelle
■ **a rubbish dump** une décharge

★ **rubbish** ADJECTIVE
▷ *see also* **rubbish** NOUN
nul (FEM nulle)
□ They're a rubbish team! Cette équipe est nulle!

★ **rucksack** NOUN
le sac à dos *masc*

rude ADJECTIVE
1 impoli (FEM impolie) (*impolite*)
□ It's rude to interrupt. C'est impoli de couper la parole aux gens.
2 grossier (FEM grossière) (*offensive*)
□ a rude joke une plaisanterie grossière □ He was very rude to me. Il a été très grossier avec moi.
■ **a rude word** un gros mot

rug NOUN
1 le tapis *masc*
□ a Persian rug un tapis persan
2 la couverture *fem* (*blanket*)
□ a tartan rug une couverture écossaise

★ **rugby** NOUN
le rugby *masc*
□ I play rugby. Je joue au rugby.

★ **ruin** NOUN
▷ *see also* **ruin** VERB
la ruine *fem*
□ the ruins of the castle les ruines du château
■ **in ruins** en ruine

★ to **ruin** VERB
▷ *see also* **ruin** NOUN
1 abîmer [28]
□ You'll ruin your shoes. Tu vas abîmer tes chaussures.
2 gâcher [28]
□ It ruined our holiday. Ça a gâché nos vacances.
3 ruiner [28] (*financially*)
□ That one mistake ruined the business. Cette seule erreur a ruiné l'entreprise.

★ **rule** NOUN
1 la règle *fem*

□ the rules of grammar les règles de grammaire

■ **as a rule** en règle générale

2 le règlement *masc* (*regulation*)

□ It's against the rules. C'est contre le règlement.

to **rule out** VERB

écarter [28] (*possibility*)

□ I'm not ruling anything out. Je n'écarte aucune possibilité.

ruler NOUN

la règle *fem*

□ Can I borrow your ruler? Je peux emprunter ta règle?

rum NOUN

le rhum *masc*

★ **rumour** (US **rumor**) NOUN

la rumeur *fem*

□ It's just a rumour. Ce n'est qu'une rumeur.

rump steak NOUN

le romsteak *masc*

★ **run** NOUN

▷ *see also* **run** VERB

le point *masc* (*in cricket*)

□ to score a run marquer un point

■ **to go for a run** courir [16] □ I go for a run every morning. Je cours tous les matins.

■ **I did a ten-kilometre run.** J'ai couru dix kilomètres.

■ **on the run** en fuite □ The criminals are still on the run. Les criminels sont toujours en fuite.

■ **in the long run** à long terme

★ to **run** VERB

▷ *see also* **run** NOUN

1 courir [16]

□ I ran five kilometres. J'ai couru cinq kilomètres.

■ **to run a marathon** participer [28] à un marathon

2 diriger [45] (*manage*)

□ He runs a large company. Il dirige une grosse société.

3 organiser [28] (*organize*)

□ They run music courses in the holidays. Ils organisent des cours de musique pendant les vacances.

4 couler [28] (*water*)

□ Don't leave the tap running. Ne laisse pas couler le robinet.

■ **to run a bath** faire [36] couler un bain

5 conduire [23] (*by car*)

□ I can run you to the station. Je peux te conduire à la gare.

to **run away** VERB

s'enfuir [39]

□ They ran away before the police came. Ils se sont enfuis avant l'arrivée de la police.

to **run out** VERB

■ **Time is running out.** Il ne reste plus beaucoup de temps.

■ **to run out of something** se trouver [28] à court de quelque chose □ We ran out of money. Nous nous sommes trouvés à court d'argent.

to **run over** VERB

■ **to run somebody over** écraser [28] quelqu'un

■ **to get run over** se faire [36] écraser □ Be careful, or you'll get run over! Fais attention, sinon tu vas te faire écraser!

rung VERB ▷ *see* **ring**

★ **runner** NOUN

le coureur *masc*

la coureuse *fem*

runner beans PL NOUN

les haricots verts *masc pl*

runner-up NOUN

le second *masc*

la seconde *fem*

★ **running** NOUN

la course *fem*

□ Running is my favourite sport. La course est mon sport préféré.

run-up NOUN

■ **in the run-up to Christmas** pendant la période de préparation de Noël

runway NOUN

la piste *fem*

★ **rural** ADJECTIVE

rural (FEM rurale, MASC PL ruraux)

★ **rush** NOUN

▷ *see also* **rush** VERB

la hâte *fem*

■ **in a rush** à la hâte

★ to **rush** VERB

▷ *see also* **rush** NOUN

1 se précipiter [28] (*run*)

□ Everyone rushed outside. Tout le monde s'est précipité dehors.

2 se dépêcher [28] (*hurry*)

□ There's no need to rush. Ce n'est pas la peine de se dépêcher.

rush hour NOUN

les heures de pointe *fem pl*

□ in the rush hour aux heures de pointe

rusk NOUN

la biscotte *fem*

★ **Russia** NOUN

la Russie *fem*

■ **in Russia** en Russie

■ **to Russia** en Russie

Russian NOUN

▷ *see also* **Russian** ADJECTIVE

1 le/la Russe *masc/fem* (*person*)

2 le russe *masc* (*language*)

Russian ADJECTIVE
▷ *see also* **Russian** NOUN
russe (FEM russe)

rust NOUN
la rouille *fem*

rusty ADJECTIVE
rouillé (FEM rouillée)
□ a rusty bike un vélo rouillé □ My French is very rusty. Mon français est très rouillé.

ruthless ADJECTIVE
sans pitié

rye NOUN
le seigle *masc*
■ **rye bread** le pain de seigle

Ss

Sabbath NOUN
1 le dimanche *masc* (*Christian*)
2 le sabbat *masc* (*Jewish*)

★ **sack** NOUN
▷ *see also* **sack** VERB
le sac *masc*
■ **to get the sack** être [35] mis à la porte

★ to **sack** VERB
▷ *see also* **sack** NOUN
■ **to sack somebody** mettre [47] quelqu'un à la porte □ He was sacked. On l'a mis à la porte.

sacred ADJECTIVE
sacré (FEM sacrée)

★ **sacrifice** NOUN
le sacrifice *masc*

★ **sad** ADJECTIVE
triste (FEM triste)

saddle NOUN
la selle *fem*

saddlebag NOUN
la sacoche *fem*

sadly ADVERB
1 tristement
□ 'She's gone,' he said sadly. 'Elle est partie,' a-t-il dit tristement.
2 malheureusement (*unfortunately*)
□ Sadly, it was too late. Malheureusement, il était trop tard.

★ **safe** NOUN
▷ *see also* **safe** ADJECTIVE
le coffre-fort *masc* (PL les coffres-forts)
□ She put the money in the safe. Elle a mis l'argent dans le coffre-fort.

★ **safe** ADJECTIVE
▷ *see also* **safe** NOUN
1 sans danger
□ Don't worry, it's perfectly safe. Ne vous inquiétez pas, c'est absolument sans danger.
■ **Is it safe?** Ça n'est pas dangereux?
2 sûr (FEM sûre) (*machine, ladder*)
□ This car isn't safe. Cette voiture n'est pas sûre.
3 hors de danger (*out of danger*)
□ You're safe now. Vous êtes hors de danger maintenant.
■ **to feel safe** se sentir [77] en sécurité
■ **safe sex** les rapports (sexuels) protégés

★ **safety** NOUN
la sécurité *fem*
■ **a safety belt** une ceinture de sécurité
■ **a safety pin** une épingle à nourrice

Sagittarius NOUN
le/la Sagittaire *masc/fem*
□ I'm Sagittarius. Je suis Sagittaire.

Sahara NOUN
■ **the Sahara Desert** le Sahara

said VERB ▷ *see* **say**

★ **sail** NOUN
▷ *see also* **sail** VERB
la voile *fem*

★ to **sail** VERB
▷ *see also* **sail** NOUN
1 naviguer [28] (*travel*)
2 prendre [65] la mer (*set off*)
□ The boat sails at eight o'clock. Le bateau prend la mer à huit heures.

sailing NOUN
la voile *fem*
□ His hobby is sailing. Son passe-temps, c'est la voile.
■ **to go sailing** faire [36] de la voile
■ **a sailing boat** un voilier
■ **a sailing ship** un grand voilier

sailor NOUN
le marin *masc*
□ He's a sailor. Il est marin.

★ **saint** NOUN
le saint *masc*
la sainte *fem*

★ **sake** NOUN
■ **for the sake of** dans l'intérêt de

salad NOUN
la salade *fem*
■ **salad cream** la mayonnaise
■ **salad dressing** la vinaigrette

salami NOUN
le salami *masc*

★ **salary** NOUN
le salaire *masc*

★ **sale** NOUN
les soldes *masc pl* (*reductions*)
□ There's a sale on at the department store. Il y a des soldes dans le grand magasin.

■ **on sale** en vente
■ **The factory's for sale.** L'usine est en vente.
■ **'for sale'** 'à vendre'

sales assistant NOUN
le vendeur *masc*
la vendeuse *fem*
□ She's a sales assistant. Elle est vendeuse.

salesman NOUN
1 le représentant *masc* (*sales rep*)
□ He's a salesman. Il est représentant.
■ **a double-glazing salesman** un représentant en doubles vitrages
2 le vendeur *masc* (*sales assistant*)

sales rep NOUN
le représentant *masc*
la représentante *fem*

saleswoman NOUN
1 la représentante *fem* (*sales rep*)
□ She's a saleswoman. Elle est représentante.
2 la vendeuse *fem* (*sales assistant*)

salmon NOUN
le saumon *masc*

salon NOUN
le salon *masc*
□ a hair salon un salon de coiffure □ a beauty salon un salon de beauté

saloon car NOUN
la berline *fem*

★ **salt** NOUN
le sel *masc*

salty ADJECTIVE
salé (FEM salée)

to **salute** VERB
saluer [28]

Salvation Army NOUN
l'armée du Salut *fem*

★ **same** ADJECTIVE
même (FEM même)
□ the same primary school la même école primaire □ at the same time en même temps
■ **They're exactly the same.** Ils sont exactement pareils.
■ **It's not the same.** Ça n'est pas pareil.

★ **sample** NOUN
l'échantillon *masc*

★ **sand** NOUN
le sable *masc*

sandal NOUN
la sandale *fem*
□ a pair of sandals une paire de sandales

sand castle NOUN
le château de sable *masc* (PL les châteaux de sable)

★ **sandwich** NOUN
le sandwich *masc*
□ a cheese sandwich un sandwich au fromage

sandwich course NOUN
le cours avec stage pratique *masc*

sang VERB ▷ *see* **sing**

sanitary towel NOUN
la serviette hygiénique *fem*

sank VERB ▷ *see* **sink**

Santa Claus NOUN
le père Noël *masc*

sarcastic ADJECTIVE
sarcastique (FEM sarcastique)

sardine NOUN
la sardine *fem*

sat VERB ▷ *see* **sit**

satchel NOUN
le cartable *masc*

★ **satellite** NOUN
le satellite *masc*
□ satellite television la télévision par satellite
■ **a satellite dish** une antenne parabolique

satisfactory ADJECTIVE
satisfaisant (FEM satisfaisante)

satisfied ADJECTIVE
satisfait (FEM satisfaite)

sat nav NOUN
le GPS *masc*

★ **Saturday** NOUN
le samedi *masc*
□ on Saturday samedi □ on Saturdays le samedi □ every Saturday tous les samedis □ last Saturday samedi dernier □ next Saturday samedi prochain
■ **I've got a Saturday job.** Je travaille le samedi.

★ **sauce** NOUN
la sauce *fem*

saucepan NOUN
la casserole *fem*

saucer NOUN
la soucoupe *fem*

Saudi Arabia NOUN
l'Arabie Saoudite *fem*
■ **in Saudi Arabia** en Arabie Saoudite

sauna NOUN
le sauna *masc*

★ **sausage** NOUN
1 la saucisse *fem*
2 le saucisson *masc* (*salami*)
■ **a sausage roll** un friand à la saucisse

★ to **save** VERB
1 mettre [47] de côté (*save up money*)
□ I've saved £50 already. J'ai déjà mis cinquante livres de côté.
2 économiser [28] (*spend less*)
□ I saved £20 by waiting for the sales. J'ai économisé vingt livres en attendant les soldes.
■ **to save time** gagner [28] du temps □ We

took a taxi to save time. Nous avons pris un taxi pour gagner du temps. ◻ It saved us time. Ça nous a fait gagner du temps.

3 sauver [28] (*rescue*)
◻ Luckily, all the passengers were saved. Heureusement, tous les passagers ont été sauvés.

4 sauvegarder [28] (*on computer*)
◻ Don't forget to save your work regularly. N'oublie pas de sauvegarder ton travail régulièrement.

to **save up** VERB
mettre [47] de l'argent de côté
◻ I'm saving up for a new bike. Je mets de l'argent de côté pour un nouveau vélo.

savings PL NOUN
les économies *fem pl*
◻ She spent all her savings on a computer. Elle a dépensé toutes ses économies en achetant un ordinateur.

savoury ADJECTIVE
salé (FEM salée)
◻ Is it sweet or savoury? C'est sucré ou salé?

saw VERB ▷ *see* **see**

saw NOUN
la scie *fem*

sax NOUN
le saxo *masc* (*informal*)
◻ I play the sax. Je joue du saxo.

saxophone NOUN
le saxophone *masc*
◻ I play the saxophone. Je joue du saxophone.

★ to **say** VERB
dire [27]
◻ I say what I think. Je dis ce que je pense.
◻ You never say anything. Tu ne dis jamais rien. ◻ He says he loves me. Il me dit qu'il m'aime. ◻ What did he say? Qu'est-ce qu'il a dit? ◻ Did you hear what she said? Tu as entendu ce qu'elle a dit?
■ **Could you say that again?** Pourriez-vous répéter s'il vous plaît?
■ **That goes without saying.** Cela va sans dire.

saying NOUN
le dicton *masc*
◻ It's just a saying. C'est juste un dicton.

★ **scale** NOUN
1 l'échelle *fem* (*of map*)
◻ a large-scale map une carte à grande échelle
2 l'ampleur *fem* (*size, extent*)
◻ a disaster on a massive scale un désastre d'une ampleur incroyable
3 la gamme *fem* (*in music*)

scales PL NOUN
la balance *fem sing* (*in kitchen, shop*)
■ **bathroom scales** le pèse-personne *sing*

scampi PL NOUN
les scampi *masc pl*

★ **scandal** NOUN
1 le scandale *masc* (*outrage*)
◻ It caused a scandal. Ça a fait scandale.
2 les ragots *masc pl* (*gossip*)
◻ It's just scandal. Ce ne sont que des ragots.

Scandinavia NOUN
la Scandinavie *fem*
■ **in Scandinavia** en Scandinavie

Scandinavian ADJECTIVE
scandinave (FEM scandinave)

scar NOUN
la cicatrice *fem*

scarce ADJECTIVE
limité (FEM limitée)
◻ scarce resources des ressources limitées
■ **Jobs are scarce these days.** Il y a peu de travail ces temps-ci.

scarcely ADVERB
à peine
◻ I scarcely knew him. Je le connaissais à peine.

scare NOUN
▷ *see also* **scare** VERB
la panique *fem*
■ **a bomb scare** une alerte à la bombe

to **scare** VERB
▷ *see also* **scare** NOUN
■ **to scare somebody** faire [36] peur à quelqu'un ◻ He scares me. Il me fait peur.

scarecrow NOUN
l'épouvantail *masc*

scared ADJECTIVE
■ **to be scared** avoir [8] peur ◻ I was scared stiff. J'avais terriblement peur.
■ **to be scared of** avoir [8] peur de ◻ Are you scared of him? Est-ce que tu as peur de lui?

scarf NOUN
1 l'écharpe *fem* (*long*)
2 le foulard *masc* (*square*)

scary ADJECTIVE
effrayant (FEM effrayante)
◻ It was really scary. C'était vraiment effrayant.

★ **scene** NOUN
1 les lieux *masc pl* (*place*)
◻ The police were soon on the scene. La police est vite arrivée sur les lieux. ◻ the scene of the crime les lieux du crime
2 le spectacle *masc* (*event, sight*)
◻ It was an amazing scene. C'était un spectacle étonnant.
■ **to make a scene** faire [36] une scène

scenery NOUN
le paysage *masc* (*landscape*)

scent NOUN
le parfum *masc* (*perfume*)

★ **schedule** NOUN
le programme *masc*
□ a busy schedule un programme chargé
■ **on schedule** comme prévu
■ **to be behind schedule** avoir [8] du retard

scheduled flight NOUN
le vol régulier *masc*

scheme NOUN
1 le truc *masc* (*idea*)
□ a crazy scheme he dreamed up un truc farfelu qu'il a inventé
2 le projet *masc* (*project*)
■ **a scheme to make extra pocket money** un plan pour gagner plus d'argent de poche

scholarship NOUN
la bourse *fem*

★ **school** NOUN
l'école *fem*
■ **to go to school** aller [3E] à l'école

schoolbag NOUN
le cartable *masc*

schoolbook NOUN
le livre scolaire *masc*

★ **schoolboy** NOUN
l'écolier *masc*

★ **schoolchildren** NOUN
les écoliers *masc pl*

★ **schoolgirl** NOUN
l'écolière *fem*

★ **school uniform** NOUN
l'uniforme scolaire *masc*

★ **science** NOUN
la science *fem*

science fiction NOUN
la science-fiction *fem*

scientific ADJECTIVE
scientifique (FEM scientifique)

★ **scientist** NOUN
le chercheur *masc*
la chercheuse *fem*
■ **He trained as a scientist.** Il a une formation scientifique.

★ **scissors** PL NOUN
les ciseaux *masc pl*
□ a pair of scissors une paire de ciseaux

to **scoff** VERB
bouffer [28] (*informal: eat*)
□ My brother scoffed all the sandwiches. Mon frère a bouffé tous les sandwichs.

scone NOUN
le scone *masc*

scooter NOUN
1 le scooter *masc*
2 la trottinette *fem* (*child's toy*)

★ **score** NOUN
▷ *see also* **score** VERB
le score *masc*
□ The score was three-nil. Le score était de trois à zéro.

★ to **score** VERB
▷ *see also* **score** NOUN
1 marquer [28] (*goal, point*)
□ to score a goal marquer un but □ Our team didn't score. Notre équipe n'a pas marqué de but.
■ **to score 6 out of 10** obtenir [83] un score de six sur dix
2 compter [28] les points (*keep score*)
□ Who's going to score? Qui va compter les points?

Scorpio NOUN
le Scorpion *masc*
□ I'm Scorpio. Je suis Scorpion.

Scot NOUN
l'Écossais *masc*
l'Écossaise *fem*

Scotch tape® NOUN (US)
le scotch® *masc*

★ **Scotland** NOUN
l'Écosse *fem*
■ **in Scotland** en Écosse
■ **to Scotland** en Écosse
■ **I'm from Scotland.** Je suis écossais.

Scots ADJECTIVE
écossais (FEM écossaise)
□ a Scots accent un accent écossais

★ **Scotsman** NOUN
l'Écossais *masc*

★ **Scotswoman** NOUN
l'Écossaise *fem*

★ **Scottish** ADJECTIVE
écossais (FEM écossaise)
□ a Scottish accent un accent écossais

scout NOUN
le scout *masc*
□ I'm in the Scouts. Je suis scout.

scrambled eggs PL NOUN
les œufs brouillés *masc pl*

scrap NOUN
▷ *see also* **scrap** VERB
1 le bout *masc*
□ a scrap of paper un bout de papier
2 la bagarre *fem* (*fight*)
■ **scrap iron** la ferraille

to **scrap** VERB
▷ *see also* **scrap** NOUN
abandonner [28] (*plan*)
□ The idea was scrapped. L'idée a été abandonnée.

scrapbook NOUN
l'album *masc*

to **scratch** VERB
▷ *see also* **scratch** NOUN
se gratter [28]
□ Stop scratching! Arrête de te gratter!

scratch NOUN
▷ *see also* **scratch** VERB
l'égratignure *fem* (*on skin*)
■ **to start from scratch** partir [57E] de zéro

★ **scream** NOUN
▷ *see also* **scream** VERB
le hurlement *masc*

★ to **scream** VERB
▷ *see also* **scream** NOUN
hurler [28]

★ **screen** NOUN
l'écran *masc*

screw NOUN
la vis *fem*

screwdriver NOUN
le tournevis *masc*

to **scribble** VERB
griffonner [28]

to **scrub** VERB
récurer [28]
□ to scrub a pan récurer une casserole

sculpture NOUN
la sculpture *fem*

★ **sea** NOUN
la mer *fem*

★ **seafood** NOUN
les fruits de mer *masc pl*
□ I don't like seafood. Je n'aime pas les fruits de mer.

seagull NOUN
la mouette *fem*

seal NOUN
▷ *see also* **seal** VERB
1 le phoque *masc* (*animal*)
2 le cachet *masc* (*on letter*)

to **seal** VERB
▷ *see also* **seal** NOUN
1 sceller [28] (*document*)
2 coller [28] (*letter*)

seaman NOUN
le marin *masc*

★ to **search** VERB
▷ *see also* **search** NOUN
fouiller [28]
□ They searched the woods for her. Ils ont fouillé les bois pour la trouver.
■ **to search for something** chercher [28] quelque chose □ He searched for evidence. Il cherchait des preuves.

★ **search** NOUN
▷ *see also* **search** VERB
la fouille *fem*

search engine NOUN
le moteur de recherche *masc*

search party NOUN
l'expédition de secours *fem*

seashore NOUN
le bord de la mer *masc*
□ on the seashore au bord de la mer

seasick ADJECTIVE
■ **to be seasick** avoir [8] le mal de mer

★ **seaside** NOUN
le bord de la mer *masc*
□ at the seaside au bord de la mer

★ **season** NOUN
la saison *fem*
□ What's your favourite season? Quelle est ta saison préférée?
■ **out of season** hors saison □ It's cheaper to go there out of season. C'est moins cher d'y aller hors saison.
■ **during the holiday season** en période de vacances
■ **a season ticket** une carte d'abonnement

★ **seat** NOUN
le siège *masc*

seat belt NOUN
la ceinture de sécurité *fem*

sea water NOUN
l'eau de mer *fem*

seaweed NOUN
les algues *fem pl*

★ **second** ADJECTIVE
▷ *see also* **second** NOUN
deuxième (FEM deuxième)
□ on the second page à la deuxième page
■ **to come second** (*in race*) arriver [5E] deuxième
■ **the second of March** le deux mars

★ **second** NOUN
▷ *see also* **second** ADJECTIVE
la seconde *fem*
□ It'll only take a second. Ça va prendre juste une seconde.

★ **secondary school** NOUN
1 le collège *masc*
2 le lycée *masc*

DID YOU KNOW...?
In France, pupils go to a **collège** between the ages of 11 and 15, and then to a **lycée** until the age of 18.

second-class ADJECTIVE, ADVERB
1 de seconde classe (*ticket, compartment*)
■ **to travel second class** voyager [45] en seconde
2 à tarif réduit (*stamp, letter*)
□ to send something second class envoyer quelque chose à tarif réduit

secondhand ADJECTIVE
d'occasion
□ a secondhand car une voiture d'occasion

secondly ADVERB
deuxièmement
■ **firstly ... secondly ...** d'abord ... ensuite ...
□ Firstly, it's too expensive. Secondly, it wouldn't work anyway. D'abord, c'est trop cher. Ensuite, ça ne marcherait pas de toute façon.

★ **secret** ADJECTIVE
▷ *see also* **secret** NOUN
secret (FEM secrète)
□ a secret mission une mission secrète

★ **secret** NOUN
▷ *see also* **secret** ADJECTIVE
le secret *masc*
□ It's a secret. C'est un secret. □ Can you keep a secret? Tu sais garder un secret?
■ **in secret** en secret

★ **secretary** NOUN
le/la secrétaire *masc/fem*
□ She's a secretary. Elle est secrétaire.

secretly NOUN
secrètement

★ **section** NOUN
la section *fem*

★ **security** NOUN
la sécurité *fem*
□ a feeling of security un sentiment de sécurité □ a campaign to improve airport security une campagne visant à améliorer la sécurité dans les aéroports
■ **job security** la sécurité de l'emploi

security guard NOUN
1 l'agent de sécurité *masc* (*in building, shop*)
2 le garde chargé de la sécurité *masc* (*on guard*)
3 un convoyeur de fonds (*transporting money*)

sedan NOUN (US)
la berline *fem*

★ to **see** VERB
voir [92]
□ I see her every day. Je la vois tous les jours. □ You see things clearly. Tu vois les choses clairement. □ He sees them at weekends. Il les voit le week-end. □ I can't see. Je n'y vois rien. □ I saw him yesterday. Je l'ai vu hier. □ Have you seen him? Est-ce que tu l'as vu?
■ **See you!** Salut!
■ **See you soon!** À bientôt!
■ **to see to something** s'occuper [28] de quelque chose □ Can you see to lunch, please? Tu peux t'occuper du déjeuner, s'il te plaît?

★ **seed** NOUN
la graine *fem*
□ sunflower seeds des graines de tournesol

to **seek** VERB
chercher [28]
■ **to seek help** chercher [28] de l'aide

★ to **seem** VERB
avoir [8] l'air
□ She seems tired. Elle a l'air fatiguée. □ The shop seemed to be closed. Le magasin avait l'air d'être fermé.
■ **That seems like a good idea.** Ce n'est pas une mauvaise idée.
■ **It seems that ...** Il paraît que ... □ It seems she's getting married. Il paraît qu'elle va se marier.
■ **There seems to be a problem.** Il semble y avoir un problème.

seen VERB ▷ *see* **see**

seesaw NOUN
la balançoire à bascule *fem*

see-through ADJECTIVE
transparent (FEM transparente)

seldom ADVERB
rarement

★ to **select** VERB
sélectionner [28]

★ **selection** NOUN
la sélection *fem*

self-assured ADJECTIVE
sûr de soi (FEM sûre de soi)
□ He's very self-assured. Il est très sûr de lui.

self-catering ADJECTIVE
■ **a self-catering apartment** un appartement de vacances

self-centred (US **self-centered**) ADJECTIVE
égocentrique (FEM égocentrique)

self-confidence NOUN
la confiance en soi *fem*
□ He hasn't got much self-confidence. Il n'a pas très confiance en lui.

self-conscious ADJECTIVE
■ **to be self-conscious** **1** (*embarrassed*) être [35] mal à l'aise □ She was really self-conscious at first. Elle était vraiment mal à l'aise au début. **2** (*shy*) manquer [28] d'assurance □ He's always been rather self-conscious. Il a toujours un peu manqué d'assurance.

self-contained ADJECTIVE
■ **a self-contained flat** un appartement indépendant

self-control NOUN
le sang-froid *masc*

self-defence (US **self-defense**) NOUN
l'autodéfense *fem*
□ self-defence classes les cours d'autodéfense
■ **She killed him in self-defence.** Elle l'a tué en légitime défense.

self-discipline NOUN
l'autodiscipline *fem*
self-employed ADJECTIVE
■ **to be self-employed** travailler [28] à son compte □ He's self-employed. Il travaille à son compte.
■ **the self-employed** les travailleurs indépendants
selfie NOUN
le selfie *masc*
selfie stick NOUN
la perche *fem* à selfie
selfish ADJECTIVE
égoïste (FEM égoïste)
□ Don't be so selfish. Ne sois pas si égoïste.
self-respect NOUN
l'amour-propre *masc*
self-service ADJECTIVE
■ **It's self-service.** (*café, shop*) C'est un self-service.
■ **a self-service restaurant** un restaurant self-service
★ to **sell** VERB
vendre [88]
□ He sold it to me. Il me l'a vendu.
to **sell off** VERB
liquider [28]
to **sell out** VERB
se vendre [88]
□ The tickets sold out in three hours. Les billets se sont tous vendus en trois heures.
□ The show didn't quite sell out. Ce spectacle ne s'est pas très bien vendu.
■ **The tickets are all sold out.** Il ne reste plus de billets.
sell-by date NOUN
la date limite de vente *fem*
selling price NOUN
le prix de vente *masc*
Sellotape® NOUN
le scotch® *masc*
semi NOUN
la maison jumelée *fem*
□ We live in a semi. Nous habitons dans une maison jumelée.
semicircle NOUN
le demi-cercle *masc*
semicolon NOUN
le point-virgule *masc*
semi-detached house NOUN
la maison jumelée *fem*
□ We live in a semi-detached house. Nous habitons dans une maison jumelée.
semi-final NOUN
la demi-finale *fem*
semi-skimmed milk NOUN
le lait demi-écrémé *masc*

★ to **send** VERB
envoyer [33]
□ She sent me a birthday card. Elle m'a envoyé une carte d'anniversaire.
to **send back** VERB
renvoyer [33]
to **send off** VERB
1 envoyer [33] (*goods, letter*)
2 renvoyer [33] du terrain (*in sports match*)
□ He was sent off. On l'a renvoyé du terrain.
■ **to send off for something** **1** (*free*) se faire [36] envoyer quelque chose □ I've sent off for a catalogue. Je me suis fait envoyer un catalogue. **2** (*paid for*) commander [28] quelque chose par correspondance □ She sent off for a new passport. Elle a commandé un nouveau passeport.
to **send out** VERB
envoyer [33]
■ **to send out for** commander [28] par téléphone □ Shall we send out for a pizza? Et si on commandait une pizza par téléphone?
sender NOUN
l'expéditeur *masc*
l'expéditrice *fem*
★ **senior** ADJECTIVE
haut placé (FEM haut placée)
■ **senior management** les cadres supérieurs
■ **senior school** le lycée
■ **senior pupils** les grandes classes
senior citizen NOUN
la personne du troisième âge *fem*
sensational ADJECTIVE
sensationnel (FEM sensationnelle)
★ **sense** NOUN
1 le bon sens *masc* (*wisdom*)
□ Use your common sense! Un peu de bon sens, voyons!
■ **It makes sense.** C'est logique.
■ **It doesn't make sense.** Ça n'a pas de sens.
2 le sens *masc* (*faculty*)
□ the five senses les cinq sens
■ **the sense of touch** le toucher
■ **the sense of smell** l'odorat *masc*
■ **the sixth sense** le sixième sens
■ **sense of humour** le sens de l'humour
□ He's got no sense of humour. Il n'a aucun sens de l'humour.
senseless ADJECTIVE
insensé (FEM insensée)
★ **sensible** ADJECTIVE
raisonnable (FEM raisonnable)
□ Lara is a very sensible girl. Lara est une jeune fille très raisonnable.
■ **That wasn't a sensible idea.** Cela n'était pas une idée judicieuse

BE CAREFUL!
Do not translate **sensible** by the French word **sensible**.

★ **sensitive** ADJECTIVE
sensible (FEM sensible)
□ She's very sensitive. Elle est très sensible.

sensuous ADJECTIVE
sensuel (FEM sensuelle)

sent VERB ▷ *see* **send**

★ **sentence** NOUN
▷ *see also* **sentence** VERB
1 la phrase *fem*
□ What does this sentence mean? Que veut dire cette phrase?
2 la peine *fem* (*punishment*)
□ the death sentence la peine de mort
■ **He got a life sentence.** Il a été condamné à la réclusion à perpétuité.

★ to **sentence** VERB
▷ *see also* **sentence** NOUN
condamner [28]
■ **to sentence somebody to life imprisonment** condamner [28] quelqu'un à la réclusion à perpétuité
■ **to sentence somebody to death** condamner [28] quelqu'un à mort

sentimental ADJECTIVE
sentimental (FEM sentimentale, MASC PL sentimentaux)

★ **separate** ADJECTIVE
▷ *see also* **separate** VERB
séparé (FEM séparée)
□ I wrote it on a separate sheet. Je l'ai écrit sur une feuille séparée.
■ **The children have separate rooms.** Les enfants ont chacun leur chambre.
■ **on separate occasions** à différentes reprises

★ to **separate** VERB
▷ *see also* **separate** ADJECTIVE
1 séparer [28]
2 se séparer [28] (*married couple*)
□ My parents are separated. Mes parents sont séparés.

separately ADVERB
séparément

separation NOUN
la séparation *fem*

★ **September** NOUN
septembre *masc*
■ **in September** en septembre

sequel NOUN
la suite *fem* (*book, film*)

sequence NOUN
1 l'ordre *masc*
■ **in sequence** par ordre
■ **a sequence of events** une succession d'événements
2 la séquence *fem* (*in film*)

sergeant NOUN
1 le sergent *masc* (*army*)
2 le brigadier *masc* (*police*)

serial NOUN
le feuilleton *masc*

★ **series** NOUN
1 la série *fem*
□ a TV series une série télévisée
2 la suite *fem* (*of numbers*)

★ **serious** ADJECTIVE
1 sérieux (FEM sérieuse)
□ You look very serious. Tu as l'air sérieux.
■ **Are you serious?** Sérieusement?
2 grave (FEM grave) (*illness, mistake*)

★ **seriously** ADVERB
sérieusement
□ No, but seriously ... Non, mais sérieusement ...
■ **to take somebody seriously** prendre [65] quelqu'un au sérieux
■ **seriously injured** gravement blessé
■ **Seriously?** Sérieusement?

sermon NOUN
le sermon *masc*

servant NOUN
le/la domestique *masc/fem*

★ to **serve** VERB
▷ *see also* **serve** NOUN
1 servir [78]
□ Dinner is served. Le dîner est servi. □ It's Murray's turn to serve. C'est à Murray de servir.
2 purger [45] (*prison sentence*)
■ **to serve time** être [35] en prison
■ **It serves you right.** C'est bien fait pour toi.

★ **serve** NOUN
▷ *see also* **serve** VERB
le service *masc* (*tennis*)
■ **It's your serve.** C'est à toi de servir.

server NOUN
le serveur *masc* (*computing*)

★ to **service** VERB
▷ *see also* **service** NOUN
réviser [28] (*car, washing machine*)

★ **service** NOUN
▷ *see also* **service** VERB
1 le service *masc*
□ Service is included. Le service est compris.
2 la révision *fem* (*of car*)
3 l'office *masc* (*church service*)
■ **the Fire Service** les sapeurs-pompiers
■ **the armed services** les forces armées

service area NOUN
l'aire de service *fem*

service charge NOUN
le service *masc*
□ There's no service charge. Le service est compris.

serviceman NOUN
le militaire *masc*
□ He's a serviceman. Il est militaire.

service station NOUN
la station-service *fem* (PL les stations-service)

servicewoman NOUN
la femme soldat *fem*
□ She's a servicewoman. Elle est femme soldat.

serviette NOUN
la serviette *fem*

session NOUN
la séance *fem*

★ **set** NOUN
▷ *see also* **set** VERB
1 le jeu *masc* (PL les jeux)
□ a set of keys un jeu de clés □ a chess set un jeu d'échecs
■ **a train set** un train électrique
2 le set *masc* (*in tennis*)

★ to **set** VERB
▷ *see also* **set** NOUN
1 mettre [47] à sonner (*alarm clock*)
□ I set the alarm for 7 o'clock. J'ai mis le réveil à sonner pour sept heures.
2 établir [38] (*record*)
□ The world record was set last year. Le record du monde a été établi l'année dernière.
3 se coucher [28] (*sun*)
□ The sun was setting. Le soleil se couchait.
■ **The film is set in Morocco.** L'action du film se déroule au Maroc.
■ **to set sail** prendre [65] la mer
■ **to set the table** mettre [47] le couvert

to **set off** VERB
partir [57E]
□ We set off for Newcastle at 9 o'clock. Nous sommes partis pour Newcastle à neuf heures.

to **set out** VERB
partir [57E]
□ We set out for Newcastle at 9 o'clock. Nous sommes partis pour Newcastle à neuf heures.

settee NOUN
le canapé *masc*

★ to **settle** VERB
1 résoudre [70] (*problem*)
2 régler [34] (*argument, account*)
■ **to settle on something** opter [28] pour quelque chose

to **settle down** VERB
se calmer [28] (*calm down*)
■ **Settle down!** Du calme!

to **settle in** VERB
s'installer [28]

★ **seven** NUMBER
sept
□ She's seven. Elle a sept ans.

★ **seventeen** NUMBER
dix-sept
□ He's seventeen. Il a dix-sept ans.

★ **seventeenth** ADJECTIVE
dix-septième (FEM dix-septième)
□ her seventeenth birthday son dix-septième anniversaire □ the seventeenth floor le dix-septième étage
■ **the seventeenth of August** le dix-sept août

★ **seventh** ADJECTIVE
septième (FEM septième)
□ the seventh floor le septième étage
■ **the seventh of August** le sept août

★ **seventy** NUMBER
soixante-dix

★ **several** ADJECTIVE, PRONOUN
plusieurs
□ several schools plusieurs écoles
■ **several of them** plusieurs □ I've seen several of them. J'en ai vu plusieurs.

to **sew** VERB
coudre [15]

to **sew up** VERB
recoudre [15] (*tear*)

sewing NOUN
la couture *fem*
□ I like sewing. J'aime faire de la couture.
■ **a sewing machine** une machine à coudre

sewn VERB ▷ *see* **sew**

sex NOUN
le sexe *masc*
■ **to have sex with somebody** coucher [28] avec quelqu'un
■ **sex education** l'éducation sexuelle *fem*

sexism NOUN
le sexisme *masc*

sexist ADJECTIVE
sexiste (FEM sexiste)

sexual ADJECTIVE
sexuel (FEM sexuelle)
□ sexual discrimination la discrimination sexuelle □ sexual harassment le harcèlement sexuel

sexuality NOUN
la sexualité *fem*

sexy ADJECTIVE
sexy (FEM+PL sexy)

shabby ADJECTIVE
miteux (FEM miteuse)

★ **shade** NOUN
1 l'ombre *fem*
■ **in the shade** à l'ombre □ It was 35 degrees in the shade. Il faisait trente-cinq à l'ombre.
2 la nuance *fem* (*colour*)
□ a shade of blue une nuance de bleu

★ **shadow** NOUN
l'ombre *fem*

★ to **shake** VERB
1 secouer [28]
□ She shook the rug. Elle a secoué le tapis.
2 trembler [28] (*tremble*)
□ He was shaking with cold. Il tremblait de froid.
■ **to shake one's head** (*in refusal*) faire [36] non de la tête
■ **to shake hands with somebody** serrer [28] la main à quelqu'un □ They shook hands. Ils se sont serré la main.

DID YOU KNOW...?
Boys shake hands with their friends or kiss them on the cheek when they arrive at school in the morning.

shaken ADJECTIVE
secoué (FEM secouée)
□ I was feeling a bit shaken. J'étais un peu secoué.

shaky ADJECTIVE
tremblant (FEM tremblante) (*hand, voice*)

★ **shall** VERB
■ **Shall I shut the window?** Vous voulez que je ferme la fenêtre?
■ **Shall we ask him to come with us?** Si on lui demandait de venir avec nous?

shallow ADJECTIVE
peu profond (FEM peu profonde) (*water, pool*)

shambles NOUN
la pagaille *fem*
□ It's a complete shambles. C'est la pagaille complète.

★ **shame** NOUN
la honte *fem*
□ The shame of it! Quelle honte!
■ **What a shame!** Quel dommage!
■ **It's a shame that ...** C'est dommage que ...

c'est dommage que has to be followed by a verb in the subjunctive.

□ It's a shame he isn't here. C'est dommage qu'il ne soit pas ici.

★ **shampoo** NOUN
le shampooing *masc*
□ a bottle of shampoo une bouteille de shampooing

shandy NOUN
le panaché *masc*

shan't = **shall not**

★ **shape** NOUN
la forme *fem*

★ **share** NOUN
▷ *see also* **share** VERB
1 l'action *fem* (*in company*)
□ They've got shares in the company. Ils ont des actions dans la société.
2 la part *fem*
□ Everybody pays their share. Tout le monde paie sa part.

★ to **share** VERB
▷ *see also* **share** NOUN
partager [45]
□ to share a room with somebody partager une chambre avec quelqu'un

to **share out** VERB
distribuer [28]
□ They shared the sweets out among the children. Ils ont distribué les bonbons aux enfants.

shark NOUN
le requin *masc*

★ **sharp** ADJECTIVE
1 tranchant (FEM tranchante) (*razor, knife*)
2 pointu (FEM pointue) (*spike, point*)
3 intelligent (FEM intelligente) (*clever*)
□ She's very sharp. Elle est très intelligente.
■ **at two o'clock sharp** à deux heures pile

to **shave** VERB
se raser [28] (*have a shave*)
■ **to shave one's legs** se raser [28] les jambes

shaver NOUN
■ **an electric shaver** un rasoir électrique

shaving cream NOUN
la crème à raser *fem*

shaving foam NOUN
la mousse à raser *fem*

★ **she** PRONOUN
elle
□ She's very nice. Elle est très gentille.

★ **shed** NOUN
la remise *fem*

she'd = **she had, she would**

★ **sheep** NOUN
le mouton *masc*

sheepdog NOUN
le chien de berger *masc*

sheer ADJECTIVE
pur (FEM pure)
□ It's sheer greed. C'est de l'avidité pure.

★ **sheet** NOUN
le drap *masc* (*on bed*)
■ **a sheet of paper** une feuille de papier

shelf NOUN
1 l'étagère *fem* (*in house*)
2 le rayon *masc* (*in shop*)

★ **shell** NOUN
1 le coquillage *masc* (*on beach*)
2 la coquille *fem* (*of egg, nut*)
3 l'obus *masc* (*explosive*)

she'll = **she will**

shellfish NOUN
les fruits de mer *masc pl*

shell suit NOUN
le survêtement *masc*

★**shelter** NOUN
■ **to take shelter** se mettre [47] à l'abri
■ **a bus shelter** un arrêt d'autobus

shelves PL NOUN ▷ *see* **shelf**

shepherd NOUN
le berger *masc*

sheriff NOUN
le shérif *masc*

sherry NOUN
le xérès *masc*

she's = **she is, she has**

Shetland NOUN
les îles Shetland *fem pl*

shield NOUN
le bouclier *masc*

shift NOUN
▷ *see also* **shift** VERB
le service *masc*
□ His shift starts at 8 o'clock. Il prend son service à huit heures. □ the night shift le service de nuit
■ **to do shift work** faire [36] les trois-huit

to **shift** VERB
▷ *see also* **shift** NOUN
déplacer [12] (*move*)
□ I couldn't shift the wardrobe on my own. Je n'ai pas pu déplacer l'armoire tout seul.
■ **Shift yourself!** Pousse-toi de là! (*informal*)

shifty ADJECTIVE
1 louche (FEM louche) (*person*)
□ He looked shifty. Il avait l'air louche.
2 fuyant (FEM fuyante) (*eyes*)

shin NOUN
le tibia *masc*

to **shine** VERB
briller [28]
□ The sun was shining. Le soleil brillait.

shiny ADJECTIVE
brillant (FEM brillante)

★**ship** NOUN
1 le bateau *masc* (PL les bateaux)
2 le navire *masc* (*warship*)

shipbuilding NOUN
la construction navale *fem*

shipwreck NOUN
le naufrage *masc*

shipwrecked ADJECTIVE
■ **to be shipwrecked** faire [36] naufrage

shipyard NOUN
le chantier naval *masc*

★**shirt** NOUN
1 la chemise *fem* (*man's*)
2 le chemisier *masc* (*woman's*)

to **shiver** VERB
frissonner [28]

★**shock** NOUN
▷ *see also* **shock** VERB
le choc *masc*
■ **to get a shock** 1 (*surprise*) avoir [8] un choc 2 (*electric*) recevoir [67] une décharge
■ **an electric shock** une décharge

★to **shock** VERB
▷ *see also* **shock** NOUN
1 bouleverser [28] (*upset*)
□ They were shocked by the tragedy. Ils ont été bouleversés par la tragédie.
2 choquer [28] (*scandalize*)
□ I was rather shocked by her attitude. J'ai été assez choqué par son attitude. □ He'll be shocked if you say that. Tu vas le choquer si tu dis ça.

shocking ADJECTIVE
choquant (FEM choquante)
□ It's shocking! C'est choquant!
■ **a shocking waste** un gaspillage épouvantable

★**shoe** NOUN
la chaussure *fem*

shoelace NOUN
le lacet *masc*

shoe polish NOUN
le cirage *masc*

shoe shop NOUN
le magasin de chaussures *masc*

shone VERB ▷ *see* **shine**

shook VERB ▷ *see* **shake**

★to **shoot** VERB
1 abattre [9] (*kill*)
□ He was shot by a police officer. Il a été abattu par un policier.
2 fusiller [28] (*execute*)
□ He was shot at dawn. Il a été fusillé à l'aube.
3 tirer [28] (*gun*)
□ Don't shoot! Ne tirez pas!
■ **to shoot at somebody** tirer [28] sur quelqu'un
■ **He shot himself with a revolver.** (*dead*) Il s'est suicidé d'un coup de revolver.
■ **He was shot in the leg.** (*wounded*) Il a reçu une balle dans la jambe.
■ **to shoot an arrow** envoyer [33] une flèche
4 tourner [28] (*film*)
□ The film was shot in Prague. Le film a été tourné à Prague.
5 shooter [28] (*in football*)

shooting NOUN
1 les coups de feu *masc pl*
□ They heard shooting. Ils ont entendu des coups de feu.
■ **a shooting** une fusillade □ a drive-by shooting une fusillade au volant d'une voiture

2 la chasse *fem* (*hunting*)

□ to go shooting aller à la chasse

★ **shop** NOUN

le magasin *masc*

□ a sports shop un magasin de sports

★ **shop assistant** NOUN

le vendeur *masc*

la vendeuse *fem*

□ She's a shop assistant. Elle est vendeuse.

★ **shopkeeper** NOUN

le commerçant *masc*

la commerçante *fem*

□ He's a shopkeeper. Il est commerçant.

shoplifting NOUN

le vol à l'étalage *masc*

★ **shopping** NOUN

les courses *fem pl* (*purchases*)

□ Can you get the shopping from the car? Tu peux aller chercher les courses dans la voiture?

■ **I love shopping.** J'adore faire du shopping.

■ **to go shopping** 1 (*to buy food*) faire [36] des courses 2 (*for pleasure*) faire [36] du shopping

■ **a shopping bag** un sac à provisions

■ **a shopping centre** un centre commercial

shop window NOUN

la vitrine *fem*

shore NOUN

le rivage *masc*

■ **on shore** à terre

★ **short** ADJECTIVE

1 court (FEM courte)

□ a short skirt une jupe courte □ short hair les cheveux courts

■ **too short** trop court □ It was a great holiday, but too short. C'étaient des vacances super, mais trop courtes.

2 petit (FEM petite) (*person, period of time*)

□ She's quite short. Elle est assez petite. □ a short break une petite pause □ a short walk une petite promenade

■ **to be short of something** être [35] à court de quelque chose □ I'm short of money. Je suis à court d'argent.

■ **at short notice** au dernier moment

■ **In short, the answer's no.** Bref, la réponse est non.

shortage NOUN

la pénurie *fem*

□ a water shortage une pénurie d'eau

short cut NOUN

le raccourci *masc*

□ I took a short cut. J'ai pris un raccourci.

shorthand NOUN

la sténo *fem*

★ **shortly** ADVERB

bientôt

shorts PL NOUN

le short *masc sing*

■ **a pair of shorts** un short

short-sighted ADJECTIVE

myope (FEM myope)

short story NOUN

la nouvelle *fem*

★ **shot** VERB ▷ *see* **shoot**

★ **shot** NOUN

1 le coup de feu *masc* (*gunshot*)

2 la photo *fem* (*photo*)

□ a shot of Edinburgh Castle une photo du château d'Édimbourg

3 le vaccin *masc* (*vaccination*)

shotgun NOUN

le fusil de chasse *masc*

★ **should** VERB

When 'should' means 'ought to', use **devoir**.

devoir [26]

□ You should take more exercise. Vous devriez faire plus d'exercice. □ He should be there by now. Il devrait être arrivé maintenant. □ That shouldn't be too hard. Ça ne devrait pas être trop difficile.

■ **should have** avoir dû □ I should have told you before. J'aurais dû te le dire avant.

When 'should' means 'would', use the conditional tense.

□ I should go if I were you. Si j'étais vous, j'irais. □ I should be so lucky! Ça serait trop beau!

★ **shoulder** NOUN

l'épaule *fem*

■ **a shoulder bag** un sac à bandoulière

shouldn't = **should not**

★ to **shout** VERB

▷ *see also* **shout** NOUN

crier [19]

□ Don't shout! Ne criez pas! □ 'Go away!' he shouted. 'Allez-vous-en!' a-t-il crié.

★ **shout** NOUN

▷ *see also* **shout** VERB

le cri *masc*

shovel NOUN

la pelle *fem*

★ **show** NOUN

▷ *see also* **show** VERB

1 le spectacle *masc* (*performance*)

2 l'émission *fem* (*programme*)

3 le salon *masc* (*exhibition*)

★ to **show** VERB

▷ *see also* **show** NOUN

1 montrer [28]

■ **to show somebody something** montrer [28] quelque chose à quelqu'un □ Have I shown you my new trainers? Je t'ai montré mes nouvelles baskets?

2 faire [36] preuve de

□ She showed great courage. Elle a fait preuve de beaucoup de courage.

■ **It shows.** Ça se voit. □ I've never been riding before. — It shows. Je n'ai jamais fait de cheval. — Ça se voit.

to **show off** VERB

frimer [28] *(informal)*

to **show up** VERB

se pointer [28] *(turn up)*

□ He showed up late as usual. Il s'est pointé en retard comme d'habitude.

★ **shower** NOUN

1 la douche *fem*

■ **to have a shower** prendre [65] une douche

2 l'averse *fem (of rain)*

showerproof ADJECTIVE

imperméabilisé (FEM imperméabilisée)

showing NOUN

la projection *fem (of film)*

shown VERB ▷ *see* **show**

show-off NOUN

le frimeur *masc*

la frimeuse *fem*

shrank VERB ▷ *see* **shrink**

to **shriek** VERB

hurler [28]

shrimps PL NOUN

les crevettes *fem pl*

to **shrink** VERB

rétrécir [38] *(clothes, fabric)*

Shrove Tuesday NOUN

le mardi gras *masc*

to **shrug** VERB

■ **to shrug one's shoulders** hausser [28] les épaules

shrunk VERB ▷ *see* **shrink**

to **shudder** VERB

frissonner [28]

to **shuffle** VERB

■ **to shuffle the cards** battre [9] les cartes

★ to **shut** VERB

fermer [28]

□ What time do you shut? À quelle heure est-ce que vous fermez? □ What time does the left-luggage office shut? À quelle heure est-ce que la consigne ferme?

to **shut down** VERB

fermer [28]

□ The cinema shut down last year. Le cinéma a fermé l'année dernière.

to **shut up** VERB

1 fermer [28] *(close)*

2 se taire [82] *(be quiet)*

□ Shut up! Tais-toi!

shutters NOUN

les volets *masc pl*

shuttle NOUN

la navette *fem*

shuttlecock NOUN

le volant *masc (badminton)*

shy ADJECTIVE

timide (FEM timide)

Sicily NOUN

la Sicile *fem*

■ **in Sicily** en Sicile

■ **to Sicily** en Sicile

★ **sick** ADJECTIVE

1 malade (FEM malade) *(ill)*

□ He was sick for four days. Il a été malade pendant quatre jours.

2 de mauvais goût *(joke, humour)*

□ That's really sick! C'est vraiment de mauvais goût!

■ **to be sick** *(vomit)* vomir [38]

■ **I feel sick.** J'ai envie de vomir.

■ **to be sick of something** en avoir [8] assez de quelque chose □ I'm sick of your jokes. J'en ai assez de tes plaisanteries.

sickening ADJECTIVE

écœurant (FEM écœurante)

sick leave NOUN

le congé maladie *masc*

sickness NOUN

la maladie *fem*

sick note NOUN

1 le mot d'absence *masc (from parents)*

2 le certificat médical *masc (from doctor)*

sick pay NOUN

l'indemnité de maladie *fem*

★ **side** NOUN

1 le côté *masc (of object, building, car)*

□ He was driving on the wrong side of the road. Il roulait du mauvais côté de la route.

2 le bord *masc (of pool, river, road)*

□ by the side of the lake au bord du lac

3 le flanc *masc (of hill)*

4 l'équipe *fem (team)*

■ **He's on my side.** **1** *(on my team)* Il est dans mon équipe. **2** *(supporting me)* Il est de mon côté.

■ **side by side** côte à côte

■ **the side entrance** l'entrée latérale

■ **to take sides** prendre [65] parti □ She always takes his side. Elle prend toujours son parti.

sideboard NOUN

le buffet *masc*

side-effect NOUN

l'effet secondaire *masc*

side street NOUN

la petite rue transversale *fem*

sidewalk NOUN (US)
le trottoir *masc*

sideways ADVERB
1 de côté (*look, be facing*)
2 de travers (*move*)
■ **sideways on** de profil

sieve NOUN
la passoire *fem*

sigh NOUN
▷ *see also* **sigh** VERB
le soupir *masc*

to **sigh** VERB
▷ *see also* **sigh** NOUN
soupirer [28]

★**sight** NOUN
1 la vue *fem*
□ to have poor sight avoir une mauvaise vue
■ **to know somebody by sight** connaître [14] quelqu'un de vue
2 le spectacle *masc*
□ It was an amazing sight. C'était un spectacle étonnant.
■ **in sight** visible
■ **out of sight** hors de vue
■ **the sights** (*tourist spots*) les attractions touristiques
■ **to see the sights of Rome** visiter [28] Rome

★**sightseeing** NOUN
le tourisme *masc*
■ **to go sightseeing** faire [36] du tourisme

★**sign** NOUN
▷ *see also* **sign** VERB
1 le panneau *masc* (PL les panneaux) (*notice*)
□ There was a big sign saying 'private'. Il y avait un grand panneau indiquant 'privé'.
■ **a road sign** un panneau
2 le signe *masc* (*gesture, indication*)
□ There's no sign of improvement. Il n'y a aucun signe d'amélioration.
■ **What sign are you?** (*star sign*) Tu es de quel signe?

★to **sign** VERB
▷ *see also* **sign** NOUN
signer [28]

to **sign on** VERB
s'inscrire [30] au chômage (*as unemployed*)

★**signal** NOUN
▷ *see also* **signal** VERB
le signal *masc* (PL les signaux)

★to **signal** VERB
▷ *see also* **signal** NOUN
■ **to signal to somebody** faire [36] un signe à quelqu'un

signature NOUN
la signature *fem*

significance NOUN
l'importance *fem*

★**significant** ADJECTIVE
important (FEM importante)

sign language NOUN
le langage des signes *masc*

signpost NOUN
le poteau indicateur *masc*

★**silence** NOUN
le silence *masc*

silencer NOUN
le silencieux *masc*

★**silent** ADJECTIVE
silencieux (FEM silencieuse)

silicon chip NOUN
la puce électronique *fem*

silk NOUN
▷ *see also* **silk** ADJECTIVE
la soie *fem*

silk ADJECTIVE
▷ *see also* **silk** NOUN
en soie
□ a silk scarf un foulard en soie

silky ADJECTIVE
soyeux (FEM soyeuse)

★**silly** ADJECTIVE
bête (FEM bête)

★**silver** NOUN
l'argent *masc*
□ a silver medal une médaille d'argent

★**similar** ADJECTIVE
semblable (FEM semblable)
■ **similar to** semblable à

★**simple** ADJECTIVE
simple (FEM simple)
□ It's very simple. C'est très simple.

★**simply** ADVERB
simplement
□ It's simply not possible. Ça n'est tout simplement pas possible.

simultaneous ADJECTIVE
simultané (FEM simultanée)

sin NOUN
▷ *see also* **sin** VERB
le péché *masc*

to **sin** VERB
▷ *see also* **sin** NOUN
pécher [28]

★**since** PREPOSITION, ADVERB, CONJUNCTION
1 depuis
□ since Christmas depuis Noël □ since then depuis ce moment-là □ I haven't seen him since. Je ne l'ai pas vu depuis.
■ **ever since** depuis ce moment-là
2 depuis que
□ I haven't seen her since she left. Je ne l'ai pas vue depuis qu'elle est partie.
3 puisque (*because*)
□ Since you're tired, let's stay at home. Puisque tu es fatigué, restons à la maison.

sincere ADJECTIVE
sincère (FEM sincère)

sincerely ADVERB
▪ **Yours sincerely ...** **1** (*in business letter*) Veuillez agréer l'expression de mes sentiments les meilleurs ... **2** (*in personal letter*) Cordialement ...

★ to **sing** VERB
chanter [28]
▫ He sang out of tune. Il chantait faux. ▫ Have you ever sung this tune before? Vous avez déjà chanté cet air-là?

★ **singer** NOUN
le chanteur *masc*
la chanteuse *fem*

singing NOUN
le chant *masc*

★ **single** ADJECTIVE
▷ *see also* **single** NOUN
célibataire (FEM célibataire) (*unmarried*)
▪ **a single room** une chambre pour une personne
▪ **not a single thing** rien du tout

★ **single** NOUN
▷ *see also* **single** ADJECTIVE
l'aller simple *masc* (*ticket*)
▫ A single to Toulouse, please. Un aller simple pour Toulouse, s'il vous plaît.

single parent NOUN
▪ **She's a single parent.** Elle élève ses enfants toute seule.
▪ **a single-parent family** une famille monoparentale

singles PL NOUN
le simple *masc sing* (*in tennis*)
▫ the women's singles le simple dames

singular NOUN
le singulier *masc*
▫ in the singular au singulier

sinister ADJECTIVE
sinistre (FEM sinistre)

★ **sink** NOUN
▷ *see also* **sink** VERB
l'évier *masc*

★ to **sink** VERB
▷ *see also* **sink** NOUN
couler [28]

★ **sir** NOUN
monsieur *masc*
▪ **Yes sir.** Oui, Monsieur.

siren NOUN
la sirène *fem*

★ **sister** NOUN
1 la sœur *fem*
▫ my little sister ma petite sœur
2 l'infirmière en chef *fem* (*nurse*)

sister-in-law NOUN
la belle-sœur *fem* (PL les belles-sœurs)

★ to **sit** VERB
s'asseoir [6]
▪ **to sit on something** s'asseoir [6] sur quelque chose ▫ She sat on the chair. Elle s'est assise sur la chaise.
▪ **to be sitting** être [35] assis
▪ **to sit an exam** passer [58] un examen

to **sit down** VERB
s'asseoir [6]

sitcom NOUN
la comédie de situation *fem*

site NOUN
1 le site *masc*
▫ an archaeological site un site archéologique
▪ **the site of the accident** le lieu de l'accident
2 le camping *masc* (*campsite*)
▪ **a building site** un chantier

sitting room NOUN
le salon *masc*

situated ADJECTIVE
▪ **to be situated** être [35] situé ▫ The village is situated on a hill. Le village est situé sur une colline.

★ **situation** NOUN
la situation *fem*

★ **six** NUMBER
six
▫ He's six. Il a six ans.

★ **sixteen** NUMBER
seize
▫ He's sixteen. Il a seize ans.

★ **sixteenth** ADJECTIVE
seizième (FEM seizième)
▫ the sixteenth floor le seizième étage
▪ **the sixteenth of August** le seize août

★ **sixth** ADJECTIVE
sixième (FEM sixième)
▫ the sixth floor le sixième étage
▪ **the sixth of August** le six août

sixth form NOUN
le lycée *masc*

★ **sixty** NUMBER
soixante

★ **size** NOUN
1 la taille *fem* (*of object, clothing*)
▫ What size do you take? Quelle taille est-ce que vous faites?
▪ **I'm a size ten.** Je fais du trente-huit.
2 la pointure *fem* (*of shoes*)
▪ **I take size six.** Je fais du trente-neuf.

DID YOU KNOW...?
France uses the European system to show clothing and shoe sizes.

to **skate** VERB
1 faire [36] du patin à glace (*ice-skate*)
2 faire [36] du patin à roulettes (*roller-skate*)

skateboard NOUN
le skateboard *masc*

skateboarding NOUN
le skateboard *masc*
□ to go skateboarding faire du skateboard

skates NOUN
les patins *masc pl*

skating NOUN
le patin à glace *masc*
□ to go skating faire du patin à glace
■ **a skating rink** une patinoire

skeleton NOUN
le squelette *masc*

sketch NOUN
▷ *see also* **sketch** VERB
le croquis *masc* (*drawing*)

to **sketch** VERB
▷ *see also* **sketch** NOUN
■ **to sketch something** faire [36] un croquis de quelque chose

★ **ski** NOUN
▷ *see also* **ski** VERB
le ski *masc*
■ **ski boots** les chaussures de ski *fem pl*
■ **a ski lift** un remonte-pente
■ **ski pants** le fuseau *sing*
■ **a ski pole** un bâton de ski
■ **a ski slope** une piste de ski
■ **a ski suit** une combinaison de ski

★ to **ski** VERB
▷ *see also* **ski** NOUN
skier [19]
□ Can you ski? Tu sais skier?

to **skid** VERB
déraper [28]

skier NOUN
le skieur *masc*
la skieuse *fem*

★ **skiing** NOUN
le ski *masc*
■ **to go skiing** faire [36] du ski
■ **to go on a skiing holiday** aller [3E] aux sports d'hiver

skilful ADJECTIVE
adroit (FEM adroite)

★ **skill** NOUN
le talent *masc*
□ He played with great skill. Il a joué avec beaucoup de talent.

skilled ADJECTIVE
■ **a skilled worker** un ouvrier spécialisé

skimmed milk NOUN
le lait écrémé *masc*

skimpy ADJECTIVE
1 minuscule (FEM minuscule) (*clothes*)
2 maigre (FEM maigre) (*meal*)

★ **skin** NOUN
la peau *fem* (PL les peaux)
■ **skin cancer** le cancer de la peau

skinhead NOUN
le/la skinhead *masc/fem*

skinny ADJECTIVE
maigre (FEM maigre)

skin-tight ADJECTIVE
collant (FEM collante)

skip NOUN
▷ *see also* **skip** VERB
la benne *fem* (*container*)

to **skip** VERB
▷ *see also* **skip** NOUN
sauter [28]
□ to skip a meal sauter un repas
■ **to skip a lesson** sécher [34] un cours

★ **skirt** NOUN
la jupe *fem*

skittles NOUN
les quilles *fem pl*
□ to play skittles jouer aux quilles

to **skive** VERB
tirer [28] au flanc (*be lazy*)

to **skive off** VERB
sécher [34] (*informal*)
□ to skive off school sécher les cours

skull NOUN
le crâne *masc*

★ **sky** NOUN
le ciel *masc*

Skype® NOUN
▷ *see also* **Skype** VERB
Skype® *masc*

to **Skype** VERB
▷ *see also* **Skype** NOUN
skyper [28]

skyscraper NOUN
le gratte-ciel *masc* (PL les gratte-ciel)

slack ADJECTIVE
1 lâche (FEM lâche) (*rope*)
2 négligent (FEM négligente) (*person*)

to **slag off** VERB
■ **to slag somebody off** dire [27] du mal de quelqu'un

to **slam** VERB
claquer [28]
□ The door slammed. La porte a claqué. □ She slammed the door. Elle a claqué la porte.

slang NOUN
l'argot *masc*

slap NOUN
▷ *see also* **slap** VERB
la claque *fem*

to **slap** VERB
▷ *see also* **slap** NOUN
■ **to slap somebody** donner [28] une claque à quelqu'un

slate NOUN
l'ardoise *fem*

sledge NOUN
la luge *fem*

sledging NOUN
■ **to go sledging** faire [36] de la luge

★ **sleep** NOUN
▷ *see also* **sleep** VERB
le sommeil *masc*
■ **I need some sleep.** J'ai besoin de dormir.
■ **to go to sleep** s'endormir [29]

★ to **sleep** VERB
▷ *see also* **sleep** NOUN
dormir [29]
□ I couldn't sleep last night. J'ai mal dormi la nuit dernière.
■ **to sleep with somebody** coucher [28] avec quelqu'un

to **sleep in** VERB
1 ne pas se réveiller [28] (*accidentally*)
□ I'm sorry I'm late, I slept in. Désolé d'être en retard: je ne me suis pas réveillé.
2 faire [36] la grasse matinée (*on purpose*)

to **sleep together** VERB
coucher [28] ensemble

★ **sleeping bag** NOUN
le sac de couchage *masc*

sleeping car NOUN
le wagon-lit *masc* (PL les wagons-lits)

sleeping pill NOUN
le somnifère *masc*

sleepy ADJECTIVE
■ **to feel sleepy** avoir [8] sommeil □ I was feeling sleepy. J'avais sommeil.
■ **a sleepy little village** un petit village tranquille

sleet NOUN
▷ *see also* **sleet** VERB
la neige fondue *fem*

to **sleet** VERB
▷ *see also* **sleet** NOUN
■ **It's sleeting.** Il tombe de la neige fondue.

sleeve NOUN
la manche *fem*
□ long sleeves les manches longues □ short sleeves les manches courtes

sleigh NOUN
le traîneau *masc* (PL les traîneaux)

slept VERB ▷ *see* **sleep**

★ **slice** NOUN
▷ *see also* **slice** VERB
la tranche *fem*

★ to **slice** VERB
▷ *see also* **slice** NOUN
couper [28] en tranches

slick NOUN
■ **an oil slick** une marée noire

★ **slide** NOUN
▷ *see also* **slide** VERB
1 le toboggan *masc* (*in playground*)
2 la diapositive *fem* (*photo*)
3 la barrette *fem* (*hair slide*)

★ to **slide** VERB
▷ *see also* **slide** NOUN
glisser [28]

★ **slight** ADJECTIVE
léger (FEM légère)
□ a slight problem un léger problème □ a slight improvement une légère amélioration

★ **slightly** ADVERB
légèrement

★ **slim** ADJECTIVE
▷ *see also* **slim** VERB
mince (FEM mince)

★ to **slim** VERB
▷ *see also* **slim** ADJECTIVE
faire [36] un régime (*be on a diet*)
□ I'm slimming. Je fais un régime.

sling NOUN
l'écharpe *fem*
□ She had her arm in a sling. Elle avait le bras en écharpe.

★ **slip** NOUN
▷ *see also* **slip** VERB
1 l'erreur *fem* (*mistake*)
2 le jupon *masc* (*underskirt*)
3 la combinaison *fem* (*full-length underskirt*)
■ **a slip of paper** un bout de papier
■ **a slip of the tongue** un lapsus

★ to **slip** VERB
▷ *see also* **slip** NOUN
glisser [28]
□ He slipped on the ice. Il a glissé sur le verglas.

to **slip up** VERB
faire [36] une erreur (*make a mistake*)

slipper NOUN
le chausson *masc*
■ **a pair of slippers** des chaussons

slippery ADJECTIVE
glissant (FEM glissante)

slip-up NOUN
l'erreur *fem*

slope NOUN
la pente *fem*

sloppy ADJECTIVE
1 bâclé (FEM bâclée) (*work*)
2 négligé (FEM négligée) (*person, appearance*)

English-French

S

slot NOUN
la fente *fem*

slot machine NOUN
1 la machine à sous *fem* (*for gambling*)
2 le distributeur automatique *masc* (*vending machine*)

★ **slow** ADJECTIVE
lent (FEM lente)
□ We are behind a very slow lorry. On est derrière un camion très lent.
■ **My watch is slow.** Ma montre retarde.

to **slow down** VERB
ralentir [38]

★ **slowly** ADVERB
lentement

slug NOUN
la limace *fem*

slum NOUN
1 le quartier insalubre *masc* (*area*)
2 le taudis *masc* (*house*)

slush NOUN
la neige fondue *fem*

sly ADJECTIVE
rusé (FEM rusée) (*person*)
■ **a sly smile** un sourire sournois

smack NOUN
▷ *see also* **smack** VERB
la tape *fem*

to **smack** VERB
▷ *see also* **smack** NOUN
■ **to smack somebody** donner [28] une tape à quelqu'un

★ **small** ADJECTIVE
petit (FEM petite)
■ **small change** la petite monnaie

WORD POWER
You can use a number of other words instead of **small** to mean 'little':
miniature miniature
□ a miniature version une version miniature
minute infime
□ a minute chance une chance infime
tiny minuscule
□ a tiny garden un jardin minuscule

★ **smart** ADJECTIVE
1 chic (FEM+PL chic) (*elegant*)
2 intelligent (FEM intelligente) (*clever*)
■ **a smart idea** une idée astucieuse

smartphone NOUN
le smartphone *masc*

★ **smash** NOUN
▷ *see also* **smash** VERB
l'accident *masc*

★ to **smash** VERB
▷ *see also* **smash** NOUN
1 casser [28] (*break*)
□ I've smashed my watch. J'ai cassé ma montre.
2 se briser [28] (*get broken*)
□ The glass smashed into tiny pieces. Le verre s'est brisé en mille morceaux.

★ **smell** NOUN
▷ *see also* **smell** VERB
l'odeur *fem*
■ **the sense of smell** l'odorat *masc*

★ to **smell** VERB
▷ *see also* **smell** NOUN
1 sentir [77] mauvais
□ That old dog really smells! Qu'est-ce qu'il sent mauvais, ce vieux chien!
■ **to smell of something** sentir [77] quelque chose □ It smells of petrol. Ça sent l'essence.
2 sentir [77] (*detect*)
□ I can't smell anything. Je ne sens rien.

smelly ADJECTIVE
qui sent mauvais
□ He's got smelly feet. Il a les pieds qui sentent mauvais.

smelt VERB ▷ *see* **smell**

★ **smile** NOUN
▷ *see also* **smile** VERB
le sourire *masc*

★ to **smile** VERB
▷ *see also* **smile** NOUN
sourire [74]

smiley NOUN
l'émoticon *masc*

★ **smoke** NOUN
▷ *see also* **smoke** VERB
la fumée *fem*

★ to **smoke** VERB
▷ *see also* **smoke** NOUN
fumer [28]
□ I don't smoke. Je ne fume pas. □ He smokes cigars. Il fume le cigare.

smoker NOUN
le fumeur *masc*
la fumeuse *fem*

★ **smoking** NOUN
■ **to give up smoking** arrêter [28] de fumer
■ **Smoking is bad for you.** Le tabac est mauvais pour la santé.
■ **'no smoking'** 'défense de fumer'

★ **smooth** ADJECTIVE
1 lisse (FEM lisse) (*surface*)
2 mielleux (FEM mielleuse) (*person*)

SMS NOUN
le SMS *masc*
□ I'll send you an SMS. Je t'enverrai un SMS.

smudge NOUN
la bavure *fem*

smug ADJECTIVE
suffisant (FEM suffisante)

to **smuggle** VERB
passer [58] en fraude (*goods*)
□ to smuggle drugs into a country faire passer de la drogue en fraude dans un pays
■ **They managed to smuggle him out of prison.** Ils ont réussi à le faire sortir de prison clandestinement.

smuggler NOUN
le contrebandier *masc*
la contrebandière *fem*

smuggling NOUN
la contrebande *fem*

snack NOUN
l'en-cas *masc* (PL les en-cas)
■ **to have a snack** prendre [65] un en-cas

snack bar NOUN
le snack-bar *masc*

snail NOUN
l'escargot *masc*

snake NOUN
le serpent *masc*

★ to **snap** VERB
casser [28] net (*break*)
□ The branch snapped. La branche a cassé net.
■ **to snap one's fingers** faire [36] claquer ses doigts

snap fastener NOUN
le bouton-pression *masc* (PL les boutons-pression)

snapshot NOUN
la photo *fem*

to **snarl** VERB
gronder [28] (*animal*)

to **snatch** VERB
■ **to snatch something from somebody** arracher [28] quelque chose à quelqu'un □ He snatched the keys from my hand. Il m'a arraché les clés des mains.
■ **My bag was snatched.** On m'a arraché mon sac.

to **sneak** VERB
■ **to sneak in** entrer [32E] furtivement
■ **to sneak out** sortir [79E] furtivement
■ **to sneak up on somebody** s'approcher [28] de quelqu'un sans faire de bruit

to **sneeze** VERB
éternuer [28]

to **sniff** VERB
1 renifler [28]
□ Stop sniffing! Arrête de renifler!
2 flairer [28]
□ The dog sniffed my hand. Le chien m'a flairé la main.

snob NOUN
le/la snob *masc/fem*

snooker NOUN
le billard *masc*
□ to play snooker jouer au billard

snooze NOUN
le petit somme *masc*
□ to have a snooze faire un petit somme

to **snore** VERB
ronfler [28]

★ **snow** NOUN
▷ *see also* **snow** VERB
la neige *fem*

★ to **snow** VERB
▷ *see also* **snow** NOUN
neiger [45]
□ It's snowing. Il neige.

snowball NOUN
la boule de neige *fem*

snowflake NOUN
le flocon de neige *masc*

snowman NOUN
le bonhomme de neige *masc*
□ to build a snowman faire un bonhomme de neige

★ **so** CONJUNCTION, ADVERB
1 alors
□ The shop was closed, so I went home. Le magasin était fermé, alors je suis rentré chez moi. □ So, have you always lived in Cambridge? Alors, vous avez toujours vécu à Cambridge?
■ **So what?** Et alors?
■ **It rained, so I got wet.** Il pleuvait, donc j'ai été mouillé.
2 tellement (*very*)
□ It was so heavy! C'était tellement lourd!
□ He was talking so fast I couldn't understand. Il parlait tellement vite que je ne comprenais pas.
■ **It's not so heavy!** Ça n'est pas si lourd que ça!
■ **How's your father? — Not so good.** Comment va ton père? — Pas très bien.
■ **so much** (*a lot*) tellement □ I love you so much. Je t'aime tellement.
■ **so much ...** tellement de ... □ I've got so much work. J'ai tellement de travail.
■ **so many ...** tellement de ... □ I've got so many things to do today. J'ai tellement de choses à faire aujourd'hui.
3 aussi (*in comparisons*)
□ He's like his sister but not so clever. Il est comme sa sœur mais pas aussi intelligent.
■ **so do I** moi aussi □ I love horses. — So do I. J'aime les chevaux. — Moi aussi.
■ **so have we** nous aussi □ I've been to Ireland twice. — So have we. Je suis allé en Irlande deux fois. — Nous aussi.
■ **I think so.** Je crois.

■ **I hope so.** J'espère bien.
■ **That's not so.** Ça n'est pas le cas.
■ **so far** jusqu'à présent □ It's been easy so far. Ça a été facile jusqu'à présent.
■ **so far so good** jusqu'ici ça va
■ **ten or so people** environ dix personnes
■ **at five o'clock or so** à environ cinq heures

to **soak** VERB
tremper [28]

soaked ADJECTIVE
trempé (FEM trempée)
□ By the time we got back we were soaked. Nous sommes rentrés trempés.

soaking ADJECTIVE
trempé (FEM trempée)
□ By the time we got back we were soaking. Nous sommes rentrés trempés.
■ **soaking wet** trempé □ Your shoes are soaking wet. Tes chaussures sont trempées.

★ **soap** NOUN
le savon *masc*

soap opera NOUN
le feuilleton à l'eau de rose *masc*

soap powder NOUN
la lessive *fem*

to **sob** VERB
sangloter [28]
□ She was sobbing. Elle sanglotait.

sober ADJECTIVE
sobre (FEM sobre)

to **sober up** VERB
dessoûler [28]

★ **soccer** NOUN
le football *masc*
□ to play soccer jouer au football
■ **a soccer player** un joueur de football

★ **social** ADJECTIVE
social (FEM sociale, MASC PL sociaux)
□ a social class une classe sociale
■ **I have a good social life.** Je vois beaucoup de monde.
■ **social media** médias sociaux

socialism NOUN
le socialisme *masc*

socialist ADJECTIVE
▷ *see also* **socialist** NOUN
socialiste (FEM socialiste)

socialist NOUN
▷ *see also* **socialist** ADJECTIVE
le/la socialiste *masc/fem*

social network NOUN
le réseau social *masc*

social security NOUN
1 l'aide sociale *fem* (*money*)
■ **to be on social security** recevoir [67] des aides sociales
2 la sécurité sociale *fem* (*organization*)

social worker NOUN
1 l'assistant social *masc* (FEM assistante sociale)
□ She's a social worker. Elle est assistante sociale.
2 le travailleur social *masc*
□ He's a social worker. Il est travailleur social.

society NOUN
1 la société *fem*
□ We live in a multi-cultural society. Nous vivons dans une société multiculturelle.
2 le club *masc*
□ a drama society un club de théâtre

sociology NOUN
la sociologie *fem*

sock NOUN
la chaussette *fem*

socket NOUN
la prise de courant *fem*

soda NOUN
le soda *masc* (*soda water*)

soda pop NOUN (US)
le soda *masc*

sofa NOUN
le canapé *masc*

★ **soft** ADJECTIVE
1 doux (FEM douce) (*fabric, texture*)
2 mou (FEM molle) (*pillow, bed*)
■ **soft cheeses** les fromages à pâte molle
3 fin (FEM fine) (*hair*)
■ **to be soft on somebody** (*be kind to*) être [35] indulgent avec quelqu'un
■ **a soft drink** une boisson non alcoolisée
■ **soft drugs** les drogues douces *fem pl*
■ **a soft option** une solution de facilité

★ **software** NOUN
le logiciel *masc*

soggy ADJECTIVE
1 trempé (FEM trempée) (*soaked*)
□ a soggy tissue un mouchoir trempé
2 mou (FEM molle) (*not crisp*)
□ soggy chips des frites molles

★ **soil** NOUN
la terre *fem*

solar ADJECTIVE
solaire (FEM solaire)
■ **a solar panel** un panneau solaire

solar power NOUN
l'énergie solaire *fem*

sold VERB ▷ *see* **sell**

★ **soldier** NOUN
le soldat *masc*
□ He's a soldier. Il est soldat.

★ **solicitor** NOUN
1 l'avocat *masc*
l'avocate *fem* (*for lawsuits*)
□ He's a solicitor. Il est avocat.
2 le notaire *masc* (*for wills, property*)
□ She's a solicitor. Elle est notaire.

solid ADJECTIVE
1 massif (FEM massive) (*not hollow*)
□ solid gold l'or massif
2 solide (FEM solide)
□ a solid wall un mur solide
■ **for three hours solid** pendant trois heures entières

solo NOUN
le solo *masc*
□ a guitar solo un solo de guitare

★**solution** NOUN
la solution *fem*

★to **solve** VERB
résoudre [70]

★**some** ADJECTIVE, PRONOUN

> When 'some' means 'a certain amount of', use **du**, **de la** or **des** according to the gender of the French noun that follows it. **du** and **de la** become **de l'** when they are followed by a noun starting with a vowel.

1 du
□ Would you like some bread? Voulez-vous du pain?
de la
□ Would you like some lemonade? Voulez-vous de la limonade?
de l'
□ Would you like some water? Voulez-vous de l'eau?
des
□ I've got some crisps. J'ai des chips.
■ **Some people say that ...** Il y a des gens qui disent que ...
■ **some day** un de ces jours
■ **some day next week** un jour la semaine prochaine
2 certains (FEM certaines) (*some but not all*)
□ Are these mushrooms poisonous? — Only some. Est-ce que ces champignons sont vénéneux? — Certains le sont.
■ **some of them** quelques-uns □ I only sold some of them. J'en ai seulement vendu quelques-uns.
■ **I only took some of it.** J'en ai seulement pris un peu.
■ **I'm going to buy some sweets. Do you want some too?** Je vais acheter des bonbons. Tu en veux aussi?
■ **Would you like some coffee? — No thanks, I've got some.** Tu veux du café? — Non merci, j'en ai déjà.

★**somebody** PRONOUN
quelqu'un
□ Somebody stole my purse. Quelqu'un a volé mon porte-monnaie.

★**somehow** ADVERB
■ **I'll do it somehow.** Je trouverai le moyen de le faire.
■ **Somehow I don't think he believed me.** Quelque chose me dit qu'il ne m'a pas cru.

★**someone** PRONOUN
quelqu'un
□ Someone stole my purse. Quelqu'un a volé mon porte-monnaie.

someplace ADVERB (US)
quelque part

★**something** PRONOUN
quelque chose
□ something special quelque chose de spécial
□ Wear something warm. Mets quelque chose de chaud. □ That's really something! C'est vraiment quelque chose! □ It cost £100, or something like that. Ça a coûté cent livres, ou quelque chose comme ça. □ His name is Pierre or something. Il s'appelle Pierre, ou quelque chose comme ça.

sometime ADVERB
un de ces jours
□ You must come and see us sometime. Passez donc nous voir un de ces jours.
■ **sometime last month** dans le courant du mois dernier

★**sometimes** ADVERB
quelquefois
□ Sometimes I think she hates me. Quelquefois j'ai l'impression qu'elle me déteste.

★**somewhere** ADVERB
quelque part
□ I left my keys somewhere. J'ai laissé mes clés quelque part. □ I'd like to go on holiday somewhere sunny. J'aimerais aller en vacances, quelque part où il y a du soleil.

★**son** NOUN
le fils *masc*

★**song** NOUN
la chanson *fem*

son-in-law NOUN
le gendre *masc*

★**soon** ADVERB
bientôt
□ very soon très bientôt
■ **soon afterwards** peu après
■ **as soon as possible** aussitôt que possible

sooner ADVERB
plus tôt
□ Can't you come a bit sooner? Tu ne peux pas venir un peu plus tôt?
■ **sooner or later** tôt ou tard

soot NOUN
la suie *fem*

soppy ADJECTIVE
sentimental (FEM sentimentale, MASC PL sentimentaux)

soprano NOUN
le/la soprano *masc/fem* (*singer*)

sorcerer NOUN
le sorcier *masc*

sore ADJECTIVE
▷ *see also* **sore** NOUN
■ **My feet are sore.** J'ai mal aux pieds.
■ **It's sore.** Ça fait mal.
■ **That's a sore point.** C'est un point sensible.

sore NOUN
▷ *see also* **sore** ADJECTIVE
la plaie *fem*

★ **sorry** ADJECTIVE
désolé (FEM désolée)
□ I'm really sorry. Je suis vraiment désolé.
□ I'm sorry, I haven't got any change. Je suis désolé, je n'ai pas de monnaie. □ I'm sorry I'm late. Je suis désolé d'être en retard.
■ **sorry!** pardon!
■ **sorry?** pardon?
■ **I'm sorry about the noise.** Je m'excuse pour le bruit.
■ **You'll be sorry!** Tu le regretteras!
■ **to feel sorry for somebody** plaindre [17] quelqu'un

★ **sort** NOUN
la sorte *fem*
□ What sort of bike have you got? Quelle sorte de vélo as-tu?

to **sort out** VERB
1 ranger [45] (*objects*)
2 résoudre [70] (*problems*)

so-so ADVERB
comme ci comme ça
□ How are you feeling? — So-so. Comment est-ce que tu te sens? — Comme ci comme ça.

sought VERB ▷ *see* **seek** VERB

soul NOUN
1 l'âme *fem* (*spirit*)
2 la soul *fem* (*music*)

★ **sound** NOUN
▷ *see also* **sound** VERB, ADJECTIVE, ADVERB
1 le bruit *masc* (*noise*)
□ Don't make a sound! Pas un bruit! □ the sound of footsteps des bruits de pas
2 le son *masc*
□ Can I turn the sound down? Je peux baisser le son?

★ to **sound** VERB
▷ *see also* **sound** NOUN, ADJECTIVE, ADVERB
■ **That sounds interesting.** Ça a l'air intéressant.
■ **It sounds as if she's doing well at school.** Elle a l'air de bien travailler à l'école.
■ **That sounds like a good idea.** C'est une bonne idée.

★ **sound** ADJECTIVE, ADVERB
▷ *see also* **sound** NOUN, VERB
bon (FEM bonne)
□ That's sound advice. C'est un bon conseil.
■ **sound asleep** profondément endormi

soundtrack NOUN
la bande sonore *fem*

★ **soup** NOUN
la soupe *fem*
□ vegetable soup la soupe aux légumes

sour ADJECTIVE
aigre (FEM aigre)

★ **south** ADJECTIVE, ADVERB
▷ *see also* **south** NOUN
1 sud (FEM+PL sud)
□ the south coast la côte sud
2 vers le sud
□ We were travelling south. Nous allions vers le sud.
■ **south of** au sud de □ It's south of London. C'est au sud de Londres.

★ **south** NOUN
▷ *see also* **south** ADJECTIVE, ADVERB
le sud *masc*
□ in the south dans le sud □ the South of France le sud de la France

South Africa NOUN
l'Afrique du Sud *fem*
■ **in South Africa** en Afrique du Sud
■ **to South Africa** en Afrique du Sud

South America NOUN
l'Amérique du Sud *fem*
■ **in South America** en Amérique du Sud
■ **to South America** en Amérique du Sud

South American NOUN
▷ *see also* **South American** ADJECTIVE
le Sud-Américain *masc*
la Sud-Américaine *fem*

South American ADJECTIVE
▷ *see also* **South American** NOUN
sud-américain (FEM sud-américaine)

southbound ADJECTIVE
■ **The southbound carriageway is blocked.** La route est bloquée en direction du sud.
■ **We were going southbound on the M1.** Nous étions sur la M1 en direction du sud.

southeast NOUN
le sud-est *masc*
□ southeast England le sud-est de l'Angleterre

★ **southern** ADJECTIVE
■ **the southern part of the island** la partie sud de l'île
■ **Southern England** le sud de l'Angleterre

South Pole NOUN
le pôle Sud *masc*

South Wales NOUN
le sud du pays de Galles *masc*

southwest NOUN
le sud-ouest *masc*
□ southwest France le sud-ouest de la France

souvenir NOUN
le souvenir *masc*
■ **a souvenir shop** une boutique de souvenirs

soya NOUN
le soja *masc*

soy sauce NOUN
la sauce de soja *fem*

★ **space** NOUN
1 la place *fem*
□ There isn't enough space. Il n'y a pas suffisamment de place.
■ **a parking space** une place de parking
2 l'espace *masc* (*universe, gap*)
□ to go into space aller dans l'espace □ Leave a space after your answer. Laissez un espace après votre réponse.
■ **a space shuttle** une navette spatiale

spacecraft NOUN
l'engin spatial *masc*

spade NOUN
la pelle *fem*
■ **spades** (*in cards*) le pique *sing* □ the ace of spades l'as de pique

★ **Spain** NOUN
l'Espagne *fem*
■ **in Spain** en Espagne
■ **to Spain** en Espagne

★ **Spaniard** NOUN
l'Espagnol *masc*
l'Espagnole *fem*

spaniel NOUN
l'épagneul *masc*

★ **Spanish** NOUN
▷ *see also* **Spanish** ADJECTIVE
l'espagnol *masc* (*language*)
■ **the Spanish** les Espagnols

★ **Spanish** ADJECTIVE
▷ *see also* **Spanish** NOUN
espagnol (FEM espagnole)
□ She's Spanish. Elle est espagnole.

to **spank** VERB
■ **to spank somebody** donner [28] une fessée à quelqu'un

spanner NOUN
la clé anglaise *fem*

★ **spare** ADJECTIVE
▷ *see also* **spare** VERB, NOUN
de rechange
□ spare batteries des piles de rechange □ a spare part une pièce de rechange
■ **a spare room** une chambre d'amis
■ **spare time** le temps libre □ What do you do in your spare time? Qu'est-ce que tu fais pendant ton temps libre?
■ **spare wheel** une roue de secours

★ to **spare** VERB
▷ *see also* **spare** ADJECTIVE, NOUN
■ **Can you spare a moment?** Vous pouvez m'accorder un instant?
■ **I can't spare the time.** Je n'ai pas le temps.
■ **There's no room to spare.** Il n'y a plus de place.
■ **We arrived with time to spare.** Nous sommes arrivés en avance.

★ **spare** NOUN
▷ *see also* **spare** ADJECTIVE, VERB
■ **a spare** un autre □ I've lost my key. — Have you got a spare? J'ai perdu ma clé. — Tu en as une autre?

sparkling ADJECTIVE
pétillant (FEM pétillante) (*water*)
■ **sparkling wine** le mousseux

sparrow NOUN
le moineau *masc* (PL les moineaux)

spat VERB ▷ *see* **spit**

★ to **speak** VERB
parler [28]
□ Do you speak English? Est-ce que vous parlez anglais?
■ **to speak to somebody** parler [28] à quelqu'un □ Have you spoken to him? Tu lui as parlé? □ She spoke to him about it. Elle lui en a parlé.

to **speak up** VERB
parler [28] plus fort
□ Speak up, we can't hear you. Parle plus fort, nous ne t'entendons pas.

★ **speaker** NOUN
1 l'enceinte *fem* (*loudspeaker*)
2 l'intervenant *masc*
l'intervenante *fem* (*in debate*)

★ **special** ADJECTIVE
spécial (FEM spéciale, MASC PL spéciaux)

★ **specialist** NOUN
le/la spécialiste *masc/fem*

speciality NOUN
la spécialité *fem*

★ to **specialize** VERB
se spécialiser [28]
□ We specialize in skiing equipment. Nous nous spécialisons dans les articles de ski.

specially ADVERB
spécialement
□ It's specially designed for teenagers. C'est spécialement conçu pour les adolescents.
■ **not specially** pas spécialement □ Do you like volleyball? — Not specially. Tu aimes le volley? — Pas spécialement.

★ **species** NOUN
l'espèce *fem*

★**specific** ADJECTIVE
1 particulier (FEM particulière) (*particular*)
□ certain specific issues certains problèmes particuliers
2 précis (FEM précise) (*precise*)
□ Could you be more specific? Est-ce que vous pourriez être plus précis?

★**specifically** ADVERB
1 spécialement
□ It's specifically designed for teenagers. C'est spécialement conçu pour les adolescents.
2 particulièrement
□ in Britain, or more specifically in England en Grande-Bretagne, ou plus particulièrement en Angleterre
■ **I specifically said that ...** J'ai clairement dit que ...

specs, spectacles PL NOUN
les lunettes *fem pl*

★**spectacular** ADJECTIVE
spectaculaire (FEM spectaculaire)

spectator NOUN
le spectateur *masc*
la spectatrice *fem*

★**speech** NOUN
le discours *masc*
□ to make a speech faire un discours

speechless ADJECTIVE
muet (FEM muette)
□ speechless with admiration muet d'admiration
■ **I was speechless.** Je suis resté sans voix.

★**speed** NOUN
la vitesse *fem*
□ a ten-speed bike un vélo à dix vitesses □ at top speed à toute vitesse

to **speed up** VERB
accélérer [34]

speedboat NOUN
la vedette *fem*

speeding NOUN
l'excès de vitesse *masc*
□ He was fined for speeding. Il a reçu une contravention pour excès de vitesse.

speed limit NOUN
la limitation de vitesse *fem*
■ **to break the speed limit** faire [36] un excès de vitesse

speedometer NOUN
le compteur *masc*

★to **spell** VERB
▷ *see also* **spell** NOUN
1 écrire [30] (*in writing*)
□ How do you spell that? Comment est-ce que ça s'écrit?
2 épeler [4] (*out loud*)
□ Can you spell that please? Est-ce que vous pouvez épeler, s'il vous plaît?
■ **I can't spell.** Je fais des fautes d'orthographe.

★**spell** NOUN
▷ *see also* **spell** VERB
■ **to cast a spell on somebody** jeter [41] un sort à quelqu'un
■ **to be under somebody's spell** être [35] sous le charme de quelqu'un

spelling NOUN
l'orthographe *fem*
□ My spelling is terrible. Je fais beaucoup de fautes d'orthographe.
■ **a spelling mistake** une faute d'orthographe

spelt VERB ▷ *see* **spell**

★to **spend** VERB
1 dépenser [28] (*money*)
2 passer [58] (*time*)
□ He spent a month in Germany. Il a passé un mois en Allemagne.

spice NOUN
l'épice *fem*

spicy ADJECTIVE
épicé (FEM épicée)

★**spider** NOUN
l'araignée *fem*

to **spill** VERB
1 renverser [28] (*tip over*)
□ He spilled his coffee over his trousers. Il a renversé son café sur son pantalon.
2 se répandre [9] (*get spilt*)
□ The soup spilled all over the table. La soupe s'est répandue sur la table.

spinach NOUN
les épinards *masc pl*

spin drier NOUN
l'essoreuse *fem*

spine NOUN
la colonne vertébrale *fem*

spinster NOUN
la célibataire *fem*

spire NOUN
la flèche *fem*

★**spirit** NOUN
1 le courage *masc* (*courage*)
■ **to be in good spirits** être [35] de bonne humeur
2 l'énergie *fem* (*energy*)

spirits PL NOUN
les alcools forts *masc pl*
□ I don't drink spirits. Je ne bois pas d'alcools forts.

★**spiritual** ADJECTIVE
religieux (FEM religieuse)
□ the spiritual leader of Tibet le chef religieux du Tibet

spit NOUN
▷ *see also* **spit** VERB
la salive *fem*

to **spit** VERB
▷ *see also* **spit** NOUN
cracher [28]
■ **to spit something out** cracher [28] quelque chose

★ **spite** NOUN
▷ *see also* **spite** VERB
■ **in spite of** malgré
■ **out of spite** par méchanceté

★ to **spite** VERB
▷ *see also* **spite** NOUN
contrarier [19]
□ He just did it to spite me. Il a fait ça juste pour me contrarier.

spiteful ADJECTIVE
1 méchant (FEM méchante) (*action*)
2 rancunier (FEM rancunière) (*person*)

to **splash** VERB
▷ *see also* **splash** NOUN
éclabousser [28]
□ Careful! Don't splash me! Attention! Ne m'éclabousse pas!

splash NOUN
▷ *see also* **splash** VERB
le plouf *masc*
□ I heard a splash. J'ai entendu un plouf.
■ **a splash of colour** une touche de couleur

splendid ADJECTIVE
splendide (FEM splendide)

splint NOUN
l'attelle *fem*

splinter NOUN
l'écharde *fem*

★ to **split** VERB
1 fendre [88] (*break apart*)
□ He split the wood with an axe. Il a fendu le bois avec une hache.
2 se fendre [88]
□ The ship hit a rock and split in two. Le bateau a percuté un rocher et s'est fendu en deux.
3 partager [45] (*divide up*)
□ They decided to split the profits. Ils ont décidé de partager les bénéfices.

to **split up** VERB
1 rompre [75] (*couple*)
□ My parents have split up. Mes parents ont rompu.
2 se disperser [28] (*group*)

to **spoil** VERB
1 abîmer [28] (*object*)
2 gâcher [28] (*occasion*)
3 gâter [28] (*child*)

spoiled ADJECTIVE
gâté (FEM gâtée)
□ a spoiled child un enfant gâté

spoilsport NOUN
le/la trouble-fête *masc/fem*

spoilt ADJECTIVE
gâté (FEM gâtée)
□ a spoilt child un enfant gâté

spoilt VERB ▷ *see* **spoil**

spoke VERB ▷ *see* **speak**

spoke NOUN
le rayon *masc* (*of wheel*)

spoken VERB ▷ *see* **speak**
■ **spoken French** le français parlé

★ **spokesman** NOUN
le porte-parole *masc* (PL les porte-parole)

spokeswoman NOUN
le porte-parole *masc* (PL les porte-parole)

sponge NOUN
l'éponge *fem*
■ **a sponge cake** un biscuit de Savoie

★ **sponsor** NOUN
▷ *see also* **sponsor** VERB
1 le donateur *masc*
la donatrice *fem*
2 le sponsor *masc*

★ to **sponsor** VERB
▷ *see also* **sponsor** NOUN
parrainer [28]
□ The festival was sponsored by ... Le festival a été parrainé par ...

spontaneous ADJECTIVE
spontané (FEM spontanée)

spooky ADJECTIVE
1 sinistre (FEM sinistre) (*eerie*)
■ **a spooky story** une histoire qui fait froid dans le dos
2 étrange (FEM étrange) (*strange*)
□ a spooky coincidence une étrange coïncidence

★ **spoon** NOUN
la cuiller *fem*

spoonful NOUN
la cuillerée *fem*
□ two spoonfuls of sugar deux cuillerées de sucre

★ **sport** NOUN
le sport *masc*
□ What's your favourite sport? Quel est ton sport préféré?
■ **a sports bag** un sac de sport
■ **a sports car** une voiture de sport

sportsman NOUN
le sportif *masc*

sportswear NOUN
les vêtements de sport *masc pl*

English-French

sportswoman NOUN
la sportive *fem*

sporty ADJECTIVE
sportif (FEM sportive)
□ I'm not very sporty. Je ne suis pas très sportif.

★ **spot** NOUN
▷ *see also* **spot** VERB
1 la tache *fem* (*mark*)
□ There's a spot on your shirt. Il y a une tache sur ta chemise.
2 le pois *masc* (*in pattern*)
□ a red dress with white spots une robe rouge à pois blancs
3 le bouton *masc* (*pimple*)
□ He's covered in spots. Il est couvert de boutons.
4 le coin *masc* (*place*)
□ It's a lovely spot for a picnic. C'est un coin agréable pour un pique-nique.
■ **on the spot** **1** (*immediately*) sur-le-champ □ They gave her the job on the spot. Ils lui ont offert le poste sur-le-champ. **2** (*at the same place*) sur place □ Luckily they were able to repair the car on the spot. Heureusement ils ont pu réparer la voiture sur place.

★ to **spot** VERB
▷ *see also* **spot** NOUN
repérer [34]
□ I spotted a mistake. J'ai repéré une faute.

spotless ADJECTIVE
immaculé (FEM immaculée)

spotlight NOUN
le projecteur *masc*
□ The universities have been in the spotlight recently. Les universités ont été sous le feu des projecteurs ces derniers temps.

spotty ADJECTIVE
boutonneux (FEM boutonneuse) (*pimply*)

spouse NOUN
l'époux *masc*
l'épouse *fem*

S

to **sprain** VERB
▷ *see also* **sprain** NOUN
■ **to sprain one's ankle** se faire [36] une entorse à la cheville

sprain NOUN
▷ *see also* **sprain** VERB
l'entorse *fem*
□ It's just a sprain. C'est juste une entorse.

★ **spray** NOUN
▷ *see also* **spray** VERB
la bombe *fem* (*spray can*)

★ to **spray** VERB
▷ *see also* **spray** NOUN
1 vaporiser [28]
□ to spray perfume on one's wrist se vaporiser du parfum sur le poignet
2 traiter [28] (*crops*)
3 peindre [60] avec une bombe (*graffiti*)
□ Somebody had sprayed graffiti on the wall. Quelqu'un avait peint des graffiti avec une bombe sur le mur.

★ **spread** NOUN
▷ *see also* **spread** VERB
■ **cheese spread** le fromage à tartiner
■ **chocolate spread** le chocolat à tartiner

★ to **spread** VERB
▷ *see also* **spread** NOUN
1 étaler [28]
□ to spread butter on a slice of bread étaler du beurre sur une tranche de pain
2 se propager [45] (*disease, news*)
□ The news spread rapidly. La nouvelle s'est propagée rapidement.

to **spread out** VERB
se disperser [28] (*people*)
□ The soldiers spread out across the field. Les soldats se sont dispersés dans le champ.

spreadsheet NOUN
le tableur *masc* (*computer program*)

★ **spring** NOUN
1 le printemps *masc* (*season*)
■ **in spring** au printemps
2 le ressort *masc* (*metal coil*)
3 la source *fem* (*water hole*)

spring-cleaning NOUN
le grand nettoyage de printemps *masc*

springtime NOUN
le printemps *masc*
■ **in springtime** au printemps

sprinkler NOUN
l'arroseur *masc* (*for lawn*)

sprint NOUN
▷ *see also* **sprint** VERB
le sprint *masc*

to **sprint** VERB
▷ *see also* **sprint** NOUN
courir [16] à toute vitesse
□ She sprinted for the bus. Elle a couru à toute vitesse pour attraper le bus.

sprinter NOUN
le sprinteur *masc*
la sprinteuse *fem*

sprouts PL NOUN
■ **Brussels sprouts** les choux de Bruxelles *masc pl*

spy NOUN
▷ *see also* **spy** VERB
l'espion *masc*
l'espionne *fem*

to **spy** VERB
▷ *see also* **spy** NOUN
■ **to spy on somebody** espionner [28] quelqu'un

Numbers in brackets refer to verb tables on pages 650 to 658

spying NOUN
l'espionnage *masc*

to **squabble** VERB
se chamailler [28]
□ Stop squabbling! Arrêtez de vous chamailler!

★ **square** NOUN
▷ *see also* **square** ADJECTIVE
1 le carré *masc*
□ a square and a triangle un carré et un triangle
2 la place *fem*
□ the town square la place de l'hôtel de ville

★ **square** ADJECTIVE
▷ *see also* **square** NOUN
carré (FEM carrée)
□ two square metres deux mètres carrés
■ **It's two metres square.** Ça fait deux mètres sur deux.

squash NOUN
▷ *see also* **squash** VERB
le squash *masc* (*sport*)
□ I play squash. Je joue au squash.
■ **a squash court** un court de squash
■ **a squash racket** une raquette de squash
■ **orange squash** l'orangeade *fem*
■ **lemon squash** la citronnade
■ **mint squash** le sirop de menthe

to **squash** VERB
▷ *see also* **squash** NOUN
écraser [28]
□ You're squashing me. Tu m'écrases.

to **squeak** VERB
1 pousser [28] un petit cri (*mouse, child*)
2 grincer [12] (*creak*)

★ to **squeeze** VERB
1 presser [28] (*fruit, toothpaste*)
2 serrer [28] (*hand, arm*)

to **squeeze in** VERB
1 trouver [28] une petite place
□ It was a tiny car, but we managed to squeeze in. La voiture était toute petite, mais nous avons réussi à trouver une petite place.
2 caser [28] (*for appointment*)
□ I can squeeze you in at two o'clock. Je peux vous caser à deux heures.

to **squint** VERB
▷ *see also* **squint** NOUN
loucher [28]

squint NOUN
▷ *see also* **squint** VERB
■ **He has a squint.** Il louche.

★ **squirrel** NOUN
l'écureuil *masc*

to **stab** VERB
poignarder [28]

★ **stable** NOUN
▷ *see also* **stable** ADJECTIVE
l'écurie *fem*

★ **stable** ADJECTIVE
▷ *see also* **stable** NOUN
stable (FEM stable)
□ a stable relationship une relation stable

stack NOUN
la pile *fem*
□ a stack of books une pile de livres

★ **stadium** NOUN
le stade *masc*

★ **staff** NOUN
1 le personnel *masc* (*in company*)
2 les professeurs *masc pl* (*in school*)

staffroom NOUN
la salle des professeurs *fem*

★ **stage** NOUN
1 la scène *fem* (*in plays*)
2 l'estrade *fem* (*for speeches, lectures*)
■ **at this stage 1** à ce stade □ at this stage in the negotiations à ce stade des négociations
2 pour l'instant □ At this stage, we can't be sure. Pour l'instant, nous n'avons aucune certitude.
■ **to do something in stages** faire [36] quelque chose étape par étape

> **BE CAREFUL!**
> Do not translate **stage** by the French word **stage**.

to **stagger** VERB
chanceler [4]

stain NOUN
▷ *see also* **stain** VERB
la tache *fem*

to **stain** VERB
▷ *see also* **stain** NOUN
tacher [28]

stainless steel NOUN
l'inox *masc*

stain remover NOUN
le détachant *masc*

stair NOUN
la marche *fem* (*step*)

staircase NOUN
l'escalier *masc*

★ **stairs** PL NOUN
l'escalier *masc sing*

stale ADJECTIVE
rassis (FEM rassie) (*bread*)

stalemate NOUN
le pat *masc* (*in chess*)

stall NOUN
le stand *masc*
□ He's got a market stall. Il a un stand au marché.
■ **the stalls** (*in theatre*) l'orchestre *masc sing*

stamina NOUN
l'endurance *fem*

stammer NOUN
le bégaiement *masc*
■ **He's got a stammer.** Il bégaie.

★to **stamp** VERB
▷ *see also* **stamp** NOUN
affranchir [38] (*letter*)
■ **to stamp one's foot** taper [28] du pied

★**stamp** NOUN
▷ *see also* **stamp** VERB
1 le timbre *masc*
□ My grandad's hobby is stamp collecting. Mon grand-père collectionne les timbres.
■ **a stamp album** un album de timbres
■ **a stamp collection** une collection de timbres
2 le tampon *masc* (*rubber stamp*)

stamped ADJECTIVE
affranchi (FEM affranchie)
□ The letter wasn't stamped. La lettre n'était pas affranchie.
■ **Enclose a stamped addressed envelope.** Joindre une enveloppe affranchie à vos nom et adresse.

★to **stand** VERB
1 être [35] debout (*be standing*)
□ He was standing by the door. Il était debout à la porte.
2 se lever [43] (*stand up*)
3 supporter [28] (*tolerate, withstand*)
□ I can't stand all this noise. Je ne supporte pas tout ce bruit.

to **stand for** VERB
1 être [35] l'abréviation de (*be short for*)
□ 'DM' stands for 'direct message'. 'DM' est l'abréviation de 'direct message'.
2 supporter [28] (*tolerate*)
□ I won't stand for it! Je ne supporterai pas ça!
■ **to stand in for somebody** remplacer [12] quelqu'un

to **stand out** VERB
se distinguer [28]
□ None of the candidates really stood out. Aucun des candidats ne s'est vraiment distingué.
■ **She really stands out in that orange coat.** Tout le monde la remarque avec ce manteau orange.

to **stand up** VERB
se lever [43] (*get up*)
■ **to stand up for** défendre [88] □ Stand up for your rights! Défendez vos droits!

★**standard** ADJECTIVE
▷ *see also* **standard** NOUN
1 courant (FEM courante)
□ standard French le français courant
2 ordinaire (FEM ordinaire) (*equipment*)
■ **the standard procedure** la procédure normale

★**standard** NOUN
▷ *see also* **standard** ADJECTIVE
le niveau *masc* (PL les niveaux)
□ The standard is very high. Le niveau est très haut.
■ **the standard of living** le niveau de vie
■ **She's got high standards.** Elle est très exigeante.

stand-by ticket NOUN
le billet stand-by *masc*

standpoint NOUN
le point de vue *masc*

stands PL NOUN
la tribune *fem sing* (*at sports ground*)

stank VERB ▷ *see* **stink**

staple NOUN
▷ *see also* **staple** VERB
l'agrafe *fem*

to **staple** VERB
▷ *see also* **staple** NOUN
agrafer [28]

stapler NOUN
l'agrafeuse *fem*

★**star** NOUN
▷ *see also* **star** VERB
1 l'étoile *fem* (*in sky*)
2 la vedette *fem* (*celebrity*)
□ He's a TV star. C'est une vedette de la télé.
■ **the stars** (*horoscope*) l' horoscope *masc*

★to **star** VERB
▷ *see also* **star** NOUN
être [35] la vedette
□ to star in a film être la vedette d'un film
■ **The film stars Kristen Stewart.** Le film a pour vedette Kristen Stewart.
■ **... starring Johnny Depp** ... avec Johnny Depp

to **stare** VERB
■ **to stare at something** fixer [28] quelque chose

stark ADVERB
■ **stark naked** complètement nu

★**start** NOUN
▷ *see also* **start** VERB
1 le début *masc*
□ It's not much, but it's a start. Ce n'est pas grand-chose, mais c'est un début.
■ **Shall we make a start on the washing-up?** On commence à faire la vaisselle?
2 le départ *masc* (*of race*)

★to **start** VERB
▷ *see also* **start** NOUN
1 commencer [12]
□ What time does it start? À quelle heure est-ce que ça commence?
■ **to start doing something** commencer [12] à faire quelque chose □ I started learning Chinese three years ago. J'ai commencé à apprendre le chinois il y a trois ans.

2 créer [18] (*organization*)
◻ He wants to start his own business. Il veut créer sa propre entreprise.
3 organiser [28] (*campaign*)
◻ She started a campaign against drugs. Elle a organisé une campagne contre la drogue.
4 démarrer [28] (*car*)
◻ He couldn't start the car. Il n'a pas réussi à démarrer la voiture. ◻ The car wouldn't start. La voiture ne voulait pas démarrer.

to **start off** VERB
commencer [12]
◻ Things started off badly. Les choses ont mal commencé. ◻ Let's start off with a reminder of what we did last week. Commençons par un rappel de ce que nous avons fait la semaine dernière. ◻ She started off by thanking everyone. Elle a commencé par remercier tout le monde.

starter NOUN
l'entrée *fem* (*first course*)

to **starve** VERB
mourir [51] de faim
◻ People were literally starving. Les gens mouraient littéralement de faim.
▪ **I'm starving!** Je meurs de faim!

★ **state** NOUN
▷ *see also* **state** VERB
l'état *masc*
▪ **He was in a real state.** Il était dans tous ses états.
▪ **the state** (*government*) l'État
▪ **the States** (*USA*) les États-Unis *masc pl*

★ to **state** VERB
▷ *see also* **state** NOUN
1 déclarer [28] (*say*)
◻ The prime minister stated that... Le Premier ministre a déclaré que...
2 donner [28] (*give*)
◻ Please state your name and address. Veuillez donner vos nom et adresse. ◻ He stated his opinion. Il a donné son avis.

stately home NOUN
le château *masc* (PL les châteaux)

★ **statement** NOUN
la déclaration *fem*

★ **station** NOUN
la gare *fem* (*railway*)
▪ **the bus station** la gare routière
▪ **a police station** un poste de police
▪ **a radio station** une station de radio

stationer's NOUN
la papeterie *fem*

station wagon NOUN (US)
le break *masc*

statue NOUN
la statue *fem*

status NOUN
le statut *masc*
◻ She's changed her status. Elle a changé son statut.

★ **stay** NOUN
▷ *see also* **stay** VERB
le séjour *masc*
◻ my stay in Switzerland mon séjour en Suisse

★ to **stay** VERB
▷ *see also* **stay** NOUN
1 rester [71E] (*remain*)
◻ Stay here! Reste ici!
2 loger [45] (*spend the night*)
◻ to stay with friends loger chez des amis
◻ Where are you staying? Où est-ce que vous logez?
▪ **to stay the night** passer [58] la nuit
▪ **We stayed in Belgium for a few days.** Nous avons passé quelques jours en Belgique.

to **stay in** VERB
rester [71E] à la maison (*not go out*)

to **stay up** VERB
rester [71E] debout
◻ We stayed up till midnight. Nous sommes restés debout jusqu'à minuit.

★ **steady** ADJECTIVE
1 régulier (FEM régulière)
◻ steady progress des progrès réguliers
2 stable (FEM stable)
◻ a steady job un emploi stable
3 ferme (FEM ferme) (*voice, hand*)
4 calme (FEM calme) (*person*)
▪ **a steady boyfriend** un copain
▪ **a steady girlfriend** une copine

steak NOUN
le steak *masc* (*beef*)
◻ steak and chips un steak frites

★ to **steal** VERB
voler [28]

★ **steam** NOUN
la vapeur *fem*
◻ a steam engine une locomotive à vapeur

★ **steel** NOUN
l'acier *masc*
◻ a steel door une porte en acier

steep ADJECTIVE
raide (FEM raide) (*slope*)

steeple NOUN
le clocher *masc*

steering wheel NOUN
le volant *masc*

★ **step** NOUN
▷ *see also* **step** VERB
1 le pas *masc* (*pace*)
◻ He took a step forward. Il a fait un pas en avant.
2 la marche *fem* (*stair*)

□ She tripped over the step. Elle a trébuché sur la marche.

★ to **step** VERB

▷ *see also* **step** NOUN

■ **to step aside** faire [36] un pas de côté

■ **to step back** faire [36] un pas en arrière

★ **stepbrother** NOUN

le demi-frère *masc*

★ **stepdaughter** NOUN

la belle-fille *fem* (PL les belles-filles)

★ **stepfather** NOUN

le beau-père *masc* (PL les beaux-pères)

stepladder NOUN

l'escabeau *masc* (PL les escabeaux)

★ **stepmother** NOUN

la belle-mère *fem* (PL les belles-mères)

★ **stepsister** NOUN

la demi-sœur *fem*

★ **stepson** NOUN

le beau-fils *masc* (PL les beaux-fils)

stereo NOUN

la chaîne *fem* (PL les chaînes)

sterling ADJECTIVE

■ **£500 sterling** cinq cents livres sterling

stew NOUN

le ragoût *masc*

★ **steward** NOUN

le steward *masc*

★ **stewardess** NOUN

l'hôtesse de l'air *fem*

★ **stick** NOUN

▷ *see also* **stick** VERB

1 le bâton *masc*

2 la canne *fem* (*walking stick*)

★ to **stick** VERB

▷ *see also* **stick** NOUN

coller [28] (*with adhesive*)

□ Stick the stamps on the envelope. Collez les timbres sur l'enveloppe.

to **stick out** VERB

sortir [79] (*project*)

□ A pen was sticking out of his pocket. Un stylo sortait de sa poche.

■ **She stuck out her tongue.** Elle a tiré la langue.

sticker NOUN

l'autocollant *masc*

stick insect NOUN

le phasme *masc*

sticky ADJECTIVE

1 poisseux (FEM poisseuse)

□ to have sticky hands avoir les mains poisseuses

2 adhésif (FEM adhésive)

□ a sticky label une étiquette adhésive

stiff ADJECTIVE, ADVERB

rigide (FEM rigide) (*rigid*)

■ **to have a stiff neck** avoir [8] un torticolis

■ **to feel stiff** avoir [8] des courbatures

■ **to be bored stiff** s'ennuyer [53] à mourir

■ **to be frozen stiff** être [35] mort de froid

■ **to be scared stiff** être [35] mort de peur

★ **still** ADVERB

▷ *see also* **still** ADJECTIVE

1 encore

□ I still haven't finished. Je n'ai pas encore fini.

□ Are you still in bed? Tu es encore au lit?

■ **better still** encore mieux

2 quand même (*even so*)

□ We lost, but it was still a good match. On a perdu, mais c'était quand même un bon match.

3 enfin (*after all*)

□ Still, it's the thought that counts. Enfin, c'est l'intention qui compte.

★ **still** ADJECTIVE

▷ *see also* **still** ADVERB

■ **Keep still!** Ne bouge pas!

■ **Sit still!** Reste tranquille!

sting NOUN

▷ *see also* **sting** VERB

la piqûre *fem*

□ a bee sting une piqûre d'abeille

to **sting** VERB

▷ *see also* **sting** NOUN

piquer [28]

□ I've been stung. J'ai été piqué.

stingy ADJECTIVE

pingre (FEM pingre)

to **stink** VERB

▷ *see also* **stink** NOUN

puer [28]

□ It stinks! Ça pue!

stink NOUN

▷ *see also* **stink** VERB

la puanteur *fem*

★ to **stir** VERB

remuer [28]

to **stitch** VERB

▷ *see also* **stitch** NOUN

coudre [15] (*cloth*)

stitch NOUN

▷ *see also* **stitch** VERB

1 le point *masc* (*in sewing*)

2 le point de suture *masc* (*in wound*)

□ I had five stitches. J'ai eu cinq points de suture.

stock NOUN

▷ *see also* **stock** VERB

1 la réserve *fem* (*supply*)

2 le stock *masc* (*in shop*)

□ in stock en stock

■ **out of stock** épuisé

3 le bouillon *masc*

□ chicken stock du bouillon de volaille

to **stock** VERB
▷ *see also* **stock** NOUN
avoir [8] (*have in stock*)
▫ Do you stock board games? Vous avez des jeux de société?

to **stock up** VERB
s'approvisionner [28]
▫ to stock up with something s'approvisionner en quelque chose

stock cube NOUN
le cube de bouillon *masc*

stocking NOUN
le bas *masc*

stole, stolen VERB ▷ *see* **steal**

★ **stomach** NOUN
l'estomac *masc*
▫ to have an upset stomach avoir l'estomac barbouillé

stomachache NOUN
■ **to have stomachache** avoir [8] mal au ventre

★ **stone** NOUN
1 la pierre *fem* (*rock*)
▫ a stone wall un mur en pierre
2 le noyau *masc* (PL les noyaux) (*in fruit*)
▫ a peach stone un noyau de pêche

DID YOU KNOW...?
In France, weight is expressed in kilos. A stone is about 6.3 kg.

■ **I weigh eight stone.** Je pèse cinquante kilos.

stood VERB ▷ *see* **stand**

stool NOUN
le tabouret *masc*

★ to **stop** VERB
▷ *see also* **stop** NOUN
1 arrêter [28]
▫ a campaign to stop whaling une campagne pour arrêter la chasse à la baleine
2 s'arrêter [28]
▫ The bus doesn't stop there. Le bus ne s'arrête pas là. ▫ I think the rain's going to stop. Je pense qu'il va s'arrêter de pleuvoir.
■ **to stop doing something** arrêter [28] de faire quelque chose ▫ to stop smoking arrêter de fumer
■ **to stop somebody doing something** empêcher [28] quelqu'un de faire quelque chose
■ **Stop!** Stop!

★ **stop** NOUN
▷ *see also* **stop** VERB
l'arrêt *masc*
▫ a bus stop un arrêt de bus
■ **This is my stop.** Je descends ici.

stopwatch NOUN
le chronomètre *masc*

store NOUN
▷ *see also* **store** VERB
1 le magasin *masc* (*shop*)
▫ a furniture store un magasin de meubles
2 la réserve *fem* (*stock, storeroom*)

BE CAREFUL!
Do not translate **store** by the French word **store**.

to **store** VERB
▷ *see also* **store** NOUN
1 garder [28]
▫ They store potatoes in the cellar. Ils gardent des pommes de terre dans la cave.
2 enregistrer [28] (*information*)

storey NOUN
l'étage *masc*
▫ a three-storey building un immeuble à trois étages

★ **storm** NOUN
1 la tempête *fem* (*gale*)
2 l'orage *masc* (*thunderstorm*)

stormy ADJECTIVE
orageux (FEM orageuse)

★ **story** NOUN
l'histoire *fem*

stove NOUN
1 la cuisinière *fem* (*in kitchen*)
2 le réchaud *masc* (*camping stove*)

★ **straight** ADJECTIVE
1 droit (FEM droite)
▫ a straight line une ligne droite
2 raide (FEM raide)
▫ straight hair les cheveux raides
3 hétéro (FEM hétéro) (*heterosexual*)
■ **straight away** tout de suite
■ **straight on** tout droit

straighteners PL NOUN
le fer à lisser *masc sing*
■ **a pair of straighteners** un fer à lisser

straightforward ADJECTIVE
simple (FEM simple)

strain NOUN
▷ *see also* **strain** VERB
le stress *masc*
■ **It was a strain.** C'était éprouvant.

to **strain** VERB
▷ *see also* **strain** NOUN
se faire [36] mal à
▫ I strained my back. Je me suis fait mal au dos.
■ **to strain a muscle** se froisser [28] un muscle

strained ADJECTIVE
froissé (FEM froissée) (*muscle*)

stranded ADJECTIVE
■ **We were stranded.** Nous étions coincés.

English-French

★ **strange** ADJECTIVE
bizarre (FEM bizarre)
□ That's strange! C'est bizarre!

stranger NOUN
l'inconnu *masc*
l'inconnue *fem*
□ Don't talk to strangers. Ne parle pas aux inconnus.
■ **I'm a stranger here.** Je ne suis pas d'ici.

to **strangle** VERB
étrangler [28]

strap NOUN
1 la courroie *fem* (*of bag, camera, suitcase*)
2 la bretelle *fem* (*of bra, dress*)
3 la lanière *fem* (*on shoe*)
4 le bracelet *masc* (*of watch*)

straw NOUN
la paille *fem*
■ **That's the last straw!** Ça, c'est le comble!

★ **strawberry** NOUN
la fraise *fem*
□ strawberry jam la confiture de fraises □ a strawberry ice cream une glace à la fraise

stray NOUN
■ **a stray cat** un chat perdu

★ **stream** NOUN
le ruisseau *masc* (PL les ruisseaux)

★ **street** NOUN
la rue *fem*
□ in the street dans la rue

streetcar NOUN (US)
le tramway *masc*

streetlamp NOUN
le réverbère *masc*

street plan NOUN
le plan de la ville *masc*

streetwise ADJECTIVE
dégourdi (FEM dégourdie)

★ **strength** NOUN
la force *fem*

★ to **stress** VERB
▷ *see also* **stress** NOUN
souligner [28]
□ I would like to stress that ... J'aimerais souligner que ...

★ **stress** NOUN
▷ *see also* **stress** VERB
le stress *masc*

★ to **stretch** VERB
1 s'étirer [28] (*person, animal*)
□ The dog woke up and stretched. Le chien s'est réveillé et s'est étiré.
2 se détendre [88] (*get bigger*)
□ My jumper stretched when I washed it. Mon pull s'est détendu au lavage.
3 tendre [88] (*stretch out*)
□ They stretched a rope between two trees. Ils ont tendu une corde entre deux arbres.
■ **to stretch out one's arms** tendre [88] les bras

stretcher NOUN
le brancard *masc*

stretchy ADJECTIVE
élastique (FEM élastique)

★ **strict** ADJECTIVE
strict (FEM stricte)

★ **strike** NOUN
▷ *see also* **strike** VERB
la grève *fem*
■ **to be on strike** être [35] en grève
■ **to go on strike** faire [36] grève

★ to **strike** VERB
▷ *see also* **strike** NOUN
1 sonner [28] (*clock*)
□ The clock struck three. L'horloge a sonné trois heures.
2 faire [36] grève (*go on strike*)
3 frapper [28] (*hit*)
■ **to strike a match** frotter [28] une allumette

striker NOUN
1 le/la gréviste *masc/fem* (*person on strike*)
2 le buteur *masc* (*footballer*)

striking ADJECTIVE
1 en grève (*on strike*)
□ striking journalists les journalistes en grève
2 frappant (FEM frappante) (*noticeable*)
□ a striking difference une différence frappante

★ **string** NOUN
1 la ficelle *fem*
□ a piece of string un bout de ficelle
2 la corde *fem* (*of violin, guitar*)

to **strip** VERB
▷ *see also* **strip** NOUN
se déshabiller [28] (*get undressed*)

strip NOUN
▷ *see also* **strip** VERB
la bande *fem*
■ **a strip cartoon** une bande dessinée

stripe NOUN
la rayure *fem*

striped ADJECTIVE
à rayures
□ a striped skirt une jupe à rayures

stripper NOUN
le strip-teaseur *masc*
la strip-teaseuse *fem*

stripy ADJECTIVE
rayé (FEM rayée)
□ a stripy shirt une chemise rayée

to **stroke** VERB
▷ *see also* **stroke** NOUN
caresser [28]

S

stroke NOUN
▷ *see also* **stroke** VERB
l'attaque *fem*
□ to have a stroke avoir une attaque

stroll NOUN
■ **to go for a stroll** aller [3E] faire une petite promenade

stroller NOUN (US)
le poussette *fem*

★ **strong** ADJECTIVE
1 fort (FEM forte)
□ She's very strong. Elle est très forte.
2 résistant (FEM résistante) (*material*)

strongly ADVERB
fortement
□ We recommend strongly that ... Nous recommandons fortement que ...
■ **He smelt strongly of garlic.** Il sentait fort l'ail.
■ **strongly built** solidement bâti
■ **I don't feel strongly about it.** Ça m'est égal.

struck VERB ▷ *see* **strike**

to **struggle** VERB
▷ *see also* **struggle** NOUN
se débattre [9] (*physically*)
□ He struggled, but he couldn't escape. Il s'est débattu, mais il n'a pas pu s'échapper.
■ **to struggle to do something** **1** (*fight*) se battre [9] pour faire quelque chose □ He struggled to get custody of his daughter. Il s'est battu pour obtenir la garde de sa fille.
2 (*have difficulty*) avoir [8] du mal à faire quelque chose □ She struggled to get the door open. Elle a eu du mal à ouvrir la porte.

struggle NOUN
▷ *see also* **struggle** VERB
la lutte *fem* (*for independence, equality*)
■ **It was a struggle.** Ça a été laborieux.

stub NOUN
le mégot *masc* (*of cigarette*)

to **stub out** VERB
écraser [28] (*cigarette*)

stubborn ADJECTIVE
têtu (FEM têtue)

stuck VERB ▷ *see* **stick**

stuck ADJECTIVE
coincé (FEM coincée) (*jammed*)
□ It's stuck. C'est coincé.
■ **to get stuck** rester [71E] coincé □ We got stuck in a traffic jam. Nous sommes restés coincés dans un embouteillage.

stuck-up ADJECTIVE
coincé (FEM coincée) (*informal*)

stud NOUN
1 la boucle d'oreille *fem* (*earring*)
2 le crampon *masc* (*on football boots*)

★ **student** NOUN
l'étudiant *masc*
l'étudiante *fem*

studio NOUN
le studio *masc*
□ a TV studio un studio de télévision
■ **a studio flat** un studio

★ to **study** VERB
1 faire [36] des études (*at university*)
□ I plan to study biology. J'ai l'intention de faire des études de biologie.
2 travailler [28] (*do homework*)
□ I've got to study tonight. Je dois travailler ce soir.

★ **stuff** NOUN
1 le truc *masc* (*substance*)
□ I need some stuff for hay fever. J'ai besoin d'un truc contre le rhume des foins.
2 les trucs *masc pl* (*things*)
□ There's some stuff on the table for you. Il y a des trucs sur la table pour toi.
3 les affaires *fem pl* (*possessions*)
□ Have you got all your stuff? Est-ce que tu as toutes tes affaires?

stuffy ADJECTIVE
mal aéré (FEM mal aérée) (*room*)
■ **It's really stuffy in here.** On étouffe ici.

to **stumble** VERB
trébucher [28]

stung VERB ▷ *see* **sting**

stunk VERB ▷ *see* **stink**

stunned ADJECTIVE
sidéré (FEM sidérée) (*amazed*)
□ I was stunned. J'étais sidéré.

stunning ADJECTIVE
superbe (FEM superbe)

stunt NOUN
la cascade *fem* (*in film*)

★ **stupid** ADJECTIVE
stupide (FEM stupide)
□ a stupid joke une plaisanterie stupide
■ **Me, go running? Don't be stupid!** Moi, faire du jogging? Ne dis pas de bêtises!

to **stutter** VERB
▷ *see also* **stutter** NOUN
bégayer [59]

stutter NOUN
▷ *see also* **stutter** VERB
■ **He's got a stutter.** Il bégaie.

★ **style** NOUN
le style *masc*
□ That's not his style. Ça n'est pas son style.

★ **subject** NOUN
1 le sujet *masc*
□ The subject of my presentation was social media. Le sujet de mon exposé, c'était les médias sociaux.

2 la matière *fem* (*at school*)
□ What's your favourite subject? Quelle est ta matière préférée?

subjunctive NOUN
le subjonctif *masc*
□ in the subjunctive au subjonctif

submarine NOUN
le sous-marin *masc*

subscription NOUN
l'abonnement *masc* (*to paper, magazine*)
■ **to take out a subscription to something** s'abonner [28] à quelque chose

subsequently ADVERB
en conséquence

to **subsidize** VERB
subventionner [28]

subsidy NOUN
la subvention *fem*

★ **substance** NOUN
la substance *fem*

★ **substitute** NOUN
▷ *see also* **substitute** VERB
le remplaçant *masc*
la remplaçante *fem* (*person*)

★ to **substitute** VERB
▷ *see also* **substitute** NOUN
substituer [28]
□ to substitute A for B substituer A à B

subtitled ADJECTIVE
sous-titré (FEM sous-titrée)

subtitles PL NOUN
les sous-titres *masc pl*
□ a French film with English subtitles un film français avec des sous-titres en anglais

subtle ADJECTIVE
subtil (FEM subtile)

to **subtract** VERB
retrancher [28]
□ to subtract 3 from 5 retrancher trois de cinq

suburb NOUN
la banlieue *fem*
□ a suburb of Paris une banlieue de Paris
■ **the suburbs** la banlieue □ They live in the suburbs. Ils habitent en banlieue.

suburban ADJECTIVE
de banlieue
□ a suburban train un train de banlieue

subway NOUN
le passage souterrain *masc* (*underpass*)

★ to **succeed** VERB
réussir [38]
□ to succeed in doing something réussir à faire quelque chose

★ **success** NOUN
le succès *masc*
□ The play was a great success. La pièce a eu beaucoup de succès.

★ **successful** ADJECTIVE
réussi (FEM réussie)
□ a successful attempt une tentative réussie
■ **to be successful in doing something** réussir [38] à faire quelque chose
■ **She's a successful designer.** C'est une designer couronnée de succès.

successfully ADVERB
avec succès

successive ADJECTIVE
■ **on four successive occasions** quatre fois de suite

★ **such** ADJECTIVE, ADVERB
si
□ such nice people des gens si gentils □ such a long journey un voyage si long
■ **such a lot of** tellement de □ such a lot of work tellement de travail
■ **such as** (*like*) comme □ hot countries, such as India les pays chauds, comme l'Inde
■ **not as such** pas exactement □ He's not an expert as such, but ... Ce n'est pas exactement un expert, mais ...
■ **There's no such thing.** Ça n'existe pas.
□ There's no such thing as the yeti. Le yéti n'existe pas.

such-and-such ADJECTIVE
tel ou tel (FEM telle ou telle)
□ such-and-such a place tel ou tel endroit

to **suck** VERB
sucer [12]
□ to suck one's thumb sucer son pouce

★ **sudden** ADJECTIVE
soudain (FEM soudaine)
□ a sudden change un changement soudain
■ **all of a sudden** tout à coup

★ **suddenly** ADVERB
1 brusquement (*stop, leave, change*)
2 subitement (*die*)
3 soudain (*at beginning of sentence*)
□ Suddenly, the door opened. Soudain, la porte s'est ouverte.

suede NOUN
le daim *masc*
□ a suede jacket une veste en daim

★ to **suffer** VERB
souffrir [54]
□ She was really suffering. Elle souffrait beaucoup.
■ **to suffer from a disease** avoir [8] une maladie □ I suffer from hay fever. J'ai le rhume des foins.

to **suffocate** VERB
suffoquer [28]

★ **sugar** NOUN
le sucre *masc*
□ Do you take sugar? Est-ce que vous prenez du sucre?

★ to **suggest** VERB
suggérer [34]
□ I suggested they set off early. Je leur ai suggéré de partir de bonne heure.

★ **suggestion** NOUN
la suggestion *fem*
□ to make a suggestion faire une suggestion

★ **suicide** NOUN
le suicide *masc*
■ **to commit suicide** se suicider [28]

suicide bomber NOUN
le/la kamikaze *masc/fem*

★ **suit** NOUN
▷ *see also* **suit** VERB
1 le costume *masc* (*man's*)
2 le tailleur *masc* (*woman's*)

★ to **suit** VERB
▷ *see also* **suit** NOUN
1 convenir [89] à (*be convenient for*)
□ What time would suit you? Quelle heure vous conviendrait?
■ **That suits me fine.** Ça m'arrange.
■ **Suit yourself!** Comme tu veux!
2 aller [3E] bien à (*look good on*)
□ That dress really suits you. Cette robe te va vraiment bien.

★ **suitable** ADJECTIVE
1 convenable (FEM convenable)
□ a suitable time une heure convenable
2 approprié (FEM appropriée) (*clothes*)
□ suitable clothing des vêtements appropriés

suitcase NOUN
la valise *fem*

suite NOUN
1 la suite *fem* (*in hotel*)
2 l'ensemble de meubles *masc*
□ a bathroom suite un ensemble de meubles de salle de bains

to **sulk** VERB
bouder [28]

sulky ADJECTIVE
boudeur (FEM boudeuse)

sultana NOUN
le raisin sec *masc* (PL les raisins secs)

★ **sum** NOUN
1 le calcul *masc* (*calculation*)
□ She's good at sums. Elle est bonne en calcul.
2 la somme *fem* (*amount*)
□ a sum of money une somme d'argent

to **sum up** VERB
résumer [28]

to **summarize** VERB
résumer [28]

summary NOUN
le résumé *masc*

★ **summer** NOUN
l'été *masc*
■ **in summer** en été
■ **summer clothes** les vêtements d'été
■ **the summer holidays** les vacances d'été
■ **a summer camp** (US) une colonie de vacances

summertime NOUN
l'été *masc*
■ **in summertime** en été

★ **summit** NOUN
le sommet *masc*

★ **sun** NOUN
le soleil *masc*
□ in the sun au soleil

to **sunbathe** VERB
se bronzer [28]

sunblock NOUN
l'écran total *masc*

sunburn NOUN
le coup de soleil *masc*

sunburnt ADJECTIVE
■ **I got sunburnt.** J'ai attrapé un coup de soleil.

★ **Sunday** NOUN
le dimanche *masc*
□ on Sunday dimanche □ on Sundays le dimanche □ every Sunday tous les dimanches □ last Sunday dimanche dernier □ next Sunday dimanche prochain

Sunday school NOUN
le catéchisme *masc*
□ to go to Sunday school aller au catéchisme

sunflower NOUN
le tournesol *masc*
□ sunflower seeds des graines de tournesol

sung VERB ▷ *see* **sing**

sunglasses PL NOUN
les lunettes de soleil *fem pl*

sunk VERB ▷ *see* **sink**

sunlight NOUN
le soleil *masc*

sunny ADJECTIVE
ensoleillé (FEM ensoleillée)
□ a sunny morning une matinée ensoleillée
■ **It's sunny.** Il y a du soleil.
■ **a sunny day** une journée ensoleillée

sunrise NOUN
le lever du soleil *masc*

sunroof NOUN
le toit ouvrant *masc*

sunscreen NOUN
la crème solaire *fem*

sunset NOUN
le coucher du soleil *masc*

sunshine NOUN
le soleil *masc*

sunstroke NOUN
l'insolation *fem*
□ to get sunstroke attraper une insolation

suntan NOUN
le bronzage *masc*
■ **suntan lotion** la crème solaire

★**super** ADJECTIVE
formidable (FEM formidable)

★**superb** ADJECTIVE
superbe (FEM superbe)

★**supermarket** NOUN
le supermarché *masc*

supernatural ADJECTIVE
surnaturel (FEM surnaturelle)

superstitious ADJECTIVE
superstitieux (FEM superstitieuse)

to **supervise** VERB
surveiller [28]

supervisor NOUN
1 le surveillant *masc*
la surveillante *fem* (*in factory*)
2 le chef de rayon *masc* (*in department store*)

supper NOUN
le dîner *masc*

supplement NOUN
le supplément *masc*

supplies PL NOUN
les vivres *masc pl* (*food*)

★to **supply** VERB
▷ *see also* **supply** NOUN
fournir [38] (*provide*)
■ **to supply somebody with something** fournir [38] quelque chose à quelqu'un □ The centre supplied us with all the equipment. Le centre nous a fourni tout l'équipement.

★**supply** NOUN
▷ *see also* **supply** VERB
la provision *fem*
□ a supply of paper une provision de papier
■ **the water supply** (*to town*) l'approvisionnement en eau *masc*

supply teacher NOUN
le remplaçant *masc*
la remplaçante *fem*

★to **support** VERB
▷ *see also* **support** NOUN
1 soutenir [83]
□ My mum has always supported me. Ma mère m'a toujours soutenu.
2 être [35] supporter de
□ What team do you support? Tu es supporter de quelle équipe?
3 subvenir [89] aux besoins de (*financially*)
□ She had to support five children on her own. Elle a dû subvenir toute seule aux besoins de cinq enfants.

BE CAREFUL!
Do not translate **to support** by the French word **supporter**.

★**support** NOUN
▷ *see also* **support** VERB
le soutien *masc* (*backing*)

★**supporter** NOUN
1 le supporter *masc*
□ a Liverpool supporter un supporter de Liverpool
2 le sympathisant *masc*
la sympathisante *fem*
□ a supporter of the Labour Party un sympathisant du parti travailliste

★to **suppose** VERB
imaginer [28]
□ I suppose he's late. J'imagine qu'il est en retard. □ Suppose you won the lottery. Imaginez que vous gagniez à la loterie.
■ **I suppose so.** J'imagine.
■ **to be supposed to do something** être [35] censé faire quelque chose □ You're supposed to show your passport. On est censé montrer son passeport.

supposing CONJUNCTION
si
□ Supposing you won the lottery ... Si tu gagnais à la loterie ...

surcharge NOUN
la surcharge *fem*

★**sure** ADJECTIVE
sûr (FEM sûre)
□ Are you sure? Tu es sûr?
■ **Sure!** Bien sûr!
■ **to make sure that ...** vérifier [19] que ...
□ I'm going to make sure the door's locked. Je vais vérifier que la porte est fermée à clé.

★**surely** ADVERB
■ **Surely you haven't forgotten?** Tu n'as sûrement pas oublié, n'est-ce pas?
■ **She will get into university, surely?** J'imagine qu'elle ira à l'université, non?

surf NOUN
▷ *see also* **surf** VERB
le ressac *masc*

to **surf** VERB
▷ *see also* **surf** NOUN
surfer [28]
■ **to go surfing** faire [36] du surf
■ **to surf the Net** surfer [28] sur le Net

★**surface** NOUN
la surface *fem*

surfboard NOUN
la planche de surf *fem*

surfing NOUN
le surf *masc*
□ to go surfing faire du surf

surgeon NOUN
le chirurgien *masc*
□ She's a surgeon. Elle est chirurgien.

★**surgery** NOUN
le cabinet médical *masc* (*doctor's surgery*)
■ **surgery hours** les heures de consultation *fem pl*

surname NOUN
le nom de famille *masc*

★**surprise** NOUN
la surprise *fem*

★**surprised** ADJECTIVE
surpris (FEM surprise)
□ I was surprised to see him. J'ai été surpris de le voir.

★**surprising** ADJECTIVE
surprenant (FEM surprenante)

★to **surrender** VERB
capituler [28]

surrogate mother NOUN
la mère porteuse *fem*

★to **surround** VERB
encercler [28]
□ The police surrounded the house. La police a encerclé la maison.
■ **surrounded by** entouré de □ The house is surrounded by trees. La maison est entourée d'arbres.

surroundings PL NOUN
le cadre *masc sing*
□ a hotel in beautiful surroundings un hôtel situé dans un beau cadre

★**survey** NOUN
l'enquête *fem* (*research*)

surveyor NOUN
1 l'expert en bâtiment *masc* (*of buildings*)
2 le/la géomètre *masc/fem* (*of land*)

survivor NOUN
le survivant *masc*
la survivante *fem*
□ There were no survivors. Il n'y a pas eu de survivants.

★to **suspect** VERB
▷ *see also* **suspect** NOUN
soupçonner [28]

★**suspect** NOUN
▷ *see also* **suspect** VERB
le suspect *masc*
la suspecte *fem*

to **suspend** VERB
1 exclure [13] (*from school, team*)
□ He's been suspended. Il s'est fait exclure.
2 suspendre [88] (*from job*)

suspenders PL NOUN (US)
les bretelles *fem pl* (*braces*)

suspense NOUN
1 l'attente *fem* (*waiting*)
□ The suspense was terrible. L'attente a été terrible.
2 le suspense *masc* (*in story*)
□ a film with lots of suspense un film avec beaucoup de suspense

suspension NOUN
1 l'exclusion *fem* (*from school, team*)
2 la suspension *fem* (*from job*)

suspicious ADJECTIVE
1 méfiant (FEM méfiante)
□ He was suspicious at first. Il était méfiant au début.
2 louche (FEM louche) (*suspicious-looking*)
□ a suspicious person un individu louche

to **swallow** VERB
avaler [28]

swam VERB ▷ *see* **swim**

swan NOUN
le cygne *masc*

to **swap** VERB
échanger [45]
□ Do you want to swap? Tu veux échanger?
□ to swap A for B échanger A contre B

to **swat** VERB
écraser [28]

to **sway** VERB
osciller [28]

to **swear** VERB
jurer [28] (*make an oath, curse*)

swearword NOUN
le gros mot *masc*

sweat NOUN
▷ *see also* **sweat** VERB
la transpiration *fem*

to **sweat** VERB
▷ *see also* **sweat** NOUN
transpirer [28]

sweater NOUN
le pull *masc*

sweatshirt NOUN
le sweat *masc*

sweaty ADJECTIVE
1 en sueur (*person, face*)
□ I'm all sweaty. Je suis en sueur.
2 moite (FEM moite) (*hands*)

★**Swede** NOUN
le Suédois *masc*
la Suédoise *fem* (*person*)

swede NOUN
le rutabaga *masc* (*vegetable*)

★**Sweden** NOUN
la Suède *fem*
■ **in Sweden** en Suède
■ **to Sweden** en Suède

★**Swedish** NOUN
▷ *see also* **Swedish** ADJECTIVE
le suédois *masc* (*language*)

★ **Swedish** ADJECTIVE
▷ *see also* **Swedish** NOUN
suédois (FEM suédoise)
□ She's Swedish. Elle est suédoise.

★ to **sweep** VERB
balayer [59]
■ **to sweep the floor** balayer [59]

★ **sweet** NOUN
▷ *see also* **sweet** ADJECTIVE
1 le bonbon *masc* (*candy*)
□ a bag of sweets un paquet de bonbons
2 le dessert *masc* (*pudding*)
□ What sweet did you have? Qu'est-ce que vous avez mangé comme dessert?

★ **sweet** ADJECTIVE
▷ *see also* **sweet** NOUN
1 sucré (FEM sucrée) (*not savoury*)
2 gentil (FEM gentille) (*kind*)
□ That was really sweet of you. C'était vraiment gentil de ta part.
3 mignon (FEM mignonne) (*cute*)
□ Isn't she sweet? Comme elle est mignonne!
■ **sweet and sour chicken** le poulet à la sauce aigre-douce

sweetcorn NOUN
le maïs doux *masc*

sweltering ADJECTIVE
■ **It was sweltering.** Il faisait une chaleur étouffante.

swept VERB ▷ *see* **sweep**

to **swerve** VERB
faire [36] une embardée
□ He swerved to avoid the cyclist. Il a fait une embardée pour éviter le cycliste.

★ **swim** NOUN
▷ *see also* **swim** VERB
■ **to go for a swim** aller [3E] se baigner

★ to **swim** VERB
▷ *see also* **swim** NOUN
nager [45]
□ Can you swim? Tu sais nager?
■ **She swam across the river.** Elle a traversé la rivière à la nage.

swimmer NOUN
le nageur *masc*
la nageuse *fem*
□ She's a good swimmer. C'est une bonne nageuse.

★ **swimming** NOUN
la natation *fem*
□ Do you like swimming? Tu aimes la natation?
■ **to go swimming** (*in a pool*) aller [3E] à la piscine
■ **a swimming cap** un bonnet de bain
■ **a swimming costume** un maillot de bain
■ **a swimming pool** une piscine
■ **swimming trunks** le maillot de bain

★ **swimsuit** NOUN
le maillot de bain *masc*

★ **swing** NOUN
▷ *see also* **swing** VERB
la balançoire *fem* (*in playground, garden*)

★ to **swing** VERB
▷ *see also* **swing** NOUN
1 se balancer [12]
□ A bunch of keys swung from his belt. Un trousseau de clés se balançait à sa ceinture.
■ **Sam was swinging an umbrella as he walked.** Sam balançait son parapluie en marchant.
2 virer [28]
□ The canoe swung round sharply. Le canoë a viré brusquement.

★ **Swiss** NOUN
▷ *see also* **Swiss** ADJECTIVE
le/la Suisse *masc/fem* (*person*)
■ **the Swiss** les Suisses

★ **Swiss** ADJECTIVE
▷ *see also* **Swiss** NOUN
suisse (FEM suisse)
□ Sabine's Swiss. Sabine est suisse.

★ **switch** NOUN
▷ *see also* **switch** VERB
le bouton *masc* (*for light, radio etc*)

★ to **switch** VERB
▷ *see also* **switch** NOUN
changer [45] de
□ We switched partners. Nous avons changé de partenaire.

to **switch off** VERB
1 éteindre [60] (*electrical appliance*)
2 arrêter [28] (*engine, machine*)

to **switch on** VERB
1 allumer [28] (*electrical appliance*)
2 mettre [47] en marche (*engine, machine*)

★ **Switzerland** NOUN
la Suisse *fem*
■ **in Switzerland** en Suisse

swollen ADJECTIVE
enflé (FEM enflée) (*arm, leg*)

to **swop** VERB
échanger [45]
□ Do you want to swop? Tu veux échanger? □ to swop A for B échanger A contre B

sword NOUN
l'épée *fem*

swore, sworn VERB ▷ *see* **swear**

swot NOUN
▷ *see also* **swot** VERB
le bûcheur *masc*
la bûcheuse *fem*

 Numbers in brackets refer to verb tables on pages 650 to 658

to **swot** VERB
▷ *see also* **swot** NOUN
bosser [28] dur
□ I'll have to swot for my maths exam. Je vais devoir bosser dur pour mon examen de maths.

swum VERB ▷ *see* **swim**

swung VERB ▷ *see* **swing**

syllabus NOUN
le programme *masc*
□ on the syllabus au programme

★ **symbol** NOUN
le symbole *masc*

sympathetic ADJECTIVE
compréhensif (FEM compréhensive)

BE CAREFUL!
Do not translate **sympathetic** by the French word **sympathique**.

to **sympathize** VERB
■ **to sympathize with somebody**
comprendre [65] quelqu'un

★ **sympathy** NOUN
la compassion *fem*

★ **symptom** NOUN
le symptôme *masc*

syringe NOUN
la seringue *fem*

★ **system** NOUN
le système *masc*

Tt

★**table** NOUN
la table *fem*
□ to lay the table mettre la table
tablecloth NOUN
la nappe *fem*
tablespoon NOUN
la grande cuillère *fem*
▪ **two tablespoons of sugar** deux cuillerées à soupe de sucre
tablet NOUN
1 le comprimé *masc* (*medicine*)
2 la tablette *fem* (*computer*)
table tennis NOUN
le ping-pong *masc*
□ to play table tennis jouer au ping-pong
tabloid NOUN
le tabloïd *masc*
★**tackle** NOUN
▷ *see also* **tackle** VERB
1 le tacle *masc* (*in football*)
2 le plaquage *masc* (*in rugby*)
▪ **fishing tackle** le matériel de pêche
★to **tackle** VERB
▷ *see also* **tackle** NOUN
1 tacler [28] (*in football*)
2 plaquer [28] (*in rugby*)
▪ **to tackle a problem** s'attaquer [28] à un problème
tact NOUN
le tact *masc*
tactful ADJECTIVE
plein de tact (FEM pleine de tact)
tactics PL NOUN
la tactique *fem sing*
tactless ADJECTIVE
▪ **to be tactless** manquer [28] de tact □ a tactless remark une remarque qui manque de tact
tadpole NOUN
le têtard *masc*
tag NOUN
l'étiquette *fem* (*label*)
★**tail** NOUN
la queue *fem*
▪ **Heads or tails?** Pile ou face?
tailor NOUN
le tailleur *masc*
la tailleuse *fem*
★to **take** VERB
1 prendre [65]
□ Are you taking your new camera? Tu prends ton nouvel appareil photo? □ He took a plate from the cupboard. Il a pris une assiette dans le placard. □ It takes about an hour. Ça prend environ une heure.
2 emmener [43] (*person*)
□ When will you take me to London? Quand est-ce que tu vas m'emmener à Londres?
▪ **to take something somewhere** emporter [28] quelque chose quelque part □ Do you take your exercise books home? Vous emportez vos cahiers chez vous? □ Don't take anything valuable with you. N'emportez pas d'objets de valeur. □ I'm going to take my coat to the cleaner's. Je vais donner mon manteau à nettoyer.
3 demander [28] (*effort, skill*)
□ That takes a lot of courage. Cela demande beaucoup de courage.
▪ **It takes a lot of money to do that.** Il faut beaucoup d'argent pour faire ça.
4 supporter [28] (*tolerate*)
□ He can't take being criticized. Il ne supporte pas d'être critiqué.
5 passer [58] (*exam, test*)
□ Have you taken your driving test yet? Est-ce que tu as déjà passé ton permis de conduire?
6 faire [36] (*subject*)
□ I decided to take French instead of German. J'ai décidé de faire du français au lieu de l'allemand.
to **take after** VERB
ressembler [28] à
□ She takes after her mother. Elle ressemble à sa mère.
to **take apart** VERB
▪ **to take something apart** démonter [28] quelque chose
to **take away** VERB
1 emporter [28] (*object*)
2 emmener [43] (*person*)
▪ **to take something away** (*confiscate*) confisquer [28] quelque chose
▪ **pizza to take away** pizzas à emporter

to **take back** VERB
rapporter [28]
□ I took it back to the shop. Je l'ai rapporté au magasin.
■ **I take it all back!** Je retire ce que j'ai dit!

to **take down** VERB
1 enlever [43] *(poster, sign)*
2 décrocher [28] *(painting, curtains)*
3 démonter [28E] *(tent, scaffolding)*
4 prendre [65] en note *(make a note of)*
□ He took down the details in his notebook. Il a pris tous les détails en note dans son carnet.

to **take in** VERB
comprendre [65] *(understand)*
□ I didn't really take it in. Je n'ai pas bien compris.

to **take off** VERB
1 décoller [28] *(plane)*
□ The plane took off twenty minutes late. L'avion a décollé avec vingt minutes de retard.
2 enlever [43] *(clothes)*
□ Take your coat off. Enlevez votre manteau.

to **take out** VERB
sortir [79] *(from container, pocket)*
■ **He took her out to the theatre.** Il l'a emmenée au théâtre.

to **take over** VERB
prendre [65] la relève
□ I'll take over now. Je vais prendre la relève.
■ **to take over from somebody** remplacer [12] quelqu'un

takeaway NOUN
le plat à emporter *masc (meal)*
■ **a Chinese takeaway** un restaurant chinois qui vend des plats à emporter

taken VERB ▷ *see* **take**

takeoff NOUN
le décollage *masc (of plane)*

talcum powder NOUN
le talc *masc*

★ **tale** NOUN
le conte *masc (story)*

★ **talent** NOUN
le talent *masc*
□ She's got lots of talent. Elle a beaucoup de talent.
■ **to have a talent for something** être [35] doué pour quelque chose □ He's got a real talent for languages. Il est vraiment doué pour les langues.

talented ADJECTIVE
■ **She's a talented pianist.** C'est une pianiste de talent.

★ **talk** NOUN
▷ *see also* **talk** VERB
1 l'exposé *masc (speech)*
□ She gave a talk on rock climbing. Elle a fait un exposé sur la varappe.
2 la conversation *fem (conversation)*
□ I had a talk with my mum about it. J'ai eu une conversation avec ma mère à ce sujet.
3 les racontars *masc pl (gossip)*
□ It's just talk. Ce sont des racontars.

★ to **talk** VERB
▷ *see also* **talk** NOUN
parler [28]
□ to talk about something parler de quelque chose
■ **to talk something over with somebody** discuter [28] de quelque chose avec quelqu'un

talkative ADJECTIVE
bavard (FEM bavarde)

★ **tall** ADJECTIVE
1 grand (FEM grande) *(person, tree)*
■ **to be 2 metres tall** mesurer [28] deux mètres
2 haut (FEM haute) *(building)*

tame ADJECTIVE
apprivoisé (FEM apprivoisée) *(animal)*
□ They've got a tame hedgehog. Ils ont un hérisson apprivoisé.

tampon NOUN
le tampon *masc*

tan NOUN
le bronzage *masc*
□ She's got an amazing tan. Elle a un bronzage superbe.

tangerine NOUN
la mandarine *fem*

tangle NOUN
1 l'enchevêtrement *masc (ropes, cables)*
2 le nœud *masc (hair)*
■ **to be in a tangle** **1** *(ropes, cables)* être [35] enchevêtré **2** *(hair)* être [35] emmêlé

tank NOUN
1 le réservoir *masc (for water, petrol)*
2 le char d'assaut *masc (military)*
■ **a fish tank** un aquarium

tanker NOUN
1 le pétrolier *masc (ship)*
■ **an oil tanker** un pétrolier
2 le camion-citerne *masc (truck)*
■ **a petrol tanker** un camion-citerne

★ **tap** NOUN
1 le robinet *masc (water tap)*
2 la petite tape *fem (gentle blow)*

tap-dancing NOUN
les claquettes *fem pl*
□ I do tap-dancing. Je fais des claquettes.

★ **tape** NOUN
le scotch® *masc (sticky tape)*

tape measure NOUN
le mètre à ruban *masc*

★ **target** NOUN
la cible *fem*

tarmac NOUN
le macadam *masc* (*on road*)

tart NOUN
la tarte *fem*
□ an apple tart une tarte aux pommes

tartan ADJECTIVE
écossais (FEM écossaise)
□ a tartan scarf une écharpe écossaise

★ **task** NOUN
la tâche *fem*

★ **taste** NOUN
▷ *see also* **taste** VERB
le goût *masc*
□ It's got a really strange taste. Ça a un goût vraiment bizarre. □ a joke in bad taste une plaisanterie de mauvais goût
■ **Would you like a taste?** Tu veux goûter?

★ to **taste** VERB
▷ *see also* **taste** NOUN
goûter [28]
□ Would you like to taste it? Vous voulez y goûter?
■ **to taste of something** avoir [8] un goût de quelque chose □ It tastes of fish. Ça a un goût de poisson.
■ **You can taste the garlic in it.** Ça a bien le goût d'ail.

tasteful ADJECTIVE
de bon goût

tasteless ADJECTIVE
1 fade (FEM fade) (*food*)
2 de mauvais goût (*in bad taste*)
□ a tasteless remark une remarque de mauvais goût

tasty ADJECTIVE
savoureux (FEM savoureuse)

tattoo NOUN
le tatouage *masc*

taught VERB ▷ *see* **teach**

Taurus NOUN
le Taureau *masc*
□ I'm Taurus. Je suis Taureau.

★ **tax** NOUN
1 les impôts *masc pl* (*on income*)
2 la taxe *fem* (*on goods, alcohol*)

taxi NOUN
le taxi *masc*
■ **a taxi driver** un chauffeur de taxi

taxi rank NOUN
la station de taxis *fem*

TB NOUN
la tuberculose *fem*

★ **tea** NOUN
1 le thé *masc*
□ a cup of tea une tasse de thé
■ **a tea bag** un sachet de thé
2 le dîner *masc* (*evening meal*)
■ **We were having tea.** Nous étions en train de dîner.

> **DID YOU KNOW...?**
> In France, it is more common to have lemon with your tea.

★ to **teach** VERB
1 apprendre [65]
□ My sister taught me to swim. Ma sœur m'a appris à nager. □ That'll teach you! Ça t'apprendra!
2 enseigner [28] (*in school*)
□ She teaches physics. Elle enseigne la physique.

★ **teacher** NOUN
1 le professeur *masc* (*in secondary school*)
□ a maths teacher un professeur de maths
□ She's a teacher. Elle est professeur.
2 l'instituteur *masc*
l'institutrice *fem* (*in primary school*)
□ He's a primary school teacher. Il est instituteur.

teacher's pet NOUN
le chouchou *masc*
la chouchoute *fem*

teaching assistant NOUN
l'aide-éducateur *masc*
l'aide-éducatrice *fem*

tea cloth NOUN
le torchon *masc*

★ **team** NOUN
l'équipe *fem*
□ a football team une équipe de football
□ She was in my team. Elle était dans mon équipe.

teapot NOUN
la théière *fem*

★ **tear** NOUN
la larme *fem*
□ She was in tears. Elle était en larmes.

★ to **tear** VERB
1 déchirer [28]
□ Be careful or you'll tear the page. Fais attention, tu vas déchirer la page.
2 se déchirer [28]
□ It won't tear, it's very strong. Ça ne se déchire pas, c'est très solide.

to **tear up** VERB
déchirer [28]
□ He tore up the letter. Il a déchiré la lettre.

tear gas NOUN
le gaz lacrymogène *masc*

to **tease** VERB
1 tourmenter [28] (*unkindly*)
□ Stop teasing that poor animal! Arrête de tourmenter cette pauvre bête!

2 taquiner [28] (*jokingly*)
□ He's teasing you. Il te taquine.
■ **I was only teasing.** Je plaisantais.

teaspoon NOUN
la petite cuillère *fem*
■ **two teaspoons of sugar** deux cuillerées à café de sucre

teatime NOUN
l'heure du dîner *fem* (*in evening*)
□ It was nearly teatime. C'était presque l'heure du dîner.

tea towel NOUN
le torchon *masc*

★ **technical** ADJECTIVE
technique (FEM technique)

technician NOUN
le technicien *masc*
la technicienne *fem*

★ **technique** NOUN
la technique *fem*

techno NOUN
la techno *fem* (*music*)

technological ADJECTIVE
technologique (FEM technologique)

★ **technology** NOUN
la technologie *fem*

teddy bear NOUN
le nounours *masc*

teenage ADJECTIVE
1 pour les jeunes
□ a teenage magazine un magazine pour les jeunes
2 adolescent (FEM adolescente) (*boys, girls*)
□ She has two teenage daughters. Elle a deux filles adolescentes.

★ **teenager** NOUN
l'adolescent *masc*
l'adolescente *fem*

teens PL NOUN
■ **She's in her teens.** C'est une adolescente.

tee-shirt NOUN
le tee-shirt *masc*

teeth PL NOUN
les dents *fem pl*

to **teethe** VERB
faire [36] ses dents

teetotal ADJECTIVE
■ **I'm teetotal.** Je ne bois jamais d'alcool.

telecommunications PL NOUN
les télécommunications *fem pl*

★ **telephone** NOUN
le téléphone *masc*
□ on the telephone au téléphone
■ **a telephone box** une cabine téléphonique
■ **a telephone call** un coup de téléphone
■ **a telephone number** un numéro de téléphone

telesales PL NOUN
la vente par téléphone *fem sing*
■ **She works in telesales.** Elle est télévendeuse.

telescope NOUN
le télescope *masc*

★ **television** NOUN
la télévision *fem*
■ **on television** à la télévision
■ **a television licence** une redevance de télévision
■ **a television programme** une émission de télévision

★ to **tell** VERB
dire [27]
■ **to tell somebody something** dire [27] quelque chose à quelqu'un □ Did you tell your mother? Tu l'as dit à ta mère? □ I told him that I was going on holiday. Je lui ai dit que je partais en vacances.
■ **to tell somebody to do something** dire [27] à quelqu'un de faire quelque chose □ He told me to wait a moment. Il m'a dit d'attendre un moment.
■ **to tell lies** dire [27] des mensonges
■ **to tell a story** raconter [28] une histoire
■ **I can't tell the difference between them.** Je n'arrive pas à les distinguer.

to **tell off** VERB
gronder [28]

telly NOUN
la télé *fem*
□ to watch telly regarder la télé
■ **on telly** à la télé

temper NOUN
le caractère *masc*
□ He's got a terrible temper. Il a un sale caractère.
■ **to be in a temper** être [35] en colère
■ **to lose one's temper** se mettre [47] en colère □ I lost my temper. Je me suis mis en colère.

★ **temperature** NOUN
la température *fem* (*of oven, water, person*)
■ **The temperature was 30 degrees.** Il faisait trente degrés.
■ **to have a temperature** avoir [8] de la fièvre

★ **temple** NOUN
le temple *masc*

temporary ADJECTIVE
temporaire (FEM temporaire)

to **tempt** VERB
tenter [28]
□ I'm very tempted! Je suis très tenté!
■ **to tempt somebody to do something** persuader [28] quelqu'un de faire quelque chose

temptation NOUN
la tentation *fem*

tempting ADJECTIVE
tentant (FEM tentante)

★ **ten** NUMBER
dix
□ She's ten. Elle a dix ans.

tenant NOUN
le locataire *masc*
la locataire *fem*

to **tend** VERB
■ **to tend to do something** avoir [8] tendance à faire quelque chose □ He tends to arrive late. Il a tendance à arriver en retard.

tender ADJECTIVE
1 tendre (FEM tendre) (*food*)
2 sensible (FEM sensible) (*part of body*)
□ My feet are really tender. J'ai les pieds très sensibles.

★ **tennis** NOUN
le tennis *masc*
□ Do you play tennis? Vous jouez au tennis?
■ **a tennis ball** une balle de tennis
■ **a tennis court** un court de tennis
■ **a tennis racket** une raquette de tennis

tennis player NOUN
le joueur de tennis *masc*
la joueuse de tennis *fem*
□ He's a tennis player. Il est joueur de tennis.

tenor NOUN
le ténor *masc*

tenpin bowling NOUN
le bowling *masc*
□ to go tenpin bowling jouer au bowling

tense ADJECTIVE
▷ *see also* **tense** NOUN
tendu (FEM tendue)

tense NOUN
▷ *see also* **tense** ADJECTIVE
■ **the present tense** le présent
■ **the future tense** le futur

tension NOUN
la tension *fem*

tent NOUN
la tente *fem*
■ **a tent peg** un piquet de tente
■ **a tent pole** un montant de tente

★ **tenth** ADJECTIVE
dixième (FEM dixième)
□ the tenth floor le dixième étage
■ **the tenth of August** le dix août

★ **term** NOUN
1 le trimestre *masc* (*at school*)
2 le terme *masc*
□ a short-term solution une solution à court terme
■ **to come to terms with something** accepter [28] quelque chose

terminal ADJECTIVE
▷ *see also* **terminal** NOUN
incurable (FEM incurable) (*illness, patient*)

terminal NOUN
▷ *see also* **terminal** ADJECTIVE
un terminal (*of computer*)
■ **an oil terminal** un terminal pétrolier
■ **an air terminal** une aérogare

terminally ADVERB
■ **to be terminally ill** être [35] condamné

terrace NOUN
1 la terrasse *fem* (*patio*)
2 la rangée de maisons *fem* (*row of houses*)
■ **the terraces** (*at stadium*) les gradins *masc pl*

terraced ADJECTIVE
■ **a terraced house** une maison mitoyenne

★ **terrible** ADJECTIVE
épouvantable (FEM épouvantable)
□ My French is terrible. Mon français est épouvantable.

terribly ADVERB
1 terriblement
□ He suffers terribly. Il souffre terriblement.
2 vraiment
□ I'm terribly sorry. Je suis vraiment désolé.

terrier NOUN
le terrier *masc*

terrific ADJECTIVE
super (FEM+PL super) (*wonderful*)
□ That's terrific! C'est super!
■ **You look terrific!** Tu es superbe!

terrified ADJECTIVE
terrifié (FEM terrifiée)
□ I was terrified! J'étais terrifié!

terrorism NOUN
le terrorisme *masc*

★ **terrorist** NOUN
le/la terroriste *masc/fem*
■ **a terrorist attack** un attentat terroriste

★ **test** NOUN
▷ *see also* **test** VERB
1 l'interrogation *fem* (*at school*)
□ I've got a test tomorrow. J'ai une interrogation demain.
2 l'essai *masc* (*trial, check*)
□ nuclear tests les essais nucléaires
3 l'analyse *fem* (*medical*)
□ a blood test une analyse de sang □ They're going to do some more tests. Ils vont faire d'autres analyses.
■ **driving test** l'examen du permis de conduire □ He's got his driving test tomorrow. Il passe son permis de conduire demain.

★ to **test** VERB
▷ *see also* **test** NOUN
1 essayer [59]
□ to test something out essayer quelque chose
2 interroger [45] (*class*)
□ He tested us on the vocabulary. Il nous a interrogés sur le vocabulaire.
■ **She was tested for drugs.** On lui a fait subir un contrôle antidopage.

test match NOUN
le match international *masc*

test tube NOUN
l'éprouvette *fem*

tetanus NOUN
le tétanos *masc*
□ a tetanus injection un vaccin contre le tétanos

★ **text** NOUN
▷ *see also* **text** VERB
1 le texte *masc*
2 le SMS *masc* (*on mobile phone*)

★ to **text** VERB
▷ *see also* **text** NOUN
■ **to text someone** envoyer [33] un SMS à quelqu'un

textbook NOUN
le manuel *masc*
□ a French textbook un manuel de français

★ **text message** NOUN
le SMS *masc*

Thames NOUN
la Tamise *fem*

★ **than** CONJUNCTION
que
□ She's taller than me. Elle est plus grande que moi. □ I've got more books than him. J'ai plus de livres que lui.
■ **more than ten years** plus de dix ans
■ **more than once** plus d'une fois

★ to **thank** VERB
remercier [19]
□ Don't forget to thank them. N'oublie pas de les remercier.
■ **thank you** merci
■ **thank you very much** merci beaucoup

thanks EXCLAMATION
merci!
■ **thanks to** grâce à □ Thanks to him, everything went OK. Grâce à lui, tout s'est bien passé.

★ **that** ADJECTIVE, PRONOUN, CONJUNCTION

> Use **ce** when 'that' is followed by a masculine noun, and **cette** when 'that' is followed by a feminine noun. **ce** changes to **cet** before a vowel and before most words beginning with 'h'.

1 ce
□ that book ce livre
cet
□ that man cet homme
cette
□ that woman cette femme □ that road cette route
■ **THAT road** cette route-là
■ **that one** **1** celui-là *masc* □ This man? — No, that one. Cet homme-ci? — Non, celui-là. **2** celle-là *fem* □ Do you like this photo? — No, I prefer that one. Tu aimes cette photo? — Non, je préfère celle-là.
2 ça
□ You see that? Tu vois ça?
■ **What's that?** Qu'est-ce que c'est?
■ **Who's that?** Qui est-ce?
■ **Is that you?** C'est toi?
■ **That's ...** C'est ... □ That's my teacher. C'est mon prof. □ That's what he said. C'est ce qu'il a dit.

> In relative phrases use **qui** when 'that' refers to the subject of the sentence, and **que** when it refers to the object.

3 qui
□ the man that saw us l'homme qui nous a vus □ the man that spoke to us l'homme qui nous a parlé
4 que
□ the man that we saw l'homme que nous avons vu □ the man that we spoke to l'homme à qui nous avons parlé

> **que** changes to **qu'** before a vowel and before most words beginning with 'h'.

□ the dog that she bought le chien qu'elle a acheté □ He thought that Henri was ill. Il pensait qu'Henri était malade. □ I know that she likes chocolate. Je sais qu'elle aime le chocolat.
■ **It was that big.** Il était grand comme ça.
■ **It's about that high.** C'est à peu près haut comme ça.
■ **It's not that difficult.** Ça n'est pas si difficile que ça.

★ **the** ARTICLE

> Use **le** with a masculine noun, and **la** with a feminine noun. Use **l'** before a vowel and most words beginning with 'h'. For plural nouns always use **les**.

le
□ the boy le garçon
l'
□ the man l'homme *masc* □ the air l'air *masc*
□ the habit l'habitude *fem*
la
□ the girl la fille
les
□ the children les enfants

English-French

★ **theatre** (US **theater**) NOUN
le théâtre *masc*

theft NOUN
le vol *masc*

★ **their** ADJECTIVE
leur (PL leurs)
□ their house leur maison □ their parents leurs parents

★ **theirs** PRONOUN
le leur + *masc noun*
□ It's not our garage, it's theirs. Ce n'est pas notre garage, c'est le leur.
la leur + *fem noun*
□ It's not our car, it's theirs. Ce n'est pas notre voiture, c'est la leur.
les leurs + *pl noun*
□ They're not our ideas, they're theirs. Ce ne sont pas nos idées, ce sont les leurs.
■ **Is this theirs?** **1** (*masculine owners*) C'est à eux? **2** (*feminine owners*) C'est à elles? □ This car is theirs. Cette voiture est à eux. □ Whose is this? — It's theirs. C'est à qui? — À eux.

★ **them** PRONOUN
1 les
□ I didn't see them. Je ne les ai pas vus.

Use **leur** when 'them' means 'to them'.

2 leur
□ I gave them some brochures. Je leur ai donné des brochures. □ I told them the truth. Je leur ai dit la vérité.

Use **eux** or **elles** after a preposition.

3 eux *masc pl*
□ It's for them. C'est pour eux.
elles *fem pl*
□ Layla and Sophie came — Louis was with them. Layla et Sophie sont venues — Louis était avec elles.

theme NOUN
le thème *masc*

theme park NOUN
le parc d'attractions *masc*

★ **themselves** PRONOUN
1 se
□ Did they hurt themselves? Est-ce qu'ils se sont fait mal?
2 eux-mêmes *masc*
elles-mêmes *fem*
□ They did it themselves. Ils l'ont fait eux-mêmes.

★ **then** ADVERB, CONJUNCTION
1 ensuite (*next*)
□ I get dressed. Then I have breakfast. Je m'habille. Ensuite je prends mon petit déjeuner.
2 alors (*in that case*)
□ My pen's run out. — Use a pencil then! Il n'y a plus d'encre dans mon stylo. — Alors utilise un crayon!
3 à l'époque (*at that time*)
□ There was no electricity then. Il n'y avait pas l'électricité à l'époque.
■ **now and then** de temps en temps □ Do you play chess? — Now and then. Vous jouez aux échecs? — De temps en temps.
■ **By then it was too late.** Il était déjà trop tard.

★ **therapy** NOUN
la thérapie *fem*

★ **there** ADVERB
1 là
□ Put it there, on the table. Mets-le là, sur la table.
■ **over there** là-bas
■ **in there** là
■ **on there** là
■ **up there** là-haut
■ **down there** là-bas
■ **There he is!** Le voilà!
2 y
□ He went there on Friday. Il y est allé vendredi. □ Brussels? I've never been there. Bruxelles? Je n'y suis jamais allé.
■ **There is ...** Il y a ... □ There's a factory near my house. Il y a une usine près de chez moi.
■ **There are ...** Il y a ... □ There are five people in my family. Il y a cinq personnes dans ma famille.
■ **There has been an accident.** Il y a eu un accident.
■ **Will there be a buffet?** Est-ce qu'il y aura un buffet?

★ **therefore** ADVERB
donc

there's = **there is, there has**

thermometer NOUN
le thermomètre *masc*

Thermos® NOUN
le thermos® *masc*

★ **these** ADJECTIVE, PRONOUN
1 ces
□ these shoes ces chaussures
■ **THESE shoes** ces chaussures-là
2 ceux-ci *masc*
□ I want these! Je veux ceux-ci!
celles-ci *fem*
□ I'm looking for some sandals. Can I try these? Je cherche des sandales. Je peux essayer celles-ci?

★ **they** PRONOUN

Check if 'they' stands for a masculine or feminine noun.

ils
□ Are there any tickets left? — No, they're sold out. Est-ce qu'il reste des billets? — Non, ils sont tous vendus.
elles

t

□ Do you like those shoes? — No, they're horrible. Tu aimes ces chaussures? — Non, elles sont affreuses.
■ **They say that ...** On dit que ...

they'd = **they had, they would**

they'll = **they will**

they're = **they are**

they've = **they have**

★ **thick** ADJECTIVE
1 épais (FEM épaisse) (*not thin*)
■ **The walls are one metre thick.** Les murs font un mètre d'épaisseur.
2 bête (FEM bête) (*stupid*)

★ **thief** NOUN
le voleur *masc*
la voleuse *fem*
■ **Stop thief!** Au voleur!

thigh NOUN
la cuisse *fem*

★ **thin** ADJECTIVE
1 mince (FEM mince) (*person, slice*)
2 maigre (FEM maigre) (*skinny*)

> **WORD POWER**
> You can use a number of other words instead of **thin** to mean 'skinny':
> **lanky** dégingandé
> □ a lanky boy un garçon dégingandé
> **skinny** maigre
> □ a skinny dog un chien maigre
> **slim** mince
> □ a slim girl une fille mince

★ **thing** NOUN
1 la chose *fem*
□ beautiful things de belles choses
2 le truc *masc* (*thingy*)
□ What's that thing called? Comment s'appelle ce truc?
■ **my things** (*belongings*) mes affaires *fem pl*
■ **You poor thing!** Mon pauvre!

★ to **think** VERB
1 penser [28] (*believe*)
□ I think you're wrong. Je pense que vous avez tort. □ What do you think about the war? Que pensez-vous de la guerre?
2 réfléchir [38] (*spend time thinking*)
□ Think carefully before you reply. Réfléchis bien avant de répondre. □ I'll think about it. Je vais y réfléchir.
■ **What are you thinking about?** À quoi tu penses?
3 imaginer [28] (*imagine*)
□ Just think — tomorrow we'll be on holiday! T'imagines: demain, on sera en vacances!
■ **I think so.** Oui, je crois.
■ **I don't think so.** Je ne crois pas.
■ **I'll think it over.** Je vais y réfléchir.

★ **third** ADJECTIVE
▷ *see also* **third** NOUN
troisième (FEM troisième)
□ the third day le troisième jour □ the third time la troisième fois □ I came third. Je suis arrivé troisième.
■ **the third of March** le trois mars

★ **third** NOUN
▷ *see also* **third** ADJECTIVE
le tiers *masc*
□ a third of the population un tiers de la population

thirdly ADVERB
troisièmement

★ **Third World** NOUN
le tiers-monde *masc*

thirst NOUN
la soif *fem*

★ **thirsty** ADJECTIVE
■ **to be thirsty** avoir [8] soif

★ **thirteen** NUMBER
treize
□ I'm thirteen. J'ai treize ans.

★ **thirteenth** ADJECTIVE
treizième (FEM treizième)
□ her thirteenth birthday son treizième anniversaire □ the thirteenth floor le treizième étage
■ **the thirteenth of August** le treize août

★ **thirty** NUMBER
trente

★ **this** ADJECTIVE, PRONOUN

> Use **ce** when 'this' is followed by a masculine noun, and **cette** when 'this' is followed by a feminine noun. **ce** changes to **cet** before a vowel and before most words beginning with 'h'.

1 ce
□ this book ce livre
cet
□ this man cet homme
cette
□ this woman cette femme □ this road cette route
■ **THIS road** cette route-ci
■ **this one** 1 celui-ci *masc* □ Pass me that pen. — This one? Passe-moi ce stylo. — Celui-ci? 2 celle-ci *fem* □ Of the two photos, I prefer this one. Des deux photos, c'est celle-ci que je préfère.
2 ça
□ You see this? Tu vois ça?
■ **What's this?** Qu'est-ce que c'est?
■ **This is my mother.** (*introduction*) Je te présente ma mère.
■ **This is Izzy speaking.** (*on the phone*) C'est Izzy à l'appareil.

thistle NOUN
le chardon *masc*

★ **thorough** ADJECTIVE
minutieux (FEM minutieuse)
□ She's very thorough. Elle est très minutieuse.

thoroughly ADVERB
à fond (*examine*)

★ **those** ADJECTIVE, PRONOUN
1 ces
□ those shoes ces chaussures
■ **THOSE shoes** ces chaussures-là
2 ceux-là *masc*
□ I want those! Je veux ceux-là!
celles-là *fem*
□ I'm looking for some sandals. Can I try those? Je cherche des sandales. Je peux essayer celles-là?

★ **though** CONJUNCTION, ADVERB
bien que
□ Though it's raining ... Bien qu'il pleuve ...

bien que has to be followed by a verb in the subjunctive.

■ **He's a nice person, though he's not very clever.** Il est sympa, mais pas très malin.

★ **thought** VERB ▷ *see* **think**

★ **thought** NOUN
l'idée *fem* (*idea*)
□ I've just had a thought. Je viens d'avoir une idée.
■ **It was a nice thought, thank you.** C'est gentil de ta part, merci.

thoughtful ADJECTIVE
1 pensif (FEM pensive) (*deep in thought*)
□ You look thoughtful. Tu as l'air pensif.
2 prévenant (FEM prévenante) (*considerate*)
□ She's very thoughtful. Elle est très prévenante.

thoughtless ADJECTIVE
■ **He's completely thoughtless.** Il ne pense absolument pas aux autres.

★ **thousand** NUMBER
■ **a thousand** mille □ a thousand euros mille euros
■ **£2000** deux mille livres
■ **thousands of people** des milliers de personnes

thousandth ADJECTIVE, NOUN
le millième *masc*

thread NOUN
le fil *masc*

★ **threat** NOUN
la menace *fem*

★ to **threaten** VERB
menacer [12]
□ to threaten to do something menacer de faire quelque chose

★ **three** NUMBER
trois
□ She's three. Elle a trois ans.

three-dimensional ADJECTIVE
à trois dimensions

threw VERB ▷ *see* **throw**

thrifty ADJECTIVE
économe (FEM économe)

thrill NOUN
l'émotion *fem* (*excitement*)

thrilled ADJECTIVE
■ **I was thrilled.** (*pleased*) J'étais absolument ravi.

thriller NOUN
le thriller *masc*

thrilling ADJECTIVE
palpitant (FEM palpitante)

★ **throat** NOUN
la gorge *fem*
□ to have a sore throat avoir mal à la gorge

to **throb** VERB
■ **a throbbing pain** un élancement
■ **My arm's throbbing.** J'ai des élancements dans le bras.

throne NOUN
le trône *masc*

★ **through** PREPOSITION, ADJECTIVE, ADVERB
1 par
□ through the window par la fenêtre □ I know her through my sister. Je la connais par ma sœur. □ to go through Birmingham passer par Birmingham
■ **to go through a tunnel** traverser [28] un tunnel
2 à travers
□ through the mist à travers la brume
□ through the crowd à travers la foule
■ **a through train** un train direct
■ **'no through road'** 'impasse'

★ **throughout** PREPOSITION
■ **throughout Britain** dans toute la Grande-Bretagne
■ **throughout the year** pendant toute l'année

★ to **throw** VERB
lancer [12]
□ He threw the ball to me. Il m'a lancé le ballon.
■ **to throw a party** organiser [28] une soirée
■ **That really threw him.** Ça l'a décontenancé.

to **throw away** VERB
1 jeter [41] (*rubbish*)
2 perdre [61] (*chance*)

to **throw out** VERB
1 jeter [41] (*throw away*)
2 mettre [47] à la porte (*person*)
□ I threw him out. Je l'ai mis à la porte.

 Numbers in brackets refer to verb tables on pages 650 to 658

to **throw up** VERB
vomir [38]

thug NOUN
le voyou *masc*

thumb NOUN
le pouce *masc*

thumb tack NOUN (US)
la punaise *fem*

to **thump** VERB
■ **to thump somebody** donner [28] un coup de poing à quelqu'un

thunder NOUN
le tonnerre *masc*

thunderstorm NOUN
l'orage *masc*

thundery ADJECTIVE
orageux (FEM orageuse)

★ **Thursday** NOUN
le jeudi *masc*
□ on Thursday jeudi □ on Thursdays le jeudi □ every Thursday tous les jeudis □ last Thursday jeudi dernier □ next Thursday jeudi prochain

thyme NOUN
le thym *masc*

tick NOUN
▷ *see also* **tick** VERB
1 la coche *fem* (*mark*)
2 le tic-tac *masc* (*of clock*)
■ **I'll be back in a tick.** J'en ai pour une seconde.

to **tick** VERB
▷ *see also* **tick** NOUN
1 cocher [28]
□ Tick the correct answer. Cochez la bonne réponse.
2 faire [36] tic-tac (*clock*)

to **tick off** VERB
1 cocher [28] (*check*)
□ He ticked off our names on the list. Il a coché nos noms sur la liste.
2 passer [58] un savon à (*tell off*)
□ She ticked me off for being late. Elle m'a passé un savon à cause de mon retard.

★ **ticket** NOUN

> **BE CAREFUL!**
> Be careful to choose correctly between **le ticket** and **le billet**.

1 le ticket *masc* (*for bus, tube, cinema, museum*)
□ an underground ticket un ticket de métro
2 le billet *masc* (*for plane, train, theatre, concert*)
■ **a parking ticket** un P.-V.

ticket inspector NOUN
le contrôleur *masc*
la contrôleuse *fem*

ticket office NOUN
le guichet *masc*

to **tickle** VERB
chatouiller [28]

ticklish ADJECTIVE
chatouilleux (FEM chatouilleuse)
□ Are you ticklish? Tu es chatouilleux?

★ **tide** NOUN
la marée *fem*
■ **high tide** la marée haute
■ **low tide** la marée basse

★ **tidy** ADJECTIVE
▷ *see also* **tidy** VERB
1 bien rangé (FEM bien rangée) (*room*)
□ Your room's very tidy. Ta chambre est bien rangée.
2 ordonné (FEM ordonnée) (*person*)
□ She's very tidy. Elle est très ordonnée.

★ to **tidy** VERB
▷ *see also* **tidy** ADJECTIVE
ranger [45]
□ Go and tidy your room. Va ranger ta chambre.

to **tidy up** VERB
ranger [45]
□ Don't forget to tidy up afterwards. N'oubliez pas de ranger après.

★ **tie** NOUN
▷ *see also* **tie** VERB
la cravate *fem* (*necktie*)
■ **It was a tie.** (*in sport*) Ils ont fait match nul.

★ to **tie** VERB
▷ *see also* **tie** NOUN
1 nouer [28] (*ribbon, shoelaces*)
■ **to tie a knot in something** faire [36] un nœud à quelque chose
2 faire [36] match nul (*in sport*)
□ They tied three all. Ils ont fait match nul, trois à trois.

to **tie up** VERB
1 ficeler [4] (*parcel*)
2 attacher [28] (*dog, boat*)
3 ligoter [28] (*prisoner*)

tiger NOUN
le tigre *masc*

★ **tight** ADJECTIVE
1 moulant (FEM moulante) (*tight-fitting*)
□ tight clothes les vêtements moulants
2 juste (FEM juste) (*too tight*)
□ This dress is a bit tight. Cette robe est un peu juste.

to **tighten** VERB
1 tendre [88] (*rope*)
2 resserrer [28] (*screw*)

tightly ADVERB
fort (*hold*)

English-French

t

tights PL NOUN
le collant *masc sing*

tile NOUN
1 la tuile *fem* (*on roof*)
2 le carreau *masc* (PL les carreaux) (*on wall, floor*)

tiled ADJECTIVE
1 en tuiles (*roof*)
2 carrelé (FEM carrelée) (*wall, floor, room*)

★**till** NOUN
▷ *see also* **till** PREPOSITION, CONJUNCTION
la caisse *fem*

★**till** PREPOSITION, CONJUNCTION
▷ *see also* **till** NOUN
1 jusqu'à
□ I waited till ten o'clock. J'ai attendu jusqu'à dix heures.
■ **till now** jusqu'à présent
■ **till then** jusque-là
2 avant

> Use **avant** if the sentence you want to translate contains a negative such as 'not' or 'never'.

□ Till last year I'd never been to France. Avant l'année dernière, je n'étais jamais allé en France. □ It won't be ready till next week. Ça ne sera pas prêt avant la semaine prochaine.

★**time** NOUN
1 l'heure *fem* (*on clock*)
□ What time is it? Quelle heure est-il? □ What time do you get up? À quelle heure tu te lèves? □ It was two o'clock, French time. Il était deux heures, heure française.
■ **on time** à l'heure □ He never arrives on time. Il n'arrive jamais à l'heure.
2 le temps *masc* (*amount of time*)
□ I'm sorry, I haven't got time. Je suis désolé, je n'ai pas le temps.
■ **from time to time** de temps en temps
■ **in time** à temps □ We arrived in time for lunch. Nous sommes arrivés à temps pour le déjeuner.
■ **just in time** juste à temps
■ **in no time** en un rien de temps □ It was ready in no time. Ça a été prêt en un rien de temps.
■ **It's time to go.** Il est temps de partir.
■ **a long time** longtemps □ Have you lived here for a long time? Vous habitez ici depuis longtemps?
3 le moment *masc* (*moment*)
□ This isn't a good time to ask him. Ce n'est pas le bon moment pour lui demander.
■ **for the time being** pour le moment
4 la fois *fem* (*occasion*)
□ this time cette fois-ci □ next time la prochaine fois □ two at a time deux à la fois
■ **How many times?** Combien de fois?
■ **at times** parfois
■ **in a week's time** dans une semaine □ I'll come back in a month's time. Je reviendrai dans un mois.
■ **Come and see us any time.** Venez nous voir quand vous voulez.
■ **to have a good time** bien s'amuser [28]
□ Did you have a good time? Vous vous êtes bien amusés?
■ **2 times 2 is 4** deux fois deux égalent quatre

time bomb NOUN
la bombe à retardement *fem*

time off NOUN
le temps libre *masc*

timer NOUN
le minuteur *masc*

time-share NOUN
l'appartement en multipropriété *masc*

★**timetable** NOUN
1 l'horaire *masc* (*for train, bus*)
2 l'emploi du temps *masc* (*at school*)

time zone NOUN
le fuseau horaire *masc*

★**tin** NOUN
1 la boîte *fem*
□ a tin of soup une boîte de soupe □ a biscuit tin une boîte à biscuits
2 la boîte de conserve *fem*
□ The bin was full of tins. La poubelle était pleine de boîtes de conserve.
3 l'étain *masc* (*type of metal*)

tinned ADJECTIVE
en boîte (*food*)
□ tinned peaches des pêches en boîte

tin opener NOUN
l'ouvre-boîte *masc*

tinsel NOUN
les guirlandes de Noël *fem pl*

tinted ADJECTIVE
teinté (FEM teintée) (*spectacles, glass*)

★**tiny** ADJECTIVE
minuscule (FEM minuscule)

★**tip** NOUN
▷ *see also* **tip** VERB
1 le pourboire *masc* (*money*)
□ Shall I give him a tip? Je lui donne un pourboire?
2 le tuyau *masc* (PL les tuyaux) (*advice*)
□ a useful tip un bon tuyau (*informal*)
3 le bout *masc* (*end*)
□ It's on the tip of my tongue. Je l'ai sur le bout de la langue.
■ **a rubbish tip** une décharge
■ **This place is a complete tip!** Quel fouillis!

★to **tip** VERB
▷ *see also* **tip** NOUN
donner [28] un pourboire à
□ Don't forget to tip the taxi driver. N'oubliez

pas de donner un pourboire au chauffeur de taxi.

tipsy ADJECTIVE
pompette (FEM pompette)

tiptoe NOUN
■ **on tiptoe** sur la pointe des pieds

★ **tired** ADJECTIVE
fatigué (FEM fatiguée)
□ I'm tired. Je suis fatigué.
■ **to be tired of something** en avoir [8] assez de quelque chose

tiring ADJECTIVE
fatigant (FEM fatigante)

★ **tissue** NOUN
le kleenex® *masc*
□ Have you got a tissue? Tu as un kleenex®?

★ **title** NOUN
le titre *masc*

title role NOUN
le rôle principal *masc*

★ **to** PREPOSITION

à + le changes to **au**. **à + les** changes to **aux**.

1 à
□ to go to Lyon aller à Lyon □ to go to school aller à l'école □ a letter to his mother une lettre à sa mère □ the answer to the question la réponse à la question
au
□ to go to the theatre aller au théâtre
aux
□ We said goodbye to the neighbours. Nous avons dit au revoir aux voisins.
■ **ready to go** prêt à partir
■ **ready to eat** prêt à manger
■ **It's easy to do.** C'est facile à faire.
■ **something to drink** quelque chose à boire
■ **I've got things to do.** J'ai des choses à faire.
■ **from ... to ...** de ... à ... □ from nine o'clock to half past three de neuf heures à trois heures et demie

2 de
□ the train to Carlisle le train de Carlisle □ the road to Edinburgh la route d'Édimbourg □ the key to the front door la clé de la porte d'entrée
■ **It's difficult to say.** C'est difficile à dire.
■ **It's easy to criticize.** C'est facile de critiquer.

When referring to someone's house, shop or office, use **chez**.

3 chez
□ to go to the doctor's aller chez le docteur
□ to go to the butcher's aller chez le boucher
□ Let's go to Max's house. Si on allait chez Max?

When 'to' refers to a country which is feminine, use **en**; when the country is masculine, use **au**.

4 en
□ to go to France aller en France
au
□ to go to Portugal aller au Portugal

5 jusqu'à (*up to*)
□ to count to ten compter jusqu'à dix

6 pour (*in order to*)
□ I did it to help you. Je l'ai fait pour vous aider.
□ She's too young to go to school. Elle est trop jeune pour aller à l'école.

toad NOUN
le crapaud *masc*

toadstool NOUN
le champignon vénéneux *masc*

★ **toast** NOUN
1 le pain grillé *masc*
□ a piece of toast une tranche de pain grillé
2 le toast *masc* (*speech*)
□ to drink a toast to somebody porter un toast à quelqu'un

toaster NOUN
le grille-pain *masc* (PL les grille-pain)

toastie NOUN
le sandwich chaud *masc*
■ **a cheese and ham toastie** un croque-monsieur

tobacco NOUN
le tabac *masc*

tobacconist's NOUN
le bureau de tabac *masc* (PL les bureaux de tabac)

toboggan NOUN
la luge *fem*

tobogganing NOUN
■ **to go tobogganing** faire [36] de la luge

★ **today** ADVERB
aujourd'hui
□ What did you do today? Qu'est-ce que tu as fait aujourd'hui?

toddler NOUN
le bambin *masc*

★ **toe** NOUN
le doigt de pied *masc*

toffee NOUN
le caramel *masc*

★ **together** ADVERB
1 ensemble
□ Are they still together? Ils sont toujours ensemble?
2 en même temps (*at the same time*)
□ Don't all speak together! Ne parlez pas tous en même temps!
■ **together with** (*with person*) avec

★ **toilet** NOUN
les toilettes *fem pl*

toilet paper NOUN
le papier hygiénique *masc*

toiletries PL NOUN
les articles de toilette *masc pl*

toilet roll NOUN
le rouleau de papier hygiénique *masc* (PL les rouleaux de papier hygiénique)

token NOUN
▪ **a gift token** un bon-cadeau

told VERB ▷ *see* **tell**

tolerant ADJECTIVE
tolérant (FEM tolérante)

toll NOUN
le péage *masc* (*on bridge, motorway*)

★ **tomato** NOUN
la tomate *fem*
□ tomato sauce la sauce tomate □ tomato soup la soupe à la tomate

tomboy NOUN
le garçon manqué *masc*
□ She's a real tomboy. C'est un vrai garçon manqué.

★ **tomorrow** ADVERB
demain
□ tomorrow morning demain matin
□ tomorrow night demain soir
▪ **the day after tomorrow** après-demain

★ **ton** NOUN
la tonne *fem*
□ That old bike weighs a ton. Ce vieux vélo pèse une tonne.

> **DID YOU KNOW...?**
> In France, measurements are in metric tonnes rather than tons. A ton is slightly more than a **tonne**.

★ **tongue** NOUN
la langue *fem*
▪ **to say something tongue in cheek** dire [27] quelque chose en plaisantant

tonic NOUN
le Schweppes® *masc* (*tonic water*)
▪ **a gin and tonic** un gin tonic

★ **tonight** ADVERB
1 ce soir (*this evening*)
□ Are you going out tonight? Tu sors ce soir?
2 cette nuit (*during the night*)
□ I'll sleep well tonight. Je dormirai bien cette nuit.

tonsillitis NOUN
l'angine *fem*

tonsils PL NOUN
les amygdales *fem pl*

★ **too** ADVERB
1 aussi (*as well*)
□ My sister came too. Ma sœur est venue aussi.
2 trop (*excessively*)
□ The water's too hot. L'eau est trop chaude.
□ We arrived too late. Nous sommes arrivés trop tard.
▪ **too much** **1** (*with noun*) trop de □ too much noise trop de bruit **2** (*with verb*) trop □ At Christmas we always eat too much. À Noël nous mangeons toujours trop. **3** (*too expensive*) trop cher □ Fifty euros? That's too much. Cinquante euros? C'est trop cher.
▪ **too many** trop de □ too many hamburgers trop de burgers
▪ **Too bad!** Tant pis!

took VERB ▷ *see* **take**

★ **tool** NOUN
l'outil *masc*
▪ **a tool box** une boîte à outils

★ **tooth** NOUN
la dent *fem*

★ **toothache** NOUN
le mal de dents *masc*
□ to have toothache avoir mal aux dents

★ **toothbrush** NOUN
la brosse à dents *fem*

★ **toothpaste** NOUN
le dentifrice *masc*

★ **top** NOUN
▷ *see also* **top** ADJECTIVE
1 le haut *masc* (*of page, ladder, garment*)
□ at the top of the page en haut de la page
□ She wore jeans and a top. Elle portait un jean et un haut.
▪ **a bikini top** un haut de bikini
2 le sommet *masc* (*of mountain*)
3 le dessus *masc* (*of table*)
▪ **on top of** (*on*) sur □ on top of the fridge sur le frigo
▪ **You need to pay a tip on top of that.** Il faut payer un pourboire en plus.
▪ **from top to bottom** de fond en comble □ I searched the house from top to bottom. J'ai fouillé la maison de fond en comble.
4 le couvercle *masc* (*of box, jar*)
5 le bouchon *masc* (*of bottle*)

★ **top** ADJECTIVE
▷ *see also* **top** NOUN
grand (FEM grande) (*first-class*)
□ a top surgeon un grand chirurgien
▪ **a top model** un top model
▪ **He always gets top marks in chemistry.** Il a toujours d'excellentes notes en chimie.
▪ **the top floor** le dernier étage □ on the top floor au dernier étage

topic NOUN
le sujet *masc*
□ The essay can be on any topic. Cette

 Numbers in brackets refer to verb tables on pages 650 to 658

dissertation peut être sur n'importe quel sujet.

topical ADJECTIVE
d'actualité
□ a topical issue un sujet d'actualité

torch NOUN
la lampe de poche *fem*

tore, torn VERB ▷ *see* **tear**

tortoise NOUN
la tortue *fem*

★ **torture** NOUN
▷ *see also* **torture** VERB
la torture *fem*
□ It was pure torture. C'était une vraie torture.

to **torture** VERB
▷ *see also* **torture** NOUN
torturer [28]
□ Stop torturing that poor animal! Arrête de torturer cette pauvre bête!

Tory ADJECTIVE
▷ *see also* **Tory** NOUN
conservateur (FEM conservatrice)
□ the Tory government le gouvernement conservateur

Tory NOUN
▷ *see also* **Tory** ADJECTIVE
le conservateur *masc*
la conservatrice *fem*
■ **the Tories** les conservateurs

to **toss** VERB
■ **to toss pancakes** faire [36] sauter les crêpes
■ **Shall we toss for it?** On joue à pile ou face?

★ **total** ADJECTIVE
▷ *see also* **total** NOUN
total (FEM totale, MASC PL totaux)
■ **the total amount** le total

★ **total** NOUN
▷ *see also* **total** ADJECTIVE
le total *masc* (PL les totaux)
■ **the grand total** le total

totally ADVERB
complètement
□ He's totally useless. Il est complètement nul.

★ **touch** NOUN
▷ *see also* **touch** VERB
■ **to get in touch with somebody** prendre [65] contact avec quelqu'un
■ **to keep in touch with somebody** rester [71E] en contact avec quelqu'un
■ **Keep in touch!** Donne-moi de tes nouvelles!
■ **to lose touch** se perdre [61] de vue
■ **to lose touch with somebody** perdre [61] quelqu'un de vue

★ to **touch** VERB
▷ *see also* **touch** NOUN
toucher [28]
■ **Don't touch that!** N'y touche pas!

touchdown NOUN
l'atterrissage *masc*

touched ADJECTIVE
touché (FEM touchée)
□ I was really touched. Ça m'a beaucoup touché.

touching ADJECTIVE
touchant (FEM touchante)

touchline NOUN
la ligne de touche *fem*

touchpad NOUN
le pavé tactile *masc*

touchy ADJECTIVE
susceptible (FEM susceptible)
□ She's a bit touchy. Elle est susceptible.

★ **tough** ADJECTIVE
1 dur (FEM dure)
□ It was tough, but I managed OK. C'était dur, mais je m'en suis tiré. □ It's a tough job. C'est dur.
■ **The meat's tough.** La viande est coriace.
2 solide (FEM solide) (*strong*)
□ tough leather gloves de solides gants en cuir
□ She's tough. She can take it. Elle est solide. Elle tiendra le coup.
3 dangereux (FEM dangereuse) (*rough, violent*)
■ **He thinks he's a tough guy.** Il se prend pour un gros dur.
■ **Tough luck!** C'est comme ça!

toupee NOUN
le postiche *masc*

★ **tour** NOUN
▷ *see also* **tour** VERB
1 la visite *fem* (*of town, museum*)
□ We went on a tour of the city. Nous avons visité la ville.
■ **a package tour** un voyage organisé
2 la tournée *fem* (*by singer, group*)
□ on tour en tournée
■ **to go on tour** faire [36] une tournée

★ to **tour** VERB
▷ *see also* **tour** NOUN
■ **Rihanna is touring Europe.** Rihanna est en tournée en Europe.

tour guide NOUN
le/la guide *masc/fem*

tourism NOUN
le tourisme *masc*

★ **tourist** NOUN
le/la touriste *masc/fem*
■ **tourist information office** l'office du tourisme *masc*

English-French

t

★ **tournament** NOUN
le tournoi *masc*

tour operator NOUN
le tour-opérateur *masc*

★ **towards** PREPOSITION
1 vers (*in the direction of*)
□ He came towards me. Il est venu vers moi.
2 envers (*of attitude*)
□ my feelings towards him mes sentiments envers lui

★ **towel** NOUN
la serviette *fem*

★ **tower** NOUN
la tour *fem*
■ **a tower block** une tour

★ **town** NOUN
la ville *fem*
□ a town plan un plan de ville
■ **the town centre** le centre-ville
■ **the town hall** la mairie

tow truck NOUN (US)
la dépanneuse *fem*

★ **toy** NOUN
le jouet *masc*
□ a toy shop un magasin de jouets
■ **a toy car** une petite voiture

trace NOUN
▷ *see also* **trace** VERB
la trace *fem*
□ There was no trace of the robbers. Il n'y avait pas de trace des voleurs.

to **trace** VERB
▷ *see also* **trace** NOUN
décalquer [28] (*draw*)

tracing paper NOUN
le papier calque *masc*

track NOUN
1 le chemin *masc* (*dirt road*)
2 la voie ferrée *fem* (*railway line*)
3 la piste *fem* (*in sport*)
□ two laps of the track deux tours de piste
4 la chanson *fem* (*song*)
□ This is my favourite track. C'est ma chanson préférée.
5 les traces *fem pl* (*trail*)
□ They followed the tracks for miles. Ils ont suivi les traces sur des kilomètres.

to **track down** VERB
■ **to track somebody down** retrouver [28] quelqu'un □ The police never tracked down the thief. La police n'a jamais retrouvé le voleur.

★ **tracksuit** NOUN
le jogging *masc*

tractor NOUN
le tracteur *masc*

trade NOUN
le métier *masc* (*skill, job*)
□ to learn a trade apprendre un métier

trade union NOUN
le syndicat *masc*

trade unionist NOUN
le/la syndicaliste *masc/fem*

★ **tradition** NOUN
la tradition *fem*

★ **traditional** ADJECTIVE
traditionnel (FEM traditionnelle)

★ **traffic** NOUN
la circulation *fem*
□ The traffic was terrible. Il y avait une circulation épouvantable.

traffic circle NOUN (US)
le rond-point *masc* (PL les ronds-points)

traffic jam NOUN
l'embouteillage *masc*

★ **traffic lights** PL NOUN
les feux *masc pl*

traffic warden NOUN
le contractuel *masc*
la contractuelle *fem*

tragedy NOUN
la tragédie *fem*

tragic ADJECTIVE
tragique (FEM tragique)

trailer NOUN
1 la remorque *fem* (*vehicle*)
2 la bande-annonce *fem* (*film advert*)

★ **train** NOUN
▷ *see also* **train** VERB
1 le train *masc*
■ **a train set** un train électrique
2 la rame *fem* (*on underground*)

★ to **train** VERB
▷ *see also* **train** NOUN
s'entraîner [28] (*sport*)
□ to train for a race s'entraîner pour une course
■ **to train as a teacher** suivre [81] une formation d'enseignant
■ **to train an animal to do something** dresser [28] un animal à faire quelque chose

trained ADJECTIVE
■ **She's a trained nurse.** Elle est infirmière diplômée.

trainee NOUN
1 le/la stagiaire *masc/fem* (*in profession*)
□ She's a trainee. Elle est stagiaire.
2 l'apprenti *masc*
l'apprentie *fem* (*apprentice*)
□ a trainee plumber un apprenti plombier

trainer NOUN
1 l'entraîneur *masc* (*sports coach*)

2 le dompteur *masc*
la dompteuse *fem* (*of animals*)

★ **trainers** PL NOUN
les baskets *fem pl*
□ a pair of trainers une paire de baskets

★ **training** NOUN
1 la formation *fem*
□ a training course un stage de formation
2 l'entraînement *masc* (*sport*)

tram NOUN
le tramway *masc*

tramp NOUN
le clochard *masc*
la clocharde *fem*

trampoline NOUN
le trampoline *masc*

transfer NOUN
la décalcomanie *fem* (*sticker*)

transfusion NOUN
la transfusion *fem*

transistor NOUN
le transistor *masc*

transit NOUN
le transit *masc*
□ in transit en transit

transit lounge NOUN
la salle de transit *fem*

to **translate** VERB
traduire [23]
□ to translate something into English traduire quelque chose en anglais

translation NOUN
la traduction *fem*

translator NOUN
le traducteur *masc*
la traductrice *fem*
□ Anita's a translator. Anita est traductrice.

transparent ADJECTIVE
transparent (FEM transparente)

transplant NOUN
la greffe *fem*
□ a heart transplant une greffe du cœur

★ **transport** NOUN
▷ *see also* **transport** VERB
le transport *masc*
□ public transport les transports en commun

★ to **transport** VERB
▷ *see also* **transport** NOUN
transporter [28]

trap NOUN
le piège *masc*

trash NOUN (US)
les ordures *fem pl*
■ **the trash can** la poubelle

trashy ADJECTIVE
nul (FEM nulle)
■ **a really trashy film** un film vraiment ringard

traumatic ADJECTIVE
traumatisant (FEM traumatisante)
□ It was a traumatic experience. Ça a été une expérience traumatisante.

★ **travel** NOUN
▷ *see also* **travel** VERB
les voyages *masc pl*

★ to **travel** VERB
▷ *see also* **travel** NOUN
voyager [45]
□ I prefer to travel by train. Je préfère voyager en train.
■ **I'd like to travel round the world.** J'aimerais faire le tour du monde.
■ **We travelled over 800 kilometres.** Nous avons fait plus de huit cents kilomètres.
■ **News travels fast!** Les nouvelles circulent vite!

travel agency NOUN
l'agence de voyages *fem*

travel agent NOUN
■ **She's a travel agent.** Elle travaille dans une agence de voyages.

traveller (US **traveler**) NOUN
1 le voyageur *masc*
la voyageuse *fem* (*on bus, train, plane*)
2 le/la nomade *masc/fem* (*gypsy*)

travelling (US **traveling**) NOUN
■ **I love travelling.** J'adore les voyages.

travel sickness NOUN
le mal des transports *masc*

tray NOUN
le plateau *masc* (PL les plateaux)

to **tread** VERB
marcher [28]
□ to tread on something marcher sur quelque chose

treasure NOUN
le trésor *masc*

★ **treat** NOUN
▷ *see also* **treat** VERB
1 le petit cadeau *masc* (PL les petits cadeaux) (*present*)
2 la gâterie *fem* (*food*)
■ **to give somebody a treat** faire [36] plaisir à quelqu'un

★ to **treat** VERB
▷ *see also* **treat** NOUN
traiter [28] (*well, badly*)
■ **to treat somebody to something** offrir [54] quelque chose à quelqu'un □ He treated us to an ice cream. Il nous a offert une glace.

★ **treatment** NOUN
le traitement *masc*

English-French

t

to **treble** VERB
tripler [28]
□ The cost of living there has trebled. Le coût de la vie là-bas a triplé.

★ **tree** NOUN
l'arbre *masc*

to **tremble** VERB
trembler [28]

tremendous ADJECTIVE
énorme (FEM énorme)
□ a tremendous success un succès énorme

trend NOUN
1 la mode *fem* (*fashion*)
□ to set a trend lancer [12] une mode
2 la tendance *fem* (*tendency*)
□ a downward trend in exam results une tendance à la baisse dans les résultats aux examens.

trendy ADJECTIVE
branché (FEM branchée)

★ **trial** NOUN
le procès *masc* (*in court*)

triangle NOUN
le triangle *masc*

tribe NOUN
la tribu *fem*

★ **trick** NOUN
▷ *see also* **trick** VERB
1 le tour *masc*
□ to play a trick on somebody jouer un tour à quelqu'un
2 le truc *masc* (*knack*)
□ It's not easy: there's a trick to it. Ce n'est pas facile: il y a un truc.

★ to **trick** VERB
▷ *see also* **trick** NOUN
■ **to trick somebody** rouler [28] quelqu'un

tricky ADJECTIVE
délicat (FEM délicate)

tricycle NOUN
le tricycle *masc*

trifle NOUN
le diplomate *masc* (*dessert*)

to **trim** VERB
▷ *see also* **trim** NOUN
1 égaliser [28] (*hair*)
2 tondre [69] (*grass*)

trim NOUN
▷ *see also* **trim** VERB
la coupe d'entretien *fem* (*haircut*)
□ to have a trim se faire rafraîchir la coupe

★ **trip** NOUN
▷ *see also* **trip** VERB
le voyage *masc*
□ to go on a trip faire un voyage □ Have a good trip! Bon voyage!
■ **a day trip** une excursion d'une journée

★ to **trip** VERB
▷ *see also* **trip** NOUN
trébucher [28] (*stumble*)

triple ADJECTIVE
triple (FEM triple)

triplets PL NOUN
les triplés *masc pl*
les triplées *fem pl*

trivial ADJECTIVE
insignifiant (FEM insignifiante)

trod, trodden VERB ▷ *see* **tread**

trolley NOUN
le chariot *masc*

trombone NOUN
le trombone *masc*
□ I play the trombone. Je joue du trombone.

troops PL NOUN
les troupes *masc pl*
□ British troops les troupes britanniques

trophy NOUN
le trophée *masc*
□ to win a trophy gagner un trophée

tropical ADJECTIVE
tropical (FEM tropicale)
□ The weather was tropical. Il faisait une chaleur tropicale.

to **trot** VERB
trotter [28]

★ **trouble** NOUN
le problème *masc*
□ The trouble is, it's too expensive. Le problème, c'est que c'est trop cher.
■ **to be in trouble** avoir [8] des ennuis
■ **What's the trouble?** Qu'est-ce qui ne va pas?
■ **stomach trouble** troubles gastriques
■ **to take a lot of trouble over something** se donner [28] beaucoup de mal pour quelque chose
■ **Don't worry, it's no trouble.** Mais non, ça ne me dérange pas du tout.

troublemaker NOUN
l'élément perturbateur *masc*

★ **trousers** PL NOUN
le pantalon *masc sing*
□ a pair of trousers un pantalon

trout NOUN
la truite *fem*

truant NOUN
■ **to play truant** faire [36] l'école buissonnière

★ **truck** NOUN
le camion *masc*

truck driver NOUN
le camionneur *masc*
la conductrice de camion *fem*
□ He's a truck driver. Il est camionneur.

★ **true** ADJECTIVE
vrai (FEM vraie)
■ **That's true.** C'est vrai.
■ **to come true** se réaliser [28] □ I hope my dream will come true. J'espère que mon rêve se réalisera.
■ **true love** le grand amour

truly ADVERB
vraiment
□ It was a truly remarkable victory. C'était vraiment une victoire remarquable.

trumpet NOUN
la trompette *fem*
□ She plays the trumpet. Elle joue de la trompette.

trunk NOUN
1 le tronc *masc* (*of tree*)
2 la trompe *fem* (*of elephant*)
3 la malle *fem* (*luggage*)
4 le coffre *masc* (US: *of car*)

trunks PL NOUN
■ **swimming trunks** le maillot de bain
■ **a pair of trunks** un maillot de bain

★ **trust** NOUN
▷ *see also* **trust** VERB
la confiance *fem*
□ to have trust in somebody avoir confiance en quelqu'un

★ to **trust** VERB
▷ *see also* **trust** NOUN
■ **to trust somebody** faire [36] confiance à quelqu'un □ Don't you trust me? Tu ne me fais pas confiance? □ Trust me! Fais-moi confiance!

trusting ADJECTIVE
confiant (FEM confiante)

★ **truth** NOUN
la vérité *fem*

truthful ADJECTIVE
■ **She's a very truthful person.** Elle dit toujours la vérité.

★ **try** NOUN
▷ *see also* **try** VERB
l'essai *masc*
□ his third try son troisième essai
■ **to have a try** essayer [59]
■ **It's worth a try.** Ça vaut la peine d'essayer.
■ **to give something a try** essayer [59] quelque chose

★ to **try** VERB
▷ *see also* **try** NOUN
1 essayer [59] (*attempt*)
□ to try to do something essayer de faire quelque chose
■ **to try again** refaire [36] un essai
2 goûter [28] (*taste*)
□ Would you like to try some? Voulez-vous goûter?

to **try on** VERB
essayer [59] (*clothes*)

to **try out** VERB
essayer [59]

T-shirt NOUN
le tee-shirt *masc*

★ **tube** NOUN
le tube *masc*
■ **the Tube** (*underground*) le métro

tuberculosis NOUN
la tuberculose *fem*

★ **Tuesday** NOUN
le mardi *masc*
□ on Tuesday mardi □ on Tuesdays le mardi
□ every Tuesday tous les mardis □ last Tuesday mardi dernier □ next Tuesday mardi prochain
■ **Shrove Tuesday** (*Pancake Tuesday*) le mardi gras

tug-of-war NOUN
la lutte à la corde *fem*

tuition NOUN
les cours *masc pl*
■ **private tuition** les cours particuliers

tulip NOUN
la tulipe *fem*

tumble dryer NOUN
le sèche-linge *masc* (PL les sèche-linge)

tummy NOUN
le ventre *masc*

tuna NOUN
le thon *masc*

★ **tune** NOUN
l'air *masc* (*melody*)
■ **to play in tune** jouer [28] juste
■ **to sing out of tune** chanter [28] faux

Tunisia NOUN
la Tunisie *fem*
■ **in Tunisia** en Tunisie

★ **tunnel** NOUN
le tunnel *masc*
■ **the Channel Tunnel** le tunnel sous la Manche

Turk NOUN
le Turc *masc*
la Turque *fem*

Turkey NOUN
la Turquie *fem*
■ **in Turkey** en Turquie
■ **to Turkey** en Turquie

turkey NOUN
1 la dinde *fem* (*meat*)
2 le dindon *masc* (*live bird*)

English-French

t

★ = core vocabulary

English-French

Turkish NOUN
▷ *see also* **Turkish** ADJECTIVE
le turc *masc* (*language*)

Turkish ADJECTIVE
▷ *see also* **Turkish** NOUN
turc (FEM turque)

★ **turn** NOUN
▷ *see also* **turn** VERB
1 le tournant *masc* (*bend in road*)
■ **'no left turn'** 'défense de tourner à gauche'
2 le tour *masc* (*go*)
□ It's my turn! C'est mon tour!

★ to **turn** VERB
▷ *see also* **turn** NOUN
1 tourner [28]
□ Turn right at the lights. Tournez à droite aux feux.
2 devenir [25E] (*become*)
□ to turn red devenir rouge
■ **to turn into something** se transformer [28] en quelque chose □ The frog turned into a prince. La grenouille s'est transformée en prince.

to **turn back** VERB
faire [36] demi-tour
□ We turned back. Nous avons fait demi-tour.

to **turn down** VERB
1 refuser [28] (*offer*)
2 baisser [28] (*radio, TV, heating*)
□ Shall I turn the heating down? Je baisse le chauffage?

to **turn off** VERB
1 éteindre [60] (*light, radio*)
2 fermer [28] (*tap*)
3 arrêter [28] (*engine*)

to **turn on** VERB
1 allumer [28] (*light, radio*)
2 ouvrir [55] (*tap*)
3 mettre [47] en marche (*engine*)

to **turn out** VERB
■ **It turned out to be a mistake.** Il s'est avéré que c'était une erreur.
■ **It turned out that she was right.** Il s'est avéré qu'elle avait raison.

t

to **turn round** VERB
1 faire [36] demi-tour (*car*)
2 se retourner [72] (*person*)

to **turn up** VERB
1 arriver [5E] (*arrive*)
2 monter [48] (*heater*)
■ **Could you turn up the radio?** Tu peux monter le son de la radio?

turning NOUN
■ **It's the third turning on the left.** C'est la troisième à gauche.
■ **We took the wrong turning.** Nous n'avons pas tourné au bon endroit.

turnip NOUN
le navet *masc*

turquoise ADJECTIVE
turquoise (FEM+PL turquoise) (*colour*)

turtle NOUN
la tortue *fem*

tutor NOUN
le professeur particulier *masc* (*private teacher*)

tuxedo NOUN (US)
le smoking *masc*

★ **TV** NOUN
la télé *fem*

tweet NOUN
▷ *see also* **tweet** VERB
le tweet *masc* (*on Twitter*)

to **tweet** VERB
▷ *see also* **tweet** NOUN
tweeter [28] (*on Twitter*)

tweezers PL NOUN
la pince à épiler *fem sing*

★ **twelfth** ADJECTIVE
douzième (FEM douzième)
□ the twelfth floor le douzième étage
■ **the twelfth of August** le douze août

★ **twelve** NUMBER
douze
□ She's twelve. Elle a douze ans.
■ **twelve o'clock 1** (*midday*) midi
2 (*midnight*) minuit

★ **twentieth** ADJECTIVE
vingtième (FEM vingtième)
□ the twentieth time la vingtième fois
■ **the twentieth of May** le vingt mai

★ **twenty** NUMBER
vingt
□ He's twenty. Il a vingt ans.
■ **in twenty fourteen** en deux mille quatorze

★ **twice** ADVERB
deux fois
■ **twice as much** deux fois plus □ He gets twice as much pocket money as me. Il a deux fois plus d'argent de poche que moi.

★ **twin** NOUN
le jumeau *masc* (MASC PL les jumeaux)
la jumelle *fem*
■ **my twin brother** mon frère jumeau
■ **her twin sister** sa sœur jumelle
■ **identical twins** les vrais jumeaux
■ **a twin room** une chambre à deux lits

twinned ADJECTIVE
jumelé (FEM jumelée)
□ Stroud is twinned with Châteaubriant. Stroud est jumelée avec Châteaubriant.

★ to **twist** VERB
1 tordre [49] (*bend*)
2 déformer [28] (*distort*)

□ You're twisting my words. Tu déformes ce que j'ai dit.

twit NOUN

le crétin *masc*

la crétine *fem*

Twitter® NOUN

Twitter®

★ **two** NUMBER

deux

□ She's two. Elle a deux ans.

★ **type** NOUN

▷ *see also* **type** VERB

le type *masc*

□ What type of smartphone have you got? Quel type de smartphone as-tu?

★ to **type** VERB

▷ *see also* **type** NOUN

taper [28] à la machine

typewriter NOUN

la machine à écrire *fem*

★ **typical** ADJECTIVE

typique (FEM typique)

□ That's just typical! C'est typique!

tyre NOUN

le pneu *masc*

Uu

UFO NOUN
l'OVNI *masc* (= *objet volant non identifié*)

ugh EXCLAMATION
pouah!

★**ugly** ADJECTIVE
laid (FEM laide)

★**UK** NOUN (= *United Kingdom*)
le Royaume-Uni *masc*
■ **from the UK** du Royaume-Uni
■ **in the UK** au Royaume-Uni
■ **to the UK** au Royaume-Uni

ulcer NOUN
l'ulcère *masc*
■ **a mouth ulcer** un aphte

Ulster NOUN
l'Irlande du Nord *fem*
■ **in Ulster** en Irlande du Nord

ultimate ADJECTIVE
suprême (FEM suprême)
□ the ultimate challenge le défi suprême
■ **It was the ultimate adventure.** C'était la grande aventure.

ultimately ADVERB
au bout du compte
□ Ultimately, it's your decision. Au bout du compte, c'est votre décision.

★**umbrella** NOUN
1 le parapluie *masc*
2 le parasol *masc* (*for sun*)

umpire NOUN
1 l'arbitre *masc* (*in cricket*)
2 le juge de chaise *masc* (*in tennis*)

UN NOUN (= *United Nations*)
l'ONU *fem* (= *Organisation des Nations Unies*)

★**unable** ADJECTIVE
■ **to be unable to do something** ne pas pouvoir [64] faire quelque chose □ I was unable to come. Je n'ai pas pu venir.

unacceptable ADJECTIVE
inacceptable (FEM inacceptable)

unanimous ADJECTIVE
unanime (FEM unanime)
□ a unanimous decision une décision unanime

unattended ADJECTIVE
■ **to leave something unattended** laisser [28] quelque chose sans surveillance □ Never leave pets unattended in your car. Ne laissez jamais d'animaux domestiques sans surveillance dans votre voiture.

unavoidable ADJECTIVE
inévitable (FEM inévitable)

unaware ADJECTIVE
■ **to be unaware** **1** (*not know about*) ignorer [28] □ I was unaware of the regulations. J'ignorais le règlement. **2** (*not notice*) ne pas se rendre [7] compte □ She was unaware that she was being filmed. Elle ne se rendait pas compte qu'on la filmait.

unbearable ADJECTIVE
insupportable (FEM insupportable)

unbeatable ADJECTIVE
imbattable (FEM imbattable)

unbelievable ADJECTIVE
incroyable (FEM incroyable)

unborn ADJECTIVE
■ **the unborn child** le fœtus

unbreakable ADJECTIVE
incassable (FEM incassable)

uncanny ADJECTIVE
étrange (FEM étrange)
□ That's uncanny! C'est étrange!
■ **an uncanny resemblance** une ressemblance troublante

uncertain ADJECTIVE
incertain (FEM incertaine)
□ The future is uncertain. L'avenir est incertain.
■ **to be uncertain about something** ne pas être [35] sûr de quelque chose

uncivilized ADJECTIVE
barbare (FEM barbare)

★**uncle** NOUN
l'oncle *masc*
□ my uncle mon oncle

★**uncomfortable** ADJECTIVE
pas confortable (FEM pas confortable)
□ The seats are rather uncomfortable. Les sièges ne sont pas très confortables.

unconscious ADJECTIVE
sans connaissance

uncontrollable ADJECTIVE
incontrôlable (FEM incontrôlable)

unconventional ADJECTIVE
peu conventionnel (FEM peu conventionnelle)

★**under** PREPOSITION
1 sous
□ The cat's under the table. Le chat est sous la table. □ The tunnel goes under the Channel. Le tunnel passe sous la Manche.
■ **under there** là-dessous □ What's under there? Qu'est-ce qu'il y a là-dessous?
2 moins de (*less than*)
□ under 20 people moins de vingt personnes
□ children under 10 les enfants de moins de dix ans

underage ADJECTIVE
■ **He's underage.** Il n'a pas l'âge réglementaire.

undercover ADJECTIVE, ADVERB
secret (FEM secrète)
□ an undercover agent un agent secret
■ **She was working undercover.** Elle travaillait sous une fausse identité.

to **underestimate** VERB
sous-estimer [28]
□ I underestimated her. Je l'ai sous-estimée.

to **undergo** VERB
subir [38] (*operation, examination, change*)
■ **to be undergoing repairs** être [35] en réparation

★**underground** ADJECTIVE, ADVERB
▷ *see also* **underground** NOUN
1 souterrain (FEM souterraine)
□ an underground car park un parking souterrain
2 sous terre
□ Moles live underground. Les taupes vivent sous terre.

★**underground** NOUN
▷ *see also* **underground** ADJECTIVE, ADVERB
le métro *masc*
□ Is there an underground in Lille? Est-ce qu'il y a un métro à Lille?

to **underline** VERB
souligner [28]

underneath PREPOSITION, ADVERB
1 sous
□ underneath the carpet sous la moquette
2 dessous
□ I got out of the car and looked underneath. Je suis descendu de la voiture et j'ai regardé dessous.

underpaid ADJECTIVE
sous-payé (FEM sous-payée)
□ I'm underpaid. Je suis sous-payé.

underpants PL NOUN
le slip *masc sing*

underpass NOUN
1 le passage souterrain *masc* (*for people*)
2 le passage inférieur *masc* (*for cars*)

undershirt NOUN (US)
le maillot de corps *masc*

underskirt NOUN
le jupon *masc*

★to **understand** VERB
comprendre [65]
□ Do you understand? Vous comprenez? □ I don't understand this word. Je ne comprends pas ce mot. □ Is that understood? C'est compris?

★**understanding** ADJECTIVE
compréhensif (FEM compréhensive)
□ She's very understanding. Elle est très compréhensive.

understood VERB ▷ *see* **understand**

undertaker NOUN
l'entrepreneur des pompes funèbres *masc*

underwater ADJECTIVE, ADVERB
sous l'eau
□ This sequence was filmed underwater. Cette séquence a été filmée sous l'eau.
■ **an underwater camera** un appareil photographique de plongée
■ **underwater photography** la photographie subaquatique

★**underwear** NOUN
les sous-vêtements *masc pl*

underwent VERB ▷ *see* **undergo**

to **undo** VERB
1 défaire [36] (*buttons, knot*)
2 déballer [28] (*parcel*)

to **undress** VERB
se déshabiller [28] (*get undressed*)
□ The doctor told me to undress. Le médecin m'a dit de me déshabiller.

uneconomic ADJECTIVE
pas rentable (FEM pas rentable)

★**unemployed** ADJECTIVE
au chômage
□ He's unemployed. Il est au chômage. □ He's been unemployed for a year. Ça fait un an qu'il est au chômage.
■ **the unemployed** les chômeurs *masc pl*

★**unemployment** NOUN
le chômage *masc*

★**unexpected** ADJECTIVE
inattendu (FEM inattendue)
□ an unexpected visitor un visiteur inattendu

unexpectedly ADVERB
à l'improviste
□ They arrived unexpectedly. Ils sont arrivés à l'improviste.

★**unfair** ADJECTIVE
injuste (FEM injuste)

□ It's unfair to girls. C'est injuste pour les filles.

unfamiliar ADJECTIVE
■ **I heard an unfamiliar voice.** J'ai entendu une voix que je ne connaissais pas.

unfashionable ADJECTIVE
démodé (FEM démodée)

unfit ADJECTIVE
■ **I'm rather unfit.** Je ne suis pas en très bonne condition physique.

to **unfold** VERB
déplier [19]
□ She unfolded the map. Elle a déplié la carte.

unforgettable ADJECTIVE
inoubliable (FEM inoubliable)

★ **unfortunately** ADVERB
malheureusement
□ Unfortunately, I arrived late. Malheureusement, je suis arrivé en retard.

to **unfriend** VERB
supprimer [28] de sa liste d'amis
□ Her brother has unfriended her on Facebook. Son frère l'a supprimée de sa liste d'amis sur Facebook.

unfriendly ADJECTIVE
pas aimable (FEM pas aimable)
□ The waiters are a bit unfriendly. Les serveurs ne sont pas très aimables.

ungrateful ADJECTIVE
ingrat (FEM ingrate)

★ **unhappy** ADJECTIVE
malheureux (FEM malheureuse)
□ He was very unhappy as a child. Il était très malheureux quand il était petit.
■ **to look unhappy** avoir [8] l'air triste

unhealthy ADJECTIVE
1 maladif (FEM maladive) (*person*)
2 malsain (FEM malsaine) (*place, habit*)
3 pas sain (FEM pas saine) (*food*)

uni NOUN
la fac *fem* (*university*)
□ to go to uni aller à la fac

★ **uniform** NOUN
l'uniforme *masc*
□ school uniform l'uniforme scolaire

> **DID YOU KNOW...?**
> Most French children don't wear school uniform.

uninhabited ADJECTIVE
inhabité (FEM inhabitée)

union NOUN
le syndicat *masc* (*trade union*)

Union Jack NOUN
le drapeau du Royaume-Uni *masc*

unique ADJECTIVE
unique (FEM unique)

unit NOUN
1 l'unité *fem*
□ a unit of measurement une unité de mesure
2 l'élément *masc* (*piece of furniture*)
□ a kitchen unit un élément de cuisine

★ **United Kingdom** NOUN
le Royaume-Uni *masc*

United Nations NOUN
les Nations Unies *fem pl*

★ **United States** NOUN
les États-Unis *masc pl*
■ **in the United States** aux États-Unis
■ **to the United States** aux États-Unis

★ **universe** NOUN
l'univers *masc*

★ **university** NOUN
l'université *fem*
□ She's at university. Elle va à l'université.
□ Do you want to go to university? Tu veux aller à l'université? □ Lancaster University l'université de Lancaster

unleaded ADJECTIVE
■ **unleaded petrol** l' essence sans plomb *fem*

unleaded petrol NOUN
l'essence sans plomb *fem*

★ **unless** CONJUNCTION
■ **unless he leaves** à moins qu'il ne parte □ I won't come unless you phone me. Je ne viendrai pas à moins que tu ne me téléphones.

unlike PREPOSITION
contrairement à
□ Unlike him, I really enjoy flying. Contrairement à lui, j'adore prendre l'avion.

★ **unlikely** ADJECTIVE
peu probable (FEM peu probable)
□ It's possible, but unlikely. C'est possible, mais peu probable.

to **unload** VERB
décharger [45]
□ We unloaded the car. Nous avons déchargé la voiture. □ The lorries go there to unload. Les camions y vont pour être déchargés.

to **unlock** VERB
ouvrir [55]
□ He unlocked the door of the car. Il a ouvert la portière de la voiture.

★ **unlucky** ADJECTIVE
■ **to be unlucky** **1** (*number, object*) porter [28] malheur □ They say thirteen is an unlucky number. On dit que le nombre treize porte malheur. **2** (*person*) ne pas avoir [8] de chance □ Did you win? — No, I was unlucky. Vous avez gagné? — Non, je n'ai pas eu de chance.

unmarried ADJECTIVE
célibataire (FEM célibataire) (*person*)
■ **an unmarried couple** un couple non marié

Numbers in brackets refer to verb tables on pages 650 to 658

unnatural ADJECTIVE
pas naturel (FEM pas naturelle)

unnecessary ADJECTIVE
inutile (FEM inutile)

unofficial ADJECTIVE
1 non officiel (FEM non officielle) (*meeting, leader*)
2 sauvage (FEM sauvage) (*strike*)

to **unpack** VERB
1 défaire [36]
□ I unpacked my suitcase. J'ai défait ma valise.
2 déballer [28] ses affaires
□ I went to my room to unpack. Je suis allé dans ma chambre pour déballer mes affaires. □ I haven't unpacked my clothes yet. Je n'ai pas encore déballé mes affaires.

unpleasant ADJECTIVE
désagréable (FEM désagréable)

to **unplug** VERB
débrancher [28]

unpopular ADJECTIVE
impopulaire (FEM impopulaire)

unpredictable ADJECTIVE
imprévisible (FEM imprévisible)

unreal ADJECTIVE
incroyable (FEM incroyable) (*incredible*)
□ It was unreal! C'était incroyable!

unrealistic ADJECTIVE
peu réaliste (FEM peu réaliste)

unreasonable ADJECTIVE
pas raisonnable (FEM pas raisonnable)
□ Her attitude was completely unreasonable. Son attitude n'était pas du tout raisonnable.

unreliable ADJECTIVE
pas fiable (FEM pas fiable) (*car, machine*)
□ It's a nice car, but a bit unreliable. C'est une belle voiture, mais elle n'est pas très fiable.
■ **He's completely unreliable.** On ne peut pas du tout compter sur lui.

to **unroll** VERB
dérouler [28]

unsatisfactory ADJECTIVE
insatisfaisant (FEM insatisfaisante)

to **unscrew** VERB
dévisser [28]
□ She unscrewed the top of the bottle. Elle a dévissé le bouchon de la bouteille.

unshaven ADJECTIVE
mal rasé

unskilled ADJECTIVE
■ **unskilled worker** le manœuvre

unstable ADJECTIVE
instable (FEM instable)

unsteady ADJECTIVE
mal assuré (FEM mal assurée) (*walk, voice*)
■ **He was unsteady on his feet.** Il marchait d'un pas mal assuré.

unsuccessful ADJECTIVE
vain (FEM vaine) (*attempt*)
■ **to be unsuccessful** ne pas réussir [38]
□ an unsuccessful artist un artiste qui n'a pas réussi

unsuitable ADJECTIVE
inapproprié (FEM inappropriée) (*clothes, equipment*)

untidy ADJECTIVE
1 en désordre
□ My bedroom's always untidy. Ma chambre est toujours en désordre.
2 débraillé (FEM débraillée) (*appearance, person*)
□ He's always untidy. Il est toujours débraillé.
3 désordonné (FEM désordonnée) (*in character*)
□ He's a very untidy person. Il est très désordonné.

to **untie** VERB
1 défaire [36] (*knot, parcel*)
2 détacher [28] (*animal*)

★ **until** PREPOSITION, CONJUNCTION
1 jusqu'à
□ I waited until ten o'clock. J'ai attendu jusqu'à dix heures.
■ **until now** jusqu'à présent □ It's never been a problem until now. Ça n'a jamais été un problème jusqu'à présent.
■ **until then** jusque-là □ Until then I'd never been to France. Jusque-là je n'étais jamais allé en France.
2 avant

> Use **avant** if the sentence you want to translate contains a negative, such as 'not' or 'never'

□ It won't be ready until next week. Ça ne sera pas prêt avant la semaine prochaine. □ Until last year I'd never been to France. Avant l'année dernière, je n'étais jamais allé en France.

★ **unusual** ADJECTIVE
1 insolite (FEM insolite)
□ an unusual shape une forme insolite
2 rare (FEM rare)
□ It's unusual to get snow at this time of year. Il est rare qu'il neige à cette époque de l'année.

unwilling ADJECTIVE
■ **to be unwilling to do something** ne pas être [35] disposé à faire quelque chose □ He was unwilling to help me. Il n'était pas disposé à m'aider.

to **unwind** VERB
se détendre [88] (*relax*)

unwise ADJECTIVE
imprudent (FEM imprudente) (*person*)
□ That was rather unwise of you. C'était plutôt imprudent de votre part.

unwound VERB ▷ *see* **unwind**

to **unwrap** VERB

déballer [28]

□ After the meal we unwrapped the presents. Après le repas nous avons déballé les cadeaux.

★ **up** PREPOSITION, ADVERB

For other expressions with 'up', see the verbs 'go', 'come', 'put', 'turn' etc.

en haut

□ up on the hill en haut de la colline

■ **up here** ici

■ **up there** là-haut

■ **up north** dans le nord

■ **to be up** (*out of bed*) être [35] levé □ We were up at 6. Nous étions levés à six heures. □ He's not up yet. Il n'est pas encore levé.

■ **What's up?** Qu'est-ce qu'il y a? □ What's up with her? Qu'est-ce qu'elle a?

■ **to get up** (*in the morning*) se lever [43] □ What time do you get up? À quelle heure est-ce que tu te lèves?

■ **to go up** monter [48E] □ The bus went up the hill. Le bus a monté la colline.

The verb **monter** uses **avoir** in the perfect tense instead of **être** when talking about a person or thing moving up something (for example, up the hill).

■ **to go up to somebody** s'approcher [28] de quelqu'un □ She came up to me. Elle s'est approchée de moi.

■ **up to** (*as far as*) jusqu'à □ to count up to fifty compter jusqu'à cinquante □ up to three hours jusqu'à trois heures □ up to now jusqu'à présent

■ **It's up to you.** C'est à vous de décider.

upbringing NOUN

l'éducation *fem*

uphill ADVERB

■ **to go uphill** monter [48E]

to **upload** VERB

télécharger [45]

upper ADJECTIVE

supérieur (FEM supérieure)

□ on the upper floor à l'étage supérieur

upright ADJECTIVE

■ **to stand upright** se tenir [83] droit

★ **upset** NOUN

▷ *see also* **upset** ADJECTIVE, VERB

■ **a stomach upset** une indigestion

★ **upset** ADJECTIVE

▷ *see also* **upset** NOUN, VERB

contrarié (FEM contrariée)

□ She's still a bit upset. Elle est encore un peu contrariée.

■ **I had an upset stomach.** J'avais l'estomac dérangé.

★ to **upset** VERB

▷ *see also* **upset** NOUN, ADJECTIVE

■ **to upset somebody** contrarier [19] quelqu'un

upside down ADVERB

à l'envers

□ That painting is upside down. Ce tableau est à l'envers.

upstairs ADVERB

en haut

□ Where's your coat? — It's upstairs. Où est ton manteau? — Il est en haut.

■ **to go upstairs** monter [48E]

uptight ADJECTIVE

tendu (FEM tendue)

□ She's really uptight. Elle est très tendue.

★ **up-to-date** ADJECTIVE

1 moderne (FEM moderne) (*car, stereo*)

2 à jour (*information*)

□ an up-to-date timetable un horaire à jour

■ **to bring something up to date** moderniser [28] quelque chose

upwards ADVERB

vers le haut

□ to look upwards regarder vers le haut

★ **urgent** ADJECTIVE

urgent (FEM urgente)

□ Is it urgent? C'est urgent?

urine NOUN

l'urine *fem*

★ **US** NOUN

les USA *masc pl*

★ **us** PRONOUN

nous

□ They helped us. Ils nous ont aidés. □ They gave us a map. Ils nous ont donné une carte.

★ **USA** NOUN

les USA *masc pl*

USB stick NOUN

la clé USB *fem*

★ **use** NOUN

▷ *see also* **use** VERB

■ **It's no use.** Ça ne sert à rien. □ It's no use shouting, she's deaf. Ça ne sert à rien de crier, elle est sourde.

■ **It's no use, I can't do it.** Il n'y a rien à faire, je n'y arrive pas.

■ **to make use of something** utiliser [28] quelque chose

★ to **use** VERB

▷ *see also* **use** NOUN

utiliser [28]

□ Can we use a dictionary in the exam? Est-ce qu'on peut utiliser un dictionnaire à l'examen?

■ **Can I use your phone?** Je peux téléphoner?

■ **to use the toilet** aller [3E] aux W.C.

■ **I used to live in London.** J'habitais à Londres autrefois.

■ **I didn't use to like maths, but now I do.** Avant, je n'aimais pas les maths, mais maintenant je les aime.

■ **to be used to something** avoir [8] l'habitude de quelque chose □ **He wasn't used to getting up early.** Il n'avait pas l'habitude de se lever tôt. □ **Don't worry, I'm used to it.** Ne t'inquiète pas, j'ai l'habitude.

■ **a used car** une voiture d'occasion

to **use up** VERB

1 finir [38]

□ **We've used up all the paint.** Nous avons fini la peinture.

2 dépenser [28] (*money*)

★ **useful** ADJECTIVE

utile (FEM utile)

★ **useless** ADJECTIVE

nul (FEM nulle)

□ **This app is just useless.** Cette appli est vraiment nulle. □ **You're useless!** Tu es nul!

■ **It's useless!** Ça ne sert à rien!

★ **user** NOUN

l'utilisateur *masc*

l'utilisatrice *fem*

user-friendly ADJECTIVE

facile à utiliser (FEM facile à utiliser)

username NOUN

le nom d'utilisateur *masc*

■ **What's your username?** Quel est ton nom d'utilisateur?

★ **usual** ADJECTIVE

habituel (FEM habituelle)

■ **as usual** comme d'habitude

★ **usually** ADVERB

1 en général (*generally*)

□ **I usually get to school at about half past eight.** En général, j'arrive à l'école vers huit heures et demie.

2 d'habitude (*when making a contrast*)

□ **Usually I don't wear make-up, but today is a special occasion.** D'habitude je ne me maquille pas, mais aujourd'hui c'est spécial.

utility room NOUN

la buanderie *fem*

U-turn NOUN

le demi-tour *masc*

□ **to do a U-turn** faire demi-tour

Vv

vacancy NOUN
1 le poste vacant *masc* (*job*)
2 la chambre disponible *fem* (*room in hotel*)

vacant ADJECTIVE
libre (FEM libre)

vacation NOUN (US)
les vacances *fem pl*
□ to be on vacation être en vacances □ to take a vacation prendre des vacances

to **vaccinate** VERB
vacciner [28]

to **vacuum** VERB
passer [58] l'aspirateur
□ to vacuum the hall passer l'aspirateur dans le couloir

vacuum cleaner NOUN
l'aspirateur *masc*

vagina NOUN
le vagin *masc*

vague ADJECTIVE
vague (FEM vague)

vain ADJECTIVE
vaniteux (FEM vaniteuse)
□ He's so vain! Qu'est-ce qu'il est vaniteux!
■ **in vain** en vain

Valentine card NOUN
la carte de la Saint-Valentin *fem*

Valentine's Day NOUN
la Saint-Valentin *fem*

valid ADJECTIVE
valable (FEM valable)
□ This ticket is valid for three months. Ce billet est valable trois mois.

★ **valley** NOUN
la vallée *fem*

★ **valuable** ADJECTIVE
1 de valeur
□ a valuable picture un tableau de valeur
2 précieux (FEM précieuse)
□ valuable help une aide précieuse

valuables PL NOUN
les objets de valeur *masc pl*
□ Don't take any valuables with you. N'emportez pas d'objets de valeur.

★ **value** NOUN
la valeur *fem*

★ **van** NOUN
la camionnette *fem*

vandal NOUN
le/la vandale *masc/fem*

vandalism NOUN
le vandalisme *masc*

to **vandalize** VERB
saccager [45]

vanilla NOUN
la vanille *fem*
□ vanilla ice cream la glace à la vanille

to **vanish** VERB
disparaître [56]

to **vape** VERB
vapoter [28]

vaping NOUN
le vapotage *masc*
le vape *fem*

variable ADJECTIVE
variable (FEM variable)

varied ADJECTIVE
varié (FEM variée)

★ **variety** NOUN
la variété *fem*

★ **various** ADJECTIVE
plusieurs
□ We visited various villages in the area. Nous avons visité plusieurs villages de la région.

to **vary** VERB
varier [19]

vase NOUN
le vase *masc*

VAT NOUN (= *value added tax*)
la TVA *fem* (= *taxe sur la valeur ajoutée*)

veal NOUN
le veau *masc*

vegan NOUN
le/la végane *masc/fem* (*diet and lifestyle*)
le végétalien *masc* (*diet only*)
la végétalienne *fem* (*diet only*)
□ I'm a vegan. Je suis végétalien.

★ **vegetable** NOUN
le légume *masc*
□ vegetable soup la soupe aux légumes

★ **vegetarian** ADJECTIVE
▷ *see also* **vegetarian** NOUN
végétarien (FEM végétarienne)
□ I'm vegetarian. Je suis végétarien.
□ vegetarian lasagne les lasagnes végétariennes *fem pl*

★ **vegetarian** NOUN
▷ *see also* **vegetarian** ADJECTIVE
le végétarien *masc*
la végétarienne *fem*
□ I'm a vegetarian. Je suis végétarien.

★ **vehicle** NOUN
le véhicule *masc*

vein NOUN
la veine *fem*

velvet NOUN
le velours *masc*

vending machine NOUN
le distributeur automatique *masc*

Venetian blind NOUN
le store vénitien *masc*

verb NOUN
le verbe *masc*

★ **verdict** NOUN
le verdict *masc*

vertical ADJECTIVE
vertical (FEM verticale, MASC PL verticaux)

vertigo NOUN
le vertige *masc*
□ I get vertigo. J'ai le vertige.

★ **very** ADVERB
très
□ very tall très grand □ not very interesting pas très intéressant
■ **very much** beaucoup

vest NOUN
1 le maillot de corps *masc* (*underclothing*)
2 le gilet *masc* (US: *waistcoat*)

vet NOUN
le/la vétérinaire *masc/fem*
□ She's a vet. Elle est vétérinaire.

★ **via** PREPOSITION
en passant par
□ We went to Paris via Boulogne. Nous sommes allés à Paris en passant par Boulogne.

vicar NOUN
le pasteur *masc*
□ He's a vicar. Il est pasteur.

★ **vice** NOUN
l'étau *masc* (*for holding things*)

vice versa ADVERB
vice versa

vicious ADJECTIVE
1 brutal (FEM brutale, MASC PL brutaux)
□ a vicious attack une agression brutale
2 méchant (FEM méchante) (*dog, person*)
■ **a vicious circle** un cercle vicieux

★ **victim** NOUN
la victime *fem*
□ He was the victim of a mugging. Il a été victime d'une agression.

★ **victory** NOUN
la victoire *fem*

★ to **video** VERB
▷ *see also* **video** NOUN
filmer [28] (*with video camera*)

★ **video** NOUN
▷ *see also* **video** VERB
la vidéo *fem* (*film*)
□ to watch a video regarder une vidéo □ a video of my family on holiday une vidéo de ma famille en vacances
■ **a video camera** une caméra vidéo
■ **a video game** un jeu vidéo □ He likes playing video games. Il aime les jeux vidéo.

Vietnam NOUN
le Viêt-Nam *masc*
■ **in Vietnam** au Viêt-Nam

Vietnamese ADJECTIVE
vietnamien (FEM vietnamienne)

★ **view** NOUN
1 la vue *fem*
□ There's an amazing view. Il y a une vue extraordinaire.
2 l'avis *masc* (*opinion*)
□ in my view à mon avis

★ **viewer** NOUN
le téléspectateur *masc*
la téléspectatrice *fem*

viewpoint NOUN
le point de vue *masc*

vile ADJECTIVE
dégoûtant (FEM dégoûtante) (*smell, food*)

villa NOUN
la villa *fem*

★ **village** NOUN
le village *masc*

villain NOUN
1 le malfrat *masc* (*criminal*)
2 le méchant *masc* (*in film*)

vine NOUN
la vigne *fem*

★ **vinegar** NOUN
le vinaigre *masc*

vineyard NOUN
le vignoble *masc*

viola NOUN
l'alto *masc*
□ I play the viola. Je joue de l'alto.

★ **violence** NOUN
la violence *fem*

★ **violent** ADJECTIVE
violent (FEM violente)

★ **violin** NOUN
le violon *masc*
□ I play the violin. Je joue du violon.

violinist NOUN
le/la violoniste *masc/fem*

viral ADJECTIVE
viral (FEM virale, MASC PL viraux)
■ **a viral video** une vidéo virale

virgin NOUN
la vierge *fem*
□ to be a virgin être vierge

Virgo NOUN
la Vierge *fem*
□ I'm Virgo. Je suis Vierge.

virtual reality NOUN
la réalité virtuelle *fem*

★ **virus** NOUN
le virus *masc* (*also computing*)

visa NOUN
le visa *masc*

visible ADJECTIVE
visible (FEM visible)

★ **visit** NOUN
▷ *see also* **visit** VERB
1 la visite *fem* (*to museum*)
2 le séjour *masc* (*to country*)
□ Did you enjoy your visit to France? Ton séjour en France s'est bien passé?
■ **my last visit to my grandmother** la dernière fois que je suis allé voir ma grand-mère

★ to **visit** VERB
▷ *see also* **visit** NOUN
1 rendre [7] visite à (*person*)
□ to visit somebody rendre visite à quelqu'un
2 visiter [28] (*place*)
□ We'd like to visit the castle. Nous voudrions visiter le château.

★ **visitor** NOUN
1 le visiteur *masc*
la visiteuse *fem* (*tourist*)
2 l'invité *masc*
l'invitée *fem* (*guest*)
■ **to have a visitor** avoir [8] de la visite

visual ADJECTIVE
visuel (FEM visuelle)

to **visualize** VERB
imaginer [28]

★ **vital** ADJECTIVE
vital (FEM vitale, MASC PL vitaux)

★ **vitamin** NOUN
la vitamine *fem*

vivid ADJECTIVE
vif (FEM vive) (*colour*)
■ **to have a vivid imagination** avoir [8] une imagination débordante

vocabulary NOUN
le vocabulaire *masc*

vocational ADJECTIVE
professionnel (FEM professionnelle)
■ **a vocational course** un stage de formation professionnelle

vodka NOUN
la vodka *fem*

★ **voice** NOUN
la voix *fem* (PL les voix)

voice mail NOUN
la boîte vocale *fem*

volcano NOUN
le volcan *masc*

volleyball NOUN
le volley-ball *masc*
□ to play volleyball jouer au volley-ball

volt NOUN
le volt *masc*

voltage NOUN
le voltage *masc*

★ **voluntary** ADJECTIVE
volontaire (FEM volontaire) (*contribution, statement*)
■ **to do voluntary work** travailler [28] bénévolement

★ **volunteer** NOUN
▷ *see also* **volunteer** VERB
le/la volontaire *masc/fem*

★ to **volunteer** VERB
▷ *see also* **volunteer** NOUN
■ **to volunteer to do something** se proposer [28] pour faire quelque chose

to **vomit** VERB
vomir [38]

★ to **vote** VERB
voter [28]

voucher NOUN
le bon *masc*
□ a gift voucher un bon d'achat

vowel NOUN
la voyelle *fem*

vulgar ADJECTIVE
vulgaire (FEM vulgaire)

Ww

wafer NOUN
la gaufrette *fem*

★ **wage** NOUN
le salaire *masc*
□ He collected his wages. Il a retiré son salaire.

waist NOUN
la taille *fem*

waistcoat NOUN
le gilet *masc*

★ to **wait** VERB
attendre [7]
■ **to wait for something** attendre [7] quelque chose
■ **to wait for somebody** attendre [7] quelqu'un □ I'll wait for you. Je t'attendrai.
■ **Wait for me!** Attends-moi!
■ **Wait a minute!** Attends!
■ **to keep somebody waiting** faire [36] attendre quelqu'un □ They kept us waiting for hours. Ils nous ont fait attendre pendant des heures.
■ **I can't wait for the holidays.** J'ai hâte d'être en vacances.
■ **I can't wait to see him again.** J'ai hâte de le revoir.

to **wait up** VERB
attendre [7] pour se coucher
□ My mum always waits up till I get in. Ma mère attend toujours que je rentre pour se coucher.

★ **waiter** NOUN
le serveur *masc*
■ **Waiter!** Excusez-moi!

waiting list NOUN
la liste d'attente *fem*

waiting room NOUN
la salle d'attente *fem*

★ **waitress** NOUN
la serveuse *fem*

to **wake up** VERB
se réveiller [28]
□ I woke up at six o'clock. Je me suis réveillé à six heures.
■ **to wake somebody up** réveiller [28] quelqu'un □ Please would you wake me up at seven o'clock? Pourriez-vous me réveiller à sept heures?

★ **Wales** NOUN
le pays de Galles *masc*
■ **in Wales** au pays de Galles
■ **to Wales** au pays de Galles
■ **I'm from Wales.** Je suis gallois.
■ **the Prince of Wales** le prince de Galles

★ to **walk** VERB
▷ *see also* **walk** NOUN
1 marcher [28]
□ He walks fast. Il marche vite.
2 aller [3E] à pied (*go on foot*)
□ Are you walking or going by bus? Tu y vas à pied ou en bus? □ We walked 10 kilometres. Nous avons fait dix kilomètres à pied.
■ **to walk the dog** promener [43] le chien

★ **walk** NOUN
▷ *see also* **walk** VERB
la promenade *fem*
□ to go for a walk faire une promenade
■ **It's 10 minutes' walk from here.** C'est à dix minutes d'ici à pied.

walking NOUN
la randonnée *fem*
□ I did some walking in the Alps last summer. J'ai fait de la randonnée dans les Alpes l'été dernier.

walking stick NOUN
la canne *fem*

★ **wall** NOUN
le mur *masc*

wallet NOUN
le portefeuille *masc*

wallpaper NOUN
1 le papier peint *masc*
2 le fond d'écran *masc* (*for phone, PC*)

walnut NOUN
la noix *fem* (PL les noix)

to **wander** VERB
■ **to wander around** flâner [28] □ I just wandered around for a while. J'ai flâné un peu.

★ to **want** VERB
vouloir [93]
□ Do you want some cake? Tu veux du gâteau?
■ **to want to do something** vouloir [93] faire quelque chose □ I want to go to the cinema. Je veux aller au cinéma. □ What do you want to

do tomorrow? Qu'est-ce que tu veux faire demain?

★ **war** NOUN
la guerre *fem*

ward NOUN
la salle *fem* (*room in hospital*)

warden NOUN
le directeur *masc*
la directrice *fem* (*of youth hostel*)

wardrobe NOUN
l'armoire *fem* (*piece of furniture*)

warehouse NOUN
l'entrepôt *masc*

★ **warm** ADJECTIVE
1 chaud (FEM chaude)
□ warm water l'eau chaude
■ **It's warm in here.** Il fait chaud ici.
■ **to be warm** (*person*) avoir [8] chaud □ I'm too warm. J'ai trop chaud.
2 chaleureux (FEM chaleureuse)
□ a warm welcome un accueil chaleureux

to **warm up** VERB
1 s'échauffer [28] (*for sport*)
2 réchauffer [28] (*food*)
□ I'll warm up some pasta for you. Je vais te réchauffer des pâtes.

★ to **warn** VERB
prévenir [89]
□ Well, I warned you! Je t'avais prévenu!
■ **to warn somebody to do something** conseiller [28] à quelqu'un de faire quelque chose

warning NOUN
l'avertissement *masc*

Warsaw NOUN
Varsovie

wart NOUN
la verrue *fem*

was VERB ▷ *see* **be**

★ **wash** NOUN
▷ *see also* **wash** VERB
■ **to have a wash** se laver [28] □ I had a wash. Je me suis lavé.
■ **to give something a wash** laver [28] quelque chose □ He gave the car a wash. Il a lavé la voiture.

★ to **wash** VERB
▷ *see also* **wash** NOUN
1 laver [28]
□ to wash something laver quelque chose
2 se laver [28] (*have a wash*)
□ Every morning I get up, wash and get dressed. Tous les matins je me lève, je me lave et je m'habille.
■ **to wash one's hands** se laver [28] les mains
■ **to wash one's hair** se laver [28] les cheveux

to **wash up** VERB
faire [36] la vaisselle

washbasin NOUN
le lavabo *masc*

washcloth NOUN (US)
le gant de toilette *masc*

DID YOU KNOW...?
The French traditionally wash with a towelling glove rather than a flannel.

washing NOUN
le linge *masc*
□ dirty washing du linge sale
■ **Have you got any washing?** Tu as du linge à laver?
■ **to do the washing** faire [36] la lessive

washing machine NOUN
la machine à laver *fem*

washing powder NOUN
la lessive *fem*

★ **washing-up** NOUN
■ **to do the washing-up** faire [36] la vaisselle

washing-up liquid NOUN
le produit à vaisselle *masc*

wasn't = **was not**

wasp NOUN
la guêpe *fem*

★ **waste** NOUN
▷ *see also* **waste** VERB
1 le gaspillage *masc*
□ It's such a waste! C'est vraiment du gaspillage!
■ **It's a waste of time.** C'est une perte de temps.
2 les déchets *masc pl* (*rubbish*)
□ nuclear waste les déchets nucléaires

★ to **waste** VERB
▷ *see also* **waste** NOUN
gaspiller [28]
□ I don't like wasting money. Je n'aime pas gaspiller de l'argent.
■ **to waste time** perdre [61] du temps
□ There's no time to waste. Il n'y a pas de temps à perdre.

wastepaper basket NOUN
la corbeille à papier *fem*

★ **watch** NOUN
▷ *see also* **watch** VERB
la montre *fem*

★ to **watch** VERB
▷ *see also* **watch** NOUN
1 regarder [28]
□ to watch television regarder la télévision
□ Watch me! Regarde-moi!
2 surveiller [28] (*keep a watch on*)
□ The police were watching the house. La police surveillait la maison.

to **watch out** VERB
faire [36] attention
■ **Watch out!** Attention!

★**water** NOUN
▷ *see also* **water** VERB
l'eau *fem*

★to **water** VERB
▷ *see also* **water** NOUN
arroser [28]
□ He was watering his garden. Il arrosait son jardin.

waterfall NOUN
la cascade *fem*

watering can NOUN
l'arrosoir *masc*

watermelon NOUN
la pastèque *fem*

waterproof ADJECTIVE
imperméable (FEM imperméable)
□ Is this jacket waterproof? Ce blouson est-il imperméable?
■ **a waterproof watch** une montre étanche

water-skiing NOUN
le ski nautique *masc*
□ to go water-skiing faire du ski nautique

★**wave** NOUN
▷ *see also* **wave** VERB
1 la vague *fem* (*in water*)
2 le signe *masc* (*of hand*)
□ We gave him a wave. Nous lui avons fait signe.

★to **wave** VERB
▷ *see also* **wave** NOUN
faire [36] un signe de la main
□ to wave at somebody faire un signe de la main à quelqu'un
■ **to wave goodbye** faire [36] au revoir de la main □ I waved her goodbye. Je lui ai fait au revoir de la main.

wavy ADJECTIVE
ondulé (FEM ondulée)
□ wavy hair les cheveux ondulés

wax NOUN
la cire *fem*

★**way** NOUN
1 la façon *fem* (*manner*)
□ She looked at me in a strange way. Elle m'a regardé d'une façon étrange.
■ **This website tells you the right way to do it.** Ce site Internet explique comment il faut faire.
■ **You're doing it the wrong way.** Ce n'est pas comme ça qu'il faut faire.
■ **in a way ...** dans un sens ...
■ **a way of life** un mode de vie
2 le chemin *masc* (*route*)
□ I don't know the way. Je ne connais pas le chemin.
■ **on the way** en chemin □ We stopped on the way. Nous nous sommes arrêtés en chemin.
■ **It's a long way.** C'est loin. □ Sydney is a long way from London. Sydney est loin de Londres.
■ **Which way is it?** C'est par où?
■ **The supermarket is this way.** Le supermarché est par ici.
■ **Do you know the way to the station?** Vous savez comment aller à la gare?
■ **He's on his way.** Il arrive.
■ **'way in'** 'entrée'
■ **'way out'** 'sortie'
■ **by the way ...** au fait ...

★**we** PRONOUN
nous
□ We're staying here for a week. Nous restons une semaine ici.

★**weak** ADJECTIVE
faible (FEM faible)

wealthy ADJECTIVE
riche (FEM riche)

★**weapon** NOUN
l'arme *fem*

★to **wear** VERB
porter [28] (*clothes*)
□ She was wearing a sweatshirt and leggings. Elle portait un sweat-shirt et un legging.
■ **She was wearing black.** Elle était en noir.

★**weather** NOUN
le temps *masc*
□ What was the weather like? Quel temps a-t-il fait? □ The weather was lovely. Il a fait un temps magnifique.

★**weather forecast** NOUN
la météo *fem*

web NOUN
1 la toile *fem* (*spider*)
2 le Web *masc* (*World Wide Web*)

web address NOUN
l'adresse web *fem*

web browser NOUN
le navigateur *masc*

★**webcam** NOUN
la webcam *fem*

★**website** NOUN
le site web *masc*

webzine NOUN
le webzine *masc*

we'd = we had, we would

★**wedding** NOUN
le mariage *masc*
■ **wedding anniversary** l'anniversaire de mariage *masc*
■ **wedding dress** la robe de mariée

★ **Wednesday** NOUN
le mercredi *masc*
□ on Wednesday mercredi □ on Wednesdays le mercredi □ every Wednesday tous les mercredis □ last Wednesday mercredi dernier □ next Wednesday mercredi prochain

weed NOUN
la mauvaise herbe *fem*
□ The garden's full of weeds. Le jardin est plein de mauvaises herbes.

★ **week** NOUN
la semaine *fem*
□ last week la semaine dernière □ every week toutes les semaines □ next week la semaine prochaine □ in a week's time dans une semaine
■ **a week on Friday** vendredi en huit

weekday NOUN
■ **on weekdays** en semaine

★ **weekend** NOUN
le week-end *masc*
□ at weekends le week-end □ last weekend le week-end dernier □ next weekend le week-end prochain

to **weep** VERB
pleurer [28]

★ to **weigh** VERB
peser [43]
□ How much do you weigh? Combien est-ce que tu pèses? □ First, weigh the flour. Tout d'abord, pesez la farine.
■ **to weigh oneself** se peser [43]

★ **weight** NOUN
le poids *masc*
■ **to lose weight** maigrir [38]
■ **to put on weight** grossir [38]

weightlifter NOUN
l'haltérophile *masc/fem*

weightlifting NOUN
l'haltérophilie *fem*

weird ADJECTIVE
bizarre (FEM bizarre)

★ **welcome** NOUN
▷ *see also* **welcome** VERB
l'accueil *masc*
□ They gave her a warm welcome. Ils lui ont fait un accueil chaleureux.
■ **Welcome!** Bienvenue! □ Welcome to France! Bienvenue en France!

★ to **welcome** VERB
▷ *see also* **welcome** NOUN
■ **to welcome somebody** accueillir [22] quelqu'un
■ **Thank you! — You're welcome!** Merci! — De rien!

★ **well** ADJECTIVE, ADVERB
▷ *see also* **well** NOUN

1 bien
□ You did that really well. Tu as très bien fait ça.
■ **to do well** réussir [38] bien □ She's doing really well at school. Elle réussit vraiment bien à l'école.
■ **to be well** (*in good health*) aller [3E] bien □ I'm not very well at the moment. Je ne vais pas très bien en ce moment.
■ **get well soon!** remets-toi vite!
■ **well done!** bravo!

2 enfin
□ It's enormous! Well, quite big anyway. C'est énorme! Enfin, c'est assez grand.
■ **as well** aussi □ I decided to have dessert as well. J'ai décidé de prendre aussi un dessert.
□ We went to Chartres as well as Paris. Nous sommes allés à Paris et à Chartres aussi.

★ **well** NOUN
▷ *see also* **well** ADJECTIVE, ADVERB
le puits *masc* (PL les puits)

we'll = **we will**

well-behaved ADJECTIVE
sage (FEM sage)

well-dressed ADJECTIVE
bien habillé (FEM bien habillée)

wellingtons PL NOUN
les bottes en caoutchouc *fem pl*

★ **well-known** ADJECTIVE
célèbre (FEM célèbre)
□ a well-known film star une vedette de cinéma célèbre

well-off ADJECTIVE
aisé (FEM aisée)

★ **Welsh** NOUN
▷ *see also* **Welsh** ADJECTIVE
le gallois *masc* (*language*)

★ **Welsh** ADJECTIVE
▷ *see also* **Welsh** NOUN
gallois (FEM galloise)
□ She's Welsh. Elle est galloise.
■ **Welsh people** les Gallois *masc pl*

★ **Welshman** NOUN
le Gallois *masc*

★ **Welshwoman** NOUN
la Galloise *fem*

went VERB ▷ *see* **go**

wept VERB ▷ *see* **weep**

were VERB ▷ *see* **be**

we're = **we are**

weren't = **were not**

★ **west** NOUN
▷ *see also* **west** ADJECTIVE, ADVERB
l'ouest *masc*
□ in the west dans l'ouest

★ **west** ADJECTIVE, ADVERB
▷ *see also* **west** NOUN

1 ouest (FEM+PL ouest)
◻ the west coast la côte ouest
■ **west of** à l'ouest de ◻ Stroud is west of Oxford. Stroud est à l'ouest d'Oxford.
2 vers l'ouest
◻ We were travelling west. Nous allions vers l'ouest.
■ **the West Country** le sud-ouest de l'Angleterre

westbound ADJECTIVE
■ **The truck was westbound on the M5.** Le camion roulait sur la M5 en direction de l'ouest.
■ **Westbound traffic is moving very slowly.** La circulation en direction de l'ouest est très ralentie.

★ **western** NOUN
▷ *see also* **western** ADJECTIVE
le western *masc* (*film*)

★ **western** ADJECTIVE
▷ *see also* **western** NOUN
■ **the western part of the island** la partie ouest de l'île
■ **Western Europe** l'Europe de l'Ouest

West Indian NOUN
▷ *see also* **West Indian** ADJECTIVE
l'Antillais *masc*
l'Antillaise *fem* (*person*)

West Indian ADJECTIVE
▷ *see also* **West Indian** NOUN
antillais (FEM antillaise)
◻ She's West Indian. Elle est antillaise.

West Indies PL NOUN
les Antilles *fem pl*
■ **in the West Indies** aux Antilles

★ **wet** ADJECTIVE
mouillé (FEM mouillée)
◻ wet clothes les vêtements mouillés
■ **to get wet** se faire [36] mouiller
■ **dripping wet** trempé
■ **wet weather** le temps pluvieux
■ **It was wet all week.** Il a plu toute la semaine.

wetsuit NOUN
la combinaison de plongée *fem*

we've = **we have**

whale NOUN
la baleine *fem*

★ **what** ADJECTIVE, PRONOUN
1 quel (FEM quelle) (*which*)
◻ What subjects are you studying? Quelles matières est-ce que tu fais? ◻ What colour is it? C'est de quelle couleur? ◻ What's the capital of Turkey? Quelle est la capitale de la Turquie? ◻ What a mess! Quel fouillis!
2 qu'est-ce que
◻ What are you doing? Qu'est-ce que vous faites? ◻ What did you say? Qu'est-ce que vous avez dit? ◻ What is it? Qu'est-ce que c'est? ◻ What's the matter? Qu'est-ce qu'il y a?
3 qu'est-ce qui
◻ What happened? Qu'est-ce qui s'est passé? ◻ What's bothering you? Qu'est-ce qui te préoccupe?

In relative phrases use **ce qui** or **ce que** depending on whether 'what' refers to the subject or the object of the sentence.

4 ce qui (*subject*)
◻ I saw what happened. J'ai vu ce qui est arrivé. ◻ I know what's bothering you. Je sais ce qui te préoccupe.
ce que (*object*)
◻ Tell me what you did. Dites-moi ce que vous avez fait. ◻ I heard what he said. J'ai entendu ce qu'il a dit.
■ **What?** (*what did you say*) Comment?
■ **What!** (*shocked*) Quoi!

wheat NOUN
le blé *masc*

★ **wheel** NOUN
la roue *fem*
■ **the steering wheel** le volant

wheelchair NOUN
le fauteuil roulant *masc*

★ **when** ADVERB, CONJUNCTION
quand
◻ When did he go? Quand est-ce qu'il est parti? ◻ She was reading when I came in. Elle lisait quand je suis entré.

★ **where** ADVERB, CONJUNCTION
où
◻ Where's Emma today? Où est Emma aujourd'hui? ◻ Where do you live? Où habites-tu? ◻ Where are you going? Où vas-tu? ◻ a shop where you can buy croissants un magasin où l'on peut acheter des croissants

★ **whether** CONJUNCTION
si
◻ I don't know whether to go or not. Je ne sais pas si je dois y aller ou non.

★ **which** ADJECTIVE, PRONOUN
1 quel (FEM quelle)
◻ Which flavour do you want? Quel parfum est-ce que tu veux?

When asking 'which one' use **lequel** or **laquelle**, depending on whether the noun is masculine or feminine.

■ **I know his brother. — Which one?** Je connais son frère. — Lequel?
■ **I know his sister. — Which one?** Je connais sa sœur. — Laquelle?
■ **Which would you like?** Lequel est-ce que vous voulez?

■ **Which of these are yours?** Lesquels sont à vous?

In relative phrases use **qui** or **que** depending on whether 'which' refers to the subject or the object of the sentence.

2 qui (*subject*)
□ the film which is on TV now le film qui passe en ce moment à la télé
que (*object*)
□ the film which I saw yesterday le film que j'ai vu hier

★**while** CONJUNCTION
▷ *see also* **while** NOUN
1 pendant que
□ You hold the torch while I look inside. Tiens la lampe électrique pendant que je regarde à l'intérieur.
2 alors que
□ Abby is very dynamic, while Kay is more laid-back. Abby est très dynamique, alors que Kay est plus relax.

★**while** NOUN
▷ *see also* **while** CONJUNCTION
le moment *masc*
□ after a while au bout d'un moment
■ **a while ago** il y a un moment □ He was here a while ago. Il était là il y a un moment.
■ **for a while** pendant quelque temps □ I lived in London for a while. J'ai vécu à Londres pendant quelque temps.
■ **quite a while** longtemps □ quite a while ago il y a longtemps □ I haven't seen him for quite a while. Ça fait longtemps que je ne l'ai pas vu.

★**whip** NOUN
▷ *see also* **whip** VERB
le fouet *masc*

★to **whip** VERB
▷ *see also* **whip** NOUN
1 fouetter [28] (*person, animal*)
2 battre [9] (*eggs*)

whipped cream NOUN
la crème fouettée *fem*

whisk NOUN
le fouet *masc*

whiskers PL NOUN
les moustaches *fem pl*

whisky NOUN
le whisky *masc* (PL les whiskies)

★to **whisper** VERB
chuchoter [28]

whistle NOUN
▷ *see also* **whistle** VERB
le sifflet *masc*
■ **The referee blew his whistle.** L'arbitre a sifflé.

to **whistle** VERB
▷ *see also* **whistle** NOUN
siffler [28]

★**white** ADJECTIVE
blanc (FEM blanche)
□ He's got white hair. Il a les cheveux blancs.
■ **white wine** le vin blanc
■ **white bread** le pain blanc
■ **white coffee** le café au lait
■ **a white man** un Blanc
■ **a white woman** une Blanche
■ **white people** les Blancs

whiteboard NOUN
le tableau blanc *masc*
□ an interactive whiteboard un tableau blanc interactif

Whitsun NOUN
la Pentecôte *fem*

★**who** PRONOUN
1 qui
□ Who said that? Qui a dit ça? □ Who is Emmanuel Macron? Qui est Emmanuel Macron?

In relative phrases use **qui** or **que** depending on whether 'who' refers to the subject or the object of the verb.

2 qui (*subject*)
□ the man who saw us l'homme qui nous a vus □ the man who spoke to us l'homme qui nous a parlé
que (*object*)
□ the man who we saw l'homme que nous avons vu □ the man who she married l'homme qu'elle a épousé

★**whole** ADJECTIVE
▷ *see also* **whole** NOUN
tout (FEM toute)
□ the whole class toute la classe □ the whole afternoon tout l'après-midi
■ **a whole box of chocolates** toute une boîte de chocolats
■ **the whole world** le monde entier

★**whole** NOUN
▷ *see also* **whole** ADJECTIVE
■ **The whole of Wales was affected.** Le pays de Galles tout entier a été touché.
■ **on the whole** dans l'ensemble

wholemeal ADJECTIVE
complet (FEM complète)
■ **wholemeal bread** le pain complet

wholewheat ADJECTIVE (US)
complet (FEM complète)

★**whom** PRONOUN
qui
□ Whom did you see? Qui avez-vous vu? □ the man to whom I spoke l'homme à qui j'ai parlé

★**whose** PRONOUN, ADJECTIVE
1 à qui
□ Whose is this? À qui est-ce? □ I know whose it is. Je sais à qui c'est. □ Whose necklace is this? À qui est ce collier?

2 dont (*after noun*)
□ the girl whose picture was in the paper la jeune fille dont la photo était dans le journal

★ **why** ADVERB
pourquoi
□ Why did you do that? Pourquoi avez-vous fait ça? □ That's why he did it. Voilà pourquoi il a fait ça. □ Tell me why. Dis-moi pourquoi.
■ **I haven't done my homework. — Why not?** Je n'ai pas fait mes devoirs. — Pourquoi?
■ **All right, why not?** D'accord, pourquoi pas?

★ **wicked** ADJECTIVE
1 méchant (FEM méchante) (*evil*)
2 génial (FEM géniale, MASC PL géniaux) (*really great*)

wicket NOUN
le guichet *masc* (*stumps*)

★ **wide** ADJECTIVE, ADVERB
large (FEM large)
□ a wide road une route large
■ **wide open** grand ouvert □ The door was wide open. La porte était grande ouverte.
□ The windows were wide open. Les fenêtres étaient grandes ouvertes.
■ **wide awake** complètement réveillé

widow NOUN
la veuve *fem*
□ She's a widow. Elle est veuve.

widower NOUN
le veuf *masc*
□ He's a widower. Il est veuf.

width NOUN
la largeur *fem*

★ **wife** NOUN
la femme *fem*
□ She's his wife. C'est sa femme.

Wi-Fi NOUN
le wifi *masc*

wig NOUN
la perruque *fem*

★ **wild** ADJECTIVE
1 sauvage (FEM sauvage) (*not tame*)
□ a wild animal un animal sauvage
2 fou (FEM folle) (*crazy*)
□ She's a bit wild. Elle est un peu folle.

> fou changes to fol before a vowel and most words beginning with 'h'.

wildlife NOUN
la nature *fem*
□ I'm interested in wildlife. Je m'intéresse à la nature.

★ **will** NOUN
▷ *see also* **will** VERB
le testament *masc*
□ He left me some money in his will. Il m'a laissé de l'argent dans son testament.

★ **will** VERB
▷ *see also* **will** NOUN
■ **I'll show you your room.** Je vais te montrer ta chambre.
■ **I'll give you a hand.** Je vais t'aider.

> Use the French future tense when referring to the more distant future.

■ **I will finish it tomorrow.** Je le finirai demain.
■ **It won't take long.** Ça ne prendra pas longtemps.
■ **Will you wash up? — No, I won't.** Est-ce que tu peux faire la vaisselle? — Non.
■ **Will you help me?** Est-ce que tu peux m'aider?
■ **Will you be quiet!** Voulez-vous bien vous taire!
■ **That will be the postman.** Ça doit être le facteur.

★ **willing** ADJECTIVE
■ **to be willing to do something** être [35] prêt à faire quelque chose

★ to **win** VERB
▷ *see also* **win** NOUN
gagner [28]
□ Did you win? Est-ce que tu as gagné?
■ **to win a prize** remporter [28] un prix

★ **win** NOUN
▷ *see also* **win** VERB
la victoire *fem*

★ to **wind** VERB
▷ *see also* **wind** NOUN
1 enrouler [28] (*rope, wool, wire*)
2 serpenter [28] (*river, path*)
□ The road winds through the valley. La route serpente à travers la vallée.

★ **wind** NOUN
▷ *see also* **wind** VERB
le vent *masc*
□ There was a strong wind. Il y avait beaucoup de vent.
■ **a wind farm** un parc éolien
■ **a wind instrument** un instrument à vent
■ **wind power** l'énergie éolienne *fem*
■ **a wind turbine** une éolienne

windmill NOUN
le moulin à vent *masc*

★ **window** NOUN
1 la fenêtre *fem* (*of building*)
2 la vitre *fem* (*in car, train*)
■ **a shop window** une vitrine
3 le carreau *masc* (PL les carreaux) (*window pane*)
□ to break a window casser un carreau □ a broken window un carreau cassé

windscreen NOUN
le pare-brise *masc* (PL les pare-brise)

windscreen wiper NOUN
l'essuie-glace *masc* (PL les essuie-glace)

windshield NOUN (US)
le pare-brise *masc* (PL les pare-brise)

windshield wiper NOUN (US)
l'essuie-glace *masc* (PL les essuie-glace)

windy ADJECTIVE
venteux (FEM venteuse) (*place*)
■ **It's windy.** Il y a du vent.

★ **wine** NOUN
le vin *masc*
□ a bottle of wine une bouteille de vin □ a glass of wine un verre de vin
■ **white wine** le vin blanc
■ **red wine** le vin rouge
■ **a wine bar** un bar à vin
■ **a wine glass** un verre à vin
■ **the wine list** la carte des vins

★ **wing** NOUN
l'aile *fem*

to **wink** VERB
■ **to wink at somebody** faire [36] un clin d'œil à quelqu'un □ He winked at me. Il m'a fait un clin d'œil.

★ **winner** NOUN
le gagnant *masc*
la gagnante *fem*

★ **winning** ADJECTIVE
■ **the winning team** l'équipe gagnante
■ **the winning goal** le but décisif

★ **winter** NOUN
l'hiver *masc*
■ **in winter** en hiver

winter sports PL NOUN
les sports d'hiver *masc pl*

★ to **wipe** VERB
essuyer [53]
■ **to wipe one's feet** s'essuyer [53] les pieds □ Wipe your feet! Essuie-toi les pieds!

to **wipe up** VERB
essuyer [53]

★ **wire** NOUN
le fil de fer *masc*

wireless ADJECTIVE
sans fil
□ wireless technology la technologie sans fil

wisdom tooth NOUN
la dent de sagesse *fem*

★ **wise** ADJECTIVE
sage (FEM sage)

★ to **wish** VERB
▷ *see also* **wish** NOUN
■ **to wish for something** souhaiter [28] quelque chose □ What more could you wish for? Que pourrais-tu souhaiter de plus?
■ **to wish to do something** désirer [28] faire quelque chose □ I wish to make a complaint. Je désire porter plainte.
■ **I wish you were here!** Si seulement tu étais ici!
■ **I wish you'd told me!** Si seulement tu m'en avais parlé!

★ **wish** NOUN
▷ *see also* **wish** VERB
le vœu *masc* (PL les vœux)
□ to make a wish faire un vœu
■ **'best wishes'** **1** (*on greetings card*) 'meilleurs vœux' **2** (*at the end of email, letter*) 'bien amicalement'

wit NOUN
l'esprit *masc* (*humour*)

★ **with** PREPOSITION
1 avec
□ Come with me. Venez avec moi. □ He walks with a stick. Il marche avec une canne.
■ **a woman with blue eyes** une femme aux yeux bleus
2 chez (*at the home of*)
□ We stayed with friends. Nous avons logé chez des amis.
3 de
□ green with envy vert de jalousie □ to shake with fear trembler de peur □ Fill the jug with water. Remplis la carafe d'eau.

★ **within** PREPOSITION
■ **The shops are within easy reach.** Les magasins sont à proximité.
■ **within the week** avant la fin de la semaine

★ **without** PREPOSITION
sans
□ without a coat sans manteau □ without speaking sans parler

witness NOUN
le témoin *masc*
□ There were no witnesses. Il n'y avait pas de témoins.

witty ADJECTIVE
spirituel (FEM spirituelle)

wives PL NOUN ▷ *see* **wife**

woke up, woken up VERB ▷ *see* **wake up**

wolf NOUN
le loup *masc*

★ **woman** NOUN
la femme *fem*

won VERB ▷ *see* **win**

★ to **wonder** VERB
se demander [28]
□ I wonder why she said that. Je me demande pourquoi elle a dit ça. □ I wonder what that means. Je me demande ce que ça veut dire. □ I wonder where Caroline is. Je me demande où est Caroline.

★ **wonderful** ADJECTIVE

formidable (FEM formidable)

won't = will not

★ **wood** NOUN

le bois *masc* (*timber, forest*)

□ It's made of wood. C'est en bois. □ We went for a walk in the wood. Nous sommes allés nous promener dans le bois.

★ **wooden** ADJECTIVE

en bois

□ a wooden chair une chaise en bois

woodwork NOUN

la menuiserie *fem*

□ My hobby is woodwork. Je fais de la menuiserie.

wool NOUN

la laine *fem*

□ It's made of wool. C'est en laine.

★ **word** NOUN

le mot *masc*

□ a difficult word un mot difficile

■ **What's the word for 'shop' in French?** Comment dit-on 'shop' en français?

■ **in other words** en d'autres termes

■ **to have a word with somebody** parler [28] avec quelqu'un

■ **the words** (*lyrics*) les paroles *fem pl* □ I really like the words of this song. J'adore les paroles de cette chanson.

word processing NOUN

le traitement de texte *masc*

word processor NOUN

le traitement de texte *masc*

wore VERB ▷ *see* **wear**

★ **work** NOUN

▷ *see also* **work** VERB

le travail *masc* (PL les travaux)

□ She's looking for work. Elle cherche du travail. □ He's at work at the moment. Il est au travail en ce moment.

■ **It's hard work.** C'est dur.

■ **to be off work** (*sick*) être [35] malade

□ He's been off work for a week. Il est malade depuis une semaine.

■ **He's out of work.** Il est sans emploi.

★ to **work** VERB

▷ *see also* **work** NOUN

1 travailler [28] (*person*)

□ She works in a shop. Elle travaille dans un magasin. □ to work hard travailler dur

2 marcher [28] (*machine, plan*)

□ The heating isn't working. Le chauffage ne marche pas. □ My plan worked perfectly. Mon plan a marché impeccablement.

to **work out** VERB

1 faire [36] de l'exercice (*exercise*)

□ I work out twice a week. Je fais de l'exercice deux fois par semaine.

2 marcher [28] (*turn out*)

□ In the end it worked out really well. Au bout du compte, ça a très bien marché.

3 arriver [5E] à comprendre (*figure out*)

□ I just couldn't work it out. Je n'arrivais pas du tout à comprendre.

■ **It works out at £10 each.** Ça fait dix livres chacun.

★ **worker** NOUN

l'ouvrier *masc*

l'ouvrière *fem* (*in factory*)

■ **He's a factory worker.** Il est ouvrier.

■ **She's a good worker.** Elle travaille bien.

work experience NOUN

le stage *masc*

□ I'm going to do work experience in an office. Je vais faire un stage dans un bureau.

working-class ADJECTIVE

ouvrier (FEM ouvrière)

□ a working-class family une famille ouvrière

workman NOUN

l'ouvrier *masc*

works NOUN

l'usine *fem* (*factory*)

worksheet NOUN

la feuille d'exercices *fem*

workshop NOUN

l'atelier *masc*

□ a drama workshop un atelier de théâtre

workspace NOUN

l'espace de travail *masc* (*computing*)

workstation NOUN

le poste de travail *masc*

★ **world** NOUN

le monde *masc*

■ **He's the world champion.** Il est champion du monde.

worm NOUN

le ver *masc*

worn VERB ▷ *see* **wear**

worn ADJECTIVE

usé (FEM usée)

□ The carpet is a bit worn. La moquette est un peu usée.

■ **worn out** (*tired*) épuisé (FEM épuisée)

★ **worried** ADJECTIVE

inquiet (FEM inquiète)

□ She's very worried. Elle est très inquiète.

■ **to be worried about something** s'inquiéter [34] pour quelque chose □ I'm worried about the exams. Je m'inquiète pour les examens.

■ **to look worried** avoir [8] l'air inquiet □ She looks a bit worried. Elle a l'air un peu inquiète.

★ to **worry** VERB

s'inquiéter [34]

■ **Don't worry!** Ne t'inquiète pas!

★ **worse** ADJECTIVE, ADVERB

1 pire (FEM pire)

□ It was even worse than that. C'était encore pire que ça. □ My results were bad, but his were even worse. Mes notes étaient mauvaises, mais les siennes étaient encore pires.

2 plus mal

□ I'm feeling worse. Je me sens plus mal.

to **worship** VERB

vénérer [34] (*God*)

■ **He really worships her.** Il est en adoration devant elle.

★ **worst** ADJECTIVE

▷ *see also* **worst** NOUN

■ **the worst** le plus mauvais □ the worst student in the class le plus mauvais élève de la classe □ He got the worst mark in the whole class. Il a eu la plus mauvaise note de toute la classe.

■ **my worst enemy** mon pire ennemi

■ **Maths is my worst subject.** Je suis vraiment nul en maths.

★ **worst** NOUN

▷ *see also* **worst** ADJECTIVE

le pire *masc*

□ The worst of it is that ... Le pire c'est que ...

■ **at worst** au pire

■ **if the worst comes to the worst** au pire

★ **worth** ADJECTIVE

■ **to be worth** valoir [87] □ It's worth a lot of money. Ça vaut très cher. □ How much is it worth? Ça vaut combien?

■ **It's worth it.** Ça vaut la peine. □ Is it worth it? Est-ce que ça vaut la peine? □ It's not worth it. Ça ne vaut pas la peine.

★ **would** VERB

■ **Would you like a biscuit?** Vous voulez un petit gâteau?

■ **Would you like to go and see a film?** Est-ce que tu veux aller voir un film?

■ **Would you close the door please?** Vous pouvez fermer la porte, s'il vous plaît?

■ **I'd like ...** J'aimerais ... □ I'd like to go to America. J'aimerais aller en Amérique. □ Shall we go and see a film? — Yes, I'd like that. Si on allait voir un film? — Oui, j'aimerais bien.

■ **I said I would do it.** J'ai dit que je le ferais.

■ **If you asked him he'd do it.** Si vous le lui demandiez, il le ferait.

■ **If you had asked him he would have done it.** Si vous le lui aviez demandé, il l'aurait fait.

wouldn't = **would not**

★ **wound** NOUN

▷ *see also* **wound** VERB

la blessure *fem*

★ to **wound** VERB

▷ *see also* **wound** NOUN

blesser [28]

□ He was wounded in the leg. Il a été blessé à la jambe.

★ to **wrap** VERB

emballer [28]

□ She's wrapping her Christmas presents. Elle est en train d'emballer ses cadeaux de Noël.

■ **Can you wrap it for me please?** (*in shop*) Vous pouvez me faire un papier cadeau, s'il vous plaît?

to **wrap up** VERB

emballer [28]

wrapping paper NOUN

le papier cadeau *masc*

wreck NOUN

▷ *see also* **wreck** VERB

1 le tas de ferraille *masc* (*vehicle, machine*)

□ That car is a wreck! Cette voiture est un tas de ferraille!

2 la loque *fem* (*person*)

□ After the exams I was a complete wreck. Après les examens j'étais une véritable loque.

to **wreck** VERB

▷ *see also* **wreck** NOUN

1 démolir [38] (*building, vehicle*)

□ The explosion wrecked the whole house. L'explosion a démoli toute la maison.

2 ruiner [28] (*plan, holiday*)

□ The trip was wrecked by bad weather. Le voyage a été ruiné par le mauvais temps.

wreckage NOUN

1 les débris *masc pl* (*of vehicle*)

2 les décombres *masc pl* (*of building*)

wrestler NOUN

le lutteur *masc*

la lutteuse *fem*

wrestling NOUN

la lutte *fem*

wrinkled ADJECTIVE

ridé (FEM ridée)

wrist NOUN

le poignet *masc*

★ to **write** VERB

écrire [30]

□ to write a letter écrire une lettre

■ **to write to somebody** écrire [30] à quelqu'un □ I'm going to write her an email in French. Je vais lui écrire un mail en français.

to **write down** VERB

noter [28]

□ I wrote down the address. J'ai noté l'adresse.

■ **Can you write it down for me, please?** Vous pouvez me l'écrire, s'il vous plaît?

★ **writer** NOUN

l'écrivain *masc*

□ She's a writer. Elle est écrivain.

★ **writing** NOUN

l'écriture *fem*

□ I can't read your writing. Je n'arrive pas à lire ton écriture.

■ **in writing** par écrit

★ **written** VERB ▷ *see* **write**

★ **wrong** ADJECTIVE, ADVERB

1 faux (FEM fausse) (*incorrect*)

□ The information they gave us was wrong. Les renseignements qu'ils nous ont donnés étaient faux.

■ **the wrong answer** la mauvaise réponse

■ **You've got the wrong number.** Vous vous êtes trompé de numéro.

2 mal (*morally bad*)

□ I think hunting is wrong. Je trouve que c'est mal de chasser.

■ **to be wrong** (*mistaken*) se tromper [28]

□ You're wrong about that. Tu te trompes.

■ **to do something wrong** se tromper [28]

□ You've done it wrong. Tu t'es trompé.

■ **to go wrong** (*plan*) mal tourner [28] □ The robbery went wrong and they got caught. Le cambriolage a mal tourné et ils ont été pris.

■ **What's wrong?** Qu'est-ce qui ne va pas?

■ **What's wrong with her?** Qu'est-ce qu'elle a?

wrote VERB ▷ *see* **write**

WWW NOUN (= *World Wide Web*)

le Web *masc*

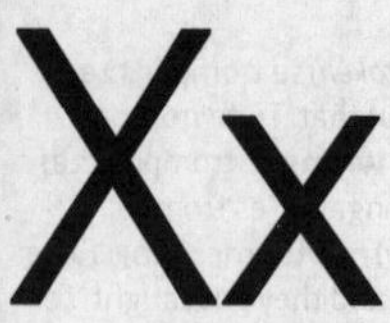

Xmas NOUN (= *Christmas*)
Noël

to **X-ray** VERB
▷ *see also* **X-ray** NOUN
■ **to X-ray something** faire [36] une radio de quelque chose □ They X-rayed my arm. Ils ont fait une radio de mon bras.

X-ray NOUN
▷ *see also* **X-ray** VERB
la radio *fem*
□ to have an X-ray passer une radio

★**yacht** NOUN
1 le voilier *masc* (*sailing boat*)
2 le yacht *masc* (*luxury motorboat*)

★**yard** NOUN
1 la cour *fem* (*of building*)
□ in the yard dans la cour
2 le mètre *masc*

DID YOU KNOW...?
In France, measurements are in metres rather than yards. A yard is slightly less than a metre.

to **yawn** VERB
bâiller [28]

★**year** NOUN
l'an *masc*
□ last year l'an dernier □ next year l'an prochain
■ **to be 15 years old** avoir [8] quinze ans
■ **an eight-year-old child** un enfant de huit ans

DID YOU KNOW...?
In French secondary schools, years are counted from the **sixième** (youngest) to **première** and **terminale** (oldest).

□ year 7 la sixième □ year 8 la cinquième
□ year 9 la quatrième □ year 10 la troisième
□ year 11 la seconde
■ **She's in year 11.** Elle est en seconde.
■ **He's a first-year.** Il est en sixième.

to **yell** VERB
hurler [28]

★**yellow** ADJECTIVE
jaune (FEM jaune)

★**yes** ADVERB
1 oui
□ Do you like it? — Yes. Tu aimes ça? — Oui.
■ **Would you like a cup of tea? — Yes please.** Voulez-vous une tasse de thé? — Je veux bien.
2 si

Use **si** when answering negative questions.

□ Don't you like it? — Yes! Tu n'aimes pas ça? — Si! □ You're not Swiss, are you? — Yes I am! Tu n'es pas suisse, si? — Si!

★**yesterday** ADVERB
hier
□ yesterday morning hier matin □ yesterday afternoon hier après-midi □ yesterday evening hier soir □ all day yesterday toute la journée d'hier

★**yet** ADVERB
encore
■ **not yet** pas encore □ It's not finished yet. Ce n'est pas encore fini.
■ **not as yet** pas encore □ There's no news as yet. Nous n'avons pas encore de nouvelles.
■ **Have you finished yet?** Vous avez fini?

to **yield** VERB (US)
céder [34] le passage (*on road sign*)

yob NOUN
le loubard *masc*

★**yoghurt** NOUN
le yaourt *masc*

yolk NOUN
le jaune d'œuf *masc*

★**you** PRONOUN

Only use **tu** when speaking to one person you know well or who is your own age or younger. If in doubt use **vous**.

1 vous (*polite form or plural*)
□ Do you like football? Est-ce que vous aimez le football? □ Can I help you? Est-ce que je peux vous aider? □ It's for you. C'est pour vous.
2 tu (*familiar singular*)
□ Do you like athletics? Tu aimes l'athlétisme?

vous never changes, but **tu** has different forms. When 'you' is the object of the sentence use **te** not **tu**. **te** becomes **t'** before a vowel sound.

3 te
□ I know you. Je te connais. □ I gave it to you. Je te l'ai donné.
t'
□ I saw you. Je t'ai vu. □ I'll help you. Je vais t'aider.
4 toi

toi is used instead of **tu** after a preposition and in comparisons.

□ It's for you. C'est pour toi. □ I'll come with you. Je viens avec toi. □ She's younger than you. Elle est plus jeune que toi.

★ **young** ADJECTIVE
jeune (FEM jeune)
■ **young people** les jeunes

younger ADJECTIVE
plus jeune (FEM plus jeune)
□ He's younger than me. Il est plus jeune que moi.
■ **my younger brother** mon frère cadet
■ **my younger sister** ma sœur cadette

youngest ADJECTIVE
plus jeune (FEM plus jeune)
□ my youngest brother mon plus jeune frère □ She's the youngest. C'est la plus jeune.

★ **your** ADJECTIVE

Only use **ton/ta/tes** when speaking to one person of your own age or younger. If in doubt use **votre/vos**.

1 votre (FEM votre) (*polite form or plural*)
□ your house votre maison
vos *pl*
□ your seats vos places
2 ton *masc* (*familiar singular*)
□ your brother ton frère
ta *fem*
□ your sister ta sœur
tes *pl*
□ your parents tes parents

ta becomes **ton** before a vowel sound

■ **your friend** **1** (*male*) ton ami **2** (*female*) ton amie

Do not use **votre/vos** or **ton/ta/tes** with parts of the body.

□ Would you like to wash your hands? Est-ce que vous voulez vous laver les mains? □ Do you want to wash your hair? Tu veux te laver les cheveux?

★ **yours** PRONOUN

Only use **le tien/la tienne/les tiens/les tiennes** when talking to one person of your own age or younger. If in doubt use **le vôtre/la vôtre/les vôtres**. The same applies to **à toi** and **à vous**.

1 le vôtre + *masc noun*
□ I've lost my pen. Can I use yours? J'ai perdu mon stylo. Je peux utiliser le vôtre?
la vôtre + *fem noun*
□ I like that car. Is it yours? J'aime cette voiture-là. C'est la vôtre?
les vôtres + *pl noun*
□ my parents and yours mes parents et les vôtres
■ **Is this yours?** C'est à vous? □ This book is yours. Ce livre est à vous. □ Whose is this? — It's yours. C'est à qui? — À vous.
■ **Yours sincerely ...** Veuillez agréer l'expression de mes sentiments les meilleurs ...
2 le tien + *masc noun*
□ I've lost my pen. Can I use yours? J'ai perdu mon stylo. Je peux utiliser le tien?
la tienne + *fem noun*
□ I like that car. Is it yours? J'aime cette voiture-là. C'est la tienne?
les tiens + *masc pl noun*
□ my parents and yours mes parents et les tiens
les tiennes + *fem pl noun*
□ My hands are dirty, yours are clean. Mes mains sont sales, les tiennes sont propres.
■ **Is this yours?** C'est à toi? □ This book is yours. Ce livre est à toi. □ Whose is this? — It's yours. C'est à qui? — À toi.

★ **yourself** PRONOUN

Only use **te** when talking to one person of your own age or younger; use **vous** to everyone else. If in doubt use **vous**.

1 vous (*polite form*)
□ Have you hurt yourself? Est-ce que vous vous êtes fait mal? □ Tell me about yourself! Parlez-moi de vous!
2 te (*familiar form*)
□ Have you hurt yourself? Est-ce que tu t'es fait mal?
3 toi (*familiar form*)

After a preposition, use **toi** instead of **te**.

□ Tell me about yourself! Parle-moi de toi!
4 toi-même
□ Do it yourself! Fais-le toi-même!
5 vous-même
□ Do it yourself! Faites-le vous-même!

★ **yourselves** PRONOUN
1 vous
□ Did you enjoy yourselves? Vous vous êtes bien amusés?
2 vous-mêmes
□ Did you make it yourselves? Vous l'avez fait vous-mêmes?

youth club NOUN
le centre de loisirs *masc*

youth hostel NOUN
l'auberge de jeunesse *fem*

Zz

zany ADJECTIVE
loufoque (FEM loufoque)

zebra NOUN
le zèbre *masc*

zebra crossing NOUN
le passage clouté *masc*

★ **zero** NOUN
le zéro *masc*

Zimbabwe NOUN
le Zimbabwe *masc*
▪ **in Zimbabwe** au Zimbabwe

Zimmer frame® NOUN
le déambulateur *masc*

zip NOUN
la fermeture éclair® *fem* (PL les fermetures éclair®)

zip code NOUN (US)
le code postal *masc*

zipper NOUN (US)
la fermeture éclair® *fem* (PL les fermetures éclair®)

zit NOUN
le bouton *masc*

zodiac NOUN
le zodiaque *masc*
□ the signs of the zodiac les signes du zodiaque

★ **zone** NOUN
la zone *fem*

★ **zoo** NOUN
le zoo *masc*

zoom lens NOUN
le zoom *masc*

zucchini NOUN (US)
la courgette *fem*

Contents

French verb tables

This section is designed to help you find all the verb forms you need in French. From pages 629–649 you will find 21 very common regular and irregular verbs shown in full, with example phrases.

From pages 650–658 you will see a list of 93 regular and irregular verbs with full conjugation of their main forms.

How to find the verb you need

Most of the French verbs on both sides of the dictionary, when they appear in the infinitive form (-**er**, -**ir** or -**re**), are followed by a number in square brackets. Each of these numbers corresponds to a verb in this section. For example:

> ★ **regarder** VERB [28]
> **1** to look at

Here, the number [28] after the verb **regarder** means that **regarder** follows the same pattern as verb number 28 in the list at the end of this section, which is **donner**. This is one of the very common verbs shown in full at the start of this section. For other verbs, a summary of the main forms is given. For example:

> **avancer** VERB [12]
> **1** to move forward

Here, **avancer** follows the same pattern as verb number [12] in the list at the end of this section, which is **commencer**. On page 650 of this section, you can see that the main forms of **commencer** are given to show you how this verb (and others like it) works.

In the full verb tables, you will find examples of regular verbs: a regular -**er** verb (**donner**), a regular -**ir** verb (**finir**) and a regular -**re** verb (**vendre**). Regular verbs follow one of three set patterns. When you have learnt these patterns, you will be able to form any regular verb.

You will also find **avoir** (to have) and **être** (to be) in the full verb tables. These are very important verbs which must be learnt. You use them when you want to say 'I have' *etc* or 'I am' *etc*. The present tense of **avoir** or **être** is also used to form the **perfect tense**. In most cases, **avoir** is used to form the perfect, but reflexive verbs like **se taire** (to stop talking) and verbs of movement like **aller** (to go) and **venir** (to come) use **être** – for example, the French for both 'he's gone' and 'he went' is **il *est* allé**, not **il *a* allé**.

On the French side of the dictionary, where a verb uses **être** to form the **perfect tense**, this is shown after the verb number. For example:

★ **tomber** VERB [84, *aux* être]
to fall

On the English side, the symbol ^{E} after the verb number in the translation shows which verbs use **être** in the **perfect tense**. For example:

★ to **arrive** VERB
arriver [5^{E}]

Verb tenses

The present tense

The present tense is used to talk about what is true at the moment, what happens regularly and what is happening now, for example, 'I'm a student'; 'He works as a consultant'; 'I'm studying French'.

There is more than one way to express the present tense in English. For example, you can either say 'I give', 'I am giving' or occasionally 'I do give'. In French, you use the same form **je donne** for all these.

In English you can also use the present to talk about something that is going to happen in the near future. You can do the same in French.

J'emménage à la fin du mois.	**I'm moving in** at the end of the month.
On sort avec Aurélie ce soir.	**We're going out** with Aurélie tonight.

The future tense

The future tense is used to talk about something that will happen or will be true. There are several ways to express the future tense in English: you can use the future tense ('I'll ask him on Tuesday'), the present tense ('I'm not working tomorrow'), or 'going to' followed by an infinitive ('She's going to study in France for a year'). In French you can also use the future tense, the present tense, or the verb **aller** (to go) followed by an infinitive.

Elle ne rentrera pas avant minuit.	**She won't be back** before midnight.
Il arrive dans dix minutes.	**He's coming** in ten minutes.
Je vais me faire couper les cheveux.	**I'm going to** have my hair cut.

The imperfect tense

The imperfect tense is one of the tenses used to talk about the past, especially in descriptions, and to say what used to happen, for example 'I used to work in Manchester'; 'It was sunny yesterday'.

Je ne faisais rien de spécial.	**I wasn't doing anything** special.
C'était une super fête.	**It was** a great party.
Avant, **il était** professeur.	**He used to be** a teacher.

The perfect tense

The perfect tense is made up of two parts: the present tense of **avoir** or **être**, and the French past participle (like 'given', 'finished' and 'done' in English).

Most verbs form the perfect tense with **avoir**. There are two main groups of verbs which form their perfect tense with **être** instead of **avoir**: all reflexive verbs (see **s'asseoir** page 631 and **se taire** page 645) and a group of verbs that are mainly used to talk about movement or a change of some kind, including:

aller	to go
venir	to come
arriver	to arrive, to happen
partir	to leave, to go
descendre	to go down, to come down, to get off
monter	to go up, to come up
entrer	to go in, to come in
sortir	to go out, to come out
mourir	to die
naître	to be born
devenir	to become
rester	to stay
tomber	to fall

Richard **est parti** de bonne heure.	Richard **left** early.
Tu es sortie hier soir?	**Did you go out** last night?
On est resté trois jours à Toulouse.	**We stayed** in Toulouse for three days.

Some verbs can use either **avoir** *or* **être** in the perfect tense, depending on their meaning. These verbs are marked in the dictionary as '*aux* **avoir** *or* **être**' after the verb number, with an explanatory note about which to use and when.

The imperative

An imperative is a form of the verb used when giving orders and instructions, for example, 'Be quiet!', 'Don't forget your passport!', 'Please fill in this form'.

In French, there are several forms of the imperative that are used to give instructions or orders to someone. These correspond to **tu**, **vous** and **nous**. The **nous** form means the same as 'let's' in English. For regular verbs, the imperative is the same as the **tu**, **nous** and **vous** forms of the present tense, except that you do not say the pronouns **tu**, **nous** and **vous**. Also, in the **tu** form of -**er** verbs like **donner**, the final -**s** is dropped.

Arrête de me faire rire!	**Stop** making me laugh!
Venez déjeuner chez nous.	**Come** round to ours for lunch.
Allons voir ce qu'ils font.	**Let's go** and see what they're up to.

The subjunctive

The subjunctive is a verb form that is used in certain circumstances to express some sort of feeling, or to show there is doubt about whether something will happen or something is true. It is used after certain structures in French, for example, **il faut que** and **il faudrait que**.

Il faut que je rentre.	**I have to** get back.
Il faudrait qu'on loue une voiture.	**We should** hire a car.
Je veux que tu viennes avec moi.	**I want** you to come with me.

The conditional

The conditional is a verb form used to talk about things that would happen or that would be true under certain conditions, for instance, 'I would help you if I could'. It is also used to say what you would like or need, for example, 'Could you give me the bill?'.

Je voudrais deux billets.	**I'd like** two tickets.
Si j'étais toi, **je téléphonerais**.	**I'd call** if I were you.

acquérir (to acquire)

PRESENT		PRESENT SUBJUNCTIVE	
j'	**acquiers**	j'	**acquière**
tu	**acquiers**	tu	**acquières**
il/elle/on	**acquiert**	il/elle/on	**acquière**
nous	**acquérons**	nous	**acquérions**
vous	**acquérez**	vous	**acquériez**
ils/elles	**acquièrent**	ils/elles	**acquièrent**

PERFECT		IMPERFECT	
j'	**ai acquis**	j'	**acquérais**
tu	**as acquis**	tu	**acquérais**
il/elle/on	**a acquis**	il/elle/on	**acquérait**
nous	**avons acquis**	nous	**acquérions**
vous	**avez acquis**	vous	**acquériez**
ils/elles	**ont acquis**	ils/elles	**acquéraient**

FUTURE		CONDITIONAL	
j'	**acquerrai**	j'	**acquerrais**
tu	**acquerras**	tu	**acquerrais**
il/elle/on	**acquerra**	il/elle/on	**acquerrait**
nous	**acquerrons**	nous	**acquerrions**
vous	**acquerrez**	vous	**acquerriez**
ils/elles	**acquerront**	ils/elles	**acquerraient**

PRESENT PARTICIPLE

acquérant

PAST PARTICIPLE

acquis

IMPERATIVE

acquiers / acquérons / acquérez

EXAMPLE PHRASES

Elle **a acquis** la nationalité française en 2013. She acquired French nationality in 2013.

je/j' = I **tu** = you **il** = he/it **elle** = she/it **on** = we/one **nous** = we **vous** = you **ils/elles** = they

aller (to go)

	PRESENT		PRESENT SUBJUNCTIVE
je	**vais**	j'	**aille**
tu	**vas**	tu	**ailles**
il/elle/on	**va**	il/elle/on	**aille**
nous	**allons**	nous	**allions**
vous	**allez**	vous	**alliez**
ils/elles	**vont**	ils/elles	**aillent**

	PERFECT		IMPERFECT
je	**suis allé(e)**	j'	**allais**
tu	**es allé(e)**	tu	**allais**
il/elle/on	**est allé(e)**	il/elle/on	**allait**
nous	**sommes allé(e)s**	nous	**allions**
vous	**êtes allé(e)(s)**	vous	**alliez**
ils/elles	**sont allé(e)s**	ils/elles	**allaient**

	FUTURE		CONDITIONAL
j'	**irai**	j'	**irais**
tu	**iras**	tu	**irais**
il/elle/on	**ira**	il/elle/on	**irait**
nous	**irons**	nous	**irions**
vous	**irez**	vous	**iriez**
ils/elles	**iront**	ils/elles	**iraient**

PRESENT PARTICIPLE

allant

PAST PARTICIPLE

allé

IMPERATIVE

va / allons / allez

EXAMPLE PHRASES

Vous **allez** au cinéma? Are you going to the cinema?
Je **suis allé** à Londres. I went to London.
Est-ce que tu **es** déjà **allé** en Allemagne? Have you ever been to Germany?

je/j' = I **tu** = you **il** = he/it **elle** = she/it **on** = we/one **nous** = we **vous** = you **ils/elles** = they

s'asseoir (to sit down)

	PRESENT		PRESENT SUBJUNCTIVE
je	**m'assieds/m'assois**	je	**m'asseye**
tu	**t'assieds/t'assois**	tu	**t'asseyes**
il/elle/on	**s'assied/s'assoit**	il/elle/on	**s'asseye**
nous	**nous asseyons/ nous assoyons**	nous	**nous asseyions**
vous	**vous asseyez/ vous assoyez**	vous	**vous asseyiez**
ils/elles	**s'asseyent/s'assoient**	ils/elles	**s'asseyent**

	PERFECT		IMPERFECT
je	**me suis assis(e)**	je	**m'asseyais**
tu	**t'es assis(e)**	tu	**t'asseyais**
il/elle/on	**s'est assis(e)**	il/elle/on	**s'asseyait**
nous	**nous sommes assis(es)**	nous	**nous asseyions**
vous	**vous êtes assis(e(s))**	vous	**vous asseyiez**
ils/elles	**se sont assis(es)**	ils/elles	**s'asseyaient**

	FUTURE		CONDITIONAL
je	**m'assiérai**	je	**m'assiérais**
tu	**t'assiéras**	tu	**t'assiérais**
il/elle/on	**s'assiéra**	il/elle/on	**s'assiérait**
nous	**nous assiérons**	nous	**nous assiérions**
vous	**vous assiérez**	vous	**vous assiériez**
ils/elles	**s'assiéront**	ils/elles	**s'assiéraient**

PRESENT PARTICIPLE

s'asseyant

PAST PARTICIPLE

assis

IMPERATIVE

assieds-toi / asseyons-nous / asseyez-vous

EXAMPLE PHRASES

Assieds-toi, Nicole. Sit down Nicole.
Asseyez-vous, les enfants. Sit down children.
Je peux **m'assoir**? May I sit down?
Je **me suis assise** sur un chewing-gum! I've sat on some chewing gum!

je/j' = I **tu** = you **il** = he/it **elle** = she/it **on** = we/one **nous** = we **vous** = you **ils/elles** = they

avoir (to have)

	PRESENT		PRESENT SUBJUNCTIVE
j'	**ai**	j'	**aie**
tu	**as**	tu	**aies**
il/elle/on	**a**	il/elle/on	**ait**
nous	**avons**	nous	**ayons**
vous	**avez**	vous	**ayez**
ils/elles	**ont**	ils/elles	**aient**

	PERFECT		IMPERFECT
j'	**ai eu**	j'	**avais**
tu	**as eu**	tu	**avais**
il/elle/on	**a eu**	il/elle/on	**avait**
nous	**avons eu**	nous	**avions**
vous	**avez eu**	vous	**aviez**
ils/elles	**ont eu**	ils/elles	**avaient**

	FUTURE		CONDITIONAL
j'	**aurai**	j'	**aurais**
tu	**auras**	tu	**aurais**
il/elle/on	**aura**	il/elle/on	**aurait**
nous	**aurons**	nous	**aurions**
vous	**aurez**	vous	**auriez**
ils/elles	**auront**	ils/elles	**auraient**

PRESENT PARTICIPLE

ayant

PAST PARTICIPLE

eu

IMPERATIVE

aie / ayons / ayez

EXAMPLE PHRASES

Il **a** les yeux bleus. He's got blue eyes.
Quel âge **as**-tu? How old are you?
Il **a eu** un accident. He's had an accident.
J'**avais** faim. I was hungry.
Il y **a** beaucoup de monde. There are lots of people.

je/j' = I **tu** = you **il** = he/it **elle** = she/it **on** = we/one **nous** = we **vous** = you **ils/elles** = they

croire (to believe)

	PRESENT		PRESENT SUBJUNCTIVE
je	**crois**	je	**croie**
tu	**crois**	tu	**croies**
il/elle/on	**croit**	il/elle/on	**croie**
nous	**croyons**	nous	**croyions**
vous	**croyez**	vous	**croyiez**
ils/elles	**croient**	ils/elles	**croient**

	PERFECT		IMPERFECT
j'	**ai cru**	je	**croyais**
tu	**as cru**	tu	**croyais**
il/elle/on	**a cru**	il/elle/on	**croyait**
nous	**avons cru**	nous	**croyions**
vous	**avez cru**	vous	**croyiez**
ils/elles	**ont cru**	ils/elles	**croyaient**

	FUTURE		CONDITIONAL
je	**croirai**	je	**croirais**
tu	**croiras**	tu	**croirais**
il/elle/on	**croira**	il/elle/on	**croirait**
nous	**croirons**	nous	**croirions**
vous	**croirez**	vous	**croiriez**
ils/elles	**croiront**	ils/elles	**croiraient**

PRESENT PARTICIPLE

croyant

PAST PARTICIPLE

cru

IMPERATIVE

crois / croyons / croyez

EXAMPLE PHRASES

Je ne te **crois** pas. I don't believe you.
J'**ai cru** que tu n'allais pas venir. I thought you weren't going to come.
Elle **croyait** encore au père Noël. She still believed in Santa.

je/j' = I **tu** = you **il** = he/it **elle** = she/it **on** = we/one **nous** = we **vous** = you **ils/elles** = they

devoir (to have to; to owe)

	PRESENT		PRESENT SUBJUNCTIVE
je	**dois**	je	**doive**
tu	**dois**	tu	**doives**
il/elle/on	**doit**	il/elle/on	**doive**
nous	**devons**	nous	**devions**
vous	**devez**	vous	**deviez**
ils/elles	**doivent**	ils/elles	**doivent**

	PERFECT		IMPERFECT
j'	**ai dû**	je	**devais**
tu	**as dû**	tu	**devais**
il/elle/on	**a dû**	il/elle/on	**devait**
nous	**avons dû**	nous	**devions**
vous	**avez dû**	vous	**deviez**
ils/elles	**ont dû**	ils/elles	**devaient**

	FUTURE		CONDITIONAL
je	**devrai**	je	**devrais**
tu	**devras**	tu	**devrais**
il/elle/on	**devra**	il/elle/on	**devrait**
nous	**devrons**	nous	**devrions**
vous	**devrez**	vous	**devriez**
ils/elles	**devront**	ils/elles	**devraient**

PRESENT PARTICIPLE

devant

PAST PARTICIPLE

dû (*NB*: due, dus, dues)

IMPERATIVE

dois / devons / devez

EXAMPLE PHRASES

Je **dois** aller faire les courses ce matin. I have to do the shopping this morning.
À quelle heure est-ce que tu **dois** partir? What time do you have to leave?
Il **a dû** faire ses devoirs hier soir. He had to do his homework last night.
Il **devait** prendre le train pour aller travailler. He had to go to work by train.

je/j' = I **tu** = you **il** = he/it **elle** = she/it **on** = we/one **nous** = we **vous** = you **ils/elles** = they

dire (to say)

PRESENT		PRESENT SUBJUNCTIVE	
je	**dis**	je	**dise**
tu	**dis**	tu	**dises**
il/elle/on	**dit**	il/elle/on	**dise**
nous	**disons**	nous	**disions**
vous	**dites**	vous	**disiez**
ils/elles	**disent**	ils/elles	**disent**

PERFECT		IMPERFECT	
j'	**ai dit**	je	**disais**
tu	**as dit**	tu	**disais**
il/elle/on	**a dit**	il/elle/on	**disait**
nous	**avons dit**	nous	**disions**
vous	**avez dit**	vous	**disiez**
ils/elles	**ont dit**	ils/elles	**disaient**

FUTURE		CONDITIONAL	
je	**dirai**	je	**dirais**
tu	**diras**	tu	**dirais**
il/elle/on	**dira**	il/elle/on	**dirait**
nous	**dirons**	nous	**dirions**
vous	**direz**	vous	**diriez**
ils/elles	**diront**	ils/elles	**diraient**

PRESENT PARTICIPLE
disant

PAST PARTICIPLE
dit

IMPERATIVE
dis / disons / dites

EXAMPLE PHRASES

Qu'est-ce qu'elle **dit**? What is she saying?
"Bonjour!", **a**-t-il **dit**. "Hello!" he said.
Ils m'**ont dit** que le film était nul. They told me that the film was rubbish.
Comment ça **se dit** en anglais? How do you say that in English?

je/j' = I **tu** = you **il** = he/it **elle** = she/it **on** = we/one **nous** = we **vous** = you **ils/elles** = they

donner (to give)

	PRESENT		**PRESENT SUBJUNCTIVE**
je	**donne**	je	**donne**
tu	**donnes**	tu	**donnes**
il/elle/on	**donne**	il/elle/on	**donne**
nous	**donnons**	nous	**donnions**
vous	**donnez**	vous	**donniez**
ils/elles	**donnent**	ils/elles	**donnent**

	PERFECT		**IMPERFECT**
j'	**ai donné**	je	**donnais**
tu	**as donné**	tu	**donnais**
il/elle/on	**a donné**	il/elle/on	**donnait**
nous	**avons donné**	nous	**donnions**
vous	**avez donné**	vous	**donniez**
ils/elles	**ont donné**	ils/elles	**donnaient**

	FUTURE		**CONDITIONAL**
je	**donnerai**	je	**donnerais**
tu	**donneras**	tu	**donnerais**
il/elle/on	**donnera**	il/elle/on	**donnerait**
nous	**donnerons**	nous	**donnerions**
vous	**donnerez**	vous	**donneriez**
ils/elles	**donneront**	ils/elles	**donneraient**

PRESENT PARTICIPLE

donnant

PAST PARTICIPLE

donné

IMPERATIVE

donne / donnons / donnez

EXAMPLE PHRASES

Donne-moi la main. Give me your hand.
Est-ce que je t'**ai donné** mon adresse? Did I give you my address?
L'appartement **donne** sur la place. The flat overlooks the square.

je/j' = I **tu** = you **il** = he/it **elle** = she/it **on** = we/one **nous** = we **vous** = you **ils/elles** = they

être (to be)

PRESENT		PRESENT SUBJUNCTIVE	
je	**suis**	je	**sois**
tu	**es**	tu	**sois**
il/elle/on	**est**	il/elle/on	**soit**
nous	**sommes**	nous	**soyons**
vous	**êtes**	vous	**soyez**
ils/elles	**sont**	ils/elles	**soient**

PERFECT		IMPERFECT	
j'	**ai été**	j'	**étais**
tu	**as été**	tu	**étais**
il/elle/on	**a été**	il/elle/on	**était**
nous	**avons été**	nous	**étions**
vous	**avez été**	vous	**étiez**
ils/elles	**ont été**	ils/elles	**étaient**

FUTURE		CONDITIONAL	
je	**serai**	je	**serais**
tu	**seras**	tu	**serais**
il/elle/on	**sera**	il/elle/on	**serait**
nous	**serons**	nous	**serions**
vous	**serez**	vous	**seriez**
ils/elles	**seront**	ils/elles	**seraient**

PRESENT PARTICIPLE
étant

PAST PARTICIPLE
été

IMPERATIVE
sois / soyons / soyez

EXAMPLE PHRASES

Mon père **est** professeur. My father's a teacher.
Quelle heure **est**-il? – Il **est** dix heures. What time is it? – It's 10 o'clock.
Ils ne **sont** pas encore arrivés. They haven't arrived yet.

je/j' = I **tu** = you **il** = he/it **elle** = she/it **on** = we/one **nous** = we **vous** = you **ils/elles** = they

faire (to do; to make)

	PRESENT		**PRESENT SUBJUNCTIVE**
je	**fais**	je	**fasse**
tu	**fais**	tu	**fasses**
il/elle/on	**fait**	il/elle/on	**fasse**
nous	**faisons**	nous	**fassions**
vous	**faites**	vous	**fassiez**
ils/elles	**font**	ils/elles	**fassent**

	PERFECT		**IMPERFECT**
j'	**ai fait**	je	**faisais**
tu	**as fait**	tu	**faisais**
il/elle/on	**a fait**	il/elle/on	**faisait**
nous	**avons fait**	nous	**faisions**
vous	**avez fait**	vous	**faisiez**
ils/elles	**ont fait**	ils/elles	**faisaient**

	FUTURE		**CONDITIONAL**
je	**ferai**	je	**ferais**
tu	**feras**	tu	**ferais**
il/elle/on	**fera**	il/elle/on	**ferait**
nous	**ferons**	nous	**ferions**
vous	**ferez**	vous	**feriez**
ils/elles	**feront**	ils/elles	**feraient**

PRESENT PARTICIPLE

faisant

PAST PARTICIPLE

fait

IMPERATIVE

fais / faisons / faites

EXAMPLE PHRASES

Qu'est-ce que tu **fais**? What are you doing?
Qu'est-ce qu'il **a fait**? What has he done? *or* What did he do?
J'**ai fait** un gâteau. I've made a cake *or* I made a cake.
Il **s'est fait** couper les cheveux. He's had his hair cut.

je/j' = I **tu** = you **il** = he/it **elle** = she/it **on** = we/one **nous** = we **vous** = you **ils/elles** = they

finir (to finish)

	PRESENT		PRESENT SUBJUNCTIVE
je	**finis**	je	**finisse**
tu	**finis**	tu	**finisses**
il/elle/on	**finit**	il/elle/on	**finisse**
nous	**finissons**	nous	**finissions**
vous	**finissez**	vous	**finissiez**
ils/elles	**finissent**	ils/elles	**finissent**

	PERFECT		IMPERFECT
j'	**ai fini**	je	**finissais**
tu	**as fini**	tu	**finissais**
il/elle/on	**a fini**	il/elle/on	**finissait**
nous	**avons fini**	nous	**finissions**
vous	**avez fini**	vous	**finissiez**
ils/elles	**ont fini**	ils/elles	**finissaient**

	FUTURE		CONDITIONAL
je	**finirai**	je	**finirais**
tu	**finiras**	tu	**finirais**
il/elle/on	**finira**	il/elle/on	**finirait**
nous	**finirons**	nous	**finirions**
vous	**finirez**	vous	**finiriez**
ils/elles	**finiront**	ils/elles	**finiraient**

PRESENT PARTICIPLE

finissant

PAST PARTICIPLE

fini

IMPERATIVE

finis / finissons / finissez

EXAMPLE PHRASES

Finis ta soupe! Finish your soup!
J'ai **fini**! I've finished!
Je **finirai** mes devoirs demain. I'll finish my homework tomorrow.

je/j' = I **tu** = you **il** = he/it **elle** = she/it **on** = we/one **nous** = we **vous** = you **ils/elles** = they

mettre (to put)

	PRESENT		PRESENT SUBJUNCTIVE
je	**mets**	je	**mette**
tu	**mets**	tu	**mettes**
il/elle/on	**met**	il/elle/on	**mette**
nous	**mettons**	nous	**mettions**
vous	**mettez**	vous	**mettiez**
ils/elles	**mettent**	ils/elles	**mettent**

	PERFECT		IMPERFECT
j'	**ai mis**	je	**mettais**
tu	**as mis**	tu	**mettais**
il/elle/on	**a mis**	il/elle/on	**mettait**
nous	**avons mis**	nous	**mettions**
vous	**avez mis**	vous	**mettiez**
ils/elles	**ont mis**	ils/elles	**mettaient**

	FUTURE		CONDITIONAL
je	**mettrai**	je	**mettrais**
tu	**mettras**	tu	**mettrais**
il/elle/on	**mettra**	il/elle/on	**mettrait**
nous	**mettrons**	nous	**mettrions**
vous	**mettrez**	vous	**mettriez**
ils/elles	**mettront**	ils/elles	**mettraient**

PRESENT PARTICIPLE

mettant

PAST PARTICIPLE

mis

IMPERATIVE

mets / mettons / mettez

EXAMPLE PHRASES

Mets ton manteau! Put your coat on!
Où est-ce que tu **as mis** les clés? Where have you put the keys?
J'**ai mis** le livre sur la table. I put the book on the table.
Elle **s'est mise** à pleurer. She started crying.

je/j' = I **tu** = you **il** = he/it **elle** = she/it **on** = we/one **nous** = we **vous** = you **ils/elles** = they

ouvrir (to open)

	PRESENT		PRESENT SUBJUNCTIVE
j'	**ouvre**	j'	**ouvre**
tu	**ouvres**	tu	**ouvres**
il/elle/on	**ouvre**	il/elle/on	**ouvre**
nous	**ouvrons**	nous	**ouvrions**
vous	**ouvrez**	vous	**ouvriez**
ils/elles	**ouvrent**	ils/elles	**ouvrent**

	PERFECT		IMPERFECT
j'	**ai ouvert**	j'	**ouvrais**
tu	**as ouvert**	tu	**ouvrais**
il/elle/on	**a ouvert**	il/elle/on	**ouvrait**
nous	**avons ouvert**	nous	**ouvrions**
vous	**avez ouvert**	vous	**ouvriez**
ils/elles	**ont ouvert**	ils/elles	**ouvraient**

	FUTURE		CONDITIONAL
j'	**ouvrirai**	j'	**ouvrirais**
tu	**ouvriras**	tu	**ouvrirais**
il/elle/on	**ouvrira**	il/elle/on	**ouvrirait**
nous	**ouvrirons**	nous	**ouvririons**
vous	**ouvrirez**	vous	**ouvririez**
ils/elles	**ouvriront**	ils/elles	**ouvriraient**

PRESENT PARTICIPLE

ouvrant

PAST PARTICIPLE

ouvert

IMPERATIVE

ouvre / ouvrons / ouvrez

EXAMPLE PHRASES

Elle **a ouvert** la porte. She opened the door.
Est-ce que tu pourrais **ouvrir** la fenêtre? Could you open the window?
Je me suis coupé en **ouvrant** une boîte de conserve. I cut myself opening a tin.
La porte **s'est ouverte**. The door opened.

je/j' = I **tu** = you **il** = he/it **elle** = she/it **on** = we/one **nous** = we **vous** = you **ils/elles** = they

pouvoir (to be able)

	PRESENT		**PRESENT SUBJUNCTIVE**
je	**peux**	je	**puisse**
tu	**peux**	tu	**puisses**
il/elle/on	**peut**	il/elle/on	**puisse**
nous	**pouvons**	nous	**puissions**
vous	**pouvez**	vous	**puissiez**
ils/elles	**peuvent**	ils/elles	**puissent**

	PERFECT		**IMPERFECT**
j'	**ai pu**	je	**pouvais**
tu	**as pu**	tu	**pouvais**
il/elle/on	**a pu**	il/elle/on	**pouvait**
nous	**avons pu**	nous	**pouvions**
vous	**avez pu**	vous	**pouviez**
ils/elles	**ont pu**	ils/elles	**pouvaient**

	FUTURE		**CONDITIONAL**
je	**pourrai**	je	**pourrais**
tu	**pourras**	tu	**pourrais**
il/elle/on	**pourra**	il/elle/on	**pourrait**
nous	**pourrons**	nous	**pourrions**
vous	**pourrez**	vous	**pourriez**
ils/elles	**pourront**	ils/elles	**pourraient**

PRESENT PARTICIPLE

pouvant

PAST PARTICIPLE

pu

IMPERATIVE

not used

EXAMPLE PHRASES

Je **peux** t'aider, si tu veux. I can help you if you like.
J'ai fait tout ce que j'**ai pu**. I did all I could.
Je ne **pourrai** pas venir samedi. I won't be able to come on Saturday.

je/j' = I **tu** = you **il** = he/it **elle** = she/it **on** = we/one **nous** = we **vous** = you **ils/elles** = they

savoir (to know)

	PRESENT		PRESENT SUBJUNCTIVE
je	**sais**	je	**sache**
tu	**sais**	tu	**saches**
il/elle/on	**sait**	il/elle/on	**sache**
nous	**savons**	nous	**sachions**
vous	**savez**	vous	**sachiez**
ils/elles	**savent**	ils/elles	**sachent**

	PERFECT		IMPERFECT
j'	**ai su**	je	**savais**
tu	**as su**	tu	**savais**
il/elle/on	**a su**	il/elle/on	**savait**
nous	**avons su**	nous	**savions**
vous	**avez su**	vous	**saviez**
ils/elles	**ont su**	ils/elles	**savaient**

	FUTURE		CONDITIONAL
je	**saurai**	je	**saurais**
tu	**sauras**	tu	**saurais**
il/elle/on	**saura**	il/elle/on	**saurait**
nous	**saurons**	nous	**saurions**
vous	**saurez**	vous	**sauriez**
ils/elles	**sauront**	ils/elles	**sauraient**

PRESENT PARTICIPLE

sachant

PAST PARTICIPLE

su

IMPERATIVE

sache / sachons / sachez

EXAMPLE PHRASES

Tu **sais** ce que tu vas faire l'année prochaine? Do you know what you're doing next year?
Je ne **sais** pas. I don't know.
Elle ne **sait** pas nager. She can't swim.
Tu **savais** que son père était pakistanais? Did you know her father was Pakistani?

je/j' = I **tu** = you **il** = he/it **elle** = she/it **on** = we/one **nous** = we **vous** = you **ils/elles** = they

sentir (to smell; to feel)

	PRESENT		PRESENT SUBJUNCTIVE
je	**sens**	je	**sente**
tu	**sens**	tu	**sentes**
il/elle/on	**sent**	il/elle/on	**sente**
nous	**sentons**	nous	**sentions**
vous	**sentez**	vous	**sentiez**
ils/elles	**sentent**	ils/elles	**sentent**

	PERFECT		IMPERFECT
j'	**ai senti**	je	**sentais**
tu	**as senti**	tu	**sentais**
il/elle/on	**a senti**	il/elle/on	**sentait**
nous	**avons senti**	nous	**sentions**
vous	**avez senti**	vous	**sentiez**
ils/elles	**ont senti**	ils/elles	**sentaient**

	FUTURE		CONDITIONAL
je	**sentirai**	je	**sentirais**
tu	**sentiras**	tu	**sentirais**
il/elle/on	**sentira**	il/elle/on	**sentirait**
nous	**sentirons**	nous	**sentirions**
vous	**sentirez**	vous	**sentiriez**
ils/elles	**sentiront**	ils/elles	**sentiraient**

PRESENT PARTICIPLE

sentant

PAST PARTICIPLE

senti

IMPERATIVE

sens / sentons / sentez

EXAMPLE PHRASES

Ça **sentait** mauvais. It smelt bad.
Je n'**ai** rien **senti**. I didn't feel a thing.
Elle ne **se sent** pas bien. She's not feeling well.

je/j' = I **tu** = you **il** = he/it **elle** = she/it **on** = we/one **nous** = we **vous** = you **ils/elles** = they

se taire (to stop talking)

	PRESENT		PRESENT SUBJUNCTIVE
je	**me tais**	je	**me taise**
tu	**te tais**	tu	**te taises**
il/elle/on	**se tait**	il/elle/on	**se taise**
nous	**nous taisons**	nous	**nous taisions**
vous	**vous taisez**	vous	**vous taisiez**
ils/elles	**se taisent**	ils/elles	**se taisent**

	PERFECT		IMPERFECT
je	**me suis tu(e)**	je	**me taisais**
tu	**t'es tu(e)**	tu	**te taisais**
il/elle/on	**s'est tu(e)**	il/elle/on	**se taisait**
nous	**nous sommes tu(e)s**	nous	**nous taisions**
vous	**vous êtes tu(e)(s)**	vous	**vous taisiez**
ils/elles	**se sont tu(e)s**	ils/elles	**se taisaient**

	FUTURE		CONDITIONAL
je	**me tairai**	je	**me tairais**
tu	**te tairas**	tu	**te tairais**
il/elle/on	**se taira**	il/elle/on	**se tairait**
nous	**nous tairons**	nous	**nous tairions**
vous	**vous tairez**	vous	**vous tairiez**
ils/elles	**se tairont**	ils/elles	**se tairaient**

PRESENT PARTICIPLE

se taisant

PAST PARTICIPLE

tu

IMPERATIVE

tais-toi / taisons-nous / taisez-vous

EXAMPLE PHRASES

Il **s'est tu**. He stopped talking.
Taisez-vous! Be quiet!
Sophie, **tais-toi**! Be quiet Sophie!

je/j' = I **tu** = you **il** = he/it **elle** = she/it **on** = we/one **nous** = we **vous** = you **ils/elles** = they

vendre (to sell)

	PRESENT		PRESENT SUBJUNCTIVE
je	**vends**	je	**vende**
tu	**vends**	tu	**vendes**
il/elle/on	**vend**	il/elle/on	**vende**
nous	**vendons**	nous	**vendions**
vous	**vendez**	vous	**vendiez**
ils/elles	**vendent**	ils/elles	**vendent**

	PERFECT		IMPERFECT
j'	**ai vendu**	je	**vendais**
tu	**as vendu**	tu	**vendais**
il/elle/on	**a vendu**	il/elle/on	**vendait**
nous	**avons vendu**	nous	**vendions**
vous	**avez vendu**	vous	**vendiez**
ils/elles	**ont vendu**	ils/elles	**vendaient**

	FUTURE		CONDITIONAL
je	**vendrai**	je	**vendrais**
tu	**vendras**	tu	**vendrais**
il/elle/on	**vendra**	il/elle/on	**vendrait**
nous	**vendrons**	nous	**vendrions**
vous	**vendrez**	vous	**vendriez**
ils/elles	**vendront**	ils/elles	**vendraient**

PRESENT PARTICIPLE

vendant

PAST PARTICIPLE

vendu

IMPERATIVE

vends / vendons / vendez

EXAMPLE PHRASES

Il m'**a vendu** son vélo pour 50 euros. He sold me his bike for 50 euros.
Est-ce que vous **vendez** des piles? Do you sell batteries?
Elle voudrait **vendre** sa voiture. She would like to sell her car.

je/j' = I **tu** = you **il** = he/it **elle** = she/it **on** = we/one **nous** = we **vous** = you **ils/elles** = they

venir (to come)

PRESENT		PRESENT SUBJUNCTIVE	
je	**viens**	je	**vienne**
tu	**viens**	tu	**viennes**
il/elle/on	**vient**	il/elle/on	**vienne**
nous	**venons**	nous	**venions**
vous	**venez**	vous	**veniez**
ils/elles	**viennent**	ils/elles	**viennent**

PERFECT		IMPERFECT	
je	**suis venu(e)**	je	**venais**
tu	**es venu(e)**	tu	**venais**
il/elle/on	**est venu(e)**	il/elle/on	**venait**
nous	**sommes venu(e)s**	nous	**venions**
vous	**êtes venu(e)(s)**	vous	**veniez**
ils/elles	**sont venu(e)s**	ils/elles	**venaient**

FUTURE		CONDITIONAL	
je	**viendrai**	je	**viendrais**
tu	**viendras**	tu	**viendrais**
il/elle/on	**viendra**	il/elle/on	**viendrait**
nous	**viendrons**	nous	**viendrions**
vous	**viendrez**	vous	**viendriez**
ils/elles	**viendront**	ils/elles	**viendraient**

PRESENT PARTICIPLE
venant

PAST PARTICIPLE
venu

IMPERATIVE
viens / venons / venez

EXAMPLE PHRASES

Elle ne **viendra** pas cette année. She won't be coming this year.
Fatou et Malik **viennent** du Sénégal. Fatou and Malik come from Senegal.
Je **viens** de manger. I've just eaten.

je/j' = I **tu** = you **il** = he/it **elle** = she/it **on** = we/one **nous** = we **vous** = you **ils/elles** = they

voir (to see)

	PRESENT		PRESENT SUBJUNCTIVE
je	**vois**	je	**voie**
tu	**vois**	tu	**voies**
il/elle/on	**voit**	il/elle/on	**voie**
nous	**voyons**	nous	**voyions**
vous	**voyez**	vous	**voyiez**
ils/elles	**voient**	ils/elles	**voient**

	PERFECT		IMPERFECT
j'	**ai vu**	je	**voyais**
tu	**as vu**	tu	**voyais**
il/elle/on	**a vu**	il/elle/on	**voyait**
nous	**avons vu**	nous	**voyions**
vous	**avez vu**	vous	**voyiez**
ils/elles	**ont vu**	ils/elles	**voyaient**

	FUTURE		CONDITIONAL
je	**verrai**	je	**verrais**
tu	**verras**	tu	**verrais**
il/elle/on	**verra**	il/elle/on	**verrait**
nous	**verrons**	nous	**verrions**
vous	**verrez**	vous	**verriez**
ils/elles	**verront**	ils/elles	**verraient**

PRESENT PARTICIPLE

voyant

PAST PARTICIPLE

vu

IMPERATIVE

vois / voyons / voyez

EXAMPLE PHRASES

Venez me **voir** quand vous serez à Paris. Come and see me when you're in Paris.
Je ne **vois** rien sans mes lunettes. I can't see anything without my glasses.
Est-ce que tu l'**as vu**? Did you see him? *or* Have you seen him?
Est-ce que cette tache **se voit**? Does that stain show?

je/j' = I **tu** = you **il** = he/it **elle** = she/it **on** = we/one **nous** = we **vous** = you **ils/elles** = they

vouloir (to want)

PRESENT		PRESENT SUBJUNCTIVE	
je	**veux**	je	**veuille**
tu	**veux**	tu	**veuilles**
il/elle/on	**veut**	il/elle/on	**veuille**
nous	**voulons**	nous	**voulions**
vous	**voulez**	vous	**vouliez**
ils/elles	**veulent**	ils/elles	**veuillent**

PERFECT		IMPERFECT	
j'	**ai voulu**	je	**voulais**
tu	**as voulu**	tu	**voulais**
il/elle/on	**a voulu**	il/elle/on	**voulait**
nous	**avons voulu**	nous	**voulions**
vous	**avez voulu**	vous	**vouliez**
ils/elles	**ont voulu**	ils/elles	**voulaient**

FUTURE		CONDITIONAL	
je	**voudrai**	je	**voudrais**
tu	**voudras**	tu	**voudrais**
il/elle/on	**voudra**	il/elle/on	**voudrait**
nous	**voudrons**	nous	**voudrions**
vous	**voudrez**	vous	**voudriez**
ils/elles	**voudront**	ils/elles	**voudraient**

PRESENT PARTICIPLE

voulant

PAST PARTICIPLE

voulu

IMPERATIVE

veuille / veuillons / veuillez

EXAMPLE PHRASES

Elle **veut** un vélo pour Noël. She wants a bike for Christmas.
Ils **voulaient** aller au cinéma. They wanted to go to the cinema.
Est-ce que tu **voudrais** une tasse de thé? Would you like a cup of tea?

je/j' = I **tu** = you **il** = he/it **elle** = she/it **on** = we/one **nous** = we **vous** = you **ils/elles** = they

French verb forms

	PRESENT	PERFECT	IMPERFECT	FUTURE	PRESENT SUBJUNCTIVE
1 **acheter**	j' ach**è**te	j' ai acheté	j' achetais	j' ach**è**terai	j' ach**è**te
to buy	tu ach**è**tes	tu as acheté	tu achetais	tu ach**è**teras	tu ach**è**tes
	il/elle ach**è**te	il/elle a acheté	il/elle achetait	il/elle ach**è**tera	il/elle ach**è**te
	nous achetons	nous avons acheté	nous achetions	nous ach**è**terons	nous achetions
	vous achetez	vous avez acheté	vous achetiez	vous ach**è**terez	vous achetiez
	ils/elles ach**è**tent	ils/elles ont acheté	ils/elles achetaient	ils/elles ach**è**teront	ils/elles ach**è**tent
2 **acquérir** to acquire	see full verb table page 629				
3 **aller** to go	see full verb table page 630				
4 **appeler**	j' appe**ll**e	j' ai appelé	j' appelais	j' appe**ll**erai	j' appe**ll**e
to call	tu appe**ll**es	tu as appelé	tu appelais	tu appe**ll**eras	tu appe**ll**es
	il/elle appe**ll**e	il/elle a appelé	il/elle appelait	il/elle appe**ll**era	il/elle appe**ll**e
	nous appelons	nous avons appelé	nous appelions	nous appe**ll**erons	nous appelions
	vous appelez	vous avez appelé	vous appeliez	vous appe**ll**erez	vous appeliez
	ils/elles appe**ll**ent	ils/elles ont appelé	ils/elles appelaient	ils/elles appe**ll**eront	ils/elles appe**ll**ent
5 **arriver**	j' arrive	je suis arrivé(e)	j' arrivais	j' arriverai	j' arrive
to arrive	tu arrives	tu es arrivé(e)	tu arrivais	tu arriveras	tu arrives
	il/elle arrive	il/elle est arrivé(e)	il/elle arrivait	il/elle arrivera	il/elle arrive
	nous arrivons	nous sommes arrivé(e)s	nous arrivions	nous arriverons	nous arrivions
	vous arrivez	vous êtes arrivé(e)(s)	vous arriviez	vous arriverez	vous arriviez
	ils/elles arrivent	ils/elles sont arrivé(e)s	ils/elles arrivaient	ils/elles arriveront	ils/elles arrivent
6 **s'asseoir** to sit down	see full verb table page 631				
7 **attendre**	j' attends	j' ai attendu	j' attendais	j' attendrai	j' attende
to wait	tu attends	tu as attendu	tu attendais	tu attendras	tu attendes
	il/elle attend	il/elle a attendu	il/elle attendait	il/elle attendra	il/elle attende
	nous attendons	nous avons attendu	nous attendions	nous attendrons	nous attendions
	vous attendez	vous avez attendu	vous attendiez	vous attendrez	vous attendiez
	ils/elles attendent	ils/elles ont attendu	ils/elles attendaient	ils/elles attendront	ils/elles attendent
8 **avoir** to have	see full verb table page 632				
9 **battre**	je bats	j' ai battu	je battais	je battrai	je batte
to beat	tu bats	tu as battu	tu battais	tu battras	tu battes
	il/elle bat	il/elle a battu	il/elle battait	il/elle battra	il/elle batte
	nous battons	nous avons battu	nous battions	nous battrons	nous battions
	vous battez	vous avez battu	vous battiez	vous battrez	vous battiez
	ils/elles battent	ils/elles ont battu	ils/elles battaient	ils/elles battront	ils/elles battent
10 **boire**	je bois	j' ai bu	je b**uv**ais	je boirai	je boi**v**e
to drink	tu bois	tu as bu	tu b**uv**ais	tu boiras	tu boi**v**es
	il/elle boit	il/elle a bu	il/elle b**uv**ait	il/elle boira	il/elle boi**v**e
	nous b**uv**ons	nous avons bu	nous b**uv**ions	nous boirons	nous b**uv**ions
	vous b**uv**ez	vous avez bu	vous b**uv**iez	vous boirez	vous b**uv**iez
	ils/elles boi**v**ent	ils/elles ont bu	ils/elles b**uv**aient	ils/elles boiront	ils/elles boi**v**ent
11 **bouillir**	je bous	j' ai bouilli	je bouillais	je bouillirai	je bouille
to boil	tu bous	tu as bouilli	tu bouillais	tu bouilliras	tu bouilles
	il/elle bout	il/elle a bouilli	il/elle bouillait	il/elle bouillira	il/elle bouille
	nous bouillons	nous avons bouilli	nous bouillions	nous bouillirons	nous bouillions
	vous bouillez	vous avez bouilli	vous bouilliez	vous bouillirez	vous bouilliez
	ils/elles bouillent	ils/elles ont bouilli	ils/elles bouillaient	ils/elles bouilliront	ils/elles bouillent
12 **commencer**	je commence	j' ai commencé	je commen**ç**ais	je commencerai	je commence
to start	tu commences	tu as commencé	tu commen**ç**ais	tu commenceras	tu commences
	il/elle commence	il/elle a commencé	il/elle commen**ç**ait	il/elle commencera	il/elle commence
	nous commen**ç**ons	nous avons commencé	nous commencions	nous commencerons	nous commencions
	vous commencez	vous avez commencé	vous commenciez	vous commencerez	vous commenciez
	ils/elles commencent	ils/elles ont commencé	ils/elles commen**ç**aient	ils/elles commenceront	ils/elles commencent

Letters in bold indicate a significant change in spelling from the infinitive form.

	PRESENT	PERFECT	IMPERFECT	FUTURE	PRESENT SUBJUNCTIVE
13 conclure	je conclus	j' ai conclu	je concluais	je conclurai	je conclue
to conclude	tu conclus	tu as conclu	tu concluais	tu concluras	tu conclues
	il/elle conclut	il/elle a conclu	il/elle concluait	il/elle conclura	il/elle conclue
	nous concluons	nous avons conclu	nous concluions	nous conclurons	nous concluions
	vous concluez	vous avez conclu	vous concluiez	vous conclurez	vous concluiez
	ils/elles concluent	ils/elles ont conclu	ils/elles concluaient	ils/elles concluront	ils/elles concluent
14 connaître	je connais	j' ai connu	je connaissais	je conna**î**trai	je conna**iss**e
to know	tu connais	tu as connu	tu connaissais	tu conna**î**tras	tu conna**iss**es
	il/elle connaît	il/elle a connu	il/elle connaissait	il/elle conna**î**tra	il/elle conna**iss**e
	nous connaissons	nous avons connu	nous connaissions	nous conna**î**trons	nous conna**iss**ions
	vous connaissez	vous avez connu	vous connaissiez	vous conna**î**trez	vous conna**iss**iez
	ils/elles connaissent	ils/elles ont connu	ils/elles connaissaient	ils/elles conna**î**tront	ils/elles conna**iss**ent
15 coudre	je couds	j' ai cou**s**u	je cou**s**ais	je coudrai	je cou**s**e
to sew	tu couds	tu as cou**s**u	tu cou**s**ais	tu coudras	tu cou**s**es
	il/elle coud	il/elle a cou**s**u	il/elle cou**s**ait	il/elle coudra	il/elle cou**s**e
	nous cou**s**ons	nous avons cou**s**u	nous cou**s**ions	nous coudrons	nous cou**s**ions
	vous cou**s**ez	vous avez cou**s**u	vous cou**s**iez	vous coudrez	vous cou**s**iez
	ils/elles cou**s**ent	ils/elles ont cou**s**u	ils/elles cou**s**aient	ils/elles coudront	ils/elles cou**s**ent
16 courir	je cours	j' ai couru	je courais	je courrai	je coure
to run	tu cours	tu as couru	tu courais	tu courras	tu coures
	il/elle court	il/elle a couru	il/elle courait	il/elle courra	il/elle coure
	nous courons	nous avons couru	nous courions	nous courrons	nous courions
	vous courez	vous avez couru	vous couriez	vous courrez	vous couriez
	ils/elles courent	ils/elles ont couru	ils/elles couraient	ils/elles courront	ils/elles courent
17 craindre	je crains	j' ai craint	je crai**gn**ais	je craindrai	je crai**gn**e
to fear	tu crains	tu as craint	tu crai**gn**ais	tu craindras	tu crai**gn**es
	il/elle craint	il/elle a craint	il/elle crai**gn**ait	il/elle craindra	il/elle crai**gn**e
	nous crai**gn**ons	nous avons craint	nous crai**gn**ions	nous craindrons	nous crai**gn**ions
	vous crai**gn**ez	vous avez craint	vous crai**gn**iez	vous craindrez	vous crai**gn**iez
	ils/elles crai**gn**ent	ils/elles ont craint	ils/elles crai**gn**aient	ils/elles craindront	ils/elles crai**gn**ent
18 créer	je crée	j' ai créé	je créais	je créerai	je crée
to create	tu crées	tu as créé	tu créais	tu créeras	tu crées
	il/elle crée	il/elle a créé	il/elle créait	il/elle créera	il/elle crée
	nous créons	nous avons créé	nous créions	nous créerons	nous créions
	vous créez	vous avez créé	vous créiez	vous créerez	vous créiez
	ils/elles créent	ils/elles ont créé	ils/elles créaient	ils/elles créeront	ils/elles créent
19 crier	je crie	j' ai crié	je criais	je crierai	je crie
to cry	tu cries	tu as crié	tu criais	tu crieras	tu cries
	il/elle crie	il/elle a crié	il/elle criait	il/elle criera	il/elle crie
	nous crions	nous avons crié	nous criions	nous crierons	nous criions
	vous criez	vous avez crié	vous criiez	vous crierez	vous criiez
	ils/elles crient	ils/elles ont crié	ils/elles criaient	ils/elles crieront	ils/elles crient
20 croire to believe		see full verb table page 633			
21 croître	je cro**î**s	j' ai cr**û**	je croissais	je croîtrai	je croisse
to grow	tu cro**î**s	tu as cr**û**	tu croissais	tu croîtras	tu croisses
	il/elle croît	il/elle a cr**û**	il/elle croissait	il/elle croîtra	il/elle croisse
	nous croissons	nous avons cr**û**	nous croissions	nous croîtrons	nous croissions
	vous croissez	vous avez cr**û**	vous croissiez	vous croîtrez	vous croissiez
	ils/elles croissent	ils/elles ont cr**û**	ils/elles croissaient	ils/elles croîtront	ils/elles croissent
22 cueillir	je cueille	j' ai cueilli	je cueillais	je cueillerai	je cueille
to pick	tu cueilles	tu as cueilli	tu cueillais	tu cueilleras	tu cueilles
	il/elle cueille	il/elle a cueilli	il/elle cueillait	il/elle cueillera	il/elle cueille
	nous cueillons	nous avons cueilli	nous cueillions	nous cueillerons	nous cueillions
	vous cueillez	vous avez cueilli	vous cueilliez	vous cueillerez	vous cueilliez
	ils/elles cueillent	ils/elles ont cueilli	ils/elles cueillaient	ils/elles cueilleront	ils/elles cueillent

Letters in bold indicate a significant change in spelling from the infinitive form.

	PRESENT	PERFECT	IMPERFECT	FUTURE	PRESENT SUBJUNCTIVE
23 cuire	je cuis	j' ai cuit	je cuisais	je cuirai	je cuise
to cook	tu cuis	tu as cuit	tu cuisais	tu cuiras	tu cuises
	il/elle cuit	il/elle a cuit	il/elle cuisait	il/elle cuira	il/elle cuise
	nous cuisons	nous avons cuit	nous cuisions	nous cuirons	nous cuisions
	vous cuisez	vous avez cuit	vous cuisiez	vous cuirez	vous cuisiez
	ils/elles cuisent	ils/elles ont cuit	ils/elles cuisaient	ils/elles cuiront	ils/elles cuisent
24 descendre to go down	je descends	je suis descendu(e)/ j' ai descendu	je descendais	je descendrai	je descende
	tu descends	tu es descendu(e)/ tu as descendu	tu descendais	tu descendras	tu descendes
	il/elle descend	il/elle est descendu(e)/ il/elle a descendu	il/elle descendait	il/elle descendra	il/elle descende
	nous descendons	nous sommes descendu(e)s/ nous avons descendu	nous descendions	nous descendrons	nous descendions
	vous descendez	vous êtes descendu(e)(s)/ vous avez descendu	vous descendiez	vous descendrez	vous descendiez
	ils/elles descendent	ils/elles sont descendu(e)s/ ils/elles ont descendu	ils/elles descendaient	ils/elles descendront	ils/elles descendent
25 devenir	je deviens	je suis devenu(e)	je devenais	je deviendrai	je devienne
to become	tu deviens	tu es devenu(e)	tu devenais	tu deviendras	tu deviennes
	il/elle devient	il/elle est devenu(e)	il/elle devenait	il/elle deviendra	il/elle devienne
	nous devenons	nous sommes devenu(e)s	nous devenions	nous deviendrons	nous devenions
	vous devenez	vous êtes devenu(e)(s)	vous deveniez	vous deviendrez	vous deveniez
	ils/elles deviennent	ils/elles sont devenu(e)s	ils/elles devenaient	ils/elles deviendront	ils/elles deviennent
26 devoir to have to; to owe		see full verb table page 634			
27 dire to say		see full verb table page 635			
28 donner to give		see full verb table page 636			
29 dormir	je dors	j' ai dormi	je dormais	je dormirai	je dorme
to sleep	tu dors	tu as dormi	tu dormais	tu dormiras	tu dormes
	il/elle dort	il/elle a dormi	il/elle dormait	il/elle dormira	il/elle dorme
	nous dormons	nous avons dormi	nous dormions	nous dormirons	nous dormions
	vous dormez	vous avez dormi	vous dormiez	vous dormirez	vous dormiez
	ils/elles dorment	ils/elles ont dormi	ils/elles dormaient	ils/elles dormiront	ils/elles dorment
30 écrire	j' écris	j' ai écrit	j' écri**v**ais	j' écrirai	j' écri**v**e
to write	tu écris	tu as écrit	tu écri**v**ais	tu écriras	tu écri**v**es
	il/elle écrit	il/elle a écrit	il/elle écri**v**ait	il/elle écrira	il/elle écri**v**e
	nous écri**v**ons	nous avons écrit	nous écri**v**ions	nous écrirons	nous écri**v**ions
	vous écri**v**ez	vous avez écrit	vous écri**v**iez	vous écrirez	vous écri**v**iez
	ils/elles écri**v**ent	ils/elles ont écrit	ils/elles écri**v**aient	ils/elles écriront	ils/elles écri**v**ent
31 émouvoir	j' ém**eu**s	j' ai ému	j' émouvais	j' émouvrai	j' ém**eu**ve
to move	tu ém**eu**s	tu as ému	tu émouvais	tu émouvras	tu ém**eu**ves
	il/elle ém**eu**t	il/elle a ému	il/elle émouvait	il/elle émouvra	il/elle ém**eu**ve
	nous émouvons	nous avons ému	nous émouvions	nous émouvrons	nous émouvions
	vous émouvez	vous avez ému	vous émouviez	vous émouvrez	vous émouviez
	ils/elles ém**eu**vent	ils/elles ont ému	ils/elles émouvaient	ils/elles émouvront	ils/elles ém**eu**vent
32 entrer to come in; to go in	j' entre	je suis entré(e)/ j' ai entré	j' entrais	j' entrerai	j' entre
	tu entres	tu es entré(e)/ tu as entré	tu entrais	tu entreras	tu entres
	il/elle entre	il/elle est entré(e)/ il/elle a entré	il/elle entrait	il/elle entrera	il/elle entre
	nous entrons	nous sommes entré(e)s/ nous avons entré	nous entrions	nous entrerons	nous entrions
	vous entrez	vous êtes entré(e)(s)/ vous avez entré	vous entriez	vous entrerez	vous entriez
	ils/elles entrent	ils/elles sont entré(e)s/ ils/elles ont entré	ils/elles entraient	ils/elles entreront	ils/elles entrent

Letters in bold indicate a significant change in spelling from the infinitive form.

	PRESENT	PERFECT	IMPERFECT	FUTURE	PRESENT SUBJUNCTIVE
33 envoyer to send	j' envoie	j' ai envoyé	j' envoyais	j' enve**rr**ai	j' envoie
	tu envoies	tu as envoyé	tu envoyais	tu enve**rr**as	tu envoies
	il/elle envoie	il/elle a envoyé	il/elle envoyait	il/elle enve**rr**a	il/elle envoie
	nous envoyons	nous avons envoyé	nous envoyions	nous enve**rr**ons	nous envoyions
	vous envoyez	vous avez envoyé	vous envoyiez	vous enve**rr**ez	vous envoyiez
	ils/elles envo**i**ent	ils/elles ont envoyé	ils/elles envoyaient	ils/elles enve**rr**ont	ils/elles envo**i**ent
34 espérer to hope	j' esp**è**re	j' ai espéré	j' espérais	j' espérerai	j' esp**è**re
	tu esp**è**res	tu as espéré	tu espérais	tu espéreras	tu esp**è**res
	il/elle esp**è**re	il/elle a espéré	il/elle espérait	il/elle espérera	il/elle esp**è**re
	nous espérons	nous avons espéré	nous espérions	nous espérerons	nous espérions
	vous espérez	vous avez espéré	vous espériez	vous espérerez	vous espériez
	ils/elles esp**è**rent	ils/elles ont espéré	ils/elles espéraient	ils/elles espéreront	ils/elles esp**è**rent
35 être to be		see full verb table page 637			
36 faire to do; to make		see full verb table page 638			
37 falloir to have to	il f**au**t	il a fallu	il fallait	il f**aud**ra	il f**aill**e
38 finir to finish		see full verb table page 639			
39 fuir to flee; to drip	je fuis	j' ai fui	je fu**y**ais	je fuirai	je fuie
	tu fuis	tu as fui	tu fu**y**ais	tu fuiras	tu fuies
	il/elle fuit	il/elle a fui	il/elle fu**y**ait	il/elle fuira	il/elle fuie
	nous fu**y**ons	nous avons fui	nous fu**y**ions	nous fuirons	nous fu**y**ions
	vous fu**y**ez	vous avez fui	vous fu**y**iez	vous fuirez	vous fu**y**iez
	ils/elles fuient	ils/elles ont fui	ils/elles fu**y**aient	ils/elles fuiront	ils/elles fuient
40 haïr to hate	je hais	j' ai haï	je haïssais	je haïrai	je haïsse
	tu hais	tu as haï	tu haïssais	tu haïras	tu haïsses
	il/elle hait	il/elle a haï	il/elle haïssait	il/elle haïra	il/elle haïsse
	nous haïssons	nous avons haï	nous haïssions	nous haïrons	nous haïssions
	vous haïssez	vous avez haï	vous haïssiez	vous haïrez	vous haïssiez
	ils/elles haïssent	ils/elles ont haï	ils/elles haïssaient	ils/elles haïront	ils/elles haïssent
41 jeter to throw (away)	je je**tt**e	j' ai jeté	je jetais	je je**tt**erai	je je**tt**e
	tu je**tt**es	tu as jeté	tu jetais	tu je**tt**eras	tu je**tt**es
	il/elle je**tt**e	il/elle a jeté	il/elle jetait	il/elle je**tt**era	il/elle je**tt**e
	nous jetons	nous avons jeté	nous jetions	nous je**tt**erons	nous jetions
	vous jetez	vous avez jeté	vous jetiez	vous je**tt**erez	vous jetiez
	ils/elles je**tt**ent	ils/elles ont jeté	ils/elles jetaient	ils/elles je**tt**eront	ils/elles je**tt**ent
42 joindre to join	je joins	j' ai joint	je joi**gn**ais	je joindrai	je joi**gn**e
	tu joins	tu as joint	tu joi**gn**ais	tu joindras	tu joi**gn**es
	il/elle joint	il/elle a joint	il/elle joi**gn**ait	il/elle joindra	il/elle joi**gn**e
	nous joi**gn**ons	nous avons joint	nous joi**gn**ions	nous joindrons	nous joi**gn**ions
	vous joi**gn**ez	vous avez joint	vous joi**gn**iez	vous joindrez	vous joi**gn**iez
	ils/elles joi**gn**ent	ils/elles ont joint	ils/elles joi**gn**aient	ils/elles joindront	ils/elles joi**gn**ent
43 lever to raise	je l**è**ve	j' ai levé	je levais	je l**è**verai	je l**è**ve
	tu l**è**ves	tu as levé	tu levais	tu l**è**veras	tu l**è**ves
	il/elle l**è**ve	il/elle a levé	il/elle levait	il/elle l**è**vera	il/elle l**è**ve
	nous levons	nous avons levé	nous levions	nous l**è**verons	nous levions
	vous levez	vous avez levé	vous leviez	vous l**è**verez	vous leviez
	ils/elles l**è**vent	ils/elles ont levé	ils/elles levaient	ils/elles l**è**veront	ils/elles l**è**vent
44 lire to read	je lis	j' ai lu	je lisais	je lirai	je lise
	tu lis	tu as lu	tu lisais	tu liras	tu lises
	il/elle lit	il/elle a lu	il/elle lisait	il/elle lira	il/elle lise
	nous lisons	nous avons lu	nous lisions	nous lirons	nous lisions
	vous lisez	vous avez lu	vous lisiez	vous lirez	vous lisiez
	ils/elles lisent	ils/elles ont lu	ils/elles lisaient	ils/elles liront	ils/elles lisent
45 manger to eat	je mange	j' ai mangé	je mangeais	je mangerai	je mange
	tu manges	tu as mangé	tu mangeais	tu mangeras	tu manges
	il/elle mange	il/elle a mangé	il/elle mangeait	il/elle mangera	il/elle mange
	nous mangeons	nous avons mangé	nous mangions	nous mangerons	nous mangions
	vous mangez	vous avez mangé	vous mangiez	vous mangerez	vous mangiez
	ils/elles mangent	ils/elles ont mangé	ils/elles mangeaient	ils/elles mangeront	ils/elles mangent

Letters in bold indicate a significant change in spelling from the infinitive form.

	PRESENT	PERFECT	IMPERFECT	FUTURE	PRESENT SUBJUNCTIVE
46 maudire	je maudis	j'ai maudit	je maudissais	je maudirai	je maudisse
to curse	tu maudis	tu as maudit	tu maudissais	tu maudiras	tu maudisses
	il/elle maudit	il/elle a maudit	il/elle maudissait	il/elle maudira	il/elle maudisse
	nous maudissons	nous avons maudit	nous maudissions	nous maudirons	nous maudissions
	vous maudissez	vous avez maudit	vous maudissiez	vous maudirez	vous maudissiez
	ils/elles maudissent	ils/elles ont maudit	ils/elles maudissaient	ils/elles maudiront	ils/elles maudissent
47 mettre to put	see full verb table page 640				
48 monter	je monte	je suis monté(e)/ j' ai monté	je montais	je monterai	je monte
to go up	tu montes	tu es monté(e)/ tu as monté	tu montais	tu monteras	tu montes
	il/elle monte	il/elle est monté(e)/ il/elle a monté	il/elle montait	il/elle montera	il/elle monte
	nous montons	nous sommes monté(e)s/ nous avons monté	nous montions	nous monterons	nous montions
	vous montez	vous êtes monté(e)(s)/ vous avez monté	vous montiez	vous monterez	vous montiez
	ils/elles montent	ils/elles sont monté(e)s/ ils/elles ont monté	ils/elles montaient	ils/elles monteront	ils/elles montent
49 mordre	je mords	j'ai mordu	je mordais	je mordrai	je morde
to bite	tu mords	tu as mordu	tu mordais	tu mordras	tu mordes
	il/elle mord	il/elle a mordu	il/elle mordait	il/elle mordra	il/elle morde
	nous mordons	nous avons mordu	nous mordions	nous mordrons	nous mordions
	vous mordez	vous avez mordu	vous mordiez	vous mordrez	vous mordiez
	ils/elles mordent	ils/elles ont mordu	ils/elles mordaient	ils/elles mordront	ils/elles mordent
50 moudre	je mouds	j'ai mou**l**u	je mou**l**ais	je moudrai	je mou**l**e
to grind	tu mouds	tu as mou**l**u	tu mou**l**ais	tu moudras	tu mou**l**es
	il/elle moud	il/elle a mou**l**u	il/elle mou**l**ait	il/elle moudra	il/elle mou**l**e
	nous mou**l**ons	nous avons mou**l**u	nous mou**l**ions	nous moudrons	nous mou**l**ions
	vous mou**l**ez	vous avez mou**l**u	vous mou**l**iez	vous moudrez	vous mou**l**iez
	ils/elles mou**l**ent	ils/elles ont mou**l**u	ils/elles mou**l**aient	ils/elles moudront	ils/elles mou**l**ent
51 mourir	je m**eu**rs	je suis mort(e)	je mourais	je mourrai	je m**eu**re
to die	tu m**eu**rs	tu es mort(e)	tu mourais	tu mourras	tu m**eu**res
	il/elle m**eu**rt	il/elle est mort(e)	il/elle mourait	il/elle mourra	il/elle meure
	nous mourons	nous sommes mort(e)s	nous mourions	nous mourrons	nous mourions
	vous mourez	vous êtes mort(e)(s)	vous mouriez	vous mourrez	vous mouriez
	ils/elles m**eu**rent	ils/elles sont mort(e)s	ils/elles mouraient	ils/elles mourront	ils/elles m**eu**rent
52 naître	je nais	je suis n**é**(e)	je naissais	je naîtrai	je naisse
to be born	tu nais	tu es n**é**(e)	tu naissais	tu naîtras	tu naisses
	il/elle naît	il/elle est n**é**(e)	il/elle naissait	il/elle naîtra	il/elle naisse
	nous naissons	nous sommes n**é**(e)s	nous naissions	nous naîtrons	nous naissions
	vous naissez	vous êtes n**é**(e)(s)	vous naissiez	vous naîtrez	vous naissiez
	ils/elles naissent	ils/elles sont n**é**(e)s	ils/elles naissaient	ils/elles naîtront	ils/elles naissent
52 nettoyer	je nettoie	j'ai nettoyé	je nettoyais	je nettoierai	je nettoie
to clean	tu nettoies	tu as nettoyé	tu nettoyais	tu nettoieras	tu nettoies
	il/elle nettoie	il/elle a nettoyé	il/elle nettoyait	il/elle nettoiera	il/elle nettoie
	nous nettoyons	nous avons nettoyé	nous nettoyions	nous nettoierons	nous nettoyions
	vous nettoyez	vous avez nettoyé	vous nettoyiez	vous nettoierez	vous nettoyiez
	ils/elles nettoient	ils/elles ont nettoyé	ils/elles nettoyaient	ils/elles nettoieront	ils/elles nettoient
54 offrir	je offre	j'ai offert	je offrais	je offrirai	je offre
to offer	tu offres	tu as offert	tu offrais	tu offriras	tu offres
	il/elle offre	il/elle a offert	il/elle offrait	il/elle offrira	il/elle offre
	nous offrons	nous avons offert	nous offrions	nous offrirons	nous offrions
	vous offrez	vous avez offert	vous offriez	vous offrirez	vous offriez
	ils/elles offrent	ils/elles ont offert	ils/elles offraient	ils/elles offriront	ils/elles offrent
55 ouvrir to open	see full verb table page 641				

Letters in bold indicate a significant change in spelling from the infinitive form.

	PRESENT	PERFECT	IMPERFECT	FUTURE	PRESENT SUBJUNCTIVE
56 paraître	je parais	j' ai paru	je paraissais	je paraîtrai	je paraisse
to seem	tu parais	tu as paru	tu paraissais	tu paraîtras	tu paraisses
	il/elle paraît	il/elle a paru	il/elle paraissait	il/elle paraîtra	il/elle paraisse
	nous paraissons	nous avons paru	nous paraissions	nous paraîtrons	nous paraissions
	vous paraissez	vous avez paru	vous paraissiez	vous paraîtrez	vous paraissiez
	ils/elles paraissent	ils/elles ont paru	ils/elles paraissaient	ils/elles paraîtront	ils/elles paraissent
57 partir	je pars	je suis parti(e)	je partais	je partirai	je parte
to leave	tu pars	tu es parti(e)	tu partais	tu partiras	tu partes
	il/elle part	il/elle est parti(e)	il/elle partait	il/elle partira	il/elle parte
	nous partons	nous sommes parti(e)s	nous partions	nous partirons	nous partions
	vous partez	vous êtes parti(e)(s)	vous partiez	vous partirez	vous partiez
	ils/elles partent	ils/elles sont parti(e)s	ils/elles partaient	ils/elles partiront	ils/elles partent
58 passer	je passe	j' ai passé/ je suis passé(e)	je passais	je passerai	je passe
to pass	tu passes	tu as passé/ tu es passé(e)	tu passais	tu passeras	tu passes
	il/elle passe	il/elle a passé/ il/elle est passé(e)	il/elle passait	il/elle passera	il/elle passe
	nous passons	nous avons passé/ nous sommes passé(e)s	nous passions	nous passerons	nous passions
	vous passez	vous avez passé/ vous êtes passé(e)(s)	vous passiez	vous passerez	vous passiez
	ils/elles passent	ils/elles ont passé/ ils/elles sont passé(e)s	ils/elles passaient	ils/elles passeront	ils/elles passent
59 payer	je paie ***or*** paye	j' ai payé	je payais	je paierai	je paie ***or*** paye
to pay	tu paies ***or*** payes	tu as payé	tu payais	tu paieras	tu paies ***or*** payes
	il/elle paie ***or*** paye	il/elle a payé	il/elle payait	il/elle paiera	il/elle paie ***or*** paye
	nous payons	nous avons payé	nous payions	nous paierons	nous payions
	vous payez	vous avez payé	vous payiez	vous paierez	vous payiez
	ils/elles paient ***or*** payent	ils/elles ont payé	ils/elles payaient	ils/elles paieront	ils/elles paient ***or*** payent
60 peindre	je peins	j' ai peint	je pei**gn**ais	je peindrai	je pei**gn**e
to paint	tu peins	tu as peint	tu pei**gn**ais	tu peindras	tu pei**gn**es
	il/elle peint	il/elle a peint	il/elle pei**gn**ait	il/elle peindra	il/elle pei**gn**e
	nous pei**gn**ons	nous avons peint	nous pei**gn**ions	nous peindrons	nous pei**gn**ions
	vous pei**gn**ez	vous avez peint	vous pei**gn**iez	vous peindrez	vous pei**gn**iez
	ils/elles pei**gn**ent	ils/elles ont peint	ils/elles pei**gn**aient	ils/elles peindront	ils/elles pei**gn**ent
61 perdre	je perds	j' ai perdu	je perdais	je perdrai	je perde
to lose	tu perds	tu as perdu	tu perdais	tu perdras	tu perdes
	il/elle perd	il/elle a perdu	il/elle perdait	il/elle perdra	il/elle perde
	nous perdons	nous avons perdu	nous perdions	nous perdrons	nous perdions
	vous perdez	vous avez perdu	vous perdiez	vous perdrez	vous perdiez
	ils/elles perdent	ils/elles ont perdu	ils/elles perdaient	ils/elles perdront	ils/elles perdent
62 plaire	je plais	j' ai plu	je plaisais	je plairai	je plaise
to please	tu plais	tu as plu	tu plaisais	tu plairas	tu plaises
	il/elle plaît	il/elle a plu	il/elle plaisait	il/elle plaira	il/elle plaise
	nous plaisons	nous avons plu	nous plaisions	nous plairons	nous plaisions
	vous plaisez	vous avez plu	vous plaisiez	vous plairez	vous plaisiez
	ils/elles plaisent	ils/elles ont plu	ils/elles plaisaient	ils/elles plairont	ils/elles plaisent
63 pleuvoir to rain	il pleut	il a plu	il pleuvait	il pleuvra	il pleuve
64 pouvoir to be able		see full verb table page 642			
65 prendre	je prends	j' ai pris	je prenais	je prendrai	je pre**nn**e
to take	tu prends	tu as pris	tu prenais	tu prendras	tu pre**nn**es
	il/elle prend	il/elle a pris	il/elle prenait	il/elle prendra	il/elle pre**nn**e
	nous prenons	nous avons pris	nous prenions	nous prendrons	nous prenions
	vous prenez	vous avez pris	vous preniez	vous prendrez	vous preniez
	ils/elles pre**nn**ent	ils/elles ont pris	ils/elles prenaient	ils/elles prendront	ils/elles pre**nn**ent

Letters in bold indicate a significant change in spelling from the infinitive form.

	PRESENT	PERFECT	IMPERFECT	FUTURE	PRESENT SUBJUNCTIVE
66 protéger	je prot**è**ge	j' ai protégé	je protégeais	je protégerai	je prot**è**ge
to protect	tu prot**è**ges	tu as protégé	tu protégeais	tu protégeras	tu prot**è**ges
	il/elle prot**è**ge	il/elle a protégé	il/elle protégeait	il/elle protégera	il/elle prot**è**ge
	nous protégeons	nous avons protégé	nous protégions	nous protégerons	nous protégions
	vous protégez	vous avez protégé	vous protégiez	vous protégerez	vous protégiez
	ils/elles prot**è**gent	ils/elles ont protégé	ils/elles protégeaient	ils/elles protégeront	ils/elles prot**è**gent
67 recevoir	je re**ç**ois	j' ai re**ç**u	je recevais	je recevrai	je re**ç**oive
to receive	tu re**ç**ois	tu as re**ç**u	tu recevais	tu recevras	tu re**ç**oives
	il/elle re**ç**oit	il/elle a re**ç**u	il/elle recevait	il/elle recevra	il/elle re**ç**oive
	nous recevons	nous avons re**ç**u	nous recevions	nous recevrons	nous recevions
	vous recevez	vous avez re**ç**u	vous receviez	vous recevrez	vous receviez
	ils/elles re**ç**oivent	ils/elles ont re**ç**u	ils/elles recevaient	ils/elles recevront	ils/elles re**ç**oivent
68 rentrer	je rentre	je suis rentré(e)/ j' ai rentré	je rentrais	je rentrerai	je rentre
to come in	tu rentres	tu es rentré(e)/ tu as rentré	tu rentrais	tu rentreras	tu rentres
	il/elle rentre	il/elle est rentré(e)/ il/elle a rentré	il/elle rentrait	il/elle rentrera	il/elle rentre
	nous rentrons	nous sommes rentré(e)s/ nous avons rentré	nous rentrions	nous rentrerons	nous rentrions
	vous rentrez	vous êtes rentré(e)(s)/ vous avez rentré	vous rentriez	vous rentrerez	vous rentriez
	ils/elles rentrent	ils/elles sont rentré(e)s/ ils/elles ont rentré	ils/elles rentraient	ils/elles rentreront	ils/elles rentrent
69 répondre	je réponds	j' ai répondu	je répondais	je répondrai	je réponde
to answer	tu réponds	tu as répondu	tu répondais	tu répondras	tu répondes
	il/elle répond	il/elle a répondu	il/elle répondait	il/elle répondra	il/elle réponde
	nous répondons	nous avons répondu	nous répondions	nous répondrons	nous répondions
	vous répondez	vous avez répondu	vous répondiez	vous répondrez	vous répondiez
	ils/elles répondent	ils/elles ont répondu	ils/elles répondaient	ils/elles répondront	ils/elles répondent
70 résoudre	je résous	j' ai réso**lu**	je réso**lv**ais	je résoudrai	je réso**lve**
to resolve	tu résous	tu as réso**lu**	tu réso**lv**ais	tu résoudras	tu réso**lve**s
	il/elle résout	il/elle a réso**lu**	il/elle réso**lv**ait	il/elle résoudra	il/elle réso**lve**
	nous réso**lv**ons	nous avons réso**lu**	nous réso**lv**ions	nous résoudrons	nous réso**lv**ions
	vous réso**lv**ez	vous avez réso**lu**	vous réso**lv**iez	vous résoudrez	vous réso**lv**iez
	ils/elles réso**lv**ent	ils/elles ont réso**lu**	ils/elles réso**lv**aient	ils/elles résoudront	ils/elles réso**lv**ent
71 rester	je reste	je suis resté(e)	je restais	je resterai	je reste
to stay	tu restes	tu es resté(e)	tu restais	tu resteras	tu restes
	il/elle reste	il/elle est resté(e)	il/elle restait	il/elle restera	il/elle reste
	nous restons	nous sommes resté(e)s	nous restions	nous resterons	nous restions
	vous restez	vous êtes resté(e)(s)	vous restiez	vous resterez	vous restiez
	ils/elles restent	ils/elles sont resté(e)s	ils/elles restaient	ils/elles resteront	ils/elles restent
72 retourner	je retourne	je suis retourné(e)/ j' ai retourné	je retournais	je retournerai	je retourne
to go back	tu retournes	tu es retourné(e)/ tu as retourné	tu retournais	tu retourneras	tu retournes
	il/elle retourne	il/elle est retourné(e)/ il/elle a retourné	il/elle retournait	il/elle retournera	il/elle retourne
	nous retournons	nous sommes retourné(e)s/ nous avons retourné	nous retournions	nous retournerons	nous retournions
	vous retournez	vous êtes retourné(e)(s)/ vous avez retourné	vous retourniez	vous retournerez	vous retourniez
	ils/elles retournent	ils/elles sont retourné(e)s/ ils/elles ont retourné	ils/elles retournaient	ils/elles retourneront	ils/elles retournent
73 revenir	je reviens	je suis revenu(e)	je revenais	je reviendrai	je revienne
to come back	tu reviens	tu es revenu(e)	tu revenais	tu reviendras	tu reviennes
	il/elle revient	il/elle est revenu(e)	il/elle revenait	il/elle reviendra	il/elle revienne
	nous revenons	nous sommes revenu(e)s	nous revenions	nous reviendrons	nous revenions
	vous revenez	vous êtes revenu(e)(s)	vous reveniez	vous reviendrez	vous reveniez
	ils/elles reviennent	ils/elles sont revenu(e)s	ils/elles revenaient	ils/elles reviendront	ils/elles reviennent

Letters in bold indicate a significant change in spelling from the infinitive form.

	PRESENT	PERFECT	IMPERFECT	FUTURE	PRESENT SUBJUNCTIVE
74 **rire**	je ris	j' ai ri	je riais	je rirai	je rie
to laugh	tu ris	tu as ri	tu riais	tu riras	tu ries
	il/elle rit	il/elle a ri	il/elle riait	il/elle rira	il/elle rie
	nous rions	nous avons ri	nous riions	nous rirons	nous riions
	vous riez	vous avez ri	vous riiez	vous rirez	vous riiez
	ils/elles rient	ils/elles ont ri	ils/elles riaient	ils/elles riront	ils/elles rient
75 **rompre**	je romps	j' ai rompu	je rompais	je romprai	je rompe
to break	tu romps	tu as rompu	tu rompais	tu rompras	tu rompes
	il/elle rompt	il/elle a rompu	il/elle rompait	il/elle rompra	il/elle rompe
	nous rompons	nous avons rompu	nous rompions	nous romprons	nous rompions
	vous rompez	vous avez rompu	vous rompiez	vous romprez	vous rompiez
	ils/elles rompent	ils/elles ont rompu	ils/elles rompaient	ils/elles rompront	ils/elles rompent
76 **savoir** to know		see full verb table page 643			
77 **sentir** to smell; to feel		see full verb table page 644			
78 **servir**	je sers	j' ai servi	je servais	je servirai	je serve
to serve	tu sers	tu as servi	tu servais	tu serviras	tu serves
	il/elle sert	il/elle a servi	il/elle servait	il/elle servira	il/elle serve
	nous servons	nous avons servi	nous servions	nous servirons	nous servions
	vous servez	vous avez servi	vous serviez	vous servirez	vous serviez
	ils/elles servent	ils/elles ont servi	ils/elles servaient	ils/elles serviront	ils/elles servent
9 **sortir**	je sors	je suis sorti(e)/ j' ai sorti	je sortais	je sortirai	je sorte
to go out	tu sors	tu es sorti(e)/ tu as sorti	tu sortais	tu sortiras	tu sortes
	il/elle sort	il/elle est sorti(e)/ il/elle a sorti	il/elle sortait	il/elle sortira	il/elle sorte
	nous sortons	nous sommes sorti(e)s/ nous avons sorti	nous sortions	nous sortirons	nous sortions
	vous sortez	vous êtes sorti(e)(s)/ vous avez sorti	vous sortiez	vous sortirez	vous sortiez
	ils/elles sortent	ils/elles sont sorti(e)(s)/ ils/elles ont sorti	ils/elles sortaient	ils/elles sortiront	ils/elles sortent
o **suffire**	je suffis	j' ai suffi	je suffisais	je suffirai	je suffise
to be enough	tu suffis	tu as suffi	tu suffisais	tu suffiras	tu suffises
	il/elle suffit	il/elle a suffi	il/elle suffisait	il/elle suffira	il/elle suffise
	nous suffisons	nous avons suffi	nous suffisions	nous suffirons	nous suffisions
	vous suffisez	vous avez suffi	vous suffisiez	vous suffirez	vous suffisiez
	ils/elles suffisent	ils/elles ont suffi	ils/elles suffisaient	ils/elles suffiront	ils/elles suffisent
1 **suivre**	je suis	j' ai suivi	je suivais	je suivrai	je suive
to follow	tu suis	tu as suivi	tu suivais	tu suivras	tu suives
	il/elle suit	il/elle a suivi	il/elle suivait	il/elle suivra	il/elle suive
	nous suivons	nous avons suivi	nous suivions	nous suivrons	nous suivions
	vous suivez	vous avez suivi	vous suiviez	vous suivrez	vous suiviez
	ils/elles suivent	ils/elles ont suivi	ils/elles suivaient	ils/elles suivront	ils/elles suivent
se taire to stop talking		see full verb table page 645			
tenir	je tiens	j' ai tenu	je tenais	je tiendrai	je tienne
to hold	tu tiens	tu as tenu	tu tenais	tu tiendras	tu tiennes
	il/elle tient	il/elle a tenu	il/elle tenait	il/elle tiendra	il/elle tienne
	nous tenons	nous avons tenu	nous tenions	nous tiendrons	nous tenions
	vous tenez	vous avez tenu	vous teniez	vous tiendrez	vous teniez
	ils/elles tiennent	ils/elles ont tenu	ils/elles tenaient	ils/elles tiendront	ils/elles tiennent
tomber	je tombe	je suis tombé(e)	je tombais	je tomberai	je tombe
to fall	tu tombes	tu es tombé(e)	tu tombais	tu tomberas	tu tombes
	il/elle tombe	il/elle est tombé(e)	il/elle tombait	il/elle tombera	il/elle tombe
	nous tombons	nous sommes tombé(e)s	nous tombions	nous tomberons	nous tombions
	vous tombez	vous êtes tombé(e)(s)	vous tombiez	vous tomberez	vous tombiez
	ils/elles tombent	ils/elles sont tombé(e)s	ils/elles tombaient	ils/elles tomberont	ils/elles tombent

Letters in bold indicate a significant change in spelling from the infinitive form.

	PRESENT	PERFECT	IMPERFECT	FUTURE	PRESENT SUBJUNCTIVE
85 traire to milk	je trais	j' ai trait	je trayais	je trairai	je traie
	tu trais	tu as trait	tu trayais	tu trairas	tu traies
	il/elle trait	il/elle a trait	il/elle trayait	il/elle traira	il/elle traie
	nous tra**y**ons	nous avons trait	nous tra**y**ions	nous trairons	nous tra**y**ions
	vous tra**y**ez	vous avez trait	vous tra**y**iez	vous trairez	vous tra**y**iez
	ils/elles traient	ils/elles ont trait	ils/elles tra**y**aient	ils/elles trairont	ils/elles traient
86 vaincre to defeat; to overcome	je vaincs	j' ai vaincu	je vain**qu**ais	je vaincrai	je vain**que**
	tu vaincs	tu as vaincu	tu vain**qu**ais	tu vaincras	tu vain**que**s
	il/elle vainc	il/elle a vaincu	il/elle vain**qu**ait	il/elle vaincra	il/elle vain**que**
	nous vain**qu**ons	nous avons vaincu	nous vain**qu**ions	nous vaincrons	nous vain**qu**ions
	vous vain**qu**ez	vous avez vaincu	vous vain**qu**iez	vous vaincrez	vous vain**qu**iez
	ils/elles vain**qu**ent	ils/elles ont vaincu	ils/elles vain**qu**aient	ils/elles vaincront	ils/elles vain**qu**ent
87 valoir to be worth	je v**aux**	j' ai valu	je valais	je v**aud**rai	je v**aill**e
	tu v**aux**	tu as valu	tu valais	tu v**aud**ras	tu v**aill**es
	il/elle v**aut**	il/elle a valu	il/elle valait	il/elle v**aud**ra	il/elle v**aill**e
	nous valons	nous avons valu	nous valions	nous v**aud**rons	nous valions
	vous valez	vous avez valu	vous valiez	vous v**aud**rez	vous valiez
	ils/elles valent	ils/elles ont valu	ils/elles valaient	ils/elles v**aud**ront	ils/elles v**aill**ent
88 vendre to sell	see full verb table page 646				
89 venir to come	see full verb table page 647				
90 vêtir to dress	je vêts	j' ai vêtu	je vêtais	je vêtirai	je vête
	tu vêts	tu as vêtu	tu vêtais	tu vêtiras	tu vêtes
	il/elle vêt	il/elle a vêtu	il/elle vêtait	il/elle vêtira	il/elle vête
	nous vêtons	nous avons vêtu	nous vêtions	nous vêtirons	nous vêtions
	vous vêtez	vous avez vêtu	vous vêtiez	vous vêtirez	vous vêtiez
	ils/elles vêtent	ils/elles ont vêtu	ils/elles vêtaient	ils/elles vêtiront	ils/elles vêtent
91 vivre to live	je vis	j' ai vécu	je vivais	je vivrai	je vive
	tu vis	tu as vécu	tu vivais	tu vivras	tu vives
	il/elle vit	il/elle a vécu	il/elle vivait	il/elle vivra	il/elle vive
	nous vivons	nous avons vécu	nous vivions	nous vivrons	nous vivions
	vous vivez	vous avez vécu	vous viviez	vous vivrez	vous viviez
	ils/elles vivent	ils/elles ont vécu	ils/elles vivaient	ils/elles vivront	ils/elles vivent
92 voir to see	see full verb table page 648				
93 vouloir to want	see full verb table page 649				

Letters in bold indicate a significant change in spelling from the infinitive form.